March 12–16, 2016
Delft, Netherlands

I0027443

Association for Computing Machinery

Advancing Computing as a Science & Profession

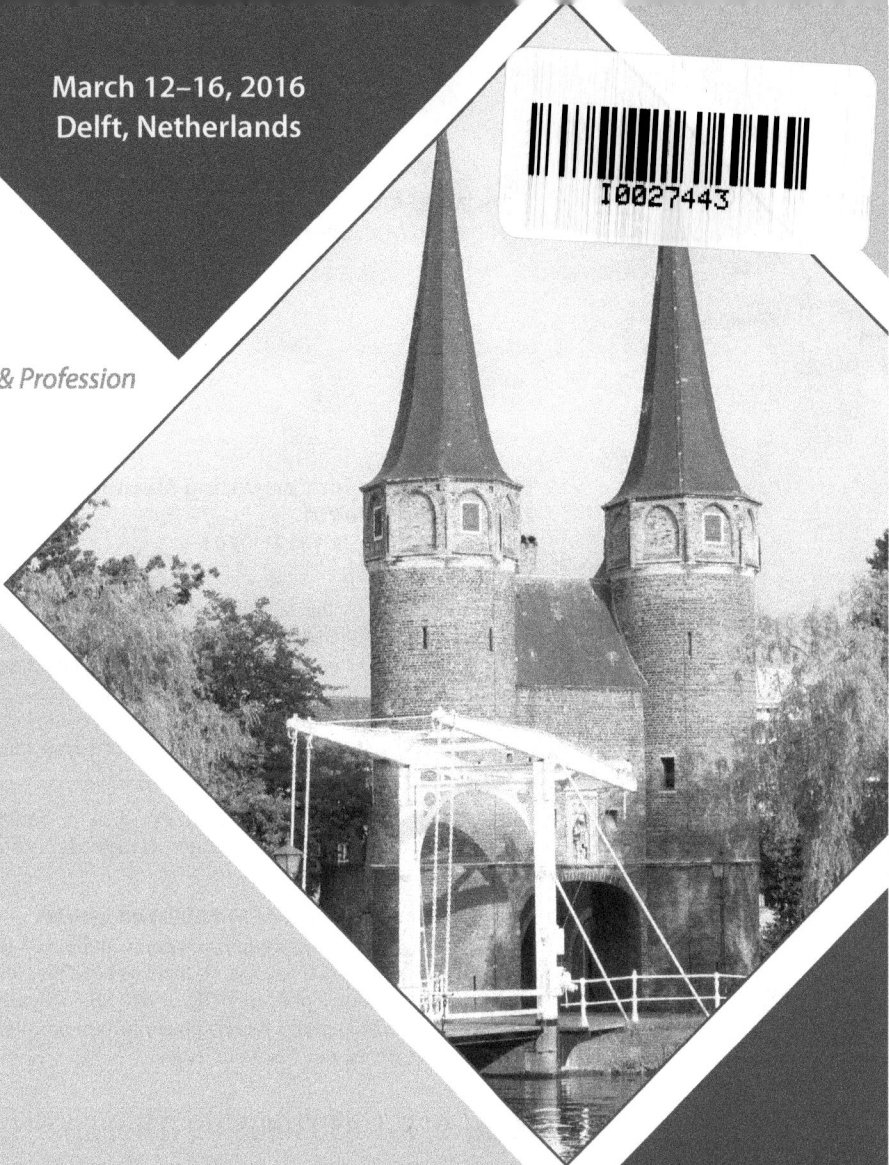

ICPE'16

Proceedings of the 2016 ACM/SPEC
**International Conference
on Performance Engineering**

Sponsored by:
ACM SIGMETRICS, ACM SIGSOFT, and SPEC

Supported by:
Delft University of Technology and SPEC Research

Association for Computing Machinery

Advancing Computing as a Science & Profession

The Association for Computing Machinery
2 Penn Plaza, Suite 701
New York, New York 10121-0701

Notice to Past Authors of ACM-Published Articles
ACM intends to create a complete electronic archive of all articles and/or other material previously published by ACM. If you have written a work that has been previously published by ACM in any journal or conference proceedings prior to 1978, or any SIG Newsletter at any time, and you do NOT want this work to appear in the ACM Digital Library, please inform permissions@acm.org, stating the title of the work, the author(s), and where and when published.

ISBN: 978-1-4503-4080-9 (Digital)

ISBN: 978-1-4503-4471-5 (Print)

Additional copies may be ordered prepaid from:

ACM Order Department
PO Box 30777
New York, NY 10087-0777, USA

Phone: 1-800-342-6626 (USA and Canada)
+1-212-626-0500 (Global)
Fax: +1-212-944-1318
E-mail: acmhelp@acm.org
Hours of Operation: 8:30 am – 4:30 pm ET

Printed in the USA

ICPE 2016 - General Chairs' Welcome

It is our great pleasure to welcome you to the 7th ACM/SPEC International Conference on Performance Engineering (ICPE) and to the beautiful city of Delft. If one looks at the ancient canals lined with merchants' houses, the old churches, and the splendid town hall, one sees that Delft's rich history is still very much alive. At the same time, though, it is a very modern and vibrant city. More than ten percent of its 100,000 inhabitants are students and the university has attracted a large number of technology-oriented companies. The Delft University of Technology is the oldest technical university in the Netherlands, with an excellent international reputation for its engineering and scientific results, and with diverse and international faculty and students. The Distributed Systems group, who co-organized ICPE 2016 on behalf of the Delft University of Technology, fits into this profile of excellence.

This year's ICPE continues its tradition of being the premier forum for the integration of theory and practice in the field of performance engineering. ICPE is an annual joint meeting that has grown out of the ACM Workshop on Software Performance (WOSP) and the SPEC International Performance Engineering Workshop (SIPEW). It brings together researchers and industry practitioners to share ideas, discuss challenges, and present results of both work-in-progress and state-of-the-art research on performance engineering of software and systems.

Putting together *ICPE'16* was a team effort. We first thank the authors for providing the content of the program. We are grateful to the PC Chairs and to the program committee who worked very hard in reviewing papers and providing feedback for authors. We also thank the chairs of the other tracks of the conference, the dissemination and proceedings chairs, the web site chair, the finance chair, the numerous other helpers, and the local organizers. Finally, we thank our hosting University, the Delft University of Technology, and our lead sponsors, ACM SIGMETRICS, ACM SIGSOFT, and SPEC.

We hope that you will find this program interesting and thought-provoking and that the conference will provide you with a valuable opportunity to share ideas with other researchers and practitioners from institutions around the world and to learn about Delft rich history.

Alberto Avritzer
ICPE'16 General Chair
Sonatype, Inc., MD, USA

Alexandru Iosup
ICPE'16 General Chair
Delft University of Technology,
the Netherlands

ICPE 2016 – Program Chairs' Welcome

The 7th ACM/SPEC International Conference on Performance Engineering (ICPE 2016) takes place in Delft in The Netherlands in March 2016. The conference grew out of the ACM Workshop on Software Performance (WOSP since 1998) and the SPEC International Performance Engineering Workshop (SIPEW since 2008), with the goal of integrating theory and practice in the field of performance engineering. It is a great pleasure for us to offer an outstanding technical program this year, which we believe will allow researchers and practitioners to present their visions and latest innovation, and to exchange ideas within the community.

Overall, we received 89 high quality submissions across all three tracks. The main Research Track attracted 57 submissions with 19 accepted (33% acceptance rate) for presentation at the conference. Among them were 16 full papers and three short papers. Each paper received at least three reviews from experienced program committee members. In the Work-In-Progress and Vision Track, six out of 15 contributions were selected. The Industry and Experience Track received 17 submissions, of which seven were selected for inclusion in the program. The accepted papers were organized into five research track sessions, two industry track sessions, and one WiP and vision track session. Three best paper candidates were also selected: two research papers and one industry paper.

We are proud to have three excellent keynote speakers as part of our technical program:

- Bianca Schroeder from University of Toronto, Canada, presenting "Case studies from the real world: The importance of measurement and analysis in building better systems"

- Wilhelm Hasselbring from Kiel University, Germany, discussing "Microservices for Scalability"

- Angelo Corsaro, Chief Technology Officer at PrismTech, talking about "Cloudy, Foggy and Misty Internet of Things"

In addition, the program includes four tutorials, a doctoral symposium, a poster and demo track, the SPEC Distinguished Dissertation Award, and three interesting workshops, including the International Workshop on Large-Scale Testing (LT), the 2nd International Workshop on Performance Analysis of Big data Systems (PABS), and the 2nd Workshop on Challenges in Performance Methods for Software Development (WOSP-C).

The program covers traditional ICPE topics such as software and systems performance modeling and prediction, analysis and optimization, characterization and profiling, as well as application of performance engineering theory and techniques to several practical fields, including distributed systems, cloud computing, storage, energy, big data, virtualized systems and containers.

We'd like to thank all the authors who submitted their innovative work to ICPE this year. In addition, we thank all the program committee members and subreviewers for volunteering their time for the benefit of the community and their hard work in providing quality reviews for the submitted papers. Finally, we'd like to thank all the participants who will attend ICPE in person this year, since we will rely on you to make this event interactive, engaging, and thought-provoking for everyone involved.

We look forward to meeting all of you in Delft in March 2016!

Steffen Becker

ICPE 2016 Program Co-Chair Chemnitz University of Technology, Germany

Xiaoyun Zhu

ICPE 2016 Program Co-Chair Futurewei Technologies, USA

Jerry Rolia

ICPE 2016 Industrial Co-Chair Hewlett Packard Labs, USA

Manoj Nambiar

ICPE 2016 Industrial Co-Chair Tata Consultancy Services, India

Table of Contents

Keynote Address

Best Paper Candidate 1

Performance Modelling

Industry Track 1

Work-In-Progress and Vision Papers

Doctoral Symposium

Demos and Posters

Keynote 2

Best Paper Candidate 2

Industry Track 2

Distributed Systems & Cloud

Best Paper Candidate 3

Characterization and Profiling

Keynote 3

Monitoring and Analysis

Data Intensive Computing

Tutorials

Author Index

ICPE 2016 Conference Organization

General Chairs: Alberto Avritzer *(Sonatype, Inc., USA)*
Alexandru Iosup *(Delft University of Technology, the Netherlands)*

Program Chairs: Xiaoyun Zhu *(Futurewei Technologies, USA)*
Steffen Becker *(Chemnitz University of Technology, Germany)*

Industrial Chairs: Jerry Rolia *(Hewlett Packard Labs, USA)*
Manoj Nambiar *(TCS Innovation Labs, India)*

Tutorial Chair: Andre van Hoorn *(University of Stuttgart, Germany)*
Mihai Capota *(Intel Labs, USA)*

Workshop Chair: Ana Varbanescu *(University of Amsterdam, the Netherlands)*

Demos and Posters Chair: Radu Prodan *(University of Innsbruck, Austria)*

Doctoral Symposium Chair: Dick Epema *(TU Delft, the Netherlands)*

Proceedings Chair: Catia Trubiani *(Gran Sasso Science Institute, Italy)*

Finance Chair: Anne Koziolek *(Karlsruhe Institute of Technology, Germany)*

Web Chair: Tim Hegeman *(TU Delft, the Netherlands)*

Publicity Chair: Daniel Sadoc Menasche *(Federal University of Rio de Janeiro, Brazil)*
Dorina Petriu *(Carleton, Canada)*
Vanish Talwar *(HP Labs, USA)*
Alexander Wert *(NovaTec GmbH, Germany)*
Timothy Wood *(George Washington University, USA)*
Yu Hua *(Huazhong University of Science and Technology, China)*

Steering Committee: Andre B. Bondi (Co-Chair) *(Siemens Corporate Research, USA)*
Samuel Kounev (Co-Chair) *(University of Würzburg, Germany)*
Meikel Poess (Secretary) *(Oracle Corporation, USA)*
J. Nelson Amaral *(University of Alberta, Canada)*
Vittorio Cortellessa *(Università di L'Aquila, Italy)*
Klaus-Dieter Lange *(Hewlett-Packard Company, USA)*
Raffaela Mirandola *(Politecnico di Milano, Italy)*
Jerry Rolia *(HP Labs, UK)*
Kai Sachs *(SAP AG, Germany)*
Bran Selic *(ObjecTime Limited, Canada)*

Program Committee	Ana Lucia Varbanescu *(University of Amsterdam, the Netherlands)*
(Research Track,	Marco Vieira *(University of Coimbra, Portugal)*
Work-in-Progress	Katinka Wolter *(Freie Universitaet zu Berlin, Germany)*
& Vision Track)	Timothy Wood *(The George Washington University, USA)*
(continued):	Murray Woodside *(Carleton University, Ottawa, Canada)*
	Ming Zhao *(Arizona State University, USA)*

Program Committee	Lydia Y. Chen *(IBM Research Zurich Lab, Switzerland)*
(Industrial Track):	Cloyce Spradling *(Oracle, USA)*
	Klaus-Dieter Lange *(Hewlett-Packard, USA)*
	Meikel Poess *(Oracle, USA)*
	Bronis de Supinski *(Lawrence Livermore National Laboratory, USA)*
	Avadh Patel *(Oracle, USA)*
	Mike Tricker *(Microsoft, USA)*
	Heiko Koziolek *(ABB Corporate Research, Germany)*
	Alberto Avritzer *(Siemens SCR, USA)*
	Rean Griffith *(VMware, USA)*
	Daniel Gmach *(HP Labs, USA)*
	Christos Kartsaklis *(Oak Ridge National Lab, USA)*

Additional reviewers:	Nuno Antunes *(University of Coimbra, Portugal)*
	Martin Arlitt *(Hewlett Packard Labs, USA)*
	Raul Barbosa *(University of Coimbra, Portugal)*
	Vincenzo De Maio *(University of Innsbruck, Austria)*
	Daniel Dubois *(Imperial College, London)*
	Henning Groenda *(FZI Research Center FOR Information Technology, Germany)*
	Philipp Gschwandtner *(University of Innsbruck, Austria)*
	Lukas Iffländer *(University of Würzburg, Germany)*
	Pooyan Jamshidi *(Imperial College, London)*
	Matthias Janetschek *(University of Innsbruck, Austria)*
	Jeyhun Karimov
	Mehdi Khouja
	Dragi Kimowski
	Isaac Lera *(University of the Balearic Islands, Spain)*
	Roland Matha *(University of Innsbruck, Austria)*
	Alexander Milenkoski *(University of Würzburg, Germany)*
	Tiffany M. Mintz *(Oak Ridge National Lab, USA)*
	Armin Moebius *(IBAK, Germany)*
	Rasha Osman
	Andrea Rosà *(Università della Svizzera Italiana, Switzerland)*
	Piotr Rygielski *(University of Würzburg, Germany)*

Luca Salucci *(Università della Svizzera Italiana, Switzerland)*
Nishant Saurabh *(University of Innsbruck, Austria)*

ICPE 2016 Sponsors & Supporters

Sponsors:

Supporters:

Delft University of Technology

Case Studies from the Real World: The Importance of Measurement and Analysis in Building Better Systems

Bianca Schroeder
University of Toronto
Department of Computer Science
Toronto, Canada
bianca@cs.toronto.edu

ABSTRACT

At the core of the "Big Data" revolution lie frameworks and systems that allow for the massively parallel processing of large amounts of data. Ironically, while they have been designed for processing large amounts of data, these systems are at the same time major producers of data: to support the administration and management of these huge-scale systems, they are configured to generate detailed log and monitoring data, periodically capturing the system state across all nodes, components and jobs in the system. While such logging information is used routinely by sysadmins for ad-hoc trouble-shooting and problem diagnosis, we point out that there is a tremendous value in analyzing such data from a research point of view. In this talk, we will go over several case studies that demonstrate how measuring and analyzing measurement data from production systems can provide new insights into how systems work and fail, and how these new insights can help in designing better systems.

BIO

Bianca is an associate professor and Canada Research Chair in the Computer Science Department at the University of Toronto. Before joining UofT, she spent 2 years as a post-doc at Carnegie Mellon University working with Garth Gibson. She received her doctorate from the Computer Science Department at Carnegie Mellon University under the direction of Mor Harchol-Balter. She is an Alfred P. Sloan Research Fellow, the recipient of the Outstanding Young Canadian Computer Science Prize of the Canadian Association for Computer Science, an Ontario Early Researcher Award, an NSERC Accelerator Award, a two-time winner of the IBM PhD fellowship and her work has won four best paper awards and one best presentation award. She has co-chaired the TPCs of Usenix FAST'14, ACM Sigmetrics'14 and IEEE NAS'11, and is an associate editor for IEEE TDSC. Her work on hard drive reliability and her work on DRAM reliability have been featured in articles at a number of news sites, including Computerworld, Wired, Slashdot, PCWorld, StorageMojo and eWEEK.

ICPE'16 March 12-18, 2016, Delft, Netherlands

© 2016 Copyright held by the owner/author(s).

ACM ISBN 978-1-4503-4080-9/16/03.

DOI: http://dx.doi.org/10.1145/2851553.2858660

Maximum Likelihood Estimation of Closed Queueing Network Demands from Queue Length Data

Weikun Wang   Giuliano Casale
Department of Computing
Imperial College London
London, UK
{weikun.wang11,
g.casale}@imperial.ac.uk

Ajay Kattepur   Manoj Nambiar
Performance Engineering Research Center
TCS Innovation Labs
Mumbai, India
{ajay.kattepur,m.nambiar}@tcs.com

ABSTRACT

Resource demand estimation is essential for the application of analyical models, such as queueing networks, to real-world systems. In this paper, we investigate maximum likelihood (ML) estimators for service demands in closed queueing networks with load-independent and load-dependent service times. Stemming from a characterization of necessary conditions for ML estimation, we propose new estimators that infer demands from queue-length measurements, which are inexpensive metrics to collect in real systems. One advantage of focusing on queue-length data compared to response times or utilizations is that confidence intervals can be rigorously derived from the equilibrium distribution of the queueing network model. Our estimators and their confidence intervals are validated against simulation and real system measurements for a multi-tier application.

CCS Concepts

•Software and its engineering → Model-driven software engineering; Software performance;

Keywords

Queueing Network; Demand Estimation; Maximum likelihood

1. INTRODUCTION

Guaranteeing Quality-of-Service (QoS) is an important concern for cloud providers and software vendors in order to minimize service-level agreement violations. Performance models such as queueing networks are commonly used for performance analysis and prediction and therefore can support engineers in coping with these problems. Closed queueing networks, in particular, are often used for software systems [20] since real applications are layered and thus operate under pooling constraints that limit the maximum

ICPE'16, March 12-18, 2016, Delft, Netherlands
© 2016 ACM. ISBN 978-1-4503-4080-9/16/03...$15.00
DOI: http://dx.doi.org/10.1145/2851553.2851565

parallelism level at each layer and the underpinning hardware resources. For instance, Layered Queueing Networks (LQN), which describe the nested structure of softwares, are based on closed queueing networks [9] and has applications in a wide rang of distributed systems. However, despite solution methods for these models have been systematically investigated, their parametrization from real measurements is often difficult, but still it is essential to obtain accurate predictions [32]. Among these parameters, the *resource demand*, i.e., the cumulative time a request seizes from a server excluding contention overheads, is particularly challenging to estimate, since demands are difficult to measure directly without introducing substantial overheads. Statistical inference can therefore be used to determine accurate estimates from indirect measurements, such as throughputs, utilizations, queue-length, or response time data [4, 15, 18, 19, 22, 24, 38] .

Linear regression methods that use CPU utilization and request throughputs have attracted much attention in the last decade for demand estimation. However, these methods are known to suffer from the multicollinearity problem leading to biased estimates [13]. On the other hand, the idea of exploiting response time measurements has recently been investigated in a number of works [15,24,38]. Nonetheless, collecting response time may pose a large overhead to the application system, especially if one needs to instrument separate layers of a multi-tier application. In this paper, we therefore investigate a different approach to obtain the demand estimates, where we attempt to exploit queue-length samples, i.e., measurements of the number of executing requests at each resource. Compared to response time, according to BCMP theorem [2] queue-length samples are rather insensitive to scheduling policies and to the moments of service times higher than the mean. Therefore, queue-length based fitting appears more applicable and less error-prone than response-time based fitting. Recent research [35] has also explored this problem, however the resulting algorithm based on Gibbs sampling is computationally expensive for large models, thus restraining its use to offline analysis.

Stemming from the above considerations, in this paper we investigate the problem of *efficiently* estimating demands from queue-length measurements. Using the equilibrium distribution of product-form closed queueing networks, we develop a characterization of necessary conditions for maximum likelihood solutions to the demand estimation problem. We then provide tractable expressions for the Hessian matrix that can be used to verify if a stationary point is indeed a maximum. Furthermore, we show that the Hessian matrix readily provides the confidence intervals associated to the (local) maximum likelihood estimator.

In addition to the above contributions, we show that our method applies also to load-dependent systems, which is a distinctive advantage of our approach compared to other methods. While most existing demand estimation methods are limited to load-independent models, i.e., models where the service demand remains constant irrespectively of the number of requests running at a resource, our conditions to identify maximum likelihood estimators readily extend to load-dependent models, where demands are functions of the current queue-length. Real-world systems typically exhibit a load dependent behavior, often as a result of parallelism of multi-core servers or caching and shared data structures in enterprise web applications [5]. Therefore the ability to estimate how a request demand varies with the load is essential for predicting performance of real applications where these aspects are critical for performance. The work in [16] is to our knowledge the first attempt to estimate the demand in a load-dependent queueing network, however it only applies to open models and requires prior knowledge of a parametric expression for the load-dependent function. Instead, the estimation technique presented in this paper generalizes to *closed* load-dependent models, making demand estimation viable also for this class of models. While the method we propose is also more efficient if prior knowledge of the load dependent function is available, our expressions are general and can work also without this assumption.

We illustrate the efficiency and accuracy of the proposed estimators using simulated data and a real-world enterprise application. We also compare against existing demand estimation algorithms showing our approach to be effective. We show the applicability of our methodology against a real world case study of a multi-tier application by comparing the performance of the system with the predictions of a queueing network that uses the estimated demands. In particular, we show that predictions with demands estimated at low-load can be quite effective in characterizing high-load behaviour, even in presence of load-dependence.

Summarizing, the main contribution of this paper are:

- Novel estimators of resource demands for load-independent and load-dependent closed queueing networks;

- Confidence interval expressions for the proposed estimators in both classes of models;

- An experimental study based on simulated and real system data showing the effectiveness of the estimation methods.

This paper extends a preliminary work published as an extended abstract in [36]. Compared to our initial investigation, in this paper we generalize our results to load-dependent networks and include formal proofs for all the results, which were not given in [36].

The rest of the paper is organized as follows. Section 2 reviews the previous work on demand estimation while Section 3 presents the background information. In Section 4 a motivating example is illustrated. Later, Section 5 and 6 presents the proposed algorithms of demand estimation for load-independent and load-dependent models. Finally, evaluation of the algorithms are given in Section 7 followed by the conclusion remarks.

2. RELATED WORK

Existing work for characterizing resource demand are based on statistical inference of indirect measurements, among which CPU utilization, throughput and response time are the most popular ones. In particular, methods for regressing CPU utilization and throughput to obtain service demand have gained much attention [22,27,28,38]. Later [4] has proposed an approach for robust demand estimation, based on a Least Trimmed Squares regression technique. However regression methods suffer from known problems, such as multicollinearity [13] that can lead to biased estimates. To overcome this shortcoming, various algorithms based on machine learning has been proposed. Kalman filters [34,37,39,40] have shown to be effective in parameter tracking. Other methods including clustering [6, 7], pattern recognition [11, 14], independent component analysis [31] have also been explored to estimate service demands. However, these methods require CPU utilization measurements which are not always available or reliable, especially in cloud environments. Compared to these algorithms, our proposed methods rely on queue-length samples, which are easier to collect since they only require to monitor the number of running worker threads in a system and the identity of the running request.

Besides CPU utilization, response times have also been used for estimating service demand. The work in [18] defines a quadratic programming using end-to-end response time and CPU utilization together with request throughputs. The methods introduced in [15] and [29] employ response time values as well, but they only apply to FCFS servers. The work in [19] focuses on estimating demands for some simple queueing systems through optimization programs that use response time data. Recent work [24] also proposes new algorithms based on regression and maximum likelihood methods for response time data. However, collecting response data may pose additional overhead to the system compared to queue-length monitoring, since both arrivals and departures need to be continuously tracked and response time based fitting algorithm are more sensitive to the scheduling policy.

In spite of the above mentioned measurements, queue-length samples have also been exploited for demand estimation. The study in [35] uses Gibbs sampling and Bayesian estimation methods to obtain service demands. The method also allows for prior information in the estimation. However, it is computationally expensive, with running times often exceeds many tens of minutes or even hours. This makes the technique difficult to apply to online systems. The authors in [33] have also developed an algorithm based on Bayesian inference, which has been shown to be robust to missing data. A Ornstein-Uhlenbeck diffusion is used for demand estimation in [29] also using queue-length samples. Compared to the present work, the methods in [33] and [29] are limited to open models, whereas we focus here on closed models.

Finally, the above mentioned techniques do not provide confidence interval for the estimates. The work in [12] proposes an approach to estimate resource demand with confidence through linear programming. Nonetheless, it does not apply to load-dependent networks. The other work for obtaining confidence interval is introduced in [17]. However this method is limited to single-class models only and does not work for load-dependent networks.

3. REFERENCE MODEL

We consider product-form closed queueing networks, under the assumptions of the BCMP theorem [2]. Models have R job classes, M queues, a think time of θ_{0j} for job class j, a service demand θ_{ij} at queue i for class j, and a population of N_j jobs of class j. Indexes range in $1 \leq i, k \leq M, 1 \leq j, h \leq R$. When needed, we will explicit the dependence of the above metrics on the demand vector $\boldsymbol{\theta} = (\theta_{01}, \ldots, \theta_{MR})$.

Let n_{0j} be the total number of class j jobs in thinking state and let n_{ij} be the number of jobs of class j at station i. Define $n_i = \sum_{j=1}^{R} n_{ij}$ to be the total number of jobs at station i. Then the probability of observing state $\boldsymbol{n} = (n_{01}, \ldots, n_{0R}, n_{11}, \ldots, n_{1R}, \ldots, n_{MR})$ at equilibrium is known from the BCMP theorem to be

$$\mathbb{P}(\boldsymbol{n}|\boldsymbol{\theta}, \boldsymbol{\gamma}) = \left(\prod_{j=1}^{R} \frac{\theta_{0j}^{n_{0j}}}{n_{0j}!} \right) \prod_{i=1}^{M} n_i! \prod_{j=1}^{R} \frac{\theta_{ij}^{n_{ij}}}{n_{ij}! G(\boldsymbol{\theta})} \prod_{u=1}^{n_i} \gamma_i(u), \quad (1)$$

where $\gamma_i(u)$ is the load-dependent function that scales the demand for station i when its queue-length is u and $G(\boldsymbol{\theta})$ is the normalizing constant that assures $\sum_{\boldsymbol{n} \in \mathcal{S}} \mathbb{P}(\boldsymbol{n}|\boldsymbol{\theta}) = 1$, being $\mathcal{S} = \{\sum_{i=0}^{M} n_{ij} = N_j, n_{ij} \geq 0\}$ the state space. The case $\gamma_i(u) = 1, 1 \leq u \leq n_i$, in which each demand is independent of the station queue-length state, is referred to as the load-independent case. Class switching is a special case of BCMP queueing networks [2], but we do not consider it in this paper and leave it for future work.

In order to perform a demand estimation, let us consider independent state samples $\boldsymbol{n}^l \in \boldsymbol{D}$, being $\boldsymbol{D}$ a dataset of empirical observations of L vectors $\boldsymbol{n}^l$. The problem of estimating the true demands $\boldsymbol{\theta}$ and scaling factors $\boldsymbol{\gamma} = (\gamma_i(u))$ may be solved by considering a maximum likelihood (ML) estimator

$$(\hat{\boldsymbol{\theta}}, \hat{\boldsymbol{\gamma}}) = \arg \max_{(\boldsymbol{\theta}, \boldsymbol{\gamma}) \in \boldsymbol{\Theta}} \mathcal{L}(\boldsymbol{\theta}) = \arg \max_{(\boldsymbol{\theta}, \boldsymbol{\gamma}) \in \boldsymbol{\Theta}} \prod_{l=1}^{L} \mathbb{P}(\boldsymbol{n}^l|\boldsymbol{\theta}, \boldsymbol{\gamma}) \quad (2)$$

where $\mathcal{L}(\cdot)$ is the likelihood function, $\mathbb{P}(\cdot|\boldsymbol{\theta}, \boldsymbol{\gamma})$ is defined as in (1), and $\boldsymbol{\Theta}$ is the parameter space composed by the candidate demands $\boldsymbol{\theta}$ and scaling factors $\boldsymbol{\gamma}$. We have also observed in real web traces that the assumption of independence of state samples is typically acceptable for estimation purposes, with the autocorrelation function of samples quickly decreasing as the time spacing between samples increases.

4. MOTIVATING EXAMPLE

In this section, we provide a motivating example that compares properties of three state-of-the-art demand estimation algorithms and illustrates their limitations. We consider utilization-based regression (UBR) (e.g., [38]), Gibbs Sampling for Queue Lengths (GQL) [35] and Extended Regression for Processor Sharing (ERPS) [24]. UBR is based on multivariate linear regression of CPU utilization against request throughput. GQL combines Bayesian estimation and Gibbs sampling to obtain service demands from queue length data. GQL is an iterative algorithm along each dimension of the demand vector and thus computationally expensive. ERPS is a regression-based method that relies on response time and arrival queue length measurements as input for the analysis.

We generate random queueing models with $M = 2$ queues and $R = 4$ classes of requests and assume that the total

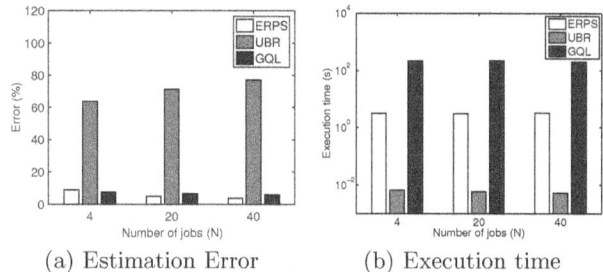

(a) Estimation Error (b) Execution time

Figure 1: Various estimation methods

number of users N varies in $\{4, 20, 40\}$. We generate 80 submodels by randomly choosing N_j and θ_{ij}. The think time is assumed to be known and it is set in all random models to $\theta_{0j} = 1, \forall j$. All service processes are load independent. The required data for each algorithm is generated via simulation using the methodology described later in Section 7. $500,000$ service completions are simulated and the results collected.

Figure 1 illustrates the mean relative absolute error and the execution time for the above algorithms. It can be noticed that UBR shows a bad estimation accuracy, likely due to problems such as multicollinearity, which lead to degraded results. Figure 1(a) instead shows that GQL and ERPS achieve good accuracy, but Figure 1(b) reveals that the execution time of GQL is fairly large and probably unacceptable for online use. ERPS performs well considering both the accuracy and execution time, nonetheless it requires response time data, which assumes the ability to track the state of individual requests, which may not be possible at server-side without introducing substantial overheads (e.g., instrumentation of worker threads at milli-second or microsecond timescales). Besides, none of the above algorithms offers confidence intervals to characterize the quality of the generated estimates. In a real system study, when the exact demands are unknown, such confidence intervals can provide guidance on the reliability of the inferred demand values and the associated predictions.

5. LOAD-INDEPENDENT NETWORKS

In this section, we focus on demand estimation for load-independent models, thus we ignore scaling factors since $\gamma_i(u) = 1, \forall i, u$ and focus on deriving estimators for the service demand vector $\boldsymbol{\theta}$. In addition, we derive the analytical expressions of the confidence intervals for the $\boldsymbol{\theta}$ estimates. Finally, we introduce a closed-form approximate formula that simplifies the task of obtaining an approximate, but accurate, estimate.

5.1 Necessary conditions

We begin with assuming that the parameter space $\boldsymbol{\Theta}$ is a compact set and that the think time θ_{0j} are known and strictly positive. Under the above conditions, it is simple to show that the likelihood function is continuous and that a ML estimator exists [23]. We also assume that $\boldsymbol{\Theta}$ is large enough for the true demand $\boldsymbol{\theta}^*$ to be an interior point of this set. A consequence of this assumption is that our results do not cover the estimation of demands with true value $\theta_{ij}^* = 0$. This is equivalent to say that we assume a-priori knowledge of what classes of jobs can visit a given resource, which seems a realistic assumption in many practical situations.

Under the above assumptions, we can give the following characterization of the ML estimator in (2).

THEOREM 1. *Given a dataset $\boldsymbol{D}$, a necessary condition for an interior point of Θ to be an ML estimator $\hat{\boldsymbol{\theta}}$ of the service demand is that*

$$Q_{ij}(\hat{\boldsymbol{\theta}}) = \widetilde{Q}_{ij}(\boldsymbol{D}), \qquad \forall i, j,$$

where $\widetilde{Q}_{ij}(\boldsymbol{D}) = \sum_{l=1}^{L} n_{ij}^l / L$ are the empirical mean queue-lengths calculated over the dataset $\boldsymbol{D}$.

The proof of this theorem and the following ones are given in the Appendix. Note that the predicted mean queue lengths $Q_{ij}(\hat{\boldsymbol{\theta}})$ can be computed, for example, using the MVA algorithm [2].

The main contribution of Theorem 1 is to provide theoretical support to the idea that the estimation of demands in load-independent models may be simply performed by matching theoretical predictions of mean queue-lengths to the observed mean values in the real system, without need for correction terms. Furthermore, it states the less obvious fact that the demand estimation depends only on the *mean* queue-length, even though the maximum-likelihood function is probabilistic in nature. That is, if one can find a vector $\boldsymbol{\theta}$ that generates by the MVA algorithm mean queue-length predictions that are identical to the observed values, then this vector will satisfy the necessary condition to be a ML estimator. Clearly, even if Theorem 1 does not prove $\hat{\boldsymbol{\theta}}$ to be the ML estimator, the condition of the theorem ensures that $\hat{\boldsymbol{\theta}}$ will achieve correct performance predictions that reproduce the training data. Hence, while in principle several vectors $\boldsymbol{\theta}$ may satisfy the same necessary condition, any of these will be a suitable choice for reproducing the observations.

The main requirement for Theorem 1 to be a sufficient condition is the availability of results that prove that a given set of queue-length values $Q_{ij}(\boldsymbol{\theta})$ can be obtained by a unique vector $\boldsymbol{\theta}$. This appears intuitive, but we are not aware of any such formal characterization in the literature of product-form models, presumably due to the complex non-linear nature of the MVA equations. Therefore, in order to support a deeper analysis of the demand vectors obtained from (1), we derive the expression of the Hessian matrix for the underpinning closed queueing network that can be used to verify that a candidate vector is indeed a local maximum for (2).

THEOREM 2. *The Hessian matrix of $\mathcal{L}(\hat{\boldsymbol{\theta}})$ at $\hat{\boldsymbol{\theta}}$ is a $MR \times MR$ matrix with elements*

$$\boldsymbol{H}(\hat{\boldsymbol{\theta}})_{ij,kh} = \begin{cases} \frac{L}{\hat{\theta}_{ij}^2}(Q_{kh}(\hat{\boldsymbol{\theta}})(Q_{kh}(\hat{\boldsymbol{\theta}}) - Q_{kh}^{+i}(\hat{\boldsymbol{\theta}}, \boldsymbol{N} - \boldsymbol{1}_j)) - \widetilde{Q}_{kh}), & i = k, j = h \\ \frac{L Q_{ij}(\hat{\boldsymbol{\theta}})}{\hat{\theta}_{ij}\hat{\theta}_{kh}}(Q_{kh}(\hat{\boldsymbol{\theta}}) - Q_{kh}^{+i}(\hat{\boldsymbol{\theta}}, \boldsymbol{N} - \boldsymbol{1}_j)), & otherwise \end{cases}$$

where $\boldsymbol{N} = (N_1, \ldots, N_R)$, L is the total number of samples, and $Q_{kh}^{+i}(\hat{\boldsymbol{\theta}}, \boldsymbol{N} - \boldsymbol{1}_j)$ is the mean queue length in a model obtained by adding an identical replica of queue i to the closed network under study and removing a job of class j from it.

With the Hessian matrix at $\hat{\boldsymbol{\theta}}$, we can easily check if the generated estimate is a local minimum, a local maximum or a saddle point. In particular, if $\boldsymbol{H}(\hat{\boldsymbol{\theta}})$ is invertible and $\boldsymbol{H}(\hat{\boldsymbol{\theta}})$ is positive definite, i.e. all eigenvalues are positive, then $\hat{\boldsymbol{\theta}}$ is a local minimum. If $\boldsymbol{H}(\hat{\boldsymbol{\theta}})$ is negative definite, i.e. all eigenvalues are negative, then $\hat{\boldsymbol{\theta}}$ is a point of local maximum and therefore a local maximum likelihood estimator.

We also remark that Theorem 1 does not specify how one can find the demand vector $\hat{\boldsymbol{\theta}}$, since the expression of $\hat{\boldsymbol{\theta}}$ is given there in implicit form. An explicit approximation for $\hat{\boldsymbol{\theta}}$ is developed later in Section 5.3.

5.2 Exact confidence intervals

In this section, we assume that the vector $\hat{\boldsymbol{\theta}}$ has been obtained and we give a characterization of the resulting confidence intervals. As shown in the proof of the next theorem, this result follows from the fact that we have found that the Fisher information matrix $\boldsymbol{I}$ can be explicitly computed for a closed queueing network, since this is simply the negative Hessian matrix at $\hat{\boldsymbol{\theta}}$. For the confidence interval, we assume the critical value c is given, which determines the confidence level (e.g. $c = 1.96$ means 95% confidence).

COROLLARY 1. *Assume that $\hat{\boldsymbol{\theta}}$ satisfies the standard regularity conditions for asymptotic normality. The confidence interval for the ML estimator is then given by*

$$\hat{\theta}_{ij} \pm c \sqrt{(\boldsymbol{I}(\hat{\boldsymbol{\theta}})^{-1})_{ij,ij}}$$

where $\boldsymbol{I}(\hat{\boldsymbol{\theta}})$ is the negative Hessian matrix, i.e. $\boldsymbol{I}(\hat{\boldsymbol{\theta}}) = -\boldsymbol{H}(\hat{\boldsymbol{\theta}})$.

The above expression for the confidence intervals can assist in evaluating the ML estimation accuracy. The main result is that, similarly to the ML estimator, also confidence intervals can be computed using the standard MVA algorithm, since this involves evaluating models where some queues are replicated, i.e., where we add new stations having identical demands. As we show later in this paper, the situation is more complex in load-dependent models.

5.3 Approximate Closed-Form Expression

We now turn our attention to obtaining numerically an estimator $\hat{\boldsymbol{\theta}}$ that satisfies the necessary conditions of Theorem 1. One simple possibility is to apply search method such as numerical optimization and fixed point iteration to find a vector $\hat{\boldsymbol{\theta}}$ that matches the empirical mean queue-lengths. However, this turns out to be expensive in the case of numerical optimization. Moreover, we were unable to find fixed point iteration schemes that were converging on all instances.

To cope with the above problems, we develop in this section an accurate approximation of $\hat{\boldsymbol{\theta}}$ using the Bard-Schweitzer (BS) approximation [1, 30]. Our idea is to relax the necessary condition of the theorem by requiring that the queue-length $Q_{ij}(\hat{\boldsymbol{\theta}})$ is computed not by exact methods, but by the BS approximate mean-value analysis, which leads to a simple analytical form for $Q_{ij}(\hat{\boldsymbol{\theta}})$. Such approximation is fairly accurate for multiclass models, except in some contrived examples, and therefore the error of the approximation of the necessary condition is quite limited.

THEOREM 3. *Assume $\sum_{k=1}^{M} \widetilde{Q}_{kj} \neq N_j$, $\forall j$. Let $\boldsymbol{\theta}^{bs}$ be an interior point of Θ and $Q_{ij}^{bs}(\boldsymbol{\theta}^{bs}) = \widetilde{Q}_{ij}(\boldsymbol{D})$, where $Q_{ij}^{bs}(\cdot)$ is the Bard-Schweitzer approximation of $Q_{ij}(\cdot)$. Then*

$$\theta_{ij}^{bs} = \frac{\widetilde{Q}_{ij}(\boldsymbol{D})}{(N_j - \sum_{k=1}^{M} \widetilde{Q}_{kj}(\boldsymbol{D}))} \frac{\theta_{0,j}}{(1 + \sum_{h=1}^{R} \widetilde{Q}_{ih}(\boldsymbol{D}) - \widetilde{Q}_{ij}(\boldsymbol{D})/N_j)} \quad (3)$$

It can be noted that Theorem 3 is a closed-formula that can be readily computed using the empirical mean queue lengths. This makes it suitable for online use. For ease of reference, we refer to the demand vector $\boldsymbol{\theta}$ obtained with (3) as the *QMLE* demand estimator.

6. LOAD-DEPENDENT NETWORK

In this section, we illustrate how the previous results generalize to the load-dependent case. Here the problem is more complex since one needs to estimate not just the demands θ_{ij}, but also the scaling factors $\gamma_i(u)$, which together define the mean demand $\theta_{ij}(u) = \theta_{ij}\gamma_i(u)$ for station i when it has u enqueued jobs. Recall that we have denoted by $\boldsymbol{\gamma}$ the vector that includes the scaling factors $\gamma_i(u)$, $\forall i, u$. Here we present the ML estimates for the service demand vector $\boldsymbol{\theta}$ as well as for the scaling function $\boldsymbol{\gamma}$. We then introduce a technique to identify the initial points that help in efficiently searching for the optimal estimates.

6.1 Necessary conditions

We take similar assumptions for the parameters set as for the load-independent case, with the main difference being that the scaling factors $\gamma_i(u)$ are unknown. We assume these terms $\gamma_i(u)$ to be bounded and, without loss of generality, we take $\gamma_i(1) = 1$ so that $\theta_{ij}(1) = \theta_{ij}$. These conditions guarantee existence of the estimators [21].

THEOREM 4. *Given a dataset $\boldsymbol{D}$, a necessary condition for a point $\hat{\boldsymbol{\chi}} = (\hat{\boldsymbol{\theta}}, \hat{\boldsymbol{\gamma}})$ in the interior point of $\boldsymbol{\Theta}$ to be a ML estimator of demands and scaling factors is that*

$$Q_{ij}(\hat{\boldsymbol{\chi}}) = \widetilde{Q}_{ij}(\boldsymbol{D}), \qquad \forall i, j,$$

and

$$\mathbb{P}(n_k = v | \hat{\boldsymbol{\chi}}) = \mathbb{P}(\widetilde{n}_k = v | \boldsymbol{D}), \qquad \forall k, v$$

where $\mathbb{P}(\widetilde{n}_k = v | \boldsymbol{D})$ are the empirical marginal queue length probabilities obtained from the dataset $\boldsymbol{D}$.

The Hessian matrix for the load-dependent case is generalized as follows.

THEOREM 5. *The Hessian matrix of $\mathcal{L}(\hat{\boldsymbol{\chi}})$ at the ML estimates $\hat{\boldsymbol{\chi}}$ is given as*

$$H(\hat{\boldsymbol{\chi}})_{ij,i'j'} = \begin{cases} \frac{L}{\hat{\theta}_{ij}^2}(Q_{ij}(\hat{\boldsymbol{\chi}})^2 - E[n_{ij}^2|\hat{\boldsymbol{\chi}}] + Q_{ij}(\hat{\boldsymbol{\chi}}) - \widetilde{Q}_{ij}(\boldsymbol{D})) & \text{if } i=i', j=j' \\ \frac{L(Q_{ij}(\hat{\boldsymbol{\chi}})Q_{i'j'}(\hat{\boldsymbol{\chi}}) - E[n_{ij}n_{i'j'}|\hat{\boldsymbol{\chi}}])}{\hat{\theta}_{ij}\hat{\theta}_{i'j'}} & \text{otherwise} \end{cases}$$

$$H(\hat{\boldsymbol{\chi}})_{ij,kv} = L\frac{Q_{ij}(\hat{\boldsymbol{\chi}})\mathbb{P}(n_k \geq v|\hat{\boldsymbol{\chi}}) - E[n_{ij}|\hat{\boldsymbol{\chi}}, n_k \geq v]}{\hat{\theta}_{ij}\hat{\gamma}_k(v)}$$

$$H(\hat{\boldsymbol{\chi}})_{kv,k'v'} = \begin{cases} L\frac{\mathbb{P}(n_k \geq v|\hat{\boldsymbol{\chi}})^2 - \mathbb{P}(\widetilde{n}_k \geq v|\boldsymbol{D})}{\hat{\gamma}_k(v)^2} & \text{if } k=k', v=v' \\ \frac{L(\mathbb{P}(n_k \geq v|\hat{\boldsymbol{\chi}})\mathbb{P}(n_{k'} \geq v'|\hat{\boldsymbol{\chi}}) - \mathbb{P}(n_k \geq v, n_{k'} \geq v'|\hat{\boldsymbol{\chi}}))}{\hat{\gamma}_k(v)\hat{\gamma}_{k'}(v')} & \text{otherwise} \end{cases}$$

The result is qualitatively similar to the one in Theorem 1, and analogous considerations apply. An optimization program can be formulated by minimizing the difference between theoretical and the observed mean queue lengths and marginal probabilities. In particular, the load-dependent MVA algorithm [2] can be used in an optimization program to find vectors $\hat{\boldsymbol{\theta}}$ and $\hat{\boldsymbol{\gamma}}$ that satisfy the mean queue-length necessary condition of Theorem 4. However, load-dependent MVA is known to be computationally expensive as the model size grows, having $O(MRN \prod_{r=1}^{R} N_r)$ time and $O(MN\sqrt{\prod_{r=1}^{R} N_r})$ storage requirements [3], being N the

total population in the model and R the number of classes. Therefore, these methods experience early memory bottlenecks when the model size grows. This means that even for small models with a few queues, load-dependent MVA is difficult to use in an optimization program due to its large computational requirements. Moreover, efficient computation of the marginal probability $\mathbb{P}(\widetilde{n}_k \geq v | \boldsymbol{D})$ is also required by Theorem 4. To alleviate this computational bottleneck, we define a method to locate a good initial point for the optimization program.

Similar as the discussion in Section 5.2, we are able to use the above expression to determine if the generated estimates are local maximum or not. The confidence interval of load-dependent network can be characterized in the same way as in Corollary 1. Differently from the load-independent case, computing confidence intervals here requires to obtain the second-order moments of marginal queue-length, i.e., the terms $E[n_{ij}n_{i'j'}|\hat{\boldsymbol{\chi}}]$, for determining the Hessian matrix. This assumes the availability of efficient computational algorithms for such moments, which yet do not exist in the load-dependent setting. Moreover, marginal probability and mean queue-length is also required to compute the confidence intervals. Therefore, without specialized algorithms, the applicability of confidence intervals will be limited to models with a small or a medium-sized population, where these moments can be obtained by direct computation over the state space. It is therefore an interesting line of future research in closed queueing networks to develop efficient algorithms that can determine such joint moments.

6.2 Initialization heuristic

As introduced in Section 6.1, an optimization program can be formulated to obtain the ML estimates from Theorem 4. However, the heavy computational requirement of MVA restricts its application to large models. Therefore, here we develop an algorithm to alleviate this problem by identifying a good initial point for the optimization program.

Noticing that the structure of (1) allows us to apply logarithms, we write

$$\log(\mathbb{P}(\boldsymbol{n}|\boldsymbol{\theta}, \boldsymbol{\gamma})) = \sum_{i=1}^{M} \sum_{j=1}^{R} n_{ij} \log(\theta_{ij}) + \sum_{u=1}^{n_i} \log(\gamma_i(u))$$
$$- \log(G(\boldsymbol{\theta})) + \sum_{j=1}^{R} n_{0j} \log(\theta_{0j}) \qquad (4)$$
$$+ \sum_{i=1}^{M} \log(n_i!) - \sum_{i=0}^{M} \sum_{j=1}^{R} \log(n_{ij}!)$$

For each observed state $\widetilde{\boldsymbol{n}} \in S'$, where S' is the observed state space, we can rewrite (4) as

$$\log(\mathbb{P}(\widetilde{\boldsymbol{n}}|\boldsymbol{D})) = \sum_{i=1}^{M} \sum_{j=1}^{R} \widetilde{n}_{ij} \log(\theta_{ij}) + \sum_{u=1}^{\widetilde{n}_i} \log(\gamma_i(u)) \qquad (5)$$
$$- \log(G(\boldsymbol{\theta})) + I$$

where I is constant and $I = \sum_{j=1}^{R} \widetilde{n}_{0j} \log(\theta_{0j}) + \sum_{i=1}^{M} \log(\widetilde{n}_i!) - \sum_{i=0}^{M} \sum_{j=1}^{R} \log(\widetilde{n}_{ij}!)$.

It is now possible to observe that by treating $\log(\mathbb{P}(\widetilde{\boldsymbol{n}}|\boldsymbol{D}))$ as response variable and $\log(\boldsymbol{\theta})$, $\log(\boldsymbol{\gamma})$ and the normalizing constant $\log(G(\boldsymbol{\theta}))$ as unknown variables, we can easily solve (5) as a multivariate linear regression. This therefore provides an initial guess for the demands $\boldsymbol{\theta}$ and scaling factors $\boldsymbol{\gamma}$, without the need for computing the most expensive term, i.e., the normalizing constant $G(\boldsymbol{\theta})$. The above approach can therefore assist in the optimization program in identifying a suitable initial point in negligible computational time. As we show later in the validation, this initial point substantially improves the optimization compared to the use of a random initial point.

7. NUMERICAL VALIDATION

We now present the validation methodology for evaluating the proposed algorithms. We have evaluated the algorithms using randomly generated queueing models. Service completions data are simulated from the underlying Markov Chain of a closed network, which is described in [2]. From these data, we have generated typical monitoring measurements such as response time, CPU utilization, throughput and queue-length samples. In particular, to obtain queue-length samples, we have first computed the steady state probability from the simulation events. Then we have sampled from it by generating random numbers between 0 and 1 and determining which sample fits in the cumulative probability. This is also known as the inverse transform sampling.

Our experiments have been run on a desktop machine with an Intel Core i7-2600 CPU, running at 3.4GHz with 16 GB of memory. We use the mean absolute percentage error as the evaluation criteria.

7.1 Load-independent network

7.1.1 QMLE evaluation

We begin with evaluating the proposed algorithm for load-independent network. For comparison, we have also implemented several other demand estimation algorithms. They are CI [24], UBR [38], GQL [35] and ERPS [24]. UBR, ERPS and GQL have been already introduced in Section 4. CI requires the complete sample path of the requests for analysis. The input data for these algorithms is generated from the same simulation events as of the queue-length samples. 500,000 service completions are simulated.

The parameters for the random models are $M \in \{2, 4, 8\}$, $R \in \{2, 3, 4\}$, $K = \sum_j N_j \in \{4, 20, 40\}$, $\theta_{0j} \in \{1, 5, 10\}$. For each generated model, 80 sub-models are defined by randomly generating N_j and θ_{ij} from the uniform distribution. Without loss of generality, demands are normalized so that $\sum_{j=1}^{R} \theta_{ij} = 1$. Here, we limit to assess the QMLE estimator in Theorem 3 since it is much more practical to compute than the exact one in Theorem 1.

Figure 2 presents a sensitivity analysis of the considered algorithms. The result of UBR is not included since the error is around 100% due to multicollinearity. From the figure, it can be noticed that CI is the most accurate method since it relies on the knowledge of the complete sample path. However, this method cannot be applied in production systems, where only sample measurements are available. The error of QMLE and GQL is almost the same, around 5%, which shows the effectiveness of QMLE since GQL is defined using a much more complex algorithm featuring Gibbs sampling and iterative approximation of the normalising constant $G(\boldsymbol{\theta})$. ERPS is worse in terms of accuracy, but generally still quite accurate. As expected, the accuracy of QMLE and GQL increases as the number of observed queue-length samples increases. However, with only 500 queue-length

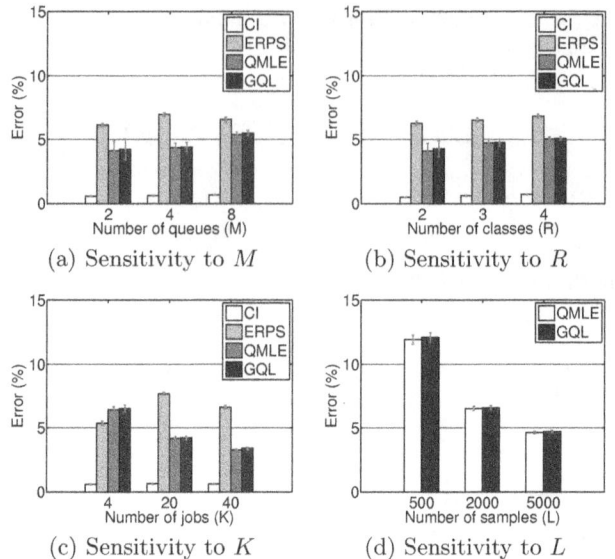

(a) Sensitivity to M (b) Sensitivity to R

(c) Sensitivity to K (d) Sensitivity to L

Figure 2: Sensitivity analysis of the estimators

samples QMLE already achieves a small 10% error.

Figure 3(a) shows the execution time of each method. Clearly the proposed QMLE is orders magnitude better than the other algorithms with average 0.0002 second against 1400 (CI), 3 (ERPS) and 148 (GQL) seconds.

7.1.2 Confidence Interval validation

Validation on the confidence interval requires computing the maximum likelihood estimates of the service demand $\hat{\boldsymbol{\theta}}$. For this purpose, we have implemented a fixed point iteration method based on Theorem 1 to estimate $\hat{\boldsymbol{\theta}}$. The test is based on a queueing model with $M = 2, R = 3, K = 4$. Each test consists of H experiments with a queue-length dataset $\boldsymbol{D}$ of $L = \{500, 2000, 5000\}$ entries generated from the same model. Each experiment has a different queue-length dataset which is generated from the same simulation events. We use 95% confidence intervals.

Figure 3(b) shows the confidence interval validation result. H is set to $\{100, 500, 1000\}$. The vertical axis shows the percentage of the cases that the exact demand lies in the confidence interval of the estimated demand. For different L and H, results suggest that the confidence interval is correct.

7.2 Load-dependent network

7.2.1 Exact analysis

For the evaluation of load-dependent queueing networks, we have used the MATLAB *fmincon* solver to estimate $\hat{\boldsymbol{\theta}}$ and $\hat{\gamma}_i(t)$ based on Theorem 4. We consider the following scaling factors $\gamma_i(t)$: $\gamma_i(t) = 1/t$ and $\gamma_i(t) = 1/\min(t, C_i)$, where C_i is the number of CPUs at queueing node i. These two represent the most typical load-dependent scenarios, e.g. think time and multi-core feature of servers.

The random models generated here consider $M = 2$ queues, $R = 2$ classes, $K = 8$ jobs, think time $\theta_{0j} \in \{1, 5, 10\}$ and $C_i \in \{2, 3, 4\}$. This is a very small model, but we are limited in scalability by the cost of load-dependent MVA. We generate 8 sub-models considering the high computational cost and randomly generate the number of jobs and the demands

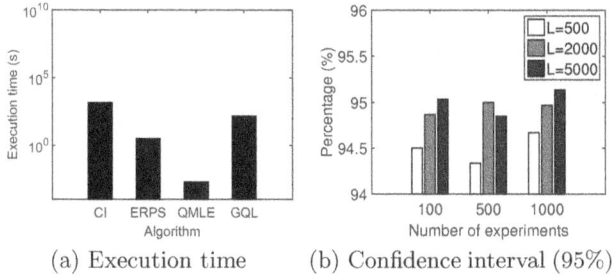

(a) Execution time   (b) Confidence interval (95%)

Figure 3: Execution time and confidence interval validation

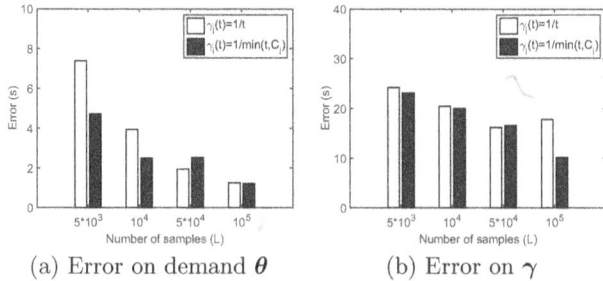

(a) Error on demand θ (b) Error on γ

Figure 4: Load-dependent experiment result

using a uniform distribution. Figure 4 shows the result for different scaling factors. It is easy to observe that the error drops as the number of observed queue-length samples L increases since the average queue-length and marginal probability becomes more accurate. Given $L = 5000$ samples the error for the demands is already below 10% and the error on scaling factors around 20%.

7.2.2 Confidence interval validation

We here present the confidence interval validation based on Section 6.1. The exact demand is computed in the same way as in the previous section. The test is based on a queueing model with $M = 2$ queues, $R = 2$ classes, $K = 4$ jobs. We explicitly consider the multi-core load-dependent behavior here with $C_i = 2$. Each test consists of H experiments with a queue length dataset D of $L = \{2000, 5000, 10000\}$ entries generated from the same model. We use 95% confidence intervals. The result is presented in Figure 5. Clearly, it shows the computed confidence interval is correct given the estimates for different L and H.

7.2.3 Initial value determination

Here, we present the evaluation for the proposed method

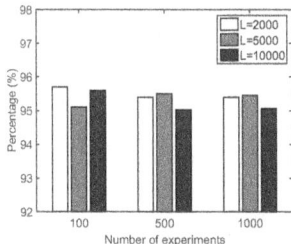

Figure 5: Confidence interval validation (95%)

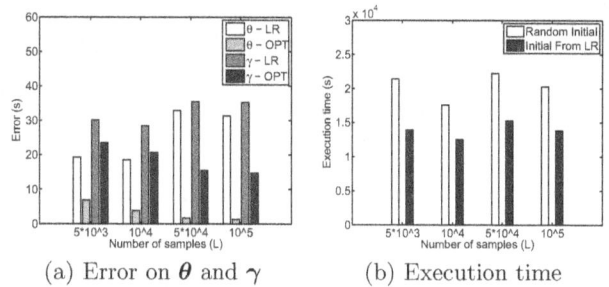

(a) Error on θ and γ (b) Execution time

Figure 6: Error and execution time with initial points

in Section 6.2 to determine the initial point for the optimization program and the impact on the evaluation process.

The random queueing models are generated with $M = 2$, $R = 2$, $K = 4$, $C \in \{2, 3, 4\}$, $\theta_{0j} \in \{1, 5, 10\}$. 8 sub-models are generated. Figure 6 presents the evaluation result. In Figure 6(a), we demonstrate the error on the demands θ and γ comparing both the initial points (referred to as LR) and the estimates from the optimization program (referred to as OPT). Clearly the initial points already output very accurate estimates, which are useful to guide the optimization program. Figure 6(b) shows the execution time of the optimization program for using random initial points and the initial points returned from LR. It can be noticed the execution time drops significantly with the heuristic initials. We do not include the execution time of LR since it is based on linear regression and takes less than 0.1 second.

8. CASE STUDY

In this section, we present a case study based on a real application.

8.1 Experimental setting

The benchmarking application chosen is MyBatis JPet-Store[1], an open source version of Sun's J2EE pet store application. It is an e-commerce application that allows customers to login, browse pet categories, select pets and checkout payments. A single end-to-end transaction is considered, with customers visiting all the application pages sequentially. 5GB of data (2,000,000 items) for viewing and selection by customers is used in the testbed.

Two tiers of servers are used, with both the Web/Application and Database servers consisting of 4-core Intel Xeon E5620 CPUs with 8 GB of memory. The Grinder[2] open source testing framework is used for load injection, with each test lasting 10 minutes to eliminate transient values. The experiment setup is listed in Table 3, with Database server CPU utilization values listed corresponding to tested concurrency values. As bottlenecks are observed at the Database server CPU (maximum contribution to overall service demands), these metrics are used in the performance analysis (i.e., network, memory and disk effects are negligible).

8.2 Explaining observed performance

Considering that in real system the exact demand is unknown, we evaluate the proposed algorithm by comparing

---

[1]https://github.com/mybatis/jpetstore-6
[2]http://grinder.sourceforge.net/

Table 1: Performance prediction with same dataset where demands are estimated

Z(s)	Metric	LD-LR	BS				AMVA-QD			
			CI	ERPS	GQL	QMLE	CI	ERPS	GQL	QMLE
0.1	X	13.6	9.6	10.6	13.5	11.1	_2.3_	3.5	4.2	5.7
	Q	9.7	9.6	9.5	13.9	8.3	3.4	3.3	7.0	_2.2_
	CN	19.8	13.6	15.0	22.2	16.3	_1.6_	3.3	10.1	7.2
0.5	X	6.1	7.5	8.8	9.3	7.6	_3.9_	7.0	4.4	4.2
	Q	14.0	64.0	41.0	39.4	39.8	12.3	10.6	17.7	_10.6_
	XN	15.8	40.8	40.2	45.9	41.9	_8.3_	8.8	15.0	10.1
1	X	_3.6_	3.7	9.4	4.1	4.4	3.6	12.3	4.2	4.9
	Q	17.7	43.4	44.4	45.3	40.1	14.6	21.1	18.3	_14.4_
	CN	18.8	43.9	58.3	46.2	41.1	_12.0_	39.2	18.4	15.5
5	X	4.8	_2.3_	17.9	3.9	3.0	3.8	20.0	5.7	5.4
	Q	37.5	63.0	161.3	44.4	60.2	37.1	177.4	_12.0_	14.6
	CN	38.9	62.6	443.0	46.2	59.9	36.0	464.6	_14.2_	14.9
All	X	7.0	5.8	11.7	7.7	6.5	_3.4_	10.7	4.6	5.1
	Q	19.7	45.0	64.1	35.8	37.1	16.8	53.1	13.7	_10.4_
	CN	23.3	40.2	139.1	40.1	39.8	14.5	129.0	14.4	_11.9_

Table 3: Experiment setup with Think Time, Concurrency and Database server CPU Utilization.

Think time	Number of jobs	CPU Utilization
0.1s	$\{1, 3, 5, 10, 15\}$	$\{0.12, 0.38, 0.58, 0.90, 0.95\}$
0.5s	$\{1, 3, 5, 10, 20\}$	$\{0.03, 0.14, 0.23, 0.44, 0.79, 0.93\}$
1s	$\{1, 2, 5, 10, 20, 40\}$	$\{0.04, 0.06, 0.14, 0.26, 0.51, 0.88\}$
5s	$\{1, 10, 20, 40\}$	$\{0.01, 0.06, 0.12, 0.22\}$

the observed performance metrics and the theoretical ones computed with the estimated demands. Here, the algorithms considered are the proposed linear regression method for determining the initial values, which is referred as *LD-LR*, as well as the QMLE approach. The load-independent algorithms introduced in Section 7.1 are also included.

The performance metrics considered here are average throughput (X), average queue length (Q) and average response time (CN). To produce these metrics, we consider using both the Bard-Schweitzer (BS) approximation, which we already used in Section 5.3 and the recently proposed AMVA-QD method, which is an approximate algorithm for mean performance metrics in load-dependent models [5]. For the previous case, we scale the demands by the minimum of the number of jobs and number of CPUs to approximate the multi-core behavior of the server. For the latter case, we explicitly use the *softmin* function, which is defined as

$$\gamma_i(u) = \frac{u e^{\alpha u} + C_i e^{\alpha C_i}}{e^{\alpha u} + e^{\alpha C_i}} u$$

This is an approximation of the multi-core function and converges to the exact value as $\alpha \to -\infty$. We set α to be $\alpha = -10$ throughout the experiment. For load-independent demand estimation algorithms, we assume the number of CPUs is given. For *LD-LR*, we use the Piecewise Cubic Hermite interpolation method [10] to fit the estimated γ and then use AMVA-QD to estimate the performance.

Table 1 presents the analysis result. From the table, it can first be noticed that evaluation with AMVA-QD returns much accurate result than using AMVA-BS for all the algorithms. In addition, compared to CI and GQL, QMLE outputs stable and accurate performance for all different kind of models. Finally, the linear regression method produces

accurate result as well except the case with $Z = 5$, which is caused by the large K in that experiment. Considering that this method does not have a-priori knowledge of how many cores the server has, the finding is more significant than the others.

8.3 Performance prediction

Here we study another common problem which is to predict the performance of the application using benchmarked dataset. In particular, the demand is first estimated for the benchmarked dataset, then it is used to predict the performance for a number of requests that is different from the one used for demand fitting. For ease of comparison, we assume the think time is the same as the one of the experiment on which the demand was fitted.

Evaluation results are given in Table 2 focusing on the case $Z = 0.1s$. For each dataset, we first estimate the demands and predict the performance for $K \in \{1, 3, 5, 10, 15\}$ and obtain the average error. We limit our study to load-independent algorithms only for demand estimation since it is unfair to use methods such as the *LD-LR* to predict the performance considering for small K there is not enough information on γ. From the table, in general algorithms with AMVA-QD performs much better than the ones with AMVA-BS method. The proposed QMLE method with AMVA-QD is able to predict the performance with less than 9% error.

9. CONCLUSION

In this paper, we have proposed a class of maximum likelihood estimator for resource demand in closed queueing networks with both load-independent and load-dependent service. After identifying necessary conditions for an estimator to be a maximizer of the likelihood function, we derived explicit and tractable expressions for the confidence interval of the estimates. For load-independent models, a closed form formula has been presented for demand estimation, which allows to obtain good estimates very quickly. Moreover, a heuristic method is proposed to accelerate searching for the estimates in load-dependent networks. Finally, evaluation based on simulation data and traces of a multi-tier applica-

Table 2: Performance prediction with different datasets

K	Metric	BS				AMVA-QD			
		CI	ERPS	GQL	QMLE	CI	ERPS	GQL	QMLE
1	X	18.5	18.5	37.6	13.2	8.2	8.2	25.2	3.7
	Q	15.5	15.5	27.1	11.9	7.9	7.9	18.1	5.0
	CN	25.0	25.0	45.0	19.7	13.1	13.1	33.9	7.7
3	X	14.1	14.2	13.1	15.2	6.7	6.9	3.7	5.4
	Q	10.0	10.0	11.6	13.0	3.7	3.7	4.8	5.8
	CN	21.2	21.4	19.1	21.9	9.1	9.6	7.1	9.9
5	X	14.4	14.5	13.6	14.2	7.8	8.0	4.1	6.9
	Q	9.9	9.9	12.2	10.0	3.8	3.8	5.2	3.7
	CN	22.3	22.5	20.3	21.4	11.2	11.7	8.3	9.6
10	X	13.3	14.2	13.2	13.7	4.1	7.0	3.7	5.3
	Q	11.2	10.0	11.9	10.4	4.4	3.7	4.9	3.8
	CN	18.9	21.5	19.6	19.9	6.9	9.7	7.6	7.8
15	X	13.1	13.1	13.6	13.8	3.8	3.8	4.8	5.6
	Q	11.6	11.6	10.7	10.3	4.7	4.7	4.1	3.8
	CN	18.9	21.5	19.6	19.9	7.1	7.1	7.4	8.1
All	X	14.7	14.9	18.2	14.0	6.1	6.8	8.3	5.4
	Q	11.7	11.4	14.7	11.1	4.9	4.8	7.4	4.4
	CN	21.3	22.4	24.7	20.6	9.5	10.2	12.9	8.6

tion demonstrate the applicability of the proposed methods to demand estimation in real software systems.

Acknowledgment

The research of Weikun Wang was supported by the European Union under grant agreements FP7-318484 (MODA-Clouds) and H2020-644869 (DICE). Giuliano Casale was supported by the EPSRC grant EP/M009211/1 (OptiMAM). The data used in this paper is available at http://dx.doi.org/10.5281/zenodo.35321.

10. REFERENCES

[1] Y. Bard. Some extensions to multiclass queueing network analysis. In *Proc. of SPECTS*, pages 51–62. 1979.

[2] G. Bolch, S. Greiner, H. de Meer, and K. S Trivedi. *Queueing networks and Markov chains: modeling and performance evaluation with computer science applications.* John Wiley & Sons, 2006.

[3] S. Bruell, G. Balbo and PV. Afshari. Mean value analysis of mixed, multiple class BCMP networks with load dependent service stations. *Perf. Eval.*, 4(4):241–260, 1984.

[4] G. Casale, P. Cremonesi, and R. Turrin. Robust workload estimation in queueing network performance models. In *Proc. of IEEE PDP*, pages 183–187. 2008.

[5] G. Casale, J. F Pérez, and W. Wang. QD-AMVA: Evaluating systems with queue-dependent service requirements. *Perf. Eval.*, 91:80–98, 2015.

[6] P. Cremonesi, K. Dhyani, and A. Sansottera. Service time estimation with a refinement enhanced hybrid clustering algorithm. In *Proc. of ASMTA*, pages 291–305. Springer, 2010.

[7] P. Cremonesi and A. Sansottera. Indirect estimation of service demands in the presence of structural changes. *Perf. Eval.*, 73:18–40, 2014.

[8] E. De Souza e Silva and R. R Muntz. Simple relationships among moments of queue lengths in product form queueing networks. *IEEE TC*, 37(9):1125–1129, 1988.

[9] G. Franks, T. Al-Omari, M. Woodside, O. Das and S. Derisavi. Enhanced modeling and solution of layered queueing networks. *IEEE TSE*, 35(2):148–161, 2009.

[10] F. N Fritsch and R. E Carlson. Monotone piecewise cubic interpolation. *SIAM SINUM*, 17(2):238–246, 1980.

[11] D. Gmach, J. Rolia, L. Cherkasova, and A. Kemper. Workload analysis and demand prediction of enterprise data center applications. In *Proc. of IEEE IISWC*, pages 171–180. 2007.

[12] A. Kalbasi, D. Krishnamurthy, J. Rolia, and S. Dawson. Dec: Service demand estimation with confidence. *IEEE TSE*, 38(3):561-578, 2012.

[13] A. Kalbasi, D. Krishnamurthy, J. Rolia, and M. Richter. Mode: Mix driven on-line resource demand estimation. In *Proc. of IEEE CNSM*, pages 1–9. 2011.

[14] A. Khan, X. Yan, S. Tao, and N. Anerousis. Workload characterization and prediction in the cloud: A multiple time series approach. In *Proc. of IEEE NOMS*, pages 1287–1294. 2012.

[15] S. Kraft, S. Pacheco-Sanchez, G. Casale, and S. Dawson. Estimating service resource consumption from response time measurements. In *Proc. of ValueTools*, page 48. 2009.

[16] D. Kumar, L. Zhang, and A. Tantawi. Enhanced inferencing: Estimation of a workload dependent performance model. In *Proc. of ValueTools*, page 47. 2009.

[17] S. S. Lavenberg and G. S. Shedler. Derivation of confidence intervals for work rate estimators in a closed queuing network. *SIAM Journal on Computing*, 4(2):108–124, 1975.

[18] Z. Liu, L. Wynter, C. H Xia, and F. Zhang. Parameter

inference of queueing models for it systems using end-to-end measurements. *Perf. Eval.*, 63(1):36–60, 2006.

[19] D. A Menascé. Computing missing service demand parameters for performance models. In *Int. CMG Conference*, pages 241–248, 2008.

[20] D. A Menascé, V. AF Almeida, L. W Dowdy and L. Dowdy. *Performance by design: computer capacity planning by example*. Prentice Hall, 2004.

[21] I.J. Myung. Tutorial on maximum likelihood estimation. *JMP*, 47 (1):90–100, 2003.

[22] G. Pacifici, W. Segmuller, M. Spreitzer, and A. Tantawi. CPU demand for web serving: Measurement analysis and dynamic estimation. *Perf. Eval.*, 65(6):531–553, 2008.

[23] Y. Pawitan. *In all likelihood: statistical modelling and inference using likelihood*. Oxford University Press, 2001.

[24] J. F Perez, G. Casale, and S. Pacheco-Sanchez. Estimating computational requirements in multi-threaded applications. *IEEE TSE*, 41(3):264–278, 2015.

[25] M. Reiser and H. Kobayashi. On the convolution algorithm for separable queuing networks. In *Proc. of ACM SIGMETRICS*, pages 109–117. 1976.

[26] M. Reiser and S. S Lavenberg. Mean-value analysis of closed multichain queuing networks. *JACM*, 27(2):313–322, 1980.

[27] J. Rolia and V. Vetland. Parameter estimation for performance models of distributed application systems. In *Proc. of CASCON*, page 54. 1995.

[28] J. Rolia and V. Vetland. Correlating resource demand information with arm data for application services. In *Proc. of ACM WOSP*, pages 219–230. 1998.

[29] J. V Ross, T. Taimre, and P. K Pollett. Estimation for queues from queue length data. *Queueing Systems*, 55(2):131–138, 2007.

[30] P. J. Schweitzer. Approximate analysis of multiclass closed networks of queues. In *Proc. of Inter. Conf. on Stoc. Cont. and Opti.*, pages 25–29. 1979.

[31] A. B Sharma, R. Bhagwan, M. Choudhury, L. Golubchik, R. Govindan, and G. M Voelker. Automatic request categorization in internet services. *ACM SIGMETRICS PER*, 36(2):16–25, 2008.

[32] S. Spinner, G. Casale, F. Brosig, and S. Kounev. Evaluating Approaches to Resource Demand Estimation. *Perf. Eval.*, 92:51–71, 2015.

[33] C. Sutton and M. I Jordan. Bayesian inference for queueing networks and modeling of internet services. *The Annals of Applied Statistics*, pages 254–282, 2011.

[34] W. Wang, X. Huang, X. Qin, W. Zhang, J. Wei, and H. Zhong. Application-level cpu consumption estimation: Towards performance isolation of multi-tenancy web applications. In *Proc. of IEEE CLOUD*, pages 439–446. IEEE, 2012.

[35] W. Wang and G. Casale. Bayesian service demand estimation using Gibbs sampling. In *Proc. of IEEE MASCOTS*, pages 567–576. 2013.

[36] W. Wang and G. Casale. Maximum likelihood estimation of closed queueing network demands from queue length data. *ACM SIGMETRICS PER*,

43(2):45–47, 2015.

[37] X. Wu and M. Woodside. A calibration framework for capturing and calibrating software performance models. In *Computer Performance Engineering*, pages 32–47. Springer, 2008.

[38] Q. Zhang, L. Cherkasova, and E. Smirni. A regression-based analytic model for dynamic resource provisioning of multi-tier applications. In *Proc. of IEEE ICAC*, pages 27–27. 2007.

[39] T. Zheng, M. Woodside, and M. Litoiu. Performance model estimation and tracking using optimal filters. *IEEE TSE*, 34(3):391–406, 2008.

[40] T. Zheng, J. Yang, M. Woodside, M. Litoiu, and G. Iszlai. Tracking time-varying parameters in software systems with extended Kalman filters. In *Proc. of CASCON*, pages 334–345. IBM Press, 2005.

Appendix

Proof of Theorem 1

A sufficient condition for existence of a ML estimator is that the parameter space is compact and the likelihood function continuous. Observe that the parameter space is compact since $\boldsymbol{\theta}$ is assumed bounded. Since the normalising constant is continuous in $\boldsymbol{\theta}$ and $G(\mathbf{0}) \neq 0$ since $\theta_{0,j} > 0$, then $\mathcal{L}(\boldsymbol{\theta})$ is also continuous in $\boldsymbol{\theta}$.

Given existence, we now determine the ML estimator. Recall the following relationship proved in [8]

$$\frac{\partial G(\boldsymbol{\theta})}{\partial \theta_{ij}} = \frac{Q_{ij}(\boldsymbol{\theta})}{\theta_{ij}} G(\boldsymbol{\theta}) \qquad (6)$$

This allows us to take the first derivative of the likelihood function as follows

$$\begin{aligned} \frac{d\mathcal{L}(\boldsymbol{\theta})}{d\theta_{ij}} &= \frac{\partial}{\partial \theta_{ij}} \Big[\prod_{l=1}^{L} \frac{1}{G(\boldsymbol{\theta})} \prod_{i=1}^{M} n_i^l! \prod_{j=1}^{R} \frac{\theta_{ij}^{n_{ij}^l}}{n_{ij}^l!} \Big] \\ &= \sum_{l=1}^{L} \left(-\frac{Q_{ij}(\boldsymbol{\theta})}{\theta_{ij}} + \frac{n_{ij}^l}{\theta_{ij}} \right) \mathcal{L}(\boldsymbol{\theta}) \end{aligned} \qquad (7)$$

A stationarity point is then found at

$$-Q_{ij}(\boldsymbol{\theta})L + \sum_{l=1}^{L} n_{ij}^l = 0$$

which implies the condition $Q_{ij}(\hat{\boldsymbol{\theta}}) = \widetilde{Q}_{ij}$. This completes the proof. □

Proof of Theorem 2

Given the maximum likelihood estimator $\hat{\boldsymbol{\theta}}$, the Hessian matrix is defined as

$$\boldsymbol{H}(\boldsymbol{\theta})_{ij,kh} = \frac{\partial^2 \log \mathcal{L}(\boldsymbol{\theta})}{\partial \theta_{ij} \partial \theta_{kh}} \Big|_{\boldsymbol{\theta}=\hat{\boldsymbol{\theta}}} \qquad (8)$$

Using (7), the partial derivative of $\log \mathcal{L}(\boldsymbol{\theta})$ with respect to θ_{ij} is

$$\frac{\partial \log \mathcal{L}(\boldsymbol{\theta})}{\partial \theta_{ij}} = \frac{1}{\mathcal{L}(\boldsymbol{\theta})} \frac{\partial \mathcal{L}(\boldsymbol{\theta})}{\partial \theta_{ij}} = L \frac{\widetilde{Q}_{ij} - Q_{ij}(\boldsymbol{\theta})}{\theta_{ij}} \qquad (9)$$

It can be seen from (9) that in order to obtain the Hessian the partial derivative of $Q_{ij}(\boldsymbol{\theta})$ is required. According to [25]

$$Q_{ij}(\boldsymbol{\theta}) = \frac{\theta_{ij} G^{+i}(\boldsymbol{\theta}, \boldsymbol{N} - \boldsymbol{1}_j)}{G(\boldsymbol{\theta}, \boldsymbol{N})}$$

where $\boldsymbol{1}_j$ is a vector has all components zeros except for j and $G^{+i}(\cdot)$ refers to a model with an additional queue identical to queue i in the original model (i.e. same demands).

If $i = k$ and $j = h$, we then have

$$
\begin{aligned}
\frac{\partial Q_{ij}(\boldsymbol{\theta})}{\partial \theta_{ij}} &= \frac{G^{+i}(\boldsymbol{\theta}, \boldsymbol{N} - \boldsymbol{1}_j)}{G(\boldsymbol{\theta}, \boldsymbol{N})} - \frac{\theta_{ij} G^{+i}(\boldsymbol{\theta}, \boldsymbol{N} - \boldsymbol{1}_j) Q_{ij}(\boldsymbol{\theta})}{\theta_{ij} G(\boldsymbol{\theta}, \boldsymbol{N})} \\
&\quad + \frac{\theta_{ij}}{G(\boldsymbol{\theta}, \boldsymbol{N})} \frac{Q_{ij}^{+j}(\boldsymbol{\theta}, \boldsymbol{N} - \boldsymbol{1}_j)}{\theta_{ij}} G^{+j}(\boldsymbol{\theta}, \boldsymbol{N} - \boldsymbol{1}_j) \\
&= \frac{G^{+i}(\boldsymbol{\theta}, \boldsymbol{N} - \boldsymbol{1}_j)}{G(\boldsymbol{\theta}, \boldsymbol{N})}(1 + Q_{ij}^{+i}(\boldsymbol{\theta}, \boldsymbol{N} - \boldsymbol{1}_j) - Q_{ij}(\boldsymbol{\theta})) \\
&= \frac{Q_{ij}(\boldsymbol{\theta})}{\theta_{ij}}(1 + Q_{ij}^{+i}(\boldsymbol{\theta}, \boldsymbol{N} - \boldsymbol{1}_j) - Q_{ij}(\boldsymbol{\theta}))
\end{aligned}
\tag{10}
$$

For the other cases, we have

$$
\begin{aligned}
\frac{\partial Q_{ij}(\boldsymbol{\theta})}{\partial \theta_{kh}} &= \frac{\theta_{ij}}{G(\boldsymbol{\theta}, \boldsymbol{N})} \frac{Q_{kh}^{+i}(\boldsymbol{\theta}, \boldsymbol{N} - \boldsymbol{1}_j)}{\theta_{kh}} G^{+i}(\boldsymbol{\theta}, \boldsymbol{N} - \boldsymbol{1}_j) \\
&\quad - \frac{\theta_{ij} G^{+i}(\boldsymbol{\theta}, \boldsymbol{N} - \boldsymbol{1}_j) Q_{kh}(\boldsymbol{\theta})}{\theta_{kh} G(\boldsymbol{\theta}, \boldsymbol{N})} \\
&= \frac{\theta_{ij} G^{+i}(\boldsymbol{\theta}, \boldsymbol{N} - \boldsymbol{1}_j)}{\theta_{kh} G(\boldsymbol{\theta}, \boldsymbol{N})}(Q_{kh}^{+i}(\boldsymbol{\theta}, \boldsymbol{N} - \boldsymbol{1}_j) - Q_{kh}(\boldsymbol{\theta})) \\
&= \frac{Q_{ij}(\boldsymbol{\theta})}{\theta_{kh}}(Q_{kh}^{+i}(\boldsymbol{\theta}, \boldsymbol{N} - \boldsymbol{1}_j) - Q_{kh}(\boldsymbol{\theta}))
\end{aligned}
\tag{11}
$$

Combine (10)(11) with (7) and (8), the diagonal elements of the Hessian matrix is

$$
\begin{aligned}
\boldsymbol{H}(\hat{\boldsymbol{\theta}})_{ij,ij} &= \frac{\partial^2 \mathcal{L}(\hat{\boldsymbol{\theta}})}{\partial \hat{\theta}_{ij} \partial \hat{\theta}_{ij}} = L \frac{Q_{ij}(\hat{\boldsymbol{\theta}}) - \widetilde{Q}_{ij}}{\hat{\theta}_{ij}^2} - \frac{L}{\hat{\theta}_{ij}} \frac{\partial Q_{ij}(\hat{\boldsymbol{\theta}})}{\partial \hat{\theta}_{ij}} \\
&= L \frac{Q_{ij}(\hat{\boldsymbol{\theta}})(Q_{ij}(\hat{\boldsymbol{\theta}}) - Q_{ij}^{+i}(\hat{\boldsymbol{\theta}}, \boldsymbol{N} - \boldsymbol{1}_j)) - \widetilde{Q}_{ij}}{\hat{\theta}_{ij}^2}
\end{aligned}
$$

The non-diagonal elements are

$$
\begin{aligned}
\boldsymbol{H}(\hat{\boldsymbol{\theta}})_{ij,kh} &= \frac{\partial^2 \log \mathcal{L}(\hat{\boldsymbol{\theta}})}{\partial \hat{\theta}_{ij} \partial \hat{\theta}_{kh}} = -\frac{L}{\hat{\theta}_{ij}} \frac{\partial Q_{ij}(\hat{\boldsymbol{\theta}})}{\partial \hat{\theta}_{kh}} \\
&= \frac{L Q_{ij}(\hat{\boldsymbol{\theta}})}{\hat{\theta}_{ij} \hat{\theta}_{kh}}(Q_{kh}(\hat{\boldsymbol{\theta}}) - Q_{kh}^{+i}(\hat{\boldsymbol{\theta}}, \boldsymbol{N} - \boldsymbol{1}_j))
\end{aligned}
$$

which completes the proof. $\square$

Proof of Corollary 1

According to [23, Chapter 9], the distribution of the maximum likelihood estimator $\boldsymbol{\theta}$ is asymptotically normal with mean $\hat{\boldsymbol{\theta}}$ and the covariance matrix being approximated by the inverse of the Fisher Information matrix $\boldsymbol{I}(\hat{\boldsymbol{\theta}})$.

The corresponding confidence interval for $\hat{\theta}_{ij}$ is

$$\hat{\theta}_{ij} \pm c\sqrt{\boldsymbol{I}(\hat{\boldsymbol{\theta}})_{ij,ij}^{-1}}$$

where c is the appropriate z critical value (e.g. 1.96 for 95% confidence). The Fisher Information for unknown parameters $\boldsymbol{\theta}$ is a matrix $\boldsymbol{I}(\boldsymbol{\theta})$ defined by elements

$$\boldsymbol{I}(\boldsymbol{\theta})_{ij,kh} = -\mathbb{E}\left[\frac{\partial^2 \log \mathcal{L}(\boldsymbol{\theta})}{\partial \theta_{ij} \partial \theta_{kh}}\right]$$

According to [23, Chapter 2], for the maximum likelihood estimator $\hat{\boldsymbol{\theta}}$, it can be further simplified to

$$\boldsymbol{I}(\hat{\boldsymbol{\theta}})_{ij,kh} = -\frac{\partial^2 \log \mathcal{L}(\hat{\boldsymbol{\theta}})}{\partial \hat{\theta}_{ij} \partial \hat{\theta}_{kh}}\Big|_{\theta=\hat{\theta}} = -\boldsymbol{H}(\hat{\boldsymbol{\theta}})_{ij,kh}$$

The Fisher Information matrix for the maximum likelihood estimates is also referred to as the observed Fisher Information matrix. This completes the proof. $\square$

Proof of Theorem 3

By the Arrival Theorem [26] we have:

$$\theta_{ij} = \frac{Q_{ij}(\boldsymbol{\theta})}{X_j(\boldsymbol{\theta})(1 + A_{ij}(\boldsymbol{\theta}))}$$

where $A_{ij} = \sum_{r=1}^{R} Q_{ir}(\boldsymbol{\theta}, \boldsymbol{N} - \boldsymbol{1}_j)$. Since Little's law on a closed network implies $X_j(\boldsymbol{\theta})\theta_{0,ij} + \sum_{i=1}^{M} Q_{ij}(\boldsymbol{\theta}) = N_j$, we get

$$\theta_{ij} = \frac{Q_{ij}(\boldsymbol{\theta})}{(N_j - \sum_{i=1}^{M} Q_{ij}(\boldsymbol{\theta}))} \frac{X_j(\boldsymbol{\theta})\theta_{0,j}}{X_j(\boldsymbol{\theta})(1 + A_{ij}(\boldsymbol{\theta}))}$$

Direct substitution can be used to check that his expression holds also for the Bard-Schweitzer fixed point. Simplifying we can write

$$\theta_{ij} = \frac{Q_{ij}^{bs}(\boldsymbol{\theta})}{(N_j - \sum_{i=1}^{M} Q_{ij}^{bs}(\boldsymbol{\theta}))} \frac{\theta_{0,j}}{(1 + Q_i^{bs}(\boldsymbol{\theta}) - Q_{ij}^{bs}(\boldsymbol{\theta})/N_j)}$$

for all demand vectors $\boldsymbol{\theta}$. For the Bard-Schweitzer estimator, the last expression becomes (3) since $Q_{ij}(\boldsymbol{\theta}^{bs}) = \widetilde{Q}_{ij}$. This completes the proof. $\square$

Proof of Theorem 4

Similar to the proof of Theorem 1, it is not difficult to verify the existence of the ML estimator. From [8], the relationship in (6) still holds for the load-dependent queueing network. Define $\boldsymbol{\chi} = (\boldsymbol{\theta}, \boldsymbol{\gamma})$, therefore considering θ_{ij}, we have

$$\frac{d\mathcal{L}(\boldsymbol{\chi})}{d\theta_{ij}} = \sum_{l=1}^{L} \left(-\frac{Q_{ij}(\boldsymbol{\chi})}{\theta_{ij}} + \frac{n_{ij}^l}{\theta_{ij}}\right) \mathcal{L}(\boldsymbol{\chi})$$

which implies the condition $Q_{ij}(\hat{\boldsymbol{\chi}}) = \widetilde{Q}_{ij}$.

For $\gamma_k(v)$, we have

$$
\begin{aligned}
\frac{\partial \log \mathcal{L}(\boldsymbol{\chi})}{\partial \gamma_k(v)} &= \frac{1}{\mathcal{L}(\boldsymbol{\chi})} \frac{\partial \mathcal{L}(\boldsymbol{\chi})}{\partial \gamma_k(v)} \\
&= \frac{L\mathbb{P}(\widetilde{n}_k \geq v)}{\gamma_k(v)} - \frac{L}{G(\boldsymbol{\chi})} \frac{\partial G(\boldsymbol{\chi})}{\partial \gamma_k(v)} \\
&= L \frac{\mathbb{P}(\widetilde{n}_k \geq v) - \mathbb{P}(n_k \geq v|\boldsymbol{\chi})}{\gamma_k(v)}
\end{aligned}
\tag{12}
$$

The stationarity point is $\mathbb{P}(\widetilde{n}_k \geq v) = \mathbb{P}(n_k \geq v|\hat{\boldsymbol{\chi}})$ which further simplifies to $\mathbb{P}(\widetilde{n}_k = v) = \mathbb{P}(n_k = v|\hat{\boldsymbol{\chi}})$. $\square$

Proof of Theorem 5

Similar as the proof of Theorem 2, derivation of Hessian matrix $\boldsymbol{H}(\hat{\boldsymbol{\chi}})$ requires the evaluation of second-order partial derivatives. First, we consider the partial derivative of $\log \mathcal{L}(\boldsymbol{\chi})$ regarding θ_{ij}

$$\frac{\partial \log \mathcal{L}(\boldsymbol{\chi})}{\partial \theta_{ij}} = \frac{1}{\mathcal{L}(\boldsymbol{\chi})} \frac{\partial \mathcal{L}(\boldsymbol{\chi})}{\partial \theta_{ij}} = L \frac{\widetilde{Q}_{ij}(\boldsymbol{D}) - Q_{ij}(\boldsymbol{\chi})}{\theta_{ij}} \tag{13}$$

The following computes the partial derivative of $Q_{ij}(\boldsymbol{\chi})$ regarding $\theta_{i'j'}$. if $i = i', j = j'$, we have

$$
\begin{aligned}
\frac{\partial Q_{ij}(\boldsymbol{\chi})}{\partial \theta_{i'j'}} &= \frac{\partial \sum_{\boldsymbol{n}\in S} n_{ij}\mathbb{P}(\boldsymbol{n}|\boldsymbol{\chi})}{\partial \theta_{ij}} \\
&= \frac{\sum_{\boldsymbol{n}\in S} n_{ij}\mathbb{P}(\boldsymbol{n}|\boldsymbol{\chi})(n_{ij} - Q_{ij}(\boldsymbol{\chi}))}{\theta_{ij}} \\
&= \frac{\sum_{\boldsymbol{n}\in S} n_{ij}^2 \mathbb{P}(\boldsymbol{n}|\boldsymbol{\chi}) - Q_{ij}(\boldsymbol{\chi}) \sum_{\boldsymbol{n}\in S} n_{ij}\mathbb{P}(\boldsymbol{n}|\boldsymbol{\chi})}{\theta_{ij}} \\
&= \frac{E[n_{ij}^2|\boldsymbol{\chi}] - Q_{ij}^2(\boldsymbol{\chi})}{\theta_{ij}}
\end{aligned} \tag{14}
$$

Otherwise, we have

$$
\begin{aligned}
\frac{\partial Q_{ij}(\boldsymbol{\chi})}{\partial \theta_{i'j'}} &= \frac{\partial \sum_{\boldsymbol{n}\in S} n_{ij}\mathbb{P}(\boldsymbol{n}|\boldsymbol{\chi})}{\partial \theta_{i'j'}} \\
&= \frac{\sum_{\boldsymbol{n}\in S} n_{ij}\mathbb{P}(\boldsymbol{n}|\boldsymbol{\chi})(n_{i'j'} - Q_{i'j'}(\boldsymbol{\chi}))}{\theta_{i'j'}} \\
&= \frac{\sum_{\boldsymbol{n}\in S} n_{ij} n_{i'j'}\mathbb{P}(\boldsymbol{n}|\boldsymbol{\chi}) - Q_{i'j'}(\boldsymbol{\chi}) \sum_{\boldsymbol{n}\in S} n_{ij}\mathbb{P}(\boldsymbol{n}|\boldsymbol{\chi})}{\theta_{i'j'}} \\
&= \frac{E[n_{ij} n_{i'j'}|\boldsymbol{\chi}] - Q_{ij}(\boldsymbol{\chi}) Q_{i'j'}(\boldsymbol{\chi})}{\theta_{i'j'}}
\end{aligned} \tag{15}
$$

Substituting (14) and (15) into (13), for $\boldsymbol{H}(\hat{\boldsymbol{\chi}})_{ij,ij}$ we have

$$
\begin{aligned}
\boldsymbol{H}(\hat{\boldsymbol{\chi}})_{ij,ij} &= \frac{\partial^2 \log \mathcal{L}(\hat{\boldsymbol{\chi}})}{\partial \hat{\theta}_{ij} \partial \hat{\theta}_{ij}} \\
&= L \frac{Q_{ij}(\hat{\boldsymbol{\chi}}) - \widetilde{Q}_{ij}(\boldsymbol{D})}{\hat{\theta}_{ij}^2} - \frac{L}{\hat{\theta}_{ij}} \frac{\partial Q_{ij}(\hat{\boldsymbol{\chi}})}{\hat{\theta}_{ij}} \\
&= \frac{L}{\hat{\theta}_{ij}^2}\left(Q_{ij}^2(\hat{\boldsymbol{\chi}}) - E[n_{ij}^2|\hat{\boldsymbol{\chi}}] + Q_{ij}(\hat{\boldsymbol{\chi}}) - \widetilde{Q}_{ij}(\boldsymbol{D})\right)
\end{aligned}
$$

for $\boldsymbol{H}(\hat{\boldsymbol{\chi}})_{ij,i'j'}$, we have

$$
\begin{aligned}
\boldsymbol{H}(\hat{\boldsymbol{\chi}})_{ij,i'j'} &= \frac{\partial^2 \log \mathcal{L}(\hat{\boldsymbol{\chi}})}{\partial \hat{\theta}_{ij} \partial \hat{\theta}_{i'j'}} = -\frac{L}{\hat{\theta}_{ij}} \frac{\partial Q_{ij}(\hat{\boldsymbol{\chi}})}{\hat{\theta_{i'j'}}} \\
&= L \frac{Q_{ij}(\hat{\boldsymbol{\chi}}) Q_{i'j'}(\hat{\boldsymbol{\chi}}) - E[n_{ij} n_{i'j'}|\hat{\boldsymbol{\chi}}]}{\hat{\theta}_{ij} \hat{\theta}_{i'j'}}
\end{aligned}
$$

For computing $\frac{\partial^2 \log \mathcal{L}(\boldsymbol{\chi})}{\partial \gamma_k(v) \partial \theta_{ij}}$, $\frac{\partial \log \mathcal{L}(\boldsymbol{\chi})}{\partial \gamma_k(v)}$ is already given in (12). Noticing that

$$
\begin{aligned}
\frac{\partial \mathbb{P}(n_k \geq v|\boldsymbol{\chi})}{\partial \theta_{ij}} &= \sum_{\boldsymbol{n}\in S, n_k \geq v} \frac{\partial \mathbb{P}(\boldsymbol{n}|\boldsymbol{\chi})}{\partial \theta_{ij}} \\
&= \frac{1}{\theta_{ij}} \sum_{\boldsymbol{n}\in S, n_k \geq v} \mathbb{P}(\boldsymbol{n}|\boldsymbol{\chi})(n_{ij} - Q_{ij}(\boldsymbol{\chi})) \\
&= \frac{1}{\theta_{ij}}\left(E[n_{ij}|\boldsymbol{\chi}, n_k \geq v] - Q_{ij}(\boldsymbol{\chi})\mathbb{P}(n_k \geq v|\boldsymbol{\chi})\right)
\end{aligned}
$$

Therefore we have

$$
\begin{aligned}
\boldsymbol{H}(\hat{\boldsymbol{\chi}})_{ij,kv} &= \frac{\partial \log \mathcal{L}(\hat{\boldsymbol{\chi}})}{\partial \hat{\gamma}_k(v) \partial \hat{\theta}_{ij}} \\
&= L \frac{Q_{ij}(\hat{\boldsymbol{\chi}})\mathbb{P}(n_k \geq v|\hat{\boldsymbol{\chi}}) - E[n_{ij}|\hat{\boldsymbol{\chi}}, n_k \geq v]}{\hat{\chi}_{ij}\hat{\gamma}_k(v)}
\end{aligned}
$$

Finally, we consider to compute $\frac{\partial^2 \log \mathcal{L}(\boldsymbol{\chi})}{\partial \gamma_k(v) \partial \gamma'_k(v')}$. If $k =$ $k', v = v'$

$$
\begin{aligned}
\frac{\partial \mathbb{P}(n_k \geq v|\boldsymbol{\chi})}{\partial \gamma_k(v)} &= \sum_{\boldsymbol{n}\in S, n_k \geq v} \frac{\partial \mathbb{P}(\boldsymbol{n}|\boldsymbol{\chi})}{\partial \gamma_k(v)} \\
&= \sum_{\boldsymbol{n}\in S, n_k \geq v} \frac{\mathbb{P}(\boldsymbol{n}|\boldsymbol{\chi})}{\gamma_k(v)} - \frac{\mathbb{P}(\boldsymbol{n}|\boldsymbol{\chi})}{G(\boldsymbol{\chi})}\frac{\partial G(\boldsymbol{\chi})}{\partial \gamma_k(v)} \\
&= \sum_{\boldsymbol{n}\in S, n_k \geq v} \frac{1}{\gamma_k(v)}\mathbb{P}(\boldsymbol{n}|\boldsymbol{\chi})(1 - \mathbb{P}(n_k \geq v|\boldsymbol{\chi})) \\
&= \frac{1 - \mathbb{P}(n_k \geq v|\boldsymbol{\chi})}{\gamma_k(v)}\mathbb{P}(n_k \geq v|\boldsymbol{\chi})
\end{aligned}
$$

For cases otherwise

$$
\begin{aligned}
\frac{\partial \mathbb{P}(n_k \geq v|\boldsymbol{\chi})}{\partial \gamma_{k'}(v')} &= \sum_{\boldsymbol{n}\in S, n_k \geq v} \frac{\partial \mathbb{P}(\boldsymbol{n}|\boldsymbol{\chi})}{\partial \gamma_{k'}(v')} \\
&= \sum_{\boldsymbol{n}\in S, n_k \geq v, n_{k'} \geq v'} \frac{\mathbb{P}(\boldsymbol{n}|\boldsymbol{\chi})}{\gamma_{k'}(v')} - \sum_{\boldsymbol{n}\in S, n_k \geq v} \frac{\mathbb{P}(\boldsymbol{n}|\boldsymbol{\chi})}{G(\boldsymbol{\chi})}\frac{\partial G(\boldsymbol{\chi})}{\gamma_{k'}(v')} \\
&= \frac{\mathbb{P}(n_k \geq v, n_{k'} \geq v'|\boldsymbol{\chi})}{\gamma_{k'}(v')} - \sum_{\boldsymbol{n}\in S, n_k \geq v} \frac{\mathbb{P}(\boldsymbol{n}|\boldsymbol{\chi})\mathbb{P}(n_{k'} \geq v'|\boldsymbol{\chi})}{\gamma_{k'}(v')} \\
&= \frac{\mathbb{P}(n_k \geq v, n_{k'} \geq v'|\boldsymbol{\chi}) - \mathbb{P}(n_k \geq v|\boldsymbol{\chi})\mathbb{P}(n_{k'} \geq v'|\boldsymbol{\chi})}{\gamma_{k'}(v')}
\end{aligned}
$$

Therefore, for $\boldsymbol{H}(\hat{\boldsymbol{\chi}})_{kv,kv}$ we have

$$
\begin{aligned}
\boldsymbol{H}(\hat{\boldsymbol{\chi}})_{kv,kv} &= \frac{\partial^2 \log \mathcal{L}(\hat{\boldsymbol{\chi}})}{\partial \hat{\gamma}_k(v) \partial \hat{\gamma}_k(v)} \\
&= L \frac{\mathbb{P}(n_k \geq v|\hat{\boldsymbol{\chi}}) - \mathbb{P}(\widetilde{n}_k \geq v|\boldsymbol{D})}{\hat{\gamma}_k(v)^2} \\
&\quad - L\mathbb{P}(n_k \geq v|\hat{\boldsymbol{\chi}})\frac{1 - \mathbb{P}(n_k \geq v|\hat{\boldsymbol{\chi}})}{\hat{\gamma}_k(v)^2} \\
&= L \frac{\mathbb{P}(n_k \geq v|\hat{\boldsymbol{\chi}})^2 - \mathbb{P}(\widetilde{n}_k \geq v|\boldsymbol{D})}{\hat{\gamma}_k(v)^2}
\end{aligned}
$$

For $\boldsymbol{H}(\hat{\boldsymbol{\chi}})_{kv,k'v'}$

$$
\begin{aligned}
\boldsymbol{H}(\hat{\boldsymbol{\chi}})_{kv,k'v'} &= \frac{\partial \log \mathcal{L}(\hat{\boldsymbol{\chi}})}{\partial \hat{\gamma}_k(v) \partial \hat{\gamma}_{k'}(v')} \\
&= L \frac{\mathbb{P}(n_k \geq v|\hat{\boldsymbol{\chi}})\mathbb{P}(n_{k'} \geq v'|\hat{\boldsymbol{\chi}}) - \mathbb{P}(n_k \geq v, n_{k'} \geq v'|\hat{\boldsymbol{\chi}})}{\hat{\gamma}_k(v)\hat{\gamma}_{k'}(v')}
\end{aligned}
$$

which completes the proof. $\square$

A Cost/Benefit Approach to Performance Analysis

David Maplesden
Dept. of Computer Science
The University of Auckland
dmap001@aucklanduni.ac.nz

Ewan Tempero
Dept. of Computer Science
The University of Auckland
e.tempero@auckland.ac.nz

John Hosking
Faculty of Science
The University of Auckland
j.hosking@auckland.ac.nz

John C. Grundy
School of Software and Electrical Engineering
Swinburne University of Technology
jgrundy@swin.edu.au

ABSTRACT

Most performance engineering approaches focus on understanding the use of runtime resources. However such approaches do not quantify the *value* being provided in return for the consumption of these resources. Without such a measure it is not possible to compare the *efficiency* of these components (that is whether the runtime cost is reasonable given the benefit being provided). We have created an empirical approach that measures the value being provided by a code path in terms of the *visible* data it generates for the rest of the application. Combining this with traditional performance cost data, creates an efficiency measure for every code path in the application. We have evaluated our approach using the DaCapo benchmark suite, demonstrating our analysis allows us to quantify the efficiency of the code in each benchmark and find real optimisation opportunities, providing improvements of up to 36% in our case studies.

General Terms

Performance,Measurement

Keywords

efficiency analysis, blended analysis, profiling, runtime bloat

1. INTRODUCTION

Performance is a vital yet elusive attribute for much of the software developed today. Software engineering practices that focus on increasing developer productivity and software reuse have inevitably led to software built upon generalised frameworks and libraries. This often results in software with many layers of abstractions and very complex runtime behaviour. For example an enterprise Java service-oriented application may implement SOAP web services using the Axis web services framework in front of a Hibernate backend accessing a relational database and be deployed in

ICPE'16, March 12–18, 2016, Delft, Netherlands.
Copyright is held by the owner/author(s). Publication rights licensed to ACM.
ACM 978-1-4503-4080-9/16/03...$15.00.
DOI: http://dx.doi.org/10.1145/2851553.2851558.

a J2EE application server. This approach means that even simple requests induce a chain of furious activity requiring hundreds, maybe thousands, of method calls and data transformations to complete [13]. The tendency of modern applications to engage excessive activity to complete straightforward tasks has become known as runtime bloat [11, 21].

Most performance engineering approaches focus on understanding an application's *cost* i.e. its use of runtime resources. However understanding cost alone does not necessarily help find optimisation opportunities. One piece of code may take longer than another simply because it is performing more necessary work. For example it would be no surprise that a routine that sorted a list of elements took longer than a routine that returned the number of elements in the list. The fact that the costs of the two routines are different does not help us understand which may represent an optimisation opportunity. However if we had two different routines which both achieved the same result e.g. two different sorting algorithms, then determining which is the more efficient solution becomes a simple cost comparison.

The key is to understand the runtime *value* provided by a piece of code. Without this understanding it is not possible to compare different branches of code to find the superfluous activity that characterises runtime bloat. Existing performance analysis approaches generally do not measure value, traditionally this has been left to the engineer to determine through experience, intuition or guesswork. The challenge of intuitively divining value becomes much more difficult in modern, large-scale applications. Large-scale applications have thousands of methods interacting to implement runtime behaviours with millions of code paths[6]. Establishing the value provided by each method via manual inspection is not practical with such numbers of method calls. If we were able to empirically measure runtime value then we could combine this with traditional runtime cost information to establish the *efficiency* of each code path in the application.

This then is the key idea presented in this paper, we describe an approach to empirically quantify the runtime value of all code paths in an application so we can measure their efficiency. This allows us to find the most inefficient code paths in the application and analyse them for optimisation opportunities.

The main contributions of this paper are:

- We introduce the concept of focussing on the efficiency rather than purely on the cost of runtime behaviour.

- We describe *blended efficiency analysis*, a blended analysis approach to measuring code efficiency.
- We empirically evaluate our approach over standard benchmarks to characterise typical efficiency attributes.
- We demonstrate the utility of blended efficiency analysis in several case studies.

The remainder of this paper is structured as follows. Section 2 motivates our work and presents background information. Section 3 covers related work. Section 4 describes our approach. Section 5 presents an evaluation using the DaCapo benchmark suite and several case studies. Section 6 discusses the results of our evaluation and areas of future work. We conclude in Section 7.

2. MOTIVATION AND BACKGROUND

Traditional profiling tools typically record measurements of execution cost per method call. The costs are usually captured with calling context information, that is, the hierarchy of active methods calls leading to the current call, and are aggregated in a calling context tree (CCT) [1].

A CCT is a data structure that records all distinct calling contexts of a program. Each node in the tree has a method label representing the method call at that node and has a child node for each unique method invoked from that calling context. Therefore the method labels on the path from a node to the root of the tree describe a complete and distinct calling context.

Figure 1 in Section 4 shows an example CCT. Each node records the aggregated execution costs for a specific calling context. The execution cost recorded at a node does not include the cost of any child method calls, therefore it is known as the *exclusive* cost. The *inclusive* cost at a node does include the cost of child method calls and is the sum of the exclusive costs of all the children in the sub-tree rooted at the node.

The difficulty in analysing a CCT profile is that large-scale applications tend to have runtime costs that are thinly distributed across thousands of methods, meaning there are few obvious hotspots to target [21]. Table 1 shows the top ten hot methods from the **h2** DaCapo benchmark and illustrates the typical challenges. Five of the ten hot methods are low level utility methods from the Java system library, methods that are typically very difficult to optimise or avoid. Four of the remaining five methods (numbers 2, 4, 7 & 9) are core routines in the H2 implementation that are again both simple and widely used, e.g. `Row.getValue()` is a basic getter method that occurs in over 3000 locations in the CCT. This leaves only `TPCC.calculateSumDB`, which we discuss in Section 5.1.1, as a realistic optimisation opportunity from the top ten hot methods.

Intuitively then nine of the ten hot methods are hot simply because they are being frequently executed and not because they are inherently inefficient. In our experience this is typical of many large-scale object oriented programs. However within the **h2** benchmark there exist a number of optimisation opportunities not easily discoverable from the traditional performance profile, in fact over 10% of the benchmark's cost is spent in methods that achieve nothing at all.

An example of one of these **no effect** methods is `JdbcResultSet.checkColumnIndex()`, which is called every time a field is retrieved from a result set. It is responsible for raising a suitable exception should the column index not be in

Table 1: Top 10 Hot Methods — h2

Method	%Cost
org.dacapo.h2.TPCC.calculateSumDB(String, int)	08.011
org.h2.index.BaseIndex.compareRows(Row, Row)	06.159
java.lang.String.charAt(int)	05.767
org.h2.index.BaseIndex.compareValues(Value, Value, int)	04.063
java.lang.Integer.getChars(int, int, char[])	03.922
java.lang.System.arraycopy(Object, int, Object, int, int)	02.967
org.h2.table.TableFilter.next()	02.954
java.lang.String.length()	02.473
org.h2.result.Row.getValue(int)	02.321
java.lang.AbstractStringBuilder.append(String)	01.964

the valid range for the result set. However it also checks that both the underlying JDBC statement and connection are still open. In the course of our benchmark run these conditions were always satisfied, so in practice the method never raised an exception and hence its runtime value was zero – it was making no practical contribution to the benchmark processing. Reviewing the implementation we found that the checks on the statement and connection were unnecessary as neither were used during a field access. All field data is loaded into memory when the result set cursor is advanced to the current row via `JdbcResultSet.next()`. Both the statement and connection are confirmed to be open at this point, making the repeated checking on every field access redundant. We were able to refactor the checks performed on every field access and almost completely eliminate their runtime cost. This change reduced the total amount of benchmark code that was having no effect by over 75% and reduced the overall benchmark time by 8%.

3. RELATED WORK

There is a large body of work into investigating software performance that we cannot adequately describe here due to space limitations. We discuss the most closely related work below but a full review of relevant empirical performance analysis approaches can be found in our review paper [9].

3.1 Runtime Bloat Analysis

The body of work that most closely matches ours in its motivation is the existing research into runtime bloat [21]. Generally the research has focussed on memory bloat (excessive memory use)(e.g. [5, 2]) or they have taken a data-flow centric approach [12, 13], looking for patterns of inefficiently created or used data structures, collections and objects [17, 19, 22, 18, 20, 23, 14]. Most of these approaches are looking for optimisation opportunities of a similar nature to those we are searching for, but our more generalised notion of understanding the *value* provided by all code paths in an application, rather than focussing primarily on understanding the use of data structures, allows us to discover a variety of different optimisation opportunities. Our previous work [10] on subsuming methods analysis aimed to finding compact repeated patterns of method calls that represented a significant hotspot and optimisation opportunity.

3.2 Blended Analysis

Blended analysis (a term first coined by Dufour et al in their work on blended escape analysis [7, 8]) is a combination of dynamic and static analysis, where the dynamic analysis determines the program region over which the static analysis is performed. With the notable exception of the work by Dufour et al, very little existing performance analysis research uses either static or blended analysis to aid in the gathering or interpretation of performance data [9]. In particular the majority of the runtime bloat research instead uses pure dynamic analysis in the form of specialised profiling implemented by modifying an open-source research JVM, often incurring very high runtime overheads.

We have implemented our efficiency analysis as a blended analysis, leveraging both dynamic profiling information and an intra-procedural forward data flow static analysis. Using blended analysis allows us to leverage the benefits of both static and dynamic analysis. To quote from Dufour et al [8]:

> Blended analysis offers many advantages compared to a purely static or dynamic analysis. First, blended analysis limits the scope of the static analysis to methods in the program that actually were executed, thus dramatically reducing the cost of a very precise static analysis by reducing its focus, allowing achievement of high precision over an interesting portion of the program. Second, blended analysis only requires a lightweight dynamic analysis, thus limiting the amount of overhead and perturbation during execution.

We gained the same advantages, allowing us to implement an offline analysis that could measure the runtime value of all code paths captured by a lightweight dynamic profile. Where the focus of Dufour et al's work was to understand the use of temporary objects our more general focus was to appreciate the value being provided by the code paths captured in an application profile.

4. BLENDED EFFICIENCY ANALYSIS

We wish to quantify the efficiency of the code in an application. Our approach to achieving this is to calculate a measure of value for every node in a captured calling context tree profile. We can then trivially combine this with the traditional cost measures captured in the profile to calculate the efficiency at every calling context:

$$CC_{eff} = CC_{value}/CC_{cost}$$

We can also similarly calculate the efficiency of any method using the aggregated method value and cost. Our measure of value at each calling context is an inclusive measure for the entire sub-tree rooted at that node. Therefore the efficiency measure is not just for the activity in the method at that node but all the activity in the sub-tree.

Our approach to quantifying value is to measure the volume of data created by a method that becomes visible to the rest of the application i.e. it escapes the context of the method. Our rationale is that the value a method is providing can only be imparted by the data it creates that is subsequently visible outside of the method. Intermediate objects and calculations that are created during processing but then discarded do not contribute to this final value. Intuitively two method calls that produce identical results (given the same arguments) and have no other side effects, are providing the same value, regardless of their internal implementation.

Specifically we track the number of object field updates that ultimately escape their enclosing method. An object field update is any assignment to an object field or array element e.g. `foo.value = 1` or `bar[0] = 1`. For brevity we will refer to such an assignment as a *write*. Writes to static fields are handled as a special case of an object field write that is being applied to a special global object. Assignments to primitive local variables are **not** recorded as writes as they hold only intermediate values that must be copied to an object field in order to escape the current calling context.

To escape the current calling context, a write must be applied to either:

- a globally accessible field or object (globally escaping)
- a method operand (operand or argument escaping)
- an object returned from the method (returned)

To these traditional escape states we also track when an object has been passed to an IO output routine (output escaping) as the data has escaped to an external source.

Our concept of escaping writes is similar to *object escape analysis*[4]. Escape analysis is a method of characterising the effective lifetime of objects, it calculates whether newly created objects become visible outside of the method which created them. Our tracking of writes rather than objects gives us a more fine-grained view of the work being done and our concept of output escaping writes has no parallel in object escape analysis.

Each write that occurs at a calling context we call a *local* write. The *total* writes for a calling context is the sum of the total writes of its child methods plus its local writes. Therefore the sum of the local writes in any sub-tree will equal the total writes for the node at the root of the sub-tree. Each one of the total writes either *escapes* the calling context or we say it is *non-escaping*. Escaping writes are categorised as *global*, *operand*, *returned* or *output* depending on how they escape. An escaping write may satisfy more than one of these classifications simultaneously. For example a write to an object that is both an operand and returned will be counted as both an operand and returned write, but only a single escaping write.

Operand and returned writes may be *captured* by a parent context if, for example, an object created and returned by one method is then discarded by the calling method. Global and output writes however are globally escaping, they can never be captured. To be exact the *captured* writes for a calling context is the number of local and child escaping writes that do not escape the context. This definition means the sum of the captured writes in any sub-tree will equal the non-escaping writes for the node at the root of the sub-tree.

Finally the *value* for each calling context is the number of escaping writes at the node plus, for methods with primitive non-void return types, we add the method invocation count. This ensures they have a value of at least one for each invocation, to reflect the value of the primitive they return.

Example 1 lists some examples from Java library code:

- `Arrays.copyOf()` – has only returned writes as it returns the new array object it creates and populates. There are no operand, global, output or captured writes.
- `String.getChars()` – has only operand writes as it simply populates the buffer passed as its third operand
- `AbstractStringBuilder.expandCapacity()` – has only operand writes, as it only updates the state of the **this** object to create a new larger internal buffer
- `AbstractStringBuilder.append(String)` — has both operand and returned writes as it updates its internal state and then returns a reference to itself

Example 1 Selected Java library methods

```
1: public class AbstractStringBuilder {
2:   public AbstractStringBuilder append(String str) {
3:     if (str == null) str = "null";
4:     int len = str.length();
5:     ensureCapacityInternal(this.count + len);
6:     str.getChars(0, len, this.value, this.count);
7:     this.count += len;
8:     return this;
9:   }

10:   private void ensureCapacityInternal(int minimumCapacity) {
11:     if (minimumCapacity - this.value.length > 0)
12:       expandCapacity(minimumCapacity);
13:   }

14:   void expandCapacity(int minimumCapacity) {
15:     int newCapacity = this.value.length * 2 + 2;
16:     if (newCapacity - minimumCapacity < 0)
17:       newCapacity = minimumCapacity;
18:     if (newCapacity < 0) {
19:       if (minimumCapacity < 0) // overflow
20:         throw new OutOfMemoryError();
21:       newCapacity = Integer.MAX_VALUE;
22:     }
23:     value = Arrays.copyOf(this.value, newCapacity);
24:   }
25: }

26: public class String {
27:   public void getChars(int bgn,int end, char dst[],int pos) {
28:     System.arraycopy(this.value, bgn, dst, pos, end - bgn);
29:   }
30: }

31: public class Arrays {
32:   public static char[] copyOf(char[] orig, int len) {
33:     char[] c = new char[len];
34:     System.arraycopy(orig,0,c,0,Math.min(orig.length,len));
35:     return c;
36:   }
37: }
```

Our blended efficiency analysis consists of three phases:

- the capturing of a dynamic calling context tree profile during the execution of an application
- a pure intra-procedural static analysis for each method captured in the dynamic profile
- a final analysis phase where the results of the static analysis are combined with the dynamic profile to build a complete inter-procedural write analysis

Our implementation is built to work with Java applications, but the concepts are easily transferable to any object-oriented language.

4.1 Profiling

We used the JP2 profiler developed at the University of Lugano [15, 16] to capture our CCT profiles. JP2 is an instrumentation based profiler that captures basic block level profiles in a calling context tree data structure. Each node has an array of invocation counts, one for each basic block in the method. JP2 calculates the runtime cost for each node as the number of bytecode instructions executed. This platform independent metric appealed to us for our experiments because it was portable and reproducible.

We made one extension to JP2 to support our specific profiling needs. `System.arraycopy()` is a native method used to copy array content from a source array to a destination array and it is passed a length parameter which defines the number of elements copied. We felt it important to be able to record its activity, because it is a very frequently invoked

method whose sole purpose is to populate an array i.e. create writes. Because it is a native method we cannot record its activity using normal bytecode instrumentation. Therefore we augmented JP2 to record the length parameter at runtime and aggregate it into a cumulative count kept alongside the basic block counts for each `System.arraycopy()` node in the CCT. This allows us to know precisely how many writes have been performed at each of these nodes in the CCT.

4.2 Static Write Analysis

The static analysis we use is an intra-procedural forward data flow analysis (implemented using the ASM 5.0.4 bytecode manipulation library[1]) that tracks the origin of each object reference utilised within the method. We first find and record the basic blocks within the method before then performing the data flow analysis. Like all forward data flow analyses our analysis simulates all execution paths through the method and maintains a complete stack frame for each instruction representing the possible values of all local variables and method operands after that instruction. The key implementation points of our analysis are:

- Each object reference has a value (we call its *origin value*) indicating its possible origin, being one of:
  - `Operand` – a method operand
  - `Local` – a new locally created object
  - `ReturnValue` – the result of a child method call
  - `Global` – retrieved from a global (static) field
  - `Output` – an operand to an IO output method
  - a composite value made up of a set of the above values
- The initial stack frame is initialised with `Operand` values for the method operands
- New `Local`, `ReturnValue` and `Global` values are created in response to the *new object*, *invoke method* and *get static field* instructions respectively
- The result of referencing an object field (via the get field instruction) is the value of the parent object e.g. the field of a `Local` is a `Local`
- For each *put field* instruction we record a *write* against the current basic block with the origin value of both the updated field and the value being put
- We also record a *write* for each newly created object or array so that new objects, even with no explicit field puts, have a non-zero write count
- Arrays are handled the same way as objects, with the *new array* instruction creating a new `Local` value and getting or setting of an array element being treated the same as an object field get or put
- For each child method call instruction we record the origin values of the method operands used for the call
- For each return instruction we record against the current basic block the origin value of the returned object

At the completion of the analysis we have recorded for each method:

- the child method call information, including the origin value for every operand to those calls
- the basic blocks in the method, and for each basic block:
  - every field write, including the origin value of both the updated and put objects
  - the origin value of any return instruction (there can be at most one in a basic block)

---

[1]http://asm.ow2.org/

This information gives us the static escape information for each potential write performed by the method. However it is not until we combine it with the runtime profile information that we can determine how many writes were performed and what the escape status of those writes is.

For example the static information for `Arrays.copyOf()` from Example 1 can tell us that:

- There is one new object (an array) created at line 33, which we denote `Local[33]`
- There is one method call made to `System.arraycopy()` where we pass `Operand[0]` as the first parameter and `Local[33]` as the third parameter
- We return `Local[33]`

At this intra-procedural static analysis phase we do not know what, if any, writes `System.arraycopy()` may perform and therefore we do not know the actual number of returned writes in `Local[33]` or operand writes applied to `Operand[0]`.

4.3 Inter-Procedural Write Analysis

The final stage of the blended analysis completes the inter-procedural write analysis using a post-order (i.e. child-first) traversal of the CCT to merge the dynamic profile data with the static write information. The essence of the process is to use the basic block count information from the dynamic profile to determine which statically recorded writes actually occurred. We use this write information to construct an *object update graph* that represents which objects are assigned to the fields of which other objects. This allows us to account for situations such as when a write is applied to a `Local` object which is then put into an `Operand` object. The initial write has been propagated to an operand and needs to be counted as operand escaping.

The actual steps performed for each node in the CCT are:

- find the node's runtime return value
- build the node's object update graph
- use the object update graph to find the escape status for each occurring write and record these writes
- aggregate the write information from the child nodes to complete the write counts at this node

We also need to *resolve* any `ReturnValue` origin values from the static analysis phase. *Resolving* an origin value is the process of determining a concrete runtime origin value for `ReturnValue` types i.e. whether it is in fact a `Local`, `Global` or `Operand` object. We do this by finding the actual child in the CCT associated with the method call from the `ReturnValue` origin value and using the runtime return value from that node. If this runtime return value refers to an `Operand` origin value we then need to use our recorded child call information to determine the value of the operand when the method was called. So consider resolving the call to `StringBuilder.append(String)` at line 4 (we denote this as `ReturnValue[append()@4]`) in the method below:

```
1:  public static String buildString() {
2:    final StringBuilder sb = new StringBuilder();
3:    return sb.append("Hello")
4:            .append("World").toString();
5:  }
```

We know that `StringBuilder.append(String)` returns `this` so the child node in the CCT will have a return value of `Operand[0]`. Looking at the static call information for the `[append()@4]` method call we can see that operand 0

for that call is `ReturnValue[append()@3]` i.e. the result of the append on line 3. So we then resolve the call to `ReturnValue[append()@3]`. The associated child node will again have a return value of `Operand[0]` but this time the static call information for `[append()@3]` tells us that operand 0 is `Local[2]` (the new `StringBuilder` created at line 2 assigned to the `sb` variable). Therefore the final resolved value for `ReturnValue[append()@4]` is `Local[2]`.

The complete algorithm for resolving values is listed in Algorithm 1. Note that when processing the child return value *cv* there is no need to handle `ReturnValue` types as these child return values have themselves already been resolved i.e. they cannot have a `ReturnValue` type.

Algorithm 1 Resolve Value
_____
function RESOLVE(OriginValue *v*, CCTNode *node*)
  if ISCOMPOSITE(*v*) **then**
    OriginValue *result* ← null
    for all OriginValue *next* in *v.values* **do**
      OriginValue *r* ← RESOLVE(*next*, *node*)
      result ← MERGE(*result*, *r*)
    return result
  else if ISRETURNVALUE(v) **then**
    CCTNode *child* ← *node*.GETCHILD(*v.call.method*)
    OriginValue *cv* ← *child.returnValue*
    OriginValue *result* ← null
    if ISOPERAND(*cv*) **then**
      OriginValue *op* ← *v.call.arg[cv.opIndex]*
      OriginValue *r* ← RESOLVE(*op*, *node*)
      result ← MERGE(*result*, *r*)
    if ISLOCAL(*cv*) **then**
      result ← MERGE(*result*, Local)
    if ISGLOBAL(*cv*) **then**
      result ← MERGE(*result*, Global)
    return *result*
  else
    return *v*
_____

The algorithm for finding the runtime return value for a node is listed in Algorithm 2. The basic idea is that we merge together the possible return values from the basic blocks with non-zero invocation counts. Any basic block with a zero invocation count has not been executed and therefore we can exclude it from the runtime return value for the current node. Finally we resolve this merged runtime value (using Algorithm 1) to remove any references to `ReturnValue` types giving us a runtime return value purely in terms of `Local`, `Global` and `Operand` origin values.

Algorithm 2 Runtime Return Value
_____
function FINDRUNTIMERETURNVALUE(CCTNode *node*)
  OriginValue *result* ← null
  int *i* ← 0
  for all BasicBlock *bb* in *node.method.blocks* **do**
    if *node.blockCount[i]* > 0 **then**
      result ← MERGE(*result*, *bb.returnValue*)
    i ← *i* + 1
  return RESOLVE(*result*, *node*)
_____

An overview of the algorithm used to build the object update graph is listed in Algorithm 3. In the first stage we iterate over every recorded write from a basic block with a non-zero invocation count and add an edge from the putted value to the updated value. In the second stage we iterate over the child nodes in the CCT and merge in the parts of their object update graphs that impact the objects in the current node. That is every edge in the child graph that leaves an operand type or the returned object. When we merge edges from the child graphs we need to resolve operand types in the child to their values in the parent using the recorded child call information. In the final stage, if the method at the current node is an IO output method, we add an edge from each output operand to the special `Output` origin value type.

Algorithm 3 Building the Object Update Graph

---

function BUILDUPDATEGRAPH(CCTNode *node*)
  Graph *result ← new* Graph
  int *i ← 0*
  for all BasicBlock *bb* in *node.method.blocks* **do**
    if *node.blockCount*[*i*] > 0 **then**
      for all Write *w* in *bb.writes* **do**
        OriginValue *from ←*RESOLVE(*w.putted*, *node*)
        OriginValue *to ←*RESOLVE(*w.updated*, *node*)
        graph.ADDEDGE(*from*, *to*)
    i ← i + 1
  for all CCTNode *child* in *node.children* **do**
    for all OriginValue *from* in *child.graph* **do**
      if ISOPERAND(*from*) **then**
        Call *call ← node.method*.GETCALL(*child.method*)
        OriginValue *op ← call.arg*[*from.opIndex*]
        OriginValue *value ←* RESOLVE(*op*, *node*)
        for all OriginValue *to* in *child.graph* **do**
          if *child.graph*.HASPATH(*from*,*to*) **then**
            if ISOPERAND(*to*) **then**
              to ← call.arg[*to.opIndex*]
              to ← RESOLVE(*to*, *node*)
              graph.ADDEDGE(*value*, *to*)
            if ISGLOBAL(*to*) **then**
              graph.ADDEDGE(*value*, Global)
            if ISOUTPUT(*to*) **then**
              graph.ADDEDGE(*value*, Output)
            if *child*.ISRETURNED(*to*) **then**
              graph.ADDEDGE(*value*, Local)
  if ISOUTPUT(*node.method*) **then**
    for all int *op* in *node.method.operands* **do**
      if ISOUTPUTARGUMENT(*op*) **then**
        graph.ADDEDGE(Operand[*op*], Output)
  return *graph*

Once the object update graph has been built it is straightforward to count the object writes performed at the current node. We iterate again over the writes from the basic blocks with non-zero counts. For each write we use the object update graph to determine the escape status of the write and then account for the write accordingly.

The final stage of the process is to aggregate the child write information so that we have at each node the complete aggregate write information for the sub-tree. Total, global, output and non-escaping writes can be aggregated directly from the child nodes as for each of these types of writes the status is preserved from the child to the parent e.g. a global write in the child will always be a global write in the parent. The difficulty comes in determining the status of the operand and returned writes from the child, whether they escape the parent or are captured.

To accurately aggregate the child escaping write information we replay the operand and returned writes recorded by the child node, after again resolving the operands to their appropriate origin values in the current node using the recorded child call information. This allows us to evaluate the escape status for these writes in the current node and account for them accordingly. When we account for a write at a given node we keep a record of that accounting so that the parent can later use it to replay the operand and returned writes. These *write records* include the relevant writes from all child nodes, therefore a node only needs to

check the write records of its direct children and not all the nodes further down the sub-tree.

The final task is to calculate a value for each CCT node. This is simply the number of escaping writes at the node plus an adjustment for methods with primitive non-void return types. For these methods we added the method invocation count to the value, effectively giving them a value of at least one for each invocation, to reflect the primitive data value they return.

4.4 Example - Time Formatting

Consider the example code listed in Example 2. The CCT with the calculated write information for this code is shown in Figure 1 and the final write statistics aggregated by method are shown in Table 2.

Example 2 Time formatting

```
 1:  public static void outputTime(OutputStream out) {
 2:      final StringBuilder sb = new StringBuilder();
 3:      formatTime(sb, 123456789, false);
 4:      out.write(sb.toString().getBytes());
 5:  }

 6:  public static void formatTime(StringBuilder sb, long time,
 7:                              boolean appendMillis) {
 8:      long seconds = time / 1000;
 9:      long minutes = seconds / 60;
10:      long hours = minutes / 60;
11:
12:      sb.append(zeroPad(4, hours)).append(" hours ");
13:      sb.append(zeroPad(2, minutes % 60)).append(" minutes ");
14:      sb.append(zeroPad(2, seconds % 60));
15:      if (appendMillis) {
16:          sb.append(".").append(zeroPad(3, time % 1000));
17:      }
18:      sb.append(" seconds");
19:  }

20:  public static String zeroPad(int 1, long v) {
21:      String result = "" + v;
22:      while (result.length() < 1) {
23:          result = "0" + result;
24:      }
25:      return result;
26:  }
```

This code outputs a formatted time string to the given `OutputStream`. The code as written with the hard-coded value of 123456789 outputs the string "0034 **hours** 17 **minutes** 36 **seconds**" (32 characters). We begin our analysis with the `zeroPad` method. This method constructs a zero-padded string representation of a `long` that is at least a given minimum length. On every invocation the statement on line 21 creates a new `StringBuilder` and calls `append(long)` and then `toString()` on it. When the result needs to be zero-padded, the statement on line 23 creates an additional `StringBuilder` (this time via the `<init>(String)` constructor) and more calls to `append(String)` and `toString()`. In our example `zeroPad` is invoked 3 times, and on one of these invocations it twice iterates around the zero-pad loop, so in total we have 5 calls to `toString()` which cumulatively have 33 returned writes. The return value for `zeroPad` is the result of these `toString()` calls so the number of returned writes for `zeroPad` is 33. These are the only escaping writes for the method, all writes generated by the use of the `StringBuilder` objects are captured by the method.

The `formatTime` method populates a `StringBuilder` object (passed as operand 0) with a formatted time string for a given `long` value. It calls `append(String)` 6 times, 3 times

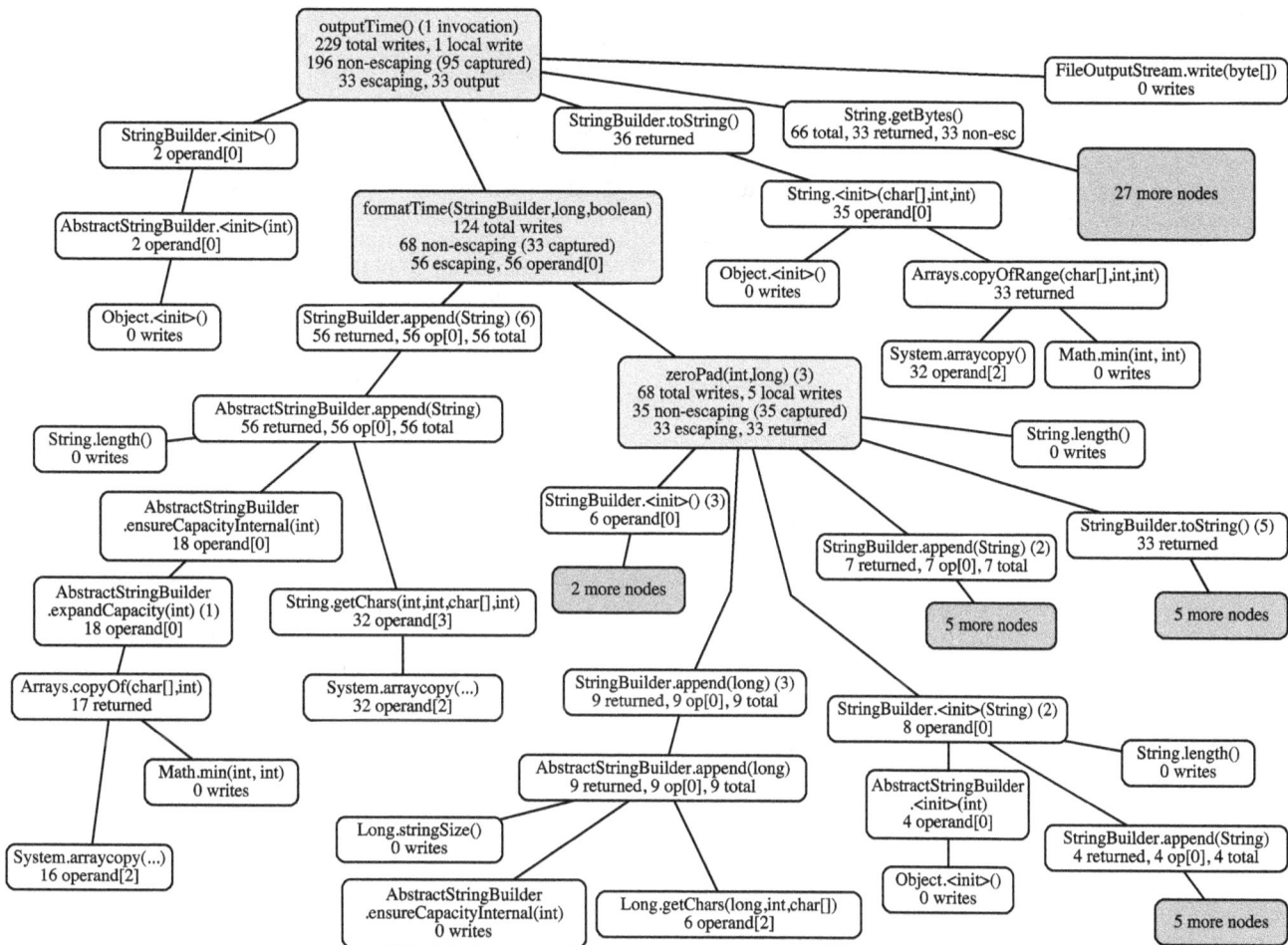

Figure 1: CCT annotated with write information for Example 2

The shaded blocks represent sub-trees that have been truncated for simplicity, most of these are shown in full elsewhere in the tree. The number in parentheses is the node's invocation count, where it is not shown the invocation count is the same as for the parent node. All non-zero write counts for each node are also shown, where a count for a particular type of write is not given it can be taken as 0.

Table 2: Aggregated Method Write Counts - Example 2

Method	Inv.	Cost	Value	Efficiency	Total	Esc	Non-Esc	Cap	Out	Ret	Op	Local
outputTime(OutputStream)	1	3563	33	00.926	**229**	33	**196**	95	33	0	0	1
System.arraycopy(...)	18	924	132	14.285	132	132	0	0	0	0	132	132
formatTime(StringBuilder,long,boolean)	1	2100	56	02.666	124	56	68	33	0	0	56	0
StringBuilder.toString()	6	675	75	11.111	69	69	0	0	0	69	0	6
zeroPad(IJ)	3	1291	36	02.788	68	33	35	35	0	33	0	5
StringBuilder.append(String)	10	1069	67	06.267	67	67	0	0	0	67	67	0
AbstractStringBuilder.append(String)	10	1009	67	06.640	67	67	0	0	0	67	67	10
String.getBytes()	1	1121	33	02.943	66	33	33	0	0	33	0	0
StringEncoder.encode(char[],int,int)	1	906	33	03.642	66	33	33	33	0	33	0	1
String.<init>(char[],int,int)	6	621	63	10.144	63	63	0	0	0	0	63	12
Arrays.copyOfRange(char[],int,int)	6	477	51	10.691	51	51	0	0	0	51	0	6
String.getChars(int,int,char[],int)	10	473	39	08.245	39	39	0	0	0	0	39	0
Arrays.copyOf(byte[],int)	1	243	33	13.580	33	33	0	0	0	33	0	1
UTF_8$Encoder.encode(char[],int,int,byte[])	1	603	33	05.472	32	32	0	0	0	0	32	32
AbstractStringBuilder.expandCapacity(int)	1	153	18	11.764	18	18	0	0	0	0	18	1
AbstractStringBuilder.ensureCapacityInternal(int)	13	247	18	07.287	18	18	0	0	0	0	18	0
Arrays.copyOf(char[],int)	1	132	17	12.878	17	17	0	0	0	17	0	1
AbstractStringBuilder.<init>(int)	6	42	12	28.571	12	12	0	0	0	0	12	12
AbstractStringBuilder.append(long)	3	414	9	02.173	9	9	0	0	0	9	9	3
StringBuilder.append(long)	3	432	9	02.083	9	9	0	0	0	9	9	0
StringBuilder.<init>(String)	2	186	8	04.301	8	8	0	0	0	0	8	0
StringBuilder.<init>()	4	44	8	18.181	8	8	0	0	0	0	8	0
Long.getChars(long,int,char[])	3	228	6	02.631	6	6	0	0	0	0	6	6
String.length()	17	68	17	25.000	0	0	0	0	0	0	0	0
Math.min(int,int)	9	47	9	19.148	0	0	0	0	0	0	0	0
Long.stringSize(long)	3	78	3	03.846	0	0	0	0	0	0	0	0
Totals								196				**229**

with the result of a call to `zeroPad` and 3 times with string literal values. These 6 calls induce 56 operand escaping writes to the `StringBuilder` made up of:

- 32 individual character writes
- 6 writes (one per call) to the builder's count variable
- 18 further writes that occur when the builder needs to expand the capacity of its internal buffer - this expansion creates a new buffer (1 write), copies the existing 16 characters into it and assigns it (1 more write) to its buffer variable

The 33 returned writes from `zeroPad` are all captured by `formatTime` as the strings returned from `zeroPad` do not escape `formatTime`. Therefore we have 68 non-escaping writes (the 33 captured by `formatTime` plus the 35 captured by `zeroPad`), 56 escaping writes and 124 writes in total.

The `outputTime` method creates a `StringBuilder`, passes it to `formatTime`, then calls `toString()` and finally `getBytes()` on the result to create a byte array it can pass to the given `OutputStream`. The writes associated with the builder (3 from its construction and 56 operand writes from `formatTime`) plus the 36 writes returned from `toString()` make up the 95 captured writes as neither of these objects escape the method. The 33 returned writes from `getBytes()` are output escaping because the returned byte array is passed to our IO output method. There are 33 returned writes for our 32 length byte array because of the one write allocated for each newly constructed object, in this case the byte array itself. The `getBytes` call also has 33 non-escaping writes because the string encoder does not know the exact length of the byte array to allocate ahead of time. Therefore it needs to encode into an oversized byte array and copy the array when it is finished to return an array of the exact size.

Even from this simple example there are some points of note in the method write statistics in Table 2.

- The methods with the most obvious inefficiencies (such as `zeroPad` and `formatTime`) had high numbers of captured writes and low efficiency values.
- The difference in efficiency between the builder's `append(String)` and `append(long)` methods shows how much more work has to be done to convert a two's complement form value into a string when compared to simply copying existing character data.
- `System.arraycopy` was the root source of more than half of all the writes in our example. Whilst this is a contrived example this was a trend we also noticed in our later experiments.

5. EVALUATION

In order to evaluate our blended efficiency analysis we have conducted experiments with the 14 benchmark applications in the DaCapo-9.12-bach suite [3]. Using the results of those experiments we have undertaken:

- A study of the characteristics of application efficiency
- Three detailed case studies that describe real optimisations we made in the benchmark applications based upon our efficiency analysis results

All benchmarks were run with their default input size. All experiments were run on a quad-core 2.4 GHz Intel Core i7 with 8 GB 1600 MHz DDR3 memory running Mac OS X 10.9.3. We used Oracle's Java SE Runtime Environment (build 1.7.0_71-b14) with the HotSpot 64-Bit Server VM (build 24.71-b01, mixed mode).

We profiled the benchmarks in the same manner that we conducted our experiments in our previous paper [10]. That is we executed the majority of the benchmarks in the fashion outlined in the most recent JP2 paper [15], but for the client/server benchmarks (`tomcat`, `tradebeans` and `tradesoap`) and the benchmarks with background worker threads (`eclipse` and `xalan`) we used our own wrapper which activated profiling for the entire run of the benchmark. We also had to disable intrinsic methods (a feature of the JIT compiler) in order to obtain complete profiles as otherwise our instrumentation was by-passed for these methods.

Once we had obtained our captured profiles we ran our offline blended analysis over the profiles to analyse the runtime behaviour and efficiency of the benchmarks. Our results are summarised in Table 3. The table shows for each benchmark:

- the size of the captured CCT
- the number of unique methods in the CCT
- the cost – the number of bytecode instructions executed
- the number of IO output writes
- the efficiency rating, this is $output/cost$

The next three columns show the percentage of the total benchmark activity that had certain properties:

- had no side effects – no output, operand or global writes
- had no effect – no side effects and no return value
- had low efficiency – when $value/cost < 0.1$

We were also interested in the distribution of inefficient behaviour within the benchmarks. Therefore we analysed the percentage of the captured writes across each benchmark that were attributed to different locations, specifically:

- the top single capturing node in the CCT
- the top capturing method
- the ten top capturing methods

To analyse the importance of `System.arraycopy` we calculated the percentage of writes for which it is responsible. Finally we list the time taken for the analysis to complete.

The results show that across the benchmarks, using median values:

- 42.2% of all activity was side effect free
- 2.0% of all activity **had no effect**
- 25.3% of all writes were caused by `System.arraycopy`
- 78.4% of all captured writes came from the top ten capturing methods

5.1 Case Studies

To evaluate the full potential of our blended efficiency analysis we investigated several of the benchmarks in more detail. For each we used the results of our analysis to identify several optimisation opportunities. We implemented improvements for these opportunities and re-ran the benchmarks to confirm the improvement. Here we present the results of the first case study in some detail, before summarising the other case studies[2].

5.1.1 Case Study: h2

The `h2` benchmark runs a series of SQL load tests using the H2 pure Java relational database implementation. We ran our blended efficiency analysis and reviewed the top ten:

- side effect free methods (Table 4)

---

[2]`https://www.cs.auckland.ac.nz/~dmap001/efficiency` has more details and complete results.

Table 3: Results for DaCapo benchmarks

Benchmark	CCT Nodes	Method Count	Cost millions	Output thousands	Effncy	Side Effect Free	Effect Free	Low Effncy	Captured Writes 1 Node	Captured Writes 1 Meth	Captured Writes 10 Meth	System arraycopy	Analysis Time (s)
lusearch	127,386	2,592	9,131	421,942	04.621	22.07%	00.86%	05.85%	46.77%	46.77%	98.34%	24.75%	2.8
avrora	271,610	3,448	8,434	600	00.007	26.22%	05.07%	06.34%	00.67%	00.69%	01.75%	00.88%	12.9
luindex	279,484	3,435	2,869	92,555	03.226	28.37%	03.01%	10.93%	42.31%	44.57%	97.18%	12.31%	6.2
h2	412,539	4,580	13,934	11,108	00.079	75.83%	10.25%	72.49%	44.80%	54.42%	96.42%	24.01%	7.9
sunflow	432,017	4,473	50,430	17	00.000	21.15%	00.80%	18.17%	14.24%	79.98%	99.27%	00.14%	9.4
xalan	506,441	4,545	9,218	237,653	02.578	36.24%	01.59%	14.40%	02.39%	28.62%	82.36%	21.78%	21.4
batik	782,742	7,645	2,549	18,339	00.719	14.33%	00.48%	05.19%	27.93%	27.93%	73.94%	16.27%	26.8
fop	814,713	7,572	1,015	16,642	01.639	46.60%	02.69%	21.82%	09.85%	14.81%	76.50%	40.67%	365.0
tomcat	3,360,093	13,802	5,488	92,593	01.687	41.24%	01.40%	17.85%	13.63%	17.00%	67.73%	57.46%	361.5
pmd	5,314,934	5,425	2,630	65	00.002	43.24%	03.34%	31.17%	01.69%	36.82%	85.96%	25.88%	129.9
tradebeans	9,859,665	29,764	28,187	85,040	00.301	63.53%	04.26%	31.48%	02.88%	27.05%	78.76%	47.54%	575.4
tradesoap	10,558,423	30,387	31,993	284,125	00.888	50.16%	02.01%	21.10%	03.41%	16.24%	71.72%	50.22%	569.9
eclipse	22,720,671	17,124	99,268	2,271,788	02.288	63.25%	01.15%	31.82%	05.04%	20.23%	77.96%	47.97%	1,579.6
jython	26,501,991	9,082	15,879	863	00.005	70.36%	01.97%	36.33%	05.72%	12.03%	64.74%	56.55%	1,264.1
Minimum						14.33%	00.48%	05.19%	00.67%	00.69%	01.75%	00.14%	
Median						**42.24%**	**01.99%**	**19.63%**	**07.79%**	**27.49%**	**78.36%**	**25.32%**	
Maximum						75.83%	10.25%	72.49%	46.77%	79.98%	99.27%	57.46%	

- effect free methods (Table 5)
- low efficiency methods (Table 6), and
- capturing methods (Table 7)

From these methods we targeted the following opportunities:

`JdbcResultSet.checkColumnIndex()` — The top four no effect methods are all closely related in that `checkColumnIndex` calls `checkClosed` on the result set which in turn calls `checkClosed` on the connection. We discussed the improvement we were able to make to `checkColumnIndex` in our motivating example in Section 2. We were able to almost completely eliminate the cost of `checkColumnIndex`.

Much of the remaining effect free cost is due to `TraceObject.debugCodeCall()`, which uses debug logging to record the value of every API method call. This method is effect free when debug level logging is disabled. This cost could be trivially eliminated from a production build if trace logging was never to be used in production.

`TPCC.calculateSumDB()` — This method was the top low efficiency method and the second highest capturing method in the benchmark. This is part of the DaCapo benchmark harness that generates the SQL load against the database. The method calculates a checksum for the database state so that it can be verified the database has been reset between each benchmark iteration. It uses a very inefficient procedure for creating the checksum, converting every field retrieved from the database into a string before processing the strings into a digested checksum. We were able to change the implementation to avoid this conversion into strings for number and timestamp fields, reducing the cost of `calculateSumDB` by 62%.

`ConditionAndOr.getValue()` — The third and fourth top low efficiency methods are part of the database engine that evaluates conditional matching clauses in SQL statements. The profile for these methods shows a very large proportion of their cost was being spent doing string comparisons. We changed the string comparison code to only perform a full comparison if the strings hashcode values matched, reducing the cost of `ConditionAndOr.getValue()` by 19%. This was effective because:

- the vast majority of comparisons are between strings that do not match, meaning the hashcode check can be used to cheaply avoid most full comparisons
- H2 internally caches and reuses string values, so the cost of calculating the hashcode value is amortised over the number of times the string is compared

`JdbcResultSet.getColumnIndex()` – Internally H2 stores the result set data in indexed arrays, so `getColumnIndex()` is used to convert a column or alias name into an index to retrieve the appropriate data. To do this efficiently the implementation builds a map from the column and alias names to column index values the first time it is called. However, because H2 uses case-insensitive column names, it blindly converts all column and alias names to upper case before storing them in the map. It therefore needs to convert the passed column name to upper case on every subsequent method call so it can check the map for the correct index. We found it much more efficient to instead use the map as a cache of index values for previously seen column names, and search for the column index by brute force when it is not found in the map. This avoids the need for the converting of strings to

Table 4: Top 10 No Side Effect Methods — h2

Method	%Cost
org.h2.index.BaseIndex.compareRows(SeachRow,SeachRow)	18.057
org.h2.value.ValueTimestamp.getString()	14.745
java.sql.Timestamp.toString()	14.585
org.h2.index.BaseIndex.compareValues(Value,Value,int)	10.068
org.h2.expression.Expression.getBooleanValue(Session)	09.535
org.h2.expression.ConditionAndOr.getValue(Session)	08.396
org.h2.expression.Comparison.getValue(Session)	08.133
org.h2.index.TreeIndex.findFirstNode(SearchRow,boolean)	08.006
org.h2.jdbc.JdbcResultSet.checkClosed()	06.183
org.h2.jdbc.JdbcResultSet.checkColumnIndex(int)	06.142

Table 5: Top 10 No Effect Methods — h2

Method	%Cost
org.h2.jdbc.JdbcResultSet.checkClosed()	06.183
org.h2.jdbc.JdbcResultSet.checkColumnIndex(int)	06.142
org.h2.jdbc.JdbcConnection.checkClosed(boolean)	03.547
org.h2.jdbc.JdbcConnection.checkClosed()	01.936
org.h2.message.TraceObject.debugCodeCall(String,long)	01.166
org.h2.message.TraceObject.debugCodeCall(String)	00.121
org.h2.command.Prepared.checkParameters()	00.075
org.h2.command.CommandContainer.recompileIfRequired()	00.017
org.h2.table.Column.updateSequenceIfRequired(Session,Val)	00.015
org.h2.table.TableData.checkRowCount(Session,Index,int)	00.015

Table 6: Top 10 Low Efficiency Methods — h2

Method	%Cost
org.dacapo.h2.TPCC.calculateSumDB(String,int)	48.969
org.dacapo.h2.TPCC.calculateSumDB()	48.969
org.h2.expression.ConditionAndOr.getValue(Session)	08.396
org.h2.expression.Comparison.getValue(Session)	08.133
org.h2.index.TreeIndex.findFirstNode(SearchRow,boolean)	08.006
org.h2.jdbc.JdbcResultSet.checkClosed()	06.183
org.h2.jdbc.JdbcResultSet.checkColumnIndex(int)	06.142
org.h2.expression.ExpressionColumn.getValue(Session)	04.998
org.h2.jdbc.JdbcConnection.checkClosed()	03.547
org.h2.result.Row.getValue(int)	02.321

Table 7: Top 10 Capturing Methods — h2

Method	Captured
java.sql.Timestamp.toString()	85,455,479
org.dacapo.h2.TPCC.calculateSumDB(String,int)	54,946,291
org.h2.jdbc.JdbcResultSet.getColumnIndex(Strg)	4,939,507
java.math.BigInteger.toString(int)	1,047,292
org.h2.jdbc.JdbcSQLException.buildMessage()	993,060
java.text.MessageFormat.applyPattern(String)	935,691
java.math.BigDecimal.divideAndRound(...)	814,314
org.apache.derbyTesting .system.oe.direct.Standard.payment(...)V	813,290
java.math.BigInteger.pow(I)	776,589
java.text.Format.format(Object)	698,562

upper case and the up front caching of every column name, when only a few columns may be requested. This change reduced the cost of `getColumnIndex` by 80%.

`JdbcSQLException.buildMessage()` — This method on the `JdbcSQLException` class is used to generate the message string returned from its `getMessage()` method. However `buildMessage` was often called multiple times during the construction of an exception as different pieces of information about the exception were added to the exception object, and then often the expensively constructed message was never used by the exception handler that ultimately received the exception. We changed the implementation to instead lazily construct the message if and when it was first requested. This change completely eliminated all calls to `buildMessage()` in the benchmark.

With these combined changes we were able to reduce the total runtime cost of the benchmark by 36%.

5.1.2 Case Study: fop

The `fop` benchmark uses the Apache FOP library to apply an XSL-FO stylesheet to an XML document to create a PDF document.

`AbstractLayoutManager.addChildLM` — The top capturing write method in the benchmark is responsible for adding a child layout manager to an existing parent. However the method constructs a string for a trace level logging call that was not guarded by a check that trace level logging was enabled, so the string was expensively constructed on every call even though in practice it was never used. We guarded the construction of the string with a `log.isTraceEnabled()` call and reduced the cost of this method by 97%.

`Glyphs.charToGlyphName` — The top six low efficiency methods recorded in the benchmark were all related to this one method that is used during the postscript header generation. During the encoding of font information in the postscript header several common character sets are encoded using information loaded from text files. This encoding in-

formation was loaded into a number of large arrays which were then searched in a brute force manner for the correct encoding information, resulting in many thousands of string comparisons. We loaded the encoding information into maps instead, resulting in a much more efficient lookup process, reducing the cost of this method by 99%.

`PSRenderer.renderText` – The second top capturing write location is responsible for generating the correct postscript command for generating a specific piece of text. This method takes an input string and constructs another (usually very similar) string from it, applying font mapping and postscript character escaping. For many values the input text was unchanged. We added code to handle this common case much more efficiently, falling back to the original behaviour when necessary, reducing the cost of method by 89%.

With these three changes we were able to reduce the overall runtime cost of the benchmark by 28%.

5.1.3 Case Study: luindex

The `luindex` benchmark uses the Apache Lucene library to index a set of text documents.

`Token.initTermBuffer` — The top effect free method in the benchmark is responsible for checking and maintaining a consistent internal state in the `Token` data structure. This data structure is used to represent a string and some additional meta data about the context in which the string occurred. The string value can be initialised as either a Java `String` or char `[]` and the data structure has different fields that store these values respectively. The `initTermBuffer` method is used internally to convert the Java `String` value (if it exists) to the equivalent char `[]` value as necessary. The majority of the methods on `Token` wish to process the string value as a char `[]` and therefore `initTermBuffer` is called very frequently to ensure the char `[]` value is available. Given that the value is almost always a char `[]` already, often this work is unnecessary. We changed the implementation to convert the Java `String` value to a char `[]` when the value was initialised so that we then never had to check a later point if the char `[]` value existed. This removed the cost of this method entirely from the benchmark and reduced the overall cost of the benchmark by 4%.

6. DISCUSSION

The overall results show that there is a significant proportion of the activity in the benchmarks that is side effect free, effect free or has low efficiency. This is important because each of these represent potential optimisation opportunities. With side effect free activity the implementation can be treated as a black box that can have its results cached or be completely replaced. Effect free methods represent behaviour that could potentially be eliminated completely as it is having no practical benefit. Low efficiency methods have a poor cost / benefit ratio, meaning they too represent potential optimisation opportunities, albeit ones that are more difficult to realise than with either side effect free or effect free methods.

Interpreting the overall application efficiency measure for the benchmarks needs to be done with caution. Whilst we feel that our chosen measure has value for many real-world applications it is not appropriate for some of the benchmarks (e.g. `avrora`, `pmd` and `jython`) that are not focussed on producing output. In the other benchmarks it perhaps gives some insight into the nature of the benchmark rather than being a fair absolute measure of efficiency. For example the low efficiency number for sunflow is understandable given the computational nature of graphics rendering. The overall efficiency measure is useful when comparing similar applications, or different releases of the same application.

As was evident in the case studies, measuring and comparing efficiency at the individual method level within an application is more valid. Activity within a single application is more homogeneous, making efficiency outliers more unusual and interesting.

In our case studies we highlighted a selection of the optimisation opportunities we found and how we were able to effectively address them. These were not the only optimisation opportunities that we discovered, there were numerous others, and in analysing these we noted a number of trends.

String processing is often inefficient – Many of the optimisation opportunities we found involved the processing and manipulation of strings. There seemed to be two root causes for many of these problems:

1) Transcoding between the JVM's UTF-16 based char representation and the most common 8-bit character sets (e.g. ISO-8859-1 or UTF-8). Frequently input data would be received as UTF-8, be decoded to a Java string, passed around and manipulated before being encoded back to UTF-8 on output. If the underlying representation of a string in Java had been based on UTF-8 rather than UTF-16 then much of this transcoding would be unnecessary.

2) APIs that use Java strings instead of mutable `String-Builder` objects. There are many routines that build up a large text results out of smaller values but many of these accept and return the immutable Java `String` object as values. Consequently when the results of these methods are composed the character content is copied into a new string object each time. If more of these methods accepted `String-Builder` or `CharBuffer` objects then much of this repeated copying could be avoided.

No effect methods are common – We found a great number of methods that were having no practical effect. In almost all cases the method would check some condition to determine whether or not to take an action, and in practice the condition never held true. The most common examples were assertion checkers such as `ArrayList.rangeCheck()`, responsible for raising an exception if some condition did not hold, and debug logging methods. Often these can be eliminated with the trade-off of less flexible logging or less precise exception reporting.

Captured write locations are often quick wins – Through our analysis we were able to find different types of optimisation opportunities but often the top captured write methods were the easiest to address. Locations with a high number of captured writes naturally contained code that performed work that was then discarded. Often it was possible to quickly understand what work was being wasted and could be somehow avoided or reused.

Inefficient activity is very localised – Our results show that the top ten capturing methods accounted for a median value of 78.4% of all captured writes in each benchmark. This means that an engineer often has only a very few, usually high value, locations to inspect to attempt to substantially improve efficiency.

System.arraycopy is the source of many writes – Across our benchmarks `System.arraycopy` accounted for a median value of just over 25% of all writes. For the benchmarks most similar to many real world applications (`tomcat`, `tradebeans`, `tradesoap`, and `eclipse`) this was even higher, accounting for at least 47% of all writes. This is important because it shows that `arraycopy` is a significant hotspot for many applications and yet in our experience most Java profilers fail to show this, probably because it is a native method. In our experiments we had no evidence that `arraycopy` was such an important source of activity until we specifically customised the JP2 profiler to record its writes.

6.1 Threats to Validity

The most obvious threat to validity for our analysis is that our measure of value may not accurately reflect a true measure of value. In our case studies we have found the concept of escaping writes to be intuitive and useful. It seems to naturally quantify the amount of useful work a method is producing and also works well to explain (via captured writes) how work done by some methods is then wasted by a calling method. Our value measure however does not reflect the complexity of the data escaping a method. For example a method which compresses a large byte array before returning it would be valued less than one that did not, even though intuitively the results are equivalent.

There are also some sources of imprecision in our analysis which can lead us to overstate the value being provided by a particular execution path.

Our analysis does not account for situations where a single field is being repeatedly overwritten with new values. In this case the actual amount of new data escaping a method may be less than the number of writes the method is performing. Ideally we would like to classify the writes that are overwritten as being captured.

The approach we take to handling object field references again means that we can overstate the value provided by many methods. A future improvement would be to more precisely model the use of field references so we can track the escape status of writes to individual fields. Presently all writes to any field of an object are regarded as escaping a method if any other field in the object escapes the method.

We do not distinguish between different types of output. For example debug logging being sent to a file on disk is categorised in a similar manner to an HTTP response being sent over the network. It is likely that these two types of output would be valued differently by an engineer investigating the performance of their application.

Despite these sources of imprecision causing us to overvalue some execution paths we were still able to find real optimisation opportunities. Our analysis is deliberately conservative so that none of these problems cause us to understate the value of a method. Therefore we can take our current measures for the percentage of activity that is side effect free, effect free and low efficiency as lower bounds on their real values. Future work to help improve the accuracy of our analysis should make it even more effective.

Finally we would like to evaluate our efficiency analysis on real world large scale object oriented software. We are encouraged by the results we have achieved with the Da-Capo benchmarks, which we believe are representative of many Java applications and therefore we are confident that our results are applicable for many real world applications. However we would like to validate our approach with a real world case study.

7. CONCLUSION

Existing performance analysis tools and approaches focus on understanding the distribution of runtime costs in an application. However without understanding the value being provided in return for this expense it is difficult to establish where effort is being wasted and where optimisation opportunities might truly exist. In this paper we present a blended analysis approach to quantifying the value provided by all execution paths in an application, thereby enabling an analysis of their efficiency and a practical cost/benefit approach to performance analysis. This allows the discovery of new optimisation opportunities not readily apparent from the original profile data. The results of our experiments and the performance improvements we made in our case studies demonstrate that efficiency analysis is an effective technique that can be used to complement existing performance engineering approaches.

8. ACKNOWLEDGMENTS

David Maplesden is supported by a University of Auckland Doctoral Scholarship.

9. REFERENCES

[1] G. Ammons, T. Ball, and J. R. Larus. Exploiting hardware performance counters with flow and context sensitive profiling. *Proc. of the Conf. on Prog. Language Design and Impl.*, pages 85–96, 1997.

[2] S. Bhattacharya, M. G. Nanda, K. Gopinath, and M. Gupta. Reuse, Recycle to De-bloat Software. *Lecture Notes in Comp. Sci.*, 6813:408–432, 2011.

[3] S. M. Blackburn, R. Garner, C. Hoffmann, A. M. Khan, K. S. McKinley, R. Bentzur, A. Diwan, D. Feinberg, D. Frampton, S. Z. Guyer, M. Hirzel, A. Hosking, M. Jump, H. Lee, J. E. B. Moss, A. Phansalkar, D. Stefanovic, T. VanDrunen, D. von Dincklage, and B. Wiedermann. The DaCapo Benchmarks: Java Benchmarking Development and Analysis. *Proc. of the Conf. on Object Oriented Prog. Systems Languages and App.*, pages 169–190, 2006.

[4] B. Blanchet. Escape analysis for object-oriented languages: application to java. *Proc. of the Conf. on Object Oriented Prog. Systems Languages and App.*, pages 20–34, 1999.

[5] A. E. Chis, N. Mitchell, E. Schonberg, G. Sevitsky, P. O. Sullivan, T. Parsons, and J. Murphy. Patterns of Memory Inefficiency. *Lecture Notes in Comp. Sci.*, 6813:383–407, 2011.

[6] D. C. D'Elia, C. Demetrescu, and I. Finocchi. Mining hot calling contexts in small space. *Proc. of the Conf. on Prog. Language Design and Impl.*, pages 516–527, 2011.

[7] B. Dufour, B. G. Ryder, and G. Sevitsky. Blended analysis for performance understanding of framework-based applications. *Proc. of the Int'l Symp. on Soft. Testing and Analysis*, pages 118–128, 2007.

[8] B. Dufour, B. G. Ryder, and G. Sevitsky. A scalable technique for characterizing the usage of temporaries in framework-intensive Java applications. *Proc. of the 16th Int'l Symp. on Foundations of Soft. Eng.*, pages 59–70, 2008.

[9] D. Maplesden, E. Tempero, J. Hosking, and J. C. Grundy. Performance Analysis for Object-Oriented Software: A Systematic Mapping. *IEEE Transactions on Soft. Eng.*, 41(7):691–710, 2015.

[10] D. Maplesden, E. Tempero, J. Hosking, and J. C. Grundy. Subsuming Methods: Finding New Optimisation Opportunities in Object-Oriented Software. *6th ACM/SPEC Int'l Conf. on Performance Engineering*, pages 175–186, 2015.

[11] N. Mitchell, E. Schonberg, and G. Sevitsky. Four Trends Leading to Java Runtime Bloat. *IEEE Software*, 27(1):56–63, 2010.

[12] N. Mitchell, G. Sevitsky, and H. Srinivasan. The diary of a datum: an approach to modeling runtime complexity in framework-based applications. *Library-Centric Software Design*, page 85, 2005.

[13] N. Mitchell, G. Sevitsky, and H. Srinivasan. Modeling Runtime Behavior in Framework-Based Applications. *Lecture Notes in Comp. Sci.*, 4067:429–451, 2006.

[14] K. Nguyen and G. Xu. Cachetor: detecting cacheable data to remove bloat. *Proc. of the 9th Joint Meeting on Foundations of Soft. Eng.*, pages 268–278, 2013.

[15] A. Sarimbekov, A. Sewe, W. Binder, P. Moret, and M. Mezini. JP2: Call-site aware calling context profiling for the Java Virtual Machine. *Science of Computer Programming*, 79:146–157, 2014.

[16] A. Sarimbekov, A. Sewe, W. Binder, P. Moret, M. Schoeberl, and M. Mezini. Portable and accurate collection of calling-context-sensitive bytecode metrics for the Java virtual machine. *Proc. of the Int'l Conf. on Principles and Practice of Prog. in Java*, page 11, 2011.

[17] O. Shacham, M. Vechev, and E. Yahav. Chameleon: Adaptive Selection of Collections. *Proc. of the Conf. on Prog. Language Design and Impl.*, pages 408–418, 2009.

[18] G. Xu. Finding reusable data structures. *Proc. of the Conf. on Object Oriented Prog. Systems Languages and App.*, page 1017, 2012.

[19] G. Xu, N. Mitchell, M. Arnold, A. Rountev, E. Schonberg, and G. Sevitsky. Finding low-utility data structures. *Proc. of the Conf. on Prog. Language Design and Impl.*, pages 174–186, 2010.

[20] G. Xu, N. Mitchell, M. Arnold, A. Rountev, E. Schonberg, and G. Sevitsky. Scalable Runtime Bloat Detection Using Abstract Dynamic Slicing. *ACM Transactions Soft. Eng. Methodology*, 23(3):23:1–23:50, 2014.

[21] G. Xu, N. Mitchell, M. Arnold, A. Rountev, and G. Sevitsky. Software Bloat Analysis: Finding, Removing, and Preventing Performance Problems in Modern Large-Scale Object-Oriented Applications. *Proc. of the FSE/SDP Workshop on the Future of Soft. Eng. Research*, pages 421–425, 2010.

[22] G. Xu and A. Rountev. Detecting inefficiently-used containers to avoid bloat. *Proc. of the Conf. on Prog. Language Design and Impl.*, pages 160–173, 2010.

[23] D. Yan, G. Xu, and A. Rountev. Uncovering performance problems in Java applications with reference propagation profiling. *Int'l Conf. on Soft. Eng.*, pages 134–144, 2012.

Automated Extraction of Network Traffic Models Suitable for Performance Simulation

Piotr Rygielski
Institute of Computer Science
University of Würzburg,
Germany
piotr.rygielski
@uni-wuerzburg.de

Viliam Simko
FZI Forschungszentrum
Informatik
Haid-und-Neu-Straße 10–14,
76131 Karlsruhe, Germany
simko@fzi.de

Felix Sittner
Zentrum für Telematik e.V.
97218 Gerbrunn, Germany
felix.sittner
@telematik-zentrum.de

Doris Aschenbrenner
Zentrum für Telematik e.V.
97218 Gerbrunn, Germany
doris.aschenbrenner
@telematik-zentrum.de

Samuel Kounev
Institute of Computer Science
University of Würzburg,
Germany
samuel.kounev
@uni-wuerzburg.de

Klaus Schilling
Institute of Computer Science
University of Würzburg,
Germany
schi@informatik.uni-
wuerzburg.de

ABSTRACT

Data centers are increasingly becoming larger and dynamic due to virtualization. In order to leverage the performance modeling and prediction techniques, such as Palladio Component Model or Descartes Modeling Language, in such a dynamic environments, it is necessary to automate the model extraction. Building and maintaining such models manually is not feasible anymore due to their size and the level of details. This paper is focused on traffic models that are an essential part of network infrastructure. Our goal is to decompose real traffic dumps into models suitable for performance prediction using Descartes Network Infrastructure modeling approach. The main challenge was to efficiently encode an arbitrary signal in the form of simple traffic generators while maintaining the shape of the original signal. We show that a typical 15 minute long *tcpdump* trace can be compressed to $0.4 - 15\%$ of its original size whereas the relative median of extraction error is close to 0% for the most of the 69 examined traces.

1. INTRODUCTION

Modern IT data center systems have increasingly complex layered architectures composed of loosely-coupled components deployed in virtualized environments. The use of virtualization provides increased flexibility and efficiency by enabling the sharing of resources among independent applications. The computing resources are connected by virtualized network infrastructure that spans across the virtual machines and servers. However, management of the performance of such complex infrastructures is challenging. It is difficult to follow the dynamic changes of the virtual infrastructures without any proper representation or model.

The following questions may arise during operation: How the user-caused workloads affect the load of the data center network? How such operations as e.g., migration of VMs, provisioning and deprovisioning of extra resources affect the performance of data center network? Which part of the data center network is a bottleneck if any? How a network reconfiguration would affect the Service Level Agreements (SLAs) provided to the end-user? To answer such questions it is necessary to predict the network performance during operation and observe the influences of the network to the other parts of the system when the workloads change.

Existing approaches to network performance prediction are mostly based on coarse-grained performance models, that treat the network components as black-boxes additionally abstracting the link to the computing infrastructure and the architecture of the applications running in the data center. On the other hand, there exist many fine grained simulation models for network performance but such models usually capture only selected specific aspects of the network infrastructure whereas other aspects are abstracted. The Descartes Network Infrastructures (DNI) modeling approach [11] addresses the gap between the coarse-grained and simulation models. However, the process of model extraction remains challenging for a DNI model as well as for the other network performance models [20].

Usually, a performance model must represent the structure of the modeled system, its performance-relevant variables, and the workload. Building such performance models that capture different aspects of system behavior is a challenging, error-prone, and time-consuming task when applied manually to real-size systems [8]. The data about the network topology, configuration, and deployment of software may be fragmented between different engineers, obsolete or not documented at all. Fortunately, both, the static or slowly-changing parameters, such as: topology, configuration, and software deployment can be automatically extracted out of a running system assuming that the access to the system is permitted. However, the model of the network workload (network traffic) remains the challenging part mainly due to the high dynamism and large volume of the data transmitted via network in every second.

Techniques for automated model extraction based on observation of the system at run-time are highly desirable given the high costs of manual modeling of the network traffic, high dynamism of network traffic profiles, large volumes of data, and the importance of the traffic model for performance modeling. To address

ICPE'16, March 12-18, 2016, Delft, Netherlands
© 2016 ACM. ISBN 978-1-4503-4080-9/16/03... $15.00
DOI: http://dx.doi.org/10.1145/2851553.2851570

the challenges of network traffic model extraction, in this paper we contribute:
- a novel **tool** for workload characterization that is based on *Multi-scale time-series decomposition* (MSD),
- a **flexible algorithm** (MSD) for extracting traffic profiles from *tcpdump* traces (practically, from any time series),
- **optimization routine**, so that the level-of-details of the extracted model can be tuned,
- **set of tools** that implement the presented approach and automatically create instances of the DNI model (the traffic part) out of a set of *tcpdump* traces.

The main novelties of our approach are the following:
- we do not extract aggregated statistical models, but a set of deterministic *traffic generator* models that can be understood by non-experts,
- the granularity of the extracted model can be defined manually to fit the level of details required by a given use-case,
- the extracted and optimized traffic model is much compacter than the original trace so it can be simulated faster and even manually corrected by human operator if needed,
- the extraction and optimization process (compacting the extracted model) is automated and does not require human attention,
- the extracted models can be directly used for performance prediction using automatically-generated simulations (using DNI model),
- using the extracted information in the *traffic generator* form can be used for the purpose of traffic patterns analysis, network dimensioning, or debugging.

The rest of this paper is organized as follows. In Section 2, we introduce the traffic generator model that we use as an intermediate step of the extraction. Section 3 describes in detail the MSD (Multi-Scale-Decomposition) algorithm and the optimizations applied to the extracted model. The description is enriched with toy examples and partially evaluated to demonstrate the effects of various fine-tuning parameters. In Section 4, we present the robot tele-maintenance case study that we use for evaluation of the proposed approach. Also in Section 4, we describe the evaluation procedure, characterize the traces and present selected representative extraction results along with discussion. Section 5 presents the related work in the field of network traffic models and model extraction. Finally, we conclude the paper and present possible future work directions in Section 6.

2. EXTRACTED TRAFFIC MODEL

In our approach, the extraction of a network traffic model is divided into two coarse steps: (a) extraction and optimization of the traffic generators, and (b) transformation of the traffic generators into an instance of the DNI meta-model. The first step is tailored to simplify the second step, however the output of the first extraction step is not bound to the DNI model and can be used for other models as well. The details about the extraction and optimization using the proposed Multi-scale Decomposition (MSD) algorithm are presented later in Section 3.

2.1 Network Traffic Generator Model

Before we explain the extraction pipeline and signal decomposition, it is necessary to summarize important assumptions about the network traffic. Typically, in a network traffic dump, we can identify multiple communicating parties based on IP addresses, ports or other parameters. For example, inside the communication from a single server we can identify two applications by the TCP port, albeit the IP address is always the same. In this paper, we assume that

a pre-processing step takes place to isolate individual sessions that are worth modeling. We assume that the network traffic is represented as a univariate time-series with one-second time granularity and positive values (packets with negative size do not make sense).

In reality, we may observe regular and periodic data transfers but also irregular and highly asymmetric signals depending on the application. Therefore, our decomposition algorithm has to handle irregular signals well and to take advantage of regularities whenever possible.

The last assumption in our approach concerns the DNI model and the simulation models that can be automatically generated from a DNI model. Network traffic in simulators generated by DNI (e.g., SimQPN[14] or OMNeT++) has to be modeled as a collection of traffic generators emitting packets with a certain frequency. The information about packets emitted is encoded into DNI *flows* that are later transformed into entities used in the respective simulation (e.g., packets in OMNeT++ or tokens in SimQPN). There is not much room for implementing arbitrary real-value functions, which also hinders the application of Fourier and Wavelet transforms as explained further in Section 3.1.

2.1.1 Model of a simple traffic generator

In this paper, we assume the model of a simple traffic generator as depicted in Figure 1.

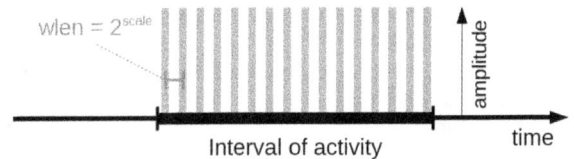

Figure 1: Model of a simple traffic generator

A simple traffic generator is a tuple:

$$Generator = (scale, amplitude, begin, end)$$

where:
- **scale**: How frequently the generator emits packets; every $wlen = 2^{scale}$ seconds.
- **amplitude**: Size of the packet to be emitted.
- **begin**: Beginning of the interval when the generator is active.
- **end**: End of the activity interval.

The extracted set of generators is saved in a text format for further processing. We parse the generator descriptions and build a DNI model but the data can be used also for other models. Figure 2 demonstrates the idea behind the decomposition into activity of simple traffic generators and the corresponding fragment of the DNI model.

2.1.2 Examples of Network Traffic

Figure 3 shows four examples of a recorded network traffic. The first time-series represents data transfer during 60 minutes of video streaming with occasional caching. The second example represents an irregular data transfer with a heat-up phase containing several small data transfers, followed by a continuous transfer reaching the link capacity. The third example represents a signal with several outliers — an example of multiple applications transferring data in parallel. The fourth time-series represents a regular signal.

2.1.3 Clustering of the traffic

We observe that the traffic rates can be efficiently clustered because an application usually transfers data in packets of certain

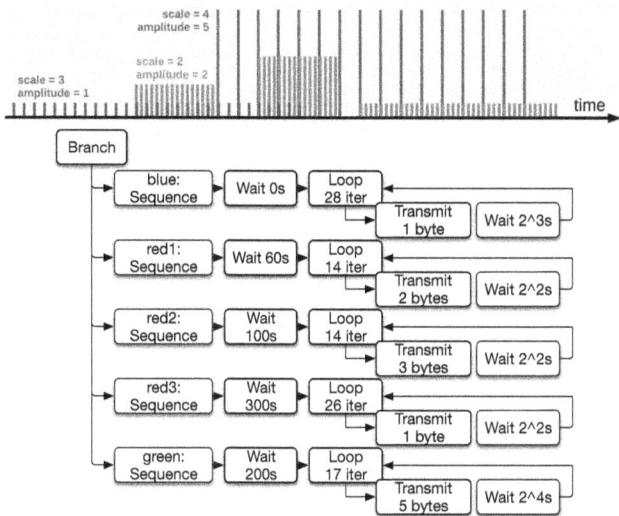

Figure 2: A toy example: decomposition into traffic generators at different scales and amplitudes and the corresponding instance of a DNI traffic model.

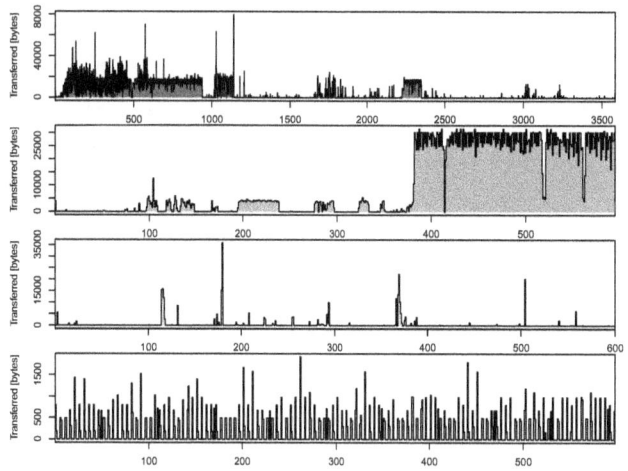

Figure 3: Four examples of typical traffic dumps (60, 10, 10, 10 minutes). X-axis represents time in seconds, Y-axis represents bytes transferred per second.

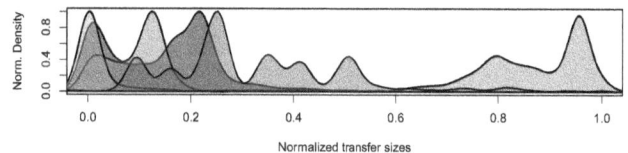

Figure 4: Normalized kernel density plots of transferred bytes from the example traffic dumps.

sizes. This can be seen in Figure 4. We plotted the kernel density plot for each of our example traffic dumps showing the amount of different transfer sizes. In order to compare all the densities, we applied normalization and plotted them together in a single diagram. Each local maximum in the diagram represents a cluster candidate. From Figure 4 we observed that a good estimate for our clustering is between 3 and 7 clusters.[1] Similar behavior can also be observed in other network traces, such as those made available publicly by the LBNL/ICSI Enterprise Tracing Project.[2]

2.2 Traffic Model in DNI

The generators extracted from the traffic traces are meant to be represented in DNI model. Here, we revise how the DNI meta-model represents the network traffic. More information about the DNI meta-model can be found in [11, 12, 10].

In the DNI meta-model, network traffic is generated by traffic sources originating from software components that are deployed on so-called end nodes (e.g., servers, VMs). Each traffic source generates traffic flows that have exactly one source and possibly multiple destinations. The flow destinations are software components that are located in nodes and can be uniquely identified by a set of protocol-level addresses. Flows can be composed in a workload model that defines how each flow is generated (e.g., with sequences, loops, or branches). For the purpose of this paper, we describe a flow by specifying the amount of transferred data (so called *GenericFlow*). Graphically, the traffic part of the DNI meta-model is depicted in Figure 5.

Besides the network traffic information, the DNI model represents also the network topology and its configuration. We say, that the extracted model is partial because we focus on traffic model extraction. In fact, we derive simplified models of network topology

and the deployment of software on nodes, but this information is incomplete as its extraction is not the goal of this paper (e.g., in the extracted model we assume that all nodes are connected with a star topology which is not always the case in general).

3. APPROACH

In Figure 6, we present the high-level overview of the approach, i.e. the extraction pipeline. The process starts by recording real traffic on multiple interfaces within the network (e.g., using *tcpdump*). A single traffic dump (here depicted as *tcpdump.log*) is treated as a univariate irregular time-series and goes into the *Multiscale decomposition* step (explained in detail in Section 3.1), which in turn produces the *Decomposition Matrix*.

Each row of the matrix is a separate regularized time-series. First column represent the original signal (for debugging purposes), while the other columns represent packets emitted by simple traffic generators operating at different frequencies and amplitudes. The Decomposition Matrix is then further transformed into the *Configuration for generators*. This is a sequence of tuples in the form of $(scale, amplitude, begin, end)$ as already explained above. Finally, the DNI model is produced which reflects the decomposition.

3.1 Multi-scale time-series decomposition

Our *Multi-scale time-series decomposition* (MSD) is loosely inspired by Wavelets, in particular by Discrete Wavelet Transform (DWT) [16]. In DWT, the signal is processed at multiple scales: $Scales = (1, \ldots, maxscale)$ where: $maxscale = log_2 |signal|$ The DWT software packages, such as wavethresh in R, expect the input signal length to be a power of two. For each scale $s \in Scales$, the signal has got half the size of the signal at the pre-

---

[1]We also provide an mechanism for estimating the optimal number of clusters automatically, tailored for a given signal.

[2]Packet header traces of LBNL's internal enterprise traffic: ftp: //ftp.bro-ids.org/enterprise-traces/hdr-traces05/, last accessed January 8, 2016

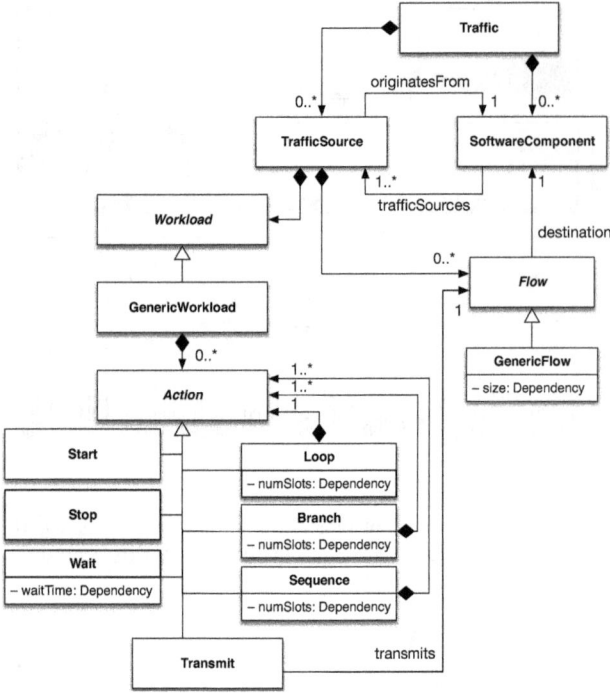

Figure 5: DNI Meta-model of network traffic

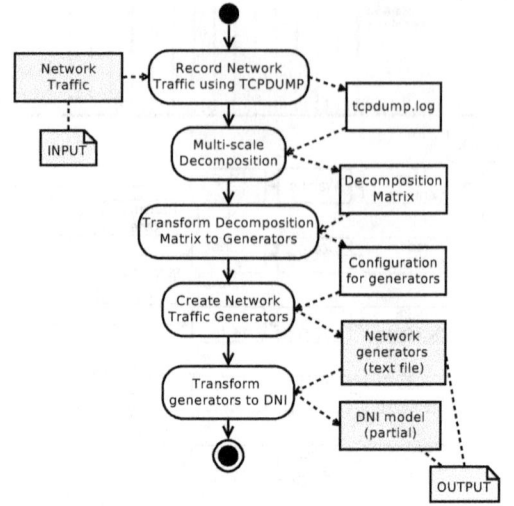

Figure 6: The overview of the extraction pipeline. (Rectangles represent data, ovals represent actions)

vious scale $(s-1)$, i.e.: $|signal_s| = |signal_{s-1}|/2$. Scale 0 represents the original signal, i.e. $signal = signal_0$. Roughly speaking, at each scale $s \in Scales$, DWT computes the interference between the $signal_s$ and a particular wave (stretched and shifted *mother wavelet*). This yields a vector of coefficients $Coef_s = (c_1^s, \ldots, c_{|signal_s|}^s)$. All scales together form a pyramid which can be represented as a single linear vector:

$$ Coef = \bigcup_{s \in Scales} Coef_s $$

The DWT coefficients represent the original signal in a new space of functions. It should be noted that the time complexity of DWT is $O(|signal|)$, the length of the original signal and the length of $Coef$ vector are the same:

$$ |Coef| = |signal| $$

In a similar way, the original signal can be reconstructed by a process which uses DWT coefficients $Coef$ and stretched/shifted wavelets in an inverse manner.

The applications of DWT usually involve manipulation of DWT coefficients, such as removing all coefficients from a particular scale $Coef_s$ (e.g. for compression). However, there are many other application areas of science and engineering – noise reduction, edge detection, time/frequency analysis, ...

Unfortunately, for the purpose of traffic modeling with DNI[3], we realized that DWT is not particularly useful. Although it makes frequency analysis at different bands possible, DWT coefficients cannot be directly mapped to simple traffic generators. Remember that a DWT coefficient represents the *strength* of interference between the signal and a wavelet at a particular time (shift) and frequency band (scale). A single coefficient can well be a negative

---

[3]Currently, DNI supports automated transformation to OMNeT++ simulation and Queueing Petri nets (using SimQPN simulator [14])

---

number. This makes sense for inverse DWT, when multiple functions are summed together forming the original signal, but has little use when modeling a simple traffic generator that can only produce *positive* traffic. Even after several attempts, we were not able to get convincing results with DWT, thus we opted for a custom DWT-inspired transformation instead — the aforementioned MSD.

Similarly to DWT, the notion of scales is preserved in MSD, however, the scales are processed in reversed order: $maxscale, \ldots, 1$. Instead of a pyramid of DWT coefficients, MSD transforms the signal into a matrix of *Emits*. Each scale s corresponds to a vector $Emits_s$ of equal length:

$$ |Emits_1| = \ldots = |Emits_{maxscale}| = |signal| $$

Before the actual MSD loop, the input time-series needs to be preprocessed as follows:

1. Regularization, i.e. every second should be represented by a single value. Gaps in the signal are replaced by zeroes, while multiple values are aggregated using the *sum* function. (Figure 7: *Read Input*)

2. The signal length is padded with zeroes to the nearest power-of-two (e.g. signal with the size of 4000 samples is padded to 4096 samples)

3. Values in the signal are clustered. As already explained, we can efficiently apply clustering of values using k-means. We can either manually set the number of clusters (e.g. 6 clusters) or we can use an automated estimation approach. (Figure 7: *Estimate Optimal Number of Clusters*) We compute total within-cluster sum of squares for up to 25 clusters. Then we pick the lowest number such that a higher number would only differ by less than a preselected cutoff value (10% by default). After k-means clustering of values, a new signal is generated where original values are replaced by the cluster centers.

Such a preprocessed signal then goes into the MSD loop, where it is passed through a sieve which subtracts certain sub-signal in each iteration until only "noise" remains. The subtracted sub-signal (a vector of Emits) is such a traffic that can be generated by a simple

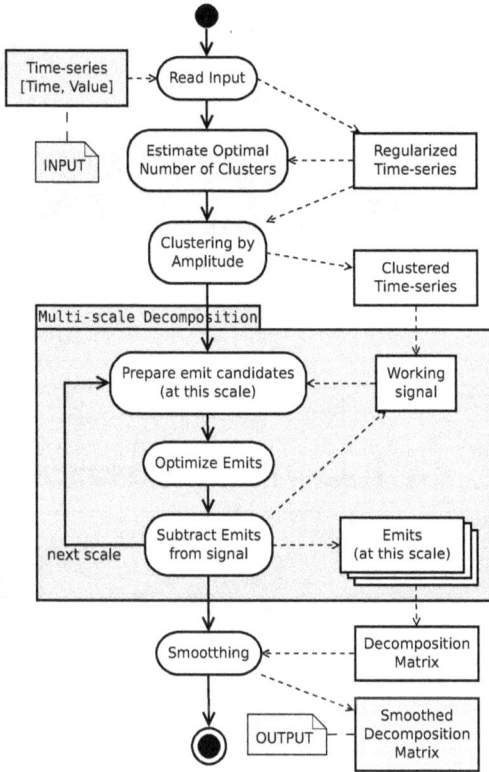

Figure 7: Multi-scale decomposition algorithm. (Rectangles represent data, ovals represent actions)

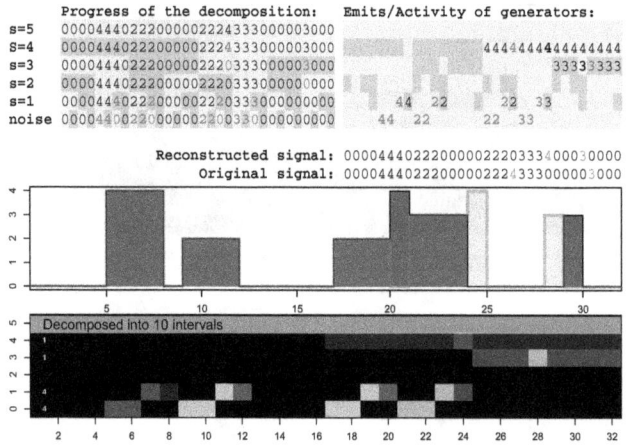

Figure 8: Example decomposition explained step-by-step.

1. Small sequences of equivalent consecutive emits are removed. The reason for this is to prevent isolated peaks to become emits at higher scales. Example:

$$001\mathbf{11}00\mathbf{2}01110 \rightarrow 000\mathbf{000}00\mathbf{0}01110$$

2. Small gaps are removed in order to achieve higher compression. Example:

$$000111\mathbf{2}11100 \rightarrow 000\mathbf{111111}00$$

Time complexity of MSD is $O(n.log(n))$, $n = |signal|$. After Emits from all scales were collected, vector of Emits at each scale can be further smoothed (This is an optional step, Figure 7: *Smoothing*).

3.2 Decomposition of a real signal

We have demonstrated in Figure 8 the result of decomposition on a toy signal consisting of 32 samples. Let us now take a look at decomposition of a real network traffic (10 minutes sampled at 1 second, total 600 samples). This signal has already been presented in Figure 3 (second diagram from the top). Without any optimization nor clustering, MSD decomposes the signal into 253 intervals as depicted in Figure 9.

The top diagram shows the original and reconstructed signal combined. To provide more insight into the decomposition algorithm, we use three visual tools for comparing signals from the frequency-content point of view:

1. *Periodogram* [3] compares spectra of the original signal(solid line) and reconstructed signal (dashed line) as given by the Fourier Transform. From left to right are shown densities of all frequencies (from lower to higher) in the signals' spectra.

2. *Squared Coherency* [3] diagram estimates the percentage of variance in the original signal that is predictable from the reconstructed signal at the same frequency band. The higher the value, the more similar the reconstructed signal to the original is.

3. *Scaleograms* [17] represent signals in a time/frequency domain as given by the continuous wavelet transform using the *Paul* mother-wavelet.

traffic generator with a frequency corresponding to the particular scale.

An example decomposition of a short signal is depicted in Figure 8 (without any clustering nor optimization). Signal in this example consists of 32 samples which is then processed at 5 scales. To derive the Emits at each scale, we have to:

1. Split the remaining signal into equal intervals.

2. Extract a single emit candidate from each interval. (Figure 7: *Prepare emit candidates*)

3. Optimize the vector of emit candidates. (Figure 7: *Optimize Emits*)

Ad. 1, at a given scale s, the working signal is split into intervals $(I_1, \ldots, I_{wtimes})$ of equal length $wlen$.

$$\begin{aligned} wlen &= 2^{scale} \\ wtimes &= |signal|/wlen \end{aligned}$$

Ad. 2, for each interval I_i, a single emit candidate is selected that has the highest value such that it appears only once inside the interval.

$$Emits = \bigcup_{i \in 1}^{wtimes} select(I_i)$$

If no such a candidate exists, the *select* function returns 0 as a candidate.

Ad. 3, the $Emits$ vector is then optimized as follows:

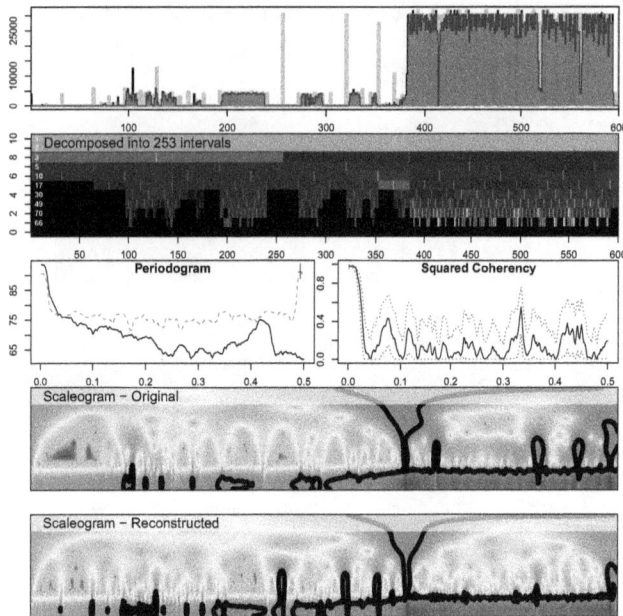

Figure 9: Decomposition example: 10 minutes of traffic without optimization.

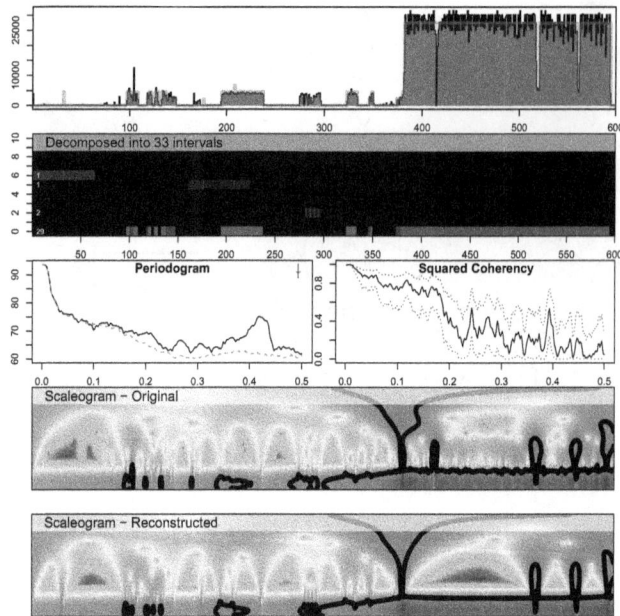

Figure 10: Decomposition example: 10 minutes of traffic with moderate optimization.

When we reconstruct the signal, we can see that it matches its original with an exception of few isolated peaks and some additional high-frequency content. Frequency, however, is not the main criterion for evaluating the quality of the decomposition. More important is the overall shape of the signal that plays the major role later in the simulation phase.

With a moderate optimization, as depicted in Figure 10, we were able to reduce the number of intervals to 33 (i.e., 13%). At the same time, the reconstructed signal still preserves the shape of the original. The tradeoff between the reconstruction accuracy and the model size can be fine-tuned using the following parameters: (1) Number of clusters, (2) reduction of gaps and isolated peaks in emit vectors, and (3) final smoothing of emit vectors.

In Section 4, we set the parameters of the extraction process and further evaluate the quality of extraction on different traffic traces using a real-world case study.

4. EVALUATION

In Section 3, we evaluated the extraction and optimization method using selected traces from online repositories to demonstrate the features of the approach. In this Section, we evaluate the proposed approach using traces from the robot telemaintenance scenario. The traces include mainly two types of network traffic: small control instructions or sensor readings and large flows of video streams from cameras that observe the work of a robot. The traces have been captured in a data center where the devices were controlled from. We have recorded the *tcpdump* trace from the server that acting as a switch (see Fig/ 11b). It was equipped with a four port network card. For the need on the experiment the server was replacing a standard gigabit data center switch.

4.1 Robot Telemaintenance Scenario

The Industry 4.0 initiated by German government[4] comprises among other things the introduction of the Internet to the manu-

---
[4]Similarly *Industrial Internet* was framed in the US

facturing process. In the research project *MainTelRob*[2] different industry 4.0 approaches have been tested for telemaintenance of a plant in a working production line [4]. Figure 11 depicts the project setting. The costumer production site of Braun, which belongs to Procter & Gamble, consists of a six-axis Cartesian industrial robot by KUKA Industries, a two-component injection molding system and an assembly unit. The plant produces plastic parts for electric toothbrushes. On the upper half there is a telemaintenance center from which an engineer—the *expert*—who provides technical expertise to the local repair personnel (the facility technician). Next to the plant, the facility contains telemaintenance equipment: a computer, multiple cameras for video streaming and a mobile device. Center and facility are connected over the Internet. The main prerequisite is to provide the expert with a good view of the situation on-site. This insight can be offered by a specifically orchestrated combination of services: Remote access to machinery data in combination with video streaming and communication services, e.g., text chat and Voice-over-IP (VoIP). In addition, visual Augmented Reality (AR) overlays inserted into the camera pictures or video view are used to provide guidance. As the targeted environment includes the service technician repairing the machinery on-site, the industrial telemaintenance system should additionally provide modern means of communication.

4.2 Traffic Modeling in the Telemaintenance

For the presented scenario, the proposed extraction method delivered insight in the patterns of the data exchange between the components of the system. Although the main goal of the proposed method is to use the extracted models for performance prediction, here, the robot operator can observe the patterns of traffic. The analysis of the data exchange patterns may be used (additionally to the performance prediction) for the following purposes: (1) analyzing compact representation of control signals for debugging purposes (instead of, e.g., analyzing textual *wireshark* traces), (2) understanding the data exchange for network dimensioning.

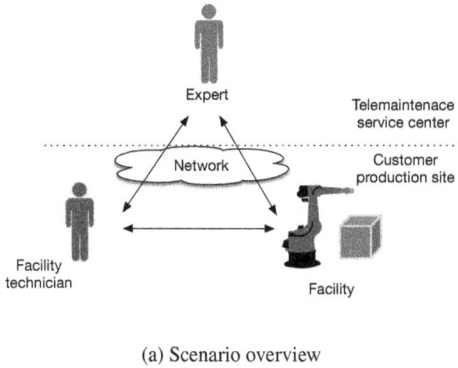

(a) Scenario overview

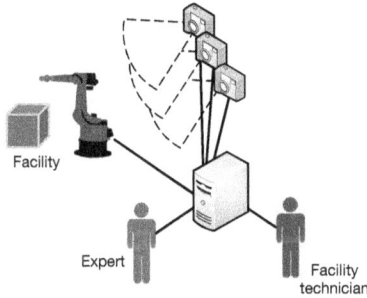

(b) Network topology with central server, robot, surveillance cameras, and maintenance staff.

Figure 11: Robot telemaintenance scenario. The remote expert and the local facility technician use mobile devices to observe the production facility.

4.3 Assessing Model Extraction Errors

We evaluate the model extraction accuracy by computing the relative errors for each pair of time intervals in the extracted model instance and the original trace. We stress, that the maximal model accuracy and the size of the extracted model are the trade-offs and the model should not tend towards one of these extremes. During evaluation of the size of the extracted models, we assume that the original trace represents as many *transmit* actions as many lines the original *tcpdump* file contains.

We selected 69 traffic traces from the robot telemaintenance scenario. Average trace size was similar among the four types and amounts about 22000 data samples. The traces were captured within a 15-minute measurement period. For each trace we picked arbitrary parameters of the extraction algorithm (smoothing 0, maximal number of clusters 25, cut-off for clustering 0.1, and intervals reduction parameter to 0.0004). We repeated the analysis of the 69 files 30 times and collected the following metrics: (1) median of relative error; the error was calculated between the original and extracted trace for every second (the aggregation function over one-second bins was sum) (2) mean relative error, (3) relative error of the total data transmitted in a trace (4) compression of the modeled signal (the modeled signal requires only x% of generators of the original signal). For the four metrics, we calculated the 5th, 50th, and 95th percentiles and presented the results in Table 1.

We divided the traces into four types based on the values of the obtained metrics. To the first type we account the traces with the three relative errors lower than 10%. There are 43 traces of this

type what shows that the proposed method can extract models of the most traces with good accuracy and good compression—the extracted models are 40–200 times smaller than original (compressed to 0.4%–2.3% of the original size).

The traces assigned to the second type are characterized with good relative median error and relative total data error but higher values of the relative mean error. We investigated the discrepancies among the traces and the extracted models. The higher mean error rates are caused mainly by shift in a extracted signal—a workload peak shifted in time doubles the error: first because a real peak is not discovered and second because an artificial peak is produced whereas no peak exists in a real signal. An example of the described situation is depicted in Figure 12a). Few peaks of type 2 were also influenced by non-ideal set of extraction parameters of extracted model (see traces categorized as type 3).

The traces of the third type are described by low errors of relative total data error but higher relative median and mean. We name this type "extraction parameters" as the parameters of the extraction and optimization process were not optimal for the traces (reminder: for the whole scenario we select parameter values arbitrarily). The higher errors are caused mainly by two factors: time-shifted peaks and outliers in the extracted signal caused by lower fit of the extracted model. We selected one trace affected by lower quality extraction and depicted it in Figure 12b). We observe, that the extraction was generally correct, but there are several periods where the data is not generated although the original trace behaves differently. This low extraction accuracy is caused by the fixed set of parameters selected for the method. One could optimize the accuracy by fine tuning the algorithm parameters or use less optimization for the compression. Although the median and mean errors vary from 13% to 30% the total amount of transmitted data is accurate and the compression ratio is good 7–125. Comparing the traces of type 2 against type 3, we observed that the ratio of time-shifted peaks to lower quality of extraction is higher in type 2; in type 3 the situation is opposite: there are more cases of lower quality extraction.

The fourth traces of type four do not fit to any other type. In this experiment the relative mean error and total data error are above the arbitrarily selected 10% threshold. The relative median error is low and the compression ratio vary from 7 to 12. There were only two traces of type 4 in the dataset. We depicted a selected trace of type 4 in Figure 12c). The errors are mainly caused by outliers introduced by suboptimal selection of extraction method parameters. We observe that the main shape of data trace was extracted correctly.

5. RELATED WORK

As noticed by Adas, "Traffic models are at the heart of any performance evaluation of telecommunications networks" [1]. On the other hand, the authors of [7] claim that "there is not much work on measurement, analysis, and characterization of datacenter traffic" suggesting that more focus should be put to modern data centers and the intra-data-center traffic characterization.

There exist many related work on modeling general network traffic [5, 9, 6, 13]. However, most of the works focus on probabilistic models that were meant to approximate the characteristics of network traffic when aggregated or to preserve self-similar nature of the traffic. Goals of this work are different. We want to represent the traffic deterministically to analyze the traffic exactly from the time it was recorded and not to generalize the model to larger time scales. Due to that, we: (1) decompose the traffic profile into a set of generators (on-off traffic sources) with defined start and end of their activity, (2) flexibly compress the model of the network traffic at the same time being able to control the loss of the charac-

Table 1: Results for the 69 analyzed traces divided into 4 groups

Type	Traces	Relative median error % percentile			Relative mean error % percentile			Relative total data error % percentile			Compressed to % percentile		
		.05	.50	.95	.05	.50	.95	.05	.50	.95	.05	.50	.95
1	43	0	0	2.9	0	0.1	8.4	−1.2	0	1.7	0.4	0.8	2.3
2 (shifted peaks)	13	0	0	7.5	12.6	16.4	36.7	−4.4	1.5	6.6	1.6	7.8	15
3 (extraction parameters)	11	13.5	21.8	32.4	13	17.1	23	0	0.3	2.6	0.8	1.6	13.3
4 (rest)	2	0.8	1.2	1.7	24.1	26.1	28.2	10.9	11.7	12.5	8.1	10.9	13.7

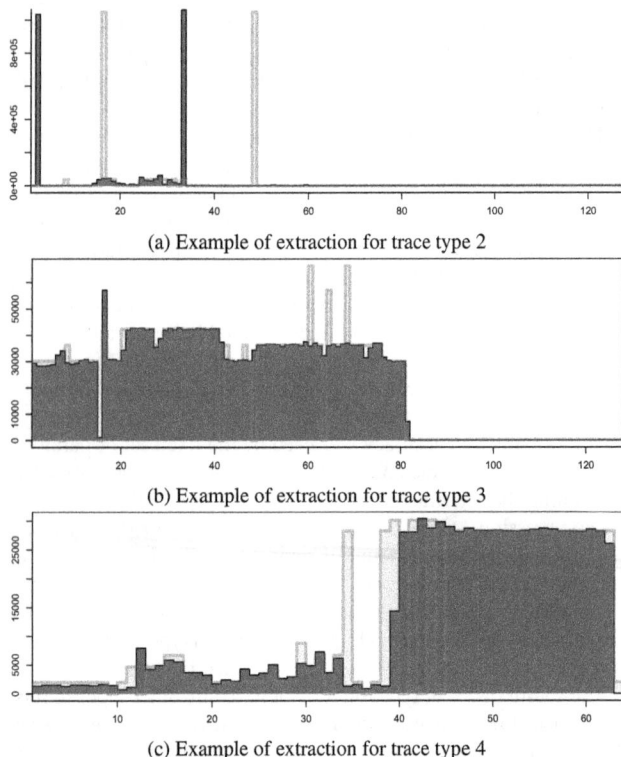

(a) Example of extraction for trace type 2

(b) Example of extraction for trace type 3

(c) Example of extraction for trace type 4

Figure 12: Representative traces of type, 2, 3, and 4 (in grey) and their extracted models (red).

teristics of the original trace (some simulators cannot accept large detailed inputs, for example: SimQPN [14]), (3) support any traffic aggregation interval, whereas the trace driven simulations use usually packet as a smallest unit of traffic and due to that produce fine-grained models with predefined, constant granularity.

The authors of [19] propose a similar approach to ours. They propose a tool that extract workload profiles (not network traces but rather service requests) and decompose them into patterns. The decomposed traces are stored in an ecore-based models [15] and are used mainly for workload forecasting and replaying modified traces in benchmark environments (e.g., replaying an original trace but with amplified burstiness). Although the approach is similar, the details clearly separate the work from ours. First, the workload model that LIMBO extracts is different to DNI Traffic model so the extraction procedure needs to be different. We extract sets of traffic generators whereas LIMBO looks for patterns like, for example: seasonal, trend, burst. Second, we focus on network traffic models extraction by considering time series of data transferred; LIMBO defines workload at the level of requests that can be mapped to var-

ious data sizes. And finally, LIMBO depends strongly on seasonality of the workload as the first step of their extraction procedure searches for data seasonal patterns (e.g., sine-shape). Our approach also supports seasonal patterns (see network traffic generator model in Section 2.1), however any other traffic characteristic can be modeled as well using the network traffic generator representation.

Regarding the approaches to model extraction, the most of the approaches calculate traffic statistics from the traces and represent the traffic statistically, for example using packet size distributions and packet inter-arrival times. As already discussed, such approaches cannot be applied in our case, as we aim to discover relatively compact set of traffic generators to represent the trace. Other works, for example [18], do model the structural information about the traffic, but this is usually represented as users, sessions, connections and packets causing the approach to be application-specific. Additionally, in [18], there is no intention for flexibility of representation of the traffic so that the trade-off between model size and accuracy of representation cannot be selected. In our approach, we allow the user to tune the parameters of the MSD algorithm to provide different level of details in the representation.

6. CONCLUSION AND FUTURE WORK

The nature of the data center network traffic is still not well known due to large variety of virtualized applications running in modern environments that can be provisioned and deprovisioned with resources on the fly. In this paper we addressed the problem of microscopic deterministic analysis of the network traffic traces for performance modeling purposes. We provided a flexible algorithm (MSD — Multi-Scale-Decomposition) for extracting traffic profiles from any time series (e.g., *tcpdump* traces). Moreover, we showed that the extracted traffic models, represented as set of traffic generators, can be optimized to reduce the size of the model but sill accurately model the characteristics of the original trace. We showed that the model with reduced size can be as small as about 0.5% of the original while still accurately represent the original traffic characteristics (relative errors can be as low as 0.1%). Furthermore, the extraction and the optimization procedure can be fine-tuned to extract even long and complicated traces—without the fine tuning, we may observe relative extraction errors up to 30% in the worst case. The parametrized extraction causes that the procedure is flexible with respect to the demanded level of details in the extracted models. The models can be larger but more detailed or more compressed but coarser. Finally, we implemented the method as a set of tools that can be freely used for extraction of the traffic generator models as well as the DNI meta-model instances. We stress, that the extracted model in form of the *traffic generator* model is not explicitly designed for DNI, but may be also used *as-it-is* for traffic pattern analysis, debugging, or network dimensioning purposes. The auxiliary materials (including the MSD decomposition) are available online under http://go.uni-wuerzburg.de/aux.

As a part of our future work, we see several possible directions.

First is the improvement of the automatic selection of extraction parameters (described in Section 3.2) so that more traces can be analyzed with lower extraction errors automatically. Second, we think that the approaches to automatic model extraction should be compared with the manual-built models crafted by humans. In such evaluation the human caused errors could be compared with the imperfections of the MSD extraction algorithm. Such evaluations are challenging and time consuming (mainly due to the involvement of the human factor), however the results would be interesting. Finally, the proposed approach was tailored (but not limited) to extract traffic models in a DNI-friendly format. The scope could be extended and also the extraction of other traffic models could be added.

7. REFERENCES

[1] A. Adas. Traffic Models in Broadband Networks. *Communications Magazine, IEEE*, 35(7):82–89, Jul 1997.

[2] D. Aschenbrenner, F. Sittner, M. Fritscher, M. Krauss, and K. Schilling. Teleoperation of an Industrial Robot in an Active Production Line. In *Proceedings of 2nd IFAC Conference on Embedded Systems, Computational Intelligence and Telematics in Control (CESCIT)*, 2015.

[3] P. Bloomfield. *Fourier Analysis of Time Series: An Introduction*. Wiley, 1976.

[4] S. Chowdhury and A. Akram. E-Maintenance: Opportunities and Challenges. In *Proceedings of the 34th Information Systems Research Seminar in Scandinavia (IRIS)*, pages 68–81, 2011.

[5] V. Frost and B. Melamed. Traffic Modeling for Telecommunications Networks. *Communications Magazine, IEEE*, 32(3):70–81, March 1994.

[6] A. Grzech and P. Świątek. Parallel Processing of Connection Streams in Nodes of Packet-switched Computer Communication Systems. *Cybernetics and Systems*, 39(2):155–170, 2008.

[7] S. Kandula, S. Sengupta, A. Greenberg, P. Patel, and R. Chaiken. The nature of data center traffic: Measurements & analysis. In *Proceedings of the 9th ACM SIGCOMM Conference on Internet Measurement Conference*, IMC '09, pages 202–208, New York, NY, USA, 2009. ACM.

[8] S. Kounev. Performance Modeling and Evaluation of Distributed Component-Based Systems using Queueing Petri Nets. *IEEE Transactions on Software Engineering*, 32(7):486–502, July 2006.

[9] L. Qian, A. Krishnamurthy, Y. Wang, Y. Tang, P. Dauchy, and A. Conte. A new traffic model and statistical admission control algorithm for providing qos guarantees to on-line traffic. In *Global Telecommunications Conference, 2004. GLOBECOM '04. IEEE*, volume 3, pages 1401–1405 Vol.3, Nov 2004.

[10] P. Rygielski and S. Kounev. Descartes Network Infrastructures (DNI) Manual: Meta-models, Transformations, Examples. Technical Report v.0.3, Chair of Software Engineering, University of Würzburg, Sep. 2014.

[11] P. Rygielski, S. Kounev, and P. Tran-Gia. Flexible Performance Prediction of Data Center Networks using Automatically Generated Simulation Models. In *Proceedings of the Eighth EAI International Conference on Simulation Tools and Techniques (SIMUTools 2015)*, August 2015.

[12] P. Rygielski, S. Kounev, and S. Zschaler. Model-Based Throughput Prediction in Data Center Networks. In *Proceedings of the 2nd IEEE International Workshop on Measurements and Networking (M&N 2013)*, pages 167–172, October 2013.

[13] M. Z. Shafiq, L. Ji, A. X. Liu, and J. Wang. Characterizing and Modeling Internet Traffic Dynamics of Cellular Devices. *SIGMETRICS Perform. Eval. Rev.*, 39(1):265–276, 2011.

[14] S. Spinner, S. Kounev, and P. Meier. Stochastic Modeling and Analysis using QPME: Queueing Petri Net Modeling Environment v2.0. In S. Haddad and L. Pomello, editors, *Proceedings of the 33rd International Conference on Application and Theory of Petri Nets and Concurrency (Petri Nets 2012)*, volume 7347 of *Lecture Notes in Computer Science (LNCS)*, pages 388–397, June 2012. Springer.

[15] D. Steinberg, F. Budinsky, M. Paternostro, and E. Merks. *EMF: Eclipse Modeling Framework 2.0*. Addison-Wesley Professional, 2nd edition, 2009.

[16] M. Stéphane, editor. *A Wavelet Tour of Signal Processing (Third Edition)*. Academic Press, Boston, 2009.

[17] C. Torrence and G. P. Compo. A practical guide to wavelet analysis. *Bulletin of the American Meteorological Society*, 79:61–78, 1998.

[18] K. V. Vishwanath and A. Vahdat. Realistic and responsive network traffic generation. In *Proceedings of the 2006 Conference on Applications, Technologies, Architectures, and Protocols for Computer Communications*, SIGCOMM '06, pages 111–122, New York, NY, USA, 2006. ACM.

[19] J. von Kistowski, N. R. Herbst, D. Zoller, S. Kounev, and A. Hotho. Modeling and Extracting Load Intensity Profiles. In *Proceedings of the 10th International Symposium on Software Engineering for Adaptive and Self-Managing Systems (SEAMS 2015)*, May 2015.

[20] F. Willnecker, M. Dlugi, A. Brunnert, S. Spinner, S. Kounev, and H. Krcmar. Comparing the Accuracy of Resource Demand Measurement and Estimation Techniques. In *Computer Performance Engineering — Proceedings of the 12th European Workshop (EPEW 2015)*, volume 9272 of *Lecture Notes in Computer Science*, pages 115–129. Springer, 2015.

Learning from Source Code History to Identify Performance Failures

Juan Pablo Sandoval Alcocer
PLEIAD Lab
DCC, University of Chile
jsandova@dcc.uchile.cl

Alexandre Bergel
PLEIAD Lab
DCC, University of Chile
abergel@dcc.uchile.cl

Marco Tulio Valente
Federal University of Minas
Gerais, Brazil
mtov@dcc.ufmg.br

ABSTRACT

Source code changes may inadvertently introduce performance regressions. Benchmarking each software version is traditionally employed to identify performance regressions. Although effective, this exhaustive approach is hard to carry out in practice. This paper contrasts source code changes against performance variations. By analyzing 1,288 software versions from 17 open source projects, we identified 10 source code changes leading to a performance variation (improvement or regression). We have produced a cost model to infer whether a software commit introduces a performance variation by analyzing the source code and sampling the execution of a few versions. By profiling the execution of only 17% of the versions, our model is able to identify 83% of the performance regressions greater than 5% and 100% of the regressions greater than 50%.

Keywords

Performance variation; performance analysis; performance evolution

1. INTRODUCTION

Software evolution refers to the dynamic change of characteristics and behavior of the software over time [17]. These progressive changes may negatively decrease the quality of the software and increase its complexity [3, 15]. Such deterioration may also affect the application performance over time [20]. Testing software continuously helps detect possible issues caused by source code changes [2, 8].

Diverse approaches have been proposed to detect performance regressions along software evolution [5, 18, 22, 26]. The most commonly employed technique is exhaustively executing all benchmarks over all versions: comparing the performance metrics of the recently released version with the previous ones are then used to spot performance variations [5, 11]. However, such approaches are highly time consuming because benchmarks can take days to execute [12]. Furthermore, there are a number of factors (e.g., garbage

ICPE'16, March 12-18, 2016, Delft, Netherlands
© 2016 ACM. ISBN 978-1-4503-4080-9/16/03...$15.00
DOI: http://dx.doi.org/10.1145/2851553.2851571

collection, JIT compiler) that can affect the measurements and benchmarks need to be executed multiple times to reduce the measurement bias [22]. For this reason, testing software performance periodically (e.g., daily or per release basis) is an expensive task. It has been shown that by identifying the relations between source code changes and performance variations, it is possible to estimate whether a new software version introduces a performance regression or not; without executing the benchmarks [12].

Existing research [12, 13, 24, 30] predominantly categorizes recurrent performance bugs and fixes by analyzing a random sample of performance bug reports. These studies voluntary ignore performance related issues that are not reported as a bug or bug fix. Therefore, in this paper, we aim to bridge this gap by conducting a comprehensive study of real-world performance variations detected by analyzing the performance evolution of 17 open source projects along 1,288 software versions. The two research questions addressed in this study are:

- RQ1 – *Are performance variations mostly caused by modifications of the same methods?* This question is particularly critical to understanding what performance variation stems from. Consider a method m that causes a performance regression when it is modified. It is likely that modifying m once more will impact the performance. Measuring the proportion of such "risky" methods is relevant for statically predicting the impact a code revision may have.

- RQ2 – *What are the recurrent source code changes that affect performance along software evolution?* More precisely, we are interested in determining which source code changes mostly affect program performance along software evolution and in which context. If performance variations actually do match identified source code changes, then it is possible to judge the impact of a given source code change on performance.

Findings. Our experiments reveal a number of facts for the source code changes that affect the performance of the 17 open source systems we analyzed:

- Most performance variations are caused by source code changes made in different methods. Therefore, keeping track of methods that participated in previous performance variations is not a good option to detect performance variations.

- Most source code changes that cause a performance variation are directly related to method call addition, deletion or swap.

Based on the result of our study, we propose *horizontal profiling*, a sampling technique to statically identify versions that may introduce a performance regression. It collects run-time metrics periodically (*e.g.*, every k versions) and uses these metrics to analyze the impact of each software version on performance. *Horizontal profiling* assigns a cost to each source code change based on the run-time history. The goal of *horizontal profiling* is to reduce the performance testing overhead, by benchmarking just software versions that contain costly source code changes. Assessing the accuracy of horizontal profiling leads to the third research question:

- RQ3 – *How well can horizontal profiling prioritize the software versions and reduce the performance testing overhead?* This question is relevant since the goal of *horizontal profiling* is to reduce the performance regression testing overhead by only benchmarking designated versions. We are interested in measuring the balance between the overhead of exercising *horizontal profiling* and the accuracy of the prioritization.

We evaluate our technique over 1,125 software versions. By profiling the execution of only 17% of the versions, our model is able to identify 83% of the performance regressions greater than 5% and 100% of the regressions greater than 50%. These figures are therefore comparable with the related work: Huang *et al.* [12] have proposed a static approach and identify 87% (without using program slicing) of regression with 14% of software versions. However, by using a dedicated profiling technique, our cost model does not require painful manual tuning, and it performs well, independently of the performance regression threshold. Moreover, our hybrid technique (static and dynamic) is applicable to a dynamically typed and object-oriented programming languages.

Outline. Section 2 describes the projects under study and the benchmarks used to detect performance variations. Section 3 contrasts source code changes with the performance variations. Section 4 presents and evaluates the cost model based on the run-time history. Section 5 discusses threats to validity we face and how we are addressing them. Section 6 overviews related work. Section 7 concludes and presents an overview of our future work.

2. EXPERIMENTAL SETUP

2.1 Project under Study

We conduct our study around the Pharo programming language[1]. Our decision is motivated by a number of factors: First, Pharo offers an extended and flexible reflective API, which is essential to iteratively execute benchmarks over multiple application versions and executions. Second, application instrumentation and monitoring its execution are also cheap and with a low overhead. Third, the computational model of Pharo is uniform and very simple, which means that applications for which we have no knowledge are easy to download, compile and execute.

---

[1]http://pharo.org

Table 1: Projects under Study.

Project	Versions	LOC	Classes	Methods
Morphic	214	41,404	285	7,385
Spec	270	10,863	404	3,981
Nautilus	214	11,077	173	2012
Mondrian	145	12,149	245	2,103
Roassal	150	6,347	227	1,690
Rubric	83	10,043	173	2,896
Zinc	21	6,547	149	1,606
GraphET	82	1,094	51	464
NeoCSV	10	8,093	9	125
XMLSupport	22	3,273	118	1,699
Regex	13	4,060	39	309
Shout	16	2,276	18	320
PetitParser	7	2,011	63	578
XPath	10	1,367	93	813
GTInspector	17	665	17	128
Soup	6	1,606	26	280
NeoJSON	8	700	16	139
Total	**1,288**	**130,386**	**2,106**	**26,528**

We pick 1,288 release versions of 17 software projects from the Pharo ecosystem stored on the Pharo forges (*Squeak-Source*[2], *SqueakSource3*[3] and *SmalltakHub*[4]). The set of considered project have a broad range of application: user interface frameworks (Morphic and Spec), a source code highlighter (Shout), visualization engines (Roassal and Mondrian), a HTTP networking tool (Zinc), parsers (PetitParser, NeoCSV, XMLSupport, XPath, NeoJSON and Soup), a chart builder (GraphET), a regular expression checker (Regex), an object inspector (GTInspector) and code browsers and editors (Nautilus and Rubric).

Table 1 summarizes each one of these projects and gives the number of defined classes and methods along software evolution. It also shows the average lines of code (LOC) per project.

These applications have been selected for our study for a number of reasons: (i) they are actively supported and represent relevant assets for the Pharo community. (ii) The community is friendly and interested in collaborating with researchers. As a result, developers are accessible in answering our questions about their projects.

2.2 Source Code Changes

Before reviewing variation of performance, we analyze how source code changes are distributed along all the methods of each software project. Such analysis is important to contrast performance evolution later on.

Let M be the number of times that a method is modified along software versions of each software project. Figure 1 gives the distribution of variable M of all projects under study. The y-axis is the percentage of methods, and x-axis is the number of modifications. One method has been modified 14 times. In total, 83% of the methods are simply defined without being modified in subsequent versions of the application ($M = 0$).

There are 2,846 methods (11%) modified only once ($M = 1$) in the analyzed versions. Only 6% of the methods are modified more than once ($M > 1$). Table 2 gives the number of methods that: i) are not modified ($M = 0$), ii) are modified only once ($M = 1$), and iii) are modified more than once ($M > 1$) for each software project. We have found that in all

---

[2]http://www.squeaksource.com/
[3]http://ss3.gemstone.com/
[4]http://smalltalkhub.com/

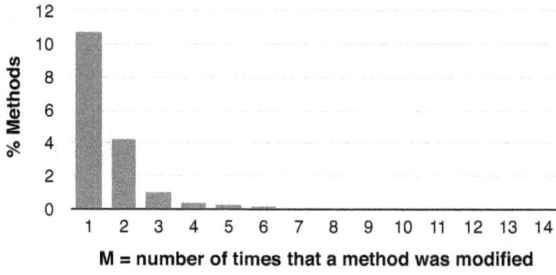

Figure 1: Source Code Changes histogram at method level.

but one project, the number of methods that are modified more than once are relatively small compared to the number of methods that are modified once. The Mondrian project is clearly an outlier since 28% of its methods are modified twice or more. A discussion with the authors of Mondrian reveals the application went through long and laborious maintenance phases on a reduced set of particular classes.

Table 2: M = number of times that a method is modified.

Project	Methods	M = 0	M = 1	M >1
Morphic	7,385	6,810 (92%)	474 (6%)	101 (1%)
Spec	3,981	2,888 (73%)	730 (18%)	363 (9%)
Rubric	2,896	2,413 (83%)	362 (13%)	121 (4%)
Mondrian	2,103	1,361 (65%)	146 (7%)	596 (28%)
Nautilus	2,012	1,646 (82%)	248 (12%)	118 (6%)
XMLSupport	1,699	1,293 (76%)	276 (16%)	130 (8%)
Roassal	1,690	1,379 (82%)	232 (14%)	79 (5%)
Zinc	1,606	1,431 (89%)	139 (9%)	36 (2%)
XPath	813	780 (96%)	33 (4%)	0 (0%)
PetitParser	578	505 (87%)	66 (11%)	7 (1%)
GraphET	464	354 (76%)	70 (15%)	40 (9%)
Shout	320	304 (95%)	12 (4%)	4 (1%)
Regex	309	303 (98%)	5 (2%)	1 (0%)
Soup	280	269 (96%)	11 (4%)	0 (0%)
NeoJSON	139	131 (94%)	7 (5%)	1 (1%)
GTInspector	128	119 (93%)	0 (0%)	9 (7%)
NeoCSV	125	84 (67%)	35 (28%)	6 (5%)
Total	**26,528**	**22,070 (83%)**	**2,846 (11%)**	**1,612 (6%)**

Similarly, we analyzed the occurrence of class modification: 59% of the classes remain unmodified after their creation, 14% of the classes are modified once (*i.e.,* at least one method has been modified), and 27% of the classes are modified more than once.

2.3 Benchmarks

In order to get reliable and repeatable execution footprints, we select a number of benchmarks for each considered application. Each benchmark represents a representative execution scenario that we will carefully measure. Several of the applications already come with a set of benchmarks. If no benchmarks were available, we directly contacted the authors and they kindly provided benchmarks for us. Since these benchmarks have been written by the authors, they are likely to cover part of the application for which its performance is crucial.

At that stage, some benchmarks have to be worked or adapted to make them runnable on a great portion of each application history. The benchmarks we considered are therefore generic and do not directly involve features that have

been recently introduced. Identifying the set of benchmarks runnable over numerous software versions is particularly time consuming since we had to test each benchmark over a sequence of try-fix-repeat. We have 39 executable benchmarks runnable over a large portion of the versions.

All the application versions and the metrics associated to the benchmarks are available online[5].

3. UNDERSTANDING PERFORMANCE VARIATIONS OF MODIFIED METHODS

A software commit may introduce a scattered source code change, spread over a number of methods and classes. We found 4,458 method modifications among 1,288 analyzed software versions. Each software version introduces 3.46 method modifications on average. As a consequence, a performance variation may be caused by multiple method source code changes within the same commit.

3.1 Performance Variations of Modified Methods

We carefully conducted a quantitative study about source code changes that directly affect the method performance. Let V be the number of times that a method is modified and becomes slower or faster after the modification. We consider that the execution time of a method varies if the absolute value of the variation of the accumulated execution time between two consecutive versions of the method is greater than a threshold. In our situation, we consider *threshold = 5%* over the total execution time of the benchmark. Below 5%, it appears that the variations may be due to technical consideration, such as inaccuracy of the profiler [4].

Figure 2 gives the distribution of V for all methods of the projects under study. In total, we found 150 method modifications where the modified method becomes slower or faster. These modifications are made over 111 methods; 91 methods are modified only once ($V = 1$) and 20 more than once ($V > 1$). Table 3 gives the number of methods for each software project.

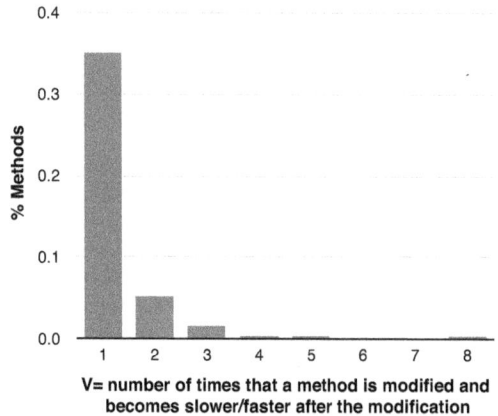

Figure 2: Performance Variations of Modified Methods (threshold = 5%), 111 methods are here reported.

[5]http://users.dcc.uchile.cl/~jsandova/hydra/

Table 3: V= number of times that a method is modified and becomes slower/faster after the modification. (threshold = 5%).

Project	Methods	V = 0	V = 1	V >1
Morphic	7,385	7,382 (100%)	2 (0%)	1 (0%)
Spec	3,981	3,944 (99%)	24 (1%)	13 (0%)
Rubric	2,896	2,896 (100%)	0 (0%)	0 (0%)
Mondrian	2,103	2,091 (99%)	11 (1%)	1 (0%)
Nautilus	2,012	2,008 (100%)	4 (0%)	0 (0%)
XMLSupport	1,699	1,689 (99%)	10 (1%)	0 (0%)
Roassal	1,690	1,675 (99%)	14 (1%)	1 (0%)
Zinc	1,606	1,597 (99%)	7 (0%)	2 (0%)
XPath	813	813 (100%)	0 (0%)	0 (0%)
PetitParser	578	566 (98%)	12 (2%)	0 (0%)
GraphET	464	459 (99%)	3 (1%)	2 (0%)
Shout	320	320 (100%)	0 (0%)	0 (0%)
Regex	309	309 (100%)	0 (0%)	0 (0%)
Soup	280	280 (100%)	0 (0%)	0 (0%)
NeoJSON	139	138 (99%)	1 (1%)	0 (0%)
GTInspector	128	128 (100%)	0 (0%)	0 (0%)
NeoCSV	125	119 (95%)	5 (4%)	1 (1%)
Total	**26,528**	**26,417(99.6%)**	**91(0.33%)**	**20(0.07%)**

Table 4: Method modifications that affect method performance (R= regression, I= improvement, R/I = regression in some benchmarks and Improvement in others).

Project	Method Modifications				Involved Methods	Mod. by Method
	R	I	R/I	Total		
Spec	19	9	0	28	16	1.75
Roassal	7	5	0	12	11	1.09
Zinc	2	1	4	7	7	1.00
Mondrian	5	3	0	8	7	1.14
XMLSupport	6	0	0	6	6	1.00
GraphET	4	3	0	7	5	1.4
NeoCSV	0	5	0	5	5	1.00
PetitParser	5	0	0	5	5	1.00
Morphic	2	1	0	3	2	1.50
Nautilus	2	0	0	2	2	1.00
NeoJSON	0	1	0	1	1	1.00
Total	**52**	**28**	**4**	**84**	**67**	**1.25**

False Positive. However, not all these 150 modifications are related to the method performance variations because there are a number of false-positives. Consider the change made in the open method on the class ROMondrianViewBuilder:

```
ROMondrianViewBuilder>>open
  | whiteBox realView |
  self applyLayout.
  self populateMenuOn: viewStack.
-   ^ stack open
+   ^ viewStack open
```

This modification is only a variable renaming: the variable stack has been renamed into viewStack. Our measurement indicates that this method is now slower, which is odd since a variable renaming should not be the culprit of a performance variation. A deeper look at the method called by open reveals that the method applyLayout is also slower. Therefore, we conclude that open is slower because of a slower dependent method, and not because of its modification. Such a method is a false positive and its code modification should not be considered as the cause of the performance variation.

Example code with a leading "-" is from the previous version, while code with a leading "+" is in the current version. Unmarked code (without a leading "-" or "+") is in both versions.

Manually Cleaning the Data. We manually revised the 150 method variations by comparing the call-graph (obtained during the execution) and the source code modification. We then manually revised the source code (as we just did with the method open). In total, we found 66 method modifications (44%) that are not related with the method performance variation. The remaining 84 method modifications (56%) cause a performance variation in the modified method. These modifications are distributed along 11 projects; table 4 gives the distribution by project.

Summary. Are performance variations mostly caused by modifications of the same methods? We found that 84 method modifications that cause a performance variation (regression or improvement) were done over 67 methods, which means 1.25 modifications per method. Table 4 shows the ratio between method modifications and methods is less than two in all projects. In addition, we found that the these methods

were modified a number of times along source code evolution without causing a performance variation.

> Most performance variations were caused by source code changes made in different methods. Therefore, keeping track of methods that participated in previous performance variations is not a good option to detect performance variations.

3.2 Understanding the Root of Performance Regressions

Accurately identifying the root of a performance regression is difficult. We investigate this by surveying authors of method modifications causing a regression. From the 84 method modifications mentioned in Section 3.1, we obtained author feedback for 21 of them. Each of 21 method modifications is the cause of a regression greater than 5%. We also provided the benchmarks to the authors since it may be that the authors causing a regression are not aware of the application benchmarks. These methods are spread over four projects (Roassal, Mondrian, GraphET, and PetitParser). Each author was contacted by email and we discussed about the method modification causing a regression.

For 6 (29%) of these 21 modifications, the authors were aware of the regression at the time of the modification. The authors therefore consciously and intentionally made the method slower by adding or improving functionalities. We also asked them whether the regression could be avoided while preserving the functionalities. They answered that they could not immediately see an alternative to avoid or reduce the performance regression.

For 5 (24%) of the modifications, authors did not know that their new method revision caused a performance regression. However, authors acknowledged the regressions and were able to propose an alternative method revision that partially or completely removes the regression.

For the 10 remaining modifications, author did not know that they caused a performance regression and no alternative could be proposed to improve the situation.

This is a preliminary result and we can not draw any strong conclusion from only 21 method modifications. However, this small and informal survey of practitioners indicates that a significant number of performance regressions are apparently inevitable. On the other hand, such incertitude expressed by the authors regarding the presence of a regression and providing change alternative highlights the relevance of our study and research effort.

3.3 Categorizing Source Code Changes That Affect Method Performance

This section analyzes the cause of all source code changes that affect method performance. We manually inspected the method source code changes and the corresponding performance variation. We then classify the source code changes into different categories based on the abstract syntax tree modifications and the context in which the change is used. In our study, we consider only code changes that are the culprits for performance variation (regression or improvement), ignoring the other non-related source code changes.

Subsequently, recurrent or significant source code changes are described. Each source code change has a title, a brief description, followed by one source code example taken from the examined projects.

Method Call Addition. This source code change adds expensive method calls that directly affect the method performance. This situation occurs 24 times (29%) in our set of 84 method modifications, all these modifications cause performance regressions. Consider the following example:

```
GETDiagramBuilder>>openIn: aROView
  self diagram displayIn: aROView.
  + self relocateView
```

The performance of openIn: dropped after having inserted the call to relocateView.

Method Call Swap. This source code change replaces a method call with another one. Such a new call may be either more or less expensive than the original call. This source change occurs 24 times (29%) in our set of 84 method modifications; where 15 of them cause a performance regression and 9 a performance improvement.

```
MOBoundedShape>>heightFor: anElement
  ^ anElement
  - cachedNamed: #cacheheightFor:
  - ifAbsentInitializeWith: [ self computeHeightFor:
    anElement ]
  + cacheNamed: #cacheheightFor:
  + of: self
  + ifAbsentInitializeWith: [ self computeHeightFor:
    anElement ]
```

The performance of heightFor: dropped after having swapped the call to cacheNamed:ifAbsentInitializeWith by cacheNamed: of:ifAbsentInitializeWith.

Method Call Deletion. This source code change deletes expensive method calls in the method definition. This pattern occurs 14 times (17%) in our set of 84 method modifications - all these modifications cause performance improvements.

```
MOGraphElement>>resetMetricCaches
  - self removeAttributesMatching: ''cache*''
  + cache := nil.
```

This code change follows the intuition that removing a method call makes the application faster.

Complete Method Change. This category groups the source code changes that cannot be categorized in one of these situations, because there are many changes in the method that contribute to the performance variation (*i.e.,* a combination of method call additions and swaps). We have seen 9 complete method rewrites (11%) among the 84 considered method modifications.

Loop Addition. This source code change adds a loop (*i.e.,* while, for) and a number of method calls that are frequently executed inside the loop. We have seen 5 occurrences of this pattern (6%) - all of them cause a performance regression.

```
ROMondrianViewBuilder>>buildEdgeFrom:to:for:
  | edge |
  edge := (ROEdge on: anObject from: fromNode to:
    toNode) + shape.
  + selfDefinedInteraction do: [:int | int value: edge ].
  ^ edge
```

Change Object Field Value. This source code change sets a new value in an object field causing performance variations in the methods that depend on that field. This pattern occurs 2 times in the whole set of method modifications have analyzed.

```
GETVerticalBarDiagram>>getElementsFromModels
  ^ rawElements with: self models do: [ :ele :model |
    + ele height: (barHeight abs).
    count := count + 1].
```

On this example, the method height: is a variable accessor for the variable height defined on the object ele.

Conditional Block Addition. This source code change adds a condition and a set of instructions. These instructions are executed upon the condition. This pattern occurs 2 times in the whole set of method modifications we analyzed. Both of them cause a performance improvement.

```
ZnHeaders>>normalizeHeaderKey:
  + (CommonHeaders includes: string) ifTrue: [ ^ string ].
  ^ (ZnUtils isCapitalizedString: string)
    ifTrue: [ string ]
    ifFalse: [ ZnUtils capitalizeString: string ]
```

Changing Condition Expression. This source code change modifies the condition of a conditional statement. This change could introduce a variation by changing the method control flow and/or the evaluation of the new condition expression is faster/slower. This pattern occurs 2 times in the whole set of method modifications we have analyzed.

```
NeoCSVWriter>>writeQuotedField:
  | string |
  string := object asString.
  writeStream nextPut: $".
  string do: [ :each |
  -   each = $"
  +   each == $"
      ifTrue: [ writeStream nextPut: $"; nextPut: $" ]
      ifFalse: [ writeStream nextPut: each ] ].
  writeStream nextPut: $"
```

The example above simply replaces the equal operation = by the identity comparison operator ==. The latter is significantly faster.

Change Method Call Scope. This source code change moves a method call from one scope to another executed more or less frequently. We found 1 occurrence of this situation

Table 5: Source code changes that affect method performance (R= Regression, I= Improvement, R/I = Regression in some benchmarks and Improvement in others).

Source Code Changes		R	I	R/I	Total
1	Method call additions	23	0	1	24 (29%)
2	Method call swaps	15	9	0	24 (29%)
3	Method call deletion	0	14	0	14 (17%)
4	Complete method change	6	0	3	9 (11%)
5	Loop Addition	5	0	0	5 (6%)
6	Change object field value	2	0	0	2 (2%)
7	Conditional block addition	0	2	0	2 (2%)
8	Changing condition expression	0	2	0	2 (2%)
9	Change method call scope	1	0	0	1 (1%)
10	Changing method parameter	0	1	0	1 (1%)
	Total	52	28	4	84 (100%)

in the whole set of method modifications. Such a change resulted in a performance improvement.

```
GETCompositeDiagram>>transElements
  self elements do: [ :each | | trans actualX |
    + pixels := self getPixelsFromValue: each getValue.
    (each isBig)
      ifTrue: [ | pixels |
        − pixels := self getPixelsFromValue: each
      getValue.
        ...
      ifFalse: [ ^ self ].
    ...
  ]
```

Changing Method Parameter. The following situation changes the parameter of a method call. We found only 1 occurrence of this situation in the whole set of method modifications.

```
ROMondrianViewBuilder>>buildEdgeFrom:to:for:
  | edge |
  edge := (ROEdge on: anObject from: fromNode to:
    toNode) + shape.
  − selfDefinedInteraction do: [:int | int value: edge ].
  + selfDefinedInteraction do: [:int | int value: (Array with:
    edge) ].
  ^ edge'
```

Table 5 gives the frequency of each previously presented source code change.

Categorizing Method Calls. Since most changes that cause a performance variation (patterns 1,2,3) involve a method call. We categorize the method call additions, deletions and swaps (totaling 62) in three different subcategories:

- *Calls to external methods:* 10% of the method calls correspond to method of external projects (*i.e.,* dependent projects).

- *Calls to recently defined methods:* 39% of the method calls correspond to method that are defined in the same commit. For instance, a commit that defines a new method and adds method calls to this method.

- *Calls to existing project methods:* 51% of the method calls correspond to project methods that were defined in previous versions.

Summary. *RQ2: What are the most common types of source code changes that affect performance along software evolution?* We found, in total, that 73% of the source code changes

that cause a performance variation are directly related to method call addition, deletion or swap (patterns 1,2,3). This percentage varies between 60% and 100% in all projects, with the only exception of the Zinc project that has a 29%; most Zinc performance variations were caused by complete method changes.

> Most source code changes that cause a performance variation are directly related to method call addition, deletion or swap.

3.4 Triggering a Performance Variation

To investigate whether a kind of change could impact the method performance we compare changes that caused a performance variation with those that do not cause a performance variation. For this analysis, we consider the source code changes: loop addition, method call addition, method call deletion and method call swap [6].

To fairly compare between changes that affect performance and changes that do not affect performance, we consider changes in methods that are executed by our benchmark set. Table 6 shows the number of times that a source code change was done along software versions of all projects (Total), and the number of times that a source code change cause a performance variation (Perf. Variation) greater than 5% over the total execution time of the benchmark.

Table 6: Comparison of source code changes that cause a variation with the changes that do not cause a variation (R= regression, I= improvement, R/I = regression in some benchmarks and Improvement in others).

Source Code Changes	Total	Perf. Variations			
		R	I	R/I	Total
Method call additions	231	23	0	1	24(10.39%)
Method call deletions	119	0	14	0	14(11.76%)
Method call swap	321	15	9	0	24 (7.48%)
Loop additions	8	5	0	0	5(62.5%)

Table 6 shows that these four source code changes are frequently done along source code evolution; however just a small number of instances of these changes cause a performance variation. After manually analyzing all changes that cause a variation, we conclude that there are mainly two factors that contribute to the performance variation:

- *Method call executions.* The number of times that a method call is executed plays an important role to determine if this change can cause a performance regression. We found that 92% of source code changes were made over a frequently executed source code section.

- *Method call cost.* The cost of a method call is important to determine the grade of performance variation. We found that 7 (8%) method calls additions/deletions were only executed once and cause a performance regression greater than 5%. In the other 92% the performance vary depending on how many times the method call is executed and the cost of each method call execution.

---

[6]These changes correspond the top-4 most common changes, with the exception of "Complete method change" which we did not consider in the analysis since it is not straightforward to detect this pattern automatically.

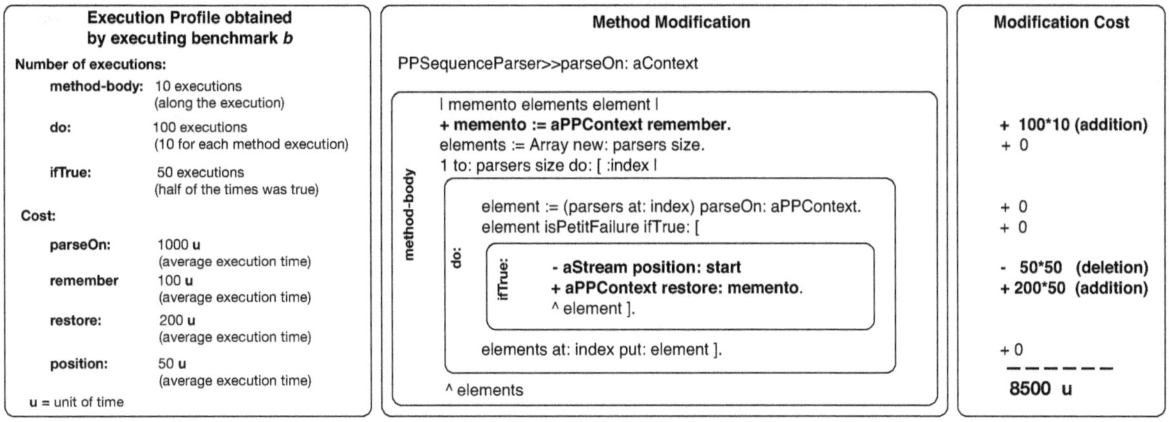
Execution Profile obtained by executing benchmark b
Number of executions:
method-body: 10 executions (along the execution)
do: 100 executions (10 for each method execution)
ifTrue: 50 executions (half of the times was true)
Cost:
parseOn: 1000 u (average execution time)
remember 100 u (average execution time)
restore: 200 u (average execution time)
position: 50 u (average execution time)
u = unit of time
Method Modification
PPSequenceParser>>parseOn: aContext
| memento elements element |
+ memento := aPPContext remember.
elements := Array new: parsers size.
1 to: parsers size do: [:index |
element := (parsers at: index) parseOn: aPPContext.
element isPetitFailure ifTrue: [
- aStream position: start
+ aPPContext restore: memento.
^ element].
elements at: index put: element].
^ elements
method-body
do:
ifTrue:
Modification Cost
+ 100*10 (addition)
+ 0
+ 0
+ 0
- 50*50 (deletion)
+ 200*50 (addition)
+ 0
8500 u

Figure 3: LITO cost model example

We believe these factors are good indicators to decide when a source code change could introduce performance variation. We support this assumption by using this criteria to detect performance regressions, as we describe in the following sections.

4. HORIZONTAL PROFILING

We define *horizontal profiling* as a technique to statically detect performance regressions based on benchmark execution history. The rationale behind *horizontal profiling* is that if a software execution becomes slow for a repeatedly identified situation (*e.g.*, particular method modification), then the situation can be exploited to reduce the performance regression testing overhead.

4.1 LITO: A Horizontal Profiler

We built LITO to (mostly) statically identify software versions that introduce a performance regressions. LITO takes as input (i) the source code of a software version V_n and (ii) the profile (obtained from a traditional code execution profiler) of the benchmarks execution on a previous software version V_m. LITO identifies source code changes in the analyzed software version V_n, and determines if that version is likely to introduce a performance regression or not.

The provided execution profile is obtained from a dedicated code execution profiler and is used to infer components dependencies and loop invariants. As discussed later on, LITO is particularly accurate even if V_m is a version distant from V_n.

Using our approach, practitioners prioritize the performance analysis in the selected versions by *LITO*, without the need to carry out costly benchmark executions for all versions. The gain here is significant since LITO helps identify software commits that may or may not introduce a performance variation.

Execution Profile. LITO runs the benchmarks each k versions to collect run-time information (*e.g.*, each ten versions, $k = 10$). Based on the study presented in previous sections, LITO considers three aspects to collect run-time information in each sample:

- *Control flow* – LITO records sections of the source code and method calls that are executed. This allows LITO to ignore changes made in source code sections that are not executed by the benchmarks (*e.g.*, a code block associated to an if condition or a method that is never executed).
- *Number of executions* – As we presented in the previous sections, the method call cost itself is not enough to detect possible performance regressions. Therefore LITO records the number of times that methods and loops are executed.
- *Method call cost* – LITO associates the average execution time of each method as the cost of executing each method call. Note that LITO does not estimate the execution time variation itself, it uses this average as a metric to detect possible performance regressions.
- *Method execution time* – LITO estimates for each method m (i) the accumulated total execution time and (ii) the average execution time for calling m once during the benchmarks executions.

LITO Cost Model. LITO abstracts all source code changes as a set of method calls additions and/or deletions. To LITO, a *method call swap* is abstracted as a method call addition and deletion. *Block additions*, such as loops and conditional blocks, are abstracted as a set of method call additions.

The LITO cost model is illustrated in Figure 3. Consider the modification made in the method parseOn: in the class PPSequenceParser. In this method revision, one line has been removed and two have been added: two method call additions (remember and restore:) and one deletion (position:). In order to determine whether the new version of parseOn: is slower or faster than the original version, we need to estimate how the two call additions compare with the call deletion in terms of execution time. This estimation is based on an execution profile.

The LITO cost model assesses whether a software version introduces a performance regression for a particular benchmark. The cost of each call addition and deletion depends therefore on the benchmark b when the execution profile is produced.

We consider an execution profile obtained from the execution of a benchmark on the version of the application that contains the original definition of parseOn:. LITO determines whether the revised version of parseOn: does or does not introduce a performance regression based on the execution profile of the original version of parseOn:.

The execution profile indicates the number of times that each block contained in the method parseOn: is executed. It further indicates the number of executions of the code block contained in the iteration (*i.e.*, do: [:index | ...]). The profile also gives the number of times the code block contained in the ifTrue: statement is executed. In Figure 3, the method parseOn: is executed 10 times, the iteration block is executed 100 times (*i.e.*, 10 times per single execution of parseOn: on average) and the conditional block is executed 50 times (*e.g.*, 0.5 time per single execution of parseOn: on average).

LITO uses the notion of *cost* [12] as a proxy of the execution time. We denote u as the unit of time we use in our cost model. In our setting, u refers to the number of times the send message bytecode is executed by the virtual machine. We could have used a direct time unit as milliseconds, however it has been shown that counting the number of sent messages is significantly more accurate and this metric is more stable than estimating the execution time [4]. On the example, the method parseOn: costs 1000u, and remember 100u, implying that remember is 10 times faster to execute than parseOn:.

The modification cost estimates the cost difference between the new version and original version of a method. On the example, the modification cost of method parseOn: is 8500u, meaning that the method parseOn: spends 8500u more than previous version for a given benchmark b. For instance, if the benchmark b execution time is 10,000u, then the new version of the method parseOn: results in a performance regression of 85%.

The average cost of calling each method is obtained by dividing the total accumulated cost of a method m by the number of times m has been executed during a benchmark execution. In our example, calling remember has an average cost of 100u. The theoretical cost of a method call addition m is assessed by multiplying the cost of calling m and the number of times that it would be executed based on the execution profile (Figure 3 right hand).

Let A_i be a method call addition of a given method modification and D_j a method call deletion. Let be $cost_b$ a function that returns the average cost of a method call when executing benchmark b, and $exec_b$ a function that returns the number of times a method call is executed. Both functions lookup the respective information in the last execution sample gathered by LITO.

Let $MC_b(m)$ be the cost of modify the method m for a benchmark b, na the number of method call additions and nd the number of method call deletions. The method modification cost is the sum of the cost of all method call additions less the cost of all method call deletions.

$$MC_b(m) = \sum_{i=1}^{na} cost_b(A_i) * exec_b(A_i) - \sum_{j=1}^{nd} cost_b(D_j) * exec_b(D_j).$$

Let C be the cost of all method modifications of a software version, and m the number of modified methods, we therefore have:

$$C[v,b] = \sum^{m \in v} MC_b(m)$$

In case we have $C[v,b] > 0$ for a particular version v and a benchmark b, we then consider that version v introduces a performance regression.

New Method, Loop Addition, and Conditions. Not all the methods may have a computed cost. For example, a new method, for which no historical data is available, may incur a regression. In such a case, we statically determine the cost for code modification with no historical profiling data.

We qualify as fast a method that is returning a constant value, an accessor / mutator, or doing arithmetic or logic operations. A fast method receives the lowest method cost obtained from the previous execution profile. All other methods receive a high cost, the maximal cost of all the methods in the execution profile.

In case a method is modified with a new loop addition or a conditional block, no cost has been associated to it. LITO hypothesizes that the conditional block will be executed and the loop will be executed the same number of times as the most recently executed enclosing loop in the execution profile.

The high cost we give to new methods, loop additions, and conditions is voluntarily conservative. It assumes that these additions may trigger a regression. As we show in Table 5, loop and conditional block additions represent 6% and 2%, respectively, of the source code changes that affect software performance.

Project Dependencies. An application may depend on externally provided libraries or frameworks. As previously discussed (Section 3), a performance regression perceived by using an application may be in fact located in a dependent and external application. LITO takes such analysis into account when profiling benchmark executions. The generated profile execution contains runtime information not only of the profiled application but also of all the dependent code.

During our experiment, we had to ignore some dependencies when analyzing the Nautilus project. Nautilus depends on two external libraries: ClassOrganizer and RPackage. LITO uses these two libraries. We exclude these two dependencies in order to simplify our analysis and avoid unwanted hard-to-trace recursions. In the case of our experiment, any method call toward ClassOrganizer or RPackage is considered costly.

4.2 Evaluation

For the evaluation, we use the project versions where at least one benchmark can be executed. In total, we evaluate LITO over 1,125 software versions. We use the following 3-steps methodology to evaluate LITO:

S1. We run our benchmarks for all 1,125 software versions and measure performance regressions.

S2. We pick a sample of the benchmark executions, every k versions, and apply our cost model on all the 1,125 software versions. Our cost model identifies software versions that introduce a performance regression.

S3. Contrasting the regressions found in S1 and S2 will measure the accuracy of our cost model.

Step S1 - Exhaustive Benchmark Execution. Consider two successive versions, v_i and v_{i-1} of a software project P and a benchmark b. Let $\mu[v_i, b]$ be the mean execution time to execute benchmark b multiple times on version v_i.

Table 7: Detecting performance regressions with LITO using a threshold=5% and a sample rate of 20.

Project	Versions	Selected Versions	Performance Regressions	Detected Perf. Reg.	Undetected Perf. Reg.	Performance Evolution by benchmark
Spec	267	43(16%)	11	8 (73%)	3	
Nautilus	199	64 (32%)	5	5 (100%)	0	
Mondrian	144	9 (6%)	2	2 (100%)	0	
Roassal	141	26 (18%)	3	3 (100%)	0	
Morphic	135	8 (6%)	2	1 (50%)	1	
GraphET	68	20 (29%)	5	4 (80%)	1	
Rubric	64	2 (3%)	0	0 (100%)	0	
XMLSupport	18	8 (44%)	4	4 (100%)	0	
Zinc	18	2 (11%)	0	0 (100%)	0	
GTInspector	16	1 (6%)	1	1 (100%)	0	
Shout	15	0 (0%)	1	0 (0%)	1	
Regex	12	1 (8%)	1	1 (100%)	0	
NeoCSV	9	3 (33%)	0	0 (100%)	0	
NeoJSON	7	0 (0%)	0	0 (100%)	0	
PetitParser	6	1 (17%)	1	1 (100%)	0	
Soup	4	0 (0%)	0	0 (100%)	0	
XPath	2	0 (0%)	0	0 (100%)	0	
Total	1125	188 **(16.7%)**	36	30 **(83.3%)**	6 **(16.7%)**	

The execution time is measured in terms of sent messages (u unit, as presented earlier). Since this metric has a great stability [4], we executed each benchmark only 5 times and took the average number of sent messages. It is known that the number of sent messages is linear to the execution time in Pharo [4].

We define the time difference between versions v_i and v_{i-1} for a given benchmark b as:

$$D[v_i, b] = \mu[v_i, b] - \mu[v_{i-1}, b] \qquad (1)$$

Consequently, the time variation is defined as:

$$\Delta D[v_i, b] = \frac{D[v_i, b]}{\mu[v_{i-1}, b]} \qquad (2)$$

For a given *threshold*, we say v_i introduces a performance regression if it exists a benchmark b_j such that $\Delta D[v_i, b_j] \geq$ *threshold*.

Step S2 - Applying the Cost Model. Let $C[v_i, b]$ be the cost of all modifications made in version v_i from v_{i-1}; using the run-time history of benchmark b.

$$\Delta C[v_i, b] = \frac{C[v_i, b]}{\mu[v_j, b]} \qquad (3)$$

We have j, the closest inferior version number that has been sampled at an interval k. If $C[v_i, b] \geq$ *threshold* in at least one benchmark, then LITO considers that version v_i may introduce a performance regression.

Step S3 - Contrasting $\Delta C[v_i, b]$ with $\Delta D[v_i, b]$. The cost model previously described (Section 4.1) is designed to favor the identification of performance regression. Such design

is reflected in the high cost given to new methods, loop additions, and conditions. We therefore do not consider performance optimizations in our evaluation.

Results. We initially analyze the software versions with LITO and collect the run-time information each $k = 20$ versions, and a *threshold* of 5%. LITO is therefore looking for all the versions that introduce a performance regression of at least 5% in one of the benchmarks. These benchmarks are executed every 20 software versions to produce execution profiles that are used for all the software versions. LITO uses the cost model described previously to assess whether a software version introduces a regression or not.

Table 7 gives the results of each software project. During this process LITO selected 189 costly versions that represent 16.7% of total of analyzed versions. These selected versions contain 83.3% of the versions that effectively introduce a performance regression greater than 5%. In other words, based on the applications we have analyzed, practitioners could detect 83.3% of the performance regressions by running the benchmarks on just 16.8% of all versions, picked at a regular interval from the total software source code history.

Table 8 shows that LITO has a high recall (83.3%) despite having a low precision (15.95%). This high recall indicates that LITO helps practitioners to identify a great portion of the performance regressions by running the benchmarks over a few software versions.

Threshold. To understand the impact of the threshold in our cost model, we carry out the experiment described above but using different thresholds (5, 10, 15, 20, 25, 30, 35, 40, 45, and 50). Figure 4 shows the percentage of selected versions and detected performance regressions by LITO. Figure 4 shows that LITO detects all regressions greater than 50%

Table 8: Precision and recall of LITO to detect performance regressions greater than 5%(threshold) using a sample-rate of 20. (TP = true-positive, TN = true-negative, FP = false-positive, FN = false-negative, Prec. = Precision).

Project	TP	FP	FN	TN	Prec.	Recall
Spec	8	35	3	221	0.19	0.73
Nautilus	5	59	0	135	0.08	1
Mondrian	2	7	0	135	0.22	1
Roassal	3	23	0	115	0.12	1
Morphic	1	7	1	126	0.13	0.5
GraphET	4	16	1	47	0.2	0.8
Rubric	0	2	0	62	0	-
XMLSupport	4	4	0	10	0.5	1
Zinc	0	2	0	16	0	-
GTInspector	1	0	0	15	1	1
Shout	0	0	1	14	-	0
Regex	1	0	0	11	1	1
NeoCSV	0	3	0	6	0	-
NeoJSON	0	0	0	7	-	-
PetitParser	1	0	0	5	1	1
Soup	0	0	0	4	-	-
XPath	0	0	0	2	-	-
Total	30	158	6	931	15.95%	83.33%

(totaling ten). Figure 4 also shows that the number of selected versions decreases as the threshold increases, meaning that LITO safely discards more versions because their cost is not high enough to cause a regression with a greater threshold.

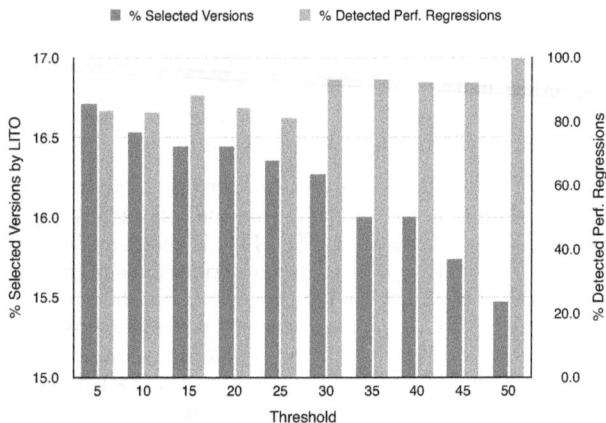

Figure 4: The effect of the threshold on the percentage of detected performance regressions and the percentage of selected versions by LITO (> threshold).

By profiling the execution of only 17% of the versions, our model is able to identify 83% of the performance regressions greater than 5% and 100% of the regressions greater than 50%. Such versions are picked at a regular interval from the software source code history.

Sample Rate. To understand the effect of the sample rate, we repeated the experiment using different tree sample rates 1, 20 and 50. Figure 5 shows the percentage of performance regressions by LITO with the different sample rates. As it was expected, the accuracy of LITO increment when we take a sample of the execution every version (sample rate

= 1). Consequently the accuracy get worse when we take a sample each 50 versions. Figure 5 shows that sampling a software source code history each 50 versions make LITO able to detect a great portion of the performance regression, for any threshold lower than 50%.

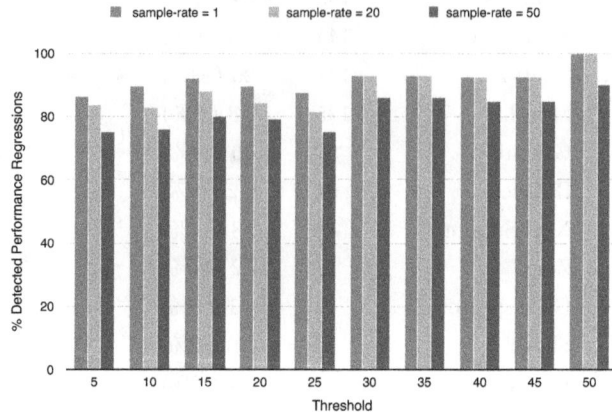

Figure 5: Evaluating LITO with sample rates of 1, 20, and 50.

Overhead. Statically analyzing a software version with LITO takes 12 seconds (on average). It is considerably cheaper than executing the benchmarks in a software version. However, each time that LITO collects the run-time information is seven times (on average) more expensive than executing the benchmarks. LITO instruments all method projects, and executed twice the benchmarks: the first one to collect the average time of each method and the second one to collect the number of executions of each source code section. Even with this, the complete process of prioritizing the versions and executing a performance testing over the prioritized versions is far less expensive than executing the benchmarks over all application versions.

For instance, in our experiment, the process to do an exhaustive performance testing in all software versions takes 218 hours; on the other hand, the process of prioritize the versions and executed the benchmarks only in the prioritized versions takes 54 hours (25%).

5. THREATS TO VALIDITY

To structure the threats to validity, we follow the Wohlin et al. [29] validity system.

Construct Validity. The method modifications we have manually identified may not be exhaustive. We analyzed method modifications that cause performance variations greater than 5%, over the total execution time of the benchmark. Analyzing small performance variations, such as the one close to 5%, is important since it may sum up over multiple software revisions. Detecting and analyzing variations smaller variation is difficult, because many factors may distort variance to the observable performance, such as inaccuracy of the profiler [4].

External Validity. This paper is voluntarily focused on the Pharo ecosystem. We believe this study provides relevant findings about the performance variation in the studied projects. We cannot be sure of how much the results generalize to other software projects beyond the specific scope this study was conducted. As future work, we plan to replicate our experiments for the Javascript and Java ecosystem. In addition, we plan to analyze how LITO performs with multi-thread applications.

Internal Validity. We cover diverse categories of software projects and representative software systems. To minimize the potential selection bias, we collect all possible release versions of each software project, without favoring or ignoring any particular version. We manually analyze twice each method modification: the first time to understand the root-cause of the performance variation and the second time to confirm the analysis.

6. RELATED WORK

Performance Bug Empirical Studies. Empirical studies over performance bug reports [13, 24] provide a better understanding of the common root causes and patterns of performance bugs. These studies help practitioners save manual effort in performance diagnosis and bug fixing. These performance bug reports are mainly collected from the tracking system or mailing list of the analyzed projects.

Zaman *et al.* [30] study the bug reports for performance and non-performance bugs in Firefox and Chrome. They studied how users perceive the bugs, how bugs are reported, what developers discuss about the bug causes and the bug patches. Their study is similar to that of Nistor *et al.* [23] but they go further by analyzing additional information for the bug reports. Nguyen *et al.* [21] interviewed the performance engineers responsible for an industrial software system, to understand these regression-causes.

Sandoval *et al.* [1] have studied performance evolution against software modifications and have identified a number of patterns from a semantic point of view. They describe a number of scenarios that affect performance over time from the intention of a software modification (vs the actual change as studied in this paper).

We focus our research on performance variations. In this sense we consider performance drops and improvements that are not reported as a bug or a bug-fix. We contrast the performance variations with the source code changes at method granularity. In addition, we analyze what kind of source code changes cause performance variations in a large variety of applications.

Performance Bug Detection and Root-Cause Analysis. Great advances have been made to automate the performance bug detection and root-cause analysis [10, 19, 27]. Jin *et al.* [13] propose a rule-based performance-bug detection using rules implied by patches to found unknown performance problems. Nguyen *et al.* [21] propose the mining of a regression-causes repository (where the results of performance tests and causes of past regressions are stored) to assist the performance team in identifying the regression-cause of a newly-identified regression. Bezemer *et al.* [6] propose an approach to guide performance optimization processes and to help developers find performance bottlenecks via execution profile comparison. Heger *et al.* [11] propose an approach based on bisection and call context tree analysis to isolate the root cause of a performance regression caused by multiple software versions.

We improve the performance regression overhead by prioritizing the software versions. We believe that our work complements these techniques in order to help developers address performance related issues. We do not attempt to detect performance regression bugs or provide root-cause diagnosis.

Performance Regression Testing Prioritization. Different strategies have been proposed in order to reduce the functional regression testing overhead, such as test case prioritization [9, 25] and test suite reduction [7, 14, 16, 31]. However, few projects have been able to reduce the performance regression testing overhead.

Huang *et al.* [12] propose a technique to measure the risk given to a code commit in introducing performance regressions. Their technique uses a full static approach to measure the risk of a software version based on worst case analysis. They automatically categorize the source code change (*i.e.,* extreme, high, and low) and assign a risk score to each category; these scores may require an initial tuning. However, a fully static analysis may not accurately assess the risk of performance regression issues in dynamic languages. For instance, statically determining the loop boundaries may not be possible without special annotations [28]. Dynamic features of programming languages such as dynamic dispatching, recursion and reflexion make this task more difficult.

In this paper we propose a hybrid (dynamic and static) technique to automatically prioritize the performance testing; it uses the run-time history to track the control flow and the loop boundaries. Our technique reduces a number of limitations of a fully static approach and does not need an initial tuning. We believe that these techniques can complement each other to provide a good support for developers and reduce the overhead of performance regression testing.

7. CONCLUSION

This paper studies the source code changes that affect software performance of 17 software projects along 1,288 software versions. We have identified 10 source code changes leading to a performance variation (improvement or regression). Based on our study, we propose a new approach, *horizontal profiling*, to reduce the performance testing overhead based on the run-time history.

As future work, we plan to extend our model to prioritize benchmarks and generalize *horizontal profiling* to identify memory and energy performance regressions.

8. ACKNOWLEDGMENTS

Juan Pablo Sandoval Alcocer is supported by a Ph.D. scholarship from CONICYT, Chile. CONICYT-PCHA/Doctorado Nacional para extranjeros/2013-63130199. We also thank the European Smalltalk User Group (www.esug.org) for the sponsoring. This work has been partially sponsored by the FONDECYT 1160575 project and STICAmSud project 14STIC-02.

9. REFERENCES

[1] Juan Pablo Sandoval Alcocer and Alexandre Bergel. Tracking down performance variation against source code evolution. In *Proceedings of the 11th Symposium on Dynamic Languages*, DLS 2015. ACM.

[2] Len Bass, Ingo Weber, and Liming Zhu. *DevOps: A Software Architect's Perspective*. Addison-Wesley Professional, jun 2015.

[3] L. A. Belady and M. M. Lehman. A model of large program development. *IBM Syst. J.*, 15(3):225–252, September 1976.

[4] Alexandre Bergel. Counting messages as a proxy for average execution time in pharo. In *Proceedings of ECOOP'11*.

[5] C. Bezemer, E. Milon, A. Zaidman, and J. Pouwelse. Detecting and analyzing i/o performance regressions. *Journal of Software: Evolution and Process*, 26(12):1193–1212, 2014.

[6] C. Bezemer, E. Milon, A. Zaidman, and J. Pouwelse. Detecting and analyzing i/o performance regressions. *Journal of Software: Evolution and Process*, 26(12):1193–1212, 2014.

[7] Jennifer Black, Emanuel Melachrinoudis, and David Kaeli. Bi-criteria models for all-uses test suite reduction. In *Proceedings of ICSE '04*. IEEE.

[8] Paul Duvall, Steve Matyas, and Andrew Glover. *Continuous Integration: Improving Software Quality and Reducing Risk*. Addison-Wesley Professional, first edition, 2007.

[9] Sebastian Elbaum, Alexey G. Malishevsky, and Gregg Rothermel. Prioritizing test cases for regression testing. *SIGSOFT Softw. Eng. Notes*, 25(5):102–112, August 2000.

[10] Shi Han, Yingnong Dang, Song Ge, Dongmei Zhang, and Tao Xie. Performance debugging in the large via mining millions of stack traces. In *Proceedings of ICSE 2012*.

[11] Christoph Heger, Jens Happe, and Roozbeh Farahbod. Automated root cause isolation of performance regressions during software development. In *Proceedings of ICPE '13*.

[12] Peng Huang, Xiao Ma, Dongcai Shen, and Yuanyuan Zhou. Performance regression testing target prioritization via performance risk analysis. In *Proceedings of ICSE '14*.

[13] Guoliang Jin, Linhai Song, Xiaoming Shi, Joel Scherpelz, and Shan Lu. Understanding and detecting real-world performance bugs. *SIGPLAN Not.*, 47(6):77–88, June 2012.

[14] Jung-Min Kim and Adam Porter. A history-based test prioritization technique for regression testing in resource constrained environments. In *Proceedings of ICSE '02*.

[15] M M. Lehman, J F. Ramil, P D. Wernick, D E. Perry, and W M. Turski. Metrics and laws of software evolution - the nineties view. In *Proceedings of the 4th International Symposium on Software Metrics*, METRICS '97, pages 20–32. IEEE Computer Society.

[16] Zheng Li, M. Harman, and R.M. Hierons. Search algorithms for regression test case prioritization. *IEEE Transactions on Software Engineering*, 33(4):225–237, April 2007.

[17] Nazim H. Madhavji, Juan Fernandez-Ramil, and Dewayne E. Perry. *Software Evolution and Feedback: Theory and Practice*. Wiley, Chichester, UK, 2006.

[18] H. Malik, Zhen Ming Jiang, B. Adams, A.E. Hassan, P. Flora, and G. Hamann. Automatic comparison of load tests to support the performance analysis of large enterprise systems. In *14th European Conference on Software Maintenance and Reengineering (CSMR)*, 2010.

[19] D. Maplesden, E. Tempero, J. Hosking, and J.C. Grundy. Performance analysis for object-oriented software: A systematic mapping. *IEEE Transactions on Software Engineering*, 41(7):691–710, July 2015.

[20] Ian Molyneaux. *The Art of Application Performance Testing: Help for Programmers and Quality Assurance*. O'Reilly Media, Inc., 1st edition, 2009.

[21] Thanh H. D. Nguyen, Meiyappan Nagappan, Ahmed E. Hassan, Mohamed Nasser, and Parminder Flora. An industrial case study of automatically identifying performance regression-causes. In *Proceedings of MSR '14*.

[22] Thanh H.D. Nguyen, Bram Adams, Zhen Ming Jiang, Ahmed E. Hassan, Mohamed Nasser, and Parminder Flora. Automated detection of performance regressions using statistical process control techniques. In *Proceedings of ICPE '12*.

[23] Adrian Nistor, Tian Jiang, and Lin Tan. Discovering, reporting, and fixing performance bugs. In *Proceedings of MSR '13*.

[24] Adrian Nistor, Linhai Song, Darko Marinov, and Shan Lu. Toddler: Detecting performance problems via similar memory-access patterns. In *Proceedings of ICSE '13*.

[25] G. Rothermel, R.H. Untch, Chengyun Chu, and M.J. Harrold. Test case prioritization: an empirical study. In *Proceedings of ICSM '99*.

[26] Wei Shang, Ahmed E. Hassan, Mohamed Nasser, and Parminder Flora. Automated detection of performance regressions using regression models on clustered performance counters. In *Proceedings of ICPE '15*.

[27] Du Shen, Qi Luo, Denys Poshyvanyk, and Mark Grechanik. Automating performance bottleneck detection using search-based application profiling. In *Proceedings of ISSTA '15*.

[28] Reinhard Wilhelm, Jakob Engblom, Andreas Ermedahl, Niklas Holsti, Stephan Thesing, David Whalley, Guillem Bernat, Christian Ferdinand, Reinhold Heckmann, Tulika Mitra, Frank Mueller, Isabelle Puaut, Peter Puschner, Jan Staschulat, and Per Stenström. The worst-case execution-time problem; overview of methods and survey of tools. *ACM Trans. Embed. Comput. Syst.*, 7(3):36:1–36:53, May 2008.

[29] Claes Wohlin, Per Runeson, Martin Höst, Magnus C. Ohlsson, Björn Regnell, and Anders Wesslén. *Experimentation in Software Engineering*. Kluwer Academic Publishers, 2000.

[30] Shahed Zaman, Bram Adams, and Ahmed E. Hassan. A qualitative study on performance bugs. In *Proceedings of MSR '12*.

[31] Hao Zhong, Lu Zhang, and Hong Mei. An experimental comparison of four test suite reduction techniques. In *Proceedings of ICSE '06*.

Resource and Performance Distribution Prediction for Large Scale Analytics Queries

Alireza Khoshkbarforoushha
Australian National University & CSIRO
Canberra, Australia
a.khoshkbarforoushha@anu.edu.au

Rajiv Ranjan
Newcastle University, UK
raj.ranjan@ncl.ac.uk

ABSTRACT

Efficient resource consumption and performance estimation of data-intensive workloads is central to the design and development of workload management techniques. Recent work has explored the efficacy of using distribution-based estimation of workload performance as opposed to single point prediction for a number of workload management problems such as query scheduling, admission control, and the like. However, the proposed approaches lack an efficient workload performance distribution prediction in that they simply assume that the probability distribution function (pdf) of the target value is already available. This paper aims to address this problem for an inseparable portion of big data analytics workloads, Hive queries. To this end, we combine knowledge of Hive query executions with the novel usage of mixture density networks to predict the whole spectrum of resource and performance as probability density functions. We evaluate our technique using the TPC-H benchmark, showing that it not only produces accurate pdf predictions but outperforms the state of the art single point techniques in half of experiments.

Keywords

Query performance prediction; Distribution prediction; Hive

1. INTRODUCTION

Data-intensive workload management strategies including resource provisioning, workload scheduling, and admission control need the cost of a request to be specified a priori. Recent studies [14, 5, 4] detailed the advantages of distribution-based estimation as opposed to single point prediction of workload performance for profit-oriented admission control [14], efficient query scheduling [5], and cost-optimized cloud resource provisioning [4]. These studies simply assume that the probability distribution function (pdf) of the target value (e.g. CPU, Response time, etc.) is already available. On the other hand, the state of the art

©2016 Association for Computing Machinery. ACM acknowledges that this contribution was authored or co-authored by an employee, contractor or affiliate of a national government. As such, the Government retains a nonexclusive, royalty-free right to publish or reproduce this article, or to allow others to do so, for Government purposes only.

ICPE'16, March 12-18, 2016, Delft, Netherlands

© 2016 ACM. ISBN 978-1-4503-4080-9/16/03. . . $15.00

DOI: http://dx.doi.org/10.1145/2851553.2851578

estimators [2, 6, 7, 12, 8] model resource and performance of data-intensive workload as a single point value.

This leaves us with one key question to answer in this paper: *How can we predict the resource and performance distribution of data-intensive workloads?* Answering this question is important for the increasingly common data-intensive platforms where efficient resource usage prediction is a key operating criterion for proper cluster and resource utilization and service level agreement (SLA) management.

Moreover, in a shared multi-system cluster, having a mix of different applications and workloads (e.g. Pig, Hive) running concurrently is a trivial practice to utilize resources cost efficiently, while challenging accurate workload performance prediction. In this context, we argue that with distribution-based prediction of data-intensive workloads we are able to tackle properly the inevitable performance variances in the presence of resource contention.

To this end, in the subsequent section we derive an optimal proposal model for *CPU* and *Runtime* distribution prediction of the major big data workloads, Hive queries. Apache Hive (https://hive.apache.org/) is a data warehouse infrastructure built on top of Hadoop that facilitates querying and managing large datasets residing in distributed storage. It provides a mechanism to project structure onto this data and query the data using a SQL-style language, HiveQL.

1.1 Overview of the Proposed Approach

Our approach combines knowledge of Hive query processing with Mixture Density Networks (MDN) [3], a flexible technique to modelling real-valued distributions with neural networks. For this purpose, we firstly execute training Hive workloads and log their CPU usage and runtime values along with predefined query features. Secondly, we input the query features to the MDN model. Finally, the MDN statistically analyses the feeding features' numbers and actual observation of the resource consumption and runtime of training data and predicts the probability distribution parameters (i.e. mean, variance, and mixing coefficients) over target values (i.e. CPU and query execution time).

To illustrate the gains possible by using the proposed approach, consider Fig. 1 which displays two sample predicted pdfs for CPU usage and runtime for one of the experiments conducted on TPC-H queries (www.tpc.org/tpch/) in this paper. The predicted pdfs correspond to a test input from Template-7 (Q7) of TPC-H against 100GB database size. To demonstrate the whole possible range of performance values under Q7, the histograms for 30 instance queries based on Q7 from the test set are shown as well.

As we can see, the predicted pdfs properly estimate the

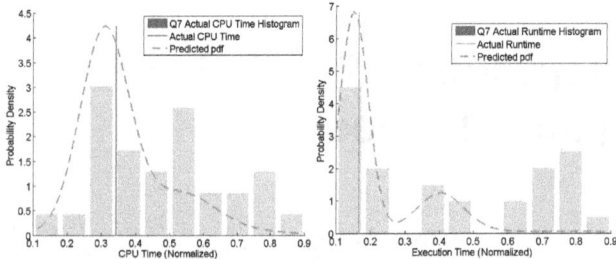

Figure 1: Two sample predicted distributions for (a) CPU and (b) Execution Time for a sample input from Q7 of TPC-H. The histograms show respectively the actual CPU and Runtime values for 30 different instance queries generated based on template-7 and executed in the cluster.

CPU and Runtime distribution in which they show high probability around the target value. More importantly, they provide information about the whole spectrum of performance and resource usage. Specifically, the predicted pdf in Fig. 1(b) shows highly probable Runtime in ranges (0.1, 0.2) and (0.3, 0.5) which are consistent with the actual distribution, though the predicted pdf corresponds to one input, meaning that the resulting uncertainty of pdf for the range (0.8, 0.9) is defensible. Similarly, the predicted pdf for CPU time (Fig. 1a) provides a complete description of the statistical properties of the CPU usage through which we are not only able to capture the observation point, but the different range of resource usage. In contrast, a best prediction from existing single point techniques [8, 2, 12] merely estimates the point which is visualized by solid vertical line through which, unlike the pdf, we are not able to directly extract valuable statistical measures including variance, expectation, and confidence interval about the target.

1.2 Contributions

Distribution-Based Prediction: This paper transfers solid techniques from other computer science fields to the distributed systems community. Although other approaches such as Conditional Density Estimation Network and Random Vector Functional Link are also available to estimate the pdf, the benefit of using MDN is its ability to model unknown distributions. Put differently, the MDN does not hold any assumption about the final shape of resource and performance distribution of workloads.

Resource Modelling of Hive Queries: We develop a set of black-box models for predicting CPU and runtime distribution of Hive query workloads. The models are trained based on a set of SQL and MapReduce specific features and the corresponding data input statistics appeared in the HiveQL query execution plan.

Evaluation: We evaluate our approach on the TPC-H state of the art decision support benchmark, showing that it approximates accurate pdf predictions using proper error metrics for evaluating distribution predictions.

2. RELATED WORK

Query processing runtime and resource usage estimation has been investigated in the context of DBMS or MapReduce [2, 7, 12, 8, 1, 6]. In the majority of related work, different statistical ML techniques are applied for query performance estimation. Specifically, techniques such as Kernel Canonical Correlation Analysis (KCCA), Multiple Additive Regression-Trees, and Support Vector Machine (SVM) have

been respectively built upon query plan features [7] operator level features [2, 12] or both [2]. These approaches build statistical models using past query executions and a representative set of query features which have high predictive power in terms of resource or performance estimation.

In terms of concurrent workloads, [1] uses various regression models to predict the completion times of batch query workloads when multiple queries are running concurrently. Along similar lines, [6] argues that the buffer access latency metric is correlated with the query runtime, and they use linear regression techniques for mapping buffer access latency to the execution times. Though the above approaches primarily use statistical ML techniques, they apply fine-grained models in a different context, that of massively parallel data processing in the MapReduce environment.

Another related paper applies KCCA to the Hive workload using two different set of features [8]. In their initial job feature vector they consider features corresponding to the number of occurrences of each operator in a job's execution plan. The obtained results suggest that Hive operator occurrence counts are insufficient for modelling Hive query *runtime* which is somehow consistent with what we will report and discuss in 4.4 (Fig. 4b and 5b). Following that, they include another set of low level features pertaining to Hive query execution such as the number of maps and reduces, bytes read locally, bytes read from HDFS, and bytes input to the map stage, which lead to good prediction accuracy. However, the provided low level features are not available before the query is executed, so that it can not be used for performance prediction of new incoming queries.

Note that all of the above studies approximate the performance of workload as a single point value which is neither expressive enough nor does it capture performance variances.

3. PERFORMANCE MODELLING OF HIVE

To approach the problem of resource and performance distribution prediction of Hive workloads, we use knowledge of Hive query execution in Hadoop combined with statistical machine learning (ML) techniques.

3.1 Query Execution in HiveQL

A key to the accuracy of a prediction model is choosing the most predictive features from the available set of features to train the model. Therefore, we need to identify a set of potential features that would affect the performance and the query resource usage. To identify the potential features we need to dissect the way a HiveQL statement is being executed on top of a Hadoop cluster.

Once a Hive query is submitted against the chunks of data residing in distributed file systems (e.g. HDFS, GFS), the Hive engine compiles it to workflows of MapReduce jobs, in which the SQL operators are plugged into map and reduce functions of the job. At the end of each map and reduce phase, the intermediate results are materialized on disk. During a Hive query execution, SQL specific operators (e.g. table scan, select) which are implemented inside map and reduce functions along with MapReduce specific tasks (e.g. read, spill, shuffle, write) are the main computation tasks which use cluster resources and impact the query completion latency. The overhead of the latter is in fact the function of the number of mappers and reducers spawned across a cluster to execute the query's operators against the data blocks. This number is itself dependent on input data to each query processing stage, job configurations, and available free resources in a multi-system cluster.

As we aim at resource and runtime distribution prediction of Hive queries before any actual execution takes place, we inevitably need to stick with the data provided by the Hive query execution plan. Unlike conventional database systems, the Hive execution plan is an intermediate step before determining the number of mappers and reducers to be executed as a MapReduce job. However, assuming constant configuration, the estimated input data size is a proper predictive feature for alleviating the issue of mappers/reducers numbers and their corresponding Hadoop phases (e.g. reading, spilling, shuffling, writing). Thus, our feature set includes SQL and MapReduce operator counts along with the input record number and data size as specified in Table 1.

Table 1: Feature set for resource modelling of Hive queries.

Feature Name	Description
SQL Operator No	Number of SQL operators (e.g. Table Scan) which appear in the HiveQL query plan.
SQL Operator Input Records	Input Row Numbers for each operator as per the query plan.
SQL Operator Input Byte	Input Data Size to SQL operator.
MapReduce Operator No	Number of MapReduce operators (e.g. Reduce Output Operator), appear in the HiveQL query plan.
MapReduce Operator Input Records	Input Row Numbers for each operator as per the query plan.
MapReduce Operator Input Byte	Input Data Size to the MapReduce specific operator.

We note that the resource contention among different concurrent workloads will impact the performance and following its estimation. However we put forward the claim that with distribution prediction of data-intensive workloads, we are able to tackle properly the inevitable performance variances in the presence of resource contention and runtime configurations. We will discuss this issue in detail in 4.4 and 5.

3.2 Mixture Density Networks

One of the challenging decisions when using statistical models is the choice of the underlying ML technique itself. This is why identifying the most accurate prediction model without training and testing multiple models is hardly possible. Nevertheless, the focus of our work which is conditional probability density prediction, alleviates the problem of picking the right model. We use Mixture Density Networks as an underlying ML technique in the proposed approach. Our decision is backed up by i) its successful applications in speech synthesis or meteorological domain, and ii) its flexibility in capturing skewed and multi-modal distributions, as exhibited by runtime and resource usage distributions in a multi-system cluster.

A classic MDN fuses a Gaussian mixture model (GMM) with multilayer perceptron (MLP). In MDN, the distribution of the outputs t is described by a parametric model whose parameters are determined by the output of a neural network, which takes x as inputs. Fig. 2 gives an overview of MDN in which the neural network is responsible for mapping the input vector x to the parameters of the mixture

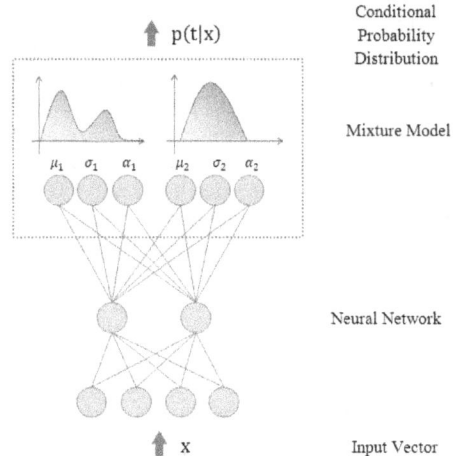

Figure 2: MDN approximates distribution parameters, conditioned on the input vector.

model $(\alpha_i, \mu_i, \sigma^2)$, which in return provides the conditional distribution. An MDN, in fact, maps input features x to the parameters of a GMM: mixture weights α_i, mean μ_i, and variance σ^2, which in turn produces the full *pdf* of an output feature t, conditioned on the input vector $p(t|x)$. Thus, the conditional density function takes the form of GMM:

$$p(t|x) = \sum_{i=1}^{M} \alpha_i(x)\phi_i(t|x) \qquad (1)$$

where M is the number of mixture components, ϕ_i is the ith Gaussian component's contribution to the conditional density of the target vector t as follows:

$$\phi_i(t|x) = \frac{1}{(2\pi)^{c/2}\sigma_i(x)^c} exp\left\{-\frac{||t-\mu_i(x)||^2}{2\sigma_i(x)^2}\right\} \qquad (2)$$

The MDN approximates the GMM as:

$$\alpha_i = \frac{exp(z_i^\alpha)}{\sum_{j=1}^{M} exp(z_j^\alpha)} \qquad (3)$$

$$\sigma_i = exp(z_i^\sigma) \qquad (4)$$

$$\mu_i = z_i^\mu \qquad (5)$$

where z_i^α, z_i^σ, and z_i^μ are the outputs of the neural network corresponding to the mixture weights, variance, and mean for the ith Gaussian component in the GMM, given x [3]. To constrain the mixture weights to be positive and sum to unity, a softmax function is used in Eq. 3 which associates the output of corresponding units in the neural network to the mixing coefficients. Similarly, the variance parameters (Eq. 4) are related to the outputs of the neural network which constrains the standard deviations to be positive.

4. EXPERIMENTAL EVALUATION

4.1 Experimental Setup

Infrastructure Setup. We evaluate our models on CSIRO Big Data cluster. The cluster comprises of 14 worker nodes connected with fast Infiniband network, each featuring 2 x Intel Xeon E5-2660 @ 2.20 GHz CPU (8 cores), 128 GB RAM and 12 x 2 TB NL-SAS HD making up the total disk space of 240 TB. All experiments were run on top of HiveQL 0.13.1, and Hadoop 2.3.0 in Yarn mode on.

Workloads. We test our approach on TPC-H benchmark. We execute TPC-H queries on six scaling factors: 2, 5, 25, 50, 75, and 100 GB. All databases are generated in Apache Parquet data file format. The TPC-H workload consists of all queries except the queries that are either super slow (including Q2, Q8, Q9) or failed (e.g. Q19[1]), thereby we run the super slow queries for solely 2 and 5 GB database size to keep the overall experiment duration under control.

There are approximately 11 queries from each template in six databases. Thus, the resulting data set we used contains 995 queries. Note that our cluster is shared by multiple users in the organization who submit different ranges of applications (e.g. Spark, MapReduce) for processing. Moreover, queries are either run *sequentially* or in *parallel* without any pre-defined ordering to simulate real world conditions as much as possible.

Training and Testing Settings. To assess how the result of a predictive model would be generalized to an independent data set, we divide the TPC-H workload randomly into training and testing datasets with 66% and 34% respectively. Before training and testing, the input and output features are normalized using z-score and min-max normalization with range (0.1-0.9). For training and testing, we use a Netlab toolbox [13] which is designed for the simulation of neural network algorithms and related models, in particular MDN. The implemented MDN model uses the MLP as a feed forward neural network.

4.2 Error Metrics

To determine whether a probabilistic model performs well, we need to implement a set of appropriate error metrics. Therefore, in the following subsection three error metrics including continuous ranked probability score (CRPS), negative log predictive density (NLPD), and root mean-square error (RMSE) are defined. The first two measures are proper metrics for evaluating the accuracy of a distribution prediction. We also use RMSE to compare the MDN with the state of the art single point prediction techniques.

The goal of a probabilistic prediction is to maximize the sharpness of the predictive distributions subject to calibration [9]. Sharpness refers to the concentration of the predictive distributions. Calibration refers to the statistical consistency between the pdfs. The objective is to predict pdfs that closely estimate the region in which the target lies with proper sharpness. Thus, the CRPS [9] is a proper metric to evaluate the accuracy of pdfs. The CRPS takes the whole distribution into account when measuring the error:

$$CRPS(F,t) = \int_{-\infty}^{\infty} \left[F(x) - O(x,t) \right]^2 dx \qquad (6)$$

where F and O are the cumulative distribution functions (cdfs) of prediction and observation distributions respectively. $O(x,t)$ is a step function that attains the value of 1 if $x \geq t$ and the value of 0 otherwise.

To calculate CRPS both the prediction and the observation are converted to cumulative distribution functions. The CRPS compares the difference between cumulative distributions of prediction and observation as given by the hatched area in Fig. 3. It can be seen that the area gets smaller if the prediction distribution concentrates probability mass near the observation, i.e. the better it approximates the step

---

[1]This issue is also reported by users in https://issues.apache.org/jira/browse/HIVE-600

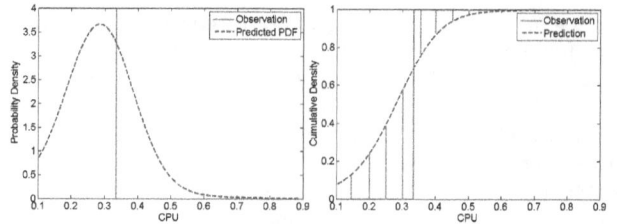

Figure 3: (a) predicted pdf and the observation (b) schematic sketch of the CRPS as the difference between cdfs of prediction and observation.

function. Moreover, the small CRPS value shows that the prediction captures the sharpness of prediction accurately.

After calculating the CRPS for each prediction, we need to average the values to evaluate the whole input set:

$$CRPS = \frac{1}{n} \sum_{i=1}^{n} CRPS(F_i, t_i) \qquad (7)$$

To evaluate the spread of predictive density in which our targets lie, the average NLPD [10] error metric is used. Note that unlike CRPS, it is not sensitive to distance:

$$NLPD = \frac{1}{n} \sum_{i=1}^{n} -log(p(t_i|x_i)) \qquad (8)$$

where n is the number of observations. The NLPD evaluates the amount of probability that the model assigns to targets and penalizes both over- and under-confident predictions.

The last metric is the RMSE:

$$RMSE = \sqrt{\frac{1}{n} \sum_{i=1}^{n} (t_i - m_i)^2} \qquad (9)$$

where m refers to the mean of the pdfs as point predictions for the MDNs. This metric allows us to compare the proposed estimation technique with single point competitors.

4.3 State of the Art Techniques

In order to compare the performance of distribution-based prediction with single point estimators, we study REPTree, SVM, and MLP as the alternative techniques. REPTree and SVM are the main prediction techniques used in [14] and [2] respectively. Moreover, [12] also uses a variant of regression trees as a core predictor. Since classical MDN uses MLP in its neural network layer, we can expect that MDN as a single point prediction shows almost the same performance and accuracy as MLP. Thus, we report and discuss the results under MLP as well. These three algorithms are implemented in the well-known Weka package [11].

4.4 Evaluation: Single Point Estimators

Before presenting and discussing the results under the MDN technique, let us first investigate how accurately the Hive query performance and resource usage could be estimated in terms of the proposed feature set (Table 1) using well-established ML techniques.

Fig. 4 displays the performance of REPTree in CPU and runtime estimation of Hive workloads where it approximates resource usage more successfully than runtime. We will discuss this issue later in this section, by then we are interested in the performance of other competing techniques as well. Because, in general, identifying the most accurate prediction model without training and testing multiple models is

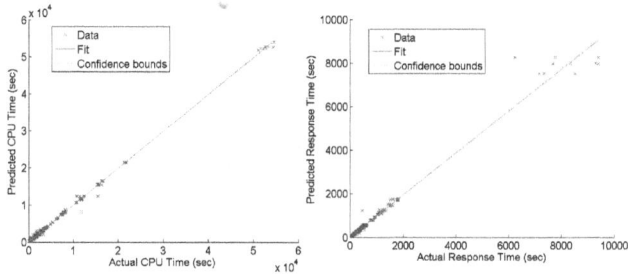

Figure 4: (a) CPU and (b) Response time prediction for Hive queries, modelled using the Table 1 feature set.

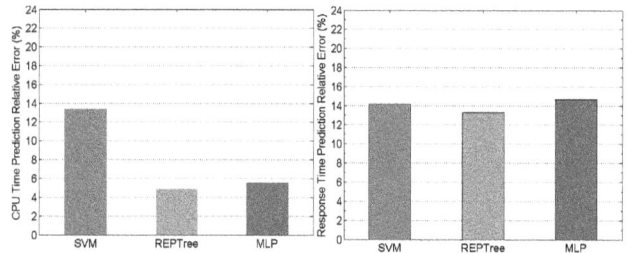

Figure 5: Relative error (%) for (a) CPU and (b) Response time prediction using SVM, REPTree, and MLP techniques.

hardly possible, thereby the Relative Error (%) of CPU and Runtime estimation of ~ 1000 Hive queries using all three alternative techniques (i.e. REPTree, SVM, and MLP) are evaluated and shown in Fig. 5.

As we can see, REPTree outperforms the other predictors in both CPU and Response Time estimation with relative errors of 4.83% and 13.28% respectively. More importantly, our classifiers are more successful in resource estimation than runtime. The main reason behind this observation is the *resource contention* issue in a shared cluster of machines. As stated earlier, our cluster is shared by multiple users and various applications concurrently processing GBs or TBs of data. Therefore, when multiple jobs and queries are submitted to the cluster, they compete for common resources such as disk, memory, or CPU which might negatively impact the performance. In terms of resource modelling, the contention is not a challenge because our models capture the CPU time which is the amount of time for which CPUs are used for processing instructions, as opposed to, for example, waiting for I/O operations. In contrast, interference of other workloads inevitably hit the query runtime.

We argue that with the distribution of query performance we are able properly to capture and express the whole spectrum of performance (i.e. here response time) and any possible variances in presence of resource contention. To capture the impact of the concurrency and interference in performance, there are some proposals [1, 6] for query executions in DBMSs. However, the proposed techniques are not applicable to the Hive workloads in a multi-system cluster due to i) different abstraction level of query processing in Hive, and ii) lack of control on the type of concurrent workloads in a cluster where they typically hold some assumptions about the mixture of queries running concurrently. Nevertheless, our approach relaxes such constraints and more importantly it is able to estimate the performance while the concurrent workloads are not even from the same platform, for example, where a certain Hive query is competing with Spark jobs for the CPU shares.

4.5 Evaluation: Distribution-Based Prediction

We now discuss the accuracy of the proposed approach. The results for both the proposed approach using MDN and the single point estimators under CRPS, NLPD, and RMSE metrics are shown in Table 2. Note that the number of Gaussian components is a hyper-parameter in MDN and needs to be specified beforehand. To do so, we report the results under 1, 3, and 5 mixture components (M).

All three metrics are negatively oriented scores; hence the smaller the value the better. Let us first study the accuracy of the MDN per se using CRPS and NLPD metric errors. As the small numbers under CRPS and NLPD indicate, the

proposed model is an appropriate estimator for both CPU and Runtime distribution prediction of Hive workloads. Unlike single point estimators, the MDN shows slightly better performance in Runtime prediction rather CPU. Another interesting observation is that in the TPC-H workload sophisticated MDN architecture with 3 and 5 mixture components led to increased fidelity of results.

To compare the proposed approach with the competing techniques, we need to treat it as a single point estimator, thereby we use RMSE metric error for comparison. According to Table 2, the MDN outperforms SVM in CPU prediction, albeit REPTree has the lowest RMSE value. Similarly, REPTree outperforms the others in Response Time (RT) estimation. However, this is not the whole story.

Taking the output corresponding to the mean of the predicted pdfs is almost equivalent to using an MLP with linear output activation function, trained with a least-squares error function. It means that the MLP classifier accuracy is comparable to the MDN. A closer look at the data indicates that the RMSE values under the MLP are in between SVM and REPTree. This observation is consistent with what we saw in RMSE values for MDN.

However, the question may arise *"Why tharee RMSE values under MDN and MLP totally different?"*. This observation is sourced from the different normalization and configuration parameters used in MLP implementation in Netlab toolbox [13] and Weka [11] which are respectively employed for the MDN and MLP (as a standalone technique) training. To test our hypothesis, we replaced the default MLP configuration of Weka with what is used in Netlab, observing almost the same RMSE errors.

In summary, our approach outperforms the state of the art single point techniques in 2 out of 4 experiments conducted using SVM and REPTree. This result is quite promising because it shows that our approach is not only able to predict the full distribution over targets accurately, it is also a reliable single point estimator.

4.6 Training Times and Overhead

Table 3 denotes the training times regarding different workload sizes. As the results indicate, the training cost is very

Table 2: MDN performance compared with its competitors.

		MDN			REPT.	SVM	MLP
Targ.	M	CRPS	NLPD	RMSE	RMSE	RMSE	RMSE
CPU	1	0.093	-1.2	**0.077**			
	3	0.091	-2.54	0.08	0.005	0.08	0.048
	5	**0.024**	**-2.65**	0.081			
RT	1	0.064	-1.1	**0.077**			
	3	0.031	-2.68	0.079	0.01	0.073	0.031
	5	**0.017**	**-3.2**	0.08			

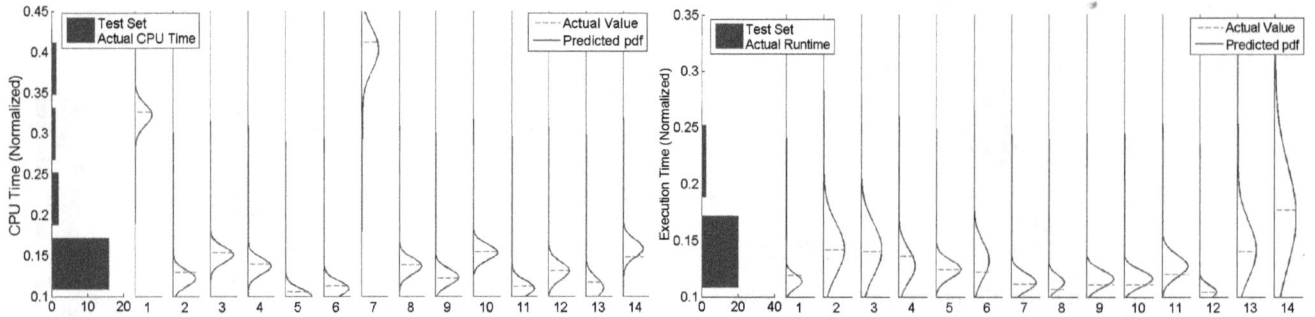

Figure 6: Sample pdf predictions for (a) CPU and (b) Execution Time of Hive queries based on TPC-H workload.

small and it grows linearly in terms of the training set size.

Table 3: Training times in seconds with regard to different workload sizes for 500 iterations.

Workload Size	1K	2K	4K	8K	16K
Elapsed Time (sec)	1.47	1.9	2.63	3.84	7.83

Apart from reasonable training time, low overhead in invoking a trained model at runtime is yet another critical parameter because it has to be quick enough to get the estimates ready in time for decision making modules of the workload management strategies at runtime, where unreasonable delays may lead to SLA misses. To this end, we measured the elapsed time for evaluating an MDN model for a given input feature set on a 2.80GHz Intel Core i7, and obtained an overhead of about 0.2 ms for each call. To put these numbers in perspective, the execution plan generation in Hive (using EXPLAIN command) for say Q1 of TPC-H takes 4.97 seconds, meaning that invoking the MDN model for each new incoming query would not be a significant factor in the overall workload management cost.

5. PREDICTION UTILIZATION

This section provides a clear picture of how the provided prediction could be utilized and employed in workload management of data-intensive applications. We have visualized some sample predicted pdfs from the test set of the TPC-H workload as shown in Fig. 6. In particular, the figure plots 14 random sample predicted pdfs for CPU and execution time. The histograms show the actual CPU and runtime values for the whole test dataset. Each pdf may (not) belong to different queries as they were randomly selected from the test set, meaning they are conditioned on different inputs. The dotted vertical line shows the observation value.

As the figures show, the pdfs accurately approximate the resource usage and performance distributions which are primarily within the range (0.1, 0.4) and (0.1, 0.25) for CPU and runtime respectively. In a consistent manner, the models for CPU and execution time beyond the values 0.5 and 0.3 are much more uncertain. Put differently, the tendency of all CPU and runtime pdfs is to the right hand side of diagram and this is consistent with the plotted histograms of actual resource and performance values in which, for example, we hardly face resource demand above 0.5.

These sample pdfs demonstrate that the MDN is also a reliable classifier in the classic point estimate sense, where the pdfs cover the observation points with high probability in all figures but pdfs number 14 in 6(a) and 8 in 6(b). However, they locate the shape of distributions precisely.

We also argue that distribution-based prediction gives the

resource and workload management systems a concise yet lucid way of interpreting workload behaviour. Such capability is crucial for a number of resource management activities such as run-time performance isolation or diagnosis inspection. In particular, upper and lower bounds of resource usage simplify the task of performance isolation, since for example our predictions in all figures capture the dominant CPU time precisely. When it comes to performance inspection, diagnosing abnormal behaviour as per the predicted numbers is also viable. Specifically, Fig. 6(a) reports that for a given set of queries we will not face peak CPU time (>0.5) very often, hence a higher peak CPU time indicates the possible presence of a fault in the software or cluster.

6. CONCLUSIONS AND FUTURE WORK

This work presented a novel approach of using mixture density networks for CPU and runtime distribution prediction of large-scale analytics queries. We evaluated our approach on TPC-H, showing that it outperforms the state of the art techniques in half of experiments. For future work, we plan to devise a distribution-based admission control and query scheduler on top of Apache Yarn to avoid resource usage spikes on busy clusters.

7. REFERENCES

[1] M. Ahmad et al. Predicting completion times of batch query workloads using interaction-aware models and simulation. In *EDBT*, pages 449–460. ACM, 2011.
[2] M. Akdere et al. Learning-based query performance modeling and prediction. In *ICDE*, pages 390–401. IEEE, 2012.
[3] C. M. Bishop. Mixture density networks. 1994.
[4] S. Chaisiri et al. Optimization of resource provisioning cost in cloud computing. *TSC*, 5(2):164–177, 2012.
[5] Y. Chi et al. Distribution-based query scheduling. *VLDB*, 6(9):673–684, 2013.
[6] J. Duggan et al. Performance prediction for concurrent database workloads. In *SIGMOD*, pages 337–348. ACM, 2011.
[7] A. Ganapathi et al. Predicting multiple metrics for queries: Better decisions enabled by machine learning. In *ICDE*, pages 592–603. IEEE, 2009.
[8] A. Ganapathi et al. Statistics-driven workload modeling for the cloud. In *ICDEW*, pages 87–92. IEEE, 2010.
[9] T. Gneiting and A. E. Raftery. Strictly proper scoring rules, prediction, and estimation. *Journal of the American Statistical Association*, 102(477):359–378, 2007.
[10] I. J. Good. Rational decisions. *Journal of the Royal Statistical Society. Series B (Methodological)*, pages 107–114, 1952.
[11] M. Hall et al. The weka data mining software: an update. *SIGKDD*, 11(1):10–18, 2009.
[12] J. Li et al. Robust estimation of resource consumption for sql queries using statistical techniques. *VLDB*, 5(11):1555–1566, 2012.
[13] I. Nabney. *NETLAB: algorithms for pattern recognition*. Springer Science & Business Media, 2002.
[14] P. Xiong et al. Activesla: a profit-oriented admission control framework for database-as-a-service providers. In *SoCC*, page 15. ACM, 2011.

Automatic Performance Modelling from Application Performance Management (APM) Data:
An Experience Report

Paul Brebner

CTO, Performance Assurance Pty Ltd

www.performance–assurance.com.au

Canberra, Australia

paul@performance-assurance.com.au

ABSTRACT

Traditional testing approaches for enterprise systems are no longer possible, agile enough, affordable, or accurate in many cases. This is due to ongoing changes, reduced time between production updates and the inability to test all system components because of third party services and the expense of maintaining a test environment. One alternative approach has been to manually build predictive performance models to mitigate performance risk. Even this has become impractical and cannot keep pace with changes in complex enterprise systems.

In response to these challenges we have developed a way to automatically build and parameterize performance models for large scale enterprise systems from Application Performance Management (APM) data. This industry experience report summaries our experiences with automatically building performance models for commercial customers over the last two years. For each project we summarize the problem context, the performance risks to be addressed, the automatic modelling process, the range in complexity of the resulting models, the accuracy of the predictions, and the benefits and limitations of the models in practice.

Keywords

Modelling; measurement; performance; scalability; automatic; APM

1. Introduction

Since 2007 we have developed a software performance modelling tool and applied it to a variety of different enterprise technologies and performance problems [15-27]. For the last 2 years we have been delivering performance modelling in a purely commercial context which has necessitated a change from manually built performance models to automatically built models. We have found that manually built models cannot be built with sufficient speed, reliability, accuracy or complexity, to satisfy the business

and technical constraints of commercial performance model delivery. However, many customers now have increasingly sophisticated APM tools installed, from a decreasing number of vendors, which provide a valuable source of data for automatic model building, particularly if the investment in building tools for conversion from APM tools to a modelling platform can be maximized by reuse for multiple customers.

Previous work in automated performance modelling explores a variety of approaches for data capture (including modelling from architecture and design artefacts, source code, code instrumentation, JVM, logs, and monitoring data), and application domains (e.g. enterprise software, HPC) [1-10].

Because we are working in a commercial enterprise application context we have focused on a few APM vendors who provide monitoring solutions which include: Large-scale monitoring of heterogeneous software stacks; End-to-end transaction flow data for every transaction and every sub-system called; a rich variety of per transaction metrics; and means of obtaining the data from the APM system (e.g. export facilities or REST APIs).

Our performance modelling tool is model driven and supports a meta-model of software performance based around SOA concepts of workloads, composite and simple services, and servers. These can be used to model business processes, workflows, and internal software processes and services to an arbitrary level of detail. Our tool provides a graphical user interface to build, parameterize and visualize performance models. The performance models are solved with a discrete event simulation engine and performance metrics computed and displayed graphically for analysis. Models can be changed and predictions easily compared. The tool is currently hosted as a SaaS to reduce costs and increase ease of use by customers. Previously we parameterized models from a variety of data sources depending on availability such as SLAs, sub-system time budgets, benchmarks, experimental in-house test-bed results, log files, custom monitoring solutions, and older APM products. Such data was often substandard in terms of quality and quantity and coverage of the target systems.

We have developed an automatic model building pipeline for one main APM vendor, and experimented with variation of it for several others. The pipeline can ingest data from files obtained from customer copies of the APM tool, or it can use REST API calls to obtain data remotely or from a local copy of the APM tool. Once the raw APM data is read it, several processing steps occur including parsing, format/structure/semantic conversion and transformation steps into our internal normalized APM data format, error checking, statistics calculations, initial internal model building and analytical simulation (for more sophisticated validation), and finally generation of the performance model and upload to the SaaS tool where simulations can be run and changes made to the models. Depending on the amount and type of APM data available, and the purpose of modelling, different models types can be automatically generated. Typically the tradeoff is between model simplicity and complexity, modelling for capacity vs. performance predictions, and availability of detailed transactional data from the APM tools. Being able to build different model types from the same data is also valuable for research purposes and we easily investigate the pros/cons of different model types and the impact on accuracy, power of the models, and ease of use and understandability. Changes (additions, deletions, modifications, aggregation) can also be introduced at different phases of the pipeline with different pros/cons including in the APM tool before data is imported into our system, in the data itself before or during processing, in the pre-processing tool either before, during or after internal model generation, in the outputted model, or in the SaaS modelling tool.

The bulk of the paper will focus on our experiences with automatic model building for three projects. However, two aspects of modelling that are discussed in the project summaries are first introduced in more detail to provide sufficient background. These are: Model Calibration, and Model Complexity.

1.1 Model calibration

By default our performance models are parameterized with measured data (metric time distributions). They are more accurate at loads closer to the average load that the APM data was collected at, but tend to produce optimistic predictions for response times, capacity and resource requirements at significantly higher loads. For more accurate predictions models can be calibrated with load test results, however, such calibrations are dependent on the availability, correctness, and interpretability of load test data, and are context specific as they depend on the actual load and specific server resources available. Moreover, if part of the system saturates first (which is inevitable for real world systems) then the calibrations are likely to be inaccurate for the as yet unsaturated sub-systems. In theory it is be possible to obtain 0% model error using calibration data, however, in practice we have found that this is unachievable for commercial systems due to factors such as: problems running and interpreting load test result; differences in transactions and transaction mixes in load tests and models; and ambiguity around the modelling, allocation and setting resource limits for servers for detailed time breakdown metrics available from some APM tools, e.g. CPU (user/system), I/O, suspension, wait, and synchronization times. Introducing load dependent scaling (e.g. using linear or non-linear regression analysis) to model times under varying loads is a typical solution used to increase the predictive accuracy. However, it depends on having a sufficiently large sample of data from a large enough range of loads to be significant, extrapolation beyond the measured load range is risky, and it is difficult to apply to complex models which are parameterized with response time distributions, as in many cases load dependency is specific to each transaction, service and server combination. Hence, for the reported projects most of the models could not be calibrated to 0% error.

1.2 Model complexity

Model complexity is a simplified estimate of the upper number of components in a model and is computed as *complexity = (transactions * services) + services + servers*. Transactions are the number of transaction types (not individual transactions). Services appear twice as there is one model component per transaction type per service for the probability of the service being called and the time distribution, and another component per service per model representing the deployment of that service on a server. Servers is the number of physical or virtual servers the services are deployed to. Actual models may be simpler as not all services are called for each transaction, but more complex in that this formula does not take account into account relationships between components. Automatically built models can also include other system aspects such as Entry points (where a transaction enters the system), APIs, Classes and even method calls, which all have the potential for dramatically increasing the complexity but also the utility of models. Our previously manually constructed and parameterized models were practically limited to a maximum complexity of around 100, but automatically built models can have orders of magnitude higher complexity. We summarize the automatically built models for the projects below in terms of minimum (aggregated transactions) and maximum (all transaction types represented) complexities.

2. Projects
2.1 Project 1

The context of project 1 was the migration of multiple different applications from a legacy physical infrastructure that was soon to be retired, to a new virtualized infrastructure. There were a large number of poorly understood legacy applications, with different performance characteristics, and the client wanted to be able to assure their customers (who owned and used these applications) that they would still perform on the new infrastructure well in advance of migration. They also wanted to know if the sizing of the new infrastructure was sufficient and also efficient from a cost perspective. The plan was to take an example application (the first application to be migrated), install an APM tool on the physical infrastructure, deploy the application on both platforms, and run load tests on each application and platform to determine the maximum capacity. The next step was to build models from the APM data on the physical platform, and then demonstrate that given the APM data and model for the application on the physical platform, the performance, capacity and resource requirements for the application on the new virtualized platform could be predicted, and that this was a repeatable process for other applications to be migrated in the future.

Our methodology was to run a load test multiple times for each application/platform, and ramp up the load gradually until maximum throughput was observed. Load test and APM data was captured for each test and the results used to build a model and validate the predictions. The high level results are as follows. For the old physical platform, the maximum measured capacity was 14TPS. Models were built for the lowest and the highest loads. The lowest and highest load models predicted an optimistic maximum theoretical capacity of 92TPS and 63TPS respectively, both obviously higher than the actual measured capacity.

For the new virtualized platform, the maximum measured capacity was higher at 38TPS. The low load model from the physical platform was calibrated for the lowest and the highest loads on the virtualized platform, and predicted a closer maximum theoretical capacity of 45TPS and 49TPS respectively, with an error of 21% and 33% respectively.

The uncertainty in these predictions is due to a combination of factors including using only load independent models which don't take into account increasing times with increasing load, uncertainty over how to allocate and accurately model capacity of time metric breakdowns (User and system CPU/IO, and other times), and simplifications made in calibrating the models (using scaling factors computed using average times for each server at the maximum load divided by the average times for the same components at the minimum load. To be more accurate, calibration is ideally done per transaction type/service).

Another metric was also computed which we call "efficiency". It is computed as $efficiency = TP/RT/cores$. Higher efficiency is better. The old physical platform was actually faster than the new virtualized platform, although the new virtualized platform had higher concurrency (16 cores c.f. 12). The efficiency of the old physical platform was better (7.8) than the efficiency of the new virtualized platform (5.8). The metric TP/RT is referred to in the literature as "power" [11, 12].

The business goal of this project was to reuse the methodology to assist with migrating multiple applications. However, there was a problem with repeatability with our approach, as in theory the calibration factors used to scale the model of the application on the legacy platform to make accurate capacity predictions for the new platform first needs to be obtained from load tests of the application on the new virtualized platform – but the application has to be first deployed on the new platform. The calibration factors are likely to be specific to application, hardware, virtualization technology, cores per VM, load, etc. However, a few more complete iterations with multiple application examples would produce more calibration examples. It may then be possible to calibrate models with a range and average values obtained from previous examples, to provide sufficient assurance before decisions are made to migrate the applications to the new virtualized platform.

The project 1 application was relatively simple, having 40 transaction types, 2-3 services, and 3-4 servers. The model complexity for the application on the physical platform was 85 and for the virtualized platform the model complexity was 127. We used 24k transactions from the APM tool to build the model on the physical platform, and 67k on the virtualized platform. On the physical platform the average metric breakdown percentages were 44% for DB time, 2% user CPU, and 53% system CPU/IO. On the virtualized platform the average metric percentages were 11% for DB time, 1% user CPU, 87% system CPU/IO. In absolute terms both DB time and system CPU/IO times were greater on the virtualized platform, probably due to the overhead of virtualization.

2.2 Project 2
The context of project 2 was the migration of a large scale mission critical application to a web-based system, and migration to new infrastructure to support it. There was a hard deadline for the migration to occur by, and the client wanted assistance in assuring that the migrated application had adequate performance and scalability, and that the new infrastructure was sufficient but not substantially over resourced, as there was a significant cost overhead and time delay for server provisioning. The development and testing and user acceptance testing of the new system was conducted on different platforms to the new production infrastructure, and the focus of testing was functional rather than performance or load testing. However, all the systems were monitored by a commercial APM tool which provided detailed per transaction metrics per service/sub-system, including a breakdown of metric times (user and system CPU, I/O, wait, synchronization and suspension) and server metrics including CPU utilization and number of cores. Due to the timetable of the migration and when data from the various testing activities was available, we had a very limited amount of time to obtain the APM data, build models, and make capacity and resource predictions.

The earliest APM data available was from functional testing in an Amazon Web Services (AWS) Cloud environment. The tests were performed in a planned order, exercising a subset of transaction types at a time over a period of weeks. We therefore needed to obtain the APM data for a significant range of the test period to obtain as many transaction types as possible. This gave us 104k transaction samples to work with. Once we had the data we analyzed it to check for quality prior to modelling, revealing that there were a large number of errors and unhandled exceptions, and the majority of time was spent in synchronization and I/O+System CPU (50% synchronization, 25% I/O+System CPU, 20% User CPU). There were 2114 transaction types in the test data, significantly less than expected, leading us to suspect that the data was not giving us complete coverage of the application. It was also unlikely that the transaction ratios from test were representative of a production mixture. After filtering out some of the worst transactions, we automatically built and parameterized a performance model from the remaining data. The most complex model that we built from this data (including all 2214 transaction types, 27 services, and 46 hosts) had a complexity of 59k, and the simplest (using a single aggregated transaction, which is adequate for capacity prediction) had a complexity of only 100. Using only the CPU time breakdowns the model predicted a total minimum number of cores at the target load of 240.

Given the potentially problematic results from the AWS environment, the client decided to accelerate production deployment, and deployed a subset of the final functionality onto a smaller production environment earlier than planned. We obtained 80k transactions over 5 days of APM data from this environment. We noticed that the percentage of User CPU time had gone up to 50% (but absolutely was a lot less), I/O+system CPU time was 20%, synchronization time had dropped below 1%). There was also a substantial reduction in errors and unhandled exceptions. The number of transactions types had increased to 7771 so more functionality was being measured. The model automatically built from this data predicted a total minimum number of cores at the target load of 74, significantly less than the original prediction. The client had meanwhile arranged for a cheaper/more flexible provisioning option and proceeded to fully deploy the application in production with 152 cores (approximately double the minimum predicted cores) to reduce the risk of performance and scalability issues. Once the production system had been deployed and running for several weeks we obtained a final 220k transaction sample. The final number of transaction types was 13k, with 30 servers and 46 servers. The most complex model had 402k components, but the simplest had 106 components. The final model predicted a minimum of 72 cores at the target load, close to the 2nd prediction. However, we noticed that the percentage of user CPU time had dropped to 13%, synchronization and suspension times had risen to 3%, but I/O+system CPU had risen to 74%. Given that the application was consuming significant non-user CPU resources, and that as the load increased some of these times would increase due to load dependence, we redid the prediction including these times, giving a more pessimistic minimum number of cores at the target load of 134, closer to the number the client had used in production (15% error).

This project exposed some difficulties of building performance models from APM data which was skewed in multiple ways (e.g. exceptions, incomplete functionality, un-representative transaction ratios, from different infrastructures, at low load compared to the target load). The main challenge was calibrating the model for accurate capacity predictions at significantly higher target loads than measured. The average measured load from the three samples of APM data was 12k, 8k and 30 times less than the target load, so the potential calibration error was substantial. Even though it was possible to rapidly build performance models to assist with capacity prediction, project 2 suggests that having high quality representative APM data is desirable for improved accuracy of results. In practice it is also becoming common practice to have a more flexible and dynamic provisioning approach (in terms of costs, initial and ongoing billing periods, VM sizes, provisioning times, elastic spin up of VMs, etc), and this will better manage unknowns, variations, and spikes in loads.

Note that as this project was focused on capacity prediction the simplest possible models (a single aggregated transaction) were used. The more complex models mentioned were built as a proof of concept to show that it was possible to build models that could also be useful for predicting response times for each transaction type.

2.3 Project 3

The business goals for project 3 were to demonstrate that we could build performance models automatically from a proprietary APM solution. The models had to be accurate for the baseline systems, and we had to demonstrate that we could model a number of alternatives of relevance to the customer. The system was a mission critical distributed system with many types of online users (employees and users, in different locations, on different platforms), it had well defined SLAs for the internal processing time for the system (excluding network time), and performed risk assessment processing in real-time. Risk assessment was performed by a sub-system which supported multiple types of assessment services, consuming different amounts of resources, and called with a large range of different frequencies per day. The challenges for the client were: to support a growing number of users over time; different peaks per day depending on the time of year; to develop, test, and put into production increasing numbers of risk assessment services at a faster rate than before; to explore alternative deployment options, all while understanding the impact of changes on performance, scalability and resources.

We have previously had experience of automatically building performance models from an APM product which provided detailed application independent per transaction metrics in a variety of data formats including XML and CSV, for which we developed a pre-processor (Projects 1 and 2). However, the semantics, structure and format of the data from this clients' APM tool were different. We developed a solution in Apache Hive [28] to pre-process the client APM data and transform it into the semantics, structure and format that could be consumed by our automatic model building pipeline. The main challenge was that the times from the APM tool were provided for "profile points" (times which were captured by developers in their code using the APM tool harness, basically a way of registering the time between two arbitrary points in the code). These times were developed for assurance, testing and business purposes rather than performance modelling, and therefore sometimes crossed sub-system and server boundaries, requiring extra processing to determine the breakdown of times for each sub-system and server.

Once the new enhanced APM modelling pipeline was developed and tested we were able to repeatably build baseline models from a day or more of production or test data. The baseline model response time performance predictions were accurate to less than 10% error for the baseline average daily load giving us and the client confidence that modelling alternatives would be useful. We have a number of different ways of modelling alternatives with this type of automatic model building pipeline including: deleting, changing or adding to the input APM performance data (e.g. by increasing the number of some type of transactions, by introducing new transactions and times, etc); by introducing transformations into the model building phase (e.g. categorizing or aggregating transactions differently, scaling times, or changing the service to server deployment mappings, or by changing the number or CPU on servers); or by manually or semi-automatically changing the resulting models. For this project all of these approaches were trialed. Some simple alternative models produced included: Calling the risk-assessment services either synchronously or asynchronously, calling some sub-systems sequentially or concurrently (if allowed by the business logic), adding new risk-assessment services (given the expected frequency of calls per day and average response time).

A more complex alternative scenario was to model the impact of splitting the risk assessment services across multiple different servers. The default deployment was for each service to be deployed on multiple servers, but the number and type of services was close to the upper limit that could be supported with the existing infrastructure due mainly to RAM consumption. The client was interested in modelling the impact of deploying a subset of the services on different numbers of servers. This is actually an optimization problem, comparable to the box packing problem with multiple variables (number of services, number of servers, CPUs per server, memory use per service, response time distribution per service, and frequency of calls per service - average and peak). The client had determined a possible split of services to servers, but it was apparent from the initial base model that we had built that some services were substantially more demanding than others (in terms of Service Demand), which they had not taken into account.

As an aside, we recently noticed [personal email to Samuel Kounev and Andreas Brunnert, 1/9/2015] that (based on upwards of five client examples of APM data) the service demand of components, sub-systems, services, etc of large scale distributed systems typically approximates Zipf's law. That is, a few components are more demanding that all the others put together. A graph of log10 of *rank* of service demand for each component vs. log10 of service demand for each component gives a straight line with a gradient close to -1.0. Zipf's law has been explored for word frequency, city sizes, animal species, the internet, and performance evaluation, etc [13, 14]. This relationship has potentially interesting/useful implications for software performance and modelling. For example, the scalability and resource usage of a system may be critically dependent on the very few most demanding components. Also, if you can measure the demand on the most demanding component, and estimate the total number of components, Zipf's law can be used to estimate the total service demand of the system (e.g. in the same way that given the weight of just the largest animal and the number of species on Noah's Ark, you can estimate the total mass of animals on the Ark).

We modelled the impact of locating only the most demanding four risk assessment services on one server, and all others (approximately thirty) on another server. This resulted in a predicted 50:50 resource split so was optimal in terms of resource load balancing. Even though it doesn't measure the impact for all the variables, it does demonstrate the possibility of significant problems with performance and scalability if the wrong subsets of assessment services are deployed on the same server. For example, scalability and therefore response times under higher loads will be impacted if too many high demand services are deployed to one server only. Response times (potentially even at lower loads) may be impacted if services with very long and very short response times are deployed on the same server. We have therefore proposed a future work plan to the client to address this risk. They will provide us with: details of service performance metrics (including number, memory use, response times, and frequency of use), and possible deployment scenarios. We will optimize the deployment of the services for 1-n servers with different numbers of CPUs, and model the most promising deployments and predict response time distributions and resource usage/scalability and tell them which ones pass/fail SLAs.

There were a couple of challenges to producing an accurate capacity model for this project. The 1st was that the APM tool did not give us a breakdown of time metrics, just response time. If breakdown times are available we have previously found that it is possible to calibrate models for best and worst case capacity predictions, and at least for simple (e.g. linear) load dependence. However, the APM data did give us explicit Garbage Collection times (because GC was one of the profile points), which revealed that GC was a significant overhead for the system (33% of the total service demand). Consequently a simple tactic to improve resource usage was to explore more efficient GC strategies, such as the use of multiple object pools to enable objects used in only a single transactional context to be efficiently deleted.

The 2nd problem related to the limited range of load data. The baseline model was built from a typical day's production data. The peak load of the day was close to the expected absolute peak load for the application, there was not much variation in load across the day, and there was still substantial headroom available on the servers. It was therefore difficult to calibrate the model for load dependent behavior to accurately predict response times and resource demands at significantly higher loads using techniques such as regression. Instead we relied on the client conducting a

stress to break load test. However, the test itself had problems with performance and resource problems (increased response time, increased CPU utilization, increased errors) well before the final eventual stable measured maximum capacity was reached. Nevertheless, using the final measured maximum throughput we calibrated our baseline model to predict the maximum throughput accurately, resulting in a reduction in error margin from 60% to 10%.

One of the unexpected difficulties with the APM data for this project was that for some likely modelling alternatives a model will be needed which accurately captures the different transaction types. We have successfully built detailed transaction type models from other APM data, however it was unavailable for this application and APM combination. Instead we attempted to infer the transaction types from the available APM data, using a combination of parameter values visible in the data and services called. We were able to automatically produce multiple possible transaction categories, however producing the exact required category was unachievable as in practice the resulting categories were either too few or too many.

The baseline model was finally built from several days of data (170k transactions), with half of the data used to build the model, and half to validate it. The simplest model had 1 transaction type, 44 services and 7 servers, giving a model complexity of 95, and the most complex had 183 inferred transaction types giving a much higher model complexity of 8k. The initial APM data size was 2GB, so the size of each transaction was 11.8KB on average. The output from Hive pre-processing was 34MB, and the model size (XML size before upload to our SaaS modelling tool) was 235KB, giving an overall size reduction of 8,510 times. This shows quantitatively the power of abstraction due to modelling, even simply at the level of the data compression ratio from raw APM data to a model.

As part of proposal for providing ongoing modelling services for this client we estimated the likely ROI of using a hybrid testing and modelling approach. We assumed that each load test takes 1 week and costs $10,000, and that the initial performance model also takes 1 week and costs $10,000. Evaluating alternatives using the performance model are much faster and cheaper, taking only 1 day and costing $2,000. A testing only approach can only complete 4 tests per month at a cost of $40,000. A hybrid testing/modelling approach, allowing for 1 initial model build, 4 alternatives modelled and evaluated, and 1 load test to confirm the most promising alternative, would cost $28,000 and take 2 weeks and 4 days. Better cost and time savings can be achieved as the effort to build initial and updated models decreases over time (potentially reducing to a single day), and with increasing numbers of alternatives modelled. This increased efficiency is likely to have agility benefits as decisions can be made earlier based on modelling results, even in the business and development phases.

3. Conclusions

Table 1 shows a summary of the projects including minimum and maximum model complexity, and the smallest error % for each.

Table 1 Summary of model complexity and smallest error

	Minimum Complexity	Maximum Complexity	Smallest Error %
Manual models	3	100	<= 100%
Project 1	85	127	21%
Project 2	100	60k	15%
Project 3	95	8k	10%

Some issues we discovered include: lack of standards for APM data resulting in differences in metrics available, different metric semantics and names, differences in metric structure and availability of transactional metrics. Accurate and automatic calibration of models for load dependency and maximum capacity is an outstanding problem. Some of the models quickly become very complex, making it difficult to visualize them and make manual changes. The benefits of automatic model building are significant. We demonstrated that we can build models automatically for a variety of application types and from several APM tools. The use of detailed transaction metrics including response time distributions rather than just averages results in models with accurate response time distribution predictions. Models are useful, accurate enough in practice, and can be built fast and reliably enough to solve real business problems on a commercial basis.

3.1 Future work

We discovered that some APM tools and applications capture a very large amount of data per transaction. Consequently one of the significant issues we encountered was the long time taken to obtain data for large numbers of transactions from the APM tool. In the worst case we could only extract 10 transactions per second from the APM REST API. We did not need all the data captured about each transaction to build performance models, but there was no way to request only the required data, which may have increased the throughput. However, once the data was obtained from the APM tool our automatic model building program worked very quickly (in the order of seconds, rather than hours to get the data in the first place). Apart from obvious potential improvements to the APM APIs to improve throughput, another solution we have considered is sampling. For some APMs it may be possible to obtain summary data for all the transactions of interest very quickly (including transaction type, start and end time of transaction, total response time, and transaction id). In this case it is often possible to obtain detailed transaction data for specific transactions by request. Some sampling strategies we have either experimented with or are considering for the future include: model building from a small fixed or percentage random sample of transactions (using complete data), and testing against the remainder (using summary data only); incrementally building models starting from very small sizes and then increasingly the sample size until there is no observed benefit from including more samples; filtering transactions to remove problematic samples with errors or exceptions; filtering transactions based on load ranges or thresholds, e.g. to remove samples with long response times, or when server or thread resources are saturated; and requesting samples of specific transaction types to ensure that each transaction type has sufficient representation to be statistically significant. Note that some APM tools provide ways

of filtering the transactions in advance of (or as part of) the external service calls to obtain the data.

Some of these approaches will also be applicable for use in DevOps when there is a continuous stream of APM data available. Models could be built periodically, incrementally or even continuously. Full or incremental or continuous model building, or partial updates to models, could be triggered by changes to components in the monitored environment (e.g. transaction types, services or servers coming or going) and once significant differences between model predictions and APM measurements are detected. Models could be quickly rebuilt once a potential problem is detected using the most recent data only, and then used to compare with previous model results.

We are also investigating the use of automatic decisions about possible model types based on analysis of the APM data and model purpose. This could also result in automatic retrieval of more, better or selected data on demand to achieve modelling purposes with the least effort and most agility.

We also suggest that it would be valuable to the wider performance engineering community to conduct more in-depth experiments and comparisons of different APM tools on the same application, with the purpose of evaluating what types and accuracy of models can be built from each, what data is essential or optional, and overall what the pros and cons of each APM tool are for automatic model building. To facilitate this we have developed a draft evaluation framework based on knowledge of four APM tools which begins to capture important similarities and differences.

4. REFERENCES

[1] Torsten Hoefler, "Towards fully automated interpretable performance models", PASAC16, June 2016, http://icl.cs.utk.edu/newsletter/presentations/2015/Hoefler-Towards-Fully-Automated-Interpretable-Performance-Models-2015-07-01.pdf

[2] Michael Hauck, "Automated Experiments for Deriving Performance-relevant Properties of Software Execution Environments", KIT Scientific Publishing, February 2014.

[3] A Mizan, G Franks, "Automated Performance Model Construction through Event Log Analysis", ICST2012, http://ieeexplore.ieee.org/xpl/articleDetails.jsp?arnumber=6200164

[4] Ludmila Cherkasova, Kivanc Ozonat, Ningfang Mi, Julie Symons, and Evgenia Smirni. 2009. Automated anomaly detection and performance modeling of enterprise applications. *ACM Trans. Comput. Syst.* 27, 3, Article 6 (November 2009), 32 pages. DOI=10.1145/1629087.1629089 http://doi.acm.org/10.1145/1629087.1629089

[5] Andreas Brunnert, Christian Vögele, Helmut Krcmar: "Automatic Performance Model Generation for Java Enterprise Edition (EE) Applications", EPEW 2013: 74-88

[6] Felix Willnecker, Andreas Brunnert, Wolfgang Gottesheim, and Helmut Krcmar. 2015. Using Dynatrace Monitoring Data for Generating Performance Models of Java EE Applications. In *Proceedings of the 6th ACM/SPEC International Conference on Performance Engineering* (ICPE '15). ACM, New York, NY, USA, 103-104.

DOI=10.1145/2668930.2688061
http://doi.acm.org/10.1145/2668930.2688061

[7] Markus Dlugi, Andreas Brunnert, and Helmut Krcmar. 2015. Model-based performance evaluations in continuous delivery pipelines. In *Proceedings of the 1st International Workshop on Quality-Aware DevOps* (QUDOS 2015). ACM, New York, NY, USA, 25-26. DOI=10.1145/2804371.2804376 http://doi.acm.org/10.1145/2804371.2804376

[8] Wu, Xingfu, Valerie Taylor, and Joseph Paris. "A web-based prophesy automated performance modeling system." *the International Conference on Web Technologies, Applications and Services (WTAS2006)*. 2006.

[9] Tauseef A. Israr, Danny H. Lau, Greg Franks, and Murray Woodside. 2005. Automatic generation of layered queuing software performance models from commonly available traces. In *Proceedings of the 5th international workshop on Software and performance* (WOSP '05). ACM, New York, NY, USA, 147-158. DOI=http://doi.acm.org/10.1145/1071021.1071037

[10] Murray Woodside, "Performance Data and Performance Models", Keynote, First SPEC Int. Performance Evaluation Workshop, 2008, http://www.sipew2008.org/presentations/SIPEW08-Keynote-Woodside.pdf

[11] Dror G. Feitelson and Larry Rudolph. 1998. Metrics and Benchmarking for Parallel Job Scheduling. In *Proceedings of the Workshop on Job Scheduling Strategies for Parallel Processing* (IPPS/SPDP '98), Dror G. Feitelson and Larry Rudolph (Eds.). Springer-Verlag, London, UK, UK, 1-24. http://www.cs.huji.ac.il/~feit/parsched/jsspp98/p-98-1.pdf

[12] L. Kleinrock, "Power and deterministic rules of thumb for probabilistic problems in computer communications". In Intl. Conf. Communications, vol. 3, pp. 43.1.1-43.1.10, Jun 1979.

[13] Zipf's law, references: http://ccl.pku.edu.cn/doubtfire/NLP/Statistical_Approach/Zip_law/references%20on%20zipf's%20law.htm

[14] Mark Crovella. 2000. Performance Evaluation with Heavy Tailed Distributions. In *Proceedings of the 11th International Conference on Computer Performance Evaluation: Modelling Techniques and Tools* (TOOLS '00), Boudewijn R. Haverkort, Henrik C. Bohnenkamp, and Connie U. Smith (Eds.). Springer-Verlag, London, UK, UK, 1-9.

[15] Brebner, P. C. 2012. Experiences with early life-cycle performance modeling for architecture assessment. In *Proceedings of the 8th international ACM SIGSOFT Conference on Quality of Software Architectures* (Bertinoro, Italy, June 25 - 28, 2012). QoSA '12. ACM, New York, NY, 149-154. DOI= http://doi.acm.org/10.1145/2304696.2304721

[16] Brebner, P. C. 2012. A performance modeling "blending" approach for early life-cycle risk mitigation. In *Proceedings of the 3rd ACM/SPEC international Conference on Performance Engineering* (Boston, Massachusetts, USA, April 22 - 25, 2012). ICPE '12. ACM, New York, NY, 271-274. DOI= http://doi.acm.org/10.1145/2188286.2188336

[17] Brebner, P. C. 2012. Is your cloud elastic enough?: performance modelling the elasticity of infrastructure as a service (IaaS) cloud applications. In *Proceedings of the 3rd ACM/SPEC international Conference on Performance*

Engineering (Boston, Massachusetts, USA, April 22 - 25, 2012). ICPE '12. ACM, New York, NY, 263-266. DOI= http://doi.acm.org/10.1145/2188286.2188334

[18] Brebner, P. C. 2011. Real-world performance modelling of enterprise service oriented architectures: delivering business value with complexity and constraints (abstracts only). *SIGMETRICS Perform. Eval. Rev.* 39, 3 (Dec. 2011), 12-12. DOI= http://doi.acm.org/10.1145/2160803.2160813

[19] Brebner, P. C. 2011. Real-world performance modelling of enterprise service oriented architectures: delivering business value with complexity and constraints. In *Proceedings of the 2nd ACM/SPEC international Conference on Performance Engineering* (Karlsruhe, Germany, March 14 - 16, 2011). ICPE '11. ACM, New York, NY, 85-96. DOI= http://doi.acm.org/10.1145/1958746.1958762

[20] Brebner, P. and Liu, A. 2011. Performance and cost assessment of cloud services. In *Proceedings of the 2010 international Conference on Service-Oriented Computing* (San Francisco, CA, December 07 - 10, 2010). Springer-Verlag, Berlin, Heidelberg, 39-50.

[21] Paul Brebner, Is your Cloud Elastic Enough? Part 1. CMG Measure IT, Issue 2, 2011. http://www.cmg.org/wp-content/uploads/2011/08/m_82_3.pdf

[22] Paul Brebner, Is your Cloud Elastic Enough? Part 2. CMG Measure IT, Issue 3, 2011. http://www.cmg.org/wp-content/uploads/2011/10/m_84_3.pdf

[23] Brebner, P. 2009. Service-Oriented Performance Modeling the MULE Enterprise Service Bus (ESB) Loan Broker Application. In *Proceedings of the 2009 35th Euromicro Conference on Software Engineering and Advanced Applications* (August 27 - 29, 2009). IEEE Computer Society, Washington, DC, 404-411. DOI= http://dx.doi.org/10.1109/SEAA.2009.57

[24] Paul Brebner, Liam O'Brien, Jon Gray: "Performance modeling evolving Enterprise Service Oriented Architectures". In *Software Architecture, 2009 & European Conference on Software Architecture. WICSA/ECSA 2009. Joint Working IEEE/IFIP Conference on*. 14-17 Sept. 2009. 71 – 80. DOI=http://dx.doi.org/10.1109/WICSA.2009.5290793

[25] Brebner, P., O'Brien, L, Gray, J., "Performance modeling power consumption and carbon emissions for Server Virtualization of Service Oriented Architectures (SOAs)". EDOCW 2009. 13th. 92-99.

[26] Paul Brebner, Liam O'Brien, Jon Gray. "Performance Modeling for e-Government Service Oriented Architectures (SOAs)", ASWEC (Australasian Software Engineering Conference) Proceedings (Perth, March, 2008), 130-138.

[27] Paul C. Brebner. 2008. Performance modeling for service oriented architectures. In *Companion of the 30th international conference on Software engineering* (ICSE Companion '08). ACM, New York, NY, USA, 953-954. DOI=http://dx.doi.org/10.1145/1370175.1370204

[28] A. Thusoo, J. S. Sarma, N. Jain, Z. Shao, P. Chakka, N. Zhang, S. Anthony, H. Liu, and R. Murthy. Hive - A Petabyte Scale Data Warehouse Using Hadoop. In ICDE, 2010.

Analyzing the Efficiency of a Green University Data Center

Patrick Pegus II*, Benoy Varghese†, Tian Guo*, David Irwin*, Prashant Shenoy*
Anirban Mahanti†, James Culbert‡, John Goodhue‡, Chris Hill§
*University of Massachusetts Amherst, †NICTA, ‡MGHPCC, §Massachusetts Institute of Technology

ABSTRACT

Data centers are an indispensable part of today's IT infrastructure. To keep pace with modern computing needs, data centers continue to grow in scale and consume increasing amounts of power. While prior work on data centers has led to significant improvements in their energy-efficiency, detailed measurements from these facilities' operations are not widely available, as data center design is often considered part of a company's competitive advantage. However, such detailed measurements are critical to the research community in motivating and evaluating new energy-efficiency optimizations. In this paper, we present a detailed analysis of a state-of-the-art 15MW green multi-tenant data center that incorporates many of the technological advances used in commercial data centers. We analyze the data center's computing load and its impact on power, water, and carbon usage using standard effectiveness metrics, including PUE, WUE, and CUE. Our results reveal the benefits of optimizations, such as free cooling, and provide insights into how the various effectiveness metrics change with the seasons and increasing capacity usage. More broadly, our PUE, WUE, and CUE analysis validate the green design of this LEED Platinum data center.

1. INTRODUCTION

Data centers form the backbone of our increasingly IT-driven economy, and are commonly used by enterprises to run their IT infrastructure. In recent years, the number and scale of data centers has grown rapidly. While small data centers may host a few thousand servers, the largest ones now host hundreds of thousands of servers. The energy consumed by these servers and their associated IT and network infrastructure is significant—globally, recent estimates attribute 2% of U.S. electricity consumption to data centers [12]. The largest data centers now consume over 100MW and incur monthly energy bills in the millions of dollars [8].

Thus, improving data center energy-efficiency has emerged as both an important academic research topic, as well as a pressing industry need. Over the past fifteen years, there has been much work on improving the energy-efficiency of the servers housed in data centers, e.g.,[6, 3, 19, 4]. More recently, researchers have fo-

cused on optimizing the efficiency of data center cooling systems, e.g., by using free cooling from the outside air with air-side economizers [9, 13], since cooling servers consumes a significant fraction of data center energy. Collectively, these advances have led to a steady decrease in the Power Usage Effectiveness (PUE) metric commonly used to quantify data center energy-effectiveness.[1] Recent studies show that older enterprise data centers have PUEs of 1.7 or higher [21], while newer data centers that incorporate energy optimizations for servers and their cooling infrastructure have PUEs near 1.1 [10].

While industry groups and companies, including Google, Microsoft, Facebook, Amazon, and Apple, have published average PUE values across their data centers, detailed energy measurements are not widely available. For example, the published PUE values are typically averages across many data centers over a long period, e.g., the past year, and do not break PUE down spatially, temporally, or across subsystems. Facebook has taken strides to increase access to such data through its OpenCompute project, which includes both hardware and facility designs for its data centers, as well as a public dashboard showing their real-time PUE and Water Usage Effectiveness (WUE) [14] (although without a detailed breakdown). Detailed access to such operational data can enable important insights into data center operations that motivate new research directions. Unfortunately, detailed data on internal data center operations is typically kept confidential, since most companies view data center design as a competitive advantage. Thus, only the few researchers at each company with access to the data are able to identify the real problems that affect the energy-efficiency of data center operations. Our goal is, in part, to democratize research in data center energy-efficiency to enable a much broader set of researchers to make contributions in this area. To do so, this paper presents and analyzes detailed energy measurements from a state-of-the-art 15MW multi-tenant ("colo") university data center.

While our measurements, analysis, and insights should prove useful to systems researchers, our study is particularly interesting since our data center—the Massachusetts Green High Performance Computing Center (MGHPCC)—is specifically designed to be a "green" facility, and thus incorporates many of same technological advances employed by recent state-of-the-art commercial data centers. The facility uses renewable cooling and renewable hydro-electric power, and is one of only 13 data centers in the country (and the only university data center) to receive a LEED Platinum rating [1]. The data center is jointly owned and operated by a consortium of universities in Massachusetts, including UMass, MIT,

---

[1]PUE is a widely used metric that quantifies the effectiveness with which a data center cools and delivers power to servers. It is not a measure of energy-efficiency, since the performance of the servers is not included in the PUE computation.

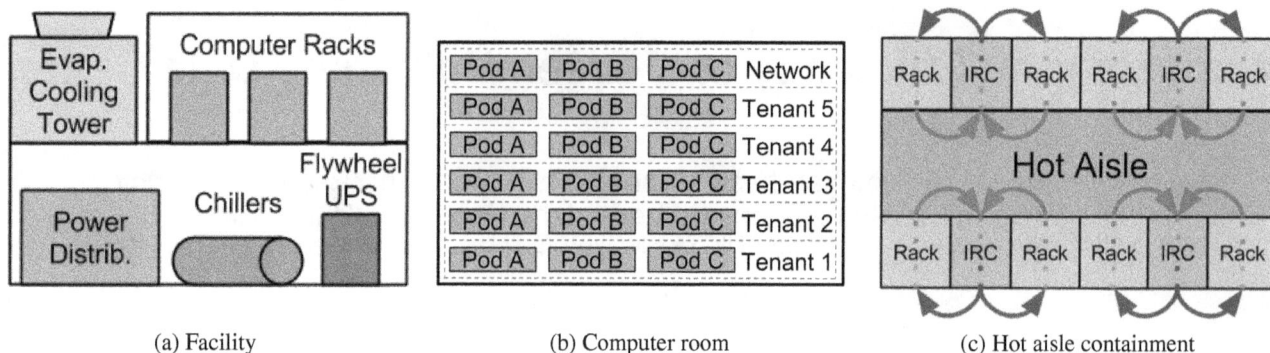

|(a) Facility|(b) Computer room|(c) Hot aisle containment|

Figure 1: Physical layout of the MGHPCC.

Harvard, Boston University, and Northeastern. The data center is primarily used for research-oriented computing with batch workloads; each university in the consortium is a tenant, which allocates its reserved space within the data center as its own colo facility to house compute clusters owned by various research groups on each campus.

In this paper, we analyze detailed facility-level data, e.g., of energy and water use, from the second year of the MGHPCC's operation. In doing so, we aim to address the following questions.

- Since the data center's workload is primarily batch-oriented, how much do the time-of-day and seasonal effects influence the workload's intensity? What are the implications for many previously proposed energy-efficiency optimizations, which often focus on exploiting these effects?

- What is the facility's overall PUE and what is the contribution/overhead from each subsystem?

- How does the PUE vary over time and how is it affected by changing weather and the seasons?

- How does the PUE vary spatially across tenants and clusters and what causes such variations?

- What is the WUE of the facility?

- Given its use of renewable energy sources, what is the Carbon Usage Effectiveness (CUE) of the facility?

Unlike prior work on improving data center energy efficiency, we focus on detailed measurements and analysis of data from the facility itself, rather than from individual servers or clusters. While direct access to such data has largely been restricted to facility managers, it is important in developing energy optimizations for multi-tenant data centers. While data centers controlled by a single entity have access to the underlying servers and network infrastructure and are able to implement many previously proposed cluster-level energy optimizations, multi-tenant data centers do not. Thus, these data centers must apply optimizations at the facility-level, similar to how a multi-tenant commercial building generally cannot control the energy usage of its tenants. As a result, facility-level energy optimizations for data centers have more in common with building energy-efficiency optimizations than the server-centric optimizations that have largely been the focus of prior work. In answering the questions above, this paper makes the following contributions.

Detailed Design Overview and Data Collection. In Section 2, we describe details of the design and operation of a medium-sized data center facility, as well the instrumentation available for facility data collection. The design applies many of the advanced techniques used in recent state-of-the-art commercial data centers. We gather and analyze data from over 900 sensors in the facility to both better understand its operation, and provide a baseline for other re-

searchers studying the efficiency of data centers at the facility level. **Temporal and Spatial PUE Analysis**. In Section 3, we then analyze both the temporal and spatial PUE of the data center over the past year. To estimate per-tenant spatial PUE, we develop a model for partitioning the energy usage of the data center's centralized cooling system across different pods of racks based on their load. **CUE and WUE Analysis**. Based on our data, we also analyze the WUE in Section 4 and the CUE in Section 5. Our results indicate that, even at low capacity utilization, the data center's WUE is better than published numbers for an average data center, while its CUE is near the published CUEs of the best commercial data centers.

2. BACKGROUND AND GREEN DESIGN

In this section, we present general background on the MGHPCC, including the design of its power and cooling infrastructure.

Overview. Our study focuses on the MGHPCC, a green data center built by a consortium of universities in Massachusetts for research computing. The data center is located in Holyoke, Massachusetts. The location was chosen based on the availability of abundant and cheap renewable hydroelectric power in Holyoke, the proximity to fibre-optic network backbones, and inexpensive real-estate. Massachusetts has a relatively cool climate with mean summer and winter temperatures of 23°C and -3°C, respectively, although summers months can be hot and humid; this cool climate enables the facility to employ renewable cooling, as explained later.

The data center became operational in November 2012 at the location of a former industrial mill site. The facility has 90,000 square feet of computing space and is provisioned for a 15MW peak load. The present utilization of the data center is less than 10% of its peak load, with an approximate compute load of 1MW and a non-compute load of 0.3 MW. As we discuss later, the compute load is steadily ramping up over time as new colo clusters are installed, and is expected to reach full capacity in a few years.

The data center is jointly operated by the university consortium and is structured as a multi-tenant facility with space pre-allocated to each member university. Each university uses its space to co-locate compute clusters owned by various research groups and units on their campus. The multi-tenant colo data center houses a growing number of clusters for research computing with workloads that are primarily *batch-oriented* with different clusters running scientific batch jobs of various flavors.

Green Design The MGHPCC was designed as a green facility, and was the first university data center to achieve a LEED Platinum rating. As noted earlier, the facility is largely powered using renewable hydroelectric power, and employs a number of modern techniques to increase its energy-efficiency and minimize its power usage, as discussed below. For example, the data center employs

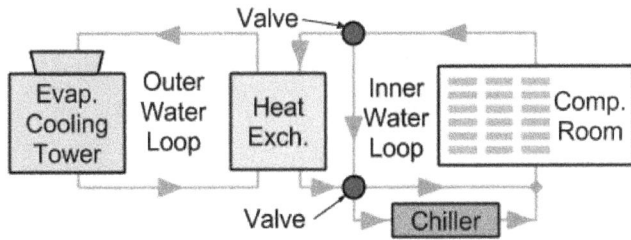

Figure 2: The MGHPCC's cooling infrastructure leverages free evaporative cooling and backup chillers.

hot aisle containment and uses renewable free cooling from outside air whenever possible to reduce its cooling-related energy usage. Finally, the facility employed a number of sustainable practices during the construction process and continues to do so during its operations (described in more detail here [1]).

Physical Layout Figure 1 depicts the physical layout of the data center. As shown in Figure 1(a), the data center comprises of two levels. The lower level contains the main power infrastructure, including a utility sub-station and flywheel-based uninterruptible power supply (UPS) system, and cooling infrastructure including chillers and water pumps. The upper level mainly contains racks for hosting the computing infrastructure. Evaporative cooling towers are housed on the roof of the first floor, adjacent to the computer floor. The data center also includes backup diesel generators that provide power for a fraction of the facility in case of a utility outage. The UPS system minds the gap between an outage and the activation of the diesel generators to prevent servers from losing power. Figure 1(b) shows the layout of the computer floor. There are five main aisles of racks, one for each tenant. A sixth aisle is the "networking aisle" and houses networking equipment to connect each tenant's computing infrastructure to the incoming fibre optic lines. Each tenant's aisle has three groups of racks, each referred to as a pod. Racks in each pod are designed for hot aisle containment as shown in Figure 1(c).

Power Infrastructure. The power infrastructure for the data center resembles a small-scale distribution network in the electric grid. The infrastructure comprises of substations, feeders, transformers, and switchboards that feed power to the computing and cooling infrastructure. Electricity enters the facility at 13.8kV where it is distributed from the main switchboard, transformed to 230V before entering the switchboards at the lowest levels, and is finally delivered to the busplugs that feed the power distribution units (PDUs) in each server rack.

Since power conversion losses can be a key source of higher PUEs in data centers, the data center uses a number of techniques to reduce such losses. First, the facility uses high voltage, and low current, to deliver power, which reduces losses due to power conversion and heat generation. Higher distribution voltages also make it possible to eliminate an entire tier of transformers from the distribution network, further reducing transformer losses. Second, energy losses due to the UPS system are another source of higher PUEs.

Since the data center houses research computing infrastructure, not all of which is "mission critical", only a fraction (roughly 20%) of each tenant's racks are backed up by the centralized UPS system. The tenants are then able to choose how to partition their compute infrastructure between UPS and non-UPS racks. The remaining racks are not connected to the centralized UPS system, which naturally avoids UPS losses for the 80% of the racks in the data center. Third, in many data centers, the UPS system for UPS-backed

racks normally operates in a double conversion mode, which incurs losses in both directions when converting from AC to DC and from DC to AC. Double conversion is often useful in conditioning the incoming power to provide a consistent high-quality AC power signal, i.e., a "tight" 60Hz sine wave, for mission-critical applications. At the MGHPCC, most workloads are not mission-critical and the hydroelectric power offered by the local utility is already high-quality. Thus, UPS systems in the MGHPCC are configured to operate in direct mode, where power is fed directly to racks, rather than through the UPS, and there is a near instantaneous transfer (within tens of milliseconds) to UPS systems when a power failure is detected.

Finally, the facility's UPS system stores energy kinetically in spinning flywheels, which is more environmentally-friendly than storing energy chemically in batteries that often contain harmful chemicals, such as lead in lead-acid batteries. The data center is provisioned for 18 seconds of UPS power in case of an outage, and standby diesel generators take over within this time period.

Cooling Infrastructure. Traditionally data centers have used chillers to cool the servers in the facility. However, chillers consume a significant amount of energy and their use is a key contributor to high data center PUEs. Thus, modern data centers have begun using alternative technologies to cool their servers and lower their PUEs. The MGHPCC leverages "free cooling" (also known as "renewable cooling") to cool servers. Specifically the data center uses evaporative cooling technology that essentially uses the outside air to cool servers. Figure 2 depicts the two cooling water loops used in the data center.

The water in the outer loop is cooled using evaporative cooling towers whenever the temperature of the outside air permits it. The inner water loop circulates water through the computer room racks. The water loop is used to extract heat from the hot air ejected by the server, which cools the air. The hot water in the inner loop is then sent to the heat exchanger, where the heat from this water is exchanged with the cold water in the outer water loop. Doing so, transfers the heat from the servers to the outer loop, cooling the water in the inner loop, which is sent back to the computer racks. The hot water in the outer loop is sent to the evaporative cooling tower where it is cooled again using the outside air, through an evaporative process, and circulated back to the heat exchangers.

The cooler climate in Massachusetts permits the use of this free cooling approach for over 70% of the year. Evaporative cooling becomes less feasible or infeasible during the warmer, and more humid, summer months. During these months, the data center falls back on using chillers to cool water in the inner loop. A hybrid mode is also possible where water is partly cooled using evaporative cooling and then cooled further using chillers (when the weather permits part, but not full, free cooling).

Each tenant's rack is configured to use hot aisle containment to prevent hot and cold air from mixing together, which increases the efficiency of the cooling system by focusing cold air on servers. The cold air in the inner water loop is circulated through in-row chillers (IRCs), which are deployed adjacent to racks, to cool the hot air extracted from the servers and produce cool air. The use of in-row chillers allows for a close coupling of the cooling with the computing heat load—the controls of the in-row chillers actively adjust fan speeds and chilled water flow to closely match the computing heat load on nearby racks, thereby enhancing efficiency.

Finally, the data center maintains the computer floor temperature at 80°F, which is a higher temperature than traditional data centers; doing so, reduces the amount of cooling required, which in turn improves cooling efficiency without impacting the reliability of modern server hardware.

Dataset	Description	Resolution
Power	All IT and non-IT power usage	20 second
Mechanical	Cooling equipment usage	1 minute
Water	Water usage	Monthly
Weather	Temperature, humidity	5 minute

Table 1: Description of our datasets.

Compute Infrastructure. As noted earlier, the data center is a multi-tenant facility, with each university tenant treating its allocated racks as a co-location facility to house research computing clusters from on-campus groups. Thus, the data center does not own, or exercise direct control, over the type of servers deployed at the facility. Consequently, all energy optimizations "stop" at the rack and the data center cannot mandate the use of any specific server model. This is in contrast to companies, such as Facebook or Google, that are capable of deploying optimizations anywhere in the data center, including energy-optimized severs that may be DC powered, use power supplies optimized for their load levels, or employ local on-board batteries rather than a centralized UPS system.

The compute load has been increasing steadily as new clusters are deployed by each tenant. One consequence of the presently low capacity utilization is that the current PUE of the facility is higher than it would be at full utilization, largely because the cooling infrastructure is sized for a much higher load and is less efficient at lower loads (since it is not energy proportional).

Monitoring Infrastructure. The data center is highly instrumented to monitor all aspects of its operation and has several thousand points of instrumentation that provide real-time data on power, cooling, and water usage within the facility. Note that this facility-level data is separate from the type of data monitored at the level of individual servers and clusters; facility-level data is monitored by the data center staff, while the server and cluster-level data is accessible only to tenants (who own the compute infrastructure), and not to the facility staff.

Table 1 depicts the various datasets that we have gathered from the facility and form the basis of our study in this paper. At the facility level, the power distribution infrastructure is monitored by over 900 networked electric meters that monitor power usage at different levels of the distribution network at 20 second granularity. These meters monitor the average power usage of individual racks, as well as the aggregate usage at higher levels of power distribution hierarchy. There are also separate meters to monitor the power usage of the cooling infrastructure, including its associated pumps, chillers, and in-row chillers.

The facility's mechanical systems, which are primarily associated with the cooling infrastructure, are also monitored by a conventional building management system. The available data includes water pump flow levels at various points in the water loops, as well as data from in-row chillers, such as fan speed, water inlet and outlet temperature, and water flow data. This data is generally recorded and available at a one-minute granularity. The temperature and humidity of the computer room floor is extensively monitored using sensors that are deployed on the hot and cold sides of each rack. The outside weather data is monitored using a weather station (we also use data from Weather Underground), and the facility's overall water usage is recorded by a water meter.

Datasets: We use the datasets in Table 1 gathered over a 12 month period from May 2014 to April 2015, which roughly corresponds to the second year of the data center's operation. As shown in the table, we use four different datasets in our analysis. The power data is gathered from the 900 electric meters deployed within the power distribution system. This data is gathered at 20 second resolution and includes the average power usage data of individ-

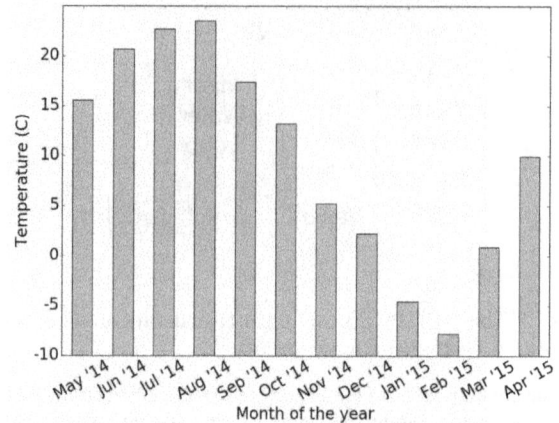

Figure 3: Average monthly temperature at the data center.

ual racks, UPS-backed rack usage, aggregate in-row chiller power usage, and the power usage of the cooling infrastructure such as chillers and water pumps.[2] The mechanical data comprises primarily data from in-row chillers, which includes fan speed, water flow speed, as well water inlet and outlet temperature. Our water usage data includes the monthly water usage of the facility. Finally, weather data consists of outside temperature and humidity at the facility over the year (see Figure 3). Inside temperature data monitored at hot and cold side of individual racks is also available, but not directly used in our analysis. Data collection is ongoing and will last several years to enable a long-term efficiency study of the MGHPCC.

3. PUE ANALYSIS

In this section, we analyze in detail the power usage of the MGH-PCC. We first analyze the IT load, e.g., of the server and networking equipment, over different time scales to quantify its impact on the facility's PUE. We also analyze the various factors contributing to the observed PUE, and consider the impact of seasons on PUE to quantify the benefits of free cooling. In addition to analyzing temporal PUE, we perform a spatial analysis to compute per-tenant PUEs and analyze how the PUE varies across tenants and why.

3.1 IT Load Analysis

Figure 4 depicts the IT power usage of the data center at the time scale of months, a week and a day. The IT power usage is derived by combining the electricity meter data for only those meters that supply power directly to the computing and networking racks. Figure 4(a) depicts the mean monthly IT load from May 2014 to April 2015. As the figure shows, the IT load steadily rose over the one year period, largely due to new colo compute clusters being commissioned at a steady rate by the various tenants. The figure also shows that the mean IT load is less than 1MW, which is less than 10% of the peak provisioned power capacity. Thus, we expect the increasing trend in IT load to continue for the foreseeable future.

As a research computing facility, the workload of the data center is primarily batch-oriented. Hence, analyzing the IT load over the time scales of a week and a day are instructive in determining whether the workload exhibits the time-of-day and week-of-day effects that are common in commercial data centers that host interactive Internet workloads. Figure 4(b) depicts the mean daily IT load for different days of the week for the month of April 2015, while Figure 4(c) shows the load for different hours of the day. The

---

[2]Some older power data is only available at an 8 hour resolution, while all recent data is archived at 20s granularity.

(a) Monthly (b) Daily (c) Hourly

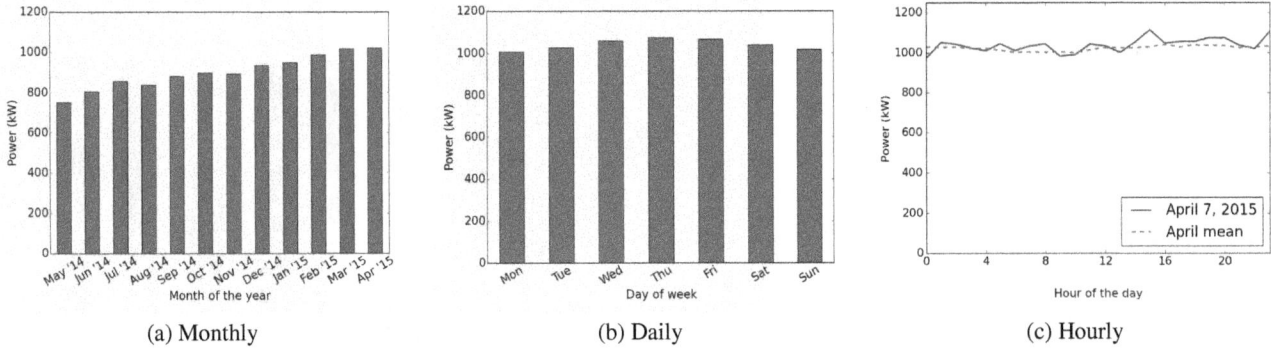

Figure 4: Variation in IT Power load at time scales of months, days and hours. The load has been increasing steadily over the course of the year, but the batch-oriented load does not show any significant day-of-the-week or time-of-day effects.

figures show that, unlike interactive workloads, the batch workload of the data center does not show pronounced time-of-day or day-of-the-week effects. As Figure 4(b) shows, there is only a very modest rise in the load in the middle of the week, but no significant weekday-weekend effects. Similarly, 4(c) shows that long-running batch jobs or batch schedulers with a queue of jobs cause the compute load to remain high across both the day and the night. While there is a very small drop ($\sim 2.5\%$) in load in the early hours of the day (4am to 7am), possibly due to the completion of overnight batch jobs, it does not yield any perceptible time-of-day effects.

Result: The explicit goal of many server- and cluster-level energy optimizations is to exploit such time-of-day and day-of-week effects, e.g., by powering down servers when the workload drops to make them more energy-proportional [4, 22]. Our data indicates that these types of energy optimizations are not as applicable to the MGHPCC, as it does not experience significant time-of-day and day-of-week effects.

3.2 Temporal PUE Analysis

We next analyze the PUE of the data center over the course of the year. The PUE metric is computed as ratio of the facility's total power usage to the power usage of the IT equipment, e.g., servers and switches. The total power usage is monitored directly by a networked meter that measures the power entering the facility from the grid, while the IT power usage is computed as outlined in the previous section. Figure 5 depicts the monthly PUE of the data center over the course of the year. The figure shows that the PUE varies between 1.285 and 1.509 over the year. We note that a mean PUE value of 1.377 is significantly lower than the average PUE value of 1.7 (or higher) that is common in enterprise data centers in the industry [21]. However, the value is not as low as the PUEs near 1.1 reported by the newest (and most effective) data centers built by large Internet companies, such as Facebook and Google [17, 10].

We analyze the key contributors to our PUE in more detail below. We note that the data center's cooling infrastructure is sized for a much greater load than the present server room occupancy produces and is not energy proportional. Hence, we believe the facility will achieve further reductions in PUE as its IT load increases to full utilization. Thus, the PUE values we report here are conservative in that the facility's design is more effective than its current PUE values indicate.

Second, the figure shows a reduction in the PUE from May 2014 to April 2015. This reduction can be attributed to two possible factors. First, since the IT power load has risen during this period, the cooling infrastructure, which is not energy proportional, becomes *relatively* more efficient with increased IT load, yielding a lower PUE. Second, free cooling is feasible only during cooler months

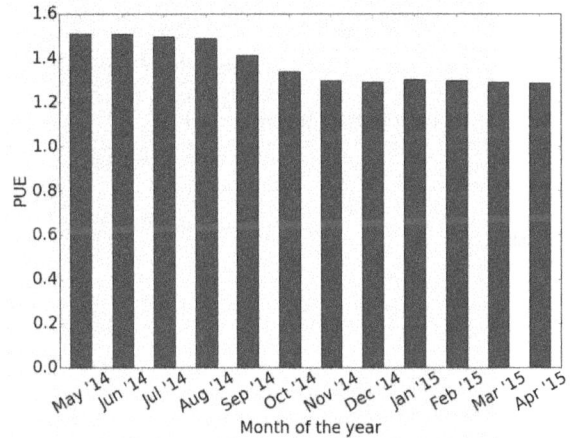

Figure 5: Temporal variations in the monthly PUE.

of the year and the data center needs chillers to cool the facility in warmer months. This use of chillers will cause a higher PUE in warmer months (May to September), and the PUE is lower for the remaining months when free cooling is used.

Our analysis shows that the second factor dominates, since turning off chillers yields a greater reduction in PUE than the increase in IT power load during this period (since the total IT power load is relatively low, its impact on the PUE is much smaller). Figure 6(a) confirms that chillers are used during the months of May to September and that they consume a significant amount of energy (thereby contributing to a higher PUE in those months). The lack of chiller energy use in other months stems from the use of free cooling during those months, yielding a lower PUE. This result shows the PUE of the data center is 1.413 when chillers are in use and 1.301 when free cooling is used; in other words, PUE decreases 0.112 when not using chillers even at this low capacity utilization.

Next, we analyze the non-IT load of the data center, which in turn reveals the various factors contributing to the PUE. Conventional wisdom has held that there are two main sources of overhead that contribute to the non-IT power load: cooling infrastructure and power distribution losses, including UPS losses. Figure 6 depicts the power usage of various non-IT loads in the data center. As the figure shows, roughly half of the non-compute load can be attributed to cooling and other mechanical systems; a quarter can be attributed to power losses; and another quarter can be attributed to other factors, including measurement error. The measurement error is only a few tens of kilowatts (of the multi-megawatt power usage), but it is almost a quarter of the current non-IT load, since the overall capacity utilization is low. This error will become negligible once the data center becomes fully utilized.

67

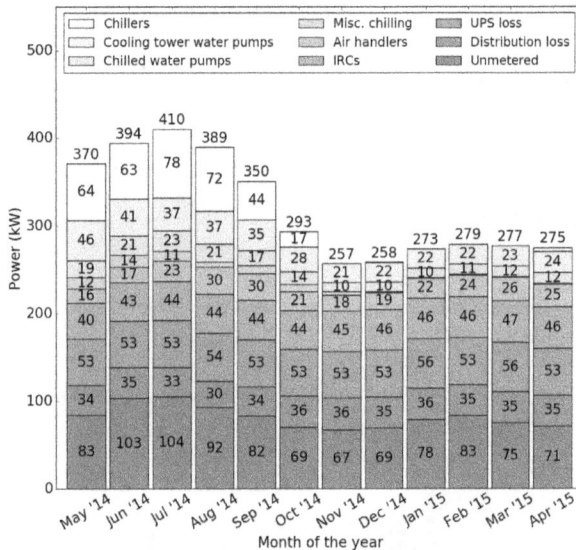

(a) Factors contributing to the PUE.

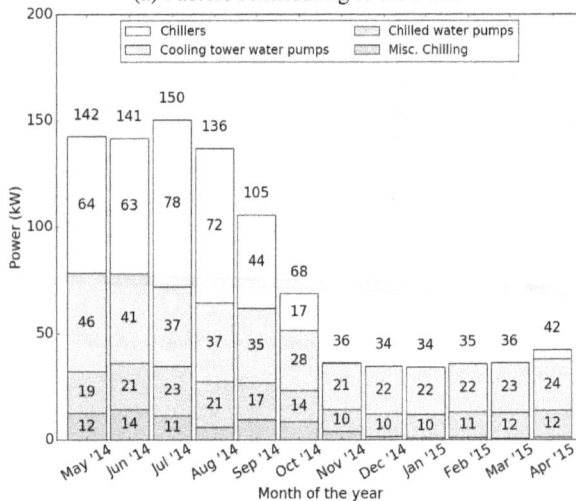

(b) Cooling factors contributing to the PUE

Figure 6: Various factors contributing to the PUE, including cooling energy use and power losses.

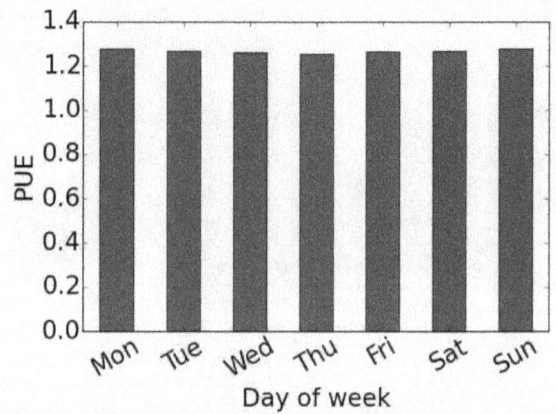

(a) Daily

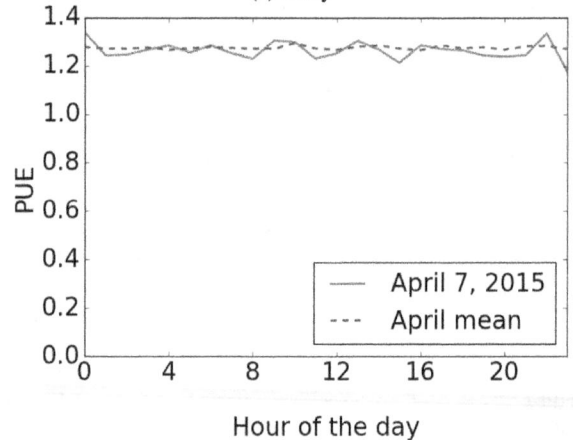

(b) Hourly

Figure 7: Daily and hourly variations in the data center PUE.

The cooling load, which is roughly half or more of the total non-IT power load, comprises of (i) chillers, (ii) cooling tower ("outer loop") water pumps, (iii) chilled water ("inner loop") water pumps, (iv) air handlers, (v) in-row chillers, and (vi) miscellaneous cooling equipment. As shown in Figure 6, chillers are the largest component whenever they are operating in the warmer months. Thus, eliminating the use of chillers by using free cooling yields a significant reduction in both cooling power usage and PUE. [3]

The power losses consist of two key components: power distribution losses that occur when the incoming power flows through various components of the data center's distribution network, and UPS losses that occur in all UPS systems. The data center has optimized UPS losses by not using UPS systems in double conversion mode, which results in losses from AC to DC and DC to AC con-

version; instead power is directly fed to the computing racks with a fast fail-over to UPS upon detecting a power loss or fluctuation. Further, since only 20% of the racks have a UPS backup, this naturally cuts down on the total UPS losses in the facility.

Finally, Figure 7 depicts the daily and hourly variations in the PUE for the different days of the week in April and a particular day in April 2015, respectively. As Figure 7(a) shows, the PUE is mostly flat over the course of a week, as the corresponding IT load seen during different days of the week, shown in Figure 4(b), is nearly flat without any week of the day effects. The hourly PUE in Figure 7(b) shows small fluctuations caused by corresponding variations in the instantaneous hourly IT load; the hourly PUE is mostly flat when averaged over the month, as expected, since the hourly IT load is similarly flat without any significant time-of-day effects.

Result: The MGHPCC's PUE is 1.3773, even at a low 10% capacity utilization, a figure generally considered to by quite competitive, although not as low as some of the most effective data centers in industry. We note that this relatively low PUE is achieved in a multi-tenant colo facility where the data center has no direct ability to optimize server hardware (unlike, say, Google or Facebook data centers where end-to-end optimizations that include the server tier are feasible). Free cooling yields a significant reduction in PUE over periods when chillers have to be deployed, demonstrating the benefits of optimizing the cooling infrastructure on lowering the PUE. Finally, an interesting artifact of our batch workloads is that

---

[3] As shown in Figure 6(b), cooling tower pumps used more power in the months of May and June than in warmer summer months such as July; this is due to use of hybrid cooling to partially cool water first and then use chillers to cool the rest. As seen, this mode uses more power than using chillers alone in warmer months; facility managers are currently optimizing pump controls to enhance the efficiency of hybrid cooling.

they do not exhibit typical time-of-day or weekend effects, pointing to the possibility of higher server utilizations throughout the day.

3.3 Per-tenant PUE Analysis

The previous section shows that the overall PUE of the data center is between 1.285 and 1.509. As noted earlier, the data center is a multi-tenant facility, with each tenant operating an entire aisle of racks independently of the other tenants. Thus, analyzing and comparing the PUE of each tenant to the facility's overall PUE is useful. Further, different tenants are in different stages of their roll-out of computing equipment at the data center, and per-tenant PUE analysis can provide insights into how the PUE might vary when the racks are at different capacity utilizations.

There is no well-known method to compute the per-tenant PUE. While the IT load is directly metered on a per-rack (and per-tenant) basis, the non-IT load is not. The cooling infrastructure including the evaporative cooling towers and chillers are facility-wide equipment and not deployed on a per-tenant basis. Thus, to compute PUE on a per-tenant basis, we must determine how to apportion to non-IT (and particularly cooling) loads across individual tenants.

Fortunately, in our case, each tenant operates an entirely separate aisle of racks, such that the racks do not mix computing equipment from multiple tenants. Thus, determining the compute and cooling load of all racks in a given aisle is equivalent to determining the computing and cooling load due to that tenant. In other words, spatial analysis of PUE across racks and aisles in our case also yields the PUE of the various tenants.

3.3.1 Per-tenant PUE and IRC Power Models

To determine the PUE of an aisle of racks, or more precisely a pod of racks, we make the following assumptions.

First, we assume that the hot air containment used by the racks to isolate the hot air from cold air is perfect [18]. That is, the hot air from the racks is fully contained and does not impact the temperature, or associated cooling, of the racks in other aisles.

Second, while the cooling infrastructure, such as chillers and cooling towers, are facility-wide equipment, the in-row chillers are deployed to locally cool adjacent racks and represent per-pod (and per-tenant) cooling equipment. Further, in-row chillers directly remove the heat generated by racks in each pod, and hence, the power consumed by in-row chillers is an indirect measure of the cooling needs of that pod. Hence, we can use power consumed by the in-row chillers of a pod to apportion the remaining non-IT load across pods. We note that such a method is an approximation since neither the in-row chillers nor the facility-wide cooling equipment are energy-proportional, i.e., a linear increase in heat generated *does not* result in a proportionate linear increase in power usage of the IRCs or the cooling equipment.

Given these assumptions, the PUE of a pod is given below.

$$PUE_{pod} = \frac{P_{total}^{pod}}{P_{IT}^{pod}} = \frac{P_{IT}^{pod} + P_{non-IT}^{pod}}{P_{IT}^{pod}} \quad (1)$$

In the equation, P_{total}^{pod} denotes the total power usage of a pod, while P_{IT}^{pod} and P_{non-IT}^{pod} denote the IT and non-IT power used by the pod. The IT power consumed by each rack is directly measured, while the non-IT power used by the pod must be estimated. Based on the assumption above, the non-IT power usage of a pod is assumed to be proportional to the power consumed by the pod's in-row chillers, which itself depends on local cooling demands.

Thus, we estimate the non-IT power usage of the pod below.

$$P_{non-IT}^{pod} = \frac{P_{IRC}^{pod}}{P_{IRC}^{total}}(P_{total} - P_{IT}) \quad (2)$$

Here, P_{IRC}^{pod} and P_{IRC}^{total} denote the power consumed by the IRCs of a pod and the total power consumed by IRC across all aisles and pods, and P_{total} and P_{IT} denotes the total facility power and the total IT power across all tenants (the difference between the two is the total non-IT power usage). If each in-row chiller were individually metered, all of the quantities in the above equation would be known. However, the data center meters IRC power consumption in the aggregate (for groups of IRCs) and thus the power used by individual IRCs is not directly monitored. However, our mechanical dataset monitors the fan speeds of the in-row chillers and it is well known (from IRC manuals) that power consumption of an IRC is a cubic function of its fan speed. Thus, we use a model to estimate IRC power usage from its monitored fan speed, as shown below.

$$P_{IRC} = \alpha \cdot x^3 + \beta \quad (3)$$

Here, α and β are constants that depend on a specific model of an IRC and x denotes the fan speed. Since the aggregate power consumed by a group of IRCs is metered and known, the following relationship holds for power consumed by IRCs in each metered group at time instant t.

$$P_{IRC}^1 + P_{IRC}^2 + \ldots + P_{IRC}^n = P_{IRC}^{total} + \epsilon \quad (4)$$

Here, P_{IRC}^i denotes the power consumed by the ith IRC within a metered group and P_{IRC}^{total} denotes the total power consumed by all IRCs within that group. ϵ is a term that captures the measurement error. By substituting Equation 3 for each individual IRC into Equation 4, we obtain a set of equations, one for each measurement interval t, for the unknown constants α and β.

We can then use regression on this set of equations to derive the α and β that minimize the error term ϵ. By deriving α and β, the regression then yields an IRC power model where the power consumed by the IRC is a function of the fan speed x with known constants α and β. That is, $P_{IRC} = \alpha \cdot x^3 + \beta$. Since fan speeds are directly measured and available to us, the power usage of a pod can be estimated using this approach, and this value can be substituted in Equation 2 to estimate the non-IT power usage of a pod P_{non-IT}^{pod}. Since the IT power usage of each pod is directly measured and known, we can compute the PUE of each pod.

We ran the regression on the measured values of IRC fan speeds and the total IRC power consumption to derive the IRC power model as discussed above. Figure 8 depicts the model we learned for the IRC power consumption as a function of the IRC fan speed. To validate our model, we compute the power consumed by individual IRCs using measured fan speeds, and then compare the sum of the computed individual IRC power values to the total IRC power as measured by the electric meter. Figure 9 depicts the estimated IRC power consumption from the model and the actual values from the metered data. As can be seen, there is a close match between the model estimates and the actual values.

3.3.2 Spatial PUE Analysis.

Given our models above to estimate the per-IRC power consumption and the per-pod PUE, we next analyze the *spatial* distribution of computing load and the resulting PUE on a pod-by-pod and tenant-by-tenant basis. We note at the outset that the spatial distribution of servers across racks can impact the PUE, similar to how prior work has shown the spatial distribution of compute load influences cooling costs [16]. To illustrate, consider two different deployments of ten servers, one where all ten servers are housed in a single rack and another where each individual server is deployed on a separate rack, i.e., a "depth-first" versus "breadth-first" deployment. Although the IT power load of these ten servers is independent of how they are placed on the racks, the cooling load

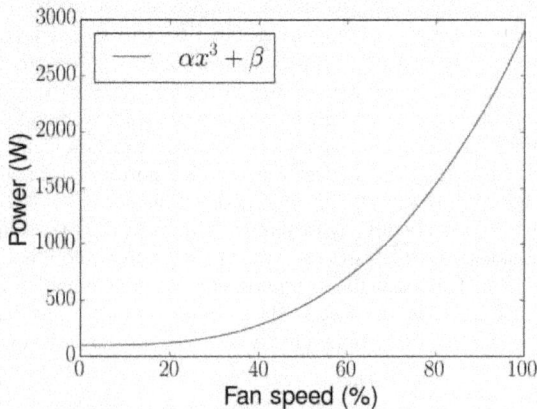

Figure 8: IRC power model learned via regression: the model is cubic in fan speed with parameters $\alpha = 0.00279$ and $\beta = 97.7$.

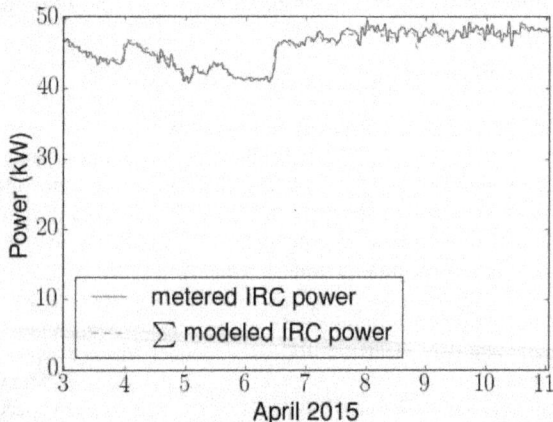

Figure 9: We validate our IRC power model by comparing the fit of total modeled IRC power to the aggregate meter values.

depends on the spatial distribution of servers. In the former case, the cooling load is concentrated in one rack and a single IRC can handle the cooling of the servers while the remaining IRCs in the pod can remain idle. In the latter case, the cooling load is spread across multiple racks, and multiple IRCs will need to absorb this spatially by spreading out the cooling load. Thus, the two deployments will result in different PUE values even though both have the same IT load. This toy example illustrates that two pods with identical IT loads may have different PUEs if they have different spatial distributions of servers across racks.

Figure 10(a) depicts the spatial distribution of the IT power usage of server racks in each pod across different pods and tenants. Recall that each tenant has an aisle dedicated to them, and each aisle is partitioned into three pods of racks; let T_i denote tenant i, and the suffix A, B or C denote the three pods allocated to that tenant. The sixth row, denoted by N, houses network equipment to connect the tenants to various network/fibre backbones. As shown, different tenants are at different stages of deployment of their research clusters—the IT load of a pod varies from 2kW to 214kW. Many pods—those with usage of less than 5kW—remain empty. A few pods are moderately loaded and have IT loads of 50-100kW. Only one pod (pod A for tenant 2) is nearing capacity and has a current load of nearly 220kW. The pods housing networking gear also remain lightly utilized.

Using these IT power loads and our models, we compute the PUE of each pod, which is depicted as a heat-map in Figure 10(b). The data shown is for April 3-11, 2015, where the overall PUE of

the data center was 1.28. To compute this figure, we used a more refined PUE model than the one discussed in Section 3.3.1 where the UPS power losses are only attributed to pods with UPS backup power, rather than being uniformly spread across both UPS and non-UPS racks. The figure reveals the following insights.

As expected, the pods that have low utilization also have high PUEs. However, these PUE values are not meaningful since they are associated with an IT load that is close to zero. In general, we observe that the PUE of a pod is inversely proportional to the IT load: as the IT load increases, its associated PUE value falls. Thus, lightly and moderately loaded pods have PUEs that are higher than the facility-wide PUE, while more heavily loaded pods have lower PUEs than than the overall PUE. This trend is not surprising, since the cooling equipment and in-row chillers are not energy proportional and operate at optimal efficiency levels at near-peak loads, and are much less efficient at lower loads. Hence, the PUE is much lower (and better) for more heavily loaded pods.

Interestingly, pod B for tenant 4 and pod C for tenant 2 have roughly similar IT load, i.e., 70kW, but have different PUE values of 1.28 and 1.21, respectively. This is a real-world depiction of the toy example above, and demonstrates that the spatial distribution of servers in a pod does matter and can impact a pod's PUE, i.e., two pods with identical compute loads but different spatial distribution of servers can yield different PUEs.

4. WUE ANALYSIS

In addition to consuming significant amounts of power, data centers also typically consume significant amounts of water, mainly as part of their cooling infrastructure. While there has been significant emphasis on measuring and optimizing the power usage using metrics such as PUE, there has been less attention on measuring the efficiency of water usage. Recently a new metric to capture the effectiveness of water usage has been proposed. The WUE of a data center is defined as below.

$$\text{WUE} = \frac{\text{Water Usage (liters)}}{\text{IT Energy Usage (kWh)}} \quad (5)$$

Intuitively, WUE is defined as liters of water used per kilowatt-hour (kWh) of energy used by the IT equipment. Unlike its better known PUE counterpart, there is little data published on WUE of data centers. Recently Facebook released data indicating that the WUE of their Prineville data center was 0.28 L/kWh and their Forest City data center was 0.34 L/kWh [7]. In contrast, an average 15MW data center (similar in size of our MGHPCC data center) may consume as much as 360,000 gallons of water each day [15]. Assuming a moderate PUE of 1.5, a fully utilized 15MW data center has an IT load of 10MW, which translates into a WUE of 5.67 L/kWh. In contrast, GreenGrid published a report indicating the average data center has a WUE of 1 L/kWh but did not provide details [11].

Figure 11(a) depicts the monthly water usage of the data center over a 12 month period. The present water usage varies between 1000 kL and 2000 KL per month depending on the season of the year. As the figure shows, the water usage is higher in the warmer months and lower in cooler months. This is not surprising since warmer months lead to more evaporative water loss and the use of chillers in these months consumes more water. In contrast, the data center relies on free cooling in cooler months, resulting in lower water usage in those months. Next, Figure 11(b) depicts the WUE of our data center over a 12 month period. As shown, the WUE values vary between 1.5 L/kWh and 3.0 L/kWh over the course of the year. The WUE rises in the warmer months and falls in the

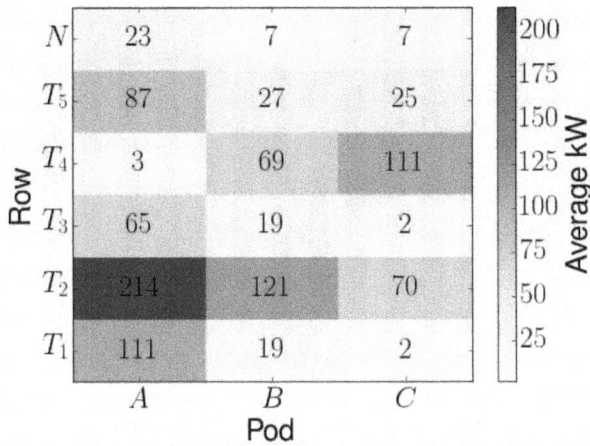

(a) IT power consumption

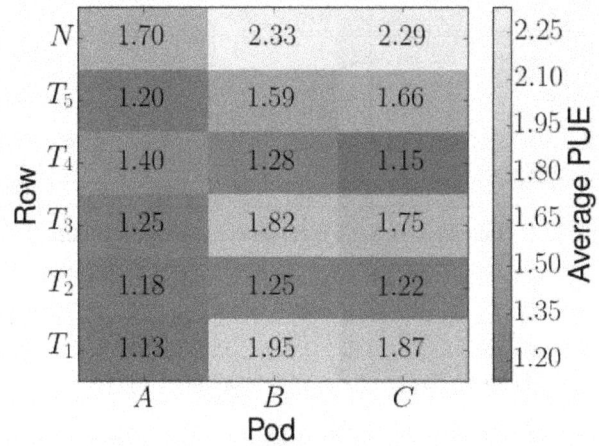

(b) pod PUE

Figure 10: Heat-maps showing the mean IT power consumption and mean pod PUE of different pods and tenants across our multi-tenant data center. Data shown is for April 3-11, 2015.

cooler months. We attribute this trend to two factors: rising IT load over the course of the year results in more effective use of water and a fall in WUE, and seasonal effects where there is less loss from evaporative cooling in cooler months.

While a WUE between 1.5 and 3.0 L/kWh is already lower than the average WUE of 5.67 hinted in [15], it is higher than the Green-Grid value of 1. There is little real-world data available to provide a meaningful comparison. We note, however, that the MGHPCC is presently operating at only 10% capacity, and we expect a significant fall in WUE as the capacity ramps up, in line with the trends observed in the initial months of 2015. Thus, our hypothesis is that, in the long run, the WUE of the MGHPCC will be significantly lower than the "typical" data center, and in line with its green design goal. Although not shown here, the data center uses a number of other measures to optimize its water footprint, including the use of water filtration techniques to maximize the circulation of water in the two water loops as well as use of recycled water for many auxiliary purposes, e.g., for landscaping.

5. CUE ANALYSIS

Our final analysis focuses on the carbon impact of the MGHPCC, since ultimately it is designed to be a green facility. While there are many methodologies to compute the operational carbon footprint of a building, the new CUE metric has been defined explicitly to compute the carbon effectiveness of data centers [5]. The CUE of a data center is defined as below

$$\text{CUE} = \frac{\text{CO}_2 \text{ emmissions from the total data center energy}}{\text{IT equipment energy}} \quad (6)$$

$$= \frac{\text{kg CO}_2}{\text{kWh}} \cdot \frac{\text{Total data center energy}}{\text{IT equipment energy}} = \frac{\text{kg CO}_2}{\text{kWh}} \cdot \text{PUE}$$

As shown, the CUE depends significantly on the carbon emissions due to the electricity consumed by the data center. The carbon emissions of the electricity consumption, in turn, depend on the generation source mix of the electric utility that supplies power to the data center. In the event that the data center uses on-site or contracted renewable energy, that portion must also be considered in the overall electricity mix as well.

The MGHPCC does not use any on-site renewables and depends entirely on the local utility company for its power needs. The local utility, Holyoke Gas and Electric (HG&E), generates a large

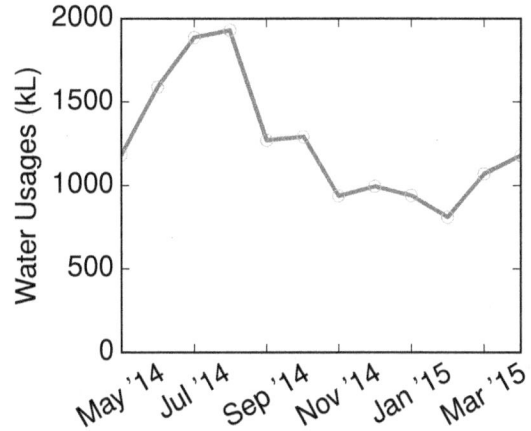

(a) Monthly water usage

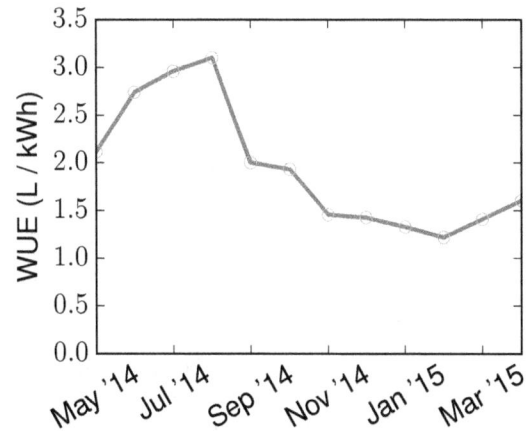

(b) Monthly WUE

Figure 11: Monthly water usage and WUE of our data center.

Fuel Type	Energy (MWh)	Energy (%)	CO_2 (kg)	CO_2 (%)
Oil	1724	0.4	1476897	16.3
Hydro	261691	66.7	0	0
Nuclear	61310	15.6	0	0
Solar	6105	1.6	0	0
Contracted (carbon free)	40800	10.4	0	0
Contracted (other)	20592	5.3	7584064	83.7
Total	392222	100	9060054	100

Table 2: Holyoke Gas & Electric power generation sources.

Utility	HG&E	U.S grid		
		mean	min	max
$\frac{kg\ CO_2}{kWh}$	0.0231	0.559	0.203	0.860

Table 3: Power producer carbon intensity [2].

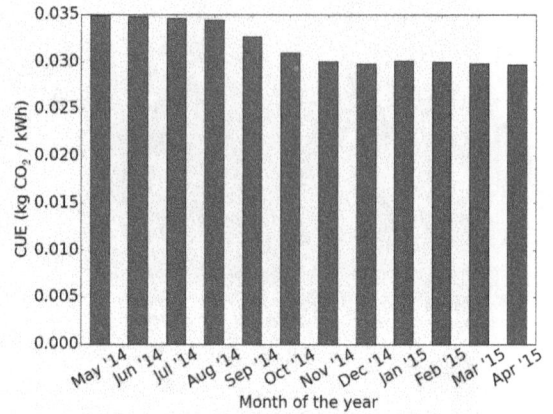

Figure 12: Monthly CUE of the data center.

fraction of its electricity using hydroelectric power from a sophisticated canal system. This hydro-electric power is not only inexpensive, but also a clean source of renewable energy. The mix of generation sources used by HG&E to generate power for its customers is shown in Table 2. As the table shows, HG&E generates or purchases 94.3% of the electricity from carbon-free sources, two-thirds of which derives from the local canal system. In addition, HG&E operates one of the largest solar deployments in New England, totaling 5.3MW of installed capacity. In addition, 15% of its power derives from nuclear power plants, which are also carbon free. HG&E also purchases electricity in the wholesale electricity market through a variety of contracts. Roughly 16% of its needs are met from these contracted sources, of which 10.4% comes from carbon-free sources. Thus, their high fraction (94.3%) of carbon-free electricity in their generation mix yields a low ratio (of 0.0231) in the amount of kilograms of CO_2 emitted per kWh of energy generated. This ratio, which is nearly an order of magnitude lower than the most carbon efficient region in the U.S., is shown in Table 3.

Consequently, 94.3% of electricity consumed by the MGHPCC is carbon-free. Figure 12 depicts the monthly CUE of the data center. The CUE varies from 0.0297 to 0.0349 with an annual average of 0.0318. By way of comparison, an "average" data center that draws power form the "average" utility mix in the U.S. will have $25\times$ higher CUE at the same PUE level (and an even higher CUE at higher typical values of 1.8 PUE). Recently, Apple claimed that 100% of its data centers are powered using renewables and Google has followed a similar strategy of using contracted wind energy for its data centers. Our data center compares favorably to these state-of-the-art data centers in terms of CUE, but has achieved its low CUE by careful choice of location and utility rather than building or contracting renewable energy.

6. CONCLUDING REMARKS

In this paper, we present an empirical analysis of the efficiency of a green academic data center. The data center we study, the MGHPCC, is a multi-tenant facility that is designed to house colo research clusters running batch-oriented workloads. Our temporal PUE analysis reveals that the data center has PUE values that range from 1.285 to 1.509, with higher PUEs in warmer summer months. We show that free cooling, which avoids the use of chillers can reduce PUE by as much as 0.224 in cool seasons. Our spatial multi-tenant analysis reveals the non-proportional nature of the cooling equipment, which causes its efficiency to increase as each pod of racks becomes fully utilized, yielding lower PUEs. Our water usage analysis shows that the WUE of the data center is between 1.5 and 3 L/kWh. Finally, we show that data center has a CUE of 0.03,

which is $25\times$ lower than a typical data center. The low CUE is mainly due to the large portion of renewable energy within the electricity mix supplied by the local utility. Overall, our results validate the green design of the data center and point to further efficiencies in the future at higher utilizations.

This work is a first effort in a long-term efficiency study of the MGHPCC. In the future, we will examine energy efficiency at the server level. By calculating metrics, such as Energy-Agility proposed in a companion work [20], we will account for server efficiency that is beyond the scope of PUE. Additionally, we will develop data driven models that will learn the relationship between various control parameters and their impact on electricity and cooling demands. We will use these models to determine inefficient settings and tune these parameters to enhance day-to-day operational efficiency.

Acknowledgements. We would like to thank our shepherd Klaus-Dieter Lange and the anonymous reviewers for their astute comments that improved this paper. This work is supported in part by the UMass Clean Energy Extension, NEAGEP/IMSD Fellowship, and NSF grants CNS-1405826, CNS-1422245, and ACI-1339839.

7. REFERENCES

[1] Massacusetts Green High Performance Computing Center: Green Design. http://www.mghpcc.org/about/green-design/.

[2] U. E. P. Agency. eGRID 9th edition Version 1.0 Year 2010 GHG Annual Output Emission Rates. http://www.epa.gov/cleanenergy/documents/egridzips/ eGRID_9th_edition_V1-0_year_2010_GHG_Rates.pdf.

[3] D. Andersen, J. Franklin, M. Kaminsky, A. Phanishayee, L. Tan, and V. Vasudevan. FAWN: A Fast Array of Wimpy Nodes. In *SOSP*, October 2009.

[4] L. Barroso and U. Hölzle. The Case for Energy-Proportional Computing. *Computer*, 40(12), December 2007.

[5] C. Belady, D. Azevedo, M. Patterson, J. Pouchet, and R. Tipley. Carbon Usage Effectiveness (CUE): A Green Grid Data Center Sustainability Metric. *White Paper*, 32, 2010.

[6] J. S. Chase, D. C. Anderson, P. N. Thakar, A. M. Vahdat, and R. P. Doyle. Managing Energy and Server Resources in Hosting Centers. In *SOSP*, October 2001.

[7] Facebook. OpenCompute Project: Energy-Efficiency. http://www.opencompute.org/about/energy-efficiency/.

[8] K. Fehrenbacher. The Era of the 100MW Data Center. In *Gigaom*, January 31 2012.

[9] I. Goiri, T. D. Nguyen, and R. Bianchini. CoolAir:

Temperature- and Variation-Aware Management for Free-Cooled Datacenters. In *ASPLOS*, March 2015.

[10] Google. Efficiency: How we do it. http://www.google.com/about/datacenters/efficiency/internal/.

[11] GreenGrid. Water Usage Effectiveness (WUE): A Green Grid Data Center Sustainability Metric. http://www.thegreengrid.org/en/Global/Content/white-papers/WUE.

[12] J. Koomey. Growth in Data Center Electricity Use 2005 to 2010. In *Analytics Press*, Oakland, California, August 2011.

[13] I. Manousakis, I. Goiri, S. Sankar, T. D. Nguyen, and R. Bianchini. CoolProvision: Underprovisioning Datacenter Cooling. In *SoCC*, August 2015.

[14] L. McTiernan. Open Sourcing PUE/WUE Ddashboards. https://code.facebook.com/posts/272417392924843/open-sourcing-pue-wue-dashboards/, March 2014.

[15] R. Miller. Data Centers Move to Cut Water Waste. In *Data Center Knowledge*, April 9th 2009.

[16] J. Moore, J. Chase, P. Ranganathan, and R. Sharma. Making Scheduling "Cool": Temperature-Aware Workload Placement in Data Centers. In *USENIX*, June 2005.

[17] J. Parr. Designing a Very Efficient Data Center. https://www.facebook.com/notes/facebook-engineering/designing-a-very-efficient-data-center/10150148003778920, April 2011.

[18] A. O. Rabassa III. Economic performance of modularized hot-aisle contained datacenter PODs utilizing horizontal airflow cooling. http://hdl.handle.net/1721.1/90248.

[19] S. Rivoire, M. Shah, and P. Ranganathan. JouleSort: A Balanced Energy-Efficient Benchmark. In *SIGMOD*, June 2007.

[20] S. Subramanya, Z. Mustafa, D. Irwin, and P. Shenoy. Beyond Energy-Efficiency: Evaluating Green Datacenter Applications for Energy-Agility. In *ICPE*, March 2016.

[21] Y. Sverdlik. Survey: Industry Average Data Center PUE Stays Nearly Flat Over Four Years. In *Data Center Knowledge*, June 2nd 2014.

[22] N. Tolia, Z. Wang, M. Marwah, C. Bash, P. Ranganathan, and X. Zhu. Delivering Energy Proportionality with Non-Energy-Proportional Systems: Optimizing the Ensemble. In *HotPower*, December 2008.

Interconnect Emulator for Aiding Performance Analysis of Distributed Memory Applications

Qi Wang[1,2], Ludmila Cherkasova[1], Jun Li[1], Haris Volos[1]

[1]Hewlett Packard Labs [2]The George Washington University

interwq@gwu.edu, lucy.cherkasova@hpe.com, jun.li@hpe.com, haris.volos@hpe.com

ABSTRACT

Many modern large graph and Big Data processing applications operate on datasets that do not fit into DRAM of a single machine. This leads to a design of scale-out applications, where the application dataset is partitioned and processed by a cluster of machines. Typically, these applications rely on high speed interconnects which employ Remote Direct Memory Access (RDMA) technology to provide fast and high bandwidth communications. Distributed memory applications exhibit complex behavior: they tend to interleave computations and communications, use bursty transfers, and utilize global synchronization primitives. This makes it difficult to analyze the impact of communication layer on the application performance and answer the questions: how interconnect latency or bandwidth characteristics may change the application performance? will the application performance scale when processed by a larger system? In this work,[1] we introduce a novel emulation framework, called *InterSense*, which is implemented on top of existing high-speed interconnect, such as InfiniBand, and which provides two performance knobs for changing the (today's) interconnect bandwidth and latency. This approach offers an easy-to-use framework for a sensitivity analysis of complex distributed applications to communication layer performance instead of creating customized and time-consuming application models to answer the same questions. We evaluate the emulator accuracy with popular OSU MPI benchmark suite and two clusters with different generation InfiniBand interconnects (DDR and FDR): *InterSense* emulates the specified *bandwidth and latency* values with less than 2% error between the expected and measured values. *InterSense* supports an efficient emulation of a wide range of interconnect latencies and bandwidth characteristics for enabling performance and scalability analysis of Big Data applications, deriving and interpolating their requirements for performance characteristics of the underlying communication layer. To demonstrate the *InterSense*'s ease of use, we present a case study, where we apply *InterSense* for

sensitivity analysis of four applications and benchmarks for getting non-trivial insights.

Keywords: Performance emulation; InfiniBand; MPI; distributed shared memory; benchmarking; profiling

1. INTRODUCTION

Exponential increase in online data and a corresponding proliferation of data-centric applications (Big Data analytics) forces system architects to revisit assumptions and requirements of the future system design, and at the same time, it challenges the application designers to tune and optimize their applications' implementation to efficiently utilize underlying hardware and its performance characteristics.

As a working set size of modern applications grows, to hold the entire dataset in main memory requires more than a single machine. This leads to a scale-out, distributed application implementation on a cluster of machines, where each server handles a portion of the complete dataset, and needs to communicate with each other to synchronize the main processing phases. Message passing interface (MPI) is a popular and widely used programming paradigm for scale-out, distributed memory applications. Performance of distributed memory applications inherently depends on performance of communication layer in the cluster. One can execute MPI programs using a traditional TCP/IP based network. However, over last decade, traditional networking often gets replaced by high-speed interconnects with Remote Direct Memory Access (RDMA) technology for optimizing performance of distributed memory applications. During last couple years, many Big Data applications, such as Hadoop, Spark, Memcached, etc., were re-written to take advantage of high-performance RDMA-capable interconnects [22, 23, 14, 13] which provide fast and high-bandwidth communications. The application analysis of potential performance improvements due to faster and higher bandwidth interconnects is a challenging task. Does the existing application implementation take a full advantage of the underlying interconnect or not? Will the application performance get worse if the interconnect has X% increased latency or Y% lower bandwidth?

With MPI, a distributed memory application runs on multiple machines as separate computation processes. These processes are also responsible for handling the communications, which can be a significant portion of the execution. In a new, popular, large graph processing benchmark Graph 500 [2], MPI communications could easily consume more than 50% of the program execution time (for larger graphs and smaller cluster sizes). Moreover, depending on the performance characteristics of the underlying interconnect, dif-

---

[1]This work was originated and largely completed during Qi Wang' summer internship at Hewlett Packard Labs.

ICPE 2016, March 12-18, 2016, Delft, Netherlands.
© 2016 ACM. ISBN 978-1-4503-4080-9/16/03 ...$15.00
DOI: http://dx.doi.org/10.1145//2851553.2851574.

ferent implementation decisions on communication style and size of transfers are made as a part of program optimization [12, 11, 18]. Many other scale-out applications [7, 13, 4] are also reported to be sensitive to either communication latency or communication bandwidth.

Complex MPI-based programs might interleave communication portions with computational ones in different patterns which makes it difficult to perform an accurate analysis of a communication layer impact on application performance and predict scaling properties of these programs. Building an accurate application model for predicting the application performance as a function of bandwidth and latency of underlying interconnect could be a very challenging and time-consuming task. Typically, such customized application model requires deep understanding of application functionality and its implementation, and could additionally necessitate detailed application profiling. Currently, it is practically impossible to analyze the application sensitivity to performance characteristics of the underlying interconnect and to answer the question: what impact the changed interconnect latency or/and bandwidth may have on performance of these applications?

To enable the analysis of an application dependency on performance characteristics of the underlying interconnect, we aim to offer an emulation framework, called *InterSense*, with *two performance knobs* for changing the interconnect perceived *bandwidth* and *latency*. Our earlier short paper [21] sketches the initial design of the interconnect performance emulator and provides preliminary evidence of its effectiveness. Here, we provide a complete description of our implementation along with discussion of different design alternatives and implementation challenges related to these choices. In the paper, we discuss technical subtleties of implementing the low-overhead emulation for high-speed interconnects and for decoupling latency and bandwidth emulations. We evaluate the emulator accuracy and the imposed overhead with popular OSU MPI benchmark suite [6] and two cluster-testbeds deployed with different generation InfiniBand interconnects (DDR and FDR): *InterSense* emulates the specified *bandwidth and latency* values with less than 2% error between the expected and measured values. To demonstrate the *InterSense*'s ease of use, we present a case study, where we apply *InterSense* for sensitivity analysis of modern applications and popular benchmarks, such as *Memcached* application [13], *NAS Parallel Benchmarks suite* [7], *RandomAccess memory benchmark (GUPS)* [4], and *Graph 500* benchmark [2].

Forward-looking projects like Firebox [9] and HP's The Machine [3] envision future scale-out computing architectures with enormous amount of non-volatile memories (NVMs) and with nodes connected via a high-speed interconnect. While the slowed-down interconnect appears to emulate a slower communication layer, *InterSense* can be used as a tool to predict the performance of future higher-performance systems. Intuitively, these future systems will have a higher computation-to-communication ratio than today's systems. Our tool can assist system designers in useful assessment of computation-to-communication ratio ranges that could support expected (or desired) performance of popular applications. We believe that the designed emulator can be used for conducting application sensitivity analysis, interpolating the application scalability, and projecting its performance on future interconnects with different performance characteristics.

The remainder of the paper is organized as follows. Section 2 provides background on MPI programming, outlines our approach to the emulator design, and discusses implementation challenges. Section 3 introduces our approach to bandwidth emulation and subtleties of its implementation. Section 4 outlines the latency control in our emulator, possible implementation choices, and our solution. Section 5 presents the evaluation study: assessment of emulator accuracy and its ease of use. Section 6 describes a review of related work. Finally, Section 7 provides summary and future work directions.

2. INTERCONNECT PERFORMANCE EMULATOR: ITS DESIGN AND IMPLEMENTATION CHALLENGES

Message Passing Interface (MPI) offers a language-independent communications protocol for implementing parallel and distributed memory applications. The MPI paradigm is attractive due to its wide portability: it can be used for communication by distributed-memory and shared-memory multiprocessors, as well as by clusters of servers. The MPI framework is applicable in different settings, it is independent of network speed or memory architecture. **Figure 1** shows the underlying communication methods available and used in MPI libraries over different media (that utilize different protocols). We use this diagram in order to explain the communication layer addressed by our interconnect emulator.

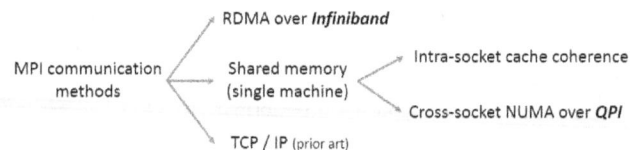

Figure 1: MPI Communication Methods

One can execute MPI programs using a *traditional TCP/IP based network* (the *bottom branch*). This communication style is based on a traditional (slow) networking, and therefore, one can apply some existing software-based networking emulators (e.g., *ModelNet, Netbed*, or *netem* [20, 8, 24]) that were designed and actively exploited for controlling network performance characteristics in the analysis of their impact on the application performance.

There are two branches (top and middle ones) that rely on a much faster and efficient media. The *middle branch* supports MPI program implementation on *shared memory* machines. There are two different sub-cases:

- different MPI processes are assigned and executed on the same socket (e.g., executed by different cores of the same processor). This communication style and its implementation relies on *intra-socket cache coherence* protocol for sending messages across MPI processes;
- different MPI processes are assigned and executed by different sockets (e.g., executed by different cores of different processors). This communication style and its implementation relies on *inter-socket or cross-socket (NUMA) cache coherence* protocol and QPI (Quick Path Interconnect between the processors) for sending messages across MPI processes.

The *top branch* is related to a cluster of machines connected via InfiniBand. This configuration allows implementing large distributed memory (combined across all the machines) and communications between the machines (i.e., between MPI processes residing on different machines) is done by using Remote Direct Memory Access over InfiniBand (*RDMA over InfiniBand*). The MPI communications performed over InfiniBand is the target of our work.

InfiniBand is the state of the art approach for high-speed interconnect between multiple machines. Different from QPI interconnect which requires CPU involvement in transmission, InfiniBand adapter is RDMA enabled and accepts requests actively. This enables the transmission to be asynchronous and without consuming CPU processing power. Based on the performance/features of InfiniBand, we choose it to study performance of future *RDMA-like devices*.

The large-scale Internet environment and high-speed interconnects have substantially different characteristics. For example, InfiniBand achieves bandwidth above 100 Gb/s and latency lower than 1 microsecond. These performance characteristics differences prevent the use of existing networking emulators for the interconnect emulation due to their high overhead. The high-speed interconnect emulation poses a number of challenges:

- Because of the high-speed nature of interconnect, the emulation overhead needs to be minimized. Imposing an additional software layer (e.g., TCP/IP protocol) or extra hardware (e.g., *ModelNet core node*) is not acceptable for interconnect emulation because of the overhead.

- Latency and bandwidth characteristics of the interconnect emulation need to be orthogonal to each other, i.e., the emulation mechanism of one characteristic should not interfere with the other. Therefore, separate latency and bandwidth emulation mechanisms are required.

- There is no bandwidth or latency control support in existing hardware, e.g., there are no hardware knobs in InfiniBand adapters/switches that can be used for emulation of different performance characteristics. By the way, the QPI situation is similar.

To implement the low-overhead emulation and to decouple latency and bandwidth emulations, we designed the following software techniques for a bandwidth and latency control as summarized in Figure 2:

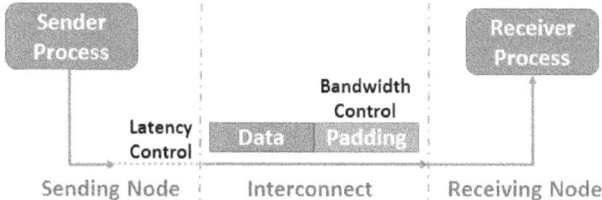

- *For bandwidth emulation*, we add padding packets to reduce an effective bandwidth for applications.
- *For latency emulation*, we insert a software emulated delay before sending the application's messages.

Figure 2: Emulation Mechanism Overview.

One additional interesting point to note here is that the latency emulation approach described later in Section 4 can be also applied to control the latency via shared memory (middle branch shown in Figure 1).

3. BANDWIDTH EMULATION

For emulating interconnect with different bandwidth characteristics, we impact effective bandwidth of the interconnect by sending extra padding packets. The ratio between padding packets and data packets determines the effective bandwidth for applications. It is defined in a software emulation layer so that we can achieve a fine-grained control over effective bandwidth. There are multiple layers in software, where bandwidth can be impacted:

1. an application,
2. the communication library, i.e., MPI library, and
3. a device driver.

Figure 3 summarizes advantages and disadvantages of each layer for bandwidth throttling.

Padding Layer	Pluses and Minuses
Application	- : Application specific - : Modification complexity
MPI library	+ : Portable for MPI applications + : MPI library support – MPI information available - : High complexity of MPI implementations
IB driver library	+ : Accuracy – padding right before sending - : Complexity – missing high-level library support - : Non-portable – device specific

Figure 3: Bandwidth Control Layer.

If we implement an interconnect bandwidth emulation in the *application layer* this requires only modification to the application itself. However, this may cause many lines of changes to the application code (and in many cases, the application source code might not be available). Also, for some MPI operations that perform both computation and communication, e.g., *MPI_Allreduce*, it is not possible to impact the interconnect bandwidth accurately because the communication pattern, implemented in the underlying MPI library, is transparent to the application.

On the other end, in the *device driver layer* (e.g., driver library of InfiniBand adapters), we would communicate with devices directly. However, at this layer, we are losing a higher level operation view, and have no information from MPI library. In addition, the driver library is *device specific*, and the process of setting up and sending of padding packets are two rather complex operations. This means that if the bandwidth control is done in the driver layer, migrating (re-implementing) the emulation platform to a different hardware would be difficult.

We believe the **MPI library layer** offers the *best trade-off* among portability, accuracy and complexity: it works for all MPI-based applications, it is close to hardware (right above the driver layer), and it provides additional flexibility of seeing the MPI operators used by the program. This information can be used in the emulator for exploiting different bandwidth values across the interconnect links to mimic special interconnect topologies or resources available to the program.

To emulate correct bandwidth impact on packet latencies, a padding packet is sent before the corresponding data packet. Bandwidth does have a natural impact on the latency of larger packets. By sending the padding packets before the actual data packets we aim to correctly capture the bandwidth characteristic (i.e., latency of the large packets will increase with lower bandwidth). To avoid impacting the latency of small packets, their padding packets are batched (combined together) until the total size reaches a pre-defined threshold (64 KB in our experiments). The threshold parameter should be large enough to amortize software overhead, while not too large that bandwidth is not controlled in time. We found that for InfiniBand FDR interconnect with 56 Gbits/sec, 64 KB threshold is sufficient to ensure both no latency interference for small packets and the accurate bandwidth control.

We implement bandwidth control in a widely-used MPI implementation: MVAPICH2 [5]. To send padding packets, memory buffer needs to be allocated as for sending and receiving padding packets.

There are a few padding buffer allocation options:

- *Naive approach*: allocate a buffer with a size equal to the largest application message multiplied by a padding ratio. However, this may result in a very high memory requirement for padding buffers: the maximum application message size could be very large and its size is unknown to the MPI library.

- *Buffer-reusable approach*: allocate a buffer with a size equal to the largest MPI packet segmentation size. Since MPI library does packet segmentation internally (with a fixed maximum segmentation size: 4MB in our case), the size of packets at the interconnect level will not be greater than the segmentation size. Based on this, we can point all the padding packets to the same memory region. This requires the minimal amount of memory for padding buffer. We use this approach in our emulator.

Moreover, inside the MPI library, there are a few implementation choices, where adding of padding packets can be done: high-level interface layer (closer to MPI's user API) or low-level device API layer (closer to hardware, e.g., InfiniBand Verbs API). We prototyped and compared these two implementation alternatives for the interconnect bandwidth control:

- *High-level MPI interface layer* approach – it requires no deep modification of MPI library. A new *padding_send* operation is attached to each *send*-based MPI operation to consume desired bandwidth. For example, *MPI_Send()* will send a separate padding packet along with the data packet. To avoid unnecessary receiving calls for padding packets, which add overhead and prevent batching for small packets, one-sided communication is used to send padding packets.

  However, the considered MPI's user API level imposes the following implementation requirement: the described "padding" modification should be introduced for **all** API functions. Unfortunately, there are MPI functions with a high complexity (e.g., *MPI_Allreduce*) that cannot be easily modified to impact bandwidth accurately. This makes the high-level API approach less promising for achieving an accurate interconnect bandwidth throttling outcome.

- *Low-level MPI Verbs-based layer* – it needs modifications at a deeper level inside the MPI library, such as InfiniBand Verbs layer. For InfiniBand, the *padding_send* operation is attached to each *ibv_post_send()* invocation. The operating level here is closer to hardware, i.e., right before communicating with hardware driver. In such a way, this low-level approach is much more compact and provides a *unified method* for handling bandwidth characteristics across **all** high-level MPI operations.

Therefore, for implementing the interconnect bandwidth control, we add padding packets at a low-level Verbs layer of MPI library. For emulating the correct bandwidth impact on large packet latencies, the padding packet is sent before the corresponding data packet.

4. LATENCY EMULATION

Since high-speed interconnects have an ultra low native latency (e.g., 1 μs for InfiniBand), the emulation overhead needs to be very low as well. This means that expensive operations like context switches cannot be involved. Our approach for emulating the interconnect latency is to generate an additional delay by *spinning*, i.e., by introducing an extra *idle time* for desired latency. A spinning approach has the following advantages:

1. a high accuracy (close to 10ns),
2. a low implementation complexity, and
3. a low overhead (no other operations are needed).

The only disadvantage is that a spinning process results in additional consumption of CPU computation cycles [2]. However, we believe that the computation cycles spent on spin is acceptable because the desirable emulation targets of the interconnect latency emulation are at nanosecond or microsecond level (depending on the interconnect).

Similar to the bandwidth control implementation, multiple layers in the software stack can be used for impacting the interconnect latency. Figure 4 summarizes advantages and disadvantages of each layer.

For latency control of InfiniBand, because of the spin implementation simplicity, we choose the **driver library layer**. In addition, this approach aims to maximize the emulation accuracy (despite the driver's portability limitation). When migrating the emulation to a different hardware platform, the effort of re-implementing the spin-based latency control in a different driver library is minimal – it is approximately 20 lines of code in our case.

When a driver specific modification is not preferred, the latency control can also be done in a *low-level MPI library layer* (i.e., before calling *ib_verb* API) to achieve an MPI-portable implementation. However, there is a *limitation* of this approach: the delay inserted in the MPI library layer could be invalid when *multithreading is enabled* in the MPI library because multiple threads could be contending for locks in a driver after inserting their delays.

For latency control over shared memory (a middle branch in

---

[2]One can use dedicated resources for spinning (e.g., spinning cores) to alleviate competing with application for the same CPU cycles. However, it has a different complication: in order to inform the spin cores about the packet, message passing is required, e.g., using lock-free ring buffers. A message between cores itself has a rather high overhead (approx. 100ns per message within a socket), and it goes up dramatically when there is a contention. So, this approach will reduce the spin cycle consumption (minus the message overhead), but will cause an extra cache coherency traffic.

Delay Insertion Layer	Pluses and Minuses
Application	+: Trivial to implement - : Application specific - : Inaccurate for asynchronous requests
MPI library	+: Portable for MPI applications - : High complexity of MPI implementations - : Not close to hardware (Infiniband)
IB driver library	+: Accuracy – delay right before sending - : Non-portable – device specific

Figure 4: Latency Control Layer.

Figure 1) a similar approach can be applied. The communication latency over shared memory and/or QPI can be controlled in the MPI library layer: right before writing to shared memory (since no driver is needed for QPI communication due to direct memory operations using a shared memory protocol). When using this approach one needs to remember a granularity of introduced additional delay relative to a basic latency.

5. EVALUATION

In this section, we evaluate the emulator accuracy and demonstrate its ease of use for application sensitivity analysis by presenting a case study with four distributed-memory applications and benchmarks.

5.1 Experimental Testbeds and Workloads

We evaluate the effectiveness and accuracy of our emulator by using a popular OSU MPI benchmark suite [6] and two clusters with different generation interconnects: DDR InfiniBand (20 Gbits/s) and FDR InfiniBand (56 Gbits/s):

- *Cluster_1* with 4 nodes, where each node is based on HP DL380 servers (two sockets Xeon E5-2697 with 12 cores per socket), and connected with FDR InfiniBand (56 Gbits/s);
- *Cluster_2* with 8 nodes, where each node is based on HP Proliant BL460c servers (two sockets Xeon E5345 with 12 cores per socket), and connected with DDR InfiniBand (20 Gbits/s).

The Ohio MPI Microbenchmark suite [6] is a collection of independent MPI message passing performance microbenchmarks developed and provided as an open source by the Network-Based Computing Laboratory of the Ohio State University. In particular, it includes some simple benchmarks for performance measurements of latency and bandwidth for basic MPI communications.

5.2 Emulator Accuracy

OSU MPI bandwidth test is implemented by having a sender sending out a fixed number (equal to a window size) of back-to-back messages to a receiver and then waiting for a reply from the receiver. The receiver sends the reply only after receiving all the messages. This process is repeated for several iterations and the bandwidth is calculated based on the elapsed time (from the time sender sends the first message until the time it receives the re-

ply back from the receiver) and the number of bytes sent by the sender. The objective of this bandwidth test is to determine the maximum sustained data rate that can be achieved at the network level. Thus, non-blocking version of MPI functions (*MPI_Isend* and *MPI_Irecv*) are used in the test.

Figure 5 (a) shows the bandwidth emulation results measured with OSU MPI benchmark executed on the FDR InfiniBand-based Cluster_1 (with 56 Gbits/s links). The X-axis shows the target, emulated bandwidth (aimed between the sender and receiver), while Y-axis reports on the measured bandwidth. We have executed benchmark runs with default parameters of the bandwidth test program: each configuration is run for 20×64 iterations. From the

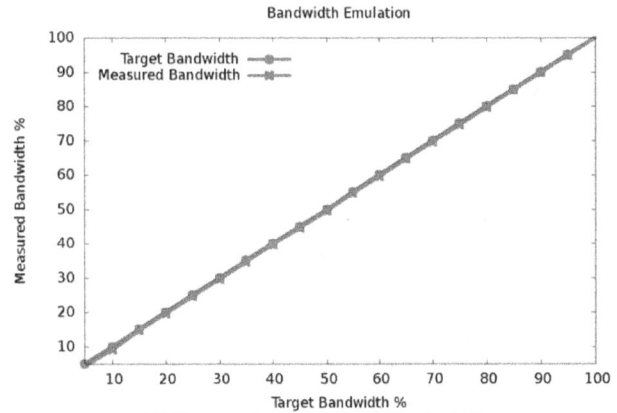

(a) Expected vs Measured Bandwidth.

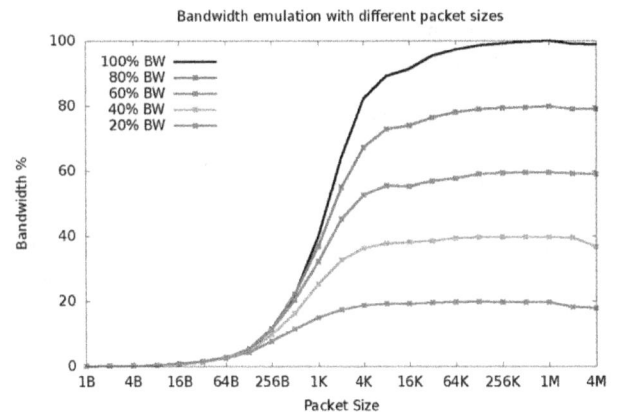

(b) Bandwidth Control for Packets with Different Sizes.

Figure 5: OSU benchmark: Evaluating Accuracy of Interconnect Bandwidth Emulation.

experimental results, we observe that the interconnect *bandwidth emulation* is supported with a high accuracy: less than 2% error between the expected, emulated interconnect bandwidth and the measured interconnect bandwidth in the experiments (packet size = 1 MB).

Moreover, the bandwidth control works correctly for packets with different sizes as shown in **Figure 5 (b)**: large packets are impacted by bandwidth control, while small packets are not impacted because they are not limited by bandwidth.

- The large packets (i.e., packets $\geq$ 128 KB) are capable of fully utilizing the available interconnect bandwidth. We can

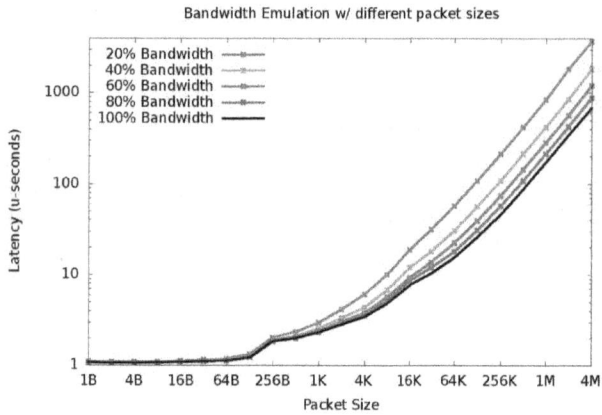

Figure 6: Bandwidth Impact on Packet Latency.

see that when 100% of bandwidth is available, the large packets are able to saturate and utilize 100% of interconnect bandwidth (top line). If only 80% of bandwidth is available, the large packets are utilizing 80% of bandwidth, etc. Therefore transfers of large packets are impacted correctly by bandwidth control.

- The small size packet transfers (less than 256 bytes) are not impacted by bandwidth emulation. Their transfers are not limited by the interconnect bandwidth (small packets are not capable of utilizing the available bandwidth). Small size transfers are limited by the interconnect message rate. Therefore, the achievable bandwidth for small size packets is practically the same under different emulation values of interconnect bandwidth as shown in the left side of **Figure 5 (b)**.

We also measure the latency of different size packets under different emulated interconnect bandwidth. We find that these packets are controlled accurately in the emulator, and the bandwidth emulation is orthogonal to latency emulation. **Figure 6** shows that small packets (not limited by bandwidth) have no latency change under different emulated interconnect bandwidth control, while the latency of large packets (limited by bandwidth) is impacted correctly.

OSU MPI latency test is carried out in a ping-pong fashion. A sender sends a message with a certain data size to a receiver and waits for a reply from the receiver. The receiver receives the message from the sender and sends back a reply with the same data size. Many iterations of this ping-pong test are carried out and average one-way latency numbers are obtained. Synchronous version of MPI functions (*MPI_Send* and *MPI_Recv*) are used in the tests.

Figure 7 shows the latency emulation results measured with OSU MPI benchmark executed on the FDR InfiniBand-based Cluster_1 (with 56 Gbits/s links).

The *latency emulation* results, measured with OSU MPI benchmark, again show high accuracy: $\leq 2\%$ error between expected (emulated) latency and measured one as shown in **Figure 7 (a)**. Moreover, the designed mechanism works effectively for packets with different sizes as demonstrated in **Figure 7 (b)**. The bottom line on this graph shows the measured latency of different size packets. As we can see, when we emulate the increased intercon-

nect latency (i.e., *latency+2μs*, *latency+4μs*, etc.) the measured packet latency closely follows the original latency pattern. It means that the designed latency emulation mechanism does not impact the interconnect bandwidth, and therefore the emulation mechanisms for latency and bandwidth do not interfere with each other.

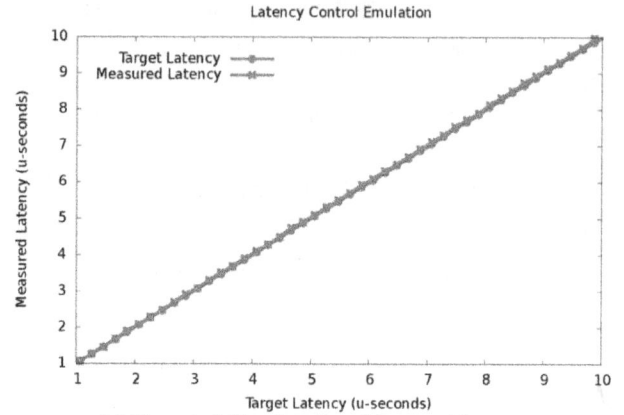

(a) Expected (Emulated) vs Measured Latency.

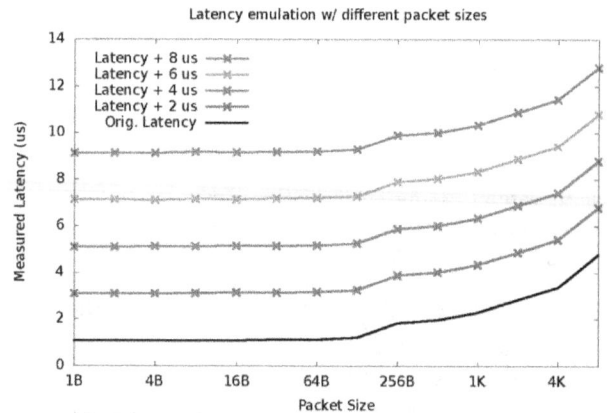

(b) Latency Emulation with Different Packet Sizes.

Figure 7: OSU benchmark: Evaluating Accuracy of Interconnect Latency Emulation.

The results obtained in the DDR InfiniBand-based Cluster_2 (with 20 Gbits/s links) show similar accuracy results. We omit them due to a paper space limitation.

5.3 Application Sensitivity Analysis with InterSense

Complex MPI-based programs might interleave communication portions with computational ones in different patterns which makes it difficult to analyze the communication layer impact on application performance and predict scaling properties of the program. Currently, it is extremely challenging to analyze the application sensitivity to performance characteristics of the underlying interconnect and to answer the question: what impact the changed interconnect latency or/and bandwidth may have on performance of these applications?

To demonstrate the *InterSense*'s ease of use, we present a case study, where we apply *InterSense* for a sensitivity analysis of modern applications and popular benchmarks, such as *Memcached* application [13], *RandomAccess memory benchmark (GUPS)* [4], *NAS Parallel Benchmarks suite* [7], and *Graph 500* benchmark [2]. Note, that the only other way to get the results below is to build customized performance models of these benchmarks and applications as a function of interconnect latency and bandwidth, which is a difficult and challenging task even for a skilled performance analysts.

Figure 8 shows performance of *Memcached* application [13] as a function of emulated (increased) interconnect latency. *Memcached* is a key-value distributed memory application used in the data-center environment for caching results of database calls, API calls, etc. This application is redesigned for RDMA capable networks instead of traditional BSD Sockets implementation. It shows an extremely low response time for small requests, and therefore, it is very sensitive to any increase in the interconnect latency, which directly impacts the application performance as shown in Figure 8 (a).

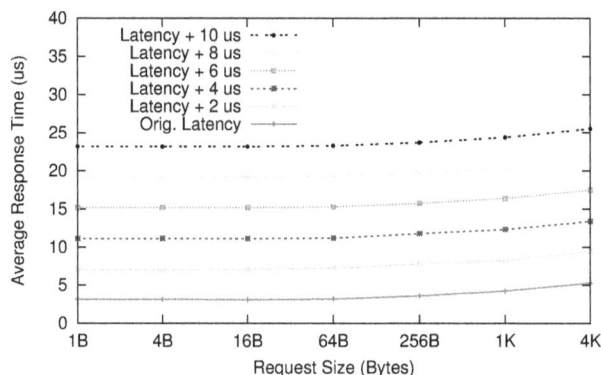

(a) Memcached Response Time under Different Emulated Latency and Small Request Sizes.

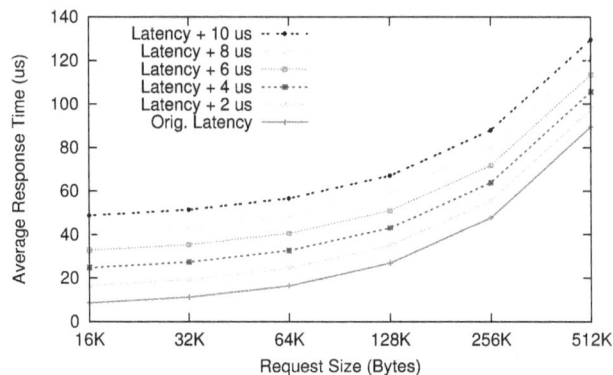

(b) Memcached Response Time under Different Emulated Latency and Large Request Sizes.

Figure 8: Memcached Response Time under Different Emulated Latency and Larger Request Sizes.

For example, an additional latency of $2\mu s$ via interconnect increases the response time of small requests ($\leq 4KB$) almost twice. For larger requests the relative impact of increased latency diminishes as shown in Figure 8 (b).

Another interesting point is that for small requests (≤ 4 KB), when interconnect latency is increased by N μs, the response time increases by $2 \times N$ μs as we can see in Figure 8 (a) because of a single round-trip communication that is required to serve this request. While for large requests (≥ 16 KB) shown in Figure 8 (b), the response time increases by $4 \times N$ μs, because two round-trip communications are required for large requests: first one for setting up the memory buffer and the second one for actual data transfer. For small requests the data is embedded in the first packet. These differences are not obvious without understanding application implementation. However, our tool can discover this easily without having a deep knowledge of the application.

Figure 9 shows a sensitivity of *RandomAccess memory benchmark (GUPS)* to the interconnect latency. *GUPS* is a new benchmark proposed by IBM Research [19] a few years ago for measuring how frequently a computer can issue updates to randomly generated RAM locations. Giga-updates per second (*GUPS*) is a measure of random memory access capability of multicores platforms. *GUPS* is latency sensitive, but in a very special way. Its sensitivity is defined by the number of outstanding concurrent requests. If the number of outstanding requests is limited ($\leq 1K$) then *GUPS* performance is 30-100% worse with increased interconnect latency. However, for outstanding requests $\geq 4K$ there is no difference in performance: the pipeline of processed requests is constantly full, and it hides the increased interconnect latency.

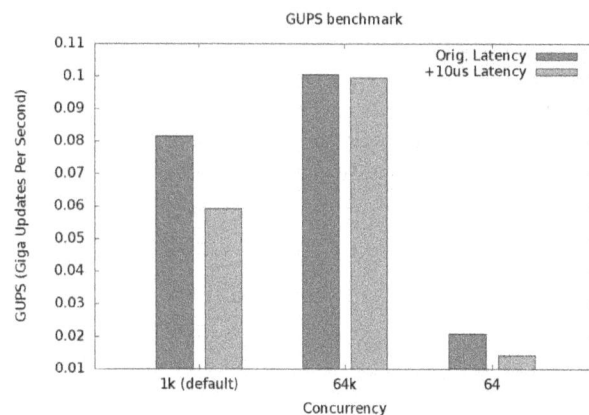

Figure 9: GUPS: Emulated Latency.

Both *Memcached* and *GUPS* are not bandwidth sensitive in our experiments: they operate with very small size requests and cannot utilize the available interconnect bandwidth in our *Cluster_1* testbed. Small size transfers are limited by the interconnect message rate.

Figure 10 shows performance of a popular *NAS Parallel Benchmarks suite* [7] as a function of emulated bandwidth. *NAS Parallel Benchmarks* are used for the evaluation and comparison of parallel supercomputers. This suite includes seven diverse applications with different computation and communication patterns. The bandwidth sensitivity among benchmarks is very different: *LU, MG, SP,* and *BT* show 20-40% increase in the execution time at 2.8 Gb/s available bandwidth (i.e., at 5% of the original interconnect bandwidth). However, *CG* and *FT* react to diminished bandwidth in a more extreme way: their execution time increases by more than 300%. These applications are extremely bandwidth sensitive for delivering good performance and this dependency impacts the applications' scalability on a larger cluster. Finally, *EP* application

(*Embarrassingly Parallel*) is not sensitive to bandwidth at all. None of the NAS studied benchmarks is sensitive to the increased interconnect latency (up to 10x latency in our experiments) because they use extensively the asynchronous communications which hide the impact of communication latency.

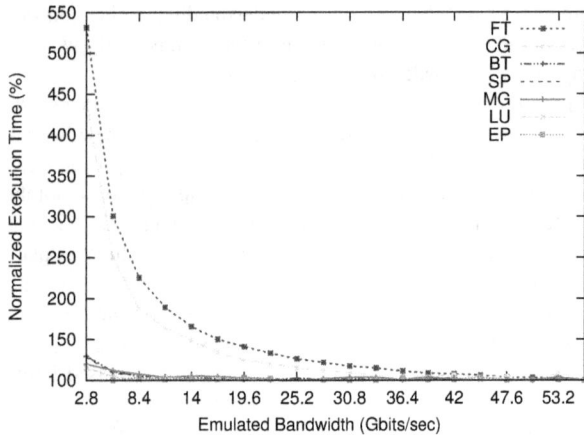

Figure 10: NAS parallel Benchmarks: Emulated Bandwidth.

Figure 11 shows performance of *Graph 500* benchmark [2] with emulated interconnect bandwidth. *Graph 500* is a benchmark implementing a *Breadth First Search* algorithm on large graphs and used for assessing system performance based on processing efficiency of their memory and interconnect. Producing winning results is a goal for many companies with leading hardware and system design.

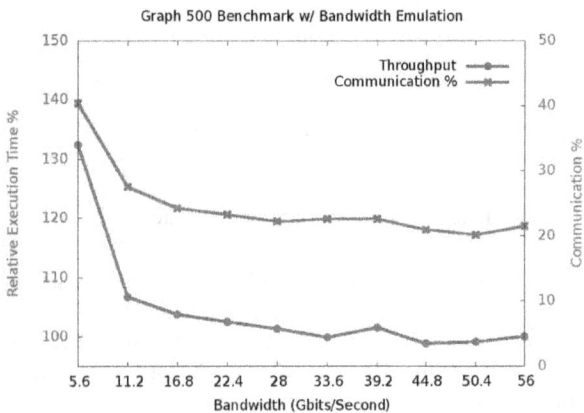

Figure 11: Graph500: Emulated Bandwidth.

Figure 11 shows that only 30% of FDR InfiniBand bandwidth is effectively used (for selected graph and cluster sizes). With 10% of interconnect bandwidth, the execution time (red line) is increased by 30%, and a fraction of communication time (blue line) is doubled. This type of sensitivity analysis is very useful for understanding the cost/performance trade-offs. *InterSense* can help answering capacity planning questions which require careful estimates of the available "remaining" interconnect capacity for supporting a higher load/volume service without compromising its performance.

Graph 500 was not sensitive to a higher (10x) interconnect latency in our experiments (due to using asynchronous communication and high messaging volume).

This concludes our case study with *InterSense*. The goal of this study was to show the ease of tool use and the appeal of the designed interconnect emulator for performing the sensitivity analysis of emerging benchmarks and modern applications instead of creating customized and time-consuming application models to answer the same questions.

6. RELATED WORK

Many previous efforts explored emulation environments for evaluating the networking impact on their applications [10, 15, 17, 25]. However, the initial attempts were targeting static and relatively small scale systems. Later, more advanced efforts [20, 24, 16, 8] offered a variety of flexible TCP/IP-based emulation approaches to support a broad range of research efforts for evaluating the Internet and data center environments.

ModelNet [20] is a large-scale network emulator that allows users to evaluate distributed networked systems and analyze performance of their applications in the Internet-like environments. It employs virtualization and routes packets through control nodes (*ModelNet* core) to emulate desired delay, bandwidth and loss rate. It further performs full hop-by-hop network emulation, allowing it to capture the effects of contention and bursts in the middle of the network.

Another closely related to this approach is *Netbed* [24] (a descendant of *Emulab* [1]). This tool allows users to configure and access integrated network resources composed of emulated, simulated and wide-area nodes and links for distributed systems and networking experiments.

However, large-scale Internet environment and high-speed interconnect have substantially different characteristics: for Internet infrastructure, bandwidth and latency performance is hundred times worse than the InfiniBand ones. In addition, the scale, security, reliability issues are often of concern as well. These performance characteristics differences prevent the *ModelNet* approach from being applied for high-speed interconnect emulation. For example, the high overhead coming from virtualization and re-routing is not suitable for the interconnect emulation.

Another effort [16] applies the emulation for evaluating a variety of effects in wide-area network on web server performance. The authors advocate emulating network performance characteristics at end hosts rather than in the network core for improved and simplified scalability. While this approach requires appropriate emulation software on the edge nodes and must share each host CPU between the emulation and the target application, this approach is attractive due to its flexibility and simplicity. Our *InterSense* emulator follows a similar approach that offers performance knobs for controlling the interconnect latency and bandwidth at the end points.

netem [8] is an open source network emulation tool that is enabled in the Linux kernel. However, it also focuses on wide area networks like Internet, which makes it unfit for the interconnect emulation. Other related tools are available for QoS management over TCP/IP based network. But they all suffer from high protocol overhead, when running on a high-speed interconnect, such as IP over IB (IPoIB).

The network-related emulation tools are traditionally designed around TCP/IP protocol, which functionality is significantly different compared to RDMA over InfiniBand. The designed *Inter-Sense* emulator offers unique capabilities for analysis of scale-out distributed memory applications.

7. CONCLUSION AND FUTURE WORK

In this work, we introduce novel bandwidth and latency control mechanisms for performance emulation of the high-speed interconnects. We built a prototype of a new emulator and carefully evaluated its performance, efficiency, and accuracy. *InterSense* can assist researchers and engineers in emulating a variety of performance characteristics of future large-scale interconnects and conducting the application sensitivity and scalability analysis dependent on these characteristics.

We are working on augmenting the proposed approach with additional profiling, modeling, and prediction technique. By performing the emulation in small deployments with increased interconnect latency and decreased bandwidth we aim to derive the predictive models for application performance when processing larger data amounts in large-scale distributed environments. We believe that the *InterSense* ability to accurately indicate the *needed* interconnect bandwidth for achieving the user-defined application performance objectives and to reflect the application sensitivity to the increased interconnect latency will help in applications' optimization and redesign.

8. REFERENCES

[1] Emulab - Network Emulation Testbed, http://www.emulab.net/.

[2] Graph 500 Benchmark. www.graph500.org/.

[3] HP Labs. The Machine: A new kind of computer. http://www.hpl.hp.com/research/systems-research/.

[4] HPCC RandomAccess (GUPS) Benchmark. http://icl.cs.utk.edu/projectsfiles/hpcc/RandomAccess/.

[5] MVAPICH: MPI over InfiniBand, 10GigE/iWARP and RoCE. http://mvapich.cse.ohio-state.edu/.

[6] MVAPICH Ohio State University Micro benchmark. http://mvapich.cse.ohio-state.edu/benchmarks/.

[7] NAS Parallel Benchmarks. http://www.nas.nasa.gov/publications/npb.html.

[8] netem, http://www.linuxfoundation.org/collaborate/workgroups/networking/netem.

[9] K. Asanovic. FireBox: A Hardware Building Block for 2020 Warehouse-Scale Computers. In *Proc. of FAST*, 2014.

[10] G. Banga, J. C. Mogul, and P. Druschel. A scalable and Explicit Event Delivery Mechanism for UNIX. In *Proc. of the USENIX Annual Technical Conference*, 1999.

[11] F. Checconi and F. Petrini. Traversing Trillions of Edges in Real Time: Graph Exploration on Large-Scale Parallel Machines. In *Proc. of Intl. Parallel and Distributed Processing Symposium, IPDPS'14*, 2014.

[12] F. Checconi, F. Petrini, J. Willcock, A. Lumsdaine, A. R. Choudhury, and Y. Sabharwal. Breaking the Speed and Scalability Barriers for Graph Exploration on Distributed-Memory Machines. In *Proc. of Conference on High Performance Computing Networking, Storage and Analysis, SC'12,*, 2012.

[13] J. Jose, H. Subramoni, M. Luo, M. Zhang, J. Huang, M. Wasi-ur Rahman, N. S. Islam, X. Ouyang, H. Wang, S. Sur, and D. K. Panda. Memcached Design on High Performance RDMA Capable Interconnects. In *Proc. of the 2011 International Conference on Parallel Processing*, ICPP '11, 2011.

[14] X. Lu, M. Wasi-ur Rahman, N. S. Islam, D. Shankar, , and D. K. D. Panda. Accelerating Spark with RDMA for Big Data Processing: Early Experiences. In *Proc. of Hot Interconnects*, 2014.

[15] R. P. Martin, A. M. Vahdat, D. E. Culler, and T. E. Anderson. Effects of Communication Latency, Overhead, and Bandwidth in a Cluster Architecture. In *Proc. of the 24th Annual International Symposium on Computer Architecture*, ISCA '97, 1997.

[16] E. M. Nahum, M.-C. Rosu, S. Seshan, and J. Almeida. The Effects of Wide-area Conditions on WWW Server Performance. In *Proc. of the 2001 ACM SIGMETRICS International Conference on Measurement and Modeling of Computer Systems*, SIGMETRICS '01, 2001.

[17] B. D. Noble, M. Satyanarayanan, G. T. Nguyen, and R. H. Katz. Trace-Based Mobile Network Emulation. In *Proc. of SIGCOMM*, 1997.

[18] X. Que, F. Checconi, and F. Petrini. Performance Analysis of Graph Algorithms on P7IH. In *Proc. of the 29th Intl. Conference on Supercomputing, ISC'14*, 2014.

[19] V. Saxena, Y. Sabharwal, and P. Bhatotia. Performance evaluation and optimization of random memory access on multicores with high productivity. In *Proc. of Intl. Conference on High Performance Computing (HiPC)*, 2010.

[20] A. Vahdat, K. Yocum, K. Walsh, P. Mahadevan, D. Kostić, J. Chase, and D. Becker. Scalability and accuracy in a large-scale network emulator. *SIGOPS Oper. Syst. Rev.*, 36(SI), Dec. 2002.

[21] Q. Wang, L. Cherkasova, J. Li, and H. Volos. InterSense: Interconnect Performance Emulator for Future Scale-out Distributed Memory Applications. In *Intl. Symposium on Modelling, Analysis and Simulation of Computer and Telecommunication Systems (MASCOTS)*, 2015.

[22] M. Wasi-ur Rahman, N. S. Islam, X. Lu, J. Jose, H. Subramoni, H. Wang, and D. K. D. Panda. High-Performance RDMA-based Design of Hadoop MapReduce over InfiniBand. In *Proc. of the 2013 IEEE 27th International Symposium on Parallel and Distributed Processing Workshops and PhD Forum*, IPDPSW '13, 2013.

[23] M. Wasi-ur-Rahman, X. Lu, N. S. Islam, R. Rajachandrasekar, and D. K. Panda. MapReduce over Lustre: Can RDMA-Based Approach Benefit? In *Proc. of the 20th International Conference EuroPar*, 2014.

[24] B. White, J. Lepreau, L. Stoller, R. Ricci, S. Guruprasad, M. Newbold, M. Hibler, C. Barb, and A. Joglekar. An Integrated Experimental Environment for Distributed Systems and Networks. *SIGOPS Oper. Syst. Rev.*, 36(SI), Dec. 2002.

[25] H. Yu and A. Vahdat. The Costs and Limits of Availability for Replicated Services. In *Proc. of the 18th ACM Symposium on Operating Systems Principles (SOSP)*, 2001.

Parallel Graph Processing: Prejudice and State of the Art

Assaf Eisenman[1,2], Ludmila Cherkasova[2], Guilherme Magalhaes[3], Qiong Cai[2],
Paolo Faraboschi[2], Sachin Katti[1]

[1]Stanford University, [2]Hewlett Packard Labs, [3]Hewlett Packard Enterprise

assafe@stanford.edu, {lucy.cherkasova, guilherme.magalhaes, qiong.cai, paolo.faraboschi}@hpe.com,
skatti@stanford.edu

Abstract

Large graph processing has attracted much renewed attention due to its increased importance for a social network analysis. The efficient parallel graph processing faces a set of software and hardware issues, discussed in literature. The main cause of these challenges is the "irregularity" of graph computations and related difficulties in efficient parallelization of graph processing. Unbalanced computations, caused by uneven data partitioning, can affect application scalability. Moreover, the issue of poor data locality is another major concern, that makes the graph processing applications memory-bound. In this paper[1], we aim to profile how large, parallel graph applications (based on Galois framework) utilize modern systems, in particular, memory subsystem. We found that modern graph processing frameworks executed on the latest Intel multi-core systems (a single node server) exhibit a good data locality and achieve a good speedup with an increased number of cores, contrary to traditional past stereotypes. The application processing speedup is highly correlated with utilized memory bandwidth. At the same time, our measurements show that the memory bandwidth is not a bottleneck, and the analyzed graph applications are memory-latency bound. These new insights can help us in matching the resource demands of the graph processing applications to future system design parameters.

Categories and Subject Descriptors: C.4 [Computer System Organization] Performance of Systems, D.2.6.[Software] Programming Environments.

General Terms: Measurement, Performance, Design.

Keywords: Parallel graph processing, benchmarking, profiling, hardware performance counters.

1. INTRODUCTION

The interest to large graph processing has gained momentum over last years due to the increased importance of efficient graph processing for the analysis and problem solving in social networks, data mining, and machine learning. The steep increase in volume of data being produced led to a renewed interest in parallel graph

---

[1]This work was originated and largely completed during A. Eisenman' internship at Hewlett Packard Labs in summer 2015.

processing. The rise of multi-core processors and their dominance in modern Data Centers offers new challenges and opportunities for efficient use of this platform for large graph processing. Unfortunately, most of the graph algorithms have some inherent characteristics that make them difficult to parallelize and execute efficiently.

The detailed survey paper [14] on challenges in parallel graph processing lists a set of software and hardware issues that limit graph processing performance. Among them the **"irregularity"** of graph computations, which makes it difficult to parallelize graph processing by either partitioning the algorithm computation or partitioning the graph data. Moreover, unbalanced computations, caused by uneven data partitioning, can affect and **limit the achievable scalability**. Finally, the issue of **poor data locality** during graph processing is another major concern and challenge described in [14]. All these challenges are side effects of the "irregular" algorithms, which are typically data-driven, with dependencies between tasks and computations defined at runtime.

To better understand the design points of the various future hardware and software components, we have to analyze and investigate a set of workloads that can drive the system design and implementation. In this paper, we aim to profile how large parallel graph applications utilize underlying resources in modern systems (a single server, based on Intel Xeon Ivy Bridge processor). We are especially interested in performance analysis of the memory subsystem and related system bottlenecks caused by parallel graph processing. This understanding can help us in matching the resource demands of the graph processing applications to future system design parameters.

For our study we have chosen the Galois system [18, 11], which was specially designed for parallel processing of irregular algorithms. The Galois framework was successfully applied for parallelizing graph algorithms, which exhibit similar properties. Our profiling approach takes advantage of hardware performance counters implemented in the Ivy Bridge processor. It leverages performance events from the processor Performance Monitoring Units (PMUs), both inside the core (i.e., execution units, L1 and L2 caches) and outside the cores (i.e., L3 cache, Memory Controller).

We analyzed five popular graph algorithms executed on two large datasets. We found that some of the traditional stereotypes portrayed in the literature do not hold, and that many irregular algorithms processing issues have been successfully tackled by a novel run-time support and task scheduling introduced in Galois. This makes the Galois' approach even more attractive and interesting for parallel graph processing. The key findings are the following:

- The available *memory bandwidth is not a bottleneck*: it is not fully utilized;
- Applications achieve a *good processing speedup* with an increased number of cores in a socket;
- The *speedup (scalability)* of graph applications is highly correlated with utilized memory bandwidth;

- The analysis of execution stall cycles in the system shows that graph processing is *memory-latency bound*;
- Graph applications exhibit *high L1 hit rates* and *significant Last-Level Cache (LLC) hit rates*. This reflects a good data locality that could be efficiently exploited.

The remainder of the paper presents our results in more detail.

2. OUR PROFILING APPROACH

In this section, we motivate why we have chosen Galois graph processing framework, outline a set of selected graph algorithms, describe details of our experimental testbed, and introduce our profiling approach based on hardware performance counters.

2.1 Parallel Graph Processing Framework

Why Galois?.

Out of many available graph processing frameworks (e.g., GraphChi[10], GraphLab [12], Apache Giraph [1], and Ligra [22], just to name a few) we chose Galois [18], which was designed as a system for automated parallelization of irregular algorithms. Since graph processing highly resembles irregular algorithms Galois system can be efficiently applied for large graph processing and diverse graph analytics. Galois is a task based parallelization framework, with a graph computation expressed in either vertex or edge based style. It implements coordinated and autonomous execution of these tasks and allows application-specific control of scheduling policies (application-specific task priorities). In the recent study [21], conducted by independent researchers, graph algorithms implemented in Galois have been shown as highly competitive compared to a manually crafted and optimized code (only 1.1-2.5 times performance difference for a diverse set of popular graph algorithms executed on a variety of large datasets).

Selected Graph Applications.

For our profiling study, we selected five popular graph algorithms implemented in Galois [18] with different characteristics: some of them are *i)* traversal, i.e., topology driven, or *ii)* data-driven. Below is a short summary of these algorithms:

- **PageRank:** this algorithm is used by search engines to rank websites for displaying the output results. PageRank offers a way of measuring the importance and popularity of website pages.
- **Breadth First Search (BFS):** this is a typical graph traversal algorithm performed on an undirected, unweighted graph. A goal is to compute a distance from a given source vertex s to each vertex in the graph, i.e., finding all the vertices which are "one hop" away, "two hops" away, etc.
- **Betweenness Centrality (BC):** this algorithm measures the importance of a node in a graph. In social networks analysis, it is actively used for computing the user "influence" index. The vertex index reflects the fraction of shortest paths between all vertices that pass through a given vertex.
- **Connected Components (CC):** this algorithm identifies the maximal sets of vertices reachable from each other in an undirected graph.
- **Approximate Diameter (DIA):** the graph diameter is defined as a maximum length of the shortest paths between any pair of vertices in the graph. The precise (exact) computation of a graph diameter can be prohibitively expensive for large graphs, and this is why many implementations rather provide a diameter approximation.

We chose these graph applications in Galois for a few reasons: *i)* these problems represent popular graph kernels (they can be utilized as modules for solving more complex graph problems), and

ii) the Galois implementation of these kernels was optimized and tuned by the Galois team to produce an efficient code as shown in [18, 21]. Using an optimized and tuned code in our study is very important for profiling and understanding the real system bottlenecks during large graph processing (rather than discovering the bottlenecks related to an inefficiently written code).

2.2 Experimental hardware platform

In our profiling experiments, we use a dual-socket system representing one of the latest Intel Xeon-based processor families:

- **Intel Xeon E5-2660 v2 with Ivy Bridge processor**: each socket supports 10 *two-way hyper-threaded* cores running at 2.2 GHz and 25 MB of last level cache. The system is equipped with 128 GB DDR3-1866 DRAM (i.e., with 4 DDR3 channels).

There are a few challenges in using hardware performance counters for accurately measuring the system hardware memory access latencies and characterizing memory performance. Performance counter measurements are provided in cycles, e.g., stall cycles. However, for energy efficiency many processors are applying DVFS (Dynamic Voltage and Frequency Scaling), where the processor frequency can be increased or decreased dynamically during workload processing depending on the system utilization. Therefore, to preserve a fixed ratio of cycles per time unit we **disable** Turbo Boost and DVFS feature.

We **disable** hyper-threading in our experiments in order to analyze application performance as a function of an increased number of physical cores assigned to application processing. We are especially interested in understanding how these added compute resources translate in the application speedup, and how it changes utilized memory bandwidth in the system.

In this work, we are concentrating on the bottleneck analysis of Galois applications executed on a **single multi-core socket**. In such a way, we can see the best possible multi-threaded code execution with its performance not being impacted by coherency traffic and NUMA considerations[2].

2.3 Profiling system resource usage with hardware performance counters

As a part of our profiling approach we leverage the Performance Monitoring Units (**PMUs**) implemented in Ivy Bridge processors. We select a group of performance events for our analysis as shown in Table 1, using PMUs located inside and outside the cores. Last column provides an exact Intel event names, while the 2nd column shows mnemonic, short names for these events used in the paper.

The first two counters in Table 1 refer to events found in the integrated Memory Controller (**MC**). These events are read for each memory channel. $DRAM_{reqs}$ is used to count the number of outgoing MC requests issued to DRAM, while MC_{cycles} are used for measuring the run time.

Counter 3 measures the number of occupied Line Fill Buffers (**LFB**) in each cycle, from which we deduce the *average LFB occupancy*. LFBs accommodate outstanding memory references (which missed in the L1 data cache) until the corresponding data is retrieved from the memory hierarchy (caches or memory). Hence LFBs may limit the number of cache misses handled by the core.

Counters 4-5 are used to compute achievable *Instructions per Cycle (IPC)*.

Counters 6-11 are used for the analysis of *hit/miss rates in data caches L1,L2, and LLC*.

Counter 12 provides the total number of execution stall cycles

---

[2]Evaluating an additional NUMA impact on the performance of graph processing applications, analyzing bottlenecks and utilized memory bandwidth in multi-socket configuration is a direction for our future work.

incurred by the system. Counter 13 is used to measure the execution stall cycles caused by waiting for the memory system to return data (including caches), while counters 14 and 15 are used to categorize them into stall cycles caused by misses in the data caches L1 and L2, respectively.

Because stores typically do not delay other instructions directly, counters 6-15 concentrate on loads.

1	$DRAM_{reqs}$	ivbep_unc_imc0::UNC_M_CAS_COUNT:ALL
2	MC_{cycles}	ivbep_unc_imc0::UNC_M_DCLOCKTICKS
3	$FB_{occupancy}$	L1D_PEND_MISS:PENDING
4	$Instructions$	ix86arch::INSTRUCTION_RETIRED
5	$Cycles$	ix86arch::UNHALTED_CORE_CYCLES
6	$L1_{loads}$	perf::L1-DCACHE-LOADS
7	$L1_{misses}$	perf::L1-DCACHE-LOAD_MISSES
8	$L2_{loads}$	L2_RQSTS:ALL_DEMAND_DATA_RD
9	$L2_{hits}$	L2_RQSTS:DEMAND_DATA_RD_HIT
10	LLC_{loads}	perf::LLC-LOADS
11	LLC_{misses}	perf::LLC-LOAD-MISSES
12	$Stalls_{total}$	CYCLE_ACTIVITY:CYCLES_NO_EXECUTE
13	$Stalls_{mem}$	CYCLE_ACTIVITY:STALLS_LDM_PENDING
14	$Stalls_{L1}$	CYCLE_ACTIVITY:STALLS_L1D_PENDING
15	$Stalls_{L2}$	CYCLE_ACTIVITY:STALLS_L2_PENDING

Table 1: Selected performance events in Ivy Bridge processor family and memory subsystem.

In order to read performance counters, we use the PAPI [3] framework. PAPI provides a fully programmable, low level interface for dealing with processor hardware counters. We instrumented PAPI into the algorithm's source code in such a way that it initializes the counters when the algorithm starts the computation part (after the setup period). Due to a limited number of programmable PMU events per run, we execute these experiments multiple times for collecting and profiling different event sets.

We use $DRAM_{reqs}$ to count the number of outgoing MC requests issued to DRAM. Modern Intel processors have a memory line size of 64 bytes, thus we multiply the sum of $DRAM_{reqs}$ over the 4 memory channels by 64 to get the byte traffic sent to DRAM. We then calculate memory bandwidth with the following formula:

$$Memory\_BW(bytes/s) = \frac{MEM\_LINE\_SIZE * \sum_{i=0}^{3} DRAM_{reqs}[i]}{Time}$$

For the *memory-bound* application characterization, we use similar definitions to those described in the Intel Optimization Manual [2]. We define the memory bound metric as the cycles where the execution is stalled and there is at least one outstanding memory demand load:

$$Memory\_bound = \frac{Stalls_{mem}}{Cycles}$$

Because Ivy Bridge does not have a counter for the number of execution stalls that happen due to LLC pending loads, we use the following formula for defining $DRAM\_Bound$ metric. This formula approximates the number of cycles where the execution is stalled and there is at least one outstanding memory reference in DRAM:

$$DRAM\_Bound = \frac{Stalls_{L2} * LLC\_miss\_fraction}{Cycles}$$

We utilize LLC_{misses} to estimate $LLC\_miss\_fraction$. We apply a correction factor $WEIGHT$ to reflect the latency ratios between DRAM and LLC. For the Ivy Bridge processor, the empirical factor value is 7 as defined in [2]:

$$LLC\_miss\_fraction = \frac{WEIGHT * LLC_{misses}}{LLC_{hits} + WEIGHT * LLC_{misses}}$$

3. SYSTEM PERFORMANCE CHARACTERIZATION

In order to analyze system bottlenecks while executing graph applications, we need to set realistic expectations on achievable performance (peak resource usage) of the system under study. In particular, we need to measure peak achievable memory bandwidth and memory latency, as well as to characterize how the memory bandwidth and memory access latency change under increased memory traffic issued by multiple cores.

In many traditional cases, peak memory bandwidth is measured using the STREAM benchmark [5]. These measurements characterize memory bandwidth achievable under the *sequential access pattern*. However, real graph applications, processed by current multi-core systems, exhibit a quite different access pattern, where concurrent threads, executed on different cores, utilize the memory system by issuing a set of *independent* memory references. We need to measure the ability of the memory system to serve a high number of *concurrent, random access memory operations* present in current multi-core systems and identify the related system bottlenecks.

To achieve this goal, we utilize an open source *pChase benchmark* [4] which was originally introduced by Pase and Enckl [20] to measure the memory latency and bandwidth of IBM systems. The enhanced version of pChase benchmark was successfully used for characterizing and modeling memory performance of modern multi-core and multi-socket systems [15]. pChase benchmark enables measuring both memory latency and throughput under controlled degree of issued concurrent memory references.

pChase is a memory-latency bound pointer-chasing benchmark. The benchmark creates a pointer chain, such that the content of each element dictates which memory location is read next. This ensures that the next memory reference cannot be issued until the result of the previous one is returned. The benchmark can create *multiple* independent chains per thread, with memory references from different chains issued concurrently.

pChase allocates a pointer chain in a page by page manner: each page is filled before proceeding to the next page. Using this pattern helps in minimizing TLB misses, which is important for accurate measurements of memory access latencies. Inside a page, it creates a chain between all its cache lines (data blocks) in a semi-random manner. However, this pattern is still partly prefetchable because there are partial strides. Only after finishing the page, pChase goes to the next page (it creates 64 pointers with size of 8 bytes in each 4 KB page). For accurate measurements of memory latency, we need to guarantee that all issued pointers are served from memory. To avoid prefetching and caching side effects it is important that **hardware prefetching is disabled** during pChase experiments in the system.

Figure 1 (a) shows achievable memory bandwidth (Y-axis) measured with hardware performance counters as described in Section 2.3. Five different lines reflect measurement results of pChase benchmark executed with a different number of threads (1, 2, 4, 8, and 10), which are processed by available cores in a socket, i.e., 1, 2, 4, 8, and 10 cores. Each thread is executed with an increased number of concurrent chains (X-axis).

The results show that a single pChase thread (executed by 1 core) achieves maximum memory bandwidth of 5.5 GB/s with approximately 9-10 concurrent pointer chains. This result makes sense because for each load miss in L1 cache a Line Fill Buffer (LFB) should be allocated. Modern Intel processors (Sandy Bridge, Ivy Bridge, Haswell) have 10 LFBs per core, and therefore, **a single core is limited to issuing 10 concurrent memory references**.

Figure 1 (a) shows that with two pChase threads and two cores achievable memory bandwidth increases perfectly to 11 GB/s, i.e., 2 times higher. However, for four pChase threads and four cores

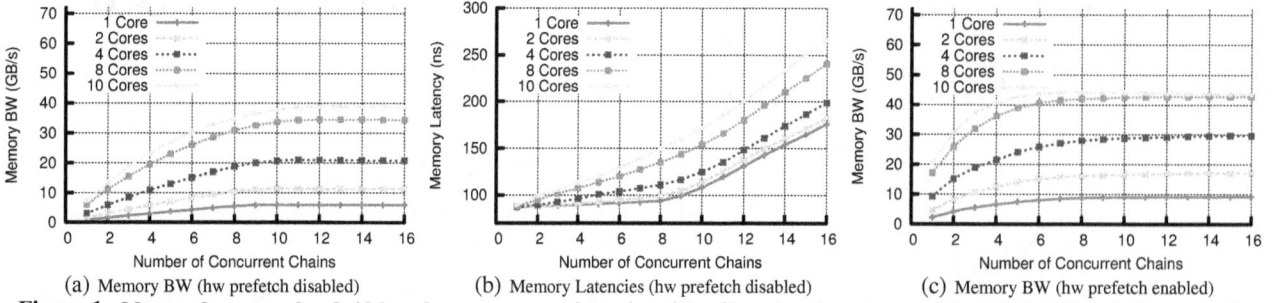

(a) Memory BW (hw prefetch disabled) (b) Memory Latencies (hw prefetch disabled) (c) Memory BW (hw prefetch enabled)

Figure 1: Measured memory bandwidth and memory access latencies with pChase benchmark executed on 1, 2, 4, 8, and 10 cores, where each thread is configured with increasing number of concurrent pointer chains.

Dataset	Brief Description	# Vertices	# Edges	Source	Reference
Twitter	Twitter Follower Graph	61.5 M	1,458 M	http://an.kaist.ac.kr/traces/WWW2010.html	[9]
PLD	Web Hyperlink Graph	39 M	623 M	http://webdatacommons.org/hyperlinkgraph/2012-08/download.html	[16]

Table 2: Datasets: graphs used in the algorithm evaluation.

the peak memory bandwidth is 20 GB/s, and for 10 cores, it is 39 GB/s. This shows that when four cores are issuing memory references at their "maximum speed" an additional system *bottleneck starts to form in the memory subsystem*, most likely in the memory controller. This bottleneck could be related to memory requests queueing on existing 4 memory channels in DDR3.

Figure 1 (b) shows measured memory access latencies by pChase threads (1, 2, 4, 8, and 10 threads) with concurrent pointer chains. A line with a single pChase thread clearly shows the power of memory level parallelism (MLP): memory references from 9-10 concurrent chains could be processed with the same access latency of 86 ns by memory system. After all 10 LFBs are used, the core is stalled until the issued memory references are served by DRAM and the core's LFBs are released and made available for processing next outstanding memory references. Figure 1 (b) exhibits significantly increased memory latencies for pChase configurations with more than 4 concurrent threads. It is indicative of the increased contention in the memory system when a high number of cores are issuing concurrent memory loads. When 10 cores are issuing a maximum number of concurrent requests (with 10 LFBs full) the measured memory access latency is almost doubled. This increased memory latency and contention in memory system explains lower memory bandwidth scaling for higher number of cores in pChase benchmark as shown in Figure 1 (a).

Now, we demonstrate the importance of understanding and evaluating the **performance impact of hardware prefetching** that causes increased memory bandwidth usage as a result. Figure 1 (c) shows the achievable memory bandwidth (Y-axis) measured by pChase benchmark executed with a different number of threads (1, 2, 4, 8, and 10), and a different number of concurrent chains per thread (X-axis). It shows almost double memory bandwidth for pChase executed with a single thread (on 1-core configuration) compared to Figure 1 (a) with hardware prefetch disabled. For a higher number of pChase threads (cores) the amount of additional prefetch memory traffic decreases. Overall, hardware prefetching increases the achievable socket memory bandwidth (when all 10 cores execute pChase threads) by 12.8% and it reaches 44 GB/s.

4. EVALUATION

Graph Datasets.

In this section, we analyze the profiling results of five selected graph applications that are executed using two datasets described in Table 2.

Performance of graph applications may significantly depend on the structure and properties of the graphs used for processing. In this study, we choose to concentrate on processing graphs that belong to a category of *social networks*. Social networks are difficult to partition because they come from non-spatial sources. They are often called "small-world" graphs due to a low diameter. In "small-world" graphs, most nodes can be reached from each other by a limited number of hops. Another property of "small-world" graphs is that their degree distribution follows a power-law, at least asymptotically. Thus, there is a group of vertices with a very high number of connections (edges), while majority of vertices are connected to fewer neighbors. Both datasets *Twitter* and *PLD*, shown in Table 2 and used in the evaluation study, are small-world graphs.

Utilized Memory Bandwidth.

First, we analyze memory bandwidth used by applications under study. We execute the selected graph applications with an increased number of cores in the configuration and profile the utilized memory bandwidth in the system. Figures 2 (a)-(b) show four bars for each profiled application. These bars represent average memory bandwidth measured during the application processing in configurations with 1, 4, 8, and 10 cores on two datasets: *Twitter* and *PLD* respectively. PageRank achieves highest memory bandwidth on both datasets: 27-28 GB/s. BFS and Betweenness Centrality

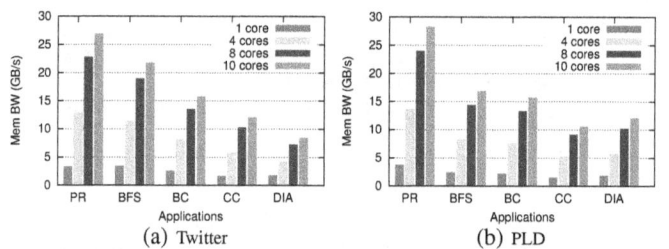

(a) Twitter (b) PLD

Figure 2: Average memory bandwidth (with prefetch enabled).

utilize 16-22 GB/s, followed by Connected Components and Approximate Diameter applications. Our memory characterization with pChase benchmark in Section 3 demonstrates 44 GB/s peak bandwidth on 10 cores with hardware prefetch enabled. Therefore, apparently all five graph applications *do not fully utilize available memory bandwidth* in the system.

While two datasets used in the study are quite different, the measured memory bandwidth scales in a similar way for selected graph applications processed with an increased number of cores. For 10 cores, memory bandwidth is increased 7-8 times compared to 1-core configuration.

Table 3 presents the average LFB occupancy (across configurations with 1, 4, 8, and 10 cores and two processed datasets respectively). Clearly, this data shows that LFBs are not a system bottleneck. Here, they do not cause the memory bandwidth not being fully utilized.

Metrics	PR	BFS	BC	CC	DIA
LFB occupancy	4.7-5.5	3.3-3.5	1.8 -2.2	1.4-1.6	0.2-1
IPC	0.5-0.6	0.5-0.8	0.6-0.9	0.7-1	0.7-1.2

Table 3: **Average LFB occupancy and IPC across 1, 4, 8, and 10 cores configurations and two datasets** *Twitter* **and** *PLD*.

The IPC metric (Instructions per Cycle) is used to assess the computation efficiency of a processor by the application. The achieved IPC is low for all five applications. It is not-surprising: memory-bound applications typically have lower IPC.

Data Locality.

Table 4 presents surprising and unexpected results on measured cache hit rates for L1 and LLC. The measurements are performed with hardware prefetch disabled in order to observe the cache hit rates caused by application memory loads only. We can see that graph applications exhibit *high L1* and *significant LLC hit rates* that indicates a good data locality that could be efficiently exploited [3].

Metrics	PR	BFS	BC	CC	DIA
L1 hit rates	74-77%	89-90%	93-98%	95-96%	96-98%
LLC hit rates	35-39%	34-37%	30-33%	29-31%	10-22%

Table 4: **Cache Hit Rates (L1 and LLC) across 1, 4, 8, and 10 cores configurations and two datasets** *Twitter* **and** *PLD*.

These are very interesting results reflecting that traditional stereotypes about poor data locality do not hold for modern graph processing frameworks executed on the latest Intel multi-core systems. [4].

Application Scalability.

Figures 3 (a)-(b) show the application speedup for processing in configurations with 1, 4, 8, and 10 cores on two datasets: *Twitter* and *PLD* respectively. All the applications (except DIA on *Twitter*) show a very good speedup: 6-8 times is achieved on 10 cores compared to 1 core performance. The analyzed applications do *show a good scalability* as a function of increased compute resources.

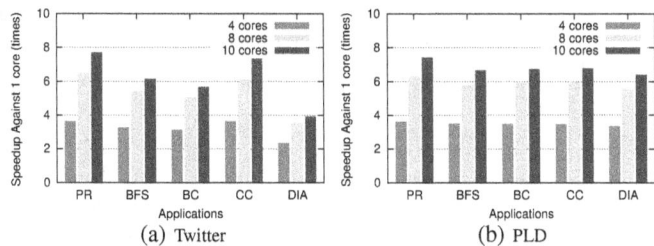

Figure 3: **Application scalability: speedup compared to 1 core-configuration performance (with prefetch enabled).**

By comparing the memory bandwidth scaling trends in Figure 2 with application speedup shown in Figure 3, one can see that these trends are correlated. Figures 4 (a)-(b) show memory bandwidth scaling vs application speedup. X-axis reflect memory bandwidth scaling with respect to 1 core-configuration, while Y-axis show the corresponding application speedup under the same configuration.

The red line in Figures 4 (a)-(b) shows the ideal correlation between memory bandwidth scaling and application speedup. Note, that all the points in these figures follow closely the diagonal line.

---

[3]L2 cache counters had some issues, and we omit reporting their results.

[4]In our experimental system, the size of LLC is 25 MB. Therefore, the application working set for both graphs in Table 2 cannot be cached since they significantly exceed available LLC size.

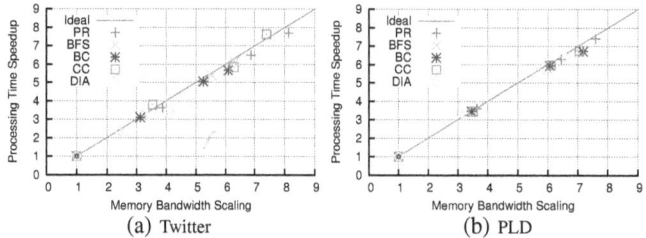

Figure 4: **Memory bandwidth scaling vs application speedup (with prefetch enabled).**

This shows a *very strong (almost ideal) correlation between memory bandwidth scaling and application speedup*.

This leads us to a natural question: does this mean that the application performance is memory bandwidth-bound?

Memory bandwidth-bound or memory latency-bound.

In order to answer this question, we analyze the percentage of execution stall cycles during the application computation, and provide stall cycles' breakdown with respect to system functionality that caused the observed stalls. Figures 5 (a)-(b) show three bars for each profiled application. The red bar represents the total per-

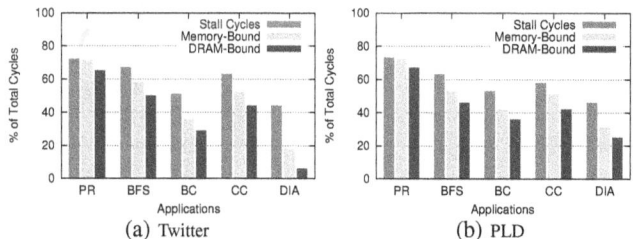

Figure 5: **Execution Stall Cycles (10 cores, with prefetch enabled).**

centage of execution stall cycles during the application processing, i.e., cycles when the corresponding processor core executes nothing. The percentage of stall cycles is high across all the applications: reaching 71% for PageRank and being above 60% for BFS and CC. The next green bar shows that most execution stall cycles are caused by the memory subsystem (except DIA execution on the *Twitter* dataset). We refer the reader to Section 2.3 for definitions of memory-bound and DRAM-bound metrics.

Note, that the memory hierarchy includes a set of caches (L1, L2, and LLC) and DRAM. The last blue bar provides an additional insight that execution stall cycles due to outstanding DRAM references represent the majority of stall cycles in the memory hierarchy (the DIA execution on the *Twitter* dataset suffers from the unbalanced processing across the cores, and the measured averages do not convey the accurate story).

The earlier results (shown in Figures 2 (a)-(b)) indicate that all five graph applications utilize memory bandwidth significantly less than 60% of its peak. Combining these observations with the analysis of stall cycles breakdown, we can conclude that considered graph applications *are not memory bandwidth-bound (as often assumed in literature)* but are rather *memory latency-bound*.

5. RELATED WORK

In the past few years, graph algorithms have received much attention and have become increasingly important for meaningful analysis of large datasets. A number of different graph processing frameworks [1, 10, 12, 18, 22] were offered for optimized parallel and distributed graph processing. This caused multiple efforts [18, 21, 8] in research community to compare the efficiency of these frameworks in order to understand their benefits, applicability, and performance optimization opportunities. For setting a reasonable base for performance expectations, the authors in [21] provide a native, hand-optimized implementation of four algorithms and use them as a reference point. According to the paper results, the Galois system (which we chose for our study) shows very close to optimal performance. In this study [21], the authors refer to either memory system or network being a bottleneck for different frameworks and their configurations. In related studies [13, 6], the authors strive towards creating a benchmark for comparing graph-processing platforms. While many evaluation studies hint on the memory system being a bottleneck, they do not provide a detailed workload analysis of how a memory subsystem is used and what are the causes of system inefficiencies during large graph processing. Our paper aims to provide this missing analysis and insights.

In [17], the authors share a view that graph analytics algorithms exhibit little locality and therefore present significant performance challenges. They asssume that graph-processing algorithms are memory-latency bound and the efficient system for processing large graphs should be able to tolerate higher latencies with higher concurrency. They outline a high-level system design, where multiple nodes (based on commodity processors) communicate over an InfiniBand network, manage high number of concurrent threads, and may efficiently serve memory requests to the global memory space shared across the nodes. The latest HP Labs project "The Machine" [19] promotes a similar high-level system design. The authors in [17] justify the proposed solution by evaluating achievable performance with pointer chasing benchmark, which is similar to pChase that we use in our study for assessing memory processing capabilities. As we have shown in our paper, concurrent independent memory chains generated by pChase could deliver much higher memory bandwidth compared to real graph processing applications that have additional dependencies limiting the available parallelism in the program.

The authors of the paper [7] follow a similar intuition that multithreading should help in hiding memory latency. At the same time, by studying IBM Power7 and Sun Niagara2 they make observations that the number of hardware threads in either platform is not sufficient to fully mask memory latency. Our experiments with graph processing on modern Ivy Bridge-based servers expose a similar behavior that the available concurrency cannot efficiently hide the incurred memory latency in the system.

6. CONCLUSION AND FUTURE WORK

In this paper, we discuss a set of software and hardware challenges accompanying the efficient parallel graph processing, which were highlighted in earlier literature. The core of these issues is the "irregularity" of graph computations which makes the efficient parallelization of graph processing more difficult.

By careful profiling with hardware performance counters available in modern Intel processors, we analyzed how parallel implementation of graph applications use resources of modern multi-core system, in particular a memory system.

We found that Galois graph processing framework executed on latest Intel Ivy Bridge multi-core processor exhibits a good data locality and achieves a good application speedup with an increased number of cores, contrary to traditional past stereotypes, and that a memory bandwidth is not a bottleneck. In our current work, the focus was on the multi-core processor performance and its memory subsystem. In our future work, we plan to analyze a multi-socket configuration and its bottlenecks, as well as the impact of non-unified memory access (NUMA) latencies on performance of large graph processing applications,

Acknowledgements

We are extremely grateful to the Galois team (Andrew Lenharth, Muhammad Amber Hassaan, and Roshan Dathathri) for their generosity in sharing the graph applications' code and patiently answering our numerous questions over the cause of the project. Our sincere thanks to Anirban Mandal, Rob Fowler, and Allan Porterfield (the authors of [15]) for sharing the pChase code and their help with related scripts and questions for measuring the memory system performance.

7. REFERENCES

[1] Apache Giraph. http://giraph.apache.org/.

[2] Intel 64 and ia-32 architectures optimization reference manual. http://www.intel.com/content/dam/www/public/us/en/documents/manuals/64-ia-32-architectures-optimization-manual.pdf.

[3] PAPI: Performance Application Programming Interface. http://icl.cs.utk.edu/papi/.

[4] pChase. https://github.com/maleadt/pChase.

[5] STREAM benchmark. http://www.cs.virginia.edu/stream/.

[6] M. Capotă, T. Hegeman, A. Iosup, A. Prat-Pérez, O. Erling, and P. Boncz. Graphalytics: A big data benchmark for graph-processing platforms. In *Proc. of the GRADES'15*, 2015.

[7] G. Cong and K. Makarychev. Optimizing large-scale graph analysis on a multi-threaded, multi-core platform. In *Proc. of the 2011 IEEE Intl. Parallel & Distributed Processing Symposium (IPDPS)*, 2011.

[8] Y. Guo, A. L. Varbanescu, A. Iosup, C. Martella, and T. L. Willke. Benchmarking graph-processing platforms: A vision. In *Proc. of the 5th ACM/SPEC Intl. Conference on Performance Engineering (ICPE)*, 2014.

[9] H. Kwak, C. Lee, H. Park, and S. Moon. What is Twitter, a Social Network or a News Media? In *Proc. of the 19th International Conference on World Wide Web*, 2010.

[10] A. Kyrola, G. Blelloch, and C. Guestrin. GraphChi: Large-Scale Graph Computation on Just a PC. In *Proc. of the 10th USENIX Symposium on Operating Systems Design and Implementation (OSDI)*, 2012.

[11] A. Lenharth and K. Pingali. Scaling Runtimes for Irregular Algorithms to Large-Scale NUMA Systems . *IEEE Computer Journal*, Aug, 48, 2015.

[12] Y. Low, D. Bickson, J. Gonzalez, C. Guestrin, A. Kyrola, and J. M. Hellerstein. Distributed GraphLab: A Framework for Machine Learning and Data Mining in the Cloud. *Proc. VLDB Endow.*, 5(8), Apr. 2012.

[13] Y. Lu, J. Cheng, D. Yan, and H. Wu. Large-scale Distributed Graph Computing Systems: An Experimental Evaluation. *Proc. VLDB Endow.*, 8(3), 2014.

[14] A. Lumsdaine, D. Gregor, B. Hendrickson, and J. Berry. Challenges in Parallel Graph Processing. *Parallel Processing Letters*, 17(1), 2007.

[15] A. Mandal, R. Fowler, and A. Porterfield. Modeling Memory Concurrency for Multi-Socket Multi-Core Systems. In *Proc. of Intl. Symposium on Performance Analysis of Systems and Software (ISPASS)*, 2010.

[16] R. Meusel, O. Lehmberg, C. Bizer, and S. Vigna. Extracting the Hyperlink Graphs from the Common Crawl. http://webdatacommons.org/hyperlinkgraph.

[17] J. Nelson, B. Myers, A. H. Hunter, P. Briggs, L. Ceze, C. Ebeling, D. Grossman, S. Kahan, and M. Oskin. Crunching large graphs with commodity processors. In *Proc. of the 3rd USENIX Conference on Hot Topic in Parallelism*, 2011.

[18] D. Nguyen, A. Lenharth, and K. Pingali. A lightweight infrastructure for graph analytics. In *Proc.of the 24th Symposium on Operating Systems Principles, (SOSP)*, 2013.

[19] K. Packard. The Machine Architecture. http://keithp.com/blogs/the_machine_architecture.

[20] D. M. Pase and M. A. Eckl. Performance of the IBM System x3755. *Technical Report, IBM, August*, 2006.

[21] N. Satish, N. Sundaram, M. M. A. Patwary, J. Seo, J. Park, M. A. Hassan, S. Sengupta, Z. Yin, and P. Dubey. Navigating the Maze of Graph Analytics Frameworks Using Massive Graph Datasets. In *Proc. of Intl. Conference on Management of Data, (SIGMOD)*, 2014.

[22] J. Shun and G. E. Blelloch. Ligra: A Lightweight Graph Processing Framework for Shared Memory. In *Proc. of the 18th ACM SIGPLAN Symposium on Principles and Practice of Parallel Programming, (PPoPP)*, 2013.

Asking "What?", Automating the "How?": The Vision of Declarative Performance Engineering

Jürgen Walter
University of Würzburg
97074 Würzburg Germany

Andre van Hoorn
University of Stuttgart
70569 Stuttgart Germany

Heiko Koziolek
ABB Corporate Research
68526 Ladenburg Germany

Dušan Okanović
University of Stuttgart
70569 Stuttgart Germany

Samuel Kounev
University of Würzburg
97074 Würzburg Germany

ABSTRACT

Over the past decades, various methods, techniques, and tools for modeling and evaluating performance properties of software systems have been proposed covering the entire software life cycle. However, the application of performance engineering approaches to solve a given user concern is still rather challenging and requires expert knowledge and experience. There are no recipes on how to select, configure, and execute suitable methods, tools, and techniques allowing to address the user concerns. In this paper, we describe our vision of Declarative Performance Engineering (DPE), which aims to decouple the description of the user concerns to be solved (performance questions and goals) from the task of selecting and applying a specific solution approach. The strict separation of "what" versus "how" enables the development of different techniques and algorithms to automatically select and apply a suitable approach for a given scenario. The goal is to hide complexity from the user by allowing users to express their concerns and goals without requiring any knowledge about performance engineering techniques. Towards realizing the DPE vision, we discuss the different requirements and propose a reference architecture for implementing and integrating respective methods, algorithms, and tooling.

1. INTRODUCTION

During the life cycle of a software system, performance analysts continuously need to provide answers to and act on performance-relevant questions about response times, resource utilization, bottlenecks, trends, anomalies, etc. Their everyday work includes questions such as [7]: *"What performance would a new service or application deployed on the infrastructure exhibit and how much resources should be allocated to it?", "What would be the performance impact of adding a new component or upgrading an existing component as services and applications evolve?", "If an application experiences a load spike or a change of its workload profile, how would this affect the system performance?", "What would be the effect of migrating a service or an application component from one physical server to another?".* Despite advances in measurement-based and model-based performance engineering (concerning compatibility, reuse, and modeling convenience)[3, 5], it is still challenging to apply such tools in practice without having extensive knowledge and experience in performance engineering. Additionally, the performance of a software system may be evaluated with different techniques over time, each having specific parameters and capabilities. Searching for solutions, performance analysts typically follow the process depicted in Figure 1 to find an answer to a given performance query. Starting with a performance query (specifying a specific question that needs to be answered), the process consists of the choice of an analysis approach, its parametrization, processing, result filtering and interpretation. The application of the process to answer such queries is complex, time-consuming and error-prone—even for performance experts. To illustrate this, we consider a software service evolution example, focusing on the response time of a single service. At system design-time, predicting the response time of the service involves complex decisions such as the selection of a suitable modeling formalism (predictive formalisms, like layered queueing networks or queueing Petri nets, or architecture-level modeling languages, such as UML MARTE, PCM [2], or DML [11], or

ICPE'16, March 12 - 18, 2016, Delft, Netherlands

© 2016 Copyright held by the owner/author(s). Publication rights licensed to ACM.
ISBN 978-1-4503-4080-9/16/03...$15.00

DOI: http://dx.doi.org/10.1145/2851553.2858662

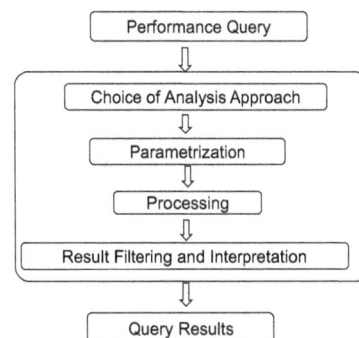

Figure 1: Performance Query Answering Process

even intermediate approaches like CSM [16] or KLAPER [8]), the choice of modeling granularity (e.g., black box, coarse-grained, or fine-grained), solvers and solution technique (e.g., Markovian analytical solvers, product-form solution or simulation-based solvers [4]), and the derivation of model parameters. These decisions affect the modeling accuracy, as well as the speed and overhead of the analysis, and require a lot of expert knowledge. At system testing and deployment time, there is the opportunity to evaluate the service response time by conducting performance measurements on the real system. However, again complex decisions about the measurement configuration have to be made, for example regarding sufficient experiment run length, the configuration of ramp-up time, and the choice of an appropriate instrumentation granularity allowing to obtain the required measurement data. During system operation, it is often also required to predict the effects of possible system reconfigurations or the expected impact of an increased or varied workload mix. This enables proactive resource management but requires modeling techniques that support predicting future system states. The response time query remains the same, however, the analysis approach and parametrization have to be tuned for a fast response. Another source for answering performance queries are historical monitoring logs. The answering process then parameterizes a database request.

In this paper, we describe our vision of Declarative Performance Engineering (DPE) aiming to provide a simplified and unified performance engineering interface. The idea is to use a declarative language allowing to specify performance queries independent of the various approaches that can be applied in the context of the considered system to obtain the required information. The processing of a performance query can be automated and optimized, while hiding complexity from the user. Besides the setup challenges described in the example, the filtering and interpretation of results provided by applying performance engineering techniques can be automated. Further, our approach enables a convergence of model-based and measurement-based analysis as demanded in [15]. Agile software development processes—including the DevOps paradigm—have received increasing attention in the last years [1]. Their implied shorter release cycles raise the need for novel unified interfaces for applying performance engineering techniques that hide complexity from the user and automate the performance analysis process, such that performance engineering techniques can be applied efficiently by developers throughout the software engineering life cycle [5]. Our vision, described in this paper, proposes an approach for addressing this need.

The remainder of this paper is organized as follows: At first, Section 2 formulates the problem statement, which is the basis for our DPE vision described in Section 3. After discussing the vision, we propose a realization approach analyzing the various requirements and proposing a possible architecture for building DPE tools in Section 4. Section 5 reviews our previous work and related work that will serve as foundation of DPE. Finally, Section 6 provides a conclusion and an outlook.

2. PROBLEM STATEMENT

Existing performance engineering techniques require expert knowledge to apply them correctly. Different performance analysis techniques are applicable at the various stages of the software life cycle. For performance engineering, currently there is no generalized layer or a unified interface that provides:

- A high-level language allowing to specify goals and queries independent of the solution approach (e.g., using measurement-based or model-based techniques)
- Decision support for the selection of an appropriate performance engineering technique and tool for answering a performance query, considering functional and non-functional requirements (e.g., system perturbation) as part of the selection and parametrization of performance engineering techniques

3. THE VISION OF DECLARATIVE PERFORMANCE ENGINEERING

The high-level objective of Declarative Performance Engineering (DPE) is to support system developers and administrators in performance-relevant decision making. Performance analysts formulate their concerns using a declarative domain-specific language. We aim to reduce the currently huge abstraction gap between the level on which performance-relevant concerns are formulated and the level on which performance engineering techniques are typically applied. The goal of DPE is to enable the formulation and answering of performance-relevant questions and goals for a software system in a human-understandable manner by using a high-level *declarative language* to interact with performance engineering tools. The proposed language processing exploits a high degree of automation through a corresponding interpretation and execution infrastructure, which builds on established low-level performance evaluation methods, techniques, and tools. The core characteristics of the DPE vision are:

- Enabling the performance analyst to *declaratively* specify *what* performance-relevant questions need to be answered without being concerned about *how* they should be answered. Particularly, the declarative language is independent of the performance evaluation approach. This enables the integration of both, measurement-based and model-based analysis.
- Hiding complexity from the user by automating the selection and execution of a solution approach, which may involve the application of multiple performance engineering techniques. For maximum flexibility, it should be possible to process the results from the various applied techniques manually, semi-automatically, or by using full automation.
- Supporting the whole software system life cycle, including design, operation, and evolution. In particular, we consider modern software development paradigms, where development and operation merge (DevOps) [1].
- Supporting extensibility of the declarative language and the implementation platform and respective tools.

4. DPE APPROACH

The DPE vision requires an architecture for building frameworks and tools that allow to reach the targeted goals. Figure 2 provides an overview of our envisioned DPE archi-

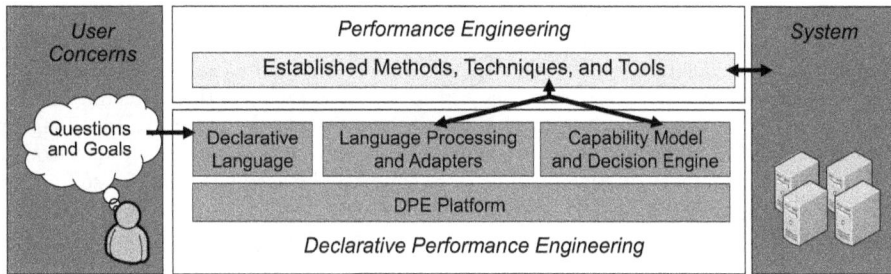

Figure 2: Declarative Performance Engineering Architecture

tecture. It comprises a declarative performance evaluation language, a capability model and a decision engine for solution techniques, as well as language processing algorithms all being part of the DPE platform. In the following, we explain the specific objectives for these components in more detail.

4.1 Declarative Language

The DPE language should be easy to adopt and understandable by software developers and administrators, as well as by non-technicians. We aim to cover a wide range of performance concerns. In particular, we plan to support the following types of language statements:

- **System element queries** enable self-description of the system concerning its elements, e.g., *"What services or resources are provided by the system?"*.
- **User-controlled queries** enable asking questions about the system performance.
  1. *Basic queries* (e.g., *"What is the response time of service x [for workload y] [at time z]?"*)
  2. *Degree-of-freedom queries* or exploration space queries (e.g., *"What is the utilization of server x for [100, 150 or 200] users?"*)
  3. *Exploration space search queries* (e.g., scalability questions about the maximum number of users without SLA violation or bottleneck detection)
- **Temporal queries** enable asking questions concerning observations based on monitoring the system over an extended period of time, e.g., trends, forecasting, and anomaly detection.
- **Sensitivity queries** evaluate the effect/influence of a service or resource, e.g., *"influence of service x on the utilization of resource y"*.
- **Goal definitions** allow to describe user level goals. They provide a basis to derive concrete actions in order to achieve a specified goal. Goals can be in conflict to each other. Hence, the optional specification of priorities or criticality levels should be supported.

For some scenarios, it is not sufficient to solely specify the desired result but also to constrain the way of how results are obtained. This is important given that system perturbation, solution time, and accuracy may differ significantly depending on the applied performance engineering technique. Measuring the performance of a system may have side effects on the system operation. While for some scenarios, it may be acceptable to generate additional load on the system for better measurement precision, in others it may be required to minimize overheads. Hence, the language should support expressing such *tradeoffs*.

4.2 Language Processing and Adapters

To process performance queries expressed using the declarative language, the DPE platform should support plugging in adapters for different performance evaluation approaches. The adapter interface shall be generic and centered around the needs of the language. The adapters control any monitoring or processing required by the respective performance evaluation approach. The requirements on the adapter design are:

- **Automated processing**: Experiment design, load script generation, and experiment execution are carried out automatically.
- **Optimized processing**: The performance query processing shall be efficiently parameterized for the specific scenario. It should take into account user concerns about accuracy, time-to-result, and system perturbation.
- **Light-weight design**: The complexity of tool adapters shall be minimized. Therefore, the generic composition of complex results out of sub-results should be integrated into the language processing.

4.3 Capability Model and Decision Engine

The idea of DPE is to integrate multiple solution adapters. At a first step, it has to be evaluated if an adapter is able to deduce the requested metrics. In case multiple adapters are capable to solve a given query, the choice should be based on a matching of tool and query capabilities. For model-based analysis, there exist many analysis approaches optimized for certain model capabilities (e.g., independence of model subparts, open or closed workload, applied queueing strategies, etc.). Furthermore, the best solution technique also depends on the requested metric. For example, if the performance analyst is solely interested in aggregated values, faster approaches, like product-form solutions, can be applied. Besides improving efficiency under the constraint of preserving accuracy, there are approximation procedures, like fluid analysis, which trade off analysis speed versus the cost of accuracy.

We propose to introduce a *decision engine* that, for a given language statement, automatically selects from the set of plugged in tool adapters, an appropriate one to solve the respective query. The aim of the decision engine is to decide based on matching statement requirements against the tool capabilities. This requires a *capability model* of each tool, capturing its functional and non-functional properties. In particular, capturing information relevant for the aforementioned tradeoffs between accuracy, time-to-result, and system perturbation shall be supported. The capability model will be designed using a hierarchical structure. We propose the use of at least one abstract capability layer where a general model, e.g., for monitoring tools, can be specified. Then, a capability model for a concrete monitoring tool instance can inherit from the abstract monitoring capability model. This enables the reuse of capability specifications for other monitoring tools. The abstract capability models can be overwritten by a concrete tool capability model in case an adapter is not yet implemented.

5. RELATED WORK

In our previous work, we proposed initial query languages and frameworks to automate the application of performance analysis techniques and to parameterize, execute, and filter results accordingly. These are MAMBA [6] for measurement-based analysis and DQL [7] for model-based analysis. However, they consider measurement and model-based analysis separately, instead of, for example, using measurements where available, while resorting to model predictions where measurements are not feasible. Further, these languages currently only support basic queries, no complex or composite queries, e.g., for bottleneck analysis. Besides expressing performance queries, system goal specifications can be declaratively described in the form of service level agreements (SLAs), e.g., based on standards such as WSLA, WSOL, WS-Agreement, SLA⋆, and SLAng [13]. Some of the named approaches assess the SLA conformity of runtime performance properties based on reactive approaches. However, these SLA languages are not yet connected to proactive reconfiguration mechanisms that prevent SLA violations, as done in our preliminary work in [10]. Further, we intend to include several related approaches for implementing our vision, from which we want to name a few. To reduce the overhead of creating model transformations in performance engineering, intermediate models like CSM [16] and KLAPER [8] address the N-to-M problem. Obviously, experiment automation like initialization bias detection [9] should be included. Moreover, degrees-of-freedom exploration can be optimized. Efficient experiment selection can reduce the total number of experimental setups to analyze as performed in [14].

6. CONCLUSION AND NEXT STEPS

Throughout the past decades, various established methods, techniques, and tools for modeling and evaluating performance properties have been proposed. However, the application of performance engineering techniques to address a given user concern is challenging and requires expert knowledge. In this vision paper, we described the Declarative Performance Engineering (DPE) paradigm aiming to decouple the description of user concerns to be solved (performance questions and goals) from the various possible techniques and solution approaches. We envision an automated selection and execution of a performance engineering approach tailored to address a given user concern. Towards accomplishing the DPE vision, we discussed the major requirements and proposed a possible architecture for building respective analysis tools and frameworks. We expect DPE to impact all fields in computer science where performance plays an important role, especially for real-time systems and cloud computing. Our architecture enables to already use sub parts, e.g., the decision support, the au-

tomated parametrization, or the result filtering. As next steps, we will continue our joint work on DPE based on a project funded by the German Research Foundation (DFG). Further, we will continue pushing the DPE vision within the SPEC DevOps community. In a long term perspective, the tools to answer performance questions and to process concerns can be used as a basis for self-aware computing systems [12].

Acknowledgments: This work is supported by the German Research Foundation (DFG) in the Priority Programme "DFG-SPP 1593: Design For Future—Managed Software Evolution" (HO 5721/1-1 and KO 3445/15-1) and by the Research Group of the Standard Performance Evaluation Corporation (SPEC).

7. REFERENCES

[1] L. Bass, I. Weber, and L. Zhu. *DevOps: A Software Architect's Perspective.* Addison-Wesley Professional, 2015.

[2] S. Becker, H. Koziolek, and R. Reussner. The Palladio component model for model-driven performance prediction. *Elsevier Journal of Systems and Software (JSS)*, 2009.

[3] A. B. Bondi. *Foundations of Software and System Performance Engineering: Process, Performance Modeling, Requirements, Testing, Scalability, and Practice.* Addison-Wesley Professional, 2014.

[4] F. Brosig, P. Meier, S. Becker, A. Koziolek, H. Koziolek, and S. Kounev. Quantitative evaluation of model-driven performance analysis and simulation of component-based architectures. *IEEE Transactions on Software Engineering (TSE)*, 41(2):157–175, 2015.

[5] A. et al. Performance-oriented DevOps: A research agenda. Technical Report SPEC-RG-2015-01, SPEC Research Group — DevOps Performance Working Group, Standard Performance Evaluation Corporation (SPEC), 2015.

[6] S. Frey, A. van Hoorn, R. Jung, W. Hasselbring, and B. Kiel. MAMBA: A measurement architecture for model-based analysis. Technical Report TR-1112, Department of Computer Science, University of Kiel, Germany, 2011.

[7] F. Gorsler, F. Brosig, and S. Kounev. Performance queries for architecture-level performance models. In *Proceedings of the 5th ACM/SPEC International Conference on Performance Engineering (ICPE 2014)*, pages 99–110. ACM, 2014.

[8] V. Grassi, R. Mirandola, and A. Sabetta. Filling the gap between design and performance/reliability models of component-based systems: A model-driven approach. *Journal of Systems and Software*, 80(4):528–558, 2007.

[9] K. Hoad, S. Robinson, and R. Davies. Automating warm-up length estimation. *Journal of the Operational Research Society*, 61(9):1389–1403, 2010.

[10] N. Huber, A. van Hoorn, A. Koziolek, F. Brosig, and S. Kounev. Modeling run-time adaptation at the system architecture level in dynamic service-oriented environments. *Service Oriented Computing and Applications Journal (SOCA)*, 8(1):73–89, 2014.

[11] S. Kounev, F. Brosig, and N. Huber. The Descartes Modeling Language. Technical report, Department of Computer Science, University of Wuerzburg, 2014.

[12] S. Kounev, X. Zhu, J. O. Kephart, and M. Kwiatkowska. Model-driven Algorithms and Architectures for Self-Aware Computing Systems (Dagstuhl Seminar 15041). *Dagstuhl Reports*, 5(1):164–196, 2015.

[13] K. Kritikos, B. Pernici, P. Plebani, C. Cappiello, M. Comuzzi, S. Benrernou, I. Brandic, A. Kertész, M. Parkin, and M. Carro. A survey on service quality description. *ACM Comput. Surv.*, 46(1):1:1–1:58, July 2013.

[14] D. Westermann, R. Krebs, and J. Happe. Efficient experiment selection in automated software performance evaluations. In *Proceedings of the 8th European Conference on Computer Performance Engineering*, EPEW'11, pages 325–339, Berlin, Heidelberg, 2011. Springer-Verlag.

[15] M. Woodside, G. Franks, and D. C. Petriu. The future of software performance engineering. In *2007 Future of Software Engineering (FOSE '07)*, pages 171–187. IEEE, 2007.

[16] M. Woodside, D. C. Petriu, D. B. Petriu, H. Shen, T. Israr, and J. Merseguer. Performance by unified model analysis (puma). In *Proceedings of the 5th International Workshop on Software and Performance (WOSP '05)*, pages 1–12. ACM, 2005.

Predicting the System Performance by Combining Calibrated Performance Models of its Components

A Preliminary Study

Thomas Begin
LIP, CNRS - ENS Lyon - UCB Lyon 1 - Inria 5668
France
DIVA Lab, University of Ottawa
Canada

Alexandre Brandwajn
Baskin School of Engineering
University of California Santa Cruz
PALLAS International Corporation
San Jose, CA, USA

ABSTRACT

In this paper we consider the problem of combining calibrated performance models of system components in order to predict overall system performance. We focus on open workload system models, in which, under certain conditions, obtaining and validating the overall system performance measures can be a simple application of Little's law. We discuss the conditions of applicability of such a simple validation methodology, including examples of successful application, as well as examples where this approach fails.

Additionally, we propose to analyze the deviations between the model predictions and system measurements, so as to decide if they correspond to "measurement noise" or if an important system component has not been correctly represented. This approach can be used as an aid in the design of validated system performance models.

Keywords

performance models; component-level models; overall system performance; validation; calibration.

1. INTRODUCTION

Faced with increasingly complex system architectures, an obvious and commonly used approach is to characterize the behavior of selected system components deemed crucial to overall system performance. These performance components have then to be combined in a global system model so as to produce the desired overall system performance characterization. A number of methods have been employed to effect such combination.

For closed system models, fixed-point iterations (e.g. [18]), state-dependent equivalence (e.g. [8]), and near- decomposability (e.g. [11]) are just a very partial list of methods that were employed in this area. The resulting overall performance model must then be validated against real or simulated system performance measurements. In an open system, under certain conditions, obtaining and validating the

overall system performance measures can be a simple application of Little's law.

In this paper, we focus on open workload system models, but several aspects of our discussion are applicable to closed systems as well. We discuss the conditions of applicability of such simple validation methodology using Little's law, including examples of successful application, as well as examples where this approach fails. Even if the applicability conditions are met, some degree of deviation between the model and the system measurements is expected. We propose to analyze these deviations, so as to decide if they correspond to simple "measurement noise" or if an important system component has not been correctly represented. As such, this approach can be used as an aid in the design of validated system performance models.

In the next section, we review related work. In Section 3 we discuss the simple use of Little's law in open models and its applicability conditions. Section 4 is devoted to examples of application of this methodology, and in Section 5 we discuss the use of this approach to discover and model hidden system components. Section 6 concludes this paper.

2. RELATED WORK

From the early days of computer system and network models, it was clear that "divide and conquer" approaches may be beneficial when dealing with complex systems. This gave rise to many flavors of decomposition approaches where different parts of a system are analyzed in isolation (X-model [14], Kühn [15], near- decomposability [11], Norton equivalent [10, 4], equivalence and decomposition, etc). For instance, it is usually considerably easier to analyze the I/O subsystem separately from the complexity of CPU priority scheduling when analyzing the performance of a computer system.

Of course, we need a way to combine the results of the analysis of decomposed subsystems to obtain the desired overall system performance metrics. Depending on the decomposition approach used, such "assembly" of the decomposed models may be accomplished by replacing a whole subsystem by a simple delay representing the average time a task spends in the subsystem (X-model). In other approaches, the performance of a subsystem may be represented as a state-dependent server (Norton, near- decomposability, equivalence and decomposition). As shown in [9], many of these approaches may be viewed in a unified way as relying (implicitly or explicitly) on the use of marginal and conditional probabilities, which provides, at least in theory,

ICPE'16, March 12–18, 2016, Delft, Netherlands.
© 2016 ACM. ISBN 978-1-4503-4080-9/16/03. . . $15.00
DOI: http://dx.doi.org/10.1145/2851553.2858658

a clean way to assemble the results of the analysis of decomposed subsystems.

Present-day systems often comprise a number of components that work together to process incoming requests. As mentioned above, it may be easier to model the performance of each individual component than directly that of the whole system. The component modeling may be performed using a constructive approach requiring knowledge and expertise, or using a "black box" approach, which parameterizes predefined models by observing the relationships between the component input and output parameters [6, 2, 3]. Several approaches have been proposed in the literature for combining component-level models into system-level performance.

In the context of disk I/O requests, a case in point is the work done by Ganger and Patt [12]. At that time, accurate and sound models have been proposed for I/O subsystem performance. But it was unclear how the improvements of subsystems will be reflected in the overall system performance. Among other things, the authors stress that looking to improve the overall system performance is not directly the same as improving the I/O subsystem performance. This is because composing the performance of subsystems is not always straightforward.

The issue of predicting performance of a system based on the behavior of its components has also been addressed in the area of autonomic systems. Harbaoui et al. have proposed a framework to predict the performance of a target configuration when planning a system reconfiguration [13]. They decompose a distributed application into black boxes, identifying the queue model for each black box and assembling these models into a queueing network according to the candidate target configuration.

More recently, Kraft et al. have studied the response times experienced by disk I/O requests in consolidated virtualized environments [16, 17]. The authors have shown how to extrapolate the model of a single Virtual Machine (VM) into a model to predict the degree of contention when multiple VMs are accessing a remote storage server.

These previous works have emphasized the need and proposed a specific-area solution to the problem of combining models of components to represent the performance of a system. In this paper, we attempt to propose a more general framework for this problem.

3. FROM LOCAL TO GLOBAL SYSTEM PERFORMANCE

We concentrate on systems in which requests (tasks, transactions, jobs) arrive from an outside source, are processed by the system and eventually depart from the system. We refer to such systems as "open systems".

The system considered consists of K known components (see Figure 1) that are deemed important with respect to a specific average performance measure F (e.g. mean number of requests in system (L), mean response time (R) or loss probability (P)). We assume that we have a set of I system-level measurement points $\{x_S^{exp}, f_S^{exp}\}, i = 1, \ldots, I$, where x_S^{exp} denotes the mean measured system throughput, i.e., the number of requests successfully processed by the system per time unit, and f_S^{exp} is the corresponding value of the selected performance measure. We use the superscript exp to refer to measured values and the superscript mod to denote values obtained from a model. We assume that calibrated models have been developed for each of the K system

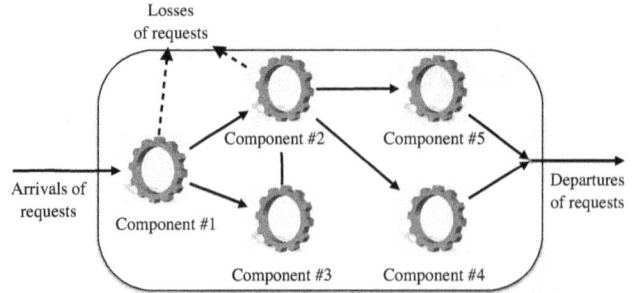

Figure 1: A system with $K = 5$ components.

components. Our K component models can be viewed as a set of K functions $f_k^{mod}(x_k^{mod})$ with $k = 1, \ldots, K$.

In order to be able to use our component models to assess overall system performance, we must know the relationship between the overall system throughput X_S and the component throughputs X_k, $k = 1, \ldots, K$. This is an essential assumption. In practice, this relationship will be known from the nature of the system or from measurements. Another essential assumption is that a given request occupies a single component at a time.

Given this assumption, obviously, if the selected performance measure is the mean number of requests L, the overall mean number of requests in the system should be equal to the sum of the mean numbers obtained from the component models for throughput levels that correspond to the measured system throughput levels $\{x_S^{exp}\}_i$.

If the selected performance measure is the mean response time R, Little's formula [7] can be used to obtain the overall mean response time for arbitrary values of system throughput x_S^{mod}:

$$r_S^{mod} = \frac{\sum_{k=1}^{K} (r_k^{mod} x_k^{mod})}{x_S^{mod}} \qquad (1)$$

Clearly, to attempt to validate this approach, we select system throughput values $x_S^{mod} = x_S^{exp}$ and we compare the mean response time values obtained from Formula (1) with those known from measurements r_S^{exp} for the same values of system throughput.

If the loss probability is the selected performance measure, the overall loss probability can be expressed as:

$$p_S^{mod} = \frac{1}{1 + \frac{x_S^{mod}}{\sum_{k=1}^{K} x_k^{mod} \cdot p_k^{mod}/(1 - p_k^{mod})}} \qquad (2)$$

Formula (2) allows us to assess the overall loss probability in terms of component-level loss probabilities and request throughputs.

As mentioned earlier, for our approach to work, we need to know the relationship between the overall system throughput and the throughputs of individual components. If this relationship is not obvious or known from the structure of the system, we may be able to determine it using measurements. To this end, we need at least one set of reasonably synchronized measurements of x_S^{exp} and x_k^{exp}, $k = 1, \ldots, K$. If only one set of synchronized measurements is available, the best one can do is to assume that the observed ratios x_k^{exp}/x_S^{exp} carry over to other workload levels, i.e., remain constant as the overall system throughput varies. With multiple measurement points, one can check if this is indeed the case or possibly try to infer a more involved relationship between throughputs.

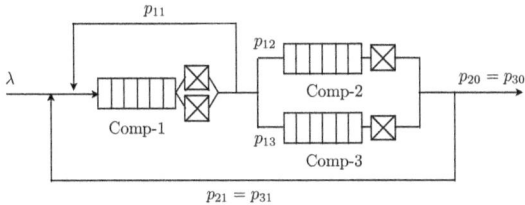

Figure 2: A centralized system architecture.

Table 1: Parameters used for Figure 2.

Comp-1	C_1	Number of servers	2
	mst_1	Mean service time	1
	cvs_1	Coefficient of variation for service time	3
	p_{11}	Probability of returning to Comp-1 upon request completion	0.3
	p_{12}	Probability of going to Comp-2 upon request completion	0.6
	p_{13}	Probability of going to Comp-3 upon request completion	0.1
Comp-2	C_2	Number of servers	1
	mst_2	Mean service time	2
	cvs_2	Coefficient of variation for service time	2
	p_{20}	Probability of leaving the system upon request completion	0.3
	p_{21}	Probability of going to Comp-1 upon request completion	0.7
Comp-3	C_3	Number of servers	1
	mst_3	Mean service time	10
	cvs_3	Coefficient of variation for service time	0.5
	p_{30}	Probability of leaving the system upon request completion	0.3
	p_{31}	Probability of going to Comp-1 upon request completion	0.7

Note that the throughput ratios discussed above are analogous to the so-called visit ratios in analytical modeling methods such as Mean Value Analysis [19, 20] or BCMP theorem [5]. With few exceptions, in general solution methods, these ratios are taken to be constant. Additionally, the general analytical solutions require specific restrictions on the types of service discipline and service time distributions in order to be applicable. On the other hand, our approach requires no specific assumptions on service disciplines and distributions or arrivals of requests (even if we may assume that the throughput ratios remain constant).

4. ILLUSTRATIVE CASES

4.1 Successful case

In this first case we focus on the mean response time, R_S, for a system with a centralized architecture and a total of $K = 3$ components, one of which, is referred to as the central server(s) and the remaining K-1 components are referred as the peripheral servers. Our goal is to study how well R_S can be determined from correctly calibrated performance models of the components.

Centralized architectures are common in telecommunication and computer network. In our example, we assume that the incoming tasks, representing the system workload, require first a burst of service from the central server(s). Upon completion of a service burst, a task may request another service burst at the central server(s) or it may need service from one of the peripheral servers. Upon completion of service at a peripheral server, a task may require another round of processing at the central server or it may leave the system.

For the sake of convenience and reproducibility, the "measured" values of the overall system performance, $\{x_S^{exp}, r_S^{exp}\}_i$, $i = 1, \ldots, I$ as well as those of its components, were obtained using a discrete-event simulation. The system simulated is the machine repairman network shown in Figure 2. The task arrivals are represented through a Poisson process of rate λ. The central server(s) and the peripherals are each represented by a single queue, labeled Comp-1, Comp-2 and Comp-3, respectively. Table 1 gives the details of the simulated system parameters. Thus, in our system: (i) 30% of tasks require another burst of service at the central server(s) after completing a service burst ($p_{11} = 0.3$), (ii) two requests can be processed simultaneously at the central servers ($C_1 = 2$), (iii) the service time of Comp-2 is considerably faster than at Comp-3 ($mst_3 = 5.mst_2$), (iv) the variability of service times is much larger for Comp-2 than for Comp-3 (although the mean time is less) ($cvs_2 = 4.cvs_3$), (v) 70% of requests return to the central servers queue upon completion of service at a peripheral server ($p_{21} = p_{31} = 0.7$).

As discussed above, we assume that accurate and calibrated models have been developed for each of the 3 components (Comp-1, Comp-2 and Comp-3) of the system. In

other words, the model of the k-th component (Comp-k) provides a function $r_k^{mod}(x_k^{mod})$ that returns a predicted level of mean response time for any given value of the mean throughput at the given component. Note that we used the high-level modeling approach [6] to find calibrated models for the components. In our case, these happen to be based on queueing theory but any other approach would work provided that the resulting models are accurate. Figure 3 illustrates the accuracy of the component models by showing the "measured" and the model-predicted performance for each system component. We observe that our component models match well the "measured" performance values throughout the range of workload values under consideration.

Having in hand a calibrated model for each of the system components, we can now use Formula (1) to determine the mean response time for the whole system as a function of the mean system throughput. All we need is to know are the throughput ratio of each component, namely x_k^{exp}/x_S^{exp}, $k = 1, \ldots, K$. These quantities may be smaller or larger than 1 as they represent the relative rate of request arrivals at component k as compared to that at the system level. In our example, it is easy to compute these ratios from the system topology (see Figure 2). The corresponding values are $\frac{1}{(1-p_{11})(1-p_{21})} = 4.762$, $\frac{p_{12}}{(1-p_{11})(1-p_{21})} = 2.857$ and $\frac{p_{13}}{(1-p_{11})(1-p_{31})} = 0.4762$ for component Comp-1, Comp-2 and Comp-3, respectively. As mentioned in Section 3, in other cases, these values can be discovered thanks to synchronized measurements of throughput. Next, in order to obtain r_S^{mod} as a function of x_S^{mod}, we simply "convert" any given value of x_S^{mod} into values of x_k^{mod}, $k = 1, \ldots, K$ by multiplying it by the respective throughput ratio, and then we call the component models to compute the values of r_k^{mod} associated to x_S^{mod}, and thereby applying Formula (1). We performed this step for many levels of workload, including low and high levels. Figure 4 shows the resulting overall system performance values obtained using this approach. Clearly, and perhaps not surprisingly, we observe that the performance of the composed model $\{x_S^{mod}, r_S^{mod}\}$ match very well those measured in the simulation $\{x_S^{exp}, r_S^{exp}\}$, validating the proposed approach for this example.

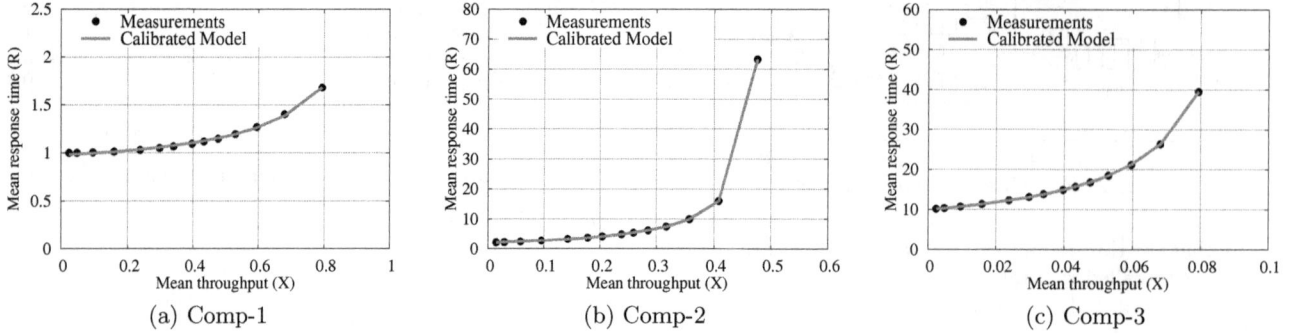

(a) Comp-1   (b) Comp-2   (c) Comp-3

Figure 3: Performance measurements and modeling for each of the 3 components of the centralized system.

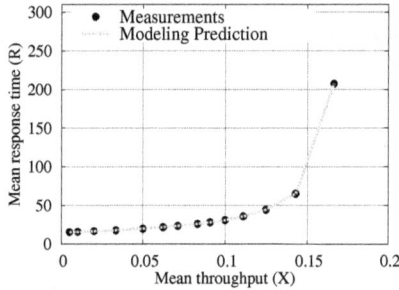

Figure 4: Predictions of system performance against measurements for the centralized system.

4.2 Cases of failure

As illustrated by examples in this section, considerably inaccurate performance predictions can be expected when the applicability conditions are not met.

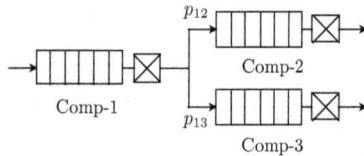

Figure 5: System with state-dependent routing.

Table 2: Parameters used for Figure 5.

Comp-1	C_1	Number of servers	1
	mst_1	Mean service time	1
	cvs_1	Coefficient of variation for service time	1
	p_{12}	Probability of going to Comp-2 upon request completion	1 or .5
	p_{13}	Probability of going to Comp-3 upon request completion	0 or .5
Comp-2	C_2	Number of servers	1
	mst_2	Mean service time	2
	cvs_2	Coefficient of variation for service time	1
Comp-3	C_3	Number of servers	1
	mst_3	Mean service time	2
	cvs_3	Coefficient of variation for service time	1

We now consider a system with 3 components in which, unlike the previous example, the routing probabilities depend on the current state of components. Such state-dependencies may occur in systems with load-balancing policies. Figure 5 illustrates the topology of our example. In this system, the incoming requests, which arrive according to a Poisson process with rate λ, go through two components. They start with Comp-1 and, if the current number of requests waiting or being served in Comp-2 is larger than 10,

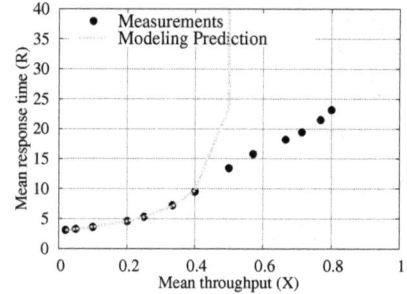

Figure 6: Predictions of system performance against measurements for the system with state-dependent routing probabilities.

they are routed to Comp-3. Otherwise, they are equally likely to be dispatched to Comp-2 and Comp-3. Table 2 summarizes the system parameters used in our simulation. Note that the buffers at each component are assumed to be large enough to avoid overflows.

Assuming we have calibrated models to capture the performance of each component, we apply the proposed approach to estimate the mean response time of the whole system as a function of the mean throughput following Formula (1). Here, the predicted values do not match well those actually observed ("measured") in the simulation. Figure 6 illustrates this discrepancy.

The reason for the discrepancy shown in Figure 6 is clear: unlike in the previous example, the throughput ratios for components Comp-2 and Comp-3 are not constant. Indeed, as the workload increases, the number of requests waiting or being served in Comp-2 increases, so that requests leaving Comp-1 become more likely to be routed to Comp-3 (up to half of them). In the proposed approach, however, the throughput ratio for each queue was derived at a lower level of workload, and it was applied for other levels of workload considered.

State-dependencies causing failure of the proposed approach can appear in seemingly different examples. Consider a system in which the arrivals and departures of requests may occur at several places in the system. Such behavior may occur in systems exhibiting internal losses of requests (e.g. due to buffer overflow, transmission errors, dynamic routing). Figure 7 shows a system where incoming requests may be routed to Comp-1 or directly to Comp-2 depending on the current number of requests waiting in Comp-1. If the number of queued requests is less than 7, then incom-

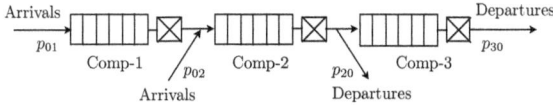

Figure 7: System with internal losses and arrivals.

Table 3: Parameters used for Figure 7.

Comp-1	C_1	Number of servers	1
	mst_1	Mean service time	2
	cvs_1	Coefficient of variation for service time	1
	p_{01}	Probability for new requests to enter at Comp-1	1 or 0
Comp-2	C_2	Number of servers	1
	mst_2	Mean service time	1
	cvs_2	Coefficient of variation for service time	1
	p_{02}	Probability for new requests to enter at Comp-2	0 or 1
	p_{20}	Probability of leaving the system upon completion of Comp-2	0 or 1
Comp-3	C_3	Number of servers	1
	mst_3	Mean service time	2
	cvs_3	Coefficient of variation for service time	1

ing requests go to Comp-1. Otherwise, they skip Comp-1 and go directly to Comp-2. Similarly, if the current number of requests at Comp-3 is less than 7, requests completed at Comp-2 are routed to Comp-3. Otherwise, upon completion at Comp-2, they skip Comp-3 and leave the system. Table 3 gives the details of the system parameters used in our simulation. As in our preceding example, request arrivals form a Poisson process and the buffer sizes at each component are assumed to be large enough to avoid overflows.

Again, with accurately calibrated performance models for each component, we apply Formula (1) to predict the mean response time of the whole system for different levels of mean system throughput. Here too, as illustrated in Figure 8, the proposed approach is doomed to failure since the throughput ratios of Comp-1 and Comp-3 are not constant.

As discussed above, the proposed approach would work if the rate of arrivals at Comp-2 and the rate of departures from Comp-2 were known in advance or if they were simply proportional to the overall system workload (as would be the case, for example, if requests departures represented transmission errors in a communication network).

In addition to cases in which the throughput ratios vary with workload levels and their variation is not known in advance, the proposed approach is not applicable for systems in which requests may simultaneously "occupy" two or more resources. For instance, in order to get fully processed by a "primary" component, the requests, while holding the component resource, need to receive service from a "secondary" component. The latter may be shared with other competing

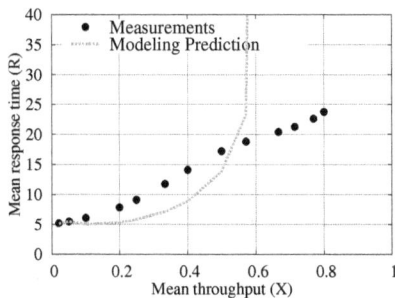

Figure 8: Predictions of system performance against measurements for the system with internal losses and arrivals.

sources of requests. Systems like databases and certain disk controllers may exhibit this behavior.

Figure 9 illustrates a simple example of a system with simultaneous resource possession. The service time in Comp-1 is represented as a two-stage process where the second stage represents the resource holding time while the request potentially waits for and accesses the shared resource at Comp-2. Here, any calibrated model of component Comp-1 is in fact a good candidate to predict the mean response time of the whole system since both coincide. Comp-1 and Comp-2 are too strongly coupled (Comp-2 can be seen as being embedded within Comp-1) and cannot be combined as described in Section 3. Similarly, systems with fork and join mechanisms would cause problems.

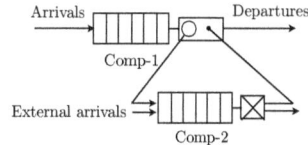

Figure 9: System with simultaneous resource possession.

5. DISCOVERY OF UNKNOWN SYSTEM COMPONENTS

Our next system of interest is similar to that discussed in Section 4.1 but it includes an additional component, viz. Comp-4. We assume that available measurements points pertain to the overall system performance as well as to components Comp-1, Comp-2 and Comp-3 with the exception of Comp-4. This latter may have been considered unimportant for the overall system performance or simply overlooked by or unknown to the performance analyst. Comp-4 may represent for example access to internal tables or buffers deemed so fast that it is unlikely to be a factor in the overall system performance. Figure 10 illustrates the corresponding system with a gray box around Comp-4. We re-use the same system parameters for components 1 through 3 as in Table 1 and indicate the parameters for Comp-4 in Table 4. The parameters for Comp-4 were chosen so that it can become a bottleneck because of the frequency with which requests visit it while each visit is very short.

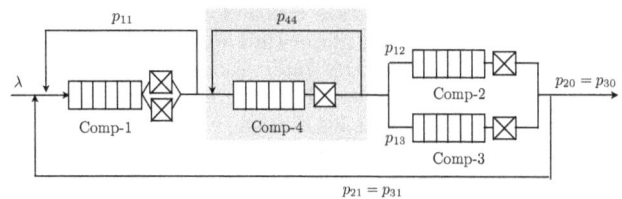

Figure 10: System with an "unknown" component.

Table 4: Parameters used for Figure 10.

Comp-4	C_4	Number of servers	1
	mst_4	Mean service time	0.1
	cvs_4	Coefficient of variation for service time	0
	p_{44}	Probability of returning to Comp-4 upon request completion	0.96

Having developed a calibrated performance model for each of the components Comp-1, Comp-2 and Comp-3, we applied the proposed method following Formula (1) to derive the performance of the whole system. Figure 11a displays the corresponding results. Clearly, the proposed approach is missing something. Now, assuming this missing something

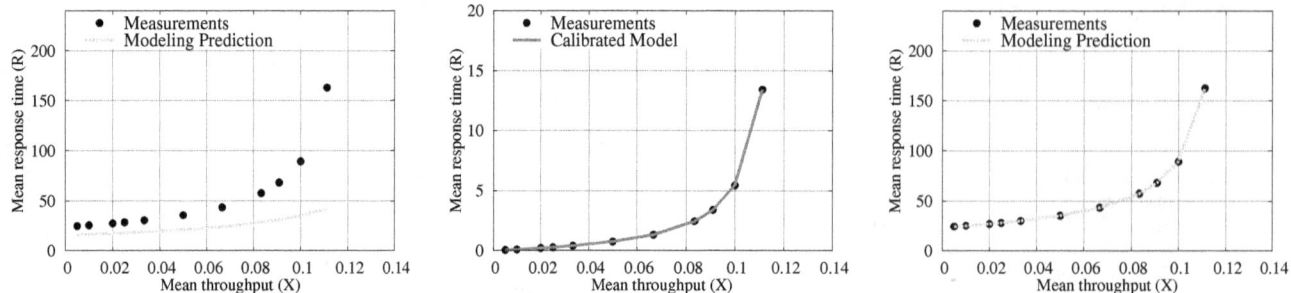

(a) Initial performance prediction   (b) Modeling the residual performance   (c) Refined performance prediction

Figure 11: Predictions of system performance against measurements for the centralized system with an unknown component.

is an additional component that was not measured (and perhaps even not instrumented) and therefore not modeled, we consider the difference in the performance metric between the system measurement points and the performance curve given by Formula (1). Given this residual pattern of performance, we apply a black-box modeling approach [6] to find a model that reproduces adequately this behavior. It turns out that a simple $M/M/1$ queue can fit the data (see Figure 11b).

If the pattern was more chaotic and could not be matched by a reasonable model, it might imply that the residual performance difference is just measurement "noise", or that something else is amiss and that the system does not comply with the set of assumptions required for the proposed approach to work. A possible approach to try to determine whether the residual performance difference is due to "measurement noise" would be to apply simple statistical tests [1].

Now, having in hand a calibrated model for each of the four system components, we can re-apply the proposed approach to forecast the system performance. The corresponding results are shown in Figure 11c and clearly, including a new component was the right choice in our case.

6. CONCLUSIONS

In this paper we consider the problem of combining calibrated performance models of individual system components into an accurate system-level performance model. We concentrate on open workload systems and we show that under certain conditions the straightforward application of Little's law allows one to effect this integration. We give examples to illustrate the successful application of the proposed approach, as well as examples that show the extent of inaccuracies if the applicability conditions are not met.

Additionally, we show that by analyzing the discrepancies between the model predictions and the measurements it may be possible to determine if an important system component has not been correctly represented. This can be of help in the design of calibrated system performance models.

As future work, the authors plan to further investigate the important issue of distinguishing "measurement noise" from errors due to missing components. Another area of investigation pertains to the extensions of the proposed framework to closed systems.

7. REFERENCES

[1] Allen, A. O. (1990). *Probability, Statistics, and Queueing Theory: With Computer Science Applications*, Academic Press.

[2] Awad, M., & Menascé, D. A. (2014). On the Predictive Properties of Performance Models Derived through Input-Output Relationships. *Computer Performance Engineering.*

[3] Awad, M., & Menascé, D. A. (2014). Dynamic Derivation of Analytical Performance Models in Autonomic Computing Environments. In Proc. of *CMG.*

[4] Balsamo, S., & Iazeolla, G. (1982). An extension of Norton's theorem for queueing networks. *IEEE Transactions on Software Engineering.*

[5] Baskett, F., Chandy, K. M., Muntz, R. R., & Palacios, F. G. (1975). Open, closed, and mixed networks of queues with different classes of customers. *Journal of the ACM.*

[6] Begin, T., Brandwajn, A., Baynat, B., Wolfinger, B. E., & Fdida, S. (2010). High-level approach to modeling of observed system behavior. *Performance Evaluation.*

[7] Bolch, G., Greiner, S., Meer, H., & Trivedi, K. (2005). *Queueing Networks and Markov Chains.*

[8] Brandwajn, A. (1974). A model of a time sharing virtual memory system solved using equivalence and decomposition methods. *Acta Informatica.*

[9] Brandwajn, A. (1985). Equivalence and decomposition in queueing systems - A unified approach. *Performance Evaluation.*

[10] Chandy, K. M., Herzog, U., & Woo, L. (1975). Parametric analysis of queuing networks. *IBM Journal of Research and Development.*

[11] Courtois, P. J. (2014). *Decomposability: queueing and computer system applications*, Academic Press.

[12] Ganger, G. R., & Patt, Y. N. (1993). The process-flow model: examining I/O performance from the system's point of view. In Proc. of *ACM SIGMETRICS.*

[13] Harbaoui, A., Salmi, N., Dillenseger, B., & Vincent, J. M. (2010). Introducing queuing network-based performance awareness in autonomic systems. In Proc. of *IEEE ICAS.*

[14] Herzog, U. (1974). Some remarks concerning the extended analytic models for system evaluation. *IBM RR 4975.*

[15] Kühn, P. (1976). Analysis of Complex Queueing Networks by Decomposition. In Proc. of *IEEE ITC.*

[16] Kraft, S., Casale, G., Krishnamurthy, D., Greer, D., & Kilpatrick, P. (2011). IO performance prediction in consolidated virtualized environments. In Proc. of *ACM SIGSOFT.*

[17] Kraft, S., Casale, G., Krishnamurthy, D., Greer, D., & Kilpatrick, P. (2013). Performance models of storage contention in cloud environments. *Software and Systems Modeling.*

[18] Marie, R. (1979). An approximate analytical method for general queueing networks. *IEEE Transactions on Software Engineering.*

[19] Reiser, M. (1979). Mean Value Analysis fo Queueing Networks - A New Look at an Old Problem. In Proc. of *IFIP PERFORMANCE.*

[20] Reiser, M., & Lavenberg, S. S. (1980). Mean-value analysis of closed multichain queuing networks. *Journal of the ACM.*

Towards Using Code Coverage Metrics for Performance Comparison on the Implementation Level

Mathias Menninghaus
mathias.menninghaus@uos.de

Elke Pulvermüller
elke.pulvermueller@uos.de

University of Osnabrück, Institute of Computer Science
Albrechtstraße 28, 49069 Osnabrück, Germany

ABSTRACT

The development process for new algorithms or data structures often begins with the analysis of benchmark results to identify the drawbacks of already existing implementations. Furthermore it ends with the comparison of old and new implementations by using one or more well established benchmark. But how relevant, reproducible, fair, verifiable and usable those benchmarks may be, they have certain drawbacks. On the one hand a new implementation may be biased to provide good results for a specific benchmark. On the other hand benchmarks are very general and often fail to identify the worst and best cases of a specific implementation. In this paper we present a new approach for the comparison of algorithms and data structures on the implementation level using code coverage. Our approach uses model checking and multi-objective evolutionary algorithms to create test cases with a high code coverage. It then executes each of the given implementations with each of the test cases in order to calculate a *cross coverage*. Using this it calculates a *combined coverage* and *weighted performance* where implementations, which are not fully covered by the test cases of the other implementations, are punished. These metrics can be used to compare the performance of several implementations on a much deeper level than traditional benchmarks and they incorporate worst, best and average cases in an equal manner. We demonstrate this approach by two example sets of algorithms and outline the next research steps required in this context along with the greatest risks and challenges.

Keywords

performance comparison, algorithm engineering, test case generation, performance tests

1. INTRODUCTION AND RELATED WORK

Developing new algorithms and data structures often starts with the analysis of the already existing approaches. A help-

ICPE'16, March 12 - 18, 2016, Delft, Netherlands

© 2016 Copyright held by the owner/author(s). Publication rights licensed to ACM.
ISBN 978-1-4503-4080-9/16/03. . . $15.00

DOI: http://dx.doi.org/10.1145/2851553.2858663

ful tool for finding drawbacks are well established benchmarks [6] for the particular problem domain. They are also used to compare the performance of the new to the performance of the existing approaches. Either type of benchmark has two major drawbacks when used for the comparison of new to previous implementations. On the one hand, an implementation may be biased to provide good results for a specific benchmark. On the other hand, benchmarks are designed to evaluate the impact of specific data sets and configurations and not for a specific implementation. They therefore do not necessarily expose the worst and best cases of an implementation.

We propose a solution to these problems by comparing implementations via performance tests which are dynamically created and can not be biased as easily as common benchmarks. Additionally our performance tests cover all aspects of an implementation in equal measure and not only those parts which where foreseen by the creators of a benchmark. [8] propose a model driven automated benchmark creator which relies on a UML 2.0 testing profile and creates benchmarks from the architecture and basic design of the software. Contrary to that, we create test sets on basis of the actual implementation and not the specification. This way, we create test sets which do not miss any part of the code and therefore our tests do not miss certain best and worst case scenarios. [2] propose WISE, a tool to automatically generate inputs which cause worst case performance using symbolic execution. Since they use the actual implementation as a basis, WISE seems to be a good start. However, it searches for a certain behavior instead of representing the overall performance conduct with one test set, which is our goal. [7] criticize the lack of coverage in performance testing and question significance if the coverage is ignored. By generating test sets with the aim of a maximized coverage, we also face this problem.

Beside the generation of test cases which cover the complete implementation, we develop a metric to compare implementations of the same algorithm or implementations of different algorithms which solve the same problem. Such a metric is useful to decide if two implementations are comparable at all. In some cases, several implementations may be used to solve the same problem but focus on different aspects of this problem. In contrast to focusing on one of the aspects and therefore specializing the comparison, we want to compare every speciality of the implementations automatically. Therefore, we need a metric which determines how different the implementations are. To our knowledge there is no other metric which examines the comparability of implementations available at present.

In order to provide complete and somehow fair performance tests we combine both aspects, the test sets with a maximized coverage and the comparability metric. Using this, we can evaluate which implementation performs generally best, independently from certain performance profiles.

We give an overview of our framework and the creation of test case sets along with the explanation of our comparability metric. Using a simple example we explain our comparison formula, which is called *combined coverage* and introduce the *weighted performance* which evaluates an implementation based on the aforementioned comparability and test cases with maximized coverage. As the framework is still work in progress we address the main risks and challenges in chapter 3 and conclude with an outlook in chapter 4.

2. PERFORMANCE TEST COMPARISON

In this chapter, we will describe the generation of test cases and the calculation of the combined coverage and weighted performance.

First, for each implementation a test case set with maximized coverage is generated. Second, each implementation is executed with each of the test case sets as parameters. The coverage and average performance of this executions is measured for each test case set. Third, using the coverage of each test case set given by an implementation, the *combined coverage* for measuring the comparability of one implementation to the others is generated. Fourth and last, using the coverage and performance of each test case set on an implementation, the *weighted performance* is generated.

As an introduction consider the four Java code-snippets as depicted in Figure 1. Each of them is an implementation of the method `public int max(int a, int b)` which returns the maximum value of the two given parameters `a` and `b`. We want to evaluate which implementation performs best in comparison to the others. It is crucial to note that two different implementations of the `max` method can be compared much better, if the test cases generated for comparison cover the whole code of both implementations. Otherwise the test cases miss uncovered sections and no valid conclusion about the overall performance can be derived. The only requirement for our procedure is that every implementation fulfills the same specification and reacts with an identical output on certain inputs. So either the same algorithm has been implemented or algorithms which solve the same problem. The framework does not test the functionality of the given implementations, but measures their comparability and performance.

The framework does not generate test cases which cover all given implementations, since that would cause a great computation overhead every time a new implementation has to be compared to the existing ones. Instead, it generates test cases for each of the given implementations. It can either use a model checking approach using Java Path Finder (JPF) [5, 3] or an evolutionary approach using the multi-objective evolutionary algorithm (MOEA) [1] framework. The first is able to find all simple paths in the control flow and therefore maximal covering test cases but fails for rather complex implementations as it faces a state-explosion and too many possible paths. The latter is not confronted with state explosions and may find an ideal implementation which has a

maximal coverage and minimal number of test cases but this depends on the given fitness function and mutation operators. An evolutionary algorithm may get stuck in an local optima and not find a good implementation. As the given examples are rather simple we use the JPF-based approach and get the test cases as depicted in Figure 1 in the second column. Another point for adjustment in our framework is the coverage metric on which the comparison weights are based. Since there are many different code coverage metrics available, the framework only provides a general interface for the implementation of additional metrics together with the major ones like statement, branch and path coverage metrics. The decision for one of the metrics should be made in respect for the intended aspect and how detailed the comparability should be determined. For the given example we simply calculate the basic block coverage not only for each of the implementations but for each implementation and each set of test cases. Each entry c_{ij} in Table 1 contains the coverage of test case set j executed on implementation i.

Table 1: Basic block coverage for each of the test case sets executed on each of the algorithms

implementation	test cases of			
	A	B	C	D
A	1.0	2/3	1.0	1.0
B	2/3	1.0	1.0	2/3
C	0.8	0.8	1.0	0.8
D	1.0	2/3	1.0	1.0

The covered paths in the control flow graphs of each implemenation when executed with the test case set generated from solution A are shown in Figure 1 in the third column. The coverage value may not exceed a maximum value and should be calculated in relation to the maximal possible coverage. In our case, the maximum is always 1.0. For some coverage metrics, which may not be fully covered or implementations which contain unreachable, *dead* code, it may be less. The coverage value is therefore adjusted to

$$cov_{ij} = \begin{cases} \frac{c_{ij}}{max_i} & \text{if } c_{ij} < max_i \\ 1 & \text{else} \end{cases} \quad (1)$$

where max_i is the maximal possible coverage on implementation i. For a proper comparison of the implementations the framework needs to combine the coverage values for each implementation. If one implementation only covers the test case set of one other implementation well, this indicates that it may be designed especially for this competitor. Therefore, some very good and very bad coverage values are worse than average coverage values only. The combined coverage should also take into account how many test case sets have been combined. A combination of only two implementations should assign a higher weight to a single coverage value than the combination of 10 values. We propose the combined coverage c_i as

$$c_i = \prod_{j=1}^{n} (cov_{ij})^{\frac{k}{n}} \quad (2)$$

where n is the total number of implementations and k is the parameter to adjust the impact of bad coverage values on the combined coverage. The combined coverages for our example are presented in table 2 in the middle column. They

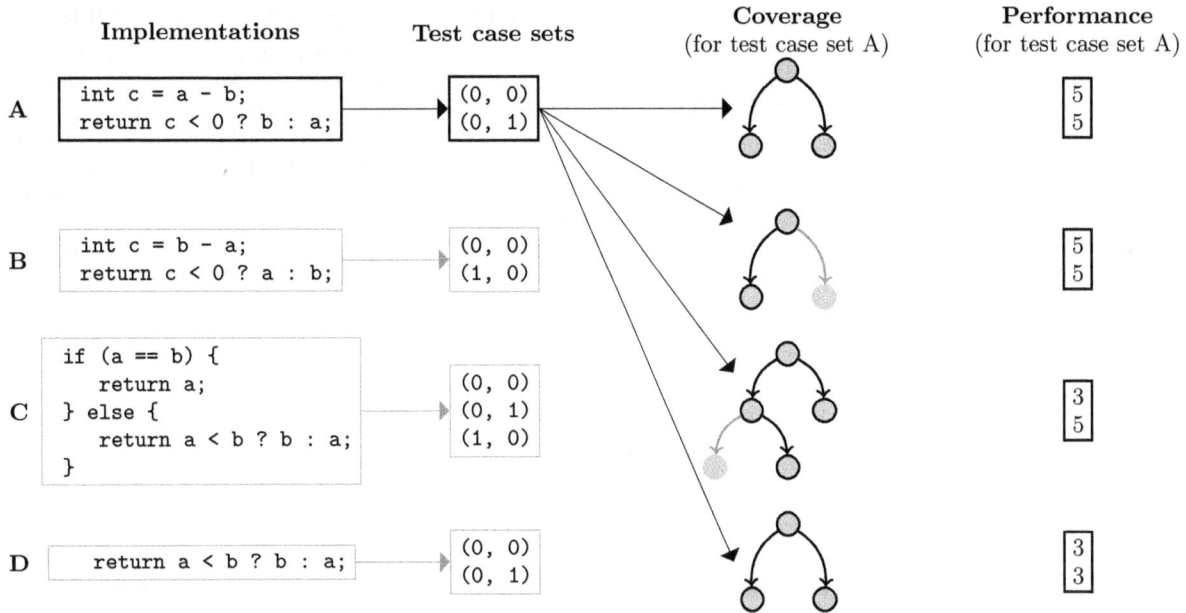

Figure 1: Overview over our framework. Sets of test cases with maximized coverage are generated from each implementation (first to second column). Each implementation is executed with each test case set and the coverage (third column) and performance (fourth column) are measured.

Table 2: Combined coverage and weighted performance with $k = 2$

implementation	combined coverage	weighted performance
A	0,816497	6,562500
B	0,666667	8,125000
C	0,715542	5,770833
D	0,816497	3,937500

can be interpreted as follows: Implementations A and D have the same control flow graph and therefore react equal on test cases. Implementation C has an additional test case, caused by the first statement, the test on the equality of parameters a and b. Therefore the test cases of C cover all other implementations, but C is not fully covered by the others. In contrast to A, C and D implementation B returns parameter b if it equals a and therefore has the least combined coverage. That means, that B can not be compared to the other implementations as good as A, C and D.

In the last step, the performance of each implementation is combined with the coverage for each test case set. In our approach a higher performance value is worse and the best possible performance is 1. To maintain a comparability we calculate the weighted performance p_i with the following definition

$$p_i = \left(\sum_{j=1}^{n} \frac{p_{ij}}{(cov_{ij})^k} \right) / n \qquad (3)$$

where p_{ij} is the average performance of implementation i when executed with the test cases from implementation j. Similar to the coverage calculation, the way the performance of the implementations is measured, has an impact on the outcome of the evaluation. For our example we use the num-

ber of bytecode load and store operations on integers as performance values. The best performing implementation is assumed to be the one with the least number of those instructions. The performance of every implementation when executed with the test cases from A is shown in Figure 1 in the right column. One may consider other performance values like the number of executed cpu cycles, the wall clock time etc., but counting the bytecode operations is sufficient for our explanation. We also disabled Java's just-in-time-compilation which has to be taken into account outside of our simple example.

As for the combined coverage, the coverage values are weighted with the parameter k in order to punish a bad coverage more than an average coverage. The weighted performance of our example is presented in table 2 in the right column. It shows that implementation D is considered to have the best weighted performance. This means, that this implementation not only has a good average performance but also is covered best by the test cases of the other implementations.

3. DISCUSSION

From this first view on our procedure we can identify several uncertainties and open issues which will be discussed in this chapter.

The performance value p_{ij} treats every test case in the same way. It does not weight very unlikely or likely test cases. On the one hand this is not fair, if one implementation has a clearly better average performance but one very unlikely worst case and the other performs worse in average but has no worst case. On the other hand, the aim of our framework is to fully compare several implementations, and not build another benchmark generator. Weighting one test case more than another would also imply knowledge of the intended use and that disagrees our introductive claim to cover all aspects of an implementation equally. Therefore, a full comparison needs to incorporate all cases in equal measure. Nonetheless, at least the graphical representation of our framework will highlight worst, best, and average case scenarios and identify often used paths and instructions. A prototype of the UI is shown in figure 2.

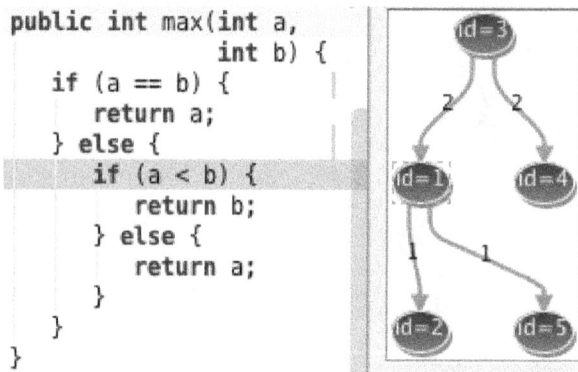

```
public int max(int a,
                int b) {
    if (a == b) {
        return a;
    } else {
        if (a < b) {
            return b;
        } else {
            return a;
        }
    }
}
```

Figure 2: UI - excerpt of our framework. Source code (left) and control nodes (right) are linked to each other. After execution, the visited paths are highlighted and the edges are labeled with the number of accesses.

In the end, the developer who uses our tools, may adjust the weights for the specific purpose after getting a complete overview about the investigated implementations.

The chosen coverage metric is essential and clearly has an impact on the overall computation. For example, we also computed the combined coverage and weighted performance for four sorting algorithms with a quadratic average computation time: BubbleSort, InsertionSort, SelectionSort and ShellSort. When using basic block coverage as metric, each implementation is fully covered by each test case set and therefore also the combined coverage for each implementation is 1.0. We also used path coverage, with the constraint that every loop should be accessed at least twice for full coverage, as metric. Although this changes the combined coverage, it does not change the general outcome for the weighted performance. As the four algorithms are very similar it is only logical that their test cases cover each other and that there is no reasonable coverage metric which would alter the weighted performance such that the performance ranking of the algorithms would change. When confronted with very different implementations, the coverage has a greater impact than for similar implementations.

Not only the way the performance and coverage are calculated, but also the generation of the test cases affects the outcome. In the previous chapter we used JPF to create relatively universal test cases which cover all control flow paths. Changing the test cases of B to (1, 0) | (0, 1) already changes the coverage for A and D but not for B and C. This has an impact on the weighted performance and even on the performance ranking. But it is rather obvious that even a slight change on one of two test cases changes the outcome. Problems which require more complex implementations than the simple `max` example in this paper will also produce more test cases per test case set and therefore be less prone to minor changes in the test cases.

4. CONCLUSIONS AND OUTLOOK

In this paper, we present a new approach for comparing the performance of algorithms and data structures on the implementation level. We provide two metrics, the combined coverage and the weighted performance which can be used to compare the coverage and the performance of different implementations. We also discuss our work in progress and state that our calculations may be altered by using different performance weights, coverage metrics and test case generators but none of the alterations let the overall reasoning behind our metrics fail.

In the next steps, we need to apply our framework on a more complex domain. Complex data structures for indexing spatio-temporal data like the R^{ST}-tree [4] are generated on the prior analyzation of their predecessors and therefore are exactly the structures we aim at. We also need to compare our framework to the already existing benchmarks and test sets for those structures or find a way to incorporate them in our performance comparison.

For more complex implementations the usage of JPF is unpractical not only because of a possible state explosion but also because JPF is not able to handle input arrays of variable length. Beside the risk of getting stuck in a local optimum, evolutionary algorithms have to be set up for every problem domain anew. Especially the definition of the fitness function and the mutation operators is crucial for the success of the evolutionary algorithms. Therefore, we need to build a simple and more general framework for the generation of test cases via evolutionary algorithms, which takes one method call as a single gene and a chromosome as one test case. After an extensive test of this evolutionary computation framework, the user will be able to use predefined mutation operators and algorithms which have proven best in previous evaluations.

5. REFERENCES

[1] MOEA Framework. pages 1–210, Jan. 2015.
[2] J. Burnim, S. Juvekar, and K. Sen. WISE: Automated test generation for worst-case complexity. *2009 IEEE 31st International Conference on Software Engineering*, pages 463–473, 2009.
[3] S. Monpratarnchai, S. Fujiwara, A. Katayama, and T. Uehara. Automated testing for Java programs using JPF-based test case generation. *ACM SIGSOFT Software Engineering Notes*, 39(1):1–5, Feb. 2014.
[4] S. Saltenis and C. S. Jensen. R-Tree Based Indexing of General Spatio-Temporal Data. 1999.
[5] W. Visser, C. S. Păsăreanu, S. Khurshid, and S. Khurshid. Test input generation with java PathFinder. *ACM SIGSOFT Software Engineering Notes*, 29(4):97–107, July 2004.
[6] J. von Kistowski, J. A. Arnold, K. Huppler, K.-D. Lange, J. L. Henning, and P. Cao. How to Build a Benchmark. In *the 6th ACM/SPEC International Conference*, pages 333–336, New York, New York, USA, 2015. ACM Press.
[7] M. Woodside, G. Franks, and D. C. Petriu. *The Future of Software Performance Engineering*. IEEE, 2007.
[8] L. Zhu, N. B. Bui, Y. Liu, and I. Gorton. MDABench: Customized benchmark generation using MDA. *Journal of Systems and Software*, 80(2):265–282, Feb. 2007.

Performance Extrapolation of IO Intensive Workloads

[Work in Progress]

Dheeraj Chahal   Rupinder Virk   Manoj Nambiar

{d.chahal|rupinder.virk|m.nambiar}@tcs.com
Performance Engineering Research centre
TCS Innovation Labs
Mumbai, India

ABSTRACT

Performance prediction of an application before migrating from a source system and deploying on the target system is a challenging but important task.

In this paper, we present a method for predicting the performance of an IO intensive multithreaded enterprise application workload on target systems connected to advanced storage devices. Our approach is an extension of well-known trace and replay method. We extract traces of IO intensive enterprise workloads representing temporal and spatial characteristics (e.g. read and write requests) on the source system where application is currently deployed. These traces are replayed on the system of interest called target system. The experimental results presented demonstrate the effectiveness and accuracy of this method.

Keywords

Performance prediction; IO traces; extrapolation

1. INTRODUCTION

Many organizations are showing interest in migrating their applications from the existing low-end hard disk based systems to a high-end hard disk or a local flash memory based Solid State Device (SSD) systems for a dual purpose of saving energy and enhancing the performance of database servers. Migrating the application to a new system and testing the performance is a non-trivial and daunting task. It requires lots of efforts to set it up and subsequently fine tune. One solution is running the synthetic workloads generated by the IO subsystem and characterization tools. The synthetic workloads have access pattern very similar to that of real application. Though this approach is relatively easier to implement but may not reproduce the characteristics of the application or the workload accurately.

IO trace replay is another popular technique that can be used for reproducing the application characteristics on a tar-

get platform. Trace replay is a commonly used technique for debugging and benchmarking I/O systems.

Traces are portable such that the trace generated under one environment can be run on the other with minimal efforts without changes in the code. Trace replay can mimic the behavior of the application with very high accuracy by capturing its characteristics without revealing the sensitive information. Moreover, trace and replay is a preferred technique for migration studies since it does not require copying the actual data on the target system because data access pattern is important than the actual data itself. Traces are deterministic and prove to be better than other methods like modeling techniques in some situations.

Unfortunately, trace capturing tools like *strace* and *blktrace* slowdown the execution of the application and cause software overhead at larger workloads. Hence capturing trace for a large workload at the source system results in time dilation and replaying the same on the target systems might not provide the correct performance estimation. One solution is to capture the traces at low concurrency levels and replay on the target system and then extrapolate the results.

Using a performance prediction method before actually migrating an IO intensive application to an advanced hard disk drive (HDD) or SSD would be helpful in capacity planning. We used trace and replay technique for predicting the performance of enterprise applications on a target system with storage systems like high-end HDD and SSD. Our approach consists of the following steps:

1) Systematically generating the IO traces of the application on the database server of the source system for varying concurrencies (no. of users).

2) Replaying the traces on the database layer of the target system and collecting the performance statistics like utilization, throughput and response time.

3) Extrapolating the data collected on the target system using an extrapolation tool.

Eventually, we should be able to answer the questions like "What is the maximum number of users that we can serve if we upgrade to a new system with an advanced storage device ?" or "What would be the performance of my application with a new storage system under different workloads ?". Also these queries shall be answered without actually going through the painful process of deploying the application on target systems with different types of storage devices.

This short paper introduces a trace and replay procedure for predicting the performance of an enterprise application

ICPE'16, March 12-18, 2016, Delft, Netherlands
© 2016 ACM. ISBN 978-1-4503-4080-9/16/03. . . $15.00
DOI: http://dx.doi.org/10.1145/2851553.2858665

in a new environment where it is to be migrated. Our contribution is a method that can be followed for pre-deployment performance estimation of mutlithreaded IO intensive applications on different target systems with advanced storage devices. We also present efficacy of this methods by testing on multiple target systems with different storage devices.

The rest of this paper is structured as follows: Section 2 describes the related work. In section 3 we discuss our approach to implement our methodology. Experimental set up is discussed in section 4. Section 5 provides the analysis of experimental results to evaluate the efficiency of our method. Conclusion and future scope is discussed in section 6.

2. RELATED WORK

The use of IO traces for application profiling has been there for many years now but its usage has found traction in recent years for predicting the performance in the cloud environment. Recently Tak et. al. developed a technique called PseudoApp[10]. Contrary to the approach followed in PseudoApp which builds an artificial workload , we run the actual trace on the target system. The former approach does not require replicating the database on target architecture but replaying the artificial workload is a complex process. Another similar work in this area is development of ROOT[12]. We have further extended the work of PseudoApp and ROOT to predict the performance of multithreaded applications for higher concurrency using our extrapolation tool called PerfExt [4].

There is a large body of work for IO trace replay mechanisms particularly for storage system evaluations for different purposes [2][3][7]. //Trace is another popular approach for parallel application. Yet another interesting research work for predicting the performance of web application on cloud is CloudProphet [9]. Though CloudProphet is capable of predicting the end-to-end performance of multiple resources with high accuracy but it is based on simple scaling which may not hold good for high concurrency.

3. OUR APPROACH

Our systems is a multi-tier system consisting of the load generator, application layer an the database layer. The http scripts of the application of interest are captured using the TCPProxy[1] plug-in. We perform randomization and parameterization of http scripts to simulate the random access pattern of the web application by different users. These test scripts are replayed with Grinder http plug-in [8] for arbitrary number of users and thinktime. Since the primary focus of this research is to study IO intensive applications, we captured and replayed traces only on the database layer. Detailed discussion on our approach is provided in our previous work [11].

3.1 IO trace recording

There are numerous methods and tools to trace the IO calls of an applications depending upon the layer they operate on e.g. kernel, user space or a combination of both. The layer at which these tools and methods execute also defines the performance overhead and the complexity involved. We preferred user mode contrary to the perception that kernel mode reduces error. The user mode requires no modification in the application or the kernel and profiling information can be captured easily. The I/O profile trace of application of interest is captured using the *strace* utility in the linux system. To reduce *strace* overhead and the size of trace file, we captured only IO related system calls: *read()*, *write()*, *pread()*, *pwrite()*, *lseek()*, *fsync()*, *open()*, *close()*. Each row in the captured trace consists of process ID, timestamp value, offset and the IO system call. To capture the trace, we first find all the thread IDs that are spawned by the MySQL and then *strace* is attached to each of these thread IDs. Thus multiple trace output files are generated. In order to maintain the same order of the execution on the target system, we merge all these files in to a single file and then sort system calls according to their timestamp value.

3.2 Trace replay

As a next step, the database files of the application are copied to a temporary directory on the target system. Any access to the database file in the trace is replaced by a path to the temporary directory. We used ioreplay [6] to replay the I/O trace captured on the test system. The replay tool executes the IO operations as recorded in the trace file. The ioreplay studies have shown that the it scales within a difference of few percent when compared with the original application [5]. One of the drawback with ioreplay is that it is single threaded. Hence replaying the trace for high concurrency is a challenge. We modified the ioreplay to support multlithreading.

One of the challenges associated with the trace-replay method is maintaining the realism of the workload when load-profile is replayed on a target system. We capture the IO system calls along with its timestamp. When the trace is replayed on the target system we ensure that IO calls are executed at the same time interval as in the original system so that workload is replicated correctly.

3.3 Extrapolation

To extrapolate the performance data of an application from a small number to a large number of users on the target system, we used PerfExt. PerfExt is a tool developed in our lab. The tool takes load testing results as input from for a small number of users in terms of throughput and resource utilization. To extrapolate throughput, PerfExt first estimates the maximum throughput based on the resource utilization information. Linear regression is used to predict the performance until throughput reaches the half of the maximum throughput and beyond that point sigmoid curve is fit in till the throughput reaches 90% of the maximum value. It uses a combination of linear regression and another statistical technique called sigmoid curve (or S curve) to predict the performance until the application encounters the first bottleneck. PerfExt has been tested successfully with a number of sample multi-tier applications and is able to provide accuracy of about 90% in the throughput and utilization metrics. However, it makes an assumptions that there in no software bottleneck in the application of interest.

For extrapolation using PerfExt, user performance data obtained by running traces for two concurrency levels on the target system is sufficient. The resource utilization for these multiple concurrencies is used in the PerfExt as input and extrapolated for higher concurrencies to obtain performance metrics like resource utilization, throughput and response time.

Storage device	Disk Model	RPM	No. of Disks	IO Scheduler	File System	Interface	System Config	Linux Kernel
Low-end HDD	Caviar SE Serial ATA drive	7200	1	CFQ	ext4	300 Mb/s Serial ATA 2.0	8 Core Xeon CPU @ 2.6 GHz,,6MB L2 cache	CentOS 6.5,2.6.32
High-end HDD	HP-GEN7	10000	1	CGQ	ext4	Dual Port,SAS 6GB/s	16 Core Xeon CPU @ 2.4 GHz,12MB L2 cache	CentOS 6.6,2.6.32
High-end HDD (VM)	HP-GEN9	10000	1	CGQ	ext4	Dual Port,SAS 6GB/s	16 Core Xeon CPU @ 2.4 GHz,12MB L2 cache	CentOS 6.6,2.6.32
SSD	Virident Systems Inc. FlashMAX Drive Micron-slc-32	-	1PCIe	Default	ext3	-	16 Core Xeon CPU @ 2.4 GHz,,12MB L2 cache	CentOS 6.6,2.6.32

Table 1: Storage systems used in our study

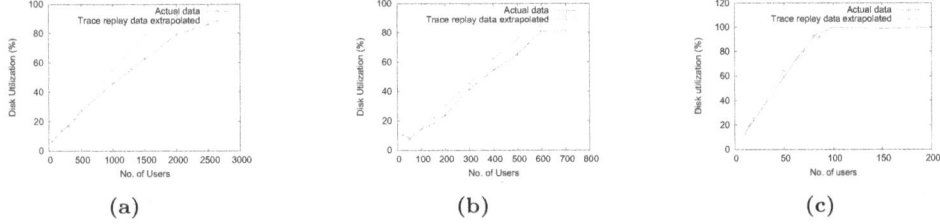

| (a) | (b) | (c) |

Figure 1: Disk utilization predictions for high-end HDD for (a)JPetStore (b) equiz(c) TPC-C

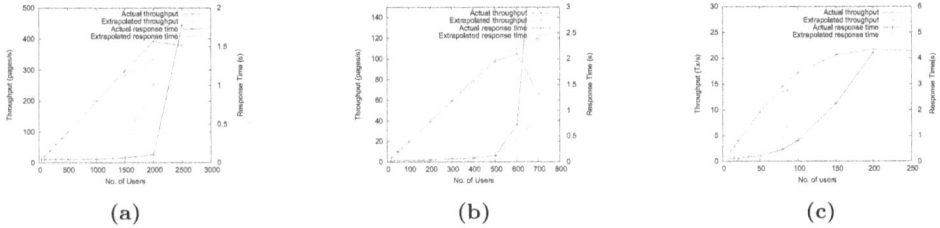

| (a) | (b) | (c) |

Figure 2: Throughput and response time prediction for high-end HDD for (a) JPetStore (b) equiz (c) TPC-C

4. EXPERIMENTAL SETUP

We have validated our methodology using industrial benchmark TPC-C and two web based applications. TPC-C is an online transaction processing (OLTP) benchmark . TPC-C is considered a popular benchmark for comparing performance across different softwares and hardware configurations. Being an IO intensive benchmark, it is an appropriate test case for us.

Other two applications used in this study are equiz and JPetStore. The equiz application is implemented with java servlets, stored procedures and includes an automatic code evaluation (ACE) framework. JPetStore is an eCommerce J2EE application benchmark which allows users to browse and search for different types of pets in five top level categories.

TPC-C is executed from the command prompt while JPetStore and equiz are deployed on apache tomcat server. MySQL 5.6 is used as backend for all the applications. The think time between the application pages is fixed at 5 sec. All the performance data metrics are mesured in the steady state of the run.

The storage system configurations that we used in our studies are are given in table 1. We used low-end HDD with source system and high-end HDD or SSD with target system. The virtual machine used in the experiment had 48 Core Xeon CPU (2.5 GHz),30MB L2 cache and CentOS 6.4.

5. RESULTS

We predicted the performance of these applications on a high end HDD and SSD storage systems using the trace generated on low-end HDD.

5.1 Low-end HDD to High-end HDD migration

Trace files were generated on the source system by running JPetStore, equiz application and TPC-C benchmark on the test system for varying workloads. JPetStore application was run on the source system with low-end HDD for 50, 100, 200, 300 users, equiz for 50,100 and 150 users and TPC-C for 10, 15, 20 users. All these trace files were replayed on the target system and performance metrics were observed. Performance data was extrapolated for higher concurrencies using PerfExt as shown in the Figure 1 and Figure 2. Extrapolation tool is modeled to predict until any of the resources (CPU, disk or memory) is 90% utilized while the application is run till average disk utilization is 98% and hence actual data trend lines are extended for larger concurrencies as compared to the extrapolated. Disk utilization (Figure 1), throughput and response time (Figure 2) are predicted accurately until 90% of the resource utilization (CPU or disk) on the database server when compared with the actual performance data. Some inaccuracy is observed in the response time prediction particularly for TPC-C at higher concurrencies. We observed that for TPC-C disk attains 90% utilization around 120 user workload but throughput and response time increases until utilization is 98% for 200 users beyond which throughput starts falling gradually.

TPC-C performance prediction was also done for VM with high-end HDD (figure 3) and results similar to physical machine are obtained upto 90% of disk utilization.

5.2 Low-end HDD to SSD migration

IO traces of JPetStore and equiz from the source system were also tested on target systems with SSD. As shown in the

107

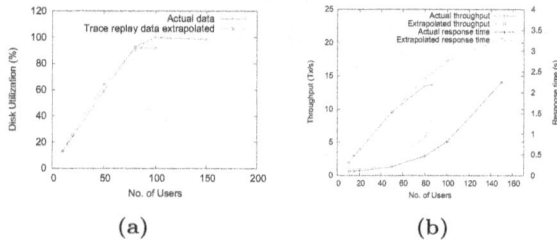

Figure 3: TPC-C throughput and response time prediction for VM with high-end HDD (a) Disk utilization (b) Throughput and response time

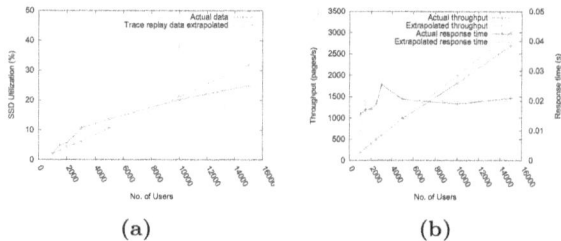

Figure 4: JPetStore application predictions for SSD (a) Device utilization (b)throughput and response time

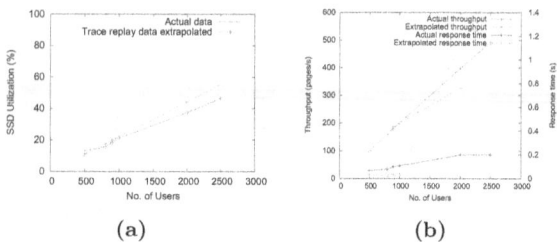

Figure 5: Equiz application prediction for SSD (a) Device utilization (b) Throughput and response time

figure 4 and figure 5, maximum device utilization for JPet-Store and equiz is 25% for 15000 and 45% for 2500 users respectively. Beyond this workload, CPU at application server becomes a bottleneck. SSD utilization, throughput and response time predictions are close to actual performance data for JPetStore (Figure 4). Utilization and throughput are predicted correctly for equiz as well (Figure 5). The incorrect response time prediction for equiz beyond 1200 users is due to our extrapolation tool considering only disk service demand for predictions while CPU service demand is dominant in this case.

6. CONCLUSION

The primary objective of our research is cross platform application performance prediction when it is migrated from one storage system to another. We predicted the performance with a high accuracy when application database is migrated from a low-end HDD to a high-end HDD (VM and physical systems) and SSD. The experimental results show that the prediction accuracy is within 10% error bound until 90% of the storage device utilization is reached.

Our future work aims to evaluate the performance predictions for CPU intensive applications using IO, network and memory traces. We also plan to conduct extensive tests for performance estimation of virtual machines running within cloud data centers.

7. REFERENCES

[1] http://grinder.sourceforge.net/g3/tcpproxy.html.
[2] E. Anderson, M. Kallahalla, M. Uysal, and R. Swaminathan. Buttress: A toolkit for flexible and high fidelity i/o benchmarking. In *Proceedings of the 3rd USENIX Conference on File and Storage Technologies*, pages 4–4. USENIX Association, 2004.
[3] A. Aranya, C. P. Wright, and E. Zadok. Tracefs: A file system to trace them all. In *FAST*, pages 129–145, 2004.
[4] S. Duttagupta and R. Mansharamani. Extrapolation tool for load testing results. In *Performance Evaluation of Computer Telecommunication Systems (SPECTS) 2011 International Symposium on*, pages 69–76, June 2011.
[5] J. Horkỳ and R. Santinelli. From detailed analysis of io pattern of the hep applications to benchmark of new storage solutions. In *Journal of Physics: Conference Series*, volume 331, page 052008. IOP Publishing, 2011.
[6] H. J. Ioapps toolkit - ioprofiler and ioreplay tools, 2010.
[7] N. Joukov, T. Wong, and E. Zadok. Accurate and efficient replaying of file system traces. In *FAST*, volume 5, pages 25–25, 2005.
[8] J. KrizÌŇanicÌĄ, A. GrguricÌĄ, M. MosÌŇmondor, and P. Lazarevski. Load testing and performance monitoring tools in use with ajax based web applications. In *MIPRO, 2010 Proceedings of the 33rd International Convention*, pages 428–434, May 2010.
[9] A. Li, X. Zong, M. Zhang, S. Kandula, and X. Yang. Cloudprophet: predicting web application performance in the cloud. *ACM SIGCOMM Poster*, 2011.
[10] B. C. Tak, C. Tang, H. Huang, and L. Wang. Pseudoapp: Performance prediction for application migration to cloud. In *Integrated Network Management (IM 2013), 2013 IFIP/IEEE International Symposium on*, pages 303–310, May 2013.
[11] R. Virk and D. Chahal. Trace replay based i/o performance studies for enterprise workload migration. In *2nd Annual Conference of CMG India*, page Online, Nov. 2015.
[12] Z. Weiss, T. Harter, A. C. Arpaci-Dusseau, and R. H. Arpaci-Dusseau. Root: Replaying multithreaded traces with resource-oriented ordering. In *Proceedings of the Twenty-Fourth ACM Symposium on Operating Systems Principles*, SOSP '13, pages 373–387, New York, NY, USA, 2013. ACM.

BFT-Bench: A Framework to Evaluate BFT Protocols

[Work-In-Progress Paper]

Divya Gupta
Univ. Grenoble Alpes, LIG
Grenoble, France
divya.gupta@imag.fr

Lucas Perronne
Univ. Grenoble Alpes, LIG
Grenoble, France
lucas.perronne@imag.fr

Sara Bouchenak
INSA Lyon, LIRIS
Lyon, France
sara.bouchenak@insa-lyon.fr

ABSTRACT

Byzantine Fault Tolerance (BFT) has been extensively studied and numerous protocols and software prototypes have been proposed. However, most BFT prototypes have been evaluated in an ad-hoc setting, considering different fault types and fault injection scenarios. In this paper, we present BFT-Bench, the first benchmarking framework for evaluating and comparing BFT protocols in practice. BFT-Bench includes different BFT protocols implementations, their automatic deployment in a distributed setting, the ability to define and inject different faulty behaviors, and the online monitoring and reporting of performance and dependability measures. Preliminary results of BFT-Bench show the effectiveness of the framework, easily allowing an empirical comparison of different BFT protocols, in various workload and fault scenarios.

Keywords

Fault Tolerance; Byzantine Faults; Fault Injection; Performance; Robustness; Benchmarking

1. INTRODUCTION

Cloud computing environments are now increasingly common. With their expansion, unpredictable events such as malicious attacks, network delays, data corruption, and other types of Byzantine faults require specific fault tolerance mechanisms. Byzantine Fault Tolerance (BFT), based on state machine replication, consists in replicating the critical service in several replicas running on different nodes, and thus, ensuring service availability despite failure occurrence [15]. When clients access the service, this is done through a specific BFT communication protocol that ensures that client requests are processed by replicas in the same order.

There has been a large amount of work on Byzantine Fault Tolerance (BFT) protocols. Early efforts have explored the practicality of Byzantine Fault Tolerance, with PBFT protocol[6]. Other efforts have been made to improve the performance of the protocols and reduce the cost they induce

due to many message rounds and cryptographic operations. Thus, some BFT protocols focus on improving performance in fault-free cases [16, 12, 11, 10, 8, 17], while other protocols improve performance in presence of failures, each one proposing and applying techniques to counter specific types of faults such as network contention, system overload, etc. [2, 7, 9, 1]. However, there has been very little in the way of empirical evaluation of BFT protocols. Evaluations of the protocols have often been conducted in an ad-hoc way, which makes them difficult to reproduce, and compare with new protocols. Moreover, it is generally admitted that BFT protocols are too complex to implement, thus, re-implementing them each time a new protocol must be compared with existing ones is not realistic.

In this paper, we present BFT-Bench, a benchmarking environment for evaluating performance and robustness of Byzantine fault tolerance systems. BFT-Bench enables the definition of various execution scenarios and faultloads, their automatic deployment in an online system, and the production of various monitoring statistics. This provides a means to analyze and compare the effectiveness of the protocols in various situations. BFT-Bench is an open framework that includes state-of-the-art BFT protocols, and may be extended with new BFT protocols. In addition, the paper presents an evaluation with BFT-Bench, empirically comparing different BFT protocols, and exhibiting their level of performance and robustness in different scenarios. The remainder of the paper is structured as follows. Section 2 presents an overview of BFT-Bench. Section 3 describes the experimental evaluation, and Section 4 concludes the paper.

2. OVERVIEW OF BFT-Bench

We present *BFT-Bench*, a novel framework for empirical evaluation and comparison of Byzantine Fault-Tolerant systems.

2.1 BFT Protocols in Consideration

BFT-Bench is intended to be an open framework, that includes BFT protocol prototypes, and that may be extended with new BFT protocols. In the following, we consider state-of-the-art BFT protocols: PBFT for being the first practical BFT protocol [6], Chain for its performance efficiency in fault-free conditions [10], and RBFT as an instance of robust protocol that minimizes performance in presence of failures [2].

PBFT is considered the baseline of BFT protocols [6]; and its communication pattern is used by many other protocols [7, 2, 4]. In PBFT, there is a primary and replicas that

ICPE'16, March 12-18, 2016, Delft, Netherlands

© 2016 ACM. ISBN 978-1-4503-4080-9/16/03. . . $15.00

DOI: http://dx.doi.org/10.1145/2851553.2858667

interact through three stages of message exchanges, before the client can commit its request. First, primary sends pre-prepare messages to other replicas with assigned sequence number to each request. The two following message stages, prepare and commit, are dedicated to the exchange and validation of the sequence numbers proposed by the primary. PBFT ensures *Safety* and *Liveness*; upon violation of these properties the primary is suspected to be faulty and thus, a primary view change is initiated by replicas.

As the name suggests, Chain has a chain-like communication pattern for replicas that greatly benefits from the batch optimization (i.e. multiple messages in one batch) [10]. Thus, Chain allows to handle a high load of requests. Chain must rely on a protocol switching mechanism when subject to failures.

RBFT is a robust protocol that strengthens the architecture of PBFT and incorporates fault adaptive mechanisms to deal with certain faulty behaviors [2]. RBFT runs $f + 1$ multiple instances of the same protocol in parallel but the requests are executed only by one of the instances called master instance while other f instances are called backup instances. Each backup instance has its own primary which orders the incoming requests in order to monitor the difference of throughput between the master instance and itself. If the performance at backup and master instances differs by a defined threshold at more than $2f + 1$ replicas, the primary replica at master instance is considered faulty and a view change is triggered, where a new primary is elected at every instance.

2.2 Faultload

Faults can occur accidentally or can be induced intentionally. Users of BFT-Bench framework can generate various faultloads involving different faulty behaviors. Each faultload contains various information which we describe below:

- **Fault Trigger Time**: The *fault trigger time* contains the time stamp at which the fault must be triggered.

- **Fault Type**: Byzantine faults encompass numerous faulty behaviors, e.g. hardware failure, software failure, network congestion, etc.

- **Fault Parameters**: Different faults may require additional fault parameters at time of fault injection. According to the type of fault to be injected, fault parameters might vary. For *replica crash, message delay & network flooding*, the location of the fault must be specified, whereas in *system overloading*, the location is irrelevant since no replica acts faulty. For *network flooding*, the size of the corrupted messages is an important factor, whereas for *message delay*, the value of the delay introduced before sending a message must be specified.

Fault types that are tackled by the considered BFT protocols are the following:
Replica Crash. Crash of a server is a common performance failure that can happens in a system. Upon crash, the server stops completely and do not participates in any further communication with the clients or the servers. Most of the industries like Salesforce, Amazon, Oracle, etc, rely on Paxos[14, 13] for handling crash but are unable to detect byzantine faults and face challenges due to disrupted

availability. BFT protocols consider crash as yet another byzantine fault.
Message Delay. Delaying the sending of messages benefits from the difficulty to distinguish a faulty replica from a slow network. When a replica starts delaying of messages, it slows down all future operations depending on these messages. As described in section 2.1, most of BFT protocols ensure the *Safety* property by reaching an agreement on the total order of execution of the requests. If the messages containing these information are delayed, then the whole protocol is delayed, thus leading to degradation in performance. This byzantine behavior is thus especially critical when it occurs at the primary.
Network Flooding. Network flooding is meant to overload both the network and the computational resources with malicious messages which cannot be said invalid until verified. This verification of messages consumes a lot of computational cycles and prevents the resources from focusing on the correct messages.
System Overload. Overloading the system with a large number of requests sent by a large number of clients can prove to be catastrophic and can affect the performance to a large extent. Although none of the servers behave malicious in this attack, but continuous increase in concurrent clients can eventually deteriorate the performance or lead to system failure.

2.3 Workload

The workload is first characterized by number of concurrent clients sending requests to the BFT system. Client requests are executed in FIFO order in a closed loop, where a client submits a request, waits for the request to get processed and receives a response, before sending another request. The workload is also characterized by the size of client request/response messages exchanged with the BFT system. It is an important parameter as large size messages affect BFT system performance, due to time consuming cryptographic operations executed by BFT protocols. BFT-Bench includes a client emulator implementing multi-client behavior, where each client process sends requests to the underlying BFT system, and receives corresponding responses.

2.4 Performance and Dependability Analysis

BFT-Bench produces statistics for performance metrics, namely *Throughput* and *Latency*. The former is the number of client requests handled by the system per unit of time, and the latter is the time elapsed from the moment a client submits a request until the complete response is received by this client. *Availability* is measured in terms of time when the service is available, i.e., the service is responding. It is the ratio of the time the service was returning responses (correct or incorrect) to the total time the service was meant to run. It is usually measured over a period of time, usually in terms of days, months or years. BFT protocols should theoretically be 100% reliable and available. The experimental evaluation (see Section 3) describes how well they perform in practice.

3. EXPERIMENTAL EVALUATION

In this section we present a preliminary comparative analysis of the three BFT protocols, PBFT, Chain and RBFT when facing different types of faults.

3.1 Experimental Setup

Our experiments were conducted on a cluster running in Grid'5000 [5] composed of 34 nodes. Each node hosts two 4-core Intel Xeon E5420 QC processors at 2.50GHz frequency with 8GB of RAM and 160GB SATA of storage space. Machines are interconnected through 1 Gigabit Ethernet and have only a single network interface. In the experiments we consider a cluster of 4 nodes ($3f + 1$) for running BFT protocol instances. We reserve 2 extra nodes, one for concurrent clients' emulator, and one for hosting BFT-Bench framework. A client requests incurs 30 ($\pm 10\%$) milliseconds emulating application computations. We use a/b micro-benchmark by Castro and Liskov [6] for evaluating throughput and latency for each faulty behavior. We used original versions of the code bases for the three protocols in consideration[1].

3.2 Replica Crash

Here, we consider the Byzantine misbehavior described by the following faultload:
<300s, replica crash, {primary}>, defining *fault trigger time*, *fault type* and *fault location*, respectively.

For our evaluation, we consider crash of primary. Since primary replica is responsible for ordering the incoming requests, its crash leads to expensive *view change protocol* initiated by other replicas, thus degrading the overall performance. In our experiments, all the backup replicas wait for 5 seconds before considering primary to be unresponsive. In case of non primary crash, protocol continues as replicas need only 2f+1 matching responses.

Figure 1 presents the performance of the prototypes when a primary crashes. In the results for PBFT, we observe a sudden increase in latency (Figure 1-a), and throughput (Figure 1-b) drops sharply upon crash of the primary. This is due to the *view change protocol* which replaces the faulty primary. Prototypes for Chain and RBFT fail to respond once the primary crashes. Upon crash, Chain cannot maintain its pipeline structure as the successor of the crashed server never receives any messages. Chain must switch to PBFT upon crash, but unfortunately this mechanism is not present in the original prototype. We would have observed the same performance as PBFT if switching was possible [3]. In RBFT, clients broadcast requests to all replicas. During crash fault, client enters an infinite request re-transmission loop while attempting to send request to the crashed replica. This is due to the absence of a crash handling mechanism at client side.

3.3 Network Flooding

Figure 2 presents the performance of PBFT & RBFT when a non-primary replica starts to flood (sends as many malicious/corrupt messages as possible) other replicas. Faultload used is as follows:
<300s, network flooding, {$Replica_2$, 4KB}>, where $Replica_2$ will start to flood other servers with corrupt messages of size 4KB at 300s.

BFT-Bench implements this behavior by forcing a replica to enter an infinite loop of continuous transmission of malicious messages to other servers until the end of the exper-

---
[1]Code base of PBFT was downloaded from http://www.pmg.csail.mit.edu/bft/#sw whereas RBFT and Chain implementations were obtained directly from authors [10, 2].

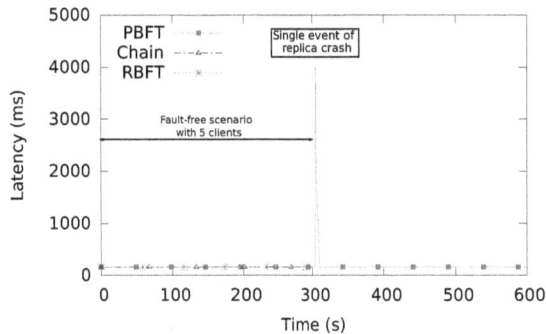

(a) Latency

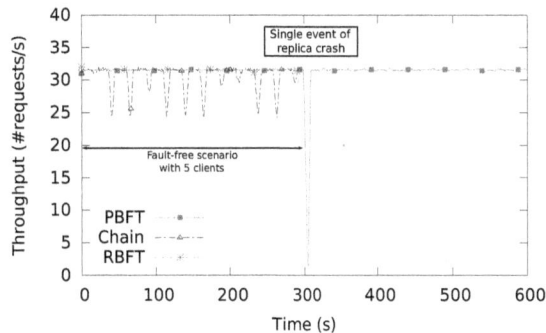

(b) Throughput

Figure 1: Evaluation in presence of replica crash

iment. We observe that any replica, either primary or non primary would impact the performance in the same way.

The results illustrate that Chain makes no progress upon fault injection while performance of PBFT becomes sporadic. This is due to the expensive time consuming cryptographic operations performed over corrupt messages by all the replicas in PBFT and successor replica in Chain. Inability to handle corrupt messages introduces a gap in the communication pattern and lack of protocol switching mechanism, holds the Chain from continuing.

RBFT uses multiple NICs to avoid malicious clients and replicas from flooding client-to-replica & replica-to-replica communications. RBFT also employs flood adaptive mechanism where non-faulty replicas can detect a flooding replica and blacklist it [2]. Flood protection enables a non-faulty replica to monitor the number of messages (including correct & malicious messages) received. If a non faulty replica receives more than a specific number of messages from a particular replica in a period of time, then it can label this replica as faulty and initiate a blacklisting protocol. When this happens, RBFT closes the NIC of the misbehaving replica for some time but after a given period it rejoins the system again. Due to this we observe slight variations in performance with upto 5% of degradation.

4. CONCLUSION

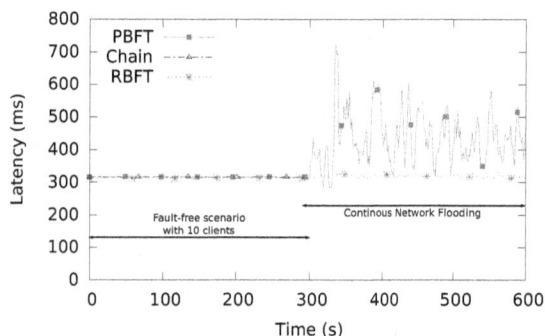

(a) Latency

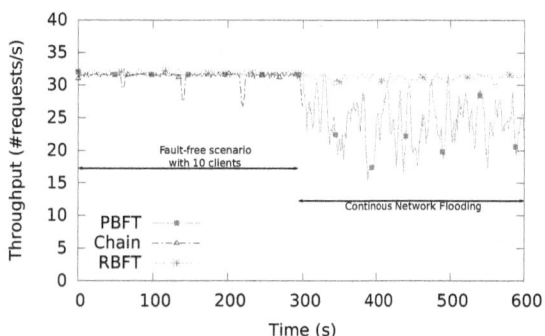

(b) Throughput

Figure 2: Evaluation in presence of network flooding

This paper presented BFT-Bench, the first framework for evaluating BFT implementations under different faulty behaviors and workloads. BFT-Bench framework includes three state-of-the-art BFT protocols, automatically deploys them, allows to generate different types of faults, injects them at different locations and different rates, and computes performance and dependability measures. The paper presented preliminary experiments conducted with BFT-Bench. The evaluation results show that BFT-Bench is able to successfully compare various BFT protocols, in various faulty behaviors. We wish to make BFT benchmarking easy to adopt by developers and end-users of BFT protocols. BFT-Bench framework aims to help researchers and practitioners to better analyze and evaluate the effectiveness and robustness of BFT systems.

Acknowledgement

This work was partly supported by AMADEOS, a collaborative project funded under the European Commission's FP7 (FP7-ICT-2013-610535). The experiments presented in the paper were conducted in Grid'5000, an experimental testbed developed under the INRIA ALADDIN development action with support from CNRS, RENATER and several Universities, as well as other funding bodies.

5. REFERENCES

[1] Y. Amir, B. A. Coan, J. Kirsch, and J. Lane. Byzantine Replication Under Attack. In *DSN*, pages 197–206, 2008.

[2] P.-L. Aublin, S. B. Mokhtar, and V. Quéma. RBFT: Redundant Byzantine Fault Tolerance. In *ICDCS*, pages 297–306, 2013.

[3] J.-P. Bahsoun, R. Guerraoui, and A. Shoker. Making BFT Protocols Adaptive.

[4] A. Bessani, J. Sousa, and E. E. Alchieri. State Machine Replication for the Masses with BFT-SMART. In *Dependable Systems and Networks (DSN), 2014 44th Annual IEEE/IFIP International Conference on*, pages 355–362. IEEE, 2014.

[5] F. Cappello, E. Caron, M. Dayde, F. Desprez, Y. Jégou, P. Primet, E. Jeannot, S. Lanteri, J. Leduc, N. Melab, et al. Grid'5000: A Large Scale and Highly Reconfigurable Grid Experimental Testbed. In *Proceedings of the 6th IEEE/ACM International Workshop on Grid Computing*, pages 99–106. IEEE Computer Society, 2005.

[6] M. Castro and B. Liskov. Practical Byzantine Fault Tolerance. In *OSDI*, pages 173–186, 1999.

[7] A. Clement, E. L. Wong, L. Alvisi, M. Dahlin, and M. Marchetti. Making Byzantine Fault Tolerant Systems Tolerate Byzantine Faults. In *NSDI*, pages 153–168, 2009.

[8] M. Correia, N. F. Neves, and P. Veríssimo. BFT-TO: Intrusion Tolerance with Less Replicas. *Comput. J.*, 56(6):693–715, 2013.

[9] G. S. V. et. al. Spin one's wheels? byzantine fault tolerance with a spinning primary.

[10] R. Guerraoui, N. Knezevic, V. Quéma, and M. Vukolic. The Next 700 BFT Protocols. In *EuroSys*, pages 363–376, 2010.

[11] R. Guerraoui, N. Knezevic, V. Quema, and M. Vukolic. Stretching BFT. Technical report, Technical Report EPFL-REPORT-149105, EPFL, 2011.

[12] R. Kotla, L. Alvisi, M. Dahlin, A. Clement, and E. L. Wong. Zyzzyva: Speculative Byzantine Fault Tolerance. *ACM Trans. Comput. Syst.*, 27(4), 2009.

[13] L. Lamport. The Part-Time Parliament. *ACM Trans. Comput. Syst.*, 16(2):133–169, 1998.

[14] L. Lamport. Paxos Made Simple. *SIGACT News*, 32(4):51–58, 2001.

[15] F. B. Schneider. Implementing Fault-tolerant Services Using the State Machine Approach: A Tutorial. *ACM Comput. Surv.*, 22(4):299–319, Dec. 1990.

[16] R. van Renesse and F. B. Schneider. Chain Replication for Supporting High Throughput and Availability. In *OSDI*, pages 91–104, 2004.

[17] G. S. Veronese, M. Correia, A. N. Bessani, L. C. Lung, and P. Veríssimo. Efficient Byzantine Fault-Tolerance. *IEEE Trans. Computers*, 62(1):16–30, 2013.

Towards Performance and Scalability Analysis of Distributed Memory Programs on Large-Scale Clusters

Sourav Medya[1,2], Ludmila Cherkasova[2], Guilherme Magalhaes[3], Kivanc Ozonat[2],
Chaitra Padmanabha[3], Jiban Sarma[3], Imran Sheikh[3]

[1]University of California, Santa Barbara, [2]Hewlett Packard Labs, [3]Hewlett Packard Enterprise

medya@cs.ucsb.edu, lucy.cherkasova@hpe.com, guilherme.magalhaes@hpe.com,
kivanc.ozonat@hpe.com, p.chaitra@hpe.com, jiban.jyoti.sarma@hpe.com, imrans@hpe.com

Abstract

Many HPC and modern Big Data processing applications belong to a class of so-called scale-out applications, where the application dataset is partitioned and processed by a cluster of machines. Understanding and assessing the scalability of the designed application is one of the primary goals during the application implementation. Typically, in the design and implementation phase, the programmer is bound to a limited size cluster for debugging and performing profiling experiments. The challenge is to assess the scalability of the designed program for its execution on a larger cluster. While in an increased size cluster, each node needs to process a smaller fraction of the original dataset, the communication volume and communication time might be significantly increased, which could become detrimental and provide diminishing performance benefits. The distributed memory applications exhibit complex behavior: they tend to interleave computations and communications, use bursty transfers, and utilize global synchronization primitives. Therefore, one of the main challenges is the analysis of bandwidth demands due to increased communication volume as a function of a cluster size. In this paper[1], we introduce a novel approach to assess the scalability and performance of a distributed memory program for execution on a large-scale cluster. Our solution involves 1) a limited set of traditional experiments performed in a medium size cluster and 2) an additional set of similar experiments performed with an "interconnect bandwidth throttling" tool, which enables the assessment of the communication demands with respect to available bandwidth. This approach enables a prediction of a cluster size, where a communication cost becomes a dominant component, at which point the performance benefits of the increased cluster lead to a diminishing return. We demonstrate the proposed approach using a popular Graph500 benchmark.

1. INTRODUCTION

In the last few years, graph algorithms have received much attention and become increasingly important for solving many problems in social networks, web connectivity, scientific computing,

---

[1]This work was originated and largely completed during S. Medya's internship at Hewlett Packard Labs in summer 2015.

ICPE 2016, March 12-18, 2016, Delft, Netherlands.
© 2016 ACM. ISBN 978-1-4503-4080-9/16/03 ...$15.00
DOI: http://dx.doi.org/10.1145/2851553.2858669.

data mining, and other domains. The numbers of vertices in the analyzed graph networks have grown from billions to tens of billions and the edges have grown from tens of billions to hundreds of billions. A traditional way for improving performance application is to store and process its working set in memory. As the problem size increases and it cannot fit into memory of a single server, the distributed computing and memory resources are required for holding the entire dataset in memory and processing it. This leads to a scale-out execution, where each machine handles a portion of the complete dataset, and needs to communicate with each other to synchronize the executions.

Message passing interface (MPI) is a standard programming paradigm for scale-out, distributed memory applications. Complex MPI-based programs interleave computations and communications in inter-tangled patterns which makes it difficult to perform an accurate analysis of communication layer impact on application performance and predict scaling properties of the program. Due to asynchronous, concurrent execution of different nodes, many communication delays between the nodes could be "hidden" (i.e., do not contribute or impact the overall application completion time). It happens when some nodes are still in their "computation-based" or "processing" portions of the code, while the other nodes already perform communication exchanges. Equally difficult is to analyze the utilized (required) interconnect bandwidth during the execution of MPI program due to a variety of existing MPI collectives and calls that could involve different sets of nodes and communication styles. At the same time, performance of such distributed memory applications inherently depends on a performance of a communication layer of the cluster.

Designing and implementing an efficient and scalable distributed memory program is a challenging task. Typically, during the initial implementation and debugging phases, a programmer is limited to experiments on a small/medium size cluster for application testing and profiling. The challenge is to assess (predict) the scalability of the designed program during its execution on a larger size cluster. This scalability problem had existed for decades and some elaborate and sophisticated ensembles of tools and simulators [11, 10, 6, 12, 5, 9, 2, 4, 1, 13, 14] were proposed by HPC community to attack this challenging problem.

In this work, we discuss a new approach for assessing the scalability and performance of distributed memory programs. We analyze a recently introduced by HPC community Graph500 benchmark [3] for measuring and comparing computer's performance in memory retrieval. It implements a Breadth First Search algorithm on graphs and uses as an input a synthetically generated scale-free graph, which could be easily scaled to extremely large sizes. Our approach is based on performing a limited set of traditional experiments in a small/medium size cluster for assessing a baseline program scalability. For deriving the interconnect bandwidth demands by the program in a larger size cluster and assessing these demands' scaling trend, we perform an additional set of similar experiments augmented with the "interconnect bandwidth throttling" tool [15], which helps to expose the communication demands of the program with respect to required (utilized) interconnect bandwidth. By combining the insights from these two complementary sets of experiments, we could project the application performance for larger cluster sizes, and in particular, the size, where a communication cost becomes a dominant component. At this point, the performance benefits of the increased cluster size provide a diminishing return. The remainder of the paper presents our approach and results in more detail.

2. WHAT MATTERS FOR APPLICATION PERFORMANCE AND SCALABILITY?

In this work, we focus on the performance and scalability analysis of distributed shared memory programs, and graph algorithms in particular. We demonstrate the problem and our approach by considering the Graph500 benchmark [3] that implements Breadth First Search (BFS) algorithm. BFS is an important algorithm as it serves a building block for many other algorithms such as computation of betweenness centrality of vertices, shortest path between two vertices, etc. Breadth First Search is a typical graph traversal algorithm performed on an undirected, unweighted graph. A goal is to compute a distance from a given source vertex s to each vertex in the graph, i.e., finding all the vertices which are "one hop" away, "two hops" away, etc. When reasoning about program performance and its execution efficiency on a large-scale distributed cluster, the following factors are critically important (see Figure 1):

1. **Selected Underlying Algorithm**: Graph problems could be implemented in many different ways in terms of graph data partitioning for parallel processing as shown in the top layer of Figure 1. Data partitioning and algorithm details play an important role in scalability analysis as it impacts algorithm's communication style and the communication volume (in a distributed scenario), and thus the application completion time. There are a few well-known data partitioning approaches (e.g., 1-D and 2-D) proposed for parallel processing of BFS [8]. The 2-D partitioning algorithm was theoretically proven to be a scalable algorithm [8].

2. **Implementation Code**: Program performance and its scalability further depends on the code that implements a selected/designed algorithm. This is the middle layer shown in Figure 1. In spite of excellent theoretical properties of the 2-D partitioning algorithm, its inefficient implementation may result in a poorly performing and badly scaling program. Therefore, the implementation details are critical part of application performance and scalability.

3. **Underlying System Hardware and Software**: Finally, the underlying system hardware, that is available and targeted for program execution, is extremely important for program performance and its scalability as shown by the bottom layer in Figure 1. Specially designed systems, such as Blue Gene and K Computer, have proprietary, custom-built interconnects which provide enhanced support for MPI collectives, and therefore, demonstrate superior performance compared to commodity clusters.

Therefore, the scalability analysis and performance prediction depends on the underlying graph problem/algorithm, its parallel implementation, and the underlying system software and hardware. Figure 1 illustrates these critical factors with some examples from each category.

In the paper, we demonstrate our approach by using the 2-D partitioning IBM implementation of BFS algorithm [3] executed on the commodity cluster (shown by the green boxes in Figure 1).

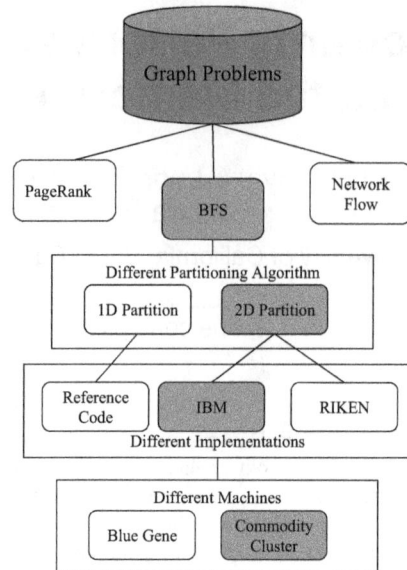

Figure 1: Performance and scalability: example of critical factors.

In our experiments, we use a **32-node cluster** connected via FDR InfiniBand (56 Gbits/s). Each node is based on HP DL360 Gen9 servers with two sockets, each with 14 cores, 2 GHz, Xeon E5-2683 v3, 35 MB last level cache size, and 256 GB DRAM per node.

3. BASE LINEAR REGRESSION MODEL

There are different ways to formulate "scaling" of a particular program. One of the classical methods is *strong scaling*. In strong scaling, the problem data size is kept fixed and the number of processors (nodes) to execute the program is increased. In a general case, the completion time of a distributed memory program can be modeled as follows:

$$CompletionTime = ProcessingTime + CommunicationTime$$

As the number of processors in the cluster is increased to p, one would expect that the *ProcessingTime* in this equation will improve by p times. With the assumption that the data is evenly distributed over the nodes, the processing time can be approximated as $O(\frac{1}{p})$.

To estimate the *CommunicationTime* of a distributed memory program as a function of number of processors p is a more challenging task. To our rescue comes a theoretical analysis of 2-D partitioning implementation [8]: its communication pattern is well known—the number of messages per processor is $O(\sqrt{p})$. We exploit this asymptotic analysis and include this factor in our model. So, the communication time can be accounted as $O(\frac{1}{\sqrt{p}})$.

Base Linear Regression Model: we can derive the formulation for *Completion Time* as linearly dependent on $\frac{1}{p}$ and $\frac{1}{\sqrt{p}}$:

$$Completion\ Time(p) = C_1 * \frac{1}{p} + C_2 * \frac{1}{\sqrt{p}} \qquad (1)$$

Figure 2 (a) shows measured completion times of Graph500 benchmark executed in our cluster for different graph sizes and number of nodes in the cluster. We configured each node in the cluster to execute 18 MPI processes, each with 1 thread. The legend "scale" denotes the size of the graph [3]. The scale s defines the graph with 2^s vertices and $16 \cdot 2^s$ edges, e.g., graph of scale 27 has 134 Million vertices and 2.1 Billion edges, graph of scale 28 has 268 Million vertices and 4.2 Billion edges, etc.

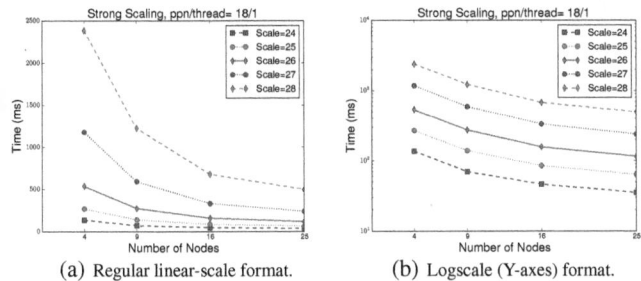

(a) Regular linear-scale format. (b) Logscale (Y-axes) format.

Figure 2: The Graph500 completion time in a strong scaling scenario.

Note, that Figure 2 (b) shows the same measurements with Y-axes in logscale format. If $CompletionTime(p)$ would scale as $O(\frac{1}{p})$ (i.e., no communication overhead) then in Figure 2 (b) one can expect a straight line with a negative slope near 1 [7]. However, it is not the case, and the communication time represents an essential component of the overall completion time of Graph500 execution.

Eq. 1 provides the formulation for $CompletionTime$ as linearly dependent on $\frac{1}{p}$ and $\frac{1}{\sqrt{p}}$, where C_1 and C_2 are constants which need to be derived from the asymptotic analysis. We aim to find these constants via linear regression. Using a medium size cluster N with n processors in total we obtain measured completion times for BFS code on all possible sub-cluster configurations with p processors, where $p \leq n$. So, we have data points as a pair, (*time, number of processors*). We use these experimental data in the set of equations (as shown below) and solve this set of equations for finding the coefficients C_1 and C_2 via linear regression:

$$CompletionTime_1(p_1) = C_0 + C_1 * \frac{1}{p_1} + C_2 * \frac{1}{\sqrt{p_1}}$$

$$CompletionTime_2(p_2) = C_0 + C_1 * \frac{1}{p_2} + C_2 * \frac{1}{\sqrt{p_2}}$$

$$\ldots \qquad \ldots \qquad \ldots \qquad \ldots$$

where $CompletionTime_i$ is the corresponding completion time when p_i processors are used. C_0 is added in regression methods to characterize noise. A popular method for solving such set of equations is Least Squares Regression, which we use here. In statistics, this is an approach for modeling the relationship between a scalar dependent variable (e.g., $CompletionTime$ here) and one or more independent variables (e.g., $\frac{1}{p}$ and $\frac{1}{\sqrt{p}}$). The set of coefficients C_0, C_1 and C_2 is the model that describes the relationship.

For a fixed problem data size in Graph500, we perform experiments with different number of nodes in our 32-node cluster (using the same configuration per node), collect measurement data, and then solve Eq. 1 with linear regression for finding constants C_0, C_1, and C_2. Figures 3 (a)-(b) show the regression results for problem scales 27 and 28 respectively. The solution is based on collected measurements of approximately 1000 data points.

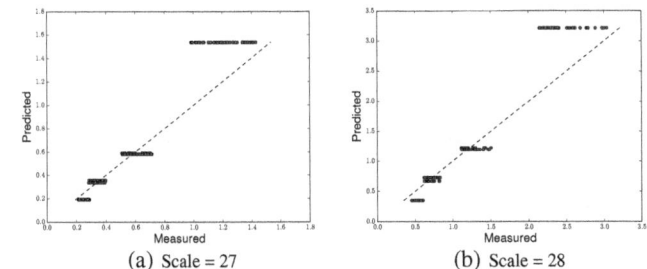

(a) Scale = 27 (b) Scale = 28

Figure 3: Computing the Constants via Regression.

Two well studied measures to show quality of regression are R^2 and "mean square" error. R^2 is better being close to 1. We get R^2 as 0.95 and 0.97 for scales 27 and 28 respectively. The corresponding "mean square" errors (close to 0 is better) are 0.04 and 0.19. Both types of errors reflect a high quality of regression results. The computed coefficient C_1 (57.67 and 102.1) is greater than C_2 (3.8 an 10.3) in both cases (for scales 27 and 28 respectively). This result shows that the processing time dominates the benchmark execution time (i.e., $CompletionTime$) in a small/medium cluster.

4. ESTIMATING THE COMMUNICATION BANDWIDTH DEMANDS

With an increased number of cluster nodes the communication volume becomes a dominant component in Eq 1. Past literature [7] shows that in a strong scaling scenario, the program performance gets additionally impacted when system interconnect bandwidth starts affecting the communication time. We need to assess the increased bandwidth demands of a communication volume as a function of the increased cluster size. Unfortunately, there are no existing tools or common approaches to analyze the utilized (required) interconnect bandwidth during the execution of general MPI program. It is a very challenging task due to a variety of existing MPI collectives and MPI calls that could involve different sets of nodes and communication styles.

To overcome this challenge, we apply *InterSense* [15] - a special interconnect emulator, which can control (throttle) the interconnect bandwidth to determine how much bandwidth the program needs before its completion time becomes impacted. It enables us to accurately estimate the required (needed) bandwidth by the program.

Figures 4 (a)-(b) show the outcome of bandwidth throttling experiments. We execute Graph500 benchmark for two different dataset scales, 27 and 28, and four different cluster sizes. Each line shows the benchmark completion times at different (controlled by *InterSense*) interconnect bandwidth percentage. These plots show that there is a non-linear relation between completion times and available interconnect bandwidth. To get accurate estimates on the required interconnect bandwidth, we experiment with 2% interval in the range from 20% to 40%. As expected, the completion times are higher with larger scales and smaller process configurations.

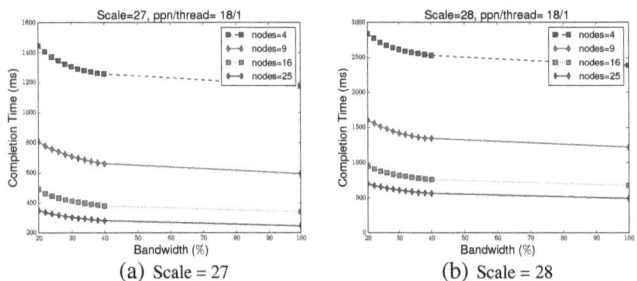

(a) Scale = 27 (b) Scale = 28

Figure 4: Bandwidth Impact on the Completion Time.

For a particular configuration, we define *Completion Time Increment* (**CTI**) at an available bandwidth (*bw*) as the increment in percentage w.r.t the completion time when 100% bandwidth is available.

$$CTI_{bw} = \frac{Completion\ Time\ at\ bw - Completion\ Time\ at\ 100}{Completion\ Time\ at\ 100} \qquad (2)$$

Bandwidth Demand ($BW_{CTI,p}$) is defined as the percentage of bandwidth required to achieve the predefined *CTI* for a particular processor configuration p.

Figure 4 shows that different cluster configurations have different completion times when the available interconnect bandwidth is varied. **The question is** how *CTI* is related to bandwidth demands in a cluster with different number of nodes? So, **the goal is** to predict the required interconnect bandwidth by Graph500 benchmark in the cluster with increased number of nodes. Then we can incorporate the impact of increased bandwidth demands into the increased communication time. As a result, we can estimate the cluster size, where a communication cost becomes a highly dominant component, at which point the performance (scalability) benefits in the further increased cluster would lead to a diminishing return.

We aim to build a model of required interconnect bandwidth for predicting these bandwidth demands in a larger size cluster. For a particular problem scale (i.e., graph size), different CTIs have similar trends as shown in Figure 5.

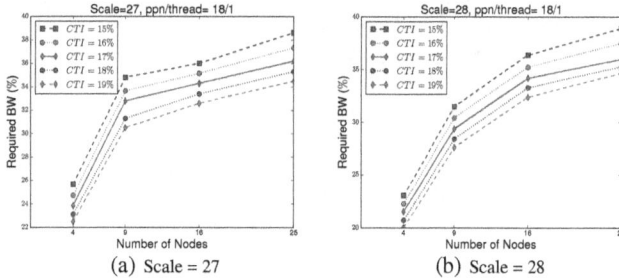

(a) Scale = 27   (b) Scale = 28

Figure 5: Interconnect Bandwidth Demands.

We compute a single *DemandConstant (DC)* for all different CTIs to predict the interconnect bandwidth demand for a larger cluster configuration. First, we determine how two processors' configurations and their required bandwidth demands are related. We follow the relation to determine a constant DC_{CTI,p_1,p_2} for a particular *CTI*, and two processors' configurations :

$$\frac{BW_{CTI,p_1}}{BW_{CTI,p_2}} = DC_{CTI,p_1,p_2} \frac{\sqrt{p_1}}{\sqrt{p_2}}$$

where $p_1 > p_2$, and p_1 and p_2 are the number of processes in the executed configurations. The intuition of the above relation comes from 2-D partitioning algorithm, where a number of messages per processor is $O(\sqrt{p})$. *DC* is taken as an average over all such DC_{p_i,p_j}. Once *DC* is computed, one can use the following equation to find the bandwidth demand ($BW_{CTI,p'}$) for a larger cluster size and a given *CTI*:

$$BW_{CTI,p'} / BW_{CTI,p*} = DC \frac{\sqrt{p'}}{\sqrt{p*}} \qquad (3)$$

where $p*$ is a number of processes in the smaller cluster size configuration available.

Next, we validate our model by executing a set of experiments with varying interconnect bandwidth, size of the graph, and number of nodes in the cluster.

Prediction Accuracy of Bandwidth Demands: We aim to predict the interconnect bandwidth demands using Eq. 3 for a 25-node cluster, and evaluate the accuracy of the designed model. Using the collected measurements for clusters with 4, 9, and 16 nodes (where each node is configured with 18 MPI processes, i.e., with 72, 162, 288 MPI processes respectively), we can obtain 3 different combinations for each considered CTI (15 in total). Actual *DC* is averaged over these 15 DC_{p_i,p_j}s. Bandwidth demands for 25 nodes (with 450 processes respectively) are computed using *DC*, Eq. 3, and $p*$ as 288 (16 nodes). The *DC* for scales 27 and 28 are 0.8 and 0.86 respectively.

Figures 6 (a)-(b) show the accuracy of the prediction. The error (difference between predicted and measured) is lower than 2% and 0.5% for scales 27 (Fig. 6 (a)) and 28 (Fig. 6 (b)) respectively.

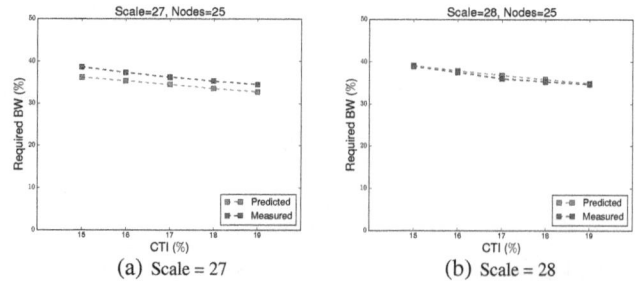

(a) Scale = 27   (b) Scale = 28

Figure 6: Prediction of Required Bandwidth Demands.

5. CONCLUSION AND FUTURE WORK

Designing and implementing an efficient and scalable distributed memory program is a challenging task. In this work, we discuss a new approach for assessing the scalability and performance of distributed memory programs by using Graph500 benchmark as a motivating example. We show a set of critical factors that needs to be taken into account for scalability analysis of a distributed memory program. Since a scalability of many distributed programs is limited by their communication volume and the available interconnect bandwidth, we show how one can derive the estimates on the required interconnect bandwidth in a larger cluster from the experiments performed in a small/medium cluster with an "interconnect bandwidth throttling" tool. By combining the outcome of these two components, we can estimate the cluster size, where a communication cost becomes a dominant component, at which point the performance benefits of the increased cluster lead to a diminishing return. In our future work, we plan to incorporate the dataset size (i.e., graph size) as a scalability problem parameter.

6. REFERENCES

[1] Dimemas: predict parallel performance using a single cpu machine. http://www.bsc.es/computer-sciences/dimemas.
[2] Extrae instrumentation package. http://www.bsc.es/computer-sciences/extrae.
[3] Graph500. http://www.graph500.org/.
[4] Paraver:Performance Analysis Tools: Details and Intelligence. http://www.bsc.es/computer-sciences/paraver.
[5] L. Adhianto, S. Banerjee, M. W. Fagan, M. Krentel, G. Marin, J. M. Mellor-Crummey, and N. R. Tallent. HPCTOOLKIT: tools for performance analysis of optimized parallel programs. *Concurrency and Computation: Practice and Experience*, 22(6), 2010.
[6] K. Barker, K. Davis, A. Hoisie, D. Kerbyson, M. Lang, S. Pakin, and J. Sancho. Using Performance Modeling to Design Large-Scale Systems. *Computer*, 42, Nov., 2009.
[7] A. Buluc and J. R. Gilbert. Parallel sparse matrix-matrix multiplication and indexing: Implementation and experiments. *SIAM Journal on Scientific Computing*, 34(4), 2012.
[8] A. Buluç and K. Madduri. Parallel breadth-first search on distributed memory systems. In *Proceedings of 2011 International Conference for High Performance Computing, Networking, Storage and Analysis*, SC '11, 2011.
[9] A. Calotoiu, T. Hoefler, M. Poke, and F. Wolf. Using Automated Performance Modeling to Find Scalability Bugs in Complex Codes. In *Proc. of Intl. Conf. for High Perf. Computing, Networking, Storage and Analysis (SC'13)*, 2013.
[10] M. Casas, R. M. Badia, and J. Labarta. Automatic Analysis of Speedup of MPI Applications. In *Proc. of the 22nd Intl. Conf. on Supercomputing*, 2008.
[11] C. Coarfa, J. M. Mellor-Crummey, N. Froyd, and Y. Dotsenko. Scalability analysis of SPMD codes using expectations. In *Procs. of the 21th Annual International Conference on Supercomputing, (ICS 2007)*, 2007.
[12] M. Geimer et al. The scalasca performance toolset architecture. *Journal on Concurr. Comput.: Pract. Exper.*, 22(6), Apr., 2010.
[13] C. Rosas, J. Gimenez, and J. Labarta. Scalability Prediction for Fundamental Performance Factors. *Journal on Supercomputing Frontiers and Innovations*, 1(2), 2014.
[14] C. Rosas, J. Gimenez, and J. Labarta. Scaling to a million cores and beyond: Using light-weight simulation to understand the challenges ahead on the road to exascale. *Journal on Future Generation Computer Systems*, 30, 2014.
[15] Q. Wang, L. Cherkasova, J. Li, and H. Volos. InterSense: Interconnect Performance Emulator for Future Scale-out Distributed Memory Applications. In *Proc. of the 23th IEEE/ACM International Symposium on Modelling, Analysis and Simulation of Computer and Telecommunication Systems (MASCOTS)*, 2015.

Empirical Analysis of Performance Problems at Code Level

David Georg Reichelt
Universität Leipzig
reichelt@informatik.uni-leipzig.de

Stefan Kühne
Universität Leipzig
stefan.kuehne@uni-leipzig.de

ABSTRACT

Performance problems are well known on architecture level. On code level their occurrences have not been systematically researched so far. Since a lot of everyday work of software developers is done on code level, methods and tools with focus on frequent performance problems are relevant.

In the presented thesis, a method for systematically evaluating the occurrence and the frequency of performance problems on code level is presented and applied to repositories. The results of this empirical research will be a classification of performance problems and a quantification of their frequency. This will raise the awareness on certain problem classes for developers and will provide a basis for the development of new performance tools for preventing performance problems.

1. INTRODUCTION

Software developers aim to choose an implementation with as little performance problems as possible. Choosing the best solution for a given problem is a non-trivial task since performance requirements are manifold, e.g. low answering time versus low memory usage, and since these requirements compete with other requirements, e.g. concerning maintainability or re-usability. Developers rely on their own experiences, ad-hoc measurements or incomplete performance problem lists to avoid performance problems, i.e. implementations with possible improvements regarding performance. A systematic, empirically founded classification of re-occurring performance problems on code level is missing. Such a classification would help developers to avoid unperformant code like regular antipatterns and would help the developer to avoid hard maintainable code.

Therefore, the research questions of the sketched PhD thesis are: (1) Which performance problem classes exist at code level? (2) How often do instances of these problem classes occur? The thesis will provide methods and tools to identify performance problems on code level and create an empirically founded problem classification gained by those

ICPE'16 March 12-18, 2016, Delft, Netherlands
© 2016 Copyright held by the owner/author(s).
ACM ISBN 978-1-4503-4080-9/16/03.
DOI: http://dx.doi.org/10.1145/2851553.2892038

methods and tools. This will help developers to decide which code patterns could be avoided. Furthermore, this contribution could be used by researchers and practitioners to tackle performance problems directly when designing tools and methods for performance improvement.

The remainder of this paper is organized as follows: First, the approach for identifying performance problems is introduced. Section 3 describes the current state of the implementation. Section 4 presents related work and explains the novelty of the approach. Section 5 presents the research plan and time schedule. Finally, a summary of the paper is provided.

2. APPROACH

The performance-optimal implementation of functional or non-functional requirements is not known a-priori. Therefore, performance problems cannot be detected from code directly. Existing code repositories contain a vast amount of performance problems which are introduced and reverted [1]. The introduction or fixture of a problem results in a measurable performance change. The set of performance changes in the code history of a software project therefore provides the basis to identify performance problems.

In the version history of a project, performance problems are present if a performance change occurs between two distinct versions and this change is not caused by a functional behaviour change[1]. If a performance change is a regression, i.e. a degradation of performance measurement values, the performance problem is located in the newer version. If the performance change is an improvement, the performance problem is located in the older version. By finding these performance problems in a sufficient number of projects and classifying them, an empirically founded classification of performance problems can be derived.

Performance changes, which are not caused by a functional behaviour change, may be due to other causes: (1) Changes trying to fulfil other performance requirements, e.g. a higher answering time may be caused by a change which decreases memory usage. (2) Changes trying to fulfil other non-functional requirements, e.g. requirements considering maintainability. The first type of change is caused by a performance trade-off and therefore no performance problem. It will not be marked as performance problem. The second type of change is a performance problem, even

---

[1]Functional behaviour changes are not equivalent to functional requirement changes. If a bug is fixed, this is not a requirement change, but a behaviour change, and it may cause a performance change.

if is caused by a reasonable trade-off between performance requirements and other requirements. Therefore, it will be marked as performance problem. A consideration whether a performance problem is acceptable due to a trade-off with other requirements is beyond the scope of this thesis.

An ideal basis for the performance analysis of a software development project would be a sufficiently documented set of load tests. Since most publicly available repositories do not maintain load tests we make the following "unit test" assumption: The performance of relevant use cases of a program correlates with the performance of at least a part of its unit tests. This assumption does hold for frameworks, in which most methods could be called in different contexts and thus become performance relevant, and for isolated backend components, where the performance of the executions themselves mainly influences the performance of the program as a whole. It does not hold for components in enterprise applications that make heavy use of other services because the performance of these services may mainly drive performance of the component.

Based on the "unit test"-assumption it is possible to detect performance changes of a program by detecting performance changes of unit tests. Therefore, this thesis will detect performance problems by comparing performance measurements of unit tests and detect changes by manually inspecting code changes that cause measurable performance changes. This method is called Performance Analysis of Software System Versions (PeASS) [12] [11]. It is planned to save detected performance problems with metadata, e.g. revision, class and expected type, into a problem database. Based on an analysis of multiple projects, a quantification of the occurrence of those problems will also be performed. These can be done based on the performance problem database created before. Furthermore, other research questions, e.g. if performance problem introduction and solving is executed by one or many committers, can be answered by the performance problem database. In the next section, the current implementation of PeASS is described.

3. STATE OF IMPLEMENTATION

Performance measurements are very time-consuming [3]. Since performance changes can only take place when called source code changes[2], measurements need only to be executed if a class called from a test case is changed. Therefore, PeASS contains the following steps: (1) determination of the tests that need to run in each version, (2) measurement of the performance of selected unit tests of selected software versions and (3) identification of performance bugs.

To determine which tests need to be run in each version, we apply change-based test selection. In the beginning, for each test, a list of classes which are called by a test is determined (I). Afterwards, for every version, it is determined based on the version control system diff whether a test has to be executed in this version (II). The test has to be executed iff the test itself or a class called from the test is changed in the current version. If the test has to be executed in the current version, the called classes of this test are re-determined since changes may introduce new called classes (IV). The construction of dependencies is done using

Kieker [15], its AspectJ instrumentation and trace analysis. This process is displayed in 1.

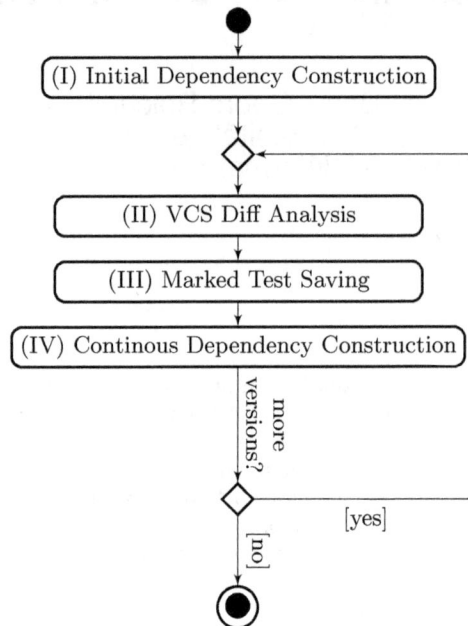

Figure 1: Steps to select the relevant tests, from: [11]

Afterwards, the performance measurement is executed. Since performance measurements are imprecise due to background processes, JIT compilation, thread scheduling and garbage collection [3], a test harness, which produces replicable results, has to be established. While jmh[3] provides such functionality, adapting performance tests for running in jmh implies considerable effort for transforming the Java source code and setting up the run environment with classpath and variable for the surefire-run without using surefire itself. Therefore, the test process with multiple sequential vm runs, test repetition for a warmup phase until a steady state is reached and the warmup executions themselves has been implemented. Currently experiments are carried out to determine the count of vm runs, warmup executions and measurement executions in order to find performance changes as fast as possible. After executing the tests, which are determined by the change-based test selection, performance changes are detected. This is done by comparison of the confidence intervals of the average values of the vm runs.

After performance changes have been identified, they are manually inspected. Every change is marked according to whether the change is necessary due to a change of a functional requirement. If it is a pure performance change, it will be classified manually. Currently, performance problem class candidates such as inefficient exception handling, inefficient exit conditions and inefficient concurrent processing have been identified based on a first run of PeASS on Apache Commons IO. With the execution of experiments with more executions and on more projects a more fine-grained classification will be gained.

---

[2]The fraction of performance problems due to other causes, e.g. changes of configuration files, is ignored. It is assumed that these changes are rare incidents.

[3]http://openjdk.java.net/projects/code-tools/jmh/

4. RELATED WORK

Work related to the PhD thesis can be found in three research fields: (1) empirical analysis of repositories for performance properties, (2) empirical analysis of documentation artifacts for performance problems and (3) work on performance antipatterns.

In order to analyse performance properties of repositories (1), several work exists analysing the performance of a version history directly [1] [5] and analysing the performance of the version history considering special properties of the software [6] [4] [10].

[1] aims at analysing the evolution of performance during software development. This goal is pursued by analysing performance changes of predefined benchmarks for projects for Pharo[4]. These benchmarks are adjusted in order to skip the call of functionalities which are not present in some of the analysed versions. The existence of performance changes during the lifecycle of a software is proven. Furthermore, they classify the changes in negative changes, like *Composing Collection Operations*, and positive changes, like *Deleting Redundant Method call*. Goal and method slightly differ from the approach of this thesis: Performance changes and not performance problems should be detected in [1], and constant benchmarks are used instead of unit tests. Since in [1] the bugs are detected in functionalities that stay stable over time, a bias may be introduced, as developers might consider performance of stable functions more relevant than performance of new functions. [5] describes a method for determining the history of energy consumption of an application over the last revisions. Therefore an hard- and software environment capable of measuring the performance of an application over several versions is defined. Only the method is presented, performance problem classes are not described.

[6] analyses the performance of a repository in order to show the applicability of Stochastic Performance Logic (SPL) for performance unit testing. Based on commit messages it is checked whether the intended performance change, i.e. an improvement of the performance, has really taken place because of a commit. This is tested by hand-written SPL unit tests. It is shown that performance does not always change as the developer beliefs. [4] shows a method to find the root cause of performance regressions in a defined range of revisions. This is a valuable part of a performance analysis of a repository. Nevertheless, an analysis itself is not carried out for all versions. [10] analyse the performance of repositories for performance issues of concurrent usage of classes. Concurrent performance tests are automatically generated using the interface of a class. Performance regressions related to behaviour under concurrent usage are detected.

Several work discusses the occurrence of performance bugs through analysis of documentation artifacts (1) [17] [7] [9] [8]. These works analyse bug tracker or commit messages in order to answer different research questions. [7] analyses 109 performance bugs and classifies them into *Uncoordinated Functions*, *Skippable Functions*, *Synchronization Issues* and *Others*. Furthermore, the introduction, exposure and fixture of performance bugs are discussed. [9] analyses the introduction and fixture of performance in repositories of established software projects. They find among others that performance bugs are found more often by reasoning on the source code than functional bugs. [17] addresses research

questions comparing performance and security bugs by an analysis of Firefox. Similar work was also done for special systems, e.g. for android applications [8]. They find that performance bugs are harder to fix than non-performance bugs and that problem effects (e.g. *Energy Leak*) and bug patterns (e.g. *Lengthy operations in main threads*) differ from other contexts. This works provide valuable findings about performance bugs in bug trackers. They may find bugs on architecture level since these bugs are also likely to be reported. Their results may lack unreported bugs. This gap is filled by PeASS which is capable of finding all performance bugs at code level which are covered by a unit test.

The work on performance antipatterns on architecture level (3) describes antipatterns and provides methods to find them in existing models. [13] analysed performance in practical projects and found 14 antipatterns ranging from the concrete *Unnecessary Processing* to the rather abstract *Falling Dominoes* which occurs when failure of one component causes the failure of another component. This is the first comprehensive listing of performance anti-patterns. Nevertheless, the performance anti-patterns have not been empirically grounded. A quantification of their occurrence has not taken place. The antipatterns described in [13] are put in a hierarchy in [16]. Furthermore, the Performance Problem Diagnostics (PDD), a method for finding performance problems in a three-tier application, is presented. PDD finds those performance problems by executing systematic experiments. It pursues a complementary approach to this thesis: Based on a-priori known problem classes, it identifies their occurrence. The performance anti-patterns are also used in [2] and [14] to detect performance problems in existing projects. [2] defines OCL queries on UML models for certain rules which formalize performance antipatterns. [14] aims at finding performance problems in Palladio Component Models. In addition, actions providing a solution to the performance problem are defined. These works define and use performance antipatterns based on real world problems. An empirical research on their occurrence has not taken place yet.

5. RESEARCH PLAN AND TIME SCHEDULE

Currently, the main process of PeASS has been implemented, including the transformation of unit tests to performance benchmarks and the statistical evaluation of their results. Furthermore, PeASS has been enriched by change-based test-selection. The remaining tasks of the thesis are: (1) The PeASS process will be finalized by determining optimal parameters for running performance experiments. Furthermore root cause analysis of performance regressions [4] will be adopted. If possible the environment for systematic experiments from DynamicSpotter[5] will be used. (2) Experiments with big repositories should be carried out. For this, open source libraries will be evaluated. It is planned to evaluate Apache Commons IO, BCEL, BeanUtils and Collections. Furthermore isolated backend components, where performance is mainly driven by unit performance, should be evaluated, if suitable software is provided. The resulting performance changes should be tagged as performance problem or as performance changes caused e.g. by functional changes. Furthermore, the resulting performance problems

---

[4]http://pharo.org/

[5]http://sopeco.github.io/DynamicSpotter/

will be classified by manual inspection. The classes should be compared to the classes created by [1] and [13]. This will be done while the experiments run. (3) Research questions arising additionally, which could be answered by the created performance problem database, e.g. about frequency and timeliness of performance problem occurrence, will be answered. (4) In the end, the thesis will be written.

The presented tasks are summarized in table 5 together with their planned time schedule.

(1)	Until 06 / 2016	Finalizing the PeASS-process
(2)	Until 03 / 2017	Running experiments, classification
(3)	Until 06 / 2017	Additional research questions
(4)	Until 09 / 2017	Finalizing thesis

Table 1: Planned time schedule of the PhD thesis

6. SUMMARY

This paper presents a thesis about the Empirical Analysis of Performance Problems at Code Level. Its main goal is to identify performance changes on code level by analysing the performance of unit tests in the version history of a project. These changes should be analysed in order to derive performance problem classes. The occurrence of those problem classes can be quantified afterwards based on measured data. Since the performance of unit tests only matters for programs where performance is mainly driven by them, this method is mainly applicable to frameworks and backend components with little outgoing calls.

The first implementation of the tool for PeASS is completed. The next steps in the PhD thesis are the completion of the tool, its application to repositories and the classification of performance problems. This classification of performance problems will assist developers to make better decisions on implementation versions regarding their performance.

Acknowledgement This work was funded by the German Federal Ministry of Education and Research within the project Competence Center for Scalable Data Services and Solutions (ScaDS) Dresden/Leipzig (BMBF 01IS14014B)

7. REFERENCES

[1] J. P. S. Alcocer and A. Bergel. Tracking down performance variation against source code evolution. In *Proceedings of the 11th Symposium on Dynamic Languages*, DLS 2015, pages 129–139, New York, NY, USA, 2015. ACM.

[2] V. Cortellessa, A. Di Marco, and C. Trubiani. Performance antipatterns as logical predicates. In *Engineering of Complex Computer Systems (ICECCS), 2010 15th IEEE International Conference on*, pages 146–156. IEEE, 2010.

[3] A. Georges, D. Buytaert, and L. Eeckhout. Statistically rigorous java performance evaluation. *ACM SIGPLAN Notices*, 42(10):57–76, 2007.

[4] C. Heger, J. Happe, and R. Farahbod. Automated root cause isolation of performance regressions during software development. In *ICPE 13*, pages 27–38, New York, USA, 2013. ACM.

[5] A. Hindle, A. Wilson, K. Rasmussen, E. J. Barlow, J. C. Campbell, and S. Romansky. Greenminer: A

[6] hardware based mining software repositories software energy consumption framework. In *MSR 2014*, pages 12–21, New York, USA, 2014. ACM.

[6] V. Horký, F. Haas, J. Kotrč, M. Lacina, and P. Tůma. Performance regression unit testing: a case study. In *Computer Performance Engineering*, pages 149–163. Springer, 2013.

[7] G. Jin, L. Song, X. Shi, J. Scherpelz, and S. Lu. Understanding and detecting real-world performance bugs. In *Proceedings of the 33rd ACM SIGPLAN PLDI*, PLDI '12, pages 77–88, New York, USA, 2012. ACM.

[8] Y. Liu, C. Xu, and S.-C. Cheung. Characterizing and detecting performance bugs for smartphone applications. In *Proceedings of the 36th ICPE*, pages 1013–1024. ACM, 2014.

[9] A. Nistor, T. Jiang, and L. Tan. Discovering, reporting, and fixing performance bugs. In *MSR 2013*, pages 237–246. IEEE Press, 2013.

[10] M. Pradel, M. Huggler, and T. R. Gross. Performance regression testing of concurrent classes. In *Proceedings of the 2014 International Symposium on Software Testing and Analysis*, pages 13–25. ACM, 2014.

[11] D. G. Reichelt and F. Scheller. Improving performance analysis of software system versions using change-based test selection. In *Symposium on Software Performance*, 2015.

[12] D. G. Reichelt and J. Schmidt. Performanzanalyse von softwaresystemversionen: Methode und erste ergebnisse. In *Software Engineering & Management 2015, Multikonferenz der GI-Fachbereiche Softwaretechnik (SWT) und Wirtschaftsinformatik (WI), FA WI-MAW, 17. März - 20. März 2015, Dresden, Germany*, pages 153–158, 2015.

[13] C. U. Smith and L. G. Williams. More new software performance antipatterns: Even more ways to shoot yourself in the foot. In *CMG Conference*, pages 717–725. Citeseer, 2003.

[14] C. Trubiani and A. Koziolek. Detection and solution of software performance antipatterns in palladio architectural models. In *ACM SIGSOFT Software Engineering Notes*, volume 36, pages 19–30. ACM, 2011.

[15] A. van Hoorn, J. Waller, and W. Hasselbring. Kieker: A framework for application performance monitoring and dynamic software analysis. In *Proceedings of the 3rd joint ACM/SPEC International Conference on Performance Engineering (ICPE 2012)*, pages 247–248. ACM, April 2012.

[16] A. Wert, J. Happe, and L. Happe. Supporting swift reaction: Automatically uncovering performance problems by systematic experiments. In *Proceedings of the 2013 ICPE*, pages 552–561. IEEE Press, 2013.

[17] S. Zaman, B. Adams, and A. E. Hassan. Security versus performance bugs: a case study on firefox. In *MSR 2011*, pages 93–102. ACM, 2011.

Sustaining Runtime Performance while Incrementally Modernizing Transactional Monolithic Software towards Microservices

Holger Knoche[*]
Software Engineering Group
Kiel University
24118 Kiel, Germany
hkn@informatik.uni-kiel.de

ABSTRACT

Microservices are a promising target architecture for the modernization of monolithic software. However, breaking up a monolith into services can have a severe impact on performance, especially transactions. Therefore, careful planning of such modernizations with respect to performance is required. This is particularly true for incremental modernizations, which release partially modernized states of the application into production. In this paper, we present a simulation-based approach for sustaining runtime performance during incremental modernizations towards Microservices.

1. INTRODUCTION

Microservices [8] have recently emerged as a promising architectural style for enterprise software. Unlike traditional service-oriented approaches, which aim at business-centric and coarsely-grained services, Microservices explicitly focus the internal structure of an application. This focus makes them a promising option for the modernization of monolithic software systems by splitting them into a set of interacting services [11].

Most monolithic software systems are too large to modernize them in a single step. As a consequence, such modernizations are carried out gradually in several steps, or increments, along a modernization path [17].[1] Since each increment is released into production, it is imperative that every single one meets the requirements of productive use, of which performance constraints are of particular importance. To ensure continuous production-readiness throughout the

---

[*]Holger Knoche is also affiliated with b+m Informatik AG, Rotenhofer Weg 20, 24109 Melsdorf, Germany.
[1]Seacord et al. use the term *modernization strategy*; however, we prefer the term modernization path to denote plans for concrete measures as strategies commonly refer to more abstract patterns.

ICPE'16 March 12-18, 2016, Delft, Netherlands
© 2016 Copyright held by the owner/author(s).
ACM ISBN 978-1-4503-4080-9/16/03.
DOI: http://dx.doi.org/10.1145/2851553.2892039

modernization, these constraints have to be considered already during the design of the modernization path.

Migrating an existing software system to services may affect runtime performance in several ways. During the migration, immediate accesses, such as native function calls or database joins, have to be substituted by service invocations. Such substitutions are known to potentially reduce performance, e.g. due to serialization and network communication [9]. Another major issue are transactions. The introduction of service invocations to existing transaction contexts increases transaction and thus lock duration, potentially leading to a reduction in transaction throughput.

There are several measures that can be taken to mitigate the performance effects of service invocations. Less rigorous transaction concepts such as explicit compensation and Try-Cancel-Confirm (TCC) [13] may help avoiding performance degradation due to transactions, and patterns like the ones presented in [4] can be applied to increase invocation performance.

Applying these measures may require significant changes on the client side, i.e. changes to the monolith. As such changes are non-trivial, they also have to be planned in advance as part of the modernization path. According to our experience, however, performance problems are tackled as they appear. Since this usually happens in late testing stages or even in production, fixes are implemented under high pressure, often jeopardizing the modernization schedule. Sometimes, modernization steps even have to be undone or postponed, because no quick fix can be devised.

In this paper, we present an approach to improve the planning of incremental modernizations by predicting the performance impact of modernization paths on use cases. The remainder of this paper is structured as follows. In Section 2, related work to our approach is discussed. The approach itself is described in detail in Section 3, and the plan for our intended research is presented in Section 4.

2. RELATED WORK

In the following section, existing work related to our proposed research is presented and shortcomings with respect to our approach are discussed.

The migration of existing software to services has been extensively researched, and a large body of literature is available on the subject. Although much of this work is concerned with traditional services, large parts can also be applied to Microservices, since both rely on similar technologies. Surveys of the existing research can be found, for instance, in [1] and [6]. In [15], a generic conceptual framework for such migrations, called SOA-MF, is presented. Based on this conceptual framework, several existing approaches are categorized into eight so-called migration families in [14]. A major shortcoming of these existing approaches is described in [16]. The authors conclude from expert interviews that migrations in industrial practice employ a similar approach, which, however, is fundamentally different from existing research approaches. While research approaches aim at fully comprehending and transforming the as-is state of the application, practical approaches focus the to-be state of the application and tend to design from scratch based on expert knowledge. Research challenges resulting from these findings are presented in [5]. Specific challenges in migrating to Microservices are discussed in [11].

Performance properties of migrations to service-oriented systems have been investigated by several authors. Performance pitfalls when migrating to Web Services are discussed in [9]. Furthermore, the author presents a performance model based on Layered Queueing Networks. Quality-of-Service issues of the migration are also discussed in [12]. A tool for performance modeling of service-oriented systems is presented in [3]. Furthermore, architectural performance models like Palladio [2] can be used for simulating performance properties of service-oriented systems. However, these approaches are created for analyzing a system at a specific point in time, and do not provide means for structural model evolution. Furthermore, the approaches do not allow to simulate the effects of transactional behavior.

3. APPROACH

In order to improve increment planning with respect to runtime performance and to address the shortcomings discussed above, we propose the following approach. Our approach assumes that the following pattern is used to separate a service from the monolith, which is based our experience from industrial projects and similar to the Branch-by-Abstraction pattern.[2] First, an existing service provided by the monolith is identified, e.g., from expert knowledge, and its to-be signature is specified. Then, implementation elements (e.g., modules, methods, or database tables) currently providing this service are localized inside the monolith, and a service implementation is provided. Note that this may be a temporary implementation wrapping or adapting the existing monolith's functionality. Once the implementation is available, accesses to the existing implementation are changed to use the new service. According to our experience, there is often a significant mismatch of the as-is and to-be signature, even to the extent that multiple services have to be invoked to substitute an existing access site. If a temporary implementation was provided earlier, it may be replaced during the substitution process. As soon as the substitution is completed and the final implementation is available, the original implementation can be retired.

Our approach targets development teams who wish to incrementally migrate a transactional, monolithic software application towards a Microservice architecture. It aims to guide and support increment planning by predicting the performance impact of the future increments. As the prediction is performed during the design phase, the findings can be an-

ticipated in the current increment. We propose an iterative approach, where each iteration consists of the eight steps described below. The process is also depicted in Figure 1.

In Step **S1**, the expected workload and performance constraints are specified based on usage scenarios. Usage scenarios are instantiations of use cases that are immediately executable using the existing application. For each usage scenario, performance constraints (response times, transaction duration, throughput) and a workload intensity distribution are defined.

Step **S2** consists of a hybrid analysis of the current evolution state of the monolith. Using dynamic analysis techniques, the usage scenarios are profiled to investigate which parts of the application take part in each scenario, and to determine current timing information. Furthermore, transaction boundaries and deployment information are recorded during the profiling. The results of the dynamic analysis can optionally be complemented with a static analysis to improve coverage. The structural information gathered by this step is stored in an Application Structure Model (ASM).

In Step **S3**, the planned modernization path alternatives are specified, where each path consists of several increment models. Each such model describes the planned changes to the application in the corresponding implementation increment. According to our experience, it is impractical to plan the entire modernization in advance, as such projects commonly take several years. Therefore, we propose that only the next few increments are modeled. We intend to use a domain-specific language (DSL) for this task, which provides a set of operations on ASMs. Currently, we envision the following operations: (i) introduction of a new service, which includes an effect specification of its implementation, (ii) substitution of an access site by one or more service invocations, (iii) replacement of a service implementation, (iv) change of deployment of a service, (v) changes of the deployment infrastructure (e.g., addition of servers), and (vi) retirement of a service.

Steps **S4** to **S6** are performed separately for each modernization path. We aim at fully automating these steps. In Step **S4**, a sequence of future ASMs is generated by applying the specified increments to the current ASM. Subsequently, a corresponding performance model is derived in Step **S5** for each of these ASMs. In Step **S6**, the increments are also applied to the traces obtained in Step **S2**. Then, the modified traces and workload distributions are used to simulate the expected performance using the performance models generated by the previous step.

Once the simulation is complete for all modernization paths, the results are checked against the defined performance constraints. In Step **S7**, the simulation results as well as the check results are presented to the developer. Based on these results, he or she may then choose to select a path for implementation, or to return to Step **S3** to improve the paths if the expected performance is deemed insufficient.

If a path has been selected for implementation, the first increment of this path is implemented in Step **S8**. We explicitly refrain from "frozen zones" during the modernization. Therefore, the changes made due to the modernization are also merged with the independent changes in the course of this step.

With the completion of Step **S8**, the iteration ends. Unless the migration is considered complete, a new iteration is started. In subsequent iterations, the existing models are

---

[2]See martinfowler.com/bliki/BranchByAbstraction.

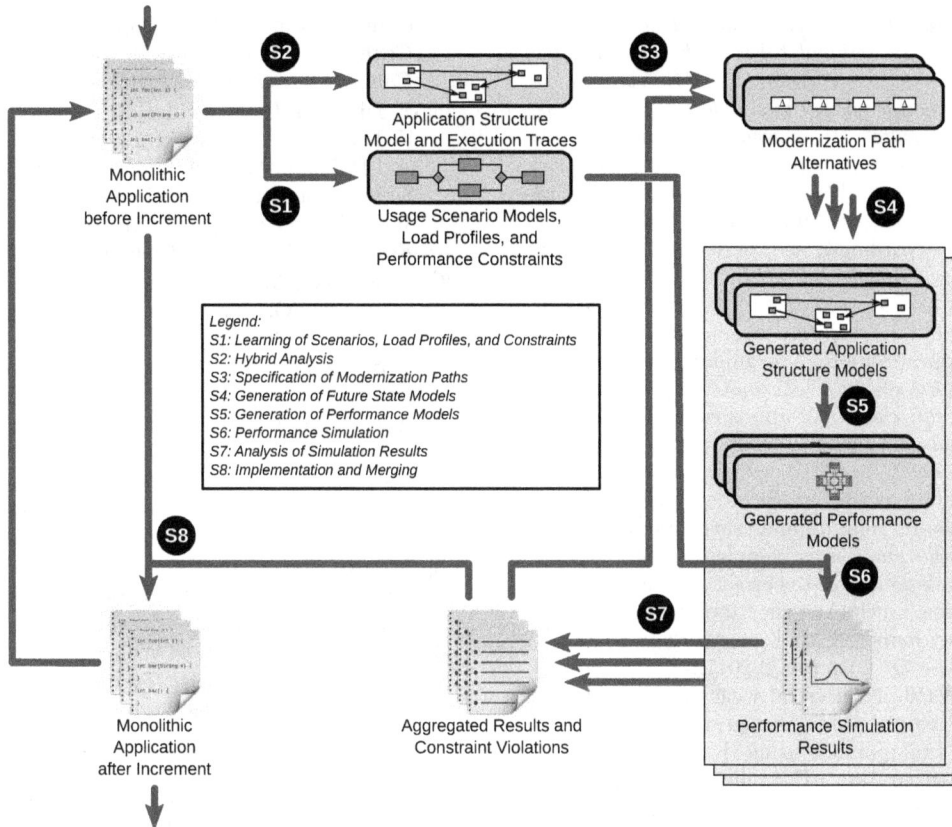

Figure 1: Overview of the proposed approach

updated to appropriately reflect the current state of the application. The first increment of the modernization path that was taken is removed, and, if applicable, a new increment is appended. The paths that were not taken are removed entirely.

4. RESEARCH PLAN

Our planned research is structured into five work packages, which are described below. For every work package, the associated research questions, intended research methods, and expected results are presented, where applicable.

The first work package, **WP1**, is almost completed and was concerned with initial research, topic development, and research planning. In addition, we were able to acquire industrial case studies for our intended research, and to initiate research collaborations for later work packages. One of these collaborations already led to a joint publication on extending the Palladio Component Model to support transactional behavior [10]. Work on this package has begun in Q4 2014, and its completion is scheduled for Q4 2015.

Work package **WP2** aims at further confirmation of the assumptions of our approach. The guiding research questions of this work package are: *What challenges exist in the transition to Microservices with respect to performance? What are common source and target architectures? What are preferred modes of transition?* To address these questions, we plan to carry out further literature research. In addition, we intend to conduct expert interviews with architects of monolithic applications to gather knowledge about common source and target architectures as well as transition modes and migration architectures. For the identification of performance challenges, we furthermore plan to perform exemplary migrations of benchmark applications in laboratory experiments. Work on this package is scheduled from Q4 2015 to Q2 2016.

Work package **WP3** is concerned with the development of the required metamodels, domain-specific languages, and tools to create and edit them. Of particular interest are the models for the specification of the modernization paths. The guiding research questions of this work package are: *Which elements and operations are required for modeling modernization paths? How can the models be efficiently created and edited? How can the models be kept in sync with the actual implementation?* To answer these questions, we intend to perform laboratory experiments with benchmark applications and our industrial case studies. To evaluate the usability of our tool set, we plan to have developers from our case studies use our tools and answer a questionnaire afterwards. For the dynamic analysis, we intend to employ Kieker [18], which also provides support for legacy languages such as COBOL [7]. Work on this work package is scheduled from Q1 2016 to Q3 2016.

Work package **WP4** is concerned with the generation of state and performance models from modernization paths, and the performance simulation thereof. The guiding research questions of this work package are: *How can ASMs and performance models be generated from modernization* path models? How can the existing execution traces be transformed? How can transactional behavior be appropriately simulated? How can patterns common to Microservice architectures (e.g., circuit breakers) be simulated? How precise are the simulation results? To answer these questions, we intend to perform laboratory experiments with benchmark application and our case studies. In order to simulate transactional behavior, we are working to extend the Palladio Component Model accordingly, as described in [10]. Work on this package is scheduled from Q2 2016 to Q4 2016.

In work package **WP5**, we plan to focus on the analysis and presentation of the simulation results, and the implementation of appropriate tools. The guiding research questions are: *How can the results be aggregated and presented so that the developer can choose an appropriate path? Which information is required to quickly locate causes for performance constraint violations?* To answer these questions, we intend to conduct experiments with developers, who are asked to analyze results from an analysis containing known violations. After the analysis is complete, it is evaluated whether the probands were able to correctly locate the cause of the violations, how much time they took to locate them, and how usable they found our tool set. Work on this package is scheduled from Q4 2016 to Q2 2017.

Work package **WP6** is concerned with the overall evaluation of our approach in industrial migration projects. We intend to evaluate the approach using three industrial case studies, a medium-sized Java EE application, a large Java EE application, and a large COBOL application. The guiding research questions are: *Is the approach and tool set scalable enough to handle industrial projects? Is it flexible and adaptable enough to handle migrations of software in different programming languages and environments? To what extent can the migration process be guided by our strategies and tools?* To answer these questions, we plan to create models of our case studies to investigate the scalability and flexibility of the tool set. In addition, we intend to migrate selected parts of the case studies using our approach to check the overall applicablility. Work on this package is scheduled from Q2 2017 to Q4 2017. In the course of the evaluation, we furthermore intend to investigate to which extent cultural aspects associated with Microservices, such as DevOps, are adopted in industrial practice.

The work packages can be mapped to the steps of the approach as follows. **WP3** addresses Steps **S1** to **S3** and **S8**, **WP4** addresses **S4** to **S6**, and **WP5** addresses **S7**. The remaining work packages cross-cut the entire approach.

5. REFERENCES

[1] A. A. Almonaies, J. R. Cordy, and T. R. Dean. Legacy System Evolution towards Service-Oriented Architecture. In *Proc. Intl. Workshop on SOA Migration and Evolution (SOAME 2010)*, 2010.

[2] S. Becker, H. Koziolek, and R. Reussner. The Palladio Component Model for Model-Driven Performance Prediction. *Journal of Systems and Software*, 82(1), 2009.

[3] P. Brebner, L. O'Brien, and J. Gray. Performance Modeling for Service Oriented Architectures. In *Companion of the 30th Intl. Conf. on Software Engineering*, 2008.

[4] U. Breitenbücher, O. Kopp, F. Leymann, M. Reiter, D. Roller, and T. Unger. Six Strategies for Building High Performance SOA Applications. In *Proc. 4th Central-European Workshop on Services and their Composition (ZEUS 2012)*, 2012.

[5] E. Di Nitto, D. Meiländer, S. Gorlatch, A. Metzger, H. Psaier, S. Dustdar, M. Razavian, D. A. Tamburri, and P. Lago. Research Challenges on Engineering Service-oriented Applications. In *Proc. 1st Intl. Workshop on European Software Services and Systems Research: Results and Challenges*, 2012.

[6] R. Khadka, A. Idu, A. Saeidi, J. Hage, and S. Jansen. Legacy to SOA Evolution: A Systematic Literature Review. In *Migrating Legacy Applications – Challenges in Service Oriented Architecture and Cloud Computing Environments*. Premier Reference Source, 2013.

[7] H. Knoche, A. van Hoorn, W. Goerigk, and W. Hasselbring. Automated Source-Level Instrumentation for Dynamic Dependency Analysis of COBOL Systems. In *Proc. 14. Workshop Software-Reengineering (WSR 2012)*, 2012.

[8] J. Lewis and M. Fowler. Microservices, 2014. http://martinfowler.com/articles/microservices.html, last accessed: 2015-09-21.

[9] M. Litoiu. Migrating to Web Services: A Performance Engineering Approach. *Journal of Software Maintenance and Evolution: Research and Practice*, 16(1-2), 2004.

[10] P. Merkle and H. Knoche. Extending the Palladio Component Model to Analyze Data Contention for Modernizing Transactional Software Towards Service-Orientation. In *Symposium on Software Performance (SSP 2015)*, 2015. To appear.

[11] S. Newman. *Building Microservices*. O'Reilly, Sebastopol, CA, 2015.

[12] L. O'Brien, P. Brebner, and J. Gray. Business Transformation to SOA: Aspects of the Migration and Performance and QoS Issues. In *Proc. 2nd Intl. Workshop on Systems Development in SOA Environments*, 2008.

[13] G. Pardon and C. Pautasso. Atomic Distributed Transactions: A RESTful Design. In *Proc. 23rd Intl. Conference on World Wide Web*, 2014.

[14] M. Razavian and P. Lago. A Frame of Reference for SOA Migration. In *Towards a Service-Based Internet*, volume 6481 of *Lecture Notes in Computer Science*. Springer, 2010.

[15] M. Razavian and P. Lago. Towards a Conceptual Framework for Legacy to SOA Migration. In *Service-Oriented Computing*, volume 6275 of *Lecture Notes in Computer Science*. Springer, 2010.

[16] M. Razavian and P. Lago. A Lean and Mean Strategy for Migration to Services. In *Proc. WICSA/ECSA 2012 Companion Volume*, 2012.

[17] R. C. Seacord, D. Plakosh, and G. A. Lewis. *Modernizing Legacy Systems: Software Technologies, Engineering Processes, and Business Practices*. Addison-Wesley, Boston, 2003.

[18] A. van Hoorn, J. Waller, and W. Hasselbring. Kieker: A Framework for Application Performance Monitoring and Dynamic Software Analysis. In *Proc. 3rd Intl. Conf. on Performance Engineering (ICPE 2012)*, 2012.

PROST: Predicting Resource Usages with Spatial and Temporal Dependencies

Ji Xue
College of
William and Mary
xuejimic@cs.wm.edu

Evgenia Smirni
College of
William and Mary
esmirni@cs.wm.edu

Thomas Scherer
IBM Research
Zurich Lab
tsc@zurich.ibm.com

Robert Birke
IBM Research
Zurich Lab
bir@zurich.ibm.com

Lydia Y. Chen
IBM Research
Zurich Lab
yic@zurich.ibm.com

ABSTRACT

We present a tool, PROST, which can achieve scalable and accurate prediction of server workload time series in data centers. As several virtual machines are typically co-located on physical servers, the CPU and RAM show strong temporal and spatial dependencies. PROST is able to leverage the spatial dependency among co-located VMs to improve the scalability of prediction models solely based on temporal features, such as neural network. We show the benefits of PROST in obtaining accurate prediction of resource usage series and designing effective VM sizing strategies for the private data centers.

1. INTRODUCTION

Tools for workload characterization and prediction are key to effective resource allocation in data centers. Based on accurate predictions of upcoming workload within the next timeframe (which can be in the order of minutes, hours, or even weeks, depending on the application), proactive decisions can be made to improve the system's performance. In a cloud data center environment, for example, this information can be used to migrate and consolidate VMs to reduce the number of required physical servers and thus improve the energy efficiency, while at the same time fulfilling the service level agreement with respect to the relevant performance metrics. Depending on the capability of predicting peak load magnitudes and timings, resources can be multiplexed at various degrees across users and time.

Past work has established that resource usage at data centers exhibits strong temporal patterns [2]. Beyond temporal dependencies that are established by usage time series [4], it is common for co-located VMs to simultaneously com-

ICPE'16 March 12-18, 2016, Delft, Netherlands

© 2016 Copyright held by the owner/author(s).

ACM ISBN 978-1-4503-4080-9/16/03.

DOI: http://dx.doi.org/10.1145/2851553.2858678

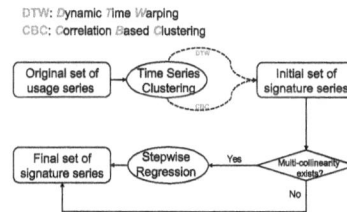

Figure 1: Overview of the PROST in obtaining signature series via the spatial dependency.

pete for the limited physical resources, essentially exhibiting strong *spatial* dependency. Indeed, in our past work we have shown that neural networks can be effectively employed for prediction [4], but their effective usage remains prohibitively expensive in practical situations as it suffers by its high training cost. In practice, in a large-scaled data center, with more than tens of thousands of physical boxes and hundreds of thousands of VMs, it is infeasible to rely on neural networks to predict future resource usage.

We solve this problem by developing a prediction framework, PROST, that discovers spatial dependencies across usage series and exploits them to develop a scalable methodology for predicting a large number of usage series. To this end, we introduce the concept of *signature VM series*, a subset of usage series that are representative of all other usage series. We are able to predict usage series not in the signatures set via a linear combination of signature VM series, which are predicted by the neural networks using their temporal dependency.

2. TOOL DESCRIPTION

The immediate obstacles of prediction given a large number of usage series of co-located VMs are accuracy, training overhead, and model scalability. Typically, temporal models [3], such as auto regressive and moving average models, are not able to capture well bursty behaviors. More sophisticated temporal models such as neural networks, capture irregular patterns better but at much higher computational overheads. Given such restrictions, it is important to come

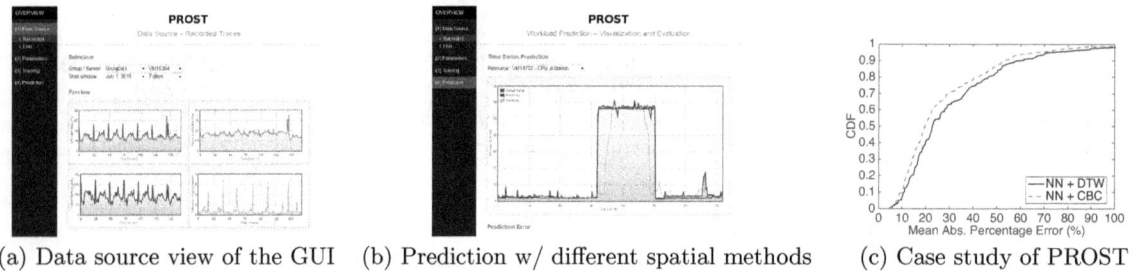

(a) Data source view of the GUI   (b) Prediction w/ different spatial methods   (c) Case study of PROST

Figure 2: Data source view of the GUI to select the servers of interest, showing a preview of the selected VM's resource utilization traces and prediction of using different spatial methods, and a case study of PROST on predicting usage series at private datacenters.

up with efficient and accurate prediction models that also scale well.

2.1 PROST Framework

Motivated by the strong spatial patterns across VCPU and VRAM, we argue that a small number of signature series as predictors can well represent the entire set of resource usages. To such an end, we propose a prediction methodology, which combines a novel correlation-based time series clustering technique, and stepwise regression. The signature series are predicted via existing time-series models exploring the auto-correlation, which unfortunately incurs very high computational overhead and storage requirement on historical data. Consequently, the linear regression model leveraging the spatial dependency can drastically reduce the computation overhead without sacrificing the accuracy.

Fig. 1 provides an overview of the PROST framework, using a two-step algorithm to identify so-called signature series (1) initial set: initial time series clustering using existing dynamic time warping (DTW) [1] or proposed correlation based clustering (CBC); (2) final set: detecting and removing multicollinearity among signature series using variance inflation factors (VIF) and stepwise regression. The second step is to fix the pitfall that though signature series appear independent combinations of certain series can well present the others in the signature set.

2.2 Implementation and Graphical User Interface

We developed a web based graphical user interface (GUI) to demonstrate the PROST framework. The PROST GUI consists of four main views to select the servers, define the model parameters, train the models, and visualize the predictions obtained via the trained models. Screenshots of the data source and prediction views are shown in Fig. 2(a)-(b).

3. EVALUATION

To test PROST, we use traces containing VCPU and VRAM utilization taken at each 15 minutes. These traces are from production data centers covering for one week 6K physical servers hosting over 80K VMs which serve various indus-

tries and use disparate operating systems such as Windows and UNIX. However, due to the computation intensity, especially of the temporal predictions, we evaluate PROST on a subset of 400 randomly selected physical servers and their hosted VMs only. We take the first five days to train the temporal models for the signature series and to train the spatial models for the non-signature series. Then, we use the models to predict the sixth day. First, we predict in one shot the signature series of the sixth day via the temporal models. Afterwards, with the predictions of signature series as input, we predict the sixth day of the non-signature series via the spatial models.

For the temporal models we consider neural networks [4], whereas for the spatial models we consider both the DTW and the CBC clustering techniques. The signature series are predicted by the neural networks, whereas the non-signature series are predicted by the linear models of signature series via DTW and CBC. We evaluate the prediction accuracy in terms of the distribution of the Absolute Percentage Error (APE). Fig. 2(c) presents the CDF of the prediction accuracy with both the DTW- and CBC-based spatial models. One can see that CBC is more precise with lower APE. Indeed, the average APEs of resources usage per physical server for using DTW and CBC to explore the spatial dependency are 31% and 23%, respectively.

Acknowledgment

This work is supported by EU commission FP7 project GENiC (grant agreement no. 608826) and the NSF under grant CCF-1218758.

4. REFERENCES

[1] D. J. Berndt and J. Clifford. Using dynamic time warping to find patterns in time series. In *KDD*, 1994.

[2] R. Birke et al. State-of-the-practice in data center virtualization: Toward a better understanding of VM usage. In *IEEE/IFIP DSN*, 2013.

[3] C. Chatfield. *The analysis of time series: an introduction.* CRC press, 2013.

[4] J. Xue et al. Practise: Robust prediction of data center time series. In *IEEE CNSM*, 2015.

126

SPEC Research Group's Cloud Working Group

[RG Cloud Group]

Alexandru Iosup[*]
Distributed Systems Group
Delft University of Technology
The Netherlands
A.Iosup@tudelft.nl

Samuel Kounev[†]
Descartes Software
Engineering Group
University of Würtzburg
Germany
Smauel.Kounev@uni-
wuertzburg.de

Kai Sachs
SAP SE
Walldorf
Germany
Kai.Sachs@sap.com

Keywords

Cloud WG; RG Cloud Group; SPEC Research Group; benchmarking; performance evaluation

1. INTRODUCTION

Classical performance evaluation and benchmarking has produced a variety of methodologies, techniques, and tools that support the design and development of systems, the procurement of IT capacity, performance engineering and tuning of operational infrastructure and applications, etc. However, new challenges in performance evaluation and benchmarking appear every year. The Research Group of the Standard Performance Evaluation Corporation (SPEC) consists of several dedicated working groups to address these challenges, by topic. In this poster, we introduce the scope, membership, activities, and an exemplary outcome of the working group focusing on challenges associated with cloud computing (RG Cloud Group).

The mission of the RG Cloud Group of SPEC is "taking a broad approach, relevant for both academia and industry, to cloud benchmarking, quantitative evaluation, and experimental analysis [...] This group focuses on novel cloud properties such as elasticity, performance isolation, dependability, and other non-functional system properties, in addition to classical performance-related metrics such as response time, throughput, scalability, and efficiency."

Current participants in the RG Cloud Group include the Delft University of Technology (Delft), the IBM T.J. Watson Research Center (USA), Lund University (Sweden), MITRE (USA), Oracle (USA), Salesforce.com (USA), SAP (Germany), Tata TCS (India), Umea University (Sweden), and the University of Wuertzburg (Germany).

Other working group are part of the SPEC Research Group, and are often collaborating with each other. The Big Data Working Group addresses the challenges of volume, vari-

ety, and veracity, and possibly also "'V'"s, by "specifying and classifying big data systems, developing rules and tools for big data benchmarking, and fostering collaboration between benchmarking efforts". The IDS Benchmarking Working Group addresses the crucial arising challenge of intrusion detection of security in datacenters and virtualized environments. The DevOps Performance Working Group addresses the challenges of "combining application performance management (APM) and model-based software performance engineering (SPE) activities for business-critical application systems".

2. SCOPE OF THE RESEARCH EFFORTS

The scope of the group is "to develop new methodological elements for gaining deeper understanding not only of cloud performance, but also of cloud operation and behavior, through diverse quantitative evaluation tools, including benchmarks, metrics, and workload generators".

Developing concepts and translating them into quantitative evaluation tools covers work on measurement of a diverse set of cloud characteristics and situations, such as elasticity, and performance variability or isolation, respectively; but also on profiling and even workload characterization. Collecting and sharing operational traces from cloud systems is also part of the scope of this group, resulting not in open-source software but in open-access data artifacts, such as the Grid Workloads Archive [4] and the Failure Trace Archive [5].

The group focuses on a broad understanding of the term performance, which includes both classical and ne performance properties, such as response times and throughput, scalability and elasticity/auto-scaling, resource- and energy-efficiency; and classical and ne dependability-related properties, such as availability, reliability, but also various risk characteristics and metrics.

The group specializes in collaborative work on evaluation prototypes and on facilitating joint research on topics related to performance, but members also develop full-blown implementations in their extensive research. For example, the Descartes Software Engineering group has developed a variety of tools, including the Descartes Modeling Language, the LIMBO Load Intensity Modeling Tool [8], the BUNGEE Cloud Elasticity Benchmark [3], and the Queueing Petri net Modeling Environment; the Delft University of Technology's group is developing the Graphalytics [1] graph analytics

Permission to make digital or hard copies of part or all of this work for personal or classroom use is granted without fee provided that copies are not made or distributed for profit or commercial advantage and that copies bear this notice and the full citation on the first page. Copyrights for third-party components of this work must be honored. For all other uses, contact the owner/author(s).

ICPE'16 March 12-18, 2016, Delft, Netherlands

© 2016 Copyright held by the owner/author(s).

ACM ISBN 978-1-4503-4080-9/16/03.

DOI: http://dx.doi.org/10.1145/2851553.2858675

benchmarking and monitoring tool for Big Data Platform-as-a-Service and Infrastructure-as-a-Service clouds; etc.

3. REPOSITORY OF PEER-REVIEWED TOOLS

Through the SPEC Research Group, the RG Cloud Group is publishing SPEC-endorsed tools addressing recurring issues in quantitative cloud evaluation and analysis. Among them,

BUNGEE is a Java-based framework focusing on cloud elasticity, especially for IaaS cloud platforms and auto-scaling environments. The tool provides load and stress-testing functionality, and automates the analysis of the quality of the elastic behavior of the system under test through several elasticity metrics [2]. Currently, BUNGEE supports CloudStack- and Amazon AWS-based deployments. The group is currently extending BUNGEE to support more cloud environments and metrics (see Section 4).

LIMBO is an Eclipse-based tool for creating, managing, and using load-intensity models. LIMBO supports different arrival rates and processes, and can be used for example for generating time series of user requests for benchmarking, or re-scaling existing traces for "what-if" scenarios.

4. THREE ACTIVE TOPICS

The RG Cloud Group members define their own joint activities. Among the research-oriented activities of the group, we detail here three:

Cloud Usage Patterns (CUPs): The goal of this activity is to define a formalism for expressing cloud usage patterns and scenarios. The joint authors, who represent seven organizations, propose [6] a simple yet expressive textual and visual formalism, which can be used by both general users and cloud experts. A key feature of the textual formalism is its conciseness; this goes in contrast to other formalisms that also focus on the executability of the specification. By expressing over ten patterns commonly seen in academic and industrial practice, the authors show that CUP is practical.

Cloud Metrics Survey and Design: This ongoing activity focuses on surveying existing cloud metrics and on the design of key missing metrics that allow the quantitative assessment and characterization of typical cloud usage scenarios. Among the key new metrics, the joint authors focus on various forms of elasticity [2] and risk-quantifying metrics [7].

Benchmarking Auto-Scaling Techniques: This activity, which various members of the RG Cloud Group are just starting, is aiming to conduct a quantitative analysis and comparison of auto-scaling techniques in virtualized environments.

The RG Cloud Group also has various presentation and service activities. It maintains a web site[1], and helps with

[1]https://research.spec.org/working-groups/rg-cloud-working-group.html

organizing various workshops and conferences, among which the flagship ACM/SPEC ICPE conference.

5. CONCLUSION

The RG Cloud Group of SPEC is an active inter-organizational research group focusing on all aspects of modern performance evaluation and benchmarking of cloud environments.

The group is actively looking for new members, to jointly develop benchmarking tools such as BUNGEE and LIMBO; to join ongoing activities such as surveying and designing cloud metrics, and benchmarking auto-scaling techniques; but also to propose new and exciting new activities.

Acknowledgments

The authors would like to thank their collaborators in the Cloud WG, and their funding agencies and organizations.

6. REFERENCES

[1] M. Capota, T. Hegeman, A. Iosup, A. Prat-Pérez, O. Erling, and P. A. Boncz. Graphalytics: A big data benchmark for graph-processing platforms. In *roceedin s o t e ird nternational or s o on ra ata ana ement eriences and ystems 2015 el ourne ustralia ay 31 - une 4 2015*, pages 7:1–7:6, 2015.

[2] N. R. Herbst, S. Kounev, and R. H. Reussner. Elasticity in cloud computing: What it is, and what it is not. In *10t nternational on erence on utonomic om utin '13 an ose une 26-28 2013*, pages 23–27, 2013.

[3] N. R. Herbst, S. Kounev, A. Weber, and H. Groenda. BUNGEE: an elasticity benchmark for self-adaptive iaas cloud environments. In *10t / nternational ym osium on o t are n ineerin or da ti e and el - ana in ystems 2015 Florence taly ay 18-19 2015*, pages 46–56, 2015.

[4] A. Iosup, H. Li, M. Jan, S. Anoep, C. Dumitrescu, L. Wolters, and D. H. J. Epema. The grid workloads archive. *Future eneration om yst*, 24(7):672–686, 2008.

[5] B. Javadi, D. Kondo, A. Iosup, and D. H. J. Epema. The failure trace archive: Enabling the comparison of failure measurements and models of distributed systems. *arallel istri om ut*, 73(8):1208–1223, 2013.

[6] A. Milenkoski, A. Iosup, S. Kounev, K. Sachs, P. Rygielski, J. Ding, W. Cirne, and F. Rosenberg. Cloud usage patterns: A formalism for description of cloud usage scenarios. *o*, abs/1410.1159, 2014. Extended article, with new core concepts, under submission.

[7] V. van Beek, J. Donkervliet, T. Hegeman, S. Hugtenburg, and A. Iosup. Self-expressive management of business-critical workloads in virtualized datacenters. *om uter*, 48(7):46–54, 2015.

[8] J. von Kistowski, N. R. Herbst, and S. Kounev. LIMBO: a tool for modeling variable load intensities. In */ nternational on erence on er ormance n ineerin '14 u lin reland arc 22-26 2014*, pages 225–226, 2014.

Integrating Faban with Docker
for Performance Benchmarking

[Demonstration Paper]

Vincenzo Ferme
Faculty of Informatics
University of Lugano (USI)
vincenzo.ferme@usi.ch

Cesare Pautasso
Faculty of Informatics
University of Lugano (USI)
cesare.pautasso@usi.ch

ABSTRACT

Reliability and repeatability are key requirements in performance benchmarking ensuring the trustworthiness of the obtained performance results. To apply a benchmark to multiple systems, the reusability of the load driver is essential. While Faban has been designed to ensure the reliability of the performance data obtained from a benchmark experiment, it lacks support for ensuring that the system under test is deployed in a known configuration. This is what Docker, a recently emerging containerization technology, excels at. In this demo paper we present how we integrated Faban with Docker as part of the BenchFlow framework to offer a complete and automated performance benchmarking framework that provides a reliable and reusable environment, ensuring the repeatability of the experiments.

Keywords

Faban, Docker, Performance Benchmarking, Repeatability

1. INTRODUCTION

Benchmarking is a well established practice for discovering application's performance pitfalls and bottlenecks [4]. A key requirement in performance testing is ensuring the reliability of the experiments [3], since important decisions will be taken based on the obtained results. Many tools for reliable performance testing exist. One of them is Faban[1], a free and open source performance workload creation and execution framework, largely used in industry standard benchmarks, such as the ones released by the Standard Performance Evaluation Corporation (SPEC)[2]. The growing complexity of modern distributed applications requires to automate their deployment with tools, such as the ones provided by the Docker ecosystem[3]. Most of the available performance test-

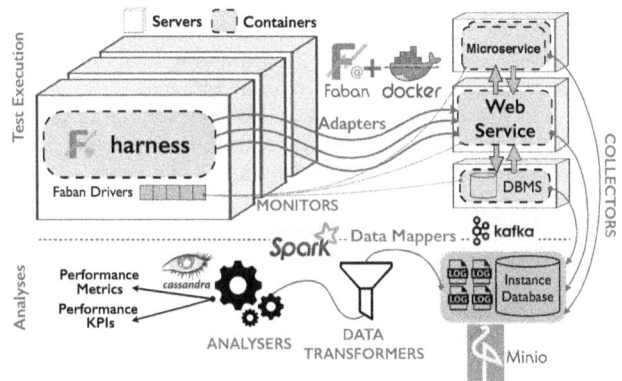

Figure 1: BenchFlow Framework

ing tools, do not provide a well defined and standard mechanism to integrate the deployment of the System Under Test (SUT) into the performance testing and benchmarking process. This is key to reduce the cost of automating the benchmarking. Additionally, this integration is necessary to enhance the repeatability [3] of the performed experiments. Additionally, given the growing complexity of the targeted deployment environment, it has become important to provide lightweight and non-invasive means to define custom performance data to be collected on the SUT side.

With BenchFlow[4] [2] we aim at solving the aforementioned limitations, as well as enhancing the reusability of the load drivers. In this demo paper we discuss the functionality and the architecture of the framework, and present a walk-through use case to demonstrate its capabilities.

2. THE BENCHFLOW FRAMEWORK

The BenchFlow framework, presented in Fig.1, is deployed in Docker containers and builds on top of Faban, to provide reliable performance benchmarking, and Docker, to ensure repeatability and reusability. The load drivers, defined by exploiting the Faban framework, are executed by the Harness, and provide the infrastructure needed to define the simulated users and their interaction with the SUT. The BenchFlow framework defines adapters between the load drivers and the SUTs. That way the same load drivers can be reused to load different systems by defining the mapping between the abstract interaction defined in the generic load drivers, and the actual implementation for each SUT. The

---

[1]http://www.faban.org
[2]https://www.spec.org
[3]https://www.docker.com

ICPE'16 March 12-18, 2016, Delft, Netherlands
© 2016 Copyright held by the owner/author(s).
ACM ISBN 978-1-4503-4080-9/16/03.
DOI: http://dx.doi.org/10.1145/2851553.2858676

[4]http://www.benchflow.inf.usi.ch

adapters guarantee the reusability of the same driver for different types of performance test [4].

The benchmark life cycle starts with SUT's deployment by exploiting the Docker containerization technology. Thus it provides for the replicability of the experiments by ensuring the SUT is always deployed in the exact same initial state. While containerization technologies introduce some overhead on system's performance, a recent reliable performance analysis of Docker [1] indicated that, if carefully configured, Docker reaches near-zero overhead. During the performance test execution, the BenchFlow framework monitors the experiment's execution state to gather resource utilization (e.g., CPU, RAM, Network) data, using the lightweight monitors of the Docker stats API. When the performance test execution is complete, a set of collectors gather the raw performance data from the distributed infrastructure on which the performance test has been performed, and send them to a central storage service, e.g., Amazon S3, or Minio[5]. We rely on a storage service, since the data have to be efficiently accessed from the components computing the metrics. To abstract from the different data formats that different SUTs might have, the performance data are then transformed to a canonical meta-model. After the transformation, the performance data are stored in a Cassandra[6] database (DB), and the performance metrics and KPIs are computed. Cassandra is a powerful DB for storing and accessing performance data from the service that computes metrics on top of them. The computation is performed by relying on Apache Spark[7], a fast, general-purpose engine for large-scale data processing. Before the computation of the metrics is triggered, the BenchFlow framework checks the logs collected from the SUT to identify execution errors and validate the experiment.

The orchestration of the performance test execution, the data collection, and the performance data analysis, is delegated to Apache Kafka[8], a publish-subscribe messaging framework. We have introduced this state-of-the-art framework to decouple the benchmark execution managed by the Faban Harness, from the performance metrics computation, and thus pipeline the gathering of performance data with the corresponding analytics, which can be performed offline.

3. GOALS OF THE DEMONSTRATION

The BenchFlow framework is currently used for benchmarking Workflow Management Systems, and has been successfully applied in different experiments [2]. In the demo we will present a walk-through use case that shows BenchFlow framework's capabilities, both from the perspective of performance researchers and performance testers. During the demo, the framework will be pre-installed on multiple servers, in a dedicated, reliable and controlled environment, which should be accessible over VPN from the conference venue. We will go through the end-to-end performance test process, by defining, submitting and monitoring the performance test, describing the SUT deployment definition, and accessing the automatically calculated performance metrics. **Defining the performance test**: the framework simplifies the definition of load drivers' behavior with Faban,

[5]https://www.minio.io
[6]http://cassandra.apache.org
[7]http://spark.apache.org
[8]http://kafka.apache.org

through load driver definition descriptors. We will define a performance test, involving a distributed system of multiple microservices and their DBs, by means of a benchmark definition file, where we can define all the performance test parameters (e.g., a load test). The framework will take care of translating the performance test definition to the actual format used internally by Faban. **Describing the SUT deployment definition**: the deployment is performed by relying on the Docker Compose tool. This ensures that each SUT deployment configuration (e.g., different amounts of RAM) and its initial state can be precisely described and executed obtaining the exact same initial conditions for the experiment. Paired with Docker Swarm[9] it is possible to automate SUT's deployment on a distributed infrastructure. **Submitting and monitoring the performance test**: we will submit the performance test we have previously defined, and monitor its execution status. The test will last 1 minute and will be repeated 3 times. **Accessing the automatically calculated performance metrics**: when the benchmark execution is complete and the performance data are ready to be explored, we will visualize them at the end of the demo.

During the demo, we aim to demonstrate the flexibility and the simplicity of using the BenchFlow framework. Once defined by means of the BenchFlow benchmark definition file and the Docker Compose deployment definition file, the experiments can be replicated multiple times in a fully automated way to obtain reliable and verified results.

4. CONCLUSIONS AND FUTURE WORK

The BenchFlow framework greatly simplifies and accelerates the definition and execution of reliable, repeatable and reusable performance tests. It does so by integrating two powerful technologies: Faban and Docker, and building on top of their functionality to provide a complete framework for automated performance test execution over a distributed environment. The next planned steps concern enabling the simplified definition of additional performance test types (e.g., spike testing), as well as providing stronger performance test validation and means for performance test result analysis and exploration. Moreover we also plan to collaborate with the ICPE and the SPEC community, to drive the framework's development and strengthen its functionality.

5. ACKNOWLEDGMENTS

This work is partially funded by the Swiss National Science Foundation with the BenchFlow - A Benchmark for Workflow Management Systems (Grant Nr. 145062) project.

6. REFERENCES

[1] W. Felter, A. Ferreira, R. Rajamony, and J. Rubio. An updated performance comparison of virtual machines and linux containers. Technical report, IBM, July 2014.

[2] V. Ferme, A. Ivanchikj, and C. Pautasso. A framework for benchmarking BPMN 2.0 workflow management systems. Proc. of BPM '15, pages 251–259, 2015.

[3] K. Huppler. The art of building a good benchmark. TPCTC 2009, pages 18–30. Springer, 2009.

[4] I. Molyneaux. *The Art of Application Performance Testing: From Strategy to Tools.* O'Reilly, 2nd edition, 2014.

[9]https://www.docker.com/docker-swarm

Which Cloud Auto-Scaler Should I Use for my Application? Benchmarking Auto-Scaling Algorithms

[Poster Paper]

Ahmed Ali-Eldin
Dept. of Computing Science
Umeå University
ahmeda@cs.umu.se

Alexey Ilyushkin
Delft University of Technology
Delft, the Netherlands
a.s.ilyushkin@tudelft.nl

Bogdan Ghit
Delft University of Technology
Delft, the Netherlands
b.i.ghit@tudelft.nl

Nikolas Roman Herbst
University of Würzburg
Würzburg, Germany
nikolas.herbst@uni-
wuerzburg.de

Alessandro
Papadopoulos
Dept. of Control
Lund University
alessandro.papadopoulos
@control.lth.se

Alexandru Iosup
Delft University of Technology
Delft, the Netherlands
A.Iosup@tudelft.nl

Rapid elasticity is one of the essential characteristics of cloud computing identified by NIST [17]. Elasticity allows resources to be provisioned and released to scale rapidly out ward and in ward according to demand. Tens – if not hundreds – of algorithms have been proposed in the literature to automatically achieve elastic provisioning [15, 23, 14, 21, 13, 20, 6, 12, 16, 10]. These algorithms are typically referred to as elasticity algorithms, dynamic provisioning techniques or autoscalers.

While trying to solve the same problem, sometimes with differing assumption, many of these algorithms are either compared to static provisioning or to a predefined QoS target, e.g., predefined response time target, with very little – or no – comparison to previously published work. This reduces the ability of an application owner or a cloud operator to choose and deploy a suitable algorithm from the literature. Many of these algorithms have been tested with one single – real or synthetic – workload in a specific use-case [13, 14, 10]. While all published algorithms are shown to work in the specific use-case they were designed for with the , typically short, workloads tested with, it is seldom the case that the real scenarios will be any thing close to the test cases for which the algorithms are shown to work. Bursts occur in workloads occasionally. Workload dynamics change over time and the load-mix of an application significantly affects how provisioning should be done [21].

This work aims to validate and better understand the literature on automated rapid elasticity algorithms under different conditions. We compare 10 auto-scalers from the state-of-the-art, namely, [23, 7, 14, 6, 5, 12, 18, 4, 13, 11, 10, 8]. We obtained the code for five of the auto-scalers from their designers and reimplemented five.

Since cloud applications are heterogeneous in nature with different resource requirements and workload characteristics [19], for this study, we choose a set of representative applications. Each of these applications stress different resources. The set of applications chosen include complex webservices, scientific workflows, big data processing, simple web services, and video streaming, Due to lack of space, we describe only two applications in more details.

1. Scientific applications and workflows. Currently, workflows are widely used to drive complex computations. A *workflow* (WF) or a *Directed Acyclic Graph* (DAG) consists of a set of *tasks* (nodes) which have precedence constraints among them. Any task can start the execution when all of its input dependencies are satisfied. The whole workflow in our setup is considered as a *job*. The popularity of workflows brings the diversity of their structures, sizes, and resource requirements. For our experiments we use three well known scientific workflows, namely, Montage, LIGO, and SIPHT. Additionally, we consider two generic workflow structures: a star (bag-of-tasks) and a chain. To schedule and execute workflows we use the KOALA scheduler [9] and OpenNebula private cloud which are deployed on the DAS-4 infrastructure [1]. The execution environment for workflow tasks consist of a single head VM and multiple worker VMs.

2. Complex Web-Services. Wikipedia, the free online encyclopedia, is one of the top 10 accessed websites on the Internet [2]. The Wikimedia foundation has open sourced MediaWiki, a custom-made, free and open-source wiki software platform written in PHP and JavaScript. MediaWiki runs using a LAMP stack (Linux, Apache, MySql, and PHP) or similar installations. This setup is similar to many cloud applications [22] including, e.g., Facebook which uses a modern version of the LAMP stack, and YouTube [1]. In our experiments, we replicate the German Wikipedia on DAS. We have chosen the German Wikipedia since it is one of the most popular Wikis in terms of number of users, and in terms of number of articles [3]. The Wikipedia server architecture deployed in their datacenters is multi-tiered with each tier deployed on a different set of servers, but in our setup, we reduce the number of layers to reduce the complexity. We have chosen to run a bare minimum setup, i.e., with the MediaWiki software, a load-balancer and a MySQL database.

ICPE'16 March 12-18, 2016, Delft, Netherlands

© 2016 Copyright held by the owner/author(s).

ACM ISBN 978-1-4503-4080-9/16/03.

DOI: http://dx.doi.org/10.1145/2851553.2858677

---

[1] www.cs.vu.nl/das4

We benchmark the performance of the selected auto-scalers with the chosen applications and quantify the performance based on the following set of metrics.

1. Average Overprovisioning $(\overline{OP})$ is the average number of overprovisioned VMs by the autoscaler per unit time. It is calculated by summing the number of overprovisioned VMs over time (OP) and dividing the number by the total time for which the autoscaler was running. A machine is considered overprovisioned if it is of no use for the next 10 minutes. This time window reduces the penalty if an algorithm predicts the future workload well in advance.

2. Average Underprovisioning $(\overline{UP})$ is the average number of underprovisioned VMs by the autoscaler per unit time. It is calculated by summing the number of underprovisioned VMs over time (UP) and dividing the number by the total time for which the autoscaler was running. Underprovisioning means that the autoscaler failed to provision the resources required to serve all requests on time.

3. Average number of Oscillations $(\overline{O})$ which is the average number of VMs started or shut-down (O) per unit time. The reason to consider $(\overline{O})$ as an important parameter is the cost of starting/stopping a VM. From our experience, starting a machine (physical or virtual) takes from one minute up to several minutes depending on the application running (almost 20 minutes for an ERP application server). This time does not include the time required to transfer the images and any data needed but is rather the time for (virtual) machine boot, network setup and application initiation. Similar time may be required when a machine is shutdown for workload migration and load balancer reconfiguration.

4. Maximum, minimum and, average time required for computing the prediction $(\overline{T})$. When possible, we also report the computational complexity of each algorithm. These values do not change significantly for the same algorithm with respect to the application managed. We thus report these values for all our experiments and comment on any anomalies in the measured times between experiments.

In addition to these general metrics, we look at application specific metrics for the applications such as response time, throughput and request drop rate for the web services, queue length for the scientific workflows and the big data workload, and jitter in the video streaming workload, The aim of our work is to provide researchers and industries with a better understanding of the current state-of-the-art.[2]

1. REFERENCES

[1] 7 Years Of YouTube Scalability Lessons In 30 Minutes. Accessed: October, 2015, URL: http://highscalability.com/blog/2012/3/26/7-years-of-youtube-scalability-lessons-in-30-minutes.html.

[2] Top Sites. Accessed: October, 2015, URL: http://www.alexa.com/topsites.

[3] Wikipedia Statistics. Accessed: October, 2015, URL: https://stats.wikimedia.org/EN/Sitemap.htm.

[4] A. Al-Shishtawy and V. Vlassov. ElastMan: Autonomic elasticity manager for cloud-based key-value stores. In *HPDC 13*, pages 115–116, 2013.

[5] A. Ali-Eldin, M. Kihl, J. Tordsson, and E. Elmroth. Efficient provisioning of bursty scientific workloads on the cloud using adaptive elasticity control. In *ScienceCloud*, pages 31–40, 2012.

[6] A. Ali-Eldin, J. Tordsson, and E. Elmroth. An adaptive hybrid elasticity controller for cloud infrastructures. In *NOMS 12*, pages 204–212, April 2012.

[7] T. Chieu, A. Mohindra, A. Karve, and A. Segal. Dynamic scaling of web applications in a virtualized cloud computing environment. In *ICEBE 09*, pages 281–286, Oct 2009.

[8] C. Delimitrou and C. Kozyrakis. Quasar: Resource-efficient and qos-aware cluster management. *ACM SIGPLAN Notices*, 49(4):127–144, 2014.

[9] L. Fei, B. Ghit, A. Iosup, and D. Epema. KOALA-C: A task allocator for integrated multicluster and multicloud environments. In *CLUSTER*, pages 57–65, 2014.

[10] H. Fernandez, G. Pierre, and T. Kielmann. Autoscaling web applications in heterogeneous cloud infrastructures. In *IC2E*, 2014.

[11] A. Gandhi, P. Dube, A. Karve, A. Kochut, and L. Zhang. Adaptive, model-driven autoscaling for cloud applications. In *ICAC*, pages 57–64, 2014.

[12] A. Gandhi, M. Harchol-Balter, R. Raghunathan, and M. A. Kozuch. AutoScale: Dynamic, robust capacity management for multi-tier data centers. *TOCS*, 30(4):14:1–14:26, Nov. 2012.

[13] N. R. Herbst, N. Huber, S. Kounev, and E. Amrehn. Self-adaptive workload classification and forecasting for proactive resource provisioning. In *ICPE*, pages 187–198, 2013.

[14] W. Iqbal, M. N. Dailey, D. Carrera, and P. Janecek. Adaptive resource provisioning for read intensive multi-tier applications in the cloud. *FGCS*, 27(6):871–879, 2011.

[15] H. C. Lim, S. Babu, J. S. Chase, and S. S. Parekh. Automated control in cloud computing: Challenges and opportunities. In *ACDC*, pages 13–18, 2009.

[16] A. H. Mahmud, Y. He, and S. Ren. Bats: Budget-constrained autoscaling for cloud performance optimization. *SIGMETRICS*, 42(1):563–564, June 2014.

[17] P. Mell and T. Grance. The nist definition of cloud computing. 2011.

[18] H. Nguyen, Z. Shen, X. Gu, S. Subbiah, and J. Wilkes. AGILE: Elastic distributed resource scaling for Infrastructure-as-a-Service. In *Proc. 10th Int. Conf. on Autonomic Computing*, ICAC 13, pages 69–82, 2013.

[19] C. Reiss, A. Tumanov, G. R. Ganger, R. H. Katz, and M. A. Kozuch. Heterogeneity and dynamicity of clouds at scale: Google trace analysis. In *SoCC*, page 7. ACM, 2012.

[20] Z. Shen, S. Subbiah, X. Gu, and J. Wilkes. CloudScale: Elastic resource scaling for multi-tenant cloud systems. In *SOCC*, pages 5:1–5:14, 2011.

[21] R. Singh, U. Sharma, E. Cecchet, and P. Shenoy. Autonomic mix-aware provisioning for non-stationary data center workloads. In *ICAC*, pages 21–30, 2010.

[22] K. Sripanidkulchai, S. Sahu, Y. Ruan, A. Shaikh, and C. Dorai. Are clouds ready for large distributed applications? *ACM SIGOPS Operating Systems Review*, 44(2):18–23, 2010.

[23] B. Urgaonkar, P. Shenoy, A. Chandra, P. Goyal, and T. Wood. Agile dynamic provisioning of multi-tier internet applications. *ACM TAAS*, 3(1):1:1–1:39, 2008.

---

[2]This project is done as a collaboration between different partners in the SPEC Cloud Research Group.

Microservices for Scalability

[Keynote Talk Abstract]

Wilhelm Hasselbring
Software Engineering Group, Kiel University, D-24098 Kiel, Germany
hasselbring@email.uni-kiel.de

ABSTRACT

Microservice architectures provide small services that may be deployed and scaled independently of each other, and may employ different middleware stacks for their implementation. Microservice architectures emphasize transaction-less coordination between services, with explicit acceptance of eventual consistency. Polyglott persistence in this context means that the individual microservices may employ multiple data storage technologies. Microservice architectures are "cloud native" allowing for automated and rapid elasticity. Fault-tolerance mechanisms achieve that failures of individual mircroservices do not affect other services thanks to container isolation. Since services can fail at any time, it is important to be able to detect the failures quickly and, if possible, automatically restore services. Essential for success in such a setting is advanced monitoring.

In this keynote, I discuss how mircoservices support scalability for both, runtime performance and development performance, via polyglott persistence, eventual consistency, loose coupling, open source frameworks, and continuous monitoring for elastic capacity management.

CCS Concepts

•Software and its engineering → Software architectures; Software performance;

Keywords

Microservices; Scalability, Monitoring

Monoliths vs. Microservices

Traditionally, information system integration [16] and enterprise application integration [2] aim at achieving high (database) integrity among heterogeneous information sources [19, 25, 26]. Federated database systems achieve high integrity via tight coupling on the schema level [20], preferably based on standards [17]. For migration and modernization [27] of (legacy) monolithic information systems, an essential design decision is how to keep old and new databases consistent [21], particularly when migrating to the cloud [5, 14, 15]. However, a great challenge with tightly integrated databases is the inherently limited horizontal scalability.

Microservice architectures intend to overcome the limited scalability of monolithic architectures. Microservices are built around business capabilities and take a full-stack implementation of software for that business area. In particular, microservices prefer letting each service manage its own database, even with different database management systems (polyglott persistence with eventual consistency). Besides data, code should not be shared among microservices to avoid dependencies; only reuse of framework code as open source software is recommended [22]. The trade-off between many small microservices and a few more coarse grained services must be considered in microservice architectures, as in any other component and system design activities [18]. To achieve an appropriate granularity, we propose a vertical decomposition along business services.

Non-functional attributes, such as scalability and fault tolerance for high availability, are addressed by microservice architectures. A consequence of using microservices as components is that applications need to be designed such that they can tolerate the failure of individual services. Since services can fail at any time, it is important to be able to detect the failures quickly and, if possible, automatically restore services. Microservice applications put a lot of emphasis on real-time monitoring of the application, checking both technical metrics (e.g. how many requests per second is the database getting) and business relevant metrics (such as how many orders per minute are received). Monitoring can provide an early warning system of something going wrong that triggers development teams to follow up. Besides Kieker [29], our ExplorViz approach [13] provides live visualization for large software landscapes introducing three hierarchical abstractions [10]. Live visualization with ExplorViz is scalable [6] and elastic in cloud environments [28]. Monitoring may provide runtime models [23] for system comprehension [9], trace visualization [4], architecture conformance checks [11], and a landscape control center [12] with performance anomaly detection [3, 24]. New perspectives on employing virtual reality [8] and physical models [7] are further explored. Regression benchmarking [31] should be integrated into continuous integration setups [30] of mircoservices. Microservices leverage techniques such as continuous integration and continuous deployment to promote DevOps [1].

ICPE'16 March 12-18, 2016, Delft, Netherlands
ACM ISBN 978-1-4503-4080-9/16/03.
DOI: http://dx.doi.org/10.1145/2851553.2858659

1. REFERENCES

[1] A. Brunnert et al. Performance-oriented DevOps: A Research Agenda. Technical report, SPEC Research Group, Aug. 2015.

[2] S. Conrad, W. Hasselbring, A. Koschel, and R. Tritsch. *Enterprise Application Integration.* Spektrum Akademischer Verlag, 2005.

[3] J. Ehlers, A. van Hoorn, J. Waller, and W. Hasselbring. Self-adaptive software system monitoring for performance anomaly localization. In *Proceedings of ICAC 2011*, pages 197–200. ACM, 2011.

[4] F. Fittkau, S. Finke, W. Hasselbring, and J. Waller. Comparing trace visualizations for program comprehension through controlled experiments. In *Proceedings of ICPC 2015*, pages 266–276. IEEE, 2015.

[5] F. Fittkau, S. Frey, and W. Hasselbring. CDOSim: Simulating cloud deployment options for software migration support. In *Proceedings of MESOCA 2012*, pages 37–46. IEEE, Sept. 2012.

[6] F. Fittkau and W. Hasselbring. Elastic application-level monitoring for large software landscapes in the cloud. In *Proceedings of ESOCC 2015*. Springer, Sept. 2015.

[7] F. Fittkau, E. Koppenhagen, and W. Hasselbring. Research Perspective on Supporting Software Engineering via Physical 3D Models. In *Proceedings of VISSOFT 2015*, pages 125–129, 2015.

[8] F. Fittkau, A. Krause, and W. Hasselbring. Exploring software cities in virtual reality. In *Proceedings of VISSOFT 2015*, pages 130–134, 2015.

[9] F. Fittkau, A. Krause, and W. Hasselbring. Hierarchical software landscape visualization for system comprehension: A controlled experiment. In *Proceedings of VISSOFT 2015*, pages 36–45, 2015.

[10] F. Fittkau, S. Roth, and W. Hasselbring. ExplorViz: Visual runtime behavior analysis of enterprise application landscapes. In *Proceedings of ECIS 2015*. AIS, 2015.

[11] F. Fittkau, P. Stelzer, and W. Hasselbring. Live visualization of large software landscapes for ensuring architecture conformance. In *Proceedings of ECSAW 2014*. ACM, Aug. 2014.

[12] F. Fittkau, A. van Hoorn, and W. Hasselbring. Towards a dependability control center for large software landscapes. In *Proceedings of EDCC 2014*, pages 58–61. IEEE, May 2014.

[13] F. Fittkau, J. Waller, C. Wulf, and W. Hasselbring. Live trace visualization for comprehending large software landscapes: The ExplorViz approach. In *Proceedings of VISSOFT 2013*, Sept. 2013.

[14] S. Frey and W. Hasselbring. The CloudMIG approach: Model-based migration of software systems to cloud-optimized applications. *International Journal on Advances in Software*, 4(3 and 4):342–353, 2011.

[15] S. Frey, W. Hasselbring, and B. Schnoor. Automatic conformance checking for migrating software systems to cloud infrastructures and platforms. *Journal of Software: Evolution and Process*, 25(10):1089–1115, Oct. 2013.

[16] W. Hasselbring. Information system integration. *Communications of the ACM*, 43(6):32–36, 2000.

[17] W. Hasselbring. The role of standards for interoperating information systems. In *Information Technology Standards and Standardization: A Global Perspective*, pages 116–130. Idea Group Pub., 2000.

[18] W. Hasselbring. Component-based software engineering. In *Handbook of Software Engineering and Knowledge Engineering*, pages 289–305. World Scientific Publishing, 2002.

[19] W. Hasselbring. Web Data Integration for E-Commerce Applications. *IEEE Multimedia*, 9(1):16–25, 2002.

[20] W. Hasselbring. Formalization of federated schema architectural style variability. *Journal of Software Engineering and Applications*, 8(2):72–92, Feb. 2015.

[21] W. Hasselbring, R. Reussner, H. Jaekel, J. Schlegelmilch, T. Teschke, and S. Krieghoff. The Dublo architecture pattern for smooth migration of business information systems. In *Proccedings of ICSE 2004*, pages 117–126. IEEE, 2004.

[22] W. Hasselbring and A. van Hoorn. Open-source software as catalyzer for technology transfer: Kieker's development and lessons learned. TR-1508, Department of Computer Science, Kiel University, Aug. 2015. http://eprints.uni-kiel.de/29463/.

[23] R. Heinrich, E. Schmieders, R. Jung, K. Rostami, A. Metzger, W. Hasselbring, R. Reussner, and K. Pohl. Integrating run-time observations and design component models for cloud system analysis. In *Proceedings of the 9th Workshop on Models@run.time*, volume 1270, pages 41–46. CEUR, Sept. 2014.

[24] N. S. Marwede, M. Rohr, A. van Hoorn, and W. Hasselbring. Automatic failure diagnosis in distributed large-scale software systems based on timing behavior anomaly correlation. In *Proceedings of CSMR 2009*, pages 47–57. IEEE, 2009.

[25] H. Niemann, W. Hasselbring, T. Wendt, A. Winter, and M. Meierhofer. Kopplungsstrategien für Anwendungssysteme im Krankenhaus. *Wirtschaftsinformatik*, 44(5):425–434, 2002.

[26] M. Roantree, J. Murphy, and W. Hasselbring. The OASIS multidatabase prototype. *ACM SIGMOD Record*, 28(1):97–103, Mar. 1999.

[27] A. van Hoorn et al. Dynamod project: Dynamic analysis for model-driven software modernization. In *Proceedings of MDSM 2011*, pages 12–13, 2011.

[28] A. van Hoorn, M. Rohr, I. A. Gul, and W. Hasselbring. An adaptation framework enabling resource-efficient operation of software systems. In *Proceedings of WUP 2009*. ACM, 2009.

[29] A. van Hoorn, J. Waller, and W. Hasselbring. Kieker: A framework for application performance monitoring and dynamic software analysis. In *Proceedings of ICPE 2012*, pages 247–248, Apr. 2012.

[30] J. Waller, N. C. Ehmke, and W. Hasselbring. Including performance benchmarks into continuous integration to enable DevOps. *SIGSOFT Softw. Eng. Notes*, 40(2):1–4, Mar. 2015.

[31] J. Waller and W. Hasselbring. A comparison of the influence of different multi-core processors on the runtime overhead for application-level monitoring. In *Proceedings of MSEPT 2012*, pages 42–53. Springer, June 2012.

Performance Modeling of Maximal Sharing

Michael J. Steindorfer
Centrum Wiskunde & Informatica
Science Park 123
1098 XG Amsterdam, The Netherlands
michael.steindorfer@cwi.nl

Jurgen J. Vinju
Centrum Wiskunde & Informatica
Science Park 123
1098 XG Amsterdam, The Netherlands
jurgen.vinju@cwi.nl

ABSTRACT

It is noticeably hard to predict the effect of optimization strategies in Java without implementing them. "Maximal sharing" (a.k.a. "hash-consing") is one of these strategies that may have great benefit in terms of time and space, or may have detrimental overhead. It all depends on the redundancy of data and the use of equality.

We used a combination of new techniques to predict the impact of maximal sharing on existing code: Object Redundancy Profiling (ORP) to model the effect on memory when sharing all immutable objects, and Equals-Call Profiling (ECP) to reason about how removing redundancy impacts runtime performance. With comparatively low effort, using the MAximal SHaring Oracle (MASHO), a prototype profiler based on ORP and ECP, we can uncover optimization opportunities that otherwise would remain hidden.

This is an experience report on applying MASHO to real and complex case: we conclude that ORP and ECP combined can accurately predict gains and losses of maximal sharing, and also that (by isolating variables) a cheap predictive model can sometimes provide more accurate information than an expensive experiment can.

Keywords

Performance modeling; maximal sharing; hash-consing; profiling; memory; optimization; Java Virtual Machine.

1. INTRODUCTION

This paper is about performance modeling of Java libraries. "Premature optimization is the root of all evil", says Donald Knuth [11]. The reason is that optimization strategies are prone to make code more complex and perhaps for no good reason because they may backfire unexpectedly.

Our question is: how can we know, a priori, that a particular optimization strategy will pay off? For most optimizations there is only one way to find out: implement an optimization and compare runtime characteristics against an unoptimized

ICPE'16, March 12-18, 2016, Delft, Netherlands
© 2016 ACM. ISBN 978-1-4503-4080-9/16/03. . . $15.00
DOI: http://dx.doi.org/10.1145/2851553.2851566

version. In reality it will often take multiple rounds of profiling and tuning before the desired effect and the promised benefit of an optimization is attained. In this paper we present the MAximal SHaring Oracle (MASHO): a prototype profiling tool that predicts the effect of the maximal sharing optimization a priori, avoiding costly and risky engineering. We report on the experience of testing MASHO and trying it out on a real and complex case.

The "maximal sharing" optimization tactic, dubbed "hash-consing" [8], entails that selected objects that are equal are not present in memory more than once at a given point in time. To make this happen a global cache is used to administrate the current universe of live objects, against which every new object is tested. There are two main expected benefits of maximal sharing: avoiding all redundancy by eliminating clones in memory, and the ability to use constant time reference comparisons instead of deep `equals` checks that are in $O(size\ of\ object\ graph)$. This is because maximal sharing enforces the following invariant among selected objects: $\forall\ objects\ x, y : x.equals(y) \Leftrightarrow x == y$, which allows any call to `equals` on shared objects to be replaced with a reference comparison. The expected overhead is the maintenance of a global cache, and for each object allocation, extra calls to the `hashcode` and `equals` methods.

Figure 1 illustrates the effect of maximal sharing on an object that is "embarrassingly redundant": a reduction from exponential to linear size (in the depth of the tree). In contrast, a tree with the same structure but all unique integer values in its leaf nodes would have no sharing potential.

Maximal sharing is associated with immutable data structures [17], since it requires objects to not change after allocation. It is applied in the context of language runtimes of functional languages [27, 10], proof assistants [5], and algebraic specification formalisms [23, 4, 6, 15, 2], compilers [26], or libraries that supply similar functionality. Especially when many incremental updates are expected during computation

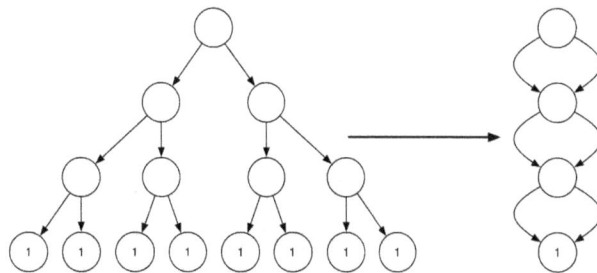

Figure 1: Good conditions for sharing: redundant objects.

(i.e., creating redundancy over time) we may expect big benefits. For example, implementations of term rewriting (reducing trees), type constraint solving (minimizing sets of solutions) and solving data flow equations (incrementally adding/removing graph edges) share these characteristics.

On the one hand, in the case of high performance implementations of term rewriting engine libraries, maximal sharing has proven to be a very successful strategy: *"It turns out the increased term construction time is more than compensated for by fast equality checking and less use of space (and hence time)"* [23]. In real cases memory savings between 52.20%–98.50% of term representations were observed [24]. On the other hand, maximal sharing can have a negative net effect on memory consumption in absence of enough redundancy, due to the overhead of the global cache.

The audience for the maximal sharing technique is library developers rather than application developers. Considering the effort associated with optimizing for maximal sharing, an often reused library is expected to have larger return on investment than a single application.

With the advance of immutable objects and functional language constructs in object-oriented languages —like Java 8 or Scala, and functional languages running on the Java Virtual Machine (JVM) like Clojure— it is now relevant to investigate if and how we can use maximal sharing to our benefit in JVM library implementations. Immutability may be a too strong requirement for any Java library in general, but if immutability comes naturally for different reasons, then the maximal sharing strategy is an important one to consider.

Potential adopters of maximal sharing suffer from a common problem: converting a library to use maximal sharing is hard and costly [22, 24, 25]: it is a cross-cutting design decision with difficult to tune implementation details. To illustrate one of many pitfalls, let us take a Java library for graph processing as example. It makes use of standard library classes for integers and sets. The hashcodes of empty sets are 0 in Java and for singleton sets the hashcodes are equal to the hashcode of the elements, because `hashCode()` of a `java.util.Set` is defined to be the sum of the hash codes of the elements in the set. Inserting such similar values in a global cache for sharing would trigger unexpected hash collisions. The success of maximal sharing depends on one hand on a broad spectrum of properties of a library, like its Application Program Interface (API) design, quality of hash codes, co-optimization of shared data structures, and on the other hand on runtime characteristics like data redundancy and the ratio between object allocations and equality checks of shared objects. Naive implementations of maximal sharing —that do not take these issues into account— are likely to slow down programs and increase their memory footprint.

1.1 Contributions and Outline

This paper does not contain an evaluation of the maximal sharing optimization technique; it does contain an evaluation of the accuracy and usefulness of a modeling and simulating technique for maximal sharing. The contribution of this paper is firstly the design of MASHO (Section 2), which includes:

- Object Redundancy Profiling (ORP): measuring the lifetime of redundant objects during a program execution, optimized to benefit from immutable data and to include the notion of data abstraction to accurately model the possible effects of maximal sharing;

- Equals-Call Profiling (ECP): capturing the recursive call-graph shapes of calls to `equals`, including a partial alias analysis;

- Maximal Sharing Model (MSM): a lightweight predictive model that uses ORP and ECP profiles to predict the behavior of a program after the application of maximal sharing.

Secondly we contribute an experience report on the use MASHO for modelling the runtime environment of a programming language. From this we learned that:

- it predicts the impact of maximal sharing on memory usage and the use of equality very accurately and so it removes the need for direct experimentation with maximal sharing, producing equivalent information for making go/no-go decisions with a mean slowdown of 7x for ORP and ECP;

- it isolates the effects of introducing maximal sharing from the effects of JVM configuration (e.g., memory bounds, garbage collector heuristics) and accidental hash collisions that would occur due to a global cache.

- for the validating experiment, a set of realistic demonstrations, implementing maximal sharing will produce good memory savings but will not lead to performance speed-up without first applying major changes to the semantics of the library. We can decide a "no-go".

In general, this experience shows how cheap predictive performance modelling can produce more actionable information than an expensive real-world experiment can since it can soundly factor our confounding factors like the Java garbage collector and reason about otherwise infeasible design alternatives. Related work is further discussed in Section 4, before we summarize in Section 5.

2. DESIGN OF THE MODELING TOOL

In the following we describe the design decisions and most important implementation details of MASHO in this order: how it is used by a library developer, its architecture and implementation choices, what its preconditions are, and then how ORP, ECP and MSM work together to predict the effect of introducing maximal sharing. We identify possible sources of inaccuracy throughout the text and evaluate these in Section 3.

2.1 Library Developer Perspective

The user first configures MASHO with a list of interesting classes or interfaces which might hypothetically benefit from maximal sharing. MASHO then instruments the library (which does not implement maximal sharing). Next, the user runs programs that use the library, while the instrumentation logs information to be analyzed. After this, MASHO analyzes the logs producing charts and tables explaining the likely effect of maximal sharing on the library in the context of the executed programs. The user interprets the charts to decide go/no-go on investing in maximal sharing, or continues tweaking the experiment's setup or the test runs.

2.2 Instrumenting a Program for Profiling

Figure 2 depicts the architecture of MASHO. A client library is instrumented using both AspectJ and the Java

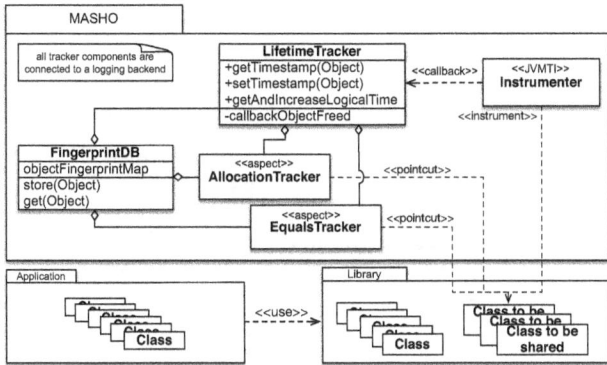

Figure 2: Class diagram and Aspect-Oriented Programming profile depicting MASHO's architecture.

Virtual Machine Tool Interface (JVMTI) for gathering the following events: object allocations, object garbage collections, and calls to `equals`. An AspectJ pointcut selects all constructor call-sites of to-be-shared classes. In an advice, which gets called whenever one of these constructors executes, MASHO performs at run-time ORP with fingerprinting (Section 2.4) and an alias-aware object graph size measurement (Section 2.5). Similarly, we use pointcuts for ECP to record the call-graph shape of `equals`-calls (Section 2.6). Bytecode Instrumentation (BCI) is used to track object allocations that are otherwise intangible for AspectJ, for example object construction via reflection. For lifetime tracking, we tag each newly allocated object with the aid of the JVMTI to get notified about an object's garbage collection.

2.3 The Precondition: Weak Immutability

Maximal sharing introduces a global cache for all designated objects and uses an object factory for creating new instances. Instead of `new Tuple(a, b)`, one would call a factory method like so: `factory.tuple(a, b)`. Whenever the factory encounters that an equal object already exists in the global cache, it returns the cached instance and forgets the temporary object. Otherwise it caches the new instance and returns it. Such a global cache introduces data dependencies between parts of the program which would normally be unrelated to each other. Consequently, maximal sharing does not work for mutable objects because it may break referential integrity: if a shared object would change, this would become observable in otherwise logically independent parts of the program.

One way to avoid breaking programs in the presence of maximal sharing is requiring full immutability of shared objects, but such a strong condition is not necessary. Therefore we define *weak immutability*, a sufficient condition under which maximal sharing can work, as follows: for any object o and its updated future value o' it holds that $o.$`equals`(o'), while observing that not necessarily all fields have to contribute to its `equals` method. Based on weak immutability, object identity can be defined by the transitive closure of immutable attributes of an object, also known as structural equality [1]. Similarly it follows that all object graphs generated from these classes, if we follow only references to fields that are used by the `equals` methods, are Directed Acyclic Graphs (DAGs).

Competitive tools [14] solely reason on the granularity of "physical" object-graph equality, while logical object equality may need some form of abstraction. For example, in case of unordered collection data structures such as hashtables, and lazily instantiated (caching) fields. We will detail in the next section, how to support those cases for better coverage.

2.4 Object Redundancy Profiling

The ORP part of MASHO takes advantage of the weak immutability of the selected classes and the fact that we are guaranteed to analyze data that could be represented as a DAG. Namely, we compute a fingerprint for each object, representing the structural identity of its value, using a bottom-up analysis of the object DAG. Fingerprinting allows us to avoid fully serializing heap objects or logging all changes of the heap to disk [20, 14]. Instead we serialize only the fingerprints that are expected to be a lot smaller in size.

The fingerprint function f, a cryptographic 256-bit SHA-2 hash function in our case, has similar goals as the normal standard 32-bit integer `hashcode` method but necessarily it has a much higher resolution to better represent object identity. For an optimal f (i.e., perfect hashing) it can be said that for any two objects o_1, o_2 it holds that $o_1.f() = o_2.f() \Leftrightarrow o_1.$`equals`$(o_2)$. The inevitable non-optimality of a cryptographic f may introduce inaccuracy in MASHO's profiles, while at the same time making the analysis feasible because we avoid a full serialization of every object.

Weakly-immutable object DAGs can only be created bottom-up, so MASHO computes a fingerprint at each allocation of a to-be-shared object. We use a fingerprint cache to efficiently refer to the fingerprints of already known objects. Therefore, fingerprinting a new composite object is always $O(shallow\ object\ size)$. We distinguish the following cases:

Leaf Objects: are objects that have no children in the immutable DAG. We serialize leaf objects and fingerprint them by applying f on the resulting byte-arrays.

Ordered Composite Objects: are objects that contain an ordered sequence of references to other shared objects. We first lookup and concatenate the fingerprints of all referenced shared objects. Then, we compute f over the concatenated hashes.

Unordered Composite Objects: are objects that contain an unordered sequence of references to other shared objects. We first lookup and concatenate the fingerprints of all referenced shared objects. Then, we reduce the set of fingerprints to a single fingerprint with the bitwise XOR operator. This commutative fingerprint computation is stable under arbitrary orderings.

In the case of unordered composite objects, arbitrary orderings of arrays, containing the same values, are to be expected for example in array-based implementations of hash-maps and hash-sets. We abstract from these arbitrary orderings in order to predict more opportunities for maximal sharing, as well as abstracting away from differences that are due to hash collision resolution tactics.

2.5 Object Graph Size Calculation

Modeling memory savings requires reasoning over which references already point to the same objects and which do not. Such aliasing is likely present in any Java application. MASHO computes the memory footprint of a to-be-shared object efficiently at object allocation time, which is sufficient only due to weak immutability. It uses Java reflection to collect fields and compute the size of all referenced objects and contained primitive values. This traversal skips nested to-be-shared objects to solely measure the overhead incurred by redundant objects. Aliases of not to-be-shared objects are detected by maintaining a lookup table that maps object identities to their memory footprints. If an object reference is already present in the table, then we have detected an alias and should not count the same object again, but simply add the size of the 32 or 64-bit reference. Note that this alias analysis is *incomplete* by design due to efficiency considerations. We distinguish two cases: *visible* and *invisible* aliases. While the former is traced accurately, the latter may introduce inaccuracy because we only partly track the heap.

Visible aliases.

I.e., references that are reachable from a to-be-shared object. For example, consider two different Java fragments which construct a tuple and its content, an atom. Both classes are to be maximally shared:

- Tuple elements are aliases:
  `Atom a = new Atom("S"); new Tuple(a, a);`

- Tuple elements are unique:
  `new Tuple(new Atom("S"); new Atom("S"));`

ORP should predict savings for the latter because it uses duplicates, whereas the former already shares the atom.

Invisible aliases.

I.e., references to library objects that are outside the interfaces that the library developer chose to track. Consider the following Java fragment: `Atom atom(String s) { return new Atom(s); }`. Atom is to be shared, whereas String is not. We attribute the size of s to the size of the first tracked object that references s. Note that s might be referenced by any other object: either from an object to be shared, or from an object that is not meant to be shared. The accuracy of MASHO is influenced by this effect (addressed by one of our evaluation questions in Section 3).

2.6 Equals-Call Profiling

The goal of ECP is to record the shape of (recursive) calls to `equals` on to-be-shared objects. Tracking the calls to `equals` requires detailed consideration to be applicable to maximal sharing. After objects are maximally shared, all calls to `equals` can be replaced by reference comparisons, but also already existing aliases have to be taken into account to not over-approximate the potential benefits of maximal sharing.

In Java it is common that `equals` implementations first check for reference equality on both arguments to short-circuit the recursion in case of aliased arguments. Using AspectJ we cannot easily capture the use of `==` or `!=`, but we can measure the difference between root calls to `equals` and recursively nested calls to `equals`. By root calls we mean invocations of `equals` that are not nested in another `equals`-call. In case `equals` implementations do not return on aliases directly, MASHO pinpoints these optimization opportunities by warning the user about them.

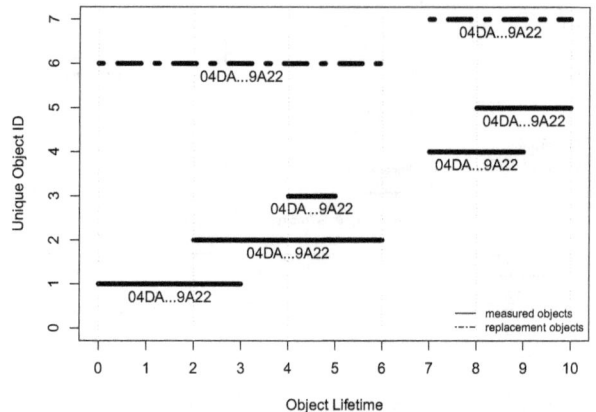

Figure 3: Overlapping lifetimes for objects with identical fingerprints. Two families of redundant alive objects are visible (solid lines) and also their possible replacement maximally shared alternatives (dashed lines).

2.7 Creating a Maximal Sharing Model

By combining the results from redundancy and `equals`-call profiling, we are able to hypothetically model the impact of maximal sharing, including changes to the heap structure, overhead introduced by a global cache, and substitutions of (recursive) `equals`-calls by reference comparisons.

Modeling memory usage.

MASHO analyzes the profiled data as follows. It reasons about redundancy that is present at each point in time. Time is measured by allocation and deallocation event timestamps. Figure 3 illustrates several objects that map to the same fingerprint $04DA\ldots9A22$. The objects with identifiers 1, 2, and 3 consecutively overlap, as well as objects 4 and 5. We call a sequence of overlapping lifetimes an "object family". In an optimal situation each family would reduce to a single object, with an extended lifetime (see dashed lines in Figure 3).

First, we replay the trace to compute the current memory usage of the profiled program for each point in time. We start from a set of object lifetime triples, $allocationTime \times deallocationTime \times uniqueSize$. We compute two lists: one with objects sorted by allocation time, and another with objects sorted by deallocation time. Then we traverse the two sorted lists and compute their running sums. At each timestamp the difference between the running sums denotes the current memory usage.

Second, we compute an estimated memory profile of the same program run as-if objects would be maximally shared. Again, we sort the aforementioned object lifetime triples on timestamps but now we also group them by their fingerprints. This artificially removes duplicate objects and extends the lifetimes of the remaining objects. The final memory usage at each point in time is computed exactly as before, but on this filtered and re-ordered set of lifetime triples. This computation predicts what memory is theoretically minimally necessary to store the observed objects. In practice of course more memory will be used because objects are now even more unlikely to be garbage collected immediately after they become unreferenced. This effect will be observable in the evaluation later.

Modeling the global cache memory overhead.

MASHO assumes a fixed bytes-per-record overhead per object reference stored in the global cache that is to be introduced. Predicting the overhead is a matter of multiplying a constant —currently 42— by the number of unique objects at any point in time. To choose its default value, we analyzed the memory overhead of an object repository that is implementable with the standard Java collections API (i.e., `WeakHashMap` with `WeakReferences` as values) and an existing and thoroughly optimized implementation from the ATerm Java library [22]. ATerm's global cache imposes a 42 bytes-per-record memory overhead, while a standard `WeakHashMap` implementation requires 79 bytes-per-record.

Modeling the global cache runtime overhead.

The expected number of newly introduced calls to the `equals` method is exactly equal to the number of redundant object allocations. The new implementation of `equals` will not have to be recursive anymore under the assumption of maximal sharing. Note that these predictions are under the assumption of optimal hash code implementations and a collision free global cache implementation.

We may also predict the maximal number of new executions of == by counting at each call to `equals` the number of immutable fields, i.e., the arity, of the object. Note that this arity depends on the definition of the original `equals` method. This is the number of fields that contribute to its implementation.

Suppose an implementation of a to-be-shared class uses arrays for storing nested objects. In this case the arity of the object is open and `equals` is in principle in $O(arity)$ even after introducing maximal sharing. The higher this arity, the lower the benefit of maximal sharing will be. This is why MASHO reports also the expected number of newly introduced reference comparisons to the library engineer.

3. EVALUATION

Does MASHO allow library engineers to model and simulate what they might get out of maximal sharing without actually implementing and tuning it? Our evaluation questions are:

Q-Accurate: does MASHO predict memory gains and the effect on `equals`-calls after maximal sharing accurately?

Q-Actionable: does MASHO give a library engineer enough information to decide upon further time investments in the maximal sharing strategy?

First, we set up a controlled experiment (Section 3.4) where we can theoretically explain the shape of the input and the shape of the resulting statistics. This is to test whether the experimental setup works reliably and accurately.

To answer **Q-Accurate** we will then compare MASHO's models to profiles obtained from realistic cases that implement maximal sharing (Section 3.5). The hypothesis is that the memory and `equals`-calls models are very accurate, i.e., within a 1% margin of error. The hypothesis assumes that the introduction of the global cache —that holds weak references to shared objects— does not (or only marginally) change the overlapping lifetimes of the object families; we will report whether or assumption holds. The output of these realistic experiments is discussed in detail as a prerequisite to assess **Q-Actionable** qualitatively.

3.1 Experience: the Program Data Base Case

We report on our experience testing and evaluating MASHO on two open-source projects: the Program Data Base (PDB),[1] a library for representing immutable facts about programs, and Rascal [10], a Domain-Specific Language (DSL) for metaprogramming. Both projects are actively developed and maintained since 2008. Rascal has 110K Source Lines of Code (SLOC) and PDB 23K SLOC. PDB is the run-time system of Rascal. All values produced and consumed by Rascal programs are instances of PDB library classes. This ranges from primitive data types, to collections, and more complex compositional data structures like arbitrary Algebraic Data Types (ADTs). PDB's basic primitive is the `IValue` interface, which every weakly-immutable data type adheres to. Thus, analyzing the usage of `IValue` in Rascal programs is comparable to analyzing how `Object` is used in Java. For the experiments below, we configured MASHO to share all objects of library classes that implement `IValue`.

The PDB classes support two forms of equality. This is common for weakly-immutable libraries with structural equality (cf. Clojure). One is implemented by `equals` satisfying weak immutability by implementing strict structural equality. The other is called `isEqual` and ignores so called "annotations". Annotations are extensions to a data value which should not break the semantics of existing code that does not know about them. The `isEqual` method does satisfy weak immutability, but if maximal sharing would be applied based on the `isEqual` semantics instead of on the `equals` semantics it could break client code: annotations would quasi-randomly disappear due to accidental order of storing (un)annotated values in the global cache. With maximal sharing in mind, annotations should not be ignored for equality.

To be able to analyse `isEqual` as well, we configured ECP to track `isEqual` calls like it tracks `equals`-calls. Note that `equals` and `isEqual` do not call each other. Furthermore, we inserted an additional rule that checks at run-time if both arguments to `isEqual` map to the same fingerprint, by performing fingerprint cache lookups. If yes, we imply that they are strictly equal to each other and do not contain annotations in their object graphs. As a consequence we model such an `isEqual` call as a reference equality, because both arguments will eventually become aliases under maximal sharing. Otherwise, if fingerprints do not match, we continue to recursively descent into the `isEqual` call.

To conclude, PDB represents a well-suited but challenging case for maximal sharing: it is not set up for tautological conclusions of our evaluation of MASHO.uality.

3.2 A Minimal Maximal Sharing Realization

For answering the **Q-Accurate** question we should verify the predictive model of MASHO against actual data from a real maximal sharing implementation. To gather memory data and to profile `equals`-calls, a fully optimized implementation is not necessary, and also absolute numbers about runtime performance are not comparable anyway due to interference of the profiler and JVM configuration. Therefore, we should abstract from absolute runtime numbers and instead evaluate the absolute reductions/increases in terms of `equals`-calls.

Figure 4 shows a class diagram of how we used AspectJ to obtain a maximally shared version of PDB. Our global cache

---

[1]https://github.com/cwi-swat/pdb.values

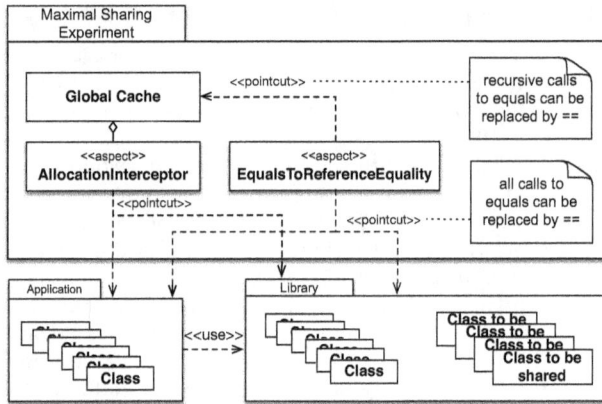

Figure 4: Using AspectJ to experiment with maximal sharing.

is implemented using a `WeakHashMap` with `WeakReference` values. We use a pointcut with *around*-advises to intercept and instrument object allocation call-sites (both in library and in application code), substituting new objects with references from the global cache, if present. We also replace all calls to `equals` outside of the central repository by reference equalities, as well as all recursive calls to `equals` called by the central repository. The recursive calls can be replaced because nested values have already been maximally shared.

3.3 Shared versus Non-Shared Measurement

We reuse MASHO's measurement facilities to measure both a shared and a non-shared version of each experimental run. In the shared version we reuse a strict subset of MASHO's measurement facilities, namely for ECP, object size calculation, and timestamping of allocation and deallocation events. The latter are services of the JVMTI. Reuse of MASHO's measurement facilities entails a threat-to-validity that is mitigated by the controlled experiment, where we can theoretically explain the shape of the data and the expected outcome. We do completely turn off ORP profiling for these experiments to avoid interference. In the presence of the maximal sharing aspect we can observe real global cache behavior and identify redundant objects based on cache hit counts.

Our first naive memory measurement method (*method 1*) is to aggregate and compare the mean memory usage from a shared library experiment against the model that is calculated from the non-shared profiles. If the difference is small, then MASHO predicts accurately. Otherwise, either the evaluation method is flawed, fingerprinting has too many collisions, or MASHO misses an important aspect in modeling maximal sharing. The hypothesis is that based on this analysis we will see only minor differences because MASHO is expected to produce an accurate model.

The previous method is naive, because we know that the Garbage Collector (GC) will influence the mean memory usage as often and perhaps as much as the optimization strategy does. It is a confounding factor. We should expect sawtooth patterns in MASHO's memory profiles caused by short-living temporary objects that could all be discarded immediately after allocation —in case of a hit in the global cache— but instead will remain in memory until the GC starts to operate. So, from the comparison of mean memory usage

we should hypothesize significant inaccuracy in predicting memory usage.

To mitigate the confounding factor introduced by the delays in garbage collection we may set the heap size setting of the JVM to a benchmark specific global minimum.[2] This would trigger the GC more often and force it to collect temporary objects. The mean memory usage then starts approaching the global minimum in memory usage. While identifying globally minimal heap sizes per benchmark could be automated with bisection search, we argue it is not precise enough for our memory measurements. Therefore we also set up a second method of comparison (*method 2*). This method is similar to the previous, but additionally we tag all short-living temporary objects —by measuring whether they cause cache hits— and subtract their sizes from the actual memory usage. The effect is that we filter noise introduced by the GC. Instead of only considering one global minimum, we now reason over a series of local minima in time. If the difference in memory usage between this minimal size and the predicted size is still large, then MASHO is inaccurate, as caused by fingerprint collisions or an unsound modeling. Otherwise it is accurate. For the sake of transparency we will discuss both the results of the naive method and the mitigated method of comparison.

Setup of JVM *Parameters.*

We use AspectJ 1.7.3 a 64-bit JVM from Oracle, Java version 1.7.0_51, running on an Intel Core i7 3720QM CPU under Mac OS X.[3] We configured the JVM with the following settings additional to the `-server` flag: with `-Xms4G -Xmx4G` we set the heap to a fixed size of 4GB and prohibit resizing; `-XX:+DisableExplicitGC` deactivates manual invocation of the GC; `-XX:+UseParallelOldGC` uses a parallel collector for new and old generations.

3.4 Controlled Experiment

Here we test-drive our evaluation method. We use two scenarios that are based on the introductory example from Figure 1: with the PDB library we first build binary trees of depth d where all leaf nodes are equal with respect to each other, and second binary trees of depth d where all leafs nodes are different from each other. We hypothesize the results of the experiment and observe whether or not these numbers are produced. This check of both an optimal case and a worst case scenario for maximal sharing would reveal obvious problems with our measurements.

3.4.1 *Expectations*

While profiling we expect from our setup that no object is garbage collected until the program ends and that both trees consume the same heap size. Zero redundancy should be measured in the redundancy-free case, and for depth d in the redundant case $2^{d+1} - d$ duplicates. When running PDB with the maximal sharing aspect, memory savings should be visible for the redundant case, and growing with increasing depth. The controlled experiment only allocates objects,

---

[2]Minimum heap size is a function of time: each program state has its own minimum. With global minimum we refer to the maximum of all minima, i.e., the lower memory bound that is sufficient to run the program.

[3]At the time of performing our experiments, the latest stable AspectJ Development Tools (AJDT) version included AspectJ 1.7.3, which only supported Java Development Kit (JDK) 7.

but does not invoke `equals`. However the maximal sharing introduces `equals`-calls by performing global cache lookups. We expect one `equals`-call per cache hit, and furthermore for each binary tree node two reference comparisons, one for the left and one for the right subtree.

3.4.2 Results

Figure 5 shows the results of profiling the creation of trees with depths from 1 to 20. The plots use logarithmic scales.

Redundant Trees.

Figure 5a focuses on redundant trees. The x-axis highlights the profiled allocation count at each depth d. Surprisingly, the measurement at $d = 0$ exhibits four allocations instead of the one expected: Manual inspection revealed that PDB's integer implementation contains an `integer(1)` constant, and further, the two boolean constants `TRUE` and `FALSE` were pre-initialized by the library.

The *profile* line shows memory usage obtained by the profiles, while the *maximum sharing model* line illustrates the predicted minimal heap usage under maximal sharing. At low object counts ($d <= 2$) the *maximum sharing model* signals a higher memory usage with maximal sharing than without, However, at $d = 5$ the measurements break even, denoting a saving potential of 66%. The saving potential stabilizes around 100% from $d = 10$.

The *sharing run (with default heap size)* line shows the heap profile with the maximal sharing aspect applied. For $d < 20$ there is no measurable difference from the *profile* line. Only at $d = 20$ with about 2M object allocations, we see a difference because temporary objects are partially collected. Performing another *sharing run (with tight heap size)*, yields results that are clearly different from the original memory profile, yet a significant error remains. The results confirm that the GC largely influences the naive *method 1*; we obtained a mean accuracy of 27%, with a range of 3–93%.

Measurements with *method 2* are not visible in the graph, because the data aligns exactly with our *maximum sharing model*. It performed with 100% accuracy at experiments with an allocation count bigger than 66; at smaller counts the three unexpected allocations reduce accuracy marginally.

The measured global cache hits (that are not listed here for brevity) are exactly off by one due to the `integer(1)` constant. Measured `equals`-calls that are caused by the global cache match exactly with the number of cache hits, as expected. Estimated reference equalities are also accurate: each cache hit of a tree node object yields two reference comparisons, one for each sub-node.

Redundancy-free Trees.

Figure 5b shows the results for trees with no shareable data. The *maximum sharing model* and *sharing run (with default heap size)* correlate. The plot illustrates the overhead of the global cache that grows linearly with each unique object. The only unexpected observation is one additional cache hit, caused by the previously mentioned `integer(1)` constant.

No hash collisions were recorded due to global cache lookups, with the exception of a single experiment ($d = 20$) that yielded 420 `false` equality comparisons in a cache with 2M cached objects. We list the number of equality checks that yielded `false` rather than full collisions to abstract from global cache implementation details.

3.4.3 Analysis

First, we observed particularities of PDB in terms of pre-allocated constants. Second, even under optimal conditions hash collisions became visible at 2M cached objects. We suspect this becoming a dominant factor in further experiments. This indicates also that the hash code quality should be an engineering priority in case of a "go" decision for maximal sharing for this kind of data.

The naive *method 1* of comparing mean memory is not able to show the effect of maximal sharing due to GC noise. In contrast, our alternative *method 2* shows accurate results that matched our model.

We may confirm **Q-Accurate** for this case: MASHO precisely analyzes potential savings and losses, our second method of memory comparison works, and also `equals`-calls are predicted accurately.

3.5 Realistic Demonstrations

In this section we report on our experience with predicting the effect of maximal sharing in the context of PDB being embedded into Rascal. We will evaluate the following benchmarks:

A: Start the Read–Eval–Print Loop (REPL) of the Rascal language interpreter, and load its prelude module.

B: Start the REPL of the Rascal language interpreter, and generate a parser for an expression grammar.

C: Start the REPL of the Rascal language interpreter, and type check a large module (5–10k lines of code).

D–H: Load serialized call-graphs and calculate the transitive closure for *JHotdraw, JWAM16FullAndreas, Eclipse-202a, jdk14v2* and *JDK140AWT*. These benchmarks are supposed to stress the influence of data shape, and the effect of redundancy in algorithmic computation.

M{E,S,T}: Peano arithmetic modulo 17 in three variations, i.e. *expression, symbolic,* and *tree*. These are standard benchmarks for term rewriting engines and are previously used to measure the effect of maximal sharing [23].

3.5.1 Results

First of all, we report that the experimental runs with the maximal sharing aspect of benchmarks B and C timed out after 30 minutes. The cause of the problem, after some manual investigation, was an enormous amount of hashing collisions in the global cache of the shared version. Using MASHO's hashcode logging feature and a Java debugger we found out that the "annotations" feature of PDB was causing trouble. For every annotated value there is a non-annotated value with the same `hashcode`, leading to as many collisions as there are annotated values. In benchmarks B and C there are many parse trees that are annotated with their source code position. To continue our experiments, we then provided an alternative `hashcode` implementations for annotated values, which only the global cache invokes for lookups. Note that altering the problematic `hashcode` method itself is not an option, because it would break the semantic of any program that uses the annotation feature. Applying the fix was necessary for continuing the evaluation, to be able to compare MASHO's models against data from a real maximal sharing implementation. However, the fix was not necessary for a priori performance modeling. We also

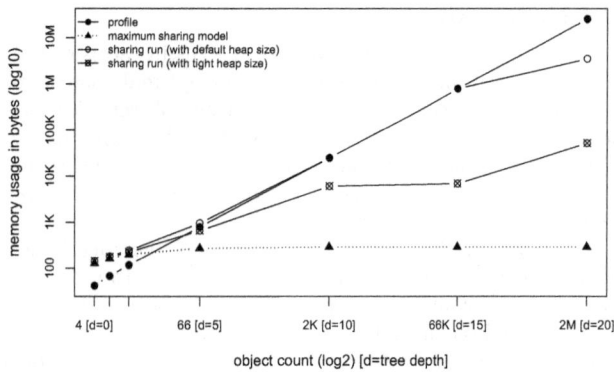

(a) results for redundant trees   (b) results for redundancy-free trees

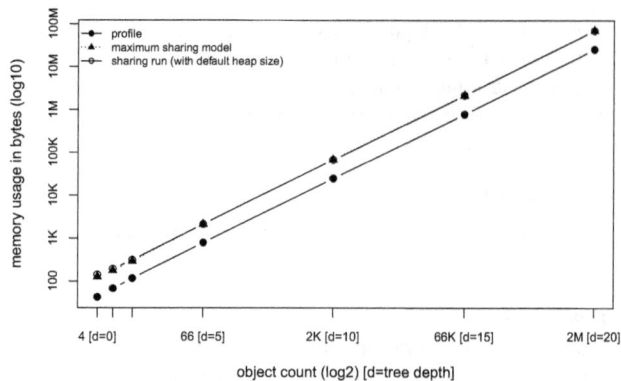

Figure 5: Calibration data: Memory usage for various test runs (without compensation for GC noise). Figure 5a illustrates that compensating for GC noise is necessary to obtain accurate memory footprint models.

noticed another `hashcode` related problem —the `hashcode` of a singleton set collides with the `hashcode` of its contained object— and fixed it analogous to the previous problem. Figure 6 finally visualizes the results for all benchmarks. We first interpret this data to subsequently answer our evaluation questions. In obtaining the results, ORP and ECP yielded a mean slowdown of 7x (range 2.5–32x).

Object Redundancy and Memory Gains.

Figure 6a illustrates *object redundancy* in relative numbers, that is how many newly allocated objects yield a hit in the global cache. Over all benchmarks, we can report a mean redundancy of 64%, with a minimum of 33%, and a high of 100% in case of the Peano arithmetic benchmarks. However, the amount of object redundancy does not imply equal gains in *mean memory reduction*. Allover, observed mean memory reductions are below the object redundancy numbers, emphasizing that the size of redundant objects matters and not only their count. In case of the algorithmic transitive closure benchmarks (D–H) we even see a negative net impact on mean memory consumption, albeit 33–58% object redundancy. The loss is attributed to the overhead of the global cache and that redundancy is mostly present in terms of small objects. Figure 6b presents another view on the *Mean Memory Reduction* data points from Figure 6a by displaying the mean memory usage of the benchmarks before and after applying maximal sharing.

Cache Hits and Negative Comparisons due to Chaining and Hash Collisions.

In Figure 6c we illustrate the number of `false` `equals`-calls that occur on average when performing a global cache lookup that eventually yields a hit. We do not further distinguish and discuss the causes of `false` `equals`-calls, which could be either attributed to implementation details of the global cache (e.g., chaining due to modulo `size` operations), or to hashcode implementations causing collisions. A high ratio should alert a library engineer to systematically explore these possible causes.

Figure 6d shows the absolute numbers for object allocations, cache hits, and collisions for all benchmarks. Benchmarks ME20, MS20, and MT20 created a high cache load —causing many negative equality checks— that in the case

of ME20 and MT20 led to substantial memory savings (cf. Figure 6b).

In our data set, on average a global cache hit triggers 1.4 nested reference comparisons. This illustrates how maximal sharing transforms the shape of `equals`-call-graphs: frequent comparisons in the global cache are shallow, and recursive `equals`-calls in the program collapse to one comparison.

Equality Profile of the Original Library.

Figure 6e highlights the mixture of equalities encountered. Surprisingly, calls to `equals` with aliased arguments occurred more frequently than calls to `equals` and `isEqual` with distinct arguments. The transitive closure benchmarks D, E and H solely perform reference comparisons. Consequently, the alias-aware analysis of ECP is necessary in our case, otherwise we would have clearly over-approximated savings under maximal sharing. With respect to the recursive call-graph shape of `equals` and `isEqual`, we observed on average 2.7 nested equality calls (other than reference equalities).

Equality Profile with Maximal Sharing.

Figure 6f shows the equality profile of the experiments with maximal sharing enabled and highlights the changes to Figure 6e. Absolute numbers of calls decrease, because each recursive `equals`-call is replaced by a single reference comparison. Recursive call-graphs for `isEqual` remain, if two objects are objects are equivalent (according to `isEqual`) but not strictly equal.

Benchmarks M{E,S,T} — Peano Arithmetic.

These benchmarks are designed to bring out best behavior for maximal sharing by generating an enormous amount of redundant terms. The results are shown for different sizes of the problem of symbolically computing $2^n \bmod 17$ in Peano arithmetic. The results show that redundancy was accurately predicted for all three benchmark versions. MS exhibited a saving potential up to 86% with increasing input size, the others up to 100%, which is in line with related work [23]. However, we do not see significant gains in use of equality. The reason is that our implementation of the benchmark uses deep pattern matching instead of direct calls to `equals` and therefore loses the benefit of $O(1)$ reference comparisons.

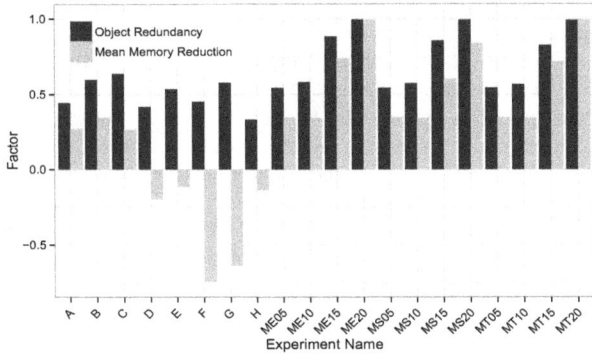

(a) Relation of Redundancy and Mean Memory Savings

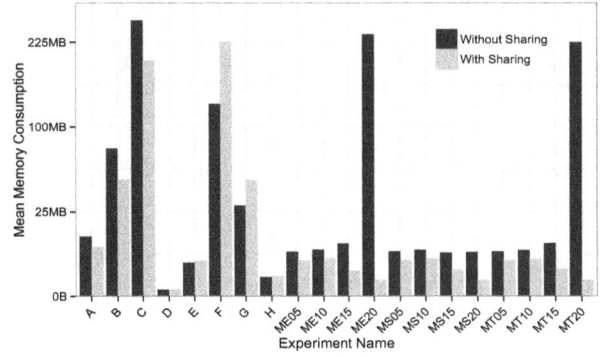

(b) Effect of Maximal Sharing on Memory Consumption

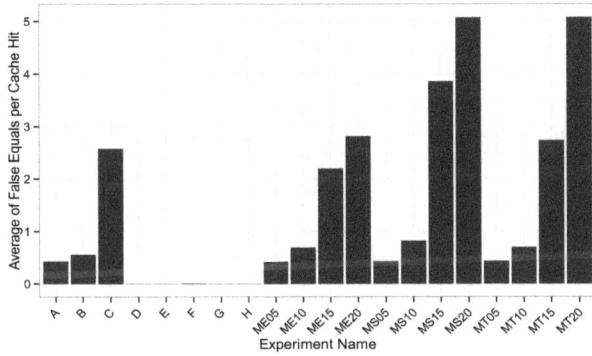

(c) Ratio of False Equality Comparisons per Cache Hit

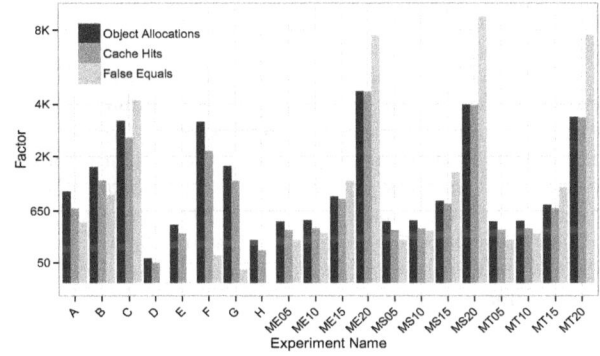

(d) Relation of Object Allocation, Cache Hits, and Collisions

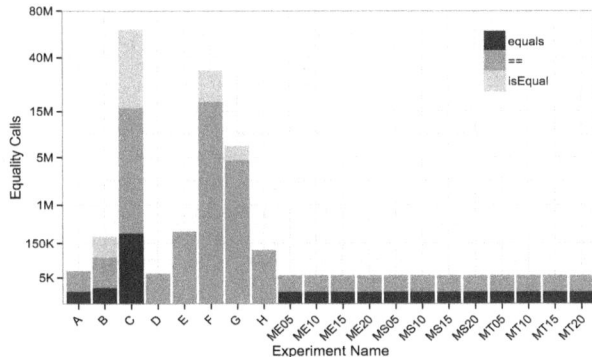

(e) Equality Profile without Maximal Sharing

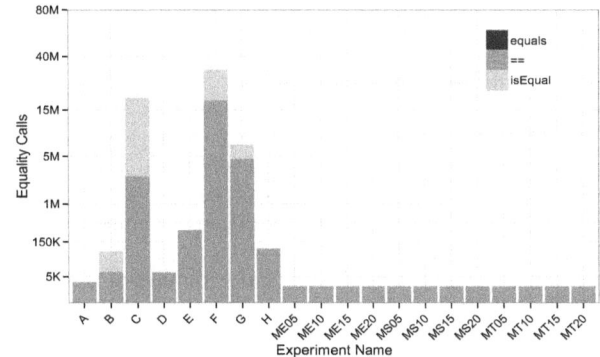

(f) Equality Profiles with Maximal Sharing

Figure 6: Realistic data: Various memory and equality aspects of the applications under test. Figures 6b and 6d use a square root scale on the y-axes, and figures 6e and 6f a double square root scale, to better accommodate the wide range of values.

3.6   Analysis

Q-Accurate.

None of the experiments showed significant differences between the predicted and the actual memory usage; the mean accuracy of *method 2* was about 99%. For all but one benchmark, calls to **equals** methods were predicted with an accuracy of at least 99%. The only outlier was benchmark B, the parser generator benchmark, that exhibited 19% more calls to **equals**, caused by an corresponding increase in global cache hits. The additional cache hits were caused by equivalent objects that were re-generated at a higher rate than the collection of the weak references from the global cache. In

the latter case, we actually under-approximated the potential savings, because the longer living weak references caused an overlap between previously disjoint object families.

We conclude that MASHO accurately models lower bounds for hypothetical heap evolution and calls to **equals** under maximal sharing for all our benchmarks. This means that 256-bit SHA-2 hashes were good enough at least for this (heterogeneous) data, and that the MASHO model is complete.

Q-Actionable.

The redundancy data clearly suggests that PDB could benefit from maximal sharing for most benchmarks. However, during profiling we figured out that PDB's annotation feature causes a substantial number of hash-collisions. Further-more, the effectiveness of maximal sharing diminished under `isEqual` that ignores annotations: many calls to `isEqual` cannot be replaced by reference comparisons. It follows that the library would require severe reengineering before maximal sharing can be applied optimally.

As compared to general memory profilers, which do not consider the specifics and preconditions of maximal sharing, we showed that the GC can hide memory savings of maximal sharing. A memory profiler will not even see substantial savings unless by trial and error global minimum heap bounds are found. Since MASHO ignores the effect of the GC, this confounding effect has become a non-issue.

The information provided by MASHO as compared to our simple maximal sharing aspect is comparable. More impor-tantly, the maximal sharing aspect suffers from arbitrary hash collisions in terms of accuracy (more `equals`-calls will be made as hash buckets become deeper) and speed (the benchmarks will run longer and longer). MASHO provides filtered information, isolating the effect of maximal sharing from the confounding effect of hash collisions.

In additional experiments simulating the semantics of re-lated memory profilers, which check for isomorphic heap graphs [18, 14], we measured that MASHO uncovers up to 14%, and at median 4%, more unique caching opportunities in the aforementioned benchmarks than the related work can provide —due to the additional abstraction facilities.

4. RELATED WORK

We position our contribution with respect to memory profiling tools and studies, programming language features, and maximal sharing libraries.

Memory profiling tools and studies.

Sewe et al. [21] investigated the differences in memory behavior between Java and Scala programs. The key findings were that objects in Scala are more likely to be immutable, small, and to have a short lifetime, compared to pure object-oriented Java programs. Ergo, the Scala community may benefit from MASHO.

Dieckmann and Hölzle [7] originally published a study about the allocation behavior of six SPECjvm98 Java pro-grams, and compared the results to Smalltalk and ML. The authors obtained allocation data by instrumenting the source code of a virtual machine and built a heap simulator.

Sartor et al. [20] discuss the limits of heap data compression by examining types and sources of memory inefficiencies. Techniques were investigated that work on a wide spectrum of granularity, ranging from object equality to stripping off empty bytes, or compressing fields and arrays. Their analysis approximates saving potentials by analyzing a series of timed heap dumps. The authors observed that deep object equality together with array sharing reduces the size of applications by 14% on average. These results also motivate our research but timed heap dumps do not provide enough detail to assess the impact of maximal sharing accurately.

Resurrector [29] is an object lifetime profiler that supports a tuneable cost settings per allocation site. For frequent calls to allocation sites, Resurrector works more precisely than garbage collector heuristics and can avoid expensive reachability analyses to identify dead objects, as used by like Merlin [9] or Elephant Tracks [19]. These more advanced lifetime profiling techniques are usually implemented inside

a Virtual Machine (VM). In contrast, MASHO uses garage collector timestamps as heuristic for object lifetime obtained standard interfaces and techniques (JVMTI and BCI) and thus works across different JVMs. MASHO predicts with almost perfect accuracy (see Section 3), so these more precise and much more expensive techniques are not necessary here.

Bhattacharya et al. [3] reduce unnecessary allocations of temporary strings or container objects inside loops, by ana-lyzing which objects can be reused after each loop iteration. MASHO reasons over redundancy of a whole program run and therefore also covers these cases, necessarily.

Nguyen and Xu [16] detect cacheable objects at allocation sites with variants of data dependence graphs, and mem-oizable functions at their call sites. Their tool, Cachetor, is implemented inside a VM and targets arbitrary mutable programs and thus leading to a 200x overhead. Redundancy profiling, as implemented by MASHO, in contrast exploits the preconditions of immutable object graphs and can thus operate at lower runtime overheads.

To optimize compilers, Lattner and Adve [12] researched a *macroscopic* approach for reasoning over pointer-intense programs, by focusing on how programs use entire logical data structures, rather than individual objects, to then segregate these objects automatically into separate memory pools.

With Object Equality Profiling (OEP), Marinov et al. [14] pinpoint groups of equivalent objects that could be replaced by a single representative instance. OEP considers every single object created during a program run. The authors use BCI to track heap activity dynamically. A post-mortem analysis calculates mergeability of objects, by checking iso-morphism of labelled graphs. OEP uses an off-line graph partitioning algorithm to process data sets that might ex-ceed main memory size in $\mathcal{O}(n \ log \ n)$ time. One of the key contributions of OEP—that makes it scalable for mutable objects but difficult to apply for modeling maximal sharing— is pre-partitioning heap graphs based on the primitive values of objects as a discriminator. In our context this causes OEP not being able to abstract from implementation details such as arbitrary ordering of elements in arrays, specialized sub-classes, and lazily initialized or cached hashcodes. For libraries based on immutable objects, this can make objects look different while they should be the same. Our exper-iments showed that MASHO uncovers up to 14%, and at median 4%, more unique sharing opportunities than OEP on the same data would. The focus on immutable objects gives MASHO both the opportunity to abstract and the ability to optimize the necessary high granularity memory profiles.

Rama and Komondoor [18] worked on an extension of OEP and introduced a tool, the Object Caching Advisor (OCA), to support introducing hash-consing at the source-code level as a refactoring. The authors reuse a fingerprinting function, introduced by Xu [28], that runs in $O(size \ of \ object \ graph)$ and yields a runtime overhead ranging from 98–2520x. In contrast, MASHO's fingerprinting, which is based on Merkle trees, operates in $O(shallow \ object \ size)$.

Language support for obviating equals and hashCode.

Vaziri et al. [26] proposed a declarative, stricter form of object identity called *relation types*. By requiring that the identity of an object never changes during runtime, the au-thors obviated potential error-prone `equals` and `hashcode` methods. A subset of immutable key fields, referred to as tuple, designates object identity. These tuples match our weak-immutability requirement (see Section 2.3). The authors formalized their programming model and proved that hash-consing preserves semantics and is a safe optimization in their model. Our contribution is nicely orthogonal: Whereas MASHO investigates maximal sharing for libraries and requires that `equals` and `hashcode` are user provided, relation types are meant to be an equality substitute at language level. Vaziri et al. contribute the language supported semantics of weak immutability, which is our a priori assumption.

Scala counters fragile `equals` and `hashcode` implementations with the concept of *case classes*. Scala shows that immutable data types that adhere to structural equality can obviate hand-written `equals` and `hashcode` implementations. The compiler —like with relation types— synthesizes their implementation, but since maximal sharing is not always beneficial it does not generate shared implementations. A recast of MASHO to Scala may help finding optimal solutions for libraries that heavily rely on case classes.

The ATerm library.
is a prime source of inspiration [22, 24, 25]. Both in C and in Java this is a successful library that employs maximal sharing for representing atomic data-types, lists and trees. Key design considerations of the ATerm library are to specialize garbage collection (in C), and (de)serialization as well based on the condition of maximal sharing and structural equality. In this paper we use benchmarks from the ATerm experience to evaluate MASHO. The reported use cases of ATerm library (specifically in the term rewriting and model checking context) indicate the possibility of great savings in memory consumption and great increases in performance, but in the general case it is unlikely that maximal sharing is always a good idea.

ShadowVM [13].
ShadowVM is a recent generic Java run-time analysis framework. It separates instrumentation from the client VM and adds asynchronous remote evaluation to increase isolation and coverage. Analyses can be written on a high level of abstraction using an open pointcut model and support bytecode instruction granularity as well. MASHO would be a good usage scenario for ShadowVM, since tracking == bytecode instructions needs bytecode instrumentation beyond the capabilities of AspectJ.

5. CONCLUSION

We introduced a new predictive performance modeling tool named MASHO— for assessing the effects of introducing the maximal sharing optimization strategy into a Java library without changing the library or client code of the library.

MASHO profiles object redundancy and calls to `equals` efficiently using object fingerprints. Under the assumption of *weak immutability*, fingerprinting leads to an accurate model efficiently. MASHO can abstract from accidental implementation details in the current version of a library, such as arbitrary array orderings which also enhances its accuracy.

The experience report focused on the accuracy of the predictions, since fingerprinting and feedback loops with garbage collection heuristics may introduce noise. This showed on a controlled case and on realistic cases that MASHO's predictions are accurate.

Predictive performance analysis with MASHO isolates the effect of maximal sharing from other noise in the measurements, in contrast to a full blown experiment where confounding effects (like garbage collection) may be prohibitive for decision making.

6. ACKNOWLEDGMENTS

The authors thank the anonymous reviewers and further Ali Afroozeh, Bas Basten, Martin Glabischnig, Davy Landman, Tijs van der Storm, and Pablo Inostroza Valdera for their valuable feedback on earlier draft versions of this paper.

7. REFERENCES

[1] H. G. Baker. Equal rights for functional objects or, the more things change, the more they are the same. *SIGPLAN OOPS Messenger*, 4(4):2–27, 1993.

[2] E. Balland, P. Brauner, R. Kopetz, P.-E. Moreau, and A. Reilles. Tom: Piggybacking rewriting on Java. In *Rewriting Theory and Applications (RTA 2007)*, LNCS. Springer, 2007.

[3] S. Bhattacharya, M. G. Nanda, K. Gopinath, and M. Gupta. Reuse, recycle to de-bloat software. In *ECOOP '11: Proceedings of the 25th European Conference on Object-oriented Programming*. Springer, 2011.

[4] P. Borovanský, C. Kirchner, H. Kirchner, P.-E. Moreau, and C. Ringeissen. An overview of ELAN. In C. Kirchner and H. Kirchner, editors, *International Workshop on Rewriting Logic and its Applications*, volume 15 of *ENTCS*. Elsevier, 1998.

[5] T. Braibant, J.-H. Jourdan, and D. Monniaux. Implementing hash-consed structures in Coq. In *Proceedings of the 4th International Conference on Interactive Theorem Proving*, LNCS. Springer, 2013.

[6] M. Clavel, F. Durán, S. Eker, P. Lincoln, N. Martí-Oliet, J. Meseguer, and J. F. Quesada. Maude: Specification and programming in rewriting logic. *Theoretical Computer Science*, 2001.

[7] S. Dieckmann and U. Hölzle. A study of the Allocation Behavior of the SPECjvm98 Java Benchmarks. In *ECOOP '99: Proceedings of the 13th European Conference on Object-oriented Programming*. Springer, 1999.

[8] E. Goto. Monocopy and Associative Algorithms in Extended Lisp. University of Toyko. Technical report, 1974.

[9] M. Hertz, S. M. Blackburn, J. E. B. Moss, K. S. McKinley, and D. Stefanović. Generating object lifetime traces with Merlin. *ACM Transactions on Programming Languages and Systems (TOPLAS)*, 28(3):476–516, 2006.

[10] P. Klint, T. van der Storm, and J. J. Vinju. EASY meta-programming with Rascal. leveraging the Extract-Analyze-SYnthesize paradigm for meta-programming. In *Proceedings of the 3rd International Summer School on Generative and Transformational Techniques in Software Engineering (GTTSE'09)*, LNCS. Springer, 2010.

[11] D. Knuth. Structured programming with Goto statements. In E. N. Yourdon, editor, *Classics in Software Engineering*. Yourdon Press, 1979.

[12] C. Lattner and V. Adve. Automatic pool allocation: improving performance by controlling data structure layout in the heap. *ACM Sigplan Notices*, 40(6):129–142, 2005.

[13] L. Marek, S. Kell, Y. Zheng, L. Bulej, W. Binder, P. Tůma, D. Ansaloni, A. Sarimbekov, and A. Sewe. ShadowVM: robust and comprehensive dynamic program analysis for the Java platform. In *GPCE '13: Proceedings of the 12th International Conference on Generative Programming: Concepts & Experiences*. ACM, 2013.

[14] D. Marinov and R. O'Callahan. Object equality profiling. In *OOPSLA '03: Proceedings of the 2003 ACM SIGPLAN International Conference on Object Oriented Programming Systems Languages & Applications*. ACM, 2003.

[15] P. D. Mosses. *CASL Reference Manual, The Complete Documentation of the Common Algebraic Specification Language*, volume 2960 of *LNCS*. Springer, 2004.

[16] K. Nguyen and G. Xu. Cachetor: Detecting cacheable data to remove bloat. In *ESEC/FSE '13: Proceedings of the 2013 9th Joint Meeting on Foundations of Software Engineering*. ACM, 2013.

[17] C. Okasaki. *Purely Functional Data Structures*. Cambridge University Press, 1999.

[18] G. M. Rama and R. Komondoor. A dynamic analysis to support object-sharing code refactorings. In *ASE '14: Proceedings of the 29th ACM/IEEE International Conference on Automated Software Engineering*. ACM, 2014.

[19] N. P. Ricci, S. Z. Guyer, and J. E. B. Moss. Elephant tracks: portable production of complete and precise GC traces. *ACM Sigplan Notices*, 48(11):109–118, 2013.

[20] J. B. Sartor, M. Hirzel, and K. S. McKinley. No bit left behind: The limits of heap data compression. In *ISMM '08: Proceedings of the 7th International Symposium on Memory Management*. ACM, 2008.

[21] A. Sewe, M. Mezini, A. Sarimbekov, D. Ansaloni, W. Binder, N. Ricci, and S. Z. Guyer. new Scala() instance of Java: a comparison of the memory behaviour of Java and Scala programs. *ACM Sigplan Notices*, 47(11):97–108, 2012.

[22] M. G. J. Van den Brand, H. A. De Jong, P. Klint, and P. A. Olivier. Efficient annotated terms. *Software: Practice and Experience*, 30(3):259–291, 2000.

[23] M. G. J. van den Brand, J. Heering, P. Klint, and P. A. Olivier. Compiling language definitions: the ASF+SDF compiler. *TOPLAS*, 24(4):334–368, 2002.

[24] M. G. J. van den Brand and P. Klint. ATerms for manipulation and exchange of structured data: It's all about sharing. *Information and Software Technology*, 49(1):55–64, 2007.

[25] M. G. J. Van Den Brand, P.-E. Moreau, and J. Vinju. A generator of efficient strongly typed abstract syntax trees in Java. *IEE Proceedings - Software Engineering*, 152(2):70–87, 2005.

[26] M. Vaziri, F. Tip, S. Fink, and J. Dolby. Declarative object identity using relation types. In *ECOOP '07: Proceedings of the 21th European Conference on Object-oriented Programming*. Springer, 2007.

[27] E. Visser. Program transformation with Stratego/XT: Rules, strategies, tools, and systems in StrategoXT-0.9. In C. Lengauer et al., editors, *Domain-Specific Program Generation*, volume 3016 of *LNCS*. Springer, 2004.

[28] G. Xu. Finding reusable data structures. In *OOPSLA '12: Proceedings of the 2012 ACM SIGPLAN International Conference on Object Oriented Programming Systems Languages & Applications*. ACM, 2012.

[29] G. Xu. Resurrector: A tunable object lifetime profiling technique for optimizing real-world programs. In *OOPSLA '13: Proceedings of the 2013 ACM SIGPLAN International Conference on Object Oriented Programming Systems Languages & Applications*. ACM, 2013.

Variations in CPU Power Consumption

Jóakim v. Kistowski
University of Würzburg
joakim.kistowski@
uni-wuerzburg.de

Hansfried Block
Fujitsu Technology Solutions
GmbH
hansfried.block@
ts.fujitsu.com

John Beckett
Dell Inc.
john_beckett@dell.com

Cloyce Spradling
Oracle
cloyce.spradling@
oracle.com

Klaus-Dieter Lange
Hewlett Packard Enterprise
klaus.lange@hpe.com

Samuel Kounev
University of Würzburg
samuel.kounev@
uni-wuerzburg.de

ABSTRACT

Experimental analysis of computer systems' power consumption has become an integral part of system performance evaluation, efficiency management, and model-based analysis. As with all measurements, repeatability and reproducibility of power measurements are a major challenge.

Nominally identical systems can have different power consumption running the same workload under otherwise identical conditions. This behavior can also be observed for individual system components. Specifically, CPU power consumption can vary amongst different samples of nominally identical CPUs. This in turn has a significant impact on the overall system power, considering that a system's processor is the largest and most dynamic power consumer of the overall system. The concrete impact of CPU sample power variations is unknown, as comprehensive studies about differences in power consumption for nominally identical systems are currently missing.

We address this lack of studies by conducting measurements on four different processor types from two different architectures. For each of these types, we compare up to 30 physical processor samples with a total sum of 90 samples over all processor types. We analyze the variations in power consumption for the different samples using six different workloads over five load levels. Additionally, we analyze how these variations change for different processor core counts and architectures.

The results of this paper show that selection of a processor sample can have a statistically significant impact on power consumption. With no correlation to performance, power consumption for nominally identical processors can differ as much as 29.6% in idle and 19.5% at full load. We also show that these variations change over different architectures and processor types.

ICPE'16, March 12 - 18, 2016, Delft, Netherlands

© 2016 Copyright held by the owner/author(s). Publication rights licensed to ACM.
ISBN 978-1-4503-4080-9/16/03. . . $15.00

DOI: http://dx.doi.org/10.1145/2851553.2851567

Keywords

Variation, SPEC, SERT, Workloads, Energy Efficiency, Metrics, Load level, Utilization

1. INTRODUCTION

Energy efficiency of computing systems has become a significant issue over the past decades. Server systems play a significant part in the overall power consumption. In 2010, the U.S. Environmental Protection Agency (U.S. EPA) estimated that 3% of the entire energy consumption in the U.S. is caused by data center power draw [20]. According to a New York Times study from 2012, data centers worldwide consume about 30 billion watts per hour. This is equivalent to the approximate output of 30 nuclear power plants [3].

Governments, manufacturers, and academic researchers are addressing this problem with various approaches. Systems benchmarking is central to these, as it helps to collect comparable information, enabling better development and purchasing decisions [19].

To ensure comparability, benchmark results must meet a number of criteria including repeatability [16], reproducibility, and verifiability [25]. As a result industry standard benchmarks, such as SPECpower_ssj2008 [18], require full disclosure of all system hardware components and software, as they can significantly affect power consumption and energy efficiency [27]. However, even nominally identical systems running the same hardware and software may produce different benchmark results. Reasons for this behavior can be found both in random measurement errors, as well as systematic errors due to minor differences in the nominally identical hardware components.

For servers, the CPU is not only the largest consumer of power, but is also responsible for most of the dynamic changes to system power consumption [10]. Consequently, it stands to reason that CPUs are also the major factor in power variation for otherwise identical systems. Many studies analyzing differences in server power consumption with focus on CPU and CPU workloads exist [5, 6]. These studies show that CPU power may vary depending on many factors, such as CPU load, workload type, used execution units, and so on. Yet none of these studies analyze the error that results from different samples of the same CPU.

In our experience, power consumption for identical CPUs can vary significantly. Yet comprehensive public studies on the size and impact of these variations are missing. Such an analysis is necessary for many fields of research even beyond benchmarking. For example, power management mechanisms and predictive power models [4] rely on low variations in power consumption for nominally identical systems and components. The actual variation in power consumption sets an upper bound for the accuracy of those approaches.

In this paper, we evaluate the power consumption and energy efficiency of four different processor types from two generations with 20 – 30 separate nominally identical physical processors (processor samples) for each of those types. In addition, as many publicly available results are not based on the publicly available final production samples of processors, we test eight separate qualification processors corresponding to two of the production batches under test. We measure energy efficiency, as well as system and CPU power consumption, for multiple workloads and load levels under two different system power management configuration. We examine the power measurements for each of the physical processor samples and compare the different distributions for the nominally identical processors. We correlate the power deviations with further measured data, such as CPU temperature and frequency.

The goal of this paper is to gain insight into the variations in power consumption for nominally identical processors and into the major impact factors contributing to these variations. The major contributions of this paper are:

1. We explore the differences in power consumption of nominally identical CPUs for multiple workloads showing that these different CPU samples exhibit statistically significant differences in power consumption.
2. We investigate correlations between the power consumption variations and additional metrics, such as throughput, CPU temperature and frequency.
3. We explore the impact of different target load levels and CPU power management configurations on variations in power consumption and energy efficiency.

Our measurements show that nominally identical processor samples can cause significant differences in CPU power consumption of up to 29.6%. This in turn propagates to a difference in system power of up tp 12.1%. These differences exhibit no significant correlation to CPU temperature and system performance. However, the actual observed variations in power consumption for nominally identical processors differ significantly depending on processor architecture.

The remainder of this paper is structured as follows: We discuss related work in Section 2. Section 3 details the experimental setup. Section 4 explores power variations during a single measurement, whereas Section 5 evaluates power variations between samples of the same processor type, and Section 6 compares measurement results and CPU sample differences over multiple processor types, deriving overall take-away lessons. We conclude the paper in Section 7.

2. RELATED WORK

A number of studies analyzing the power consumption of servers and processors exist. These studies analyze variations in power consumption for individual processors with focus on the major impact factors that can cause a difference in power consumption:

[15] and [11] analyze CPU power consumption at the circuit level. They examine individual transistors and their integration with the goal of power characterization and simulation. When analyzing power consumption of most commercially available processors, this circuit level power consumption is usually considered as a black-box, as information on processor internals is commonly not available. This black-box behavior may lead to issues with repeatability of power measurements and variations in power consumption.

[6] and [23] analyze power consumption depending on workload with a focus on the executed CPU instructions. They characterize CPU power based on performance counter data. Similarly, [8] build a power model using performance counters. As in our case, they use industry standard benchmarks, such as SPEC CPU2006 [13] for a thorough and representative analysis.

Processor power management exists at many system levels. All of these may cause variations in power consumption. [12] and [14] examine the impact of the physical location where a task is executed inside the CPU on power consumption and heat generation. Other management techniques, such as dynamic voltage and frequency scaling (DVFS) [24, 5], also have significant impact on CPU power consumption and heat. Such temperature-sensitive management techniques can add randomness to power measurements as they are influenced by environmental factors that may not be under the full control of the system's administrator.

The black-box-like behavior of some system components and the apparent randomness of environmental factors have contributed to research attempting to characterize power consumption on higher abstraction levels. Such characterizations rely on workload classifications and system level metrics, such as utilization [27, 7]. Results of these analyses are usually correlated to create full-system power models on a higher abstraction level [22, 21].

This paper addresses the power differences and variations that are caused by black-box behavior and environmental influences. We first evaluate how much the power consumption of a system can vary without any changes in the hardware, software, or system settings. We then go a step further by evaluating variations in systems that are identical in terms of technical specifications. We focus on CPUs and exchange system CPUs with nominally identical ones to analyze the impact the black-box behavior of the new sample can have on power consumption.

3. MEASUREMENT METHODOLOGY

We test four processor types on three different systems using two test suites. All systems are tested with at least 20 samples of one production processor type. Additionally, two of the systems are measured using four corresponding qualification samples with one further measurement using a mix of six qualification and six production samples. Power consumption is measured for both the entire system under test (SUT) and the processor only. Measurements are carried out following the guidelines described in the SPEC power methodology [2].

3.1 Workloads

We run two test suites on the SUT: SERT [20] and LINPACK [9]. SERT is a rating tool for analysis and evaluation of the energy efficiency of server systems, developed by the SPEC OSG Power Subcommittee. It is not intended as a benchmark for a single system energy-efficiency score, but instead runs a number of different micro workloads, called

Worklets that exercise different parts of the SUT. It features seven separate CPU Worklets that are primarily CPU bound, but may also exercise some additional parts of the SUT (such as memory). Due to the CPU focus in this paper, we chose those worklets that have been found to be the most CPU bound [27]:

1. **LU**: Implements a transaction that computes the LU factorization of a dense matrix using partial pivoting. It exercises linear algebra kernels (BLAS) and dense matrix operations. LU is almost exclusively CPU bound and scales mostly with CPU frequency.

2. **Compress**: Implements a transaction that compresses and decompresses data using a modified Lempel-Ziv-Welch (LZW) method following an algorithm introduced in [28]. It finds common substrings and replaces them with a variable size code. This is deterministic and it is done on-the-fly. Thus, the decompression procedure needs no input table, but tracks the way the initial table was built.

3. **SOR** (Jacobi Successive Over-Relaxation): Implements a transaction that exercises typical access patterns in finite difference applications, for example, solving Laplace's equation in 2D with Drichlet boundary conditions. The algorithm exercises basic "grid averaging" memory patterns. Like LU, this worklet is also mostly CPU bound. As such, we use it as our second worklet for CPU-heavy heterogeneous workloads.

4. **SHA256**: Utilizes standard Java functions to perform SHA-256 hashing and encryption/decryption transformations on a byte array. This byte array is perturbed by one byte for each transaction.

5. **Idle**: Keeps the CPU in an active idle state where it is ready to receive work.

SERT can run worklets (except Idle) at different target load levels. These are defined as the percentage of maximum throughput achievable on the SUT. To achieve a stable steady state, work units are dispatched with random exponentially distributed inter-arrival times. The mean of those inter-arrival times is selected as the inverse of the target throughput. All worklets except Idle are executed at the 25%, 50%, 75%, and 100% load levels.

LINPACK is a benchmark measuring a computer's ability to solve a system of linear equations. We run the Shared Memory Version (SHM) of the standalone LINPACK on each SUT. The server consumes a significant amount of power during its execution phase, eclipsing all of the SERT worklets in respect to power consumption. In contrast to SERT and its workloads, it does not explicitly take care to preserve a steady system state for stable energy measurements.

3.2 Systems under Test

We run our workloads on three different systems. For each of those systems, we pick a processor type and exchange samples after each run. Each system only has one socket populated to minimize multiple processor samples influencing one another. The system under test also remains identical for all samples of the same processor type. The SUTs are:

- **Fujitsu RX2540 M1** system with 4 x 16 GB RAM. We test 30 different samples of Intel's Xeon E5-2680 v3

processor on this system. It features 12 cores and a base frequency of 2.5 GHz (up to 3.3 GHz with turbo, 120 W TDP). Each sample is tested twice: Once with turbo turned on and once with turbo turned off. We also test 12 samples of the Xeon E5-2699 v3 processor on this system (six production and six qualification samples). It is an 18 core processor with a base frequency of 2.3 GHz (3.6 GHz with turbo, 145 W TDP).

- **Dell PowerEdge R730** system with 4 x 16 GB RAM. We use this system to test 20 different samples of Intel's Xeon E5-2660 v3 processor with 10 processor cores at a base frequency of 2.6 GHz (up to 3.3 GHz with turbo, 105 W TDP). We also test each sample with and without turbo on this system.

- **Sun Server X3-2** system with 4 x 4 GB RAM. This historical system is used to test 20 samples of the older Intel Xeon E5-2609 processor (80 W TDP). This processor from Intel's Sandy Bridge generation is the smallest CPU to be tested. It has four cores running at a frequency of 2.4 GHz. This system does not feature a turbo mode. Instead, we perform a series of tests with all BIOS power management disabled.

All systems run Red Hat Enterprise Linux (RHEL) 6.6 and use the Oracle Java HotSpot VM for executing SERT's Java-based worklets.

3.3 Measurement Data

For the SERT measurements, throughput data is collected on a per second resolution by SERT's Chauffeur harness [1]. Wall power is measured using the SPEC PTDaemon, which can autmatically cooperate with SERT, but can also collect data separately of any SERT execution. In addition, we measure CPU package power, temperature, and frequency using the RAPL hardware counters provided by Intel's processors. We use Intel's publicly available Performance Counter Monitor [17] to read these counters for every second during workload execution.

For system power measurements (wall power) we use Yokogawa's WT210 analyzer and the ZES Zimmer LMG95 power meter. Both report the power measurement uncertainty with a specified maximum measurement error of less than 1%. For our measurement the WT210 never exceeds 0.7% uncertainty and the LMG95 does not exceed 0.2% uncertainty.

SERT worklets are executed in intervals with measurement phases lasting 120 seconds. All power, performance, and additional data is logged at each second during the run, providing 120 data points for each worklet at each target load level. In addition to the measurement phases, SERT also runs a number of calibration, warmup, pre-measurement, and post-measurement phases, all designed to ensure a steady measurement state. These phases are explained in more detail in [26].

LINPACK also features distinct phases with the main execution phase featuring a relatively stable interval of maximum power consumption. We detect this phase and then collect all relevant data with the corresponding time stamps. As with SERT, we collect wall power using the SPEC PTDaemon and CPU package power, temperature, and frequency using the Performance Counter Monitor for each second during LINPACK execution.

4. VARIATIONS DURING A SINGLE MEASUREMENT RUN

Before analyzing the variations between different samples of the same processor, we study how power variance changes depending on workload, load level, and BIOS setting. The results of this section also help to indicate how stable power consumption can be during an interval of usage at a given stable load level. Stability in power consumption is a result of both stable CPU power management and stable workloads as part of our test suites. Both are prerequisites for the comparisons of different CPU samples in subsequent sections.

For this analysis, we choose the median sample of the Xeon E5-2680 v3 processor in the Fujitsu system, which was measured using our most accurate power analyzer. Additionally, we evaluate the impact of separate measurement runs on the same sample using the Xeon E5-2609 on the Oracle system.

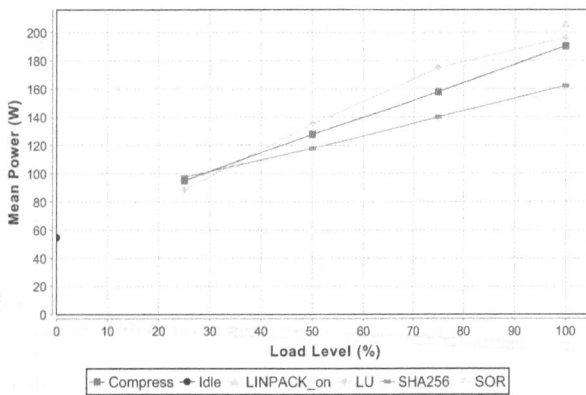

Figure 1: System power consumption of the Fujitsu server with median Xeon E5-2680 v3 processor.

System power consumption for all workloads on the Fujitsu system is shown in Figure 1. The figure displays the power consumption (in Watt) for each of the workloads over the full range of load levels. In contrast to the other workloads, Idle and LINPACK feature only one load level each. Idle power is the smallest consumer, whereas LINPACK is the largest consumer followed by LU at full load. The workloads scale almost linearly over load levels, increasing in power consumption with each additional level. The rest of this section will focus on the variances of the power measurement for each separate load level / workload combination. A thorough analysis of power scaling for the worklets over the different load levels can be found in [27].

We analyze the coefficient of variation (CV) for the power measurements. It is a normalized value defined as the ration of the standard deviation divided by the sample's mean. In contrast to a comparison of the raw standard deviation, the CV allows comparing workloads and load levels with different mean power consumption, such as Idle with a mean power consumption of 51.934 W and LINPACK with its mean power of 205.789 W on the Fujitsu system with the median CPU sample.

Table 1 shows the CV for CPU power consumption as measured by the Intel RAPL counter. It shows that variation during a 120 second measurement interval is relatively low and stable at a CV between 0.3% and 1.44%. This varia-

tion is independent of the processor's current load level and turbo setting. It is also similar for many workloads. The compression workload varies more in its power consumption. We attribute this behavior to the greater intensity of its memory access which introduces more seemingly random behavior in performance and power consumption.

	Load	Idle	Com.	LU	SHA	SOR	LIN.
Turbo on	0%	33.17					
	25%		5.63	0.53	1.20	3.63	
	50%		0.65	0.66	1.44	0.55	
	75%		0.61	0.66	1.23	0.42	
	100%		0.30	0.03	0.63	0.52	0.04
Turbo off	0%	0.84					
	25%		2.51	0.56	1.11	2.46	
	50%		0.57	0.60	1.23	0.39	
	75%		0.62	0.41	1.27	0.38	
	100%		0.38	0.40	0.61	0.05	0.04

Table 1: Coefficients of variaton (CV) in % for CPU power consumption on median Xeon E5-2680 v3 sample.

The LINPACK workload behaves differently to the SERT workloads and varies even less in its power consumption. This difference is not surprising since LINPACK work units are not dispatched using an exponentially distributed random inter-arrival process, as SERT work units are. This random arrival process for SERT transactions allows the targeting of specified load levels, but adds some variation to the power consumption.

The major outlier in Table 1 is the Idle workload. On a single idle processor sample, power consumption can vary for 35.17% with turbo on, but only 0.84% without turbo. This observation underlines our previous assertion that operating system and CPU power management may lead to variations in power consumption, as idle power minimization is a major goal of those power saving mechanisms. This variation can already be observed during the time frame of a single measurement run. We back this assertion with the correlation of CPU power consumption and frequency. For most workloads, CPU power consumption and frequency correlate little. To illustrate, LU's CPU power / frequency correlation coefficient ranges between 8.6% (25% load) and 33.3% (100% load). Other workloads are similar, as frequency remains relatively stable during the workloads' execution. The Idle workload, however, shows significant correlation. The Idle interval with the turbo setting on, in particular, exhibits a CPU power / frequency correlation coefficient of 94.2%.

Table 2 shows the variations in full system power for each measurement interval. Most CVs are smaller than their CPU power counterparts in Table 1. This indicates that a majority of the variation is caused by CPU power variations, rather than power variations due to other system components. This is especially true for the variations during system idle time. Specifically, the Idle worklet with turbo enabled features a CPU power standard deviation of 4.02 W at a mean CPU power consumption of 12.11 W, whereas the entire system features a similar standard deviation of 5.73 W at a mean power consumption of 54.07 W. The correlation coefficient of 99.93% between CPU and system power for the Idle measurement underlines this observation that CPU power directly influences system power.

LINPACK behaves differently, however. Its system power CV is significantly larger than its CPU power CV. The same

	Load	Idle	Com.	LU	SHA	SOR	LIN.
Turbo on	0%	10.47					
	25%		2.59	0.30	0.71	1.73	
	50%		0.36	0.46	0.90	0.30	
	75%		0.50	0.45	0.89	0.31	
	100%		0.36	0.19	0.29	0.33	4.14
Turbo off	0%	0.34					
	25%		1.00	0.31	0.63	1.25	
	50%		0.34	0.35	0.70	0.21	
	75%		0.39	0.30	0.82	0.25	
	100%		0.28	0.30	0.17	0.15	3.69

Table 2: Coefficients of variaton (CV) in % for system power consumption on Fujitsu system, running the median Xeon E5-2680 v3 sample.

	Load	Idle	Com.	LU	SHA	SOR	LIN.
Perf.	0%	12.93					
	25%		2.48	9.56	6.52	9.32	
	50%		10.02	9.80	7.28	9.29	
	75%		9.20	8.87	9.83	8.72	
	100%		11.00	12.12	11.21	9.19	9.03
Balanced	0%	13.62					
	25%		10.80	12.17	8.38	10.36	
	50%		11.18	8.40	8.18	19.40	
	75%		10.23	11.89	8.96	11.35	
	100%		12.43	11.98	11.72	12.91	6.21

Table 4: Second order CVs in % for system power consumption of Oracle system for measurement repeats on Xeon E5-2609 sample.

is true for the standard deviation of its power consumption. We attribute this effect the property of LINPACK to use additional system resources, especially cooling, that are not visible in the CPU power consumption.

To identify potential further stability issues with worklets that might lead to erroneous conclusions later on, we repeat our entire measurement suite 50 times on a single sample of the E5-2609 processor on the Oracle system. Specifically, we evaluate whether the variations for the median system are representative by calculating the 2nd order CVs (the CVs of the CVs) over all 50 measurement repeats. Being an older system, this system does not support turbo mode. Instead we test two different BIOS settings. We test a balanced setting (comparable to the turbo off setting for the other systems) and a performance setting with all BIOs power management disabled. The results are displayed in Tables 3 and 4. They show CPU power and system power second order CVs respectively. These 2nd order CVs show if variations between the different samples differ. Consistently high or low CVs result in a low 2nd order CV, whereas differing CVs show as high 2nd order CVs. Consequently, low values should indicate a high representativeness of our previous observations based on a single sample.

	Load	Idle	Com.	LU	SHA	SOR	LIN.
Perf.	0%	134.1					
	25%		19.15	22.35	10.87	19.87	
	50%		9.26	10.07	5.57	10.73	
	75%		7.10	20.36	3.91	13.93	
	100%		6.41	22.54	25.91	20.52	37.67
Balanced	0%	99.43					
	25%		13.36	23.51	7.84	15.76	
	50%		10.06	13.79	5.02	46.66	
	75%		8.07	22.63	7.22	10.11	
	100%		13.27	24.11	33.67	20.52	20.64

Table 3: Second order CVs in % for CPU power consumption for measurement repeats on Xeon E5-2609 sample.

Both tables show that differences between the variations for the separate measurement runs are significant, but bounded. For the balanced setting, worklet second order CPU power variations range between 8.07% for Compression at 75% load and 46.66% for SOR at 50% load. Idle is the major exception with a second order variance of 99.43%, reinforcing the previous observation that Idle can be highly volatile. System power shows smaller second order variations than CPU power. Idle features the greatest variation of variations, yet it is only 13.62%. These variations are smaller,

as system power is greater than CPU power. With the rest of the system remaining relatively stable over the different measurement runs, the differences in CPU power variations are somewhat mitigated. Idle is affected even more by this effect, as CPU power consumption during Idle is minimal and smallest in relation to the rest of the system.

Disabling BIOS power management does not significantly reduce second order variations. CPU power variations still range between 3.91% (SHA at 74% load) and 134.06% (Idle). Most notably, idle second order variation does not decrease even though a potential source of volatility inducing power management has been eliminated.

While the variations of variations are significant over multiple runs, the means of the respective measurements differ little. With balanced power management, Idle CPU power shows the smallest mean difference of 0.1 W (0.67%), ranging between 14.83 W and 14.93 W. The largest mean difference for the SERT workloads is found for LU at 50% load. However, it is only a total difference of 1.32 W (4.02%), with the minimum being 32.82 W and maximum CPU power of 34.14 W.

	Load	Idle	Com.	LU	SHA	SOR	LIN.
Perf.	0%	0.17					
	25%		0.06	0.31	0.23	0.25	
	50%		0.09	0.35	0.36	0.20	
	75%		0.11	0.59	0.41	0.15	
	100%		0.12	0.10	0.32	0.07	0.12
Balanced	0%	0.13					
	25%		0.15	0.26	0.24	0.13	
	50%		0.13	0.81	0.31	0.28	
	75%		0.11	0.60	0.31	0.21	
	100%		0.15	0.15	0.21	0.18	1.19

Table 5: CVs in % for mean CPU power consumption for measurement repeats on Xeon E5-2609 sample.

Subsequently the coefficients of variation for the measurement means in Table 5 are also very small. The greatest CV is the CV for LINPACK (which also features the greatest min / max difference) with 1.19%, the next greatest being 0.81% for LU at 50% load. These numbers do not change significantly with BIOS power management disabled. Idle min / max difference is still 0.1 W and the greatest min / max difference is LU at 75% load with an absolute difference of 0.8 W and a CV of 0.6%.

In contrast to the low CPU temperature correlation during a single measurement, repeated power measurements exhibit a correlation. All workload / load level combinations

	Load	Idle	Compress	LU	SHA256	SOR	LINPACK
Turbo on	0%	2.83 W (29.15%)					
	25%		4.92 W (13.20%)	4.87 W (15.58%)	5.53 W (13.01%)	4.28 W (11.24%)	
	50%		6.15 W (9.63%)	4.26 W (6.02%)	8.12 W (13.78%)	7.39 W (12.54%)	
	75%		9.65 W (11.22%)	7.22 W (7.02%)	11.01 W (14.43%)	10.62 W (14.09%)	
	100%		10.12 W (9.22%)	0.01 W (0.01%)	15.30 W (16.36%)	14.36 W (15.86%)	0.05 W (0.05%)
Turbo off	0%	2.32 W (23.87%)					
	25%		3.42 W (11.68%)	4.78 W (15.69%)	4.76 W (12.50%)	3.69 W (14.20%)	
	50%		5.87 W (10.55%)	5.71 W (8.78%)	5.65 W (11.12%)	5.55 W (10.95%)	
	75%		7.78 W (10.76%)	8.25 W (9.17%)	6.89 W (10.78%)	6.64 W (10.43%)	
	100%		10.78 W (12.12%)	7.44 W (6.61%)	7.75 W (10.14%)	7.47 W (10.01%)	0.04 W (0.03%)

Table 6: Min / max CPU power consumption differences over all Xeon E5-2680 v3 samples.

	Load	Idle	Compress	LU	SHA256	SOR	LINPACK
Turbo on	0%	3.34 W (6.47%)					
	25%		5.83 W (6.22%)	5.91 W (6.97%)	6.96 W (7.16%)	5.17 W (5.58%)	
	50%		8.01 W (6.28%)	5.46 W (4.10%)	10.26 W (8.74%)	9.44 W (8.04%)	
	75%		12.53 W (7.96%)	8.52 W (4.89%)	14.40 W (10.31%)	14.01 W (10.11%)	
	100%		13.73 W (7.23%)	1.01 W (0.52%)	19.64 W (12.16%)	18.66 W (11.82%)	1.56 W (0.76%)
Turbo off	0%	3.66 W (7.18%)					
	25%		4.54 W (5.43%)	5.90 W (7.04%)	6.03 W (6.61%)	4.87 W (6.22%)	
	50%		7.93 W (6.84%)	7.74 W (6.17%)	7.45 W (6.98%)	7.38 W (6.91%)	
	75%		9.72 W (6.96%)	11.02 W (7.02%)	8.59 W (6.96%)	8.37 W (6.81%)	
	100%		13.58 W (8.38%)	10.79 W (5.82%)	10.35 W (7.44%)	10.12 W (7.40%)	1.85 W (0.90%)

Table 7: Min / max system power differences for Fujitsu system over all Xeon E5-2680 v3 samples.

show a positive correlation coefficient. This coefficient is the largest at full load, with all coefficients greater than 84% with the exception of SHA256 at 55% correlation.

Concluding, we learn that power measurements are very stable both within one measurement run and in their means for multiple runs. Variations can be inconsistent over multiple runs and differ significantly, yet the mean remains very similar. The Idle workload is the odd man out. It can pose challenges as unforeseen power management may cause significant variation during single measurement intervals. However, mean idle power remains the most consistent over multiple measurements. Because of this consistency over multiple measurements and due to the importance of a processor's idle behavior, for many practical considerations, we still analyze differences in idle consumption for the upcoming sections.

5. VARIATIONS BETWEEN SAMPLES OF THE SAME CPU

Having analyzed the differences between power consumption and power variations, we analyze the power consumption differences for multiple nominally identical processor samples. We answer the question of how much power consumption can differ over multiple samples and if these differences are statistically significant beyond the power differences occurring within a single sample. We also examine variances in processor performance and how these correlate with power consumption. Finally, we take a look at additional impact factors and correlations, including temperature and frequency.

For this analysis, we must consider that the nature of outliers is different when comparing measurements on different samples, rather than comparing multiple measurement iterations from the same sample. Section 4 shows that, for single samples, variations are due to environmental conditions, such as temperature and unforeseen behavior of power management. When comparing multiple samples, differences can

also be caused by systematic differences in the integrated circuits of the samples. With this in mind, outliers gain importance as they may not be "random" flukes, but rather rare samples with a systematic difference.

Table 6 shows the differences for the mean CPU power consumption of the different Xeon E5-2680 v3 samples. These differences in power consumption of different samples are significantly larger, both absolutely and relatively, than the intra-sample differences for repeat measurements of the same sample (see Section 4). The greatest relative difference if for CPU power consumption at 29.15% with turbo and 23.87% without turbo. The greatest absolute difference is found for SHA256 at 100% load with a difference of 15.3 W with turbo. Incidentally, this is also the second highest relative variation. With turbo enabled, the smallest relative difference is 0.01% for LU at full load. Turbo disabled features the smallest relative difference of 0.03% for LINPACK. LINPACK and LU are the two biggest power consumers in our test suite. With both of these featuring the smallest differences, it stands to reason that CPU power differences between samples diminish at the highest utilization. However, this only seems to be the case for workloads that truly maximize their power consumption on the processor and is helped by BIOS settings that increase a workload's ability to maximize consumption (such as turbo). Other workloads do not manage to reach this limit, as they do not consume as much power at their highest load levels.

Table 7 shows the respective differences between minimum and maximum system power consumption for the 30 processor samples. Due to the greater base power, relative differences in power consumption decrease, even as absolute differences increase. Workloads with lower absolute CPU consumption are affected more by this. However, the increase in absolute differences indicates that an increase in CPU power consumption can lead to an increase in power consumption of secondary subsystems, such as cooling.

System power and CPU power correlate strongly. For all

workloads, the correlation coefficient for the means of those power exceeds 98%. The only exceptions are LU at high load and LINPACK. These two workloads show so little variance in CPU power consumption that the remaining system power variation is seemingly random.

	Load	Idle	Com.	LU	SHA	SOR	LIN.
Turbo on	0%	6.95					
	25%		3.34	4.06	2.74	2.72	
	50%		2.34	1.69	3.21	2.96	
	75%		2.93	1.44	3.73	3.63	
	100%		2.93	0.00	4.27	4.32	0.01
Turbo off	0%	5.93					
	25%		2.97	4.07	2.42	3.68	
	50%		2.36	1.98	2.44	2.38	
	75%		2.37	2.13	2.40	2.35	
	100%		2.73	1.96	2.37	2.33	0.01

Table 8: CVs in % for mean CPU power consumption over all Xeon E5-2680 v3 samples.

The observations from comparing min / max differences are validated by the coefficients of variation over the mean CPU power consumption of all 30 samples (see Table 8). Again, Idle has the greatest variation, whereas LINPACK and LU feature the least variation. The variation of means also helps to expose the observation that only the greatest power consumers decrease in variation at full load. With turbo enabled, SOR and SHA256 have the second and third greatest variations in power consumption at full load. These two workloads are not near the CPU power limit, with SHA-256 consuming a total average of 99.34 W and SOR a total average of 96.28 W. LINPACK and LU, on the other hand, consume 119.86 W and 119.88 W respectively.

We show the means and variations for SHA256 CPU power consumption in Figure 2. The box-plot shows the distributions of the power consumption for the separate physical CPU samples. Each colored box shows the range between first and third quartile and the horizontal line inside the boxes displays the median. The mean is shown using a filled circle. The figure shows that all CPUs vary a little with only small groups of similar samples. Means are scattered over the entire range of power differences, with some outliers at the top. The figure also shows that samples vary significantly in their internal variance. Some samples show significant variances, wheras others have all of their measured values clustered closely around their mean.

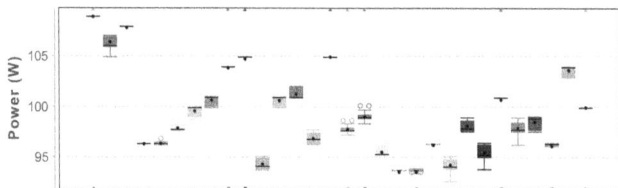

Figure 2: CPU power consumption of Xeon E5-2680 v3 processor samples running SHA256 at 100% load.

These differences in variances also show in the samples' second order coefficients of variance in Tables 9 and 10. These variances of variances are significantly greater than the intra-sample variances of Tables 3 and 4. This shows that power measurement stability is additionally affected by CPU sample properties, beyond the random errors and variances that can occur on a single sample.

Idle features the greatest variance again, regardless of turbo setting. Taking its differences in mean power consumption into account, it is safe to deduce that Idle is the by far the most volatile of all workloads. It is apparently also the state where differences between samples are the most visible, as Idle means are relatively stable for single samples, despite its volatility. Similarly, LINPACK, a workload with very small relative differences in mean power consumption, shows significant second order variances.

	Load	Idle	Com.	LU	SHA	SOR	LIN.
Turbo on	0%	183.3					
	25%		9.49	27.65	11.70	17.80	
	50%		10.44	9.47	8.98	15.91	
	75%		9.95	14.64	7.99	11.87	
	100%		53.83	35.94	43.43	49.69	156.5
Turbo off	0%	179.1					
	25%		17.80	48.77	9.65	45.35	
	50%		6.59	10.82	7.47	8.77	
	75%		11.22	7.57	5.97	10.72	
	100%		28.29	58.15	61.09	79.98	122.2

Table 9: Second order CVs in % for CPU power consumption over all Xeon E5-2680 v3 samples.

	Load	Idle	Com.	LU	SHA	SOR	LIN.
Turbo on	0%	172.8					
	25%		8.74	24.23	13.46	17.24	
	50%		212.1	6.32	11.10	26.36	
	75%		6.99	16.55	119.71	11.43	
	100%		244.7	45.40	293.57	28.17	15.56
Turbo off	0%	169.4					
	25%		105.8	39.01	10.14	34.64	
	50%		238.3	9.65	7.00	10.57	
	75%		8.64	7.60	6.84	8.13	
	100%		318.8	38.53	21.83	372.1	13.41

Table 10: Second order CVs in % for system power consumption over all Xeon E5-2680 v3 samples.

Apart from Idle, workloads seem to show their greatest second order variance at their highest load levels and smaller second order variances at the 50% and 75% load levels. The major exception to this rule is Compression which has a second order variation of coefficients of 212.05% at the 50% load level.

In Section 4 we found that power consumption differences for repeated measurements on a single sample are strongly correlated with CPU temperature. This correlation is not nearly as strong when comparing different samples. CPU power and temperature correlate for some workloads, but not all. SHA256 and SOR feature an 80% / 82% correlation between CPU power consumption per sample and CPU temperature. However, at the 25% and 50% load levels no workload exceeds a correlation of 53%. Most importantly, the workload with the highest relative CPU power difference between samples (Idle) features only a correlation of 19.8%. This leads us to conclude that differences in power consumption of multiple samples are also significantly influenced by effects other than CPU temperature.

Finally, we evaluate the variances in performance and how those relate to the power variances for the respective samples. We compare the throughput (in s^{-1}) for the SERT

	Load	Compress	LU	SHA256	SOR
T. on	25%	207.64 s^{-1} (3.42%)	683.24 s^{-1} (4.38%)	16.66 s^{-1} (1.70%)	33.42 s^{-1} (0.35%)
	50%	411.63 s^{-1} (3.40%)	1338.75 s^{-1} (4.29%)	25.75 s^{-1} (1.31%)	59.92 s^{-1} (0.31%)
	75%	620.06 s^{-1} (3.41%)	2008.15 s^{-1} (4.29%)	37.19 s^{-1} (1.26%)	74.70 s^{-1} (0.26%)
	100%	982.51 s^{-1} (4.07%)	2575.86 s^{-1} (4.18%)	37.05 s^{-1} (0.94%)	59.39 s^{-1} (0.15%)
T. off	25%	94.20 s^{-1} (1.73%)	200.66 s^{-1} (1.32%)	13.22 s^{-1} (1.57%)	30.82 s^{-1} (0.37%)
	50%	164.30 s^{-1} (1.50%)	362.76 s^{-1} (1.19%)	24.06 s^{-1} (1.42%)	49.47 s^{-1} (0.30%)
	75%	223.87 s^{-1} (1.36%)	581.34 s^{-1} (1.27%)	25.96 s^{-1} (1.02%)	44.51 s^{-1} (0.18%)
	100%	286.50 s^{-1} (1.31%)	1852.97 s^{-1} (3.11%)	31.21 s^{-1} (0.92%)	55.80 s^{-1} (0.17%)

Table 11: Min / max throughput differences for Fujitsu system over all Xeon E5-2680 v3 samples.

worklets at their respective load levels. We do not analyze Idle and LINPACK, as Idle does not have a throughput and LINPACK does not log any. The min / max differences between the worklet throughputs is shown in Table 11. Note that the absolute values can not be compared across the different worklets, as work unit sizes differ. The relative throughput differences are significantly smaller than the relative power differences. The greatest difference is the 4.38% min / max difference for LU at 25% load, which is only slightly greater than the relative differences for LU at all other load levels. The turbo setting also affects throughput in a different way than it does power consumption. System power differences (see Table 7) were affected only minimally by the turbo. It did affect only two worklets at high loads. Turbo's effect on throughput variations, however, is both significant and consistent. All worklets, with the exception of SOR at high loads, show significantly less performance variation with turbo disabled.

Not only do performance and power behave differently across the samples and power settings, they also do not correlate. Only LU at 25% load shows a correlation greater than 50% (51.4% with turbo). All other workloads show smaller correlation coefficients in the interval between -50% and 50% correlation.

In conclusion, we find that different samples of a nominally identical processor can exhibit a significantly different power consumption. These differences are most visible during the Idle state and at high load before hitting the processor's power limit. Once this limit is reached, samples behave very similarly and differences in power consumption disappear. CPUs also show great differences in the variances of power consumption a single sample can produce during the course of a measurement run. Again, Idle is the most extreme case displaying these differences. Finally, we find that the power differences correlate little with differences in sample temperatures during measurements and not at all with the sample's performance.

6. VARIATION DIFFERENCES BETWEEN PROCESSOR TYPES

We compare the power variances of the Xeon E5-2680 v3 processors from Section 5 with results of 20 samples of the Xeon E5-2660 v3 processor running on a Dell server. The processors are nearly identical, save for a 100 MHz difference in frequency and two less cores for the E5-2660 v3. Using these processors we investigate if a reduced number of cores has an impact on the CPU power variations. Next, we compare those results to results from 20 samples of the Intel Xeon E5-2609 processor. These results will help indicate if differences between processor generations exist. Finally,

we analyze processor qualification samples, which are often used for system design and analysis at early stages of a processor's product line life cycle.

6.1 Core Count

The Intel Xeon E5-2660 v3 processor running on our Dell PowerEdge R730 system is a 10-core CPU with a base frequency of 2.6 GHz. It has fewer cores than the 12-core E5-2680 v3 from our previous measurements and a 100 MHz higher base frequency. The turbo frequency of the two processors is identical at 3.3 GHz. As a result, both processors move in a similar frequency range as long as turbo is enabled. We use the Dell system to determine if a lower core count affects the variation of processor power consumption across multiple samples.

We show the min / max CPU power differences over the 20 samples in Table 12. As this processor is smaller than the E5-2680 v3 it consumes less total power. Consequently absolute min /max differences are also smaller. However, the same is true for the relative differences. With a few exceptions, all worklets have a lower relative min / max difference on the E5-2660 v3. Idle with turbo is one of the exceptions, displaying an almost identical relative min / max difference of 29.63%. Yet overall, the mean min / max power consumption difference of the E5-2680 v3 samples (11.8%) is 25.7% greater than the difference amongst the E5-2660 v3 samples (9.4%). With turbo disabled, the overall relative difference using an E5-2680 v3 (11.1%) is 25.1% greater than using an E5-2660 v3 (8.9%). With turbo disabled, some worklets go against the trend, as Compress, SHA256, and SOR at 100% load have a greater relative min / max difference with the E5-2660 v3 than with the E5-2680 v3.

	Load	Idle	Com.	LU	SHA	SOR	LIN.
Turbo on	0%	6.59					
	25%		2.71	3.37	2.13	3.07	
	50%		1.92	1.78	2.18	2.24	
	75%		1.84	1.30	2.92	2.31	
	100%		1.60	0.05	2.54	2.76	0.00
Turbo off	0%	5.50					
	25%		2.82	3.18	2.12	3.08	
	50%		2.24	1.90	2.21	2.36	
	75%		2.12	2.30	2.41	2.07	
	100%		2.21	0.10	2.32	2.42	0.01

Table 13: CVs in % for mean CPU power consumption over all Xeon E5-2660 v3 samples.

The coefficients of variation for the 10-core Xeon E5-2660 v3 samples' power consumption in Table 13 show that the cases in which relative min / max differences exceed those of the 12 core E5-2680 v3 are outliers. The CVs over all samples are always smaller for the processor with fewer cores. With

154

	Load	Idle	Compress	LU	SHA256	SOR	LINPACK
Turbo on	0%	2.73 W (29.63%)					
	25%		2.88 W (9.83%)	3.40 W (11.96%)	2.48 W (7.59%)	2.84 W (10.97%)	
	50%		3.45 W (6.89%)	3.82 W (7.05%)	3.77 W (8.18%)	3.69 W (8.19%)	
	75%		4.95 W (7.37%)	4.37 W (5.76%)	10.09 W (14.31%)	5.57 W (9.85%)	
	100%		5.67 W (5.68%)	0.18 W (0.17%)	10.15 W (11.97%)	10.92 W (13.57%)	0.02 W (0.02%)
Turbo off	0%	1.49 W (16.19%)					
	25%		2.75 W (9.95%)	3.31 W (11.69%)	2.34 W (7.52%)	2.77 W (11.24%)	
	50%		3.80 W (8.06%)	3.81 W (7.15%)	3.68 W (8.51%)	3.44 W (8.13%)	
	75%		5.70 W (9.05%)	7.25 W (9.92%)	6.82 W (11.01%)	4.52 W (8.50%)	
	100%		8.79 W (10.00%)	0.47 W (0.45%)	8.19 W (11.07%)	7.62 W (10.91%)	0.02 W (0.01%)

Table 12: Min / max system power differences for Dell system over all Xeon E5-2660 v3 samples.

turbo, the CV of means shows a relative difference of 29.0% between the processor types. Without turbo, this relative difference is reduced to 13.3%. The latter relative difference is smaller than the difference with turbo enabled, supporting the assertion that disabling turbo reduces the differences between the processor types' variations.

	Load	Idle	Com.	LU	SHA	SOR	LIN.
Turbo on	0%	236.1					
	25%		9.10	17.43	7.59	9.89	
	50%		8.34	19.67	8.68	9.88	
	75%		11.40	25.30	8.31	7.67	
	100%		98.10	8.99	89.02	61.38	15.81
Turbo off	0%	20.03					
	25%		9.06	17.96	6.78	15.88	
	50%		9.32	12.91	4.77	9.10	
	75%		6.31	21.96	50.22	8.99	
	100%		47.78	40.52	80.58	82.33	20.07

Table 14: Second order CVs in % for system power consumption over all Xeon E5-2660 v3 samples.

The differences in variations over the respective samples do not differ as much between the two processor types, as long as turbo is enabled. With a mean second order CV of all E5-2680 v3 samples of 37.7% only differs slightly from the mean second order CV of the E5-2660 v3 samples (36.3%). Disabling turbo increases the differences in variations significantly, as mean CVs decrease for the E5-2660 v3 samples, but not for the larger E5-2680 v3. Most of this can be attributed to the great second order variations of LINPACK and Idle measurements on the 10 core processor.

We conclude that decreasing the number of processor cores reduces the relative variation in CPU power. The turbo settings affects this decrease, as it is more significant with turbo enabled than with a disabled turbo. Our analysis of the second order variations of CPU power consumption returns conflicting results and remains inconclusive.

6.2 Processor Architecture

The 20 Intel Xeon E5-2609 CPU samples running on Oracle's Sun Server X3-2 are older quad-core CPUs of Intel's Sandy Bridge generation. It is the CPU with the least cores in our analysis and the only CPU of a non-Haswell architecture. Measurements using these CPUs are not only intended to confirm the observations on variation differences due to core counts, but may also indicate differences due to changes to the CPU architecture and semi conductor size. Due to its age, this SUT does not feature a turbo setting. As a result, we compare the results with the "turbo off" runs of the other processor types.

Table 15 shows the min / max mean CPU power consumption differences for the 20 E5-2609 samples. LINPACK behaves differently on this processor, as it varies stronger than for the Haswell CPUs in the previous Sections. The min / max difference over the Xeon E5-2609 samples is 8.91 W (19.45%), a significant increase compared to the 0.04 W of the other CPUs. The variations also scale differently with increasing load. Measurements using the Haswell processors showed no clear link between load level and difference in sample power consumption. However, the Sandy Bridge samples do. CPU power consumption differences between samples increase with rising load for all workloads. These results indicate a significant impact of processor architecture on inter sample power variation. This assumption is further compounded by the observation that even without the LINPACK result the 9.5% mean min / max difference over the quad-core E5-2609 samples is very similar to the 9.4% min / max difference of the 10 core E5-2660 v3, although the latter is a significantly larger processor.

	Load	Idle	Com.	LU	SHA	SOR	LIN.
Balanced	0%	1.39					
	25%		1.32	1.35	1.61	1.34	
	50%		1.98	2.30	1.94	2.04	
	75%		2.33	2.61	2.35	2.45	
	100%		2.58	2.63	2.52	2.60	4.92

Table 16: CVs in % for mean CPU power consumption over all Xeon E5-2609 samples.

Table 16 shows that the observations based on the min / max differences are systematic and not due to outliers. The coefficients of variation over all 20 CPU power means lead to the same conclusions. In contrast to the Haswell-based measurements, LINPACK's power consumption varies the most. It does not show signs of hitting a power limit and throttling to a similar power consumption over all samples. Similarly, the CVs also support the observation that power variations increase with load levels. This includes a relatively low variation for the Idle workload, which is in stark contrast to Idle's volatility on the newer processors.

	Load	Idle	Com.	LU	SHA	SOR	LIN.
Balanced	0%	243.3					
	25%		11.66	26.71	5.76	16.49	
	50%		8.10	11.84	7.17	12.28	
	75%		5.71	21.54	6.50	8.44	
	100%		24.91	26.95	25.22	25.53	99.98

Table 17: Second order CVs in % for CPU power consumption over all Xeon E5-2609 samples.

	Load	Idle	Compress	LU	SHA256	SOR	LINPACK
Balanced	0%	0.97 W (6.75%)					
	25%		1.27 W (6.36%)	1.13 W (5.67%)	1.54 W (7.45%)	1.12 W (5.89%)	
	50%		2.38 W (8.70%)	2.97 W (9.79%)	2.25 W (8.72%)	2.43 W (9.39%)	
	75%		3.49 W (10.51%)	4.57 W (12.45%)	3.23 W (10.78%)	3.44 W (11.22%)	
	100%		4.48 W (12.00%)	5.09 W (12.19%)	3.79 W (11.18%)	3.99 W (11.71%)	8.91 W (19.45%)

Table 15: Min / max system power differences for Oracle (Sun) system over all Xeon E5-2609 samples.

Second order CVs in Table 17 are also overall smaller than for the other processors, but few exceptions remain. Despite being volatile with its means, Idle still features significant differences in the size of its variations. LINPACK, on the other hand, shows more volatility than on the E5-2660 v3, but less than on the E5-2680 v3. No other workload exceeds 27%, whereas they pass it multiple times on the newer CPUs.

Concluding, we find that CPU architecture has a significant impact on the variances in power CPU power consumption over multiple CPU samples. As power scales differently over load levels, so do the differences for the samples. Specifically, differences for the Sandy Bridge CPUs increase with load levels and show no sign of throttling at high load. They also do not vary as much during idle times. Also, note that the measurement results over all Xeon E5-2609 samples differ significantly from repeated measurements on a single sample in Section 4, supporting the observations and conclusions of that section.

6.3 Qualification Samples

Finally, we test qualification samples for our Haswell-based processors. Qualification samples are often used in product testing and development before final production samples are available. We test if power measurement results obtained from qualification samples can be transferred to the final production samples. This would be the case if qualification sample power consumption resulted from the same distribution as production sample power.

We run all workloads on four qualification samples, corresponding to the Xeon E5-2680 v3 production processors and LINPACK on four qualification samples corresponding to the Xeon E5-2660 v3 processors. In addition, we test a total of 12 samples of the Xeon E5-2699 v3 processor (six production and six qualification samples). Our comparison focuses on the workloads with the least and most variations, namely LINPACK, Idle, and SOR at 100% load. We choose SOR at 50% load as an additional workload to focus on, representing workloads with average variations.

Figures 3 and 4 show the Idle CPU power consumption of the E5-2680 v3 production and qualification samples with turbo enabled. For the Idle workload, qualification sample results are in the same range as production sample results. There seems to be no significant difference between the sample batches. Consequently, the CPU power means for the samples from the two batches also fail the Student's T Test, as the 95% difference confidence interval includes 0. Disabling turbo does not change anything. The qualification samples still fall into the lower range of the overall distribution, but do not differ in a statistically significant way.

The qualification samples' CPU power does not differ significantly for the other worklets either. With turbo enabled, CPU power means for the qualification processors are always included in the min / max interval of the production means, regardless of load level or workload. This is even

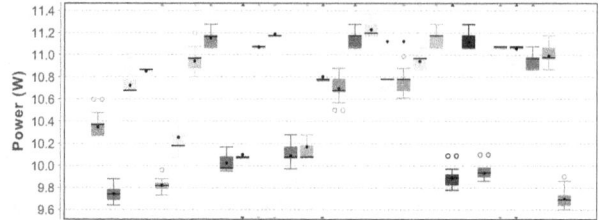

Figure 3: CPU power consumption of Xeon E5-2680 v3 production samples running Idle.

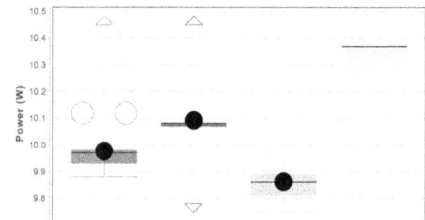

Figure 4: CPU power of qualification samples corresponding to Xeon E5-2680 v3, running Idle.

true for LINPACK, although this workload features only a CPU power range of 0.05 W (0.05%) over all production samples. Despite this tiny window, no qualification sample strays beyond it.

Disabling turbo changes this behavior for some workloads. Idle and LINPACK do not change, as min / max intervals of the production samples still include the qualification samples. SOR, on the other hand, features qualification outliers on all load levels. To illustrate, at 50% load one of the qualification samples has a mean power consumption that is 2.3 W less than the best production sample. However, these outliers are still not statistically significant and fail the 95% confidence level T test. This statistical indifference is repeated for the Xeon E5-2660 v3 and the corresponding qualification processors.

Sample variations are difficult to compare, due to the qualification batch's small sample size. Yet even with this small sample size, coefficients of variation across sample means are very similar for qualification and production samples. Idle features the greatest variation (7.3% for production and 7.0% for qualification samples, turbo on), followed by SOR at full load (4.5% and 4.3%). LINPACK features the smallest CVs without turbo (0.1% and 0.0%), and is surpassed slightly by LU at full load with turbo (0% for both production and qualification samples).

Measurements on the Xeon E5-2699 v3 samples confirm these observations. Qualification and production samples are not distinguishable based on their power consumption. Again, some qualification samples use slightly less power than the production samples, yet not enough for any statistical significance. Other qualification samples consume

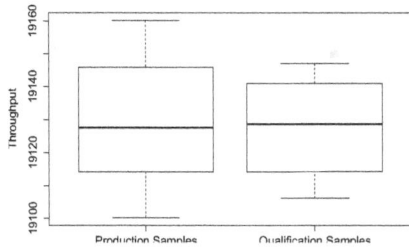

Figure 5: Throughput distribution of qualification and production Xeon E5-2680 v3 samples, running SOR at 50% load.

more power and behave similarly to some of the less energy efficient production samples. Figure 6 shows the power consumption of all samples for SOR at 50% load, visualizing that qualification samples behave like "good" production samples, but not in a statistically significant manner.

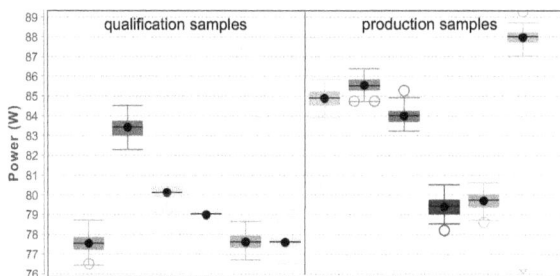

Figure 6: CPU power of Xeon E5-2699 v3 running SOR at 50% load.

Performance is also very similar for both qualification and production processors. Throughput means for the qualification samples are always in the min / max interval of the corresponding production sample throughputs. Figure 5 illustrates this using the throughput distributions for the Xeon E5-2680 v3 processor running SOR at 50% load.

Concluding, qualification samples' performance and power consumption does not differ significantly from the performance and power of their corresponding production processors. Our few qualification samples appear to have the properties of "good" production samples, consuming relatively little energy at similar performance. Yet, they do not feature any significant difference to other good production samples and are not different enough to conclude any systematic difference.

7. CONCLUSIONS

In this paper, we demonstrate that identical systems, containing nominally identical processors can exhibit significant power consumption differences that do not correlate significantly with CPU temperature and system performance. The differences are most significant during two system states: idle and high load. Idle is the most volatile state for power measurements. Different processor samples exacerbate this problem, leading to differences in mean idle power consumption of up to 29.6%. The state with the second highest power differences is high load. Older systems exhibit their greatest variations here. Newer systems feature advanced throttling mechanisms that minimize differences at the processor's temperature and power limit. They reach their greatest

absolute differences just before this limit is reached. Power consumption variations during other states is still significant. At 50% load, for instance, relative differences in CPU power can be as high as 12.5%.

The results and conclusions of this paper are not only of interest to benchmarking and standardization bodies. Benchmarking features the challenge of uncertainty when dealing with measurement results as only a comparison with other samples on an identical system can show if a measured result was measured using a "good" or "bad" processor. Beyond benchmarking, power prediction for power management and modeling is affected. The variations presented in this paper show a boundary of how accurate any power prediction mechanism for a nominally known system can be. E.g., a power prediction might be off by 10% or more entirely because an unfavorable processor sample was used for the predicted system.

This paper prompts future research as methods must be found to identify whether a given processor sample is a better or worse compared to other existing nominally identical samples. This is challenging as only a very small number (usually one) of processor samples is available to most users. The ability to identify the type of sample would enable more accurate comparisons of systems and classifications of measurement results.

8. ACKNOWLEDGMENTS

The authors also wish to acknowledge current and past members of the SPECpower Committee who have contributed to the design, development, testing, and overall success of SERT: Sanjay Sharma, Nathan Totura, Mike Tricker, Greg Darnell, Karl Huppler, Van Smith, Ashok Emani, Paul Muehr, David Ott, Cathy Sandifer, Jason Glick, and Dianne Rice, as well as the late Alan Adamson and Larry Gray.

SPEC and the names SERT, SPEC PTDaemon, and SPECpower_ssj are registered trademarks of the Standard Performance Evaluation Corporation. Additional product and service names mentioned herein may be the trademarks of their respective owners.

9. REFERENCES

[1] SPEC Chauffeur WDK. http://spec.org/chauffeur-wdk/.

[2] SPEC Power and Performance Benchmark Methodology. http://spec.org/power/docs/SPEC-Power_and_Performance_Methodology.pdf.

[3] C. Babcock. NY Times data center indictment misses the big picture. 2012.

[4] R. Basmadjian, N. Ali, F. Niedermeier, H. de Meer, and G. Giuliani. A Methodology to Predict the Power Consumption of Servers in Data Centres. In *Proceedings of the 2nd International Conference on Energy-Efficient Computing and Networking*, e-Energy '11, pages 1–10, New York, NY, USA, 2011. ACM.

[5] R. Basmadjian and H. De Meer. Evaluating and modeling power consumption of multi-core processors. In *Future Energy Systems: Where Energy, Computing and Communication Meet (e-Energy), 2012 Third International Conference on*, pages 1–10, May 2012.

[6] F. Bellosa. The Benefits of Event: Driven Energy Accounting in Power-sensitive Systems. In *Proceedings of the 9th Workshop on ACM SIGOPS European*

Workshop: Beyond the PC: New Challenges for the Operating System, EW 9, pages 37–42, New York, NY, USA, 2000. ACM.

[7] F. Chen, J. Grundy, Y. Yang, J.-G. Schneider, and Q. He. Experimental Analysis of Task-based Energy Consumption in Cloud Computing Systems. In *Proceedings of the 4th ACM/SPEC International Conference on Performance Engineering*, ICPE '13, pages 295–306, New York, NY, USA, 2013. ACM.

[8] G. Contreras and M. Martonosi. Power prediction for Intel XScale reg; processors using performance monitoring unit events. In *Low Power Electronics and Design, 2005. ISLPED '05. Proceedings of the 2005 International Symposium on*, pages 221–226, Aug 2005.

[9] J. J. Dongarra. The linpack benchmark: An explanation. In *Supercomputing*, pages 456–474. Springer, 1988.

[10] X. Fan, W.-D. Weber, and L. A. Barroso. Power Provisioning for a Warehouse-sized Computer. In *The 34th ACM International Symposium on Computer Architecture*, 2007.

[11] B. George, G. Yeap, M. Wloka, S. Tyler, and D. Gossain. Power analysis for semi-custom design. In *Custom Integrated Circuits Conference, 1994., Proceedings of the IEEE 1994*, pages 249–252, May 1994.

[12] M. Gomaa, M. D. Powell, and T. N. Vijaykumar. Heat-and-run: Leveraging SMT and CMP to Manage Power Density Through the Operating System. In *Proceedings of the 11th International Conference on Architectural Support for Programming Languages and Operating Systems*, ASPLOS XI, pages 260–270, New York, NY, USA, 2004. ACM.

[13] J. L. Henning. SPEC CPU2000: measuring CPU performance in the New Millennium. *Computer*, 33(7):28–35, Jul 2000.

[14] S. Heo, K. Barr, and K. Asanovic. Reducing power density through activity migration. In *Low Power Electronics and Design, 2003. ISLPED '03. Proceedings of the 2003 International Symposium on*, pages 217–222, Aug 2003.

[15] C. X. Huang, B. Zhang, A.-C. Deng, and B. Swirski. The design and implementation of powermill. In *Proceedings of the 1995 International Symposium on Low Power Design*, ISLPED '95, pages 105–110, New York, NY, USA, 1995. ACM.

[16] K. Huppler. The Art of Building a Good Benchmark. In R. Nambiar and M. Poess, editors, *Performance Evaluation and Benchmarking*, volume 5895 of *Lecture Notes in Computer Science*, pages 18–30. Springer Berlin Heidelberg, 2009.

[17] Intel. Intel Performance Counter Monitor. https://software.intel.com/en-us/articles/intel-performance-counter-monitor.

[18] K.-D. Lange. Identifying Shades of Green: The SPECpower Benchmarks. *Computer*, 42(3):95–97, March 2009.

[19] K.-D. Lange and K. Huppler, editors. *Server Efficiency: Metrics for Computer Servers and Storage.* ASHRAE, January 2015.

[20] K.-D. Lange and M. G. Tricker. The Design and Development of the Server Efficiency Rating Tool (SERT). In *Proceedings of the 2nd ACM/SPEC International Conference on Performance Engineering*, ICPE '11, pages 145–150, New York, NY, USA, 2011. ACM.

[21] A. Lewis, S. Ghosh, and N.-F. Tzeng. Run-time Energy Consumption Estimation Based on Workload in Server Systems. In *Proceedings of the 2008 Conference on Power Aware Computing and Systems*, HotPower'08, pages 4–4, Berkeley, CA, USA, 2008. USENIX Association.

[22] S. Rivoire, P. Ranganathan, and C. Kozyrakis. A Comparison of High-level Full-system Power Models. In *Proceedings of the 2008 Conference on Power Aware Computing and Systems*, HotPower'08, pages 3–3, Berkeley, CA, USA, 2008. USENIX Association.

[23] J. Russell and M. Jacome. Software power estimation and optimization for high performance, 32-bit embedded processors. In *Computer Design: VLSI in Computers and Processors, 1998. ICCD '98. Proceedings.*, pages 328–333, Oct 1998.

[24] J. H. Schönherr, J. Richling, M. Werner, and G. Mühl. Event-driven processor power management. In *Proceedings of the 1st International Conference on Energy-Efficient Computing and Networking*, e-Energy '10, pages 61–70, New York, NY, USA, 2010. ACM.

[25] J. von Kistowski, J. A. Arnold, K. Huppler, K.-D. Lange, J. L. Henning, and P. Cao. How to Build a Benchmark. In *Proceedings of the 6th ACM/SPEC International Conference on Performance Engineering (ICPE 2015)*, ICPE '15, New York, NY, USA, February 2015. ACM.

[26] J. von Kistowski, J. Beckett, K.-D. Lange, H. Block, J. A. Arnold, and S. Kounev. Energy Efficiency of Hierarchical Server Load Distribution Strategies. In *Proceedings of the IEEE 23nd International Symposium on Modeling, Analysis and Simulation of Computer and Telecommunication Systems (MASCOTS 2015)*. IEEE, October 2015.

[27] J. von Kistowski, H. Block, J. Beckett, K.-D. Lange, J. A. Arnold, and S. Kounev. Analysis of the Influences on Server Power Consumption and Energy Efficiency for CPU-Intensive Workloads. In *Proceedings of the 6th ACM/SPEC International Conference on Performance Engineering (ICPE 2015)*, ICPE '15, New York, NY, USA, February 2015. ACM.

[28] T. Welch. A Technique for High-Performance Data Compression. *Computer*, 17(6):8–19, June 1984.

End-to-End Java Security Performance Enhancements for Oracle SPARC Servers

Luyang Wang
Oracle
4180 Network Circle
Santa Clara, CA 95054, USA
luyang.wang@oracle.com

Pallab Bhattacharya[1]
Facebook
1 Hacker Way
Menlo Park, CA 94025, USA
pllb@fb.com

Yao-Min Chen
Oracle
4180 Network Circle
Santa Clara, CA 95054, USA
yaomin.chen@oracle.com

Shrinivas Joshi
Oracle
4180 Network Circle
Santa Clara, CA 95054, USA
shrinivas.joshi@oracle.com

James Cheng
Oracle
4180 Network Circle
Santa Clara, CA 95054, USA
james.cheng@oracle.com

ABSTRACT

In this paper we investigate the performance of cryptographic operations, when used in Java applications. We demonstrate the advantage of using built-in hardware accelerator for cryptographic operations on SPARC servers. In particular, we demonstrate the advantage of hardware cryptographic instructions invoked via AES and SHA intrinsics, implemented in the Java Virtual Machine (JVM), over the more traditional Java Native Interface (JNI) calls. For the purpose of our study, we modified the SPECweb2005 benchmark by adding modern banking requirements, and created a new workload which we call the End-to-End Java Security (EEJS) workload. Using the workload, we compare different Java Cryptographic Service Providers (CSPs) and arrive at the conclusion that hardware cryptography has significant performance advantage for Java applications. With the EEJS workload, we also identify several enhancements applicable to the Java Secure Socket Extension (JSSE).

General Terms

Performance, Security.

Keywords

Java Security; Java Cryptography Performance; SPARC Processors; JVM Intrinsics; RSA; AES; SHA; JSSE; SPECweb2005.

1. INTRODUCTION

There were a few recent customer cases where the performance of security operations on the SPARC servers was deemed critical to customer applications. These cases raised the necessity of an in-house tool to model customer application scenarios and identify performance issues and optimization opportunities. This external "push" also aligned well with the internal "pull" to evaluate the

new way of doing cryptographic acceleration since SPARC T4, which uses instructions rather than coprocessors. The two reasons combined have motivated the need to study the cryptography performance from an end-to-end perspective.[1]

Before delving into the end-to-end performance study, we briefly describe the history of SPARC cryptography acceleration. The Oracle SPARC line of processors have a history of supporting cryptographic operations at hardware level starting with the first Niagara Processor [1]. Its many generations consistently work towards adding support for more cryptographic algorithms and improving the performance of cryptographic operations. A key motivation for this effort is that certain cryptographic computations are inefficient if done in software, requiring many instructions when using a conventional instruction set. The earlier cryptographic acceleration (e.g., the implementations in UltraSPARC T2, T2 Plus and T3 [2][3]) is mostly delivered via a coprocessor mechanism, which requires device drivers or system calls to use these new capabilities, but also adds software overhead. In later generations (SPARC T4, T5 and onwards), non-privileged instructions are implemented, which avoid the overhead of traps into the kernel. With SPARC T4, new algorithms are also developed to replace old, more vulnerable algorithms as well as to address new security and usability requirements.[2]

The new hardware cryptographic instructions have been evaluated via numerous micro benchmarks. However, when they are used in a real-world application setting, sometimes the advantage is not immediate. This could be due to the fact that the software (security middleware) has not used the hardware cryptography in an effective way, or the fact that there is a bottleneck in the software. We need a tool to identify such software-hardware integration issues. Towards this end, we have devised the End-to-End Java Security (EEJS) workload. It is based on SPECweb2005 Banking Workload [4][5],[3] with enhancements to incorporate

---

[1] All work by Pallab Bhattacharya for this article was performed prior to his employment at Facebook.

[2] The newer processors, SPARC T5, M6 and M7, are similar to SPARC T4 in terms of cryptographic processing.

[3] The SPECweb2005 benchmark has been retired by SPEC.

modern banking requirements. [4] We have learned these requirements from customer engagements.

A key area of our performance study is related to the Java Native Interface (JNI) calls when executing the cryptographic instructions. JNI calls involve copying of data and flushing of register windows, making them expensive and less suitable for small messages. A new approach, called *intrinsics*, eliminates the JNI overhead. The EEJS workload is an effective tool to compare the implementation based on intrinsics and the more traditional implementation that leverages JNI.

This paper makes the following contributions. First, we demonstrate that the best performance on SPARC servers comes from using the hardware cryptographic instructions. Second, with Java Development Kit (JDK) 8u40 and later, accessing the hardware cryptography via intrinsics shows advantage over going through the JNI. Third, we have identified enhancements in the Java Secure Socket Extension (JSSE). The effects of the performance improvements are quantified in terms of response time, number of simultaneous user sessions, and intensity of user activities such as page views, just to name a few.

For the remainder of the paper, in Section 2 we describe EEJS benchmark in detail. In Section 3 we cover the experiment setup and the cryptographic service providers offered in JDK on Solaris operating system. In Section 4, we present and evaluate the performance data. This is followed by Section 5 where we describe the JSSE enhancements along with their contributions to performance improvement. Finally we conclude the paper by summarizing our results in Section 6.

2. BACKGROUND

In this section, we first discuss the SPECweb2005 Banking workload and then introduce the EEJS enhancements.

2.1 SPECweb2005

SPECweb2005 Banking workload was developed after conducting extensive research in the financial sector, specifically focusing on the Web transaction types, the business logic, the payload size and the cipher-suite specification that was prevalent at the time. From the study, RSA1024_RC4_MD5/SSLv3 was most popular *circa* 2005, thus it was chosen for SPECweb2005 as the cipher used for securing communication between the clients and the banking application.

The overall structure of the SPECweb2005 Banking workload is illustrated in Figure 1. On the left hand side of the figure, the drivers simulate the browsers or mobile apps used by the banking customers. The drivers implement load generators that inject load into the client application, which in turn sends HTTPS requests to and receives HTTPS responses from the server [4].

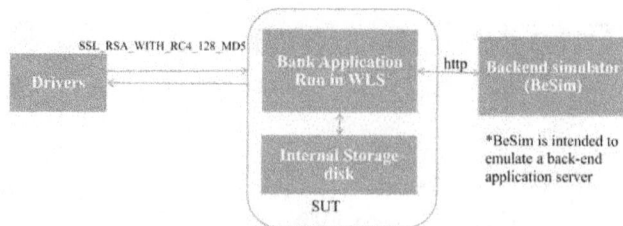

Figure 1 SPECweb2005 Banking Workload

The server is a bank application running on a hardware platform referred to as System Under Test (SUT). The application accesses static content such as check images that are hosted by the internal storage disk on the SUT. The server works with a backend simulator (BeSim) to serve the client requests. BeSim is intended to emulate a back-end application server that the bank application must communicate with to retrieve specific information (customer data, for example) needed to complete a transaction request from the customer. The communication between bank application and BeSim is over TCP and uses the HTTP protocol.

There are two quality-of-service (QoS) parameters, TIME_GOOD and TIME_TOLERABLE, which are used to define the performance metrics of the benchmark. Specifically, the performance metric SIMULTANEOUS_USERS is the maximum number of user connections that can be supported such that 1) TIME_GOOD QoS requirement can be met by at least 95% of the page requests and 2) TIME_TOLERABLE QoS requirement can be met by at least 99% of the page requests. Here, based on end-user experience [4], TIME_GOOD is set at 2 seconds and TIME_TOLERABLE is set at 4 seconds.

2.2 EEJS

The overall structure of the EEJS workload is shown in Figure 2. We had a few goals in mind when we developed the workload. First, we eliminated the heavy disk usage caused by the large document root required in the original SPECweb2005 benchmark. In our use case, we would like to focus on the security processing requirements, not to be bogged down by the disk IO performance on the SUT. There are a few ways to alleviate the disk IO bottleneck such as using faster storage (e.g., SSDs) or storage devices front ended with large amount of DRAM for caching. We opt for a software solution of implementing a small document root with a finite set of check images. Secondly, as SSLv3 has been deprecated and RC4 and MD5 are now considered insecure, we have modified the workload to use secure SSL ciphers (TLS_RSA_WITH_AES_128_CBC_SHA256 and TLS_RSA_WITH_AES_128_GCM_SHA256, for example). Additionally, we have changed the protocol between the bank application and BeSim to be HTTPS, reflecting what we have learned from bank customers. This is accomplished by replacing the BeSim client (as part of the bank application) with the Apache HTTP client [7]. Finally, to simulate realistic use cases, each request from the bank application to BeSim makes a new HTTPS connection.

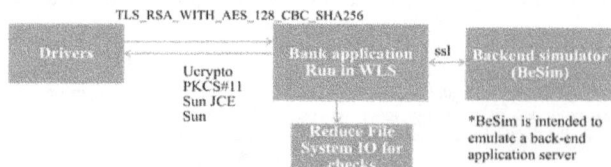

Figure 2 EEJS Workload

---

[4] It should be noted that results from our modified benchmark are not compliant with SPECweb2005 run rules and cannot be compared with published results. However, the use of SPECweb2005 benchmark conforms to SPEC Fair Use Rule for research use [6].

EEJS inherits the QoS parameters from SPECweb2005, namely, TIME_GOOD (2 seconds) and TIME_TOLERABLE (4 seconds). Instead of reporting the SIMULTANEOUS_USERS performance metric, we use the number of simultaneous user sessions to control the load driven by the SUT. For example, fixing the load at N simultaneous user sessions, we measure the average response time, the percentage of responses within the TIME_GOOD limit, and the percentage of responses within the TIME_TOLERABLE limit.

A key characteristic of the workload is that there are significant SSL handshake operations. From our experiments, more than 30% of the requests involve full handshake. Therefore, this workload stresses the cryptographic processing capability of the SUT, which serves quite well our need to address recent customer cases referred to in Section 1.

From our experience, EEJS has proven to be an effective tool. In a series of experiments described in Section 4, it is used to demonstrate the performance advantage of hardware cryptography acceleration over conventional SPARC instructions. Furthermore, we compare different ways of accessing hardware cryptography, via the different Cryptographic Service Providers (CSPs). EEJS also helped identify a number of software enhancements, which can be applied to improve JSSE. These enhancements will be described in Section 5.

3. EXPERIMENT SETUP

Here we will first introduce CSPs, what they are and how they are configured. Then we will describe the hardware and software setups.

3.1 Cryptographic Service Providers

Cryptography implementations in the JDK are provided via several different CSPs. For example, with SPARC servers there are OracleUcrypto, SunPKCS11, SUN, SunJSSE, SunJCE and SunRsaSign providers [8]. Each CSP provides a package or set of packages that supply concrete implementation of a subset of the JDK Security API security features. Each JDK installation has one or more providers installed and configured by default [8] . These built-in providers and their usage priorities are listed in a configuration file named *java.security.* [5]

OracleUcrypto provider is a Solaris specific CSP that leverages the Solaris Ucrypto library to offload and delegate cryptographic operations to hardware supported by Oracle SPARC T4 and later processor based on-core cryptographic instructions [9]. Among other ciphers, RSA [10], AES [11] and SHA [12] ciphers are available in the OracleUcrypto provider. SunPKCS11 provider is supported on Solaris (SPARC and x86) and Linux (x86), in both 32-bit and 64-bit Java processes [13]; it supports algorithms including RSA, AES and SHA. The SunJCE and SUN providers are "pure Java" CSPs in the sense that the cryptographic algorithms are implemented entirely in the JDK API classes without relying on any native libraries.

For SPARC T4 and later Oracle SPARC servers, we have embedded assembly instruction level implementation of AES and SHA ciphers in the Java side code generation logic of the JVM. These assembly code implementations leverage appropriate hardware cryptography instructions. Such JVM embedded assembly implementations are also termed as JVM Intrinsics. A

key advantage of intrinsics is that they avoid the JNI overhead associated with accessing hardware cryptography instructions via native libraries such as the Solaris Ucrypto library. AES intrinsics are available since JDK 8u20, via the SunJCE provider. SHA intrinsics are available since JDK 8u40, via the SUN provider.

EEJS has been used to evaluate the performance gain of the intrinsics, in comparison with OracleUcrypto and SunPKCS11 providers. The comparisons will be described in Subsection 4.1.

3.2 Hardware and Software Setups

Refer to Figure 2 for the following description of our experiment setup. The SUT is a recently announced SPARC T7-1 server, running Solaris 11 Update 3 Build 27. The T7-1 server has 32 cores and 480 GB of DRAM. On the SUT, we run the bank application with 4 cores of the server. Oracle WebLogic application server (WLS) running on the SUT is configured to use the following JVM flags: -Xms16g -Xmx16g -Xmn8g -XX:+PrintGCTimeStamps -XX:+PrintGCDetails. We use WLS version 12.2.1 in our experiments.

We have used JDK 8u40 and 8u60 for the Java runtime. As mentioned before, both AES and SHA intrinsics are available since JDK 8u40 for SPARC.

We deploy the bank application on WLS, which is also responsible for catering application-specific static content such as check images from the internal storage disk. The workload drivers are run on two Oracle X2-2 servers. Each X2-2 has two Intel Westmere CPUs and 48GB of DRAM. BeSim is run on an Oracle X3-2 server, which has two Intel SandyBridge CPUs and 128GB of DRAM. All the systems, i.e., the hosts running the drivers, WLS and BeSim, are connected by a 10Gb Ethernet private network.

For our experiments, we focus on the comparison between OracleUcrypto, SunPKCS11 and intrinsics. With JDK 8 on SPARC servers, OracleUcrypto is the default first priority CSP. We can edit the java.security file to change CSP priorities from OracleUcrypto to SunPKCS11. To exercise AES intrinsics, we need to disable AES in ucrypto-solaris.cfg or sunpkcs11-solaris.cfg, depending on the chosen provider. In this way, the AES intrinsics implemented for SunJCE CSP will be used. Similarly, to use SHA intrinsics implemented for SUN CSP, one needs to disable SHA in ucrypto-solaris.cfg or sunpkcs11-solaris.cfg. One can certainly use both AES and SHA intrinsics together, with appropriate changes in the ucrypto-solaris.cfg or sunpkcs11-solaris.cfg configuration files.

For the connection between the driver and the bank application, cipher suite TLS_RSA_WITH_AES_128_CBC_SHA256 is used. This cipher suite uses RSA for key exchange. Note that RSA consists of key encryption/decryption, as well as key generation. With the default OracleUcrypto provider, SunPKCS11 is used for key generation. When SunPKCS11 is disabled in file java.security, key generation falls through to the next available provider which, in our case, is SunJCE.

4. PERFORMANCE EVALUATION WITH EEJS

In this section, we provide examples of how EEJS is used for performance evaluation. The examples here include comparing different CSPs and comparing hardware cryptography acceleration with software implementation of cryptographic algorithms.

---

[5] For a SPARC server running Solaris OS, the path to the file is $JAVA_HOME/jre/lib/security/java.security.

We started out with the exact setup described in the previous section. However, we soon realized that there were a few software bottlenecks that had to be alleviated before we could move to performance comparisons of cryptography operations. The bottlenecks stemmed from the large number of connections between the bank application and BeSim (the SSL connections on the right hand side of Figure 2). To work around these bottlenecks we temporarily reverted back to plain-text HTTP connections, as were used in SPECweb2005. The data reported in this section is based on this workaround. In Section **5** we will describe how to address the discovered software bottlenecks. Identifying and addressing these bottlenecks is a major contribution of the EEJS workload analysis work.

4.1 Comparison of CSPs

We first compare the efficiency of different cryptographic service providers. Towards this end, we control the number of simultaneous user sessions and compare 1) the average response time, 2) the number of successful requests, 3) the percentage of requests that meet TIME_GOOD threshold, called *good requests,* and 4) CPU utilization including system and user times. Here, a request is considered successful if the response for it is fulfilled within the TIME_TOLERABLE interval.

Table 1: The 5 CSP Configurations Used in the Performance Comparison

CSP Configuration	A	B	C	D	E
RSA Encryption and Decryption	SunPKCS11	OracleUcrypto	SunPKCS11	OracleUcrypto	OracleUcrypto
RSA Key Generation	SunPKCS11	SunPKCS11	SunPKCS11	SunPKCS11	SunJCE
AES	SunPKCS11	OracleUcrypto	SunJCE with AES intrinsics	SunJCE with AES intrinsics	SunJCE with AES intrinsics
SHA	SunPKCS11	OracleUcrypto	SUN with SHA intrinsics	SUN with SHA intrinsics	SUN with SHA intrinsics

Table 1 shows five different configurations (A, B, C, D and E) that have been evaluated here. Under each configuration are the CSPs used for the different cryptographic operations involved. For example, with Configuration A, SunPKCS11 is used for encrypting and decrypting keys as part of RSA; so is RSA key generation, AES and SHA. By contrast, with Configuration E, OracleUcrypto is used for encrypting and decrypting keys in the RSA, while SunJCE is used for key generation, and intrinsics within SunJCE and SUN are used for AES and SHA respectively. As mentioned in Section 3.1, both AES and SHA intrinsics are assembly-level implementations of the underlying methods and are embedded in the JVM code generation logic. JVM emits this assembly code while executing appropriate intrinsified methods from the JDK API. The other configurations B, C and D are self-explanatory. Note that, Configuration B is the current out-of-box default configuration for JDK8 on SPARC servers.

The results shown in Figure 3 are from the set of experiments with 1,000 simultaneous user sessions. For each configuration, we run the load with 3 minutes ramp-up, 5 minutes warm-up, 10 minutes steady-state and 3 minutes ramp-down phases. The performance metrics are collected during the steady-state period of the run. Figure 3 shows the measured performance metrics, expressed in terms of the relative ratio to the default configuration (Configuration B).

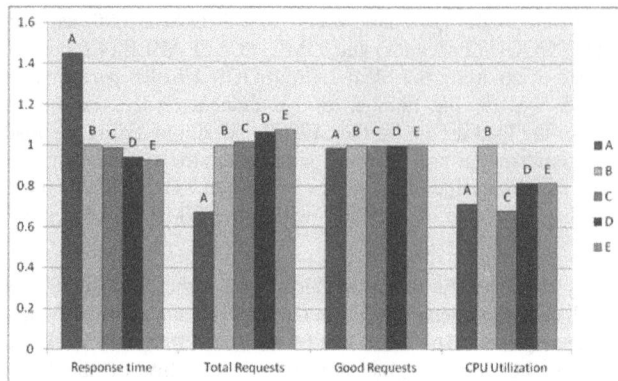

Figure 3: Performance Comparison between CSP Configurations

In the bar chart of Figure 3, lower is better for 'Response Time' and 'CPU Utilization' metrics and higher is better for 'Total Requests' and 'Good Requests' metrics.

Note that the configurations are chosen mainly to explore: 1) the performance advantages of current default configuration over the more traditional PKCS11 provider (Configuration A) and 2) the effect of using AES and SHA intrinsics. We observe that Configuration E provides the lowest average response time and highest total requests. It also has better QoS in the sense that it has higher percentage of good requests.[6] Note that the performance of Configuration E is achieved with better CPU efficiency; it uses less CPU than Configuration B.

From Figure 3, we see that Configuration B outperforms Configuration A. This is mainly because OracleUcrypto CSP's usage of Solaris Ucrypto library accesses unprivileged cryptography instructions directly from user space, which should be compared with PKCS11 that is based on system calls. By contrast, Configuration D outperforms Configuration B because AES and SHA intrinsics avoid the JNI overhead that is inherent in the OracleUcrypto provider. Configuration C stands in the middle between Configurations B and D; its use of intrinsics makes it more efficient in terms of AES and SHA, while its use of PKCS11 for RSA makes it less efficient in comparison to using Ucrypto library for RSA.

The performance contrast between Configurations D and E is an interesting one. They differ only in the CSP used for key generation. Configuration D uses SunPKCS11, while Configuration E uses SunJCE. When SunJCE is used for key generation, SHA intrinsics are used in a critical step (SecureRandom) of the key generation, which leads to better performance than using SunPKCS11 for key generation. JDK bug report JDK-8044659 [7] has the description of the key generation process in this case.

---

[6] The five configurations are virtually indistinguishable in terms of the percentage of good requests, with only Configuration A slightly lower.

[7] The notation JDK-*nnnnnnn* refers to a bug ID in the OpenJDK bug tracking system.

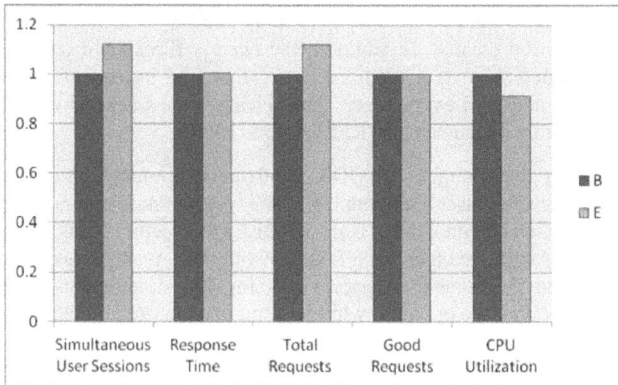

Figure 4: Capacity Comparison between Configurations B and E

With the results in hand, we proceed to verify that the CPU efficiency of Configuration E can be translated into higher number of user sessions. Figure 4 summarizes our results. Here, we increase the number of simultaneous user sessions for Configuration E until the QoS metrics match those for Configuration B. We can see that Configuration E can support 12% more simultaneous user sessions, while keeping the average response time on par with Configuration B. Moreover, Configuration E achieves this with lower CPU utilization.

From the results in this subsection, one can conclude that there is a combination that leads to best EEJS performance among the configurations tested. The combination consists of 1) OracleUcrypto for RSA encryption and decryption, 2) SunJCE for RSA key generation, 3) SunJCE for AES, and 4) SUN for SHA. Note that 2), 3) and 4) directly benefit from intrinsics. There is ongoing effort to make the best combination the default in future JDK releases.

4.2 Advantage of Cryptography Instructions

Configuration E can be further compared with a "pure software" configuration where we intentionally disable crypto intrinsics based hardware acceleration. To test a pure software configuration, we disable AES intrinsics from SunJCE, using "-XX:-UseAESIntrinsics" JVM command line flag. We also disable SHA intrinsics from the SUN provider using "-XX:-UseSHA1Intrinsics -XX:-UseSHA256Intrinsics -XX:-UseSHA512Intrinsics" JVM flags. In addition, we swap in SunJCE provider for RSA encryption and decryption. We add this "pure software" configuration to our configuration mix and call it Configuration F.

From Figure 5 we see that hardware cryptography instructions with Configuration E provide very significant performance advantage over the implementation using regular ISA ("pure software") instructions, as in Configuration F. Configuration F is not able to support the required QoS requirements, while CPU is close to 100%. By contrast, Configuration E has half the response time, utilizing only half of the CPU as that of Configuration F.

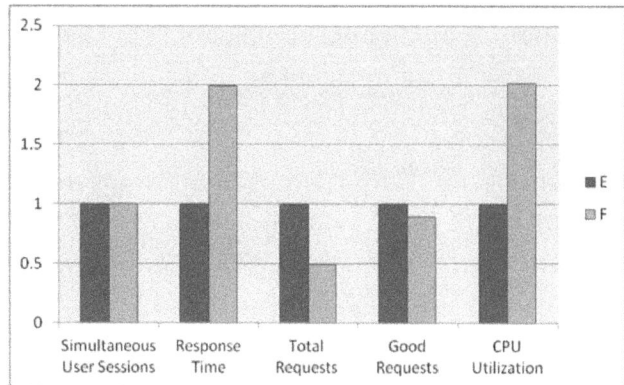

Figure 5: Comparing the implementation using cryptography instructions (Configuration E) with the software-only implementation (Configuration F)

5. PERFORMANCE OPTIMIZATIONS WITH EEJS

By analyzing performance characteristics of EEJS workload we have identified enhancements in JSSE. This section describes the associated performance bottlenecks and possible enhancements. Before describing the JSSE enhancements we provide a brief introduction of JSSE.

The Java Secure Socket Extension (JSSE) enables secure Internet communications. It provides a framework and an implementation for a Java version of the SSL and TLS protocols. It includes functionality for data encryption, server authentication, message integrity, and optional client authentication [14]. JSSE provides both an application programming interface (API) framework and an implementation of that API. The JSSE API supplements the core network and cryptographic services defined by the `java.security` and `java.net` packages by providing extended networking socket classes, trust managers, key managers, SSL contexts, and a socket factory framework for encapsulating socket creation behavior [14].

EEJS enables the performance study of related Java packages in an end-to-end application setting. It helps us identify a few enhancements that can help improve performance.

5.1 Buffered Reading of Trusted Certificates

The primary responsibility of the `TrustManager` is to determine whether the presented authentication credentials should be trusted. If the credentials are not trusted, the connection will be terminated [14]. To authenticate the remote identity of a secure socket peer, an `SSLContext` object will be initialized with one or more `TrustManager` objects. If a null `TrustManager` object is passed into the `SSLContext` initialization, a new `TrustManager` will be created.

Running EEJS with JDK 8u40, we noticed high system CPU time (around 70%) on the SUT, as well as high response time, when a null `TrustManager` was passed into the `SSLContext` initialization. During the initialization, a new `TrustManager` was created and initialized with a source of certificate authorities and related trust material, which was obtained by reading from the *cacerts*[8] file and loading the trusted certificates.

---

[8] $JAVA_HOME/jre/lib/security/cacerts

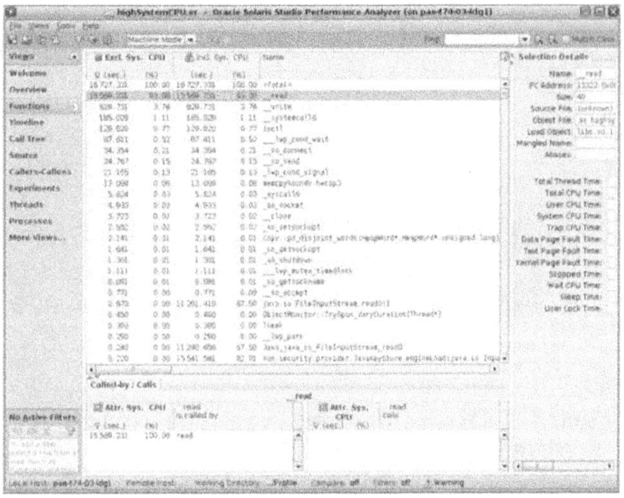

Figure 6: Functions ordered by exclusive system CPU time

Further analyzing the Oracle Studio Performance Analyzer [15] profiles as shown in Figure 6, we observed that 93% of the system CPU time was caused by the __read() system call, which, in turn, was called by the read() system call. To identify what was being read, we looked at the truss [16] output and observed that reading from the *cacerts* file was done on a single byte basis, as follows. The first four bytes of *cacerts* were the signature bytes, which were obtained by calling readInt() of the DataInputStream. Inside readInt(), it made four calls to read(). Similarly, the next four bytes representing the version of the *cacerts* file, as well as the subsequent four bytes representing the number of trusted certificate entries, were read one byte at a time. Furthermore, for each trusted certificate entry, the alias of the certificate, the certificate creation date, and the trusted certificate were also read on a single byte basis.

Performance is improved with a fix for JDK bug JDK-8129634 delivered by Java Engineering team. The fix wraps the DataInputStream representing the *cacerts* file in a BufferedInputStream object. Instead of retrieving single byte from *cacerts* file, the BufferedInputStream object buffers 8192 bytes at a time and the read from the SSLContext initialization is now from this buffer. With JDK 8u60 that includes this bug fix, system CPU time drops to around 20% (from the previous 70%). Reducing the number of reads thus makes a significant difference in system CPU utilization.

5.2 Consolidation of the Cacerts Keystore

A keystore is a database for storing key management related data. Information residing in a keystore can be grouped into two categories: key entries and trusted certificate entries [14]. With EEJS running, we observed from the truss output that the *cacerts* file was opened for read repetitively and frequently. The frequency of the file open operations coincided with the frequency of SSL handshakes. We analyzed the call stack and associated source code and made the following observation. A new thread was created for each handshake. Each new thread started a new SSLContext initialization. During the SSLContext initialization, each TrustManager instance read the *cacerts* file and created a KeyStore instance. When there were multiple threads, each establishing its own SSLContext, there were multiple KeyStore instances accessing the common *cacerts* file, causing synchronization and memory overheads.

To optimize the performance here, only one KeyStore instance needs to be created. In addition, the *cacerts* file should only be read when there is a modification in this file, instead of being opened and read every time. These changes are tracked by JDK Request for Enhancement (RFE) JDK-8129988.

Without the change, with JDK 8u60 the maximum number of simultaneous user sessions is 490 while maintaining the TIME_GOOD and TIME_TOLERABLE QoS requirements. With the prototype changes for JDK-8129988, the average response time and the number of page views for 490 simultaneous user sessions improve by 9.5%, while meeting the QoS requirements.

5.3 Elimination of Hot Locks

5.3.1 sun.security.ssl.CipherSuite$BulkCipher.isAvailable()

When a socket is created between WLS and BeSim server, WLS gets the default cipher suite list and iterates over the list to check the availability of individual ciphers. From the jstack output of WLS server threads, we noticed that a number of server threads are blocked in the BulkCipher.isAvailable() method. It is a synchronized method which checks the availability of a bulk cipher. It is called when a cipher suite list is requested at the initial phase of a handshake. Since each new connection between WLS and BeSim Server involves a full handshake, this method is frequently called.

Within the method, there is a cache, implemented with a hash map. The cache is used to map the bulk cipher to its availability status. However, with JDK 8u60, even though the cache exists, it is cleared every time the method tries to get the cipher suite list, defeating the purpose of the cache. By not clearing the hash map cache the average response time and the number of page views have improved by additional 3% for 490 simultaneous user sessions, and there is an additional 3% improvement on the percentage of TIME_GOOD responses. This change is tracked in JDK RFE JDK-8133070.

5.3.2 SecureRandom.nextBytes()

The SecureRandom class provides the functionality of a Random Number Generator (RNG). It differs from the java.lang.Random class in that it produces cryptographically strong random numbers. Random numbers are used throughout cryptography, such as for generating cryptographic keys, algorithmic parameters, and so on [8]. There are several different algorithms for SecureRandom: PKCS11, NativePRNG, SHA1PRNG, NativePRNGBlocking and NativePRNGNonBlocking. The PKCS11 algorithm is provided by the SunPKCS11 provider, while the others are provided by the SUN provider. If the entropy gathering device in java.security file is set to file /dev/urandom or file /dev/random, then NativePRNG is preferred to SHA1PRNG. Otherwise, SHA1PRNG is preferred [9]. In this study, NativePRNG is used to generate secure random bytes.

A synchronized method is used to generate the secure random bytes. This method employs a global shared buffer for storing the random numbers read from the /dev/random file. The shared buffer is implemented using a byte array. When a fixed size of secure random bytes is requested, the method first checks if there are any bytes remaining in the buffer. If there are, it reads the requested number of bytes from the buffer and does a 'xor'

164

operation with the input random bytes.[9] If there are not enough bytes remaining in the buffer, the synchronized method replenishes the buffer by reading random numbers from /dev/random. As the buffer is a global shared variable, the 'xor' operation between the buffer and the input has to be synchronized, leading to hot locks. The locks can be alleviated by using a finer grained synchronization.

This change, which is tracked by JDK RFE JDK-8098581, helps improve the throughput of a secure random micro benchmark by more than three times. With this change, the average response time and the number of page views improve by additional 19% for the configuration with 490 simultaneous users.

5.3.3 Registration of CSP Services

We also noticed a hot lock when getting services from a CSP. By design, there is a map maintaining the services offered by each CSP, and the constructor for a CSP object should record the supported services in this map. When an application gets service from a particular CSP, it looks up the map to find the supported services. However, in our EEJS experiments, we found that with the exception of the PKCS11 provider, other CSPs do not register the services in their respective constructor. As a consequence, when an application looks up the map, it always returns a null map. When the application finds a null map, it falls back to check a legacy map for services. It first checks a `transient` variable to see if the legacy map has been modified and then get the services from the legacy map.

Ideally, a single map should suffice. When service map is null, falling back to legacy map incurs the overhead of exercising extra code path. In addition, as the method for getting services is synchronized, it causes performance regression when multiple threads are involved. This issue is currently tracked by JDK RFE JDK-8133906.

5.4 Performance Optimization Results

We measured the combined effect of all the changes mentioned in Section 5. With the officially released binaries of JDK 8u60, 490 simultaneous user sessions can be achieved while maintaining QoS requirements. With the changes described in this section, 800 simultaneous user sessions can be achieved. This is a 1.6 times improvement in terms of throughput. Table 2 shows these performance optimization results. If we restrict the load to 490 simultaneous user sessions, the aforementioned changes lead to an improvement of 34.6% in average response time, 34.6% improvement in page views, and 2.36 times improvement in login latency.

6. SUMMARY

In this paper, we describe the motivation of EEJS workload, its use in conducting performance evaluation, and the performance optimization results from it. Performance evaluations using JDK 8u40 running on SPARC servers lead to the conclusion that using JVM intrinsics for AES and SHA ciphers and using OracleUcrypto for RSA encryption and decryption provides the best performance among the configurations evaluated. There is ongoing work around out-of-the-box CSP configuration to provide the best combination of CSPs based on the underlying platform.

---

[9] The input random bytes were generated from an earlier operation invoking a secure random algorithm such as SHA1PRNG.

Table 2: Performance results comparison between JDK 8u60 and improvements from Section 5

	JDK 8u60	With the changes mentioned in Section 5.2, Section 5.3.1, and Section 5.3.2
Normalized Response time	1	0.742
Normalized total number of requests	1	1.345
Normalized login latency	1	0.423
Good	95.6%	99%
Tolerable	99.6%	99.8%
Fail	0.4%	0.2%

Since the EEJS workload is heavy on the SSL handshakes, it is also used to demonstrate the clear advantage of hardware cryptography acceleration. This is accomplished by comparing a configuration using hardware cryptography with one that uses conventional instruction set.

We have identified a number of JSSE enhancements by analyzing performance characteristics of EEJS workload. Several of these enhancements are in the process of being incorporated into future JDK releases.

7. ACKNOWLEDGMENTS

The authors would like to thank Oracle Java Security team and Solaris Security team for their support and encouragement, and our colleagues Jan-Lung Sung, Richard Smith and Andy Bowers for their valuable critiques to improve the paper. We would also like to thank the anonymous reviewers for their constructive feedback to help further improve the paper.

8. REFERENCES

[1] Kongetira, P. 2004. A 32-way Multithreaded SPARC Processor. In *Hot Chips 16*.

[2] Spracklen, L. 2009. Sun's 3rd generation on-chip UltraSPARC security accelerator. In *Hot Chips 21*.

[3] Shoaib Bin Altaf, M. and Wood, D.A. 2014. LogCA: A Performance Model for Hardware Accelerators. In *Computer Architecture Letters*. Volume: PP, Issue: 99 (Sep. 2014).

[4] SPECweb2005 Release 1.20 Benchmark Design Document. https://www.spec.org/web2005/docs/designdocument.html

[5] Trademark for the SPEC Benchmark. https://www.spec.org/spec/trademarks.html

[6] SPEC Fair Use Rule. Academic/research usage. http://www.spec.org/fairuse.html#Academic

[7] Apache HTTP Client. https://hc.apache.org/httpcomponents-client-ga/

[8] Java Cryptography Architecture (JCA) Reference Guide. https://docs.oracle.com/javase/8/docs/technotes/guides/security/crypto/CryptoSpec.html

[9] Java Cryptography Architecture Oracle Providers Documentation for JDK 8. http://docs.oracle.com/javase/8/docs/technotes/guides/security/SunProviders.html

[10] Rivest, R.; Shamir, A.; Adleman, L., 1978. A Method for Obtaining Digital Signatures and Public-Key Cryptosystems. Communications of the ACM 21 (2): 120–126.

[11] Announcing the ADVANCED ENCRYPTION STANDARD (AES). Federal Information Processing Standards Publication

197. United States National Institute of Standards and Technology (NIST). October, 2012.

[12] FIPS 180-4: Secure Hash Standard. United States National Institute of Standards and Technology (NIST). August 2015.

[13] JDK 8 PKCS#11 Reference Guide. http://docs.oracle.com/javase/8/docs/technotes/guides/security/p11guide.html

[14] Java Secure Socket Extension (JSSE) Reference Guide. https://docs.oracle.com/javase/8/docs/technotes/guides/security/jsse/JSSERefGuide.html

[15] Oracle Solaris Studio Performance Analyzer. http://www.oracle.com/technetwork/server-storage/solarisstudio/features/performance-analyzer-2292312.html

[16] Man pages for truss. http://docs.oracle.com/cd/E23823_01/html/816-5165/truss-1.html

Accelerating The Optimal Trade-Off Circular Harmonic Function Filter Design on Multicore Systems

Anubhav Jain
Center of Excellence for Parallelization &
Optimization
Tata Consultancy Services, New Delhi
anubhav.jain1@tcs.com

Amit Kalele
Center of Excellence for Parallelization &
Optimization
Tata Consultancy Services, Pune
kalele.amit@tcs.com

ABSTRACT

Optimal correlation filters are widely used in signal processing and pattern recognition applications. Correlation filters are a set of synthesized spatial filters that produce controlled response with sharp peaks. While providing excellent discrimination capabilities correlation filters offer shift, rotation and scale invariance for 2D images. Correlation filters are optimized to enhance the recognition of consistent parts while suppressing the varying patterns. Synthesizing the correlation filters for pattern recognition applications involves several complex mathematical operations and requires high computation resources especially for high resolution images and videos. In this paper, we show that near real time performance can be achieved for the design of the OTCHF filter with help of optimization and parallelization on multicore GPUs and CPUs.

Keywords

Correlation filter, Circular Harmonic Function Filter, Muticore CPU, GPU, Performance Optimization, Parallel Computing, HPC

1. INTRODUCTION

Correlation filters finds their application in variety of pattern recognition applications such as image and video watermarking, fingerprint, iris and face detection. Their ability to discriminate under several variations such as shift, scale, in-plane rotations, occlusion makes them extremely suitable for such applications and classification tasks. These filters are also robust to noise and illumination variations .

Correlation filtering is a process of correlating a digital image or a signal with a precomputed template (filter) optimized to return expected response [12, 3]. The expected magnitude response in correlation filtering are sharp peak(s) in the correlation output at locations where there is a match between the template and the signal satisfying the constraints of the template design. Advanced correlation filters have

been applied with significant success in image recognition applications [16, 6, 2]. This success is mainly attributed to:

- The advent of the modern high-speed multicore processors with the massive parallel processing abilities which can meet the computational demands imposed by correlation based methods.

- The correlation filters can be optimized for the desired response for a set of predetermined constraints.

Correlation filters are designed with the help of a set of training data containing images or frames. This training data represents the anticipated set of distortions yielding pre-determined responses to these training images.

In this paper, we consider the Optimal trade-off circular harmonic function filters (OTCHF), which are designed to account in-plane rotation distortion in pattern recognition application such as face recognition [13, 3], target detection, iris recognition etc [1].

The design of OTCHF filter allows us to specify the desired response for a range of in-plane rotations. The optimization task involves maximizing the expected correlation filter output level at the origin where the match occurs, while minimizing the correlation function levels elsewhere. The optimization procedure of the template considers all or at least some of the possible variations of the pattern to recognized, these variations include rotation, scaling and translation.

For pattern recognition applications whose input is a video, the number of frames and the resolution of the videos could impose huge computational workload. The training procedure is amenable to parallel processing. The modern day CPUs and GPUs are extremely powerful machines, equipped with multiple compute cores, they are capable of performing multiple tasks or same task on multiple data in parallel. Exploiting their parallel processing capabilities, with performance optimization techniques and usage of optimal libraries for FFTs and linear algebra routines [8, 7], could lead to many fold improvement in the performance.

In this paper, we present an optimal and parallel implementation of design of the OTCHF on Intel and Nvidia multicore platforms and report significant improvements in the performance.

ICPE'16, March 12 - 18, 2016, Delft, Netherlands

© 2016 Copyright held by the owner/author(s). Publication rights licensed to ACM.
ISBN 978-1-4503-4080-9/16/03...$15.00

DOI: http://dx.doi.org/10.1145/2851553.2851579

---

[1] The work reported in this paper was carried out for a video water marking application

2. RELATED WORK

Several methods have been proposed for obtaining different kinds of distortion invariance, most of them based on the use of filters partially matched to the target.

For rotation invariance, a suitable approach is to use the circular-harmonic functions (CHF's) of the image $f(r, \theta)$ in polar coordinate domain. Rosen and Shamir [12] proposed rotation invariant circular-harmonic component filter for automatic target detection.

Ryan et. al. [6] developed a scale-invariant correlation filter design based on the Mellin radial harmonic (MRH) transform. Minimum average correlation energy (MACE) MRH filters can approximates a user-specified scale response. Some applications where multiple scale responses are required, multiple correlation filters are used to account scale changes. Each correlation filter providing a unique scale response.

The GPUs are widely used in audio, image and signal processing and in correlation filtering [5, 14, 15] and [10]. However, to the best of our knowledge, a parallel implementation of the OTCHF filter design for pattern recognition on GPUs is not reported in the published literature.

3. OPTIMAL TRADEOFF CIRCULAR HARMONIC FUNCTION FILTER

Applications such as face recognition, fingerprint recognition, digital watermarking and other common pattern recognition tasks requires classification performance to be invariant to small in-plane rotation, shift and scaling. The optimal tradeoff circular harmonic function filters (OTCHF) or the correlation filters are designed for in-plane rotation distortion, allows us to specify the desired response for a range of in-plane rotations and also enable shift invariance. Certain level of scale invariance can also be achieved by appropriate training. The trade off parameters for this filter are noise variance and peak sharpness.

An optimized correlation filter would yield similar correlation outputs in response to test images that are from the same class as the training images while providing distortion-tolerant correlation outputs.

We utilize the circular harmonic decomposition in the frequency domain rather than in the space domain. We used finite impulse response (FIR) filter design methods to determine the CHF coefficients. Specifically, the luminance channel is used for computing correlation filter. In this paper, we have implemented the correlation filter for a video which consists of several frames where each frame is considered as an image. The steps involved in the filter design are as follows:

1. Compute the two dimensional Fourier transform $F(u, v)$ of each training image $f(x, y)$.

2. Compute the index matrix which maps the Fourier transformed image $F(u, v)$ to the polar coordinates to obtain $F(\rho, \phi)$, where $\rho = \sqrt{(u^2 + v^2)}$ and $\phi = tan^{-1}(\frac{v}{u})$.

3. Compute the harmonic function $F(\rho)$ by operating Fourier transom along the ρ axis on $F(\rho, \phi)$.

4. Define the 'desired correlation function matrix by setting '1' at locations the response should be maximum and '0' at other location in the matrix where the response must be minimal.

5. Obtain the optimal circular harmonic function (CHF) weights/coefficients (C_k) by computing Fourier transform of the above matrix.

6. Compute P_{FOM}, the figure of merit.

7. Compute the filter harmonics $H_k(\rho)$ [2] with inputs matrices P_{FOM}, C_k, index matrix and training images, $F(\rho)$ etc. as

$$H_k(\rho) = \lambda_k \cdot \frac{F_k(\rho)}{P_{FOM}(\rho)}$$

where $\lambda_k = C_k / \int_0^\infty |F_k(\rho)|^2 / P_{FOM}(\rho)\rho d\rho$

For the given m training images, sequence of matrix operations are performed to get the filter harmonics $H_k(\rho)$. We assume that each frame consist of $n \times n$ pixels. We assume that the matrices P_{FOM}, C_k and index matrix ID are computed and stored. The algorithm for computing the correlation filter $H(\rho, \phi)$ is as follows:

1. for $j = 0$ to $n - 1$

    (a) j^{th} harmonic of each frame ($=j^{th}$ column) is extracted and a $n \times m$ temporary matrix $tmpF_k$ is formed as depicted in Figure 1.

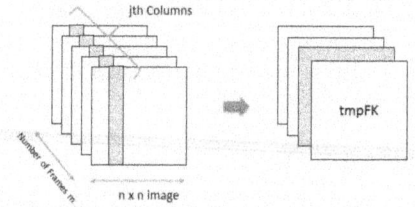

Figure 1: Formation of tmpFK matrices

    (b) Compute ($n \times m$) matrix $\text{TP}_2[i, k] = \frac{tmpF_k[i,k]}{P_{FOM}[i,k]}$, element by element division.

    (c) Compute ($n \times m$) matrix $\text{TP}_3[i, k] = \text{TP}_2[i, k] \times ID[i, k]$, element by element multiplication.

    (d) Compute complex conjugate transpose $tmpF_k^*$.

    (e) Compute the product $V = tmpF_k^* \times \text{TP}_3$.

    (f) Compute inverse of matrix V as V^{-1}

    (g) Compute $\text{TP}_4 = \text{TP}_2 \times V^{-1}$

    (h) Extract the jth column of the C_k and compute j^{th} column of filter harmonic $H_k(\rho) = \text{TP}_4 \times C_{kj}^*$, where * denotes complex conjugate.

2. end for

3. Compute the correlation filter $H(\rho, \phi)$ by taking the inverse Fourier transform of $H_k(\rho)$ and converting it back to cartesian form.

The $H_k(\rho)$ computation involves frequent matrix-matrix, matrix-vector operations and matrix inversions (done using standard factoring techniques). For larger, higher resolution and longer duration videos and images, it becomes a cumbersome computational task. We observed that for a 49 frame

Table 1: Time consumed by each step

Steps	Time in seconds
step(a) tmpFk Formation	3.791
step(b) matrix TP_2 computation	1.950
step(c) matrix TP_3 computation	0.292
step(d) conjugate transpose	0.157
step(e) compute V	39.225
step(f) compute V^{-1}	1.013
step(g) compute TP_4	27.429
step(h) compute $H_k(\rho)$	1.177
Total	**74.34**

video (with resolution of 2112×2112 pixels), the time spent for computing $H_k(\rho)$ on the single core sequential implementation was approximately 75 sec ($> 90\%$ of the over all time). The sequential implementation was developed using `OpenCV` library [9] and `FFTW` library [4]. The table 1 represents the breakup of time consumed by individual step(from step (a) to step (h)). These operations are amenable for parallelization and it is possible to achieve significant improvement in the execution speed.

4. PARALLEL IMPLEMENTATION

With the advent of multicore CPUs and many core GPUs, compute intensive applications have much to gain with parallel computing. The GPUs, which were primarily designed for graphical operations, are also proved to be equally effective in general purpose computing. Figure 2 represents general architecture of modern multicore CPUs and GPUs.

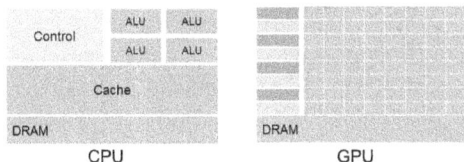

Figure 2: Multicore CPU-GPU architecture

As shown in the figure above, the GPUs have large number of light weight cores compared to multicore CPUs. Unlike CPU cores, the GPU cores are designed to carry out same instruction at a time but on different data. This enables huge data parallel through-put. On the other hand, CPUs have much more powerful cores, which are capable of carrying out different tasks at the same time at very high speeds. A typical CPU-GPU setup is shown in Figure 3. The CPU works as a master and offloads compute intensive work to GPU. The data transfer between CPU and GPU happens over PCI bus, which was often proved to be a performance bottleneck. However, this has not been the case with today's PCI express buses.

With this brief overview of today's multicore systems, we now present our approach for parallel implementation of correlation filter $H(\rho, \phi)$. In the following section, we describe the GPU implementation of the algorithm (1) mentioned in the previous section.

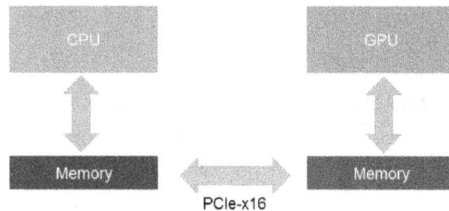

Figure 3: CPU-GPU over PCIe

4.1 Experimental Setup

In this section we present the details of all the hardware setup (CPUs/GPUs) used for the performance tuning and running the benchmarks. All the performance figures, reported in this paper, were obtained on the following hardware.

- GPU systems:
  - **Device1:** The Nvidia's Fermi $C2075$ GPU with 1.1 GHz 448 cores, 5.5GB RAM.
  - **Host1:** The Intel Westmere 2.93 GHz 4 cores with 24GB RAM.
  - **Device2:** The Nvidia's Kepler $K20x$ GPU with 796 MHz 2496 cores, 5GB RAM.
  - **Host2:** The Intel Ivy Bridge 2.1 GHz, dual socket, 6 cores/socket, 16GB RAM.

- Multicore CPU system: The Intel Xeon E5 2650 v2, Ivy Bridge 2.6 GHz dual socket, 8 cores/socket, 24GB RAM.

4.2 Correlation filter on GPU

The correlation filter computation involves number of matrix operations, which are extremely suitable for GPU computation. In this section we present the details of our implementation and measures taken for performance optimization. This implementation was specific to Nvidia platforms and was carried out in CUDA C. Though many CUDA kernels were implemented from scratch, some of the matrix computations were implemented with the help of routines/functions available in the highly optimized cuBLAS library for GPUs. The parallel algorithm implemented on the GPU is as follows:

1. Partition the total frames into $nPart$. Each partition is processed in sequence. Then for each part do:

2. Create n OpenMP threads. Each thread extracts m/n columns from each input frame to form m/n $tmpF_k$ matrices, where m is the width of input frames, and creates m/n number of $tmpF_k$ matrices in parallel.

3. Create nSt CUDA streams.

4. The $tmpF_k$ matrices are copied in batches to GPU asynchronously in each stream.

5. Carry out steps (b) to step (h) on each batch of $tmpF_k$ in each of the nSt stream.

6. Each stream computes a batch of $H_k(\rho)$ columns.

The following points were the main highlights of the implementation.

- **Accelerating matrix operations with cuBLAS:** The cuBLAS is a highly optimized CUDA C library for the linear algebra and matrix operations provided by the Nvidia. The $H_k(\rho)$ computations require matrix-matrix multiplication (step (e) and step (g)), matrix inversion in step (f) and matrix-vector multiplication in step (h). The cuBLAS also supports batch mode for matrix-matrix multiplication (`cublas< t >gemmBatched()`). The matrix inversion was computed using `cublas< t >getrfBatched` (computes LU factorization) and `cublas< t >getriBatched` (computes inverse of matrices with forward and backward triangular solvers) respectively.

- **Multi-level parallelism for higher GPU utilization:** To exploit the full potential of large number of the cores on GPU, it is required that the problem must be broken into large number of fine data parallel computations. It is observed that the `for loop` in the step 1 is amenable to parallelization. Multiple columns from the training images in step (a) were extracted and multiple $tmpF_k$ matrices were formed in parallel. This was achieved using multiple threads with the help of OpenMP on host or CPU.

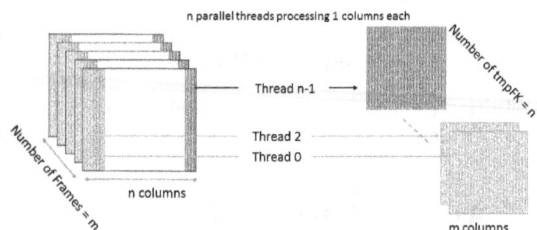

Figure 4: Parallel formation of tmpFK matrices

Similarly multiple $tmpF_k$ were processed in parallel i.e. the operations from step (b) to step (h) were carried out on multiple $tmpF_k$ concurrently on GPU. This was termed as batch processing. Secondly, each step within the loop was also parallelized. The matrix operation in step (b) to step (h) for each $tmpF_k$ are carried out in parallel. This two level parallelism effectively consumes huge compute power of the GPU.

- **Minimizing CPU-GPU data transfers:** Though today's PCI express buses are fast and support very good data transfer bandwidth, but they still fall short of compute speed and main memory (i.e. RAM) access speed by huge margins. The algorithm required the $tmpF_k$ matrices in step (b) and step (e), which in tern require same data transfer to GPU twice. For a high resolution video or large number of training images, this becomes and expensive operation. To avoid this twice data transfer, two copies of $tmpF_k$ matrices were maintained in the GPU. This significantly improved the performance but at the cost of double memory foot print.

- **Multi-Stream Computations:** The GPUs are typically high latency devices. But they support multiple stream computation, which allows hiding latencies by overlapping computations with data transfers. Streams can be imagined as concurrent compute pipelines which enable better utilization of the GPUs. To minimize the data transfers between host and device, two copies of $tmpF_k$ were maintained. The data was further divided into multiple batches and processed in multiple streams as shown in Figure 5. All the stream are launched simultaneously which results in overlapped computations and data transfers across streams. This multi-stream implementation provided further boost in the over all performance.

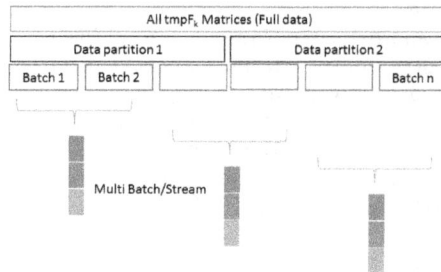

Figure 5: Multi-Batch & Multi-Stream computational

- **Coalesced data access:** The global memory load/store efficiency on GPU mostly depends on the data access pattern of the application. If the neighboring threads accessed global memory in strides then it results in poor load/store efficiency, which translates into poor performance. The data for $tmpF_k$ matrices, P_{FOM} matrix and index matrix ID is arranged to achieve coalesced data access pattern. This resulted in $\approx 85\%$ global load/store efficiency.

With all the above performance optimization, a significant speed up was achieved for correlation function computation. We report $\approx 35\times$ gain on Nvidia's $C2075$ GPU (see Figure 6).

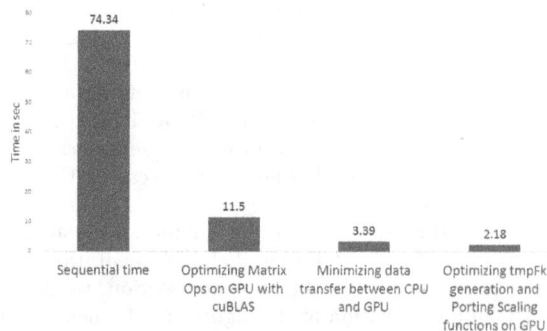

Figure 6: Performance on C2075 GPU

The modern GPUs are extremely capable machines. Figure 6 illustrates how well correlation filter design problem scales for above discussed optimizations.

4.3 Correlation filter on multicore CPU

Modern day CPUs are also equally efficient parallel processing machines. Equipped with less in number but more powerful compute cores, these CPUs also deliver high performance. We have also carried out parallel implementation on Intel multicore system. The `pthread` library [11] was used for multi-threaded application and the `OpenCV` library [9] was used for various image processing and matrix algorithms.

The parallelization approach adopted here was straightforward. The loop `for j = 0 to n-1` described in section 3 was parallelized with `pthreads`. The total number of frames, $tmpF_k$, were equally divided among all the available compute threads. Each thread processes $tmpF_k/N$ frames, where N is the number of threads. Further, parallelization of individual steps (a) to (h) was also implemented. It was observed that the overall performance degraded when inner multi-threading was enabled. This can be attributed to the lack of compute resources to accommodate nested parallelism. The readings presented here were obtained with internal parallelization turned off.

The following figure illustrates that correlation filter generation time decreases almost linearly as we increase number of the compute threads.

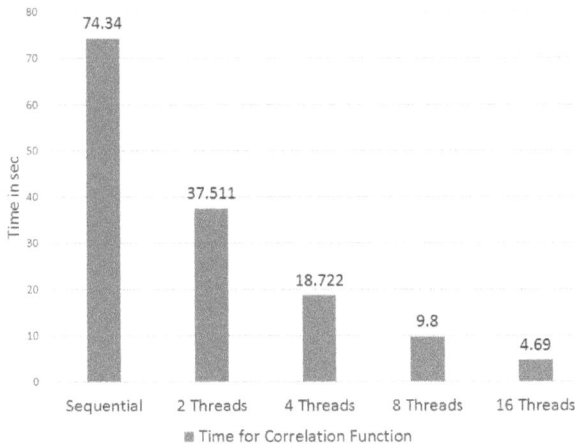

Figure 7: Performance on 16 core CPU

Compared to the sequential execution, scale up of $\approx 16\times$ was achieved on 16 physical core CPU system.

5. PERFORMANCE RESULTS

The results presented in the section 4.2 were obtained on the older Fermi C2075 GPU. The optimized GPU code was then executed on the latest Kepler series K20 GPU. This further boosted the performance. Figure 8 summarizes overall application performance gain achieved with parallelization. It also includes the energy savings while computations along with compute time.

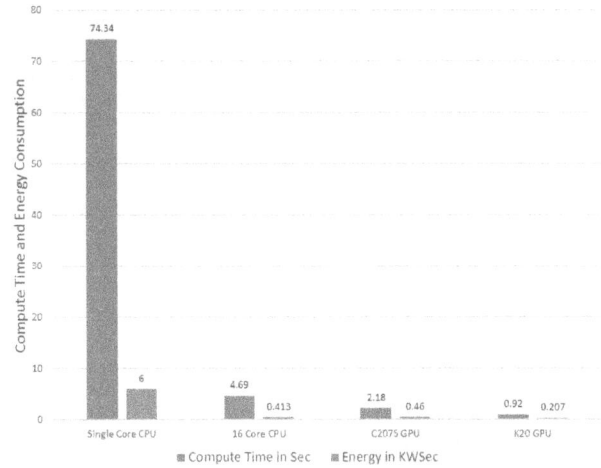

Figure 8: Performance gained on different multicore systems

6. CONCLUDING REMARKS

The OTCHF filters are widely used in many applications. A fast implementation would be desirable for large number of applications in pattern recognition, signal and image processing, which does not seem to be reported in previously published literature. The implementation reported in this paper can be easily adopted for other applications in correlation filtering.

We considered the OTCHF filter design problem on modern day multicore systems such as CPUs and GPUs. Both platforms delivered high performance with parallel processing and performance optimizations. We achieved $\approx 16\times$ and $41\times$ speed up on CPUs and GPUs respectively. Although GPUs performed better than 16 core CPU, huge effort was required in terms of changes done at design level and implementation level. Performance optimizations like exploiting two level parallelism, multi-stream computations and minimizing data transfers were the key factor in achieving the high performance on GPUs. On the other hand, parallelization on CPU required minimalistic code changes as compared to the GPU implementation.

The computational cost, in terms of energy consumption, was also drastically reduced with compute time. This enables scope for doing more simulations with in same duration and same cost, which effectively provides better results.

We conclude this paper on the note that, modern day CPUs and GPUs are extremely capable machines, however best results can only be obtained with performance optimizations.

7. ACKNOWLEDGMENTS

The authors are thankful to Srinivas Chalamala, TCS Innovation Lab Hyderabad, for many insightful discussions on the topic of pattern recognitions and its application in water marking.

8. REFERENCES

[1] A. M. B. V. K. Vijaya Kumar and R. Juday. Correlation pattern recognition. Cambridge University Press, 2005.

[2] A. M. B. V. K. Vijaya Kumar and A. Takessian. Optimal tradeoff circular harmonic function correlation filter methods providing controlled in-plane rotation response. In *IEEE Transactions On Image Processing*, volume 15, pages 84–89. IEEE, June 2000.

[3] M. B. V. K. Vijaya Kumar, Savvides. Correlation pattern recognition for face recognition. In *Proceeding of IEEE*, volume 94, pages 145–152. IEEE, November 2006.

[4] FFTW. Fftw library. www.fftw.org/, 2014.

[5] P. Irofti. Gpu parallel implementation of the approximate k-svd algorithm using opencl. In *Proceedings of European signal processing conference*, volume 15, pages 84–89. EUSIPCO, June 2014.

[6] R. A. Kerekes and B. V. K. V. Kumar. Correlation filters with controlled scale response. *IEEE Transactions on image processing*, 15(7):4012–4015, July 2006.

[7] Nvidia. cublas library. https://developer.nvidia.com/cuBLAS, 2008.

[8] Nvidia. cufft library. https://developer.nvidia.com/cuFFT, 2008.

[9] OpenCV. Opencv library. http://opencv.org/, 2008.

[10] K. Picos and V. H. Diaz-Ramirez. Object tracking under non uniform illumination conditions. GPU Technology Conference, 2014.

[11] Pthreads. Pthread library. https://computing.llnl.gov/tutorials/pthreads/, 2014.

[12] J. Rosen and J. Shamir. Circular harmonic phase filters for efficient rotation-invariant pattern recognition. *App. Opt.*, 15(5):2895–2899, November 1998.

[13] M. Savvides and B. V. K. V. Kumar. Efficient design of advanced correlation filters for robust distortion-tolerant face recognition. In *IEEE Conference on Advanced Video and Signal Based Surveillance*, volume 15, pages 45–52. IEEE, June 2003.

[14] F. Trebien. An efficient gpu-based implementation of recursive linear filters and its application to realistic real-time re-synthesis for interactive virtual worlds, July 2009.

[15] M. J. Yousri Ouerhani and A. Alfalou. Fast face recognition approach using a graphical processing unit gpu. https://hal.archives-ouvertes.fr/hal-00782740/document, 2001.

[16] H. H. A. Yuan-Neng Hsu and G. April. Rotation-invariant digital pattern recognition using circular harmonic expansion. *OSA*, 21(22):4012–4015, November 1982.

A Resource Contention Analysis Framework for Diagnosis of Application Performance Anomalies in Consolidated Cloud Environments

Tatsuma Matsuki
Software Laboratory
FUJITSU LABORATORIES LTD.
Kawasaki, Japan
matsuki.tatsuma@jp.fujitsu.com

Naoki Matsuoka
Software Laboratory
FUJITSU LABORATORIES LTD.
Kawasaki, Japan
matsuoka.naoki@jp.fujitsu.com

ABSTRACT

Cloud services have made large contributions to the agile developments and rapid revisions of various applications. However, the performance of these applications is still one of the largest concerns for developers. Although it has created many performance analysis frameworks, most of them have not been efficient for the rapid application revisions because they have required performance models, which may have had to be remodeled whenever application revisions occurred.

We propose an analysis framework for diagnosis of application performance anomalies. We designed our framework so that it did not require any performance models to be efficient in rapid application revisions. That investigates the Pearson correlation and association rules between system metrics and application performance. The association rules are widely used in data-mining areas to find relations between variables in databases.

We demonstrated through an experiment and testing on a real data set that our framework could select causal metrics even when the metrics were temporally correlated, which reduced the false negatives obtained from cause diagnosis. We evaluated our framework from the perspective of the expected remaining diagnostic costs of framework users. The results indicated that it was expected to reduce the diagnostic costs by 84.8% at most, compared with a method that only used the Pearson correlation.

Keywords

Cloud computing, Performance diagnosis, Correlation analysis, Association rule

1. INTRODUCTION

Cloud services have created many benefits to application and service developers. One of the main benefits of the cloud has been brought about by its agility. Cloud services can quickly provide application developers on-demand computational resources (e.g., virtual machines (VMs)), which allows them to agilely develop, easily revise, and scale out their applications, which accelerates their business growth. The advantage of the cloud has recently been changing the software industry, which is shifting from traditional plan-based developments to agile developments. That has also created a new term called *lean startup* [21]. Agilely developed applications in lean startups are repeatedly delivered to users for earlier feedbacks. Such agile features of applications in the cloud is leading to an era with more rapid revisions of businesses as well as applications.

While cloud services enable the agile developments of applications, the performance of applications in the cloud is still one of the prime concern for application developers. A physical server in the cloud typically hosts several VMs and these share resources (e.g., CPUs, memories, disks, and networks) on the same server. This resource sharing enables more efficient and flexible resource management, which, however, can lead to problems with the performance of applications [15]. When resource contentions between VMs occur, applications on the VMs can suffer from performance degradation due to a lack of resources. Application developers (cloud service users) and cloud service providers have to address these performance issues, which includes having to detect and diagnose them. However, these processes often involve excessive costs because of the complexity and large scale of applications and clouds.

Many researchers have proposed performance analysis tools or frameworks [25] in cloud environments and datacenters to reduce the costs. Most of them [2, 5, 14, 22, 24] have used the model-based approach, which models the performance of applications or problems using techniques such as machine learning with a training data set. However, they are inefficient for the rapid application revisions because agile revisions may cause frequent remodeling or outputting many adverse results.

This paper proposes a framework for the diagnosis of application performance anomalies caused by resource contentions in the consolidated cloud. Our framework was designed so that it did not require any performance models to work efficiently for the agile application revisions. Our framework diagnoses the performance anomalies of applications by correlating the application performance (e.g., response times) with performance metrics (e.g., CPU usage, network throughput, and disk I/O) obtained from the cloud

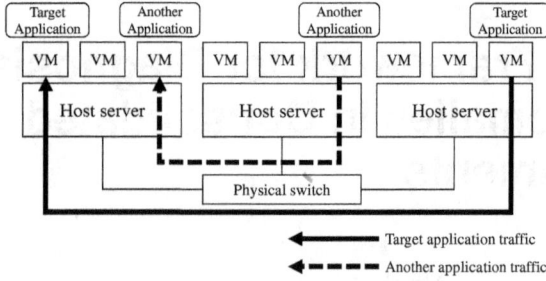

Figure 1: **Target scenario for application performance anomalies in this paper: Performance degradation of *target application* occurs due to anomalous network traffic of *another application***

infrastructure. The correlated performance metrics could provide useful information for pinpointing the root causes of the application performance anomalies as some previous studies [9, 17, 29] indicated.

Our three main contributions in this paper are:

1. We propose a model-less framework for the diagnosis of application performance anomalies caused by the resource contentions (bottlenecks) in the cloud. Our diagnosis not only includes the diagnosis of the application performance bottlenecks but also the causes of these bottlenecks.

2. We also propose a method to mine association rules [1] between application performance and individual metrics to complement the drawbacks of the standard Pearson correlation. Association rules are widely used in data-mining areas to find relations between variables in databases. The approach using association rules reduces false negatives when there are temporal correlations between a metric and application performance.

3. We further investigated the effectiveness of the proposed technique of diagnosis using the data obtained from an experimental environment and a real data set. We also evaluated our framework from the perspective of not only the accuracy and coverage but also the expected remaining diagnostic costs to our framework users.

The rest of this paper is organized as follows. We explain our performance diagnosis framework in Section 2. Section 3 details how we evaluated it in an experimental environment. Section 4 clarifies how we tested our framework on a real data set and confirmed its effectiveness. Section 5 discusses some of its limitations. Section 6 introduces some related work. Finally, we conclude the paper in Section 7.

2. SYSTEM DESIGN

2.1 Diagnosis approach

The main objective of our framework is to select (1) the subset of metrics and their associated VMs that may have caused bottlenecks (application performance anomalies) and (2) the bottleneck attributes of performance anomalies (e.g., *CPU*, *network*, and *disk*). We expect that these two outputs will easily motivate cloud administrators to deal with performance anomalies by performing operations such as VM

migration [4]. Metrics are selected by finding the correlation between individual metrics and application performance (e.g., response times). In the scenario in Figure 1, where a network resource contention occurs between a *target application* and *another application*, the causal VMs are those that host *another application* and the causal attribute is *network*. These outputs can motivate the administrator to migrate the VM to another host or set a limit for its usage of network bandwidth.

Let us now estimate the remaining diagnosis costs to our framework users and determine the main direction of our approach. It is almost impossible for diagnosis frameworks to achieve an optimal result (i.e., no false positives and no false negatives). They leave higher or lower costs for framework users. We assumed that framework users have the ability to correctly determine whether each metric is related to a performance anomaly or not, and once a related metric is found, they can address the performance issue. The cost of diagnosing a cause is then proportional to the number of metrics that is obtained from the cloud infrastructure. Denote the total number of metrics as $\aleph$. The cost, X, is represented as $X = \alpha\aleph$, where α is determined by depending on the skills of users. Assume that a cause diagnosis framework has *precision* p ($0 \le p \le 1$) and *recall* r ($0 \le r \le 1$), which are defined as

$$p = \frac{\text{\# of true positives}}{\text{\# of true positives} + \text{\# of false positives}} \quad (1)$$

and

$$r = \frac{\text{\# of true positives}}{\text{\# of true positives} + \text{\# of false negatives}}, \quad (2)$$

where p represents accuracy and r represents the comprehensiveness of diagnosis. We assumed that the diagnosis framework selected a subset of metrics whose size is $\aleph^*$. We then calculated the expected remaining cost of the diagnosis when a user utilizes the framework as:

$$X^* = \alpha\aleph^*(1-p) + \alpha(\aleph - \aleph^*)(1-r) \quad (3)$$

Note that we here assumed that p and r have probabilistic meanings. If the selected metrics include all correct metrics, the expected cost is $\alpha\aleph^*(1-p)$ because the selected metrics include false positives with the probability, $1-p$. If the selected metrics do not include the correct metrics, the cost expands by $\alpha(\aleph - \aleph^*)$ because the user has to additionally investigate the other $\aleph - \aleph^*$ metrics. The total expected remaining cost is calculated with Eq. (3) because the probability that the selected metrics will include the correct metrics is r. Even though p and r, in fact, mean the ratio in Eq. (1) and (2), the cost function (3) is intuitively accurate. When $p = 1$ and $r = 1$, the cost is $X^* = 0$, which means that an optimal diagnosis framework does not leave any diagnostic costs for users. When $r = 1$ (the results include all correct metrics), the cost is $\alpha\aleph^*(1-p)$, which means that the cost is proportional to $\aleph^*$ and the user have to investigate the cause within $\aleph^*$ metrics that have been selected by the framework. When $r = 0, p = 0$ (the results do not include any correct causes), the cost is $X^* = \alpha\aleph = X$, which means that the user has to investigate within all metrics.

We assumed $\aleph = d\aleph^*(d \geq 1)$ and transform Eq. (3) as:

$$
\begin{aligned}
X^* &= \alpha\aleph^*(1-p) + \alpha(\aleph - \aleph^*)(1-r) \\
&= \alpha\aleph - \alpha(\aleph^*p + \aleph r - \aleph^*r) \\
&= X - \alpha\aleph(\frac{d-1}{d}r + \frac{1}{d}p) \quad\quad (4)
\end{aligned}
$$

The second term in Eq. (4) represents *gain* of the diagnosis framework. We obtained an important observation from the gain function, i.e., *recall* is more important than *precision*. As d increases, the contribution of p decreases with the rate, $1/d$. When $d \to \infty$, the gain is approaching $\alpha\aleph r$ and p makes no contributions. The intuitive meaning is that when d is large, $\aleph^*$ decreases and the diagnostic costs within $\aleph^*$ metrics also decrease even when p is small.

We designed our framework from this observation to achieve better recall (fewer false negatives), while achieving acceptable precision and large d (small $\aleph^*$).

2.2 System overview

Figure 2 overviews our framework, which is configured with the Metric Collector, Application Performance Input Module, Bottleneck Diagnosis, Cause Diagnosis and Database. Our framework uses three kinds of information for the diagnosis, i.e., performance metrics in the cloud, application performance data and classification information on the metrics, which is used to limit the analyzing metrics. We will now explain the metric classification in Section 2.3.

The Metric Collector collects the metrics data from the cloud infrastructure with a fixed sampling interval (e.g., 1 min) and timestamps the data that are thus obtained. It also attaches labels to the collected metrics data. The attached labels include information from which the metrics have been collected. For example, the *PercentProcessorTime* metric collected from VM1 in host A has a label, *PercentProcessorTime;VM1;hostA*. These labels are used to associate a correlated metric with a VM or a host. The Application Performance Input Module receives the application performance data from application administrators (cloud service users). They can transfer time-stamped numerical data (i.e., time series data) to this module. This input module architecture is motivated by a cloud environmental feature. The application and cloud infrastructure are usually managed by different administrators, which may make it difficult to continuously collect application performance data especially in a cloud provided as an infrastructure-as-a-service (IaaS). Our framework has also been designed to work even when application data have temporally been obtained.

The Bottleneck Diagnosis and Cause Diagnosis in Figure 2 are modules that infer the bottleneck attributes of the application performance anomalies for the former and causal VMs for the latter. We will explain the technical details of these two modules in Sections 2.4 and 2.5. The Bottleneck Diagnosis outputs the analysis results to both the Application and cloud administrator. The results include the bottleneck attributes and associated metrics. The Cause Diagnosis, on the other hand, only outputs the analysis results (causal VMs and the associated metrics) to the cloud administrator because the application administrator should be agnostic about causal VMs.

2.3 Preliminary

This section explains two preliminaries: the classification of metrics and the creation of pair-wise data. We classified

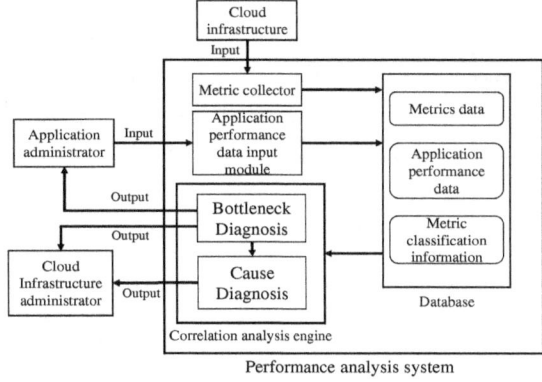

Figure 2: System overview

all the collected metrics into both of the location groups and attribute groups in advance, as summarized in Table 1, which lists the groups and the metrics examples belonging to each group. The Application VM group contains the metrics associated with VMs that the application administrator uses. The VM groups contains the metrics that do not belong to the Application VM group but that are associated with VMs. The Host group contains the metrics that is not associated with any VMs. This classification is done once in advance when our framework is installed because the kinds of collected metrics are rarely changed during the operational phase. We used this classification information for bottleneck and cause diagnosis, which will be described in Subsections 2.4 and 2.5.

Our framework evaluates the correlations between application performance and individual metrics. However, the timestamps of application performance data are different from those of metrics data. We define time units with a specific time interval $\bar{t}$ (e.g., 300 s) to adjust the timestamps. An analysis time period is determined based on input application performance data. We assume that t_s denotes the oldest timestamps of the application performance data and t_f denotes the newest. Here, we define time as absolute time such as UNIX time. Assume that the analysis start time is denoted as T_s and the end time is denoted as T_f. We then define them as $T_s = t_s - (t_s \bmod \bar{t})$ and $T_f = t_f - (t_f \bmod \bar{t}) + \bar{t}$. When T_s and T_f are represented as $T_f = T_s + N\bar{t}$, N is the number of time units in the analysis period. We denote time unit u_n as $u_n = [T_s + n\bar{t}, T_s + (n+1)\bar{t})$. A set of application performance data that have a timestamp within time unit u_n is aggregated (e.g., averaged), and we obtain a new time series as $\boldsymbol{A} = (a_0, a_1, ..., a_{N-1})$, where a_n represents the average application performance data within the time unit, u_n. We similarly obtain the new time series of metric i as $\boldsymbol{M}_i = (m_0^i, m_1^i, ..., m_{N-1}^i)$, where m_n^i represents the average metric i data within the time unit, u_n. The time series $\boldsymbol{A}$ and $\boldsymbol{M}_i$ are pair-wised, and we evaluate the correlation between them.

2.4 Bottleneck diagnosis

This section explains the technical details of how we select the bottleneck attribute, which is done by finding the metrics that are highly correlated with the application performance data. The port of *physical switch* in the scenario in Figure 1 is the bottleneck point and it is associated with a metric such as the *physical switch port packet counter*. When

Table 1: Metric classification

Location groups	Metrics	Attribute groups	Metrics
Application VM	Virtual CPUs, disks, NICs, and memories	CPU	CPUs and virtual CPUs
VM	Virtual CPUs, disks, NICs, and memories	Disk	Disks, storage, and virtual disks
Host	CPUs, disks, memories, NICs, virtual switches, physical switches and storage	Memory	Memory and virtual memories
		Network	Physical switches, NICs, virtual switches, and virtual NICs

performance degradation occurs on the target application, the *packet counter* should correlate with application performance. In order to find the correlated metrics (we call them *bottleneck metrics*), we simply used the Pearson correlation coefficient (we simply call it *correlation*). Although the correlation evaluates *linear* relationships between application performance and individual metrics, the previous work [29] has indicated that it achieves good accuracy in the bottleneck estimations. Here, we denote the set of all analysis time units as T, and calculate the correlation between A and M_i as:

$$c_i = \frac{\sum_{n \in T}(a_n - \bar{a})(m_n^i - \bar{m}_i)}{\sqrt{\sum_{n \in T}(a_n - \bar{a})^2}\sqrt{\sum_{n \in T}(m_n^i - \bar{m}_i)^2}}$$

where $\bar{a}$ and $\bar{m}_i$ are calculated as $\bar{a} = 1/N \cdot \sum_{n \in T} a_n$ and $\bar{m}_i = 1/N \cdot \sum_{n \in T} m_n^i$.

We then select a set of correlated metrics as bottleneck metrics and diagnose the bottleneck attribute. We explain the procedure for diagnosing the bottleneck attributes in Algorithm 1. All metrics belonging to the *application VM* or *host* group (summarized in Table 1) are analysis target data, which are input to Algorithm 1. All input metrics in the Algorithm 1 are sorted in decreasing order of $|c_i|$. The metrics are checked as to whether the correlation is over the threshold, T_{bot}, in order of $|c_i|$, and if so, the metrics are stored in *metr*. We use hypothesis testing of Pearson correlation with a specific significance level (e.g., 0.05) to determine threshold T_{bot}. Given the number of sample data (i.e., the number of analysis time units, N), T_{bot} is set as the critical value for testing [12]. We set a limit, l_m, for the number of selected bottleneck metrics to limit the number of selected attributes. The attributes of the correlated metrics are fetched by *attribute(i)* using the *attribute group* information in Table 1 and stored in *attr*. We finally obtain the bottleneck attributes, *attr*, and its associated metrics, *metr*.

2.5 Cause diagnosis

This section explains the technical details of cause diagnosis. We also use the correlation-based approach in causal VM diagnosis as well as bottleneck diagnosis. However, there are some difficulties in selecting metrics that are associated with causal VMs (we call them *cause metrics*). Figure 3 plots examples of bottleneck and cause metrics. We obtained the behaviors of these metrics in the experimental environment that is explained in Subsection 3.1, which is somewhat similar to the scenario in Figure 1. Figure 3 indicates the behavior of the bottleneck metric (*switch port throughput* obtained from a bottleneck point) highly correlates with the application performance (*response time*). The correlation coefficient is 0.904. The behavior of a cause metric (*virtual NIC throughput* of the causal VM), on the other hand, is less correlated with it because the cause metric has opposite behavior at some time units (e.g., time unit 14 and 19).

Algorithm 1 Bottleneck attribute diagnosis
1: Input: metrics in *application VM* group or *host* group.
2: Output: bottleneck metrics $metr \Leftarrow \phi$ and selected attributes $attr \Leftarrow \phi$
3: Threshold of correlation: T_{bot}
4: Maximum number of selected bottleneck metrics: l_m
5: Number of selected bottleneck metrics: $count = 0$
6: Set of input metrics: G

7: Calculate c_i for all metrics in G.
8: Sort $i \in G$ in decreasing order of $|c_i|$.
9: **for all** $i \in G$ **do**
10:     **if** $|c_i| > T_{\text{bot}}$ **then**
11:         $metr \Leftarrow i$
12:         **if** $attribute(i) \notin attr$ **then**
13:             $attr \Leftarrow attribute(i)$
14:         **end if**
15:         $count++$
16:         **if** $count > l_m$ **then**
17:             Break
18:         **end if**
19:     **end if**
20: **end for**
21: **return** $metr, attr$

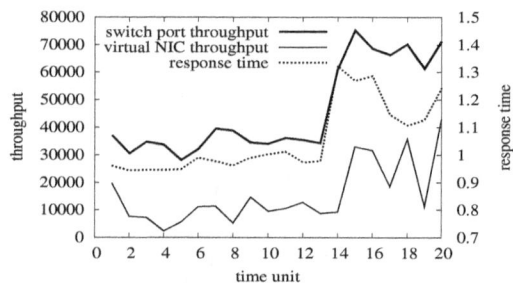

Figure 3: Examples of bottleneck and cause metrics

The correlation coefficient is 0.667. This metric is in fact one of the cause metrics because we experimentally generated a performance bottleneck using the VM. Therefore, we have to capture the cause metric by applying an additional method. Otherwise, no low-correlated cause metrics can be captured, which would lead to false negatives.

The main reason for low correlation of cause metrics is that there are multiple causes. For example, there are multiple VMs that bring about the performance bottlenecks. This means that the bottleneck metrics behave following the aggregated behavior (e.g., sum) of cause metrics. That is, each cause metric is temporally correlated with application performance. We evaluate the *association rules* [1], which has often been used in the field of data mining and previous work [9], between each metric and application performance to capture *temporal* correlations. To do this, we first have to discretize application performance and individual metrics.

We simply use a threshold in discretizing application performance and we assume that the threshold is specified by the application administrator. Given an application performance threshold, a, we discretize the application performance data as: $S_n = 0$ if $a_n \leq a$ and $S_n = 1$ otherwise. We then obtain $\boldsymbol{S} = \{S_n, n \in \boldsymbol{T}\}$. We here assume that time unit u_n is anomalous when $S_n = 1$ without losing generality.

We propose an algorithm that investigates the optimal threshold for discretizing metrics. We define the optimal threshold that maximizes *support* within a constraint of its *confidence* (denoted as T_{conf} and fixed with $T_{\mathrm{conf}} = 0.8$). Given a threshold, m^i, for metric i, we discretize metric i as: $d_n^i = 0$ if $m_n^i \leq m^i$ and $d_n^i = 1$ otherwise. We obtain the discretized data for metric i as $\boldsymbol{D}_i = \{d_n^i, n \in \boldsymbol{T}\}$. We next calculate the support and its confidence for the direction from metric i to application performance (denoted as $\mathrm{supp}(\boldsymbol{D}_i \to \boldsymbol{S}), \mathrm{conf}(\boldsymbol{D}_i \to \boldsymbol{S})$) as follows. If $|\boldsymbol{D}_i^1 \cap \boldsymbol{S}^1|/|\boldsymbol{D}_i^1| \geq |\boldsymbol{D}_i^0 \cap \boldsymbol{S}^1|/|\boldsymbol{D}_i^0|$,

$$\mathrm{supp}(\boldsymbol{D}_i \to \boldsymbol{S}) = \frac{|\boldsymbol{D}_i^1 \cap \boldsymbol{S}^1|}{|\boldsymbol{S}^1|}, \qquad (5)$$

$$\mathrm{conf}(\boldsymbol{D}_i \to \boldsymbol{S}) = \frac{|\boldsymbol{D}_i^1 \cap \boldsymbol{S}^1|}{|\boldsymbol{D}_i^1|}, \qquad (6)$$

where $\boldsymbol{D}_i^1 = \{n|d_n^i = 1, n \in \boldsymbol{T}\}, \boldsymbol{S}^1 = \{n|S_n = 1, n \in \boldsymbol{T}\}$, and if not,

$$\mathrm{supp}(\boldsymbol{D}_i \to \boldsymbol{S}) = \frac{|\boldsymbol{D}_i^0 \cap \boldsymbol{S}^1|}{|\boldsymbol{S}^1|}, \qquad (7)$$

$$\mathrm{conf}(\boldsymbol{D}_i \to \boldsymbol{S}) = \frac{|\boldsymbol{D}_i^0 \cap \boldsymbol{S}^1|}{|\boldsymbol{D}_i^0|}. \qquad (8)$$

Equations (7) and (8) are the support and confidence for negatively correlated metrics. We set m^i as m_n^i for each $n \in \boldsymbol{T}$ and examine the optimal threshold, m^{i*}, as shown in Algorithm 2. We obtain the optimal threshold as the value of *opt*, which achieves the largest support within the constraint, $\mathrm{conf}(\boldsymbol{D}_i \to \boldsymbol{S}) \geq T_{\mathrm{conf}}$. We denote the discretized metric, i, with the optimal threshold as: $d_n^{i*} = 0$ if $m_n^i \leq m^{i*}$ and $d_n^{i*} = 1$ otherwise. We then obtain $\boldsymbol{D}_i^* = \{d_n^{i*}, n \in \boldsymbol{T}\}$. When the *opt* has *null* value, we assume that there is no valid association rule between $\boldsymbol{M}_i$ and $\boldsymbol{A}$.

The support measure defined in Equations (5) and (7) indicates the degree of association between application performance and metric i. A large support means a strong association and a small support means a temporal association. For example, when $\mathrm{supp}(\boldsymbol{D}_i \to \boldsymbol{S}) = 0.5$, the half of anomalous time units ($S_n = 1$) is associated with (supported by) the metric i. Equations (6) and (8) indicate that the confidence measure is used to evaluate whether application performance is anomalous or not when the value of metric i increases (or decreases), and therefore, the confidence measure is close to one even when the correlation is temporal. The example of the temporally correlated metric in Figure 3 (*virtual NIC throughput*) is one of the metrics that has a valid association rule. When we set $a = 1.1$, its optimal discretizing threshold is set to 14,517 by Algorithm 2 and its confidence and support are calculated as 0.833 (5/6) for the former and 0.714 (5/7) for the latter.

The constraint of $T_{\mathrm{conf}} = 0.8$ indicates that 80% of the time units with $d_n^{i*} = 1$ is associated with the application

performance anomaly ($S_n = 1$). We have to set T_{conf} relatively large (e.g., ≥ 0.8) because if it is set too small, no valid association exists in the association rules. Therefore, we set $T_{\mathrm{conf}} = 0.8$, which is also the default value of the *arules* package in R language [10].

We also have to confirm *lift* measures for association rules to make the association rules valid. The lift measure for association rule $\boldsymbol{D}_i^* \to S$ is defined as:

$$\mathrm{lift}(\boldsymbol{D}_i^* \to \boldsymbol{S}) = \frac{\mathrm{conf}(\boldsymbol{D}_i^* \to \boldsymbol{S})}{|\boldsymbol{S}^1|/N} \qquad (9)$$

The lift measures generally have to be larger than one to validate association rules. The fraction of analysis time units that are anomalous ($|\boldsymbol{S}^1|/N$) therefore have to be less than 0.8 to make the lift larger than one, because we set $T_{\mathrm{conf}} = 0.8$. This means our framework requires that input application performance data have to include more than 20% of normal ($S_n = 0$) time units.

Algorithm 2 Investigate optimal discretizing threshold

1: Input: Discretized application performance $\boldsymbol{S}$ and $\boldsymbol{M}_i$
2: Output: Optimal threshold $opt = null$
3: Current max support: $max = 0$

4: **for all** $m_n^i \in \boldsymbol{M}_i$ **do**
5:     Calculate $\boldsymbol{D}_i$ with threshold m_n^i.
6:     Calculate $\mathrm{supp}(\boldsymbol{D}_i \to \boldsymbol{S})$ and $\mathrm{conf}(\boldsymbol{D}_i \to \boldsymbol{S})$.
7:     **if** $\mathrm{conf}(\boldsymbol{D}_i \to \boldsymbol{S}) \geq 0.8$ **then**
8:         **if** $\mathrm{supp}(\boldsymbol{D}_i \to \boldsymbol{S}) > max$ **then**
9:             $max = \mathrm{supp}(\boldsymbol{D}_i \to \boldsymbol{S})$, $opt = m_n^i$
10:         **end if**
11:     **end if**
12: **end for**
13: **return** opt

Let us next select a set of metrics that are associated with the causal VMs. In addition to the correlation, we use the association rules previously examined to capture the temporally correlated cause metrics. We explain the procedure for cause diagnosis in Algorithm 3. The analysis target metrics in our cause diagnosis are the metrics in the *VM* group listed in Table 1. We first remove the metrics that have no correlation with $\boldsymbol{A}$ by setting a threshold, T_{nocor}. We determine T_{nocor} as the critical value of hypothesis testing with a high significance level of $l = 0.1$, which is generally the highest. All selected cause metrics are satisfied under two conditions: i) *attr* obtained from Algorithm 1 contains its attribute and ii) its correlation is larger than T_{cor} or its support is $T_{\mathrm{supp}}(0 \leq T_{\mathrm{supp}} \leq 1)$ or above. We also determine T_{cor} by using hypothesis testing with a specific significance level of $l = 0.01$, which is set larger than T_{nocor}. We investigate the effect of the settings of T_{supp} in Section 3. The function, *extractVM*, in Algorithm 3 extracts the name of the associated VM from the index of metrics. Algorithm 3 finally outputs the cause metrics as *cause* and their associated names of VM as *causeVM*.

3. EXPERIMENTAL EVALUATION

3.1 Experimental setup

We built two types of applications on our experimental environment, i.e., a Web and virtual desktop infrastructure

Algorithm 3 Cause diagnosis

1: Input: Metrics in VM group, bottleneck attribute $attr$ from Algorithm 1, and application performance data S
2: Output: Cause metrics $cause \Leftarrow \phi$ and $causeVM \Leftarrow \phi$
3: Set of input metrics: G

4: **for all** $i \in G$ **do**
5:      Calculate c_i.
6:      **if** $|c_i| > T_{\text{nocor}}$ and $attribute(i) \in attr$ **then**
7:          Calculate D_i^* and $\text{supp}(D_i^* \to S)$.
8:          **if** ($|c_i| > T_{\text{cor}}$ or $\text{supp}(D_i^* \to S) \geq T_{\text{supp}}$) **then**
9:              $cause \Leftarrow i$
10:              **if** $extactVM(i) \notin causeVM$ **then**
11:                  $causeVM \Leftarrow extractVM(i)$
12:              **end if**
13:          **end if**
14:      **end if**
15: **end for**
16: **return** $cause, causeVM$

Table 2: Configurations of VMs

# of VMs	Usage	vCPU	MEM	vDisk
10	Virtual desktop	2	2 GB	20 GB
1	VDI benchmark	2	2 GB	20 GB
1	Web, AP server	2	2 GB	20 GB
1	Load balancer	4	8 GB	40 GB
3	DB server	4	8 GB	40 GB
3	Load generator on Host-2	8	2 GB	10 GB
1	Load generator on Host-1	2	4 GB	10 GB

(VDI), which are typical applications that require stable performance [11]. Figure 4 illustrates our experimental environment. There are two physical host servers (*Host-1* and *Host-2*) and a physical switch that connects these two servers with a local network that has 1-Gbps bandwidth. Hosts-1 and -2 have the same configuration, i.e., Intel Xeon X5680, 3.33-GHz 6 core x 2 processors, 48 GB of RAM, 278-GB SAS x 4 (RAID1 x 2, one for the host and the other for the VMs), and Windows server 2012 R2 datacenter. We installed Hyper-V [18] on the two hosts to manage the VMs. Host-1 hosts 14 VMs: 10 VMs for the VDI application, a VM for benchmarking VDI performance, a VM for the Web and application (AP) server, a VM for the load balancer of the Web application, and a VM for generating load. Host-2 hosts six VMs: three VMs for database (DB) server of the Web application and the others for generating load. Table 2 summarizes the configurations of these VMs. These 10 VDI VMs and one VDI benchmark VM were running with Windows 7 (64 bits) and the other VMs were running with CentOS-7 (64 bits).

The Web application built on our experimental environment was configured with Nginx, Kibana and ElasticSearch, which have recently been widely used for visualizing logging data [8]. We used Nginx as the Web server, Kibana as the AP server and ElasticSearch as the load balancer and DB server. We assumed that *response times* between the Web server and DB servers would provide the application performance data for the Web application, which were obtained from the access logs that were output from Nginx. We built five VMs to generate the Web access workload on another environment, each of which accessed the same Kibana dashboard with a fixed polling interval (10 s).

The 10 VDI VMs simulated a VDI service, which provided

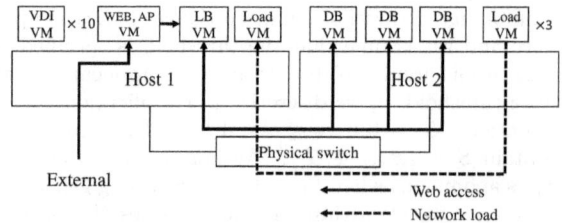

Figure 4: Experimental environment

desktop environments on Windows 7 operating system (OS). We simulated a VDI user workload that included a local Excel file open and over-write, an Excel file on an external file server open and over-write and external Web page access on each VDI VM. We wrote a script that randomly ran the above actions at random time intervals. The random intervals followed the an exponential distribution with a specific average. We set the averages as listed in Table 3. We prepared the application performance data for the VDI by measuring the experience of a VDI user. We then measured the response time of an Excel file (1 MB) open with a fixed time interval (30 s) on the VDI benchmark VM. These measures enable the disk performance of the VDI to be captured. (The disk performance is also a problem on our testing on a real data set, which will be explained in Section 4.)

Table 3: VDI workload simulation

# of VMs	Avg. interval	Actions
1	150 s	Local/remote file access, Web access
6	300 s	Local/remote file access, Web access
3	600 s	Local/remote file access, Web access

Table 4: VDI anomalous workload simulation

# of VMs	Avg. interval	Actions
1	150 s	Local/remote file access, Web access
5	300 s	Local/remote file access, Web access
4	10 s	Local file access

We used data on *Windows performance monitor* [20], which included the metrics of the host OS processor, disk, memory, network adapter, and those of VMs [28]. We obtained the data through the Windows management instrumentation (called *WMI*) [26] by running the *wmic* [27] command on the *Metric Collector* in Figure 2 with a fixed interval (60 s). We also used the simple network management protocol (SNMP) to obtain the management information base (MIB) counters of the physical switch port interfaces, which included I/O packets, bytes, and dropped packets. We obtained the MIB counters with a fixed interval (60 s). Some metrics have an cumulative feature such as a packet *counter* of a network interface and a read/write operation *counter* on a disk. Those metrics have to be calculated difference between successive data and the difference is divided by the sampling interval. These calculations are done on the *Metric Collector*. We obtained a total of 12,410 metrics from our experimental environment, which included 6,110 metrics that were associated with VMs.

3.2 Bottleneck injection

We evaluated the proposed framework with the data that contained injected performance anomalies. This section explains how performance anomalies were injected. We injected three types of resource contentions to create application performance anomalies: CPU, network, and disk.

178

CPU resource contentions were injected by the three load VMs on the host-2. This results in CPU resource shortages on DB servers, and it led to degraded performance in the Web application. We intermittently ran the *stress* [23] command on each load VM with a specific duration and the number of stressed CPU cores. The duration was randomly determined following an exponential distribution with a fixed average (10 s). The interval between two successive runs was also randomly determined following the exponential distribution with a fixed average (2 s). When the application performance was not anomalous, the number of stressed cores is set to four. When it was anomalous, we increased the number of stressed core to eight.

Network resource contentions were injected by the three load VMs on the host-2 and one load VM on host-1. We intermittently ran *iperf* [13] on all load VMs on Host-1 to generate network traffic load. The network traffic was transmitted from individual load VMs (i.e., iperf clients) on host-1 to a load VM (i.e., the iperf server) on host-2. The interval between two successive runs was also randomly determined following the exponential distribution with a fixed average (5 s). We ran *iperf* with the user datagram protocol (UDP) specifying the duration and bandwidth. The duration was randomly determined following the exponential distribution with a fixed average (10 s). When application performance was not anomalous, the bandwidth was randomly set following a uniform distribution $U(100\text{Mbps}, 300\text{Mbps})$. When it was anomalous, we switched the distribution of the determined bandwidth to $U(500\text{Mbps}, 700\text{Mbps})$ on two of the load VMs on Host-2. The increased bandwidth created response delays between the load balancer on Host-1 and DB servers on Host-2, which led to degraded performance in the Web application.

Disk resource contentions were injected by four of the ten VDI VMs. When VDI performance was anomalous, we switched the actions of four VDI VMs to only a local Excel file open/write with the small average intervals listed in Table 4. Frequent local file access caused disk I/O contentions between VDI VMs and the benchmark VM. That led to degraded VDI performance.

3.3 Experimental results

This section presents the results we obtained from the experimental evaluation that was previously explained. We injected 10 resource contentions for each CPU, network, and disk resource, which degraded application performance. We set $\bar{t} = 300$ (s) and input 10 times 18 time units (1.5 h) of application performance data, each of which included the performance degradation period.

3.3.1 Bottleneck diagnosis

Here, we present the results from bottleneck diagnosis that were obtained with Algorithm 1. The algorithm has a changeable parameter, l_m, which indicates the maximum number of bottleneck metrics that is selected by Algorithm 1. We investigated the effects of the setting of l_m as well as the evaluation of bottleneck diagnosis. We used *precision* and *recall* measures for the evaluation. Precision was defined as the fraction of selected attributes that was correct. Recall was defined that if the selected attributes contained the correct one, recall was one; if not, recall was zero.

Figure 5 plots the results obtained from evaluating the selected attributes. Note that the results are the total (i.e.,

average) results for 10 anomaly injections for each type of resource contention. When $l_m = 1$, there are some false negatives, as shown in Figure 5; the results do not include the correct attribute. Setting $l_m = 1$ means that the attribute is determined by the most correlated metric. The reason for these false negatives is that the bottleneck injections not only affect the bottleneck attribute but also others. For example, running *iperf* not only affects network metrics but also CPU and memory metrics because generating network traffic uses some CPU and memory resources. Figure 6 plots the behavior of a false positive bottleneck metric that is most correlated with application performance whose attribute is memory. As we can see from the figure, the false positive metric is highly correlated with the response time (the correlation is 0.895). If we want to remove the false positive, we have to use another method that is not correlation-based. The similar phenomena can occur in a real environment because almost all real applications use several kinds of resources. Therefore, l_m should be set relatively large. Although, the false negatives decreased and false positives increased as l_m is increased, it is important for diagnosis frameworks to reduce the number of false negatives, as was explained in Subsection 2.1.

3.3.2 Cause diagnosis

We will next discuss our evaluation of the results obtained from cause diagnosis. Note that here we assumed that the bottleneck diagnosis was accurately done (i.e., *attr* in Algorithm 3 only included an accurate attribute), so that we could evaluate our cause diagnosis without the effects of the results from the bottleneck diagnosis. We used precision and recall measures for the evaluation. Here, we define precision as the fraction of all selected cause metrics (i.e., those in *cause* in Algorithm 3) whose attributes and associated VMs are accurate. However, it is difficult to identify the exact number of metrics that have to be correlated with the application performance when resource contention is injected. We therefore used VM-level recall instead of metrics -level. We defined recall as the fraction of all causal VMs that were accurately selected (i.e., those in *causeVM* in Algorithm 3). We compared our framework with an approach using only the Pearson correlation, which selected cause metrics by hypothesis testing of the Pearson correlation with variations in significance levels of $l = 0.01, 0.05,$ and 0.1.

Figures 7 through 9 present the results in CPU, network, and disk contention cases. Each contains three graphs: (a) indicates precision, recall, and the number of selected metrics (denoted as $\aleph^*$), (b) indicates the effect of the T_{supp} setting ($T_{\text{supp}} = 0.2, 0.4, 0.6,$ and 0.8), and (c) indicates the expected remaining diagnosis cost of a framework user, which was calculated from Eq. (3) and normalized by $\alpha\aleph$. The results labeled $l = 0.01, 0.05,$ and 0.1 indicate those obtained by using the Pearson correlation with different significance levels l, and those labeled *proposal* are the results obtained from our framework with $T_{\text{supp}} = 0.2$. Note that here we have presented the total results obtained from 10 anomaly injections.

Figures 7(a), 8(a), and 9(a) indicate precision for different significance levels l has a tendency that as l increases, precision decreases and $\aleph^*$ increases. The reason for this is that the thresholds for the correlation are set large as l decreases. (When $N = 18$ and $l = 0.01, 0.05,$ and 0.1, the respective thresholds of the correlations are set to 0.589,

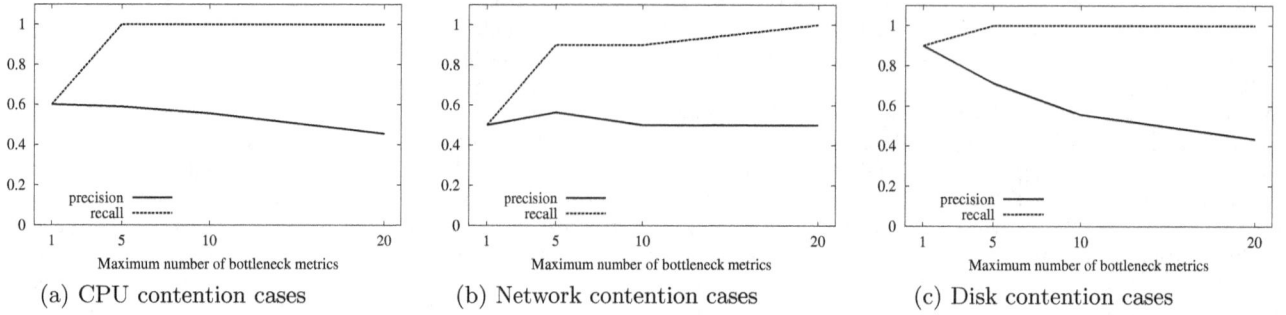

(a) CPU contention cases   (b) Network contention cases   (c) Disk contention cases

Figure 5: Total results from bottleneck diagnosis

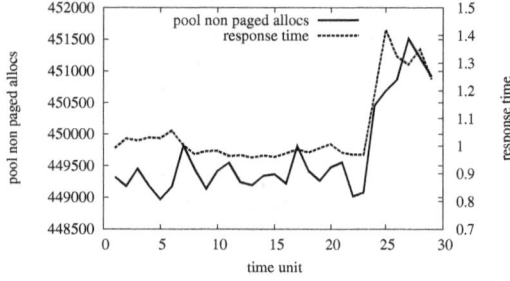

Figure 6: Example of false positive bottleneck metric

0.468, 0.400.) Higher thresholds also decrease recall because some cause metrics that have temporal correlating behaviors are not captured. As was previously explained, drops in recall may incur relatively large diagnosis costs for framework users. The framework we propose, on the other hand, achieves stable recall as well as the Pearson correlation with $l = 0.1$, which indicates that it accurately captures the metrics that have temporal and low correlation. The proposed framework achieves better precisions and smaller $\aleph^*$ for all cases of contention than that with the results using $l = 0.1$, which was used for the T_{nocor} setting. This means that even though setting $l = 0.1$ also enabled to capture temporal correlations by using low correlation thresholds, it created more false positives.

The results for the proposed framework were affected by the T_{supp} setting. As T_{supp} was set large, precision improved and $\aleph^*$ decreased as can be seen from Figures 7(b), 8(b), and 9(b). However, when $T_{\mathrm{supp}} = 0.8$, recall decreased in Fig. 8(b) and 9(b). These results indicate that some cause metrics have association rules with support of < 0.8, which means that these metrics have more temporal correlations with application performance. Therefore, T_{supp} should not be set large (e.g., ≤ 0.6) so that the temporal correlation can be captured.

Although there were tradeoffs between precision and recall in these results, we could evaluate the total performance of our framework by calculating the remaining diagnosis costs from Eq. (3). Our framework achieved better performance than those of $l = 0.01$ and 0.05 in Figs. 7(c), 8(c), and 9(c). It respectively reduced the costs, especially with $l = 0.01$, by 77.4%, 84.8%, and 79.5% for CPU, network, and disk contention case. That was caused by stable recall as was previously explained. Our framework achieves better performance in Fig. 7(c) than that in $l = 0.1$ cases. However, the cost reductions in Figs. 8(c) and 9(c) are quite small

despite the better precision of our framework. This is because $\aleph^*$ in the network and disk contention in Figs. 8(a) and 9(a) is smaller than that in the CPU contention in Fig. 7(a). That reduces the contribution of precision as was explained in Subsection 2.1.

The threshold of the Pearson correlation is also affected by the length of the analysis time period (denoted as N) because the critical value of hypothesis testing is calculated from the number of sample data. As the number of sample data increases, the critical value decreases and the correlation threshold is then set small.

Figure 10 presents the results for the remaining diagnosis costs where the analysis time period length, N, is 24 and 30. We have omitted the results for precision, recall, and $\aleph^*$ because of space limitations. The results in Fig. 10(b) have a similar tendency with the results for $N = 18$ because there are still some false negatives and recall decreases even when the correlation threshold is set small. However, the results in Figs. 10(a) and 10(c) demonstrate a different tendency. When N is large, the low correlation threshold removes false negatives and the cost is only affected by precision and $\aleph^*$. In that case, our framework achieves better performance than that of $l = 0.1$. This is because when N is large, $\aleph^*$ also increases and precision makes a larger contribution to the remaining diagnosis costs. Even though $l = 0.01$ and 0.05 achieve lower costs, there are more risks of recall-decreases, as can be seen from Fig. 10(b).

We concluded from these observations that our framework worked stably both when N was large and small. This conclusion is suitable for our framework because i) some application performance data may not be able to obtained during long periods from application administrators and ii) long periods of performance data have a greater probability of containing totally different types of causes such as disk contention and workload surge of applications. These may not be captured by the Pearson correlation because individual cause metrics should correlate with a type of anomalies but not correlate with the others, which bring about temporal correlations. Even in that situation, our framework should work well if we set T_{nocor} smaller because there can be valid association rules between individual cause metrics and application performance.

4. TESTING ON REAL DATA SET

This section explains how we adapted a prototype of our framework to a real data set and investigated the efficiency of our framework.

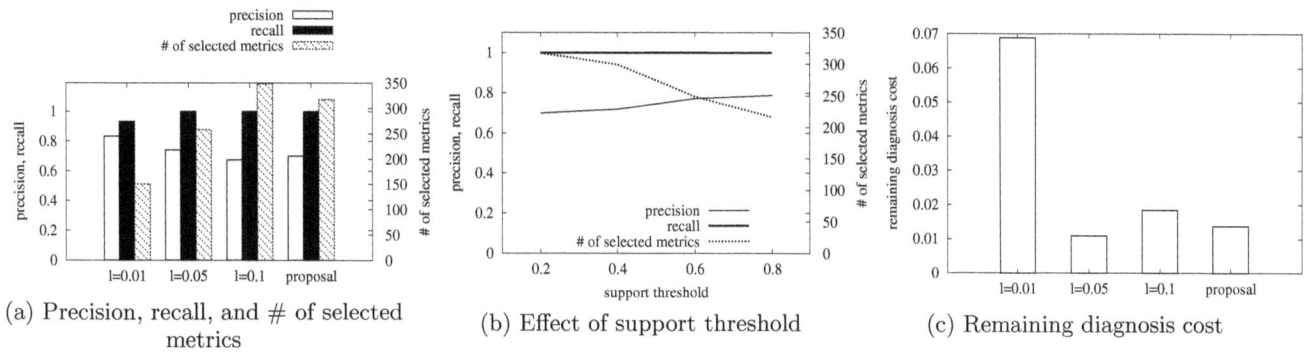

(a) Precision, recall, and # of selected metrics

(b) Effect of support threshold

(c) Remaining diagnosis cost

Figure 7: Results from cases of CPU contention

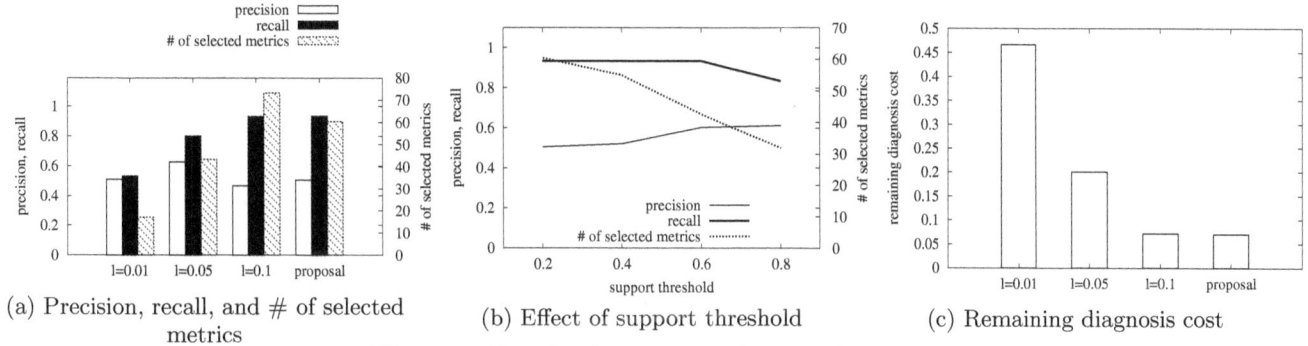

(a) Precision, recall, and # of selected metrics

(b) Effect of support threshold

(c) Remaining diagnosis cost

Figure 8: Results from cases of network contention

A. Setups

The real data set we used in this section was data that were obtained from a real VDI service, which hosted a total of 290 users (VMs). The VDI service was configured with five host servers, two FCoE 10-G physical switches, and physical storage. The five host servers had the same configuration: 256 GB of RAM, Intel Xeon E5-2695v2 2.4 GHz 12 core x 2 processors, and Windows server 2008 (Hyper-V was used for the hypervisor). Each host server used an 8-TB RAID6 volume on the physical storage, which was used for virtual disks of VMs on the host.

The metrics data were obtained by using WMI and SNMP with a fixed interval (60 s), similarly to our experimental environment explained in Subsection 3.1. We also obtained metrics from storage, which supported various kinds of private MIBs, which included metrics related to storage such as read/write response times, I/O per second, read/write throughput, and cache hits for each volume. The total number of metrics we obtained from the cloud infrastructure was approximately 49,000 (fluctuating by time), which include approximately 35,000 metrics that were associated with a specific VM. The performance of the VDI service was measured in the same way that we used in the experiment in Subsection 3.1. We ran the benchmark script on a virtual desktop and measured user-experienced performance.

When we ran the benchmark script for one week, we encountered 13 times performance anomalies. We found from additional investigations that the root cause of these performance anomalies was disk resource contentions brought about by synchronous virus scans on a large number of VMs. Therefore, the correct bottleneck attribute was the disk. However, the correct causal VMs were not identical because in order to investigate these, we have to investigate the logs obtained from virus scan software on all VMs, which was

impossible for us to do. We therefore have only presented a summary of the metrics that were selected in cause diagnosis. We input application performance data 24 time units in length. When sample data size was 24 units, the critical value of hypothesis testing was 0.344, 0.404, and 0.515 with significance levels that corresponded to 0.1, 0.05, 0.01.

B. Results

Figure 11(a) plots the results obtained from bottleneck diagnosis, where the precision (recall) has the same definition as that provided in Subsection 3.3.1. As we can see from the figure, there is the same tendency as that in the experimental results in Fig. 5(c), i.e., when l_m is set small (e.g., $l_m = 1$), there are some false negatives. Therefore, using only the most correlated metric has to be avoided in bottleneck diagnosis, which is the same conclusion that we reached in our experimental evaluation.

Figure 11(b) shows the number of selected metrics. Note its similarity with the experimental evaluation, in which we assumed that bottlenecks had been accurately diagnosed. Our framework can capture larger numbers of cause metrics than the correlation approaches ($l = 0.01$ and 0.05). Figure 11(c) shows the effect of setting T_{supp}. As can be seen from in Fig. 11(c), larger numbers of metrics are selected when T_{supp} is set small. That indicates there are large numbers of metrics that have temporal correlations. In this case, there are many temporally correlated cause metrics because the degradation in application performance is brought about by a large number of VMs.

Figure 12 plots three examples of cause metrics selected by cause diagnosis on a real data set and compares application performance. The figure indicates the *read bytes/sec* metrics of three virtual disks on VMs. These metrics (denoted *vm1*, *vm2*, and *vm3*) have temporally correlated behaviors;

181

(a) Precision, recall, and # of selected metrics

(b) Effect of support threshold

(c) Remaining diagnosis cost

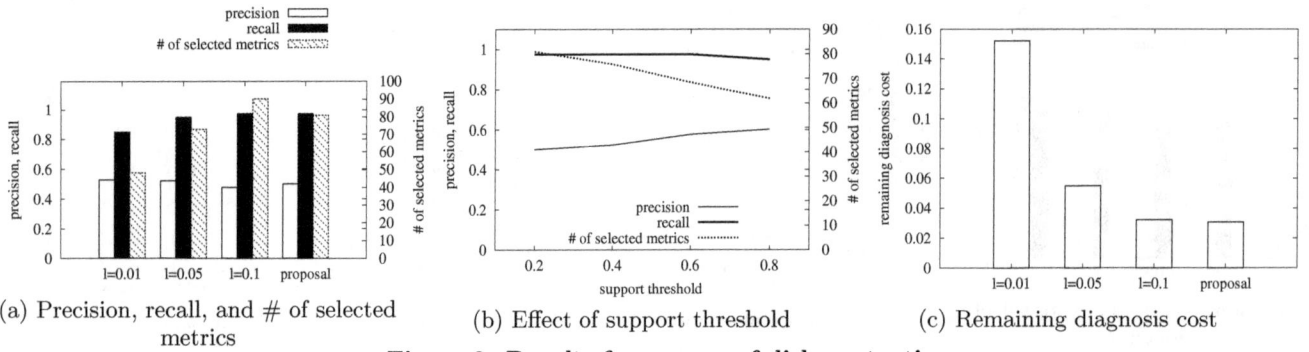

Figure 9: Results from cases of disk contention

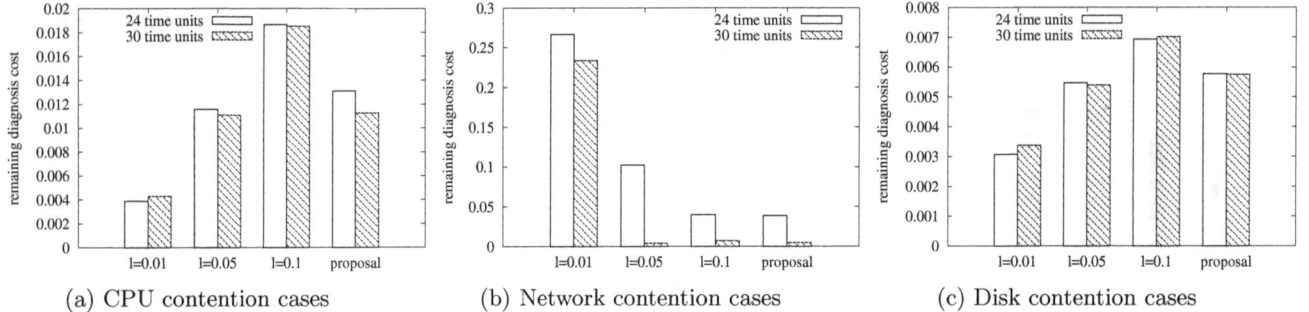

(a) CPU contention cases

(b) Network contention cases

(c) Disk contention cases

Figure 10: Effect of analysis time period length

when application performance increases at 11 through 24 time units, these three metrics increase at the subset of these time units, and they have respective correlations of 0.358, 0.478, and 0.577. Then, *vm1* is not captured by the Pearson correlation with significance levels 0.01 and 0.05, and *vm2* is also not captured by that with significance level of 0.01. Our framework, on the other hand, can capture these metrics because they have valid association rules. *vm1*, *vm2*, and *vm3* have confidence measures of 1.000, 1.000, 0.889 and support measures that correspond to 0.214, 0.357, and 0.571. Their discretizing thresholds have the same value 0.0 because that maximizes the support measure.

Our framework, however, captures some obvious false positives. Figure 13 plots the examples of false positive metrics. These metrics have negative correlations with the application performance. For example, the *vm4* metric has a confidence of 0.818, a support of 0.643, and a discretizing threshold of $4.19e^{+06}$. They do not indicate the cause of performance bottlenecks because if they indicate the cause, the *read bytes/sec* metrics of virtual disks should increase during the performance anomaly period. We inferred that these metrics, which had negative correlations, indicated VMs that suffered from degraded performance. If so, these metrics also bring to light quite useful information for cloud administrators.

5. DISCUSSION

We evaluated our framework and found that it worked well even when short periods of application performance data were obtained, which we discussed in Section 3. This feature and its model-less design will provide excellent adaptation for dynamic application revisions in the cloud. However, there were some limitations in our framework.

First, our framework only works when the cause of a per-

formance anomaly is a resource bottleneck in the cloud and the bottleneck is created by VMs. Some performance problems are brought about by anomalous host servers and hypervisors or faults on physical equipment (e.g., switches and storage). These kinds of causes can be inferred from text log data (e.g., error and warning messages) obtained from the hypervisor logs or SNMP trap data, which are managed by the cloud administrator. Those kinds of causes can be inferred with higher accuracy and coverage by using the text log data. However, no performance bottlenecks caused by VMs remain in any text logs. Therefore, our framework only focused on resolving that issue.

Second, our framework did not pinpoint the causes of performance anomalies. It required some supports from users because the results still contained some false positives. These false positives are often unavoidable because some metrics are correlated with application performance by chance. Users have to investigate the results to remove these false positives. Even though our framework was expected to reduces the cost of investigations as was explained in Section 3, the verification of the cost estimation still remains for future work.

Third, our framework needs to obtain application performance data from application administrators, who have to include performance anomaly periods. Therefore, performance anomalies have to be detected by them. They should detect performance anomalies by directly monitoring application performance such as response times or throughput because model-based or training-based approaches are not efficient for the detections in highly dynamic applications.

Finally, we will discuss the computational cost of our framework. Our framework has scalable features because the computation of correlations and association rules are independent between metrics. This means that the computation

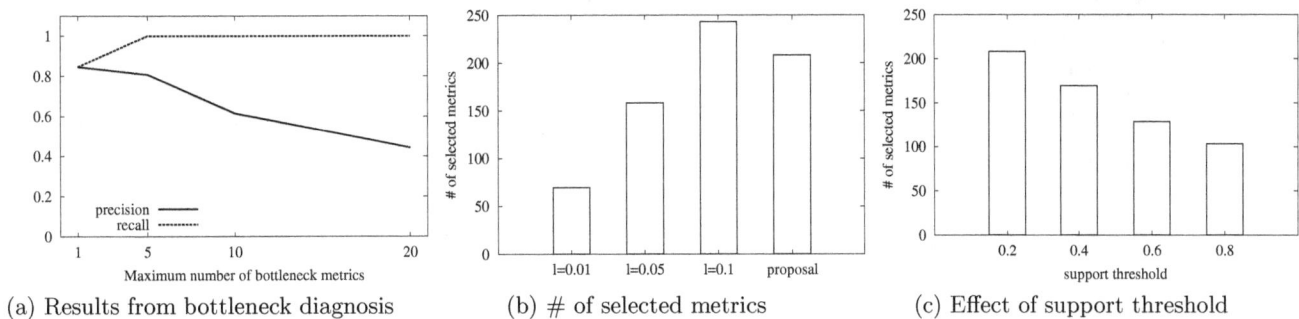

(a) Results from bottleneck diagnosis   (b) # of selected metrics   (c) Effect of support threshold

Figure 11: Results from testing on real data set

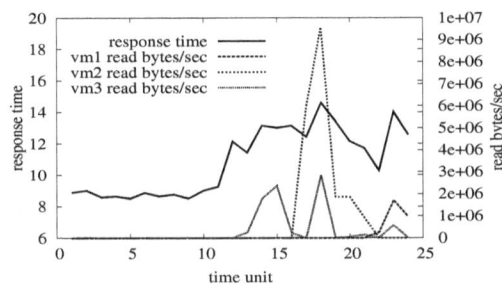

Figure 12: Examples of cause metrics on real data set

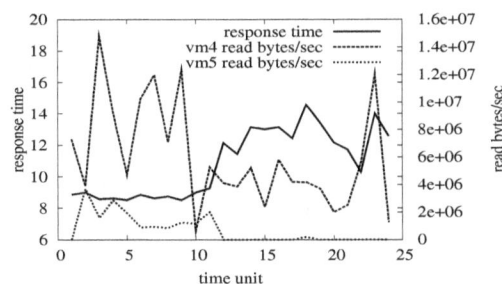

Figure 13: Examples of false positives on real data set

can be parallelized. The computational cost of our framework mainly depends on the length of analysis time periods. The computational order, especially in Algorithm 2, is two powers of the analysis period length. That may cause long computation times when excessive application performance data are input.

6. RELATED WORK

There is much existing work that has investigated the performance problems in the cloud. This section introduces some of these that are related to our work.

Several researches [3, 9, 16, 24, 30] have diagnosed the cause of performance problems by identifying which performance issues that occurred in the past were the same or closest to current performance issues. Fu et al.'s approach [9] characterizes the past performance issues based on class association rules (CARs) and identifies the metrics that will help to pinpoint the root cause of a newly encountered issue by using the CARs. These approaches require training data set and only work for recurring performance problems.

Some applications in the cloud bring about stable correlating behavior between metrics when the applications are sound. Some researchers [2, 14, 22] diagnosed the cause of

performance problems by finding breaks in the stable correlating behavior between metrics. Breaks in correlations provides a chance to predict severe performance issues and information on cause diagnosis. These approaches focus on the issues with applications, and not on resource contentions between applications in the cloud.

Xiong et al. [29] proposed a model-driven framework that builds regression models to diagnose performance bottlenecks in applications. Their approach infers the bottleneck point (e.g., a VM or a host) and its attribute (e.g., CPU or memory) from the regression models, which is similar to our bottleneck diagnosis. However, this framework does not infer VMs that created performance bottlenecks.

Resource contentions in the cloud have been addressed as problems in VM placements or scheduling in some researches [6, 7, 19]. Do et al. [7] used canonical correlation analysis (CCA) for application profiling which enables to identify dominant factors in application performance and predict resource usage of applications. The profiling helps the decisions of VM placements. These approaches assume the applications are sound and do not address application performance anomalies that are caused by anomalous resource usage in some applications.

7. CONCLUSION

We proposed an analysis framework for the cause diagnosis of application performance anomalies. Our framework captured cause metrics that had temporal correlations with application performance, which is difficult for methods that use the standard Pearson correlation, by finding association rules between each metric and application performance.

We confirmed the efficiency of our framework through our experimental evaluation. The experimental results revealed that it achieved better performance even with few application performance data. In addition to the evaluation of accuracy and coverage, we also evaluated our framework from the perspective of the remaining diagnosis cost of our framework users. Our framework was expected to reduce the cost by 84.8% at most because it reduced many false negatives. We also adapted our framework to a real data set obtained from a VDI service. The results from the real data set indicated that some cause metrics have temporal correlations, which are difficult to be captured by the Pearson correlation.

Our framework should be efficient for agile application developments and revisions because it does not involve any performance models. It works as soon as the performance data are obtained even when an application is newly developed and revised, and even when few data are obtained.

8. REFERENCES

[1] R. Agrawal, T. Imieliński, and A. Swami. Mining association rules between sets of items in large databases. In *ACM SIGMOD Record*, volume 22, pages 207–216. ACM, 1993.

[2] A.-F. Antonescu and T. Braun. Improving management of distributed services using correlations and predictions in SLA-driven cloud computing systems. In *Network Operations and Management Symposium (NOMS), 2014 IEEE*, pages 1–8. IEEE, 2014.

[3] P. Bodik, M. Goldszmidt, A. Fox, D. B. Woodard, and H. Andersen. Fingerprinting the datacenter: automated classification of performance crises. In *Proceedings of the 5th European conference on Computer systems*, pages 111–124. ACM, 2010.

[4] C. Clark, K. Fraser, S. Hand, J. G. Hansen, E. Jul, C. Limpach, I. Pratt, and A. Warfield. Live migration of virtual machines. In *Proceedings of the 2nd conference on Symposium on Networked Systems Design & Implementation-Volume 2*, pages 273–286. USENIX Association, 2005.

[5] D. J. Dean, H. Nguyen, and X. Gu. Ubl: unsupervised behavior learning for predicting performance anomalies in virtualized cloud systems. In *Proceedings of the 9th international conference on Autonomic computing*, pages 191–200. ACM, 2012.

[6] C. Delimitrou and C. Kozyrakis. Paragon: QoS-aware scheduling for heterogeneous datacenters. *ACM SIGARCH Computer Architecture News*, 41:77–88, 2013.

[7] A. V. Do, J. Chen, C. Wang, Y. C. Lee, A. Y. Zomaya, and B. B. Zhou. Profiling applications for virtual machine placement in clouds. In *Cloud Computing (CLOUD), 2011 IEEE International Conference on*, pages 660–667. IEEE, 2011.

[8] elastic. https://www.elastic.co/.

[9] Q. Fu, J.-G. Lou, Q.-W. Lin, R. Ding, D. Zhang, Z. Ye, and T. Xie. Performance issue diagnosis for online service systems. In *Reliable Distributed Systems (SRDS), 2012 IEEE 31st Symposium on*, pages 273–278. IEEE, 2012.

[10] M. Hahsler, B. Grün, and K. Hornik. arules-A computational environment for mining association rules and frequent item sets. *Journal of Statistical Software*, 14(i15), 2005.

[11] T. Hobfeld, R. Schatz, M. Varela, and C. Timmerer. Challenges of QoE management for cloud applications. *Communications Magazine, IEEE*, 50(4):28–36, 2012.

[12] Hypothesis Testing (Critical value approach). https://onlinecourses.science.psu.edu/statprogram/node/137.

[13] Iperf. http://sourceforge.net/projects/iperf/.

[14] H. Kang, H. Chen, and G. Jiang. Peerwatch: a fault detection and diagnosis tool for virtualized consolidation systems. In *Proceedings of the 7th international conference on Autonomic computing*, pages 119–128. ACM, 2010.

[15] Y. Koh, R. Knauerhase, P. Brett, M. Bowman, Z. Wen, and C. Pu. An analysis of performance interference effects in virtual environments. In *Performance Analysis of Systems and Software, 2007.*

ISPASS 2007. IEEE International Symposium on pages 200–209. IEEE, 2007.

[16] M.-H. Lim, J.-G. Lou, H. Zhang, Q. Fu, A. B. J. Teoh, Q. Lin, R. Ding, and D. Zhang. Identifying recurrent and unknown performance issues. In *Data Mining (ICDM), 2014 IEEE International Conference on*, pages 320–329. IEEE, 2014.

[17] C. Luo, J.-G. Lou, Q. Lin, Q. Fu, R. Ding, D. Zhang, and Z. Wang. Correlating events with time series for incident diagnosis. In *Proceedings of the 20th ACM SIGKDD international conference on Knowledge discovery and data mining*, pages 1583–1592. ACM, 2014.

[18] Microsoft Hyper-V Server 2012 R2. https://technet.microsoft.com/en-us/library/hh833684.aspx.

[19] R. Nathuji, A. Kansal, and A. Ghaffarkhah. Q-clouds: managing performance interference effects for QoS-aware clouds. In *Proceedings of the 5th European conference on Computer systems*, pages 237–250. ACM, 2010.

[20] Overview of Windows Performance Monitor. https://technet.microsoft.com/en-us/library/cc749154.aspx.

[21] E. Ries. *The lean startup: How today's entrepreneurs use continuous innovation to create radically successful businesses*. Random House LLC, 2011.

[22] B. P. Sharma, P. Jayachandran, A. Verma, and C. R. Das. CloudPD: problem determination and diagnosis in shared dynamic clouds. In *Dependable Systems and Networks (DSN), 2013 43rd Annual IEEE/IFIP International Conference on*, pages 1–12. IEEE, 2013.

[23] Stress. http://people.seas.harvard.edu/~apw/stress/.

[24] Y. Tan, H. Nguyen, Z. Shen, X. Gu, C. Venkatramani, and D. Rajan. Prepare: Predictive performance anomaly prevention for virtualized cloud systems. In *Distributed Computing Systems (ICDCS), 2012 IEEE 32nd International Conference on*, pages 285–294. IEEE, 2012.

[25] C. Wang, S. P. Kavulya, J. Tan, L. Hu, M. Kutare, M. Kasick, K. Schwan, P. Narasimhan, and R. Gandhi. Performance troubleshooting in data centers: an annotated bibliography? *ACM SIGOPS Operating Systems Review*, 47(3):50–62, 2013.

[26] Windows Management Instrumentation Overview. https://technet.microsoft.com/en-us/library/dn265977.aspx.

[27] WMI client. http://pkgs.org/download/wmi.

[28] WMI Performance. http://wutils.com/wmi/root/cimv2/win32_perfrawdata/#Childs.

[29] P. Xiong, C. Pu, X. Zhu, and R. Griffith. vPerfGuard: an automated model-driven framework for application performance diagnosis in consolidated cloud environments. In *Proceedings of the 4th ACM/SPEC International Conference on Performance Engineering*, pages 271–282. ACM, 2013.

[30] Q. Zhu, T. Tung, and Q. Xie. Automatic fault diagnosis in cloud infrastructure. In *Cloud Computing Technology and Science (CloudCom), 2013 IEEE 5th International Conference on*, volume 1, pages 467–474. IEEE, 2013.

Beyond Energy-Efficiency: Evaluating Green Datacenter Applications for Energy-Agility

Supreeth Subramanya, Zain Mustafa, David Irwin, and Prashant Shenoy
University of Massachusetts Amherst

ABSTRACT

Computing researchers have long focused on improving energy-efficiency under the implicit assumption that all energy is created equal. Yet, this assumption is actually incorrect: energy's cost and carbon footprint vary substantially over time. As a result, consuming energy inefficiently when it is cheap and clean may sometimes be preferable to consuming it efficiently when it is expensive and dirty. Green datacenters adapt their energy usage to optimize for such variations, as reflected in changing electricity prices or renewable energy output. Thus, we introduce *energy-agility* as a new metric to evaluate green datacenter applications.

To illustrate fundamental tradeoffs in energy-agile design, we develop GreenSort, a distributed sorting system optimized for energy-agility. GreenSort is representative of the long-running, massively-parallel, data-intensive tasks that are common in datacenters and amenable to delays from power variations. Our results demonstrate the importance of energy-agile design when considering the benefits of using variable power. For example, we show that GreenSort requires 31% more time and energy to complete when power varies based on real-time electricity prices versus when it is constant. Thus, in this case, real-time prices should be at least 31% lower than fixed prices to warrant using them.

1. INTRODUCTION

Energy-efficiency, which is defined as the amount of work, i.e., computation and I/O, done per joule of energy, has long been considered a "first class" metric for evaluating computer system performance. Energy-efficiency has become particularly important for warehouse-scale datacenter facilities, since a greater energy-efficiency reduces these facilities' large electric bills (assuming that utilities charge a constant price for energy over time) and their carbon emissions (assuming all their energy is created from carbon-based sources). Energy-efficiency for warehouse-scale datacenter facilities remains a highly active research area, as their size and number continues to grow to satisfy the demand for cloud-based

ICPE'16, March 12 - 18, 2016, Delft, Netherlands

© 2016 Copyright held by the owner/author(s). Publication rights licensed to ACM.
ISBN 978-1-4503-4080-9/16/03...$15.00

DOI: http://dx.doi.org/10.1145/2851553.2851556

services. The power requirements of the largest datacenters now exceed 100 megawatts (MW) [12], and, collectively, they are estimated to consume 1.7-2.2% of U.S. electricity [20].

To reduce energy's carbon footprint and cost, green datacenters are experimenting with generating clean power locally from renewables [5, 13] and participating in utility demand response (DR) programs [24, 40], which offer reduced rates if consumers respond to signals (often in the form of higher electricity prices) to curtail their energy usage. Both renewable energy and DR introduce the potential for variations in available power. As others have noted [19, 40], data centers are well-equipped to respond to such variations, since they i) already include sophisticated power management functions, which are remotely programmable and capable of varying power usage over a wide dynamic range, and ii) often execute non-interactive batch applications that are tolerant to some delays due to power shortages.

Unfortunately, as a metric, energy-efficiency does not account for variations in energy's cost and carbon footprint, but rather implicitly assumes i) that all energy is created equal and ii) that it is available in unlimited quantities at any time. These assumptions are not correct: in reality, all energy is not created equal—its cost and carbon footprint vary over time depending on the mix of generators used to to create it—and, as the reliance on intermittent renewable energy increases, it may not be available in unlimited quantities. Thus, just because a system is highly energy-efficient does not necessarily mean that its cost and carbon footprint is lower than a highly inefficient one. That is, an inefficient system that consumes energy at the "right" times, e.g., when renewable energy is plentiful or electricity prices are low, could be cleaner and cheaper than an energy-efficient system that uses energy at the "wrong" times, e.g., when renewable energy is scarce or electricity prices are high.

Thus, energy-efficiency is not the right metric to quantify the performance of green datacenter applications that adapt to a variable supply of power. To properly evaluate these applications, we propose a new metric, which we call *energy-agility*. While energy-efficiency is a measure of work done per joule of energy consumed by a platform, energy-agility is a measure of work done per joule of energy available to a platform, which may vary dynamically over time.

Thus, as a metric, energy-agility captures the salient characteristics above that i) energy is not always available in unlimited quantities at any time, and ii) the availability of energy may vary over time. Note that the energy available to a platform is independent of how much energy it actually consumes. Whereas energy-efficiency only depends on how much energy a platform consumes to perform a given amount of work, energy-agility applies a "use it or lose it" property to energy that incentivizes platforms to use as much energy as possible, as efficiently as possible, when it is available, or else waste it. Thus, energy-agility depends on how much energy is available to a platform to perform a given amount of work, regardless of the amount of energy that it is able to productively consume. Energy-agility captures the basic characteristic that electricity's supply and demand must be balanced at all times, and the only way to not waste unused energy is to explicitly store it for later use.

To illustrate fundamental tradeoffs in energy-agile design, we develop GreenSort, a distributed sorting system optimized for energy-agility. GreenSort is representative of the long-running, massively-parallel, data-intensive tasks that are common in datacenters and amenable to delays from power variations. Unlike short batch jobs, which a scheduler may simply defer until power is plentiful or cheap enough to complete them [16, 17], such "big data" applications must adapt their execution in real time by continuously modifying their energy usage to not exceed the available supply. In developing GreenSort, we make the following contributions.

Energy-Agility Metric. We introduce energy-agility as a new performance metric that is distinct from energy-efficiency, and motivate its importance in evaluating emerging green datacenter applications that use variable power.

GreenSort Design. We design multiple GreenSort variants to illustrate fundamental tradeoffs in energy-agile design of a prototypical datacenter application. Each variant is defined by a power management policy that performs well for a particular area of the design space, which is defined by the power signal characteristics, power state transition latencies, energy storage capacities, input data size, etc.

Implementation and Evaluation. We implement and evaluate GreenSort to quantify its performance. We demonstrate the extent to which power variations increase the time and energy to complete a task, which highlights the importance of energy-agile design when considering the benefits of using local renewables or participating in DR programs. For example, we show that GreenSort requires 31% more time and energy to complete when power varies based on real-time electricity prices versus when it is constant. Thus, in this case, real-time prices should be at least 31% lower on average than fixed prices to warrant opting into using them.

2. BACKGROUND

There has been a variety of recent research on designing green datacenter applications that adapt to power variations due to changing electricity prices or renewable energy output. For example, prior research has focused on optimizing a variety of system components for variable power, including distributed caches [32], file systems [33], virtual machines [23, 34], and batch schedulers [3, 15, 16, 17, 21]. Prior research has also investigated the use of energy storage to dampen or eliminate the effect of power variations [18, 39].

Since energy-efficiency alone does not capture the benefits of using variable power, the metric these systems measure themselves against is generally the cost of energy, as variable electricity prices are typically lower, on average, than flat prices. Thus, the "performance" benefit of prior systems is largely dependent on the absolute price of electricity: the more variable the prices, or the wider their range, the more cost savings are possible. However, energy's cost is not a sound basis for evaluation, since energy prices vary significantly by region, by time, and based on external factors. Rather, cost is only useful for assessing the monetary benefits of employing a particular system or approach at a specific point in time. Energy-agility provides a metric independent of cost to evaluate and compare the performance of such systems, similar to how the absolute cost of energy has (and should have) no bearing on a system's energy-efficiency.

2.1 Energy-agility Definition

Formally, energy-agility is a measure of the amount of work W, e.g., computation and I/O, done by a system given a *power signal* $P(t)$ that dictates an energy cap the system must adhere to over each interval $(t - \tau, t]$ for some interval length τ. Energy-agility does not dictate the underlying reason for the power variations, e.g., due to DR signals, fluctuations in renewable generation, changes in electricity prices, etc., or the characteristics of $P(t)$, which may differ widely depending on the scenario. We discuss different types of emerging scenarios and power signals in §2.2. As we show, $P(t)$'s characteristics—its average magnitude, variance, and range—have a significant influence on energy-agility design. Also, note that energy-agility incorporates energy-efficiency, and is not entirely orthogonal to it: to maximize energy-agility, at any given time t, an application is always incentivized to use the available energy as efficiently as possible.

For sorting, energy-agility translates to the number of records sorted per joule of energy *made available to* a platform over its running time, whereas energy-efficiency is the number of records sorted per joule of energy *consumed by* a platform over its running time. Thus, to complete a given amount of work, a greater energy-agility translates into a shorter running time and the need for less aggregate energy to be made available. The value τ derives from the minimum energy storage capacity necessary to enforce a platform's maximum energy cap over each τ. We assume $\tau > 0$, since platforms require some minimal energy storage capacity, as they cannot respond instantaneously to changes in power due to inherent latencies in transitioning power states. Due to energy's "use it or lose it" property, our definition dictates that application's waste any energy they cannot immediately use or store. Since storing energy incurs inverter and conversion losses, we assume an application loses a fraction L of any energy stored beyond the next interval τ. A typical value of L for lithium-ion or lead-acid batteries is 0.2.

The primary intent of energy-agility as a metric is to enable systems designers to reason about the effect of power variations on application performance. Intuitively, a more stochastic $P(t)$ increases an application's running time and, thus, the aggregate energy it requires to perform a given amount of work. As a result, even if variable energy is cheaper per kilowatt-hour (kWh), an application may not be cheaper overall to execute with variable power if it must run longer and consume more energy to complete.

Of course, the more energy storage capacity available, the more an application can dampen any power variations. Unfortunately, energy storage is highly expensive. Thus, an application that achieves the same performance using little or no energy storage, e.g., by adapting its power usage in real time, is preferable to one that uses significant energy storage. Ideally, systems would perform the same regardless of the characteristics of $P(t)$; that is, they would perform the same amount of work for a given amount of available

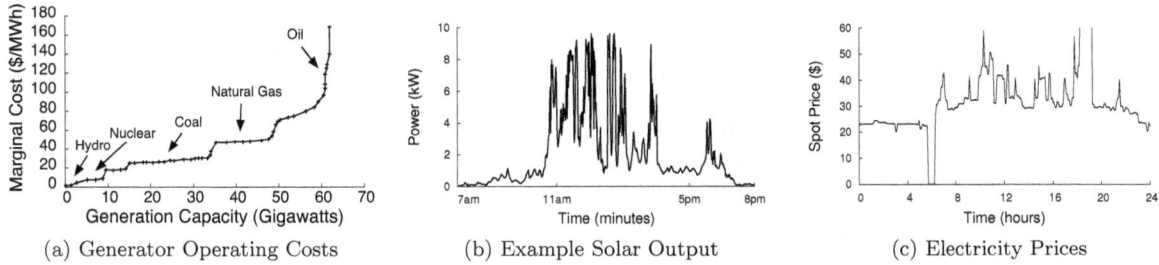

| (a) Generator Operating Costs | (b) Example Solar Output | (c) Electricity Prices |

Figure 1: The use of heterogeneous generators with different marginal costs (a) and the rising penetration of intermittent renewable energy sources (b) cause fluctuations in electricity's price every few minutes (c).

energy over time, regardless of how it varies. In practice, however, systems are not ideal: they require non-trivial latencies to toggle between numerous power states to cap their energy usage, which incurs overhead and affects application performance. Thus, quantifying the performance overhead caused by adapting to variable power is important in assessing the benefits of both energy storage and using variable power relative to its cost.

2.2 Emerging Scenarios

The motivation for energy-agility ultimately derives from the fact that all energy is *not* created equal [36]: instead, it derives from a heterogeneous mix of generators with different fuel costs, carbon emissions, and operational characteristics. For example, while solar and wind farms have variable energy output over time, they have no associated fuel costs or carbon emissions. Thus, consuming energy when renewables are generating it results in less carbon emissions than consuming it when they are not generating it. As another example, the "peaking" generators that utilities dispatch to satisfy transient demand peaks have much higher emissions and fuel costs (>10x [11]) than the baseload generators they continuously operate. Figure 1 illustrates the point by showing the disparity in marginal cost of operating various types of generators and the rapid fluctuations possible with renewable energy, which both contribute to large energy price fluctuations over time.[1] Such fluctuations are expected to intensify as renewable penetration increases in the grid.

Prior work on energy-efficient computing largely ignores how energy is actually generated in the electric grid. This is due, in part, because i) renewable energy is only now becoming a viable alternative to carbon-based energy sources and ii) utilities have historically masked variations in energy's cost and carbon footprint from consumers by charging them a fixed price for energy over time. However, there are now numerous examples of data centers using energy from local or nearby large-scale solar and wind farms [5, 13] with the most prominent example being Apple's new iCloud data center, which includes a 20MW co-located solar farm [5]. These facilities may need to vary their power usage based on renewable generation if they cannot make up the difference from other sources, e.g., energy storage or the grid.

In addition, with the mass deployment of smart electric meters, which record and transmit electricity usage in real-time at fine-granularities, e.g., every 15 minutes or less, utilities are beginning to implement more sophisticated pricing and DR mechanisms. For example, many consumers

may now opt into real-time pricing, where electricity prices change every few minutes based on supply and demand. For large industrial energy consumers like datacenters, there are other DR programs available. For example, datacenters might act as *load resources* (LRs) in the grid's ancillary service markets [40]. Somewhat like a "reverse generator," the grid controls LRs to modulate their energy "generation" by signaling them to increase and decrease power usage over time. LRs receive compensation based on their ramp time (the time required to effect a change in power) and capacity (the range of power over which they have control). Datacenters are well-suited to act as LRs, since they have short ramp times and high capacities. The grid will require more LR capacity, as renewable penetration rises, to balance an, increasingly stochastic, supply with demand.

Each of the scenarios above introduce *hard power caps* dictated by $P(t)$ with potentially different characteristics, e.g., solar power is likely more periodic and less stochastic than wind power. In contrast, prior work that is cost-oriented often assumes only soft power caps, such that, while using power may be undesirable because it is expensive or "dirty," it is always available if necessary at some price [16, 17, 24].

2.3 Power Capping Mechanisms

A prerequisite for capping energy over each τ is a mechanism to cap server power. A variety of active [7, 14] and inactive [32, 37] power capping mechanisms exist, although the specific mechanisms available are platform-dependent.

Active power capping bounds power usage by reducing servers' performance without deactivating them; it primarily focuses on reducing CPU power usage using a combination of dynamic voltage and frequency scaling (DVFS) and transitioning CPUs into low-power idle modes, e.g., ACPI's C-states. Recent research applies similar concepts to actively cap memory power [9]. While active power capping incurs low overhead, since transitions between active power states are rapid, e.g., milliseconds or less, it generally is able to lower server power usage to at most 50% of peak power [4, 37]. Unfortunately, active power capping does not reduce the power usage of other power-hungry components, such as the motherboard, disk, network card, etc. The narrow power range offered by active power capping is one reason reducing the power usage of interactive applications with low latency requirements has proven challenging [25, 27].

Inactive power capping bounds power usage by transitioning servers to an inactive power state, which deactivates a server by cutting power to nearly every component and reducing server power to near zero. For example, ACPI's Suspend-to-RAM (S3) state preserves DRAM memory state, but turns off all other components, while its Suspend-to-

---

[1]Data for Figure 1(a) is from [11]; (b) is from a 10kW home solar installation; and (c) is from a representative week in the New England five-minute spot market.

187

Disk (S4) state writes memory state to disk before turning off the server. Prior work argues that inactive power capping is more efficient than using active power capping, assuming low (<100ms) transition latencies [26]. Unfortunately, while the precise time to transition to and from an inactive power state is platform- and OS-dependent, it typically takes between tens of seconds (for S3) to a few minutes (for S4) [1, 32]. A server cluster may implement inactive power capping by either transitioning some subset of servers to the inactive state based on the available power [37], or by "blinking" servers between active and inactive states in tandem to cap power over short intervals [32]. With the latter approach, servers are inactive for some fraction of each interval based on the average power available over the interval.

In this paper, we assume that both active power capping and inactive power capping, either via deactivating or blinking servers, are available, although the precise power range and overhead of each mechanism varies widely by platform.

3. GREENSORT DESIGN

To illustrate tradeoffs in designing energy-agile applications, we develop GreenSort, a distributed sorting system optimized for energy-agility. The primary constraint Green-Sort adds to prior sorting applications is the power signal $P(t)$ that dictates an energy cap the sorting platform must adhere to over each interval $(t - \tau, t]$. We choose distributed sorting to illustrate energy-agile design for a variety of reasons. Most importantly, sorting lies at the core of many "big data" frameworks, including MapReduce [8]. Sorting is also a particularly demanding workload, as it requires shuffling its entire input dataset across all servers. A similar all-to-all shuffling phase is the bottleneck for many data-intensive applications. Finally, sorting stresses a mix of system resources: it is largely I/O-bound, but also requires non-trivial CPU time and, if distributed, network bandwidth.

GreenSort follows in a long line of sorting systems that highlight various aspects of systems design, such as I/O performance, energy-efficiency, and cost, to motivate researchers to improve upon them [35]. Insights from these prior sorting systems have influenced a broad range of systems. For instance, the notion of balance in JouleSort [31] influenced the design of energy-efficient key-value stores [4], MapReduce platforms [29], and databases [38].

Since, from an algorithmic standpoint, sorting is a solved problem with well-established tight performance bounds [2], results from prior sorting systems [31, 30, 35] primarily represent a measure of a hardware platform's capabilities combined with various software optimizations that best exploit those capabilities. GreenSort differs from prior systems in this respect: while it also represents a measure of hardware capabilities, particularly the set of available platform power states and the time to transition between them, it alters the sorting problem due to the use of inactive power states. Thus, in addition to minimizing I/O, as in conventional external sorting, GreenSort must also consider the effect of transitioning power states, which are time-consuming and may periodically render some data unavailable.

To understand how designing for energy-agility affects distributed sorting, we first summarize the design of conventional distributed sorting on an always-on cluster with no power constraints (§3.1). We then present multiple Green-Sort design variants that optimize the conventional design for energy-agility under different conditions, as defined by

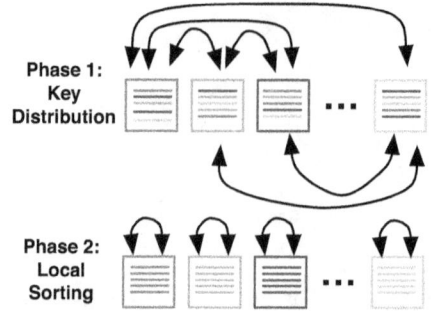

Figure 2: A conventional distributed sort has a key distribution phase followed by a local sorting phase.

the power signal, power state transition latencies, energy storage capacities, input data size, etc (§3.2).

3.1 Conventional Distributed Sorting

We assume a cluster with N homogeneous servers, each with some local storage to hold the unsorted input and the sorted output. We also assume the input data is significantly larger than the collective memory of the N servers, requiring the servers to store the input and output on disk. Thus, sort performance is largely dictated by storage I/O bandwidth, where an efficient distributed sorting implementation generally uses a large number of local disks in parallel, typically more than one per server. Initially, each server stores a random set of $1/N$th of the input records to be sorted.

Without loss of generality, we assume Indy sorting, where i) each record is 100 bytes where the first ten bytes serve as a random key and ii) keys are initially distributed uniformly across servers, mitigating the need for a separate key sampling phase to determine the distribution. The sort application divides the key space across the N servers, such that, when sorted, keys in the range $[(i-1)/N, i/N)$ are in sorted order on the ith node. The input and output are stored as files on the N servers, with the concatenation of the output files representing the sorted input.

We use the term *worker* to refer to the sorting application process on each server. Given the setup above, a conventional distributed sort may proceed in two phases [30], as depicted in Figure 2: a key distribution phase followed by a local sorting phase. During key distribution, each worker i) sequentially reads the list of keys from disk and sends them to their destination server and ii) receives keys destined for it from other workers and writes them to disk. Workers divide their key space across multiple separate files, such that each file stores a separate sub-range of the keys and fits into the workers' memory. Once each worker finishes key distribution, it locally sorts keys by reading each file into memory, sorting it with a textbook in-memory sorting algorithm, and writing it back to disk. Since our input is much larger than the servers' memory, the amount of disk I/O dictates sorting performance. This conventional design uses the theoretical minimum number of I/Os with two reads and two writes per record [2]: each record is read once at its origin server, written to a file at its destination, read again for in-memory sorting, and finally written again to the final sorted output.

3.2 Energy-Agile Distributed Sorting

As power rises and falls, an energy-agile sort must determine how to best divide the available power among the servers to finish the sort as fast as possible. Thus, in addition to workers, GreenSort also employs a *power manager* that partitions available power every τ across servers using the mechanisms from §2.3. For GreenSort's design, we focus on the key distribution phase, since workers must coordinate with each other to exchange keys during this phase. Thus, degrading the performance of one worker, e.g, via power capping, during key distribution affects the performance of the other workers. In contrast, since the local sorting phase is embarrassingly parallel, the power manager need only ensure that it allocates power to workers with work remaining.

The power manager may be able to satisfy small drops in power using active power capping without affecting the sorting application's operation. When using active power capping, the optimal strategy is to maintain *balanced progress* across all $\binom{N}{2}$ pairs of workers exchanging keys by dividing the available power equally across servers, such that each server has the same power cap. Since all workers must exchange keys with all other workers, if any worker is slower than the others, due to being in a lower power state, it will create a bottleneck by slowing the progress of all workers in distributing keys. However, significant drops in power require the sorting application to use inactive power capping, which renders some servers unavailable. Deactivating servers complicates the key distribution phase, since it disrupts the all-to-all data shuffle among servers. Below, we describe policies for capping power by deactivating servers in priority order and by blinking, as well as their advantages and disadvantages when shuffling keys across servers.

3.2.1 Priority Policy

A straightforward approach to inactive power capping is to activate and deactivate a subset of servers in priority order based on the available power. This policy uses the available power $P(t)$ each interval τ to activate servers such that it minimizes "wasted" power, while enforcing an equal allocation of power across servers to maintain balance.

We consider power as wasted if it is either below a server's minimum active power or above its maximum power necessary to run an uncapped worker. In the former case, the server has only enough power to turn on and can do no useful work, while, in the latter case, the server cannot make use of any power above some maximum value. For example, assume a power cap of 400W for a cluster of five servers, which have a minimum idle power of 50W and a maximum power of 150W when executing an uncapped worker. In this case, activating five servers at 80W wastes the most power (250W), leaving the least for useful work (150W), while activating three servers at 133W wastes the least power (150W), leaving the most for useful work (250W).

After determining how many to activate, the policy must then determine which servers to activate. To do this, the policy prioritizes servers (arbitrarily) from $1 \ldots N$, such that the highest priority server not yet completed with the key distribution phase always remains active, assuming enough power to activate one server. As power increases, the policy activates the next highest priority server(s) not yet finished exchanging keys with the current highest priority server. Likewise, as power decreases, the policy deactivates the lowest priority active servers. Once the highest priority server finishes its key distribution phase by exchanging keys with all other servers, the policy deactivates it and places it at the lowest priority, resulting in a new highest priority server.

Note that the priority policy incurs minimal overhead to transition servers to the inactive power state, since it only transitions a server to an inactive power state if i) power increases or decreases or ii) a server finishes the first phase and has no more work to do. In fact, assuming only constant power to activate k of n servers, the minimum number of transitions is $\sum_{i=0}^{\lceil \frac{n}{k-1} - 1 \rceil} (n - i(k - 1)) = O(n^2/k)$. This amount represents a lower bound on the minimum number of transitions if power varies, since increases and decreases in power may force additional transitions. Thus, for variable power, the minimum number of transitions is a function of the power signal's variability. However, as we discuss below, minimizing the transitions comes at a cost: it results in imbalanced progress and requires significant modifications to the conventional distributed sorting implementation.

Imbalanced Progress. Unlike with active power capping, the priority policy results in maximum imbalance in the progress of exchanging keys, since high priority servers finish before low priority servers have begun. While such imbalance is not an issue for constant power, since any work done is useful, it results in wasted work if power is highly variable.

To understand why, consider a simple scenario where there is enough constant power to activate two servers at all times. In this case, the priority policy cycles through each distinct combination of servers, while, each time, fully completing each pairs' key exchange. As a result, at any given time, some set of two-server combinations has completely finished exchanging keys, while the remaining two-server combinations have not yet started. Thus, if it takes $T_{exchange}$ time for two servers to finish exchanging keys *and* if power ever increases to full power (sufficient to power all N servers), then it will still take $T_{exchange}$ time to complete the key exchange for the remaining two-server combinations not yet started. Thus, any work completed at low power levels is effectively wasted: *had no servers exchanged keys until the time of the power increase, the total running time of the key distribution phase ($T_{exchange}$) would be the same.* Since the priority policy is not balanced, the remaining running time of the key distribution phase is always based on the lowest-priority pair of servers with the least progress.

Sorting Modifications. The priority policy also requires modifications to the sorting application, since servers are no longer always concurrently active. As a result, each worker running on an active server must maintain an up-to-date list of the other active workers to ensure that it only attempts to exchange keys with those workers. Of course, since input records are stored in random order on disk, an active worker that is sequentially reading records to distribute to other active workers will invariably read records destined for currently inactive servers. While a worker may be able to briefly cache these records in memory, it will ultimately have to write them to disk if the destination server does not become active in the near future.

Thus, rather than completing the key distribution phase using a single sequential scan of keys per server (with one read per key), the priority policy requires multiple passes over the keys. Even if, on the first scan, the worker stores a pointer to the location of an inactive servers' discarded keys on disk, such that only one additional read per key is required once a server becomes active, these subsequent reads will result in random, rather than sequential, I/O. Since random I/O bandwidth is generally two orders of magnitude slower than sequential I/O bandwidth, this significantly de-

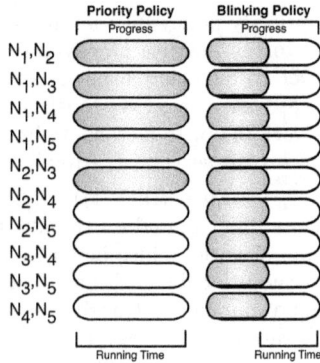

Figure 3: The priority policy causes imbalance during key distribution, while blinking does not.

grades performance of an I/O-bound distributed sort.

We address this problem in the priority policy by pre-partitioning the keys on each server before distributing them, such that the keys for a particular destination server are stored sequentially on disk. This pre-partitioning step incurs more I/O (one additional read and write) to improve performance by eliminating the need to waste I/Os by reading and discarding records destined to inactive servers. However, by sequentially storing keys destined for the same server, it increases the amount of sequential I/O during the key distribution phase.

3.2.2 Blinking Policy

The blinking policy differs from the priority policy by dividing each interval τ into an active and inactive period based on the energy available over τ [32]. For example, if τ is two minutes, the average power available over τ is 100W, and each server's active power cap is 200W, then the active and inactive periods would each be one minute. In addition, since blinking concurrently activates all servers each interval τ, it introduces a choice in setting a server's active power cap and the length of the active period each τ. To reduce wasted power, we set the active power cap to the minimum cap possible that maximizes utilization of the CPU (its most energy-efficient setting). Thus, blinking makes minimal use of active power capping, especially on balanced platforms that fully utilize the CPU. Relative to the priority policy, blinking has three main benefits.

Few Application Modifications. Unlike with the priority policy above, blinking requires few changes to the sorting application, itself, although the power manager must compute the active and inactive periods every τ and synchronously toggle servers to and from the inactive power state in tandem. The conventional distributed sort requires no changes, since inactive state transitions preserve memory state and, as before, all servers are always concurrently active

Maintains Balanced Progress. As when using active power capping, blinking servers maintains balanced progress across all workers, such that all workers distribute keys to other workers at the same rate. Since no single worker is ever a bottleneck to finishing the key distribution phase, unlike the priority policy, blinking behaves similarly regardless of the variability of the power signal. Figure 3 depicts this advantage of the blinking policy over the priority policy, where $N = 5$ and power increases to full power at the mid-point of execution. Each bar represents the progress in exchanging keys between each of the $\binom{5}{2} = 10$ distinct pairs of servers.

In this case, the figure shows that, on reaching full power, the balanced blinking policy will finish in half the time of the priority policy modulo transition overheads. Notice that imbalanced progress is only an issue if power changes, i.e., drops and then rises again, since the bottleneck only presents itself when power increases. Thus, the priority policy becomes progressively worse as power becomes more variable.

Capable of Low Power Caps. While the priority policy needs at least enough power to activate two servers during key distribution to perform useful work, the blinking policy is able to perform useful work with much less power simply by reducing the length of its active interval.

Unfortunately, blinking also has drawbacks. Most importantly, some non-trivial portion of the active time each interval τ is wasted due to transitioning power states, which may take anywhere between a few seconds to multiple minutes depending on the platform. In addition, since transitions occur at a fixed interval, the number of transitions is based on an application's running time, rather the variability in the power signal. Finally, such frequent transitions may also degrade the reliability of mechanical disks.

3.2.3 Round-robin Policy

The blinking and priority policy, represent two extremes in the energy-agility design space captured by Table 1. The blinking policy works well with small input data (resulting a short running time), short transition latencies, highly variable power, and low average power, since it incurs frequent and costly inactive power state transitions but maintains balanced progress between each pair of servers. In contrast, the priority policy works well with larger input data (resulting in longer running times), long transition latencies, less variable power, and a higher average power, since it transitions to inactive power states less but results in imbalanced progress for variable power signals.

We introduce a round-robin priority policy to mind the gap between these two extremes. This policy behaves like the priority policy, in that it assigns priorities to servers $1 \ldots N$ and activates them in order. The primary difference is the round-robin policy defines a scheduling time slice t_{sched}, which sets the maximum time any server may be active. Once a server exhausts its time, the policy deactivates the server, sets it to the lowest priority, and then activates the next highest priority inactive server. With a long time slice, the round-robin policy behaves similarly to the priority policy (with few transitions but imbalanced progress), while with a short time slice, it approximates the blinking policy (with many transitions but balanced progress).

3.2.4 Performance Modeling

We model GreenSort's performance based on its salient characteristics: the running time T when using full power with all N available nodes active, the inactive power state transition latency d, the average number of active nodes k based on the power signal $P(t)$, the time for preprocessing data on a given node T_{pre}, and the blink interval τ. M then represents the number of power state transitions required by each policy. Based on these variables, we can define the running time of Greensort under each policy as follows.

$$T * \left(\frac{N}{k}\right) + T_{pre} * \left(\frac{N}{k}\right) + d * M \qquad (1)$$

Here, the first term represents the sort's running time when only k of N nodes are active on average, since run-

Policy	Running Time (T)	Transition Latency (d)	P(t) Variability	P(t) Average
Blinking	Low	Low	High	Low
Round-Robin	↕	↕	↕	↕
Priority	High	High	Low	High

Table 1: Qualitative attributes of a distributed sort that are amenable to the blinking and priority policies. The round-robin policy's configurable time slice minds the gap between the two policies.

ning time is a linear function of the number of active servers. The second term is the time spent preprocessing input data prior to key distribution. The last term is the overhead due to power state transitions over the running time. For the blinking policy, since there is no preprocessing and nodes transition every blink interval τ, $T_{pre} = 0$ and $M = \frac{T*(N/k)}{\tau}$.

For the priority policy, the preprocessing time is proportional to the size of the input data and the network/disk I/O throughput, such that $T_{pre} = g(DataSize, I/O - throughput)$. The number of transitions then has two components. First, the minimum number of transitions assuming k of N nodes are always active, and second, any additional transitions that may occur due to variations in the power signal $P(t)$. Thus, $M = \sum_{i=0}^{\lceil \frac{n}{k-1} - 1 \rceil} (n - i(k-1)) + f(P(t))$, where $f(P(t))$ represents the number of transitions due to variations in $P(t)$.

Given the GreenSort running time above, we can derive energy-agility (in records per joule) by computing the energy E available over the running time based on $P(t)$ and then dividing the work done (in terms of the number of sorted records) by E. Thus, the overhead terms in the equations above increase the energy E in the denominator, thereby decreasing the energy-agility. Note that the model above is general and applies to any task that involves a synchronized all-to-all communication phase across all servers. By contrast, an embarrassingly-parallel task that requires no synchronization across servers, where each server must perform the same amount of work, would have a running time of only $T*(\frac{N}{k}) + d*N/k$. Here, the first term is the same as above, while the second term simply represents the transition latency incurred every time a set of k servers completes its work and activates another set of k servers.

4. IMPLEMENTATION

Our GreenSort implementation includes one worker process per server and a centralized power manager, both written in C++. The workers coordinate to sort the input data, while the power manager implements the power management policies from the previous section. We briefly discuss the worker and power manager implementations below, along with a description of our hardware platform.

Workers. We model our worker implementation after TritonSort [30], which divides the work of each sorting phase into a series of pipelined multi-threaded stages connected via producer-consumer buffers. However, since our focus is on energy-agility and not energy-efficiency, we do not optimize our workers for the highest possible efficiency on our platform. We also implement the necessary functions for workers to interact with the power manager to pause and resume its operation and report its progress with respect to other workers. Workers also include any functions necessary to support the various policies, such as pre-partitioning keys before distributing them with the priority policy.

Power Manager. The power manger monitors both server power usage and the amount of available power every τ, and then caps power by either altering servers' active power caps or activating/deactivating them. Deactivating one or more servers is a two-phase process. First, the power manager informs all workers of the servers that it is planning to deactivate. The workers on servers remaining active cleanly finish sending any outstanding buffers to the deactivating servers, while the workers on soon-to-be inactive servers cleanly finish sending all outstanding buffers to all other workers. Once finished, all workers send an acknowledgement to the power manager. The power manager subsequently deactivates servers by pausing their activity, and then remotely transitioning the server to an inactive power state. A similar two-phase process occurs when activating one or more servers. To implement our priority-based policies, the power manager also periodically polls each worker to track its progress with respect to other workers.

Platform. Our experimental platform is a set of Dell PowerEdge R720 servers, each with 32 2GHz cores, 64GB memory, and a 4TB disk. Since our platform combines a single local disk with 32 cores, it is not particularly energy-efficient for data-intensive applications, as many of its cores are largely idle during a sorting run. In particular, due the presence of only a single local disk, the servers are unable to maintain pure sequential I/O during key distribution, even when all servers are active, as the disk must concurrently read keys it sends and write keys it receives. As a result, we configure each worker to use a remote disk on a "dummy" server, as if it were another local disk, to ensure sequential I/O during key distribution. Of course, this paper's goal and the focus of our evaluation is not to construct the most efficient hardware platform, but to illustrate fundamental tradeoffs in energy-agile design.

Our servers include an external out-of-band management card that permits remote i) monitoring of server power usage every second, ii) power cycling, and iii) control of active power capping. The server's active power capping mechanism enables the power manager to set the cap between 85W (near the minimum idle power) and 285W (near the peak power). Unfortunately, the only inactive power state supported is Suspend-to-Disk (S4). The power manager transitions the server to S4 by executing a command line program, and transitions it out of S4 by remotely turning it on. The time to transition into and out of S4 has a lower bound of ~90s due to a required series of pre-boot tests.

Since our servers do not support Suspend-to-RAM (S3), which combines short power state transitions (on the order of seconds) with low power usage (~5% peak power), they impose a high overhead. S3 support is uncommon in servers; in fact, Dell makes no server that supports S3 and includes support for out-of-band management (a necessity in a remotely-managed datacenter). Due to these limitations, our power manager emulates other transition latencies by sleeping for a pre-determined amount of time when pausing and resuming servers. In addition, while we have access

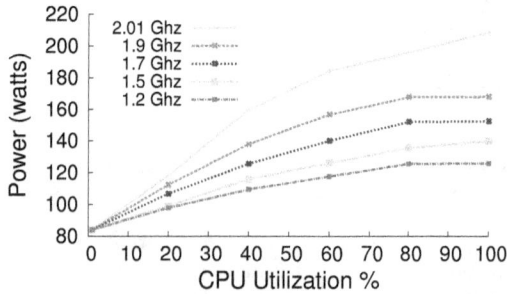

Figure 4: Power usage as a function of CPU utilization for each DVFS state on our servers.

to a shared cluster of 200 servers for experiments, we have only five dedicated servers that permit active power capping. Thus, in our evaluation, we use the cluster for experiments that focus on inactive power state transitions, and our dedicated servers for those that focus on active power capping.

5. EVALUATION

The goal of our evaluation is to use GreenSort to illustrate fundamental tradeoffs in the energy-agile design space. The design space is a function of many parameters, including the power signal characteristics, energy storage capacity, input data size, transition latency for inactive power states, etc. We first examine the limitations of using active power capping to satisfy power constraints to motivate the need for using inactive power states in our power management policies (§5.1). We then evaluate the use of inactive power states in each of our policy variants via microbenchmarks that alter the design parameters above in a controlled way to reveal their relative effect on performance (§5.2). Finally, we quantify the performance of each policy variant for real-world power traces on our platform (§5.3).

5.1 Limitations of Active Power Capping

Each of our servers permits setting an active power cap as low as 85W, which they enforce by throttling CPUs. Figure 4 shows the active power range of the servers' CPUs using DVFS, where the x-axis is the average CPU utilization across all cores (and where the network card and disk are idle). The graph shows that at 100% CPU utilization our servers' base power usage is 80W and their power usage in the highest DVFS state at 100% CPU utilization is near 215W, providing a 135W active power range for the CPU. The network interface card (NIC) and disk consume an additional 35W apiece when in use (at any utilization), resulting in an active power range (assuming any network and disk activity) of 150W to 285W. The server enforces active power caps below 150W by rapidly toggling CPUs between idle sleep modes (or C-states), which is similar, in principle, to blinking, although the C-state transitions are much faster (order of milliseconds or less).

Since our servers' CPU capacity is over-provisioned for data-intensive tasks like sorting, our workers only operate at 20% CPU utilization (averaged over all CPUs) in the lowest DVFS power state, which results in 95W CPU consumption and is already within ~15W of the platform's minimum, idle power state. Thus, the total server power, when including the NIC and disk, during key distribution is 165W. In practice, our platform has little room to use DVFS to cap power, and must use C-state throttling. Figure 5 shows the limita-

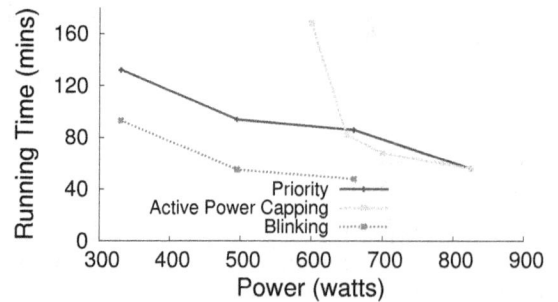

Figure 5: Sort run time for a constant power cap (on the x-axis) for different energy-agility policies.

tions of active power capping. Here, the x-axis represents a constant power cap, while the y-axis is the running time to sort 125GB of data across five servers. In one case, we keep all servers active and cap power using our server's built-in active power capping mechanism by dividing the available power equally across the five servers, while in the other case, we satisfy the cap by using either the priority policy or the blinking policy (assuming a transition latency of 30 seconds).

The figure shows that once the cap drops below 660W (or 165W per server) the performance from only keeping three servers (or less) concurrently active outperforms keeping all servers active and actively capping power below 165W. For example, a 550W cap enables three servers to be concurrently active at 183W, or five servers to be concurrently at 110W. The former case completes in 95 minutes, while the latter takes more than 23 hours. This result highlights the importance of minimizing wasted power when using active power capping. Both the priority and blinking policies generally make better use of the available power. Note that we plot running time rather than energy-agility here only for ease of exposition: since average power is the same for each run, running time is proportional to energy-agility.

By concentrating power on fewer servers, the priority and blinking policies incur much less overhead than using active power caps across five servers. The overhead arises for at least three reasons. First, the more servers that are active, the more base power is wasted. For example, consider a scenario where there are three servers active, each with an active power cap of 130W, with 105W left to distribute. Activating another server with an active power cap of 105W is less efficient than increasing the cap of the active servers by 35W each, since the new active server will only use 25W for productive work (since 80W is the base power), while the three active servers will use all 105W for productive work. Second, the more servers that are active, the more CPU and power is devoted to additional OS and worker software overhead. Finally, adhering to low power caps not satisfiable using DVFS incurs increasing overhead due to frequently toggling CPUs into and out of idle C-state sleep modes. In our experiment, with an active power cap of 110W, almost no power goes to doing productive work.

Other platforms beyond our own are similarly constrained in using active power capping. If our platform were to have ten disks, rather than one, the non-energy-proportional disks would dominate power usage, reducing the effectiveness of active CPU power states. Similarly, our platform could use a low-power CPU, such as an Intel Atom, to operate at a higher utilization when sorting. However, as before, the

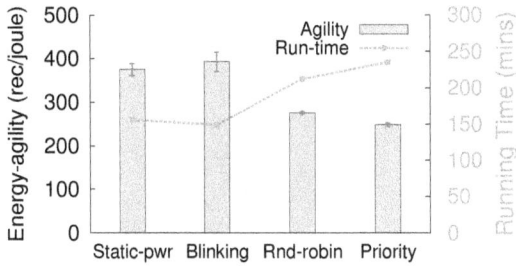

Figure 6: Baseline energy-agility (left y-axis) and running time (right y-axis) for each policy variant.

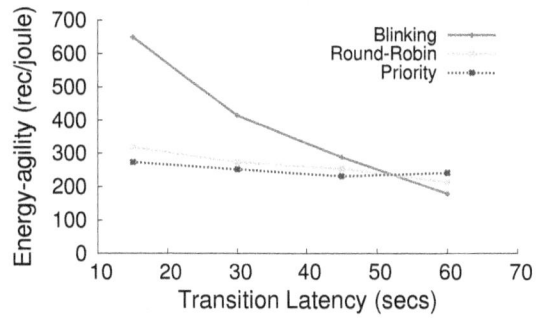

Figure 7: Transition latency's effect on agility.

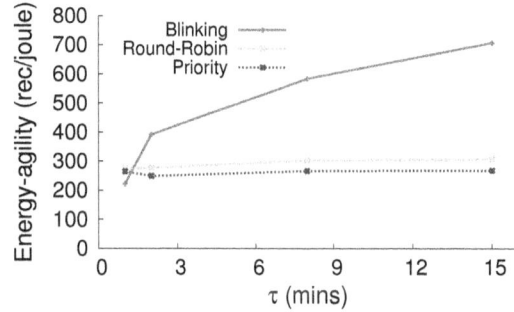

Figure 8: Power signal frequency's effect on agility (represented by energy storage capacity τ).

CPU's fraction of power would decrease relative to the non-energy-proportional disk and network card. While replacing mechanical disks with solid-state drives (SSDs) would lower the disks' fraction of power usage, low-power CPUs generally have many fewer active power states than high-power, multicore processors. For example, a low-power SuperMicro server in our lab, which has an Intel Atom processor, has no DVFS states and only a single C-state. Thus, while low-power servers may be energy-efficient, they often have a much narrower active power range than high-power servers. **Result:** *Active power capping has limited benefits for I/O-intensive applications that do not fully utilize the CPU.*

5.2 Microbenchmarks

Given active power capping's limitations, we use microbenchmarks to quantify the design space of GreenSort's policies that use inactive power capping. Our baseline microbenchmark sorts 500GB across 10 servers, assuming a latency of 30 seconds to transition to an inactive power state, and a minimum energy storage capacity capable of supporting $\tau = 2$min. We use a power signal that oscillates between 25% and 75% peak power every τ, and, for the round-robin policy, we set the time-slice to 2 minutes. From our baseline benchmark, we then vary each parameter to quantify its relative impact on performance among the policies.

To set context, Figure 6 shows the results in our baseline scenario, where the left y-axis indicates the energy-agility and the right y-axis indicates the running time of the sorting system. For each policy variant, the energy-agility (in records sorted per joule of energy available) is indicated by a bar and the running time by a point. We execute each run three times and plot the minimum, maximum, and average energy-agility, which is within 1% or less across each separate run. The graph shows that the blinking policy outperforms all other policies both in terms of being energy-agile and overall running time in our baseline case. Also, the round-robin priority policy performs better than the strict priority policy. For both the priority and round-robin policies we use the pre-partitioning optimization. Without it, the 500GB sort takes more than 20 hours to complete less than 15% of key distribution, reflecting the two orders of magnitude performance decrease from using purely random, rather than sequential, I/O. However, despite the optimization, the additional I/O required by the priority and round-robin policies in this case outweighs any additional transition overhead from the blinking policy.

Transition Latency. Figure 7 shows the performance of our three policies as the transition latency varies. The graph illustrates that the blinking policy outperforms the priority-

based policies by as much as 2X for short latencies. Even for long latencies of 45 seconds, blinking's performance remains better than priority despite the fact that blinking incurs the transition latency overhead once every $\tau = 2$ minutes. For example, with a latency of 45 seconds, the blinking policy spends 37.5% of its time simply transitioning power states. However, once the transition latency exceeds one minute, the priority policy outperforms blinking, as the overhead of transitioning begins to outweigh the benefit of blinking's fewer number of I/Os. As expected, the performance of the round-robin priority policy falls between the blinking and priority policies regardless of the latency.

Power Signal and Energy Storage. The frequency of variation in the power signal also affects performance. One way to alter the frequency is by changing the amount of minimum energy storage capacity, as represented by the length of τ. Figure 8 shows that the blinking policy's performance improves as energy storage capacity (and τ) increases from one to 15 minutes, since it reduces the frequency of blinking and its associated overhead. In contrast, energy storage does not significantly affect the priority or the round-robin policy, since they do not transition every interval τ.

We also alter the variability of the power signal without changing τ, as depicted in Figure 9. Here, the x-axis represents the length of each period of constant power, such that the power signal changes every x minutes; the higher x, the less variable the power signal. The graph shows the relative performance of the priority policy improves as the variability decreases (and the periods of constant power increase), since it reduces the impact of its imbalanced progress. In contrast, the power signal's variability does not improve the performance of blinking, since it maintains balanced progress and its transition overhead is independent of the variability.

Job Size. The length of a sorting run also affects the relative performance of the policies. While a longer running

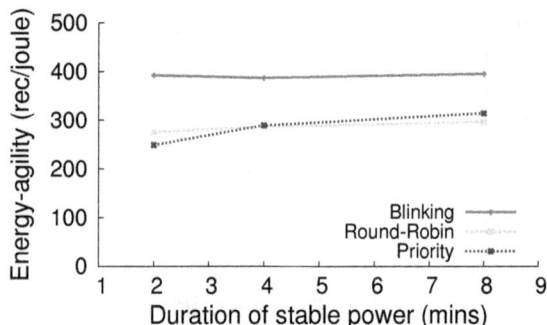

Figure 9: Power variability's effect on agility.

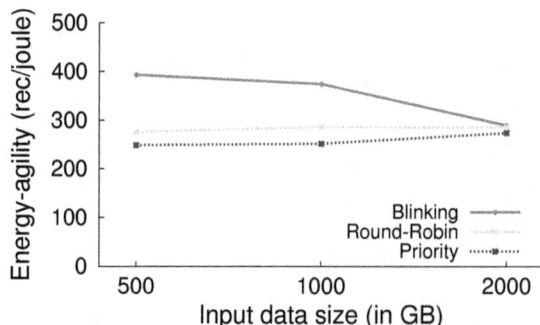

Figure 10: Input datasize's effect on agility.

time causes more transition overhead for the blinking policy, if the increase is due to fewer resources or a larger input data size, it also causes more additional I/O overhead for the priority policy. Figure 10 shows the results of increasing the input data size to sort in our baseline microbenchmark. The graph demonstrates that the larger the input data size the worse blinking (and round-robin) performs relative to the priority policy. For example, when sorting 500GB, blinking is 58% more agile, when sorting 1TB it is 48% more agile, and when sorting 2TB it is only 5% more agile. The worsening relative performance reflects the fact that blinking's transition overhead is a function of the running time, and not the variability of the power signal, as with the priority policy. Thus, as the running time becomes longer the transition overhead increasingly outweighs the additional I/O overhead due to the larger input data.

Result: *Energy-agile design is influenced by a variety of parameters, including a platform's transition latency, power signal characteristics, energy storage capacity, and job size.*

5.3 Real Power Signals

Finally, we evaluate our GreenSort policies on real power signals on our hardware platform to get a sense of performance for each policy in practice. Figure 11 shows the performance of each policy variant on the solar energy signal from Figure 1(b) and the electricity price signal from Figure 1(c). In the latter case, we set a fixed budget of 0.94¢ every five minutes for electricity (determined by the energy needed to power on five nodes at an average price of 3.27¢/kWh from our sample), which transforms the electricity price signal into a hard power cap. For comparison, we scale the solar and price traces such that they yield the same average power. In addition, we also compare our results with a uniformly random power signal and a static power signal equal to the average power of the solar and price signals. These experiments sort 1TB of data across 10 nodes.

In contrast to our microbenchmarks, the priority policy significantly outperforms the blinking policy (by more than 40% in each case). Since our actual platform has a transition latency of 90s, it restricts the blinking policy to utilizing the server for a maximum of 30s for each τ=120s cycle. As expected, the static power signal performs best since it makes maximum use of the priority policy to minimize transitions. We can compare each variable signal with this static signal to get a sense of how variations ultimately impact the running time and the energy-agility of the sorting system.

We define the energy-agility factor as the ratio of energy required to finish a sort under static power to the energy required to finish the same sort under a variable power, whose

average is same as that of the static power. For example, the uniformly random signal yields an energy-agility factor of 0.37 for the blinking policy, 0.53 for the round-robin policy, and 0.65 for the priority policy. That is, sorting under a constant power consumes only 37% of the energy provided to the blinking policy under a varying power, or 65% of the energy provided to the priority policy under a varying power. The trend is slightly worse for the blinking policy under the solar and spot price signals, since these signals are not uniformly random but have correlated periods of extended inactivity. The priority policy is 2X more agile than the blinking policy both under solar and spot price signals. We see that despite exceeding the two-read-two-write limit of distributed sorting, the priority and round-robin policies fare better than the blinking policy owing to the high transition overhead of our platform. In terms of energy agility factor, for the solar and price signals, respectively, the blinking policy yields 0.35 and 0.32, the priority policy yields 0.78 and 0.69, and the round-robin policy yields 0.71 and 0.67.

Result: *Since variations in power increase the time and energy to complete a task, energy-agile design is important when considering the benefits of using renewable energy sources or participating in demand response programs. As one example from above, sorting under a stable power will only consume 69% of the energy required by the best Green-Sort policy (priority in this case), when the power varies based on real-time electricity prices. Thus, in this case, real-time prices should be at least 31% lower than fixed prices to warrant opting into using them.*

6. RELATED WORK

Energy-agility is related to energy-proportionality [6] in that it also benefits from energy-proportional servers capable of precisely varying their power usage over a wide active power range. However, a perfectly energy-proportional server would not necessarily optimize energy-agility, as energy-proportionality only dictates that server power usage increases linearly with utilization, regardless of the energy-efficiency at a particular utilization level. In contrast, energy-agility incorporates both energy-efficiency and the ability to rapidly adapt power usage over a wide dynamic power range. In addition, unlike energy-proportionality, energy-agility is power-driven, rather than workload-driven. While energy-proportionality applies directly to web applications and batch schedulers, where the workload intensity varies over time based on user request volume, it is not applicable to long-running parallel tasks, such as distributed sorting, with no variance in the workload. Thus, recent work on energy-efficiency focuses on designing balanced systems

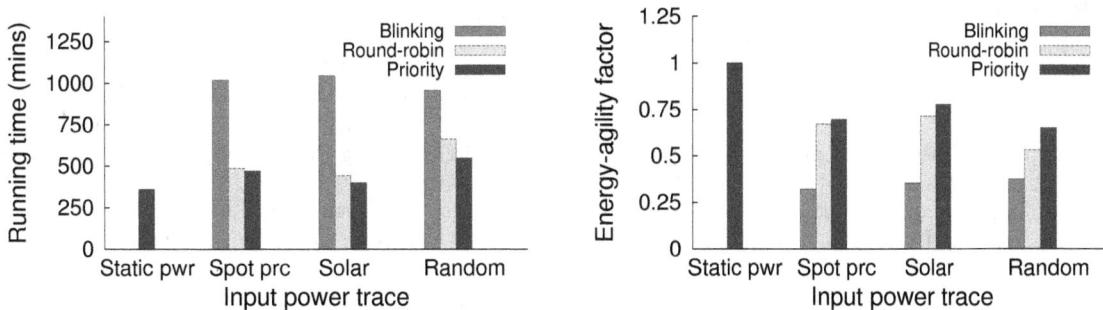

Figure 11: Performance on real power signals showing the effect on (a) running time and (b) agility.

that optimize peak performance per watt, e.g., at 100% utilization [4, 30, 31]. In contrast, energy-agility encourages applications to operate efficiently at all utilization levels.

Prior work on enforcing soft power caps generally focuses on time-shifting data center energy usage via energy storage [18, 39], workload scheduling [16, 17], or both [15] to reduce energy costs. This group of work exploits temporal and spatial variations in electricity prices to minimize costs without violating applications' quality-of-service (QoS) requirements, e.g., job deadlines or response latency requirements. In contrast, our work is not cost-oriented, but instead introduces energy-agility as a cost-independent metric to quantify an application's ability to adapt to variable power. Optimizing energy-agility is important for long-running delay-tolerant tasks, since adapting their power usage to available power is less expensive than masking power variations with energy storage [18, 39]. Long-running tasks are also less amenable to scheduling policies than short tasks, which may simply be deferred until power is cheap or plentiful [16,'17].

There has been much less prior work on adapting systems to dynamically-changing hard power caps. While a variety of power capping mechanisms exist for individual servers, these mechanisms ignore the inter-node dependencies that affect performance in distributed applications [7, 14, 22]. Thus, prior work focuses on regulating power using simplistic workloads, e.g., compute-intensive batch jobs with few data dependencies, that readily permit time-shifting workload to satisfy power caps [24]. Finally, the only prior work we are aware of that accounts for inter-node dependencies when capping power focuses on interactive services, e.g., a distributed memory cache [32] and file system [33], and not the delay-tolerant jobs that are most amenable to demand-side management. However, we show that a similar blinking abstraction applies to these workloads, albeit differently than with interactive workloads.

7. CONCLUSION

This paper introduces energy-agility as a metric to evaluate green datacenter applications that adapt to power variations, and then design GreenSort to illustrate fundamental tradeoffs in energy-agile design. While we focus on sorting, we believe our experience in designing GreenSort reveals some general lessons for energy-agile design that are applicable to a broader range of data-intensive applications, such as MapReduce [8]. We summarize these lessons below.
Inactive Power Capping is Useful, Despite its Overhead. Prior work largely focuses on active power capping [10, 25, 27, 28], since inactive power capping is not appropriate for all workloads. For example, online data-intensive (OLDI) workloads may need immediate access to data stored on any server at any time, and, thus, cannot incur the transition latency associated with inactive power capping [25, 27]. In contrast, for data-intensive, parallel batch jobs, such as sorting, we show that inactive power capping is much more efficient than using active power capping because it concentrates more power on doing useful work. This useful work offsets the transition overhead associated with inactive power capping. In addition, while applications could employ active power capping to satisfy caps as low as ~50% peak power, we find setting active caps, which slow down server progress to activate additional servers, is not beneficial due to high server idle power.
Blinking is Preferred when Coordination is Necessary. While blinking incurs high latencies at regular short intervals, it does not affect an application's pattern of remote I/O, since servers are always concurrently active for some fraction of each interval. In contrast, any policy that deactivates some fraction of servers has the potential to alter applications' remote I/O patterns and degrade performance, e.g., by changing sequential I/O to random I/O, since servers may not always be concurrently active. In addition to sorting, MapReduce and other "big data" platforms also have frequent periods of large-scale coordinated data movement. In contrast, the priority policy works well for embarrassingly parallel tasks that require no coordination, since it minimizes transition overheads.
When Deactivating Servers, Organizing Data is Beneficial. As the transition latency increases, the useful work performed when blinking decreases. At some point, minimizing this overhead by deactivating servers, as per our priority policy, becomes attractive. Since naïvely deactivating servers affects I/O patterns, actively organizing the data in conjunction with the power management policy is important. As we show, incurring additional I/O upfront to maximize sequential I/O later can improve performance. Since today's server platforms do not support ACPI's S3 state, their transition latencies warrant this approach.

Our results suggest that energy-agile design is a potentially rich area for future research, especially given the diminishing returns on improving energy-efficiency and the increasing use of variable power. Our work shows the importance of energy-agility in quantifying how power variations increase the time and energy to complete a task.

Acknowledgements. This research is funded by the National Science Foundation under grants 1422245, 1405826, and 1339839.

8. REFERENCES

[1] Y. Agarwal, S. Hodges, R. Chandra, J. Scott, P. Bahl, and R. Gupta. Somniloquy: Augmenting Network Interfaces to Reduce PC Energy Usage. In *NSDI*, April 2009.

[2] A. Aggarwal and J. Vitter. The Input/Output Complexity of Sorting and Related Problems. 1988.

[3] B. Aksanli, J. Venkatesh, L. Zhang, and T. Rosing. Utilizing Green Energy Prediction to Schedule Mixed Batch and Service Jobs in Data Centers. In *HotPower*, October 2011.

[4] D. Andersen, J. Franklin, M. Kaminsky, A. Phanishayee, L. Tan, and V. Vasudevan. FAWN: A Fast Array of Wimpy Nodes. In *SOSP*, October 2009.

[5] Apple and the Environment. http://www.apple.com/environment/renewable-energy/, Accessed November 2013.

[6] L. Barroso and U. Hölzle. The Case for Energy-Proportional Computing. *Computer*, 40(12), December 2007.

[7] R. Cochran, C. Hankendi, A. Coskun, and S. Reda. Pack & Cap: Adaptive DVFS and Thread Packing Under Power Caps. In *MICRO*, December 2011.

[8] J. Dean and S. Ghemawat. MapReduce: Simplified Data Processing on Large Clusters. In *OSDI*, December 2004.

[9] Q. Deng, D. Meisner, L. Ramos, T. Wenisch, and R. Bianchini. MemScale: Active Low-Power Modes for Main Memory. In *ASPLOS*, March 2011.

[10] X. Fan, W. Weber, and L. Barroso. Power Provisioning for a Warehouse-sized Computer. In *ISCA*, June 2007.

[11] State of the Markets Report 2008. Technical report, Federal Energy Regulatory Commission, August 2009.

[12] K. Fehrenbacher. The Era of the 100MW Data Center. In *Gigaom*, January 31 2012.

[13] K. Finley. Facebook Says its New Data Center Will Run Entirely on Wind. In *Wired*, November 13th 2013.

[14] A. Gandhi, M. Harchol-Balter, R. Das, J. Kephart, and C. Lefurgy. Power Capping via Forced Idleness. In *Weed*, June 2009.

[15] I. Goiri, W. Katsak, K. Le, T. Nguyen, and R. Bianchini. Parasol and GreenSwitch: Managing Datacenters Powered by Renewable Energy. In *ASPLOS*, March 2013.

[16] I. Goiri, K. Le, M. Haque, R. Beauchea, T. Nguyen, J. Guitart, J. Torres, and R. Bianchini. GreenSlot: Scheduling Energy Consumption in Green Datacenters. In *SC*, April 2011.

[17] I. Goiri, K. Le, T. Nguyen, J. Guitart, J. Torres, and R. Bianchini. GreenHadoop: Leveraging Green Energy in Data-Processing Frameworks. In *EuroSys*, 2012.

[18] S. Govindan, A. Sivasubramaniam, and B. Urgaonkar. Benefits and Limitations of Tapping into Stored Energy for Datacenters. In *ISCA*, June 2011.

[19] D. Irwin, N. Sharma, and P. Shenoy. Towards Continuous Policy-driven Demand Respone in Data Centers. In *GreenNets*, August 2011.

[20] J. Koomey. Growth in Data Center Electricity Use 2005 to 2010. In *Analytics Press*, Oakland, California, August 2011.

[21] A. Krioukov, C. Goebel, S. Alspaugh, Y. Chen, D. Culler, and R. Katz. Integrating Renewable Energy Using Data Analytics Systems: Challenges and Opportunities. In *Bulletin of the IEEE Computer Society Technical Committee*, March 2011.

[22] C. Lefurgy, X. Wang, and M. Ware. Server-level Power Control. In *ICAC*, February 2007.

[23] C. Li, A. Qouneh, and T. Li. iSwitch: Coordinating and Optimizing Renewable Energy Powered Server Clusters. In *ISCA*, June 2012.

[24] Z. Liu, A. Wierman, Y. Chen, B. Razon, and N. Chen. Data Center Demand Response: Avoiding the Coincident Peak via Workload Shifting and Local Generation. 70(10), 2013.

[25] D. Lo, L. Cheng, R. Govindaraju, L. Barroso, and C. Kozyrakis. Towards Energy Proportionality for Large-scale Latency-Critical Workloads. In *ISCA*, June 2014.

[26] D. Meisner, B. T. Gold, and T. F. Wenisch. PowerNap: Eliminating Server Idle Power. In *ASPLOS*, March 2009.

[27] D. Meisner, C. Sadler, L. Barroso, W. Weber, and T. Wenisch. Power Management of On-line Data Intensive Services. In *ISCA*, June 2011.

[28] P. Ranganathan, P. Leech, D. Irwin, and J. Chase. Ensemble-level Power Management for Dense Blade Servers. In *ISCA*, June 2006.

[29] A. Rasmussen, M. Conley, R. Kapoor, V. Lam, G. Porter, and A. Vahdat. Themis: An I/O-Efficient MapReduce. In *SoCC*, October 2012.

[30] A. Rasmussen, G. Porter, M. Conley, H. Madhyasthay, R. Mysore, A. Pucher, and A. Vahdat. TritonSort: A Balanced and Energy-Efficient Large-Scale Sorting System. *TOCS*, 31(1), February 2013.

[31] S. Rivoire, M. Shah, and P. Ranganathan. JouleSort: A Balanced Energy-Efficient Benchmark. In *SIGMOD*, June 2007.

[32] N. Sharma, S. Barker, D. Irwin, and P. Shenoy. Blink: Managing Server Clusters on Intermittent Power. In *ASPLOS*, March 2011.

[33] N. Sharma, S. Barker, D. Irwin, and P. Shenoy. A Distributed File System for Intermittent Power. In *IGCC*, June 2013.

[34] R. Singh, D. Irwin, P. Shenoy, and K. Ramakrishnan. Yank: Enabling Green Data Centers to Pull the Plug. In *NSDI*, April 2013.

[35] Sort Benchmark Home Page. http://sortbenchmark.org/, Accessed July 2014.

[36] C. Stewart and K. Shen. Some Joules Are More Precious Than Others: Managing Renewable Energy in the Datacenter. In *HotPower*, October 2009.

[37] N. Tolia, Z. Wang, M. Marwah, C. Bash, P. Ranganathan, and X. Zhu. Delivering Energy Proportionality with Non-Energy-Proportional Systems: Optimizing the Ensemble. In *HotPower*, December 2008.

[38] D. Tsirogiannis, S. Harizopoulos, and M. A. Shah. Analyzing the Energy Efficiency of a Database Server. In *SIGMOD*, June 2010.

[39] R. Urgaonkar, B. Urgaonkar, M. Neely, and A. Sivasubramaniam. Optimal Power Cost Management Using Stored Energy in Data Centers. In *SIGMETRICS*, March 2011.

[40] A. Wierman, Z. Liu, I. Liu, and H. Mohsenian-Rad. Opportunities and Challenges for Data Center Demand Response. In *IGCC*, June 2014.

Tackling Latency via Replication in Distributed Systems

Zhan Qiu
Department of Computing
Imperial College London
London, UK
zhan.qiu11@imperial.ac.uk

Juan F. Pérez
School of Mathematics and
Statistics
University of Melbourne
Melbourne, Australia
juan.perez@unimelb.edu.au

Peter G. Harrison
Department of Computing
Imperial College London
London, UK
pgh@imperial.ac.uk

ABSTRACT

Consistently high reliability and low latency are twin requirements common to many forms of distributed processing; for example, server farms and mirrored storage access. To address them, we consider replication of requests with canceling – i.e. initiate multiple concurrent replicas of a request and use the first successful result returned, canceling all outstanding replicas. This scheme has been studied recently, but mostly for systems with a single central queue, while server farms exploit distributed resources for scalability and robustness. We develop an approximate stochastic model to determine the response-time distribution in a system with distributed queues, and compare its performance against its centralized counterpart. Validation against simulation indicates that our model is accurate for not only the mean response time but also its percentiles, which are particularly relevant for deadline-driven applications. Further, we show that in the distributed set-up, replication with canceling has the potential to reduce response times, even at relatively high utilization. We also find that it offers response times close to those of the centralized system, especially at medium-to-high request reliability. These findings support the use of replication with canceling as an effective mechanism for both fault- and delay-tolerance.

CCS Concepts

•**Mathematics of computing** → **Markov processes;**
•**Computer systems organization** → **Reliability; Redundancy;**

Keywords

Latency-tolerance; Fault-tolerance; Matrix-analytic methods; Response time distribution; Distributed system

1. INTRODUCTION

Server farms have been widely deployed, fueled by the ever-growing demand for computation-intensive and massive-

ICPE'16, March 12-18, 2016, Delft, Netherlands

© 2016 ACM. ISBN 978-1-4503-4080-9/16/03. . . $15.00

DOI: http://dx.doi.org/10.1145/2851553.2851562

data operations, to provide cost-effective and high-performance services for organizations such as Amazon, Google, IBM, Microsoft or Yahoo, by exploiting large collections of inexpensive resources [12]. Although much effort has been spent on optimizing the performance of server farms [4, 6, 12], requests unavoidably experience failures or delays, degrading the offered quality of service. Application-level failures, which are the focus of this paper, can arise for reasons such as communication errors [13], timeouts of resources with constrained availability, or outputs exceeding latency requirements. Further, low latency, especially keeping the tail of the latency distribution short, can be difficult to achieve in the face of contention for shared resources, queueing, or hardware problems [3]. For instance, experiments at Google show that a system where each request typically responds in 1ms, has a 99th percentile latency of 10ms [3].

In this context, request replication with canceling has been proposed as a powerful mechanism to improve reliability, and to limit the response time, by initiating multiple copies of a request on separate servers and using the result from the copy that completes first [3, 16, 15]. To limit the additional load introduced by replicas, upon the successful completion of any replica, all other outstanding replicas are canceled immediately. This is achieved by allowing servers to share updates on the status of their replicas. Three key points make this approach viable. First, most clusters today are highly underutilized, with the average utilization of major data center servers being around 18% [21]; Second, much of the energy consumption is wasted at low utilization, e.g., even an idle server consumes about 65% of the power of its peak consumption [5]. Thus it is cost-effective to use these idling resources for running extra replicas of requests. Third, concurrent replication can handle unpredictable failures, as it is sufficient that one of the replicas succeeds. Further, replication has the potential to reduce both the mean and the tail of the response-time distribution, since the overall latency becomes the minimum of the delays across all the replicas [16, 15].

Although replication has been studied recently, most works focus on systems with a single central queue, while server farms exploit distributed resources for scalability and robustness. Clearly, the centralized set-up offers better performance, but the distributed set-up provides more flexibility, and in some systems holding a central queue is not possible, such as when accessing mirrored storage systems in parallel. To better understand the performance of these two settings, in this paper we develop an approximate stochastic model to determine the response-time distribution in a system with

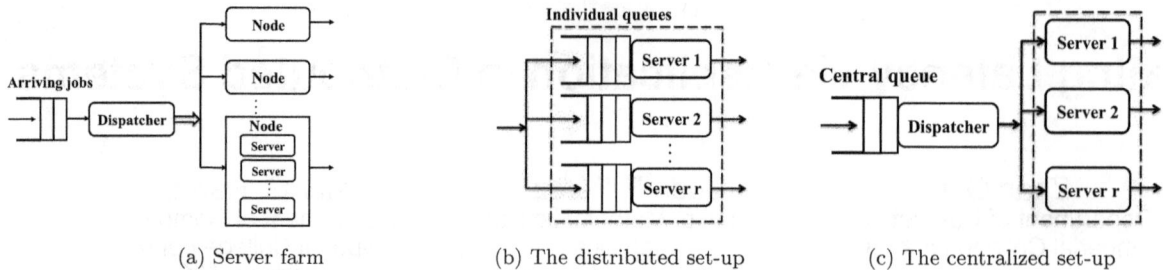

(a) Server farm   (b) The distributed set-up   (c) The centralized set-up

Figure 1: Reference models. A server farm is split in nodes, as in (a). The set-up of each node can be as in (b) or in (c).

distributed queues, and compare its performance against its centralized counterpart. Although approximate, validation results indicate that our model is accurate for not only the mean response time but also its percentiles, a significant advantage since mean response time guarantees are not sufficient in many situations, in particular for deadline-driven applications. Further, we show that in the distributed set-up replication with canceling has the potential to reduce the response times, even under relatively high utilization. The effect of replication actually depends on the specific response time percentile evaluated, especially in low-reliability scenarios. This effect is more uniform across the response-time distribution when the request reliability is high or when more than one extra replica is adopted. We also find that the distributed set-up offers response times close to those of the centralized system, especially under a medium to high request reliability. These findings support the use of replication with canceling as an effective mechanism for both fault- and delay-tolerance in server farms.

2. RELATED WORK

Concurrent replication has been considered recently as a means to reduce latency in interactive and deadline-driven applications [1, 3, 7, 16, 15, 10, 17, 20, 22]. For instance, [1] observes in trace-driven experiments that processing replicas concurrently is effective in mitigating the effect of latency. [17] explores concurrent replication with canceling as a tail-tolerant approach, and shows that this approach can be powerful in keeping the response time tail short. In particular, [7, 15, 16] evaluate the effectiveness of this approach in improving the reliability for systems with request failures. These works focus on the case with *one extra replica* for systems made up of two distributed queues [7], synchronous parallel processors [15], and for computing clusters with a central queue [16]. Among them, [16] determines the response-time distribution, while [7, 15] focus on the mean response time only. In this paper, we obtain the response-time *distribution* for systems with *both* distributed and centralized queues, and implementing *multiple* extra replicas.

3. BACKGROUND

3.1 Reference model

We consider a server farm consisting of a number of distributed, homogeneous, and independent servers, which process incoming requests with rate μ. Requests in service are subject to failures, with failure rate α. Both service and failure times are exponentially distributed, a common assumption in reliability engineering [24, 23]. In case of a failure, the request currently in service is lost, but the server

itself is not affected, and continues to serve the next request that enters. To improve the reliability, $r-1$ extra replicas are adopted for each arriving request, i.e., a total of r replicas of a request are submitted to the system. In particular, $r=1$ represents the case where no replication is adopted. We denote by *request/replica* the original request or any of its replicas, and by *job* the set of replicas for a single request, where the number of replicas r is also referred to as the *replication level*. To reduce unnecessary workload, the system replies with the result from whichever replica completes successfully first, and immediately cancels all the other outstanding replicas in the same job. The canceling overhead, which is the time to remove all the replicas in a job, is assumed to be negligible.

To take advantage of replication, we consider a server farm consisting of n distributed computing nodes, and a central scheduler that assigns jobs to the processing nodes in a round-robin or random fashion, as shown in Figure 1(a). Each node is composed of r independent and statistically identical processing servers, thus serving a job of replication level r, by processing each of the r replicas in each server. The node can have distributed queues in front of each of the servers, as shown in Figure 1(b), where each of the r replicas joins the end of the queue at one of the r servers, and is processed with first-come first-served (FCFS) scheduling. An alternative setup is to have a centralized queue in front of all the servers, as shown in Figure 1(c), where all the replicas of the incoming requests form a single queue in the order of arrival and join the next server that becomes available with FCFS scheduling. For both models, when one of the replicas in a job completes service successfully, it immediately cancels all its outstanding siblings, *either waiting or in service*. However, if a replica fails during service, it leaves the system without influencing its siblings. Analyzing the model with distributed queues is far more challenging than its counterpart with a single centralized queue, as the synchronized arrivals of replicas to all queues correlates their dynamics, while individual replicas fail asynchronously. We therefore develop an approximated model in Section 4 to cope with this setup, capturing the dynamics introduced by failures, replication and canceling. To analyze the performance of a system with a central queue, we extend our previous work [16], where we considered the $r=2$ case, to handle any number of replicas, i.e., $r \geq 2$, as described in Section 6.

3.2 Preliminaries

Motivated by the high variability and auto-correlation observed in inter-arrival times in computer systems, we utilize Markovian arrival processes (MAP) to represent inter-arrival times [14]. The continuous-time MAP [11] is a marked Markov chain (MC) with generator matrix $D = D_0 + D_1$, where matrices D_0 and D_1 hold the rates associated to transitions without and with arrivals. The diagonal entries of D_0 hold the total exit rate in each state, such that $(D_0+D_1)\mathbf{1}=\mathbf{0}$. We denote this process as $\mathrm{MAP}(m_a, D_0, D_1)$, where m_a is the number of states in the underlying MC, or arrival phases. The mean arrival rate is $\lambda = \boldsymbol{d}D_1\mathbf{1}$, where $\mathbf{1}$ is a column vector of ones, and $\boldsymbol{d}$ is the stationary distribution of the underlying MC, i.e. $\boldsymbol{d}D=0$ and $\boldsymbol{d}\mathbf{1}=1$. In the special case of Poisson arrivals, $D_0=-\lambda$ and $D_1=\lambda$.

In the next sections we show that the *job* processing time follows a Phase-type (PH) distribution, whose parameters depend on the overall system state. A PH random variable X represents the absorption time in an MC with $n+1$ states, where the states $\{1,\ldots,n\}$ are transient and state 0 is absorbing [11]. This random variable or its distribution are denoted as $\mathrm{PH}(\boldsymbol{\tau}, S)$, where the $1\times n$ vector $\boldsymbol{\tau}$ is the MC initial probability distribution for the transient states, and matrix S is the $n\times n$ sub-generator matrix holding the transition rates among the transient states. The vector $\boldsymbol{S}^*=-S\mathbf{1}$ holds the absorption rates from the transient states. Its cumulative distribution function (CDF) is $F(x)=1-\boldsymbol{\tau}\exp(Sx)\mathbf{1}$, for $x\geq 0$, and its expected value is $E[X]=-\boldsymbol{\tau}S^{-1}\mathbf{1}$.

4. THE DISTRIBUTED SETUP

In this section we introduce a stochastic model to determine the job response-time distribution offered by a single computing node that implements replication with canceling and operates with r individual queues, as in Figure 1(b). To this end we start by obtaining the waiting-time and service-time distributions separately, both of which have PH representations. For each job, composed of r replicas, the waiting time is the period between its arrival and the time the first of its replicas starts service, while the service time starts when the waiting period ends and concludes when one of the replicas completes service successfully, or when all replicas fail. In the following we refer to a period during which the server of the shortest queue is busy as an *all-busy* period, which terminates when the one server becomes idle and the queue is empty. This marks the start of a *not-all-busy* period, where at least one server is idle and terminates when a job arrives, submitting one replica to each server, initiating a not-all-busy period.

4.1 The waiting-time distribution

To determine the waiting-time distribution, we observe the queues only during the *all-busy* periods and define an *age process*, following [2, 19]. Different from [2, 19], which consider queues with service times independent of the system state, the replication and canceling mechanism introduces dependencies among the servers that cannot be analyzed by existing models. We thus define a bivariate Markov process $\{X(t), J(t)|t\geq 0\}$, where the *age* $X(t)$ is the total time-in-system of the youngest job in service at time t. The age $X(t)$ thus takes values in $[0,\infty)$, increasing linearly with rate 1 as long as no new jobs start service. Note that, during the all-busy period, a new job starts service only if the replica in service in the *shortest queue* completes service or fails. This is because for the replicas waiting in other queues, one or more of their siblings have already failed. Thus in case of a service completion or a failure in the shortest queue, a new job starts service and its age will be equal to its waiting time, thus triggering a downward jump in $X(t)$. The *phase* $J(t)=(A(t), D(t))$ holds the joint state of the arrival process

$A(t)$ and the service process $D(t)$. The arrival process is a MAP with m_a phases and parameters (D_0, D_1) as defined in Section 3.

To model the service process, we first order the queue lengths in ascending order, i.e., $(q_1, q_2, \ldots, q_r)$ with $q_i \leq q_j$ for $i<j$ and $1\leq i,j\leq r$, where the queue length includes jobs waiting and in service. During the all-busy period, the shortest queue length must be positive, i.e., $q_1>0$, while during the not-all-busy period the shortest queue must be empty, i.e., $q_1=0$. Further, we focus on the differences between two consecutive queues after ordering, defined as $(d_1,\ldots,d_{r-1})$, where $d_i=q_{i+1}-q_i$ for $1\leq i\leq r-1$. Notice that this model is closely related to the fork-join model in [18], where the difference in queue-lengths are also used to model the evolution of a set of queues. However, here we consider the replication with canceling mechanism, which displays different dynamics from the fork-join queue, and the replicas are allowed to fail, a feature not considered for the fork-join queue. Also, [18] relies on the queue-length differences with respect to the shortest queue, while here we focus on the differences between two consecutive queues after ordering. The queue-length difference is unbounded in principle, but, to keep the phase space finite, we introduce an upper bound $C<\infty$, such that the difference is at most C. As a result, the service process $D(t)$ takes values in the set $S_D = \{(d_1,\ldots,d_{r-1})|d_i \in \{1,\ldots,C\}$ for $1\leq i\leq r-1\}$, the cardinality of which is $m_s=(C+1)^{r-1}$ for a system with r queues and an upper bound of C. The phase process $J(t)$ thus takes $m=m_a m_s$ different values, where m_a is the number of arrival phases. The limit C introduces an approximation, the goodness of which depends on the system parameters. For instance, when the failure rate α is small compared to the service rate μ, the probability of a large difference d_i is small, since successful service completions are more likely to occur, activating the canceling mechanism, which keeps the queues more synchronized. With a larger failure rate, we may expect a larger difference. However, due to the canceling mechanism, the probability of large differences between queue lengths stays small, even at high loads. Section 5 evaluates the accuracy of this approximation and explores the selection of the limit C.

To determine the PH representation $(\boldsymbol{s}_{\mathrm{wait}}, S_{\mathrm{wait}})$ of the waiting-time distribution, we rely on the stationary distribution $\boldsymbol{\pi}(x)$ of the $(X(t), J(t))$ process, which has a matrix exponential representation [19] $\boldsymbol{\pi}(x)=\boldsymbol{\pi}(0)\exp(Tx)$, for $x>0$. The $m\times m$ matrix T satisfies the non-linear integral equation

$$T = S^{(\mathrm{MAP})} + \int_0^\infty \exp(Tu)A^{(\mathrm{MAP})}(u)du, \qquad (1)$$

where $S^{(\mathrm{MAP})}=S\otimes I_{m_a}$, $A^{(\mathrm{MAP})}(u)=A^{(\mathrm{jump})}\otimes \exp(D_0 u)D_1$, while I_n is the identity matrix of size n, and $\otimes$ denotes the Kronecker product. Here $S+A^{(\mathrm{jump})}$ is the generator of the marginal service phase process, where S and $A^{(\mathrm{jump})}$ are $m_s\times m_s$ matrices that hold the transition rates of the service process associated to transitions *without* and *with* the start of a new job service, respectively. As mentioned above, only the service completion or failure of the replica in service in the shortest queue triggers the start of a new *job* service, thus transitions in the shortest queue correspond to matrix $A^{(\mathrm{jump})}$, while transitions in other queues correspond to matrix S.

Table 1 shows the transition rates in S and $A^{(\mathrm{jump})}$. The first row considers the case where the replica in service in the

Table 1: Transition rates for matrices S and $A^{(\text{jump})}$

Matrix	From	To	Rate	Range
S	$(d_1,\ldots,d_i,d_{i+1},\ldots,d_{r-1})$	$(d_1,\ldots,d_i-1,d_{i+1},\ldots,d_{r-1})$	μ	$d_i>0,\, d_{i+1}>0, i\geq 1$
	$(d_1,\ldots,d_i,d_{i+1},\ldots,d_{r-1})$	$(d_1,\ldots,d_i-1,\max\{C,d_{i+1}+1\},\ldots,d_{r-1})$	α	$d_i>0,\, d_{i+1}>0, i\geq 1$
	$(d_1,\ldots,d_i,0,\ldots,0,d_k,\ldots,d_{r-1})$	$(d_1,\ldots,d_i-1,0,\ldots,0,d_k,\ldots,d_{r-1})$	$(k-i)\mu$	$d_i>0,\, d_j=0\ \ \forall i<j<k$
	$(d_1,\ldots,d_i,0,\ldots,0,d_k,\ldots,d_{r-1})$	$(d_1,\ldots,d_i-1,1,0,\ldots,0,d_k,\ldots,d_{r-1})$	$(k-i)\alpha$	$d_i>0,\, d_j=0\ \ \forall i<j<k$
$A^{(\text{jump})}$	$(d_1,d_2,\ldots,d_{r-1})$	$(d_1,d_2,\ldots,d_{r-1})$	μ	$d_1>0$
	$(d_1,d_2,\ldots,d_{r-1})$	$(\max\{C,d_1+1\},d_2,\ldots,d_{r-1})$	α	$d_1>0$
	$(0,\ldots,0,d_i,\ldots,d_{r-1})$	$(0,\ldots,0,d_i,\ldots,d_{r-1})$	$i\mu$	$d_i>0,\, d_j=0\ \ \forall j<i$
	$(0,0,\ldots,0,d_i,\ldots,d_{r-1})$	$(1,0,\ldots,0,d_i,\ldots,d_{r-1})$	$i\alpha$	$d_i>0,\, d_j=0\ \ \forall j<i$

$(i+1)^{\text{th}}$ shortest queue *completes service*, canceling its partners in all the queues longer than queue $(i+1)^{\text{th}}$, resulting in the difference between the $(i+1)^{\text{th}}$ and i^{th} shortest queues decreasing by 1, while other differences remain unaffected. The second row considers the case where the replica in the $(i+1)^{\text{th}}$ shortest queue *fails*, decreasing by 1 the difference between the $(i+1)^{\text{th}}$ and i^{th} shortest queues, while the difference between the $(i+2)^{\text{th}}$ and $(i+1)^{\text{th}}$ shortest queues increases by 1, but bounded by C. In the previous two cases we assumed that $d_{i+1}>0$, thus ensuring that the $(i+1)^{\text{th}}$ shortest queue is actually a single queue. The third and fourth rows consider the case where $d_{i+1}=\cdots=d_{k-1}=0$, such that from the $(i+1)^{\text{th}}$ to the kth shortest queues have the same length. Thus, the transition rates in the third row reflect that a service completion in any of these queues triggers the same transition. The fourth row considers the same condition for the case of replica failures. The second block in Table 1 considers similar conditions but for the matrix $A^{(\text{jump})}$. The first and second rows consider a service completion or failure of the replica in the shortest queue, thus initiating a new job service. In case of a service completion, the replica that completes service cancels all its partners, thus the differences between queue-lengths remain unchanged. On the other hand, a failure in the shortest queue leads d_1 to increase by 1, but bounded by the limit C. The last two rows consider the case where there are multiple shortest queues.

The matrix T can be found by iteratively solving Eq. (1), where each iteration involves the solution of a Sylvester matrix equation [8]. Once T has been found, we need to determine the steady state distribution $\boldsymbol{\pi}(0)$ of the phases at the beginning of an all-busy period. To find $\boldsymbol{\pi}(0)$, we need to connect the not-all-busy and the all-busy periods [2]. Compared to the all-busy period, in the not-all-busy period the shortest queue is empty, $q_1=0$, but the differences between queue-lengths can be modeled just as in the all-busy period. Thus, during the not-all-busy period we keep track of the arrival and services phases $J(t)=(A(t),D(t))$, with the service phase $D(t)$ taking values in the set S_D. We can thus follow [18] to find the stationary distribution $\boldsymbol{\pi}(0)$ that solves

$$\boldsymbol{\pi}(0)=\boldsymbol{\pi}(0)\int_0^\infty \exp(Tu)(A^{(\text{jump})}\otimes \exp(D_0u))du \qquad (2)$$
$$(S_{\text{not-all}}\oplus D_0)^{-1}(I_{m_s}\otimes D_1),$$

where the matrix $S_{\text{not-all}}$ holds all the service transition rates *between arrivals* during a not-all-busy period. Since no arrivals are allowed and the queue is empty, there are no new jobs starting service during this period and the $S_{\text{not-all}}$ matrix holds the same transition rates as the matrix S. The only difference is in the diagonal of $S_{\text{not-all}}$, which needs to be such that $S_{\text{not-all}}\mathbf{1}=\mathbf{0}$.

Let the steady state distribution of the phase during the busy period be $\boldsymbol{\pi}_{\text{busy}}=-\boldsymbol{\pi}(0)T^{-1}$, and define $\boldsymbol{\varphi}=(T-S^{(\text{MAP})})\mathbf{1}$ [2]. The PH representation of the waiting time is given by

$$\boldsymbol{s}_{\text{wait}}=\gamma\boldsymbol{\pi}_{\text{busy}}\circ\boldsymbol{\varphi}/((\boldsymbol{\pi}_{\text{busy}}\circ\boldsymbol{\varphi})\mathbf{1}),\quad S_{\text{wait}}=\Delta^{-1}T'\Delta,\ (3)$$

where $\Delta=\text{diag}(\boldsymbol{\pi}_{\text{busy}})$, and $\circ$ stands for the Hadamard product. The parameter γ is the probability that a job has to wait, and is given by $\gamma=(E[\eta_0]-1)/(E[\eta_0]-1+E[\eta_1])$, where $E[\eta_0]$ and $E[\eta_1]$ are the expected number of arrivals during an all-busy period and a not-all-busy period, respectively. Since the job that initiates the not-all-busy period does not have to wait, $E[\eta_0]-1$ is the expected number of arrivals that have to wait in a cycle of an all-busy period followed by a not-all-busy period. Further, $E[\eta_1]=1$ as an arrival during the not-all-busy period sends replicas to all queues in the node, initiating an all-busy period. Thus $\gamma=1-1/E[\eta_0]$, where $E[\eta_0]$ can be obtained as in [2, Section 6].

4.2 The service-time distribution

We now determine the job service-time distribution, which we show to be PH with parameters $(\boldsymbol{s}_{\text{ser}},S_{\text{ser}})$ that depend on the overall system state. Let $Y(t)$ be the service state of a *tagged job* in service at time t. We define $Y(t)=(R(t),D(t))$, where $R(t)$ records the number of alive replicas of the tagged job at time t, thus $R(t)\in\{1,\ldots,r\}$. The variable $D(t)$ is again the difference between queue lengths, but it focuses on the queue lengths *in front of the tagged replicas only*, ignoring any jobs that arrive after the tagged job. Thus if a tagged replica has already failed, the corresponding queue length is kept at 0. Notice that since we are interested in the service time of a tagged job, we keep track of its service phase from the moment the first tagged replica starts service, and we order the service states according to $R(t)$ in descending order. Further, when $R(t)=1$, only one tagged replica remains alive, thus it is enough to keep track of the length of the queue where this replica is located. To build the PH representation of the service-time distribution we consider the sub-generator $\bar{S}_{\text{ser}}$, and two absorbing states, S and F, representing the cases where the job completes service successfully or encounters a failure, respectively. We can then write the generator of the service-time process (ignoring the zero rows corresponding to the absorbing states) as

$$\left[\bar{S}_{\text{ser}}\quad \bar{\boldsymbol{S}}_S^*\quad \bar{\boldsymbol{S}}_F^*\right],$$

where the absorption vectors $\bar{\boldsymbol{S}}_S^*$ and $\bar{\boldsymbol{S}}_F^*$ hold the absorption rates into states S and F, respectively, and $\bar{\boldsymbol{S}}^*=\bar{\boldsymbol{S}}_S^*+\bar{\boldsymbol{S}}_F^*$.

The transitions among service phases depend not only on whether there is a successful service completion or a failure, but also on which queue this happens. The transition rates of the service process are shown in Table 2, which we

Table 2: Transition rates for $\bar{S}_{\mathrm{ser}}$, $\bar{S}_S^*$ and $\bar{S}_F^*$

From	To	Rate	Range
$m,(d_1,\ldots,d_{r-1})$	$m-1,(\max\{C,d_1+1\},\ldots,d_{r-1})$	α	$m=r$
$m,(d_1,\ldots,d_{r-1})$	S	μ	$m=r$
$m,(0,\ldots,0,d_i,\ldots,d_{r-1})$	$m-1,(1,0,\ldots,0,d_i,\ldots,d_{r-1})$	$i\alpha$	$m=r,d_i>0,d_j=0\quad\forall j<i$
$m,(0,\ldots,0,d_i,\ldots,d_{r-1})$	S	$i\mu$	$m=r,d_i>0,d_j=0\quad\forall j<i$
$m,(\ldots,d_i,d_{i+1},\ldots,d_{r-1})$	$m,(\ldots,d_i-1,d_{i+1},\ldots,d_{r-1})$	μ	$d_i>0,d_{i+1}>0,m\le r$
$m,(\ldots,d_i,d_{i+1},\ldots,d_{r-1})$	$m,(\ldots,d_i-1,\max\{C,d_{i+1}+1\},\ldots,d_{r-1})$	α	$d_i>0,d_{i+1}>0,m\le r$
$m,(\ldots,d_i,0,\ldots,0,d_k,\ldots,d_{r-1})$	$m,(\ldots,d_i-1,0,\ldots,0,d_k,\ldots,d_{r-1})$	$(k-i)\mu$	$d_i>0,d_j=0\ \forall i<j<k,m\le r$
$m,(\ldots,d_i,0,\ldots,0,d_k,\ldots,d_{r-1})$	$m,(\ldots,d_i-1,1,0,\ldots,0,d_k,\ldots,d_{r-1})$	$(k-i)\alpha$	$d_i>0,d_j=0\ \forall i<j<k,m\le r$
$m,(\mathbf{0}_{r-m-1},1,d_{r-m+1},\ldots,d_{r-1})$	$m-1,(\mathbf{0}_{r-m-1},0,\max\{C,d_{r-m+1}+1\}\ldots,d_{r-1})$	α	$d_{r-m+1}>0,1<m<r$
$m,(\mathbf{0}_{r-m-1},1,d_{r-m+1},\ldots,d_{r-1})$	S	μ	$d_{r-m+1}>0,1<m<r$
$m,(\mathbf{0}_{r-m-1},1,0,\ldots,0,d_k,\ldots,d_{r-1})$	$m-1,(\mathbf{0}_{r-m-1},0,1,0,\ldots,0,d_k,\ldots,d_{r-1})$	$(k-r+m+1)\alpha$	$1<m<r$
$m,(\mathbf{0}_{r-m-1},1,0,\ldots,0,d_k,\ldots,d_{r-1})$	S	$(k-r+m+1)\mu$	$1<m<r$
$1,(\mathbf{0}_{r-2},1)$	S	μ	$m=1$
$1,(\mathbf{0}_{r-2},1)$	F	α	$m=1$

split in four sets for clarity. The first set of rows considers the case where $R(t)=r$, i.e., none of the tagged replicas has completed service or failed, thus there is at least one tagged replica in service in one of the shortest queues. In the first two rows there is only one tagged replica in service, thus its failure, with rate α, leads d_1 to increase by 1 but bounded to C, while its service completion, with rate μ, marks the service completion of the whole job, thus entering the S state. Rows 3-4 cover a similar case, but with i tagged replicas concurrently in service. In the second set, we consider transitions in queues other than the shortest ones, which do not hold tagged replicas. The first and second rows consider the case of a service completion or a failure in the $(i+1)^{\mathrm{th}}$ queue, respectively, assuming there is a single queue with this queue length ($d_{i+1}>0$). The third and fourth rows consider a similar transition, but in this case the $(i+1)^{\mathrm{th}}$ to the kth queues have the same length, thus the transition rates are $(k-i)\mu$ and $(k-i)\alpha$, respectively. In the third set we assume that the number of tagged replicas alive is $1<m<r$, thus at least one tagged replica has already failed. In fact, the zero vector $\mathbf{0}_{r-m+1}$ in front of the state description corresponds to the queue-length differences among the $r-m$ servers where the tagged replicas have already failed. Here the first two rows correspond to the failure or service completion, respectively, of a tagged replica in the (only) shortest non-zero queue, thus assuming $d_{r-m+1}>0$. The third and fourth rows cover the same case, but considering multiple (i.e., $k-r+m-1$) shortest queues. Finally, the last set considers the case where only one tagged replica remains in service, thus its service completion marks a successful completion of the whole job, while its failure leads to the job failure.

Having obtained $\bar{S}_{\mathrm{ser}}$, we define $S_{\mathrm{ser}}=\bar{S}_{\mathrm{ser}}\otimes I_{m_a}$, which is a matrix of size m_{ser}. Since the service phase space is ordered in decreasing order according to $R(t)$, we let m_r be the number of phases where $R(t)=r$ and m_0 the remaining phases, such that $m_{\mathrm{ser}}=m_r+m_0$. We can now determine the initial probability vector $\boldsymbol{s}_{\mathrm{ser}}$, which is the stationary probability with which a job starts service in each of the phases, and following [18, Proposition 1], it is given by

$$\boldsymbol{s}_{\mathrm{ser}} = [(1-\gamma)\boldsymbol{\pi}(0) + \gamma c\boldsymbol{\pi}_{\mathrm{busy}}(T-S^{(\mathrm{MAP})}) \quad \mathbf{0}_{m_0}], \quad (4)$$

where $c^{-1}=\boldsymbol{\pi}_{\mathrm{busy}}(T-S^{(\mathrm{MAP})})\mathbf{1}$, and the zero vector correspond to phases with $R(t)<r$ as a job can only start service in phases with $R(t)=r$, since it starts with all its replicas

alive. As a result, we have that $(\boldsymbol{s}_{\mathrm{ser}},S_{\mathrm{ser}})$ is a PH representation of the service time for all jobs. For further reference we also define the corresponding exit vector $\boldsymbol{S}_S^* = \bar{\boldsymbol{S}}_S^*\otimes\mathbf{1}_{m_a}$. However, we want to focus on the successful jobs only, for which we obtain a PH representation of the service time in the following proposition, the proof of which is given in the Appendix.

PROPOSITION 1. *The service time of successful jobs follows a PH distribution with parameters $(\boldsymbol{\beta}_{ser}, B_{ser})$, where*

$$\boldsymbol{\beta}_{ser} = \boldsymbol{S}_S^{*\prime}\Pi/p_S, \quad B_{ser} = \Pi^{-1}S_{ser}'\Pi.$$

Π *is a diagonal matrix such that $\Pi\mathbf{1}=\eta'$, $\eta=-\boldsymbol{s}_{ser}S_{ser}^{-1}$ is the stationary distribution of the service phase, and $p_S = -\boldsymbol{s}_{ser}S_{ser}^{-1}\boldsymbol{S}_S^*$ is the probability that a job is successful.*

Finally, we are in a position to obtain the response-time distribution in the following theorem, the proof of which is given in the Appendix.

THEOREM 1. *The response time of successful jobs follows a PH distribution with parameters $(\boldsymbol{s}_{res}, S_{res})$, where*

$$\boldsymbol{s}_{res}=\begin{bmatrix}\boldsymbol{\beta}_{ser}^{idle} & \boldsymbol{\beta}_{ser}^{busy} & \mathbf{0}\end{bmatrix}, S_{res}=\begin{bmatrix}B_{ser}^{idle} & \mathbf{0} & \mathbf{0}\\ \mathbf{0} & B_{ser}^{busy} & (-B_{ser}^{busy}\mathbf{1})P_{s,w}\\ \mathbf{0} & \mathbf{0} & S_{wait}\end{bmatrix},$$

(5)

where $(\boldsymbol{\beta}_{ser}^{idle}, B_{ser}^{idle})$ and $(\boldsymbol{\beta}_{ser}^{busy}, B_{ser}^{busy})$ are the PH representations of the service times of successful jobs that start service immediately upon arrival and that must wait, respectively. Letting Δ_{idle} be a diagonal matrix such that $\Delta_{idle}\mathbf{1}=-(1-\gamma)(\boldsymbol{\pi}(0)S_{ser}^{-1})'$, $(\boldsymbol{\beta}_{ser}^{idle}, B_{ser}^{idle})$ are given by

$$\boldsymbol{\beta}_{ser}^{idle}=\boldsymbol{S}_S^*\Delta_{idle}/p_S, \quad B_{ser}^{idle}=\Delta_{idle}^{-1}S_{ser}'\Delta_{idle}.$$

Similarly, letting Δ_{busy} be a diagonal matrix such that $\Delta_{busy}\mathbf{1}=-\gamma(\boldsymbol{\alpha}_{busy}S_{ser}^{-1})'$, $(\boldsymbol{\beta}_{ser}^{busy}, B_{ser}^{busy})$ are given by

$$\boldsymbol{\beta}_{ser}^{busy}=\boldsymbol{S}_S^*\Delta_{busy}/p_S, \quad B_{ser}^{busy}=\Delta_{busy}^{-1}S_{ser}'\Delta_{busy}.$$

Finally, $P_{s,w}$ is an $m_{ser}\times m$ matrix given by

$$P_{s,w} = \begin{bmatrix}\tilde{P}_{s,w}\\ \mathbf{0}_{m_0\times m}\end{bmatrix},$$

where $\tilde{P}_{s,w} = \Gamma^{-1}(T-S^{(MAP)})'\Lambda$, and Γ and Λ are diagonal matrices such that $\Gamma\mathbf{1} = (T-S^{(MAP)})'\Lambda\mathbf{1}$ and $\Lambda\mathbf{1} = \boldsymbol{\alpha}_{busy}'$. Here $\boldsymbol{\alpha}_{busy} = c\boldsymbol{\pi}_{busy}(T-S^{(MAP)})$ is the initial service phase of jobs that wait, and c is a normalizing constant such that $c^{-1}=\boldsymbol{\pi}_{busy}(T-S^{(MAP)})\mathbf{1}$.

Table 3: Approximation errors compared with simulation results

r	Arr	NR-load	Measure	Err(%) - NR-reliability:10%			Err(%) - NR-reliability:50%			Err(%) - NR-reliability:90%		
				C = 5	C = 10	C = 50	C = 5	C = 10	C = 50	C = 5	C = 10	C = 50
3	Poisson	0.1	mean	<1	<1	<1	<1	<1	<1	<1	<1	<1
			R_{95}	<1	<1	<1	<1	<1	<1	<1	<1	<1
		0.5	mean	<1	<1	<1	<1	<1	<1	<1	<1	<1
			R_{95}	<1	<1	<1	<1	<1	<1	<1	<1	<1
		0.9	mean	15.16	2.62	<1	<1	<1	<1	<1	<1	<1
			R_{95}	19.55	3.53	<1	<1	<1	<1	<1	<1	<1
	MAP	0.1	mean	<1	<1	<1	<1	<1	<1	<1	<1	<1
			R_{95}	<1	<1	<1	<1	<1	<1	<1	<1	<1
		0.5	mean	31.63	11.28	<1	<1	<1	<1	<1	<1	<1
			R_{95}	28.60	9.97	<1	<1	<1	<1	<1	<1	<1
		0.9	mean	34.48	11.95	<1	1.99	<1	<1	<1	<1	<1
			R_{95}	35.08	12.78	<1	1.32	<1	<1	<1	<1	<1
2	Poisson	0.1	mean	<1	<1	<1	<1	<1	<1	<1	<1	<1
			R_{95}	<1	<1	<1	<1	<1	<1	<1	<1	<1
		0.5	mean	1.05	<1	<1	<1	<1	<1	<1	<1	<1
			R_{95}	1.01	<1	<1	<1	<1	<1	<1	<1	<1
		0.9	mean	23.89	8.17	<1	<1	<1	<1	<1	<1	<1
			R_{95}	28.28	11.32	<1	<1	<1	<1	<1	<1	<1
	MAP	0.1	mean	<1	<1	<1	<1	<1	<1	<1	<1	<1
			R_{95}	<1	<1	<1	<1	<1	<1	<1	<1	<1
		0.5	mean	39.31	22.86	<1	<1	<1	<1	<1	<1	<1
			R_{95}	35.38	18.59	<1	<1	<1	<1	<1	<1	<1
		0.9	mean	36.22	16.76	<1	3.54	<1	<1	<1	<1	<1
			R_{95}	36.51	17.16	<1	3.43	<1	<1	<1	<1	<1

4.3 The multi-node system

We conclude this section by noticing that the analysis of a single computing node can be extended to the multi-node case, and therefore to evaluate the overall performance of the server farm. This result follows by observing that, under either round-robin or random allocation, if the overall arrival process is a MAP(D_0,D_1), the arrival process to each node is also a MAP. Under round-robin allocation, the parameters are

$$C_0 = \begin{bmatrix} D_0 & D_1 & . & \cdots \\ . & D_0 & D_1 & \cdots \\ \vdots & \vdots & \ddots & \ddots \\ . & . & \cdots & D_0 \end{bmatrix}, \quad C_1 = \begin{bmatrix} 0 & 0 & \cdots & 0 \\ 0 & 0 & \cdots & 0 \\ \vdots & \vdots & \ddots & 0 \\ D_1 & 0 & \cdots & 0 \end{bmatrix}.$$

These matrices are of size nm_a, where n is the number of computing nodes in this group. Under the random allocation, the arrival process has parameters

$$C_0 = D_0 + (1 - p)D_1, \quad C_1 = pD_1,$$

where $p=1/n$. As the arrival process to each computing node is a MAP, its performance measures are readily obtained with the analytical model proposed.

5. EXPERIMENTAL VALIDATION

We now demonstrate that the proposed model is able to provide accurate results with quite moderate values of the limit C. To study its behavior, we focus on the mean response time, and the pth response time percentile, denoted as R_p, which is the maximum response time faced by $p\%$ of the successful jobs. With these two metrics, Table 3 summarizes the relative errors of the values obtained from the approximated model (finite C), against simulation results. We show the errors achieved when $r=2$ and 3, and consider different system settings. Thanks to the flexibility offered by the proposed model, we consider Poisson arrivals, and

MAPs of second order. While the Poisson case is a standard assumption, MAPs allow us to explore the effect of the variability and auto-correlation of the inter-arrival times on the accuracy of the approximation. We use the method in [9] to obtain the MAP representations, for which we set the squared coefficient of variation (SCV) to be 10 and the decay rate of the auto-correlation function to be 0.9. We denote the reliability of the system without replication by NR-reliability, which is given by $\mu/(\mu+\alpha)\%$. The service rate μ is set to be 1.0, and the failure rate α is set to achieve different NR-reliability levels, namely 10%, 50% and 90%. Further, the arrival rate is set to achieve different load levels for the system without replication, denoted as NR-load. For each configuration we consider different values of the limit C: 5, 10 and 50. For each setting, the simulations were run for 5,000 times with 500,000 samples each time, from which we obtain the mean response time and R_{95}, and their 95% confidence intervals.

Focusing first on the cases with $r=3$ and the NR-reliability of 50% and 90%, we observe that the relative error is below 1% for most test cases with C as small as 5, with the exception of the case with MAP arrivals and 0.9 load, which requires a larger C of 10 to achieve an error below 1%. Here both the load and the more variable and auto-correlated arrival process increase the likelihood of larger queues and larger differences among queue lengths, thus requiring a larger limit C. However, when the NR-reliability is just 10%, we observe significant errors for several cases with $C=5$ and 10. For instance, with MAP arrivals and 0.9 load, the error rate with $C=5$ and 10 are 34.48% and 11.95% for the mean, and 35.08% and 12.78% for R_{95}, respectively. The low NR-reliability case is more challenging as the higher likelihood of failures increases the differences among the queue lengths. Increasing the limit C to 50 allows us to obtain errors below 1%. With medium and high NR-reliability levels, failures are less frequent and the queues stay more synchronized, such that a small C is sufficient to cover most of the

Table 4: Transition rates of matrix S

From		To		Rate	Condition
$(l_r(t),\ldots,l_1(t))$	$Y(t)$	$(l_r(t),\ldots,l_1(t))$	$Y(t)$		
$(l_r,\ldots,l_i,\ldots,l_1)$	(i,j)	$(l_r,\ldots,l_{i+1}+1,l_i-1,\ldots,l_1-1)$	$(i+1,j-1)$	$l_1\beta$	$j\geq 1$
$(l_r,\ldots,l_b,\ldots,l_1)$	(i,j)	$(l_r,\ldots,l_b-1,\ldots,l_i-1,\ldots,l_{i+b}+1,\ldots,l_1)$	$(i+b,j-b)$	$bl_b\mu$	$1<b\leq r, j\geq b$
$(l_r,\ldots,l_b,\ldots,l_1)$	(i,j)	$(l_r,\ldots,l_b-1,l_{b-1}+1,\ldots,l_{i+1}+1,l_i-1,\ldots,l_1)$	$(i+1,j-1)$	$bl_b\alpha$	$1<b\leq r, j\geq 1$
$(l_r,\ldots,l_i,\ldots,l_1)$	(i,j)	$(l_r,\ldots,l_i,\ldots,l_1)$	$(i,j-1)$	$i\alpha$	$1\leq i\leq r, j\geq 1$

Table 5: Transition rates of matrix $A^{(\mathrm{jump})}$

From		To		Rate	Condition
$(l_r(t),\ldots,l_1(t))$	$Y(t)$	$(l_r(t),\ldots,l_1(t))$	$Y(t)$		
$(l_r,\ldots,l_i,\ldots,l_1)$	(i,j)	$(l_r,\ldots,l_i,\ldots,l_1)$	$(i,r-i)$	$i\mu$	$1\leq i\leq r$
$(l_r,\ldots,l_1)$	$(1,0)$	$(l_r,\ldots,l_1)$	$(1,r-1)$	β	$i=1,j=0$
$(l_r,\ldots,l_1)$	$(i,0)$	$(l_r,\ldots,l_1)$	$(1,r-1)$	$l_1\beta$	$1\leq i\leq r, j=0$
$(l_r,\ldots,l_i,\ldots,l_1)$	$(i,0)$	$(l_r,\ldots,l_i-1,l_{i-1}+1,\ldots,l_1+1)$	$(1,r-1)$	$i\alpha$	$1\leq i\leq r, j=0$
$(l_r,\ldots,l_b,\ldots,l_1)$	$(i,0)$	$(l_r,\ldots,l_b-1,l_{b-1}+1,\ldots,l_1+1)$	$(1,r-1)$	$bl_b\alpha$	$1<b\leq r$
$(l_r,\ldots,l_b,\ldots,l_1)$	(i,j)	$(l_r,\ldots,l_b-1,\ldots,l_{b-j}+1,\ldots,l_{i+j}+1,\ldots,l_i-1,\ldots,l_1)$	$(b-j,r-b+j)$	$bl_b\mu$	$1<b\leq r, j<b$

queue-length differences observed.

Considering the cases with $r=2$ we observe similar trends, with errors increasing with the load and the arrival process variability, and decreasing with the NR-reliability. However, we observe larger errors than with $r=3$ thus requiring a larger C to achieve the same level of accuracy. This can be explained by noticing that with r replicas and limit C the maximum difference allowed by the model between the shortest and the largest queues is rC. Thus a larger number of replicas allows the model to consider larger queue-length differences, given the same limit C.

6. THE CENTRALIZED SET-UP

We now consider the set-up with a centralized queue as depicted in Figure 1(c). In this case, a request is replicated such that its r copies join the central queue in a computing node, and are submitted to the next server that becomes available with FCFS scheduling. Similar to the distributed set-up, jobs are distributed to nodes with either round-robin or random scheduling, but the analysis can focus on a single computing node by appropriately modifying the arrival process. The analysis extends [16], which considered the case with $r=2$, to any number of replicas.

6.1 The waiting-time distribution

Similar to the distributed case, we define a bivariate Markov process $\{X(t),J(t)|t\geq 0\}$, where the *age* $X(t)$ is the total time-in-system of the youngest job in service at time t. Different from the distributed case, the phase $J(t)$ is defined as $J(t)=(l_r(t),\ldots,l_1(t),Y(t))$, where $l_i(t)$ is the number of jobs with i replicas in service, and $Y(t)$ holds the state of the youngest job in service. Thus, $Y(t)=(i,j)$ means that i replicas of the youngest job are in service, j replicas are waiting in the queue, and $r-i-j$ replicas already failed. $Y(t)$ therefore takes value in the set $S_Y=\{(i,j)|1\leq i+j\leq r, i\geq 1, j\geq 0\}$.

To determine the PH representation $(\boldsymbol{s}_{\mathrm{wait}},S_{\mathrm{wait}})$ of the waiting-time distribution, we follow similar steps as in Section 4, by solving Eq. (1) to find the matrix T that defines the matrix exponential representation $\boldsymbol{\pi}(x)=\boldsymbol{\pi}(0)\exp(Tx)$ of the stationary version of the process $(X(t),J(t))$. We therefore need to define the matrices S and $A^{(\mathrm{jump})}$, which hold the transition rates of the service process associated to

transitions without and with the start of a new job service, respectively, as summarized in Tables 4 and 5. For matrix S the first row considers the case where one of the l_1 jobs with a single replica in service either completes service or fails, with rate $\beta=\mu+\alpha$, allowing one of the j replicas of the youngest job in the queue to start service. In the second row, one of the l_b jobs with b replicas in service terminates successfully, canceling its siblings, and letting b new replicas to start service. Notice that the number of replicas of the youngest job waiting (j) must be at least b to ensure that no new job starts service. Similarly, if one of the b replicas of either of these l_b jobs fails, with rate α, one replica in the queue starts service. The last row for this matrix covers the case where one of the i replicas of the youngest job fails, allowing one of its siblings waiting to start service. For the $A^{(\mathrm{jump})}$ matrix we consider similar scenarios, the main difference being that the number of replicas of the youngest job waiting j is assumed to be zero in most of the cases, as this implies that the next replica to join service will be part of a new job, and the transition thus corresponds to $A^{(\mathrm{jump})}$. The only exception is in the last row, where a job with b replicas finishes successfully, and since $j<b$, this allows the j replicas of the youngest job in the queue, and $b-j$ replicas of a new job, to start service.

Using these matrices we can solve Eq. (1) to find T, and then define a similar system as that in Eq. (2) to find the $\boldsymbol{\pi}(0)$, the distribution of the phase at the beginning of an all-busy period. The main difference here is that the generator of the service process during the not-all-busy period, $S_{\mathrm{not\text{-}all}}$ in Eq. (2), requires a more detailed analysis, similar to the one developed in [16]. The key idea is that this generator has a block structure amenable for analysis, namely a level-dependent quasi-birth-and-death process [11]. Further details can be found in [16]. After finding $\boldsymbol{\pi}(0)$ we can use Eq. (3) to determine the PH representation of the waiting-time distribution $(\boldsymbol{s}_{\mathrm{wait}},S_{\mathrm{wait}})$.

6.2 The service-time distribution

The next step is to show that the service-time distribution has a PH distribution with parameters $(\boldsymbol{s}_{\mathrm{ser}},S_{\mathrm{ser}})$. For the service time, we focus on a tagged job in service, and let $Y(t)$ to be the service phase of this job at time t. Here $Y(t)$ takes values from $S_Y=\{(i,j)|1\leq i+j\leq r, i\geq 1, j\geq 0\}$, as defined be-

Table 6: Transition rates of S_{ser}

Condition	From		To		Rate	Condition
	$(l_{r-1}(t),\ldots,l_1(t))$	$Y(t)$	$(l_{r-1}(t),\ldots,l_1(t))$	$Y(t)$		
$j=0$	/	$(i,0)$	/	S	$i\mu$	$1\leq i\leq r$
	/	$(i,0)$	/	$(i-1,0)$	$i\alpha$	$1<i\leq r$
	/	$(1,0)$	/	F	α	$i=1$
$r-i=1$	/	$(r-1,1)$	/	S	$(r-1)\mu$	/
	/	$(r-1,1)$	/	$(r,0)$	β	/
	/	$(r-1,1)$	/	$(r-1,0)$	$(r-1)\alpha$	/
$r-i>1, j\geq1$	$(l_{r-1},\ldots,l_i,\ldots,l_1)$	(i,j)	/	S	$i\mu$	$1\leq i\leq r$
	$(l_{r-1},\ldots,l_1)$	(i,j)	$(l_{r-1},\ldots,l_1-1)$	$(i+1,j-1)$	$l_1\beta$	$j\geq1$
	$(l_{r-1},\ldots,l_b,\ldots,l_1)$	(i,j)	$(l_{r-1},\ldots,l_b-1,l_{b-1}+1,\ldots,l_1)$	$(i+b,j-b)$	$bl_b\mu$	$1<b\leq r, j\geq b$
	$(l_r,\ldots,l_b,\ldots,l_1)$	(i,j)	/	$(i+b,0)$	$bl_b\mu$	$1<b\leq r, j<b$
	$(l_r,\ldots,l_b,\ldots,l_1)$	(i,j)	$(l_r,\ldots,l_b-1,l_{b-1}+1,\ldots,l_1)$	$(i+1,j-1)$	$bl_b\alpha$	$1<b\leq r, 1\leq j<b$

fore. Clearly, the service time of a tagged job is affected by other jobs in service. Specifically, when the tagged job has replicas waiting in the queue, these replicas can only start service if one of the replicas in service frees a server. Thus it is essential to keep track of the states of all jobs in service, which can be done by means of $S(t)=(l_{r-1}(t),\ldots,l_1(t))$, where $l_i(t)$ is again the number of jobs with i replicas in service at time t, *but excluding the tagged job*.

Similarly to the case with individual queues, we define two absorbing states S and F that represent the cases where the job completes service successfully or encounters a failure, and describe the evolution of the service process as an MC with generator S_{ser}, given in Table 6. We split the transitions in three sets, and the first case in any of these sets considers the successful completion of the tagged job caused by a successful tagged replica. The first set considers the case where the tagged job has zero replicas waiting in the queue. Thus, if any of its i replicas in service fails (second row) the number of replicas in service decreases by one. In case there is only one tagged replica in service, $i=1$, a failure triggers the failure of the whole job (third row). The second set covers the special case where 1 tagged replica is waiting in the queue while the other $r-1$ are in service. In the second row we consider the successful completion or failure, with rate $\beta=\mu+\alpha$, of the only non-tagged replica in service, which allows the tagged replica in the queue to start service. The third row instead considers the failure of one of the tagged replicas, which also allows the tagged replica in the queue to start service. Notice that in the first two sets the evolution is independent of the state of the other jobs in service, either because there are zero tagged replicas in the queue, or because there are $r-1$ tagged replicas in execution. The other cases, which depend on the state of the non-tagged jobs in service, are described in the third set, starting with the successful completion of any of the i tagged replicas in service. In the second row, one of the l_1 jobs with a single replica in service either completes service successfully or fails, allowing one more tagged replica to start service. In the third and fourth rows, one of the l_b jobs with $b>1$ replicas in service completes successfully, allowing b new replicas to start service. If there are at least as many tagged replicas as free servers, i.e. $j\geq b$, as in the third row, we are left with $j-b$ tagged replicas waiting in queue. If not, $j<b$ as in the fourth row, all tagged replicas waiting in the queue start service and we can just focus on the tagged replicas in service, ignoring any other jobs. In the last row, one of the b replicas of the l_b jobs in service fails, with $b>1$,

allowing a new tagged replica to start service.

Having obtained S_{ser}, $\boldsymbol{\pi}(0)$ and T, we can determine the initial probability vector $\boldsymbol{s}_{\text{ser}}$ as in Eq. (4). Actually, using the block structure of the service process generator during the not-all-busy-period $S_{\text{not-all}}$, described in the previous section, we can improve this computation in a manner similar to [16]. Further, with this representation of the service time for all jobs, we can obtain the PH representation of the service-time distribution for successful jobs by directly applying Proposition 1. Finally, the PH representation of the response-time distribution $(\boldsymbol{s}_{\text{res}}, S_{\text{res}})$ is obtained by using Theorem 1.

7. EXPERIMENTAL RESULTS

In this section, we make use of the proposed model for the distributed set-up to evaluate its performance in the terms of its reliability and offered response times. We also compare against the centralized set-up and determine the performance gains obtained by keeping a central queue. Through the whole section, the service rate μ is set to 1, and the mean arrival and failure rates are set in proportion to μ to obtain different load levels and NR-reliability.

7.1 Performance of the distributed set-up

In the distributed set-up, as well as in the centralized one, the reliability, i.e. the probability that a job completes service successfully, increases with the deployment of extra replicas, and the improvement is actually independent of the queueing model implemented. For both the distributed and the centralized set-ups, with replication level $r\geq1$ the reliability achieved is $1-(\alpha/(\mu+\alpha))^r$, which simplifies to $\mu/(\mu+\alpha)$ if no replication is adopted. Beyond the evident improvement in reliability, another benefit of replication with canceling is its potential to reduce the response time by allowing the selection of the first successful result. Focusing first on the case with individual queues, we compare the response times achieved under different replication levels. We consider three different systems with r servers, mean arrival rate $r\lambda$, and replication level r, for $r=1$, 2 and 3, thus offering the same load to all systems. Figures 2, 3 and 4 show how the utilization and R_{95} change under different replication levels, under Poisson arrivals, and different NR-reliability levels (10%, 50% and 90%).

Figure 2(a) depicts how the system utilization increases as the replication level increases, although the increase is relatively minor. In this case we assume an NR-reliability of 90%. Decreasing this reliability to 50% and 10%, as de-

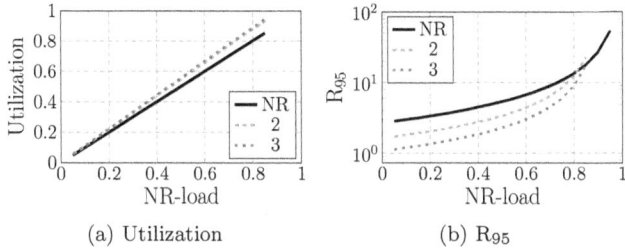

(a) Utilization

(b) R_{95}

Figure 2: Poisson arrival, NR-reliability: 90%

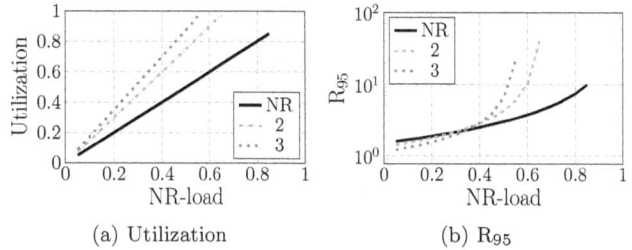

(a) Utilization

(b) R_{95}

Figure 3: Poisson arrivals, NR-reliability: 50%

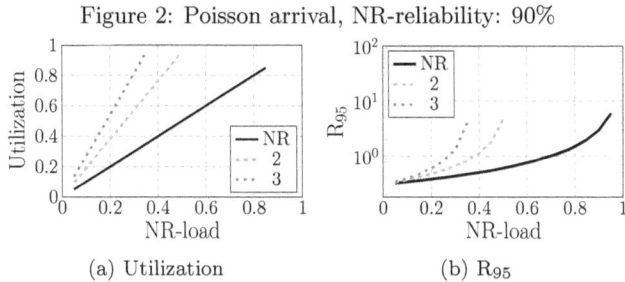

(a) Utilization

(b) R_{95}

Figure 4: Poisson arrivals, NR-reliability: 10%

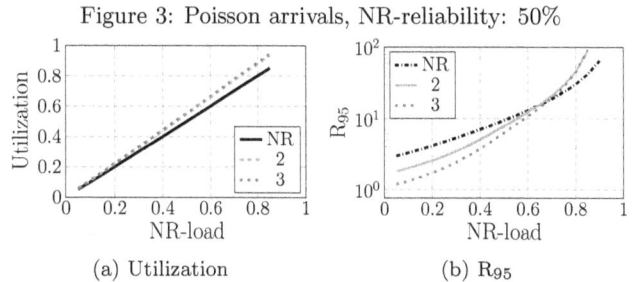

(a) Utilization

(b) R_{95}

Figure 5: MAP arrivals, NR-reliability: 90%

picted in Figures 3(a) and 4(a), the relative increase in utilization when replication is implemented is larger. For instance, when the NR-reliability is just 10%, a utilization of 0.35 without replication becomes 0.67 when $r=2$, and further increases to 0.95 when $r=3$. However, the increase in utilization does not necessarily lead to a higher delay. On the contrary, replication leads to lower response times, as long as the baseline NR-load stays below a certain threshold. For instance, Figure 2(b) shows that both replication levels achieve a lower R_{95} than without replication, when the NR-load is below 0.85. In particular, the system with 3 replicas achieves the lowest response times among the three. Although the introduction of replicas introduces extra load, which leads to an increase in the response times, at the same time it allows the selection of the first replica that finishes, potentially reducing the response times. However, the second effect weakens with a higher failure rate, as we observe in Figures 2(b), 3(b) and 4(b) that the NR-load threshold decreases with decreasing NR-reliability. In particular, when the NR-reliability is 10%, the introduction of replication increases the response times at any NR-load considered. The reason is two-fold: first, the system without replication and a low NR-reliability shows short response times since only short jobs can complete service before a failure; second, the probability that all replicas are running until the first one completes reduces with a higher failure rate, weakening the benefit of selecting the first replica that completes service.

Figure 5 shows the utilization and R_{95} obtained under MAP arrivals and an NR-reliability of 90%, while keeping the same mean arrival rate as for Poisson arrivals. We observe how the bursty workload modeled by the MAP arrivals leads to much larger response times and a lower NR-load threshold, below which replication reduces response times, compared to the case with Poisson arrivals in Figure 2. This is caused by the more variable and auto-correlated workload represented by the MAP arrivals, which limit the load range where replication is beneficial.

7.2 The Effect across the Distribution

We now look further into the effect that replication has

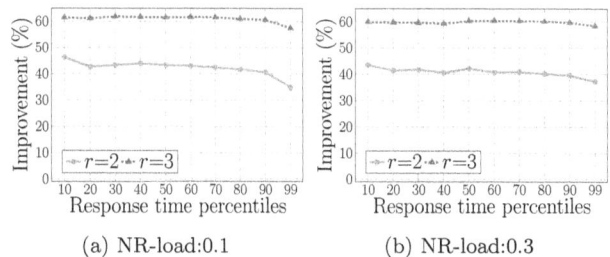

(a) NR-load:0.1

(b) NR-load:0.3

Figure 6: Improvement on R_p (Poisson, 90% NR-reliability)

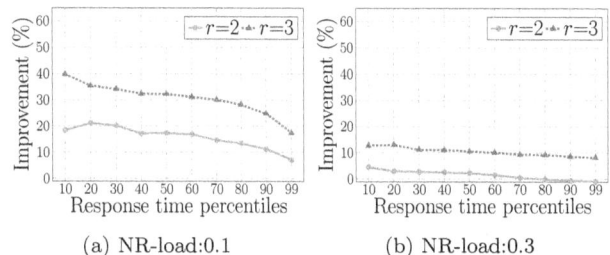

(a) NR-load:0.1

(b) NR-load:0.3

Figure 7: Improvement on R_p (Poisson, 50% NR-reliability)

across the whole response-time distribution. To this end, for each percentile p in the range $\{10, 20, \ldots, 90, 99\}$ we obtain the relative improvement $(R_p^1 - R_p^r)/R_p^1\%$, comparing the response time percentiles obtained with replication $(r=2,3)$ against those without (R_p^1). Figure 6(a)-(b) depicts the improvements for the case under Poisson arrivals with NR-reliability of 90% and NR-load levels of 0.1 and 0.3, respectively. We observe fairly stable improvements across the whole percentile range, with the exception of the improvement on the tail. For instance, when the NR-load is 0.1, and $r=2$, the improvement on the 99th percentile is 34.83%, while the improvement experienced by most percentiles is around 43%. In fact, we observe that the improvement generally decreases as the percentile considered increases. The reason for this is that a larger percentile covers longer re-

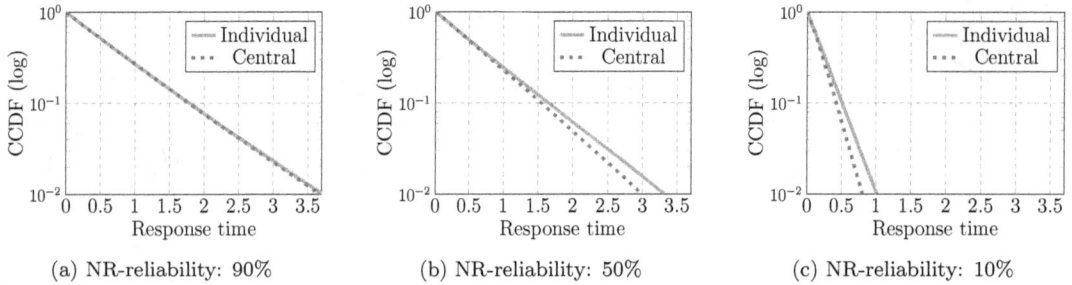

(a) NR-reliability: 90%   (b) NR-reliability: 50%   (c) NR-reliability: 10%

Figure 8: CCDFs of response times with individual queues and with a central queue (Poisson arrivals, $r=2$, NR-load:0.3)

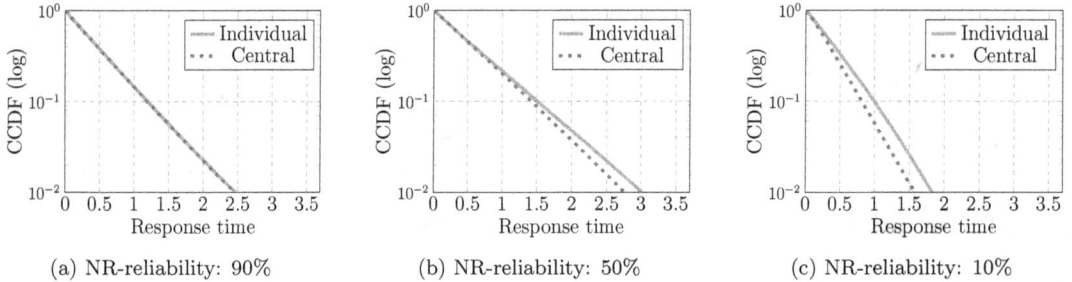

(a) NR-reliability: 90%   (b) NR-reliability: 50%   (c) NR-reliability: 10%

Figure 9: CCDFs of response times with individual queues and with a central queue (Poisson arrivals, $r=3$, NR-load:0.3)

sponse times, which are partially associated to longer service times. In a long service time there is more room for a failure to occur, in which case the system looses its ability to use the minimum of r execution times. Notice that this effect decreases if r is larger, as shown in Figure 6(a)-(b), as even if one replica fails, there are $r-1$ replicas that could execute concurrently and among which the system selects the minimum execution time. Further, this effect is stronger if the utilization is low, as confirmed when comparing Figure 6(a) and (b), since under low loads the contribution of the service time on the response time is larger as the queueing times are very short.

In the previous set-up we assumed an NR-reliability of 90%. If we reduce it to 50%, Figure 7(a)-(b) shows that the gains across the percentiles are not uniform, where we observe peaks on small percentiles, and a stronger decrease in the improvement for larger percentiles. For instance, when $r=3$ and NR-load is 0.1, the improvement of the 10th percentile is 39.64%, while it is 17.36% for the 99th percentile. This more pronounced effect is in agreement with the observation above as in this case failures are more likely and higher percentiles evaluate conditions where service times can be larger and provide more chances for failures to occur. This clearly highlights the importance of explicitly considering the response-time distribution, and not just its mean, or one percentile, when evaluating a replication strategy.

7.3 Distributed vs Centralized

Clearly, the distributed and centralized set-ups perform identically in terms of reliability, as this only depends on the replication level r, given our independence assumptions. In terms of response times, the centralized set-up must achieve lower response times than its distributed counterpart, as in the latter case it is possible for some servers to have non-zero waiting lines, while other servers remain idle. This is not possible in the centralized set-up, as all servers must be

busy if there is any job waiting to start service. To better understand this difference in performance we show in Figure 8(a) the complementary CDFs (CCDFs) of the response times achieved with 2 replicas by these two models, assuming Poisson arrivals, NR-reliability of 90%, and NR-load of 0.3 as an example. Clearly, it is hard to tell the difference between these two CCDFs. Reducing the NR-reliability to 50% and 10%, Figure 8(b)-(c) shows a more significant improvement of the centralized over the distributed set-up along the whole distribution. Increasing the replication level to $r=3$, Figure 9 shows that when the NR-reliability is high, the distributed set-up performs almost as well as the centralized one, while this difference increases when the NR-reliability decreases. Figures 8 and 9 also show that the improvement is not uniform along the distribution, and that it is more significant in the tail than in the body (e.g. second and third quartiles).

Considering different NR-load levels, Figure 10(a) examines an NR-reliability of 90%, where the centralized set-up shows a relative improvement on the R_{95} of less than 1% over the distributed case. As discussed above, Figure 10(b)-(c) shows that reducing the NR-reliability increases the advantage of the centralized set-up, and this can be over 20% for NR-load around 0.2 and $r=3$ when the NR-reliability is just 10%. If we modify the arrival process considered in Figure 10(b) from a standard Poisson to a correlated MAP, Figure 10(d) shows that the gains obtained with the centralized operation are similar in magnitude but are restricted to a smaller subset of values for the NR-load, as with MAP arrivals replication is beneficial for a more limited load range. Similar results, both in trend and magnitude, can be observed if we compare the *mean* response time or other percentiles instead of the R_{95}.

8. DISCUSSION

In the previous section we observed, as expected, that the

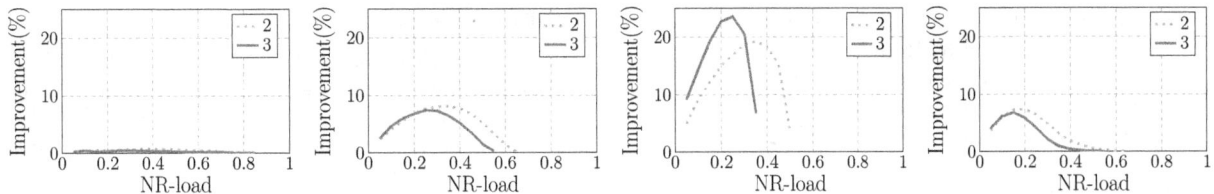

(a) Poisson, 90% NR-reliability (b) Poisson, 50% NR-reliability (c) Poisson, 10% NR-reliability (d) MAP, 50% NR-reliability

Figure 10: Improvement on R_{95} of the central model over the individual queues mode

centralized set-up achieves lower response times than the distributed case, especially at low NR-reliability. However, most large server farms dispatch incoming request to servers immediately, without holding a central queue. Replication with distributed queues is also required when accessing mirrored disks and searching distributed databases in parallel. This set-up provides more flexibility since there is no need to set up and manage a central dispatcher that keeps track of the servers state, making it easier to increase or decrease the number of servers as the load rises or falls.

A major point of our investigation is to assess the magnitude of the difference in response time between the two set-ups, to see if and when the distributed set-up suffers an excessive performance penalty. From our results, we observe that, although the centralized system performs better than the distributed set-up, this difference is quite small, under 1%, when the NR-reliability is high (90%). Even if this reliability is 50%, which is already low as it assumes that one out of two requests fail, the improvement obtained with the centralized queue is at most 8%. We therefore observe that replication not only is effective to reduce the response times in the distributed set-up, as shown in Sections 7.1 and 7.2, but it also provides a performance close to that of the centralized set-up as long as the NR-reliability is not too low. In addition, the proposed models focus on request failures, but not on server failures. While in the distributed system the replicas in a job receive service from distinct servers, in the centralized set-up several replicas in a job may be submitted to the same server as the failure of one replica allows its sibling in the queue to start at the same server, increasing the risk of failure. The distributed set-up thus offers many benefits over the centralized case, while its performance disadvantage is limited when the NR-reliability is high.

In the future, we intend to investigate other parameters that may affect the performance of the proposed approach, including the overhead of the replication and cancellation mechanisms, and the correlation between request replicas.

9. ACKNOWLEDGMENTS

The research presented in this paper was supported by the EPSRC grant EP/L00738X/1 (iBids). The research of Juan F. Pérez is supported by the ARC Centre of Excellence for Mathematical and Statistical Frontiers (ACEMS).

10. REFERENCES

[1] G. Ananthanarayanan, A. Ghodsi, S. Shenker, and I. Stoica. Why let resources idle? aggressive cloning of jobs with Dolly. *Memory*, 40:80, 2012.

[2] S. Asmussen and J. R. Møller. Calculation of the steady state waiting time distribution in GI/PH/c and MAP/PH/c queues. *Queueing Syst.*, 37:9–29, 2001.

[3] J. Dean and L. A. Barroso. The tail at scale. *CACM*, 56:74–80, 2013.

[4] A. Gandhi, M. Harchol-Balter, R. Das, and C. Lefurgy. Optimal power allocation in server farms. In *ACM SIGMETRICS PER*, pages 157–168, 2009.

[5] A. Greenberg, J. Hamilton, D. A. Maltz, and P. Patel. The cost of a cloud: research problems in data center networks. *ACM SIGCOMM CCR*, 39:68–73, 2008.

[6] B. Guenter, N. Jain, and C. Williams. Managing cost, performance, and reliability tradeoffs for energy-aware server provisioning. In *IEEE INFOCOM*, 2011.

[7] P. G. Harrison and Z. Qiu. Performance enhancement by means of task replication. In *EPEW*, 2013.

[8] Q. He. Analysis of a continuous time SM[K]/PH[K]/1/FCFS queue: Age process, sojourn times, and queue lengths. *JSSC*, 25:133–155, 2012.

[9] A. Heindl, G. Horváth, and K. Gross. Explicit inverse characterizations of acyclic MAPs of second order. In *EPEW*, 2007.

[10] G. Joshi, E. Soljanin, and G. Wornell. Efficient redundancy techniques for latency reduction in cloud systems. *arXiv preprint arXiv:1508.03599*, 2015.

[11] G. Latouche and V. Ramaswami. *Introduction to matrix analytic methods in stochastic modeling*. SIAM, 1999.

[12] I. Mitrani. Managing performance and power consumption in a server farm. *Ann. Oper. Res.*, 202:121–134, 2013.

[13] M. T. Özsu and P. Valduriez. Distributed and parallel database systems. *ACM CSUR*, 28:125–128, 1996.

[14] Parallel workloads archive. http://www.cs.huji.ac.il/labs/parallel/workload/.

[15] Z. Qiu and J. F. Pérez. Assessing the impact of concurrent replication with canceling in parallel jobs. In *IEEE MASCOTS*, 2014.

[16] Z. Qiu and J. F. Pérez. Enhancing reliability and response times via replication in computing clusters. In *IEEE INFOCOM*, 2015.

[17] Z. Qiu and J. F. Pérez. Evaluating the effectiveness of replication for tail-tolerance. In *IEEE/ACM CCGRID*, 2015.

[18] Z. Qiu, J. F. Pérez, and P. G. Harrison. Beyond the mean in fork-join queues: Efficient approximation for response-time tails. *Perform. Eval.*, 2015.

[19] B. Sengupta. Markov processes whose steady state distribution is matrix-exponential with an application

to the GI/PH/1 queue. *AAP*, 21:159–180, 1989.

[20] N. B. Shah, K. Lee, and K. Ramchandran. When do redundant requests reduce latency? In *Allerton*, 2013.

[21] B. Snyder. Server virtualization has stalled, despite the hype. http://www.infoworld.com/print/146901, 2010.

[22] A. Vulimiri, P. Godfrey, R. Mittal, J. Sherry, S. Ratnasamy, and S. Shenker. Low latency via redundancy. In *CoNEXT*, 2013.

[23] M. Wu, X.-H. Sun, and H. Jin. Performance under failures of high-end computing. In *ACM/IEEE SC*, page 48, 2007.

[24] Z. Zheng and Z. Lan. Reliability-aware scalability models for high performance computing. In *IEEE CLUSTER*, 2009.

APPENDIX

Proof of Proposition 1

Since jobs only fail during service, the failure probability is given by $p_S = \int_0^\infty \boldsymbol{s}_{\text{ser}} \exp(S_{\text{ser}}x) \boldsymbol{S}_S^* dx = -\boldsymbol{s}_{\text{ser}} S_{\text{ser}}^{-1} \boldsymbol{S}_S^*$. Thus, the probability that a job service time lasts for at most x time units and succeeds is

$$F_s(x) = \frac{1}{p_S} \int_0^x \boldsymbol{s}_{\text{ser}} \exp(S_{\text{ser}}y) \boldsymbol{S}_S^* dy$$

$$= 1 + \frac{1}{p_S} \boldsymbol{s}_{\text{ser}} S_{\text{ser}}^{-1} \exp(S_{\text{ser}}x) \boldsymbol{S}_S^*.$$

This matrix-exponential representation of the service times for successful jobs can be turned into a PH representation by defining a diagonal matrix Π such that $\Pi\boldsymbol{1}=\eta'$, where $\eta=-\boldsymbol{s}_{\text{ser}} S_{\text{ser}}^{-1}$ is the stationary distribution of the service phase. Defining $B_{\text{ser}}=\Pi^{-1} S_{\text{ser}}'\Pi$, we have

$$1 - F_s(x) = -\frac{1}{p_S} \boldsymbol{s}_{\text{ser}} S_{\text{ser}}^{-1} \Pi^{-1} \Pi \exp(S_{\text{ser}}x) \Pi^{-1} \Pi \boldsymbol{S}_S^*$$

$$= \frac{1}{p_S} \eta \Pi^{-1} \exp(B_{\text{ser}}'x) \Pi \boldsymbol{S}_S^*$$

$$= \frac{1}{p_S} \boldsymbol{S}_S^{*}{}' \Pi \exp(B_{\text{ser}}x) \boldsymbol{1}.$$

This defines a proper PH distribution as the vector $\boldsymbol{S}_S^{*}{}'\Pi/p_S$ is stochastic. This results from $\boldsymbol{S}_S^*$ and Π being non-negative, and $\boldsymbol{S}_S^{*}{}'\Pi\boldsymbol{1} = -\boldsymbol{S}_S^{*}{}'(\boldsymbol{s}_{\text{ser}} S_{\text{ser}}^{-1})' = p_S$.

Proof of Theorem 1

The proof of this result follows similar arguments as that of [18, Theorem 1], so we focus on the main differences. As in [18, Theorem 1], we rely on the fact that the PH representation of the waiting time distribution is obtained from a time-reversal argument [19], thus we also use this argument to build the PH representation of the response times. Since we focus on the *successful* jobs only, we follow Proposition 1 to obtain the PH representation of the service time distribution of successful jobs. Further, we split this representation for jobs that wait and jobs that do not. The initial service phase of jobs that wait is given by $\boldsymbol{\alpha}_{\text{busy}} = c\boldsymbol{\pi}_{\text{busy}}(T-S^{(\text{MAP})})$, as this is the distribution of the phase *just after a downward jump in* $X(t)$, and c is a normalizing constant such that $c^{-1}=\boldsymbol{\pi}_{\text{busy}}(T-S^{(\text{MAP})})\boldsymbol{1}$. Thus we apply a time-reversal by defining the diagonal matrix Δ_{busy} such that $\Delta_{\text{busy}}\boldsymbol{1}=-\gamma(\boldsymbol{\alpha}_{\text{busy}} S_{\text{ser}})'$. We then follow similar steps as in the proof of Proposition 1 to obtain the PH representation for jobs that wait $(\boldsymbol{\beta}_{\text{ser}}^{\text{busy}}, B_{\text{ser}}^{\text{busy}})$ as

$$\boldsymbol{\beta}_{\text{ser}}^{\text{busy}}=\boldsymbol{S}_S^*\Delta_{\text{busy}}/p_S, \qquad B_{\text{ser}}^{\text{busy}}=\Delta_{\text{busy}}^{-1} S_{\text{ser}}'\Delta_{\text{busy}}.$$

A similar result is obtained for jobs that do not wait, considering that in this case jobs start service according to $(1-\gamma)\boldsymbol{\pi}(0)$. We thus define Δ_{idle} as a diagonal matrix such that $\Delta_{\text{idle}}\boldsymbol{1}=-(1-\gamma)(\boldsymbol{\pi}(0)S_{\text{ser}}^{-1})'$, and the corresponding PH representation $(\boldsymbol{\beta}_{\text{ser}}^{\text{idle}}, B_{\text{ser}}^{\text{idle}})$ is given by

$$\boldsymbol{\beta}_{\text{ser}}^{\text{idle}}=\boldsymbol{S}_S^*\Delta_{\text{idle}}/p_S, \qquad B_{\text{ser}}^{\text{idle}}=\Delta_{\text{idle}}^{-1} S_{\text{ser}}'\Delta_{\text{idle}}.$$

With these PH representations for the service time, we obtain Eq. (5) by putting together the paths of jobs that do not wait, which start service with $\boldsymbol{\beta}_{\text{ser}}^{\text{idle}}$, with those of jobs that wait, which start service with $\boldsymbol{\beta}_{\text{ser}}^{\text{busy}}$. Given the time-reversal, the response time of jobs that wait is composed of a first stage of service followed by a second stage of waiting. Further, the phase in which the service stage ends determines the stage in which the waiting stage begins. The remaining of the proof follows the same steps as that of [18, Theorem 1], such that the matrix $\tilde{P}_{s,w}=\Gamma^{-1}(T-S^{(\text{MAP})})'\Lambda$ is a stochastic matrix that determines how the phase at the end of the service phase determines the phase at the beginning of the waiting phase. Once a job starts the waiting phase, it evolves according to S_{wait} until absorption. Further details can be found in [18].

Enhancing Rules For Cloud Resource Provisioning Via Learned Software Performance Models

Mark Grechanik
University of Illinois at
Chicago,
Chicago, IL, USA
drmark@uic.edu

Qi Luo,
Denys Poshyvanyk
College of William and Mary,
Williamsburg, VA, USA
{qluo,denys}@cs.wm.edu

Adam Porter
University of Maryland
College Park, MD, USA
aporter@cs.umd.edu

ABSTRACT

In *cloud computing*, stakeholders deploy and run their software applications on a sophisticated infrastructure that is owned and managed by third-party providers. The ability of a given cloud infrastructure to effectively re-allocate resources to applications is referred to as *elasticity*. To enable elasticity, programmers study the behavior of applications and write scripts that guide the cloud to provision resources for these applications. This is an imprecise, laborious, manual and expensive approach that drastically increases the cost of application deployment and maintenance in the cloud.

We propose an approach, coined as Provisioning Resources with Experimental SofTware mOdeling (PRESTO), to automatically learn behavioral models of software applications during performance testing in order to recommend programmers how to improve provisioning strategies that guide the cloud to (de)allocate resources to these applications. We applied PRESTO to two software applications and our experiments demonstrate that with PRESTO programmers can create rules for provisioning resources with a high degree of precision when the performance is about to worsen, so that the applications maintain their throughputs at the desired level.

Keywords

Cloud computing; Performance testing; Behavioral models

1. INTRODUCTION

In *cloud computing*, stakeholders deploy their software applications on a sophisticated infrastructure that is owned and managed by third-party providers (e.g., public clouds such as Amazon AWS) or in-house installations. Two fundamental properties of cloud computing include provisioning resources to applications on demand and charging their owners for pay-as-you-go resource usage [3]. The elasticity of cloud refers to its capacity to scale resources based on a real workload. Many cloud providers claim that their cloud infrastructures are *elastic*, i.e., they automatically (de/re)allocate resources, both to *scale out* and *up* – adding resources as demand increases, and to *scale in* and *down* – releasing resources as demand decreases. Using elastic clouds, stakeholders pay only for what they use, when they use it, rather than paying up-front and

ICPE'16, March 12–18, 2016, Delft, Netherlands.
ⓒ 2016 ACM. ISBN 978-1-4503-4080-9/16/03. . . $15.00
DOI: http://dx.doi.org/10.1145/2851553.2851568

continuing costs to own and maintain their hardware/software and supporting technical staff [3, 4, 23].

In practice, even the most elastic clouds are not perfectly elastic [13, 3]. Understanding when and how to reallocate resources is a hard problem, since it is generally impossible to quickly and accurately match resources to applications' needs. A recent article underscores this point as it describes its state-of-the-art supervisory system that monitors various black box metrics and then directs the cloud to initiate scaling operations based on that data [10]. As a result, some elasticity-related problems for cloud computing include *under-provisioning* applications so they lack the resources to provide appropriate quality of service, or *over-provisioning* applications so stakeholders end up holding and paying for more resources than they need. Specifically, although elasticity is a fundamental enabler of cost-effective cloud computing, existing *provisioning strategies* (i.e., rules used to (de)allocate resources to applications) are typically obtained in ad-hoc fashion by programmers who study the behavior of the application in the cloud. It is a manual, imprecise, intellectually intensive and laborious effort.

Our novel idea for *Provisioning Resources with Experimental SofTware mOdeling (PRESTO)* enhances cloud elasticity by learning and refining models of software applications through performance testing in the cloud and by using these automatically learned models to help programmers to craft application-specific resource provisioning strategies. That is, PRESTO bridges a pure black-box cloud resource provisioning to software engineering, where behavioral models of the application are re-engineered automatically as part of performance testing, and programmers use these models to create rules for provisioning of resources to these applications in the cloud. This paper makes the following contributions:

- We present a general approach for improving the performance of cloud-deployed applications by using models and artifacts automatically derived from application performance testing.

- We rely on performance models of applications and use these models to guide programmers in developing application- specific *provisioning* strategies to improve cloud elasticity.

- We evaluate PRESTO on two software applications. The results strongly suggest that PRESTO is effective and efficient. We believe that our work is the successful and early attempt at achieving precise cloud elasticity by using software engineering artifacts for guiding resource provisioning in the cloud. All experimental results are available online [28].

2. BACKGROUND AND PROBLEM STATEMENT

In this section we provide some background on behavioral models, resource provisioning and basic scaling operators, present our hypothesis, and outline the problem statement.

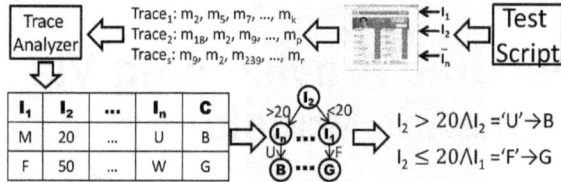

Figure 1: Learning performance rules.

2.1 Obtaining Behavioral Models

A performance model of the Application Under Test (AUT) is learned automatically during performance testing to establish under what loads and the ranges of input values the AUT loses its scalability. Creating application's performance models is fundamental to our approach for determining effective resource allocation strategies and for evaluating their costs and benefits. A recent work, FOREPOST [11], abstracts the AUT as a function that maps properties of the input data (i.e., client requests) to the classes of performance behavior of the AUT. That is, performance tests are generalized as relations (i.e., performance rules) that map input values to AUT performance behaviors.

To obtain performance rules automatically during performance testing, the AUT is executed using a test script with different values and loads for its inputs, $I_1, \ldots, I_n$ as shown in the upper right corner in Figure 1. As a result of executing the AUT, its execution traces are collected with different performance counters (e.g., elapsed execution time, memory consumption). These traces are summarized by the Trace Analyzer into a table whose columns represent input values and numbers of users who use these input values and rows correspond to the collected execution traces. The last column, C, designates the performance class of the execution trace, i.e., **G**ood or **B**ad, a summary measure of the QoS using the throughput associated with a given trace. This table is processed by a machine learning algorithm that computes a decision tree, where nodes represent the AUT inputs and their counts and the leaves represent quality of service (QoS)/throughput classes. Directed edges connect nodes and they are labeled with decisions (e.g., $I_2 > 20$) for taking a specific edge. This decision tree is translated into performance rules, examples of which are shown in Figure 1.

2.2 Resource Provisioning for Cloud Apps

In this paper, we focus on client-server data-centric applications because of their widespread use. Specifically, the front end of the application accepts requests from users (i.e., the input data), the middle tier performs some business logic computations, and the back-end encapsulates data storage. We term the set of related client requests and computations as a work unit or *transaction*. Each client request is the input data for an application, and its performance behavior depends on the type and the size of the input data, among other things. The performance of the application is typically measured as its *throughput*, i.e., the number of transactions per time interval that the application executes. Effective provisioning strategies will allocate resources to maintain a desired level of the throughput for the application.

Depending on the types of resources, their provisioning to applications has different effect on the throughput. Consider scaling up this application where more CPUs are added as new users arrive. Since the application spawns a new thread for each user, adding CPUs and assigning newly spawned threads to these CPUs will increase the throughput of the application. At the same time, adding more RAM may not necessarily help. On the other hand, if the database appears to be a main bottleneck, scaling out this application by starting its new instance or a new instance of its database may increase the throughput by parallelizing transaction process-

ing. Thus, resource provisioning in the cloud is a main technique for maintaining a desired level of the throughput to guarantee some quality of service for applications.

2.3 Scaling Operators of Cloud Computing

In a cloud computing model, software components run inside *virtual machines (VMs)*, which provide emulated physical machines [32]. In general, the cloud allocates different amounts of resources to different VMs and these resources have different costs. For example, if a VM contains more components that involve computationally intensive operations, the cloud scales it up by assigning more CPUs and memory units. Alternatively, the cloud can scale out this application by replicating VMs, thus enabling multiple requests to be processed in parallel by these VMs that run these components. The cloud uses two main scaling operators: $\text{sres}(r,a,i)$ and $\text{sinst}(a,i)$, where r is the type of a resource (e.g., memory, CPU), a is its quantity, and i is the VM identifier. The scaling operator sres (de)allocates the resource, r, in the quantity, a, to the VM, i, and the scaling operator sinst (de)allocates a instances of the VM, i. Of course, different costs are associated with these scaling operators. For example, allocating a new VM is more expensive than assigning more CPU or RAM to an already running VM. In theory, elastic clouds "know" when to apply these operators to (de)allocate resources with high precision and efficiency.

2.4 The State of the Art and Practice

Today, stakeholders typically deploy their applications in the cloud, using ad-hoc scripts in which they encode the behavior of these applications and rules on how the cloud should apply the scaling operators based on a coarse collection of performance counters and otherwise "guesstimating" on how to provision resources to their applications in the cloud. The Google Cloud, the Amazon EC2 and Microsoft Azure clouds have issued guidelines for manually load balancing their elastic clouds, directing their users to manually specifying the conditions that trigger work routing and scaling operations. The key takeaway here is that existing cloud providers understand that their users often need to manually configure the cloud. Such manual activities are tedious, error-prone and expensive, and clearly demonstrate that clouds, such as Amazon's EC2, have a long way to go in their quest for better elasticity (see http://aws.amazon.com/autoscaling/).

2.5 The Problem Statement

We address the following problem – how to enable programmers to provision resources with a high degree of precision to specific VMs to maximize the throughput of an application that runs in these VMs. Our goal is to enable stakeholders to create more precise rules for resource provisioning. In this paper we concentrate on the resource consumption by application for specific combinations of input values rather than for different loads. In order to know resource demands for an application, its performance analysis should be done, ideally, with all allowed combinations of values of the inputs. Unfortunately, this is often infeasible because of the enormous possible number of combinations. Thus, a subgoal is to approximate the performance behavior of the application.

We hypothesize that by using application-specific performance models that are re-engineered automatically during software performance testing it is possible to provision resources to specific VMs to maximize the application's throughput. To do that, it is important to know which resources affect more the performance of specific VMs that host software components. Therefore, our goal is to recommend to stakeholders what type of resources and in what quantity should be provisioned for certain types of input data, so that this information can be used to make the cloud highly elastic.

3. APPROACH

In this section, we give an overview of PRESTO and explain provisioning strategies as well as our proposed algorithm.

3.1 Overview of PRESTO

To address the problem of enhancing cloud elasticity, the cloud should provision adequate quantities of specific resources to the designated VMs using rules that are supplied by programmers. Adequate quantities of resources are those that do not lead to under- and over-provisioning. A key idea of our solution, PRESTO, is that stakeholders should create application-specific provisioning strategies using models that are obtained during performance testing in the cloud. PRESTO methodology combines obtaining application's *behavioral model* (i.e., a collection of workload profiles, constraints, performance counters, and various relations among components of the application [21, 26]) with *sensitivity analysis* that parameterizes resources and samples the parameter space to determine the types of resources that have the highest impact on the throughput of the application. Eventually, stakeholders synthesize the results of modeling and sensitivity analysis into provisioning strategies that they import into the cloud to provision resources based on specific client requests that arrive to the cloud for a given application. To summarize, provisioning strategies for the application are obtained during its performance testing. These provisioning strategies concisely describe for what types of inputs and input loads the application loses its scalability and what types of resources and in what quantities should be provisioned to maintain the application's quality of service by not allowing its throughput to fall below some level as dictated by an SLA.

3.2 Obtaining Provisioning Strategies

Using the learned model, the user of PRESTO discovers provisioning strategies that most effectively alleviate decreasing throughputs. The user searches through a space of possible cloud provisioning operations. For example, if a software component involves computationally intensive operations or requires a lot of memory, the cloud could scale-up the VM in which the component runs by giving it more CPU and memory units. If the component's performance has unacceptable latency, resulting from database interactions, then the cloud could scale-out the VM that contains this database. These strategies can be applied to the system and if additional testing shows performance improvements, then a new provisioning strategy is automatically generated.

Definition 1 *A provisioning strategy is a relation $P \Rightarrow (R \bullet R)^*$, where P is a performance rule and $R \bullet R$ is a resource provisioning scheme, where $R \in \{\mathtt{sres}, \mathtt{sinst}\}$ are resource (de)allocation operators defined in Section 2.3 and $\bullet$ stands for logical connectors* and *and* or *and $*$ is the Kleene star.*

An example representation of a provisioning strategy for this rule is $(A, \mathbb{R}) \Rightarrow \mathtt{sres}(\mathbb{P}, 3, VM_i) \wedge \mathtt{sinst}(2, VM_n)$, meaning that if we observe inputs to the application, A, then the rule $\mathbb{R}$ holds, meaning that we will triple the number of CPU units, $\mathbb{P}$, that are assigned to the VM_i (i.e., scale up), and double the number of virtual machines, VM_n that run the AUT (i.e., scale out). If this provisioning strategy is made available to the cloud in advance, then when the application, A is executed with the input values that satisfy the performance rule $\mathbb{R}$, the cloud will provision resources according to the designated provisioning strategy instead of waiting until the performance of the application demonstrably worsens as is done in existing clouds [10]. Conversely, the cloud will deallocate resources to some baseline level if no consequent is present.

3.3 PRESTO Algorithm

PRESTO's algorithm for synthesizing provisioning strategies, $\mathcal{S}$ is shown in Algorithm 1. The input to Algorithm 1 is the AUT and VM configuration that includes all VMs in which the AUT runs as well as resources assigned by the cloud to these VMs.

The algorithm builds the behavioral model using FOREPOST in line 2, outputting function $f_{\mathcal{A}}$ to represent the performance model of the AUT by learning rules to map the groups of inputs to the classes that describe different AUT performance behaviors (see details in [11]). We defined classes for behaviors: good class, where performance of the AUT is scalable and bad class, where the AUT is not scalable. But for nontrivial AUT, the range of performance behaviors is broader, thus there can be more classes. In the outer for loop between lines 4-13, the AUT is checked for each class for different loads if it loses its scalability. If it does, method GetBottleneckModel in line 5 returns types of fault models, describing violations of different properties regarding resource use, like CPU load, memory utilization, and database bottlenecks. Theses defaults are likely to cause the AUT to lose its scalability. Essentially, the method determines the consumption of resources and operations in the execution of the AUT that led to this consumption. In the for loop between lines 6-12, for each detected fault model, m, a set of allocated resources, R_m is obtained in line 7. Then, between lines 8-11, different types of allocated resources are perturbed by scaling them up or out. All the provisioning strategies, the performance rules and the corresponding AUT's behaviors are added to $\mathcal{S}$ in line 10, guiding programmers in developing provisioning strategies to improve cloud elasticity.

Algorithm 1 PRESTO Algorithm.

1: **Inputs**: AUT $\mathcal{A}$, VM Configuration Ω
2: **Behavioral Model**: $(\mathcal{A}, \Omega) \mapsto f_{\mathcal{A}} : I \to C$
3: $\mathcal{S} \leftarrow \emptyset$ {Initialize the set of provisioning strategies}
4: **for all** $c \in C \wedge \neg$ **Scalable**$(\mathcal{A}, c)$ **do**
5:     **GetBottleneckModel**$(\mathcal{A}, c) \mapsto \mathcal{M}$
6:     **for all** $m \in \mathcal{M}$ **do**
7:         **GetVMResource**$(m) \mapsto R_m$
8:         **for all** $r_m \in R_m$ **do**
9:             $\Omega_{\pm\Delta} \leftarrow$ **Perturb**(Ω, Δ_{R_m})
10:           $\mathcal{S} \leftarrow \mathcal{S} \cup$ **GetRule**$(f_{\mathcal{A},\Delta})$
11:         **end for**
12:     **end for**
13: **end for**
14: **return** $\mathcal{S}$

---

4. EXPERIMENTAL EVALUATION

In this section, we pose research questions (RQs), describe subject AUTs, explain our methodology and variables, formulate hypotheses, and discuss threats to validity.

4.1 Research Questions and Hypotheses

A main goal of our proposed work is to investigate if learned performance models of applications can enable stakeholders to create precise and effective provisioning strategies for applications running in the cloud. To do that, we will pursue and evaluate the following objectives. One objective is to show that the resulting provisioning strategies should be more effective than those strategies produced by existing state-of-the-art automated black-box approaches and manually created ad-hoc provisioning scripts (see Section 2.4). Another equally important objective is to learn these strategies quickly and automatically without placing a significant demand for resources. To better quantify these objectives, we will seek to answer the following research questions.

RQ$_1$: How effective is PRESTO in maintaining the throughput of the applications in the cloud?

RQ_2: How fast and efficient is PRESTO in learning provisioning strategies?

The rationale for RQ_1 is to determine if PRESTO strategies will enable subject applications to maintain their throughputs at some desired levels. Suppose that the application's throughput drops below some level that is dictated by an SLA for certain combinations of its input values. By applying PRESTO strategies, we expect the cloud to increase the throughput to an acceptable level. We compare how effective a cloud infrastructure using the PRESTO methodology is with respect to a cloud infrastructure without PRESTO that uses a commercial black-box application agnostic autoscaler. We introduce the following null hypothesis to evaluate how close the means are for throughputs for different approaches. We seek to evaluate the hypothesis at a 0.05 level of significance.

H_0 The primary null hypothesis is that there is no difference in throughputs of the subject applications for PRESTO and the competitive approaches.

The rationale behind the H_0 is that with PRESTO-based methodology, elastic resource provisioning will achieve the same application's throughput as the competitive approaches. We expect to reject this hypothesis to confirm our conjecture that the PRESTO-based cloud configuration will enable the cloud to provision resources to subject applications resulting in higher throughputs. The other aspect of RQ_1 is to investigate the economical aspect of autoscaling in the cloud. Recall that different resources have different costs. It is important that PRESTO can give a tradeoff between the improved throughput and its cost. To address RQ_2, we instrument our system to determine the time and resources that PRESTO needs to learn provisioning strategies. In addition, we want to establish how long it takes to converge to stable provisioning strategies.

4.2 Subjects and Cloud Configurations

We evaluate PRESTO on two three-tier Java applications, JPetStore and Dell DVD Store, which are widely used as industry performance benchmarks [30, 15]. JPetstore is a Java implementation of the PetStore benchmark. We used JPetStore 4.0.5 [18], which consists of 36 classes in 8 packages and 382 methods with the average cyclomatic complexity of ≈ 1.23. It is deployed in Tomcat 6 and uses Apache Derby as its backend database. In this paper, we only present the results for JPetStore. The experimental results for Dell DVD Store can be found in the online appendix [28].

We build a private cloud by using an open source cloud, Cloudstack 4.2.0 [7], with an integrated load balancer - NetScaler VPX 10.1[24]. NetScaler VPX is a virtual NetScaler appliance that includes load balancing/traffic management, application acceleration, application security, and offload functionality. Multiple reports and Citrix documents confirm that Netscaler is the state of the art load balancing and provisioning tool that gives us the ability to compare PRESTO with the baseline approach that is considered to be one of the best in the cloud computing industry.

4.3 Methodology

A key driver for choosing an experimental methodology is to compare the values of the dependent variable, throughput for subject applications given the following independent variables: a cloud platform, manually created resource provisioning scripts, user loads, and PRESTO. User loads are simulated for five, 15 and 30 users. An experiment involves randomly choosing client requests for transactions and measuring an average throughput. Since random URLs is unlikely to show the worst performance of the applications, we expect that an average throughput will be higher compared to the one that results from using the inputs selected in FOREPOST.

Recall that FOREPOST automatically constructs behavioral models of applications to choose inputs and user loads for which the application's throughput falls below some acceptable level. For these inputs and the predefined user loads we experiment with different provisioning strategies. Our goal is twofold: 1) we show that different provisioning strategies lead to a large variability in the resulting throughput of the applications, and 2) given that resources have different costs, we show that PRESTO can choose a provisioning strategy that reduces the cost of resource provisioning and improve the performance of the applications when they lose their throughput. We aligned our methodology with the guidelines for statistical tests to assess randomized approaches in software engineering [1, 2]. Given the high variability in the resources allocated to different applications, we execute each experiment multiple times to perform statistical tests and draw reliable conclusions from these tests.

4.3.1 Forming the Load

In JPetStore, the GUI front end is web-based and it communicates with the J2EE-based backend that accepts HTTP requests in the form of URLs. Recall that a set of URL requests is defined as a *transaction*. The backends of the subject applications can serve multiple transactions from multiple users concurrently. Test scripts are written using JMeter [16], which generates a large number of virtual users who send HTTP requests to web servers of AUTs thereby creating significant workloads. We limit the number of URLs in each transaction to 50, since we observed that users explored approximately 50 URLs before switching to other activities.

4.3.2 Experimenting With Performance Bottlenecks

To determine how well PRESTO allows the cloud to provision resources to maintain good performance of applications, we push the subject applications to worsen their throughputs by injecting computationally intensive operations into their source code. We consider CPU and database performance bottlenecks. CPU bottlenecks perform computationally intensive operations, e.g., arithmetic computations in a loop. Adding more CPUs to a VM can improve the performance of applications with CPU bottlenecks, especially if these bottlenecks are executed by multiple threads. Database bottlenecks address database locking strategies, so resources are locked and applications cannot proceed because one transaction is waiting on resources that are held by some other transactions. We randomly seeded nine CPU and nine database bottlenecks into JPetStore to create two versions (CPU and database version).

4.3.3 Resource Perturbation Modes

During performance testing, stakeholders perturb resource provisioning by applying scaling operators (see Section 2.3) to determine if the throughput of applications can be improved by assigning more resources to VMs. Baseline experiments are carried out using the basic cloud infrastructure, which was one VM with 1.0 GHz CPU and 1.0 GB memory. Different operators are shown as following. Δ_1, Δ_2 and Δ_3 are scale up operators, and Δ_4 is a scale out operator.

Δ_1: one VM with 1.0 GHz CPU and 1.5 GB RAM;
Δ_2: one VM with 1.5 GHz CPU and 1.0 GB RAM;
Δ_3: one VM, two 1.0 GHz core CPUs, 1.0 GB RAM;
Δ_4: two VMs, one 1.0 GHz CPU, 1.0 GB RAM each.

4.4 Threats to Validity

A threat to the validity is that our subject programs are relatively small; however, we used these applications since they are open-source and have been previously used for evaluating performance testing approaches [30, 15]. It is hard to obtain access to large enterprise-level applications, and increasing the size of subject applications is unlikely to affect the time and space demands of our analysis because PRESTO only considers approximations of the behaviors of these applications.

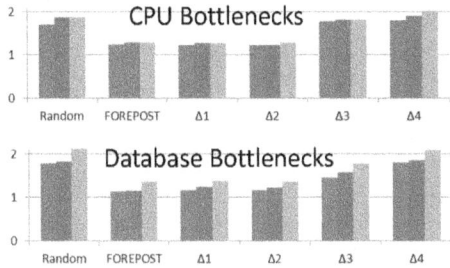

Figure 2: Throughputs for JPetStore using PRESTO on Cloud-stack. The X axis shows the throughputs (URLs per second).

A threat to validity is that application's behavioral models are easier to learn for smaller applications, however this is not a point that we address in this paper. We rely on our previously developed tool FOREPOST to learn behavioral models in this paper, however, other approaches for obtaining such models can be used in PRESTO [25, 20]. Since the focus of the paper is on provisioning strategies, we leave the work on experimenting with other approaches for deriving behavioral models for the future.

Another threat to validity relates to the fact that PRESTO uses FOREPOST for learning provisioning strategies. We do not claim that FOREPOST is able to learn sound and complete behavioral models. FOREPOST may miss some of the bottlenecks (and thus, it may miss opportunity to explore testing provisioning strategies in that context). However, in real contexts this may be less of a problem, especially when some of the "typical" usages of the application are known beforehand. Yet, we leave investigation on how undetected bottlenecks can impact performance of the applications deployed in the cloud for future work.

A threat to validity may come from relatively small loads which include at most 30 users simultaneously. However, our underlying experimental cloud platform has limited capabilities, and this threat is countered by the load chosen in a balanced way with respect to available resources. By increasing the load by five orders of magnitude, the underlying cloud platform capabilities would be increased by the same order and our experimental evaluation will stand.

5. EXPERIMENTAL RESULTS

The experimental results are shown in Figure 2. The left and right figures show experiments with CPU and database bottlenecks respectively. Experiments with the random inputs (i.e., Random) and selected input chosen in FOREPOST are common in all graphs. Other experiments are carried out for cloud configurations Δ_1-Δ_4 that we described in Section 4.3. Each experiment shows three bars. The blue, red, and green bars show throughputs for five, 15, and 30 users respectively. Exploratory performance random testing is notoriously difficult to find input types and loads to worsen an AUT's throughput below some acceptable level. Thus, we expect that the throughput for Random experiments will be higher as compared to the throughput for the selected inputs. As Fig. 2 shows, the throughput for selected-input experiments shows an average drop in performance by more than 50% as compared to an average throughput for the corresponding Random experiments, which demonstrates that FOREPOST effectively selects inputs that significantly reduce the throughput. We take the levels of throughput for selected-input experiments as baseline levels for the corresponding applications and the cloud configurations.

The experiment with selected inputs shows how the throughput falls below some unacceptable level, and the experiments for $\Delta_k, 1 \leq k \leq 4$, show how PRESTO provisions resources proactively to VMs to increase the throughput levels compared to the unacceptable level. Δ_1 scales up the VMs by 0.5GB of RAM and Δ_2 scales up the VMs by increasing the CPU speed by 0.5GHz. However, it

improves the throughput by less than 5%. Δ_3 scales up the VMs by adding one more CPU and it increases throughput by more than 40% in the CPU version and by around 30% in the database version compared to the throughput for selected-input experiments. Δ_4 allows two VMs executing requests in parallel. The throughput for Δ_4 increases almost 50% as compared to the throughput for selected-input experiments. A key here is that using the scale out operator to parallelize client request processing may achieve better throughput even with more users compared to the baseline level, thus improving the scalability of the deployed applications.

However, the scale out operator is expensive – starting and maintaining a new instance of VM leads to a higher cost compared to provisioning more RAM or CPU. Since we conduct separate experiments with CPU and database bottlenecks, our goal is to determine if PRESTO finds more economic provisioning strategies to improve the scalability of the AUTs. Note that CPU bottlenecks can be alleviated by adding more CPUs. Specifically, the scale up operator Δ_3 adds one more CPU while keeping the same quantity of RAM and the same number of VMs. On average, the difference between throughputs with Δ_3 and Δ_4 is less than 8% for CPU bottlenecks and it is over 20% for the database bottlenecks. Other scale up operators that add different quantities of RAM show little to none improvement. Naturally, PRESTO selects the configuration Δ_3 as a cheaper one for CPU bottlenecks and Δ_4 for database bottlenecks. **Our conclusion is to support RQ_1 in stating that not only does PRESTO determine effective provisioning strategies, but it also chooses them economically, so that stakeholders can balance the cost versus scalability when running applications in the cloud.**

Recall that we re-ran multiple experiments with PRESTO, since these experiments involve the random strategy. To statistically compare throughput values, we used one-way ANOVA and t-tests for paired two sample to evaluate the null hypothesis H_0 (Section 4.1). The results of t-tests showed that the applications' throughputs of PRESTO-based strategies Δ_1 and Δ_2 were comparable to the throughput of selected inputs with basic cloud infrastructure. However, for Δ_3 and Δ_4, most of other p-values were much smaller than 0.05, implying that the applications' throughputs when using other different PRESTO-based strategies were statistically significantly different as compared to the baseline approach. We also used one-way ANOVA to evaluate H_0. The results show that all p-values were substantially larger than the critical value (2.246). Hence, we reject H_0 and conclude that there is statistically significant difference in throughputs for the subject applications while using PRESTO-based strategies compared to the baseline ones.

PRESTO builds performance model for applications as a function that maps the inputs to outputs, finding performance rules that guide the input selection and pinpoint computationally intensive paths. In our experiments, it needed less than two hours to converge to stable rules for JPetStore. Once we obtained performance rules, we tried different provisioning strategies until we found the appropriate strategy that made the throughput for the application to increase to an acceptable level. There was no other manual effort needed in this process. **We support RQ_2 in stating that PRESTO is fast and efficient in learning provisioning strategies.**

Summary. Based on experimental results, we answer affirmatively to RQ_1 that the PRESTO provisioning strategies are effective in terms of improving the AUTs' performance and making them scalable. Moreover, once we obtained performance rules, it is easy to map the provisioning strategies to performance rules without much manual effort, thus we affirmatively answer RQ_2.

6. RELATED WORK

Learning rules helps stakeholders to optimize distributed systems for dynamically changing workloads [34, 31, 22]. In contrast,

PRESTO uses feedback-directed adaptive test scripts to locate most computationally intensive execution profiles and bottlenecks.

Several papers focused on improving the performance of applications deployed in the cloud [17, 27, 5, 29, 14, 6, 12, 33]. Klein et al. [19] defined a self-adaptation programming paradigm to "skip" optional functionality in the cloud-deployed applications. Frey et al. [8] used a simulation-based genetic algorithm for finding optimized cloud deployment options for the software in the cloud. An approach, ATUoCLES, allows collecting execution information for applications, which have all the logic to scale up and down automatically [9]. Spinner et al. proposed a model-based approach to improve AUT performance by adding/removing VMs [33]. However, none of these approaches analyze impact of specific inputs on the performance of deployed programs and efficient resource allocation in the cloud-based environments, which is done in PRESTO.

7. CONCLUSION AND FUTURE WORK

Our novel solution for *Provisioning Resources with Experimental SofTware mOdeling (PRESTO)* enhances cloud elasticity by learning and refining models of under-constrained applications throughout performance testing and using these models stakeholders can craft resource provisioning strategies for the cloud that are highly tailored for specific applications. Experimental results suggest that PRESTO is effective and efficient - up to 40% better response in provisioning resources on average when the AUT throughput worsened significantly. In summary, we extend the theory of cloud computing by utilizing performance testing in its load balancing and resource provisioning. We believe that our work is a successful attempt of using software engineering artifacts to guide cloud deployment of software. The future work will involve automatically searching for scaling operators to (de)allocate different resources to VMs and determining the provisioning strategies to maintain AUT's performance at an acceptable level.

Acknowledgements

This work is supported in part by the NSF IIP-1547597 and NSF CCF-1217928 grants. Any opinions, findings, and conclusions expressed herein are the authors' and do not necessarily reflect those of the sponsors.

8. REFERENCES

[1] A. Arcuri and L. Briand. A practical guide for using statistical tests to assess randomized algorithms in software engineering. In *ICSE '11*.

[2] A. Arcuri and L. Briand. A hitchhiker's guide to statistical tests for assessing randomized algorithms in software engineering. *STVR*, 2012.

[3] M. Armbrust, A. Fox, R. Griffith, A. D. Joseph, R. Katz, A. Konwinski, G. Lee, D. Patterson, A. Rabkin, I. Stoica, and M. Zaharia. A view of cloud computing. *Commun. ACM*.

[4] K. Birman, G. Chockler, and R. van Renesse. Toward a cloud computing research agenda. *SIGACT News'09*.

[5] P. C. Brebner. Is your cloud elastic enough?: Performance modelling the elasticity of infrastructure as a service (iaas) cloud applications. In *ICPE '12*.

[6] F. Brosig, N. Huber, and S. Kounev. Automated extraction of architecture-level performance models of distributed component-based systems. In *ASE'11*.

[7] Cloudstack. http://cloudstack.apache.org/.

[8] S. Frey, F. Fittkau, and W. Hasselbring. Search-based genetic optimization for deployment and reconfiguration of software in the cloud. In *ICSE '13*.

[9] A. Gambi, W. Hummer, and S. Dustdar. Automated testing of cloud-based elastic systems with autocles. In *ASE '13*.

[10] Google. Auto scaling on the google cloud platform. https://cloud.google.com/resources/articles/auto-scaling-on-the-google-cloud-platform.

[11] M. Grechanik, C. Fu, and Q. Xie. Automatically finding performance problems with feedback-directed learning software testing. In *ICSE'12*.

[12] N. Huber, A. van Hoorn, A. Koziolek, F. Brosig, and S. Kounev. Modeling run-time adaptation at the system architecture level in dynamic service-oriented environments. *SOCA'14*.

[13] S. Islam, K. Lee, A. Fekete, and A. Liu. How a consumer can measure elasticity for cloud platforms. In *ICPE '12*.

[14] P. Jamshidi, A. Ahmad, and C. Pahl. Autonomic resource provisioning for cloud-based software. In *SEAMS '14*.

[15] Z. M. Jiang, A. E. Hassan, G. Hamann, and P. Flora. Automated performance analysis of load tests. In *ICSM '09*.

[16] JMeter. https://jmeter.apache.org.

[17] K. Johnson, S. Reed, and R. Calinescu. Specification and quantitative analysis of probabilistic cloud deployment patterns. In *HVC'11*.

[18] JPetStore. http://sourceforge.net/projects/ibatisjpetstore.

[19] C. Klein, M. Maggio, K.-E. ρ Arzén, and F. Hernández-Rodriguez. Brownout: Building more robust cloud applications. In *ICSE '14*.

[20] D. Lo and S. Maoz. Scenario-based and value-based specification mining: Better together. In *ASE '10*.

[21] D. Lorenzoli, L. Mariani, and M. Pezzè. Automatic generation of software behavioral models. In *ICSE '08*.

[22] Q. Luo, A. Nair, M. Grechanik, and D. Poshyvanyk. Forepost: Finding performance problems automatically with feedback-directed learning software testing. *EMSE*, 2016.

[23] H. Mendelson. Economies of scale in computing: Grosch's law revisited. *Commun. ACM*.

[24] NetScaler. http://www.citrix.com/netscalervpx.

[25] T. Ohmann, M. Herzberg, S. Fiss, A. Halbert, M. Palyart, I. Beschastnikh, and Y. Brun. Behavioral resource-aware model inference. In *ASE '14*.

[26] T. Ohmann, K. Thai, I. Beschastnikh, and Y. Brun. Mining precise performance-aware behavioral models from existing instrumentation. In *ICSE Companion '14*.

[27] D. Perez-Palacin, R. Calinescu, and J. Merseguer. Log2cloud: Log-based prediction of cost-performance trade-offs for cloud deployments. In *SAC '13*.

[28] PRESTO. http://www.cs.wm.edu/semeru/data/ICPE16-PRESTO/.

[29] M. Sedaghat, F. Hernandez-Rodriguez, and E. Elmroth. A virtual machine re-packing approach to the horizontal vs. vertical elasticity trade-off for cloud autoscaling. In *CAC '13*.

[30] A. Shankar, M. Arnold, and R. Bodik. Jolt: Lightweight dynamic analysis and removal of object churn. In *OOPSLA '08*.

[31] D. Shen, Q. Luo, D. Poshyvanyk, and M. Grechanik. Automating performance bottleneck detection using search-based application profiling. In *ISSTA '15*.

[32] J. E. Smith and R. Nair. The architecture of virtual machines. *Computer'05*.

[33] S. Spinner, S. Kounev, X. Zhu, L. Lu, M. Uysal, A. Holler, and R. Griffith. Runtime vertical scaling of virtualized applications via online model estimation. In *SASO'14*.

[34] J. Wildstrom, P. Stone, E. Witchel, and M. Dahlin. Machine learning for on-line hardware reconfiguration. In *IJCAI'07*.

Optimized eeeBond: Energy Efficiency with non-Proportional Router Network Interfaces

Niklas Carlsson
Linköping University, Sweden
niklas.carlsson@liu.se

ABSTRACT

The recent Energy Efficient Ethernet (EEE) standard and the eBond protocol provide two orthogonal approaches that allow significant energy savings on routers. In this paper we present the modeling and performance evaluation of these two protocols and a hybrid protocol. We first present eee-Bond, pronounced "triple-e bond", which combines the eBond capability to switch between multiple redundant interfaces with EEE's active/idle toggling capability implemented in each interface. Second, we present an analytic model of the protocol performance, and derive closed-form expressions for the optimized parameter settings of both eBond and eeeBond. Third, we present a performance evaluation that characterizes the relative performance gains possible with the optimized protocols, as well as a trace-based evaluation that validates the insights from the analytic model. Our results show that there are significant advantages to combine eBond and EEE. The eBond capability provides good savings when interfaces only offer small energy savings when in short-term sleep states, and the EEE capability is important as short-term sleep savings improve.

Keywords

Energy Efficiency, EEE, eBond, Adaptive Link Rate, Energy Proportional Computing, Router Performance

1. INTRODUCTION

High energy costs associated with the operation of network equipment have prompted the development of energy efficient policies and techniques for router management [1–3]. This desire has been further compounded by the high CO_2 emissions associated with non-green energy sources and an expectation of increasing energy prices.

Energy proportionality has been expressed as a desirable energy target [4], suggesting that the energy usage of a system should be proportional to the system utilization. As Internet routers typically are over provisioned, serve highly diurnal and time varying workloads, and often operate at low utilization, there should be substantial room for energy savings. However, due to hardware limitations, the energy consumption of active router interfaces are not energy proportional, and the full energy savings are therefore often difficult to achieve in practice. For this reason, protocols and policies have been proposed to make the best possible use of the existing hardware.

Two fundamental and promising approaches to scale the energy usage based on the current traffic load is to save energy by either (i) toggle between parallel, redundant, and heterogeneous interfaces [5], or (ii) toggle each interface between an active high-power mode and a low-power idle mode, during which some interface components are put to temporary sleep [3]. eBond [5] takes the first approach. It uses redundant heterogeneous links and Ethernet's bonding feature to toggle between which interface is used. When the router is lightly loaded a low-bandwidth link (with lower energy usage) is used, allowing the regular high-bandwidth link (with higher energy usage) to be turned off. In contrast, the recent Energy Efficient Ethernet (EEE) [3] standard takes the second approach. EEE allows an individual interface to save energy by switching between a low-power idle mode and an active high-power mode. Both eBond and EEE can allow significant energy savings, but both come with shortcomings.

In this paper we make three contributions towards improving and understanding the energy savings of routers. First, we present eeeBond (pronounced "triple-e bond"), which combines eBond and EEE into a simple hybrid protocol. As shown in Table 1, eeeBond combines the eBond capability to toggle between multiple heterogeneous redundant interfaces with EEE's active/idle toggling capability implemented in each interface. Second, we present a unified analytic model of the performance of these protocols and derive closed-form expressions and explicit conditions for the optimized parameter settings of both eBond and eeeBond. Using our model we analyze and discuss the energy saving tradeoffs in both existing and future systems.

Third, we present a performance evaluation that characterizes the performance gains possible with EEE and the optimized versions of both eBond and eeeBond. Our results show that there are significant advantages to combine eBond and EEE. For current technology that often see small energy savings in short-term sleep states, the eBond capability provides most of the energy savings, whereas the EEE component (especially if combined with eBond, as in eee-Bond) provides great improvements when short-term sleep states would allow greater energy savings. The energy sav-

ICPE'16, March 12–18, 2016, Delft, Netherlands.
© 2016 ACM. ISBN 978-1-4503-4080-9/16/03. . . $15.00
DOI: http://dx.doi.org/10.1145/2851553.2851564

	Always active	Active/idle toggling
Single interface	Naive/default	EEE [3]
Multi interface	eBond [5]	eeeBond

ings with eBond, achieved through router management, are important as it is likely to be many years before we have fully proportional router hardware on the market, and the significant additional savings using eeeBond when short-term sleep states allow greater energy savings are encouraging for future systems. The conclusions based on our analytic models are complemented with a trace-based evaluation that validates the insights from the analytic model.

The remainder of the paper is organized as follows. Sections 2 and 3 presents an overview of the protocols considered in this paper, including eeeBond, and our system model, respectively. We then present our protocol optimizations (Section 4) and policy evaluation (Section 5), before concluding the paper with a discussion of related work (Section 6) and our conclusions (Section 7).

2. PROTOCOL OVERVIEW

The Energy Efficient Ethernet (EEE) [3] standard assumes a Lower Power Idle (LPI) mode and a (high-power) active mode, and defines the signaling that is required between the transmitter and the receiver when the former toggles back-and-forth between the two modes. Unfortunately, today's hardware does not allow EEE to be energy proportional. First, the interfaces often consume a significant amount of energy even when in sleep mode [5–7]. Second, there are non-negligible activation times and energy costs associated with activating an interface. For example, to achieve the suggested wakeup time (equal to the transmission time of the maximum length packet [6]) typically very few circuits in the physical layer can be turned off during the idle mode, resulting in only modest energy savings. As these hardware technologies continue to improve, and the energy usage in sleep states decrease, the expectation is that advanced hardware technologies will allow greater energy savings (up to 80%) [6].

An orthogonal approach that does not require such hardware improvements, is to leverage the use of redundant interfaces to allow one or more interfaces to go into deep sleep. As long as at least one sufficiently dimensioned interface is active, the router should be able to serve traffic demands.

This is the approach taken by eBond [5]. With eBond, the bonding protocol available and implemented in most routers is made energy-aware, such as to allow energy-aware switching between redundant heterogeneous links. For example, a low-bandwidth link can be used when the router is lightly loaded, allowing the regular high-bandwidth link to be turned off. By adapting which interface is active the capacity and energy usage can be tuned based on current traffic load.

Naturally, considering a single interface, the deep sleep modes used with eBond typically allow much greater energy savings, but comes at the cost of much longer activation times (than the sleep modes used by EEE). Therefore protocols switching between multiple redundant interfaces, must typically operate at a longer time granularity than the granularity at which EEE operates.

Motivated by eBond and EEE operating at different time

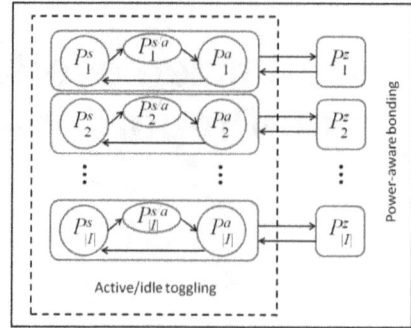

Figure 1: Router model and power states for each interface.

scales, this papers considers a simple hybrid generalization that we call eeeBond. With eeeBond, routers would have the flexibility to both (i) switch between interfaces with different capacity and energy usage, and (ii) toggle the currently used interface between active and idle mode. We expect that an eeeBond system would use energy-aware bonding (putting some interfaces to long-term deep sleep) at larger time granularity, and active/idle toggling (to/from the short-term sleep state) at a finer time granularity. For example, interface selection can be based in diurnal long-term variations in traffic volumes and active/idle toggling can be used to take into account energy saving opportunities due to short-term variations in traffic intensity.

3. SYSTEM MODEL

We consider a single router and compare policies that differ based on their capability to (i) toggle between multiple redundant links (bonding as in eBond [5]) and (ii) perform active/idle toggling (as in EEE [3]). Table 1 summarizes the four resulting candidate protocols.

- **Naive baseline:** Single interface policy that does not attempt to leverage any low-power modes.

- **EEE using single interface:** Single interface policy that uses active/idle toggling to reduce energy usage.

- **eBond:** Multi-interface policy that use energy-aware bonding to save energy.

- **eeeBond:** Multi-interface policy that use both energy-aware bonding and active/idle toggling.

Naturally, all protocols are special cases of eeeBond, and only differ in which of the two types of energy saving capabilities are implemented. To compare the relative importance and tradeoffs associated with these energy saving capabilities, we present a unified model that captures both these aspects of eeeBond and the other protocols.

3.1 General Model

Figure 1 illustrates our basic router model. For the purpose of our discussion and analysis, consider a router with $|\mathcal{I}|$ redundant interfaces, where $\mathcal{I}$ is the set of such interfaces.

Energy usage: We will consider a basic hardware model in which each interface can be in one of four power states:

- An *active* high-power state with an average power usage P_i^a in which the interface operates at full link capacity μ_i.

- A low-power *short-term (light) sleep* state with an average power usage P_i^s, which allows the interface to quickly enter the active state.

- A short *setup period* Δ_i during which the interface is activated from the short-term (light) sleep period. The average power usage during this time period is $P_i^{s/a}$.

- A low-power *long-term deep sleep* state with an average power usage P_i^z, which allows bigger energy savings than short-term sleep (i.e., $P_i^z < P_i^s$) but that require longer activation periods, and hence only can be used at coarser time granularity.

Of course, in a real system, there would also be a state bringing the interface from the active to the short-term sleep state, as well as transition states bringing the interface in and out of the deep sleep state. However, for the purpose of the analysis we do not include these states. The energy consumed in the first case can easily be accounted by adjusting the $P_i^{s/a}$ term (as there is always a corresponding activation period). For the latter case, we note that the bonding policies considered here are expected to operate at a much longer time granularity and the system therefore would only be in these transition states for a very small fraction of the total system time.

Furthermore, motivated by the above time granularity differences, we assume that, at any given point in time, one interface is responsible for the current traffic over the link. This interface is in one of the first three states (i.e., in the active, short-term sleep, or in the interface setup period) shown on left-hand side of Figure 1. All other interfaces are assumed to be in the long-term deep sleep state (right-hand side of Figure 1).

Consider the system's power usage measured over a long time period, and let the probabilities q_i^a, q_i^s, $q_i^{s/a}$, and q_i^z represent the probability of observing interface i in each of these four states (equal to the fraction of time the system would spend in each state if measured for a very long time). With this notation, the average power usage can be calculated as:

$$P_{\mathcal{I}} = \sum_{i \in \mathcal{I}} \left[q_i^a P_i^a + q_i^s P_i^s + q_i^{s/a} P_i^{s/a} + q_i^z P_i^z \right]. \quad (1)$$

Hardware comparison: For simple head-to-head policy comparison under both current and future hardware systems, we use system parameters (c_i, g_i) to capture the relative energy usage between the different states of an interface and the parameter x to capture the relative energy scaling seen between the heterogeneous interfaces' energy usage.

First, we use a constant c_i $(0 \le c_i \le 1)$ to capture the energy savings ratio $c_i = \frac{P_i^s}{P_i^a}$, of the power usage in the short-term sleep and active mode, respectively. While current systems often have a ratio between 0.8 and 1, future systems may be able to achieve much smaller ratios (e.g., 0.2) [6]. In the ideal case $c_i = 0$. Second, we define $g_i = \frac{P_i^{s/a}}{P_i^a}$ as the ratio between the power usage during the active state and during the setup period. (For most cases, we assume $g_i \approx 1$.) Finally, to allow a wide range of scaling behaviors (and to accommodate for potential future energy trends, for example) we assume that $P_i^a = f(\mu_i)$, where $f(\mu_i) = P_0^a (\frac{\mu_i}{\mu_0})^x$ and P_0^a corresponds to the power usage for a reference system with service rate μ_0. We note that this function is linear

when $x = 1$, sublinear when $x < 1$, and superlinear when $x > 1$. This model and model parameter is used to capture how the expected active power P_i^a differs between interfaces. While the energy usage clearly will vary significantly from implementation to implementation and likely will differ significantly in magnitude from the most efficient technology one decade to the most effective technology during the next decade, we expect that the current power usage typically will scale superlinearly ($x > 1$) with the service rate μ_i of the interfaces.

General per-interface delay: We extend the basic router model developed and validated using real traffic by Hohn et al. [8]. Motivated by current state of the art, only transmission delays and queueing delays on the outgoing interface are considered. Assuming a First-In-First-Out (FIFO) queueing policy and infinite buffer size (motivated by the low-loss scenario and line cards often able to accommodate up to 500 ms worth of traffic) the delay w_k experienced by the kth packet of *active* router interface i with service rate μ_i is then

$$w_k = [w_{k-1} - (t_k - t_{k-1})]^+ + \frac{l_k}{\mu_i}, \quad (2)$$

where $[y]^+ = \max(y, 0)$, and t_k is the arrival time of the kth packet of length l_k. For additional details, motivation, and validation of the model and these assumptions, we refer the interested reader to the original paper [8].

To extend this model to the case in which an interface is allowed to be in short-term sleep mode whenever there are no packets to serve, we must take into account the time Δ_i it takes to activate the link from the short-term sleep mode when a new packet arrives. The delays of such a policy can be modeled as follows:

$$w_k = \begin{cases} \Delta_i + \frac{l_k}{\mu_i}, & \text{if } t_k > t_{k-1} + w_{k-1} \\ w_{k-1} + t_{k-1} - t_k + \frac{l_k}{\mu_i}, & \text{otherwise.} \end{cases} \quad (3)$$

3.2 Steady-state Model

We next derive closed-form expressions for the expected waiting times and probabilities to be in each of the operation states. For this analysis, we consider a system in steady state, as often observed over shorter periods, for example [9]. Assuming that packets arrive according to a Poisson process (i.e., independent and exponentially distributed packet inter-arrival times) and the size of packets are mutually independent, we model the system as a $M/G/1(E, SU)$ queue with exhaustive service, multiple vacation periods, and setup time [10–13]. Under this model, the interface remains active serving packets (with expected service time $E[S_i]$) as long as there is at least one packet waiting to be served, and then goes on a "vacation" when there is no packet(s) to serve. When a new packet arrives to the interface, a setup time Δ_i is required the packet can be served. We also leverage the PASTA property that Poisson arrivals see time averages [14]. Given a packet arrival rate λ, the expected waiting time $\overline{W_i}$ for interface i can then be calculated as:

$$\overline{W_i} = E[w_k|i] = \frac{\lambda E[S_i^2]}{2(1-\rho_i)} + \frac{2E[\Delta_i] + \lambda E[\Delta_i^2]}{2(1 + \lambda E[\Delta_i])}, \quad (4)$$

where $E[S_i^2]$ is the expected service time squared, ρ_i is the expected interface utilization when interface i is active, and $E[\Delta_i]$ and $E[\Delta_i^2]$ are the expected setup times and setup-times squared, respectively. Note that the second term approaches zero as $\Delta_i \to 0$, and the expected waiting time therefore becomes equal to that of a regular $M/G/1$ queue (i.e., the first term in equation (4)) in this case.

To allow comparison of interfaces operating at different service rate, we break out the interface dependent service rates from the above expression for the expected waiting time $\overline{W_i}$. To do so, we use the following equalities: $E[S_i^2] = \frac{E[l_k^2]}{\mu_i^2}$, $\rho_i = \lambda\frac{E[l_k]}{\mu_i}$, $E[\Delta_i] = \frac{\max_k l_k}{\mu_i}$, and $E[\Delta_i^2] = \frac{\max_k l_k^2}{\mu_i^2}$. The first two equalities are true in general, whereas the last two are motivated by the EEE specifications which suggest that the setup time should be equal to the processing time of the largest packets; i.e., $\Delta_i = \max_k l_k/\mu_i$. With these observations, we can rewrite the expected waiting time as:

$$\overline{W_i} = \frac{\lambda\frac{E[l_k^2]}{\mu_i^2}}{2(1 - \lambda\frac{E[l_k]}{\mu_i})} + \frac{2\frac{\max_k l_k}{\mu_i} + \lambda\frac{\max_k l_k^2}{\mu_i^2}}{2(1 + \lambda\frac{\max_k l_k}{\mu_i})}. \quad (5)$$

To evaluate the energy usage under steady state conditions, we next calculate the state probabilities q_i^a, q_i^s, $q_i^{s/a}$, and q_i^z. Note that q_i^z simply is the long-term probability not being in an active/idle-mode state (using EEE, for example). Consider therefore the probabilities when in such active/idle mode. In this case, the busy probability can be calculated as

$$\frac{q_i^a}{1 - q_i^z} = \rho_i = \lambda\frac{E[l_k]}{\mu_i}, \quad (6)$$

the idle probability can be calculated as

$$\frac{q_i^s}{1 - q_i^z} = \frac{1 - \rho_i}{1 + \lambda E[\Delta_i]} = \frac{1 - \lambda\frac{E[l_k]}{\mu_i}}{1 + \lambda\frac{\max_k l_k}{\mu_i}}, \quad (7)$$

and finally, the setup probability can be calculated as

$$\frac{q_i^{s/a}}{1 - q_i^z} = \frac{\lambda(1 - \rho)E[\Delta_i]}{1 + \lambda E[\Delta_i]} = \frac{\lambda(1 - \lambda\frac{E[l_k]}{\mu_i})\frac{\max_k l_k}{\mu_i}}{1 + \lambda\frac{\max_k l_k}{\mu_i}}. \quad (8)$$

Here, $\rho_i = \lambda E[S] = \lambda\frac{E[l_k]}{\mu_i}$ is the utilization and $1 + \lambda E[\Delta_i] = 1 + \lambda\frac{\max_k l_k}{\mu_i}$ is the expected number of arrivals during an idle period. These probabilities can now be used with equation (1) to calculate the average power usage. For example, separating the power usage for the time period interfaces i is used and inserting the above conditional probabilities we obtain:

$$\frac{P_i - q_i^z P_i^z}{1 - q_i^z} = \left[\rho_i P_i^a + \frac{1 - \rho_i}{1 + \lambda E[\Delta_i]} P_i^s + \frac{\lambda(1 - \rho)E[\Delta_i]}{1 + \lambda E[\Delta_i]} P_i^{s/a}\right]$$
$$= \left[\lambda\frac{E[l_k]}{\mu_i} P_i^a + \frac{1 - \lambda\frac{E[l_k]}{\mu_i}}{1 + \lambda\frac{\max_k l_k}{\mu_i}} P_i^s + \frac{\lambda(1 - \lambda\frac{E[l_k]}{\mu_i})\frac{\max_k l_k}{\mu_i}}{1 + \lambda\frac{\max_k l_k}{\mu_i}} P_i^{s/a}\right]. \quad (9)$$

Equation (9) captures the energy usage of an interface using EEE as used by the interface not in low-power deep-sleep mode with eeeBond. We will use equations (5) and (9) when selecting which interface to keep active.

4. PROTOCOL OPTIMIZATION

Both the energy-delay tradeoff and the optimal policies of eBond and eeeBond differ. Definition 1 defines what we mean with an optimal policy, and in the following subsections we define the optimal eBond and eeeBond policies, and use our analytic model to provide insights to their characteristics.

DEFINITION 1. *The optimal policy always picks the interface with the lowest power usage, conditioned on also having an average waiting time W less than or equal to some threshold W^*. When no such interface exists, the policy picks the interface with the shortest expected waiting time W.*

4.1 Optimized eBond

THEOREM 1. *Given an average target waiting time W^* and an estimated packet inter arrival rate λ, the optimal eBond policy always picks the interface with the lowest service rates μ_i that can support a packet arrival rate*

$$\lambda \leq \lambda_i^* = \frac{2(W^* - E[S_i])}{E[S_i^2] + 2E[S_i](W^* - E[S_i])}, \quad (10)$$

where $E[S_i] = \frac{E[l_k]}{\mu_i}$ and $E[S_i^2] = \frac{E[l_k^2]}{\mu_i^2}$.

PROOF. (Theorem 1) First, the waiting time (for this $M/G/1$ queueing system without vacation periods) is monotonically non-decreasing. Second, we show that the energy usage of an interface with lower service rate μ_i always consumes less energy. To see this, note that we in this case have $\frac{q_i^a}{1 - q_i^z} = 1$, $\frac{q_i^s}{1 - q_i^z} = 0$, and $\frac{q_i^{s/a}}{1 - q_i^z} = 0$. With these observations, the power usage $\frac{P_i}{1 - P_i^z} = P_0^a(\frac{\mu_i}{\mu_0})^x$, clearly is monotonically non-decreasing for $x \geq 0$. To see this note that: $\frac{dP_i}{d\mu_i} = \frac{d}{d\mu_i}[P_0^a(\frac{\mu_i}{\mu_0})^x] = xP_0^a\frac{\mu_i^{x-1}}{\mu_0^x} \geq 0$. Third, we show that the expected waiting times are non-decreasing. Taking the derivative of the average waiting time in a $M/G/1$ queue (without vacations)

$$W_i = \frac{\lambda E[S_i^2]}{2(1 - \rho_i)} + E[S_i] = \frac{\lambda\frac{E[l_k^2]}{\mu_i^2}}{2(1 - \lambda\frac{E[l_k]}{\mu_i})} + \frac{E[l_k]}{\mu_i} \quad (11)$$

with regards to the service rate, we get:

$$\frac{dW_i}{d\mu_i} = -\frac{E[S_i^2]\lambda E[l_k]}{2(1 - \rho_i)^2\mu_i^2} - \frac{E[l_k]}{(1 - \rho_i)\mu_i^3} - \frac{E[l_k]}{\mu_i^2}, \quad (12)$$

which clearly is no greater than zero (as all three terms are negative) for all $0 \leq \rho_i \leq 1$. Fourth, with monotonic ordering of the energy usage and waiting times in terms of both μ_i and λ, we can obtain the threshold value λ_i^* by setting equation (11) equal to W^* and solving for λ_i^*. After minor reordering we obtain equation (10). This completes the proof. $\square$

4.2 Optimized eeeBond

Before defining and proving the optimal eeeBond policy we first identify and prove five properties of eeeBond. These are defined in the following five lemmas.

First, note that the use of a setup period causes the average waiting time W_i to be a non-monotonic function that first decreases and then increase with the packet arrival rate λ. To see this, note that the waiting time for very low arrival rates approaches Δ_i as $\lambda \to 0$, is lower for intermediate arrival rates (for which many packets may arrive with only a single packet ahead of them in the queue[1]), and then increase

---
[1]Each such packet sees a conditioned waiting time equal to the residual service time, which is smaller than the expected service time $E[W_k|1] \leq E[S_i]$, and hence also smaller than the setup time $E[S_i] = \frac{E[l_k]}{\mu_i} \leq \frac{\max_k l_k}{\mu_i} = \Delta_i$.

again as the link utilization approaches one. Our first lemma formalizes these observations and defines conditions for (i) when the waiting times are monotonically non-decreasing and (ii) when the average waiting times W_i with an arrival rate λ always is lower than that of a baseline arrival rate λ^*.

LEMMA 1. *The expected waiting time W_i is a monotonically non-decreasing function of the arrival rate λ for the region in which $W_i \geq \Delta_i$, and for any $\lambda \leq \lambda^*$ for which $W_i^* = W_i(\lambda^*) \geq \Delta_i$, the waiting time $W_i(\lambda) \leq W_i(\lambda^*)$.*

PROOF. (Lemma 1) Consider the derivative of the expected waiting time:

$$\frac{dW}{d\lambda} = \frac{E[S_i^2]}{2(1-\rho_i)^2} - \frac{\Delta_i^2}{2(1+\lambda\Delta_i)^2}. \tag{13}$$

This function is negative for $\lambda < \frac{\Delta_i^2 - E[S_i^2]}{\Delta_i E[S_i^2] + \Delta_i^2 E[S_i]}$ and positive for $\frac{\Delta_i^2 - E[S_i^2]}{\Delta_i E[S_i^2] + \Delta_i^2 E[S_i]} < \lambda$. Let $\lambda^{**} = \frac{\Delta_i^2 - E[S_i^2]}{\Delta_i E[S_i^2] + \Delta_i^2 E[S_i]}$ define the arrival rate with the minimum waiting time. With $W(\lambda) \to \Delta_i$ as $\lambda \to 0$ and a single minimum, we know that the minimum waiting time $W_i^{**} = W_i(\lambda^{**}) \leq \Delta_i$ and there exists a $\lambda^{***} \geq \lambda^{**}$ for which $W_i(\lambda^{***}) = \Delta_i$. Clearly, for $0 \leq \lambda \leq \lambda^{***}$, we have $W_i(\lambda) \leq \Delta_i \leq W_i$, and for any larger packet arrival rates $\lambda^{***} \leq \lambda$ the function is monotonically non-decreasing. This completes the proof. □

LEMMA 2. *The expected waiting time W_i is a monotonically non-increasing function of the service rate μ_i.*

PROOF. (Lemma 2) This proof is relatively straight forward. First, note that the waiting time W_i of a $M/G/1(E, SU)$ queue can be broken up into a term $W_i^{M/G/1}$ that is independent of the setup time Δ_i and a second term $W_i^{\Delta_i}$ that depends on the setup time. As for any M/G/1 system, the first term is non-increasing. For the second term we substitute $\Delta_i = \frac{\max_k l_k}{\mu_i}$ and take the derivative with regards to μ_i:

$$\frac{dW_i^{\Delta_i}}{d\mu_i} = \frac{d}{d\mu_i}\left[\frac{2\Delta_i + \lambda\Delta_i^2}{2(1+\lambda\Delta_i)}\right] = \frac{-4\frac{\Delta_i}{\mu_i} - 4\lambda\frac{\Delta_i^2}{\mu_i} - 2\lambda^2\frac{\Delta_i^3}{\mu_i}}{4(1+\lambda\Delta_i)^2} \leq 0.$$

This function is non-positive, and hence both $W_i^{\Delta_i}$ and W_i must be non-increasing with μ_i. □

LEMMA 3. *Given a target delay $W^* \geq \Delta_i$, unless there does not exist any interface with higher service rate, the optimal policy never picks a low-power interface with service rate μ_i when the packet arrival rate λ exceeds an upper bound*

$$\lambda_i^u = \frac{-a_1 + \sqrt{a_1^2 - 4a_2 a_0}}{2a_2}, \tag{14}$$

where $a_2 = \Delta_i E[S_i](2W^* - \Delta_i) + \Delta_i E[S_i^2]$, $a_1 = E[S_i^2] + 2E[S_i](W^* - \Delta_i) + \Delta_i(\Delta_i - 2W^*)$, and $a_0 = 2(\Delta - W^*)$.

PROOF. (Lemma 3) This proof follows directly from Lemmas 1 and 2. As per the monotonicity property in Lemma 1, there must exist an arrival rate λ^u such that the waiting time W_i of interface i is greater than W^* for all $\lambda > \lambda_i^u$. From Lemma 2 it also follows that in the case $\lambda > \lambda_i^u$ and $W_i \geq W^* \geq \Delta$, the waiting time of an interface with the same λ but higher service rate is no worse. Therefore, interface i should never be selected in this case. Setting equation (5) equal to W^* and rewriting the equation we obtain a

second-order equation $a_2\lambda^2 + a_1\lambda + a_0 = 0$, with the parameters a_2, a_1 and a_0 defined as in the above lemma. While such an equation has two solutions, it is easy to show that only the solution above is positive and of consideration. To see this, note that the constraint $W^* \geq \Delta_i$ directly implies that $a_2 \geq 0$ and $a_0 \leq 0$. Therefore, $\sqrt{a_1^2 - 4a_2 a_0} \geq -a_1$ and only the solution shown in the lemma is positive; completing our proof. □

LEMMA 4. *The expected power usage P_i is a monotonically non-decreasing function of the service rate μ whenever the relative energy scaling parameter x satisfies the condition:*

$$x \geq x^* = \frac{\Delta_i + E[S_i]}{G + \lambda H}, \tag{15}$$

where $G = c + (1+c)\Delta_i + (1-c)E[S_i]$, $H = \Delta_i(\Delta_i + (1-c)E[S_i])$, and $c = \frac{P_i^s}{P_i^a}$. Otherwise, the expected power usage P_i is a monotonically non-increasing function of μ.

PROOF. (Lemma 4) With the power usage during a "non-deep-sleep" period either being equal to P_i^a (active and transition mode) or P_i^s (sleep mode), we can rewrite the power usage as:

$$\frac{P_i}{1-q_i^z} = \frac{1-\lambda E[S_i]}{1+\lambda\Delta_i}P_i^s + (1 - \frac{1-\lambda E[S_i]}{1+\lambda\Delta_i})P_i^a$$
$$= \frac{c + \lambda\Delta_i + \lambda E[S_i](1-c)}{1+\lambda\Delta_i}P_i^a. \tag{16}$$

By identifying μ_i terms, we can rewrite this expression as $\frac{c + \frac{a}{\mu_i}}{1 + \frac{b}{\mu_i}}P_i^a(\mu_i)$, where $a = \lambda^2\Delta_i + \lambda^2(1-c)E[S_i]$ and $b = \lambda\mu_i\Delta_i$. With $\frac{d}{d\mu_i}(\frac{c + \frac{a}{\mu_i}}{1 + \frac{b}{\mu_i}}) = \frac{cb - a}{\mu_i^2(1 + \frac{b}{\mu_i})^2}$ and $\frac{d}{d\mu_i}P_i^a(\mu_i) = \frac{x}{\mu_i}P_i^a$, we can now calculate the derivative

$$\frac{d}{d\mu_i}(\frac{P_i}{1-q_i^z}) = \frac{cb - a}{\mu_i^2(1 + \frac{b}{\mu_i})^2}P_i^a + \frac{c + \frac{a}{\mu_i}}{1 + \frac{b}{\mu_i}}\frac{x}{\mu_i}P_i^a$$
$$= \frac{cb(1+x) + a(x-1) + cx\mu_i + \frac{abx}{\mu_i}}{\mu_i^2(1 + \frac{b}{\mu_i})^2}. \tag{17}$$

Clearly, the derivative of this function is non-negative. As this function is non-positive when $x = 0$ (as $\frac{cb - a}{\mu_i^2(1 + \frac{b}{\mu_i})^2} = \frac{-\lambda(\Delta_i + E[S_i])}{\mu_i(1 + \frac{b}{\mu_i})^2} \leq 0$) and it is trivial to find positive values for larger x (e.g., for $x = 1$ the function is $\frac{c\mu_i + \frac{ab}{\mu_i}}{\mu_i^2(1 + \frac{b}{\mu_i})^2} \geq 0$), there must therefore exist an x^* such that the function $\frac{P_i}{1-q_i^z}$ is monotonically non-decreasing function whenever $x \geq x^*$ and monotonically non-increasing otherwise. Setting equation (17) equal to zero, solving for x^*, and identifying terms, gives $x^* = \frac{A - cB}{cB + A + c + \frac{AB}{\mu_i}}$, where $A = \frac{a}{\lambda} = \lambda\Delta_i + \lambda(1-c)E[S_i]$ and $B = \frac{b}{\mu_i} = \lambda\Delta_i$. Finally, inserting the expressions for A and B and simplifying the expression (including identifying G and H), while isolating λ, completes the proof. □

Leveraging the Lemmas 1-4 we are now in a position to define and prove the optimal interface selection for eeeBond.

LEMMA 5. *Unless there does not exist another interface with higher service rate, the optimal policy never picks a low-rate, low-power interface with service rate μ_i (over an*

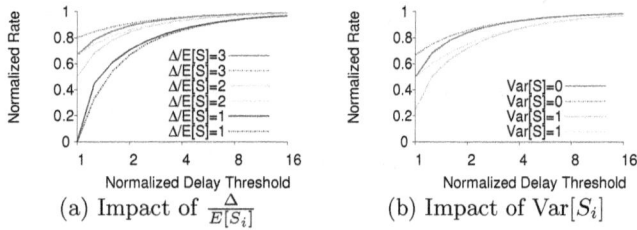

Figure 2: Normalized threshold rates calculated per equations (10) and (14) for different example scenarios.

Table 2: Normalized power usage with diurnal model.

Scenario		$\bar{u}$	x	Current $c = 0.8$			Future $c = 0.2$		
				EEE	eBond	e³B	EEE	eBond	e³B
Two		0.5	1.2	0.95	0.76	**0.73**	0.76	0.76	**0.65**
		0.25	1.2	0.90	**0.49**	0.49	0.58	0.49	**0.38**
		0.125	1.2	0.87	0.44	**0.39**	0.44	0.44	**0.25**
		0.25	0.8	0.90	0.62	**0.60**	0.58	0.62	**0.47**
		0.25	2	0.90	**0.32**	0.34	0.58	0.32	**0.27**
Three		0.5	1.2	0.95	**0.74**	0.81	0.76	0.74	**0.68**
		0.25	1.2	0.90	**0.57**	0.59	0.58	0.57	**0.45**
		0.125	1.2	0.87	**0.43**	0.47	0.44	0.43	**0.30**
		0.25	0.8	0.90	**0.66**	0.67	0.58	0.66	**0.51**
		0.25	2	0.90	**0.45**	0.48	0.58	0.45	**0.36**

interface with higher service rate) when the packet arrival rate λ is less than a lower bound

$$\lambda_i^l = \frac{1}{H}(\Delta_i + E[S_i] - xG), \tag{18}$$

where G and H are defined as in Lemma 4.

PROOF. (Lemma 5) The proof builds upon Lemmas 4 and 2. Lemma 4 implies that for a given arrival rate λ, the power usage will only be lower at the low-rate interface when $x \geq x^*$. As the targeted average waiting time conditioned on being no smaller than Δ, is a monotonically non-decreasing function (Lemma 2) of the service rate μ_i, there is therefore never an advantage in selecting the low-rate interface unless $x < x^*$. Now, taking the derivative of x^* (equation (15)), we note that the derivative $\frac{dx^*}{d\lambda} \leq 0$ is a non-positive function of λ. This shows that for any x (observed for the current technology), there exists a λ_i^l such that $x \geq x^*$ for all $\lambda \geq \lambda_i^l$. To find this λ_i^l we insert $x^* = x$ and $\lambda = \lambda_i^l$ in equation (15) and solve for λ_i^l. This completes the proof. □

THEOREM 2. *Given a target waiting time $W^* \geq \max_i \Delta_i$ and arrival rate λ, the optimal eeeBond policy picks the lowest powered interface that satisfy both (i) $\lambda_i^l \leq \lambda$, and (ii) $\lambda \leq \lambda_i^u$, where λ_i^l and λ_i^u are given by equations (18) and (14), respectively. In the case no interface satisfies both constraints, the optimal policy picks the highest capacity interface.*

PROOF. (Theorem 2) This theorem follows directly from Lemmas 3 and 5. Per these lemmas, equation (18) lower bounds the arrival rates for when an interface i is a candidate and equation (14) upper bounds the arrival rates for when interface i is a candidate. □

When applying Theorem 2 it is important to note that x typically is greater than 1 and λ_i^l therefore typically is non-positive. To see this, let us take a closer look at the lower bound (18) in Lemma 5. This expression is positive only when

$$x \leq \frac{\Delta_i + E[S_i]}{\Delta_i + E[S_i] + c(1 + \Delta_i - E[S_i])}. \tag{19}$$

With $\Delta_i \geq E[S_i]$ and $c \geq 0$, equation (19) is lower bounded by 1. Motivated by this observation, we focus on the upper bounds for eBond (equation (10)) and eeeBond (equation (14)). Figure 2 shows these two bounds as a function of the normalized delay threshold $\frac{W^*}{\Delta}$. Without loss of generality we use $E[S_i] = 1$ and measure the packet arrival rate λ in normalized units. With these normalized units, one time unit is equal to the average processing time of a packet, and the λ values shown in the figures are equal to the utilization

of the interface at the point when it is better to switch to a higher capacity interface.

We note that the rate thresholds are greatest in the cases with (i) the largest difference between the processing time of the largest packets (Δ) and average packets ($E[S_i]$), and (ii) the smallest variance in the processing time ($\text{Var}[S_i] = E[S_i^2] - E^2[S_i]$). This is to be expected as relatively small packets with small variations allow the system to operate at a higher utilization given a fixed delay threshold.

5. POLICY EVALUATION

5.1 Head-to-Head Comparison

To understand the relative performance of the four policies outlined in Section 2, we have evaluated the power usage for a wide range of scenarios. Figure 3 shows three such example scenarios. Here, we have used the packet size distributions from both edge and core traces (cf. Table 3), different power ratios $c = \frac{P_i^s}{P_i^a}$, different number of interfaces, and different service rate ratios $\frac{\mu_2}{\mu_1}$ and $\frac{\mu_3}{\mu_1}$.

We note that energy savings in sleep state typically are small today (e.g., $c = 0.8$), but are expected to improve (e.g., $c = 0.2$) in the future. While both eBond and eeeBond can achieve substantial energy savings in all scenarios, these results show that eeeBond (and EEE) perhaps have the greatest benefits as energy savings in sleep state improve (smaller c).

An interesting observation is that there are regions where eBond performs better than basic eeeBond. In these regions it is better not to shut off the low-power interface. A further improved policy would therefore try to recognize these regions, allowing us to match the bottom line (either eBond or eeeBond) in each figure.

Figure 4 shows the power usage as a function of the time of day for three example workloads. In each case, the packet arrival rate is calculated using a sinusoidal. Motivated by the light load typically seen in edge networks and somewhat heaver load in core networks, we combine the packet sizes from an edge network with a utility function with averege utility $\bar{u} = 0.25$ and the packet sizes from a core network with a utility function with average utility $\bar{u} = 0.5$. For the edge example we use a max-min ratio of 5 and for the core cases we use a max-min ratio of 9. We can again see that there are regions where both eBond and eeeBond have their respective advantages, but that they typically both significantly outperform Naive and EEE. Only when c is very small does EEE compete with eBond, and in no case does it perform better than eeeBond.

Table 2 summarizes the average normalized power usage

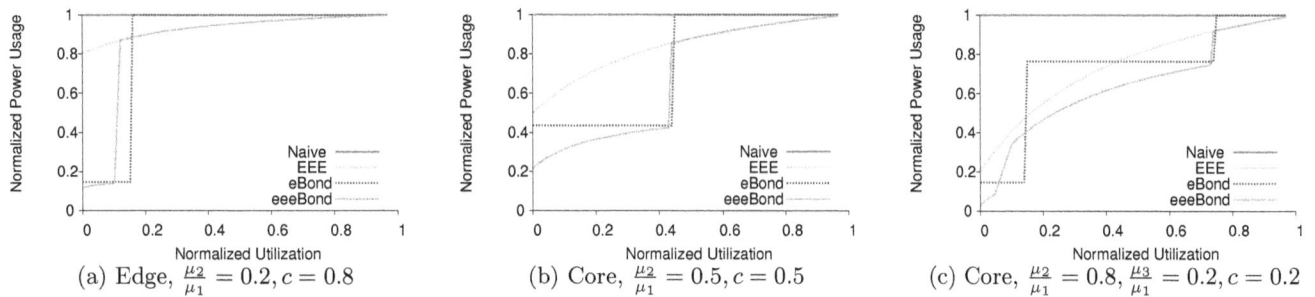

(a) Edge, $\frac{\mu_2}{\mu_1} = 0.2, c = 0.8$ (b) Core, $\frac{\mu_2}{\mu_1} = 0.5, c = 0.5$ (c) Core, $\frac{\mu_2}{\mu_1} = 0.8, \frac{\mu_3}{\mu_1} = 0.2, c = 0.2$

Figure 3: Energy usage under example scenarios. Analytic results based on packet size statistics from edge and core traces.

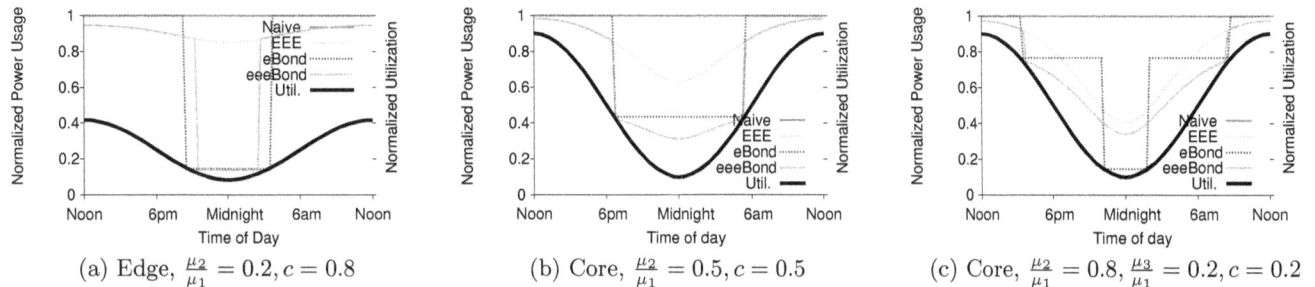

(a) Edge, $\frac{\mu_2}{\mu_1} = 0.2, c = 0.8$ (b) Core, $\frac{\mu_2}{\mu_1} = 0.5, c = 0.5$ (c) Core, $\frac{\mu_2}{\mu_1} = 0.8, \frac{\mu_3}{\mu_1} = 0.2, c = 0.2$

Figure 4: Time-of-day comparison using diurnal request rates. Switching instances calculated for optimized protocols (Section 4).

Table 3: Packet size statistics.

	$E[l_k]$	$E[l_k^2]$	$\max_k l_k$
Edge, incoming	641.817	861,414	1,514
Edge, outgoing	589.725	764,668	1,514
Core, dirA	910.32	1,271,850	1,514
Core, dirB	545.295	729,769	1,514

(across a full day) for different average utilization ($\overline{u}$) and scaling factor x for the two interface scenario in Figure 4(b) and the three interface scenario in Figure 4(c), respectively. Again, eBond is competitive (and often best) when there are little energy savings from putting the interface to sleep (large c), and eeeBond (e^3B) is by far the best when the sleep savings are greater (small c). Clearly, eeeBond and similar hybrid protocols that combine both eBond functionality and the EEE protocol, may become increasingly beneficial as sleep savings become greater (smaller c).

5.2 Trace-based evaluation

We have also evaluated the protocols using trace-based simulations. We use core traces collected at a core router (labeled *samplepoint-F*) connected to a trans-pacific link [15] and edge traces collected at an edge router (labeled Waikato VIII) of a university network [16]. Both traces were collected over a 24-hour period on January 2, 2013.

Table 3 summarizes the packet size information for the traces and Figure 5 shows the normalized traffic volume for each 15-minute period (with the peak volume that day normalized at 100%) for two of the traces. A closer look at these traces reveal that packet sizes for these traces are binomial in nature, with most packets being either small (less than 100 bytes) or large (1400-1500 bytes), and the relative fractions highly dependent on the direction.

Table 4 shows example results for the four example traces when using the same two-interface scenario as for the ana-

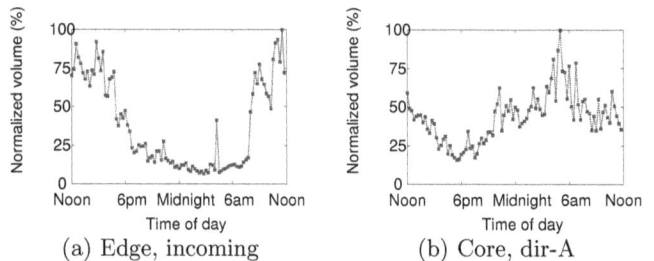

(a) Edge, incoming   (b) Core, dir-A

Figure 5: Normalized bandwidth usage. All bandwidths are normalized relative to the peak bandwidth usage during day.

Table 4: Normalized power usage with packet traces.

Scenario		Current $c = 0.8$			Future $c = 0.2$		
	Trace	EEE	eBond	e^3B	EEE	eBond	e^3B
Two	Edge, in	0.81	**0.16**	0.43	0.22	0.16	**0.13**
	Edge, out	0.81	**0.38**	0.74	0.22	0.38	**0.20**
	Core, dirA	0.81	0.15	**0.12**	0.21	0.15	**0.04**
	Core, dirB	0.82	0.15	**0.12**	0.24	0.15	**0.04**

lytic results. For this analysis, the traces are broken up into 15 minute intervals and the policies are applied on a per-15 minute granularity. Interesting future work could consider adaptive policies that apply threshold-based rules within a moving window, for example. The lower power usage for the traces is in part due to the links being lightly utilized. The results do, however, confirm that our conclusions regarding the protocols relative performance with different sleep-saving efficiency (c) are consistent also for real traces.

Finally, we note that our model easily can be extended to more closely match the traffic seen in the traces. Figure 6 shows example results from our basic model and an extended model (omitted due to lack of space), based on an $M^X/G/1(E, SU)$ system [13]. Here, the packet size statistics from a 15-minute edge trace of the incoming traffic be-

221

(a) Power usage

(b) Waiting times

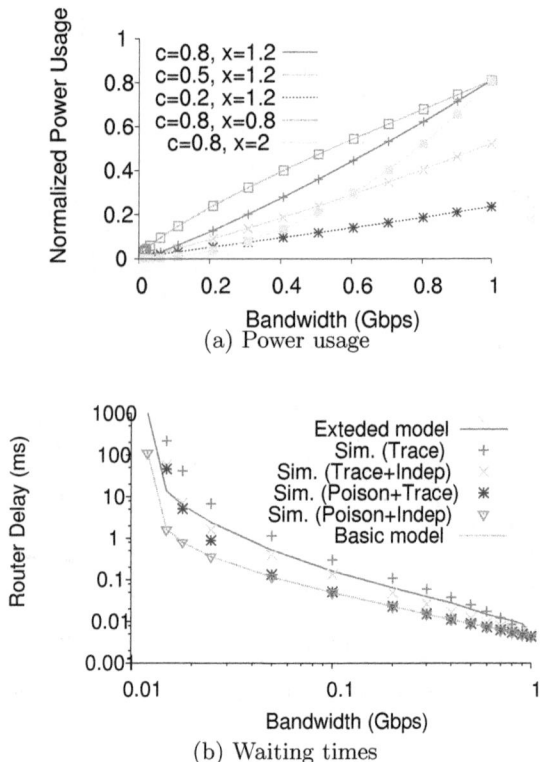

Figure 6: Comparison of model and trace-driven simulations.

tween 14:00-14:15 was used as input to the analytic model. Figure 6(a) shows that the power usage obtained using simulations (markers) and the values obtained using our analytic model (lines) provides a very good match for all example configurations (unique c and x value combination). To help understand where the errors in the waiting times (Figure 6(b)) come from we also include simulation points where we have modified the traces to introduce packet size independence (Trace+Indep), Poisson arrivals (Poisson+Trace), and both (Poisson+Indep).

6. RELATED WORK

Since the initial proposals of Adaptive Link Rate (ALR) technologies for wired networks, many protocols have been proposed [1–3]. This includes both sleep-based energy-aware traffic engineering techniques [17–20] that temporarily put interfaces to sleep within the core network, and a combination of rate switching and active/idle toggling techniques that save energy at the edge [2, 21–23].

Trace-driven simulations [2, 24] and hardware prototypes [25] have been used to study the tradeoff between switching times and energy consumption. Much attention has been given to the EEE standard [3, 6, 26]. This includes the proposal and evaluation of packet coalescaling techniques [3, 27] that increase the burstiness on the outgoing interfaces to improve the energy savings when using EEE. Trace-driven simulations have also been used to evaluate the impact that ALR techniques have on both neighboring routers [28] and end-to-end performance [29]. In contrast, we develop a queue-based model and use it to provide insights to the tradeoffs seen by four general protocol classes.

A few independent analytic models of the EEE protocol have been developed [30–33]. Although there have been some efforts to capture general inter-arrival distributions (e.g., [30]), the majority of these works, similar to ours, assume Poisson packet inter-arrival times. Poisson arrivals have also been shown to provide a good approximation over shorter time scales [9]. Our general router model presented in Section 3.1, which does not make any assumptions about packet inter-arrival times, is inspired by Hohn et al. [8]. Similar to James and Carlsson [28] we extend this model to capture the on-off pattern and energy-tradeoffs associated with EEE. In contrast to the above works, we develop a unifying model that allows us to capture the delay-energy tradeoffs and rate-switching points of both eBond [5] and eeeBond using closed-form expressions.

Finally, it should be noted that similar power saving strategies have been proposed and analyzed in many other contexts, including datacenters [34], datacenter networks [35], individual devices [36], and the wireless interfaces of mobile devices [37]. Also in these contexts hybrid approaches may be beneficial. For example, a datacenter may adjust the number of active servers through dynamic on-off switching [34], and then use speed scaling [38] to adjust the power usage of individual machines at a finer granularity.

7. CONCLUSIONS AND DISCUSSION

This paper presented a generalized protocol evaluation framework in which we perform protocol optimization and performance comparison of four general protocol classes. We first presented a general protocol and modeling framework that captures the energy-delay tradeoffs associated with two orthogonal protocol classes, which uses the on-off toggling of EEE [3, 6] and the interface switching of eBond [5], respectively, as well as a hybrid protocol class (eeeBond) that combines benefits of both protocols. Under Poisson assumptions, we then derived closed-form expressions of the energy-delay tradeoffs of each interface and of the optimal threshold of the packet arrival rates (and link utilizations) that determine the best interface for eBond and eeeBond to use. Finally, we characterized the energy savings possible with the different protocols using both our analytic model and trace-driven simulations. Our results show that eBond typically outperforms EEE, and that it even can outperform eeeBond when interfaces only offer small energy savings when in short-term sleep states (used by EEE and eeeBond). When substantial energy savings in short-term sleep states are possible, eeeBond is by far the best protocol. Interestingly, these findings and results suggest that also when sleep states would allow energy usage of high-power interfaces to become minimal in sleep state, and EEE would become close to energy proportional, the scaling factor x (typically greater than one) of peak energy usage of interfaces with different capabilities is expected to allow eeeBond to significantly outperform EEE by leveraging some slack in the maximum waiting times W^* and lower power-usage of low-power interfaces. While part of this slack also is leveraged with coalescaling techniques [3, 27], these techniques do not leverage the non-proportional advantages of low-power interfaces (and the scaling factor x). Future work includes the development of adaptive algorithms that generalize eeeBond to also turn-off its on-off toggling during times when eBond would otherwise outperform it, allowing us to minimize energy usage at all times of the day.

Acknowledgements

Financial support for this work was provided by CENIIT. The author would like thank Cyriac James for extracting the datasets and for initial discussions regarding the protocols. The author is also grateful to Sara Devenney for help with naming the protocol.

8. REFERENCES

[1] M. Gupta and S. Singh, "Greening of the Internet," in *Proc. ACM SIGCOMM*, 2003.

[2] C. Gunaratne, K. Christensen, , B. Nordman, and S. Suen, "Reducing the energy consumption of Ethernet with an adaptive link rate (ALR)," *IEEE Trans. on Comp.*, vol. 57, Apr. 2008.

[3] K. Christensen, P. Reviriego, M. Nordman, B. andBennett, M. Mostowfi, and J. Maestro, "IEEE 802.3az: the road to energy efficient Ethernet," *IEEE Comm. Magazine*, vol. 48, no. 11, pp. 50–56, 2010.

[4] L. Barroso and U. Holze, "The case for energy-proportional computing," *IEEE Computer*, vol. 40, no. 12, pp. 33–37, April 2007.

[5] M. Hähnel, B. Döbel, M. Völp, and H. Härtig, "eBond: energy saving in heterogeneous R.A.I.N." in *Proc. e-Energy*, May 2013.

[6] "IEEE 802.3az energy efficient Ethernet: Build greener networks)," *White Paper from Cisco and Intel*, 2011.

[7] Y. S. Hanay, W. Li, R. Tessier, and T. Wolf, "Saving energy and improving TCP throughput with rate adaptation in Ethernet," in *Proc. IEEE ICC*, 2012.

[8] N. Hohn, K. Papagiannaki, and D. Veitch, "Capturing router congestion and delay," *IEEE/ACM Trans. on Networking*, vol. 17, no. 3, pp. 789–802, June 2009.

[9] T. Karagiannis, M. Molle, M. Faloutsos, and A. Broido, "A nonstationary Poisson view of Internet traffic," in *Proc. IEEE INFOCOM*, Mar. 2004.

[10] N. Tian and Z. G. Zhang, *Vacation Queueing Models: Theory and Applications*. Springer, 2006.

[11] H. Levy and L. Kleinrock, "A queue with starter and a queue with vacations: Delay analysis by decomposition," *Operations Research*, vol. 34, no. 3, pp. 426–436, Jun. 1986.

[12] H. Takagi, *Queueing Analysis: A Foundation of Performance Evaluation. Vacation and Priority Systems (part 1)*. North-Holland, 1991.

[13] G. Choudhury, "An MX/G/1 queueing system with a setup period and a vacation period," *Queueing Systems*, vol. 36, pp. 23–38, 2000.

[14] R. W. Wolff, "Poisson arrivals see time averages," *Operations Research*, vol. 30, pp. 223–231, 1982.

[15] K. Cho, K. Mitsuya, and A. Kato, "Traffic data repository at the WIDE project," in *Proc. USENIX ATC*, 2000.

[16] J. G. Cleary, "Wand project at university of waikato, nz," in *Proc. HPN: Measurements and Analysis Collaborations Workshop*, 1999.

[17] L. Chiaraviglio, M. Mellia, and F. Neri, "Reducing power consumption in backbone networks," in *Proc. IEEE ICC*, 2009.

[18] J. Restrepo, C. Gruber, and C. Machoca, "Energy profile aware routing," in *Proc. IEEE GreenComm*, 2009.

[19] R. Tucker, J. Baliga, R. Ayre, K. Hinton, and W. Sorin, "Energy Consumption in IP Networks," in *Proc. ECOC*, 2008.

[20] L. Chiaraviglio, M. Mellia, and F. Neri, "Energy-aware backbone networks: A case study," in *Proc. IEEE GreenComm*, 2009.

[21] C. Gunaratne, K. Christensen, and B. Nordman, "Managing energy consumption costs in dektop PCs and LAN switches with proxying, split TCP connections, and scaling of link speed," *Int. J. of Netw. Management*, vol. 15, Sept. 2005.

[22] M. Gupta and S. Singh, "Dynamic Ethernet link shutdown for energy conservation on Ethernet links," in *Proc. IEEE ICC*, 2007.

[23] G. Ananthanarayanan and R. H. Katz, "Greening the switch," in *Proc. OSDI*, 2008.

[24] M. Gupta, S. Grover, and S. Singh, "A feasibility study for power management in LAN switches," in *Proc. IEEE ICNP*, 2004.

[25] B. Zhang, K. Sabhanatarajan, A. Gordon-Ross, and A. George, "Real-time performance analysis of adaptive link rate," in *Proc. IEEE LCN*, 2008.

[26] R. Hays, "Active/idle toggling with low-power idle," *Presentation for IEEE 802.3az Task Force*, Jan 2008.

[27] M. Mostowfi and K. Christensen, "Saving energy in LAN switches: New methods of packet coalescing for energy efficient Ethernet," in *Proc. IGCC*, July 2011.

[28] C. James and N. Carlsson, "Green domino incentives: Impact of energy-aware adaptive link rate policies in routers," in *Proc. ACM ICPE*, 2015.

[29] S. Nedevschi, L. Popa, G. Iannaccone, S. Ratnasamy, and D. Wetherall, "Reducing network energy consumption via sleeping and rate-adaptation," in *Proc. NSDI*, 2008.

[30] S. Herreria-Alonso, M. Rodriguez-Perez, M. Fernandez-Veiga, and C. Lopez-Garcia, "A GI/G/1 model for 10 Gb/s energy efficient Ethernet links," *IEEE Trans. on Comm.*, vol. 60, Nov. 2012.

[31] M. Marsan, A. Anta, V. Mancuso, B. Rengarajan, P. Vasallo, and G. Rizzo, "A simple analytical model for energy efficient Ethernet," *IEEE Comm. Letters*, vol. 15, pp. 773–775, July 2011.

[32] D. Larrabeiti, P. Reviriego, J. A. Hernandez, J. A. Maestro, and M. Uruena, "Towards an energy efficient 10 Gb/s optical Ethernet: Performance analysis and viability," *Optical Switching and Networking*, vol. 8, pp. 131–138, 2011.

[33] R. Bolla, R.Bruschi, A.Carrega, and F. Davoli, "Green network technologies and the art of trading-off," in *Proc. IEEE INFOCOM Workshops*, 2011.

[34] M. Lin, A. Wierman, L. L. Andrew, and E. Thereska, "Dynamic right-sizing for power-proportional data centers," *IEEE/ACM Transactions on Networking*, vol. 21, pp. 1378–1391, 2013.

[35] B. Heller, S. Seetharaman, P. Mahadevan, Y. Yiakoumis, P. Sharma, S. Banerjee, and N. McKeown, "ElasticTree: Saving energy in data center networks," in *Proc. NSDI*, San Jose, CA, 2010.

[36] D. Meisner, B. T. Gold, and T. F. Wenisch, "Powernap: Eliminating server idle power," in *Proc. ASPLOS*, 2009.

[37] F. R. Dogar, P. Steenkiste, and K. Papagiannaki, "Catnap: Exploiting high bandwidth wireless interfaces to save energy for mobile devices," in *Proc. MobiSys*, 2010.

[38] A. Wierman, L. Andrew, and A. Tang, "Power-aware speed scaling in processor sharing systems," pp. 2007–2015, 2009.

Communication Characterization and Optimization of Applications Using Topology-Aware Task Mapping on Large Supercomputers

Sarat Sreepathi
Oak Ridge National
Laboratory
Oak Ridge, TN, USA
sarat@ornl.gov

Ed D'Azevedo
Oak Ridge National
Laboratory
Oak Ridge, TN, USA
dazevedoef@ornl.gov

Bobby Philip
Oak Ridge National
Laboratory
Oak Ridge, TN, USA
philipb@ornl.gov

Patrick Worley
Oak Ridge National
Laboratory
Oak Ridge, TN, USA
worleyph@ornl.gov

ABSTRACT

On large supercomputers, the job scheduling systems may assign a non-contiguous node allocation for user applications depending on available resources. With parallel applications using MPI (Message Passing Interface), the default process ordering does not take into account the actual physical node layout available to the application. This contributes to non-locality in terms of physical network topology and impacts communication performance of the application. In order to mitigate such performance penalties, this work describes techniques to identify suitable task mapping that takes the layout of the allocated nodes as well as the application's communication behavior into account. During the first phase of this research, we instrumented and collected performance data to characterize communication behavior of critical US DOE (United States - Department of Energy) applications using an augmented version of the mpiP tool. Subsequently, we developed several reordering methods (spectral bisection, neighbor join tree etc.) to combine node layout and application communication data for optimized task placement. We developed a tool called mpiAproxy to facilitate detailed evaluation of the various reordering algorithms without requiring full application executions. This work presents a comprehensive performance evaluation (14,000 experiments) of the various task mapping techniques in lowering communication costs on Titan, the leadership class supercomputer at Oak Ridge National Laboratory.

Keywords

Communication Characterization; Reordering algorithms; Topology-Aware Optimization

1. INTRODUCTION

Modern leadership class supercomputers have a large number of processing elements (PEs) and the trends point to increasing complexity (beyond $O(1M)$ PEs). Moreover, such systems have a wide range of users with different requirements resulting in a plethora of job sizes and compute requirements. The job schedulers perform a critical role by allocating available resources to jobs based on numerous factors (e.g., queue type, request size, priority, wait time, other jobs etc. [11])

During typical operations, a job scheduler can assign a non-contiguous allocation to a user request depending on resource availability. In the worst case, an application could end up with an allocation where the nodes are sparsely scattered across the machine. This results in performance degradation due to long routes taken by communication messages and can be further impacted by network congestion. Even supercomputers with advanced interconnects exhibit scalability issues in such scenarios.

Task-mapping refers to the assignment of an application's tasks to available processing elements. With parallel applications using MPI (Message Passing Interface), the default task order is sequential. It does not consider the non-locality

This manuscript has been authored by UT-Battelle, LLC under Contract No. DE-AC05-00OR22725 with the U.S. Department of Energy. The United States Government retains and the publisher, by accepting the article for publication, acknowledges that the United States Government retains a non-exclusive, paid-up, irrevocable, worldwide license to publish or reproduce the published form of this manuscript, or allow others to do so, for United States Government purposes. The Department of Energy will provide public access to these results of federally sponsored research in accordance with the DOE Public Access Plan(http://energy.gov/downloads/doe-public-access-plan).

ICPE'16, March 12 - 18, 2016, Delft, Netherlands

ⓒ 2016 Copyright held by the owner/author(s). Publication rights licensed to ACM.

ACM ISBN 978-1-4503-4080-9/16/03. . . $15.00

DOI: http://dx.doi.org/10.1145/2851553.2851575

aspects of the actual physical node layout that was allocated to the application.

In order to mitigate such performance penalties, this work describes techniques to optimize task placement for the target application based on its behavior as well as network topology of the allocated nodes.

The primary contributions of this research are:

- Task mapping techniques that consider the target application's communication pattern and physical network topology to reduce communication costs (Section 2.2)

- mpiAproxy: A tool that simulates target application's communication behavior to estimate communication costs (Section 2.3).

- Detailed communication characterization of critical scientific applications from the Co-Design ecosystem and big science applications in the domains of nuclear fusion, climate and radiation diffusion. (Section 6)

The rest of the paper is organized as follows: We elaborate on the methodology for this study in Section 2. Related work is discussed in Section 3. As part of this research, we investigated communication behavior of several DOE applications. The applications are summarized in Section 4. Titan, the experiment platform is described in Section 5. We present a comprehensive performance evaluation of the various task mapping techniques along with communication characterization data in section 6 and conclude with future work.

2. METHODOLOGY

In this section, we detail the various phases of our experiment methodology. Section 2.1 presents an overview of our communication characterization tool. We discuss the details of the various reordering algorithms in section 2.2 and Section 2.3 describes the communication estimation tool that was developed to facilitate a detailed evaluation of the different methods.

2.1 Augmented mpiP Tool

For communication characterization, we used an augmented version of the mpiP [37] profiling library that was previously used in our application characterization studies [36]. We used this tool to perform a detailed analysis of an application's communication pattern. It was used to record the point-to-point communication data between communicating MPI tasks; message volume in .mpiPpv files and message counts in .mpiPpc files. Additionally, it generates histograms for the point-to-point and collective communication message sizes in .mpiPpsh and .mpiPcsh respectively.

The translation of collective operations into underlying point-to-point messages depends on the MPI implementation and the compute platform. For instance, a collection operation like MPI_Allreduce on Cray XK7 using MPICH could result in a set of point-to-point messages that could be different for the same operation on IBM BlueGene using OpenMPI. In contrast, the point-to-point communication pattern is platform-independent for a target application for a specified experiment configuration. This work focuses on on the point-to-point communication data and we intend to encompass collective communication data in the future.

2.2 Reordering Methods

Three graph based heuristics are compared for generating a mapping between the communication graph of the application and the network topology of the allocated nodes at run-time. The recursive spectral bisection and Reverse Cuthill-McKee (RCM) [17, 20] orderings were used in topology mapping in [23]. A bottom-up neigbor-join tree [24, 32] clustering heuristic commonly used in bioinformatics for the creation of phylogeneitc trees was also used. The general approach follows Hoefler and Snir [23] in generating an ordering (or permutation of the graph vertices) on the communication graph and an ordering for the network topology and matching the vertices of the two orderings to produce the topology-aware mapping.

The communication graph $C(i,j)$ is the volume of data sent from MPI process i to process j. A threshold value (e.g. 95% of total message volume) was used to ignore small transfers and obtain a sparse communication graph. The heuristics were computed using Matlab and completed in only a few seconds.

The network topology is obtained by querying the coordinates of the allocated compute nodes on the 3D torus network on Titan using rca_get_meshcoord function from Cray's Resiliency Communication Agent (RCA) library. Titan has a $25 \times 16 \times 24$ 3D torus network where 2 compute nodes share a network interface. However, the links in the "y" direction have half the bandwidth of the links in the "x" and "z" directions. The number of hops through the 3D network was used as an indicator of the communication cost with "y" direction hops being twice as costly. For details on Titan, the experiment platform see Section 5.

2.2.1 Spectral bisection techniques

The spectral bisection technique can be used to perform nested dissection reordering [21] to reduce the amount of fill-in in sparse direct Cholesky factorization of large symmetric positive matrices. The recursive spectral bisection method attempts to find a nearly equal partitioning of the graph with a small separator. The symmetrized communication graph $((C + \mathtt{transpose}(C))/2)$ or the communication hop graph was used as the weighted Laplacian graph. The eigenvector corresponding to the second smallest eigenvalue of the weighted Laplacian graph (also called the Fiedler vector) was used to partition the graph into two clusters. The spectral bisection algorithm was recursively applied to the two remaining subgraphs. The idea being clusters of nodes that exchange high volume of data should be mapped to compute nodes that have high network connectivity. The METIS library [34] was used to compute a balanced partition in [23]. Here the matlab eig() is used for small matrices ($N \leq 512$) and eigs() eigensolver based on the Lanczos algorithm was used to find the Fiedler vector.

There are two variants of the spectral methods used in this work. In SPECTRAL0, an unweighted Laplacian matrix is used where all off-diagonal entries are equal. The Fiedler eigenvector is computed from the unweighted Laplacian matrix. In SPECTRAL1, a weighted laplacian matrix is used to where the weights are related to the MPI communication graph or the network topology.

2.2.2 Reverse Cuthill-McKee (RCM) algorithm

The RCM ordering is commonly used as a heuristic for reducing the matrix band-width before performing sparse direct Cholesky factorization. It is a variant of breadth-first ordering starting from an extremal peripheral vertex in the graph. RCM was very fast but RCM ignores the numerical weight of edges and considers only the sparsity pattern of the matrix. The Matlab `rcm()` function was used.

2.2.3 Neighbor-join tree methods

The Neighbor-join tree is a bottom up clustering method where given a distance or cost matrix, the algorithm finds a hierarchical clustering of nodes to form a tree. The method find the smallest distance, say $d(x, y)$ and merge the nodes to form a new super node $[x, y]$. The cost matrix is then updated where $distance([x, y], z) = \max(d(x, z), d(y, z))$. A post-order labeling of the leaf nodes (label all left sub-tree, then right subtree) is given as the final ordering. The algorithm has $O(n^3)$ costs in the worst case.

We used two different algorithms in this family. In NJTREE1, the cost matrix is computed as the number of hops needed through the 3D torus where the hops in the y-direction has twice the cost. In NJTREE0, the cost matrix is the original network topology matrix but with negative weights so that links with high bandwidth have smaller costs.

2.3 mpiAproxy: Communication Estimation

We developed a tool called mpiAproxy to facilitate detailed evaluation of the various reordering algorithms without requiring full application executions.

The tool takes as input the detailed communication data of the application collected by the augmented mpiP tool. First, the target application is linked with the mpiP libraries and executed. This generates the point-to-point communication data; aggregate message counts and volume between communicating processes.

The mpiAproxy tool computes the average message size between communicating neighbors and simulates the communication pattern to obtain an estimate of the application's communication costs. The execution time of the tool depends on the target application it is emulating, typical runs take under a few minutes. It does this by sending a representative number of messages between communicating tasks with the relevant message size and records the time.

The tool uses an asynchronous communication protocol to avoid deadlocks. This approximation does not capture all the intricacies of a complex application but presents a broad overview for a significantly lower computation cost. For instance, it does not not reflect any load imbalances that are present in the target application. However, it facilitates extensive experimentation of task mapping layouts as the cost of each experiment is small, thereby enabling a comprehensive search for an optimal layout.

3. RELATED WORK

Finding the optimal mapping between the communication graph and network topology may be viewed as determining the graph isomorphism problem, which is $\mathcal{NP}$-hard. Thus heuristics are needed to generate the topology mapping. One approach finds the mapping as the optimization of a cost function (such as the combination of hop-byte and dilation metrics), another approach uses graph-based algorithm to find a good mapping.

Sankaran et al [33] used a genetic algorithms for optimizing the mapping for two large-scale parallel S3D and LAMMPS on the Cray XK7 machine. Bhanot et al [13]

used simulated annealing to optimize task layout of parallel applications SAGE and UMT2000 on the BlueGene/L machine. Bollinger and Midkiff [15] proposed process annealing for assigning tasks to processors and connection annealing for scheduling communication to reduce network contention.

Solomonik et al [35] considered mapping 2.5D dense matrix LU factorization algorithms onto the BlueGene/P system. However, optimization-based heuristics are quite costly and are appropriate only for applications with well characterized fixed communication pattern (such as nearest neighbor communication for stencil computation on a 2D or 3D rectangular grid or dense matrix computation) and mapping to known network partitions such as the BlueGene machine.

Another approach is to use graph-based heuristic algorithms to determine the mapping. Ercal [19] considered recursive bisection in the context of a hypercube topology where at each step the algorithm finds a minimum cut of the communication graph while maintaining approximately equal load and recursively assigns the subgraphs onto subcubes. Hoefler and Snir [23] considered heuristics based on graph similarity for irregular communication patterns. They considered several heuristics including recursive bisection, Reverse Cuthill-McKee (RCM) and a greedy heuristic for picking the node with highest communication need and paired with its closest neighbor to minimize communication cost. In his PhD thesis, Bhatele [14] considered several heuristics for general communication graphs. Deveci at al [18] proposed a geometric partitioning algorithm for task placement and demonstrated performance improvements for a structured finite difference application among others.

The breadth-first traversal (BFT) simply visit nodes by breadth-first order. Note BFT has some similarity to RCM. The max heap traversal starts with the node that has maximum number of neighbors and place it at center of 2D mesh. All unmapped neighbors are placed on the heap sorted by the number unmapped neighbors. At each step, the node with highest number of unmapped neighbors is placed close to the centroid of its mapped neighbors. Since the Cray XT batch system cannot guarantee a contiguous partition and the applications of interest (such as the XGC particle-in-cell code or climate simulation) have unstructured and not easily predictable communication patterns, the focus of this work is on exploration of fast graph-based heuristic that can be computed dynamically in a short amount of time.

4. APPLICATIONS OVERVIEW

4.1 Co-Design Benchmarks, Proxies and Applications

We have looked at a broad range of applications that are widely used in the Co-Design community. There are three Co-Design Centers under the purview of DOE, namely Exascale Co-Design Center for Materials in Extreme Environments (ExMatEx), Center for Exascale Simulation of Advanced Reactors (CESAR) and Center for and Exascale Simulation of Combustion in Turbulence (ExaCT). Additionally we studied the performance of several benchmarks associated with the CORAL (Collaboration of Oak Ridge, Argonne and Livermore)[16] acquistion effort to purchase next generation supercomputers.

4.1.1 AMG2013

AMG2013 [1] is a parallel algebraic multigrid solver for linear systems arising from problems on unstructured grids. It has been derived directly from the BoomerAMG solver in the hypre library, a large linear solver library. The default problem is a Laplace type problem on an unstructured domain with various jumps and an anisotropy in one part.

AMG2013 is a highly synchronous code. The communications and computations patterns exhibit the surface-to-volume relationship common to many parallel scientific codes.

4.1.2 BoxLibAMR

BoxLibMiniAMR is a proxy app developed by the ExaCT Co-Design center [2]. It uses a structured-grid Adaptive Mesh Refinement (AMR) approach to study combustion. It is being used to address challenges that arise in investigation of advanced low-emissions combustion systems.

4.1.3 HPCG

The HPCG (High Performance Conjugate Gradients) Benchmark project [3] is an new benchmark effort to create a more relevant metric for ranking HPC systems than the High Performance LINPACK (HPL) benchmark, that is currently used by the TOP500 listing. HPCG is designed to better match the computational, communication and data access patterns of a broad range of applications in contrast to HPL.

4.1.4 LULESH

The Livermore Unstructured Lagrange Explicit Shock Hydrodynamics (LULESH) proxy application [4, 25] is being developed at Lawrence Livermore National Laboratory. Originally developed as one of five challenge problems for the DARPA UHPC program, it has since evolved and has received widespread use in DOE research programs as a mini-app representative of simplified 3D Lagrangian hydrodynamics on an unstructured mesh.

4.1.5 MCB

Monte Carlo Benchmark (MCB) [5] is a Co-Design application developed at LLNL that is intended for use in exploring the computational performance of Monte Carlo algorithms on parallel architectures. It models the solution of a simple heuristic transport equation using a Monte Carlo technique.

4.1.6 MultiGrid_C

MultiGrid_C is a proxy app developed by the ExaCT Co-Design center [7]. It is a finite-volume multigrid solver that supports different variants.

4.1.7 Nek5000

Nek5000 [8] is a large application designed to simulate laminar, transitional, and turbulent incompressible or low Mach-number flows with heat transfer and species transport. It is also suitable for incompressible magnetohydrodynamics (MHD).

4.1.8 Nekbone

The Nekbone mini-app [9] developed by the Center for Exascale Simulation of Advanced Reactors (CESAR) is used to to study the computationally intense linear solvers that account for a large percentage of Nek5000, the full application

it is modeled after. It is also meant to emulate the communication behavior of Nek5000, specifically nearest-neighbor data exchanges and vector reductions.

4.2 Big Science Applications

In addition to benchmarks and proxy apps, we were specifically interested in large scientific applications that have intricate communication patterns that vary based on experiment configuration. Such applications manifest in hard to predict communication behavior that makes optimization efforts more challenging.

4.2.1 XGC

XGC is a whole-device modeling code, with a special strength in modeling the edge plasma (and its effect on the core plasma) in tokamak fusion reactors at first-principles level. To be precise, XGC is a full-function 5D gyro kinetic particle-in-cell (PIC)/finite element code that is uniquely capable of simulating the tokamak plasma in realistic diverted magnetic geometry, as well as covering core plasma all the way to the magnetic axis, together with neutral particle recycling at material wall surface and their Monte-Carlo transport using atomic charge-exchange and ionization cross-sections.

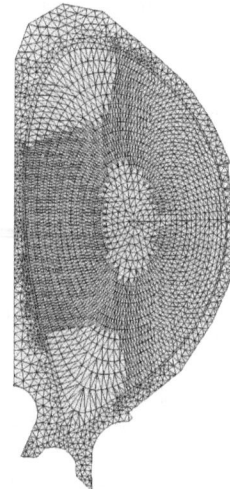

Figure 1: XGC Triangular Mesh

XGC is based upon the conventional particle-in-cell ODE solver method, with options such as electron fluid solves for kinetic-fluid hybrid physics. To be more specific, the Lagrangian ODE particle information is scattered to unstructured triangular mesh nodes on which the PDE electromagnetic force field equations are solved. The force field information is then gathered back to the particle locations for time-advancing the ODE cycle of the particles. Unlike the conventional particle-in-cell codes, all the dissipative physical processes are solved on 5D configuration-velocity space grid using finite element, finite difference schemes, which include the non-linear Fokker-Planck collisions, charge exchange, ionization, and radiation. Due to the enormity of the particle number required for full- function multiscale gyrokinetic simulation of tokamak plasma, over 95% of the computing time is spent on the ODE particle push that scales very well on extreme number of compute processors. The PDE solver parts of the code, which encapsulates the long range data dependencies in the PIC method are more demanding in extreme scale computing. One advantage of the full-function method used in XGC is that it encapsulates these global data dependencies with a small fraction of the total work: Thus, solvers currently account for less than 2% of the total computing time.

The tokamak device is partition into multiple domains by poloidal planes. Each plane consists of the identical unstructured triangular mesh (see Figure1). The mesh is used for charge deposition and the calculation of the electric field by finite element method and resulting linear systems are solved using PETSc iterative linear solvers preconditioned with Hypre multi-grid library.

The XGC code can be configure to assign MPI tasks contiguously within the same plane (called `plane major` mode) or to assign MPI tasks contiguously in the toroidal direction across planes (called `inter-plane major` mode).

4.2.2 MPAS-Ocean

The Model for Prediction Across Scales (MPAS) [6] is a collaborative project for developing atmosphere, ocean and other earth-system simulation components for use in climate, regional climate and weather studies. MPAS-Ocean, the ocean component of this effort is designed for the simulation of the ocean system across different time and spatial scales. Additionally, it is intended for the study of anthropogenic climate change.

4.2.3 NRDF

NRDF is a 3D non-equilibrium radiation diffusion code [31] that solves the time dependent non-equilibrium radiation diffusion equations that are important for solving the transport of energy through radiation in optically thick regimes with applications in several fields including astrophysics and inertial confinement fusion. The associated initial boundary value problems that are encountered often exhibit a wide range of scales in space and time and are extremely challenging to solve. The non-equilibrium radiation diffusion problem is discretized on structured adaptive mesh refinement (SAMR) hierarchies which consist of nested refinement levels with each level a union of non-overlapping patches at the same resolution. A method of lines (MOL) approach is used with a cell centered finite volume spatial discretization followed by discretization in time. To solve the nonlinear systems arising at each timestep an inexact Newton method is used with GMRES for the linear solver. The linear system is preconditioned on SAMR grids with components that involve either a multilevel Fast Adaptive Composite Grid (FAC) solver or an asynchronous version of FAC (AFACx).

The Fast Adaptive Composite grid (FAC) method [30, 29] extends techniques from multigrid on uniform grids to locally refined grids. FAC solves problems on locally refined grids by combining smoothing on refinement levels with a coarse grid solve using an approximate solver, such as a V-cycle of multigrid. On parallel computing systems, the multiplicative nature of FAC introduces synchronization points during every correction step. Moreover, there is little opportunity to overlap communication with computation. These considerations led to development of asynchronous, or additive, versions of FAC that removes these synchronization points (AFAC, AFACx) [26, 27, 28].

5. TITAN: EXPERIMENT PLATFORM

We conducted our experiments on Titan [10], a Cray supercomputer installed at Oak Ridge National Laboratory. Titan is a hybrid-architecture Cray XK7 system with a theoretical peak performance exceeding 27 petaflops. It comprises of 18,688 compute nodes, wherein each node contains 16-core AMD Opteron CPUs and NVIDIA Kepler K20X GPUs for a total of 299,008 CPU cores and 18,688 GPUs. It has a total system memory of 710 terabytes, and utilizes Cray's high-performance Gemini network. Titan has a $25 \times 16 \times 24$ 3D torus network where 2 compute nodes share a network interface. As of June 2015, it is the second fastest supercomputer in the world according to the TOP500 list [12].

The software environment for the reported experiments is as follows: Cray PGI programming environment (version 5.2.40) which uses PGI 15.3 compilers and Cray's MPICH implementation (version 7.2.2).

6. RESULTS

Large supercomputing systems exhibit a high degree of performance variability due to various factors, e.g., jitter, load imbalances, prevailing network traffic etc. Hence it is not prudent to compare best execution times or a few data points for each scenario to obtain an accurate performance comparison.

In this section, we present highlights from a large set of experiments that show the efficacy of the various reordering techniques in improving communication performance of target scientific applications. Each plot shows experiment data for 40 `mpiAproxy` executions for each reordering method (7 mappings) for a total of 280 data points.

`DEFAULT` refers to the baseline task mapping scenario where MPI ranks are sequentially assigned to the corresponding nodes. `NJTREE0`, `NJTREE1` are task mappings that are obtained from the heirarchical clustering/neighbor-join tree algorithms. `SPECTRAL0`, `SPECTRAL1` refer to the task mappings from the spectral methods. Finally, `RCM` refers to the Reverse CutHill McKee ordering and `RANDOM` is a random ordering of MPI ranks that acts a control for the experiments.

We utilized violin plots to accurately portray the efficacy, performance variability and robustness of the various scenarios to facilitate an informed comparison. The violin plots [22] are similar to box plots, except that they also show the probability density of the data at different values. The plot includes markers for the median and inter-quartile ranges of the data. Overlaid on this box plot is a kernel density estimation. The length of the violin plot reflects the degree of variability across experiments.

For each application, we present the point-to-point message volume diagram and summarize its communication behavior. Subsequently, we present the communication costs with various task mappings that are derived from the reordering algorithms. These communication costs are obtained by executing `mpiAproxy` with the target application's communication profile (point-to-point communication message count and volume data).

The first subsection focuses on the various benchmarks and proxy applications from the DOE Co-Design centers. The second section presents results for several large scientific applications.

6.1 Co-Design Benchmarks, Proxies and Applications

6.1.1 AMG2013

The communication behavior of AMG2013 is shown in Figure 2. Figure 3 shows the relative performance of the various methods. In this case, RCM performs slightly better than the default mapping.

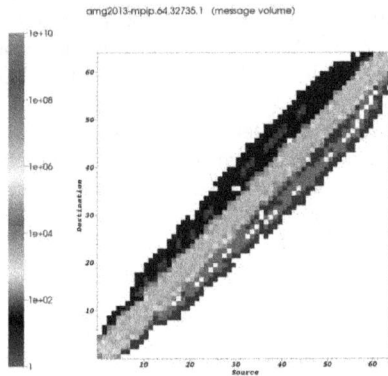

Figure 2: AMG-3dlaplace: Point-to-point communication volume pattern with 64 MPI tasks

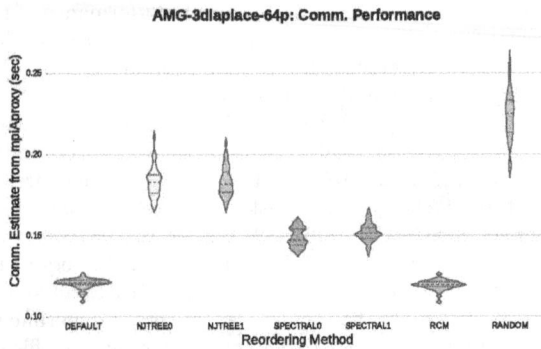

Figure 3: Task Mapping: Communication Performance of AMG-3dlaplace with 64 MPI tasks

6.1.2 BoxLibAMR

BoxLibAMR has a very dense communication pattern as shown in figure 4. Figure 5 shows the relative performance of the various methods. In this case, all methods outperform the default mapping as it is ill suited for this kind of dense communication that results in congestion.

6.1.3 HPCG

HPCG has a nearest neighbor communication pattern (Figure 6) with the dense communication concentrated along the diagonal. All reordering methods outperform the default mapping with SPECTRAL0 providing the best mapping (Figure 7).

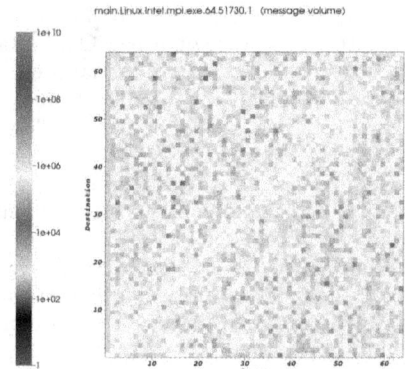

Figure 4: BoxLibMiniAMR-inputs3d: Point-to-point communication volume pattern with 64 MPI tasks

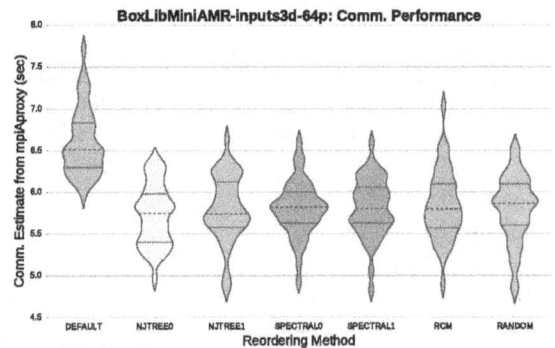

Figure 5: Task Mapping: Communication Performance of BoxLibMiniAMR-inputs3d with 64 MPI tasks

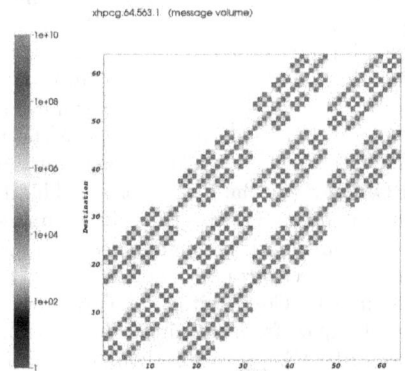

Figure 6: HPCG: Point-to-point communication volume pattern with 64 MPI tasks

6.1.4 LULESH

LULESH has a communication pattern (Figure 8) that appears similar to HPCG. The spectral methods deliver a good mapping in this scenario (Figure 9) with SPECTRAL1 providing the best results. Please note that although LULESH and

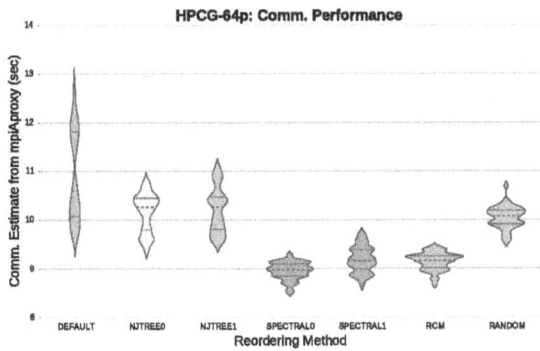

Figure 7: Task Mapping: Communication Performance of HPCG with 64 MPI tasks

HPCG *appear* to have similar patterns, the performance of the mapping algorithms differed due to the difference in the amount of off-diagonal communication.

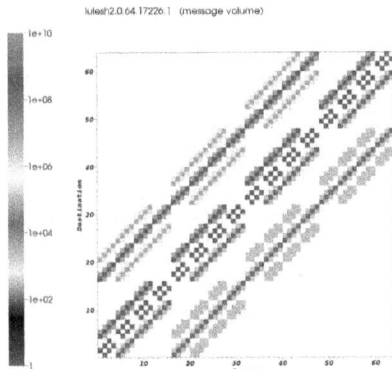

Figure 8: LULESH: Point-to-point communication volume pattern with 64 MPI tasks

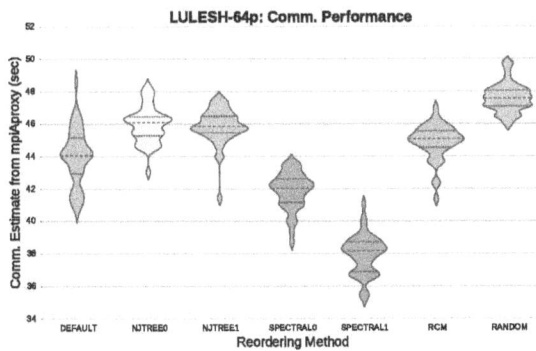

Figure 9: Task Mapping: Communication Performance of LULESH with 64 MPI tasks

6.1.5 MCB

MCB has an interesting scatter pattern originating from the origin (Figure 10). All algorithms outperform the default mapping with the spectral methods and RCM providing the best mapping (Figure 11).

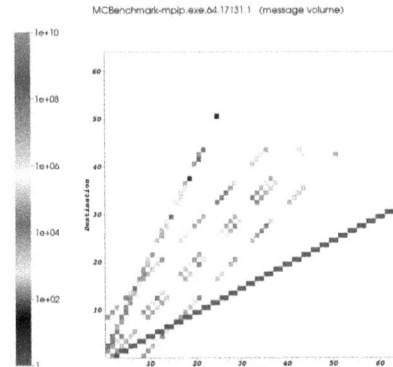

Figure 10: MCB: Point-to-point communication volume pattern with 64 MPI tasks

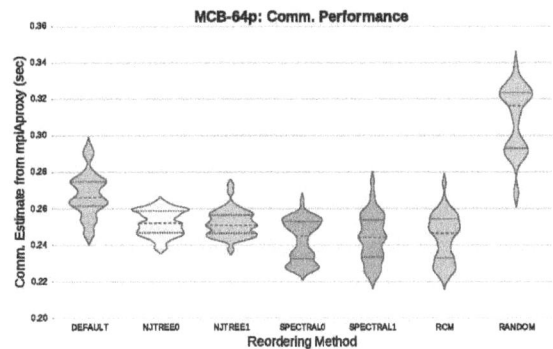

Figure 11: Task Mapping: Communication Performance of MCB with 64 MPI tasks

6.1.6 MultiGrid_C

MultiGrid_C for solving a 3d problem with 512 cells communicates mostly along the diagonal as well as pockets of nearby neighbors (Figure 12). In this case, the default mapping itself seems optimal (Figure 13).

6.1.7 Nek5000

Nek5000 communication pattern with the vortex problem configuration is shown in Figure 14. Again the default mapping itself seems optimal and at par with the spectral techniques (Figure 14)

6.1.8 NEKBONE

Figure 16 shows the communication pattern of NEKBONE with the mgrid problem. The default mapping is better for this scenario (Figure 17).

231

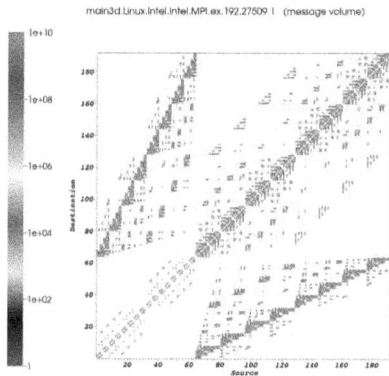

Figure 12: MultiGrid_C-3d-512cells: Point-to-point communication volume pattern with 192 MPI tasks

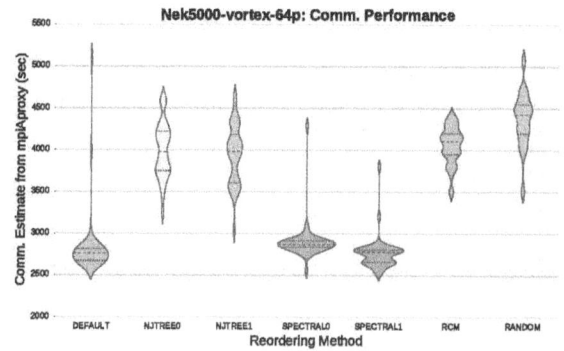

Figure 13: Task Mapping: Communication Performance of MultiGrid_C-3d-512cells with 192 MPI tasks

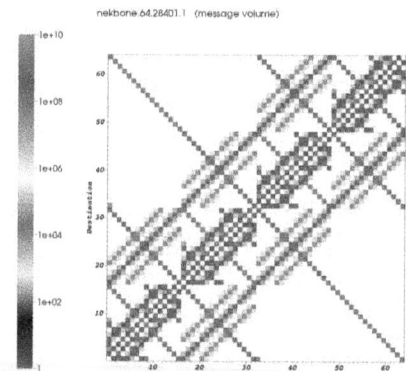

Figure 14: Nek5000-vortex: Point-to-point communication volume pattern with 64 MPI tasks

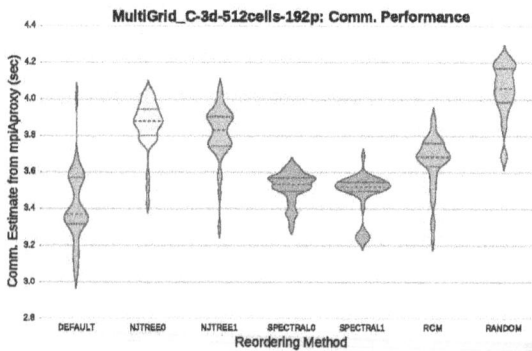

Figure 15: Task Mapping: Communication Performance of Nek5000-vortex with 64 MPI tasks

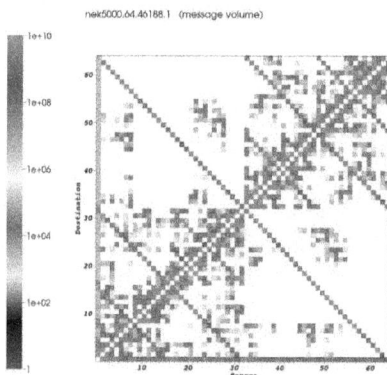

Figure 16: NEKBONE-mgrid: Point-to-point communication volume pattern with 64 MPI tasks

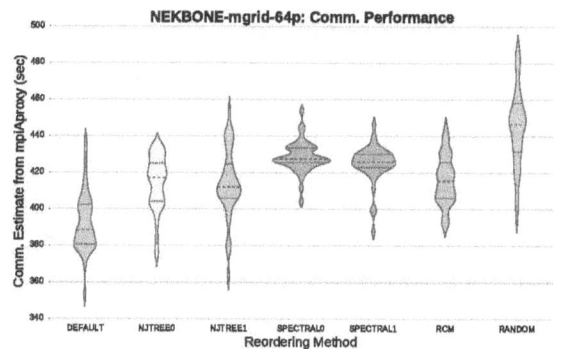

Figure 17: Task Mapping: Communication Performance of NEKBONE-mgrid with 64 MPI tasks

6.2 Big Science Applications

6.2.1 XGC

As part of this work, we have performed an in-depth analysis of a nuclear fusion code, XGC using different problem configurations (interplane/planemajor ordering and poloidal decomposition). Figure 18 shows the point-to-point communication volume without poloidal decomposition and Figure 20 with poloidal decomposition. Both experiment configurations used `interplanemajor` ordering. There is a marked increase in communication volume with poloidal decomposition.

In the first case, the tree methods perform better (Figure

232

19) whereas the spectral methods (Figure 21) fare well with poloidal decomposition. The *SPECTRAL0* method consistently provides a superior task mapping for the poloidal decomposition configuration.

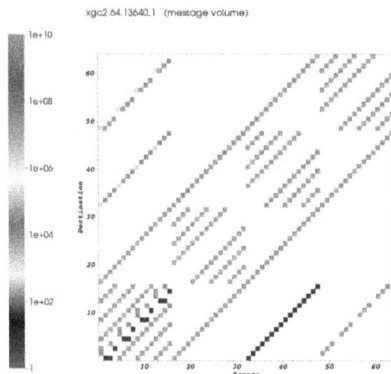

Figure 18: XGC-interplanemajor: Point-to-point communication volume pattern with 64 MPI tasks

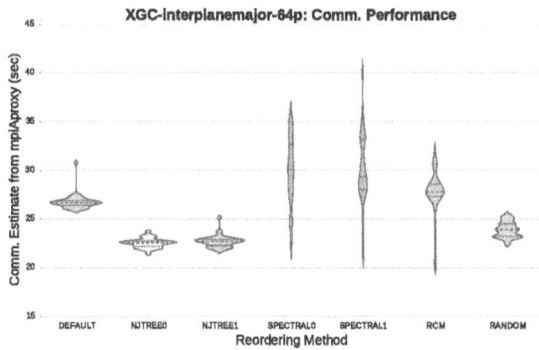

Figure 19: Task Mapping: Communication Performance of XGC-interplanemajor with 64 MPI tasks

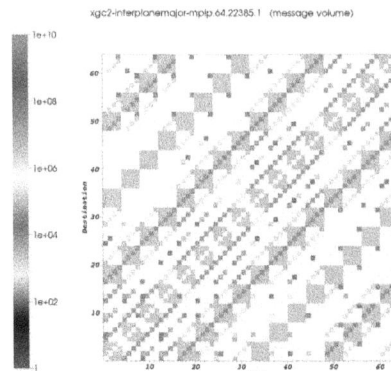

Figure 20: XGC-interplanemajor-poldecomp: Point-to-point communication volume pattern with 64 MPI tasks

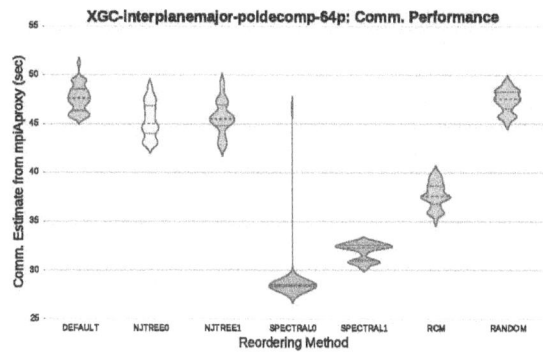

Figure 21: Task Mapping: Communication Performance of XGC-interplanemajor-poldecomp with 64 MPI tasks

At larger scale, Figure 22 shows the communication behavior at 2048 cores. Again, SPECTRAL0 provides the optimal mapping in this scenario (Figure 23).

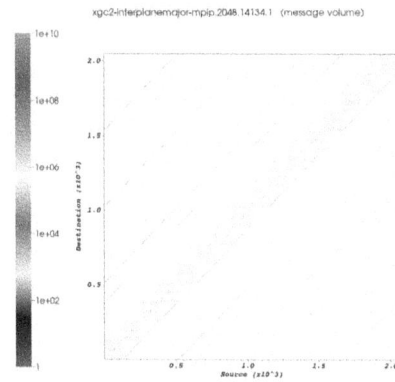

Figure 22: XGC-interplanemajor-poldecomp-10ts: Point-to-point communication volume pattern with 2048 MPI tasks

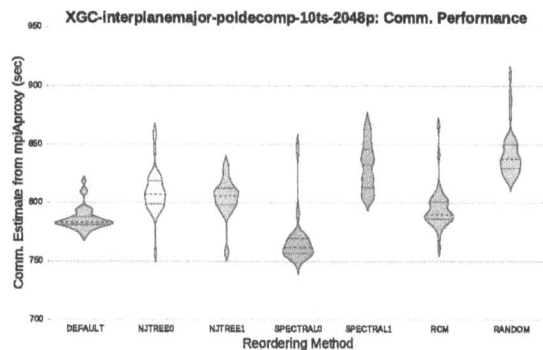

Figure 23: Task Mapping: Communication Performance of XGC-interplanemajor-poldecomp-10ts with 2048 MPI tasks

6.2.2 MPAS-Ocean

The communication behavior of MPAS-Ocean using 128 processes is shown in Figure 24. The different task mapping methods outperform the default ordering with the tree methods showing the best performance (Figure 25).

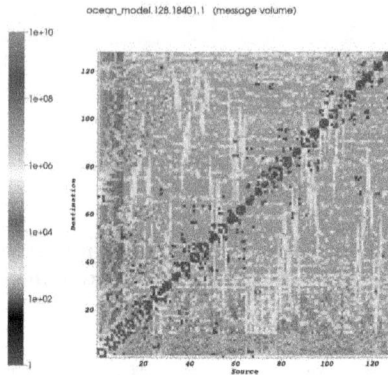

Figure 24: MPAS-default-partitioning: Point-to-point communication volume pattern with 128 MPI tasks

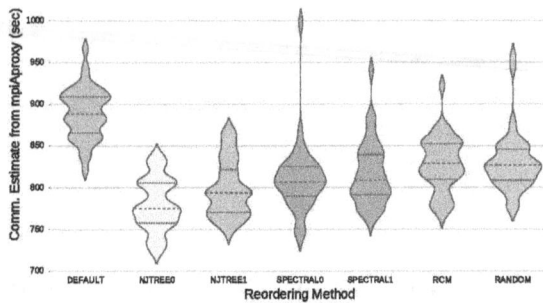

Figure 25: Task Mapping: Communication Performance of MPAS-default-part with 128 MPI tasks

At larger scale, MPAS-Ocean replicates the pattern from the smaller run with mutually exclusive subdomains (Figure 26). The tree methods still outperform other mappings (Figure 27)

6.2.3 NRDF

Finally, we did a detailed characterization of NRDF in various AMR (Adaptive Mesh Refinement) configurations. We present the highlights here. Figure 28 illustrates the communication pattern of NRDF using the AFACx algorithm in 256b3l configuration. The tree methods provide the best performance for this problem (Figure 29).

The communication pattern of NRDF using the FAC algorithm is shown in Figure 30. It is substantially different from the AFACx algorithm in the same configuration (256b3l). All reordering algorithms provide a better mapping than the default in this case (Figure 31).

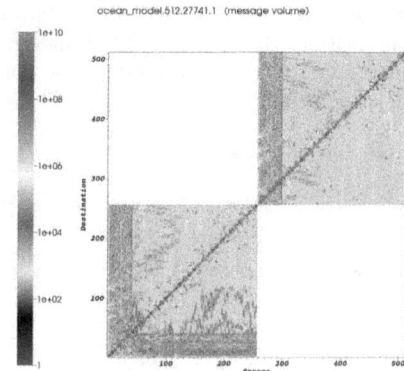

Figure 26: MPAS-60km-30d: Point-to-point communication volume pattern with 512 MPI tasks

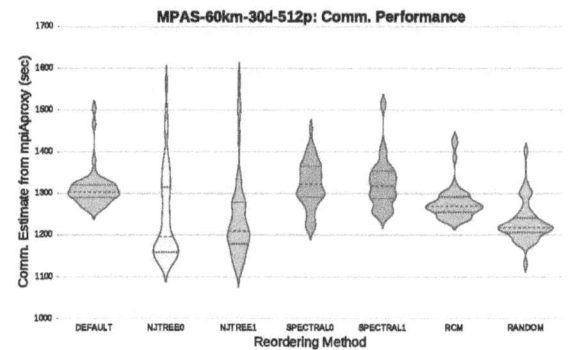

Figure 27: Task Mapping: Communication Performance of MPAS-60km-30d with 512 MPI tasks

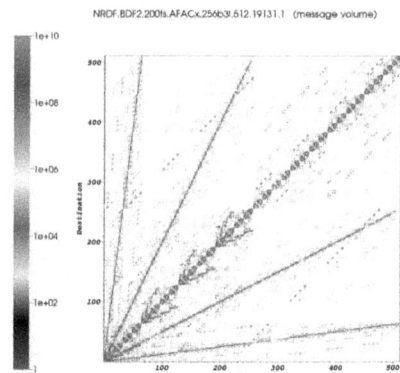

Figure 28: NRDF-AFACx-256b3l: Point-to-point communication volume pattern with 512 MPI tasks

7. CONCLUSIONS

This paper presented various task mapping algorithms that combine the insights from the application's behavior with the network topology information to provide an efficient task assignment. We developed a communication estimation tool, mpiAproxy that simulates the target application to provide a good approximation of communication

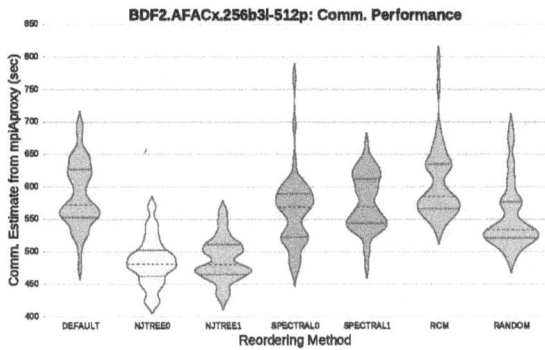

Figure 29: Task Mapping: Communication Performance of NRDF-AFACx-256b3l with 512 MPI tasks

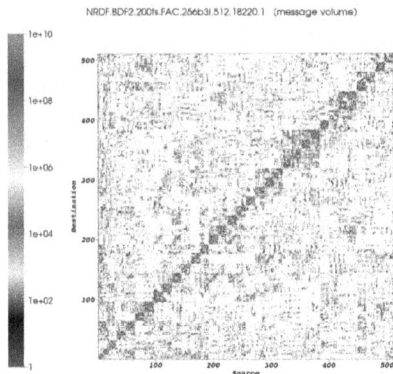

Figure 30: NRDF-FAC-256b3l: Point-to-point communication volume pattern with 512 MPI tasks

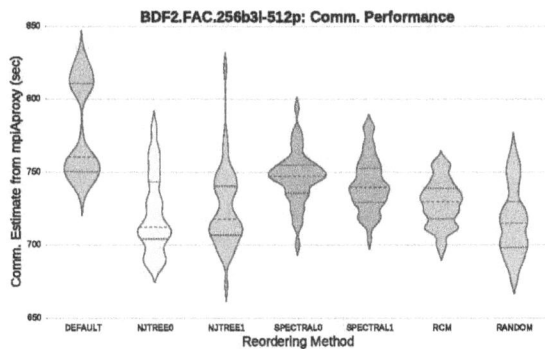

Figure 31: Task Mapping: Communication Performance of NRDF-FAC-256b3l with 512 MPI tasks

costs. We presented detailed communication characterization data for several scientific applications from the DOE Co-Design ecosystem as well as large scientific applications from the domains of nuclear fusion, climate and radiation diffusion. Finally, we presented a comprehensive performance evaluation (14,000 experiments) to understand the efficacy of the various task mapping techniques to optimize communication of our target application set.

The results demonstrate that our methods were able to extract significant performance improvements for a diverse pool of applications ranging from benchmarks and proxy apps to full scientific applications. We believe that the robustness of the techniques is amply reflected by the violin plots (that show the probability density of the data at different values) while accounting for system variability on modern supercomputers.

7.1 Future Work

We would like to extend this work to applications with multiple components that exhibit different communication patterns. For instance, the Community Earth Systems Model (CESM) comprises of several different component with vastly different communication patterns. Finding an optimal task mapping while taking the inter-component interactions into account is an open research problem.

The current implementation of our algorithms is not amenable for scaling to large core counts. We intend to address that by porting to a programming language that is more suitable for high performance computing.

During this research, we have identified several opportunities to customize algorithms specifically to a target application. Especially for NRDF, we are interested in algorithmic exploration that is intended to further reduce communication while retaining solution fidelity.

Acknowledgments

Support for this work was provided through the Scientific Discovery through Advanced Computing (SciDAC) program funded by the U.S. Department of Energy Office of Advanced Scientific Computing Research (ASCR). Early communication characterization work was partially supported by the Oxbow project, another ASCR program. Awards of computer time was provided by the Innovative and Novel Computational Impact on Theory and Experiment (INCITE) program. This research used resources of the Oak Ridge Leadership Computing Facility, which is a DOE Office of Science User Facility supported under Contract DE-AC05-00OR22725.

8. REFERENCES

[1] AMG2013 - parallel algebraic multigrid solver. https://codesign.llnl.gov/amg2013.php, 2015.

[2] BoxLibAMR- Block Structured AMR for Combusion Studies. http://exactcodesign.org/sample-page/s3dboxlib/, 2015.

[3] HPCG:High Performance Conjugate Gradients Benchmark. http://www.hpcg-benchmark.org, 2015.

[4] LULESH: Livermore Unstructured Lagrangian Explicit Shock Hydrodynamics. https://codesign.llnl.gov/lulesh.php, 2015.

[5] MCB - Monte Carlo Benchmark. https://codesign.llnl.gov/mcb.php, 2015.

[6] MPAS: Model for Prediction Across Scales. https://mpas-dev.github.io/, 2015.

[7] MultiGridC. http://exactcodesign.org/proxy-app-software/, 2015.

[8] Nek500. http://nek5000.mcs.anl.gov/, 2015.

[9] NEKBONE. https://cesar.mcs.anl.gov/content/software/thermal_hydraulics, 2015.

[10] Titan - Cray XK7 Supercomputer at Oak Ridge National Laboratory. https://www.olcf.ornl.gov/computing-resources/titan-cray-xk7/, 2015.

[11] Titan - Job Scheduling Policy. https://www.olcf.ornl.gov/kb_articles/titan-scheduling-policy/, 2015.

[12] TOP500 - Top 500 Supercomputer Sites in the World - June 2015. http://top500.org/lists/2015/06/, 2015.

[13] G. Bhanot, A. Gara, P. Heidelberger, E. Lawless, J. C. Sexton, and R. Walkup. Optimizing task layout on the Blue Gene/L supercomputer. *IBM Journal of Research and Development*, 40:489–500, 2005.

[14] A. Bhatele. *Automating topology aware mapping for supercomputers*. PhD thesis, University of Illinois at Urbana-Champaign, 2010.

[15] S. W. Bollinger and S. F. Midkiff. Processor and link assignment in multicomputers using simulated annealing. In *Proceedings of the International Conference on Parallel Processing, ICPP '88, The Pennsylvania State University, University Park, PA, USA, August 1988. Volume 1: Architecture.*, pages 1–7, 1988.

[16] CORAL Collaboration. CORAL Request for Proposal B604142, 2015.

[17] E. Cuthill and J. McKee. Reducing the bandwidth of sparse symmetric matrices. In *Proceedings of the 1969 24th National Conference*, ACM '69, pages 157–172, New York, NY, USA, 1969. ACM.

[18] M. Deveci, K. Kaya, B. Uçar, and Ü. V. Çatalyürek. Fast and high quality topology-aware task mapping. In *Proceedings of 29th IEEE International Parallel and Distributed Processing Symposium (IPDPS)*. IEEE, 2014.

[19] F. Ercal, J. Ramanujam, and P. Sadayappan. Task allocation onto a hypercube by recursive mincut bipartitioning. In *Proceedings of the 3rd Conference on Hypercube Concurrent Computers and Applications*, pages 210–221. ACM Press, 1988.

[20] A. George and J. W. Liu. *Computer Solution of Large Sparse Positive Definite*. Prentice Hall Professional Technical Reference, 1981.

[21] J. A. George. Nested dissection of a regular finite element mesh. *SIAM Journal on Numerical Analysis*, 10(2):345–363, 1973.

[22] J. L. Hintze and R. D. Nelson. Violin plots: A box plot-density trace synergism. *The American Statistician*, 52(2):181–184, May 1998.

[23] T. Hoefler and M. Snir. Generic topology mapping strategies for large-scale parallel architectures. In *Proceedings of the international conference on Supercomputing*, pages 75–84. ACM, 2011.

[24] S. C. Johnson. Hierarchical clustering schemes. *Psychometrika*, 32(3), 1967.

[25] I. Karlin, J. Keasler, and R. Neely. Lulesh 2.0 updates and changes. Technical Report LLNL-TR-641973, August 2013.

[26] B. Lee, S. McCormick, B. Philip, and D. Quinlan. Asynchronous fast adaptive composite-grid methods: numerical results. *SIAM journal on scientific computing*, 25(2), 2004.

[27] B. Lee, S. McCormick, B. Philip, and D. Quinlan. Asynchronous fast adaptive composite-grid methods for elliptic problems: Theoretical foundations. *SIAM journal on numerical analysis*, 42(1), 2005.

[28] S. McCormick and D. Quinlan. Asynchronous multilevel adaptive methods for solving partial differential equations on multiprocessors: Performance results* 1. *Parallel computing*, 12(2), 1989.

[29] S. F. McCormick. *Multilevel Adaptive Methods for Partial Differential Equations*. SIAM, Philadelphia, PA, 1989.

[30] S. F. McCormick and J. W. Thomas. The Fast Adaptive Composite grid (FAC) method for elliptic equations. *Math. Comp.*, 46:439–456, 1986.

[31] B. Philip, Z. Wang, M. Berrill, M. Birke, and M. Pernice. Dynamic implicit 3d adaptive mesh refinement for non-equilibrium radiation diffusion. *Journal of Computational Physics*, 262:17 – 37, 2014.

[32] N. Saitou and M. Nei. The neighbor-joining method: A new method for reconstructing phylogenetic trees. *Mol. Biol. Evol.*, 4(4):406–425, 1987.

[33] R. Sankaran, J. Angel, and W. M. Brown. Genetic algorithm based task reordering to improve the performance of batch scheduled massively parallel scientific applications. *Concurrency and Computation: Practice and Experience*, 2015.

[34] K. Schloegel, G. Karypis, and V. Kumar. Parallel static and dynamic multi-constraint graph partitioning. *Concurrency and Computation: Practice and Experience*, 14(3):219–240, 2002.

[35] E. Solomonik, A. Bhatele, and J. Demmel. Improving communication performance in dense linear algebra via topology aware collectives. In *Proceedings of 2011 International Conference for High Performance Computing, Networking, Storage and Analysis*, SC '11, pages 1–11, New York, NY, USA, 2011. ACM.

[36] S. Sreepathi, M. L. Grodowitz, R. Lim, P. Taffet, P. C. Roth, J. Meredith, S. Lee, D. Li, and J. Vetter. Application Characterization Using Oxbow Toolkit and PADS Infrastructure. In *Proceedings of the 1st International Workshop on Hardware-Software Co-Design for High Performance Computing*, Co-HPC '14, pages 55–63. IEEE Press, 2014.

[37] J. Vetter and C. Chambreau. mpip: Lightweight, scalable mpi profiling, 2004. URL http://mpip.sourceforge.net.

Automatically Detecting "Excessive Dynamic Memory Allocations" Software Performance Anti-Pattern

Manjula Peiris
Dept. of Computer and Information Science
Indiana University-Purdue University
Indianapolis
Indianapolis, IN, USA
tmpeiris@cs.iupui.edu

James H. Hill
Dept. of Computer and Information Science
Indiana University-Purdue University
Indianapolis
Indianapolis, IN, USA
hillj@cs.iupui.edu

ABSTRACT

This paper presents a methodology for automatically detecting the excessive dynamic memory allocation software performance anti-pattern, which is implemented in a tool named *Excessive Memory Allocation Detector (EMAD)*. To the best of author's knowledge, EMAD is the first attempt to detect excessive dynamic memory allocation anti-pattern without human intervention. EMAD uses dynamic binary instrumentation and exploratory data analysis to determine if an application (or middleware) exhibits excessive dynamic memory allocations. Unlike traditional approaches, EMAD's technique does not rely on source code analysis. Results of applying EMAD to several open-source projects show that EMAD can detect the excessive dynamic memory allocations anti-pattern correctly. The results also show that application performance improves when the detected excessive dynamic memory allocations are resolved.

Keywords

excessive dynamic memory allocation, software performance anti-pattern, dynamic binary instrumentation, detection

1. INTRODUCTION

Dynamic memory allocation [1] is the process of allocating memory "on the fly" at program runtime. In contrast to static memory allocation, programmers do not need to know the exact amount of space or the number of items (*e.g.*, size of an array) at compile time. Dynamic memory allocation operates by using *heap*, or the *free store*, of a program to allocate memory instead of the stack storage of a function. Because the *heap* is global to all scopes of a program (*e.g. classes, functions, and loops*), objects created using dynamic allocations can be shared between different scopes.

Even though dynamic memory allocations provide software developers with memory flexibility at runtime, it is an expensive operation [2]. Allocation and deallocation (*i.e.*, the process of releasing dynamically allocated memory) using standard memory allocation/deallocation functions like malloc/free (in the case of C) and new/delete (in the case of C++) require system calls. Too many dynamic memory allocations can have negative consequences on software performance. For example, Smith et al. [3] detailed how excessive dynamic memory allocations is a software performance anti-pattern. *Software performance anti-patterns* [3, 4], which we just call *anti-patterns* from this point forward, are common designs that have a negative impact on software performance.[1]

Since excessive dynamic memory allocation can negatively impact performance, there are methods to detect it. Unfortunately, the most prominent (and reliable) method for detecting and resolving excessive dynamic memory allocation—and actually any software performance anti-pattern—is (manual) source code analysis [5]. This approach, however, requires expert domain knowledge. More importantly, it requires access to the original source code to support the necessary analysis. As we know, source code may not be readily available when dealing with closed-source applications and/or third-party middleware. Lastly, software performance anti-patterns like excessive dynamic memory allocations are typically visible when a software application is running and placed into a certain state. It is therefore *hard* to identify, evaluate, and resolve the anti-pattern using source code alone.

There are also approaches for detecting software performance anti-patterns without source code. These approaches are either architecture dependent [6] or rule-based [7, 8]. Unfortunately, they do not consider the behavior of software performance anti-patterns at runtime. This makes it *hard* to detect implementation-level anti-patterns like excessive dynamic memory allocations [6].

Solution approach → Analysis supported by dynamic binary instrumentation (DBI). *Dynamic-binary instrumentation (DBI)* [9] is the process of instrumenting a software application at runtime as opposed to recompiling the software application with the instrumentation software. DBI does not require the source code of the system being instrumented because instrumentation logic is injected into the target application while the program's binary is executing. DBI also allows tracing an application and therefore capturing its behavior. DBI therefore allows us to overcome the challenges mentioned above. The remaining challenge now is understanding how to apply DBI to actually detect excessive dynamic memory allocations in an existing application, or middleware. Our proposed technique is based on the intuition that excessive dynamic

ICPE'16, March 12–18, 2016, Delft, Netherlands.
© 2016 ACM. ISBN 978-1-4503-4080-9/16/03. . . $15.00
DOI: http://dx.doi.org/10.1145/2851553.2851563

---

[1]The author Hill experienced this as a visiting researcher at EBay, Inc in 2007. The author was responsible for optimizing the backend search engine for EBay, Inc to address known performance issues. The proposed solution was to remove excessive dynamic memory allocations that were requesting 0 bytes of memory. The solution resulted in 99% improvement in performance for test scenarios that were missing their deadline and 10-15% improvement in performance for scenarios that were not missing their deadline.

memory allocations occur when the software application has many short-lived, high-frequent dynamic memory allocations.

The main contributions of this paper therefore are as follows:

- It presents a method for detecting excessive dynamic memory allocations software performance anti-pattern that has been realized in an open-source tool named *Excessive Memory Allocation Detector (EMAD)*;

- It presents an algorithm to construct a dynamic call graph of a program using an execution trace, which may be missing messages representing routine exit events correspnds to tail calls. This dynamic call graph is used to detect the excessive dynamic memory allocations anti-pattern.

- It showcases how we can apply the K-means clustering algorithm [10] and simple outlier detection techniques to the data collected from DBI to detect excessive dynamic memory allocations anti-pattern;

- It is the first attempt, to the best of the authors knowledge, of a tool that can automatically detect the excessive dynamic memory allocations software performance anti-pattern; and

- It is the first attempt, to the best of the authors knowledge, of using DBI to detect a software performance anti-pattern.

We have applied EMAD to several real open-source projects. Our results from applying EMAD to these open-source projects show that EMAD can report the correct results when the system either exhibits or does not exhibit the excessive dynamic memory allocations anti-pattern. The results also show that when EMAD reports the existence of the anti-pattern, common solutions can be used to resolve the anti-pattern and improve the performance.

Paper organization. The remainder of this paper is organized as follows: Section 2 discusses the challenges associated with detecting excessive dynamic memory allocations anti-pattern. Section 3 discusses the intuition and functionality of EMAD; Section 4 showcases the validity of our approach by applying EMAD to open source software projects. Section 5 discusses related works; and Section 6 provides concluding remarks.

2. MOTIVATION FOR EMAD

Excessive dynamic memory allocation is a common problem that can degrade the software performance. Because of this reason, many software systems and libraries adopt solutions that amortize the cost of allocating/deallocating memory, such as allocating memory from memory pools or free lists [11]. Another solution is to use the Flyweight software design pattern [12]. Although these promising solutions are available, it is *hard* to apply them if one cannot detect the excessive dynamic memory allocation anti-pattern. Unfortunately, detecting the excessive dynamic memory allocation anti-pattern poses several challenges:

1. **Inapplicability of source code analysis techniques.** As mentioned in Section 1, the prominent approach for detecting a software performance anti-pattern is source code analysis. Understanding dynamic memory allocations by just analyzing the source code, however, is *hard*. This is because key information like frequency of object allocation, the size of the object being allocated, and the lifetime of an object are hard to determine at compile time. Moreover, such analysis requires time-consuming code analysis involving experts of complex software systems [13].

Another limitation of this approach is that it requires source code to be available. Nowadays, most software systems are built using off the shelf software components and libraries. It is therefore ill-conceived to assume that source code is available for analysis at every situation. Even if the source code is available (as with open-source projects), one must still be able to understand the source code (and its intent) in order to search for excessive dynamic memory allocations.

2. **Limitations of software performance anti-pattern detection techniques based on architectural models.** Another approach for detecting software performance anti-patterns is defining rules on performance metric data (*e.g.*, response time and throughput) and/or resource usage data (*e.g.*, CPU and network usage) and then detecting rule violations [6–8]. These rules are defined on architectural models of the system and rule violations are analyzed by simulating the architectural models. Excessive dynamic memory allocation, however, happens at software implementation level. Unfortunately, it is hard to model the implementation details within architectural models [6].

On the other hand, resource usage data (*e.g.*, high memory footprint) is not a direct indicator of excessive dynamic memory allocations. This is because a function can do a large allocation at once (*e.g.*, a memory pool) and then use it subsequently throughout the entire application lifetime.

3. **Ill-defined excessive dynamic memory allocation problem.** The problem of detecting excessive dynamic memory allocations is ill defined compared to other dynamic memory associated problems like memory leak detection and invalid memory access detection. For example, memory leak detection can be defined as finding dynamic memory allocations that are no longer accessible to the program [14]. Likewise, memory access errors can be defined as detecting invalid reads/writes from/to memory locations.

```
1    struct Foo {
2      int x;
3    };
4
5    int main (int argc, char * argv[]) {
6      Foo * foo = new Foo ();
7      // Do someting with foo
8
9      return 0;
10   }
```

Listing 1: A simple program that has a potential memory leak.

Listing 1 illustrates a simple program that has a potential memory leak. As shown in the program, we can conclude that a memory leak exists by examining whether the object *foo* is, or is not, released when the main function returns. Although this examination process can be complex, the problem of detecting the memory leak is well defined.

```
1    struct Foo {
2      int x;
3    };
4
5    int main (int argc, char * argv[]) {
6      for (int i = 0; i < 1000000; i ++) {
7        Foo * foo = new Foo ();
8        // Do something with foo
9        delete foo;
10     }
11     return 0;
```

```
12    }
```

Listing 2: A simple program that has a potential excessive dynamic memory allocation.

Excessive dynamic memory allocations, however, cannot be defined in such a precise manner. The word "excessive" depends heavily on the context of the allocation. For example, Listing 2 illustrates a simple program that has a potential excessive dynamic memory allocation issue because of the high frequency at which *foo* is being created and deleted. It, however, is hard to determine whether this simple example exhibits excessive dynamic memory allocations by only examining the number of times object *foo* is being created and deleted. This is because excessive dynamic memory allocation is not only based on how many allocations/deallocations occur, but also on the lifetime of those allocated objects.

As discussed above, these challenges make it hard to create automated approaches for detecting excessive dynamic memory allocation anti-pattern. The reminder of this paper will therefore discuss how EMAD helps address these challenges–providing software developers with an improved approach to detect the excessive dynamic memory allocation anti-pattern. This will allow software developers to detect and resolve the anti-pattern problem faster and improve the performance of their software application.

3. THE DESIGN OF EMAD

Figure 1 illustrates EMAD's workflow for detecting the excessive dynamic memory allocations anti-pattern. As shown in the figure, the process consists of 3 major steps: (1) instrumenting the software application using DBI to collect an execution trace; (2) constructing a call graph of the software from the collected execution trace; and (3) analyzing the call graph to detect excessive dynamic memory allocations. We discuss each step in detail throughout the remainder of this section.

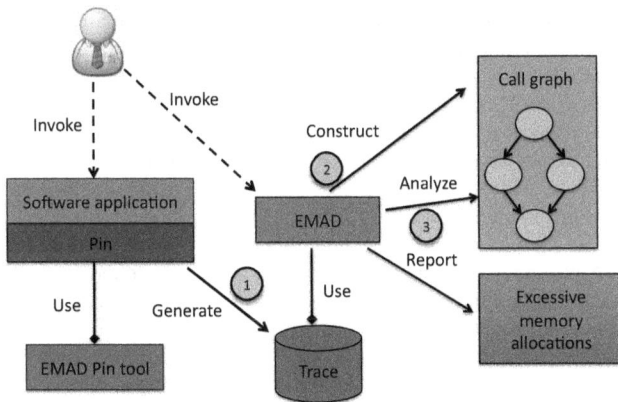

Figure 1: Conceptual overview of EMAD's workflow.

3.1 Instrumenting the Software Application

EMAD uses Pin [9] along with Pin++ [15] as the underlying DBI framework to instrument an application and collect the needed execution trace. Sidebar 1 provides a brief overview on Pin and Pin++. EMAD uses Pin++ to implement a Pintool that instruments a program at routine level. The Pintool instruments each routine call at start and at exit. The Pintool then generates an execution trace

where each message in the execution trace contains the following information:

- **Thread id.** The thread id is a unique identifier of the thread calling the routine under analysis. This is important because the caller-callee relationships between routines is determined on a per thread basis when constructing the call graph. The thread id therefore is used to uniquely identify the thread.

- **Routine id.** The routine id is a unique id of the routine assigned by Pin. This information is important because the routine name is not unique if the same routine is in different image or if it is overloaded in the same class. This allows EMAD to uniquely identify each routine it instruments.

- **Event name.** The event name represents the type of event that is occurring. For EMAD, the event name is either *start* or *exit*. Start represents the beginning of a routine call and exit represents the return of a routine call. This information is important because it determines what subprocedures (*i.e.*, the sub-procedure for receiving a start event or the sub-procedure for receiving an exit event) to call in Algorithm 1.

- **Name.** The name represents the undecorated name of the routine under instrumentation (or being analyzed). This piece of information is important because this allows EMAD to report the human readable name of a routine when it identifies the location(s) of excessive dynamic memory allocations.

> ## Sidebar 1: Pin and Pin++
>
> Pin is a DBI tool for IA-32 and X86-64 instruction-set architecture. Pin provides a framework to implement analysis tools called Pintools. Pintools analyze different aspects of a program, such as program faults, program behavior, root causes, and performance profiling. Pintools can also analyze a program at different levels of granularity: binary image level, routine level, and instruction level.
>
> Even though Pin provides several facilities to instrument programs, the Pintools implemented using Pin are fragile, rigid, hard to extend/reuse, and difficult to understand [15]. Pin++ provides an object-oriented, template meta programming approach to writing Pintools that handle the above mentioned software engineering issues. Moreover, Pintools implemented using Pin++ have a reduction in cyclomatic complexity, do not induce additional overhead, and improves the Pintools performance in certain cases. For example, Hill et al. [15] has shown that Pin++ can have a 54% reduction in complexity, increase modularity, and up to 60% reduction in instrumentation overhead when compared to traditional Pintools.

Because EMAD eventually constructs a call graph (see Section 3.2) that records dynamic memory allocations and deallocations, EMAD assumes signatures with the patterns shown in Listing 3 for dynamic memory allocation and deallocation routines. The patterns in this listing are the common signatures for most of the general-purpose memory allocation/deallocation routines in both standard libraries (*e.g.*, malloc/free and new/delete) and third-party libraries that implement custom memory management.

```
1    // Pattern expected for memory allocation routine.
2    void * [allocation_method] ( size_t size );
3
4    // Pattern expected for memory deallocation routine.
5    void [deallocation_method] ( void * location );
```

Listing 3: Allocation/Deallocation method signatures.

EMAD also collects the following additional details for allocation/deallocation routines in the execution trace:

- **Allocation size.** This is the input parameter at the start of the allocation routine, which is the size of the allocation. It is used to characterize the memory allocation.

- **Address of the allocation.** This is the return value at the exit of the allocation routine, which is the allocated memory location address. It is used to correlate memory allocations and deallocations.

- **Allocation timestamp.** This is the exiting timestamp from the allocation routine, and specifies the time when the memory allocation was active. It is used to calculate the lifetime of the corresponding memory allocation.

- **Deallocation timestamp.** This is the exiting timestamp from the deallocation routine, and specifies the time when the memory allocation was deactivated. It is used to calculate the lifetime of the corresponding memory allocation.

The execution trace (*i.e.*, the data discussed above) is recorded by the Pintool while the program under instrumentation is executing. Listing 4 shows a portion of an example execution trace the EMAD Pintool will generate. Once the execution trace is recorded, the remainder of EMAD's analysis is done offline.

```
1    0 19 start main
2    0 20 start Initialize
3    0 22 start malloc 32
4    0 22 exit malloc 842c008 141677579
5    0 20 exit Initialize
6    0 34 start operation1
7    0 22 start malloc 64
8    0 22 exit malloc 9786cd0 14167757886
9    0 35 start operation2
10   0 23 start free 9786cd0
11   0 23 exit free 14167757928
12   0 23 start free 842c008
13   0 23 exit free 14167757928
14   0 35 exit operation2
15   0 34 exit operation1
16   0 19 exit main
```

Listing 4: Example execution trace generated by EMAD

3.2 Constructing the Call Graph

EMAD uses the execution trace collected during the instrumentation step (see Section 3.1) to construct a call graph [16] of the program. The constructed call graph is a weighted directed graph. Each node in the graph represents an executed routine in the application. Each edge represents a caller-callee relationship. The edge weights represent the frequency of each routine call. The Figure 2 illustrate the call graph EMAD will be constructing for the execution trace shown in Listing 4.

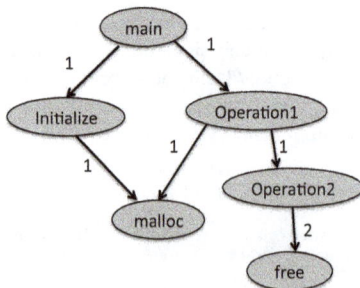

Figure 2: Call Graph for the execution trace in Listing 4.

Algorithm 1 General algorithm for constructing the call graph

```
1:  procedure CONSTRUCTCALLGRAPH(ET)
2:      ET : set of routine start/exit messages from execution trace
3:
4:      CG : Call graph
5:      CS : Set of stacks of called routines, one per each thread
6:
7:      for all ET_i ∈ ET do
8:          j ← extract_thread_id(ET_i)
9:          R ← extract_routine(ET_i)
10:         if ET_i is a routine start trace then
11:             HandleRoutineStartTrace(CG, CS_j, R)
12:         else if ET_i is a routine exit trace then
13:             HandleRoutineExitTrace(CG, CS_j, R)
14:         end if
15:     end for
16:
17:     for all k ∈ thread ids do
18:         while CS_k is not empty do
19:             R ← Top(CS_k)
20:             HandleRoutineExitTrace(CG, CS_k, R)
21:         end while
22:     end for
23:
24: end procedure
```

The constructed call graph is also a condensed graph [17]. This is because EMAD is not representing every call to a routine as its own node and edge as in a detailed call graph. Instead, EMAD is capturing how many times a routine is called. The condensed call graph reduces the amount of resources needed to construct the needed call graph of an application. More importantly, we have learned that a detailed call graph makes it hard to perform the necessary analysis to detect excessive dynamic memory allocations.

Algorithm 1 details EMAD's process for constructing the call graph from an execution trace. The algorithm consists of two sub-procedures. The first sub-procedure handles routine start messages (line 11). The second sub-procedure handles routine exit messages (line 13). It is worth noting that Algorithm 1 maintains a *called routine stack* for each thread in the application being instrumented. This is because caller-callee relationships are maintained on a per thread basis when using the condensed graph approach [17]. There, however, will be one call graph that is updated using the relationships maintained in each call stack.

The sub-procedure for handling routine start messages is shown in Algorithm 2. Whenever a routine start message is found, the corresponding routine object is pushed onto the stack. A node representing the routine object is also added into the call graph. Because EMAD is constructing a condensed call graph, the *AddNode* statement (line 7) only adds a node to the call graph if and only if the node is not in the call graph.

Algorithm 2 Procedure that handles a routine start trace.

```
1:  procedure HANDLEROUTINESTARTTRACE(CG, cs, R)
2:      CG : Call graph
3:      cs : The routine stack of a thread
4:      R : The routine
5:
6:      Push(cs, R)
7:      AddNode(CG, R)
8:  end procedure
```

The sub-procedure for handling routine exit messages is not as straightforward when compared to the sub-procedure for handling routine start messages. This is because the instrumentation of routine exits does not work reliably in the presence of tail calls or when return instructions cannot reliably be detected under Pin [18]. From our experience, a majority of the routine exit messages for the corresponding routine start messages can be found in the execution trace. When a routine exit message cannot be found in the execution trace, EMAD uses Algorithm 3 to resolve the *missing exit message* problem.

Algorithm 3 Procedure that handles a routine exit trace.

1: **procedure** HANDLEROUTINEEXITTRACE(CG, cs, R)
2:    CG : Call graph
3:    cs : The routine stack of a thread
4:    R : The routine
5:
6:    **if** cs is not empty **then**
7:        **if** $Top(cs) = R$ **then**
8:            Pop(cs)
9:            **if** cs is not empty **then**
10:                $AddEdge(CG, Top(cs), R)$
11:            **end if**
12:        **else**
13:            **while** $Top(cs) \neq R$ **do**
14:                $r \leftarrow Top(cs)$
15:                $Pop(cs)$
16:                **if** cs is not empty **then**
17:                    $AddEdge(CG, Top(cs), r)$
18:                **end if**
19:            **end while**
20:
21:            $Pop(cs)$
22:            **if** cs is not empty **then**
23:                $AddEdge(CG, Top(cs), R)$
24:            **end if**
25:        **end if**
26:    **end if**
27:
28: **end procedure**

As shown in this algorithm, it first checks whether the routine object at the stack top is the same as the routine object represented from the message. If this condition holds true, then this implies that the routine object has both start and exit messages in the execution trace. It also implies that the caller of the routine should be the stack top element once the current stack top is removed. EMAD therefore creates an edge between the two routines with the correct directionality (line 7-10) if an edge does not already exist. If an edge already exists, its weight is increased by 1. The *AddEdge* (line 17) implements this logic.

When the routine object at the top of the stack and the routine object correspond to routine exit message mismatches, it implies that the routine exit message for the routine object at the top of the stack is missing. The allocation object's caller should be current stack top's adjacent routine object. EMAD therefore saves the stack top, pops an element from the stack, and connects the new stack top with the previous stack top. EMAD continues this process until it finds the routine object represented by the current routine exit message. The sub-procedure for handling routine exit messages therefore guarantees that the correct caller-callee relationship is preserved even when routine exit messages are missing in the execution trace.

Once all messages in the execution trace are processed, there can still be routine objects remaining on the stack. EMAD explicitly calls the *HandleRoutineExitTrace* routine (line 20 of Algorithm 1) while iterating through call stacks of each thread. This is necessary because the routine exit messages of the remaining routine objects is missing. Explicitly calling *HandleRoutineExitTrace* will complete the call graph with any missing edges.

As mentioned in Section 3.1, the start/exit messages for allocation/deallocation routines contain extra details such as parameter/return values and timestamps. Algorithm 1 and its sub-procedures discussed above will extract and store this additional information in allocation/deallocation routine objects during the execution trace processing. The data associated with the allocation/deallocation routines is used to create *allocation objects*. An allocation object has three attributes, the size of the dynamic memory allocation; the routine that calls the memory allocation routine to allocate memory; and the routine that calls the memory deallocation routine. In EMAD, each dynamic memory allocation during the lifetime of the application is represented using an allocation object.

An allocation object is distinguishable from another allocation object if any of its attributes is different. One would think it should be possible to use the address of the memory allocation to uniquely represent an allocation object. This, however, is not possible because the same memory address can be reallocated several times during the lifetime of the application. The memory address of an allocation is therefore not unique once we consider the entire lifetime of the application. EMAD therefore only uses the memory address of an allocation to match the caller of the allocation routine and caller of the deallocation routine.

Each allocation object also has a frequency. The frequency specifies how many times an allocation object (with same values for above three attributes) occurs throughout the software application lifetime. For each allocation object, we can also calculate its lifetime as follows:

$$T_l = T_d - T_a \qquad (1)$$

where T_l represents the lifetime of the allocation object; T_d represents the timestamp of the deallocation exit message; and T_a represents the timestamp of the allocation exit message. Each distinct allocation object stores its average lifetime. Lastly, EMAD uses the two attributes of an allocation object, *i.e.* its frequency, its calculated average lifetime, and the constructed call graph to detect the excessive dynamic memory allocation anti-pattern.

3.3 Detecting Excessive Dynamic Memory Allocations

As mentioned in Section 1 our analysis technique for detecting excessive dynamic memory allocations is based on the intuition that this anti-pattern occurs when the software application has many short-lived high-frequent allocation objects. Our intuition comes from studying the two main solutions used to resolve the excessive dynamic memory allocation software performance anti-pattern [3].

The most common solution to resolve this anti-pattern is to use a custom memory allocator [19]. The basic idea of a custom memory allocator is to use a memory pool. When using a memory pool, a large chunk of memory is allocated during the software application initialization phase. The subsequent requirements for memory allocations are fulfilled by obtaining memory from this memory pool—thereby eliminating the system calls to allocate memory. When the allocated memory is no longer needed, it is released into the memory pool—thereby eliminating the system calls to deallocate memory.

The custom memory allocations approach will not be effective if the allocation objects are in use for long periods of time. This is because when there are many such objects, eventually the memory pool will not be able to fulfill the allocation requests. This will result in acquiring memory from the operating system and the expected performance gain may not be achieved. When the software application has high-frequent short-lived allocation objects, however, the memory pool regains the memory it has given to the application. This improves the performance by rarely allocating memory using general purpose memory allocators.

The other solution for the excessive dynamic memory allocation anti-pattern is to use the Flyweight software design pattern [20]. The Flyweight software design pattern is similar to using a custom memory allocator. Its strategy is also based on reusing the already allocated objects. The only difference is the Flyweight design pattern applies the solution at a higher level of abstraction such as reusing particular types of objects. It is also effective only when there are high-frequent short-lived object instances that are reusable.

Based on this intuition, EMAD's main goal in the detection process is to identify short-lived, high-frequent allocation objects. EMAD analyzes the frequency and average lifetime of the allocations objects annotated with the allocation/deallocation routines in the constructed call graph. To understand the analysis process, we introduce a frequency-lifetime diagram as illustrated in Figure 3. Each point in the diagram represents a unique allocation object. The x value represents the frequency of the allocation and y value represents the average lifetime of the allocation. We consider points that fall in the low-right quadrant to correspond to short-lived, high-frequent dynamic memory allocations. These are the set of points we want to identify in our analysis.

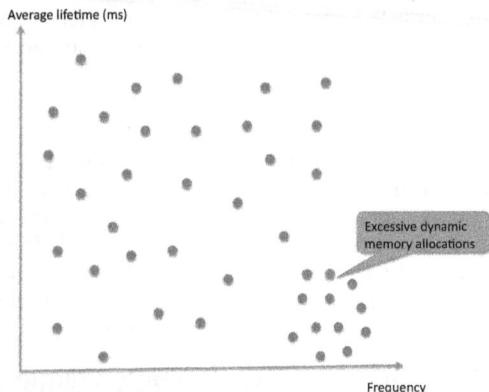

Figure 3: Frequency-lifetime diagram.

Because frequency and lifetime of allocation objects are dependent on each software application, it is hard to define thresholds to filter high-frequent, short-lived memory allocations. EMAD therefore provides two different exploratory data analysis techniques: one using K-means clustering, and the other using an outlier detection technique to identify high-frequent, short-lived memory allocations.

3.3.1 Using K-means clustering

Clustering is a non-supervised technique that can be used to partition objects based on the quantitative values of their attributes. The goal of clustering is to partition regions of points that have similarities. To accomplish this task, EMAD uses popular K-means algorithm [10] to cluster the allocation objects based on their frequency and average lifetime.

Once the allocated objects are clustered, EMAD then checks whether there is a cluster C that satisfies all the following conditions:

1. The average frequency of C's members is the highest compared to the other clusters. This information is important because if the frequency is high, then there is a potential excessive dynamic memory allocation issue.

2. The average lifetime of C's members is the lowest compared to the other clusters. This information is important because when the allocation object is a short lived object there is a potential excessive dynamic memory allocation issue.

If EMAD can find a cluster that satisfies both the conditions above, then it reports that software application has excessive dynamic memory allocation anti-pattern. The report may contain all the members of that cluster, or a user-defined number n of members. In the latter case, EMAD will report first n members in the descending order of frequency. Because the allocation objects contains the caller information of the allocation, EMAD can also report call hierarchy of the allocation similar to other dynamic memory analysis tools (e.g., Valgrind [14]). By providing the call hierarchy software developers can quickly locate the excessive dynamic memory allocations anti-pattern in the source code—eliminating tedious and time consuming source code analysis.

On the other hand, if EMAD cannot find a cluster that satisfies the conditions above, then EMAD reports that the software application does not have the excessive dynamic memory allocations anti-pattern. This is because the partitioning indicates that most of the high-frequent allocation objects have a longer lifetime, or short lived allocation objects are not frequent.

Because EMAD's analysis is based on a clustering technique, the user has to configure the parameter that controls the number of clusters. This parameter, in turn, controls the number of partitions EMAD has to create from the dataset. Unfortunately, this is one of the limitations in cluster analysis [21, 22]. Likewise, identifying the correct number of clusters may require some trial and error.

3.3.2 Using outlier detection

In this technique, we convert the two dimensional dataset into a one dimensional dataset by calculating the ratio between frequency and average lifetime of each allocation object.

Therefore, the ratio R is defined as:

$$R = \frac{frequency}{lifetime} \qquad (2)$$

According to the above equation the value of R is larger when the frequency is high and lifetime is low. Therefore we consider allocation objects that have relatively high values as potential excessive dynamic memory allocations. Based on this intuition we consider extreme outliers of this one dimensional dataset as potential excessive dynamic memory allocations. We only consider positive outliers that have larger values for R, not the outliers with lower values. To identify these extreme values we use Interquartile Range (IQR) based outlier detection technique [23]. We adopt this technique instead of standard score based outlier detection techniques because we observed that the data in our datasets are not normal distributions [24]. We consider allocation objects that have a value greater than the value obtained from the following expression as potential dynamic excessive memory allocations.

$$Q_3 + \mu \times IQR \qquad (3)$$

Here Q_3 is the third quartile, IQR is the Interquartile Range, and μ is a user provided parameter. If we increase the value of μ,

EMAD may miss potential excessive dynamic memory allocations; and a lower value for μ may cause EMAD to report several false-positives. Therefore, the user has to provide a reasonable value for μ which may requires some trial and error. A good initial value for μ is the value obtained for IQR. Another way to decide on a value for μ is to first view the datasets and see how the value of R is deviating from normal. EMAD outputs this value during the analysis. EMAD also ranks the excessive dynamic memory allocations based on the value of R. Therefore, users can get an idea about the relative significance of excessive dynamic memory allocations after seeing the results. EMAD also provide facilities to view both two dimensional (*i.e.* frequency and lifetime) and one dimensional datasets (*i.e.*, value of R) of allocation objects.

4. EVALUATION OF EMAD

This section illustrate how we validate EMAD's methodology by applying it to several real world open source systems. Validating EMAD's technique is challenging, because once EMAD reports excessive dynamic memory allocations we need to make sure it is an actual excessive dynamic memory allocation, which has an impact on system performance. We therefore validated EMAD with following types of experiments: (1) known released software version that has the anti-pattern and then a newer version of the same software without the anti-pattern; (2) software that have the anti-pattern, which is previously unknown; (3) an anti-pattern induced software version to see whether EMAD can detect the induced anti-pattern; and (4) software that does not have the anti-pattern to see if EMAD does not identify any problems. Lastly, we evaluated performance before and after resolving the anti-pattern for all experimental scenarios.

4.1 Experimental Setup

We used the following open-source projects in our experiments:

1. **SQLite** (www.sqlite.org) is a SQL database engine primarily used in embedded devices, such as mobile phones and web browsers. We selected SQLite for our experiments because we searched its release history and identified versions that were impacted by the excessive dynamic memory allocation anti-pattern. This project will evaluate if EMAD is able to identify the routine that is the source of the problem.

2. **TAO** (www.cs.wustl.edu/~schmidt/TAO) is an implementation of the CORBA specification used in distributed real-time and embedded systems. We selected TAO because its application domain values small percentages in performance improvements. Also the excessive dynamic memory allocation was not reported in TAO before applying EMAD.

3. **Axis2-C** (axis.apache.org/axis2/c/core) is a web services framework that is implemented in C using the popular Axis2 SOAP processing architecture. Axis2-C is used in some of the modern cloud computing infrastructure middleware and also in scripting language based web services engines [25]. We selected Axis2-C because we could induce the dynamic memory allocations anti-pattern. This will evaluate if EMAD can detect the induced anti-pattern.

4. **Xerces-C++** (xerces.apache.org/xerces-c) is a C++ framework for manipulating XML documents. We selected Xerces-C++ because it allows developers to integrate custom memory allocators to improve performance.

All experiments were conducted on an Intel core 2 Duo 3.33 GHz processor, with 4GB memory and running 32-bit Ubuntu 14.04 operating system. We also used Pin 2.13 and Pin++ 1.0.0-beta.

4.2 Experimental Results for SQLite

We used the Northwind database [26] for our SQLite experiments. We used a single SQL file that contained SQL statements for table creation, data insertion, table updating, and data querying. The SQLite command line interface was used to interpret the SQL file. Lastly, performance was measured by recording total time to process the Northwind database SQL file.

According to the SQLite [27] release history, SQLite had the excessive dynamic memory allocations software performance anti-pattern prior to version 3.6.1. Such versions created many number of short-lived memory allocations in each database connection. The SQLite documentation states the following related to this excessive dynamic memory allocations problem[2]:

> These small memory allocations are used to hold things such as the names of tables and columns, parse tree nodes, individual query results values, and B-Tree cursor objects. There are consequently many calls to *malloc* and *free*—so many calls that *malloc* and *free* end up using a significant fraction of the CPU time assigned to SQLite.

As a solution to this issue, SQLite developers implemented a custom memory allocator called *lookaside allocator* that preallocates a large chunk of memory and divides it to fixed size small slots inside each database connection. We therefore applied EMAD against SQLite 3.5.9. We did not use SQLite 3.6.0 because it was not a stable release.

4.2.1 Experimental results using clustering

In our experiments, EMAD detected 3 locations where SQLite 3.5.9 was performing excessive dynamic memory allocations. The 3 locations are shown in Table 1. EMAD also generated the call-tree for routines in Table 1. For example, Listing 5 illustrates the call-tree for the *sqlite3DbMallocRaw* routine. The call-tree shows the routine name and frequency (inside parentheses) of each caller-callee relationship. Although there are several call-trees for the *sqlite3DbMallocRaw* routine, Listing 5 only shows the call frequencies with maximum edge weights. Due to space limitations we discarded the other call-trees for *sqlite3DbMallocRaw* routine.

```
1    sqlite3_column_name (10659)
2    sqlite3_step (14098)
3    sqlite3VdbeExec (60800)
4    sqlite3BtreeNext (378600)
5    sqlite3VdbeMemRelease (788186)
6    sqlite3_prepare (3450)
7    sqlite3LockAndPrepare (3450)
8    sqlite3Prepare (3450)
9    sqlite3RunParser (102322)
10   sqlite3Parser (26436)
11   sqlite3Expr (26765)
12   sqlite3DbMallocRaw (45858)
```

Listing 5: Partial Call-tree for the routine *sqlite3DbMallocRaw*.

As described in the SQLite documentation, routines like *sqlite3_step* and *sqlite3_column_name* contribute to excessive dynamic memory allocations in SQLite3. As shown in Listing 5, EMAD is able to report these routines in the call-tree for *sqlite3DbMallocRaw* routine as a source of the excessive dynamic memory allocations.

Figure 4 shows the frequency-lifetime diagram for this experiment, which supports the reported excessive dynamic memory allocations. As shown in Figure 4, the 3 allocation objects that correspond to excessive dynamic memory allocations have high-frequency

---

[2]More on the quote can be found at the following location: www.sqlite.org/malloc.html#lookaside

Table 1: Excessive dynamic memory allocation locations in SQLite-3.5.9 identified by clustering method

Caller	Size	Destroyer	Freq.	Avg. Lifetime
sqlite3DbMallocRaw	68	sqlite3ExprDelete	29394	929.758
sqlite3DbMallocRaw	32	sqlite3VdbeMemRelease	12918	224.889
pager_write_size	1024	sqlite3BtreeCommitPhaseTwo	6832	1.29202

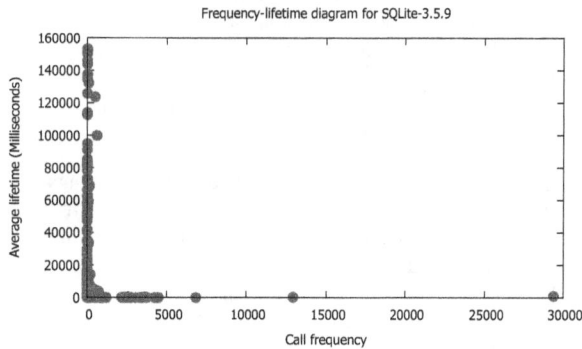

Figure 4: Frequency-lifetime diagram for SQLite-3.5.9

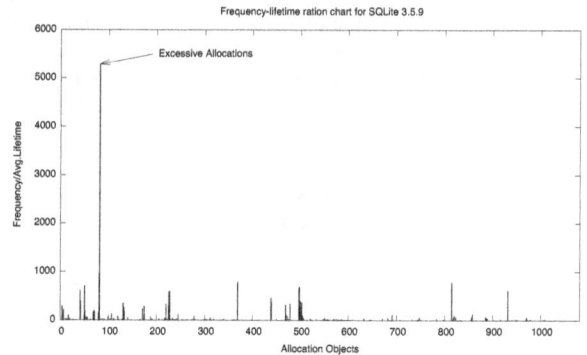

Figure 6: Frequency-lifetime ratio chart for SQLite-3.5.9

(as high as 29394) and short lifetime (as low as 1.29202ms) when compared to the other allocation objects in the figure.

SQLite releases after version SQLite 3.5.9 implement the solution to the excessive dynamic memory allocations anti-pattern. To verify this, we applied EMAD to SQLite 3.8.5. In this version, EMAD identified *memjrnlWrite* as the only location to perform excessive dynamic memory allocations. This location is related to an I/O operation that has no relation with the excessive dynamic memory allocation problem we found in SQLite 3.5.9. The frequency-lifetime digram shown in Figure 5 validates the results of EMAD. As shown in the diagram, there is only one allocation object that resides in high-frequency, short-lifetime region.

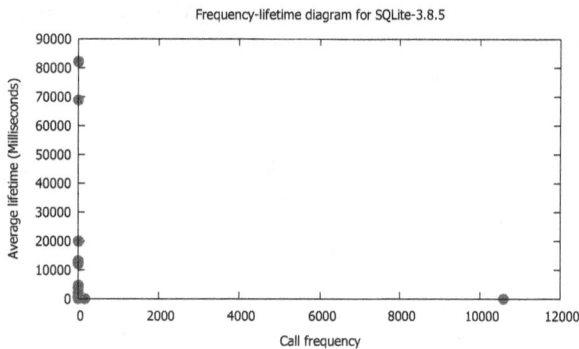

Figure 5: Frequency-lifetime diagram for SQLite-3.8.5

4.2.2 Experimental results using outlier detection

We applied EMAD to SQLite 3.5.9 after configuring EMAD to use its outlier detection technique. After using a value of 1000 for μ in Equation 3, EMAD reported *pager_write* as the only location with excessive dynamic memory allocations as shown in Figure 6.

The outlier detection technique did not categorize some of the high frequency, short-lifetime allocation objects as excessive dynamic memory allocations. This is because the IQR of the dataset is as low as 1.7211 and we had to use a value as larger as 1000 for μ

to filter the outliers. Unfortunately, a lower μ value started producing false positives. For example, when we lowered the value of μ, EMAD reported allocation objects that have a frequency of 162 and an average lifetime of 0.2075 msec as excessive dynamic memory allocations. Although the average lifetime of the allocation objects is low, the frequency is also low when compared to frequencies of excessive dynamic memory allocations. Lastly, we applied the outlier detection technique to SQLite 3.8.5. EMAD reported the same location shown in Figure 5 from the clustering technique.

4.2.3 Resolution and performance improvements

To resolve the identified problem, we used a custom memory allocator (as mentioned in the SQLite documentation) to resolve the performance anti-pattern and improve the performance. According to SQLite documentation, the custom memory allocator preallocates a chunk of memory during application initialization. To apply to solution, we re-compiled SQLite-3.8.5 with the custom memory allocator enabled. We then ran the same experiment with the enabled custom memory allocator. For our experiments, the custom memory allocator improved performance by 10%.

Table 2: Performance of different versions of SQLite

SQLite Version	Total Process Time	# of mallocs
3.5.9	475.01 ms	184859
3.8.5	338.43 ms	58441
3.8.5 w. custom allocator	308.53 ms	9706

To summarize our performance results, Table 2 shows the total processing time of the Northwind database SQL file for each version SQLite we used in our experiments. As shown in the table, the performance of SQLite improved after we applied each solution to the identifed excessive dynamic memory allocation software performance anti-pattern. For example, SQLite 3.8.5 improved approximately 30% in performance when compared to SQLite 3.5.9. Likewise, SQLite 3.8.5 with custom memory allocator improved approximately 10% when compared to SQLite 3.8.5 without the custom memory allocation. More importantly, the experiments show

EMAD was able to detect the excessive dynamic memory allocations and can assist developers in improving performance.

Lastly, Table 2 also shows the number of malloc/free routine calls invoked by each version of SQLite we used in our experiments. We collected this data using a Pintool that counts malloc/free routine calls. Our results show that when the excessive dynamic allocation anti-pattern is resolved, there are fewer system calls to malloc/free.

4.3 Experimental Results for TAO

We applied EMAD to TAO while sending 10,000 requests to its echo service example. EMAD reported two locations with excessive dynamic memory allocations[3]: (1) (*CORBA::string_alloc*, *CORBA::string_free*) and (2) (*operator »*, *IOP::ServiceContextList:: ServiceContextList*). For this experiment, both the clustering and outlier detection technique reported the same locations.

The first excessive dynamic memory allocation is coming from TAO. The second one is coming from the echo service (*i.e.,* the application) when it is echoing the received string. The frequency-lifetime diagram in Figure 7 and the frequency-lifetime ratio chart in Figure 8 confirm EMAD's findings. Apart from the two excessive dynamic memory allocations, almost all the other allocation objects have a very low frequency. Because of this, only the two data points that correspond to the excessive dynamic memory allocations are visible in the Figure 8.

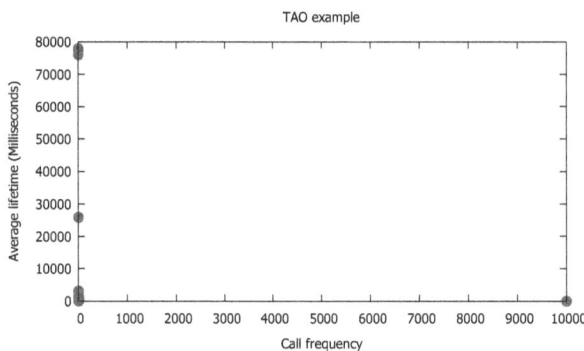

Figure 7: Frequency-lifetime diagram for TAO

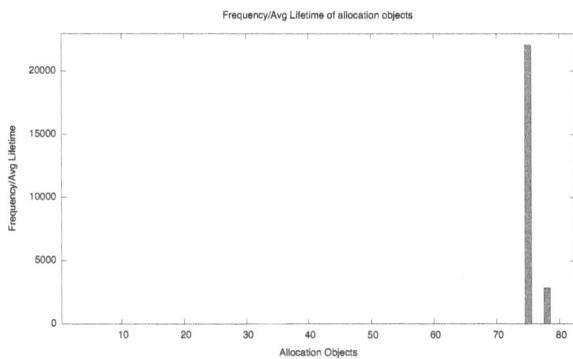

Figure 8: Frequency-lifetime ratio chart for TAO

Our focus was on resolving the identified problem that resided in TAO because it will impact all the applications that use TAO.

---

[3]We are only listing the caller and destroyer location due to space limitations

This excessive dynamic memory allocation occurs when TAO performs a zero size allocation using *operator new* to allocate a list of buffers for service context information. When the same client sends many requests, however, the buffer can be allocated only for the first request. Our simple fix was to return immediately before calling *operator new* when the requested length is 0.

After this fix we re-evaluated TAO's performance, and measured the time it takes to process n requests. We observed a 5-10% performance gain for larger number of requests. The performance results are shown in the Table 3.

Table 3: Performance of echo service example in TAO.

# of Requests	Before Fix (sec)	After Fix (sec)	Gain
10K	2.275431	2.25299	0.98%
20K	4.589058	4.491926	2.11%
30K	6.972080	6.825455	2.1%
40K	9.51474	9.419871	0.99%
50K	11.487203	11.291216	1.7%
100K	22.917998	22.587449	1.44%
200K	52.195151	45.445869	12.93%
300K	68.968680	63.624066	7.74%
400K	91.914805	85.586583	6.88%
500K	115.174436	106.963704	7.12%

We reported our findings to the TAO mailing list. The TAO developers accepted the patch as it was something they were not aware of. Although it is not a bug, they were willing to fix the problem because even a small improvement in performance is valuable in the context of distributed realtime and embedded systems.

4.4 Experimental Results for Axis2-C

Axis2-C uses Apache's memory pool routines to dynamically allocate memory. To induce the excessive dynamic memory allocations anti-pattern, we changed the Axis2-C module to use malloc/free functions. After applying the change, we used Apache Benchmark tool to send 2,000 SOAP requests to Axis2-C sample echo service deployed in an Apache Web Server, and instrumented the Apache Web Server with Axis2-C while the requests were processed. Finally, the collected execution trace was analyzed by EMAD for excessive dynamic memory allocations.

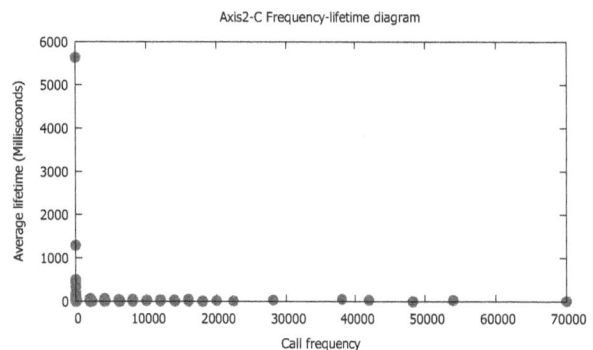

Figure 9: Frequency-lifetime diagram for Axis2-C

As shown in the frequency-lifetime (see Figure 9) and frequency-lifetime ratio (see Figure 10) diagrams, we found several locations where Axis2-C performs excessive dynamic memory allocations. The first five locations based on rank for the clustering technique was *axutil_string_create*, *axiom_node_create*, *axutil_hash_first*, *axutil_hash_find_entry*, and *axutil_string_create_assume_ownership*.

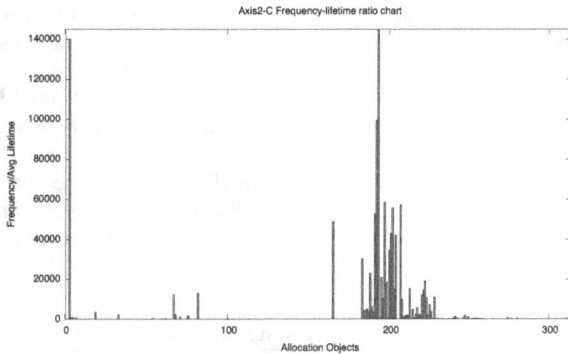

Figure 10: Frequency-lifetime ratio chart for Axis2-C

Likewise, the first five locations based on rank for the outlier technique was *guththila_get_prefix*, *axutil_hash_first*, *guththila_get_prefix*, *axutil_strdup*, and *axutil_stracat*.

From our analysis, Axis2-C's excessive dynamic memory allocations happens mainly because of deep string copies. When used with Apache Web Server, Axis2-C can still perform deep copying when necessary without sacrificing performance by leveraging Apache's memory pools. When using Apache memory pools, Axis2-C has 8% of performance improvement for processing 1 million requests as shown in Table 4. The table also shows there are 96% fewer calls to malloc when processing a single request.

Table 4: Axis2-C performance.

Item	w. memory pools	w.o. memory pools
1 million requests	280 secs	304 secs
Mallocs/request	370	11032

4.5 Experimental Results for Xerces-C++

We used Xerces-C++ Simple API for XML (SAX) command-line utility to parse a 117 KB XML file that contained 1,318 elements and 71,166 characters. We then used EMAD to collect the execution trace of the SAX command-line utility while it processed the XML file. Next, we used EMAD to generate the call graph from the execution trace and detect the presence of the excessive dynamic memory allocation software performance anti-pattern.

In this experiment, EMAD could not find any excessive dynamic memory allocations using the clustering or outlier detection technique. We also checked if previous versions of Xerces-C++ had the excessive dynamic memory allocation software performance anti-pattern. We, however, could not find any version reviewing Xerces-C++ release history.

Since Xerces-C++ supports custom memory allocators, we investigated whether we could improve Xerces-C++ performance by implementing a custom memory allocator. By default, Xerces-C++ uses the new/delete operators to allocate/deallocate memory. Our custom memory allocator is an implementation that uses a free list. At the beginning, it allocates a large chunk of memory that is partitioned into small user defined chunks. The small chunks are maintained as two linked list. The first linked list maintains the memory chunks that are being used in the program. The second linked list maintains the freely available memory chunks.

The allocation function returns a memory chunk from the free list and creates a pointer to that chunk from allocated list. The deallocation function gives back the deallocated memory chunk to the free list and removes the corresponding pointer from the allocated

list. Lastly, the memory pool calls the general-purpose memory allocation function if the allocated memory pool is not large enough to service the user request.

Table 5: Performance of Xerces-C++ with a custom memory allocator and default memory allocator.

Xerces-C++ Method	Avg. Process Time
w. default memory allocator	159 ms
w. custom memory allocator	155 ms

We measured the overall processing time for the XML file using the default memory allocator and the custom memory allocator. As presented in Table 5, even when we plugged in the custom memory allocator we could not observe much performance gain (as small as 2.5%). This is an indication that Xerces-C++ does not exhibit excessive dynamic memory allocations. Figure 11 shows the frequency-lifetime diagram for our experiments. In this figure, none of the allocation objects reside in the high-frequent, short-lifetime region of the graph. EMAD therefore does not report any excessive dynamic memory allocations.

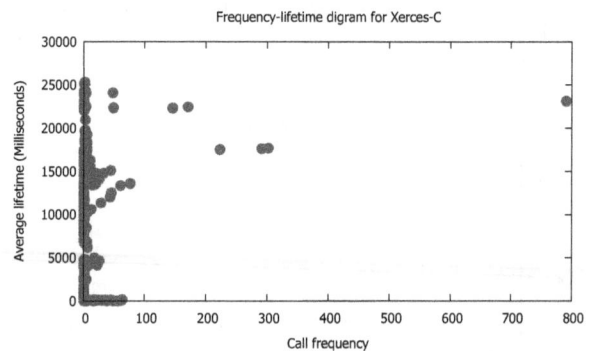

Figure 11: Frequency-lifetime ratio chart for Xerces-C

The frequency-lifetime ratio chart in Figure 12 also confirms our finding. The range of values for frequency-lifetime ratio is as low as 16. In other applications where we found excessive dynamic memory allocations, this ratio has a range as high as $150,000$.

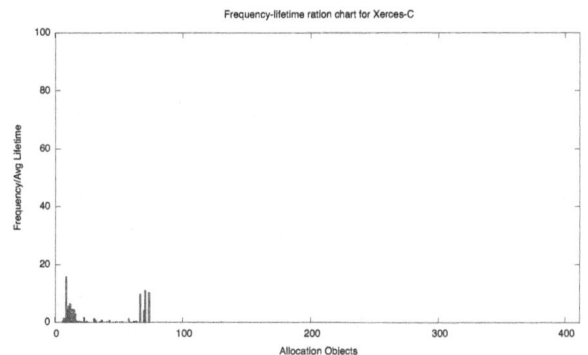

Figure 12: Frequency-lifetime ratio chart for Xerces-C

4.6 Discussion of results and threat to validity

Our experiments show the validity of EMAD's approach. EMAD was able to correctly detect and locate when a software application has, or does not have, excessive dynamic memory allocations. This kind of analysis will help software developers resolve excessive dynamic memory allocations faster. More importantly, it will eliminate the laborious process of detecting the anti-pattern via manual source code analysis.

The main advantage of the clustering technique over the outlier detection method is it does not categorize allocation objects as excessive dynamic memory allocations when it has a low frequency. In the outlier detection technique, because we consider frequency-lifetime ratio as the analytical value, it can still report extreme outliers when the frequency is low and lifetime of the allocation object is short. These low-frequent and short-lifetime values may sometime beat some high-frequent, short-lifetime objects. With the clustering technique, this kind of false positive is not possible.

When using the clustering technique, EMAD's users have to provide the number of clusters to use in the analysis phase. There are some advanced data mining techniques [22, 28] for learning this parameter from the dataset itself. EMAD, however, does not employ those techniques at the moment. Unfortunately, this can cause EMAD to provide incorrect predictions if the user does not specify a reasonable number of clusters. If the dataset has very clear separable partitions, then the impact of this parameter can still be mitigated. On the other hand, when using outlier detection technique, users have to provide μ, which may need some trial and error.

When using the clustering technique, EMAD performs quantitative analysis and detects excessive dynamic memory allocations only if high-frequent and short-lived allocation objects resides in the same cluster. A software developer, however, may still think that there are excessive dynamic memory allocations in other clusters by looking at the numbers. In this situation, EMAD's prediction may not be inline with software developer's expectation. EMAD, however, can still be helpful because the software developer can manually analyze the frequency-lifetime diagram or the frequency-lifetime ratio chart to understand the big picture. A recommended way for further analysis is to do a comparative analysis of both two-dimensional and one-dimensional datasets.

5. RELATED WORK

Automated approaches for detecting excessive dynamic memory allocations cannot be found in literature. Likewise, existing approaches for detecting software performance anti-patterns have categorized excessive dynamic memory allocations as an undetectable software performance anti-pattern [6–8]. Although there are several approaches for detecting memory leaks and memory access errors using DBI [29], the excessive dynamic memory allocation problem has not been attacked by the research community.

Chen et al. [30] have developed a tool called *MemBrush* that can be used to detect memory allocation/deallocation functions using DBI in stripped binaries. Their approach is useful in detecting memory leaks and memory access errors, but they do not discuss detecting excessive dynamic memory allocations. However, by combining the *MemBrush* approach with our approach, it may be possible to relax our assumptions about allocation/deallocation routines as EMAD expects a particular signature for those routines.

Lu et al. [31] have developed a tool called PerfBlower, which can be used to detect memory related performance problems. They have developed a domain specific language called *Instrumentation Specification Language (ISL)* that is used to specify the memory related performance issues. The application code is executed on top of a modified Java Virtual Machine (JVM) where ISL is used to modify the JVM. Although they have tried to detect several memory related performance issues, excessive dynamic memory allocation anti-pattern, related to allocation object's life time has not been considered. Moreover their approach requires recompilation of the JVM whereas our approach does not require any kind of recompilation of the target system.

DBI has been used to identify other root causes of performance anomalies. For example, Attariyan et al. [32] proposes an approach to detect root causes of performance anomalies, such as misconfigurations, using DBI. Menon et al. [33] uses DBI to diagnosis performance overheads in Xen virtual machine environments. The root causes they try to detect are related to I/O handling in virtual machine environments—particular related to TCP connections.

There are research efforts on finding the object life times in managed languages (*e.g. Java*) [34]. In managed languages the garbage collection process can happen at anytime, therefore the timestamp at which an object is deleted cannot be used alone to approximately calculate the object lifetime. We believe that by integrating precise object lifetime calculation techniques, we can extend our technique for applications created using managed languages.

6. CONCLUDING REMARKS

This paper discussed our work on a tool called EMAD, which can detect excessive dynamic memory allocations software performance anti-pattern. Our experience and results show that EMAD can correctly report the locations where the software application is performing excessive dynamic memory allocations. Based on experience gained from applying EMAD to several widely used open-source software applications, we have learned that DBI can serve as a good platform for detecting software performance anti-patterns. We therefore plan on applying DBI to detect other software performance anti-patterns [3], such as God Class, Single Lane Bridge, and Circuitous Treasure Hunt. Likewise, EMAD's current technique works only with C/C++ software applications. We plan to investigate if EMAD's approach will work on applications written in interpreted languages like Java, Python, PHP, and JavaScript.

EMAD is available in open-source format and has been integrated into the Pin++ distribution: github.com/SEDS/PinPP.

7. REFERENCES

[1] P. R. Wilson, M. S. Johnstone, M. Neely, and D. Boles, "Dynamic storage allocation: A survey and critical review," in *Memory Management*. Springer, 1995, pp. 1–116.

[2] D. Detlefs, A. Dosser, and B. Zorn, "Memory allocation costs in large c and c++ programs," *Software: Practice and Experience*, vol. 24, no. 6, pp. 527–542, 1994.

[3] C. U. Smith and L. G. Williams, "Software performance antipatterns." in *Workshop on Software and Performance*, 2000, pp. 127–136.

[4] ——, "More new software performance antipatterns: Even more ways to shoot yourself in the foot," in *Computer Measurement Group Conference*, 2003, pp. 717–725.

[5] J. Din, A. B. Al-Badareen, and Y. Y. Jusoh, "Antipatterns detection approaches in object-oriented design: A literature review," in *Computing and Convergence Technology (ICCCT), 2012 7th International Conference on*. IEEE, 2012, pp. 926–931.

[6] C. Trubiani and A. Koziolek, "Detection and solution of software performance antipatterns in palladio architectural models." in *ICPE*, 2011, pp. 19–30.

[7] V. Cortellessa, A. Di Marco, and C. Trubiani, "Performance antipatterns as logical predicates," in *Engineering of Complex Computer Systems (ICECCS), 2010 15th IEEE International Conference on*. IEEE, 2010, pp. 146–156.

[8] J. Xu, "Rule-based automatic software performance diagnosis and improvement," *Performance Evaluation*, vol. 67, no. 8, pp. 585–611, 2010.

[9] C.-K. Luk, R. Cohn, R. Muth, H. Patil, A. Klauser, G. Lowney, S. Wallace, V. J. Reddi, and K. Hazelwood, "Pin: building customized program analysis tools with dynamic instrumentation," in *Acm Sigplan Notices*, vol. 40, no. 6. ACM, 2005, pp. 190–200.

[10] J. A. Hartigan and M. A. Wong, "Algorithm as 136: A k-means clustering algorithm," *Applied statistics*, pp. 100–108, 1979.

[11] E. D. Berger, B. G. Zorn, and K. S. McKinley, "Oopsla 2002: Reconsidering custom memory allocation," *ACM SIGPLAN Notices*, vol. 48, no. 4, pp. 46–57, 2013.

[12] E. Gamma, R. Helm, R. Johnson, and J. Vlissides, *Design Patterns: Elements of Reusable Object-Oriented Software*. Reading, MA: Addison-Wesley, 1995.

[13] N. Moha, "Detection and correction of design defects in object-oriented designs," in *Companion to the 22nd ACM SIGPLAN conference on Object-oriented programming systems and applications companion*. ACM, 2007, pp. 949–950.

[14] N. Nethercote and J. Seward, "Valgrind: a framework for heavyweight dynamic binary instrumentation," *ACM Sigplan Notices*, vol. 42, no. 6, pp. 89–100, 2007.

[15] J. H. Hill and D. C. Feiock, "Pin++: an object-oriented framework for writing pintools," in *Proceedings of the 2014 International Conference on Generative Programming: Concepts and Experiences*. ACM, 2014, pp. 133–141.

[16] B. G. Ryder, "Constructing the call graph of a program," *Software Engineering, IEEE Transactions on*, no. 3, pp. 216–226, 1979.

[17] F. Eichinger, K. Böhm, and M. Huber, "Mining edge-weighted call graphs to localise software bugs," in *Machine Learning and Knowledge Discovery in Databases*. Springer, 2008, pp. 333–348.

[18] I. Corporation, "Pin 2.14 User Guide," https://software.intel.com/sites/landingpage/pintool/docs/67254/Pin/html/.

[19] E. D. Berger, B. G. Zorn, and K. S. McKinley, "Composing high-performance memory allocators," in *ACM SIGPLAN Notices*, vol. 36, no. 5. ACM, 2001, pp. 114–124.

[20] E. Gamma, R. Helm, R. Johnson, and J. Vlissides, *Design Patterns. Elements of Reusable Object-Oriented Software*. Addison-Wesley, 1997.

[21] C. Fraley and A. E. Raftery, "How many clusters? which clustering method? answers via model-based cluster analysis," *The computer journal*, vol. 41, no. 8, pp. 578–588, 1998.

[22] C. A. Sugar and G. M. James, "Finding the number of clusters in a dataset," *Journal of the American Statistical Association*, vol. 98, no. 463, 2003.

[23] V. J. Hodge and J. Austin, "A survey of outlier detection methodologies," *Artificial Intelligence Review*, vol. 22, no. 2, pp. 85–126, 2004.

[24] C. Leys, C. Ley, O. Klein, P. Bernard, and L. Licata, "Detecting outliers: do not use standard deviation around the mean, use absolute deviation around the median," *Journal of Experimental Social Psychology*, vol. 49, no. 4, pp. 764–766, 2013.

[25] M. Imran and H. Hlavacs, "Provenance in the cloud: Why and how," in *The Third International Conference on Cloud Computing, GRIDs, and Virtualization*, 2012, pp. 106–112.

[26] M. Cooperation, "Northwind database," https://northwinddatabase.codeplex.com/.

[27] SQLite, "Release History," http://www.sqlite.org/changes.html.

[28] S. Salvador and P. Chan, "Determining the number of clusters/segments in hierarchical clustering/segmentation algorithms," in *Tools with Artificial Intelligence, 2004. ICTAI 2004. 16th IEEE International Conference on*. IEEE, 2004, pp. 576–584.

[29] G. R. Luecke, J. Coyle, J. Hoekstra, M. Kraeva, Y. Li, O. Taborskaia, and Y. Wang, "A survey of systems for detecting serial run-time errors," *Concurrency and Computation: Practice and Experience*, vol. 18, no. 15, pp. 1885–1907, 2006.

[30] X. Chen, A. Slowinska, and H. Bos, "Who allocated my memory? detecting custom memory allocators in c binaries," in *Reverse Engineering (WCRE), 2013 20th Working Conference on*. IEEE, 2013, pp. 22–31.

[31] L. Fang, L. Dou, and G. Xu, "Perfblower: Quickly detecting memory-related performance problems via amplification."

[32] M. Attariyan, M. Chow, and J. Flinn, "X-ray: automating root-cause diagnosis of performance anomalies in production software," in *Proceedings of the 10th USENIX conference on Operating Systems Design and Implementation*. USENIX Association, 2012, pp. 307–320.

[33] A. Menon, J. R. Santos, Y. Turner, G. J. Janakiraman, and W. Zwaenepoel, "Diagnosing performance overheads in the xen virtual machine environment," in *Proceedings of the 1st ACM/USENIX international conference on Virtual execution environments*. ACM, 2005, pp. 13–23.

[34] M. Hertz, S. M. Blackburn, J. E. B. Moss, K. S. McKinley, and D. Stefanović, "Generating object lifetime traces with merlin," *ACM Transactions on Programming Languages and Systems (TOPLAS)*, vol. 28, no. 3, pp. 476–516, 2006.

Efficient and Viable Handling of Large Object Traces

Philipp Lengauer[1]   Verena Bitto[2]   Hanspeter Mössenböck[1]

[1]Institute for System Software
Johannes Kepler University Linz, Austria
philipp.lengauer@jku.at

[2]Christian Doppler Laboratory MEVSS
Johannes Kepler University Linz, Austria
verena.bitto@jku.at

ABSTRACT

Understanding and tracking down memory-related performance problems is a tedious task, especially when it involves automatically managed memory, i.e., garbage collection. A multitude of monitoring tools show the substantial need of developers to deal with these problems efficiently. Unfortunately, state-of-the-art tools either generate an inscrutable amount of trace data or produce only a coarse-grained view of the application's memory behavior. While the first approach generates information that is very detailed albeit difficult to handle, the second approach is more efficient but may fail to provide vital information.

In this paper, we propose a method to combine the advantages of both approaches, i.e., a method to handle fine-grained tracing information efficiently. Specifically, we present an on-the-fly compression technique for tracing data with reasonable overhead. Furthermore, we show how to overwrite old parts of the trace to circumvent its unlimited growth, but almost without losing vital information.

We also provide a detailed evaluation of our approach, showing that the introduced run-time overhead is negligible compared to similar tracing tools as well as that the information quality recovers quickly after overwriting parts of the old tracing data.

Keywords

Tracing; Trace Reduction; Garbage Collection; Java

1. INTRODUCTION

The widespread use of programming languages with automatic memory management has stressed the need for memory profiling tools. Although managed memory relieves programmers from the error-prone task of freeing memory manually, it comes at the cost of performance problems that are hard to track down. When an allocation fails due to a full heap, the subsequent garbage collection (GC) pauses the application for a hard-to-predict period of time. Depending on the application's memory behavior, garbage collections may occur frequently and, thus, may have a negative impact on the application's throughput (long overall GC time) and availability (long GC pauses).

Existing profiling tools, such as GC Spy [12], operate on memory blocks instead of objects to reduce the overhead and to make visualization easier. Consequently, these tools are only able to provide coarse-grained statistics about memory blocks, such as how many objects of a specific type are contained in it. They are unable to provide information about the origin of an object, which is crucial, for example, to track down a memory leak.

Other tools, such as the one by Ricci et al. [14] collect more fine-grained information. However, they introduce an enormous overhead of up to 14000% [7].

In Lengauer et al. [7] we introduced AntTracks, a memory profiler based on the Java Hotspot™ VM which is able to record object allocations and object movements. Although information is recorded at object level, AntTracks produces a very low run-time overhead (4.86%) compared to other state-of-the-art tools. This has been mainly achieved through white-box compression, i.e., a compact, mostly pre-compilable event format, representing object allocation events and object move events with around 5 bytes on average. No event contains redundant information. Instead all information which can be reconstructed offline is omitted. Still, the generated trace files grow large quickly. The fastest-growing trace we have observed so far (SPECjvm compiler.compiler), produces up to 200 MB of trace data per second. Considering this amount of generated data, it is obvious that we need a method to keep the trace files small in order to allow efficient analysis. Interestingly, this is a problem which seems to have been disregarded in literature so far. Every continuously tracing monitoring tool either prolonging this problem with a low granularity or seems to ignore it at all.

In this paper, we will describe the effects of black-box compression on the trace, i.e., traditional compression that does not consider individual events but rather regards the trace as a large binary stream. Black-box compression is difficult during monitoring, because it has to be done on-the-fly, resulting in a trade-off between compression rate and run-time overhead. Furthermore, black-box compression does not solve but only postpones the problem of continuously growing trace files. Although the trace will grow more slowly, it will still grow unfeasibly large for a continuously running application.

Thus, in addition to black-box compression, we describe a new method to limit the absolute size of a trace file. When the trace file starts to exceed the given limit, old events are

ICPE'16, March 12-18, 2016, Delft, Netherlands

© 2016 ACM. ISBN 978-1-4503-4080-9/16/03. . . $15.00

DOI: http://dx.doi.org/10.1145/2851553.2851555

removed from it. The trace file thus always represents only the last part of the application's memory behavior. We call this *trace rotation*.

However, rotating the trace leads to some interesting challenges, especially when considering its performance impact and a minimalistic event format. For example, as events might omit reconstructible information, they depend on previous events as described in Bitto et al. [1]. Thus, if the front of the trace is cut off, the trace cannot be processed correctly because some information may be lost.

Our scientific contributions are (1) a method to integrate on-the-fly low-overhead compression of traces into a monitoring environment, (2) a novel technique to rotate object-level trace files incrementally, and (3) methods to restore information from before the cut-off point. Furthermore, we provide (4) a detailed evaluation of both, the overall overhead, as well as the information quality, i.e., the amount of reconstructible and non-reconstructible information.

This paper is structured as follows: Section 2 provides some necessary background information about the Hotspot™ VM as well as about AntTracks; Section 3 describes both black-box compression as well as trace rotation; Section 4 provides a detailed evaluation of our techniques; Section 5 describes related work; Section 6 presents future work and Section 7 concludes this paper.

2. BACKGROUND

This section briefly discusses the basics of the Java memory management as well as AntTracks' strategies to record and encode memory events.

2.1 Memory Management in Hotspot™

Java uses garbage collection to reclaim unused memory. In its default configuration the Parallel Collector splits the heap into two generations, i.e., a young generation and an old generation. The young generation is further split into the Eden space, the survivor-from space and the survivor-to space, while the old generation consists of the old space only. Usually, objects are allocated into the Eden space until it is exhausted. In this case, the JVM triggers a *minor collection* to free unused memory in the young generation using a stop-and-copy approach. Live objects from the Eden space are copied to the empty survivor-to space. The survivor-from space contains objects that have already survived at least one collection. Depending on how many collections they have already survived, they may be either copied into the survivor-to space or into the old space. After all live objects have been evacuated, the Eden space and the survivor-from space are declared empty and the two survivor spaces are swapped. The old generation is collected during *major collections* only. Major GCs are triggered rarely, since generational collection assumes that the majority of objects in the old space are alive for a long time. Instead of copying objects to another space, the entire heap is compacted towards its beginning.

To avoid extensive synchronization in multi-threaded applications, the JVM uses thread-local allocation buffers (TLABs) for fast allocations into the Eden space and promotion-local allocation buffers (PLABs) for fast copying during minor collections. These buffers are large chunks of memory which are claimed by a single thread while locking the heap. All following allocations or copying actions of a thread can then be done without locking. Major collections

are done in parallel as well but without using PLABs. Instead the heap is divided into dedicated regions, which are collected by separate threads.

Java objects consist of two parts: the header, and the payload. The header contains meta information about the object, such as its type, its identity hash code, the lock state, and special information for the GC (such as the object's age and the mark bit). The payload contains all fields of the object.

The header is split into the mark word and the klass word, both being either 4 bytes or 8 bytes depending on the machine architecture. Figure 1 sketches the object header on a 64-bit architecture, using compressed pointers (enabled by default since Java SE 6u23). In this case, the mark word takes up 64 bits, while the klass word requires 32 bits only. The compressed klass word is made possible by storing pointers as offset from the heap base address. The mark

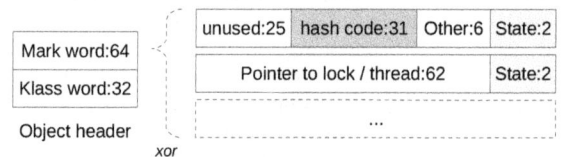

Figure 1: Object header in different object states

word is heavily over-allocated, meaning that it encodes different information depending on the object's state. The four different states are:

- neutral: The mark word contains the identity hash code and some flags regarding locking. The first 25 bits of the mark word remain unused.

- locked: The mark word holds a pointer to the native lock object.

- biased: The mark word holds a pointer to a thread towards which the object is biased. This thread may acquire the lock more efficiently.

- marked: The mark world holds a pointer to the location the object has been moved to by the GC.

Identity hash codes are generated lazily, i.e., they are initialized with zero and are generated when the identity hash is accessed for the first time. Zero is thus never a valid identity hash code.

2.2 AntTracks

AntTracks is a memory profiling tool based on the Hotspot™ VM. It records memory events, i.e., object allocations and object moves of a running Java application. The events are captured per thread as sketched in Figure 2. Each recording thread owns a private event buffer, which is fetched from a pool of empty buffers. All memory-related events of a single thread are then placed into that buffer. The size of the buffers is defined globally and is 16 kilobytes by default. The actual buffer size varies slightly to avoid multiple threads filling their buffers at the same time. Full buffers are enqueued into the flush queue which is drained by a dedicated worker thread. The worker thread undertakes the actual writing of the event buffers to the trace file. For every buffer a header is prepended, denoting the owning

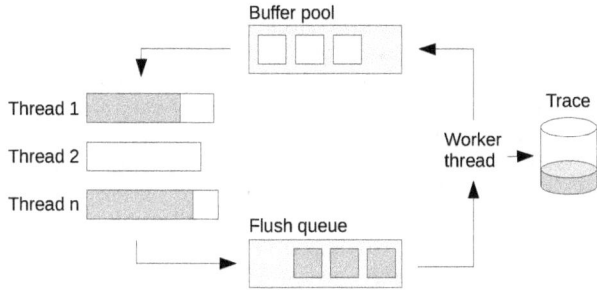

Figure 2: Event buffer management

thread and the buffer size, followed by the actual events. The processed event buffers are then returned to the buffer pool.

AntTracks has been specifically designed for low run-time overhead in order not to distort the actual memory behavior, while producing exact traces at the same time. Precisely for this reason, a lot of effort has been put into a binary, compact trace format. We omit any information from an event, which can be reconstructed offline, such that the majority of events are compile-time constants. As a result, dependencies between events arise which need to be resolved when processing the trace.

The characteristics of an object are stored in the allocation events only. For example, the *obj allocation generic* event stores the object's address, the size, the allocation site, and the allocation mode. The allocation site is defined as the location, i.e., the method and bytecode index, where the object has been allocated. The object's type can be inferred from the allocation site, and is therefore not recorded explicitly. Usually, only a single object type is allocated per allocation site. Hence, the object's size can be inferred from the allocation site as well. Only in those rare cases where this is not possible, the size is encoded into the allocation event as well. Whenever an object has been allocated into a TLAB, a *obj allocation optimized* event is fired instead, which omits the allocation address because it can be reconstructed offline by the analysis tool.

GC move events carry no explicit information about the moved objects. The *GC move generic* event (see Figure 3) contains the source address and the destination address only. The information, which object is actually moved can

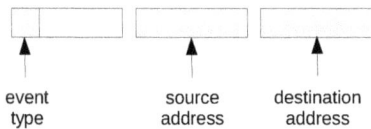

Figure 3: GC move generic event

be recovered from previous events, i.e., from the allocation address of the allocation event or from the destination address of the latest GC move event for this object. If an object is moved into a PLAB during minor collections, a *GC move optimized* event is fired, which omits the destination address. Adjacent objects, which are moved by the same offset during major collections are clustered into a single *GC move region* event. Like the *GC move generic* event, the *GC move region* event carries a source address and a destination address. However, in this case the addresses indicate only

the location of the very first object, which is moved. Additionally, the event contains the number of objects which are affected by the move. The addresses of these adjacent objects can then be inferred. A complete description of all dependencies can be found in Bitto et al. [1]. The format of all fired events has been presented in Lengauer et. al [7].

3. APPROACH

The following sections describe our approach, i.e., black-box on-the-fly compression as well as how and when to rotate the trace.

3.1 Compressing the Trace on the Fly

A common way to reduce the size of trace files is to apply conventional compression algorithms. However, since AntTracks already encodes memory events in a highly compact, binary format (as described in Section 2.2), the potential compression rate is limited. Apart from that, compression is only worthwhile if not compromising overall tracing performance. Consequently, only such algorithms are applicable which are able to encode the information on the fly, i.e., in a single-pass while the application is traced. One well-known technique which fits our criteria is the Lempel-Ziv-Welch (LZW) algorithm [16]. The LZW builds up a dictionary of commonly occurring fragments in the input data. Compression is then achieved by substituting variable-length data fragments with the corresponding indexes of the dictionary.

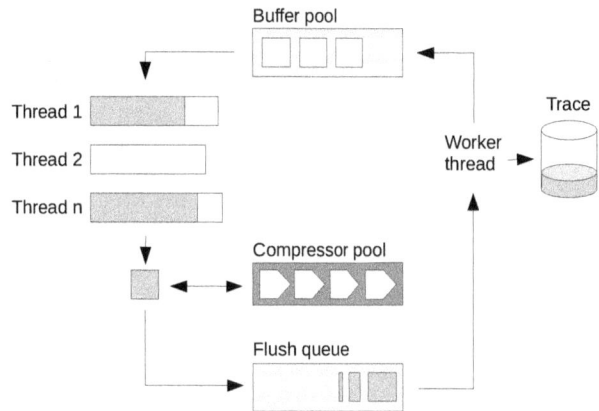

Figure 4: Event buffer management with conditional compression

We decided to introduce compression per tracing thread, i.e., a thread may compress its buffer before enqueuing it into the flush queue (see Figure 4). As a result, compression can take place in parallel without keeping the actual worker thread from writing the trace. We introduced a fixed number, i.e., the number of available cores on the machine, of compressors, each being able to compress a single buffer at a time. The compressors are retained in a dedicated compressor pool. A thread can request a compressor from that pool if he wants to compress its buffer before handing it over to the flush queue. If a compressor is available, the thread extracts it, compresses the buffer, and returns the compressor to the pool. The dictionary built by the compressor is constructed anew each time a thread retrieves a compressor from the pool, and cleared again when returning it to the pool. Though this limits compression quality, because the compressor can use its compression dictionary for a single buffer only, assigning a compressor per thread would become memory-intensive quickly.

In order to investigate the trade-off between compression rate and run time, we implemented two different strategies: (1) All event buffers are compressed given that enough compressors are available; (2) Only some event buffers are compressed. In the latter case, an event buffer is only compressed if the flush queue is filled up to a certain threshold. Otherwise the uncompressed event buffer is enqueued to prevent the worker thread from becoming idle. Both strategies are evaluated in detail in Section 4.

3.2 Rotating the Trace

Trace rotation enables limiting the absolute size of the trace, which will then never be exceeded. When the trace reaches the given size limit, old events need to be overwritten with new events. To make overwriting easier, we write n small trace files instead of one big trace file. Every trace file starts with an index number, by means of which the analysis tool can reconstruct the correct order of the individual files. When the trace is rotated, we delete the data of the oldest trace file, assign it a new index number, and continue to write the trace into that file.

Consequently, the number of rotations depends on the maximum trace size, as well as on n, i.e., the number of trace files. The absolute trace size can be specified via a VM parameter, e.g., `MaxTraceSize=16G`. In addition to that, one can specify the maximum deviation from the maximum trace size, e.g., `MaxTraceSizeDeviation=0.1`. The actual number of trace files used (n) is then calculated based on the maximum deviation. For example, a maximum size of 16 GB and a deviation of 0.25 (25%) will result in 4 trace files, where every file will be at most 4 GB in size. Thus, there will always be at least three full trace files (12 GB of data) to analyze, even if the trace has just been rotated. Figure 5 shows this example after several iterations.

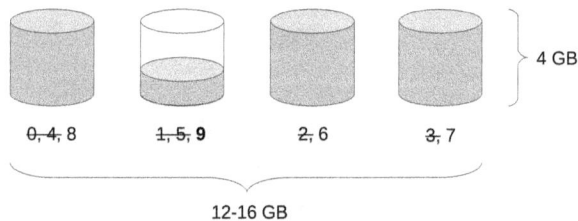

0, 4, 8   1, 5, 9   2, 6   3, 7

12-16 GB

Figure 5: Trace rotation with a maximum trace size of 16 GB and a deviation of 25% after two complete iterations

3.3 Synchronization Points

As described in Lengauer et al. [7], the trace consists of events, i.e., object allocations and object movements. Initially the analysis tool starts with an empty data structure representing the heap. It then interprets every event as an incremental change to that data structure. This assumption is usually correct because every application starts with an empty heap. However, rotating the trace invalidates this assumption, because a part of the trace is missing, meaning the heap is not empty at the start of the trace. Consequently, as every event represents an incremental change to the previous state of the heap, the resulting state will not be correct. Even more so, events may not be parsed correctly because information (that was reconstructible before) is now missing as it was located in the overwritten part of the trace file.

Thus, since every trace file may be the starting point for processing, all trace files must start with a *synchronization point* that contains enough information to reconstruct the heap as it was at that point. A synchronization point is a snapshot of the heap, containing all information that is necessary to parse the subsequent events in the trace correctly. Specifically, the analysis tool needs to know the exact location and the type of every object in the heap at that point in time.

However, iterating through the heap and creating such a snapshot is a tedious task for various reasons: (1) to get a stable snapshot, the VM needs to be suspended; (2) iterating through the entire heap costs time and destroys CPU caches; (3) a large portion of the snapshot will be useless because it is about objects that will die at the next garbage collection anyway; and (4) such a snapshot will take up a considerable amount of space in the trace file.

To cope with these problems, we use a GC (minor or major) to rotate the trace on the fly. During such a GC, we can easily extend existing GC move events (see Section 2.2) by appending an object's type information. Thus, we do not have to write any additional events. Furthermore, the VM is already suspended during a GC and the move events are only emitted for live objects. Figure 6 shows multiple trace files, including GCs and synchronization points.

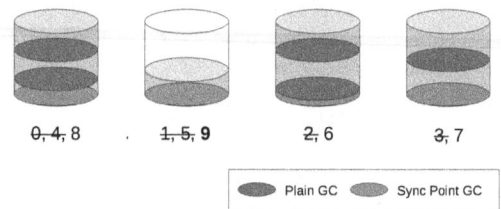

0, 4, 8   1, 5, 9   2, 6   3, 7

⬤ Plain GC   ⬤ Sync Point GC

Figure 6: Trace rotation with a maximum trace size of 16 GB and a deviation of 25% after two complete iterations, including GCs and synchronization points

Major GC.

As described in Section 2.2, a move event is written for every live object during a major GC. When we are rotating the trace file at a major GC, all move events are replaced with *GC move sync* events. Such an event (as shown in Figure 7) carries all information of a regular move event plus an additional type identifier. This type identifier will be used to reconstruct the heap data structure, if the trace starts from a synchronization point in the oldest trace file. At synchronization points that are not in the oldest trace file, only the source address and the destination address are used and the type identifier is ignored.

If possible, AntTracks clusters several adjacent objects that are moved by the same distance into a single *move region* event (cf. Section 2.2). However, the analysis tool must know the types of all objects in the region for further analysis. Thus, this optimization is only used if the GC is not a synchronization point. If the GC is a synchronization

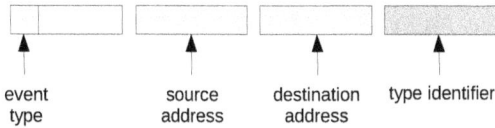

Figure 7: *GC move generic sync* event (plain *GC move generic* event with an additional field representing a type identifier)

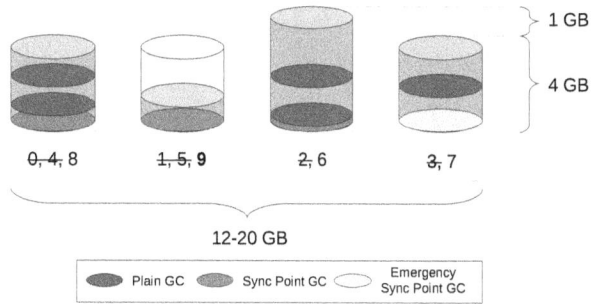

Figure 8: Trace rotation with a maximum trace size of 16 GB and a lower and upper deviation of 25% after two complete iterations, including GCs and synchronization points

point, *move region* events are split into individual *GC move sync* events to include type information.

Minor GC.

If a minor GC is a synchronization point, similarly to a major GC, every *GC move* event is replaced with a *GC move sync* event. As minor GCs use PLABs to move objects across spaces (cf. Section 2), there are also optimized events for moving objects into PLABs. Again, the original events are simply extended by a type identifier.

However, a minor GC does not collect the entire heap, but only the young generation. Consequently, after a minor GC synchronization point, the analysis tool cannot reconstruct the entire heap but only the spaces that have been collected, i.e., the Eden space, the survivor-from space, and the survivor-to space. To overcome this problem, we also iterate through the old space concurrently to the GC and create *GC sync* events for all objects there.

Using a minor GC is not as efficient as using a major GC because events for dead objects in the old generation may be created, and the run time no longer depends on the number of live objects, but on the size of the old space instead. However, it is still much more efficient than waiting for a major GC or, even worse, triggering one.

Deciding When to Rotate.

Usually, a minor GC is triggered only when the Eden space is full. Depending on the fill level of the survivor spaces and the old generation, a major GC will follow immediately or might even replace the minor GC entirely.

Consequently, there might not be the need for a GC when the trace must be rotated. In this case, we can either wait for a GC (and accept overshooting our trace size target), or rotate immediately and trigger a GC to create a synchronization point. Triggering a GC has the disadvantage that the GC behavior of the application is changed, and thus, the resulting trace is distorted.

Therefore, we use a hybrid approach by interpreting the allowed deviation not just as a lower deviation, but also as an upper deviation. For example, if the maximum trace size is 16 GB with 25% deviation (see Figure 8), this means that the trace might be somewhere between 12 GB and 20 GB. This allows us to wait for some time after reaching 16 GB in the hope that a GC will occur soon. If we reach the limit including the deviation, we trigger an emergency GC (minor) to create an artificial synchronization point.

When the trace size target has already been exceeded for a file, every allocation is adding another few bytes to an already over-full file. On the other hand, every allocation keeps filling the Eden space and thus increases the chance for triggering a GC. Thus, there is a linear relation between allocations and the probability of a GC. Therefore, if the

absolute deviation is big enough, we will never have to introduce an artificial GC and thus never distort the trace file. We will show this to be correct in Section 4.

3.4 Restoring Allocation Site Information

As described before, synchronization points contain extended events that allow the analysis tool to rebuild the heap data structure. However, these events contain only the bare minimum that is necessary to accomplish this task, i.e., the object's type. The type information is needed for inferring the size of an object. The size is crucial during trace processing in order to know how much space an object takes up in memory. Other information about objects, however, such as the allocating thread or the allocation site, is not included in *GC move sync* events.

The allocation site is the most interesting of the missing information, as it provides a clue about the origin and, thus, the purpose of an object. However, in contrast to the type, the allocation site cannot be inferred from an object. Information about the allocation site exists only during the allocation itself and is subsequently lost because it is not stored in the object.

Storing the Allocation Site.

Consequently, if we want to restore the allocation site information of an object, we need to save and store it during the allocation itself. However, finding a location to store the allocation site for every object is a challenging task.

A naïve approach would be to keep a map with object addresses as keys and allocation sites as values. Obviously, this approach is not feasible as this would require a significant amount of memory and is not trivial to maintain efficiently due to parallel allocations as well as due to the garbage collector moving objects.

The other possibility is to store the allocation site in the object itself. However, an object is already densely packed in order to fit as many objects as possible into the heap. As described in Section 2, there is neither space in the payload section nor in the header section of an object to store the allocation site. We could add an extra field in the object header to store the allocation site. However, this field would have to be at 8 bytes large to ensure proper object alignment. This would lead to an overall increase of the object size, and would thus lead to a GC time increase of at least the same magnitude.

Exploiting the Identity Hash Code.

Inspired by Odeira et al [10], we chose to exploit the identity hash code in the header. The identity hash code of an object does not have to be unique, but should only be as unique as possible to reduce hash collisions. Thus, we store the allocation site into the upper two bytes of the hash code, whereas the lower two bytes remain untouched.

Storing the allocation site into the identity hash code has two drawbacks: (1) An identity hash code must be generated eagerly for every object (usually, it is generated lazily on its first access). (2) The entropy of the identity hash code is reduced because it is now effectively only 2 bytes long.

In Section 4, we will show that the reduced entropy is negligible for the identity hash code. This is due to the fact, that most applications provide their own hash code implementation if they intend to hash objects of a specific class. Exploiting this observation, we were also able to reduce the eager generation of identity hash codes by optimistically not generating them for classes that provide a hash code implementation.

4. EVALUATION

This section provides a detailed evaluation of the black-box compression of traces as well as of their rotation in terms of overhead. Furthermore, it shows the worst-case performance as well as the performance of selected configurations.

Benchmarks.

To evaluate trace rotation, we need benchmarks that allocate a significant amount of objects. Only then, the trace is big enough so that it is rotated a number of times and the measurement can be declared to be significant.

We have examined the well-known DaCapo, DaCapo Scala, and SPECjvm (lagom) benchmark suites to evaluate whether they fit our needs. Not one of these suites had a benchmark that generates enough trace data in a single iteration (not even using the *huge* and *gargantuan* loads for DaCapo and DaCapo Scala). Thus, we have quadrupled the load of every SPECjvm benchmark. For the DaCapo and DaCapo Scala benchmarks, we chose the largest workload because only a fixed number of workloads is available. Furthermore we eliminated benchmarks, i.e., scimark.*, that did not create enough trace data.

In the following sections, we will mostly use only those benchmarks that generate enough trace data to show the impact of individual optimizations. Finally, we will show the overall overhead based on all benchmarks.

Before every measurement, we executed 20 warmups to stabilize JIT compilation. Every number shown in the following sections is the median of multiple runs. Unless otherwise noted, the standard deviation is negligible.

Setup.

All measurements were run on an Intel® Core TM i7-3770 CPU @ 3.4GHz x 4 (8 Threads) on 64-bit with 32 GB RAM and a Samsung SSD 840 PRO Series (DXM03B0Q), running Ubuntu Trusty Tahr 14.04 with the Kernel Linux 3.11.0-23-generic. All unnecessary services were disabled in order not to distort the experiments.

4.1 Compression Overhead

In Section 3.1 we proposed two strategies for enabling on-the-fly compression of the event buffers: (1) All event buffers are compressed; (2) Only some event buffers are compressed. In the latter case, an event buffer is only compressed if the flush queue is filled up to a certain degree. In the following section we provide a detailed evaluation of black-box compression.

Trace size.

The trace size is the most obvious criterion to use for measuring the effectiveness of a compression algorithm. Figure 9 shows the size of the compressed trace relative to the original trace size.

Benchmark	Trace Size Full compression / partial compression		
compiler.compiler		32.1% /	86.0%
compiler.sunflow		29.7% /	88.4%
derby		15.6% /	94.8%
serial		21.0% /	87.0%
sunflow		10.8% /	90.3%
xml.transform		25.2% /	92.1%
xml.validation		25.6% /	89.3%
mean		21.6% /	89.7%

Figure 9: Size of fully compressed trace (blue, left) and size of partially compressed trace (cyan, middle) relative to original trace size (gray, right, 100%)

The second column shows the numbers when compressing all event buffers, while the third column shows the results for partial compression. The event buffer size has been fixed to 16 kilobytes in both cases. Increasing this parameter improves the compression rate and consequently reduces the trace size further. The larger an event buffer, the longer a thread can benefit from using the same dictionary for compression. The threshold of partial compression has been set to 0.2, meaning that buffers are only compressed when the flush queue is at least filled to 20%. Increasing this parameter would worsen the compression performance, since less buffers would be compressed.

Run time.

Though the trace size can be significantly decreased when enabling full compression, the application's run time suffers dramatically. Figure 11 shows the run-time overhead of full compression and partial compression, relative to the run time without compression. While on average the run-time overhead increases about 22% (geometric mean) with full compression, partial compression comes at the cost of only about 2% (geometric mean). Further evaluation showed that the increased run time of full compression can be attributed to the time required for compressing. The reduced IO time, caused by writing less data, cannot compensate for the compression time. Consequently, full compression is impossible without compromising AntTracks' overall monitoring performance. However, partial compression proves beneficial to further reduce the trace size without worsening the application's run time considerably.

Benchmark	Run-time overhead Partial compression / full compression	
compiler.compiler		2.4% / 23.8%
compiler.sunflow		4.5% / 24.7%
derby		−0.5% / 25.8%
serial		3.7% / 24.3%
sunflow		2.0% / 15.5%
xml.transform		2.7% / 19.6%
xml.validation		1.4% / 20.1%
mean		2.3% / 21.9%

Figure 11: **Run-time overhead of full compression (blue, right) and partial compression (cyan, middle) normalized relative to the run time with disabled compression (gray, left, 100%).**

4.2 Rotation Overhead

Figure 10 shows the run-time overhead of tracing with rotation (8 GB maximum trace size with 10% deviation) relative to tracing without rotation on our selected benchmarks. Please note that these are already very allocation-intensive benchmarks, thus the average overhead is lower when using a more random set of benchmarks (see Lengauer et al. [7] and Paragraph Total Overhead Compared to Non-rotated Tracing).

We chose a relatively small maximum trace size (8 GB) intentionally to force benchmarks to rotate more often. Realistically, one would choose a much larger size, e.g, 32 GB or more. For example, doubling the maximum trace size would cut the number of synchronization points in half. Consequently, the performance can be improved by adjusting the maximum trace size. Thus, the following figures represent not the best setup but rather a minimalistic one.

The results show an average run-time overhead of 45% for rotation. This overhead can be reduced further by accepting a loss of data (cf. Paragraph Overhead without Allocation Site Information). The GC time (see right-hand side of Figure 10) is usually higher with rotation due to the additional work that has to be done for a synchronization GC.

Figure 12 reveals the ratio of synchronization GCs to plain GCs. It shows that the relatively small trace size of 8 GB is big enough for these benchmarks, as only 9.2% (geometric mean) of all GCs are synchronization points and none are emergency synchronization points. Figure 13 shows the sizes of trace data caused by garbage collections. It reveals that the required GC sync events are significantly larger than

Benchmark	Sync GC / plain GC ratio	
compiler.compiler		17.9%
compiler.sunflow		8.2%
derby		8.8%
serial		8.3%
sunflow		7.0%
xml.transform		5.0%
xml.validation		13.2%
mean		9.2%

Figure 12: **Ratio of GCs used as synchronization points (green, left) in relation to plain GCs (gray, right), when trace rotation is enabled**

Benchmark	Trace size [MB]		Sync events size overhead
	Minor GC	Major GC	
compiler.compiler	25.16	6.03	1378.7%
compiler.sunflow	11.45	-	463.5%
derby	0.22	-	22387.5%
serial	0.10	-	749.8%
sunflow	1.14	-	252.4%
xml.transform	0.61	-	756.6%
xml.validation	12.17	1.43	2087.2%

Figure 13: **Size of trace data produced by minor and major GCs, as well as sync events size overhead if a GC is used as a synchronization point**

normal GC events. In the case of derby, one minor sync GC requires about 50 MB, while a normal minor GC takes up only 0.22 MB. For compiler.compiler a minor sync GC needs about 360 MB, which means that it occupies 45% of a single 800 MB trace file.

Overhead with Storing Allocation Site Information.

In Section 3 we described how to store allocation site information into identity hash codes, thus being able to restore them after a synchronization point. However, reducing the size of the identity hash code decreases its entropy. By removing 16 bits from the 31-bit identity hash code, we reduce the number of possible values by a factor of $2^{16} = 65536$. We thus reduce the entropy of the hash to $\frac{1}{65536} = 0.0015\%$ of its original entropy. In theory, this can considerably affect the performance of an application that uses hash-based data structures. In order to estimate the worst case over-

Benchmark	Run time		GC time	
compiler.compiler		68.7%		41.6%
compiler.sunflow		36.5%		6.6%
derby		63.4%		166.9%
serial		42.8%		5.6%
sunflow		28.0%		4.9%
xml.transform		31.5%		11.1%
xml.validation		49.2%		66.9%
mean		45.0%		35.2%

Figure 10: **Run time (lower is better) of tracing with rotation relative to the run time of tracing without rotation (gray, 100%) as well as GC time (lower is better) of tracing with rotation relative to the the GC time of tracing without rotation (gray, 100%), all without saving allocation site information**

head of our approach, we designed a benchmark which puts $1 * 10^7$ plain Java objects into a `java.util.HashSet`, and subsequently queries $1 * 10^7$ times, where half of the queried objects are indeed in the HashSet. When saving allocation site information (and thus reducing the entropy of the identity hash code) the run-time overhead rises to 2291%. This overhead can be easily attributed to bad hash performance, which lets the hash map degenerate into a few long lists and thus, turns *put* and *get* into operations with linear complexity.

In practice, however, the overhead is not as bad. This is mainly because most applications make little use of the identity hash code. Figure 14 shows the run-time overhead when allocation sites are stored in objects, relative to when they are not saved.

Benchmark	Run-time overhead	
compiler.compiler		2.9%
compiler.sunflow		2.9%
derby		5.5%
serial		1.8%
sunflow		1.4%
xml.transform		6.4%
xml.validation		−0.1%
mean		2.9%

Figure 14: Run-time overhead when saving allocation sites relative to rotation without saving allocation sites

As expected, the run time slightly increases due to the decreased entropy of the hash (if the allocation site is stored), which distorts the performance of hash-based data structures, e.g., HashMaps and HashSets. Most of the benchmarks use their own implementation of hash code computation or simply do not use hash-based data structures extensively, so their run time increases only slightly. Xml.transform, however, rely on the identity hash code and thus it performance drops more significantly. This benchmark allocates a high amount of objects of class `...dom.SimpleResultTreeImpl.SimpleIterator`, which in return uses a HashMap based on identity hash codes.

Overhead with Eliminating Identity Hash Codes.

As discussed in Section 3, we can eliminate a lot of eager hash code generations by checking whether the allocated class provides its own hash code implementation. Figure 15 shows the number of eliminated hash code generations relative to the number of allocated objects. However, Figure 16 shows that there is no significant run-time reduction if the hash code generation is omitted. In case of serial, the run time even increases, because this benchmark relies on identity hash codes and the check for avoiding eager hash code generation costs some time.

Total Overhead Compared to Non-rotated Tracing.

Figure 17 shows the run-time overhead and the GC-time overhead when enabling trace rotation, storing allocation site information and eliminating hash codes, relative to our non-rotating tracing approach described in Lengauer et al. [7]. This time, not only selected benchmarks are evaluated, but we evaluate the full DaCapo, the DaCapo Scala and

Benchmark	Eliminated hashes	
compiler.compiler		41.1%
compiler.sunflow		37.7%
derby		78.0%
serial		32.6%
sunflow		0.0%
xml.transform		36.9%
xml.validation		24.7%
mean		10.0%

Figure 15: Eliminated hash code generations relative to all object allocations

Benchmark	Run-time overhead	
compiler.compiler		1.0%
compiler.sunflow		−0.4%
derby		−4.3%
serial		12.8%
sunflow		0.8%
xml.transform		−2.7%
xml.validation		0.1%
mean		0.9%

Figure 16: Run-time overhead when avoiding eager hash code generation

the SPECjvm benchmark suites. Only the SPECjvm scimark benchmarks have been excluded, since they produce traces of negligible size. Note, that especially in the DaCapo benchmark suite, some benchmarks (e.g., batik) do not fire a single GC. Nevertheless, they show a slight run-time overhead, caused from storing allocation sites, generating hash codes and eliminating hash codes. The same applies to benchmarks which are garbage collecting, but do not fire a single sync GC (cells in fourth column with 0% sync GCs ratio), because their data fit in a single trace file within one benchmark iteration. Especially DaCapo Scala kiama is sensitive to storing allocation site information into the hash code (run-time overhead of 103%, GC-time overhead of 75%), as it extensively allocates hash maps and hash entries. Comparing h2 and factorie reveals that the sync events themselves do not constitute the overhead, because although h2 generates sync event data of considerable size, this does not affect its run time negatively. On the other hand, factorie suffers most in terms of run time (about 323%), although the number of sync GCs are comparable to h2 and the size of sync event data is even smaller. However, experiments showed that if allocation site information is not stored, the overhead is reduced to 41%. This indicates that factorie makes use of identity hash codes and storing allocation sites as well as eliminating hash codes have a negative impact on performance. To achieve acceptable performance on those benchmarks, saving allocation site information and eliminating hash codes can be turned off. Benchmarks with a high amount of long-living objects, i.e,. objects which reside in the old generation, perform worse (c.f. Paragraph *Rotation Overhead*), since for every minor sync GC the old space needs to be traversed, causing the application to stall longer as needed. Consequently, how efficient trace rotation can be achieved depends mainly on the used data structures in the application and on the number of objects in the old

	Run-time overhead	GC-time overhead	Sync GC / plain GC ratio	Sync events size [MB]
DaCapo				
avrora	0.0%	0.0%	0.0%	/
batik	4.7%	/	/	/
eclipse	11.4%	/	/	/
fop	21.5%	/	/	/
h2	−2.8%	28.4%	6.4%	349.9
jython	11.8%	−14.0%	0.0%	/
luindex	0.0%	/	/	/
lusearch	3.3%	0.0%	0.0%	/
pmd	0.4%	5.5%	0.0%	/
sunflow	1.2%	6.6%	0.0%	/
tomcat	0.8%	0.0%	1.5%	3.3
tradebeans	0.4%	16.4%	6.2%	156.4
tradesoap	14.4%	1.7%	3.9%	85.6
xalan	3.9%	2.1%	0.0%	/
DaCapo Scala				
actors	−3.4%	−2.3%	1.6%	1.0
apparat	14.0%	9.3%	2.7%	26.5
factorie	323.0%	83.7%	8.8%	133.1
kiama	103.3%	75.0%	0.0%	/
scalac	3.2%	11.3%	0.0%	/
scaladoc	2.5%	−4.3%	0.0%	/
scalap	4.6%	/	/	/
scalariform	3.7%	−15.3%	0.0%	/
scalab	0.4%	−3.3%	0.0%	/
tmt	47.7%	27.7%	2.8%	3.5
SPECjvm				
compiler.compiler	75.4%	43.1%	11.7%	340.6
compiler.sunflow	39.8%	6.5%	7.4%	59.9
compress	−0.0%	0.0%	0.0%	/
crypto.aes	0.2%	0.0%	0.0%	/
crypto.rsa	1.2%	−5.0%	0.0%	/
crypto.signverify	2.9%	−1.4%	0.0%	/
derby	64.9%	204.9%	8.6%	68.4
mpegaudio	−0.1%	0.0%	0.0%	/
serial	64.1%	7.6%	7.6%	0.8
sunflow	31.0%	3.6%	6.6%	3.7
xml.transform	36.2%	7.4%	4.7%	5.7
xml.validation	49.0%	68.0%	10.7%	276.1
mean	6.5%	15.5%	5.2%	40.0

Figure 17: Run-time overhead and GC-time overhead when rotation is enabled

generation. In general, the additional overhead for rotation is low, with about 6.5% run-time overhead (geometric mean) and 15.5% GC-time overhead (geometric mean).

4.3 Information Quality after Rotations

When a truncated trace is parsed, some properties of live objects that have been allocated before the synchronization point are unknown, e.g., the allocating thread and the allocation site (if it is not saved). We call the amount of information that is available about live objects the information quality, which is defined as a value between 0 and 1, 0 meaning that there is information missing about every object in the heap, and 1 meaning that we have complete information about all objects.

Figure 18 shows the quality for every benchmark right after a synchronization point (GC #0) as well as for the following 9 GCs (which have not been used for synchronization). The general high information quality can be explained by the large number of short-lived objects resulting in very few objects surviving a GC. Compiler.sunflow, derby, and xml.transform quickly gain a quality between 83% and 93% and do not show any significant improvement over the next GCs. The lack of improvement is caused by a pool of long-living objects that are kept alive for the entire application's life cycle and thus impede a better information quality once

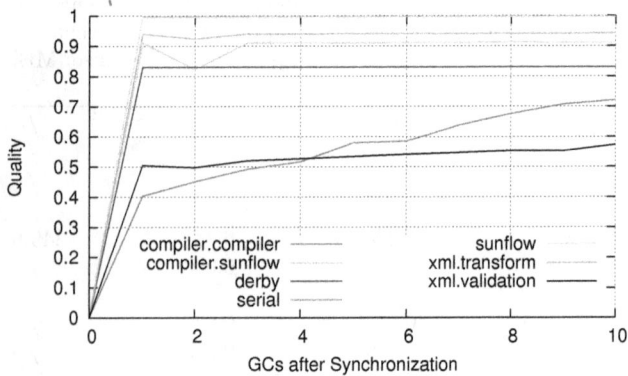

Figure 18: Information quality (percentage of objects with full information) after a synchronization point and after the following 9 GCs

their allocation is cut off. Please note the anomaly at the second GC of the compiler.sunflow benchmark in which the quality drops from 91% to 82% and rises back to 91%. This behavior is caused by a major GC collecting a large portion of objects and thus reducing the overall number of objects in the heap. In absolute numbers, the information quality is not dropping. Finally, compiler.compiler and xml.validation start off with a rather poor quality between 40% and 50%. However, as expected, the information quality increases with every GC as new objects replace old ones.

4.4 Rethinking Hash Strategies

VM implementers have spent a lot of time on thinking about good hash strategies for the identity hash code in order to increase the performance of hash-based data structures. There are multiple hash strategies of varying complexity and efficiency, such as the *Unguarded Global Park-Miller Random Number Generator (RNG)* by Park and Miller [11], the *Stable Stop-the-world (STW) with Address* hash, a *Constant Value* (for testing only), a *Global Counter* that is incremented for every object, the *Address* hash (using the lower bits of the address), and *Marsaglia's xor-shift Scheme* by Marsaglia [8]. Although the latter is the default implementation in the Hotspot™ VM, it can be overridden by setting the `-XX:hashCode` parameter.

However, when reducing the identity hash code from 31 to 15 bits, a different hash strategy might yield a better hash performance. Thus, we conducted an experiment in which we executed our synthetic worst-case benchmark (cf. Section 4.2), reduced the identity hash code to 15 bits, and tried all 6 hash code strategies mentioned above. Figure 19 shows the results of this experiment, revealing that almost all strategies perform as good as the default strategy.

The *Constant Value* strategy resulted in a timeout after taking more than 100 times as long as the default strategy, which is not surprising because it lets every hash map degenerate to a list. The *Global Counter* strategy however, resulted in a performance gain of 18.5%.

5. RELATED WORK

There is substantial work on how to record the memory behavior of applications. Chilimbi et al. [4] propose a binary trace format for allocation and deallocation events. Hertz

Hashing strategy		Run time
Park-Miller RNG		−0.1%
Stable STW w/ Address		−1.3%
Constant Value		
Global Counter		−18.5%
Address		2.5%
Marsaglia's xor-shift		base

Figure 19: Performance of our worst-case benchmark with different hash code strategies when reducing the identity hash code by 16 bits

et al. [5, 6] capture object allocations, pointer updates as well as approximate object lifetimes. Ricci et al. [13, 14] additionally record method entry, method exit and exception events. While all of these approaches produce a large amount of data, none of them reveals the size of the generated trace. Neither Hertz et al. nor Ricci et al. present strategies for reducing the trace size. Only Chilimbi et al. discuss the performance of different encoding strategies to compress a trace. Extensive work on compressing data in general has been published. Amongst others, Brown et al. [2] and Burtscher et al. [3] present algorithms for especially encoding trace data efficiently. Although compression algorithms reduce the overall size of a trace, they cannot prevent its continuous growth.

Other approaches try to find strategies for reducing the trace data altogether. In the work of Printezis and Jones [12] the live heap of a running application can be monitored and traced if requested. Users can reduce the amount of collected data by filtering the information they are interested in. However, since we strive for reproducing the entire heap, we cannot simply omit specific object allocation events or object move events. Moreover, reducing the amount of data written just delays the problem of growing traces rather than solving it. Mohror and Karavanic [9] propose to achieve trace reduction by defining similarity metrics between sections of traces. However, the reduced traces are not accurate representations of the original trace. Instead, one has to deal with the introduced error. In AntTracks, an accurate event trace is indispensable for reconstructing precise snapshots of the heap. Consequently, errors in traces cannot be accepted. Wagner and Nagel [15] present strategies for keeping events in a single memory buffer. They intend to evolve fully in-memory event traces to overcome file system interactions. However, reducing the trace once the memory buffer is exhausted, e.g., by omitting information which is least important to the user or by simply stopping recording, is hardly applicable for AntTracks. While partial information of a heap may allow detecting local performance bottlenecks, e.g., of a single thread, it is insufficient for tracking down performance degradations over time, e.g., caused by garbage collection.

6. FUTURE WORK

The work presented in this paper is part of a larger project, which precisely records the memory behavior of Java applications. We plan to further investigate this field of research. Regarding trace reduction we plan to refine our strategies to improve information quality and reduce the introduced run-time overhead even more.

Compression.

Since we face a trade-off between compression rate and run time, full compression is not favorable in AntTracks. However, partial compression can be further improved, by applying encoding more thoughtfully. One can argue that data from event buffers of mutator threads can be compressed more tightly than event buffers of GC threads. This is due to the fact, that GC move events hold more distinct data than allocation events, i.e., GC move events contain unique addresses, while allocation events from the same allocation site all look similar. Consequently, it is worthwhile to apply compression more eagerly during mutator phases and more lazily during GC phases.

Similarly, when requesting a compressor, threads that produce large amounts of trace data can be favored over others that produce less trace data. In the current implementation the compression dictionary is constructed anew each time a thread retrieves a compressor from the pool. If the compressor is returned to the pool, the compression dictionary is cleared. As a result, a thread cannot reuse patterns of multiple mutator phases or GC phases. If a thread would own its private compressor, recurrent patterns of multiple phases could be exploited for encoding. We have not implemented this strategy so far, because it gets memory-intensive quickly and potentially distorts the actual memory behavior we want to monitor. However, threads producing lots of trace data would benefit from this strategy.

Rotation.

The performance of trace rotation depends mainly on two key factors: (1) The number of objects in the old generation, which need to be traversed in the case of a minor sync GC; (2) The number of live objects for which the allocation sites is stored. While the former will affect especially the performance of applications with long-living objects, the latter harms the entropy of hash-based data structure and thus, applications relying on them. Ideally, we could omit the traversal of the old generation altogether and reduce the number of stored allocation sites.

The former could be achieved by exceeding the maximum trace size, in order to wait for an upcoming major GC. This major GC could then be exploited as synchronization GC, and thus, reduce the overall GC-time overhead as well as run-time overhead of trace rotating. This approach may be especially feasible for allocation intensive real-world applications.

The latter can be tackled by avoiding to retain allocation sites for all objects. According to generational collection, the majority of young-generation objects tend to die anyway during the next collection. To estimate, whether an object is likely to die, we can inspect the object's age field, which records the number of times an object has already been evacuated. If an allocation site creates objects that turn out to die quickly, we can refrain from storing their allocation site. This strategy would allow us to reduce the generated data while at the same time not weakening the information quality. Reducing the number or the size of sync events is also beneficial because they currently require several hundred megabytes per GC (see Section 4.2). The more space is taken up by synchronization points, the less space is left for ordinary events and the sooner another trace file is needed that requires another synchronization point. However, omitting *GC move sync* events altogether is not feasible, since our analysis tool relies on at least the object type information to obtain the object's size.

7. CONCLUSIONS

We have presented novel techniques for reducing the size of event traces, as well as for limiting their maximum growth. On the one hand, partial on-the-fly black-box compression enables us to write an even more compact trace without compromising AntTracks' overall run-time performance. On the other hand, rotating trace files allows us to overcome disk limitations.

We showed that the quality of the trace data stabilizes quickly, with an average quality of 74% after the very first GC. In general, the additional run-time overhead of rotation (6.5%) is sufficiently small considering the DaCapo, the DaCapoScala and the SPECjvm benchmark suites. For allocation intensive benchmarks (selected from the SPECjvm benchmark suites), we achieved a run-time overhead of (45%) when limiting the maximum trace size to 8 GB. Certainly, raising the maximum trace size would further improve our results.

Tracking down performance bottlenecks in large and complex Java applications is crucial. While existing tools often record only coarse-grained data or ignore the practical problem of continuously growing traces, we proposed solutions for both problems. Our approach allows a precise representation of all object allocations and object moves. With the help of trace rotation we made a first step towards continuous and almost loss-free tracing.

8. ACKNOWLEDGMENTS

This work was supported by the Christian Doppler Forschungsgesellschaft, and by Dynatrace Austria GmbH.

9. REFERENCES

[1] V. Bitto, P. Lengauer, and H. Mössenböck. Efficient rebuilding of large java heaps from event traces. In *Proc. of the 12th ACM/SPEC Int'l. Conf. on Principles and Practice of Programming on the Java Platform: virtual machines, languages, and tools*, PPPJ '15, 2015.

[2] R. Brown, K. Driesen, D. Eng, L. Hendren, J. Jorgensen, C. Verbrugge, and Q. Wang. Step: A framework for the efficient encoding of general trace data. *SIGSOFT Softw. Eng. Notes*, 28(1):27–34, Nov. 2002.

[3] M. Burtscher, I. Ganusov, S. J. Jackson, J. Ke, P. Ratanaworabhan, and N. B. Sam. The vpc trace-compression algorithms. *IEEE Trans. Comput.*, 54(11):1329–1344, Nov. 2005.

[4] T. Chilimbi, R. Jones, and B. Zorn. Designing a trace format for heap allocation events. In *Proc. of the 2nd Int'l. Symposium on Memory Management*, ISMM '00, pages 35–49, New York, NY, USA, 2000. ACM.

[5] M. Hertz, S. M. Blackburn, J. E. B. Moss, K. S. McKinley, and D. Stefanović. Error-free garbage collection traces: How to cheat and not get caught. In *Proc. of the 2002 ACM SIGMETRICS Int'l. Conf. on Measurement and Modeling of Computer Systems*, SIGMETRICS '02, pages 140–151, New York, NY, USA, 2002. ACM.

[6] M. Hertz, S. M. Blackburn, J. E. B. Moss, K. S. McKinley, and D. Stefanović. Generating object lifetime traces with merlin. *ACM Trans. Program. Lang. Syst.*, 28(3):476–516, May 2006.

[7] P. Lengauer, V. Bitto, and H. Mössenböck. Accurate and efficient object tracing for java applications. In *Proc. of the 6th ACM/SPEC Int'l. Conf. on Performance Engineering*, ICPE '15, pages 51–62, 2015.

[8] G. Marsaglia. Xorshift rngs. *Journal of Statistical Software*, 8(14):1–6, 7 2003.

[9] K. Mohror and K. L. Karavanic. Evaluating similarity-based trace reduction techniques for scalable performance analysis. In *Proc. of the Conf. on High Performance Computing Networking, Storage and Analysis*, SC '09, pages 55:1–55:12, New York, NY, USA, 2009. ACM.

[10] R. Odaira, K. Ogata, K. Kawachiya, T. Onodera, and T. Nakatani. Efficient runtime tracking of allocation sites in java. In *Proc. of the 6th ACM SIGPLAN/SIGOPS Int'l. Conf. on Virtual Execution Environments*, VEE '10, pages 109–120, 2010.

[11] S. K. Park and K. W. Miller. Random number generators: Good ones are hard to find. *Commun. ACM*, 31(10):1192–1201, Oct. 1988.

[12] T. Printezis and R. Jones. Gcspy: An adaptable heap visualisation framework. In *Proc. of the 17th ACM SIGPLAN Conf. on Object-oriented Programming, Systems, Languages, and Applications*, pages 343–358, 2002.

[13] N. P. Ricci, S. Z. Guyer, and J. E. B. Moss. Elephant tracks: Generating program traces with object death records. In *Proc. of the 9th Int'l. Conf. on Principles and Practice of Programming in Java*, PPPJ '11, pages 139–142, New York, NY, USA, 2011. ACM.

[14] N. P. Ricci, S. Z. Guyer, and J. E. B. Moss. Elephant tracks: Portable production of complete and precise gc traces. In *Proc. of the 2013 Int'l. Symposium on Memory Management*, ISMM '13, pages 109–118, New York, NY, USA, 2013. ACM.

[15] M. Wagner and W. E. Nagel. Strategies for real-time event reduction. In *Proc. of the 18th Int'l. Conf. on Parallel Processing Workshops*, Euro-Par'12, pages 429–438, Berlin, Heidelberg, 2013. Springer-Verlag.

[16] T. A. Welch. A technique for high-performance data compression. *Computer*, 17(6):8–19, June 1984.

Cloudy, Foggy and Misty Internet of Things

Angelo Corsaro, PhD
Chief Technology Officer
PrismTech / ADLink

Abstract

Early Internet of Things(IoT) applications have been build around cloud-centric architectures where information generated at the edge by the "things" in conveyed and processed in a cloud infrastructure. These architectures centralise processing and decision on the data-centre assuming sufficient connectivity, bandwidth and latency. As applications of the Internet of Things extend to industrial and more demanding consumer applications, the assumptions underlying cloud-centric architectures start to be violated as for several of these applications connectivity, bandwidth and latency to the data-centre are a challenge.

Fog and Mist computing have emerged as forms of "Cloud Computing" closer to the "Edge" and to the "Things" that should alleviate the connectivity, bandwidth and latency challenges faced by Industrial and extremely demanding Consumer Internet of Things Applications.

This keynote, will (1) introduce Cloud, Fog and Mist Computing architectures for the Internet of Things, (2) motivate their need and explain their applicability with real-world use cases, and (3) assess their technological maturity and highlight the areas that require further academic and industrial research.

Keywords: IoT; IIoT; Cloud Computing; Fog Computing

ICPE'16, March 12–18, 2016, Delft, Netherlands.
ACM ISBN: 978-1-4503-4080-9/16/03.
DOI: http://dx.doi.org/10.1145/2851553.2858661

Efficient Tracing and Versatile Analysis of Lock Contention in Java Applications on the Virtual Machine Level

Peter Hofer
peter.hofer@jku.at

David Gnedt
david.gnedt@jku.at

Andreas Schörgenhumer
andreas.schoergenhumer@jku.at

Christian Doppler Laboratory on Monitoring and Evolution of Very-Large-Scale Software Systems
Johannes Kepler University Linz, Austria

Hanspeter Mössenböck
hanspeter.moessenboeck@jku.at
Institute for System Software
Johannes Kepler University Linz, Austria

ABSTRACT

Concurrent programming has become a necessity in order to benefit from recent advances in processor design. However, implementing correct and scalable locking for accessing shared resources remains a challenge. Examining lock contention in an application at runtime is vital to determine where more sophisticated but error-prone locking pays off.

In this paper, we present a novel approach for analyzing lock contention in Java applications by tracing locking events in the Java Virtual Machine. Unlike common methods, our approach observes not only when a thread is blocked on a lock, but also which other thread blocked it by holding that lock, and records both their call chains. This reveals the causes of lock contention instead of showing only its symptoms. We describe the techniques which we use to efficiently record trace events, metadata, and call chains. We present a versatile tool for the analysis of the traces which enables users to identify locking bottlenecks and their characteristics in an effective way. We implemented our approach in the widely used HotSpot Virtual Machine, and with a mean runtime overhead of 7.8%, we consider it efficient enough to monitor production systems.

Keywords

Locking, Contention, Tracing, Java, Concurrency, Parallelism, Threading, Synchronization, Profiling, Monitoring

ICPE'16, March 12–18, 2016, Delft, Netherlands.
© 2016 ACM. ISBN 978-1-4503-4080-9/16/03. . . $15.00
DOI: http://dx.doi.org/10.1145/2851553.2851559

1. INTRODUCTION

Over decades, increasing processor clock speeds have provided software developers with almost effortless performance improvements until finally, problems with heat dissipation, power consumption and current leakage have brought this development to a halt [19]. Since then, the focus has shifted toward multi-core processors, which have become the norm from server-class machines to phones. While additional cores continue to increase the computing power of processors, software developers need to write explicitly concurrent code to benefit from these improvements.

The main challenge in concurrent programming is the synchronization of accesses to shared resources, which is typically done with locks. Subtle mistakes can cause anomalies that are difficult to detect and to debug, favoring coarse-grained locking which is easier to implement correctly. However, coarse-grained locking tends to suffer from lock contention and can neutralize any gains from parallelization. During development, it is difficult to judge in which cases more fine-grained locking would significantly improve performance and in which cases it would just make the application more complex and error-prone. Therefore, analyzing lock contention at runtime is vital to measure its effect on the performance of an application and to identify bottlenecks where more fine-grained locking would be worth the additional complexity.

Lock contention analysis is valuable not only during development, but also in production. Server applications in particular are deployed on machines with significantly more cores and memory than a developer workstation has, and must handle workloads that are often orders of magnitude larger than the workloads used for testing. Under such conditions, concurrent code can behave very differently, making it difficult to reproduce and to debug bottlenecks in locking on a smaller scale. A lock contention analysis approach that is feasible for use in a production environment should have minimal overhead while still providing information suitable to identify and comprehend bottlenecks in an effective way.

In this paper, we expand on our novel approach to Java lock contention analysis that we outlined in an earlier work-in-progress paper [7]. Our approach provides developers with exhaustive information to understand and resolve locking bottlenecks in an application, yet incurs very low overhead which makes it feasible for production use. Most notably, our approach not only records the call chains of threads that are blocked, but also accurately reports the call chains of threads that block other threads by holding a requested lock. We are capable of efficiently collecting this information because we implemented our approach directly in the OpenJDK HotSpot Virtual Machine, a popular high-performance Java Virtual Machine (VM).

The main contributions of this paper are:

1. We describe an approach for efficiently tracing fine-grained lock contention events in a Java VM, and aspects of our implementation in the HotSpot VM. Unlike other approaches, the collected traces show not just where contention occurs, but also where it is caused.

2. We describe a versatile approach for analyzing and visualizing the collected events that enables users to recognize locking bottlenecks and their characteristics in an effective way.

3. We provide an extensive evaluation of our implementation on a server-class machine, studying its overhead, the amount of generated data, the composition of traces, and the effectiveness of specific optimizations. We show that our approach has such low overhead that it is typically feasible to use it in a production environment.

The rest of this paper is organized as follows: Section 2 provides an introduction to locking in Java. Section 3 describes which events we trace and how we record them efficiently. Section 4 characterizes the analysis of our traces and the versatile aggregation and visualization of lock contentions. Section 5 evaluates the runtime overhead and other characteristics of our approach. Section 6 examines related work, and Section 7 concludes this paper.

2. LOCKING IN JAVA

Java has intrinsic support for locking, but it also provides the *java.util.concurrent* package that contains explicit locks and advanced synchronization mechanisms.

2.1 Intrinsic Locks (Monitors)

Each Java object has an intrinsic mutual-exclusion lock associated with it, which is also called the object's *monitor*. Developers can insert *synchronized blocks* in their code and specify an object to use for locking. That object's lock is then acquired before entering the block and executing its statements, and released when exiting the block. When threads contend for a lock, that is, when one thread has acquired a lock by entering a synchronized block, and other threads are trying to enter a synchronized block using the same lock, those threads are blocked until the owner exits its synchronized block and releases the lock. Developers can also declare methods as synchronized, which then acquire the lock of the *this* object when called, and release it again when returning. A notable property of synchronized blocks and synchronized methods is that a lock is guaranteed to be released in the same method and scope in which it was acquired, even when an exception is thrown.

Intrinsic locks further support conditional waiting with the *wait, notifyAll* and *notify* methods. These methods may only be called on an object while holding its lock. The *wait* method releases the lock and suspends the calling thread.

```
class BlockingQueue {
  private final List<Object> q = new LinkedList<>();
  void enqueue(Object item) {
    synchronized(q) {
      q.add(item);
      q.notifyAll();
    }
  }
  Object dequeue() {
    synchronized(q) {
      awaitNotEmpty();
      return q.remove(0);
    }
  }
  void awaitNotEmpty() {
    while (q.isEmpty()) {
      try {
        q.wait();
      } catch (InterruptedException e) { }
    }
  }
}
```

Figure 1: Blocking queue with Java intrinsic locks

When another thread calls *notifyAll* on the same object, all threads that are waiting on its lock are resumed. Each resumed thread then attempts to acquire the lock, and once successful, it continues execution. In contrast to *notifyAll*, the *notify* method wakes up only a single waiting thread. This mechanism is typically used in producer-consumer scenarios, such as threads in a thread pool that wait for tasks to execute.

Figure 1 shows an example of using intrinsic locks to implement a thread-safe blocking queue. The field *q* holds the list of queue items, and the list object's intrinsic lock is used to ensure mutually exclusive queue accesses. The *enqueue* method has a synchronized block to acquire the lock of *q* before it appends an item and calls *notifyAll* to resume any threads waiting on *q*. The *dequeue* method also uses a synchronized block and calls *awaitNotEmpty*, which invokes *wait* on *q* as long as the queue is empty. The *wait* method releases the lock of *q* and suspends the calling thread until another thread resumes it by calling *notifyAll* from *enqueue*. Alternatively, when the thread is interrupted while waiting, *wait* throws an *InterruptedException*, which we catch. In either case, *wait* attempts to reacquire the lock of *q* and once successful, execution continues in *awaitNotEmpty*, which checks again whether the list is not empty. When *awaitNotEmpty* finally returns, the list is guaranteed to be not empty, and *dequeue* can remove and return an item.

The semantics of intrinsic locks are implemented entirely in the Java VM, usually in a very efficient way so their use only incurs significant overhead when threads actually contend for locks [1, 15]. Implementations are typically *non-fair* and allow threads to acquire a recently released lock even when there are queued threads that requested that lock earlier. This increases the throughput by reducing the overhead from suspending threads, and by better utilizing the time periods between when one thread releases a lock and when a queued thread is scheduled and can acquire the lock [4].

2.2 The java.util.concurrent package

Java 5 introduced the *java.util.concurrent* package with classes that provide useful synchronization mechanisms, such as concurrent collections and read-write locks [10]. Most of

264

these classes do not use Java's intrinsic locks, but rather rely on the newly introduced *LockSupport* facility, which provides a *park* method that a thread can call to park (suspend) itself, and an *unpark* method which resumes a parked thread. Using these two methods as well as compare-and-set operations, the semantics of java.util.concurrent classes can be implemented entirely in Java. The *AbstractQueuedSynchronizer* class further provides a convenient basis for implementing synchronization mechanisms with wait queues. Because these classes are public, application developers can also implement custom synchronization mechanisms on top of them.

ReentrantLock is an example of a mutual exclusion lock in java.util.concurrent that is semantically similar to intrinsic locks, but is implemented entirely in Java on top of Abstract-QueuedSynchronizer. Code that uses ReentrantLock must explicitly call its *lock* and *unlock* methods to acquire and release the lock. ReentrantLock also supports conditional waiting by calling *await, signalAll* and *signal* on an associated *Condition* object. Unlike intrinsic locks, an arbitrary number of such condition objects can be created for each lock. Moreover, ReentrantLock has a fair mode which guarantees first-come-first-serve ordering of lock acquisitions and conditional wake-ups. This mode reduces the variance of lock acquisition times, typically at the expense of throughput.

3. LOCK CONTENTION EVENT TRACING

Analyzing lock contention in an application requires observing individual locking events and computing meaningful statistics from them. Maintaining those statistics in the synchronizing threads interferes with the execution of the application, and requires synchronization as well, so it can become a bottleneck itself. Instead, we decided to only record those events in the application threads and to analyze them later. In this section, we describe how we efficiently record events and metadata, which events we record, and how we reconstruct thread interactions from the recorded events.

3.1 Writing and Processing Events

Figure 2 shows an overview of how we write and process trace data in our approach. Naturally, we trace locking events in different application threads, and writing those events to a single shared trace buffer would require synchronization and could become a bottleneck. Therefore, each application thread T_i allocates a *thread-local trace buffer* where it can write events without synchronization. When the trace buffer is full, the thread submits it to the *processing queue* and allocates a new buffer. A *background thread* retrieves the trace buffers from the queue and processes their events. In the depicted scenario, it merges them into a single *trace file*. This trace file can be opened in an *analysis tool* for offline analysis and visualization.

We encode the events in an efficient binary representation to facilitate fast writing, to reduce the amount of generated data and to keep the memory usage of the trace buffers low. Because each buffer is written by just a single thread, we can store that thread once per buffer instead of recording it in each event. Submitting a full buffer to the queue requires synchronization, but we assign a random size between 8 KB and 24 KB to the individual buffers, which is large enough so that this is an infrequent operation. The randomization avoids that threads which perform similar tasks try to submit their buffers at the same time and contend for queue access.

Our design supports writing a trace file for offline anal-

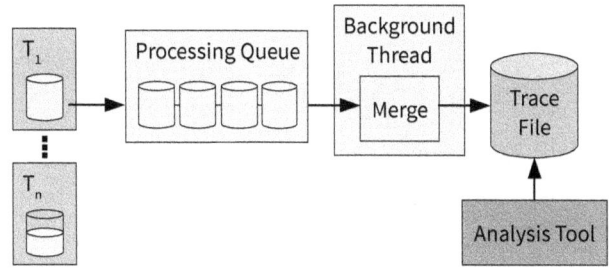

Figure 2: Writing and processing trace events

ysis as well as analyzing the recorded events online. We implemented the event processing in Java, and use a thin native code interface to dequeue the trace buffers from the processing queue and to wrap them in *DirectByteBuffer* objects, which can be read from Java without copying memory. To write trace files, we use the Java NIO subsystem [11], which can use the DirectByteBuffer objects directly. We also support fast compression of the trace data by using a Java implementation of the high-performance LZ77-type compression algorithm *Snappy* [5, 18]. Our online analysis mode currently generates a text file with statistics, but it could be extended to provide an interface for the Java Management Extensions (JMX, [13]) to configure analysis parameters and to access the produced statistics.

3.2 Tracing Intrinsic Locks

Locking causes a major performance impact when threads contend for a lock. Threads that fail to acquire a lock are suspended and cannot make progress, and a thread that releases a contended lock must also do extra work to resume a blocked thread as its successor. However, locking itself is not expensive in the HotSpot VM. An available intrinsic lock can be acquired with a single compare-and-set instruction in many cases. When a thread holds a lock only briefly, another thread that requests that lock can often still acquire it through spinning without suspending itself. Therefore, we chose to record only *lock contention* with our approach instead of recording *all* lock operations.

Conceptually, each Java object has an intrinsic lock associated with it. This lock stores its current owner thread, the threads that are blocked trying to acquire it, and the threads that are waiting for notifications on it. However, in a typical application, most Java objects are never used for locking. Therefore, the HotSpot VM assigns a lock to an object only when threads start using that object for locking. Even then, *biased locking* can avoid allocating an actual lock as long as the object is never used by more than one thread.

The act of assigning a lock to an object is called *lock inflation*. Intrinsic locks in HotSpot are data structures in native memory which are never moved by the garbage collector and can therefore be uniquely identified by their address. Whenever lock inflation happens, we record an *inflation event* with the lock's address, the object that the lock is being assigned to, and that object's class. In the trace events that follow, we record only the lock's address. When analyzing the trace, we are thus still able to infer the lock's associated object and its class from the inflation event.

When a thread cannot enter a synchronized block or method because it cannot acquire a lock, we record a *contended enter event* with the lock's address, a timestamp, and the call chain of the thread. Recording the call chain is ex-

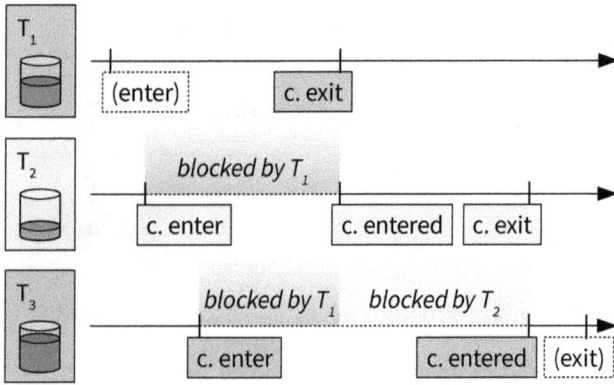

Figure 3: Events in three contending threads

pensive, but the impact on performance is moderate because the thread is unable to make progress either way. When the thread later acquires the lock, we record a *contended entered event* with only a timestamp.

With those two events, we can determine which threads were blocked when trying to acquire a lock, how long they were blocked, and what call chains they were executing. However, this information only reveals the symptoms of locking bottlenecks and not their causes. To determine the causes of contention, we record events not only in those threads that are blocked, but also in those threads which block other threads by holding a contended lock. We modified all code paths in the VM that release a lock when exiting a synchronized block or method so that they check whether any threads are currently blocked on that lock. If so, we write a *contended exit event* with a timestamp and the call chain. We delay recording the call chain and writing the event until after the lock has been released to avoid causing even more contention.

Figure 3 shows an example of events that we trace for three threads T_1, T_2 and T_3 that are executing in parallel and are contending for a single intrinsic lock. First, T_1 acquires the lock without contention, so we do not record an event. Next, T_2 tries to acquire the lock, but the lock is held by T_1, so T_2 writes a *contended enter event* in its trace buffer and suspends itself. T_3 then also fails to acquire the lock and also records a *contended enter event*. When T_1 finally releases the lock, it sees T_2 and T_3 on the lock's queue of blocked threads, so it resumes thread T_2 and writes a *contended exit event*. T_2 acquires the lock and writes a *contended entered event*. When T_2 later releases the lock, it sees T_3 on the lock's queue, resumes T_3 and writes a *contended exit event*. T_3 then acquires the lock and writes a *contended entered event*. When T_3 releases the lock, no threads are queued, and T_3 continues without writing an event. When the trace analysis later examines the events of all threads, it can infer from the *contended exit events* that T_2 and T_3 were being blocked by T_1 holding the lock, and that T_3 was subsequently being blocked by T_2. It can further compute the duration of those periods from the timestamps in the events.

Event ordering.

The trace analysis needs to arrange all events for a specific lock in their correct order to analyze them. For this purpose, we introduced a counter in HotSpot's intrinsic lock structure. When we write an event for a lock, we atomically increment

the lock's counter and record its new value in the event as its *per-lock sequence number*. Unlike timestamps, these sequence numbers have no gaps between them, which enables the analysis to determine whether it can already analyze a sequence of parsed events, or whether there are still events in a trace buffer from another thread that it has not parsed yet. This considerably simplifies and speeds up the analysis. However, when a thread records an event and then does not submit its trace buffer for a long time, it still delays the analysis of subsequent events. For this reason, we also reclaim the trace buffers of all threads during garbage collections and add them to the processing queue. The threads subsequently allocate new buffers to write further events.

Sequence numbers are also more reliable than timestamps for correctly ordering events. Although we retrieve the timestamps from a monotonic system clock, this clock typically uses a timer of the CPU or of the CPU core on which the thread is currently executing. When the timers of different CPUs or CPU cores are not perfectly synchronized, the recorded timestamps are not accurate enough to establish a happened-before relationship, while our atomically incremented sequence numbers always guarantee a correct order.

Conditional waiting.

The *wait* method temporarily releases a lock and suspends the calling thread until another thread wakes it up. When the released lock is contended, we also need to write a *contended exit event* with a call chain. However, *wait* may be called in a different method than the one that acquired the lock, as is the case with *awaitNotEmpty* in Figure 1. In this case, recording the current call chain would misrepresent the source of contention. Instead, we generate and record a *forward reference* to the call chain of the method that acquired the lock. We store the reference in the lock structure and when that method releases the lock later, we record a separate event that resolves the reference to that method's call chain.

When a thread is unable to reacquire a lock after waking up from waiting, we also record a *contended enter event,* but this form of contention is not necessarily critical. Often, only the first of several notified threads can make progress, while the other threads will find that the condition that they have been waiting on is again not met, and thus continue waiting. Therefore, we use an extra flag in the event to indicate when contention was preceded by conditional waiting. This allows us to classify this type of contention differently in analysis.

3.3 Tracing Park/Unpark Synchronization

Most synchronization mechanisms in java.util.concurrent are implemented entirely in Java. To trace them, we could instrument each class individually and generate custom trace events that are specific to the semantics of the class in question. However, what these classes have in common is that they rely on the *park* and *unpark* methods that the VM provides through the *LockSupport* class.

Figure 4 shows an outline of the *LockSupport* class. The *park* method parks (suspends) the calling thread. A parked thread remains suspended until another thread calls *unpark* on it. The methods *parkNanos* and *parkUntil* suspend the calling thread until the thread is unparked, or until a timeout has elapsed or a deadline is passed, whichever comes first. The callers of the park methods pass a *blocker object* which represents the entity that caused the thread to park. The blocker object is typically the synchronization object itself

```
class LockSupport {
  static void park(Object blocker);
  static void unpark(Thread thread);
  static void parkNanos(Object blocker, long timeout);
  static void parkUntil(Object blocker, long deadline);
  // ... variants of park without blocker argument ...
}
```

Figure 4: Methods of the LockSupport class

or an object associated with it. For example, *ReentrantLock* passes an instance of its inner class *NonfairSync* (or *FairSync*). Although passing a blocker object is optional, implementers are strongly encouraged to do so for diagnostic purposes.

When a thread cannot acquire a lock, it calls *park* to suspend itself and passes a blocker object that represents the lock. When a thread releases a contended lock, it calls *unpark* to resume a parked thread that has requested the lock. Therefore, we decided to trace the individual *park* and *unpark* calls in all threads. The class of the blocker object reveals the used type of lock (or other synchronization mechanism) and enables us to infer the exact semantic meaning of the park and unpark calls, so we can correlate them with each other and determine which threads blocked which other threads.

We also need to arrange the events for the park and unpark calls in their correct order to analyze them. Ideally, we would also generate separate sequence numbers for each lock so that the events from different locks can be ordered and analyzed independently. However, the lock is represented by the blocker object, which is only passed to *park,* not to *unpark,* and is therefore unknown when writing an unpark event. Therefore, we assign a *global sequence number* to each event, which establishes a definitive happened-before relationship between all park and unpark calls in all threads. We further use the global sequence number of an event to refer to that event from other events.

When a thread calls *park,* we record a *park begin event* with a sequence number, a timestamp, the identity of the blocker object, the object's class, and the call chain. Moreover, we include whether a timeout or deadline was specified upon which the thread would resume even without being unparked.

When a thread calls *unpark* to resume a parked thread, we record an *unpark event* with a sequence number, a timestamp, the identifier of the unparked thread, and the call chain. Moreover, we store the unpark event's sequence number to a thread-local structure of the unparked thread.

As soon as the unparked thread resumes its execution, we write a *park end event* with a sequence number and a timestamp. We retrieve the sequence number of the corresponding *unpark event* from the thread-local structure and also include it in this event, so the analysis can easily match the two events. Because a call to *park* can also end due to a timeout, we also record in the event whether this was the case.

Figure 5 shows an example of events that we record in four contending threads that use a non-fair *ReentrantLock.* Initially, T_1 is able to acquire the lock without contention. Next, T_2 tries to acquire the lock and fails, so it enters the queue of the lock and parks, and thus, we record a *park begin event.* T_4 then also fails to acquire the lock, enters the queue and parks, so we record another *park begin event.* When T_1 releases the lock, it unparks T_2 as its successor and we write an *unpark event.* However, T_3 is able to acquire the lock before T_2 resumes its execution. T_2 writes a *park end event,*

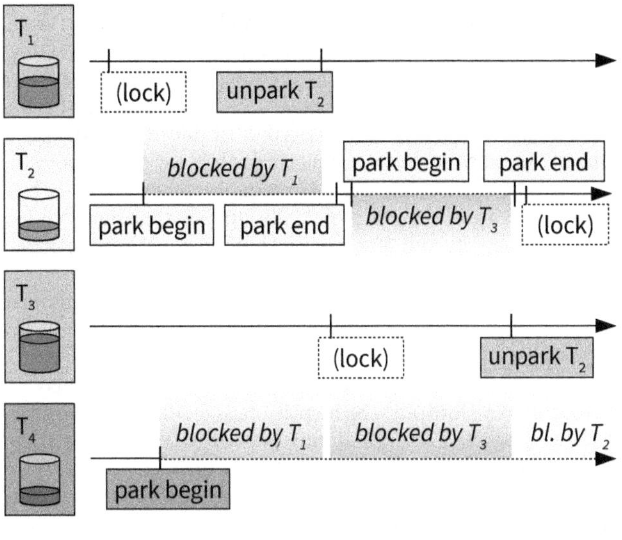

Figure 5: Park/unpark events in contending threads

but finds that the lock is still unavailable, so T_2 parks again, and we write another *park begin event.* Finally, T_3 releases the lock and unparks T_2 as its successor. When T_2 resumes its execution, we record a *park end event,* and T_2 is finally able to acquire the lock. T_4 remains parked.

During the analysis of the trace, we examine the first *park end event* of T_2, which leads us to the *unpark event* of T_1. Because a blocker object of class *ReentrantLock.NonfairSync* was recorded, we can infer that the unpark call was the consequence of an *unlock* operation, and that T_1 held the lock before the *unpark event.* The same applies to the the second unpark call, where T_3 held the lock. We can then account for the contentions in T_2 as being caused by T_1 and T_3 and their recorded call chains. Thread T_4 was also blocked by T_1 and T_3, but unpark was called only on T_2. However, because T_4 specified the same blocker object as T_2 when parking, we can infer that it was blocked by the same lock owners and also account for its contention as being caused by T_1 and T_3. Because the time between an *unpark event* and a *park end event* cannot be precisely attributed to the previous or to the next lock owner, we simply attribute such typically very short time periods to an unknown lock owner.

3.4 Metadata

Our traces contain a significant amount of repetitive data, such as the identities of threads, classes and objects, as well as call chains. Therefore, we want to collect and encode such data as efficiently as possible. However, for the data to be valuable for a user, we need to provide a meaningful representation, such as the name of a thread instead of just its numeric identifier. We decided to address this issue with *metadata events.* When we encounter an entity (such as a thread or a class) for the first time, we record a metadata event with a unique identifier for the entity and include information that is meaningful to a user. In the events that follow, we refer to that entity with only its identifier.

When the application launches a new thread, we record a *thread start event* with the thread's name and the numeric identifier that the Java runtime assigned to the thread. In future events, we refer to the thread only with that identifier. When the name of a thread is changed later, we record a *thread name change event* with the new name.

When we encounter a specific Java class for the first time, we write a *class metadata event* with the fully-qualified name of the class. HotSpot stores the metadata of a class in a data structure with a constant address, so we use that address as the unique identifier of the class. We introduced an additional field in the class metadata structures that we use to mark a class as known. Because two threads might race to write a class metadata event, we atomically update that field before writing an event, and the thread that succeeds in updating the field then writes the event.

Finding a unique identifier for Java objects is difficult. Because objects are moved by the garbage collector, their address is not suitable as an identifier. Instead, we refer to an object by recording its *identity hash code* and its class in our events. In HotSpot, the identity hash code of an object is a 31-bit integer that is randomly generated and stored with the object. In rare cases, two different objects of the same class can be assigned the same identity hash code, so that the two objects would be indistinguishable during analysis. We consider this to be an acceptable tradeoff compared to a more complex approach that involves tracking objects.

When recording call chains, we also refer to individual Java methods. Like classes, HotSpot stores the metadata of Java methods in data structures with constant addresses, which we use as unique method identifiers. When we encounter a method for the first time, we write a *method metadata event* with its identifier, the identifier of the method's class, the method's name, and the method's signature. We also use a newly introduced field to mark known methods.

Although the thread which first encounters an entity records a metadata event for it, some other thread may submit its trace buffer before that thread does. The trace analysis must be able to handle situations where events refer to an entity whose metadata event has not been processed yet, and must be able to resolve such references later.

Call chains.

We consider call chains to be vital for understanding locking bottlenecks, but walking the stack and storing them is expensive. Therefore, we have devised several techniques to record call chains more efficiently.

In a typical application, the number of call chains which use locks is limited, and many of the events that we record share identical call chains. To reduce the amount of data, we maintain a hash set of known call chains. When we record a call chain for an event, we look it up in that set. If it does not exist, we assign a unique identifier to it, insert it into the set, and write a *call chain metadata event* with its identifier and its methods. If the call chain already exists in the set, we can just record its identifier. We compute the hash code of a call chain from the instruction pointers from its methods.

Because multiple threads can access the set of call chains concurrently when recording events, those accesses require synchronization. We minimized the risk that the hash set becomes a bottleneck by implementing its operations in a *lock-free* way: when we record a call chain, we first walk the collision chain for its hash code without using any synchronization. If the call chain is found, we simply use its identifier. Otherwise, we generate a unique identifier for the call chain, and attempt to insert it into the set using a compare-and-set operation. If that operation succeeds, we record a call chain metadata event. If the compare-and-set fails, some other thread has inserted a call trace in the same collision chain,

so we start over and check if the collision chain now contains the call chain in question. Therefore, we keep the overhead of insertion to a minimum, and looking up an existing call chain incurs no synchronization overhead at all.

We also optimized the stack walk itself. A JIT-compiled Java method usually has several of its callees inlined into its compiled code, and walking the stack frame of such a method typically entails resolving which methods are inlined at the current execution position. In HotSpot, this requires decoding compressed debugging information from the compiler. Instead, we perform light-weight stack walks which do not resolve the inlined methods, and also store call chains without the inlined methods in our hash set. We resolve the inlined methods only when we encounter a new call chain for which we write a call chain metadata event.

Finally, we devised a technique to reuse parts of a call chain that were recorded earlier in the same thread. We derived this technique from our earlier research on incremental stack tracing [8]. When we walk the stack of a thread to construct its call chain, we cache the resulting call chain in a thread-local structure. We also mark the stack frame that is below the top frame by replacing its return address with the address of a code snippet, and retain the original return address in a thread-local structure. When the marked frame returns, the code snippet is executed and simply jumps to the original return address, and the marking is gone. However, as long as the marked frame does not return, we can be certain that the frames below it have not changed. When we walk the stack again later and encounter a marked frame, we can stop the stack walk and complete the call chain using the frames of the cached call chain. This technique is intended to reduce the overhead of stack walks when recording multiple events in the same method, such as a contended enter event and a contended exit event, or multiple park begin events.

Unloading of classes and compiled methods.

We refer to classes and methods by using the constant addresses of their metadata structures as identifiers. However, when HotSpot's garbage collector detects that a class loader has become unreachable, it unloads all classes loaded by that class loader and reclaims the memory occupied by their metadata. When other metadata is loaded into the same memory, the addresses that we used as identifiers in earlier events become ambiguous during the analysis of the trace.

Therefore, we need to record when identifiers become invalid. We extended the class metadata event to include the class loader, which we also identify by the address of its metadata structure. When a class loader is unloaded during garbage collection, the application is at a *safepoint*, which means that all application threads are suspended and cannot write trace events. At this point, we first reclaim the trace buffers of all threads, which can still contain references to classes that are about to be unloaded, and add them to the processing queue to ensure that they are processed first. Then we acquire a new buffer, write a single *class loader unload event* with the identifier of the class loader, and immediately submit the buffer to the processing queue. When the trace analysis processes this event, it forgets all class, method and call chain metadata that refers to the unloaded classes. Finally, we let HotSpot unload the classes.

Compiled methods are also frequently unloaded, for example when assumptions that were made during their compilation turned out to be wrong. Other code can then be

Event Parser

E

Metadata Resolver

E

Event Rearranger

IL₁ 2 → 4 → 5
IL₂ 4 → 9
G   3 → 7 → 8 → 9

E_IL   E_P

Intrinsic Lock Dispatcher   Park Thread Dispatcher

E_IL   E_IL   E_P   E_P

IL₁ Analyzer ··· IL_n Analyzer   T₁ Analyzer ··· T_n Analyzer

C   C   E_P   E_P

Park Blocker Dispatcher

E_P   E_P

B₁ Analyzer ··· B_n Analyzer

C   C

Aggregator Hierarchy

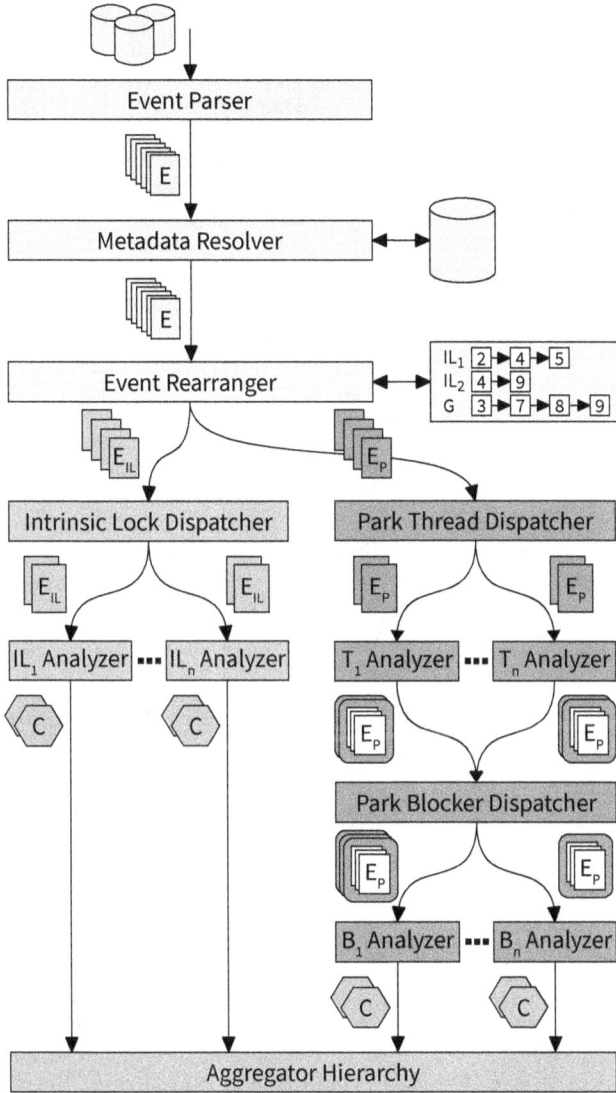

Figure 6: Processing events to identify contentions

loaded into the same memory. Because we store addresses of compiled methods in our call chains, these addresses can then become ambiguous, so we purge call chains with unloaded methods from our set of known call chains.

4. TRACE ANALYSIS

In order to identify synchronization bottlenecks effectively, we need to compute meaningful statistics from the recorded events. We accomplish this in two phases: first, we correlate events from different threads with each other to identify individual lock contentions. In the second phase, we aggregate these contentions by user-defined criteria.

4.1 Correlation and Contention Analysis

Figure 6 shows the process of extracting contentions from a trace. The *event parser* processes one trace buffer at a time. It parses the events in the buffer and forwards each event to the metadata resolver. The *metadata resolver* extracts all metadata from metadata events and keeps them in data structures. It replaces the metadata identifiers in all types of events with references to those data structures so that later

phases can access those data structures directly. The metadata resolver then passes the events to the *event rearranger*, which reorders them according to their sequence numbers. The event rearranger maintains one queue per intrinsic lock and passes each intrinsic lock's events in their correct order to the *intrinsic lock dispatcher*. For park/unpark events with a global sequence number, the event rearranger uses a single queue and passes the events to the *park thread dispatcher*.

The *intrinsic lock dispatcher* creates a *lock analyzer* for each intrinsic lock that it encounters in the events, and passes the events of that lock to its analyzer. The analyzer replays the events and keeps track of which threads were blocked and which thread held the lock, and finally generates *contention objects*. These contention objects store the duration of the contention, the thread that was blocked, the thread's call chain, the lock's associated object, and that object's class. Most importantly, the contention objects also store the cause of the contention, that is, the thread that held the lock and that thread's call chain. These contention objects are then submitted to aggregators that compute statistics, which we describe in Section 4.2.

For the park/unpark mechanism, the analysis is more complex. The *park thread dispatcher* creates a *thread analyzer* for each thread that parked or was unparked, and forwards the events of that thread to its analyzer. The thread analyzer replays the events and creates bundles of related *park begin, unpark* and *park end* events. It submits those bundles to the *park blocker dispatcher*, which creates a *blocker analyzer* for each blocker object that occurs in those bundles. We implemented different types of blocker analyzers to handle the different synchronization semantics of java.util.concurrent classes. The park blocker dispatcher chooses which type of blocker analyzer to create based on the blocker object's class. The blocker analyzer examines the event bundles that are passed to it, tracks the state of the blocker, and creates contention objects that it submits to the aggregator hierarchy. We have implemented blocker analyzers for *ReentrantLock* and for *ReentrantReadWriteLock*. ReentrantLock is very similar to intrinsic locks, and its analyzer processes events as described in the discussion of Figure 5. With a ReentrantReadWriteLock, multiple readers can share the lock at the same time without calling park or unpark, so we do not record events for those readers. Only the last reader that releases the lock calls unpark on a blocked writer and records an event. Therefore, our analyzer for ReentrantReadWriteLock cannot determine all readers which blocked a writer, but it still accurately determines which writers blocked which readers, and which writers blocked each other.

4.2 Aggregation of Contentions

To enable users to find and examine locking bottlenecks in an effective way, we devised a versatile method to aggregate the individual contentions by different aspects. These aspects of contentions are the contending thread, the contending call chain (or method), the lock owner thread, the lock owner's call chain (or method), the lock object (an intrinsic lock's associated object, or a park blocker object), and that object's class. As another aspect for aggregation, we categorize contentions into groups for intrinsic locks and for park/unpark synchronization. The user selects one or more of these aspects in a specific order. We then build a hierarchy of selectors and aggregators that break down all contentions by those aspects. An *aggregator* computes the

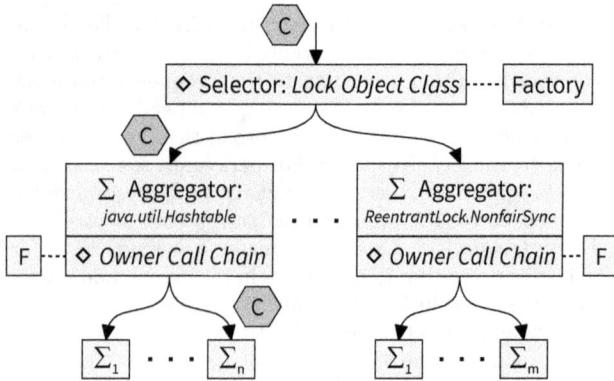

Figure 7: Aggregating events

total duration of all contentions that it processes. A *selector* distinguishes contentions by a specific aspect and forwards them to a specific aggregator according to their values.

Figure 7 shows an example in which contentions are first aggregated by the *lock object's class,* and then by the *lock owner's call chain.* When the trace analysis produces a contention object, it submits it to the hierarchy's *root selector,* which distinguishes contentions by the lock object's class. The selector has a factory that it uses to create an aggregator for each distinct lock object class that it encounters. Assuming that the submitted contention has *java.util.Hashtable* as its lock object class, the selector forwards the contention to the aggregator for that class. The aggregator then adds the contention's duration to its total duration. Because we aggregate by the lock owner's call chain next, each aggregator on this hierarchy level is coupled with a selector that distinguishes a contention by the lock owner's call chain after the aggregator has processed it. The selector also has a factory (denoted by F), which it uses to create aggregators for each encountered call chain and then forwards contentions to them. Assuming that the contention matches the call chain of aggregator Σ_n, the selector forwards the contention to that aggregator, which then adds the contention's duration to its total duration. Because there are no more aspects to aggregate by, the aggregators on that level are not coupled with selectors. The final result of aggregating multiple contentions is the tree of aggregators and the total contention times that they computed. In this example, a user might recognize from that tree that there is significant contention with *Hashtable* object locks, and that there are two call chains that cause most of these contentions. The user could then choose to optimize the code that these two call chains execute, or also select a different data structure or implementation, such as ConcurrentHashMap.

4.3 Interactive Visualization

In order to enable users to perform a comprehensive offline analysis of the generated traces, we built an interactive visualization tool. Figure 8 shows a screen capture of this tool displaying a trace file from the *avrora* benchmark, which simulates a network of microcontrollers. The main window is divided into three parts: a drill-down selection panel at the top, an aggregation tree in the center, and a detail view for the selected entry in the aggregation tree at the bottom.

In this example, the drill-down panel is configured to aggregate contentions first by group, then by the lock object's

class, next by individual lock objects, then by the lock owner's method, and finally by the lock owner's call chain. Therefore, the root level of the tree displays the different groups that we categorize events in. The first entry represents contentions from intrinsic locks, and the *Total Duration* column displays that it makes up 100% of all contentions. It also shows an absolute value of 37 seconds, which is the total time that all threads spent being blocked on intrinsic locks. The entries on the next two tree levels break down that time by lock object classes and further by individual objects, and show that 99.78% of the contention comes from locking *java.lang.Class* objects, and that all of that contention involves a single *Class* instance with identity hash code *49abf544.* The two tree levels below that display owner methods and owner call chains. With 99.32%, *SimPrinter.printBuffer* is almost always the owner of the lock when a contention occurs. The multiple owner call chains show that this method is called from more than one location, and that the amount of caused contention varies significantly by call chain. Call chains are typically too long to fit into a single line, so we show *[+n]* to denote that n calls have been omitted. However, a user can select a specific entry to view the entire call chain in the detail view below the tree.

We examined the source code of avrora and found that *SimPrinter.printBuffer* is used to log simulation events and that it calls certain static methods of class *Terminal.* To avoid that the output from different threads is interleaved, printBuffer acquires the intrinsic lock of the *Class* object of Terminal, which poses a locking bottleneck. In Figure 8, we see two call chains that cause 72.75% and 11.41% of all contention, and in both of them, printBuffer is called by *fireAfterReceiveEnd.* This method logs when a simulation node receives a network packet, which is the most frequently logged event, and its output is very large because it includes a hexadecimal representation of the packet's data. To mitigate this bottleneck, contention could be reduced by logging fewer details or fewer events, or also by queueing log events and asynchronously writing them to a file in a background thread.

Figure 8 demonstrates that our tool enables users to see the methods and call chains that caused contentions, unlike common approaches that show only which methods and call chains were blocked. However, by choosing different aspects for aggregation, users can also extract a wealth of other information, such as whether some threads caused or suffered more contention than other threads, which call chains held the lock when a specific call chain was blocked and for how long, or which contended locks were used by a specific thread, method, or call chain.

5. EVALUATION

We implemented our approach for OpenJDK 8u45 and evaluated it with synthetic workloads from a purpose-built test suite, and with real-world benchmarks.

5.1 Synthetic Workloads and Correctness

In order to verify that our approach accurately depicts the locking behavior of an application, we devised a test suite that generates predictable synthetic locking workloads. We built this test suite using the Java Microbenchmark Harness [12]. In our tests, we vary the number of threads and the number of call chains. Most importantly, we vary how long the different threads or call chains hold a lock, which changes how much contention each of them causes. We implemented those

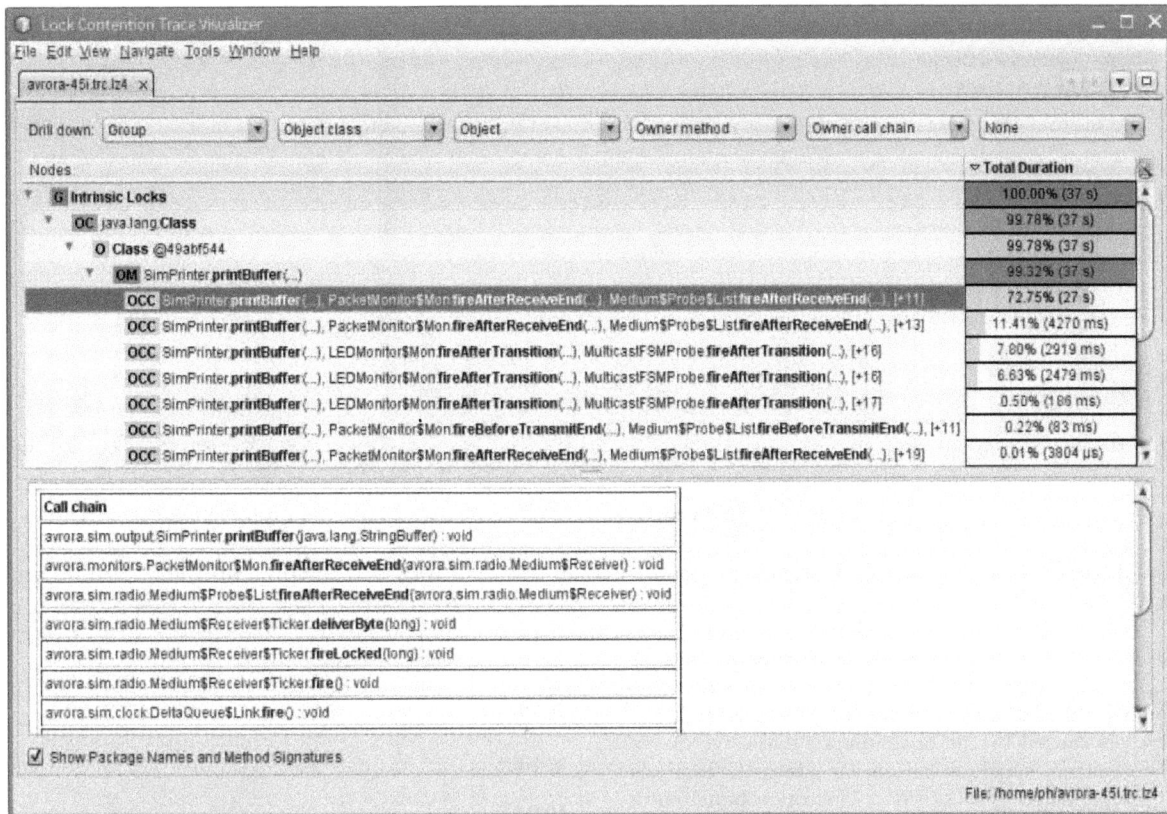

Figure 8: Visualization of a bottleneck in the *avrora* benchmark

tests for intrinsic locks and for java.util.concurrent locks and found that our generated traces match the expected amounts of contention for each test. Moreover, we verified that the recorded call chains are correct when the code throws exceptions, when the compiler inlines code, and when the code uses *wait* and *notify*.

5.2 Benchmarking

We evaluated our approach with the DaCapo 9.12 benchmark suite [2] and with the benchmarks of the Scala Benchmarking Project 0.1.0 [16]. Both suites consist of open source, real-world applications with pre-defined, non-trivial workloads.[1] We chose to execute 45 successive *iterations* of each benchmark in a single VM instance, and to discard the data from the first 35 iterations to compensate for the VM's startup phase. We tracked the start and the end of the benchmark iterations to extract the execution time and other metrics per iteration, and reinitialized event tracing at the start of each iteration. We further executed more than 10 *rounds* of each benchmark (with 45 iterations each) to ensure that the results are not biased by optimization decisions which the VM makes in its warm-up phase.

We performed all tests on a server-class system with two Intel Xeon E5-2670v2 processors with ten cores each and with hyperthreading, and thus, 40 hardware threads. The system has a total of 32 GB of memory and runs Oracle Linux 7. To get more reproducible results, we disabled dynamic frequency scaling and turbo boost, and we used a fixed Java heap size

of 16 GB. With the exception of system services, no other processes were running during our measurements.

5.3 Runtime Overhead

We measured the benchmark execution times with tracing when writing an uncompressed output file, when writing a compressed output file, and when analyzing the events online. The online analysis executes in parallel to the benchmark and aggregates the contentions by lock object class, then by contending call chain, and then by the lock owner's call chain. We compare these execution times to those of an unmodified OpenJDK 8u45 without tracing.

Figure 9 shows the median execution times of each benchmark, normalized to the median execution times without tracing. The error bars indicate the first and third quartiles. We categorized the benchmarks into multi-threaded and single-threaded benchmarks. The *G.Mean* bars show the geometric means of each category, and their error bars indicate a 50% confidence interval. For the multi-threaded benchmarks, the mean overhead of generating a trace file is 7.8%, both with and without compression. With online analysis, the mean overhead is 9.4%. For the single-threaded benchmarks, the mean overhead of generating a compressed trace file is 0.8%, and with online analysis, it is 1.2%. The overhead for single-threaded benchmarks is caused in part by the trace buffer management, and in part because the JDK itself uses multi-threading and synchronization, which we trace as well.

The overheads of the individual benchmarks correlate directly with the amount of contention that they exhibit. The benchmarks with the highest overhead are actors and

---

[1]We did not use the DaCapo suite's *batik* and *eclipse* benchmarks because they do not run on OpenJDK 8.

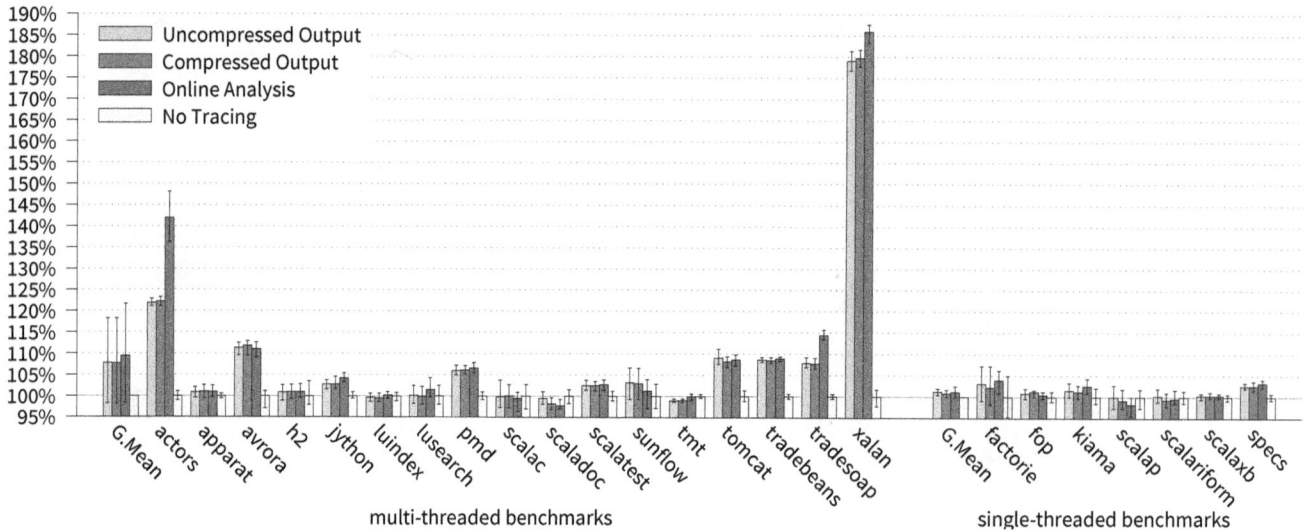

Figure 9: Overhead of tracing with uncompressed output, with compressed output, and with online analysis, relative to no tracing

xalan. *actors* is a concurrency benchmark with many fine-grained interactions between threads, and tracing them results in an overhead of 22%. Online analysis increases it to 42%, which is caused by the benchmark's extensive use of java.util.concurrent synchronization, for which the analysis is more complex and thus slower. The *xalan* benchmark transforms XML documents. It distributes work to as many threads as there are hardware threads, but all threads access a single Hashtable instance. This causes a substantial number of short contentions on our machine with 40 hardware threads, and tracing them incurs an overhead of around 80%.

For some benchmarks such as *scaladoc* or *tmt,* tracing even slightly improves the benchmark's performance. We attribute this to the delays that are introduced by recording events and call chains. David et al. found that HotSpot's locks saturate the memory bus, and that delays in lock acquisition reduce memory bus contention, which can increase performance [3]. Also, after we write a contended enter event, HotSpot's implementation of intrinsic locks retries to spin-acquire the lock while it adds the thread to the queue of blocked threads. A delay before that can increase its chances of being successful instead of suspending the thread. Additionally, the activity of the background thread in which we write the trace file or analyze the trace data influences the behavior of the garbage collector and of the thread scheduler, which can also have small beneficial effects.

The runtime overhead of our tracing is below 10% for all but three benchmarks. We consider this to be feasible for monitoring a production system. On a quad-core workstation, we measured even lower mean overheads below 3%. In future work, we intend to address cases in which the overhead is higher, in particular when tracing a substantial number of short contentions. We plan to support enabling and disabling tracing at runtime, which would allow users to analyze lock contention on a production system on demand, while causing little to no overhead when tracing is not active.

5.4 Generated Amount of Data

The amount of generated trace data is also an important factor for production use. Figure 10 shows the mean amount

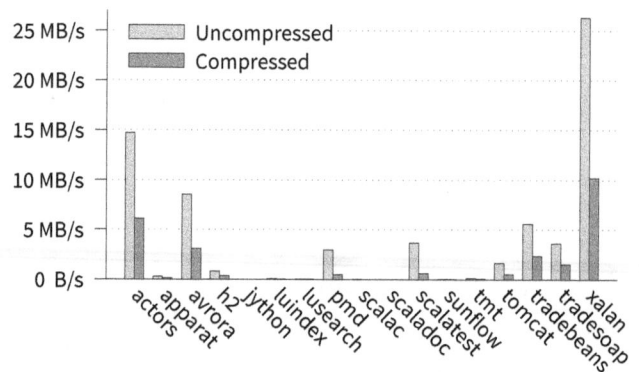

Figure 10: Trace data generated per second

of generated trace data per second for the multi-threaded benchmarks, with and without compression. Tracing *xalan,* *actors* and *avrora* generates the most uncompressed trace data at 26.3 MB/s, 14.7 MB/s, and 8.6 MB/s, respectively. For the other benchmarks, our approach generates less than 6 MB of uncompressed data per second. For those benchmarks that do not exhibit significant contention, we record less than 50 KB per second. Our on-the-fly compression typically reduces the amount of data by between 60% and 70%, and decreases the data rate of *xalan* to around 10 MB/s. Therefore, 60 minutes of trace data from a *xalan*-type application require less than 40 GB of disk space and should be more than sufficient to analyze performance problems.

We also inspected the memory footprint of the trace buffers, which have a mean capacity of 16 KB. We found that we typically use fewer than 100 buffers at any time, and hence occupy less than 2 MB of memory with trace buffers.

5.5 Trace Composition

We further examined the composition of the generated traces. Figure 11 shows the relative frequencies of individual events for the multi-threaded benchmarks. We grouped all types of metadata events for brevity. The *actors* and *apparat* benchmarks are the only ones that predominantly

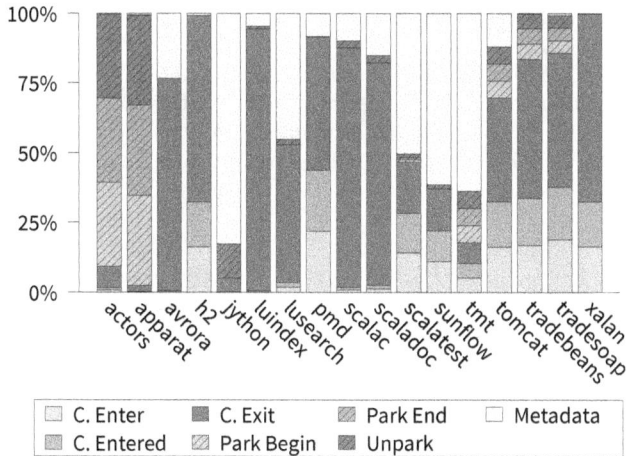

Figure 11: Frequency of trace events

rely on java.util.concurrent synchronization, with *tmt*, *tomcat*, *tradebeans* and *tradesoap* using it to some extent. As would be expected, there are typically equal numbers of park begin events, park end events, and unpark events. Surprisingly, we record only unpark events for some benchmarks, such as *jython*. This is because these benchmarks call the *Thread.interrupt* method, which always implicitly performs an unpark operation, regardless of whether the interrupted thread is currently parked.

With intrinsic locks, we record an equal number of contended enter and contended entered events, but always a significantly higher number of contended exit events. The difference is particularly large with benchmarks that acquire locks only very briefly, such as *luindex*. The reason for that is non-fair locking, with which a thread can instantly acquire an available lock even when there are queued threads, but when that thread releases the lock, it must write a contended exit event. When one of the queued threads has already been resumed and cannot acquire the lock, we do not write any additional events in that thread. With park-based synchronization, we would record another park begin event and park end event in that case, which is why the number of the three types of park events is more balanced.

For some benchmarks, metadata constitutes a relatively large portion of the trace data. Most of these benchmarks exhibit low contention, so that the amount of metadata that we record for that contention becomes relevant. In contrast to those benchmarks, *scalatest* and *tomcat* exhibit significant contention, but they generate many Java classes at runtime which use locks, so we record a large number of different call chains. *avrora* heavily uses conditional waiting with intrinsic locks, and to collect correct call chains, we must record an additional metadata event when a lock is finally released.

5.6 Call Chain Optimizations

In order to assess how much of our overhead comes from recording call chains, we also measured the tracing overhead when not recording call chains. Figure 12 compares the overheads of tracing with and without recording call chains for the multi-threaded benchmarks when writing an uncompressed trace file. When not recording call chains, the mean overhead decreases from 7.8% to 6.4%. Hence, our method of recording call chains typically constitutes less than 20% of the tracing overhead. The overhead for tracing *xalan* (which

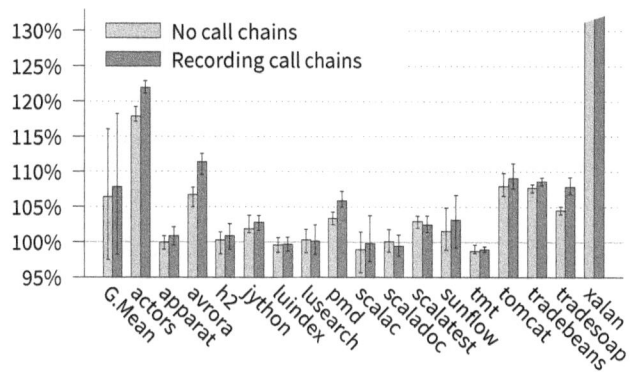

Figure 12: Overhead of recording call chains

is cut off in the chart) is reduced from 79% to 73%.

We further examined the effectiveness of reusing call chains. In all benchmarks for which we recorded more than 10,000 call chains per second, we could reuse more than 99.5% of all call chains from the set of known call chains (*pmd* is the sole exception at 89%). This reduces the amount of metadata in the trace and requires only light-weight stack walks for the lookups in the set. With our technique of marking stack frames, we further save examining between 10% and 50% of all stack frames for those same benchmarks.

6. RELATED WORK

Tallent et al. [20] describe a sampling profiler which, like our approach, identifies which threads and call chains block other threads and call chains by holding a contended lock. The profiler associates a counter with each lock and periodically takes samples. When it samples a thread that is blocked on a lock, it increases that lock's counter. When a thread releases a lock, the thread inspects the lock's counter, and if it is non-zero, the thread "accepts the blame" and records its own call chain. The profiler was implemented for C programs and is reported to have an overhead of 5%, but determines *only* which threads and call chains blocked other threads. Our approach also records which threads and call chains were blocked by a specific thread or call chain, which we consider to have diagnostic value when reasoning about performance problems that *occur* in a specific part of an application.

David et al. [3] propose a profiler that observes *critical section pressure (CSP)*, a metric which correlates the progress of threads to individual locks. When the CSP of a lock over a one-second period exceeds a threshold, the profiler records the identity of the lock and a call chain from one thread that was blocked. They implemented their profiler in HotSpot and report a measured worst-case overhead of 6%. We consider this approach complementary to ours because the CSP can be computed from the events that we record.

Inoue et al. [9] describe a sampling profiler in a Java VM which uses hardware performance counters to observe where the application acquires locks and where it blocks. It constructs call chains with a probabilistic method that uses the stack depth. The profiler is claimed to have an overhead of less than 2.2%, but it does not determine which threads and call chains block other threads and call chains.

Java Flight Recorder (JFR, [6]) is a commercial feature of the Oracle JDK that efficiently records performance-related events in an application. It collects information on blocked threads, their call chains, and the classes of lock objects. To keep the overhead low, JFR records only long contentions (more than 10ms) by default. JFR also records which thread most recently owned a lock before it could be acquired after a contention. However, although more than one thread can own a lock over that time, it considers the entire time that is spent blocking to be caused by that thread. Unlike our approach, JFR does not record call chains for threads that block other threads. It also only provides contention statistics for intrinsic locks and not for java.util.concurrent locks.

The Java VM Tool Interface (JVMTI, [14]) provides functionality to observe contention from intrinsic locks. Profilers can register callbacks for contention events and then examine the thread, the lock's associated object, and the call trace of the blocked thread. However, those events cannot be used to determine the thread which holds the lock or that thread's call chain. JVMTI also does not provide events to observe contention from java.util.concurrent locks.

Stolte et al. [17] describe *Polaris,* a system for analyzing and visualizing data in multidimensional databases. Polaris provides a visual query language for generating a range of graphical presentations, which enables users to rapidly explore the data. We believe that such a system would complement our visualization tool, and we consider implementing an export feature for the trace analyis results to a format that can be used with such systems.

7. CONCLUSIONS AND FUTURE WORK

We presented a novel approach for analyzing locking bottlenecks in Java applications by efficiently tracing lock contention in the Java Virtual Machine. We trace contention from both Java's intrinsic locks and from java.util.concurrent locks. For the analysis of the traces, we devised a versatile approach to aggregate and visualize the recorded contentions. Unlike other methods, our approach shows not only where contention occurs, but also where contention is caused. Nevertheless, our implementation in the HotSpot VM incurs a low mean overhead of 7.8%, so we consider it feasible to use our approach for monitoring production systems.

In future work, we intend to focus even further on the activities of lock owner threads while their locks are contended, for example by taking periodic samples of their call chains. We also plan to extend our analysis approach to identify connections between lock contentions, such as when a thread holds a contended lock and is then blocked when trying to acquire another lock. We further intend to collect more information about lock objects, such as the call chain where a lock object was allocated. This could provide additional information when locks are stored with data objects that are propagated to different parts of an application. Finally, we consider analyzing conditional waiting with both intrinsic locking and java.util.concurrent mechanisms. This could reveal problems such as when threads wait for each other to finish related tasks, but some tasks take significantly longer than others, leaving some threads idle.

8. ACKNOWLEDGEMENTS

This work was supported by the Christian Doppler Forschungsgesellschaft, and by Dynatrace Austria. We thank Thomas Schatzl for supporting us in evaluating our approach.

9. REFERENCES

[1] D. F. Bacon, R. Konuru, C. Murthy, and M. Serrano. Thin locks: featherweight synchronization for Java. In *ACM SIGPLAN Not.*, volume 33, pages 258–268, 1998.

[2] S. M. Blackburn et al. The DaCapo benchmarks: Java benchmarking development and analysis. OOPSLA '06, pages 169–190, 2006.

[3] F. David, G. Thomas, J. Lawall, and G. Muller. Continuously measuring critical section pressure with the free-lunch profiler. OOPSLA '14, pages 291–307, 2014.

[4] B. Goetz, T. Peierls, J. Bloch, J. Bowbeer, D. Holmes, and D. Lea. *Java concurrency in practice.* Pearson Education, 2006.

[5] Google. Snappy: a fast compressor/decompressor. http://google.github.io/snappy/, 2015.

[6] M. Hirt and M. Lagergren. *Oracle JRockit: The Definitive Guide.* Packt Publishing Ltd, 2010.

[7] P. Hofer, D. Gnedt, and H. Mössenböck. Efficient dynamic analysis of the synchronization performance of Java applications. WODA '15, pages 14–18, 2015.

[8] P. Hofer, D. Gnedt, and H. Mössenböck. Lightweight Java profiling with partial safepoints and incremental stack tracing. ICPE '15, pages 75–86, 2015.

[9] H. Inoue and T. Nakatani. How a Java VM can get more from a hardware performance monitor. OOPSLA '09, pages 137–154, 2009.

[10] D. Lea. The java.util.concurrent synchronizer framework. *Science of Computer Programming,* 58(3):293–309, 2005.

[11] Oracle. java.nio package in Java SE 8. https://docs.oracle.com/javase/8/docs/api/java/nio/package-summary.html.

[12] Oracle. OpenJDK Code Tools: Java Microbench Harness (JMH). http://openjdk.java.net/projects/code-tools/jmh/.

[13] Oracle. The Java™ Management Extensions. http://openjdk.java.net/groups/jmx/.

[14] Oracle. JVM™Tool Interface version 1.2. http://docs.oracle.com/javase/8/docs/platform/jvmti/jvmti.html, 2015.

[15] T. Pool. Lock optimizations on the HotSpot VM. Technical report, 2014.

[16] A. Sewe et al. Da Capo con Scala: design and analysis of a Scala benchmark suite for the Java virtual machine. OOPSLA '11, pages 657–676, 2011.

[17] C. Stolte, D. Tang, and P. Hanrahan. Polaris: A system for query, analysis, and visualization of multidimensional relational databases. *IEEE Trans. on Visualization and Computer Graphics,* 8(1):52–65, 2002.

[18] D. Sundstrom. Snappy in Java. https://github.com/dain/snappy, 2015.

[19] H. Sutter. The free lunch is over: A fundamental turn toward concurrency in software. *Dr. Dobb's Journal,* 30(3):202–210, 2005.

[20] N. Tallent, J. Mellor-Crummey, and A. Porterfield. Analyzing lock contention in multithreaded applications. PPoPP '10, pages 269–280, 2010.

Analysis of Overhead
in Dynamic Java Performance Monitoring

Vojtěch Horký, Jaroslav Kotrč, Peter Libič, Petr Tůma

Department of Distributed and Dependable Systems
Faculty of Mathematics and Physics, Charles University
Malostranské náměstí 25, Prague 1, 118 00, Czech Republic

first.last@d3s.mff.cuni.cz

ABSTRACT

In production environments, runtime performance monitoring is often limited to logging of high level events. More detailed measurements, such as method level tracing, tend to be avoided because their overhead can disrupt execution. This limits the information available to developers when solving performance issues at code level.

One approach that reduces the measurement disruptions is dynamic performance monitoring, where the measurement instrumentation is inserted and removed as needed. Such selective monitoring naturally reduces the aggregate overhead, but also introduces transient overhead artefacts related to insertion and removal of instrumentation. We experimentally analyze this overhead in Java, focusing in particular on the measurement accuracy, the character of the transient overhead, and the longevity of the overhead artefacts.

Among other results, we show that dynamic monitoring requires time from seconds to minutes to deliver stable measurements, that the instrumentation can both slow down and speed up the execution, and that the overhead artefacts can persist beyond the monitoring period.

Keywords

performance measurement overhead; dynamic instrumentation; Java

1. INTRODUCTION

Software performance is not only a common term, but also something of a misnomer, because it suggests performance is a property of software. In reality, software performance is a product of executing the software on a particular platform and neither the software nor the platform alone determines performance. This is also one of the reasons why performance monitoring is used – by observing the actual performance, it takes into account the software, the platform and the workload, something that is difficult to do otherwise.

ICPE'16, March 12-18, 2016, Delft, Netherlands

© 2016 ACM. ISBN 978-1-4503-4080-9/16/03. . . $15.00

DOI: http://dx.doi.org/10.1145/2851553.2851569

Technically, essential tasks of performance monitoring include data collection and data storage or data processing, or both. These tasks consume resources, giving rise to monitoring overhead. The overhead can easily range from units of percent – for example when monitoring selected methods in an enterprise benchmark application [36] – to orders of magnitude – for example when collecting calling context profile in standard application benchmarks [29]. This is obviously a practically significant factor.

Because the monitoring overhead depends on the amount of data collected, it can be reduced by collecting less data at fewer locations. Particularly interesting is dynamic monitoring, where individual components of the monitoring infrastructure are enabled and disabled, or even inserted and removed, to cater to changing monitoring demands. Dynamic monitoring support exists in many contexts, from operating systems [4, 25, 34] to enterprise application monitoring frameworks [23, 5, 7].

An important influence on dynamic monitoring overhead is exerted by probes – data collection components that are inserted directly into the monitored application. Probes can be inserted either through static instrumentation, which happens before the monitored application is executed, or through dynamic instrumentation, which happens during execution. In the former case, the probe code is always in place and contains support for enabling or disabling data collection. In the latter case, the probe code is simply inserted or removed as needed. Dynamic instrumentation is technically more challenging, because it entails modifying an executing application, but also more attractive, because it carries the implied promise of achieving zero overhead when not collecting data.

In this paper, we focus on dynamic performance monitoring in the context of Java. Starting with version 1.6, Java provides a standard support for changing the code of an executing application through mechanisms called class redefinition and class retransformation. By operating on bytecode, these mechanisms are much more portable than dynamic instrumentation based on machine code manipulation, but also much less transparent where performance overhead is concerned. We address this issue by presenting an extensive overhead study focused particularly on dynamic performance monitoring in Java.

We conduct our overhead study in the broader context of our research on performance awareness. Our general goal is to provide developers with information on software performance that is timely and relevant – that is, presented at a time and in a manner that makes it useful rather than distracting. Towards that goal, we have implemented a framework capable of both static and dynamic performance monitoring, which we use for example to answer performance related queries in the context of regression testing [3] or to provide performance information in software documentation during development [12]. Here, we therefore analyze the overhead of the framework.

The structure of the paper follows our main contributions. In Section 2, we describe our performance monitoring framework, with focus on dynamic instrumentation as the new feature. Section 3 contributes a detailed analysis of overhead sources specific to dynamic instrumentation. In Section 4, we present the experimental overhead evaluation itself. Related work discussion and concluding remarks close the paper.

2. MEASUREMENT FRAMEWORK

Figure 1 presents a high level architecture of the performance monitoring framework we use throughout this paper. The framework executes in two virtual machines – the data collection components reside in the same JVM as the measured application, the data storage and data processing components use a helper JVM. This helps minimize the framework footprint in the application JVM and provides the possibility of running the helper JVM on a separate host. It also matches the architecture of the underlying instrumentation framework we use, called DiSL [21].

The framework uses the launcher component to perform the necessary initialization and set up the connection between the application JVM and the helper JVM. Once the application executes, the measurement coordination component decides when a measurement should start – depending on circumstances, this can be in response to an interactive developer request, favorable load conditions, or other triggers. The component uses the control connection to deliver the instrumentation request to the application JVM, where the transformation agent fires a class transformation request. The application JVM reacts by asking the DiSL agent to transform the measured class, the DiSL agent in turn uses the DiSL framework in the helper JVM to perform the transformation – which in this case takes the form of inserting probe code. Once the probe code is inserted, it starts feeding measurements to the data transfer component, which uses the data connection to deliver the measurements to the helper JVM for processing. Similar process is used when removing probe code.

Listing 1 provides a compact pseudocode listing of the probe code. The code simply collects the time at the entry to and the exit from the measured method – the somewhat more complicated listing is due to the need to handle recursion. When the probe is called recursively, only the top level iteration is measured. The probe state is thread local, implemented using efficient thread local variables offered by DiSL. This minimizes synchronization.

We omit other elements of the framework, which are not essential for the purpose of this paper. These include the ability to differentiate between invocations of the same method based on the actual argument values, and the applications for regression testing and documentation generation. For more details on the performance regression testing features, refer to [3], for performance documentation generation

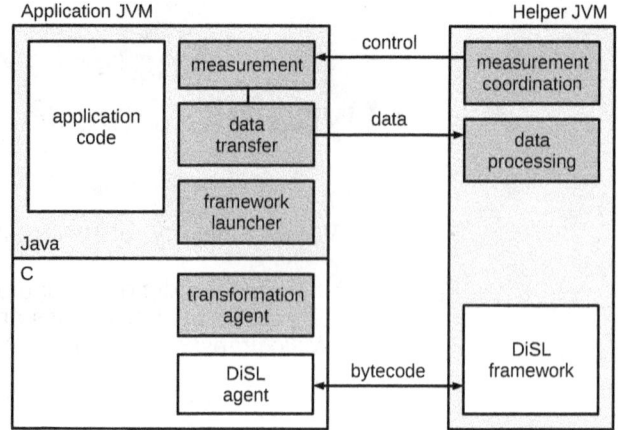

Figure 1: *High level architecture of the dynamic performance monitoring framework.*

features, refer to [12]. The framework is available as open source at http://d3s.mff.cuni.cz/software/spl.

3. OVERHEAD SOURCE ANALYSIS

A characteristic feature of contemporary computing platforms is the potential for complex interactions across multiple levels of the hardware and software stack. Dynamic measurement instrumentation influences these interactions in many ways, with the collective impact on performance forming the observed measurement overhead. Here, we discuss the sources of measurement overhead relevant to Java-like platforms – that is, platforms with applications written in a high level language, garbage collected memory, dynamic class loading and just-in-time (JIT) compilation. The discussion steers mostly clear of technical detail, available in platform-specific sources such as [14].

3.1 Probe Presence

The instrumentation inserts probes directly into the application, to be executed just before and just after the measured application code. The probe code consumes processor resources just as the application code does, introducing execution overhead.

As illustrated on Listing 1, the probe code samples time. The part of the probe code situated between the sampling points and the application code of interest will be measured together, introducing systematic measurement error. With some simplifications, the error is likely to be additive and can be possibly compensated by calibration. The remaining probe code, which resides outside the sampling points, is not measured but still counts towards the application execution time.

The systematic measurement error can grow when the measured application code is called recursively. When this is the case, the error accumulates with the depth of the recursion and, except for the top level iteration, includes the entire probe code rather than just the part of the probe between the sampling points. A similar situation arises when multiple instrumented methods call each other.

When examined in detail, the execution overhead is further influenced by interactions inside the processor microarchitecture. The probe code may or may not cause or suffer

recursion : map String to integer

▷ *Invocation local variables*
entryTime : integer
exitTime : integer
name : String

advice at method entry
   ▷ *Call is converted to constant by DiSL*
   ▷ *at class loading (weaving) time*
   name ← GetCurrentMethodName
   Increment(*recursion*[*name*])
   ▷ *Time sampled close to real entry moment*
    entryTime ← GetCurrentTime
end advice

advice at method exit
   ▷ *Time sampled close to real exit moment*
   exitTime ← GetCurrentTime
   name ← GetCurrentMethodName
   Decrement(*recursion*[*name*])
   if at top level of recursion **then**
      SendMeasurement(*name*, *entryTime*, *exitTime*)
   end if
end advice

Listing 1: *Probe pseudocode for dynamic instrumentation.*

relatively expensive events such as cache misses or branch prediction failures, whose occurrence depends on the interaction with the surrounding application code. In principle, applications that are particularly tightly tuned to the processor microarchitecture – such as numerical applications that rely on tiling to efficiently utilize caches [26] – may be disrupted significantly, however, such tight tuning is not common on platforms that do not expose memory layout to applications.

With both the application and the probe written in a high level language, control over the execution overhead is somewhat limited. Still, it is possible to minimize the overhead by structuring the probe code so that the sampling points are close to the measured application code and by avoiding potentially expensive constructs such as synchronization or polymorphic invocations. Ultimately, the overhead determines practical measurement granularity – if the overall disruption to application execution is to be reasonable, the measured application code should execute orders of magnitude longer than the probe code.

3.2 Code Manipulation

The code manipulation associated with inserting and removing probes also consumes resources. The instrumentation needs to parse the application class to be measured, insert the probe code, and have the virtual machine load the instrumented application class. In general, these are operations that are about as disruptive as other class loading activity.

As an important consequence, class manipulation during instrumentation may trigger JIT compilation. If some methods of the class were JIT compiled before instrumentation, then these compiled versions are discarded, and may be JIT compiled again after instrumentation. The impact may extend to methods of other classes whose compiled versions depend on the instrumented application class, leading to cascades of JIT compilations that reflect prior inlining decisions.

Depending on circumstances, the virtual machine may initiate JIT compilation immediately after loading the instrumented application class, at some later time, or even never. Until the JIT compilation completes, those methods whose compiled versions were discarded can execute less efficiently or even block, again in effect contributing to overhead. In general, it is not possible to tell whether some future JIT compilation will deliver a more efficient compiled version of a method, it is therefore not possible to minimize the impact on measurement simply by waiting for the compiled version. It is, however, possible to wait for JIT compilations that immediately follow instrumentation to finish – those JIT compilations should cover most hot code, where the impact on measurement is also most likely significant.

3.3 Code Optimization

The JIT compilation involves optimization decisions that may change with instrumentation. This is true even when the interaction between the probe code and the application code is kept to a minimum – most importantly, the very presence of the probe code influences the heuristics that drive method inlining. Although these heuristics may vary, they are likely to include a limit on the size of the inlined method. Inserting probe code increases code size and therefore reduces the chance of the measured methods being inlined.

Method inlining is an important optimization because it impacts the scope of most other optimizations – with JIT compilation working on methods as compilation and optimization units, inlining one method into another means the caller and the callee are optimized together. The impact of inlining on performance experiments was demonstrated in detail with JMH benchmarks [24] that can selectively disable method inlining to prevent interaction between the benchmark harness and the measured method [31]. In very general terms, we can assume that by reducing the chance of inlining, instrumentation reduces the opportunity for optimization. We can therefore expect instrumentation to introduce another systematic measurement error, due to observing possibly less optimized versions of the measured methods. Keeping probe code small, however, should make this error less likely.

The optimization decisions made during JIT compilation also depend on past application execution. Factors such as method invocation count, loop iteration count, or type variability are taken into account – it is therefore not guaranteed that the same method will be compiled in the same way at different moments in application execution. In particular, it is not guaranteed that a method will have the same compiled version after removing probes as it had before inserting probes.

3.4 Other Overhead Sources

Significant sources of measurement overhead are also associated with data storage. Whatever data a probe collects or aggregates needs to be stored in memory and then exported outside the measured application. The memory storage overhead begins with allocation – when using the application heap, additional allocations will either cause the heap to expand or the garbage collector to run more often [16, 17]. After allocation, storing data in memory consumes additional memory bandwidth, and export similarly incurs additional storage or network bandwidth. The magnitude of these effects grows with the data volume.

Because there is no principal difference between data storage overhead coming from dynamic measurement instrumentation and similar overhead from standard instrumentation or even application I/O, we do not analyze this overhead source further. A thorough analysis of the export overhead and the related measurement framework implementation issues can be found in [37].

4. EXPERIMENTAL EVALUATION

The analysis of potential overhead sources associated with dynamic measurement instrumentation directly translates into questions we want to answer using experimental evaluation:

Q1. Given that some part of the probe code is necessarily situated between the sampling points and the measured application code, what is the typical difference between the measured execution time and the actual execution time?

Q2. Does the difference between the measured execution time and the actual execution time remain stable?

Q3. Given that the measured code is potentially interacting with the probe code through code optimization decisions and other channels, is the execution time of the measured code different from the execution time with no measurement?

Q4. Given that the measured code is potentially compiled differently before and after measurement, does the execution time after measurement differ from the execution time before measurement?

Q5. What is the typical duration of JIT compilation associated with dynamic measurement instrumentation?

For completeness, we also want to answer the ever present question associated with instrumentation, even if there is no reason why the result should be significantly different from other instrumentation overhead studies:

Q6. What is the total overhead in terms of application performance that can be attributed to dynamic measurement instrumentation?

4.1 Overall Design

To answer the overhead related questions, we need to observe an application both with and without dynamic measurement instrumentation in place – in other words, we need independent observation capabilities that exist alongside the dynamic instrumentation. We employ static instrumentation deployed throughout the measured application to perform continuous measurement. From the perspective of the dynamic instrumentation, the static instrumentation is just a part of the measured application that provides baseline measurements, as outlined in Figure 2. Compared to Figure 1, the application is now augmented with the static probe code, which relies on the static measurement agent

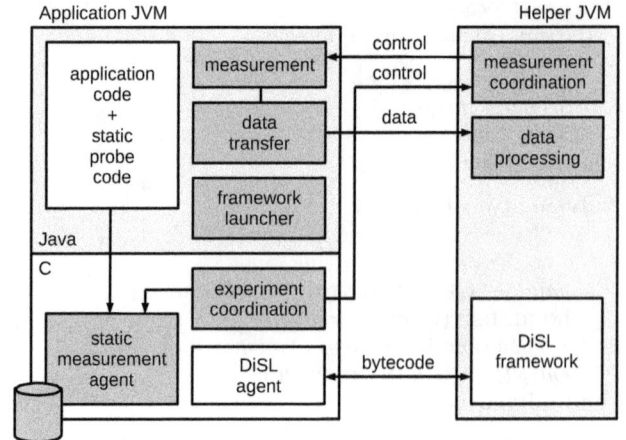

Figure 2: *High level architecture of the experiment.*

to record the baseline measurements in local storage. An experiment coordination component is introduced to direct when a measurement should start and stop, but the dynamic instrumentation remains otherwise unchanged.

With both static and dynamic instrumentation available, we pretend that we perform dynamic measurements on an application that also produces baseline measurements for comparison. We structure the experiment to model a situation where a developer chooses to observe the execution time of an arbitrary application method using dynamic instrumentation, and use the static instrumentation to measure the overhead associated with the dynamic instrumentation. To collect a representative sample, we repeatedly choose the observed methods at random. In individual steps, outlined in Figure 3, the experiment proceeds as follows:

S1. Before launch, we use static instrumentation to augment the application. The statically instrumented application continuously reports the execution times of all methods considered in the experiment and the processor utilization.

S2. We launch the application and wait for the warmup period to pass before commencing measurement.

S3. We measure and record the execution time of all methods considered in the experiment using the static instrumentation. This data describes the performance before all dynamic measurements.

S4. We choose one of the methods considered in the experiment at random to be the observed method. We use dynamic instrumentation to insert the probe code at the start and the end of the observed method and measure the time it takes the JIT compilation associated with the code manipulation to complete.

S5. At all times between inserting and removing the probe code, we measure and record the execution time of the observed method using the dynamic instrumentation. This data is the dynamic measurement sample.

S6. We measure and record the execution time of all methods considered in the experiment using the static instrumentation. This data describes the performance during dynamic measurement.

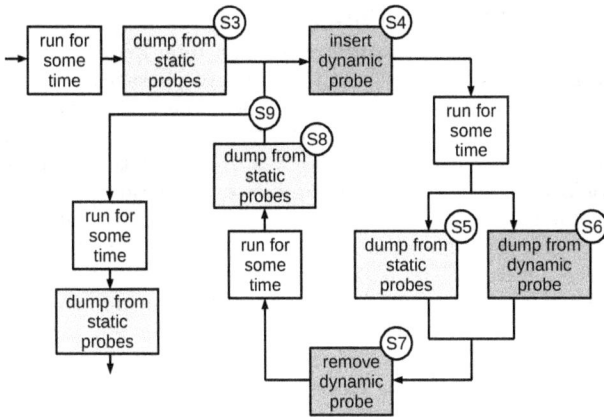

Figure 3: *Control flow of the experiment.*

S7. We use dynamic instrumentation to remove the probe code at the start and the end of the observed method and measure the time it takes the JIT compilation associated with the code manipulation to complete.

S8. We measure and record the execution time of all methods considered in the experiment using the static instrumentation. This data describes the performance after dynamic measurement.

S9. We continue with step S4 until enough methods are observed.

S10. Finally, we again measure and record the execution time of all methods considered in the experiment using the static instrumentation. This data describes the performance after all dynamic measurements.

The individual steps provide data to answer the overhead related questions – by comparing the measurements from steps S5 and S6, we evaluate the dynamic measurement accuracy ; relating the measurements from steps S6 and S8 reveals the dynamic measurement overhead ; comparing steps S3 and S10 identifies any permanent performance changes due to inserting and removing probe code, and so on.

4.2 Technical Specifics

The complete experiment implementation and configuration is available as open source, as is the performance monitoring framework. Here, we provide selected technical details necessary for interpreting the experiment results.

4.2.1 Static Probes

The static instrumentation is implemented independently of the dynamic measurement framework. AspectJ™ [1] is used to insert the probe code in the form of a `before` advice and an `after` advice. Both pieces of advice consist of a single JNI call to the actual probe code implemented natively, with statically assigned integer method identifier as the only argument. Listing 2 provides a compact pseudocode listing.

Implementing most of the static instrumentation natively provides more technical advantages including dynamic memory allocation independent of the application heap. We also obtain access to JVM state information, such as notifications about JIT compilation.

▷ *Thread local variable holding execution times of*
▷ *individual methods*
data : **array of record**
  ▷ *Individual samples*
  samples : **array of record**
    generation : integer
    entryTime : integer
    exitTime : integer
  end record
  ▷ *Index into samples*
  nextFree : integer
  ▷ *Pending call data*
  recursion : integer
  entryTime : integer
end record

procedure STARTMEASUREMENTJNI(*id* : integer)
  ▷ *Time sampled close to what dynamic probe perceives*
  ▷ *as real entry*
  now ← GETCURRENTTIME
  INCREMENT(*data*[*id*].*recursion*)
  if at top level of recursion **then**
    data[*id*].*entryTime* ← *now*
  end if
end procedure

procedure ENDMEASUREMENTJNI(*id* : integer)
  DECREMENT(*data*[*id*].*recursion*)
  if not at top level of recursion **then**
    return
  end if
  i ← *data*[*id*].*nextFree*
  ▷ *Generation indicates data validity*
  INCREMENT(*data*[*id*].*samples*[*i*].*generation*)
  data[*id*].*samples*[*i*].*entryTime* ← *data*[*id*].*entryTime*
  ▷ *Time sampled close to what dynamic probe perceives*
  ▷ *as real exit*
  data[*id*].*samples*[*i*].*exitTime* ← GETCURRENTTIME
  INCREMENT(*data*[*id*].*samples*[*index*].*generation*)
  ▷ *Overwrite oldest data if necessary*
  MODULOINCREMENT(*data*[*id*].*nextFree*, 256)
end procedure

Listing 2: *Probe pseudocode for static instrumentation.*

To avoid excessive synchronization between the probe code and the static measurement agent, which records the measurements in thread local storage, we use versioning as in sequential locks [2]. Each measurement updates the generation counter twice, the agent records only measurements whose generation counter was odd and the same both before and after access. We also take care to use the same clock source in both the static and the dynamic instrumentation (`clock_gettime` with `CLOCK_MONOTONIC`). This makes it possible to pair the static and the dynamic measurement of the same method invocation, which is used in some parts of the evaluation.

Keeping the Java part of the static probe code as simple as possible is essential to preserve a realistic interaction between the application code and the dynamic probe code that the experiment examines. We note that AspectJ™ does not simply inline the JNI call at the method entry and method

279

exit points, but uses a somewhat more complex invocation sequence that first locates the (singleton) aspect and then invokes the aspect method which contains the JNI call. The code involves monomorphic invocation and predictable conditional branching, which should optimize reasonably well. The use of JNI carries some overhead as well [10].

4.2.2 Measured Application

Because the potential overhead sources depend on interaction between the application code, the probe code, and the execution platform, we need to conduct the experiment in a reasonably realistic context. We have chosen the SPECjbb2015™ benchmark [33], a Java server business benchmark that approximates a business information system of a supermarket company.

In the experiment, we consider methods that reside in the main JAR file of the benchmark as methods that the developer of the application would be likely to observe. As a technical necessity, we omit methods of anonymous classes, which cannot be selected by static instrumentation pointcuts. This leaves us with 5628 statically instrumented methods in 957 classes. For the dynamic instrumentation, we select methods that are invoked frequently enough to provide some data in 60 s of measurement. To do this, we run the benchmark with static instrumentation for 40 min and select methods called at least 100 times in the last 10 min. This yields 1286 methods.

4.2.3 Workload Generation

The SPECjbb2015™ benchmark uses an elaborate workload generation mechanism that first identifies the request rate bounds and then generates requests with gradually increasing rate to identify the benchmark score. For our experiment, the changing workload is not practical because individual measurements would be collected at different request rates – we therefore execute the benchmark with a fixed request rate. We choose the rate to be close enough to maximum rate to maintain high utilization, because that is where the instrumentation overhead is easily visible, but low enough to make overload situations rare. On the experiment platform, this is 4000 req/s.

The workload generation mechanism of SPECjbb2015™ implements an open workload model, where individual requests arrive at the configured rate regardless of the request processing speed (except for overload situations, which are detected and reported). Hence, the instrumentation overhead does not necessarily translate to changes in request rate – instead, the processor utilization rises so that the configured request rate can be maintained. Similarly, request queueing and thread scheduling effects may mask changes in response time [22]. We therefore monitor changes in processor utilization as an indication of instrumentation overhead.

Technically, we monitor processor utilization using the processor accounting subsystem of the process control group associated with the application JVM running the benchmark. This provides accurate information at nanosecond granularity, which we express as percentage of full utilization – 0 % means no processor was executing the application JVM threads in the measurement period, 100 % means all processors were exclusively executing the application JVM threads in the measurement period.

4.3 Experiment Platform

We perform the measurements on an Intel Xeon machine with 32 logical processors (E5-2660, two packages, 8 cores per package, 2 hardware threads per core). The processors are running at 2.2 GHz, the frequency is fixed for all measurements because frequency scaling and turbo boost would otherwise distort the processor utilization measurements that we use as an indication of the instrumentation overhead. The operating system is Fedora 20, 64 bit kernel 3.19.8, OpenJDK 1.7.0-79, AspectJ 1.8.6, DiSL 1.0.

The machine has 48 GB RAM in 2 NUMA nodes. We use the default configuration for heap size and force a garbage collection cycle before each processor utilization measurement to avoid including garbage collection in data intended to characterize instrumentation overhead. As a consequence, JVM arrives at a stable heap size of less than 5 GB that reflects the allocation rate between the utilization measurements.

We use a 5 min warmup period before collecting measurements, taking care to also exercise probe code during warmup, and restart the experiment every 2 h to randomize the initial conditions [13]. Figure 4 shows the initial processor utilization, indicating that by the end of the 5 min period, the benchmark execution is stable, the same is indicated by the JIT log.

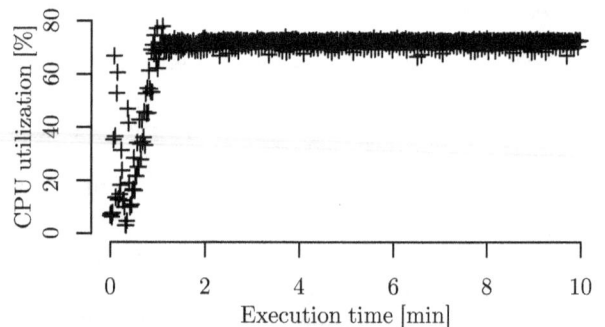

Figure 4: *Processor utilization during warmup.*

In the experiment steps that collect measurements using the static instrumentation – S3, S6, S8 and S10 – we collect the processor utilization for 30 s and the execution time of all methods for 60 s with cyclic buffers of 256 elements per thread. In the steps that wait for the JIT compilation to complete – S4 and S7 – we consider the JIT compilation complete when no new compiled method appears for 20 s, with a timeout of 60 s. We also insert a random delay of 30 s to 90 s in step S9 to prevent inadvertent synchronization between the experiment and the application.

4.4 Measurement Results

We examine the measurement results in the same order as the overhead questions. Question Q1 deals with the measurement accuracy, that is, the difference between the measured and the actual time. Figure 5 answers with a distribution of the average difference between the time reported using the static and the dynamic instrumentation in steps S5 and S6. In numbers, the minimum average difference was observed to be 76 ns, the median was 1.34 µs, the maximum was 166.09 ms.

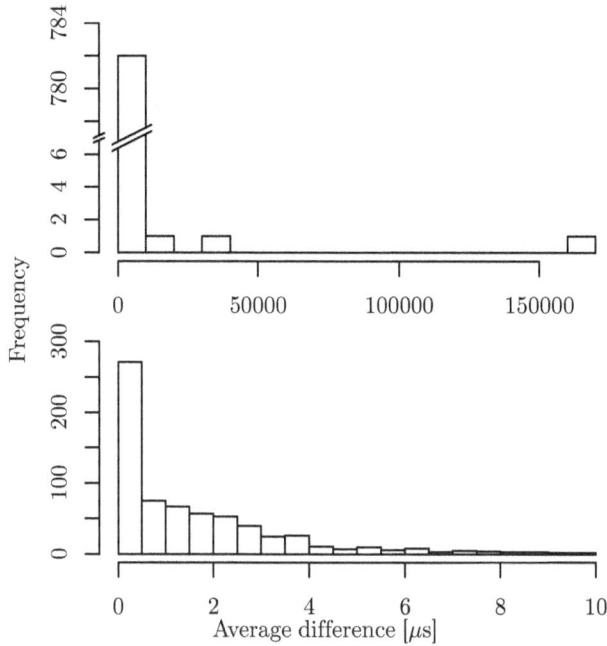

Figure 5: *Difference between measurements reported by static and dynamic instrumentation. We (1) pair static and dynamic measurements of the same invocation, (2) compute paired difference, (3) compute average difference per method, (4) plot distribution of the averages.*

Note broken scale in the top plot, the bottom plot provides a zoom in view. Results closer to zero indicate more accurate dynamic measurement, but not necessarily zero disruption due to dynamic measurement, which is examined later.

Figure 6 offers an alternative view, plotting the average ratio between the time reported using the static and the dynamic instrumentation, relative to the method execution time. The figure suggests that the relative measurement accuracy sharply declines for methods shorter than about 10 µs to 20 µs.

Figures 5 and 6 also relate to question Q2. The interquartile range of average differences is 3.33 µs, more than two times the median difference. This suggests the overhead is far from stable and therefore not easy to compensate by subtracting the average difference. We have also used one-way ANOVA to decide whether the choice of the measured method is an important factor. When ignoring the few methods with average difference over 10 µs, ANOVA returns p close to 1, suggesting that the variability does not depend on which method is measured.

Questions Q1 and Q2 concern different observations of the same invocations. In contrast, the remaining questions concern observations of different invocations, we can therefore only talk about effects on average behavior. As a consequence, outliers and fluctuations have more influence over the results. To compensate for outliers, we compute averages after discarding 2.5 % of the smallest and 2.5 % of the largest measurements for each method.

Figure 7 is related to question Q3, examining the effect of repeated JIT compilation on dynamic measurement. The

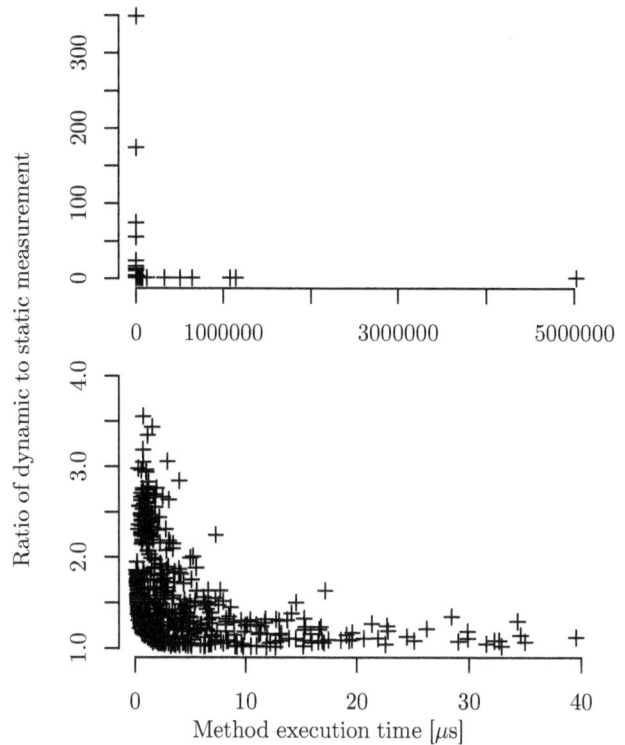

Figure 6: *Ratio between measurements reported by static and dynamic instrumentation. We (1) pair static and dynamic measurements of the same invocation, (2) compute ratio of dynamic to static measurement, (3) compute geometric average ratio per method, (4) compute average static measurement per method, (5) plot the averages of ratios relative to the averages of static measurements.*

The bottom plot provides a zoom in view. Results closer to one indicate relatively more accurate dynamic measurement, helping to identify the minimum method execution time where the relative accuracy is acceptable.

figure shows how the average method execution time, as measured by the static instrumentation, changes during dynamic measurement. Although the median rate of 1.014 indicates an intuitively reasonable small slow-down, the variability is again large, with 25 % of methods exhibiting a slow-down of more than 1.23, and, more surprisingly, 25 % of methods exhibiting a speed-up of more than 0.84. To distinguish the effects of instrumentation from normal execution time variability, we employ statistical testing with t-test – the slow-down is statistically significant at $\alpha = 0.05$ for 13.2 % of methods, and the speed-up for 18.0 % of them.

To provide more detail, Figure 8 shows a typical behaviour during dynamic measurement, from initiating the measurement in step S4 to concluding the measurement in step S8. Upon inserting the probe code, the method execution time jumps up because the compiled version of the instrumented class, and possibly other related methods, is discarded. Soon after that, the executed code is compiled again and the performance returns to normal levels. Similar behavior appears upon removing the probe code. The few other outliers that are visible throughout the measurements appear at random

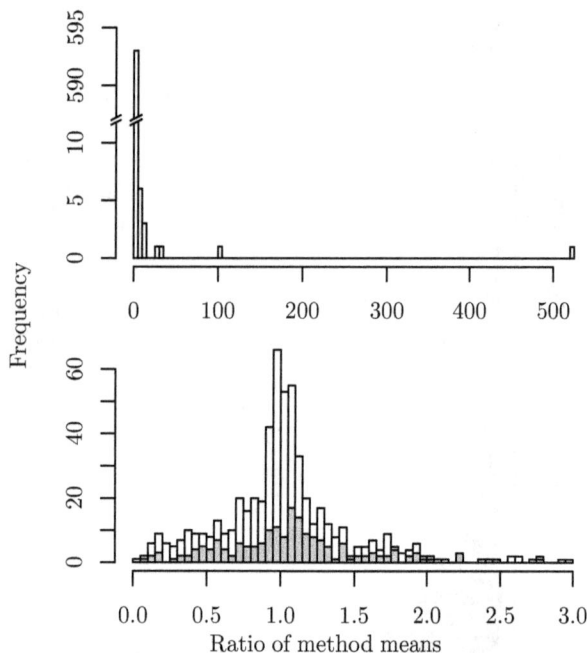

Figure 7: *Ratio between measurements reported by static instrumentation on methods during and after dynamic instrumentation. We (1) compute average static measurement per method from step S6, (2) compute average static measurement per method from step S8, (3) compute ratio of the dynamic average to the static average, (4) plot distribution of the ratios.*

Note broken scale in the top plot, the bottom plot provides a zoom in view. The gray bars denote statistically significant differences at $\alpha = 0.05$. Results smaller than one indicate methods that run faster when instrumented and vice versa.

and are probably not due to instrumentation. We have observed this behavior with most methods.

Figure 9 is related to question Q4, examining the effect of repeated JIT compilation on application outside measurement. Here, the figure shows how the average method execution time changes from near the start to near the end of the benchmark, with dynamic measurement performed in between. The median rate of 0.994 indicates a reasonably stable performance, however, at the end of the benchmark 25 % of methods are slower by a factor of over 1.12, and 25 % of methods are faster by a factor of over 0.87. The slow-down is statistically significant at $\alpha = 0.05$ for 8.9 % of methods, and the speed-up for 15.0 % of methods.

To determine whether the changes of method execution time in Figure 9 are due to dynamic measurement, Figure 10 shows how the average method execution time changes from near the start to near the end of the benchmark when no dynamic measurement is done. The median rate of 1.003, as well as the lower and upper quartiles of 0.76 and 1.16, are similar, however, the extreme values are further apart in Figure 9 than in Figure 10. We conclude that although the benchmark exhibits long term changes in the average method execution time all by itself, dynamic measurement increases the magnitude of the most extreme changes. When

no dynamic measurement is done, the slow-down is statistically significant at $\alpha = 0.05$ for 12.3 % of methods, and the speed-up for 16.2 % of methods.

By observing JIT compilation in steps S4 and S7, we also obtain statistics on the temporary disruptions due to code manipulation. As shown on Figure 11, JIT compilation takes more than 6.4 s to complete in 50 % of the probe insertion operations, and more than 3.7 s to complete in 50 % of the probe removal operations. Between 1 % and 2 % of code manipulation operations kept JIT compilation active for more than 60 s.

We conclude with Figure 12, which provides an answer to question Q6 about the total overhead associated with dynamic measurement instrumentation. The figure plots the distribution of processor utilization without dynamic instrumentation, observed in step S6, and the distribution of processor utilization with dynamic instrumentation, observed in step S8. Both cases are very similar, confirming earlier findings that small scale instrumentation does not incur significant overhead – in fact, the average utilization is 73.03 % without dynamic instrumentation and 72.17 % with dynamic instrumentation, with the difference statistically significant at $\alpha = 0.05$.

4.5 Threats To Validity

We close our results with discussing threats to validity. We focus on the threats to statistical validity, internal validity and external validity as the most relevant validity categories.

4.5.1 Statistical Validity

To guard against threats to statistical validity, we report detailed statistical properties alongside summary results. We also provide complete data at http://d3s.mff.cuni.cz/resources/icpe2016.

The statistical analysis is complicated by the fact that, for reasons inherent to the SPECjbb2015™ benchmark implementation, the individual observations of the method execution times are not necessarily independent. As a particular consequence, if too many methods exhibit sufficiently large phases in behavior, then the conclusions on the statistical significance of the results may be distorted due to observing method behavior in different phases.

4.5.2 Internal Validity

When examining internal validity, we are concerned with the possibility that the observed overhead is not due to dynamic instrumentation, and the possibility that the dynamic instrumentation introduces overhead that is not observed. Here, most dangerous are effects that can synchronize with dynamic measurement, because such effects can introduce a systematic error when measuring the overhead. We believe such systematic synchronization is unlikely, because we randomize both the choice of the measured method and the delay between measurements. Effects due to events inherent to dynamic measurement, such as dynamic code manipulation, are obviously part of the overhead by definition.

Measuring the total overhead as a change in processor utilization similarly ensures we observe all processor overhead. The benchmark is configured to perform a constant amount of work per unit of time, anything that changes the processor demand per unit of work is bound to change the processor utilization. This deserves some attention – while

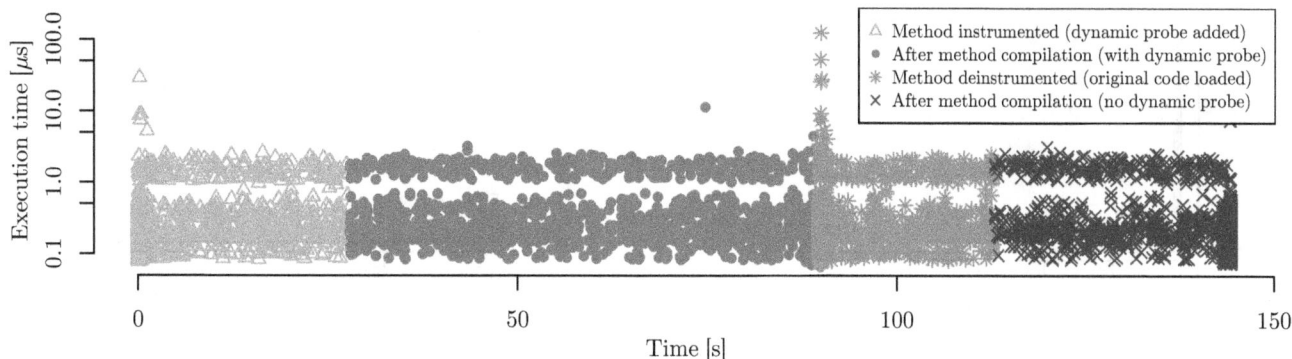

Figure 8: *Detailed measurement for the* `getArray` *method of the* `Data` *class in* `transport` *package. Method picked to demonstrate typical behavior. Note logarithmic scale.*

the benchmark does maintain a stable request rate, brief periods of increased overhead are likely to be compensated by queueing inside the benchmark. Because we perform every dynamic measurement for more than a minute, we believe we are likely to exhaust any queues that might mask the measurement overhead entirely.

As noted, we force a garbage collection cycle before each processor utilization measurement, and therefore influence the garbage collection overhead. Because utilization measurements happen much less frequently than young garbage collection cycles, we are not likely to influence the young collection overhead directly. We do make the full collection cycles more frequent, with multiple consequences – the total time spent in full collections is likely to be longer and the young collections may become more efficient because the references between generations are more likely to be live [17]. We believe this influence to be minor because no dynamic measurement instrumentation is likely to keep significant amounts of live data on the application heap for long, and the young collection overhead – which we are less likely to influence – should therefore dominate.

4.5.3 External Validity

External validity is concerned with how much the observed overhead generalizes to other dynamic instrumentation frameworks, other applications and other platforms. Much of the dynamic instrumentation framework revolves around the ability to redefine and retransform classes, frameworks that use the same mechanism are therefore likely to induce the same overhead due to code manipulation and code optimization. We note that this is pretty much the only reasonably portable dynamic instrumentation method currently available for Java, differences therefore should not be big.

Other dynamic instrumentation frameworks can also differ in their data storage and data processing implementation. There are many ways how this implementation can be optimized [37], we believe our implementation is reasonably straightforward to keep the results comparable with other probes written in Java.

To generalize to other applications, we must ask how much our measured application resembles other applications in those features that are relevant to dynamic instrumentation. Assuming the SPECjbb2015™ benchmark is reasonably rep-

resentative, we have to account for the differences introduced by static instrumentation:

– The instrumentation slows the benchmark down roughly by a factor of four. The effect is somewhat similar to using a slower platform, but the overhead is not distributed evenly – by adding similar overhead to each method, we slow down shorter methods more than longer ones in relative terms. With the measured application becoming faster, the dynamic instrumentation overhead will become relatively smaller.

– The instrumentation increases the size of all methods by a small constant amount, making compilation and inlining somewhat less likely. Examining the JIT log, we see a total of 520 kB in 24 k inlined methods and 7 k failed inline attempts for the original benchmark, and a total of 750 kB in 36 k inlined methods and 21 k failed inline attempts for the benchmark with static instrumentation.

– The instrumentation inserts JNI calls, whose impact on compiler behavior may depend on subtle memory model implementation details [15]. Hypothetically, JNI calls may require optimization barriers, leading to more conservative optimization of the measured application. We have not included a specific evaluation of this possibility into our experiment.

Given the platform specific character of our experiment, we do not make any specific claims outside our platform. We believe the platform is representative enough to account for a large percentage of existing systems, however, different platforms – especially different JVM implementations – may behave in an arbitrary manner, yielding entirely different dynamic instrumentation overhead.

5. RELATED WORK

Instrumentation overhead is an obvious concern for any measurement framework. Instrumentation can interact with the measured system, making the measured performance different from the performance exhibited otherwise. This problem is carefully explained by Malony in [18] – in this sense our work is an experimental study of performance intrusion and performance perturbation due to dynamic instrumentation in Java.

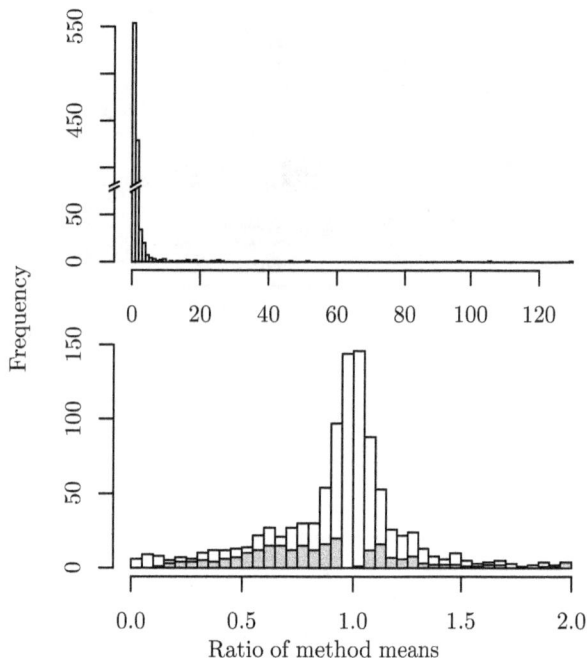

Figure 9: *Ratio between measurements reported by static instrumentation on methods before and after dynamic instrumentation. We (1) compute average static measurement per method from step S3, (2) compute average static measurement per method from step S10, (3) compute ratio of the initial average to the final average, (4) plot distribution of the ratios.*

Note broken scale in the top plot, the bottom plot provides a zoom in view. The gray bars denote statistically significant differences at $\alpha = 0.05$. Results smaller than one indicate methods that run faster at experiment startup than teardown and vice versa.

Figure 10: *Ratio between measurements reported by static instrumentation on methods at benchmark startup and before benchmark teardown without dynamic instrumentation. We (1) compute average static measurement per method from step S3, (2) compute average static measurement per method from step S10, (3) compute ratio of the initial average to the final average, (4) plot distribution of the ratios.*

Note broken scale in the top plot, the bottom plot provides a zoom in view. The gray bars denote statistically significant differences at $\alpha = 0.05$. Results smaller than one indicate methods that run faster at experiment startup than teardown and vice versa.

Malony and Shende have investigated the measurement overhead issues especially in the context of the Tau Performance System [30]. In [19], they describe a method for compensating the measurement overhead by subtracting the execution time added by the instrumentation from the individual measurements. The method assumes the computation is calibrated for particular application and platform. Our experiment is a case of such calibration that highlights the limits of accuracy in a system where the overhead of the same probe code can vary depending on the measured method, the call site, or even ephemeral compilation decisions. Our experiment extends the overhead investigation towards dynamic instrumentation, Tau focuses on more heterogeneous platforms and more distributed applications [20].

Technologically, our work is related to Java performance monitoring frameworks that collect data through instrumentation. A prominent representative is the Kieker Framework [36], which can use multiple aspect oriented instrumentation frameworks. Detailed experiments with AspectJ™ instrumentation are in [35], where a microbenchmark consisting of a single method with known execution time is used to measure the overhead of the individual instrumentation components, and two real life monitoring tasks are reported to have no observable overhead.

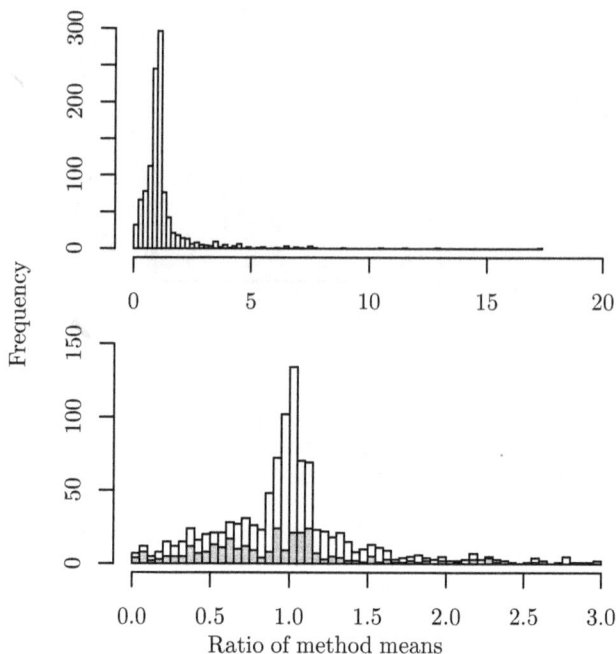

We extend the results reported in [35] in multiple directions. Some are related to the differences between static and dynamic instrumentation – in particular, we measure and examine dynamic instrumentation effects, which the static instrumentation constrains to the warmup period where the measurements are discarded. On the overall design level, we consider multiple threads, and we preserve realistic conditions for interaction between the probe code and the application code. In contrast, the microbenchmark in [35] enforces method timing by observing virtual thread time and waiting for a computed deadline [37]. This solution masks possible application timing changes due to instrumentation.

Kieker overhead experiments in [35] and [37] also very much complement our results – we do not deal in detail with overhead sources that are not unique to dynamic measurement instrumentation, in particular data storage and data processing. These are examined in detail especially in [37].

Another performance monitoring framework where our results are likely to apply is SPASS-meter [32]. SPASS-meter supports dynamic instrumentation, which can be used together with configurable monitoring scopes to restrict the instrumentation to relevant locations and therefore reduce overhead. Experiments that measure the instrumentation

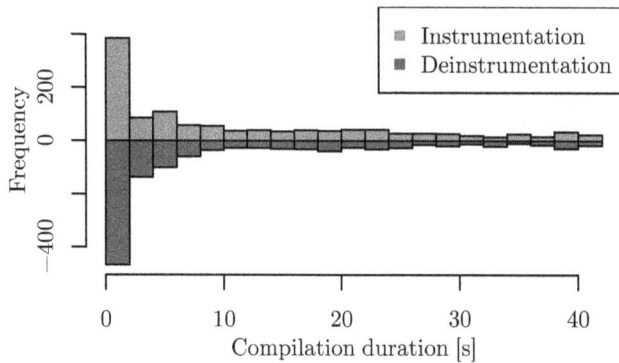

Figure 11: *Distribution of time from start of code manipulation to end of immediately following compilations.*

overhead are presented in [8], where SPECjvm2008™ is used as the benchmark application and processing overhead is defined as the change in the combined benchmark score. Again, we complement these experiments by providing a much more detailed look at the dynamic instrumentation effects, and we consider our results complemented by these experiments where the more general overhead issues are concerned.

Some monitoring framework experiments [27, 9] analyze overhead in terms of average changes to application throughput or response time, which is certainly reasonable with static instrumentation and enterprise application context. Our results are generally compatible as far as the overhead magnitude is concerned.

Instrumentation overhead is analogous to overhead introduced through aspect weaving, which is examined and attributed to particular code constructs in [6]. The need for overhead analysis in dynamic aspect weaving is advocated in [11], however, the authors performed only a limited set of experiments for dynamic aspect features supported at that time. A study examining the use of aspects for profiling of heap usage, object lifetime and execution time on the SPEC-jvm2008™ benchmark is available in [28], again with static instrumentation – in this context, we contribute experimental results relevant to dynamic aspect weaving.

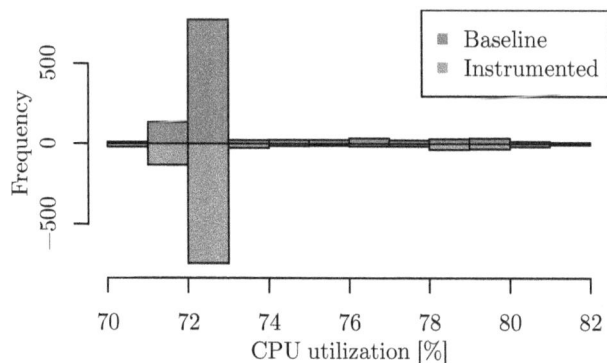

Figure 12: *Distribution of processor utilization with and without dynamic instrumentation.*

6. CONCLUSION

Dynamic performance monitoring is a promising method of reducing monitoring overhead. Coupled with dynamic instrumentation, it carries the promise of achieving zero overhead when not monitoring, because the probes that collect the monitoring data can be inserted and removed at will. On the other hand, dynamic instrumentation can interact with the execution platform in complex ways that give rise to new sources of overhead. We investigate these sources in the context of a dynamic measurement framework for Java.

Using experiments on a modified version of the SPECjbb-2015™ benchmark, we first show that the loss of measurement accuracy due to instrumentation overhead is not constant. On our platform, this limits practical measurements to methods whose execution time exceeds tens of microseconds, and also impacts the overhead compensation methods described in [19].

Next, we show that dynamic instrumentation can change the execution time of the instrumented method even when the overhead due to probes is not considered. This change can both slow down and speed up the method, sometimes significantly. We also show that the duration of the changes can vary, with short periods corresponding to compilation bursts on one end of the spectrum and periods spanning entire application execution on the other.

Looking at the compilation bursts, we show that although the code manipulation operations due to dynamic instrumentation are fast, the associated JIT compilation can last from several seconds to more than a minute. Any dynamic measurement framework looking to avoid disruptions due to JIT compilation should expect these effects to delay data collection.

Finally, we confirm that the total overhead in terms of application performance remains negligible when small scale instrumentation is deployed.

Our work is provided together with complete data and tools, available at http://d3s.mff.cuni.cz/resources/icpe2016.

Acknowledgments

This work was partially supported by Charles University Institutional Funding (SVV) and by the Research Group of the Standard Performance Evaluation Corporation (SPEC).

7. REFERENCES

[1] AspectJ, 2015. http://eclipse.org/aspectj.
[2] H. Boehm. Can seqlocks get along with programming language memory models?, 2012. http://www.hpl.hp.com/techreports/2012/HPL-2012-68.html.
[3] L. Bulej, T. Bureš, J. Keznikl, A. Koubková, A. Podzimek, and P. Tůma. Capturing performance assumptions using stochastic performance logic. In *Proc. ICPE 2012*, pages 311–322, New York, NY, USA, 2012. ACM.
[4] B. M. Cantrill, M. W. Shapiro, and A. H. Leventhal. Dynamic instrumentation of production systems. In *Proc. USENIX 2004*, 2004.
[5] A. Diaconescu, A. Mos, and J. Murphy. Automatic performance management in component based software systems. In *Proc. ICAC 2004*, 2004.

[6] B. Dufour, C. Goard, L. Hendren, O. de Moor, G. Sittampalam, and C. Verbrugge. Measuring the dynamic behaviour of AspectJ programs. In *Proc. OOPSLA 2004*, pages 150–169, New York, NY, USA, 2004. ACM.

[7] J. Ehlers, A. van Hoorn, J. Waller, and W. Hasselbring. Self-adaptive software system monitoring for performance anomaly localization. In *Proc. ICAC 2011*, pages 197–200, Karlsruhe, Germany, June 2011. ACM.

[8] H. Eichelberger and K. Schmid. Flexible resource monitoring of Java programs. *Journal of Systems and Software*, 93:163–186, July 2014.

[9] K. Govindraj, S. Narayanan, B. Thomas, P. Nair, and S. Peeru. On using AOP for application performance management. In *Proc. AOSD 2006*, pages 18–30, 2006.

[10] M. Grimmer, M. Rigger, L. Stadler, R. Schatz, and H. Mössenböck. An efficient native function interface for Java. In *Proc. PPPJ 2013*, pages 35–44, New York, NY, USA, 2013. ACM.

[11] M. Haupt and M. Mezini. Micro-measurements for dynamic aspect-oriented systems. In *Object-Oriented and Internet-Based Technologies*, number 3263 in LNCS, pages 81–96. Springer Berlin Heidelberg, 2004.

[12] V. Horký, P. Libič, L. Marek, A. Steinhauser, and P. Tůma. Utilizing performance unit tests to increase performance awareness. In *Proc. ICPE 2015*, pages 289–300, New York, NY, USA, 2015. ACM.

[13] T. Kalibera, L. Bulej, and P. Tuma. Benchmark precision and random initial state. In *Proc. SPECTS 2005*, pages 853–862. SCS, 2005.

[14] T. Kotzmann, C. Wimmer, H. Mössenböck, T. Rodriguez, K. Russell, and D. Cox. Design of the java hotspot client compiler for java 6. *ACM Transactions on Architecture and Code Optimization*, 5(1):7:1–7:32, May 2008.

[15] D. Lea. The JSR-133 cookbook for compiler writers, 2011. http://gee.cs.oswego.edu/dl/jmm/cookbook.html.

[16] P. Libič, L. Bulej, V. Horky, and P. Tůma. On the limits of modeling generational garbage collector performance. In *Proc. ICPE 2014*, pages 15–26, New York, NY, USA, 2014. ACM.

[17] P. Libič, L. Bulej, V. Horký, and P. Tůma. Estimating the impact of code additions on garbage collection overhead. In *Proc. EPEW 2015*, number 9272 in LNCS, pages 130–145. Springer International Publishing, Aug. 2015.

[18] A. D. Malony. *Performance Observability*. PhD thesis, University of Illinois at Urbana-Champaign, Champaign, IL, USA, 1990. AAI9114332.

[19] A. D. Malony and S. S. Shende. Overhead compensation in performance profiling. In *Proc. Euro-Par 2004*, number 3149 in LNCS, pages 119–132. Springer Berlin Heidelberg, Aug. 2004.

[20] A. D. Malony and S. S. Shende. Models for on-the-fly compensation of measurement overhead in parallel performance profiling. In *Proc. Euro-Par 2005*, number 3648 in LNCS, pages 72–82. Springer Berlin Heidelberg, Aug. 2005.

[21] L. Marek, A. Villazón, Y. Zheng, D. Ansaloni, W. Binder, and Z. Qi. DiSL: A domain-specific language for bytecode instrumentation. In *Proc.*

[22] T. Martinec, L. Marek, A. Steinhauser, P. Tůma, Q. Noorshams, A. Rentschler, and R. Reussner. Constructing performance model of JMS middleware platform. In *Proc. ICPE 2014*, pages 123–134, New York, NY, USA, 2014. ACM.

[23] A. Mos and J. Murphy. COMPAS: Adaptive performance monitoring of component-based systems. In *Proc. ICSE 2004 RAMSS*, 2004.

[24] Oracle. Java microbenchmark harness, 2013-2015. http://openjdk.java.net/projects/code-tools/jmh.

[25] P. Panchamukhi. Kernel debugging with kprobes, 2004. http://www.ibm.com/developerworks/library/l-kprobes/index.html.

[26] N. Park, B. Hong, and V. Prasanna. Tiling, block data layout, and memory hierarchy performance. *IEEE Transactions on Parallel and Distributed Systems*, 14(7):640–654, July 2003.

[27] T. Parsons, A. Mos, and J. Murphy. Non-intrusive end-to-end runtime path tracing for J2EE systems. *Software, IEEE Proceedings*, 153(4):149–161, Aug. 2006.

[28] D. J. Pearce, M. Webster, R. Berry, and P. H. J. Kelly. Profiling with AspectJ. *Software: Practice and Experience*, 37(7):747–777, June 2007.

[29] A. Sarimbekov, A. Sewe, W. Binder, P. Moret, and M. Mezini. JP2: Call-site aware calling context profiling for the Java Virtual Machine. *Science of Computer Programming*, 79:146–157, Jan. 2014.

[30] S. S. Shende and A. D. Malony. The Tau parallel performance system. *Int. J. High Perform. Comput. Appl.*, 20(2):287–311, May 2006.

[31] A. Shipilëv. Java Microbenchmark Harness (The Lesser of Two Evils). Presentation at Devoxx, 2013. http://shipilev.net/talks/devoxx-Nov2013-benchmarking.pdf.

[32] SPASS-meter monitoring framework, 2015. http://www.sse.uni-hildesheim.de/spass-meter.

[33] SPEC Java server business benchmark, 2015. http://www.spec.org/jbb2015.

[34] A. Tamches and B. P. Miller. Fine-grained dynamic instrumentation of commodity operating system kernels. In *Proc. OSDI 1999*, pages 117–130, Berkeley, CA, USA, 1999. USENIX Association.

[35] A. van Hoorn, M. Rohr, W. Hasselbring, J. Waller, J. Ehlers, S. Frey, and D. Kieselhorst. Continuous monitoring of software services: Design and application of the Kieker framework. Report, Department of Computer Science, Kiel University, Germany, Nov. 2009.

[36] A. van Hoorn, J. Waller, and W. Hasselbring. Kieker: A framework for application performance monitoring and dynamic software analysis. In *Proc. ICPE 2012*, pages 247–248, Boston, Massachusetts, USA, Apr. 2012. ACM.

[37] J. Waller, F. Fittkau, and W. Hasselbring. Application performance monitoring: Trade-off between overhead reduction and maintainability. In *Proceedings of the Symposium on Software Performance 2014*, pages 1–24, Stuttgart, Germany, Nov. 2014. University of Stuttgart.

The Value of Variance

Jesun Sahariar Firoz
jsfiroz@iu.edu

Martina Barnas
mbarnas@indiana.edu

Marcin Zalewski
zalewski@iu.edu

Andrew Lumsdaine
lums@iu.edu

Center for Research in Extreme Scale Technologies (CREST)
Indiana University, Bloomington, IN, USA

ABSTRACT

Measurements for distributed algorithms, such as performance results, are usually reported using averages, similarly to prevailing practice in other areas of computer science. We argue that including standard deviations offers additional information and that the minimal burden of providing standard deviations is outweighed by the benefits. We propose a new way of reporting run time speedup that incorporates standard deviation and demonstrate its usefulness in terms of two distributed graph algorithms.

Keywords

Statistical measurement; Speedup; Distributed algorithms; Performance metric; Standard deviation

1. INTRODUCTION

The increasing complexity of the software/hardware stack of modern machines, especially supercomputers, has made it hard to analyze performance of different algorithms for large-scale applications and reproduce relevant empirical results across different platforms. The variabilities incurred during reproduction of experimental results are generally acknowledged by the community and are attributed to the platform-dependent many-dimensional parameters. Considering all factors involved in experimental design, performance analysis has become an experimental science, made even more challenging due to the presence of massive irregularity and data dependency in important emerging problem areas. Hence, the baseline experimental analyses seldom incorporate uncertainty measures while reporting performance and thus lack in giving insight about an algorithm's performance.

Recently, Hoefler and Belli [14] compiled several guidelines to report results and advocated for the term *interpretability* in place of reproducibility. The authors call an experiment *interpretable* "if it provides enough information to allow scientists to understand the experiment, draw own conclusions, assess their certainty, and possibly generalize results". Many

papers in which experimental algorithms are proposed, lack the characteristic of being interpretable. In the papers reporting parallel performance, the general trend is to mention the performance of an algorithm in terms of speedup. Speedup is a metric for relative performance, defined as ratio of performance results (execution times). Typically, it is stated as a single number. However, due to different execution environments, system noise, network congestion etc., execution times are hardly deterministic. Hence, for example, a statement "algorithm A runs X times faster than algorithm B" is not always true. The speedup X should be bounded by an upper and lower limit based on the uncertainties from a set of sample runs. Some questions, for example: whether the execution times are normally distributed or not, how many runs are sufficient to predict the behavior of an algorithm, etc. remain at large and can, at least in principle, be tackled by some standard statistical methodologies (for example: Analysis of Variance (ANOVA) for the last case). However, compounding the issue is the expense of running experiments on supercomputers.

Another aspect of interpreting performance results comes from their role in aiding design of software systems. For example, our primary interest centers on designing runtime system for exascale. We use, e.g., performance of mini apps to guide the development of the runtime system. In this context, the goal is not to answer fundamental questions regarding validity of statistical approach; rather, it is to infer insight about the system such identifying bottlenecks. It is not desirable to run many experiments both due to cost and due to time it takes; on the contrary, we want to maximize insight while minimizing number of runs even if it is at the expense of rigor.

A good example to investigate the implications of proper performance reporting are irregular applications such as distributed graph algorithms. We have shown previously that for performance engineering of distributed graph algorithms, concentrating on the algorithm part of the application is not sufficient [10]. We called for more transparency in reporting results in literature, and advocated for documenting lower level runtime features that are usually overlooked [9]. This would allow us collectively construct a deeper understanding of these complex issues in order to uncover practical implications for performance engineering.

In order to be able to learn as a community, lessons learned across the field need to be generalizable and transferable. This condition is a given in hard sciences such as physics where what we know and how well we know it is inseparable. However, in computer science reporting results of

ICPE'16, March 12-18, 2016, Delft, Netherlands
© 2016 ACM. ISBN 978-1-4503-4080-9/16/03...$15.00
DOI: http://dx.doi.org/10.1145/2851553.2851573

experiments falls short of this expectation (for review, see [14]). As previously mentioned, what is typically reported are mean values without uncertainty of measurements. Thus, rigorously speaking, comparing results across different experiments or runs is not meaningful. The lack of rigor at this level percolates to undermine the ability to draw conclusions about more complex phenomena.

In this study we examine how inclusion of standard deviations of measurements illuminates performance results. For simplicity, we consider different *runs* on the same supercomputer. Each run consists of solving a set of *problem instances*. We acknowledge that methodologically, experiments in computer science are not as clear-cut as in physics, and lie somewhere in between physics and social science [17] inquiry.

Standard deviation is arguably the simplest of statistical measures, and is adequate in much of physics measurements. It is easy to implement, and we posit that it would improve the state of experiment analysis for practitioners. For these reasons, adding standard deviation as a measure of uncertainty is the focus of this present work. Moreover, standard deviation enable to expand definition of speedup, a commonly reported quantity, in a more meaningful way that allows for comparison across different runs and experiments. We refer to the expansion as *adjusted speedup equation*.

For the purpose of our study, we have chosen the prototypical irregular problem of graph traversal, in particular the single source shortest path (SSSP) problem. Graph traversal is a basic building block of other graph algorithms used in social network analytics, transportation optimization, artificial intelligence, power grids, and, in general, any problem where data consists of entities that connect and interact in irregular ways. Given a source and a destination in a graph, the SSSP problem asks to find the shortest route between the source and the destination. Specifically, we have chosen two different algorithms for finding single-source shortest paths, Δ-stepping algorithm [19] and K-level Asynchronous algorithm (KLA) [13], implementeded in two asynchronous many-task runtime systems called High Performance ParalleX 5 (HPX-5)[2] and AM++ [24]. The study was done within the context of development work of HPX-5.

The paper is organized as follows. Sec. 2 gives a summary of the method for evaluating and expressing uncertainty when multiple input quantities are involved. We then propose an adjusted speedup equation based on this discussion. Next, to make the paper self-contained, in Sec. 3, we give a brief overview of Δ-stepping and KLA based SSSP algorithms. In Sec. 4, we discuss the High Performance ParalleX 5 (HPX-5) and AM++ runtime we used to implement our SSSP algorithms. In Sec. 5, we show how including standard deviation in presenting and comparing performance results conveys valuable information that would otherwise be impossible to infer. In Sec. 6, we give a synopsis of related work. We provide our concluding remarks in Sec. 7.

2. STATISTICS OF UNCERTAINTY MEASUREMENTS

Calculation of speedup involves independent measurement of some metric (e.g., execution time, TEPS, etc.). Each of these independent performance metrics has uncertainty associated with it. When computing speedup, each of these uncertainties should be taken into account. In this section, we first recap the NIST [3] guidelines on uncertainty of measurement results, which dictate how to calculate output uncertainty when two or more independent inputs and their associated uncertainties are involved. Next, we use the NIST guidelines to propose an adjusted speedup equation, taking into consideration the associated uncertainties of performance metrics.

2.1 Background

National Institute of Standards and Technology (NIST) [3] provides guidance regarding uncertainty in physical experiments. Consider a quantity Y being measured, called the *measurand*, that can be expressed as a function of N other quantities $X_1, X_2, \ldots, X_N$.

$$Y = f(X_1, X_2, \ldots, X_N). \tag{1}$$

These quantities $X_1, X_2, \ldots, X_N$ can include other factors involved in a physical experiment, such as different observers, instruments, samples, laboratories and times at which observations are made. Consequently, the function f should contain all quantities that can contribute a significant uncertainty to the measurement result.

The *estimate of the measurand* or output quantity Y denoted by y, is derived from Eq. (1) using input estimates $x_1, x_2, \ldots, x_N$ for the values of N input quantities $X_1, X_2, \ldots, X_N$. Thus, the estimate of measurand is

$$y = f(x_1, x_2, \ldots, x_N). \tag{2}$$

The *uncertainty* of the measurement result y emerges from the component uncertainties $u(x_i)$, or u_i for brevity, of the input estimates x_i. Components of the uncertainty can be divided into two categories according to the method used to evaluate them: 1)*Type A Evaluation:* Method of evaluation of uncertainty is based on the statistical analysis of the series of observations; and 2)*Type B Evaluation:* Method of evaluation of uncertainty is based on means other than the statistical analysis of the series of observations. (These were formerly known as random and systematic uncertainty, respectively. NIST cautions against the old terminology since it can be misleading.) However evaluated, each component of uncertainty, u_i is equal to the positive square root of the estimated variance.

A useful quantity is the *relative standard uncertainty* defined as

$$u_r(x_i) = \frac{u(x_i)}{|x_i|}. \tag{3}$$

where x_i is assumed nonzero.

In this paper, we are interested in Type A evaluation. Let us consider the input quantity X_i. If we get the values for this input quantity by n independent observations $X_{i,k}$ under the same condition of measurement, then the input estimate x_i can be represented as the *sample mean*

$$x_i = \overline{X}_i = \frac{1}{n} \sum_{k=1}^{n} X_{i,k}. \tag{4}$$

An uncertainty component obtained by a Type A evaluation is represented by statistically estimated standard deviation σ_i of the sample mean, equal to the positive square root of the statistically estimated variance $\sigma_i{}^2$ and the associated number of degrees of freedom v_i. For such a component, the standard uncertainty is $u_i = \sigma_i$.

$$u(x_i) = u_i = \sigma_i = \left(\frac{1}{n(n-1)} \sum_{k=1}^{n} (X_{i,k} - \overline{X}_i)^2 \right)^{\frac{1}{2}}. \quad (5)$$

If multiple quantities $X_1, X_2, \ldots, X_N$ are involved in the calculation of estimate y, the *combined standard uncertainty of measurement results*, denoted by $\sigma(y)$, and representing the estimated standard deviation of the result, is the positive square root of the estimated variance $\sigma^2(y)$ obtained from,

$$\sigma^2(y) = \sum_{i=1}^{N} \left(\frac{\partial f}{\partial x_i} \right)^2 \sigma^2(x_i) + 2 \sum_{i=1}^{N-1} \sum_{j=i+1}^{N} \frac{\partial f}{\partial x_i} \frac{\partial f}{\partial x_j} \sigma(x_i, x_j). \quad (6)$$

Equation (6) is based on a first-order Taylor series approximation of the measurement equation Eq. (1) and is referred to as *the law of propagation of uncertainty*. The partial derivatives of f w.r.t. the X_i are called *sensitivity coefficients*, and are equal to the partial derivatives of f w.r.t the X_i evaluated at $X_i = x_i$. $\sigma(x_i)$ is the standard uncertainty associated with the input estimate x_i; and $\sigma(x_i, x_j)$ is the estimated covariance associated with x_i and x_j. If the input estimates x_i of the input quantities X_i can be assumed to be uncorrelated, then the second term vanishes.

As mentioned in [4], if the probability distribution characterized by the measurement result y and its combined standard uncertainty $\sigma(y)$ is approximately normal (Guassian), and $\sigma(y)$ is a reliable estimate of the standard deviation of y, then the interval $y - \sigma(y)$ to $y + \sigma(y)$ is expected to encompass approximately 68% of the distribution of values that could reasonably be attributed to the value of the quantity Y of which y is an estimate. This implies that it is believed with an approximate level of confidence of 68% that Y is greater than or equal to $y - \sigma(y)$ and less than or equal to $y + \sigma(y)$ which is commmonly written as $Y = y \pm \sigma(y)$.

2.2 Adjusted Speedup Equation

Let us assume that the average (mean) execution time for Algorithm A and Algorithm B is $\bar{t}_A$ and $\bar{t}_B$, respectively. Let us denote the standard deviations σ_A and σ_B, and assume that execution times for Algorithm A and Algorithm B are independent of each other. Typically, speedup S of Algorithm B over Algorithm A is calculated as a ratio of the two execution times:

$$S = \frac{\bar{t}_A}{\bar{t}_B}. \quad (7)$$

The uncertainly component, associated with $\bar{t}_A$ and $\bar{t}_B$ contributes to the calculation of combined standard uncertainty of the measurement result S. As $\bar{t}_A$ and $\bar{t}_B$ measures are uncorrelated, according to Eq. (6), the combined standard uncertainty σ of the measurement result S is

$$\sigma^2 = \frac{1}{\bar{t}_B^2} \sigma_A^2 + \frac{\bar{t}_A^2}{\bar{t}_B^4} \sigma_B^2. \quad (8)$$

Note that σ, just as the speedup S, is dimensionless while the standard deviations associated with execution times are dimensionful. We propose that speedup is reported with its uncertainty,

$$S_{adj} = S \pm \sigma, \quad (9)$$

which, combining Eq. (8) and Eq. (9), yields adjusted speedup equation in terms of observables $\bar{t}_A, \bar{t}_B, \sigma_A, \sigma_B$:

$$S_{adj} = \frac{\bar{t}_A}{\bar{t}_B} \pm \frac{1}{\bar{t}_B} \sqrt{\sigma_A^2 + \frac{\bar{t}_A^2}{\bar{t}_B^2} \sigma_B^2}. \quad (10)$$

3. OVERVIEW OF SSSP ALGORITHMS

Large scale graph processing requires distribution of the graph across multiple nodes and employing a distributed algorithm. Performance engineering for distributed graph algorithms is inherently difficult due to the irregular memory access patterns [18]. Graph algorithm performance depends not only on the algorithm logic but also on factors such as the runtime system, synchronization, lock-free data structure, processing order, etc. In this paper, we demonstrate the usefulness of including uncertainty measurement with the example of single source shortest path problem solved by two different distributed algorithms: Δ-stepping and KLA.

Conceptually, all data driven graph algorithms can be described as an *Abstract Graph Machine* (AGM) [16]. The primitive unit of processing in AGM is a *work item*, which is a tuple that has a vertex or an edge together with several *graph properties*. For example, a SSSP work item will have a vertex and distance. AGM comprises of a work item processor and a work item ordering component. The processor executes basic algorithm logic (e.g., the "relax" operation in SSSP). The ordering component partitions work items into ordered equivalence classes and feeds the smallest partition back into the processor.

Definition 1. *An **Abstract Graph Machine**(AGM) is a 5-tuple (G, WorkItems, PF, $<_{wis}$, S), where*

1. *$G = (V, E)$ is the **input graph**,*

2. *WorkItems $\subseteq (V \times P_0 \times P_1 \cdots \times P_n)$ where each P_i represents a graph property,*

3. *$PF : WorkItems \longrightarrow \mathcal{P} (WorkItems)$ is the **processing function**,*

4. *$<_{wis}$ - **Strict weak ordering relation** defined on WorkItems*

5. *$S (\subseteq WorkItems)$ - **Initial** WorkItems **set**.*

The AGM processing is driven by the *WorkItems*. The initial *WorkItems* set, $WIS_0 = S$. Let $WIS_{current}$ be the currently processing *WorkItems* set, then we calculate the next active *WorkItems* set as follows;

Input to the processing function :-
$$WIS_{in} = \text{Ordering}(WIS_{current})$$

Let, $SPF (\subseteq WorkItems) = \bigcup_{w_j \in WIS_{in}} PF(w_j)$

Now we calculate *next WorkItems* set as follows;
$$WIS_{next} = SPF \cup (WIS_{current} - WIS_{in})$$

The AGM terminates when $WIS_{next} = \{\}$.

Figure 1 depicts how ordering and processing functions interact with each other. Next we describe KLA and Δ-stepping algorithm in terms of AGM. Interestingly, most of the algorithms share a common processing function. In general the SSSP processing function ($SSSP\_PF$) can be defined as follows:

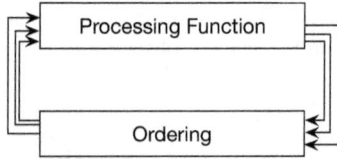

Figure 1: An Overview of *Abstract Graph Machine*

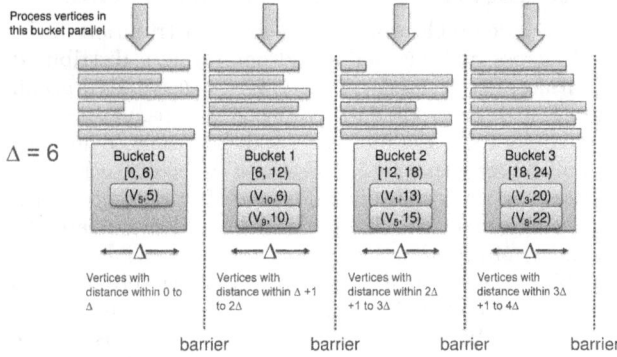

Figure 2: How Δ-stepping algorithm works

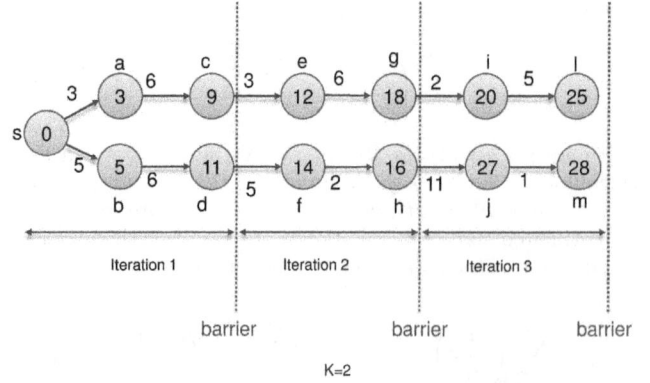

Figure 3: How algorithms progress in KLA paradigm

3.1 Δ-Stepping Algorithm

Δ-Stepping [19] arrange tasks into distance ranges (buckets) of size $\Delta(\in \mathbb{N})$ and execute buckets in order. Within a bucket, tasks are not ordered, and can be executed in any order (Fig. 2). Processing a bucket may produce extra work for the same bucket or for the successive buckets.

Definition 3. $<_\Delta$ *is a binary relation defined on SSSP WorkItems as follows; Let $w_1, w_2 \in$ SSSP Workset, then*
$$w_1 <_\Delta w_2 \text{ iff } \lfloor w_1[1]/\Delta \rfloor < \lfloor w_2[1]/\Delta \rfloor$$

Δ-Stepping algorithm partition SSSP *WorkItems* set based on relation $<_\Delta$ ($<_\Delta$ is a strict weak ordering relation.)

Proposition 1. Δ*-Stepping Algorithm is an instance of AGM where*

1. *$G = (V, E)$ is the input graph*

2. *WorkItems = SSSP WorkItems*

3. *PF = SSSP_PF*

4. *Strict weak ordering relation $<_{wis} = <_\Delta$*

5. *$S = \{<v_s, 0>\}$ where $v_s \in V$ and v_s is the source vertex.*

3.2 KLA SSSP Algorithm

The KLA SSSP algorithm [13] requires both Distance property and Level property in the *WorkItems* set. The Level property is needed to track the number of levels, k,

Definition 2. *SSSP_PF : SSSP WorkItems $\longrightarrow$ Partition $\mathcal{P}$ (SSSP WorkItems)*
$$SSSP\_PF(w) = \begin{cases} \{w_k|w_k[0] \in neighbors(w[0]) \text{ and} \\ \quad w_k[1] = w[1] + weight(w[0], w_k[0])\} \\ \quad \text{if } w[1] < distance(w[0]) \\ \{\} \quad else \end{cases}$$

asynchronously processed (Fig. 3). Therefore, we define $SSSP\ KLA\ WorkItems \subseteq (V \times Distance \times Level)$.

The processing function for KLA SSSP is defined in Definition 4.

Definition 4. *KLA_PF : SSSP KLA WorkItems $\longrightarrow$ $\mathcal{P}$ (SSSP KLA WorkItems)*
$$KLA\_PF(w) = \begin{cases} \{w_k|w_k[0] \in neighbors(w[0]) \text{ and} \\ \quad w_k[1] = w[1] + weight(w[0], w_k[0]) \\ \quad and\ w_k[2] = w[2] + 1\} \\ \quad \text{if } w[0] < distance(w[0]) \\ \\ \{\} \quad else \end{cases}$$

The strict weak ordering relation for SSSP KLA is defined in Definition 5:

Definition 5. *$<_{sssp\_kla}$ is a binary relation defined on SSSP KLA WorkItems as follows:*
Let $w_1, w_2 \in$ SSSP KLA WorkItems, then;
$$w_1 <_{sssp\_kla} w_2 \text{ iff } \lfloor w_1[2]/k \rfloor < \lfloor w_2[2]/k \rfloor$$

Note, the definition of $<_{sssp\_kla}$ is quite close to the definition of $<_\Delta$.

KLA SSSP algorithm partition SSSP *WorkItems* set based on relation $<_{sssp\_kla}$ ($<_{sssp\_kla}$ is a strict weak ordering relation.)

Proposition 2. *KLA SSSP Algorithm is an instance of AGM where;*

1. *$G = (V, E)$ is the input graph*

2. *WorkItems = SSSP WorkItems*

3. *PF = KLA_PF*

4. *Strict weak ordering relation $<_{wis} = <_{sssp\_kla}$*

5. *$S = \{<v_s, 0>\}$ where $v_s \in V$ and v_s is the source vertex.*

4. OVERVIEW OF THE RUNTIMES

We implemented two SSSP algorithms in two different runtime systems, AM++ [24] and HPX-5 [2]. HPX-5 is a high performance runtime library whose implementation is based on the the ParalleX execution model [6] targetted for exascale computing. AM++ is our legacy system centered around active messaging of the Active Pebbles [25] model.

HPX-5 comprises of a set of main components: localities, global memory, Lightweight threads and actions, Lightweight Control Objects (LCO) and parcels. These components along with the scheduler and network transport drive program execution in HPX-5. HPX-5 is intended to enable dynamic adaptive resource management and task scheduling. It creates a global name and address space (Partitioned Global Address Space (PGAS) and Active Global Address Space (AGAS)) structured through a hierarchy of processes, each of which serve as execution contexts and may span multiple nodes. It is event-driven, enabling the migration of continuations and the movement of work to data, when appropriate, based on sophisticated local control synchronization objects (e.g., futures, dataflow). HPX-5 is an evolving runtime system being employed to quantify effects of latency, overhead, contention, and parallelism. These performance parameters determine a tradeoff space within which dynamic control is performed for best performance. It is an area of active research driven by complex applications and advances in HPC architecture.

AM++ supports fine-grained parallelism of active messages with communication optimization techniques such as object-based addressing, active routing, message coalescing, message reduction, and termination detection. While less feature-rich than HPX-5, active messages share the fine-grained parallelism approach with HPX-5. In addition, AM++ is a relatively well-optimized implementation to balance the competing needs of quick delivery of work vs. minimal communication overhead.

While AM++ and HPX-5 share some features and goals, there are important differences between them. AM++ is designed for bulk processing of distributed messages, while HPX-5 is a complete system providing inter and intra-node parallelism. HPX-5 provides global address space while AM++ provides only a lightweight object-based addressing layer. In HPX-5 work is divided into first-class tasks with stacks, while AM++ only executes message handler functions on the incoming message data. These features result in significant differences in scheduling.

5. INSIGHTS FROM THE STANDARD DEVIATION

In this section we illustrate how including standard deviations provides additional insight that is not evident from the averaged quantities alone. We present weak scaling performance measurements obtained during development of HPX-5 runtime, to indicate how this way of looking at data can aid in development process. For comparison, we run the same experiments under a different, less feature rich, but comparatively well optimized runtime, AM++. We implemented KLA and Δ-stepping algorithms in these runtimes. Both of these algorithms combine asynchronous processing with a global synchronization barrier. The degree of asynchrony is regulated by a parameter (k in KLA and Δ in Δ-stepping). For the results presented here for HPX-5, we used $k = 2$ and $\Delta = 1$ which minimize the asynchronous work.[1] Even with these choices, depending on the input data, KLA can be expected to perform more asynchronous work than Δ-stepping.

---

[1] The reader is reminded that we wanted to document how the proposed methodology aids in development. We are not attempting to achieve optimal performance or to test the algorithms.

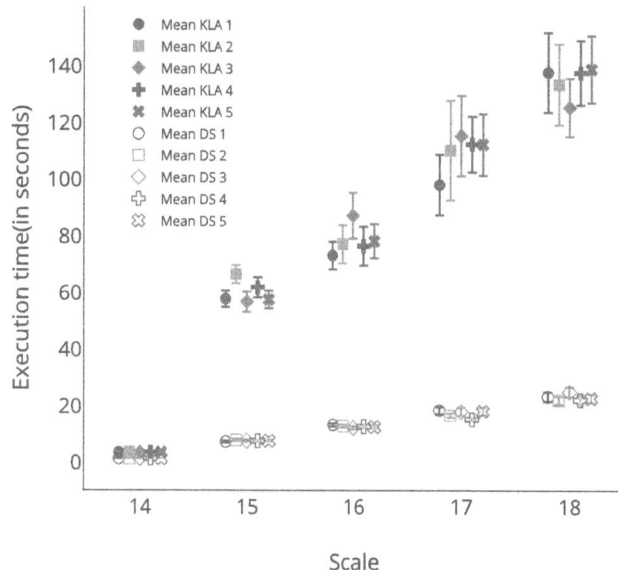

Figure 4: Weak scaling results for KLA (top) and Δ-stepping (bottom) on HPX-5 with standard deviations for 5 runs. The central point for each run is the average time for the run; the error bars show the standard deviation. Maximum edge-weight for the input graph is 255.

5.1 Experimental Setup

We conducted our experiments on Indiana University's BigRed 2 Cray XE6/XK7 supercomputer [1]. The compute nodes are connected with Gemini interconnect. Each compute node contains two AMD Opteron 16-core Abu Dhabi x86_64 CPUs and 64 GB of RAM. We used 16 threads per compute node for both AM++ and HPX-5. We compiled our program with gcc version 4.9.3 compiler with optimization flag $O3$ enabled.

For input graph generation process, we used Graph500 specification [5] with RMAT generator. Edge weights are assigned based on a pseudo-random number generator. For both AM++ and HPX-5 weak scaling results in terms of execution time and speedup, we used 1, 2, 4, 8 and 16 computing nodes for scale 14, 15, 16, 17 and 18, respectively. By scale x, we mean there are 2^x vertices in the generated graph.

Each data point at a given scale shows one run encompassing 8 different problem instances. Problem instances correspond to different starting points (sources). Both algorithms exhibit some sensitivity to the starting point. We find that the sensitivity appears to be consistent, and thus, an inconsistency suggests occurrence of a systemic effect. As evident from the figure, we measured 5 runs for each scale. We calculated the speedup by taking the ratio of execution time for KLA to Δ-stepping algorithm.

5.2 Reporting Speedup Uncertainty

5.2.1 On HPX-5 Runtime

Figs. 4 and 6 show weak scaling results on HPX-5 runtime for Δ-stepping and KLA SSSP algorithms with two different input graphs with maximum edge weight of 255 and 100, respectively. We chose two different graph inputs to verify whether the anticipated speedup plots (discussed later) have similar trends. The error bars shown correspond

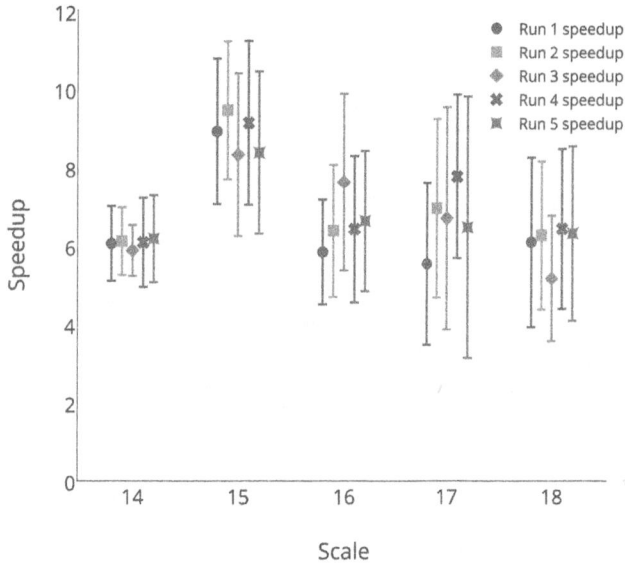

Figure 5: Adjusted speedup (ratio of KLA and Δ-stepping execution time) on HPX-5 with calculated standard deviations. Maximum edge-weight for the input graph is 255.

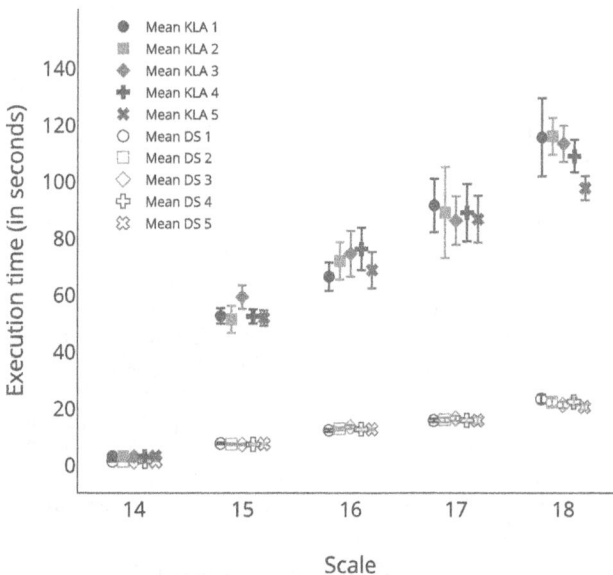

Figure 6: Weak scaling results for KLA (top) and Δ-stepping (bottom) on HPX-5 with standard deviations for 5 runs. The central point for each run is the average time for the run; the error bars show the standard deviation. Maximum edge-weight for the input graph is 100.

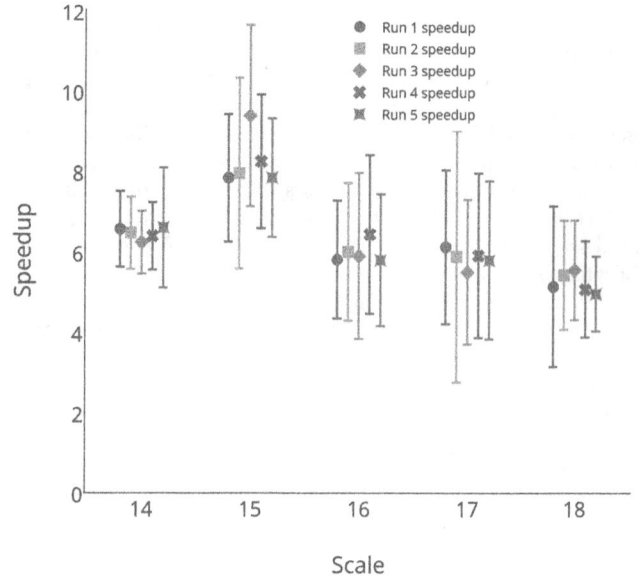

Figure 7: Adjusted speedup (ratio of KLA and Δ-stepping execution time) on HPX-5 with calculated standard deviations. Maximum edge-weight for the input graph is 100.

to the standard deviations of the average execution times. Δ-stepping algorithm is faster than KLA. The figures show that in comparison to Δ-stepping, the standard deviations from the average execution time are larger for KLA algorithm.

Although this observation is intuitive and is incorporated in practice to-date, the next related question to ask ourselves is what speedup can we anticipate when comparing the execution times for both algorithms on different runtimes or even across different runs on the same runtime? Is there a way to quantify the observable uncertainty in speedup by incorporating simple measurement like combining uncertainty measures for average execution times for both algorithms? Is saying that an algorithm runs "five times" faster good enough? We address these questions next in connection to Sec. 2.2, where we presented an equation to calculate adjusted speedup. Figures 5 and 7 present the speedup plots with standard deviations, calculated from Eq. (10). In all 5 runs, we use the same input and problem instances for a particular scale. As can be seen from the figure, the speedup can be expected to vary significantly within the approximate range of 3 to 11. But interestingly all the averages across different runs lie within the range indicated by the standard deviations for all 5 runs. For example, in Fig. 5, we can see that average speedup for run 1 centers around 6 for most cases except for scale 15, due to distributed execution on 2 nodes. But as we increase the number of nodes, the speedup again settles around 6 due to increasing network latency. Additionally, we can see that speedups across different runs cluster together pretty well. This is helpful in conjunction with the calculated deviation for speedup (Eq. (8)). Assuming that the combined uncertainty for speedup is normally distributed, Figs. 5 and 7 shows us the expected range of speedups with approximate level of confidence of 68%. Moreover Figs. 5 and 7 both show similar speedup behaviour for two different graph inputs.

5.2.2 On AM++ Runtime

Figure 8 and Fig. 9 show weak scaling results on AM++.

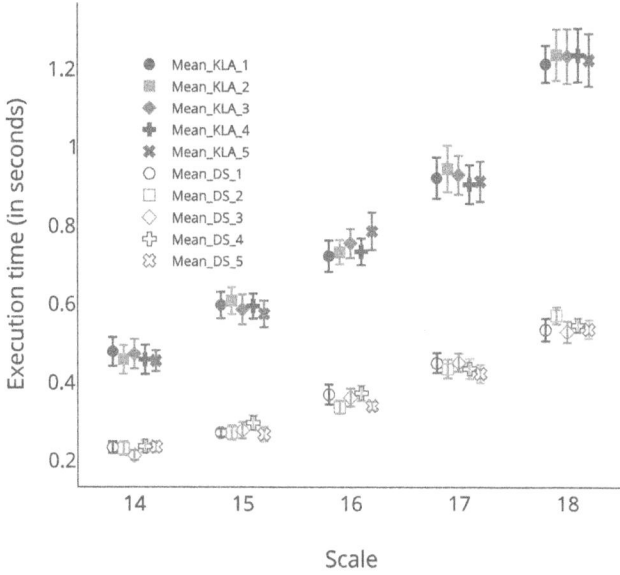

Figure 8: Weak scaling results for KLA and Δ-stepping on AM++ with standard deviations for 5 runs. The central point for each run is the average execution time for the run; error bars show the standard deviation. Maximum edge-weight for the input graph is 100.

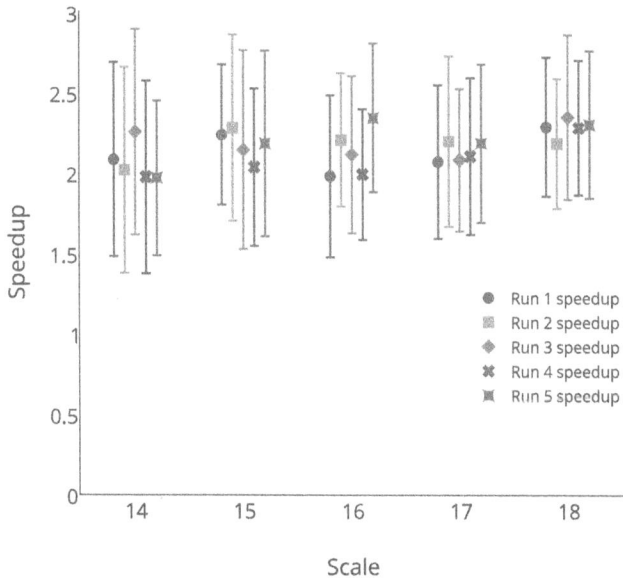

Figure 9: Adjusted speedup (ratio of KLA and Δ-stepping execution time) on AM++ with calculated standard deviations. Maximum edge-weight for the input graph is 100.

As both Δ-stepping and KLA algorithms execute faster on AM++, the standard deviations of the average of the execution time is small in AM++ compared to HPX-5. Since the execution times for both of the algorithms are significantly less, the speedup variability is also small in AM++, as can be seen from Fig. 9. This is particularly true as we increase the scale, for example scale 17 and 18.

5.2.3 Comparing Speedup Across Runtimes

More importantly, including speedup variability can give us additional information about the performance of Δ-stepping and KLA across two different runtimes AM++ and HPX-5. From Fig. 5 we can see that the speedup on HPX-5 centers around 6 and varies approximately within the range of ±3. From Fig. 9 we see that the speedup on AM++ is around 2 with an approximate range of ±1. So the variability in speedup is roughly 50% in both cases.

5.2.4 Usefulness of Relative Standard Uncertainty

We also calculate *relative standard uncertainty* (RSU) from Eq. (3). We plot the calculated RSUs in Figs. 10 to 12. These plots, based on standard deviation calculation are also useful.

For example, in Fig. 11, for scale 17 with 8 nodes, the RSU for KLA algorithm for run 2 is about 0.5. We investigated why this is the case and found out that problem instance 7 took 50% more time compared to the average execution time. Then, we looked into the execution time for problem instance 7 from other runs (for example Table 1 compares KLA algorithm execution time from run 2 and run 5). We saw that, with KLA, problem instance 7 consistently took longer time to finish across different runs. But it took the maximum time in run 2. This additional insight lend problem instance 7 for further investigation. We would have lost this valuable information if we only considered average execution time. Computing standard deviation and taking it into consideration as a measure for uncertainty empowers us with supplementary information.

We can also see that all the datapoints with maximum RSUs belong to KLA algorithm executions. This is an indication that KLA implementation in HPX-5 exercises certain runtime scheduling and network communication patterns which stress the runtime. It also tells us that KLA algorithm is more sensitive to the starting point (source vertex) of a SSSP problem. Based on this observation, we took a second look at the execution time of each individual SSSP problem instance for both Δ-stepping and KLA algorithms. We found out that Δ-stepping algorithm solves each problem instance within an average execution time of 15 seconds, having small variability in execution time for each problem instance. On the other hand, KLA execution time varies hugely among different problem instances. It is anticipated that, based on the problem instance (source) and graph input, different problem instance will take unequal time. But the execution time for Δ-stepping algorithm suggests that there is a better way to schedule tasks within runtime. This insight can be useful to optimize KLA algrithm's execution time by gathering statistics about number of exchanged network messages, scheduling polcies like number of work stealing, thread yielding, queue size of workitems etc. We leverage instrumentation infrastructure in HPX-5 for this purpose.

We have another interesting observation with reference to Fig. 12. Again, on AM++ for scale 17 with 8 nodes, we

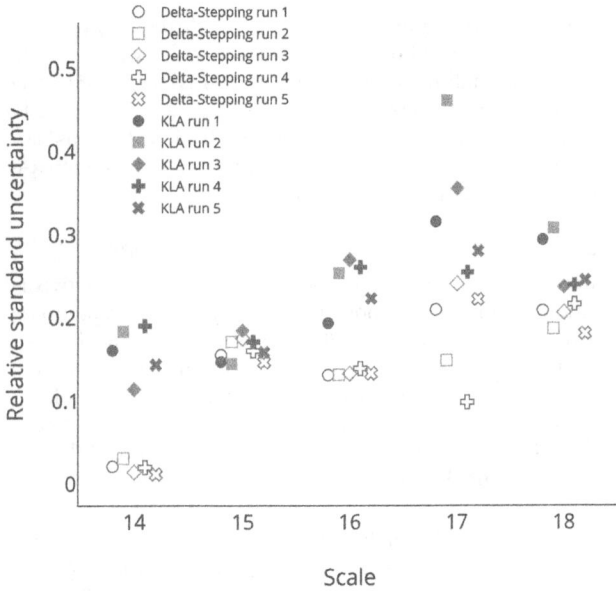

Figure 10: Relative standard uncertainty of execution time in HPX for Δ-stepping and KLA algorithms. Maximum edge-weight for the input graph is 255.

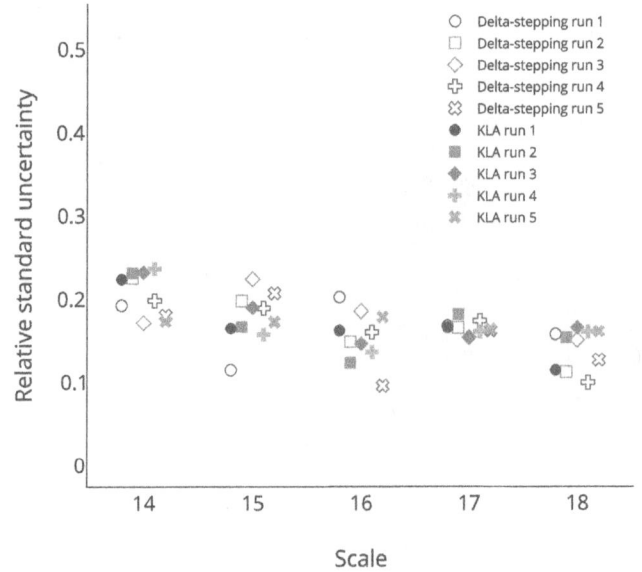

Figure 11: Relative standard uncertainty of execution time in HPX for Δ-stepping and KLA algorithms. Maximum edge-weight for the input graph is 100.

see that the RSUs are quite close for both algorithms. This also calls for further investigation.

6. RELATED WORK

Several researchers pointed out the shortcomings of presented results in computer science literature. Mytkowicz et al. [20] showed that seemingly innocuous experimental setup details, such as the UNIX environment size or the benchmark link order, can introduce a significant measurement bias in a system evaluation. Harji et al. [12] discussed about bugs and performance regressions that result as the

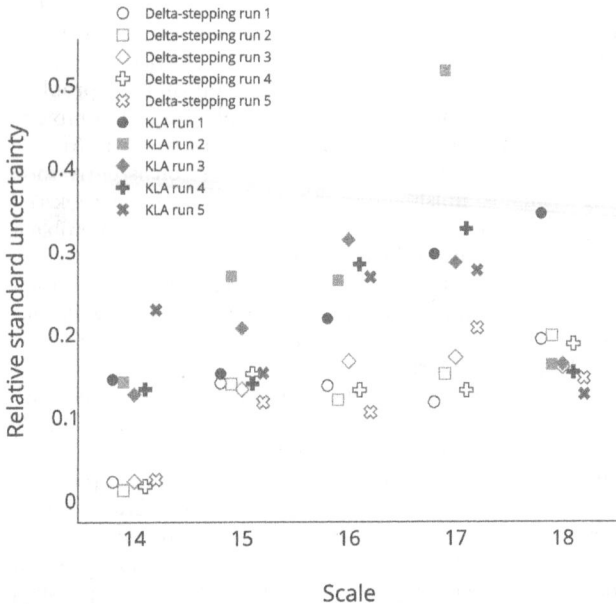

Figure 12: Relative standard uncertainty of execution time in AM++ for Δ-stepping and KLA algorithms. Maximum edge-weight for the input graph is 100.

Linux kernel evolves. For a comprehensive summary of related research see [8, 14].

A lot of attempts and proposals have been made to make computer and computational science experiments reproducible. Guerrera et al. [11] partitioned the space of computational experiments into *problem*, *method*, and *system*. Based on this partitioning, they bring forth a taxonomy for stencil benchmark results and categorized them as *replicable*, *recomputable*, and *reproducible*. Hunold and Träff [15] also urged for *reproducible* parallel computing research. Several researchers [21–23] advocated for including statistical analyses in computer science experiments. de Oliveira et al. [7] successfully demonstrated the use of quantile regression instead of ANOVA for non-normally distributed data to conduct performance evaluation. Very recently, Hoefler and Belli [14], coined the term *interpretability* and recommended a set of guidelines for scientific benchmarking based on statistical analyses. Their recommendation is based on the fact that algorithms designed for supercomputers heavily rely on particular architectures and execution environments, thus making reproducibility harder.

7. CONCLUSION

Performance engineering hinge on understanding results of conducted experiments. The key is to identify the bottlenecks and then put a concerted effort in removing these bottlenecks and optimize runtime parameters. For distributed algorithms, where complex machine architecture, network and system environment are integral part of execution, unpredictable behavior can always happen in any part of the system stack. We should account for uncertainty involved during the experiments. In this paper, we proposed a new equation to calculate speedup and showed how inclusion of standard deviation provide some insights about uncertainties associated with performance of algorithms. Under additional assumptions about the underlying distribution, the formula we introduced can become powerful tool to compare perfor-

Table 1: Execution time for KLA for different problem instances

Run	Problem Instances							
	1	2	3	4	5	6	7	8
2	67.1721137	69.1144691	58.2407584	95.0383578	81.5043034	66.1346017	196.359002	71.0783083
5	68.2187308	64.6999926	73.1340169	66.5868368	111.286377	78.3502649	127.3131639	96.6814628

mance across different set of parameters such as runtimes, algorithms etc. Any further interpretation of combined uncertainty is subject to future investigation.

8. ACKNOWLEDGMENTS

This work is supported by the NSF under grant 1111888 and grant no. 1319520 and by in part by Lilly Endowment, Inc.

References

[1] Big Red II at Indiana University. https://kb.iu.edu/d/bcqt#overview.

[2] HPX website. http://hpx.crest.iu.edu/.

[3] The NIST reference on constants, units, and uncertainty. http://physics.nist.gov/cuu/Uncertainty/basic.html, Sept. 2015.

[4] Combining uncertainty components. http://physics.nist.gov/cgi-bin/cuu/Info/Uncertainty/combination.html, Sept. 2015.

[5] The Graph500 List. http://www.graph500.org/, June 2015.

[6] ParalleX Execution Model. https://www.crest.iu.edu/projects/xpress/_media/public/parallex_v3-1_03182013.doc, June 2015.

[7] A. B. de Oliveira, S. Fischmeister, A. Diwan, M. Hauswirth, and P. F. Sweeney. Why you should care about quantile regression. *SIGARCH Comput. Archit. News*, 41(1):207–218, Mar. 2013. ISSN 0163-5964.

[8] A. B. de Oliveira, J.-C. Petkovich, T. Reidemeister, and S. Fischmeister. Datamill: Rigorous performance evaluation made easy. In *Proceedings of the 4th ACM/SPEC International Conference on Performance Engineering*, ICPE '13, pages 137–148, New York, NY, USA, 2013. ACM. ISBN 978-1-4503-1636-1.

[9] J. S. Firoz, T. A. Kanewala, M. Zalewski, M. Barnas, and A. Lumsdaine. The anatomy of large-scale distributed graph algorithms. *CoRR*, abs/1507.06702, 2015. URL http://arxiv.org/abs/1507.06702.

[10] J. S. Firoz, M. Zalewski, T. A. Kanewala, M. Barnas, and A. Lumsdaine. Importance of runtime considerations in performance engineering of large-scale distributed graph algorithms. In *Euro-Par 2015: Parallel Processing Workshops*, pages 553–564. Springer International Publishing, 2015.

[11] D. Guerrera, H. Burkhart, and A. Maffia. Reproducible experiments in parallel computing: Concepts and stencil compiler benchmark study. In *Euro-Par 2014: Parallel Processing Workshops - Euro-Par 2014 International Workshops, Porto, Portugal, August 25-26, 2014, Revised Selected Papers, Part I*, pages 464–474, 2014.

[12] A. S. Harji, P. A. Buhr, and T. Brecht. Our troubles with linux and why you should care. In *Proceedings of the Second Asia-Pacific Workshop on Systems*, APSys '11, pages 2:1–2:5, New York, NY, USA, 2011. ACM. ISBN 978-1-4503-1179-3.

[13] Harshvardhan, A. Fidel, N. M. Amato, and L. Rauchwerger. KLA: A New Algorithmic Paradigm for Parallel Graph Computations. In *Proceedings of the 23rd International Conference on Parallel Architectures and Compilation*, pages 27–38. ACM, 2014.

[14] T. Hoefler and R. Belli. Scientific Benchmarking of Parallel Computing Systems. Nov. 2015. accepted at IEEE/ACM International Conference on High Performance Computing, Networking, Storage and Analysis (SC15).

[15] S. Hunold and J. L. Träff. On the state and importance of reproducible experimental research in parallel computing. *CoRR*, abs/1308.3648, 2013. URL http://arxiv.org/abs/1308.3648.

[16] T. A. Kanewala, M. Zalewski, M. Barnas, J. S. Firoz, and A. Lumsdaine. Abstract graph algorithms with spatial-temporal execution. In preparation.

[17] J. Levin, J. A. Fox, and D. R. Forde. *Elementary statistics in social research*. Allyn & Bacon, 2010.

[18] A. Lumsdaine, D. Gregor, B. Hendrickson, and J. Berry. Challenges in parallel graph processing. *Parallel Processing Letters*, 17(1):5–20, 2007 2007.

[19] U. Meyer and P. Sanders. Δ-stepping: A Parallelizable Shortest Path Algorithm. *Journal of Algorithms*, 49(1):114–152, 2003.

[20] T. Mytkowicz, A. Diwan, M. Hauswirth, and P. F. Sweeney. Producing wrong data without doing anything obviously wrong! *SIGPLAN Not.*, 44(3):265–276, Mar. 2009. ISSN 0362-1340.

[21] L. Peterson and V. S. Pai. Experience-driven experimental systems research. *Commun. ACM*, 50(11):38–44, Nov. 2007. ISSN 0001-0782.

[22] W. F. Tichy. Should computer scientists experiment more? *Computer*, 31(5):32–40, May 1998. ISSN 0018-9162.

[23] J. Vitek and T. Kalibera. Repeatability, reproducibility, and rigor in systems research. In *Proceedings of the Ninth ACM International Conference on Embedded Software*, EMSOFT '11, pages 33–38, New York, NY, USA, 2011. ACM. ISBN 978-1-4503-0714-7.

[24] J. J. Willcock, T. Hoefler, N. G. Edmonds, and A. Lumsdaine. AM++: A Generalized Active Message Framework. In *Proce. 19th Int. Conf. on Parallel Architectures and Compilation Techniques*, pages 401–410. ACM, 2010.

[25] J. J. Willcock, T. Hoefler, N. G. Edmonds, and A. Lumsdaine. Active pebbles: a programming model for highly parallel fine-grained data-driven computations. In *Proc. 16th ACM symposium on Principles and practice of parallel programming*, pages 305–306. ACM, 2011.

Experimental Performance Evaluation of Different Data Models for a Reflection Software Architecture over NoSQL Persistence Layers

Sara Fioravanti
University of Florence
Florence, Italy
sara.fioravanti@unifi.it

Simone Mattolini
University of Florence
Florence, Italy
simone.mattolini@unifi.it

Fulvio Patara
University of Florence
Florence, Italy
fulvio.patara@unifi.it

Enrico Vicario
University of Florence
Florence, Italy
enrico.vicario@unifi.it

ABSTRACT

The recent rise of the NoSQL movement motivates investigation on the performance impact that new persistence approaches can bring in the model-driven re-engineering of a consolidated object-oriented software architecture.

We report comparative experimental performance results attained by combining a pattern-based domain logic with a persistence layer based on different paradigms and we describe how data model is persisted in various implementation based on MySQL, Neo4j, and MongoDB.

Keywords

Model-driven performance engineering, Reflection pattern, Relational databases, NoSQL databases, MySQL, MongoDB, Neo4j, Electronic Health Record (EHR) systems.

1. INTRODUCTION

Non-functional requirements of *changeability* and *adaptability* [1] have primary relevance for a large class of software intensive systems that are intended for managing great volumes of data with a high degree of variety in the structure of contents. The attainment of these qualities can be largely facilitated by the assumption of a tailored software architecture.

In particular, the *Reflection* architectural pattern [2] provides a mechanism that allows for dynamically changing data structure and system behaviour at run-time [3]. To this end, the domain logic is modeled using two different levels of abstraction: a *meta* level provides a self-representation of the system encoding knowledge about data type struc-

tures, algorithms, and relationships; besides a *base* level application logic carries concrete data whose interpretation is determined by the values of so-called *meta-objects*.

The *Observations & Measurements* analysis pattern [4] implements the reflection principle specializing the abstraction for the case of high variety in the data attributes of object types. This pattern-oriented architectural design brings a number of further benefits, mostly linked to the quality of the code, and notably to maintainability, reusability, and consolidated understanding of implementation choices and consequences.

However, design by patterns does not account for performance as first-class requirement, and naturally incurs in well-known performance anti-patterns [5, 6], which may become crucial when *volume* and *variety* must meet also *velocity* [7]. These drawbacks are largely exacerbated when the domain logic is persisted over a relational storage layer, due to the nature of the domain model and its mismatch with the relational tier [8].

In general, the persistence of a domain model with complex structure into a relational database comes with a number of performance penalties, that translate in longer time required for key persistence operations. These issues can be partially mitigated with ad-hoc optimizations in the design of the relational database [9], pertaining to the choice of a particular representation for class inheritance, the use of auxiliary tables to store additional information, and the smart use of data fetching.

The interposition of an object-relational mapping (ORM) layer between the domain logic and the storage layer can mitigate this problem. In the practice of development of Java enterprise applications, Java Persistence API (JPA) specification represents a mature and state-of-the-art ORM solution which grants many benefits [10]. First of all, it allows to persist domain classes with a minimal boilerplate code, thanks to simplified annotation facilities. Also, it provides full integration with the Java application stack, composed by other technologies such as EJB (for encapsulating the business logic) and CDI (for implementing the *Inversion of Control* pattern [11]). However, JPA further increases the degree of indirection and this can have negat-

ICPE'16, March 12-18, 2016, Delft, Netherlands

© 2016 ACM. ISBN 978-1-4503-4080-9/16/03. . . $15.00

DOI: http://dx.doi.org/10.1145/2851553.2851561

ive effects on the system performance, also due to the loss of design control on the impact that domain logic operations have on the storage process.

With the rise of the *Not Only Sql (NoSQL)* movement [12], other options in the design of the storage layer are now available, and provide various advantages, including reduced access time through the clustering of similar data [13], and increased adaptability to the variety and variability of data over time through the use of a *schemaless* structure. This motivates the investigation on engineering the performance of existing applications by changing the storage schema from a relational + ORM persistence stack to a NoSQL solution, while preserving the domain logic structure. In particular, this subtends a problem of re-modeling content representation in the schema of some NoSQL technology and quantitatively evaluating the performance gain that can be attained. In so doing, different NoSQL paradigms are more or less close to the domain model and suited for its main operations [14, 15], and a pattern-based organization of the domain logic can drive the refactoring of the data model towards more efficient performance results.

In this paper, we report on the performance engineering of a three-tier web-application focused on the replacement of a relational + ORM persistence stack through two different NoSQL technologies, describing how a reflection-based architecture can be modeled over the graph-oriented *Neo4j* [16] and the document-oriented *MongoDB* [17] databases, and comparing experimental performance results achieved by the different solutions.

To this end, in Sect. 2, we describe a reflection-based architecture that combines the *Observations & Measurements* and the *Composite* patterns to attain a high degree of adaptability and changeability and that is persisted over a relational + ORM stack (Sect. 2.1), and we describe how this was concretely exploited in the implementation of an Electronic Health Record (EHR) system [18, 19] which is in use since various years in a major Italian hospital (Sect. 2.2). In Sect. 3, we discuss how the domain model of the reflection architecture can be suitably represented over *Neo4j* and *MongoDB* databases (Sect. 3.1, 3.2) and we show how these representations are *information equivalent* to the original relational representation (Sect. 3.3). In Sect. 4 we report the result of experimentations aimed at measuring the performance gain, compared to the actual implementation, referred to a crucial application use case, applied on *real* data taken from the practice of use of the EHR system and on *synthetic* data generated so as to stress the most relevant dimensions of complexity. Performance results obtained in both datasets show a clear gain in performance by the MongoDB solution, and more generally, a better scalability of NoSQL technologies when the complexity of the data structures increases. Conclusions are drawn in Sect. 5.

2. A REFLECTION ARCHITECTURE FOR ADAPTABILITY

In this section we describe how the *Reflection* architectural principles [2] can be implemented through a powerful combination of the *Observations & Measurements* analysis pattern [4] and the *Composite* pattern [20] to implement an EHR system able to deal with medical concepts and clinical data characterized by complexity and volatility.

2.1 Exploiting the Reflection, Observations & Measurements, and Composite patterns

The *Reflection* architectural pattern [2, 3] permits the development of a domain logic with a high degree of changeability and adaptability [1] through a mechanism that allows for changing structure and behaviour of objects at run-time. To this end, the domain logic is split in two layers so as to support dynamic adaptation of the system in response to changing requirements. On the one hand, a *meta* level consists of a set of meta-objects providing information about system properties. On the other hand, a *base* level models the business logic and uses information provided by the meta level, in order to make the system more flexible when changes occur.

The *Observations & Measurements* analysis pattern [4] comprises an embodiment of the *Reflection* pattern, where meta-objects are used to create abstraction on the attributes carried by different object types. In this case, *measurements*, that allow to record quantitative information, and *observations*, that extend the expressiveness of the pattern for taking into account qualitative information, are both represented in a so-called day-to-day *operational* level. Their configuration, in terms of semantic definition, is constrained by a so-called *knowledge* level, where changes are typically more infrequent.

Hierarchical structured data resulting from repeated aggregation of basic observations and measurements can be cast in the representation through a mix-in of the *Composite* pattern [20], by allowing an observation or measurement be implemented as a collection of references to other observations or measurements.

Observations & Measurements has been frequently advocated as a scheme of great potential in the development of a variety of applications that are supposed to collect data with different structures and different versions over time. A notable class of applications, with major practical and economical impact, occurs in the creation of Electronic Health Record (EHR) systems [21]. In general, an EHR system [18] is a kind of Health Information Management (HIM) system supporting the acquisition, analysis, and maintenance of clinical information items about a patient, in digital or traditional form. For such a system, changeability and adaptability [1] are qualities of primary relevance, which largely condition the ability of a software product in fitting the needs of different medical specialities, and in accompanying their evolution over time due to changes of local organizational assumptions or even of the patient's health status.

In the rest of this Section, we describe a concrete software architecture that combines the *Observations & Measurements* pattern with the *Composite* pattern. This pattern-

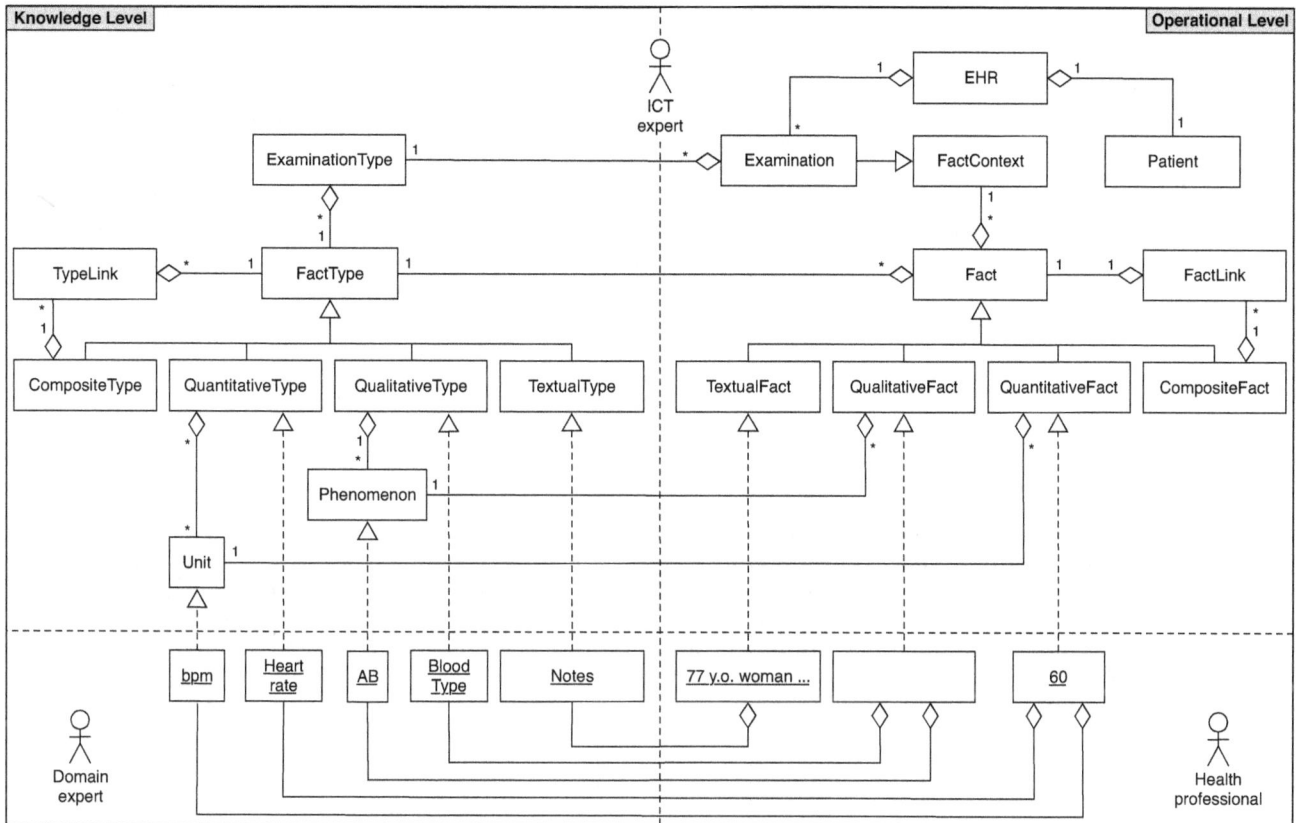

Figure 1: The domain model of the *Empedocle* EHR system based on the underlying meta-modeling paradigm, addressed in the architectural perspective by the *Reflection* pattern [2] and in the conceptual perspective by the *Observations & Measurements* pattern [4]. The meta-modeling approach allows a new medical concept to be accounted in the EHR system just through the instantiation of a new object from the class `FactType`, avoiding the need of programming new classes or class members and without any impact on the database schema or on its records. In the same manner, a new clinical concept can be recorded just through the instantiation of a new object from the class `Fact`.

based architecture was implemented within an EHR system named *Empedocle*, which is in use since more than 3 years in various units of the major hospital of Tuscany Region (Careggi hospital, in Florence). While referring to this case for the sake of experimentation concreteness, most of the subsequent discussion about the development of a graph-oriented or document-oriented database representation as well as about their impact on system performance are more generally applicable to most schemes that can be designed in the style of the *Reflection* architectural pattern.

2.2 The Empedocle EHR system

The UML class-object diagram of Fig. 1 provides a high-level specification of the domain model implemented in the core of the *Empedocle* EHR system.

At the *operational* level, an `EHR` represents a structured collection of health information items about a `Patient`, derived through a set of clinical `Examinations`. Specifically, during each `Examination`, a series of clinical information items like signs (i.e. objective evidences noticed), symptoms (i.e. subjective evidences reported by patient), and other clinical observations are captured by health professionals as instances of the `Fact` class.

Conversely, the *knowledge* level must be designed so as to accommodate the intrinsic variability of the medical domain, which depends on the evolution over time as well as on differences among medical specialities. To this end, all medical concepts can be defined directly by domain experts as instances of the `FactType` class.

The resulting high-level model abstraction allows to separate the representation of medical knowledge (i.e. the semantic of medical phenomena) from clinical data (i.e. the value assumed by a specified medical phenomenon in a specified time for a specified patient), and empower domain experts to contribute to this knowledge in the course of system life. Accordingly, four different categories of knowledge can be identified: `TextualType`, for free-text information (e.g. patient's *anamnesis*); `QualitativeType`, for values in a finite range of acceptable `Phenomena` (e.g. *blood type* with groups *A*, *B*, *AB*, and *0*); `QuantitativeType`, for quantities with a specified set of acceptable `Units` (e.g. *heart rate*, measured in *beats-per-minute*); and `CompositeType`, for composing `FactTypes` in a hierarchical structure through a *Composite* pattern implementation (e.g. *vital sign* including *temperature*, *blood pressure*, *heart* and *respiratory rate*). The same categories can be identified at the operational

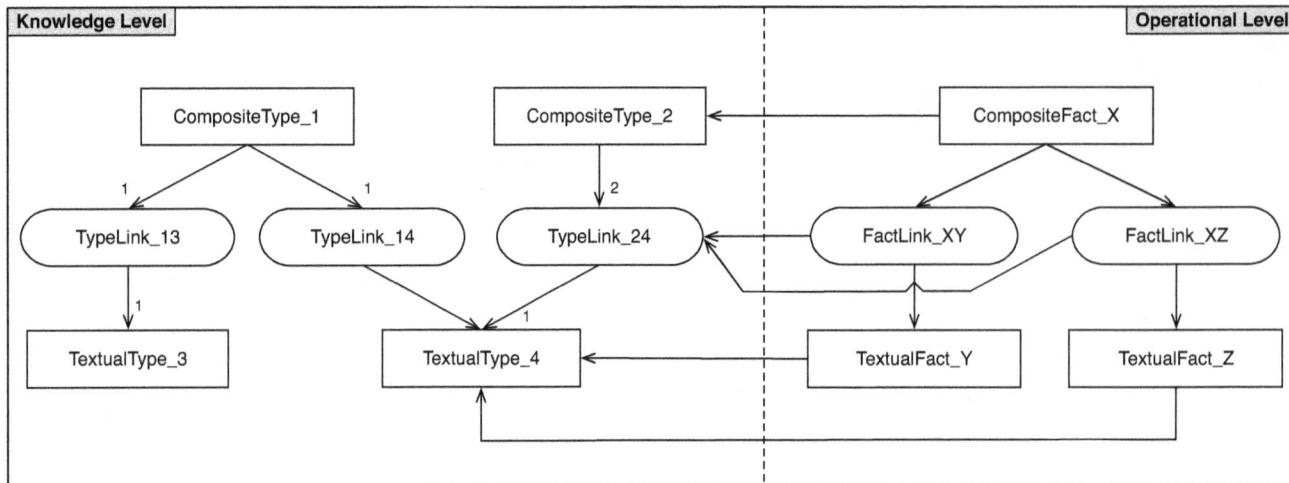

Figure 2: An example of `Examination` **structure as represented using the domain model shown in Fig. 1: on the left, a direct acyclic graph obtained composing** `FactTypes` **and** `TypeLinks`; **on the right, a tree-like structure as resulting from the composition of** `Facts` **and** `FactLinks`. **Note that rectangles represent instances of** `FactType` **and** `Fact` **classes and define, respectively, medical concepts and clinical observations that are to be taken into account during a clinical examination. Rounded boxes represent instances of** `TypeLink` **and** `FactLink` **classes and are used to increase the expressiveness of each** `Type-to-Type` **and** `Fact-to-Fact` **association (for example, through the definition of its cardinality).**

level: `TextualFact`, `QualitativeFact`, `QuantitativeFact`, and `CompositeFact`.

`ExaminationType` class represents the structure of an `Examination` in terms of which `FactTypes` (and related `Facts`) have to be considered during a medical examination; moreover, it specifies, through `TypeLink` and `FactLink` associations, the multiplicity of occurrence of each `Fact` in order to dynamically adapt the structure to multiple contexts-of-use that require a different number of instances to be recorded. In addition, the reuse of already defined *named* `FactTypes` is supported, so as to avoid their proliferation, just referencing them in multiple parts of the structure. Alternatively, *anonymous* `FactType` instances (i.e. `FactTypes` that do not need to be referenced by others) can be used, and the definition of their structures is directly included inside the parent structure. As relevant consequence, as depicted in Fig. 2, the `FactType` structure will result in a direct acyclic graph, while the derived `Fact` structure will result in a tree, usually with an increased number of nodes due to the multiplicity attribute.

This implies a more complex data model, with various drawbacks. On the one hand, while the number of `Facts` concretely recorded at run-time during a clinical session is bounded in semantic and multiplicity by the `FactType` definition, the real depth of an `Examination` cannot be known in advance, precluding the possibility to exploit optimized ad-hoc mechanisms for retrieving all the data, requiring instead to explore the entire structure. On the other hand, since the model is split in two levels, the whole `Examination` will be completely known only when both parts will be provided. For this reason, retrieving all the data collected during an `Examination` is not restricted to exploring the `Fact` tree, but requires to explore the related `FactType` graph, affecting system performances. Finally, the resulting model consists of a relative small number of classes for representing only concrete concepts; nevertheless, the high degree of abstraction

is counterbalanced by the instantiation, at run-time, of an increased number of objects required for describing the actual domain. Usually, this does not represent a problem in small and static domains, but it becomes evident in domains characterized by complexity and volatility.

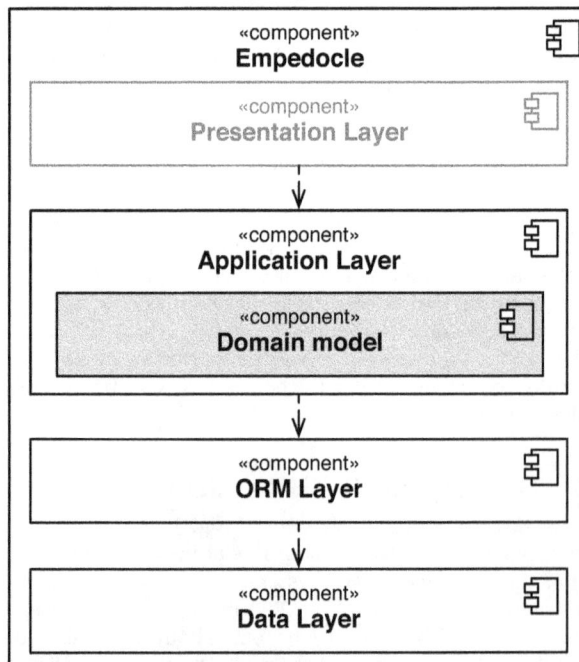

Figure 3: The software architecture of the *Empedocle* **EHR system. The** *Domain model* **component implements the domain logic through the meta-level modeling approach as described in Fig. 1.**

300

Fig. 3 shows the software architecture of the *Empedocle* EHR system, as currently deployed at the Careggi hospital, which follows the usual scheme of a 3-tier system: the *Data layer* provides mechanisms for storing and retrieving data from a relational database; the *Object-Relational Mapping (ORM) Layer*, implemented by *Hibernate*, reconciles the object/relational paradigm mismatch between objects and relational data [22]; the *Application layer* implements the domain model of Fig. 1 and other services; finally, for the sake of completeness, the *Presentation layer* implements interfaces and logic for the interaction with users, and includes a *Viewer Engine* for automated generation of EHR content GUIs.

The high degree of changeability and adaptability provided by the *Empedocle* architecture allows that user tasks and responsibilities in the context-of-use [23] be partitioned according to the summary use case diagram of Fig. 4.

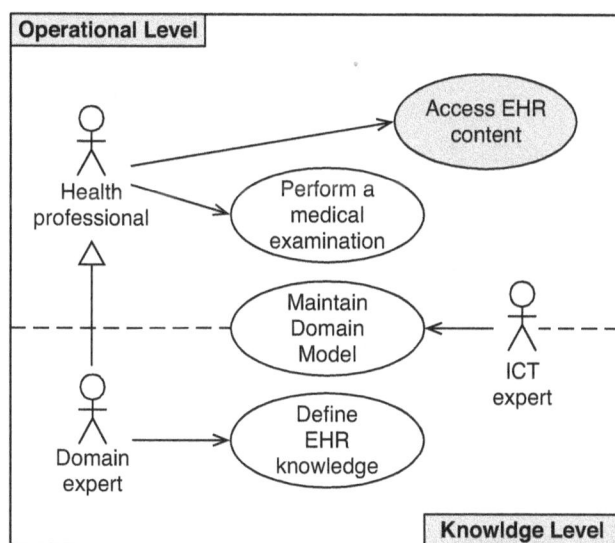

Figure 4: A typical outpatient scenario, specifying the major actors involved in the care process and their interaction with an EHR system. The highlighted use case represents a major scenario of interaction: the health professional actor accesses patient's EHR content in order to review past medical examinations and read collected clinical information.

Health professionals (e.g. general practitioner, medical specialist, registered nurse) take part to the care process at the operational level in different ways, in accordance with personal skills and specializations, including: *i)* the complete review of the patient's EHR content (e.g. clinical history, allergies, active problems, test results); *ii)* the acquisition of clinical data through a medical examination; *iii)* the formulation of the correct diagnosis; and *iv)* the development of a specific treatment plan.

Medical concepts related to clinical data collected into the EHR system are identified and steadily maintained at knowledge level by one or more *domain experts*, who are health professionals with specific domain expertise as well as aware about governmental and hospital directives, and

about factors depending on specialization of activities and scientific aims.

Finally, the *ICT expert* plays a lead role in bridging medical and informatics domains, in cases where technical skills are required for supporting health professionals through the implementation of additional system requirements that demand structural changes in the domain model, at the operational as well as the knowledge levels.

We do not report here on the characteristics of other complementary roles which are involved in the organization and enactment of the clinical process (e.g. from health direction and administrative support), but that are not directly concerned with the topic addressed in this paper.

3. MODELING REFLECTION OVER A NOSQL PERSISTENCE LAYER

In the common practice of software development, the persistence layer deals with retrieving data from and storing data to a relational data store, usually through the interposition of an ORM layer. In this kind of approach, the persistence model is largely determined by the object-oriented design of the domain logic.

By contrast, when persistence relies on a NoSQL solution, design gives space to alternative choices in the definition of the storage data model, which is, to a large extent, independent from the structure of object types. In fact, the absence of a fixed schema provides multiple options concerning the definition of the database structure, facilitating the representation of heterogeneous data characterized by high variability over time. The overall design results more flexible, but inevitably more complex and harder to understand for software developers used to deal with traditional relational databases [24]; it also requires to take into account some specific aspects so as to realize data migration in the most opportune way [13].

In the rest of this Section, we describe two new data models as implemented using different NoSQL technologies, *Neo4j* [16], and *MongoDB* [17]. The choice of these two technologies was made so as to experiment with their data structure and promising performance improvement [25, 26], and to compare graph- and document-oriented NoSQL solutions applied to the case of a reflection software architecture that combines the *Observations & Measurements* and *Composite* patterns, as described in Sect. 2. Finally, the validity of the proposed models is proved, in terms of integrity of persisted data and equivalence of data representations.

3.1 A model for Neo4j

Neo4j [16] relies on a *graph-oriented* structure, which can natively represent the domain logic of a reflection architecture, whose data structures are direct acyclic graphs and trees [27]. As a schemaless database, the data model in Neo4j is inherently defined by the *nodes* and *relationships* persisted in the database. Every node and relationship can also be characterized by an arbitrary number of *properties*.

From version 2.0, Neo4j developers tweaked its schemaless nature by introducing *labels* and *indexes*, two concepts that help modelling data in a more organized way, without losing the database original adaptability. Specifically, labels can be used to group together nodes, and each node can optionally be labeled with one or more text descriptions, and indexed

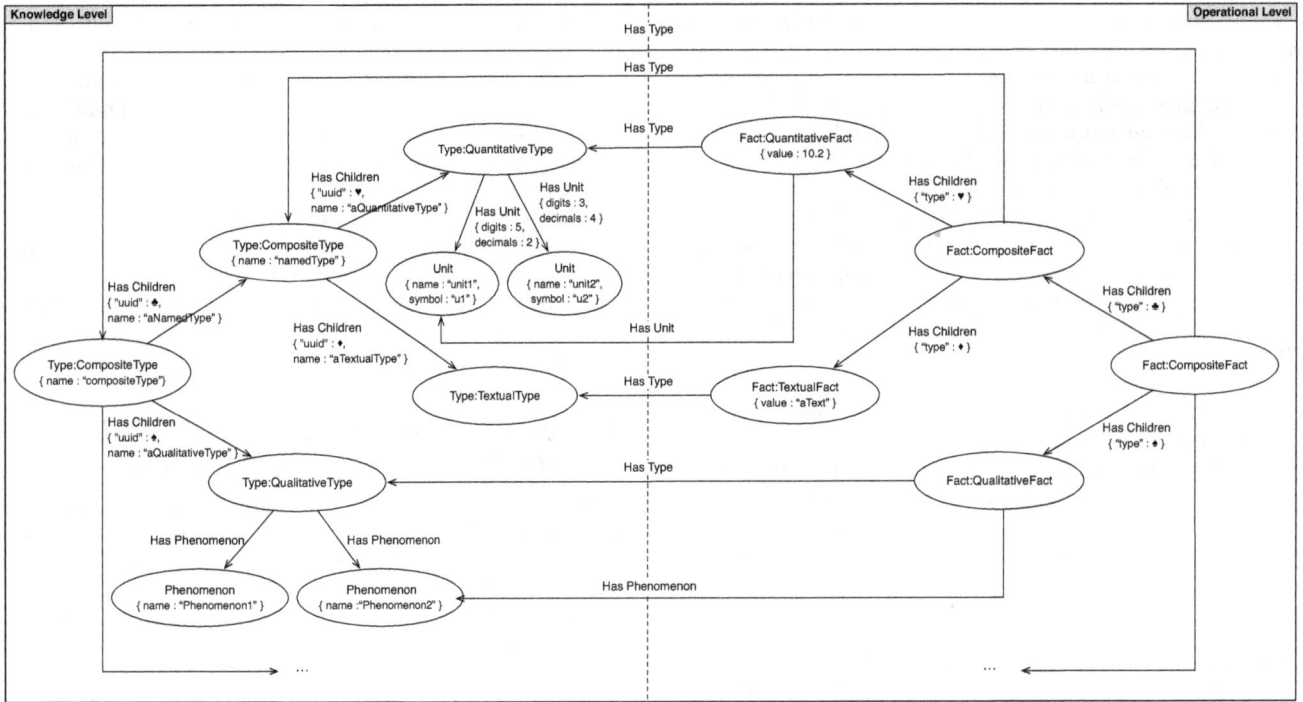

Figure 5: The representation of an instance of the domain model described in Sect. 2 on the graph model of Neo4j database. Oval shapes represent nodes, and arcs between nodes represent relationships, with labels written in bold, and properties reported between braces. For example, a *Type:CompositeType* node is characterized by multiple labels: the first one specifies that it is an instance of FactType class, the second one identifies its role in the hierarchy. The *Has Children* relationship identifies children nodes. For reasons of readability, *uuid* property values have been replaced with symbols.

to improve query expressiveness and flexibility. Moreover, indexes can be defined on properties of labelled nodes, to improve performance during query operations, similarly to the relational case. Both labels and indexes are optional.

In our concrete case, modeling the domain logic in Neo4j comes down to: *i)* identifying the node structure that forms the model; *ii)* defining the relationships between nodes; *iii)* defining the properties that characterize nodes and relationships, and *iv)* labeling with the appropriate qualifiers.

Specifically, as depicted in the schema of Fig. 5, each class that is an entity in the original model has been represented as a node in the target model (i.e. FactType and Fact hierarchy classes, and Phenomenon and Unit classes). The resulting nodes have been labeled with a correspondent qualifier and, in addition to that, nodes that are part of the FactType and Fact hierarchies contain an extra label to identify their role in the class hierarchy (e.g. *Fact:QualitativeFact* qualifies a QualitativeFact inside a Fact hierarchy).

As it can be observed in the schema, the *name* property is used for identifying, at the knowledge level, a *named* FactType. The value *property* is used to record, at the operational level, the value assumed by a TextualFact or a QuantitativeFact node: a string of text in the first case, and a double precision number in the latter case. In this model, there is basically no difference between *named* and *anonymous* FactTypes: both are modeled using a node, and the only distinction between them is the presence of the *name* property.

Another characteristic of the graph model in Fig. 5 is the capability of modeling TypeLink and FactLink classes using relationships. These two classes were introduced in the original model to represent the parent-child relationship between FactType or Fact classes. For this reason, they can be naturally represented as a relationship in a graph-oriented model. In addition, since Neo4j represents relationships as directed arcs that can be traversed in both directions, this allows to simplify the model introducing a single relationship, called *Has Children*, for modeling TypeLink and FactLink classes, without any impact on query capabilities. Note that Neo4j allows to put a relationship only between two nodes, and this precludes the possibility to use a relationship to represent the reference between TypeLink and FactLink, as in the original model. Properties have been used to solve this problem, as follows: *i)* the *uuid* property of each TypeLink is used for storing an identifier value; *ii)* the same value is copied into the *type* property of the related FactLink. Properties have been used to solve this problem without transforming these two classes from relationships to nodes. Finally, the *Has Type* relationship is used to link together Fact and FactType nodes.

The self-explanatory *Has Unit* and *Has Phenomenon* relationships are ambivalent across the knowledge and the operational level, and are used to connect a QuantitativeType or QualitativeType node with a set of possible Unit or Phenomenon nodes, and the corresponding QuantitativeFact or QualitativeFact node with the selected Unit or Phenomenon node.

Knowledge Level

db.types

```
{ "_id" : ObjectId("62e45671d4c67eba5b0e9e1a") ,
   "name" : "compositeType",
     "class" : "cmp",
       "children" : [ { "class" : "qlt",
                           "name" : "aQualitativeType",
                           "uuid" : ♠,

                           "values" : [ "Phenomenon1", "Phenomenon2" ] },
                     { "class" : "ref",
                           "name" : "aNamedType",
                           "uuid" : ♣,

                           "reference" : ObjectId("55e45670d4c67eba5b0e9e16") } ]

{ "_id" : ObjectId("55e45670d4c67eba5b0e9e16") ,
   "name" : "namedType",
     "class" : "cmp",
       "children" : [ { "class" : "txt",
                           "name" : "aTextualType",
                           "uuid" : ◆ },
                     { "class" : "qnt",
                           "name" : "aQuantitativeType",
                           "uuid" : ♥,

                           "units" : [ { "name" : "unit1",
                                           "symbol" : "u1",
                                           "format" : "5,2" },
                                       { "name" : "unit2",
                                           "symbol" : "u2",
                                           "format" : "3,4" } ] } ] }
```

Operational Level

db.facts

```
{ "_id" : ObjectId("552168dcdb77569140663ba7") ,
   "class" : "cmp",
     "typeId" : ObjectId("62e45671d4c67eba5b0e9e1a")
       "children" : [ { "class" : "qlt",
                           "type" : ♠,

                           "value" : "Phenomenon1" },
                     { "class" : "cmp",
                           "type" : ♣,

                           "children" : [ { "class" : "txt",
                                             "type" : ◆,

                                             "value" : "aText" },
                                         { "class" : "qnt",
                                             "type" : ♥,

                                             "value" : "10.2",
                                             "unit" : "u1" } ] } ] }
}
```

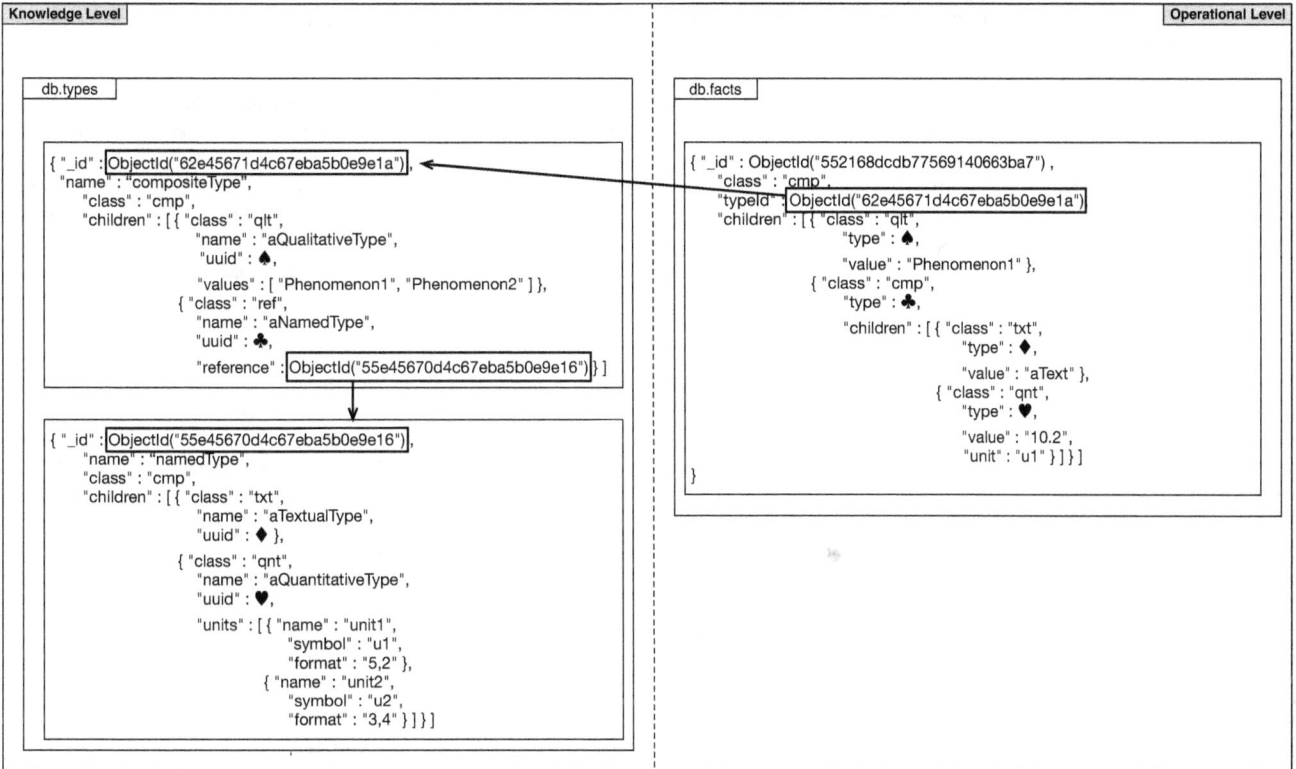

Figure 6: The representation of an instance of the domain model described in Sect. 2 on the document model of MongoDB database. The two sides of the figure show the collections used to persist FactType and Facts instances, named *db.types* and *db.facts*, respectively. At knowledge level, two *named* types have been persisted, with names *compositeType* and *namedType*. The first type includes the second one, as noted by the use of the *ObjectId* reference, and both of them include *anonymous* types as sub-documents. For reasons of readability, *uuid* property values have been replaced with symbols.

3.2 A model for MongoDB

MongoDB [17] data model is based upon a *document-oriented* structure. A document is a collection of attribute–value pairs, with values that can be basic types, array of values or nested sub-documents. Documents with similar characteristics are grouped together and stored in *collections*. Relation between documents can be represented using *references*, that produce a normalized data model, or by *embedding* related data in documents, producing denormalized models. In particular, the use of denormalization techniques [28] is promoted by document-oriented NoSQL solutions for discouraging the usage of JOIN queries, and solving typical performance issues that affect relational databases, preserving data consistency and completeness [29].

The schema of Fig. 6 illustrates the document-oriented model used in our concrete case, representing data in accordance with the domain model of Fig. 1. Usually, modeling an object-oriented domain logic using a document-based data model can be achieved in a direct way, but, in the case of study of a reflection architecture, this simplicity is weakened from the indirect structure of the model. The proposed solution attains a good balance, *mixing* together documents embedding approaches with references techniques [30] for obtaining a flexible data representation without performance degradation. In particular, the FactType hierarchy comprises a neat example of *mixed modelation*. In fact, while *named* FactType instances are persisted as documents, and are referenced by other documents using their *ObjectId*, *anonymous* FactType instances are persisted as embedded documents inside the named FactType document in which they are defined.

To efficiently recognize the subtyping-class of an instance in the FactType or Fact hierarchy, every persisted document has a property called *class* that can assume the following values: *i) txt*, for referring to a TextualType or TextualFact instance; *ii) qlt*, for referring to a QualitativeType or QualitativeFact instance; *iii) qnt*, for referring to a QuantitativeType or QuantitativeFact instance; and, *iv) cmp*, for referring to a CompositeType or CompositeFact instance. In so doing, it is sufficient to check the *class* property value of a document to recognize its nature, avoiding to pre-emptively explore its properties. In the case of *named* FactTypes, the *class* property is valued with the string value *ref*, and an additional property called *reference* contains the *ObjectId* of the *named* FactType.

This different behaviour in FactType persistence drops the need to persist the TypeLink class as a separate entity. For this reason, TypeLink and FactType classes are modeled in MongoDB as a single entity, and the *name* property of embedded documents inside CompositeType instances corresponds to the TypeLink *name* property of the original model.

303

Note that since the embedded documents are always *anonymous*, the FactType *name* property is specified only for the root document of a FactType instance.

The Fact hierarchy does not have the same need for reusability and referencing that characterize FactTypes. For this reason, Fact instances can always be represented as a single document, in which Fact children are embedded as sub-documents. In so doing, the number of queries for data retrieval is considerably limited.

Fact and related FactType instances are linked together with different strategies, based on the nature of the Fact. In the case of a Fact root document, the *typeId* property is used to store the *ObjectId* of the referenced FactType instance. Otherwise, when dealing with sub-documents of the Fact root, the *type* property is used to refer to the *uuid* value of the corresponding FactType. Consequently, for completely retrieving a Fact and its FactType, it is necessary to: *i)* query for the Fact; then, *ii)* query for the corresponding FactType using the *ObjectId* referenced by the Fact root; *iii)* link together the retrieved Fact and FactType instances using the *type* property.

For the sake of completeness, Phenomenon entities are modeled as embedded documents inside QualitativeFact and QualitativeType documents with the intent of minimizing the number of retrieval query in reading operations. In the same manner, Unit entities are modeled inside QuantitativeFact and QuantitativeType documents.

3.3 Information equivalence across data models

A comparison of the performance among different data storage implementations (i.e. from relational to a graph- or document-oriented model) requires that they are in some sense equivalent. Since data can be modeled in various ways through the use of different data structures offering the same *information capacity*, a notion of model equivalence, or hierarchy of equivalences [31], is required to be defined. In a general sense, two data structures can be considered equivalent in terms of information-capacities if they can be associated to the same number of states, such that each state of a data structure can be mapped to a *database state* of the other structure, preserving any relationship attribute value.

For the purpose of our experimentation, it is not necessary to prove the *complete* equivalence between two representations, but it is sufficient to prove the *query* equivalence of two models [32], i.e. the possibility to extract the same information from both models through query operations. Specifically, the equivalence problem consists in casting information data into structures (i.e. graphs or tree) of the same type. Comparing and matching graphs is a well-known NP-complete problem [33], and different approaches have been proposed to determine the distance between two graphs using specific heuristic [34, 35]. In our case, proving the equivalence of *Neo4j* and *MongoDB* data models with respect to the actual relational model means showing that they have the same representativeness of information. This means that the equivalence problem will be focused on showing that two data structures are exactly identical in the information they carry, rather than identifying similarities and differences between data models. Furthermore, it is not necessary to verify the *query dominance* for the new data model, but simply proving that it is possible to query the

same Examination and ExaminationType structure across different representations.

In a practical manner, we consider equivalent two data representations of the same domain logic using different persistence models when the carried information can be serialized into an equivalent string of information. In so doing, given two different persistence models, named A and B, A and B are equivalent if it is possible to generate the same string serialization for each given Examination and ExaminationType instance represented in A and B. Consequently, if A is a valid model, and A and B are equivalent, than B is also valid. Note that we assume that the actual relational model is a valid reference model, from which we want to prove the validity of the converted NoSQL models.

We have started by choosing a dataset with an arbitrary number of clinical information data persisted in the relational model. Then, we have retrieved all the Examinations and ExaminationTypes instances contained in the dataset, and we have serialized the information data in a string representation. Finally, for testing the equivalence, we have converted information data from the relational model to the target NoSQL model, serializing again the information data, and comparing the resulting string with the string obtained from the relational model at the previous step. The validation process is considered successful, if we are able to obtain an equivalence between the reference relational model and the target NoSQL model for every string of information.

Fig. 7 illustrates an example of the string produced during the serialization process applied to the information data as so represented using the models depicted in Figs. 5 and 6. The structure of the serialization is deliberately similar to a JSON document, due to its simple and readable syntax. This string serialization can be also used to verify which are the essential properties that a model must implement to be valid.

Note that the completeness of the new representation is also granted by the structures of target models. In fact, the conversion from *MySQL* to *Neo4j* model is the most natural way since it allows to maintain nodes and relationships according to the structure of the original tree or graph. Moreover, the MongoDB document representation is modeled in a way that can be considered an inverse operation of vertical decomposition during normalization process, as discussed in [32] and [36].

```
"compositeType" : {
  "aNamedType" : {
    "aQuantitativeType" : "10.2 u1"
    "aTextualType" : "aText"
  }
  "aQualitativeType" : "Phenomenon2"
}
```

Figure 7: An example of serialization of a clinical Examination. **The pattern used to serialize the information is as follows:** *type.name : fact.value.* **CompositeFact values are described by the list of values assumed by children Facts defined between braces.**

4. EXPERIMENTATION AND RESULTS

An experimentation was carried out to evaluate the performance of the three different implementations based on MySQL+Hibernate, Neo4j, and MongoDB, and their sensitivity to the characteristics of the dataset.

The evaluation was focused on the *Access EHR content* use case (see Fig. 4), in which a health professional actor access past medical examinations related to a specific patient in order to review collected clinical information. This use case has turned out to have the most relevant impact on the perceived performance in the context-of-use and, at the same time, constitutes a major scenario of interaction in EHR systems.

4.1 Methodology of experimentation

We can expect that the response time of different storage schemes be dependent on the complexity of the collection of domain logic objects that are read-from or written-to the persistence layer. Due to the pattern-based architecture of classes in the domain logic, objects are organized in an almost tree-like structure, and their complexity can thus be characterized in terms of number of nodes and depth of the tree in the examination structure.

For this reason, we experimented with two different kind of datasets: *i)* a *real* dataset of clinical examinations acquired in the *Empedocle* EHR system for which we provide a description of the statistics about the number of nodes and the depth of the tree structure; *ii)* a *synthetic* dataset for which we can control the statistics so as to stress the indexes of complexity.

The *real* dataset consists of about 13 000 examinations [1] that belong to the same medical speciality and thus share the same structure. Table 1 summarizes the complexity of the examination structure, i.e. the number of `FactTypes` included in each examination, which is the number of meta-objects in the knowledge level. The structure of the examination includes 243+110+99 fields, which are organized in a graph whose depth (intended as the maximum distance from the root node) is equal to 8, and which includes 144 `FactTypes` that act as composition nodes.

Depth	8	
Number of nodes	596	
	CompositeType	144
	QualitativeType	243
	QuantitativeType	110
	TextuaType	99

Table 1: **Characteristics of the considered examination structure in the dataset, with additional details about the distribution of type nodes contained in the structure. Of the 596 nodes that form the examination type, 452 nodes are leaf nodes, which actually contain a value.**

Note that, at the operational level, the complexity of the tree structure depends on the course of each specific examination, and its statistic is resumed in Figs. 8 and 9. Fig. 8 reports the distribution of examinations per number

---

[1] The real dataset was conveniently anonymized by omitting patients' personal information, and by obfuscating textual observations recorded during each clinical session.

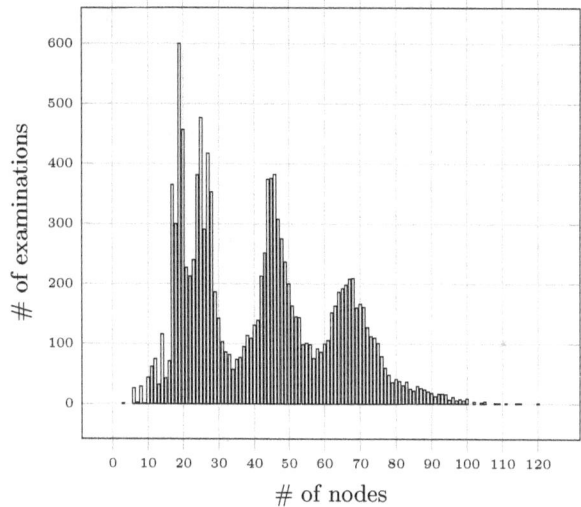

Figure 8: **The histogram describes the distribution of examinations as the number of nodes varies. Note that about 35% of the examinations in the dataset are in the neighbourhood of 23±6, with peaks in 19, 20, 25 and 27. This shows clearly how, usually, only a small part of the examination structure, comprising 596 nodes, is actually filled out by health professionals. Only about 9% of the examinations in the dataset have more than 70 nodes filled out.**

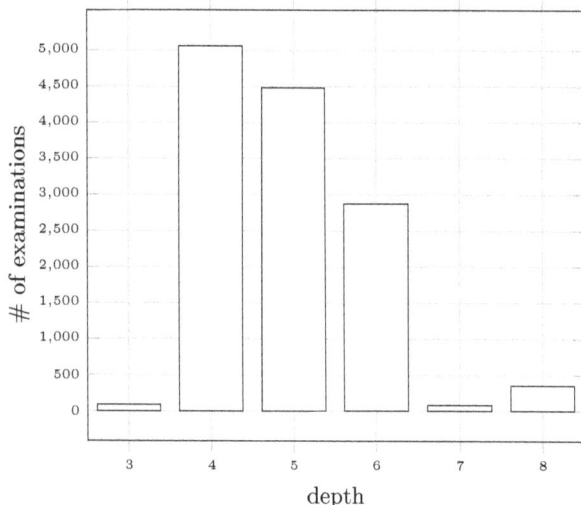

Figure 9: **The histogram describes the distribution of examinations as the depth increases. Note that 96% of the examinations in the dataset have depth comprises between 4 and 6.**

of nodes. Fig. 9 characterizes the distribution of examinations per depth of the tree structure. From these statistics, it is possible to note that the size of the tree-like structure (composed by `Facts`) is always much lower than the size of the corresponding graph structure (composed by `Fact-Types`), which depends on the fact that, during a standard clinical session, not all the observations allowed by the examination structure (≈ 600) are actually recorded.

The *synthetic* dataset contains generated examinations with a full binary tree structure, with depth ranging from 2 to 8. For each depth, a fixed number of 100 examinations has been generated. Being a full binary tree, the number of nodes n in each of the trees of depth d is given by:

$$n = 2^{d+1} - 1,$$

ranging from 3 to 511 nodes. The synthetic dataset does not correspond to a real situation in the present context-of-use of our EHR system, but it can become a possible scenario in the evolution of the use of the *Empedocle* EHR system, and, for this reason, represents a relevant part of the motivation for this performance engineering investigation. In the more general perspective of a reflection architecture, this corresponds to the case where different courses can be described on a structure with different degrees of completeness.

The evaluation has been carried out with reference to a major scenario of interaction: a health professional accesses a patient's EHR content in order to review past medical examinations and read collected clinical information. To do that, each examination in the dataset has first been retrieved and, then, a read-only operation has been performed in order to simulate the real interaction of users with the EHR system through the interfaces exposed by the *Presentation Layer*.

As a metric of performance, we evaluated the total time required to complete the selected scenario, from data retrieving to data serialization, for all compared models. Note that the examination retrieval also implies the retrieval of the associated type structure. In the process of measuring the total time, we do not distinguish time passed by the various phases of data retrieval and process: specifically, we measure the time to complete the whole use case, that comprises database retrieval operations, interactions with Java database APIs or with the ORM persistence layer present only in the relational case.

Experimental results not reported here indicate that the ORM layer, implemented by *Hibernate* in the current application stack, does not significantly impact the overall performance, since it is optimized for the underlying database technology [37, 38]. No comparison has been carried out regarding storage space requirements for the considered technologies, not representing a critical aspect for the EHR system in the case under consideration.

The experiments were conducted on a computer with the following characteristics: Debian 3.2.60 operating system, with 2 x Intel Xeon E5640 @ 2.66 GHz 64-Bit CPU, and 32 GB of RAM Memory.

4.2 Results

Table 2 reports the results of the experimentation on the real dataset, showing the mean value (μ), measured in *ms*, and the coefficient of variation (CV) of the time spent to complete the read-only operation for a single examination in the three implementations under test. These statistical indexes were evaluated by repeating the task for 100 times on all 12 953 examinations in the dataset.

In comparison with the MySQL + Hibernate implementation, Neo4j reduces the retrieval time by approximately 1.5 times, and MongoDB reduces it by more than 33 times. Performance with relational database such as MySQL are deeply linked to the number of JOIN in the executed queries. For this reason, in the considered model, the retrieval of

	μ (ms)	CV	min (ms)	max (ms)
MySQL + Hibernate	76.06	0.031	70.79	81.94
Neo4j	51.29	0.0024	50.94	51.57
MongoDB	2.27	0.064	1.82	2.57

Table 2: Comparison between MySQL+Hibernate, Neo4j, and MongoDB, evaluated using the *real* dataset comprising 12953 examinations. Table reports the mean value (μ) and the coefficient of variation (CV) for the execution of a single examination, as well as the minimum (min) and maximum (max) execution time registered during the 100 iterations for a specific technology.

specific classes of `Facts` has a different impact on the complexity of the query. In particular, since `CompositeFacts` represent hierarchical structures in the `Facts` tree, querying operations result in a higher number of JOINs, which produces a significant impact on performance, documented by [5] as "*N+1 queries*" data access anti-pattern or "*Circuitous Treasure Hunt*" problem. In a similar way, `Quantitative-Facts` and `QualitativeFacts` also produce more complex queries, since an additional JOIN operation is required to retrieve related `Phenomena` and `Units`.

Table 3 shows the results of experimentation on the *synthetic* dataset. We report the mean value (μ), measured in *ms*, and the coefficient of variation (CV) of the time spent to complete the read-only operation for a single examination in the three implementations under test, evaluated by repeating the task for 100 times on all 100 examinations in the dataset. Results indicate that MongoDB attains by far a better performance and slower sensitivity to the examination depth. It should also be noted that the MySQL + Hibernate implementation performs better than Neo4j for examination with depth lower than 7.

Depth	MySQL + Hibernate		Neo4j		MongoDB	
	μ (ms)	CV	μ (ms)	CV	μ (ms)	CV
2	6.93	0.12	18.76	0.12	1.07	0.05
3	9.54	0.11	19.41	0.09	1.2	0.06
4	12.6	0.1	21.57	0.09	1.38	0.07
5	18.87	0.09	26.04	0.08	1.64	0.07
6	28.17	0.09	33.94	0.05	2.2	0.07
7	48.18	0.08	44.03	0.05	3.05	0.08
8	121.29	0.04	72.93	0.05	4.88	0.07

Table 3: Comparison between MySQL+Hibernate, Neo4j, and MongoDB, evaluated using the *synthetic* dataset comprising 100 examinations with increasing depth. Table reports the mean value (μ) and the coefficient of variation (CV) for the execution of a single examination. Results in the table show that the MySQL + Hibernate implementation performs better than Neo4j for examination with depth lower than 7, while MongoDB attains by far a better performance and slower sensitivity to the examination depth.

5. CONCLUSIONS

In this paper we described a consolidated software architecture, pattern-based, which persistence data layer was originally based on the MySQL relational database and JPA. Using a model-driven approach we described new data persistence models based on promising NoSQL technologies, such as *Neo4j* [16] and *MongoDB* [17]. These models have been engineered to balance in the best way elements such as: ease of conversion, embedding and references, granting data integrity and equivalence in the information representation with the relational model.

We presented experimental results on performance gain achieved through the use of such databases. The comparison is based on the study of the real world scenario of our EHR system, called *Empedocle*, based on the *Observations & Measurements* [4] and *Composite* [20] patterns, where the main requirement is the structure flexibility. Since the considered NoSQL databases do not have a fixed schema, non-functional requirements of changeability and adaptability can be easily achieved. In addition, they constitute a good solution for big clusters of data which structure is subject to change over time.

Performance results obtained during experimentations in *real* and *synthetic* datasets indicate a clear gain in performance through the use of MongoDB database, and more generally, a better scalability of NoSQL solutions when the depth of the examination structures grows, due to the increased number of JOINs and reference operations affecting the MySQL solution. Moreover, both tested NoSQL technologies offer advantages in terms of flexibility in the data model, scalability and reliability.

Results also indicate a counter-intuitive conclusion: the graph-oriented data model of Neo4j allows a more natural and direct data conversion, which also permits a simpler implementation; however, the document-oriented data model of MongoDB produces by far better performance results. Specifically Neo4j, which modeling is more natural in our software architecture context, presents a performance increase of 1.5 times compared to MySQL + Hibernate. On the other hand, MongoDB, which required a bigger engineering investment to convert our data model balancing between redundancy, adaptability and performance, presents a gain of almost 33 times compared to MySQL + Hibernate.

The present investigation is completely open to explore the performances of NoSQL databases in other use cases, not only limited to read-only operations, but also extended to write and update scenarios, whose impact on the application is less relevant but nonetheless interesting to have a full comparison between the various models [39].

6. REFERENCES

[1] ISO/IEC. *ISO/IEC 9126. Software engineering – Product quality.* ISO/IEC, 2001.

[2] Frank Buschmann, Regine Meunier, Hans Rohnert, Peter Sommerlad, and Michael Stal. *Pattern-oriented Software Architecture: A System of Patterns.* John Wiley & Sons, Inc., New York, NY, USA, 1996.

[3] Joseph W Yoder, Federico Balaguer, and Ralph Johnson. Architecture and design of adaptive object-models. *ACM Sigplan Notices*, 36(12):50–60, 2001.

[4] Martin Fowler. *Analysis patterns: reusable object models.* Addison-Wesley Professional, 1997.

[5] Connie U Smith and Lloyd G Williams. Software performance antipatterns. In *Workshop on Software and Performance*, pages 127–136, 2000.

[6] Davide Arcelli, Vittorio Cortellessa, and Catia Trubiani. Antipattern-based model refactoring for software performance improvement. In *Proceedings of the 8th international ACM SIGSOFT conference on Quality of Software Architectures*, pages 33–42. ACM, 2012.

[7] Laney Douglas. 3d data management: Controlling data volume, velocity and variety. *Gartner. Retrieved*, 6, 2001.

[8] Scott Ambler. *Agile database techniques: effective strategies for the agile software developer.* John Wiley & Sons, Inc., New York, NY, USA, 2003.

[9] Baron Schwartz, Peter Zaitsev, and Vadim Tkachenko. *High performance MySQL: optimization, backups, and replication.* " O'Reilly Media, Inc.", 2012.

[10] Saleem N Bhatti, Zahid H Abro, and Farzana R Abro. Performance evaluation of java based object relational mapping tool. *Mehran University Research Journal of Engineering and Technology*, 32(2):159–166, 2013.

[11] Robert C Martin. The dependency inversion principle. *C++ Report*, 8(6):61–66, 1996.

[12] Michael Stonebraker. SQL databases v. NoSQL databases. *Communications of the ACM*, 53(4):10–11, 2010.

[13] Aaron Schram and Kenneth M Anderson. MySQL to NoSQL: data modeling challenges in supporting scalability. In *Proceedings of the 3rd annual conference on Systems, programming, and applications: software for humanity*, pages 191–202. ACM, 2012.

[14] Bogdan G Tudorica and Cristian Bucur. A comparison between several NoSQL databases with comments and notes. In *Roedunet International Conference (RoEduNet), 2011 10th*, pages 1–5. IEEE, 2011.

[15] João R Lourenço, Bruno Cabral, Paulo Carreiro, Marco Vieira, and Jorge Bernardino. Choosing the right NoSQL database for the job: a quality attribute evaluation. *Journal of Big Data*, 2(1):1–26, 2015.

[16] Neo4j the world's leading graph database. http://neo4j.com/.

[17] MongoDB for GIANT idea. https://www.mongodb.org/.

[18] ISO/TR. *ISO/TR 20514:2005. Health informatics — Electronic health record — Definition, scope and context.* ISO/TR, 2005.

[19] Paul C Tang, Joan S Ash, David W Bates, J Marc Overhage, and Daniel Z Sands. Personal health records: definitions, benefits, and strategies for overcoming barriers to adoption. *Journal of the American Medical Informatics Association*, 13(2):121–126, 2006.

[20] Erich Gamma, Richard Helm, Ralph Johnson, and John Vlissides. *Design Patterns: Elements of Reusable Object-oriented Software.* Addison-Wesley Longman Publishing Co., Inc., Boston, MA, USA, 1995.

[21] Thomas Beale, Sam Heard, Dipak Kalra, and David Lloyd. OpenEHR architecture overview. *The OpenEHR Foundation*, 2006.

[22] Christopher Ireland, David Bowers, Michael Newton, and Kevin Waugh. A classification of object-relational impedance mismatch. In *Advances in Databases, Knowledge, and Data Applications, 2009. DBKDA'09. First International Conference on*, pages 36–43. IEEE, 2009.

[23] ISO. *ISO 9241. Ergonomics of human-system interaction*. ISO, 2010.

[24] Francesca Bugiotti, Luca Cabibbo, Paolo Atzeni, and Riccardo Torlone. How I learned to stop worrying and love NoSQL databases. In *SEBD Italian Symposium on Advanced Database Systems*, 2015.

[25] Florian Holzschuher and René Peinl. Performance of graph query languages: comparison of Cypher, Gremlin and Native Access in Neo4J. In *Proceedings of the Joint EDBT/ICDT 2013 Workshops*, EDBT '13, pages 195–204, New York, NY, USA, 2013. ACM.

[26] Wei Xu, Zhonghua Zhou, Hong Zhou, Wu Zhang, and Jiang Xie. MongoDB improves big data analysis performance on Electric Health Record system. In *Life System Modeling and Simulation*, pages 350–357. Springer, 2014.

[27] Chad Vicknair, Michael Macias, Zhendong Zhao, Xiaofei Nan, Yixin Chen, and Dawn Wilkins. A comparison of a graph database and a relational database: a data provenance perspective. In *Proceedings of the 48th annual Southeast regional conference*, page 42. ACM, 2010.

[28] Anuradha Kanade, Aarthi Gopal, and Shantanu Kanade. A study of normalization and embedding in MongoDB. In *Advance Computing Conference (IACC), 2014 IEEE International*, pages 416–421. IEEE, 2014.

[29] Gansen Zhao, Qiaoying Lin, Libo Li, and Zijing Li. Schema conversion model of SQL database to NoSQL. In *P2P, Parallel, Grid, Cloud and Internet Computing (3PGCIC), 2014 Ninth International Conference on*, pages 355–362. IEEE, 2014.

[30] Ilya Katsov. NoSQL data modeling techniques. *Highly Scalable Blog*, 2012.

[31] Richard Hull. Relative information capacity of simple relational database schemata. *SIAM Journal on Computing*, 15(3):856–886, 1986.

[32] Paolo Atzeni, Giorgio Ausiello, Carlo Batini, and Marina Moscarini. Inclusion and equivalence between relational database schemata. *Theoretical Computer Science*, 19(3):267–285, 1982.

[33] Michael R. Garey and David S. Johnson. *Computers and Intractability: A Guide to the Theory of NP-Completeness*. W. H. Freeman & Co., New York, NY, USA, 1979.

[34] Sudarshan S Chawathe, Anand Rajaraman, Hector Garcia-Molina, and Jennifer Widom. Change detection in hierarchically structured information. *SIGMOD Rec.*, 25(2):493–504, June 1996.

[35] Luigi P Cordella, Pasquale Foggia, Carlo Sansone, and Mario Vento. Performance evaluation of the VF graph matching algorithm. In *Image Analysis and Processing, 1999. Proceedings. International Conference on*, pages 1172–1177. IEEE, 1999.

[36] Catriel Beeri, Philip A Bernstein, and Nathan Goodman. A sophisticate's introduction to database normalization theory. In *Proceedings of the fourth international conference on Very Large Data Bases-Volume 4*, pages 113–124. VLDB Endowment, 1978.

[37] Elizabeth J O'Neil. Object/relational mapping 2008: Hibernate and the Entity Data Model (EDM). In *Proceedings of the 2008 ACM SIGMOD international conference on Management of data*, pages 1351–1356. ACM, 2008.

[38] Qinglin Wu, Yanzhong Hu, and Yan Wang. Research on data persistence layer based on hibernate framework. In *Intelligent Systems and Applications (ISA), 2010 2nd International Workshop on*, pages 1–4. IEEE, 2010.

[39] Zachary Parker, Scott Poe, and Susan V Vrbsky. Comparing NoSQL MongoDB to an SQL db. In *Proceedings of the 51st ACM Southeast Conference*, page 5. ACM, 2013.

Optimizing the Performance-Related Configurations of Object-Relational Mapping Frameworks Using a Multi-Objective Genetic Algorithm

Ravjot Singh†, Cor-Paul Bezemer†, Weiyi Shang‡, Ahmed E. Hassan†
Software Analysis and Intelligence Lab (SAIL), Queen's University, Canada†
Department of Computer Science and Software Engineering, Concordia University, Canada‡
{rsingh, bezemer, ahmed}@cs.queensu.ca†, shang@encs.concordia.ca‡

ABSTRACT

Object-relational mapping (ORM) frameworks map low-level database operations onto a high-level programming API that can be accessed from within object-oriented source code. ORM frameworks often provide configuration options to optimize the performance of such database operations. However, determining the set of optimal configuration options is a challenging task.

Through an exploratory study on two open source applications (Spring PetClinic and ZK), we find that the difference in execution time between two configurations can be large. In addition, both applications are not shipped with an ORM configuration that is related to performance: instead, they use the default values provided by the ORM framework. We show that in 89% of the 9 analyzed test cases for PetClinic and in 96% of the 54 analyzed test cases for ZK, the default configuration values supplied by the ORM framework performed significantly slower than the optimal configuration for that test case. Based on these observations, this paper proposes an approach for automatically finding an optimal ORM configuration using a multi-objective genetic algorithm. We evaluate our approach by conducting a case study of Spring PetClinic and ZK. We find that our approach finds near-optimal configurations in 360-450 seconds for PetClinic and in 9-12 hours for ZK. These execution times allow our approach to be executed to find an optimal configuration before each new release of an application.

Keywords

object-relational mapping performance, performance configuration optimization

1. INTRODUCTION

As software becomes more complex and operates in different settings, it requires more flexibility in its underlying libraries and used frameworks. Hence, software libraries and frameworks tend to provide a high level of configurability.

ICPE'16, March 12-18, 2016, Delft, Netherlands
ⓒ2016 ACM. ISBN 978-1-4503-4080-9/16/03 ...$15.00.
DOI: http://dx.doi.org/10.1145/2851553.2851576.

On the one hand, configurability offers a great deal of flexibility. However, this flexibility comes at a cost as configuration errors can have a disastrous impact [28,31]. The potentially large impact of misconfiguration has lead to a large body of research in the area of (mis)configurability [11,15,30, 31,33,34]. Yin et al. [31] show that 27% of all reported customer issues are related to misconfiguration. Around half of these configuration issues are caused by misinterpretation of configuration options. Moreover, up to 20% of the reported cases of misconfiguration caused severe performance degradation [31]. Considering the high potential cost per issue, such as the estimated cost of 1.6 billion US dollar for a 1-second slowdown for Amazon [9], the cost of performance misconfiguration can rise to billions each year [32].

Object-relational mapping (ORM) is a technique that was introduced to provide a mapping between the higher level object-oriented model and the lower level relational model of a database management system. ORM frameworks offer a variety of configuration options that allow the user to configure how this mapping is performed statically and at run-time. Since ORM frameworks create a layer between the database and source code, their configuration can impact the performance of database operations. Chen et al. [3] show that ORM configurations can suffer from performance anti-patterns, indicating that ORM misconfiguration is a common problem.

In this paper, we first show through an exploratory study that ORM misconfigurations can indeed have a significant impact on the performance of an application. Additionally, we show that the optimal configuration performs significantly better than the configuration that is currently used by our subject applications for the analyzed workload.

The observations of our exploratory study motivate the second part of this paper, in which we propose an approach for automatically optimizing the performance-related configurations of ORM frameworks using a multi-objective genetic algorithm. We evaluate our approach through a case study of two open source applications (Spring PetClinic and ZK). Our case study shows that our approach is capable of finding configurations that are in the top 25% best-performing configurations for each studied workload. In short, we make the following contributions:

1. The observations that, in our studied subject applications:

   (a) ORM configurations have a large impact on the performance of an application

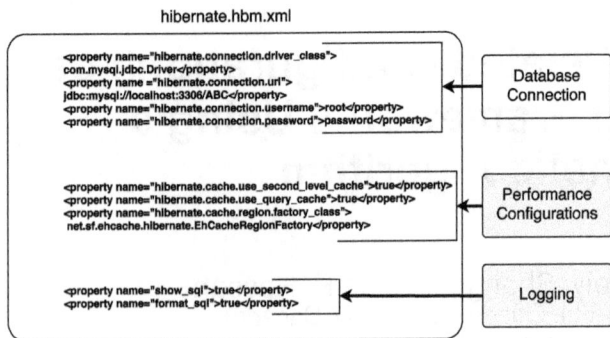

Figure 1: ORM configuration code for Hibernate

(b) The default configuration as supplied by the ORM framework performs in many cases significantly worse than the optimal configuration

2. An approach for automatically finding a near-optimal ORM configuration using a multi-objective genetic algorithm

The rest of this paper is organized as follows. Section 2 provides background information about ORM configuration. Section 3 presents the setup and results of our exploratory study. Section 4 gives an introduction to genetic algorithms. Section 5 presents our approach for automatically finding an optimal ORM configuration for an application. Section 6 and 7 describe the setup and results of the case study that we performed to evaluate our approach. Section 8 describes the threats to the validity of our work. Section 9 gives an overview of related work. Finally, Section 10 concludes the paper.

2. ORM PERFORMANCE-RELATED CONFIGURATION

ORM frameworks allow developers to perform database operations without writing boilerplate code for maintaining the connection or executing queries. One of the most popular [13] ORM frameworks is Hibernate[1] for Java. Figure 1 shows an example of the configuration code for the Hibernate framework. The configuration file *hibernate.hbm.xml* contains system-wide configuration options.

In Figure 1, the performance-related configuration specifies that caching should be used. Enabling the cache does not necessarily lead to an improvement in performance. In fact, using a cache in a situation in which data is infrequently used will lead to many cache misses, which may lead to a non-optimal performance.

Another example is the *hibernate.max_fetch_depth* configuration option. Hibernate maps database objects onto object-oriented programming objects. Data normalization is a concept heavily used in databases to keep tables small, which makes searching through them faster. An example of a simple database is depicted by Figure 2. To retrieve all information for a person, we have to perform three separate queries or one query with multiple joins. The *hibernate.max_fetch_depth* configuration option defines how Hibernate approaches such cross table queries. When set to

0, the use of joins for such queries is disabled and Hibernate will use three separate queries. When configured to a value higher than 0, Hibernate will use that value as the maximum depth of joins to perform in such a query. Using a single query with multiple joins is generally faster than using separate queries when all information returned by the query is used. However, in many situations only a part of the data is used and the overhead caused by retrieving the unnecessary data results in non-optimal performance.

The former two examples show that ORM performance-related configuration is specific to the workload and application and requires domain knowledge, which makes finding the optimal ORM configuration a challenging task. In the next section, we perform an exploratory study on the performance impact of ORM misconfiguration.

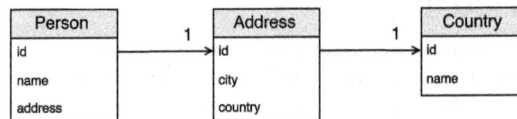

Figure 2: Database example

3. EXPLORATORY STUDY

To motivate our work, we perform an exploratory study to get an indication of how ORM configuration impacts performance.

How Does ORM Configuration Impact Performance?

By revealing the performance impact of changing the ORM configuration, we can demonstrate the importance of searching for an optimal configuration. For example, if the potential performance improvement after changing the configuration is small, it may not be worth the risk of making changes to the configuration of a stable software system.

We conducted an exploratory study with two subject applications (Spring PetClinic[2] and ZK[3]), that both use Hibernate. We selected eleven Hibernate configuration options that can influence the performance of the subject applications (see Table 3). We encode a configuration of these eleven options as a string of eleven bits. We converted the non-boolean options to boolean options by encoding their lowest allowed value as 0 and the highest allowed value as 1. This limits the total number of possible configurations to $2^{11} = 2,048$, which allows us to perform an exhaustive analysis on the solution space.

To evaluate the performance impact of changing the configuration, we need to evaluate the performance of an application when it is using that configuration. Because we do not have access to performance tests or workload generators for most systems, we use their unit tests, in particular, the ones that use ORM. To extract these tests we statically analyze the source code of a subject application and identify functions that use ORM using a list of keywords. Then we use reflection to find the unit tests that execute those functions. This process is described in more detail in Section 5.2.

We populated the database used by PetClinic and ZK with one million records that were randomly generated based on the database schema requirements. We selected 9 test cases for PetClinic and 54 for ZK. For each of the 2,048 possible

---

[1]http://hibernate.org/

[2]http://docs.spring.io/docs/petclinic.html
[3]http://zkoss.org/

Table 1: Example of the relative difference calculation

Selection	Test case	Avg. time c_1	Avg. time c_2	Diff.
#1	t_1	10	20	100%
#2	t_1	11	15	36%
#3	t_1	8	15	88%

Table 2: Default vs. optimal configuration

	PetClinic	ZK
# test cases using ORM	9	54
% test cases significantly slower than optimal	89%	96%
Effect size (only for cases that are significantly slower):		
d = small	12%	0%
d = medium	25%	71%
d = large	63%	29%

Table 3: Performance-related configuration in Hibernate [19]

Option	Value
order_updates	TRUE|FALSE
jdbc.batch_size	LOW|HIGH
order_inserts	TRUE|FALSE
connection.release_mode	TRUE|FALSE
default_batch_fetch_size	LOW|HIGH
jdbc.batch_versioned_data	TRUE|FALSE
max_fetch_depth	LOW|HIGH
id.new_generator_mappings	TRUE|FALSE
jdbc.fetch_size	TRUE|FALSE
bytecode.use_reflection_optimizer	TRUE|FALSE
cache.use_second_level_cache	TRUE|FALSE

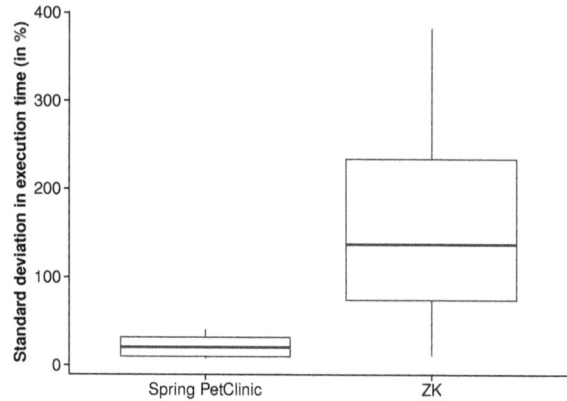

Figure 3: Standard deviation of relative difference in execution time (in %) for two randomly selected ORM configurations

configurations, we run the selected test cases 30 times to minimize variability in the performance measurements and we collect the execution time of each run for each test case.

To investigate the impact of ORM configurations on performance, we calculate the difference in execution time of the test cases when they are executed using two randomly selected configurations. We perform the following process 1,000 times for each selected test case in the subject application:

1. Randomly select two ORM configurations: c_1 and c_2

2. Take the average of the execution time of 30 runs for the test case using configuration c_1

3. Repeat step 2 using configuration c_2

4. Calculate the relative difference in execution times across both configurations

Based on the collected data, we make the following observation:

> Observation 1: Changing the ORM configuration can have a large impact on the execution time of an application.

The impact of performance-related ORM configuration options is large. Table 1 shows example output of the process we used to calculate the relative difference for one test case t_1 and three random selections of c_1 and c_2. Figure 3 shows the distribution of the standard deviation of the relative difference in execution time for two randomly selected ORM configurations across all selected test cases. For PetClinic, the median standard deviation is around 20%, while the median standard deviation for ZK is 140%.

How Does the Default ORM Configuration Perform?

Our subject applications do not include an ORM configuration. Instead, they use the default values provided by the ORM framework. We investigate the performance of this default configuration as compared to the optimal configuration.

We compared the execution times for each test case using the default configuration with the execution times using the optimal configuration for that test case using a *t-test* ($p < 0.05$). For the test cases that had a significant difference in execution time, we also calculated the effect size using *Cohen's d* [1]. Based on earlier work [14], we use the following classification for d:

$$Effect\ Size : d = \begin{cases} < 0.16 & Trivial \\ 0.16 - 0.6 & Small \\ 0.6 - 1.4 & Medium \\ > 1.4 & Large \end{cases}$$

Table 2 summarizes the results of this comparison. We observe that for 89%-96% of the test cases, their optimal configuration is significantly better than the default configuration as supplied by the ORM framework. In 88%-100%

of those cases, the difference was classified to have at least a medium effect size.

> Observation 2: For both subject applications, the default configuration as supplied by the ORM framework performs significantly worse than the test-specific optimal configuration for each test case.

Our two aforementioned observations motivate our work for finding a method that automates the configuration process. In the remainder of this paper, we will present and evaluate our approach for automatically optimizing the performance-related ORM configurations using a multi-objective genetic algorithm. First, we will give a brief introduction to genetic algorithms.

4. GENETIC ALGORITHMS

A genetic algorithm is a search-based heuristic that searches for an optimized solution in a population of solutions based

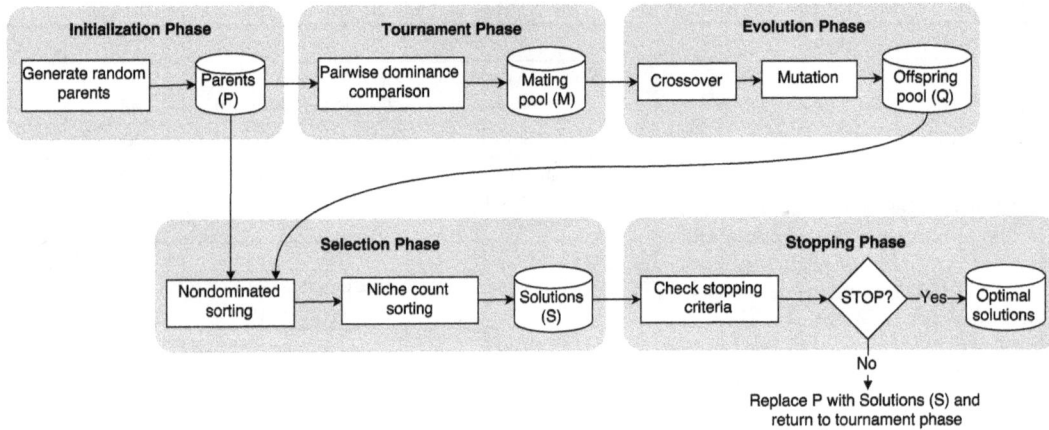

Figure 4: Phases in NSGA-II

on one or more objectives [4]. Since these objectives may be conflicting, there may be multiple optimal solutions that all have a slight bias towards one or more objectives. Genetic algorithms follow a process that closely resembles natural evolution, in particular, the 'survival of the fittest' principle. During the search, solutions that have attributes that appear to have a positive impact on one of the objectives, are selected to steer the evolution of the population. Attributes are characteristics that solutions can inherit from their parent solutions. The goal of a genetic algorithm is to improve the population during every iteration (*generation*). In our approach, we will use the non-dominated sorted genetic algorithm (NSGA-II) [5], a *multi-objective genetic algorithm* (MOGA) which aims to quickly find a set of optimal solutions. Figure 4 depicts the phases of NSGA-II, which we will explain in the remainder of this section. First, we will explain the concept of dominance and we will describe our running example that we use to demonstrate the algorithm.

4.1 Dominance

To compare two solutions that have multiple objectives, MOGAs usually rely on the concept of *dominance* [4]. A solution s_1 is said to dominate solution s_2, i.e. $s_1 \preceq s_2$, when 1) s_1 is no worse than s_2 in all objectives and 2) s_1 is strictly better than s_2 in at least one objective. By using dominance, we can compare multi-objective solutions without purposely creating a bias towards an objective.

4.2 Running Example

In a genetic algorithm, members of the population are represented as binary strings. For every member, a bit i indicates whether that member possesses the boolean attribute i. In our work, we encode configuration options as boolean attributes. In this section, we will use a running example of four boolean configuration options: { *order_updates, order_inserts, jdbc.batch_size, cache.use_second_level_cache* }. As a result, the member 1110 in the population of all combinations of these four configuration options represents the configuration in which all options except the cache are enabled. For simplicity, we will only use *execution time* as the objective in our running example. The member (1110, 50) represents that the execution time of a workload using configuration 1110 is 50 seconds. In the remainder of this section, we will explain the phases of NSGA-II using our running example.

4.3 Initialization Phase

During the initialization phase, the algorithm is started by randomly selecting a set P of members, i.e., binary strings, that will act as the initial parents in the evolution. $|P|$ represents the number of members $\in P$. The randomly selected parents in our random example are:

$$P = \{(0000, 100), (1110, 50), (1101, 100), (0111, 60)\}$$

4.4 Tournament Phase

At the start of each generation, a tournament will be held to select the best performing parents. In the tournament phase, we:

1. Randomly select two parents $P_1, P_2 \in P$ that have not been in the tournament for this generation

2. Perform a pairwise dominance comparison of P_1 and P_2 and add the dominant parent to the mating pool M

3. Repeat steps 1 and 2 until all parents $\in P$ have been in the tournament

After the tournament phase, M contains $|P|/2$ members that will be used during the evolution phase.

In our running example we compare (0000, 100) with (1110, 50) and (1101, 100) with (0111, 60). Because we have only one objective, the configurations that have a shorter execution time win the comparison. As a result,

$$M = \{(1110, 50), (0111, 60)\}$$

4.5 Evolution Phase

During the evolution phase, randomly-selected parents from the mating pool produce offspring. Evolution happens as follows:

1. Randomly select from M two parents P_1 and P_2 that have not yet evolved in this generation

2. Create an offspring that randomly inherits attributes, i.e., bits, from P_1 and P_2 (*crossover*)

3. Flip a random number of bits of the offspring (*mutation*)

312

4. Store the offspring in the offspring pool Q

In our running example we create the offspring 0110 by inheriting the first three bits from (0111, 60) and the last bit from (1110, 50) (crossover). Then, we mutate the offspring into the mutation 1111 by flipping the first and last bit. We evaluate the execution time of the workload using the mutated offspring and find that it is 40 seconds. Hence,

$$Q = \{(1111, 40)\}$$
$$P \cup Q = \{(0000, 100), (1110, 50),$$
$$(1101, 100), (0111, 60), (1111, 40)\}$$

4.6 Selection Phase

During the selection phase, members with the most positive impact on the objectives are selected. First, P and Q are combined into population X by taking their union. To select the optimal solutions, non-dominated and crowding-distance sorting are used.

During non-dominated sorting, X is ranked based on dominance: for every two members $x_i, x_j \in X$, the dominating member is assigned a higher rank than the other member, with 1 being the highest rank. We indicate the subpopulation that shares the same rank k with F_k. As a result, F_1 contains the optimal solutions found thus far, since rank 1 contains all $x_i \in X$ for which there is no $x_j \in X$ that dominates them.

Applying non-dominated sorting to X in our running example results in:

$$F_1 = (1111, 40)$$
$$F_2 = (1110, 50)$$
$$F_3 = (0111, 60)$$
$$F_4 = \{(0000, 100), (1101, 100)\}$$

To continue the evolution, we want to select $|P|$ members from the highest ranks, starting at F_1. If a rank has more members than we want to select from it, we calculate the niche count [5] between all pairs of members of the subpopulation in that rank. We calculate the niche count by counting the number of 'niche' attributes a member has compared to the other member, i.e., the number of attributes it can contribute to the population. For every two members $x_i, x_j \in X$, the member with the highest niche count has a higher niche rank, with 1 being the highest rank. We select the required number of members from the highest niche ranks. When members share a niche rank, we select random members from that rank.

(1101, 100) has a higher niche count than (0000, 100), because 1101 can contribute the first, second and fourth attribute to the population, while 0000 can contribute none. Hence, applying niche count sorting to F_4 results in:

$$F_{4,1} = (1101, 100)$$
$$F_{4,2} = (0000, 100)$$

Therefore, the set of solutions we select is:

$$Solutions = \{(1111, 40), (1110, 50), (0111, 60), (1101, 100)\}$$

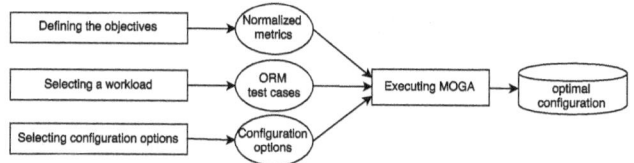

Figure 5: Finding the optimal ORM configuration

4.7 Stopping Phase

The algorithm stops when the following constraint is met: the output of the selection phase consists of members from F_1 only. If this constraint has not been satisfied, a new generation is started by using the output of the selection phase as P for the new generation. Alternatively, a generation threshold T can be specified that stops the algorithm after T generations.

5. AUTOMATIC PERFORMANCE OPTIMIZATION

In this section, we present our approach for automatically finding an optimal ORM configuration for a given application and workload. Our approach finds cross-test optimal configurations, i.e., configurations that optimize the performance for all test cases and objectives. Our approach requires three inputs: 1) the objectives that must be optimized, 2) the workload and 3) the configuration options. Figure 5 depicts the steps of our approach, which will be explained in this section.

5.1 Defining the Objectives

First, we must define the objectives that we want to optimize. Because the performance of a system has multiple, often conflicting aspects, we use a multi-objective approach. For example, optimizing both CPU usage and memory usage is a trade-off between CPU and memory. By following a multi-objective approach, we can identify the configuration that finds the optimal trade-off between conflicting objectives.

Our approach uses normalized performance metrics as objectives to avoid a bias towards objectives that have a large range of values. For example, execution time has a larger range than CPU usage, which is expressed in percentage. When optimizing execution time and CPU usage together, the algorithm may prefer the large absolute improvements a configuration can make for the execution time over the seemingly smaller improvements that can be made for CPU. In addition, normalization makes our results easier to interpret. We normalize a metric by calculating the change in percentage using a configuration compared with the performance using the current application configuration. We demonstrate the normalization process using CPU usage in n test cases for a configuration c as example below.

1. Monitor the average CPU usage for each test case i using the default configuration ($CPU_{i,current}$)

2. Monitor the average CPU usage for each test case i using c ($CPU_{i,c}$)

3. Calculate the % change for each test case i between $CPU_{i,c}$ and $CPU_{i,current}$:

$$\Delta CPU_{i,c} = \frac{CPU_{i,c} - CPU_{i,current}}{CPU_{i,current}} * 100$$

Table 4: Example CPU usage normalization

Testcase	$CPU_{i,c}$	$CPU_{i,current}$	$\Delta CPU_{i,c}$
t_1	90	100	-10
t_2	110	100	10
t_3	70	100	-30

4. Calculate the % change for all n test cases combined:

$$\Delta CPU_c = aggr(\{CPU_{t,c} | t \in \{1, .., n\}\})$$

In the last step of the process, $aggr()$ is an aggregation such as $median()$, which can be chosen based on the desired objective. As ΔCPU_c indicates the relative increase in CPU usage using configuration c as compared to the default configuration, our objective is to find the configuration c that has the smallest value for ΔCPU_c. In $CPU_{t,c}$ t is the subset of all test cases for an application which use ORM.

Table 4 shows an example of 3 test cases t_1, t_2 and t_3. The $\Delta CPU_{i,c}$ column shows that configuration c improves the CPU usage for t_1 and t_3 by 10 and 30 percent compared to the current configuration. The choice for the aggregation function influences ΔCPU_c. For example, for $median()$, $\Delta CPU_c = 10$ and for $mean()$, $\Delta CPU_c = -10$.

5.2 Selecting a Workload

To get the performance impact of a configuration compared with the default configuration, we must run a workload for the application that we want to optimize using that configuration. We propose to use a subset of the unit test suite that uses ORM. For example, we can select these test cases for Java projects as follows:

1. Define a list of keywords that identify ORM usage in functions

2. Search the subject application for functions that use ORM using the keywords

3. Collect the call hierarchy using reflection and the Eclipse JDT[4]

4. Select the unit test cases in the call hierarchy of the functions that use ORM

5.3 Selecting Configuration Options

We must define the set of configuration options that we want to use during the optimization process. This set can be selected from the documentation of the ORM framework. Every boolean configuration option can be encoded using one bit. Non-boolean options can be encoded by reserving a group of bits large enough to express the possible values. For simplicity, we use only the minimum and maximum allowed values of such options in this paper.

5.4 Executing the MOGA

After defining the objectives and selecting the workload and configuration options, we can start the MOGA as explained in Section 4. During its execution, the algorithm will generate new configurations. Every time a new configuration is generated, it is evaluated using the workload and the normalized metrics for that configuration are stored in a temporary local database, so that a configuration does not have to be reevaluated when it is encountered again during the evolution.

When the algorithm terminates, a set of optimal configurations found thus far is returned. We order these configurations based on the number of options that are changed compared to the default configuration and select a random configuration with the lowest number of changed options. Because the execution of the MOGA is fully automated, it can be integrated in a continuous integration environment to find the optimal ORM configuration for every new release. By proposing an improved configuration that requires few changes to the default configuration, we can reduce the risk of updating the configuration.

6. CASE STUDY SETUP

We evaluate our approach through a case study with two subject applications. In this section, we present the subject applications and the setup of our case study.

6.1 Subject Applications

To evaluate our approach, we use the same subject applications as used in our motivational study. Spring PetClinic is a demonstration application for the Java Spring framework. PetClinic is used regularly in performance research [3, 12, 21] as case study subject application. ZK is a web framework that assists developers in creating web GUIs. We selected ZK because of its maturity (i.e., over 22 thousand commits on GitHub) and its use of Hibernate.

6.2 Implementation

We implemented our approach in Java using the MOEA framework[5] for NSGA-II. We used SIGAR[6] to monitor the performance metrics that are used in our objectives. All test cases were executed on an Intel i7 3.6GHz quad-core processor with 16 GB RAM.

6.3 MOGA Parameters

Objectives

In our evaluation we focus on optimizing the CPU usage, memory usage and execution time. Since we express our objectives in the difference in percentage compared to the current configuration, our MOGA should search for configurations c that have minimized values for ΔCPU_c, ΔMEM_c and $\Delta EXECTIME_c$. Because our approach is multi-objective, it will search for a configuration that optimizes all these objectives together. As aggregation function for calculating ΔCPU_c, ΔMEM_c and $\Delta EXECTIME_c$ we evaluated $mean()$ and $median()$.

Workload

We selected the PetClinic and ZK unit test cases that use ORM as described in Section 5.2. This resulted in 9 (out of 13) test cases that use ORM for PetClinic and 54 (out of 55) that use ORM for ZK.

Configuration Options

We used the configuration options that are described in Table 3.

---

[4] http://www.eclipse.org/jdt/

[5] http://moeaframework.org/
[6] http://sigar.hyperic.com/

Stopping Rule

To terminate the MOGA, we run our experiments with two different stopping rules, using a t-test and the mutual dominance rate. The goal of the stopping rules is to stop the algorithm when no progress is being made in finding a better configuration.

T-test [26]: We use a t-test on each objective of all configurations generated in two consecutive generations g_i and g_j. For example, assume the solutions found in g_i are configurations a_1, a_2 and a_3 in Table 5. Likewise, b_1, b_2 and b_3 are found in g_j. In our example in Table 5, we have two objectives (CPU and MEM). Hence, we run two t-tests to compare the configurations: one on the values of ΔCPU and one on the values of ΔMEM for all configurations in both generations. When the t-tests for all objectives show insignificant differences ($p > 0.05$) for two consecutive generations, we stop the MOGA.

Mutual Dominance Rate (MDR) [16]: The mutual dominance rate is an indicator of the progress that is made by the algorithm. We introduce the number of configurations in set A that are dominated by at least one configuration in set B as dom(A,B). We define set A as the set of configurations that are found during the previous generation of the MOGA. B is the set of configurations that are found during the current generation of the MOGA. Table 5 contains two sets A and B, for which *dom()* can be calculated as follows:

$$b_1 \preceq a_2, b_1 \preceq a_3 \rightarrow dom(A, B) = \{a_2, a_3\}$$
$$a_1 \preceq b_2, a_1 \preceq b_3 \rightarrow dom(B, A) = \{b_2, b_3\}$$

Using *dom()*, the MDR is defined as:

$$MDR = \frac{|dom(A,B)|}{|A|} - \frac{|dom(B,A)|}{|B|}$$
$$MDR = \frac{2}{3} - \frac{2}{3} = 0$$

When MDR is 0, no progress is being made as both the previous set and current set of found configurations contain the same number of dominating configurations.

When MDR is -1, the solutions are actually becoming worse as the configurations in the previous set were better than in the current set (C).

$$MDR = \frac{|dom(A,C)|}{|C|} - \frac{|dom(C,A)|}{|A|}$$
$$MDR = \frac{0}{3} - \frac{3}{3} = -1$$

When MDR is 1, we know that the algorithm is progressing as there are more configurations in the current set of found configurations that are better than the configurations in the previous set. We can see that set D is better than A because:

$$MDR = \frac{|dom(A,D)|}{|A|} - \frac{|dom(D,A)|}{|D|}$$
$$MDR = \frac{3}{3} - \frac{0}{3} = 1$$

Because of the randomness in the MOGA, consecutive MDR may have alternative signs. Hence, when the MDR

Table 5: Example set A, B, C and D

	Set A			Set B	
	ΔCPU	ΔMEM		ΔCPU	ΔMEM
a_1	50	50	b_1	50	50
a_2	20	20	b_2	40	40
a_3	10	10	b_3	10	10

	Set C			Set D	
c_1	5	5	d_1	100	100
c_2	5	5	d_2	100	100
c_3	5	5	d_3	100	100

is close to zero, the MOGA can terminate.

In total, we evaluate the following 4 stopping criteria (all conditions must hold for 2 consecutive generations):

1. $STOP_t$: t-test, $p > 0.05$

2. $STOP_{0.5}$: $-0.5 < MDR < 0.5$

3. $STOP_{0.25}$: $-0.25 < MDR < 0.25$

4. $STOP_{0.1}$: $-0.1 < MDR < 0.1$

Combining the possible aggregation functions and stopping rules, we inspect a total of 8 combinations of aggregation functions and stopping rules (2 aggregation functions each evaluated with 4 stopping rules) for both studied applications during our case study. In the next section, we present our case study.

7. CASE STUDY

In this section, we discuss our case study. In particular, we focus on:

RQ1 How close are the configurations that are found by our approach to the optimal configurations? (*closeness*)

RQ2 What is the number of configurations that we need to inspect before our approach stops? (*speed*)

For both research questions, we explain the motivation behind it, our approach and our findings.

7.1 RQ1: Closeness

Motivation: The goal of our approach is to find the optimal configurations. However, limitations such as the required execution time for gathering the performance evaluation of a configuration require us to define a stopping rule. In this section, we evaluate how close the configurations found by our approach are to the optimal configurations. In addition, we evaluate how the aggregate function and stopping rule affect this closeness.

Approach: We rank all possible configurations for each subject application using non-dominated sorting, using the performance metrics that we collected during the execution of the workload (i.e., all test cases). After that, we calculate the number of configuration options that each configuration differs from the default configuration. We use this *distance*

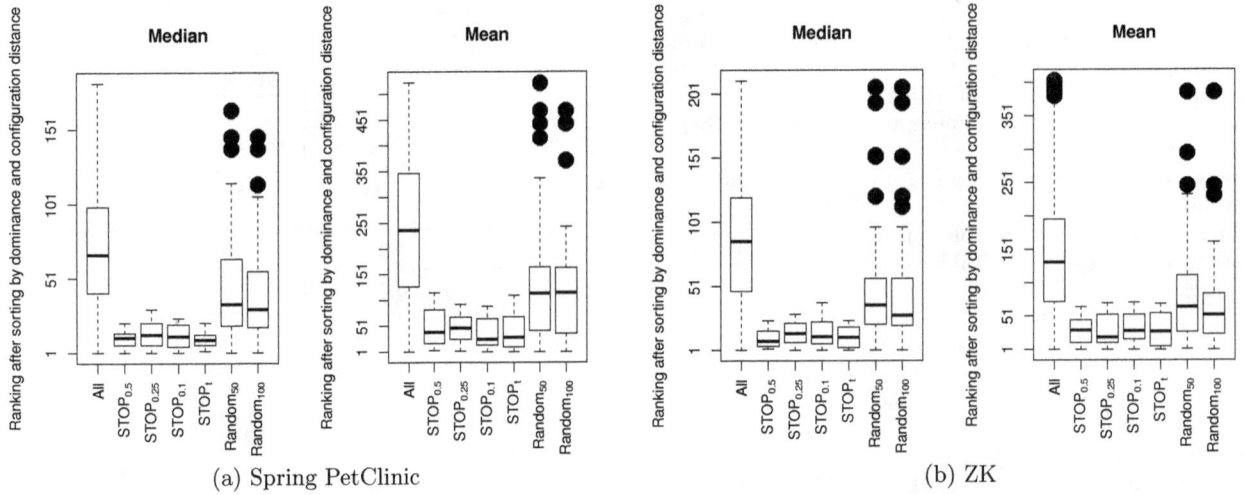

(a) Spring PetClinic   (b) ZK

Figure 6: Distribution of the ranks of all possible configurations and configurations found by our approach (rank 1 contains the optimal configuration, non-dominated and distance ranking)

to rank the configurations within a non-dominated rank. To illustrate this, Table 6 shows the top 5 ranks for PetClinic using $mean()$ as an aggregate function, $STOP_{0.25}$ as the stopping rule and 00000000000 as the default configuration. Because randomness is involved in the execution of a genetic algorithm, we execute our approach 100 times for all 8 investigated combinations of aggregation functions and stopping rules to minimize the effects of variation.

To get a baseline to compare the closeness of our approach with, we implement random selection. During the execution of our approach, we need to inspect a number of configurations n. We expect that our approach finds higher-ranked configurations as compared to when we randomly pick n configurations and select the optimal one. We perform random picking 100 times to minimize the impact of outliers. Hence, we repeat the following 100 times:

1. We select 50 ($Random_{50}$) and 100 ($Random_{100}$) configurations randomly from all possible configurations (without replacement)

2. We rank the configurations based on dominance and configuration distance and we select the configuration with the highest rank and the smallest distance

Figure 6 depicts the distribution of ranks of all possible configurations, our found solutions and the solutions that are found during our random experiments, after ranking them by dominance and configuration distance as explained.

Findings: Our approach clearly outperforms random selection for all combinations of parameters. Figure 6 shows that the rank of the worst configuration that is selected by our approach is in all cases equal to or higher (i.e., closer to 1) than the median rank of the randomly-selected configurations.

> *Case study result 1: Our approach finds configurations that are much closer to the optimal configuration than when repeatedly selecting random configurations.*

The second observation that we make in Figure 6 is that for all combinations of aggregation functions and stopping

rules, our approach finds configurations that are within the top ranked 25% of all possible configurations, i.e., the bottom of the boxplot. The boxplots in Figure 6 show that $median()$ is the best performing aggregation function.

> *Case study result 2: Our approach finds configurations that are within the top ranked 25% of all possible configurations when using all combinations of aggregation functions and stopping rules in both subject applications.*

Table 6: Top 5 ranks for PetClinic ($mean$, $STOP_{0.25}$)

Rank	Non-dominated rank	Distance	Configurations
0	0	3	00000011100 00000100110
1	0	4	00010101010 00001011001
2	0	5	10001110010 10001110001 10011001010 10001111000
3	0	6	10001111010 10010111001 00010111101 10001110101 01100111001
4	0	7	00110111011 00110011111

7.2 RQ2: Speed

Motivation: The speed with which our approach finds an optimal solution, i.e., the number of configurations it has to inspect, defines the practical applicability of our approach. Because the workload has to be executed (preferably multiple times to remove variation) in order to evaluate the performance of a configuration, the speed of our approach is dependent on the number of configurations that must be inspected.

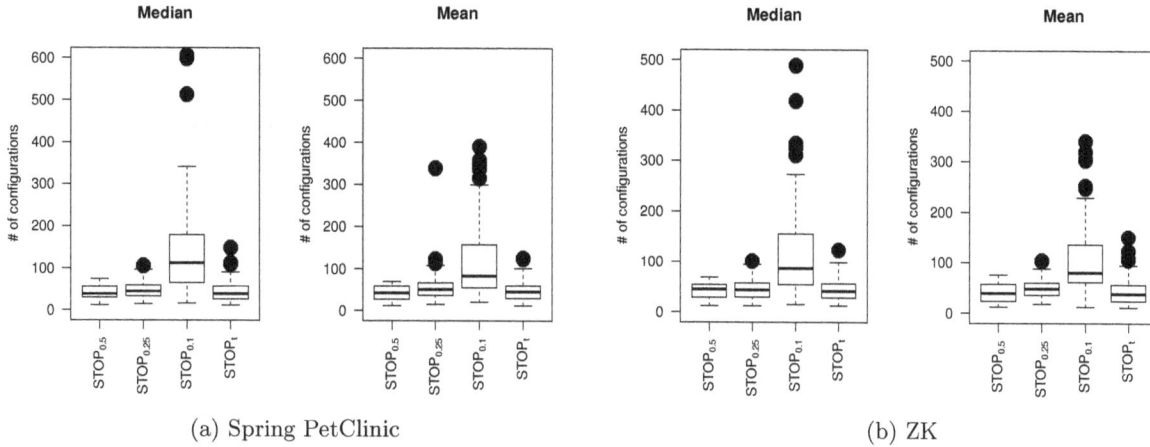

(a) Spring PetClinic   (b) ZK

Figure 7: Number of configurations generated to find an optimal configuration

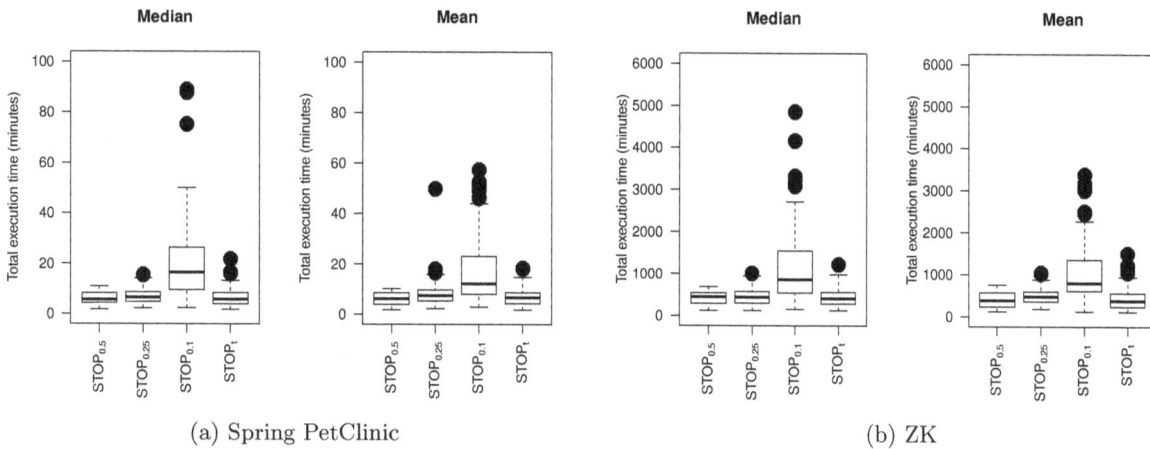

(a) Spring PetClinic   (b) ZK

Figure 8: Total execution time of our approach

Approach: To evaluate the speed with which our approach finds a solution, we monitor the number of new configurations that are generated before the algorithm terminates.

Findings: Because our approach requires the execution of the workload for every newly generated configuration, the number of new configurations generated directly influences the time in which our approach can find an optimal configuration. The execution time of the workload (i.e., all test cases executed sequentially) for PetClinic is 0.3 seconds and for ZK 28.1 seconds using the default configuration. To remove variation, we execute every workload 30 times. Hence, analyzing a new configuration for PetClinic takes 9 seconds and for ZK 843 seconds. To illustrate, analyzing all possible configurations using the subset of performance-related configuration options in Table 3 takes 5 hours for PetClinic and almost 20 days for ZK. When using a large number of configuration options, exhaustive analysis of all possible configurations is no longer feasible.

Figure 7 shows the distribution of the number of new configurations that are generated by our approach in order to find an optimal configuration for all combinations of aggregation functions and stopping rules. Figure 8 shows the

distribution of the execution time of our approach. When using $STOP_{0.5}$, $STOP_{0.25}$ or $STOP_t$ as the stopping rule, the number of analyzed configurations causes our approach to run for 360-450 seconds for PetClinic and for 9-12 hours for ZK to find an optimal configuration. This allows our approach to be run before the release of an application to find an optimal configuration.

> *Case study result 3: The execution time of our approach allows it to be executed before a new release to find an optimal configuration.*

We observe that $STOP_{0.5}$, $STOP_{0.25}$ and $STOP_t$ generate approximately the same number of configurations (40-50) before the algorithm terminates. For $STOP_{0.1}$, this number is much higher, while we observed in the previous section that the closeness does not increase. The large number of configurations generated shows that $STOP_{0.1}$ is too strict as a stopping rule.

8. THREATS TO VALIDITY

In this section, we present the threats to the validity of our work.

8.1 Internal Validity

In this paper we proposed an approach to identify the optimal ORM configuration for an application. We considered all ORM configuration options as binary values. However, some of the configuration options are non-binary values. To keep the total number of configurations low, we made these non-binary options binary by allowing only their low and high values in our motivational study and case study evaluation. This allowed us to exhaustively execute all possible configurations when evaluating the configurations that are found by our approach.

For the same reason, we selected only a subset of ORM configurations. However, the set of configuration options that are used is independent from our approach and as such, the set of configuration options can easily be adapted or extended.

During our case study we used unit test cases to evaluate the performance impact of an ORM configuration change. The advantage of using unit test cases is that they are usually readily available and repeatable in an automated fashion. In addition, the unit test cases allow us to find performance issues at the unit level. The disadvantage is that they are unlikely to be representative of a realistic workload. Our approach is agnostic to the used workload and defined objectives, making it flexible to adapt. We believe there are no limitations on the workload, other than that it should not be random, as randomness makes a fair comparison of monitored metrics impossible.

We evaluated only two different types of stopping rules (i.e. t-test and MDR). While algorithm termination is a widely researched topic in MOGA research [4, 16, 26], these two types are used regularly.

8.2 External Validity

In our case study we studied two open source projects. The evaluation of our approach may not generalize to other projects. In addition, ORM is widely adapted by enterprise applications [20]; while our studied projects are open source projects. Our findings may not generalize to enterprise applications. In future work, we plan to evaluate our approach on a large-scale industrial project.

One programming language (Java) and one ORM framework (Hibernate) is covered in our case study. Although the studied language and ORM framework are widely used in practice, the findings may be different for other programming languages and other frameworks. More case studies with more projects, especially enterprise applications, other programming languages and also other ORM frameworks, would complement our work.

9. RELATED WORK

We now describe prior research that is related to this paper. We focus on the research that aims to optimize configurations of large software systems. We discuss two types of prior research towards optimizing configurations: 1) Understanding the impact of configuration and 2) Proactive configuration optimization.

9.1 Understanding the Impact of Configuration Options

Large software systems often provide a large number of configuration options [2]. All too often, practitioners are not aware of the impact of configuration options. However, a thorough understanding of the options is essential for optimizing configurations. Prior research proposes techniques that assist in understanding the impact of configuration options.

In existing work, performance models are built that use configuration options to predict performance metrics (e.g. response time, resource utilization). Practitioners can better understand the impact of configuration options by measuring the impact of these options on the performance metrics in the model. Siegmund et al. [22] build linear regression models to understand the performance impact of configuration options. To address the challenge of having a large number of configuration options, Siegmund et al. [23] leverage forward and backward feature selection techniques to reduce the number of configuration options in the model. Guo et al. [10] leverage non-linear regression models to model system performance. Their approach automatically identifies the configuration options that have the largest impact on performance and builds models with such configuration options. As a follow-up work, Zhang et al. [34] leverage Fourier transformations on performance counters to build performance prediction models.

Statistical methodologies are often leveraged for understanding the impact of configuration options. However, to quantify the impact of each configuration option, one would need to evaluate the performance of using every possible combination of configuration options. To reduce such effort, Debnath et al. [6] assume that the impact of configuration options on performance is monotonic and there only exist single and two-factor interactions among configuration options on performance. With this assumption, Debnath et al. leverages *Plackett and Burman* statistical design methodology [25] to rank the impact of configuration options on system performance.

Prior research can assist practitioners in understanding the impact of configuration options on performance. However, even with such knowledge, practitioners may still need help in choosing the optimal configurations. Moreover, all too often, the optimal configurations depend on the specific workload. Therefore, instead of understanding the impact of configuration options on performance, this paper focuses on automatically suggesting configurations to achieve optimal performance.

9.2 Proactive Configuration Optimization

To suggest better configurations for large software systems, prior research proposes techniques that proactively optimizes the configurations of a system. These techniques do not target any particular configuration issues in the system.

Configuration optimization with optimizing algorithms. The most widely used approach to optimize configurations is through the use of an optimizing algorithm, such as hill-climbing. Duan et al. [8] proposes a framework that assists in leveraging such optimizing algorithms to find optimal configurations. The framework leverages adaptive sampling to select the experiments to evaluate performance of configurations with and performs on-line experiments in the production environment with near zero performance overhead. Xi et al. [29] optimize the configuration for the application server using sampling and a smart hill-climbing algorithm, which selects important samples for the experiment to search the optimal configuration. Lengauer et al. [15] proposes an approach that identifies the optimal configuration for the JVM garbage collector. Their approach leverages the ParamILS algorithm which performs local search iteratively. Wang et al. [27] propose an approach to optimize the configuration for Hadoop based on a hill-climbing algorithm.

To address the challenge of having a large search space for the optimal configurations, Osogami et al. [17] propose approaches that perform adaptive search to find a configuration that is better than the default configuration. Their approach only considers the configurations with minimal changes while searching for the better configuration. In addition, their approach aims to reduce the total time required for searching the best configuration by reducing the evaluation time for each configuration. A follow up work by Osogami et al. [18] improves their prior approach [17] by guessing the performance of configurations based on similarities between configurations. Instead of reducing the time of evaluating configuration performance, Thonangi et al. [24] reduces the candidates of optimal configurations by selecting a sample of configurations that most likely have the optimal performance.

In this paper, we also leverage an optimization algorithm, i.e., a multi-objective genetic algorithm, to find the optimal configurations for performance. Above mentioned techniques optimize the configurations of a system based on single objective i.e., the execution time. In contrast, our work focuses on optimizing multiple objectives at once.

Configuration optimization based on performance models. Section 9.1 presents prior research that build performance models in order to understand the impact of configurations. Such models are further leveraged to optimize configurations. Zheng et al. [35] propose an approach for optimizing configurations by traversing a configuration option dependency graph based on performance models. Diao et al. [7] monitor the CPU and memory utilization for web servers. Diao et al. model CPU and memory utilization and leverage such a model to achieve optimal configuration for an application.

Configuration optimization based on user experience. Popular large software systems often have a large user base. Experiences of choosing configuration options provide valuable information and can be generalized as guidelines of optimizing configurations of the system. Zheng et al. [36] observe that different users of a system may have the same optimal configurations and each user can have multiple near-optimal configurations. Therefore, Zheng et al. propose an approach that leverages existing configuration from different users and applies the configuration accordingly on the new software installation.

10. CONCLUSION

Object-relational mapping (ORM) provides a mapping between the higher level object-oriented model and the lower level relational model of a database management system. ORM frameworks offer a variety of configuration options that allow the user to configure how this mapping is performed in an optimal fashion.

In our motivational study we observe that ORM configurations have a large impact on the performance of an application.

Motivated by this observation, we propose an approach for automatically optimizing the performance configurations of

ORM frameworks using a multi-objective genetic algorithm (MOGA). Using a MOGA allows us to optimize the performance based on multiple, possibly conflicting, objectives. In summary, these are the most important results of this paper:

- Two randomly selected configurations can lead to a large difference in execution time

- The default configuration as supplied by the ORM framework performed in 89-96% of the analyzed test cases significantly slower than the optimal configuration for that case

- Our approach can find a near-optimal configuration in a time that makes it feasible to find such a configuration before the new release of an application

11. REFERENCES

[1] Using effect size - or why the p value is not enough. http://www.ncbi.nlm.nih.gov/pmc/articles/PMC3444174/.

[2] W. A. Babich. *Software configuration management: coordination for team productivity.* Addison-Wesley Reading, 1986.

[3] T.-H. Chen, W. Shang, Z. M. Jiang, A. E. Hassan, M. Nasser, and P. Flora. Detecting performance anti-patterns for applications developed using object-relational mapping. In *Proceedings of the 36th International Conference on Software Engineering,* pages 1001–1012. ACM, 2014.

[4] K. Deb. *Multi-objective optimization using evolutionary algorithms,* volume 16. John Wiley & Sons, 2001.

[5] K. Deb, A. Pratap, S. Agarwal, and T. Meyarivan. A fast and elitist multiobjective genetic algorithm: Nsga-ii. *Evolutionary Computation, IEEE Transactions on,* 6(2):182–197, 2002.

[6] B. K. Debnath, D. J. Lilja, and M. F. Mokbel. Sard: A statistical approach for ranking database tuning parameters. In *Data Engineering Workshop, 2008. ICDEW 2008. IEEE 24th International Conference on,* pages 11–18. IEEE, 2008.

[7] Y. Diao, J. L. Hellerstein, S. Parekh, and J. P. Bigus. Managing web server performance with autotune agents. *IBM Systems Journal,* 42(1):136–149, 2003.

[8] S. Duan, V. Thummala, and S. Babu. Tuning database configuration parameters with ituned. *Proceedings of the VLDB Endowment,* 2(1):1246–1257, 2009.

[9] K. Eaton. How one second could cost amazon $1.6 billion in sales. http://www.fastcompany.com/1825005/how-one-second-could-cost-amazon-16-billion-sales (last visited: Sep 17 2015).

[10] J. Guo, K. Czarnecki, S. Apel, N. Siegmund, and A. Wasowski. Variability-aware performance prediction: A statistical learning approach. In *Automated Software Engineering (ASE), 2013 IEEE/ACM 28th International Conference on,* pages 301–311. IEEE, 2013.

[11] F. Hutter, H. H. Hoos, K. Leyton-Brown, and T. Stützle. Paramils: an automatic algorithm configuration framework. *Journal of Artificial Intelligence Research,* 36(1):267–306, 2009.

[12] Z. M. Jiang, A. E. Hassan, G. Hamann, and P. Flora. Automatic identification of load testing problems. In *IEEE International Conference on Software Maintenance (ICSM)*, pages 307–316. IEEE, 2008.

[13] Java tools and technologies landscape for 2014. http://zeroturnaround.com/rebellabs/ java-tools-and-technologies-landscape-for-2014/ (last visited: Oct 7 2015).

[14] V. B. Kampenes, T. Dybå, J. E. Hannay, and D. I. K. Sjøberg. A systematic review of effect size in software engineering experiments. *Information and Software Technology*, 49(11-12):1073–1086, Nov 2007.

[15] P. Lengauer and H. Mössenböck. The taming of the shrew: Increasing performance by automatic parameter tuning for java garbage collectors. In *Proceedings of the 5th ACM/SPEC international conference on Performance engineering*, pages 111–122. ACM, 2014.

[16] L. Martí, J. García, A. Berlanga, and J. M. Molina. An approach to stopping criteria for multi-objective optimization evolutionary algorithms: the mgbm criterion. In *IEEE Congress on Evolutionary Computation (CEC)*, pages 1263–1270. IEEE, 2009.

[17] T. Osogami and T. Itoko. Finding probably better system configurations quickly. In *ACM SIGMETRICS Performance Evaluation Review*, volume 34, pages 264–275. ACM, 2006.

[18] T. Osogami and S. Kato. Optimizing system configurations quickly by guessing at the performance. In *ACM SIGMETRICS Performance Evaluation Review*, volume 35, pages 145–156. ACM, 2007.

[19] Red Hat Middleware, LLC. Hibernate manual: Configuration. https://docs.jboss.org/hibernate/orm/3.3/ reference/en/html/session-configuration.html (last visited: Sep 24 2015).

[20] A. R. Seddighi. *Spring Persistence with Hibernate: Build Robust and Reliable Persistence Solutions for Your Enterprise Java Application.* Packt Publishing Ltd, 2009.

[21] V. Sharma and S. Anwer. Performance antipatterns: Detection and evaluation of their effects in the cloud. In *Services Computing (SCC), 2014 IEEE International Conference on*, pages 758–765, June 2014.

[22] N. Siegmund, A. Grebhahn, S. Apel, and C. Kästner. Performance influence models for highly configurable systems. In *Proceedings of the International Symposium on Foundations of Software Engineering (FSE)*, 2015.

[23] N. Siegmund, S. S. Kolesnikov, C. Kästner, S. Apel, D. Batory, M. Rosenmüller, and G. Saake. Predicting performance via automated feature-interaction detection. In *Proceedings of the 34th International Conference on Software Engineering*, pages 167–177. IEEE Press, 2012.

[24] R. Thonangi, V. Thummala, and S. Babu. Finding good configurations in high-dimensional spaces: Doing more with less. In *Modeling, Analysis and Simulation of Computers and Telecommunication Systems, 2008. MASCOTS 2008. IEEE International Symposium on*, pages 1–10. IEEE, 2008.

[25] J. Tyssedal. Plackett–burman designs. *Encyclopedia of Statistics in Quality and Reliability*, 2008.

[26] T. Wagner, H. Trautmann, and L. Martí. A taxonomy of online stopping criteria for multi-objective evolutionary algorithms. In *Evolutionary Multi-Criterion Optimization*, pages 16–30. Springer, 2011.

[27] K. Wang, X. Lin, and W. Tang. Predatorâ̆ĂŤan experience guided configuration optimizer for hadoop mapreduce. In *Cloud Computing Technology and Science (CloudCom), 2012 IEEE 4th International Conference on*, pages 419–426. IEEE, 2012.

[28] A. Wool. A quantitative study of firewall configuration errors. *Computer*, 37(6):62–67, June 2004.

[29] B. Xi, Z. Liu, M. Raghavachari, C. H. Xia, and L. Zhang. A smart hill-climbing algorithm for application server configuration. In *Proceedings of the 13th international conference on World Wide Web*, pages 287–296. ACM, 2004.

[30] T. Xu, J. Zhang, P. Huang, J. Zheng, T. Sheng, D. Yuan, Y. Zhou, and S. Pasupathy. Do not blame users for misconfigurations. In *Proceedings of the Twenty-Fourth ACM Symposium on Operating Systems Principles*, pages 244–259. ACM, 2013.

[31] Z. Yin, X. Ma, J. Zheng, Y. Zhou, L. N. Bairavasundaram, and S. Pasupathy. An empirical study on configuration errors in commercial and open source systems. In *Proceedings of the Twenty-Third ACM Symposium on Operating Systems Principles*, pages 159–172. ACM, 2011.

[32] M. Yonkovit. The cost of not properly managing your databases. https://www.percona.com/blog/2015/04/ 06/cost-not-properly-managing-databases/ (last visited: Sep 17 2015).

[33] S. Zhang and M. D. Ernst. Automated diagnosis of software configuration errors. In *Proceedings of the 2013 International Conference on Software Engineering*, pages 312–321. IEEE Press, 2013.

[34] Y. Zhang, J. Guo, E. Blais, and K. Czarnecki. Performance prediction of configurable software systems by fourier learning. In *Proceedings of the International Conference on Automated Software Engineering (ASE)*, 2015.

[35] W. Zheng, R. Bianchini, and T. D. Nguyen. Automatic configuration of internet services. *ACM SIGOPS Operating Systems Review*, 41(3):219–229, 2007.

[36] W. Zheng, R. Bianchini, and T. D. Nguyen. Massconf: automatic configuration tuning by leveraging user community information. In *ICPE*, pages 283–288, 2011.

Building Custom, Efficient, and Accurate Memory Monitoring Tools for Java Applications

Verena Bitto
Christian Doppler Laboratory MEVSS
Johannes Kepler University Linz, Austria
verena.bitto@jku.at

Philipp Lengauer
Institute for System Software
Johannes Kepler University Linz, Austria
philipp.lengauer@jku.at

ABSTRACT

Traditional monitoring techniques can distort application behavior significantly. In this paper, we will provide an evaluation of state-of-the-art monitoring techniques and their impact on memory behavior. We will use AntTracks to show how VM-internal approaches can extract more diverse memory information at object level, vastly outperforming traditional techniques.

Keywords

Memory Monitoring; Garbage Collection; Java; Memory Monitoring Tools

1. INTRODUCTION

Higher-level programming languages like Java or C# relieve the programmer from freeing memory manually by applying automatic memory management, i.e., garbage collection (GC). Concomitantly, the actual memory behavior is hidden from the developer, making the detection of the actual source for memory anomalies a tedious task. Memory monitoring tools allow to keep track of memory internals, such as memory allocations and GC time. However, what kind of information can be tracked, at what granularity and at which costs depends mainly on the approach used for monitoring. Many existing tools impose an enormous memory footprint and run-time overhead on the monitored application, neglecting that such characteristics distort the actual memory behavior. This paper provides insights into all common monitoring strategies, i.e., *Sample-based Monitoring*, *Instrumentation-based Monitoring* and *VM-internal Monitoring*. We especially focus on VM-internal monitoring and our tool AntTracks, introduced at the ICPE'15 [3], to sketch which advantages as well as challenges custom monitoring tools implicate.

This paper is structured as follows: Section 2 describes state of the monitoring tools techniques, their benefits and drawbacks as well as their impact on the actual memory behavior; Section 3 compares all techniques by means of their information richness and information quality. Furthermore we show exemplary, which performance can be expected for different monitoring approaches; Section 4 concludes this paper.

2. STATE OF THE ART MONITORING TECHNIQUES

State-of-the-art approaches can be divided into 3 categories, i.e., *Sample-based Monitoring*, *Instrumentation-based Monitoring*, and *VM-internal Monitoring*. These approaches have fundamental differences in run-time overhead, information richness (such as the kind of data that can be captured) as well as quality (such as the accuracy of the generated results). We do not regard *Event-based Monitoring* as a distinct approach here, because one of the just mentioned approaches must be used to generate events in the first place.

The following sections will describe every approach in detail, including basic principles as well as a performance evaluation in the context of memory monitoring. We built tools according to the mentioned monitoring techniques with the aim to produce equivalent memory-related data in order to compare them accordingly. As basis for information comparison we used our tool AntTracks, since *VM-internal* techniques allow for the most diverse data to collect.

2.1 Sampling-based Monitoring

Sampling-based monitoring tools collect data periodically. In the best case, they reflect a statistically valid representation of the program under inspection. Commonly gathered information includes CPU usage information, e.g., the amount of time threads spend in specific methods, or memory information, e.g., the amount of memory data structures occupy. What kind of information can be extracted without modifying the virtual machine itself depends on the provided interface, e.g., the Java virtual machine tools interface (JVMTI) for Java or the ICorProfilerCallback interface for .NET.

A key requirement for sampling-based approaches is to sample at random time intervals. Otherwise the tool may record periodically recurring phases of a program over and over again, e.g., the stack traces of threads which are scheduled at certain intervals, while missing other phases in-between. However, randomizing sample intervals is difficult, since the program needs to be in a certain state, i.e., in safe points to pause application threads, for retrieving samples [1]. As a result, the accuracy of samples are limited by the underlying virtual machine. Consequently, different monitoring tools may deliver different results on specific metrics

ICPE'16, March 12-18, 2016, Delft, Netherlands
© 2016 ACM. ISBN 978-1-4503-4080-9/16/03...$15.00
DOI: http://dx.doi.org/10.1145/2851553.2858664

like frequently called methods, as pointed out by Mytkowicz et al. [5].

2.2 Instrumentation-based Monitoring

Instrumentation-based monitoring tools allow to modify the original code of an application such that it records the desired information. Code can be instrumented either statically or dynamically, whereupon the former inserts code at compile-time, and the latter at run-time. In the latter case, the underlying virtual machine must support retrieving the original code and exchanging it with the manipulated one, e.g., by means of the JVMTI or the ICorProfilerCallback interface. However, these interfaces only provide means to instrument at bytecode level, not at machine code level.

Compared to sampling, instrumentation-based approaches allow to record more accurate information. However, due to the modified or injected code, instrumentation may impose a significant run-time overhead on the application (1) due to the additional code itself and (2) due to the just-in-time compiler not being able to apply the same optimizations.

2.3 VM-internal Monitoring

Tools using the VM-internal monitoring approach require a modified VM to host the monitored application. The modified VM can expose internal data structures to the monitoring tool. For example, a VM may provide access to internal timers that keep track of the time of certain GC phases. Using this information, the monitoring tool may be able to explain long garbage collection times.

However, when already modifying the VM to expose additional data, one might consider to move as much as possible of the monitoring logic into the VM, because the information of interest is easier and faster to access.

In previous work (cf. Lengauer et al. [3] and Bitto et al. [2]), we have presented *AntTracks*, a custom VM able to trace object allocations and object deallocations imposing only a very small run-time overhead. Minimizing overhead is paramount to reduce the impact of the Observer Effect. Especially in the context of managed memory, a lot of adaptive heuristics and adaptive thresholds are in place to manage garbage collection. Even small changes in garbage collection time or in object allocations may lead to different choices by the GC, changing the overall garbage collection behavior and, in consequence, memory performance.

However, modifying a VM to support monitoring raises some interesting challenges if one of the primary goals is low run-time overhead and in-production use, such as (1) how to record the data, (2) how to maintain the data within the VM, (3) how to send the data to an external monitoring tool, (4) how to store the mass of data as well as (5) how to process the raw data and how to transform it to a meaningful memory representation.

Recording. The information of interest needs to be recorded, without distorting the application behavior. For example, AntTracks must fire an event for every new object by inserting code at every allocation. However, contrary to traditional instrumentation, it can insert the code during the lowering phase of the intermediate representation (i.e., in the abstract syntax tree) of the just-in-time compiler to machine code. If the allocation is optimized away, e.g., by escape analysis and scalar replacement, the allocation will not be lowered to machine code, and thus no instrumentation will be performed. Traditional bytecode instrumentation would impede escape analysis and scalar replacement, and thus change the application behavior by forcing the allocation of the object, no matter what.

Managing. The next step comprises the management of the recorded data, as we want to keep IO to a minimum and consequently do not want to process and send every event immediately. An obvious approach is to buffer data until enough has aggregated and send an entire chunk when the buffer is full, instead of firing every event one by one. However, buffering needs to be implemented carefully in order not to degrade performance. For example, when multiple threads record data in parallel, the buffer must be locked. Additionally, flushing the buffer (e.g., to a file) when it is full may block other threads for a significant amount of time. Thus, AntTracks uses thread-local buffers, i.e., every thread own its private buffer to write events to. Furthermore, when the buffer is full, the buffer is not flushed directly (which would stop the thread for too long), instead the buffer is submitted to a flush queue and a new buffer is fetched from a free list. A dedicated worker thread consumes buffers from this queue, flushes them, and submits it to the free list. Buffer sizes are randomized to avoid multiple threads with the same recording frequency to submit buffers to the flush queue at the same time.

Sending. Sending includes either storing the recorded data in a file for subsequent analysis or sending it, e.g., using a socket connection, to a tool directly. The performance of this step is heavily dependent on the underlying operating system and hardware performance.

Storing. Storing the recorded data for subsequent analysis can be challenging if the amount of data faces disk limitations. Most tools reduce their accuracy and send statistical aggregations only. However, aggregation must be done at run-time, whereupon it increases run-time overhead.

AntTracks uses a novel approach by cyclically overwriting old tracing information without losing most vital information (cf. Lengauer et al. [4]). It creates multiple trace files, clears them periodically, and starts every trace file with a synchronization point, which can be used for reattaching to the Java heap state.

Processing. Stored data is often highly compacted, keeping the storage performance and recording performance in mind. Thus, the raw data needs to be processed and transformed to meaningful memory representations. Depending on the amount of data collected, this can take up a significant amount of time.

AntTracks reconstructs thread-local heap states, and merges them at defined points in time. Thus the recorded data can be processed mostly in parallel.

3. COMPARISON

The following section compares monitoring techniques exemplary to give an estimate regarding information richness, information quality and performance. To compare the different approaches fairly, we have started from AntTracks and built tools trying to record as much of the same data as possible, once via sampling, i.e., dumping the heap periodically, and once via instrumentation at bytecode level.

Setup. All measurements were run on an Intel® Core TM i7-3770 CPU @ 3.4GHz x 4 (8 Threads) on 64-bit with 32 GB RAM and a Samsung SSD 840 PRO Series (DXM03B0Q), running Ubuntu Trusty Tahr 14.04 with the

Kernel Linux 3.11.0-23-generic. All unnecessary services were disabled in order not to distort the experiments.

3.1 Information Richness and Quality

Different monitoring techniques provide different levels of granularity of information. Figure 1 gives an overview about the different kind of traced information of the discussed monitoring strategies.

Information	Smpl. Ref.	Instr. Ref.	ET	VM AT
Object allocations	Some	All	All	All
– Size	All	All	All	All
– Type	All	All	All	All
– Pointers	All	None*	All	All
– Allocation site	None	All	All	All
– Address	None	None	None	All
– Allocating subsystem	None	None	None	All
Object deaths	Some	All	All	All
– Time unreachable	None	None	All	None
– Time collected	Some	All	None*	All
– Liveness from GC	None	None	None	All
Object lifecycle	None	None	None	All
Object movements	None	None	None	All
Heap structure	None	None	None	All
Method entries/exits	None*	None*	All	None
Temporal ordering	All	Some	All	Some
Explicit GCs triggered	None	None	All	None
Arbitrary VMs	All	Some	Some	None

Figure 1: Comparison of the capabilities of sampling-based (our reference implementation), instrumentation-based (our reference implementation as well as ElephantTracks (ET), the most similar tool to AntTracks) and VM-internal (AntTracks - AT) monitoring. (*Recording of information possible, but not implemented)

Object allocations can be tracked with every monitoring technique, although the amount of monitored information differs. Sampling stands out as the only method that may miss allocations altogether, e.g., objects may be allocated and freed in the time between two samples. Although all techniques provide basic object information like its size, its type and its pointers, only VM-based monitoring allows to collect internal information like the object's address or its allocating subsystem, i.e., the interpreter, C1 compiler or C2 compiler. Object deaths can be monitored with all techniques as well. Sampling-based approaches suffer again from incompleteness due to non-sampled time intervals. Other approaches differ in their definition of object death. ET considers the time an object becomes unreachable, while our instrumentation-based reference implementation and AT track the time an object is actually freed by the GC. The instrumentation approach uses `Phantom-References` (a more scalable variant of `WeakReferences`) to detect deallocations. Since garbage collection data is only available via VM-internal tracking, ET has to run its own reachability analysis to determine liveness of objects, by explicitly triggering additional GCs. Movements of objects, e.g., during garbage collection, are only monitored by the VM-internal approach. As a result, VM-internal techniques can reproduce the entire lifecycle of objects. This includes

changes to the object's pointers as well as its location in the heap.

Likewise, the heap structure can only be reconstructed by the VM-internal approach. This covers both object related information, e.g., the location of objects in the heap, as well as memory related information, e.g., address ranges of a specific heap region.

Method-related data cannot be monitored via sampling since heap dumps lack this kind of information. In case of AT and our sample-based reference implementation, it currently is not monitored by choice, since the hotness of methods is derived differently.

Temporal ordering concerns the chronological order of monitored information. Since AT and our instrumentation-based reference implementation record events in a thread-local manner contrary to ET, event ordering among different thread is not ensured. Sample-based approaches are by definition in order, due to the periodically drawing of samples.

Although, on the one hand, every JVM supports heap-dumps, instrumentation on the other hand requires an interface like JVMTI which is supported from JDK 5.0 onwards. VM-internal tracking requires a modified VM and therefore lacks portability.

3.2 Performance

All three approaches have major differences in terms of overhead as well as behavior distortion they introduce. Figure 2 and 3 show the run-time overhead and the GC-time overhead respectively, normalized compared to the application without any active monitoring.

To make the sampling approach comparable to the instrumentation approach and the VM-internal approach, we adjusted the sampling rate for every benchmark individually, so that the sampling approach generates as many dumps as the other approaches can reproduce a full and consistent heap state.

In terms of *run-time*, the VM-internal approach, i.e., AntTracks, outperforms all other tools. In some cases, i.e., mpegaudio, avrora, and scalaxb, the sampling strategy performs almost as good because these benchmarks only have few allocations and even fewer live objects, consequently resulting in small and fast dumps. For allocation intensive applications, however, sampling produces an overhead of at least 100%. The instrumentation approach produces the most overhead, due to impeding the scalar replacement of objects and its need for additional object allocations (phantom references).

In terms of *GC-time*, the sampling strategy performs best with only one exception (factorie) because it only introduces pauses while the application is running. Consequently, sampling shows only slight deviations regarding GC-time, due to the changed application-to-GC ratio. The instrumentation-based approach actually introduces so much GC overhead, that three benchmarks (compiler.compiler, xml.validation, factorie) crash altogether, because the VM spends more than 98% of its time on garbage collection. This overhead is caused by effectively doubling the amount of objects, i.e., one phantom reference for every object allocated, and the additional handling of those special references by the GC. In those benchmarks that do not crash, the overhead is with a minimum (with the least-allocating benchmark mpegaudio) of 2922% and a maximum of 48408% tremendous. The VM-internal approach changes the GC behavior because of

Benchmark	Sampling		Instrumentation	VM-internal (AntTracks)	
compiler.compiler		279.2% crashed			119.8%
mpegaudio		102.4%	104.2%		100.4%
xml.validation		378.2% crashed			116.7%
avrora		102.5%	113.8%		100.0%
jython		213.7%	515.0%		105.6%
factorie		377.3% crashed			126.0%
scalaxb		135.1%	255.8%		103.1%

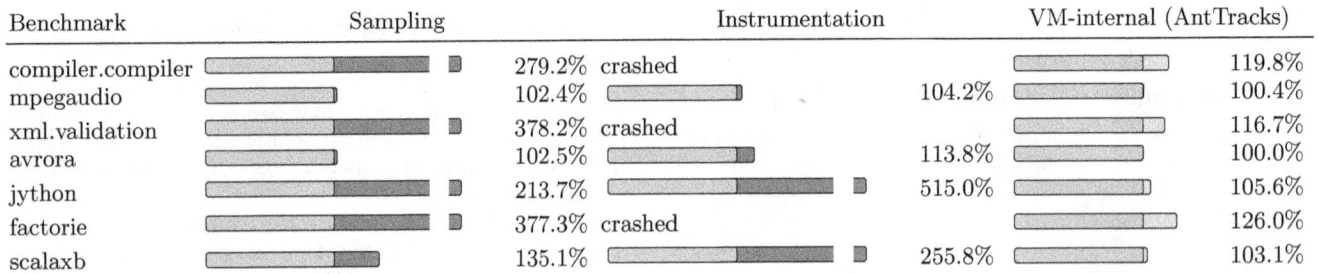

Figure 2: **Run time of all three approaches, relative to the respective application's run-time without any monitoring.**

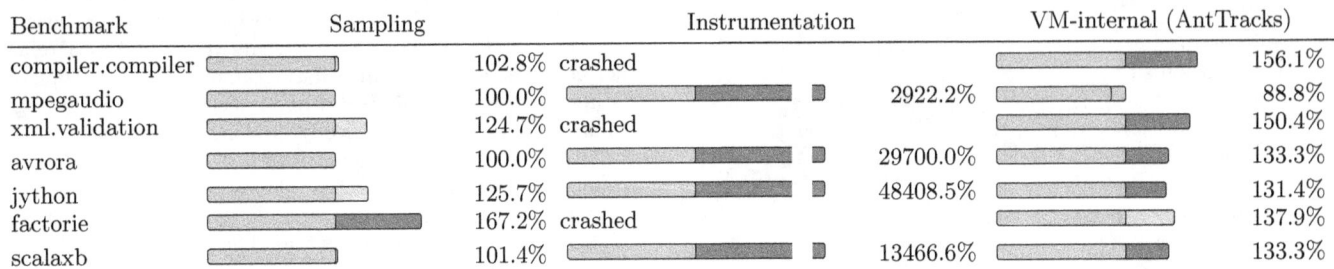

Benchmark	Sampling		Instrumentation	VM-internal (AntTracks)	
compiler.compiler		102.8% crashed			156.1%
mpegaudio		100.0%	2922.2%		88.8%
xml.validation		124.7% crashed			150.4%
avrora		100.0%	29700.0%		133.3%
jython		125.7%	48408.5%		131.4%
factorie		167.2% crashed			137.9%
scalaxb		101.4%	13466.6%		133.3%

Figure 3: **GC time of all three approaches, relative to the respective application's GC time without any monitoring.**

its internal instrumentation. Consequently, the overall GC-time is higher, however, the overhead is pretty constant and predictable compared to the other approaches.

The *data size* (bytes generated) is variable depending on the approach. In general, the instrumentation approach produces more data than the VM-internal approach, because the first has to send an event for every deallocated object, whereas the latter has to send only events for live objects. Considering that only a small portion of objects survive their first GC, the former has to generate more data. The data size of the sampling approach is highly unpredictable, depending on when a dump is taken, i.e., right before vs. right after a garbage collection.

4. CONCLUSION

In this paper, we evaluated different monitoring techniques with respect to three metrics, i.e., information quality, information richness and overhead in terms of run time, GC time, and heap memory. Although a VM-internal approach, such as AntTracks, poses more complex and VM-specific challenges to overcome, we showed that it outperforms the traditional techniques in all three metrics. Our approach incorporates new techniques for efficient monitoring, that can be easily adapted for other high-performance and almost distortion-free tools.

5. ACKNOWLEDGMENTS

This work was supported by the Christian Doppler Forschungsgesellschaft, and by Dynatrace Austria GmbH.

6. REFERENCES

[1] B. Alpern, C. R. Attanasio, J. J. Barton, M. G. Burke, P. Cheng, J.-D. Choi, A. Cocchi, S. J. Fink, D. Grove, M. Hind, S. F. Hummel, D. Lieber, V. Litvinov, M. F. Mergen, T. Ngo, J. R. Russell, V. Sarkar, M. J. Serrano, J. C. Shepherd, S. E. Smith, V. C. Sreedhar, H. Srinivasan, and J. Whaley. The jalapeño virtual machine. *IBM Syst. J.*, 39(1):211–238, Jan. 2000.

[2] V. Bitto, P. Lengauer, and H. Mössenböck. Efficient rebuilding of large java heaps from event traces. In *Proceedings of the Principles and Practices of Programming on The Java Platform*, PPPJ '15, pages 76–89, New York, NY, USA, 2015. ACM.

[3] P. Lengauer, V. Bitto, and H. Mössenböck. Accurate and efficient object tracing for java applications. In *Proc. of the 6th ACM/SPEC Int'l. Conf. on Performance Engineering*, ICPE '15, pages 51–62, 2015.

[4] P. Lengauer, V. Bitto, and H. Mössenböck. Efficient and viable handling of large object traces. In *Proc. of the 7th ACM/SPEC Int'l. Conf. on Performance Engineering*, ICPE '16, pages 51–62, 2016.

[5] T. Mytkowicz, A. Diwan, M. Hauswirth, and P. F. Sweeney. Evaluating the accuracy of java profilers. In *Proceedings of the 31st ACM SIGPLAN Conference on Programming Language Design and Implementation*, PLDI '10, pages 187–197, New York, NY, USA, 2010.

Automated Parameterization of Performance Models from Measurements

Giuliano Casale
Imperial College London
London, UK
g.casale@imperial.ac.uk

Simon Spinner
University of Würzburg
Würzburg, Germany
simon.spinner@uni-wuerzburg.de

Weikun Wang
Imperial College London
London, UK
weikun.wang11@imperial.ac.uk

ABSTRACT

Estimating parameters of performance models from empirical measurements is a critical task, which often has a major influence on the predictive accuracy of a model. This tutorial presents the problem of parameter estimation in queueing systems and queueing networks. The focus is on reliable estimation of the *arrival rates* of the requests and of the *service demands* they place at the servers. The tutorial covers common estimation techniques such as regression methods, maximum-likelihood estimation, and moment-matching, discussing their sensitivity with respect to data and model characteristics. The tutorial also demonstrates the automated estimation of model parameters using new open source tools.

Keywords

Demand Estimation; Arrival Processes

1. INTRODUCTION

The emergence of cloud computing and DevOps poses an increasing demand for tools to automatically instantiate performance models and to reduce the effort of practitioners in using them. However, it is challenging to translate performance measurements into concrete parameters of performance models. We here focus on queueing systems and networks, where the critical input parameters are service demands, which represent the cumulative amount of time a request is processed at a server before completion, and the arrival rates of requests to a queue from the external world.

Service demands, in particular, are hard to obtain as these are not explicitly tracked by log files, and deep monitoring instrumentation typically poses unacceptably large overheads, especially at high resolutions. Considering that real-world application requests can complete in a few milliseconds, individual monitoring may become too expensive to perform in a production system. Inference methods can help tackling this problem by extracting demands from partial

ICPE'16, March 12-18, 2016, Delft, Netherlands
© 2016 ACM. ISBN 978-1-4503-4080-9/16/03...$15.00
DOI: http://dx.doi.org/10.1145/2851553.2851565

measurements. To solve this problem, maximum likelihood based approaches has been developed for demand estimation problem. Maximum likelihood estimation is an optimization method that aims at finding the value of the parameters of a probabilistic model, such that the likelihood of obtaining a given set of samples is maximal. Response time and queue length data is required for this procedure.

Compared to service demands, arrival rates of requests to servers are often simple to measure, but it is difficult to estimate a representative model that captures the statistical characteristics of the arrivals, such as their time-varying patterns. Recent research has increasingly explored the fitting of arrival processes using Markovian Arrival Processes (MAPs) and Marked MAPs, which can be used in conjunction with matrix-analytic methods to predict queueing performance at servers.

In this tutorial, we overview the literature on the fitting of arrival rates and the estimation of service demands for queueing model parameterization. The tutorial covers estimation techniques and high-level paradigms for demand estimation (e.g., methods based on utilization, response-time, or queue-length) together with their sensitivity with respect to data and model characteristics. The tutorial also demonstrates the automated estimation of model parameters using open source tools, such as LibRede and FG for service demands, and M3A for arrival rates.

2. PARAMETER ESTIMATION

2.1 Service Demand Estimation

In order to quantify service demands, a dynamic analysis of the system of interest is required. Service demands are difficult to measure directly with state-of-the-art monitoring tools. Modern operating systems can only provide resource usage statistics on a per-process level. However, the mapping between operating system processes and application requests is non-trivial, because many applications serve different requests with one or more operating system processes (e.g., HTTP web servers).

The advantage of service demand estimation compared to direct measurement techniques is their general applicability and low overheads. These estimation approaches rely on coarse-grained measurements from the system (e.g., CPU utilization, and end-to-end response times), which can be easily and cheaply monitored with state-of-the-art tools without the need for fine-grained code instrumentation. These measurements are routinely collected for many applications, which makes the service demand methods applicable on systems serving production workloads. Over the years, a number of approaches to resource demand estimation have been proposed using different statistical estimation techniques (e.g., linear regression, Kalman filter, etc.) and based on different laws from queueing theory. We have surveyed and evaluated different approaches to resource demand estimation in our previous work [2]. Our evaluation shows, that one has to consider different characteristics of the estimation approach, such as the expected input parameters, its accuracy and its robustness to measurement anomalies when selecting an appropriate approach.

2.2 Arrival Process Fitting

Arrival processes of requests to queues introduce unique challenges in the estimation. Compared to service demands, which are infeasible or impractical to measure directly, inter-arrival times of requests can often be collected, either at the granularity of individual requests or in terms of aggregated arrival counts in a time period. Very often, the arrival patterns of requests exhibit temporal dependence, periodicities and non-exponential distributions that require special modelling techniques for their fitting. Markovian arrival processes (MAPs) fit an arrival process into a continuous-time Markov chain (CTMC) with marked and unmarked transitions. Upon activation of a marked transition in the chain, an arrival event occurs; conversely an unmarked transition has no associated arrival. The fitting problem is to determine the number of states, and the transition rates of marked and unmarked transitions so that the behavior of the MAP resembles as closely as possible the empirical trace. Upong addressing this problem, matrix-geometric techniques accept MAPs as descriptions of arrival processes to queueing systems and return predictions of response times and other performance metrics of interests. MAPs include as special cases renewal processes with hypo-exponential and hyper-exponential inter-arrival times and ON/OFF processes with exponential holding times, which are important to describe non-Poissonian traces. Recently, we have investigated Marked MAPs (MMAPs), which further extend the MAP model to capture a trace of multi-class arrivals [1]. Similarly to MAPs, matrix-geometric techniques enable the use of MMAPs to describe multi-class arrival processes in queueing systems. MMAPs introduce novel fitting concepts such as backward and foward moments.

3. TOOLS

The parameterization of queueing models in terms of service demands and arrival processes requires software tools to automate the process. The tutorial contemplates two tools for service demands estimation, LibReDE [4] and FG [4], and a tool for arrival process fitting, called M3A, which implements the methods in [1,5].

3.1 LibReDE

LibReDE is a library of ready-to-use implementations of state-of-the-art approaches for resource demand estimation that can be used for online and offline analysis [3]. It is the first publicly available tool for this task and aims at supporting performance engineers during performance model construction. Currently it supports different estimation approaches based on approximation, linear regression, Kalman filter and non-linear constrained optimization techniques.

LibReDE automatically checks the preconditions of different estimation approaches according to the input measurements. One or several approaches are then executed and the accuracy of the results is evaluated using cross-validation. Thus it is possible to dynamically choose the estimation approach that provides the best results for a given set of measurement data. Furthermore, LibReDE also supports the automatic derivation of a workload description (i.e., resources and workload classes) from an architecture-level performance model (e.g., Descartes Modeling Language (DML)).

3.2 Filling-the-Gap

Filling-the-Gap (FG) is a tool for continuous performance model parametrization to support Quality-of-Service (QoS) analysis [4]. It implements a set of statistical estimation algorithms to parameterize performance models from runtime monitoring data. Multiple algorithms are included, allowing for alternative ways to obtain estimates for different metrics, but with an emphasis on service demand estimation. FG tool supports advanced algorithms to estimate parameters based on response times and queue-length data, which makes the tool useful in particular for applications running in virtualized environments where utilization readings are not always available. Besides, FG also provides feedback to users by generating reports on the application performance.

3.3 M3A

M3A is a set of MATLAB functions designed for computing the statistical descriptors of MMAPs and fitting marked traces with MMAPs [1]. M3A implements a novel method to match inter-arrival time moments in a multi-class trace using a class of acyclic processes. The fitting methodology is based on moment matching and allows the fitting of traces with geometrically decaying autocorrelation functions.

Acknowledgment

Giuliano Casale is partially supported by the UK Engineering and Physical Sciences Research Council grant EP/M009211/1 (OptiMAM). Simon Spinner is partially supported by the German Research Foundation (DFG) under grant No. KO 3445/11-1. Weikun Wang is supported by the Horizon 2020 project DICE (grant agreement no. 644869).

4. REFERENCES

[1] Andrea Sansottera, Giuliano Casale, and Paolo Cremonesi. Fitting second-order acyclic marked Markovian Arrival Processes. In *Proc. of DSN*, pages 1–12. IEEE, 2013.

[2] Simon Spinner, Giuliano Casale, Fabian Brosig, and Samuel Kounev. Evaluating Approaches to Resource Demand Estimation. *Perf. Eval.*, 92:51 – 71, October 2015.

[3] Simon Spinner, Giuliano Casale, Xiaoyun Zhu, and Samuel Kounev. LibReDe: A library for resource demand estimation. In *Proc. of ICPE*, pages 227–228. ACM, 2014.

[4] Weikun Wang, Juan F Pérez, and Giuliano Casale. Filling the gap: a tool to automate parameter estimation for software performance models. In *Prod. of QUDOS*, pages 31–32. ACM, 2015.

[5] Giuliano Casale, Andrea Sansottera, and Paolo Cremonesi. Compact Markov-Modulated Models for Multiclass Trace Fitting. *Under submission*.

Incorporating Software Performance Engineering Methods and Practices into the Software Development Life Cycle

André B. Bondi
Red Bank, New Jersey
bondia@acm.org

ABSTRACT

In many software development projects, attention is only paid to performance concerns after functional testing, when it usually too late to remedy disabling performance problems. Early attention to performance concerns and early planning of performance requirements and performance testing can prevent debacles like the early rollout of healthcare.gov while addressing cross-cutting concerns such as scalability, reliability and, security. Performance engineering methods may be integrated into all phases of the software lifecycle, from the conception of a system to requirements specification, architecture, testing, and finally to production. Performance expectations can be managed by carefully specifying performance requirements. Reviewing the architecture of a system before design and implementation take place reduces the risk of designing a system that contains inherent performance vice. Performance modeling can be used to justify architectural and design decisions and to plan performance tests. The outputs of such performance tests enable us able to identify concurrent programming and other issues that would not be apparent in unit testing. Finally, risk is mitigated by avoiding design antipatterns that undermine scalability and performance.

General Terms

Performance; Measurement; Software life cycle; Architecture

Keywords

Software performance engineering; Performance measurement and testing; Software life cycle; Modeling; Architecture

1. INTRODUCTION

Historically, performance concerns about a software system have often only been addressed when system is close to being delivered for production. In a keynote speech at SIGMETRICS 1981, J. C. Browne commented that performance evaluation was usually carried out in repairman mode, i.e., when the system is in production, rather than being part of the software design process [5]. More recently, Bass *et al* presented the results of a survey showing that performance was the single biggest risk factor affecting performance [WICSA2007]. Even though Smith and Williams have emphasized that "Build it, then tune it" is a mindset that makes performance failure almost inevitable [11], there are well known cases of systems exhibiting poor performance to the point of being all but unusable. The 2013 rollout of healthcare.gov, the US government's web site for applying for health insurance, is an example. According to press reports, the demand and performance requirements of

ICPE'16, March 12 - 18, 2016, Delft, Netherlands.
Copyright is held by the owner/author(s). Publication rights licensed to ACM.
ACM 978-1-4503-4080-9/16/03...$15.00.
DOI: http://dx.doi.org/10.1145/2851553.2858668

healthcare.gov were not understood, and little time was allowed for performance testing [7].

We advocate that performance concerns be addressed from project inception to delivery, and give an overview of how performance engineering methods can be incorporated into various stages of the software development life cycle. This may be opposed by stakeholders on the ground that it takes time away from feature delivery, or that there is not enough staff time available for the purpose, among other reasons. It may be resisted by product managers who are reluctant to commit to a "performance number" because different market segments may have different performance needs.

Early involvement of a performance engineer and early use of performance engineering methods are essential to the mitigation of the business and engineering risks inherent in any large performance engineering project. The goal is to identify and address performance concerns early so as to reduce the risk of having to redo work. Early application and adoption of performance engineering practices provides insurance against the penalties, costs, and lost revenue associated with rework and late delivery.

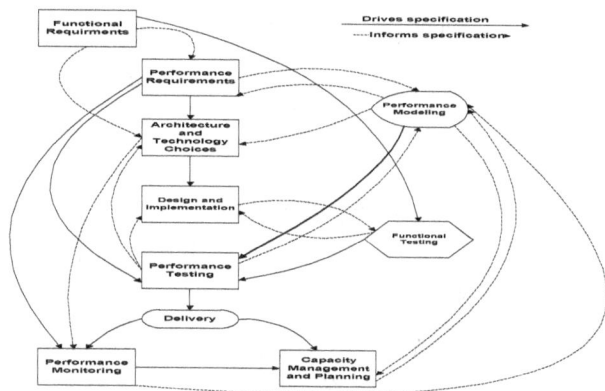

Figure 1. A performance engineering process and its relationship to a development process.

Figure 1 depicts the relationship between the steps of a performance engineering process and corresponding steps in a software development process. The functional requirements drive the form that functional testing will take. They also inform the nature of the performance requirements. The performance requirements describe how often various functions are executed, how long they will take, and the corresponding memory and secondary storage requirements. Performance requirements and performance models inform decisions about the system architecture and the technology platforms to be used as well as the planning of performance tests. When the system architecture is being mapped out, care must be taken to ensure that it will be able to meet disparate performance requirements, including those intended to meet regulatory and safety needs. This is a point at which the tradeoffs between performance and other cross-cutting concerns such as security should be identified. A performance model can help determine whether performance and security requirements and the costs of meeting them are compatible.

Performance testing usually occurs after functional testing, since there is little point in running full performance tests on a system or component that is known not to function properly. Just as functional testing is driven by functional requirements, performance test planning should be driven by performance requirements, knowledge of anticipated workloads, and the desired characteristics of performance curves. Among these characteristics is linearity of the average hardware utilizations with respect to the offered load [6]. The use of performance models to predict the capacity of a system in production is described in [6] and will not be discussed here.

2. PERFORMANCE ISSUES AT EACH LIFE CYCLE PHASE

The absence of or lack of clarity in performance requirements is a cause of unmet or unrealistic performance expectations. It is difficult to architect a system without understanding the performance requirements of various functions and the ability of various technologies to meet them. Even if performance requirements are soundly specified, poor architectural choices can undermine performance. Choices of deployment scenarios can induce foci of overloads or antipatterns such as god classes [11]. The scalability of a system might be impaired by the use of single threading when multithreaded operations could exploit multiple cores or processors. These architectural choices would be propagated into the development phase, where there are further possibilities to use performance antipatterns and poorly performing algorithms. Poorly designed performance tests might fail to reveal performance issues. Performance tests might be driven by workloads that are too small, resulting in an optimistic view of the capabilities of the system, or by workloads that are too large, with the opposite effect. Finally, lack of capacity or poor configuration in production could lead to unsatisfactory performance.

2.1 Performance Requirements

By linking performance requirements to functional requirements and to business engineering needs, one ensures that they are traceable and not superfluous. By linking them to other cross-cutting concerns such as security [10], one is driven to explore the tradeoffs between the concerns and to modify the system architecture accordingly. By insisting that performance requirements be written in measurable testable terms, we are forced to verify that instrumentation is there to provide the verification and that the performance requirements are meaningful within the context of the domain. The guidelines we suggest for writing sound performance requirements are quite similar to those for functional requirements in IEEE Standard 830 [8]. Like functional requirements, performance requirements should be traceable, so that we know why each one is there. They should be based on a well-defined and explicitly stated set of assumptions. They should be verifiable. They should also be numerically consistent. If two or more performance requirements lead to numerical inconsistency or contradict each other, the cause should be investigated before the performance requirements document is released following review. Performance modeling methods can be used to demonstrate numerical consistency or inconsistency between performance requirements. The demonstrations should be mentioned in the performance requirements documents in support

of verifiability and traceability, and, in the case of inconsistency, as triggers for correction.

2.2 Performance Engineering and Architecture

An architect should have an overview of cross-cutting concerns such as performance, reliability, scalability, availability, security, and the choices of software and hardware platforms. Architects and performance engineers can jointly assess the performance requirements to determine scalability needs and identify platform choices while bearing cross cutting concerns in mind. A performance engineer can support an architect's efforts by drawing attention to performance pitfalls during architectural reviews, clarifying performance requirements, and suggesting scheduling rules and other design choices to help meet them.

Even if not much is known with certainty about a system that does not yet exist (e.g., because performance data is lacking), a performance engineer's experience about software performance pitfalls and the properties of queueing systems and scheduling rules can be used to great effect to mitigate performance risks at this stage of the development cycle. When technological choices are being discussed, a performance engineer can have a significant impact by asking about their known performance characteristics and about how often they will be invoked. In cases of doubt, it may be prudent to defend against the possibility of a platform being too slow by recommending early performance testing and benchmarking [2], [9].

The following are among the questions that should be asked during architecture reviews to support performance needs:
- What is the end-to-end flow of information?
- What technologies and parts of the system pose the biggest risk to performance?
- Are there any object pools or other passive software objects such as lock that could become software bottlenecks?
- Does the design contain any performance antipatterns that could cause performance to degrade or that could impede scalability?
- What are the potential foci of overload?
- Can the chosen platforms handle the required actions at the desired rates and with turnaround times that are low enough to meet performance requirements?
- Is any part of the system single-threaded when multithreading could be used to exploit multiple CPUs?
- Can priority scheduling be supported if needed? Answering this question may require an understanding of the data structures and protocols that are needed to implement the system.

Rules of thumb can be used to identify performance pitfalls and antipatterns. God classes and foci of overload can be spotted by reviewing UML message sequence charts, activity and collaboration diagrams, and deployment scenarios. If a message sequence diagram shows that at least one swim lane has large numbers of arrows pointing into it or coming out of it, the corresponding object is likely to be focus of overload, a god class, or both. One-lane bridges and scheduling rules such as the museum checkroom pattern leading to deadlock [3] may be harder to spot, but the benefit of identifying them is the reduced risk of concurrent programming problems that are hard to diagnose.

2.3 Performance Engineering in Design and Implementation

The approach to taking performance considerations into account at the design and implementation stage is similar to that taken in the architectural phase, except that the focus will be on finer details than would be considered when discussing the architecture. As with the architecture, we recommend that a design review be done while keeping the risks of various performance antipatterns in mind. The implementation should avoid the use of busy waiting to implement mutual exclusion and synchronization. Scheduling rules must be free of dependencies that cause deadlocks and livelocks. A review of the implementation should flag and other activities such as insertion sorts whose processing costs are at least polynomial in the number of items involved.

2.4 Performance Testing

Functional testing can be leveraged to support performance testing, because performance tests involve the repeated invocation of the use cases exercised in the functional tests in a controlled and predictable manner. Finally, performance and resource usage monitoring in production can be combined with performance models to identify areas for performance improvement. Of course, our emphasis should be on early performance intervention rather than on measurement in production, but the latter is necessary to verify the effectiveness of and correct defects in the former.

Performance testing usually occurs towards the end of the development cycle, after functional testing. This is understandable, because performance tests of a system that does not meet functional requirements may not tell us accurately about the performance of a system that does meet them. Where an application is built on services and other building blocks, it is often useful to test those before they are built into applications. Thus, there are distinct phases of the development cycle during which performance testing is useful for containing engineering risk.

- To contain the performance risk inherent in a choice of hardware platform, software platform, programming environment, or operating system, one may subject it to synthetic loads that exercise basic functions that will be invoked frequently. This reduces the risk of building a system on the platform, only to find just before delivery that the platform is inherently unable to execute the basic functions fast enough to meet performance requirements [2], [8].
- Performance tests of the implementation of a system or of a part of the system should be done after functional testing, so that time is not wasted on testing the performance of a system that does not work. One can test the use cases of each service it is implemented. One should also test the system with multiple use cases being exercised concurrently as they would be in production.

Notice that functional tests will not usually expose concurrent programming errors, as these are usually unit tests done in single user mode. Performance tests may reveal concurrent programming errors. These can be manifested as deadlocks, livelocks, or thread safety and divisibility errors. Symptoms of thread safety and divisibility errors include the frequent transaction failures and the frequently reattempted actions, and corrupted data. Symptoms of deadlock include sudden drops in CPU utilizations and average response times that oscillate wildly over time. Symptoms of software bottlenecks include response times that grow as functions of the offered load and over time while CPU and device utilizations level off as functions of the offered load [4], [1].

Performance tests should be structured to reveal trends in utilizations, response times, and domain-related indicators such as transaction failure rates and transaction success rates. Three basic goals should be met by a performance test plan. First, one should be able to verify that a system operating under constant load will have constant average performance measures and resource utilizations between load ramp up and load ramp down. Second, one should run tests with at least three load levels to verify that utilizations are linear with respect to the offered load rate or transaction arrival rate, i.e., that the Utilization Law is satisfied. Third, one should determine that performance requirements are met by the system under test. Performance tests should be run long enough under a constant load to demonstrate that the system has reached equilibrium. Statistics on memory usage should be collected to enable the detection of memory leaks. Stress tests in which the system is subjected to a load large enough to cause a system to crash or nearly crash are of limited utility, because they reveal nothing about utilization trends and so cannot be used to predict load levels at which one or more components of the system will be saturated. They will only tell us if the system is capable of maintaining normal activity under a saturating load and of recovering from a crash once the intense load has abated. In our structured tests, if at least one of the hardware utilizations approaches 100% as the load is increased and all utilizations rise in constant ratios as predicted by the Forced Flow Law [6], we may be confident that a software bottleneck has not manifested itself. The range of transaction arrival rates and the nature of the transactions tested should be based on performance requirements, the anticipated size of the user base, as well as on functional requirements and use case specifications. A transaction rate should not be offered in a test if a modeling prediction shows that it would saturate the system.

Of necessity, the performance test lab may be a small version of a target production system that is not architecturally representative of it. This means that bottlenecks may arise in testing that might not arise in production or vice versa. To mitigate this risk, the performance test lab should be built in the light of how a system might be scaled up or down to meet the needs of various market segments while still meeting performance requirements and architectural needs.

We have found it worthwhile to conduct performance tests of the individual services of a service-oriented architecture before building and testing the applications that use them. This sort of early testing reduces the risk of having to diagnose the causes of performance problems and reworking the applications to use other services instead [1], [4].

3. SCALABILITY AND DESIGN CHOICES

Let us briefly attempt to describe our understanding of scalability and then provide illustrations of how it can be examined at the design stage. Load scalability is "the ability of a system to function gracefully, that is without undue delay and without unproductive resource consumption or resource contention, at light, moderate, or heavy loads, while making good use of available resources." A system "has space scalability if its memory requirements do not grow to intolerable levels as the number of items it supports increases." A system "may be said to have structural scalability if its implementation or standards do not impede the growth of the number of objects it encompasses, or … will not do so within a chosen time frame [3]."

Our definition of structural scalability was a precursor of a connection between scalability and performance requirements, namely that the performance requirements describe the dimensions, context and the extent of scalability that the system must support. For example, a small version of a system might be required to provide the processing power, secondary storage, memory, storage, bandwidth, and software needed to meet the performance requirements of ten users, while a large version of a system must provide them to meet the performance requirements of 100 users doing the same sort of work. Here, the dimension of scalability is the number of users, the context is the type of work they do, while the extent is ten users for the small system and 100 for the large one.

Impediments to load scalability include the occurrence of unproductive cycles (as in the case of busy waiting on locks to implement mutual exclusion rather than semaphores) and the inability to exploit parallel processing power because of serial or single-threaded processing of transactions that use disjoint data. Structural scalability can be constrained by the sizes of address spaces or of fixed-size sequence numbers. For example, the length of an array is constrained by the maximum bit length of its integer index. Questions about the impact of a design choice on load scalability can sometimes be answered by applying a simple analytic model over a wide variety of parameters. We have done this to justify the use of semaphores rather than locking instructions 1 implement mutual exclusion [3].

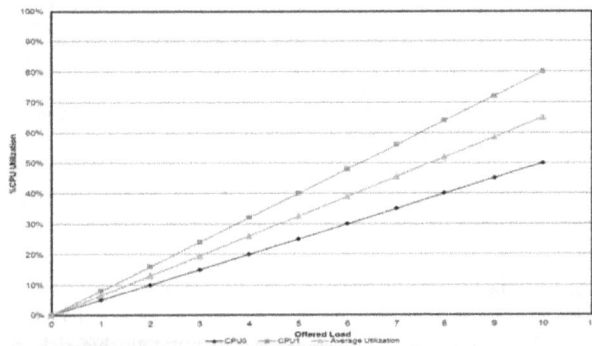

Figure 2. Unbalanced CPU loads due to serial execution via single thread.

Measurements taken during performance tests can also reveal limitations on load scalability [4]. Figure 2 illustrates contrived data representing measurements of a two-processor UNIX™-based system. The data are contrived because measurements of the actual system were not available for publication. The straight line between the upper and lower lines shows the average CPU utilization overall. Observations of the actual system were taken with *mpstat*. An examination of *ps –eLF* output taken at regular intervals revealed that activity was concentrated in two processes for which changes in the cumulative processing times corresponded to the two processor utilizations. Since cache affinity was turned on, we inferred that each process was bound to one processor, yielding test results like those shown in Figure 2. The developers explained that the more CPU-intensive process was processing disjoint sets of data sequentially. An opportunity for parallel execution had been overlooked. The maximum offered load of the system was constrained by the larger of the two CPU utilizations. Thus, the processor imbalance limited the extent of load scalability to 10 work units in unit time, while architecting the system to allow parallel execution on disjoint data sets could have increased the extent of load scalability to 12.3 units of work in unit time, in the absence of any other bottlenecks.

4. CONCLUSION
The foregoing discussion and examples illustrate how performance engineering methods can be applied to mitigate performance risk throughout the software life cycle. Clearly specified performance requirements, performance-oriented architecture reviews, and performance tests planned in the light of requirements all contribute to the mitigation of performance risk and the delivery of a product that meets performance expectations.

5. ACKNOWLEDGMENTS
The figures in this paper originally appeared in [4]. They are reproduced with the permission of the publisher. The author has benefited from frequent discussions with Alberto Avritzer and Bob Schwanke.

6. REFERENCES
[1]   Avritzer, A., and A. B. Bondi. 2012. Resilience assessment based on performance testing. In *Resilience Assessment and Evaluation of Computing Systems*, edited by K. Wolter, A. Avritzer, M .Vieira, and A. van Morsel. Springer.

[2]   Avritzer, A., and E. Weyuker. 1995. The automatic generation of load test suites and the assessment of the resulting software. *IEEE Trans. Softw. Eng.* 21(9), 705–716.

[3]   Bondi, A. B. 2000. Characteristics of scalability and their impact on performance. In *Proc. WOSP2000*, Ottawa.

[4]   Bondi, A. B. 2014. *Foundations of Software and System Performance Engineering*. Addison-Wesley, Upper Saddle River, NJ. ISBN-13: 978-0321-83382-2.

[5]   Browne, J.C. 1981. Designing systems for performance. Keynote address, ACM SIGMETRICS Conference, Las Vegas, Nevada, 1981. In *Performance Evaluation Review* 10 (1), 1, 1981.

[6]   Denning, P. J., and J. P. Buzen. 1978. The operational analysis of queueing network models. *ACM Computing Surveys* 10(3), 225–261.

[7]   Eilperin, J.2013. CGI warned of HealthCare.gov problems a month before launch, documents show. *Washington Post*, October 29, 2013.

[8]   IEEE Std 830-1998, *IEEE Recommended Practice for Software Requirements Specifications -Description*.

[9]   Masticola, S., A. B. Bondi, and M. Hettich. 2005. Model-based scalability estimation in inception-phase software architecture. In *Model Driven Engineering Languages and Systems, Lecture Notes in Computer Science* 3713, 355–366.

[10] Schwaninger, C., Wuchner, E., and Kircher, M. 2004. Encapsulating crosscutting concerns in system software. Proc. Third AOSD Workshop on Aspects, Components, and Patterns for Infrastructure Software.

[11] Smith, C.U., and Williams, L.G. 2002. *Performance Solutions*. Addison Wesley, Boston, MA.

Author Index

331

www.ingramcontent.com/pod-product-compliance
Lightning Source LLC
Chambersburg PA
CBHW080915220326
41598CB00034B/5578